CONSUMER PRICES
(1967=100)

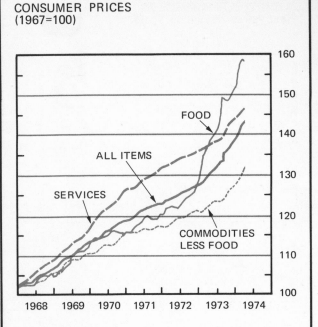

- FOOD
- ALL ITEMS
- SERVICES
- COMMODITIES LESS FOOD

160
150
140
130
120
110
100

1968 1969 1970 1971 1972 1973 1974

SOURCE: Department of Labor.

WHOLESALE PRICES
(1967=100)

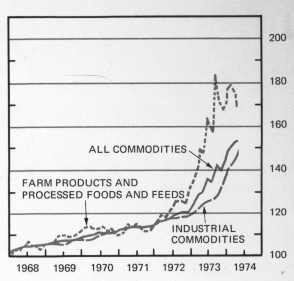

- ALL COMMODITIES
- FARM PRODUCTS AND PROCESSED FOODS AND FEEDS
- INDUSTRIAL COMMODITIES

200
180
160
140
120
100

1968 1969 1970 1971 1972 1973 1974

SOURCE: Department of Labor.

PRICES, MONEY, AND INTEREST RATES

SHORT-TERM INTEREST RATES
Percent Per Annum

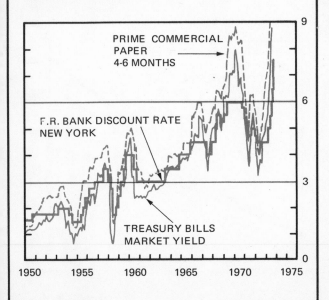

- PRIME COMMERCIAL PAPER 4-6 MONTHS
- F.R. BANK DISCOUNT RATE NEW YORK
- TREASURY BILLS MARKET YIELD

9
6
3
0

1950 1955 1960 1965 1970 1975

SOURCE: *1973 Historical Chart Book,* Federal Reserve System.

MONEY STOCK
Billions of Dollars

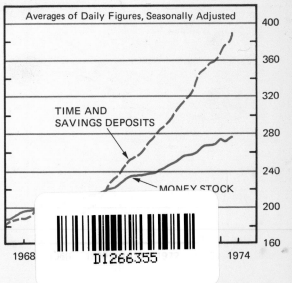

Averages of Daily Figures, Seasonally Adjusted

- TIME AND SAVINGS DEPOSITS
- MONEY STOCK

400
360
320
280
240
200
160

1968 1974

SOURCE: Board of Governors of the Federal Reserve System.

ECONOMICS

ECONOMICS

An Analysis of Principles and Policies

Second Edition

Thomas J. Hailstones

Professor of Economics
Dean, College of Business Administration
Xavier University
Cincinnati, Ohio

Michael J. Brennan

Professor of Economics
Vice President for Academic Affairs
Wesleyan University
Middletown, Connecticut

H64

Published by
SOUTH-WESTERN PUBLISHING CO.

CINCINNATI   WEST CHICAGO, ILL.   DALLAS   PELHAM MANOR, N.Y.
PALO ALTO, CALIF.   BRIGHTON, ENGLAND

ISBN: 0-538-08640-8

Library of Congress Catalog Card Number: 73-87492

1 2 3 4 5 6 K 0 9 8 7 6 5
Printed in the United States of America

Preface

In this day of rapid and dynamic change, economic issues underlie much of the political, social, cultural, and military turmoil throughout the world. Whether on a local, national, or global scale such pressing issues as poverty, unemployment, galloping inflation, energy blackouts, gyrating meat prices, gasoline rationing, housing shortages, health care needs, and national defense are all primarily economic in nature.

Throughout this text economic theory and analysis are related to the world of reality. Thus, the student can apply what is being learned to assist in making prudent judgments regarding various current economic issues even though they may have social or political overtones. We wish to emphasize that this text is written for the student—to stimulate the student, to challenge the student, and to serve as a point of departure for further inquiry into the subject matter of economics.

Since developing and writing the previous edition, the economy has changed, new problems have emerged, and others are forming on the horizon. Societal and personal interests have shifted. Consequently, our textbook format and presentation have changed to cope with these new problems and changing interests.

In Part One of this edition, for example, the first eight chapters of the previous edition have been rewritten and condensed into five chapters. This allows the reader to delve into the study of macroeconomic analysis earlier in the academic term. Moreover, each chapter of the text now contains a "Preview" which describes the main thrust of the chapter.

The analytical material on income and output determination has been brought forward into Part Two, adjacent to the chapters treating GNP, income, employment, and economic fluctuations. This presents a better understanding of the relationship of investment and saving to GNP and to the level of income and employment, and it permits students to better relate the practical with the theoretical.

In Part Three, "Economic Activity and Monetary Policy," a link has been developed showing the relationship between money and interest with the investment-saving function developed in Part Two. This serves to give us a more systematic approach in showing how the money supply, its manipulation by the Federal Reserve, its relationship to the circular flow, and the level of interest rates all relate in helping to determine the level of national income through consumption, investment, government spending, and the multiplier and accelerator effects.

"The Public Sector," Part Five, has been enlarged to take into consideration a special chapter dealing with new concepts in raising government revenues. In addition to the conventional revenue raising measures, including federal-state revenue sharing and the spreading adoption of the lottery, the value added tax and national sales tax proposals are analyzed.

Part Six, "Economic Growth and the American Experience," has been expanded with new chapters dealing with the problems of growth, the natural environment, and the establishment of economic priorities. Considered here, for example, are the problems of air, water, and solid waste pollution associated with economic growth.

A number of current economic problems are brought together in Part Ten, whose chapters consider agricultural pricing and income; urban economic issues, such as housing, mass transit, and crime; the incidence and impact of poverty; and various population and manpower problems, particularly emphasizing those of minority groups.

The parts and chapters dealing with microeconomics, the subject matter of which has better stood the test of time, received less revision attention, with the exception that more current applications were added. Parts Eleven and Twelve on world and international economics, however, were subject to many changes as a result of the turmoil and dramatic changes taking place in world resource markets and international financial centers. Realignment of national currencies associated with devaluations, revaluations, floats, expansion of SDRs, and shifting balances of payments are given special treatment, along with the role of gold in international finance.

Upon completion and assimilation of the textbook material, the student should have sufficient knowledge to analyze the economic aspects of major social, political, and business problems of the day. The student will find that many controversial issues take on new meaning in light of this economic understanding of them. In this regard the student will be better prepared to discuss these issues and to form decisions regarding their solutions. This being the case, the authors will feel that they have again accomplished their objective in writing and revising this text.

As always, the authors wish to thank their colleagues and the many users of the previous edition who gave assistance in the form of constructive criticism or suggestions for improvement of the original manuscript. A note of appreciation is due also to Mrs. Marjorie Faulhaber for her untiring stenographic assistance.

T. J. H.

M. J. B.

Contents

PART ONE

An Introduction to the
Structure and Operation
of the American Economy

1

What Is
Economics?

PREVIEW Before tackling the many facets of economics, it is important that certain fundamentals be established. These will become manifest, in more concrete terms, in the chapters that follow. They include a working definition of economics, the basic functions that must be performed in any economy, the scope of economics as an intellectual discipline, and the methods used in studying economics.

Imagine that you are standing on the main street of an American town. In the supermarket across the street, housewives are loading their pushcarts with food, toothpaste, and other household items. In the bank next door, a physician is negotiating the terms of a loan to finance the renovation of his office. Workers are hurrying to their jobs on the second shift in the furniture factory down at the end of the street. These people are engaged in what we think of as economic activities—buying, selling, or earning income.

Suppose you were to move over to the newsstand and purchase the afternoon edition of the local newspaper. You might read that in 1975 the average American is richer than ever before, yet inflation is feared. Perhaps there is an editorial on the President's proposal concerning the income tax. The paper might also carry articles on America's balance-of-payments problem, a strike by a labor union, and a decline in trading volume on the New York Stock Exchange. These, too, are what we regard as economic activities or issues that have broad social consequences.

If you were then to pause in order to reflect upon the meaning of these activities, an entire series of questions would arise. Is there some link between the actions of different individuals in the town? For example, how are household purchases in the supermarket related to employment in the furniture factory? Is the level of income in the community connected in some way to the volume of borrowing from the bank by business firms? Where does the bank get the money it lends?

Reading of the newspaper would raise questions of greater social significance. What lies behind inflationary price increases? What causes poverty? Why do periods of boom alternate with periods of depression? How do international trade and finance affect the welfare of a nation? What are the economic factors that contribute to urban blight or air pollution?

ECONOMIC ACTIVITY

We are about to embark upon an extensive study of economics. If we are not to get lost in the details (lose sight of the forest for the sake of the trees), then it is important that a sound perspective be established at the outset— and be kept constantly in mind. This perspective can be found by abstracting from the particular circumstances surrounding economic activities or issues. We begin by "rising above" the American town and taking a bird's-eye view of the action, so to speak. We do so in order to cut through a wide variety of outward manifestations and thereby to identify what is essentially common to all types of economic activities.

Economics—A Working Definition

Economics may be defined as the study of the allocation of scarce means among alternative wants. The key words in this definition are "scarce," "alternative," and "allocation."

Without *scarcity* the world would have no economic problems, and there would be no need to study economics. Each member of the human race could enjoy as much of everything as he might conceivably want. Everyone on the planet could have any amount of automobiles, clothes, books, gourmet dinners, pedicures, psychiatric consultations, sauna baths, movies, sporting events, wigs, and so on without end. Of course we do not live in such a fairyland; these goods and services are not superabundant. That is, they are scarce relative to our wants for them. Even if a person's want for a particular good could be satiated, there are still his wants for other goods that are less than completely satisfied. Such is the state of the world!

Basically, the reason why goods and services are scarce is that they have to be produced. Productive resources (land, labor, raw materials, buildings, and equipment) have to be organized in order to generate the goods and services we want. In turn, these productive resources are scarce. We do not have unlimited supplies of goods and services because we do not have unlimited supplies of human talent, natural power, and tools needed to produce them.

Since productive resources are scarce, alternative uses of available resources must be considered. Given an existing quantity of land, its use as an airport means the land cannot be put to the alternative use as a farm. If a man becomes a full-time teacher, he cannot pursue an alternative occupation, such as a full-time politician. Similarly, when all resources are employed and more are devoted to the production of residential homes, then less must be used to produce other goods, such as schools or roads.

The fundamental problem of economics is that of deciding how to allocate among alternatives. This problem underlies all economic activity. Because of scarcity, resources must be allocated among alternative employments. Once resources are allocated and a total volume of finished goods and services is produced, the output must be allocated among different users or consumers. The sharing of output determines economic welfare.

Individual Economizing

Both individuals and societies are faced with *allocation* decisions. The housewife in the supermarket must allocate a scarce (not unlimited) household income between the alternatives of saving and spending. Then she must decide how to allocate total expenditures among food, clothing, entertainment, and other goods. The physician who is negotiating a loan from the bank decides how much of the income from his practice will be used to purchase household goods and how much will be used to build up his practice. He may decide to borrow part of the funds to finance office renovations, but in doing so he allocates some of his future income to interest payments and repayment of the principal. Workers choose among alternative jobs. They also decide whether to work more or fewer hours per year. Business executives allocate the firm's sales revenue among plant maintenance and expansion, employee payroll, advertising, and other needs.

Other, less obvious, examples of economizing on the part of individuals can be brought to mind. The allocation of your scarce time between work and leisure is an economic decision. When you determine how much effort you will devote to study for each course, this too is an economic decision because it involves the allocation of scarce time among alternative uses or wants. Substitution of one expensive date for several inexpensive dates, a decision to leave the hospital and recuperate at home, a choice between driving in heavy traffic or walking, living in a city apartment as opposed to a suburban home—all of these activities entail economizing.

Social Economizing

A society also economizes. At the local or state levels of social organization, the community must determine the amount of total available resources that will be allocated to the production of goods and services that are consumed collectively, such as public education, roads, police and fire protection, and urban renewal. If provision of these services is to be financed by taxes, a tax system is determined. Given total tax revenues, expansion of one service requires that some amounts of others must be foregone. A predetermined quantity of resources is reallocated among alternative uses.

In order to solve a traffic congestion problem, a new bridge over a river is considered against the alternative of a tunnel under the river. The decision is an economic one of choosing among alternatives with different costs (absorption of scarce resources), different degrees of efficiency in handling traffic, and different esthetic characteristics. If the decision is in favor of a bridge, alternative locations and types of construction must be decided.

At the national level of government, economizing is also apparent. An expanded budget for military defense entails a reallocation of men and materials toward defense activities and away from the private sector or other public programs. The same holds true for national health insurance, agricultural support, or government-sponsored research. Some actions result in a reallocation of produced goods from the domestic to the foreign market, or the reverse. Other actions promote migration of labor from one region of the country to another.

BASIC ECONOMIC FUNCTIONS

Any economic system must perform certain basic *economic functions*. In doing so, some fundamental decisions must be made.

First, it must be decided what and how much is to be produced with the resources that are available. Should resources be diverted from the provision of entertainment to the administration of medical care? Are the citizens of the economy to have more automobiles, or are the disadvantaged to have better homes, or are both possible?

Second, the economy must provide a means of distributing among individuals whatever goods and services are produced. In other words, who is going to get a produced item and in what amount? Should each person have a minimum income with which he can purchase goods and services?

Third, a decision must be made as to whether the economy's resources and production are going to be devoted to future or current consumption. Should the economy produce a greater amount of capital goods to be used in the production of future consumable goods or more goods and services for immediate consumption?

These fundamental problems must be faced by any society. The way in which a particular society attempts to solve the problems will give rise to a type of economic organization. In turn, the economic organization is related to that society's political system.

A primitive society might place complete responsibility and authority for economic organization in the hands of a tribal chief. He would decide how many soup bowls, beads, and eggs are to be produced and how much corn shall be stored over the winter. He also decides how much effort will be devoted to these activities and how much to the production of capital goods such as wooden plows and fishing boats. Moreover, he decides who may be a hunter, who may be a turnip digger and for how long each day, and who may be a witch doctor. Finally, he must assign to each household the quantities of produced goods and services the household is entitled to consume.

When modern societies have vested authority for economic decisions in a central agency, the organization has taken the form of a military dictatorship or some system of socialism. In the former, a totalitarian political regime creates centralized institutions that direct and control the allocation of resources. Socialism—under which the means of production are controlled or regulated by the state—may be consistent with political democracy, depending upon whether the central authority is accountable to the people for its decisions. Nevertheless, a state planning agency can determine the immediate details of product and resource allocation. Communism combines socialism in the economic sphere with totalitarianism in the political sphere.

Centralization of economic decision making is common to these kinds of organizations. In contrast, an exchange or market economy—sometimes called a free enterprise or private enterprise economy—is distinguished by decentralization of most economic decisions. Instead of being delegated to a central authority, the entire system of allocation is worked out through exchange in a market. No one assigns labor to different industries, dictates the mix of capital goods and consumer goods, or distributes the proceeds of production among households. Consumers are free to choose which goods they will consume and in what amounts; businessmen are free to enter into and exit from the business of their choice; laborers may offer their services in any employment. These various decentralized decisions generate market forces of demand and supply that determine the allocation of products and resources in society.

An exchange economy is also related to a political system. A politically democratic society can function without a free enterprise economy. But a free enterprise economy—because it presupposes private property, business competition, and free exchange—cannot survive under totalitarianism.

The issue is not whether economic activity should be organized but how it should be organized. The important point is that the fundamental problems of economics are encountered by any human society. Different societies may cope with the problem of allocating scarce means among alternative wants by instituting different forms of organization. Nevertheless, the underlying problem remains.

THE SCOPE OF ECONOMICS

The subject matter embraced by economics can be divided into positive economics and normative economics. *Positive economics* is that branch of economics concerned with questions of "what is." Here we have pure analysis devoid of norms or political overtones. *Normative economics*, on the other hand, deals with a set of criteria designed to answer questions of "what ought to be." This branch of economics is concerned with value judgments, the desirability of goals or behavior, and what is best for society.

Economics as a Science

Positive economics takes as given whatever customs, goals, and values exist in society. Within this context, the study of economics centers upon discovery of systematic cause-effect relationships among variables such as prices, production, and income. The economist suspends judgment as to whether these relationships are good or bad.

Positive economics may be defined, then, as a science concerned with the production, distribution, and consumption of goods and services. Economics is considered a science because it is an organized body of knowledge coordinated, arranged, and systemized with reference to general laws or principles. The laws and principles of economics, however, are not as universal or iron-clad as are some of the laws of the physical sciences, such as physics or chemistry. Physics, for example, gives us the law of gravitation. From this law we know that every time we throw an object heavier than air, such as a baseball, into the atmosphere, it will fall to the ground. Never will the ball remain freely suspended in the air. Thus, we know what reaction we will get each time the ball or other similar objects are thrown into the air.

In economics most of the laws are general rather than universal in that they apply in most but not all cases. Take, for example, the law of saving, which states that as the income of an individual or family increases the percent of income saved will increase. This is generally true. Most of us will save a larger percent of our income as our paychecks get larger, provided our responsibilities do not become greater. There are those, however, who always manage to spend as much as, if not more than, the income they make. Therefore, our law is not universal in nature. In the physical sciences we know what reaction to anticipate from the application of a certain stimulus to a given set of physical conditions. In economics, however, we deal with individuals and groups, and circumstances may never be the same because of differences in personality, education, environment, and objectives.

Economics as a Debate

Normative economics brings in questions of bad, good, better, or best. These questions are important and, in some instances, more important than the questions posed for positive economics. A newspaper editorial may take a position on an economic issue, while an editorial in another newspaper takes a different position; each candidate for public office has an economic plank in his platform; private citizens debate the virtues of a proposed change in the tax rate or whether the distribution of income among families is equitable.

Adding to the complexity is the fact that sometimes economists or those responsible for economic decisions disagree. Generally such disagreements among economists are not about basic laws or principles, but about specific objectives or the means of attaining objectives. There may be disagreement as to whether the economy should grow at a 3 percent or a 5 percent rate or whether we should sacrifice price stability in order to achieve and to maintain full employment. Even when there is agreement regarding goals, there may be a difference of opinion concerning the best means of attaining these goals. There is general agreement that old people need medical care, but there is much disagreement as to whether or not such medical care should be provided by a government program and, if provided by the government, whether or not it should be on a voluntary or a compulsory basis.

In economics there is often no right or wrong answer. Much will depend on the judgment of the individual making the decision, based upon his intuition or experience. For example, does he believe that full employment is more important to the economy than stable prices? For noneconomic reasons a national economic adviser may recommend a tax reduction rather than an increase in total government spending in order to help the economy during a depression. He may decide that the farmer's position can be helped more by means of flexible price supports than by high, rigid price supports.

As a result of the many decisions that must be made on the basis of judgments, there are many differences of opinion on economic matters. It should be remembered that frequently the disagreements are not on basic principles but on specific objectives or on the means of accomplishing objectives. Furthermore, economic decisions are readily subject to criticism, especially by the general public. Although people hesitate to question or to criticize the decisions of the doctor, the physicist, or the engineer, because they may know very little if anything about such subjects, economics is a different matter. Every citizen feels that he knows something about economics and, in fact, he does; but, as it has often been said, a little knowledge can be a dangerous thing. Some people are inclined to forget that their knowledge of the subject matter is limited, and they fail to see or to understand many of the complexities involved in economic decision making.

Economics Related to Other Disciplines

Economics is related to other disciplines, and frequently economic analysis impinges on other fields of study. Many of the economic problems are also political in nature, such as the farm problem, the national debt, minimum wages, and social-security measures. Since some of its laws (such as the law of diminishing returns) are based on physical phenomena, economics is related to physics. A low economic level of living leads to social problems; thus, economics is related to sociology. Economics deals with human behavior when it endeavors to determine what and why people buy, how individuals react during adverse business conditions, and what consumers will do with their higher incomes. Consequently, economics shares these and other phases of its study with psychology. Because much of economics, especially at the advanced levels, is expressed and analyzed in quantitative fashion, mathematics is a useful tool for the study of economics. Since economics deals with human acts, it is also related to philosophy, and in particular to ethics, a branch of philosophy that deals with the morality of human acts. Economics is likewise related to history, since many of the events of history were caused by economic conditions and objectives. Lastly, we might keep in mind that economics is closely related to logic, the science of correct thinking, just as any study should be.

Usually when we study economics, we analyze the economic system in whole or in part as an isolated phenomenon. We find out how it works, integrate the individual parts, relate them to one another, and study the economy as a whole. From our analysis we may discover certain laws or principles and develop certain policies. After we have done this, we frequently neglect to analyze the relationship of the economy to the rest of society. For example, the economist may stress the improvement in our level of living as a prime objective. To accomplish such an objective at the expense of our political or ecological welfare, however, could prove to be highly undesirable and even dangerous. Public policy must be based upon non-economic as well as economic goals.

METHODS OF STUDYING ECONOMICS

An intellectual discipline is characterized not only by a given body of knowledge but also by the method of investigation through which the knowledge is obtained. Broadly speaking, in the study of economics we may employ one or more of three general approaches. These include the scientific, descriptive, and quantitative methods.

Scientific Method

The *scientific method* or analytical approach is an attempt to discover cause-and-effect relationships among the underlying elements that result in economic conditions and events. In the study of economics, we must do more than collect facts and memorize definitions. We need facts and many of them, but for the purpose of scientific study economic facts are important only because they help to explain the functioning of forces in the economy.

A scholar in a particular field of science may be puzzled by what he sees; but he continues to observe, and his observations lead to the collection of facts. He notes relationships by grouping and classifying these facts. He may then attempt to formulate a hypothesis; that is, he makes a scientific conjecture or assumption that explains the relationships noted. He may conduct experiments in an attempt to verify his conclusion. Unfortunately for the progress of the science of economics, however, it is difficult and usually impossible to set up experiments for the purpose of testing a hypothesis. Economics cannot be studied in a test tube or a wind tunnel. Since economics deals with human actions and variable conditions, it is often impossible to exercise effective or suitable controls over experiments.

Nevertheless, the science of economics calls for accurate, clear, and logical thinking. To think logically means that conclusions must be reached on the basis of certain ascertainable facts and premises. Such thinking requires careful evaluation of assumptions and facts before they can be accepted. In this respect we must be cautious in reasoning from a general principle to a particular application or from a particular incident to a general conclusion. It is not always safe to assume that what is true for the economy as a whole is true for any given part or, conversely, that what is true for a given part is true for the economy as a whole. To illustrate, suppose that the total amount of income in the economy had increased 10 percent last year. The fact that total, or even average, income had increased would hardly justify the conclusion that everyone was better off than he was in the previous year.

On the other hand, it is not safe to assume that what is good for the individual is good for the total economy. Suppose, for example, that Uncle Sam should send you as a gift a new Federal Reserve note for $1,000. Certainly that would be helpful to you. However, would that be equally true if the government were to send everyone in the economy that much new money? This would mean an increase of over $212 billion in our money supply, and the accompanying inflation would decrease the value of money substantially. Not only would your $1,000 buy less, but also money that had been carefully saved in previous years would lose much of its value.

Nor should we be too quick to ascribe a cause-and-effect relationship between two factors or situations. First, it is possible that two events may be coincidental; that is, they may occur together, but it is not necessarily correct to assume that one is the cause of, or dependent on, the other. For example, there is probably a high coincidence between the creation of new savings and loan institutions and spending in the economy. But one is not the cause of the other. Since they are both a function of income, it might be that the cause of each is an increase in income in the economy. Second, it does not follow logically that because one event occurs after another the former is the cause of the latter. Night follows day (or is it vice versa?) but one does not cause the other. This is known as the fallacy of *post hoc, ergo propter hoc* (after this, therefore because of this). For example, the formation of a labor union may not be the real cause of a subsequent increase in wages. Maybe it came as a result of an increase in the minimum-wage law or through the increased generosity of the employer.

Descriptive Method

The *descriptive method* of study is used in an attempt to describe the organization and functioning of institutions and policies that have economic significance. It is used, for example, in explaining the organization and function of different forms of business enterprise, the structure of the Federal Reserve System, the operation of labor unions, and the mechanics of our free enterprise capitalistic system. It is often called the *institutional approach* to the study of economics and, at one time, was very popular in many of our universities. It does have limited advantages, however, for the formulation of laws and principles unless it is coordinated with the scientific approach.

Quantitative Method

Although the *quantitative method* is a special technique of the scientific method, it is worthy of separate consideration. The entire area of economic research and the formulation of fundamental principles have been aided greatly in recent years by the use of equipment capable of absorbing, processing, integrating, relating, and storing massive quantities of economic data. Various computing devices can be used in an attempt to discover new principles and relationships and to solve practical economic and business problems.

Computer operations permit the accumulation and rapid processing of economic data in preparing the gross national product figures of the Department of Commerce, the flow-of-funds tables of the Federal Reserve, employment figures for the Bureau of Labor Statistics, and many other measures and indexes of business activity. Many firms have their own computer equipment capable of processing data at lightning speeds. One large aircraft company, for example, can complete in a few minutes on an electronic computer the calculations it would require a mathematician seven years to complete on a desk calculator. Several universities have established data processing and computer centers to provide facilities for professional research and for assisting businesses in solving their problems.

As a result of the increasing use of the quantitative method, more can be learned about the economy and industry in a shorter period of time than formerly. Existing theory can be quantified in an attempt to prove its validity, and new principles can be formulated. The new techniques developed through quantitative analysis should help improve policy and decision making by both businesses and the government.

Statistics. The quantitative method makes use of *descriptive statistics*, which refers to the collection, organization, and presentation of empirical data in the form of tables and charts. It, likewise, utilizes *analytical statistics*, which endeavors to draw general relationships or conclusions from the data. By studying and analyzing national income and employment data, we can infer certain statistical relationships, such as the conclusion that an increase in investment is related to an increase in national income and employment.

Mathematical Economics. Economic theories for many generations were expressed verbally, and for the most part they still are. It is becoming more commonplace today, however, to express economic theory in terms of mathematical symbols. For example, the relationship between price and the amount of a commodity sold can be expressed mathematically by the symbol, $q = f(p)$, which indicates that quantity sold is a function of, or is dependent on, the price of a commodity. The use of mathematical economics has a definite advantage in the analysis of complicated data. Through the use of mathematics, it is much easier to hold the constants constant and vary the variables as desired in order to reach new conclusions. On the other hand, it is difficult to explain or account for some types of economic behavior by means of mathematical equations.

Econometrics. Mathematical economics deals primarily with economic theory and expresses theoretical abstractions, whereas statistics is concerned with observed quantitative data. Mathematical economics builds its models as abstractions from reality and draws abstract conclusions. It is not immediately concerned with the random forces that might appear in the empirical statistical data. *Econometrics* bridges the gap between theory and observation by designing statistical measures of mathematical relationships and tests of hypotheses. Econometrics modifies the abstract conclusions of mathematical economics in order to show the effect of nonabstract or concrete forces. Mathematical economics, for example, expresses quantity demanded as an inverse function of price. But econometrics, through the analysis of empirical data, can supply us with a more precise relationship between a change in price and the change in quantity sold. It might, for example, reveal that for a given commodity a one percent decrease in price will result in a .5 or a 1.5 percent increase in the quantity demanded.

Model Building

Frequently the economist makes use of models in order to analyze economic behavior. In this case a model is an abstraction from reality. It is a sketch of an operation under supposed ideal or controlled conditions. *Model building* is a process of setting up a basic abstract framework that includes only the essential elements and relationships of a particular economic situation for the purpose of analysis. A model may be in the form of a verbal description, a diagram, or a mathematical expression. Although the model may not have an exact counterpart in the world of reality, a study of the model can help one to understand the underlying forces operating within a particular realistic situation. Without some type of model, it would be rather difficult to understand the operation of a real-world situation with its complexities, biases, and hidden forces. Just as it is easier to understand the operation of a complicated jet engine by first looking at a simple schematic diagram that shows how the engine draws in huge quantities of air, compresses it, adds fuel for combustion, ignites it, and shoots it out the rear so hard and fast that the aircraft is thrust forward at near sonic or supersonic speed by the reaction, so, too, it is easier to understand the complexities of competitive pricing after studying pricing under a model of perfect competition.

Once a model is constructed and understood, it can be modified in order to bring it into closer relationship with reality. This may be done in one step or through a series of approximations, each moving closer to a real-life situation. We might set up a model, for example, to explain the concept and advantages of free trade on an international scale. This model could then be modified to take into consideration the existence of tariffs, differences in exchange rates, the law of diminishing returns, political relationships, military considerations, and the economic needs of each country. In another case, the reasons for our current agricultural price-support program can be clear only if we understand how prices are determined in a model explaining the operation of the forces of supply and demand.

Although model building is extremely helpful in economic analysis and policy formulation, any principles and policies drawn therefrom must be modified before they are applied to a practical economic situation. Furthermore, a model is not an end in itself but a means to understanding actual economic relationships. Although the economist is faced with the problem of making economic decisions in a practical situation, knowledge gained through the use of economic models can assist him in making better judgments and decisions.

ECONOMIC ANALYSIS AND ECONOMIC POLICY

Economic analysis deals with the cause-and-effect relationships of economic phenomena. It aims to formulate statements or principles as to what is true or correct under assumed conditions. Economic analysis explains, for example, how price is determined under conditions of competition or monopoly, why business fluctuations occur, and what forces promote or retard economic growth.

The study of economics can be classified into two broad areas. *Microeconomics* deals with the problems of individuals, firms, and industries. It is sometimes referred to as partial equilibrium analysis since it is concerned with only a part of the total economy. It endeavors to determine what makes the individual buy one commodity rather than another. It explains price determination by the forces of supply and demand. It treats profit maximization from the viewpoint of competition and monopoly.

Macroeconomics, on the other hand, deals with the aggregates of economic analysis. It is concerned with the problems of the economy as a whole rather than those of the individual or the firm and is sometimes referred to as general equilibrium analysis. It includes such areas of study as total employment, total production, and the general price level. It describes business cycles and analyzes the use of various monetary and fiscal measures as a means of stabilizing the level of business activity. It explains inflation and analyzes the effect of changes in the rate of economic growth.

Prior to World War II, economic analysis dealt primarily with microeconomics. Since then, however, an increasing emphasis has been placed on macroeconomics. Today we study both areas.

Whereas economic analysis studies economic relationships under given circumstances, *economic policy* refers to the course of action taken under those circumstances. Thus, in periods of inflation it might be the policy of an investor to purchase stocks in preference to bonds. During a period of unemployment, it might be the policy of the Federal Reserve to lower interest rates in order to encourage business investment. The administration in office might adhere to a balanced-budget policy or favor a deficit budget during depression periods.

Unfortunately, or perhaps sometimes fortunately, economic policy does not follow the dictates of economic analysis. Sometimes economic policy must give way to other policies. Frequently we will find that economic policy is modified by political, military, or social policy. For example, economic analysis may indicate that we should maintain and even increase taxes during inflationary periods; but during an election year economic policy may yield to political pressure, and taxes are reduced in order to sway the voting public. Economists advocate free trade, but pressure groups often influence a nation to modify its stand on free trade. Free competition may be the answer to our farm problem; but because of the economic and social hardships that such a rigorous economic policy would cause, very few legislators favor the complete removal of our present farm controls and price supports.

Today a controversy exists among economists regarding the role of the economic scholar. One group maintains that, in order to remain objective and scientific, the study of economics should be limited to the realm of positive economics. They suggest that others besides economists, such as political statesmen, business executives, and labor leaders, integrating knowledge of other disciplines, such as law, philosophy, political science, sociology, and psychology, should make the decisions on what ought to be done in the economic sphere. Others, however, feel that the economist can utilize these same disciplines and that his analysis should be undertaken with certain assumed goals, rights, mores, and other criteria.

Whatever the proper role of a professional economist, a knowledge of economics is essential for everyone if we are to have a proper understanding and appreciation of the society in which we live. Economic conditions are an integral part of our social, political, and cultural environment. They are inextricably related to our military strength, and they are the basis of our foreign policy. Since we are destined to live and to work in a society so influenced by economic principles and problems, it is certainly important to learn as much about economics as possible. In addition to being of value as knowledge for the sake of knowledge, economics is of great aid in understanding our present environment. It may be studied for its practical value in the business world, as it can help the businessman better understand the internal and external factors affecting his business operations and can aid him in making more prudent business decisions. Economics also may be studied to improve our citizenship. In this respect it will give us a better understanding of current political and social issues.

A LOOK AHEAD

The remainder of this book is devoted to the many aspects of economic theory and policy. An overview of the material that lies ahead will provide both a perspective of how each part fits into the total picture as well as an idea of the path we shall follow through the analysis of economic activity.

We begin with the structure of the American economy and its three basic sectors: consumers, business firms, and government. The remainder of Part One shows how each sector performs its role in the circular flow of income. Proper insight into the interaction among these sectors is essential to an understanding of both macroeconomics and microeconomics.

Our first excursion into economic theory proper begins with macroeconomics. In Part Two the determinants of aggregate production, national income, and total employment in the economy are discussed. Part Three emphasizes the function of money in an exchange economy and the way in which changes in the total volume of money affect economic activity. The economic theory contained in Parts Two and Three is then applied and extended in Part Four to explain the relationship between economic activity and fiscal policy. The influence of government spending and taxation upon income and employment is explored in Part Five. Finally, the last section of macroeconomics, Part Six, applies these concepts and theories to the critical issues of long-run economic growth in the American economy.

Parts Seven, Eight, and Nine are concerned with microeconomics. Stress is placed upon output and employment in particular firms and industries, the determinants of product prices and resource prices, and the distribution of national income. Different types of industrial organization are analyzed, such as competitive industries and monopolies. These various concepts and theories are then applied to important domestic problems in Part Ten.

Through Part Ten our study is centered upon a single nation. In Part Eleven both macroeconomic and microeconomic principles are applied to international trade and finance. Finally, Part Twelve takes a very broad perspective in order to accomplish two purposes: It compares different economic systems—capitalism, socialism, and communism—in both technologically advanced nations and in underdeveloped nations; and, also, it opens speculations about prospects for the future.

SUMMARY

1. Economics is concerned with the allocation of scarce means among alternative wants, both the allocation of scarce productive resources among alternative employments and the allocation of produced goods and services among users or consumers.

2. The basic problems of scarcity and allocation are encountered by every society. Societies differ in the ways they organize production and consumption in order to cope with the same basic problems.

3. The study of economics may be divided into two branches: positive economics deals with "what is," and normative economics considers "what ought to be."

4. Economics is a science and as such has certain laws and principles. Its laws and principles, how-ever, usually are not universal in nature. As a result, there is room for differences of opinion and judgment in economic decision making.

5. Economics is related in various ways to many other disciplines, such as political science, psychology, sociology, mathematics, and philosophy.

6. Economics employs several different methods for obtaining knowledge, such as the scientific and descriptive methods. The quantitative method, a special technique of the scientific method, deserves special mention as a tool of economics.

7. Theoretical models are frequently used in economic analysis. Principles and policies developed therefrom serve as a basis for the formulation of economic policies.

NEW TERMS

Economics, *p. 4*
Scarcity, *p. 4*
Allocation, *p. 5*
Economic functions, *p. 6*
Positive economics, *p. 7*
Normative economics, *p. 8*
Scientific method, *p. 10*
Descriptive method, *p. 12*
Institutional approach, *p. 12*

Quantitative method, *p. 12*
Descriptive statistics, *p. 13*
Analytical statistics, *p. 13*
Econometrics, *p. 13*
Model building, *p. 14*
Economic analysis, *p. 14*
Microeconomics, *p. 15*
Macroeconomics, *p. 15*
Economic policy, *p. 15*

QUESTIONS FOR DISCUSSION AND ANALYSIS

1. Explain how you engage in economizing your income, your time, and your energy.

2. What are the basic functions performed by any economy? How do different societies perform these functions?

3. What would you consider to be three major economic issues of the present day? Why?

4. Explain how poverty is an economic, a social, and a political problem.

5. In what manner will economic considerations influence the way you will vote in the next presidential election?

6. Economics is referred to as a science. Do you agree that it should be? Why or why not?

7. Distinguish between the scientific method and the institutional approach to the study of economics. Give an example of each.

8. Show how a model can be used to explain the fundamentals of a rather complicated process, such as that by which an internal combustion engine or a Wankel (rotary) engine drives an automobile. Can models be used in the study of economics?

SUGGESTED READINGS

Economic Education in the Schools. New York: Committee for Economic Development, 1961.

Gill, Richard. *Economic Development Past and Present.* Englewood Cliffs, N.J.: Prentice-Hall, Inc., 1967.

Heilbroner, Robert L. *The Making of Economic Society*, 4th ed. Englewood Cliffs, N.J.: Prentice-Hall, Inc., 1972.

Heilbroner, Robert L., and Arthur M. Ford. *Is Economics Relevant?* Pacific Palisades, Calif.: Goodyear Publishing Co., Inc., 1971.

Keynes, John Neville. *The Scope and Method of Political Economy*, 4th ed. Clifton, N.J.: Augustus M. Kelley, Publishers, 1917.

Parsons, S. A. *How to Find Out About Economics.* Elmsford, N.Y.: Pergamon Press, Inc., 1973.

Robbins, Lionel Charles. *Essay on Nature and Significance of Economic Science*, 2d ed. New York: The Macmillan Company, 1948.

2

Our Economic System

PREVIEW In this chapter we focus on our own private enterprise, or so-called capitalistic, economy, especially as it contrasts to socialism or communism. The primary goals of the American economy are discussed. In addition, we bring to the fore several new economic goals, along with the problems and challenges they present.

We have seen that basic economic principles apply to any type of economic system. Questions of what to produce, how much, and what method to adopt in allocating goods and services are confronted by any society; but the questions are answered in different ways. We shall first consider fundamental principles and policies in terms of the American economy. Analysis of an economic environment with which you are already familiar will facilitate the later comparison of various types of economic systems.

FREE ENTERPRISE CAPITALISM

A *free enterprise system* is distinguished from other types of economic systems by the fact that the decisions as to what and how much to produce, and the manner in which goods and services are to be allocated, are made by the free actions of individuals and firms in the economy. Both socialism and communism, on the other hand, advocate a considerable degree of government direction and control of the production and distribution functions of their economies.

Under our American *capitalistic system*, capital goods are owned and used primarily by individuals and firms in the economy rather than by governmental agencies. This capital may be in the form of machinery, equipment, and buildings, or it may be represented by money that can be used to purchase these capital goods. The institution of private property is essential to a free enterprise capitalistic system. This implies more than the ownership of real estate. It means that individuals not only have the right to own, use, or sell machinery, equipment, and buildings, but they also have the right to the ownership of the fruits of their productivity. Thus, when the farmer grows cotton on his land with the use of his labor and capital, the cotton becomes his property and he can dispose of it as he sees fit. In a similar fashion, a firm that produces shoes is entitled to the ownership of the shoes and can sell them if it desires. After compensating the owners of the other resources that have contributed to the production of the shoes, the firm is entitled to what is left of the total revenue. This residual return is called profit, and profit is the incentive for obtaining and using capital goods to produce goods and services.

The Profit Incentive

Under the free enterprise system an individual may offer his services to someone else in exchange for a wage payment, let someone use his land in exchange for rent, or lend his money to another in exchange for an interest payment. On the other hand, instead of selling his productive services to another, he can combine several factors of production in order to produce goods and sell them at a profit. But to operate a business, he must produce goods or services that people want and must offer them at a price they are willing to pay. The farmer who grows cotton and sells it at a profit is benefiting not only himself but also the community by supplying a basic commodity that is needed or desired. Likewise, the shoe producer is satisfying people's wants for shoes in addition to making a profit for himself. Since the cotton grower or shoe producer may use the labor, land, and capital of others, he provides jobs and income for other members of the community. Thus, in a model situation the producer, in the process of using his property to make a profit, will increase the well-being of his fellowmen. To be successful, he must satisfy consumer demand. In some situations, however, he may suffer a loss or may exploit his fellowmen by supplying them with an inferior product or by underpaying the factors of production he utilizes.

In the operation of our economic system, the ultimate use of our manpower and resources and the allocation of goods and services are determined primarily by consumer demand. Individuals express their demand in the prices they are willing to pay. Usually the stronger the demand, other things being equal, the higher the price that consumers will pay for particular goods and services. In an effort to make a profit, businessmen cater to consumer demand. Through the prices we are willing to pay as consumers, businesses obtain the revenue necessary to purchase the manpower, resources, and capital goods necessary for producing the goods and services that are demanded. The opportunity to make profits serves as an incentive for businesses to produce these goods and services.

If the demand for a particular commodity is strong enough, it will be produced. Sometimes, however, there is such a large demand for total goods and services that we do not have sufficient manpower and capital to produce all of them. What, then, is produced? Once again, in a model system it is the consumers who decide. The firms and industries with the strongest demand for their products will have the revenues necessary to bid relatively scarce productive agents away from other uses. If consumer demand for a particular commodity is weak and the price offer is so low that it does not permit sufficient profit to the producer, few resources will be devoted to its production.

Competition

Private enterprise capitalism, resting as it does on the institution of private property and on the profit incentive, relies upon *competition* to make the system function. Business firms vie for shares of the consumer's dollar. In the markets for productive resources, they compete for scarce resources. In a centralized economy, production quotas are assigned to firms by a political leader or a planning committee. Similarly, resources are directed to employment in various industries. When allocation decisions are decentralized, however, competition serves to regulate the volume of output and the allocation of resources.

If competition is effective, the economy functions efficiently without an overseer. Through competition consumers are protected against the marketing of shoddy products and the charging of exorbitant prices. The prospect that rival firms will offer a better product at the same price or a comparable product at a lower price forces each firm to maintain quality and restrict price increases. Resource owners are protected against exploitation by the opportunity of alternative employments made available by competitive firms. The possibility open to the resource owner of selling resource services to the highest bidder prevents any one firm from keeping resources in its own employ at depressed prices. In this way effective competition regulates the power of business firms, preventing any one from dominating the market. Each firm is free to pursue its own profit without direct concern for the overall allocation of resources and products in the economy. Yet the impersonal force of competition assures the regulation of production and the flow of resources toward the most efficient firms that can afford to offer the highest prices for their services.

Of course, competition is not always effective, and it is seldom perfect. Sometimes business firms may be able to exclude others from the industry and thereby exercise almost unlimited control over price, industry output, and employment conditions. When this happens, it is deemed the responsibility of government to restore competitive conditions. Rather than taking control of the industry or assuming ownership of the means of production, the central political authority is expected to impose legal sanctions against restraint of competition or abuses that are defended in the name of competition.

The guiding principle of competitive capitalism is that privately owned business firms should produce the goods and services wanted by consumers in the quantities they wish to consume. In order that firms may satisfy consumer wants by pursuing the immediate goal of profit, competition is relied upon as a mechanism for regulating trade. Only where it is believed that competition cannot be made to work effectively—such as postal services, police and fire protection, and public utilities—does the government operate or control production. Otherwise the government is expected to create and enforce laws which assure that optimal conditions of competition will prevail.

Price as a Rationing Mechanism

Although consumer demand is the primary determinant of what and how much is produced, the decisions are by no means made unilaterally by consumers. Supply also has an influence on the price of commodities and therefore on the determination of what and how much is to be produced. Because of a shortage in the supply of particular resources (or *factors of production* as they are sometimes called), consumers may have to pay a higher price than they desire in order to obtain a particular good. Then they will have to pay the price or go without it. In a free market economy price serves as a rationing mechanism to decide who among the consumers will receive the particular good. It will be those who are willing and able to pay the highest price.

In determining what and how much to produce, our American capitalistic system works in a democratic manner based upon dollar votes. Other things being equal, the use of resources and manpower is determined by the total number of dollars spent on particular goods and services. Thus, the more dollars an individual or group accumulates in some manner or other, the greater the potential influence for determining what is to be produced. Although this is a democratic process according to dollar votes, it is not necessarily democratic as to personal preferences. In fact, since those with the most dollars have the most votes, inequities may develop. If certain individuals or groups acquire an excessive number of dollars, it could be detrimental to the economy in general as well as to other individuals in particular. For example, large amounts of dollars hoarded rather than being spent or invested could lead to a decrease in business activity and result in unemployment and loss of income for workers and lower profits for business. Even when all dollars are spent, one can envision a situation in which an economy might be producing a great number of palatial homes, high-priced cars, and yachts, while the community is deprived of much needed low-cost housing. There might be much spending on entertainment and on frivolities in the economy in general while some families are short on basic necessities and modern conveniences.

Determination of Income

Individuals through consumer demand not only determine what and how much is produced in the economy, but they also determine in part the incomes paid to the various factors of production in the form of wages, rent, interest, and profits. Revenue from the sale of commodities provides businesses with the means by which they can obtain labor, land, and capital in order to produce the goods demanded. The payment of income to the owners of these factors or resources serves as their means to purchase a certain portion of the goods and services produced by the economy. Although many other things (such as the productivity of the factor of production, its supply, government regulations, the presence or absence of a labor union and other institutional forces) have a direct bearing on the payment of income to each of the various factors, the ultimate source of income payments to the factors of production is generally the revenue from consumer demand. In a model system each factor is remunerated according to its economic contribution toward the product being made. In turn, its contribution is measured by the price that the firm was willing to pay for it, which in turn would be limited by consumer demand. Thus, our strong demand for automobiles is, in part, the reason why auto workers have historically been among the highest paid workers in the world. The income of a factor of production is affected, on the other hand, by its productivity and scarcity. If the supply of a particular type of skilled labor is limited, such workers will be able to command a higher compensation for their services than will unskilled workers.

COMMAND ECONOMIES

In our free enterprise capitalistic system, decision making is exercised by individuals and business firms in the economy. It must be remembered, however, that there are other economic systems throughout the world. Not all peoples, including some in the United States, are sold on the advantages of free enterprise capitalism. Many feel that its disadvantages, such as recurring recessions, existence of certain exploitative monopolies, wasteful use of resources in several respects, and the unequal distribution of property and income, far exceed its advantages. As a consequence, in some nations the people prefer some form of economy other than free enterprise capitalism. In other nations leaders prefer a more centralized type of economy because it is easier to exercise dictatorial control. Thus, in many parts of the world various forms of socialism, fascism, and communism exist. In contrast to exchange or market economies, these might be called *command economies*.

Socialism

Socialism is an economic system in which the means of production are controlled or regulated by the government. In such an economy capital does exist, and it is responsible for a large part of the total output of the nation. In fact, most socialistic systems stress the importance of capital formation as a means of improving production in the future. In a socialistic economy, however, unlike a free enterprise system, capital is generally owned or regulated by the government instead of by individuals and business firms. In total socialism the government not only owns but also operates the industries. In partial socialism the government owns and operates some industries, especially the basic industries, leaving the others to private enterprise. Consequently, private property exists in a socialistic economy to a greater or lesser extent, depending on the degrees of state ownership and control. Various degrees of socialism exist throughout the world, such as those in Egypt, Burma, Great Britain, Sweden, and Denmark.

Communism

Communism is a political-economic ideology that implies socialism for the economic system and totalitarianism in the political sphere with the individual subservient to the state. Communism as established in the Soviet Union is nearly complete socialism. Private property as we know it does not exist, and industrial production is carried on through approximately 200,000 large and small state enterprises, each with a government-appointed manager. In addition, in the Soviet economy there are 36,000 collective farms compared to 2.8 million privately owned farms in the United States. The number of collective farms has been reduced substantially in the past decade as a result of consolidation. Large-scale units now average nearly 17,000 acres. In the collective farm the buildings and equipment are owned jointly or collectively by the many families living on the farm, but production is supervised by the state. There are also 12,700 state farms owned and operated directly by the government.

Total and detailed production plans for the Soviet economy are formulated by a Central Planning Commission (Gosplan) in Moscow. After being forwarded to the Council of Ministers for their approval, these plans are implemented at the industry and enterprise level. In this system the plant manager must produce what is assigned to him, workers do not have complete freedom to move from one job to another, and consumers must buy the goods offered at retail outlets or go without. Only recently have consumer desires been given direct consideration. In fact, there is frequently a shortage of consumer goods and services because the Central Planning Commission puts great stress on capital formation, which currently has been amounting to 20 to 25 percent of total production compared to approximately 15 to 20 percent in the United States.

Actually, the American and Soviet economies differ not so much in economic institutions but in the degree to which economic decisions are made arbitrarily by the state or the Central Planning Commission. In the Russian economy only minor decisions are made by persons other than the planners. Decisions regarding what is to be produced, how much is to be produced, and who gets what, historically have been made by state agencies with reference to a single central plan.

During the later half of the 1960s, however, the Soviet planners and economists adopted, in part, a profit and flexible pricing system as a means of eliminating waste and inefficiencies in the Soviet economy. Under the recently adopted profit reform system, prices fluctuate with consumer demand, and the efficiency of some enterprise is measured by its profit. Bonuses, both positive and negative, for managers of the limited number of state-owned enterprises operating under the profit reform system are based on profit rather than on the production quota system. Soviet planners approved of the experimentation of the profit system by some of its enterprises in 1964. Subsequently they have extended the profit concept to more of their enterprises. They are by no means, however, ready to adopt Western style capitalism. Under the Soviet reform, profits serve as a measure of efficiency for the business enterprise; but all of the profits are subject to control by the state.[1]

GOALS OF THE AMERICAN ECONOMY

Various forms of government control over the economy have been exercised in many countries. In Turkey, for example, profit margins are limited; in Norway much government control of prices, wages, and profits exists; in Bolivia the tin mines have been nationalized; in Mainland China communes have been established; in Cuba the government has seized many industries and firms; and even in Britain eight basic industries have been nationalized at one time or another. In fact, outside the United States and Canada free enterprise capitalism as we know it is rather rare. Even in these two countries there has been an increasing amount of government control in the past several decades.

What is the future of American capitalism? Will it be able to win acceptance over other economic systems in the new nations that are being formed? Will the underdeveloped nations throughout the world move toward free enterprise or socialism in their search for economic growth. Will capitalism

[1] See Chapter 46 for a more detailed discussion of the Soviet economy.

be able to withstand the internal forces which are working to change our economic system? Or will it be modified in the future? The answers to these questions may very well depend not only on how smoothly the free enterprise system functions but also on how well it satisfies the people by attaining certain major goals or objectives.

Primary Goals

Although there may be differences of opinion as to what some of the goals of the American economy should be, let us look at the more important or generally accepted goals. First, there are three broad, primary domestic goals that the economy seeks to attain: (1) full employment, (2) stable prices, and (3) economic growth.

Full Employment. We have a labor force of 91 million people who are either employed or are seeking employment. It is generally conceded that there will always exist a certain amount of *frictional unemployment* as a result of individuals quitting their jobs, being discharged, and not being able to find jobs that fit their qualifications. The amount of frictional unemployment is usually considered to be about 4 percent of the labor force. Thus, we consider the economy to be in a state of *full employment* for all practical purposes when 4 percent or less of the labor force is unemployed. In order to have full employment, it is implicit that we have stable economic activity at a high level.

The average worker or businessman does not cherish a situation that gives him an abundance of income in some years and a dearth of goods, services, and income in others. Planning is much easier, business more fruitful, and employees more content under conditions of stability at high levels of business activity. On the other hand, intense fluctuations in production, employment, and income can discourage business enterprise, reduce worker initiative, and retard economic growth. The Employment Act of 1946, with its directive for the government to use measures at its disposal to create conditions favorable to a high level of employment, certainly makes full employment a decided goal for our economy.

Not only is it desirable to hold unemployment to a minimum, but it also is economical to reduce underemployment. What is the difference between unemployment and underemployment? *Unemployment* refers to the number of workers not employed, whereas underemployment refers to the utilization of the workers. *Underemployment* occurs when a worker is employed but is not working to his full capacity. It is possible for the economy to be in a state of full employment and yet be underemployed. Such would be the case if large numbers of workers were on jobs that did not require their full skill or productivity. For example, situations are found in which engineers are doing clerical work, artists are painting signs, mechanics are sweeping floors, or skilled secretaries are doing filing work. Annually many individuals are trained for skilled jobs but fail to find job openings. Often college graduates with tremendous potential never reach their full productive capacity. Although much has been done to prevent and to eliminate unemployment, very little has been done on a nationwide scale to reduce underemployment.

Stable Prices. Individuals who work hard and save a portion of their income for future use do not like to see the purchasing power of their savings depreciate. Others who put money into annuities, insurance policies, and pension plans do not like to have the value of these funds deteriorate as a result of substantial increases in prices over a period of time. It is difficult for a firm to plan pension funds for employees or for workers to plan for their old age if there is uncertainty about the value of the income to be received upon retirement.

If an economy is to operate smoothly, therefore, there must be a certain amount of price stability. This fact has become more apparent since the end of World War II. In the 20-year period, 1939-1958, prices more than doubled. In the 1940s and the 1950s, inflation replaced unemployment as the primary economic problem of the day. At that time many economists suggested that price stability be made a dual objective (along with a high level of employment) of the Employment Act of 1946.

Between 1958 and 1965, concern about price stability and inflation lessened considerably. During this period, consumer prices increased less than 1.5 percent annually compared to the 5 percent average annual increase in 1939-1958; and the wholesale price index remained practically stable. Consequently, problems other than inflation—such as nagging unemployment, the gold outflow, and the economic growth rate—occupied the minds of economists and others. Since 1966, however, prices have increased again at an average annual rate of 5 percent, and inflation has been in the forefront.

Economic Growth. Once a level of prosperity has been reached, it is not enough to maintain the existing levels of employment and production; we must continue to increase production if we are to prevent unemployment from increasing. The reason for this is twofold. First, we add more than 1.5 million workers annually to our labor force. This means that we must produce more if we are to have jobs for these new entrants coming into the labor force. Second, the productivity of the labor force increases about 3 percent per year. Because of this rise in productivity, the same level of output can be produced with fewer and fewer workers as the years pass, and unemployment will result unless compensating forces take place. Thus, if we merely try to maintain a certain level of output instead of increasing it, we have two forces tending toward unemployment.

Experience indicates, for example, that with a real growth rate of 3 percent or less, the American economy suffers from nagging unemployment and limited gains in per capita output and income. Unemployment at the end of 1969, for example, was 2.8 million, or 3.5 percent of the labor force. But by the end of 1970, unemployment was 4.1 million, or 4.9 percent of the civilian labor force. This occurred simply because the real output of goods and services, instead of growing, declined by a fraction of a percent in 1970. Consequently, we failed to absorb all the new entrants into the labor force plus some of those who were displaced because of technological development and automation. Furthermore, a sizeable number of workers withdrew from the labor force because they were unable to find work.

Reduced unemployment and substantial per capita gains, however, seem to occur when the economic growth rate exceeds 4 percent. In 1973, for example, the GNP in real terms grew at a rate of nearly 6 percent, and unemployment declined from 5.6 percent to 4.9 percent, as shown in Table 2-1. The potential annual growth rate of the American economy is currently 4.5 percent, reflecting a 1.5 to 2.0 percent increase in available man-hours and a 2.5 to 3.0 percent rise in output per man-hour. Unfortunately while output rose 13 percent in the five-year period from 1966 to 1971, unemployment climbed from 2.9 million, or 3.8 percent, to 5.0 million, or 5.9 percent. In short, the economy grew during the period, but it did not grow sufficiently to maintain what is usually considered to be a fully employed economy.

TABLE 2-1

PRODUCTION, EMPLOYMENT, AND UNEMPLOYMENT

1965-1973

Year	Total Production * (Billions)	GNP Growth Rate	Civilian Labor Force (Millions)	Employ- ment (Millions)	Unemploy- ment (Millions)	Rate of Unemployment
1965	$618	—	74.5	71.1	3.4	4.5%
1966	$658	6.5%	75.8	72.9	2.9	3.8%
1967	$675	2.6%	77.3	74.4	3.0	3.8%
1968	$707	4.7%	78.7	75.9	2.8	3.6%
1969	$726	2.7%	80.7	77.9	2.8	3.5%
1970	$722	−0.6%	82.7	78.6	4.1	4.9%
1971	$745	3.2%	84.1	79.1	5.0	5.9%
1972	$791	6.2%	86.5	81.7	4.8	5.6%
1973	$837	5.8%	88.7	84.4	4.3	4.9%

SOURCE: *Economic Report of the President*, 1974.

* Total Production (GNP) in 1958 constant dollars.

The growth rate has become an important competitive factor in the struggle between free enterprise capitalism and communism in the underdeveloped nations throughout the world. Since the Soviet Union and Mainland China both claim a greater economic growth rate than the

United States or other capitalistic nations, the Communists use this as a selling point for the adoption of their system. It must be pointed out, however, that their greater growth rate results in large part from the fact that their current levels of economic activity are relatively low. Thus, any substantial absolute increase appears to be a rather large percentage increase. In the United States, where the absolute level of production is nearly three times greater than that of Soviet Russia, a given absolute increase in production will naturally be a smaller percentage increase than it would be in a smaller economy. Whether the communistic nations can maintain their current rates of growth when they reach high levels of economic activity remains to be seen. Frequently in a newly developed nation it is easier to make quick progress by dictatorial economic methods than it is by relying on the free forces of private enterprise. As a result, if the underdeveloped nations are going to accept free enterprise capitalism, they must be sold on its long-run merits.

If the American free enterprise capitalistic system is to continue to satisfy the public need for goods and services in the future, if it is to provide ample income and employment, if it is to prove its superiority over other economic systems, and if it is to provide for adequate national defense in the future, it must achieve the growth objective. Whether an average growth rate of 4 percent is adequate or whether we should have a 4.5 or 5 percent annual growth rate is a debatable question. If the greater rates are desired, should government participation, either directly or indirectly, be used to attain the desired rate of economic growth?

Supplementary Goals

In addition to the three major goals of the economy, several supplementary goals deserve attention. These include: (1) greater equality of opportunity; (2) a rising level of living; (3) equitable distribution of income; (4) improved economic security; (5) a proper balance between private and social production; and (6) economic freedom.

Greater Equality of Opportunity. Our economy should provide greater equality of economic opportunity to all its citizens regardless of race, color, sex, or creed. This includes the opportunity for higher education, freedom in the choice of occupation, no undue restrictions on the right to engage in a business, and an opportunity to assume a position of public office in our economy. It implies freedom from discrimination in education, employment, business, and government.

Rising Level of Living. With the expected growth in our economy, a rising level of living becomes a logical goal. As long as productivity continues to increase faster than the rate of population, per capita real income will increase and a higher level of living is possible. This can take the form of an increase in purchasing power, a reduction in working hours, or a combination of both. The benefits of increased productivity ideally can be channeled in three directions—toward lower prices for the consumer, higher wages for the worker, and greater profits for business.

Equity in the Distribution of Income. Although perfect equality in the distribution of income is not considered necessary or desirable, a further raising of the lower levels of income is desirable. In spite of the fact that we have the highest per capita personal income of any major nation in the world, many families still live on minimum incomes. In the United States affluence and poverty exist side by side. According to standards established by the Council of Economic Advisers for President Lyndon Johnson's 1964 *Economic Report*, nearly one fifth of our American families were poor. Nearly one half of all nonwhites lived in poverty according to the Council's classification. Forty percent of all farm families were poor. Poverty is related to a lack of education insofar as 60 percent of the heads of all poor families had only grade school educations. From a geographic point of view, less than half of the poor were in the South; but a southerner's chance of being poor was roughly twice that of a person living elsewhere in the nation.

President Johnson made the elimination of poverty a national goal, and the Economic Opportunity Act passed by Congress in 1964 provided the Administration with nearly a billion dollars annually in financial support to help wage its "war on poverty." It should be mentioned, however, that normal growth and development in the economy is reducing poverty somewhat. The incidence of family poverty has been reduced from more than 30 percent in the 1920s to 26 percent in 1947 and down to less than 15 percent by 1974.

Economic Security. With growing productivity and a better understanding of our economic system, more security can be provided by our economy. The worker desires security against unemployment, primarily through steady employment. If this is not forthcoming, however, improvement in state unemployment compensation programs and private industrial supplementary unemployment benefits will help ease the burden of unemployment. Improvement in federal old-age and survivors benefits has been a help to the older generation. Medical care for the aged became an important goal during the 1960s, and the concept of a guaranteed annual income has become a major economic issue of the 1970s. Also, a program of some type is needed to make use of the skills, labor, and energy of our senior citizens. This would contribute to our total productivity and give them a greater sense of responsibility and usefulness to society.

Proper Balance Between Private and Social Production. It is important that the economy continue to satisfy consumer demand. Even though production should be in accordance with consumer demand, a certain amount of social production is required in the economy. This is generally attained through government spending. We need food, clothing, shelter, automobiles, and entertainment; but we also need schools, police protection, parks, medical care, and roads. As the economy expands, the need for social production will increase. Whether we are channeling a sufficient amount of our production in this direction is a current and controversial question. Exactly what the balance between the two should be now and in the future will continue to be an important issue in the years to come.

Economic Freedom. In considering other goals for the economy, we must not lose sight of one of our most important goals—the preservation of economic freedom. The individual desires freedom in the choice of a job or business, freedom to spend or to save his money, freedom to buy from one seller rather than another, and freedom to support or to oppose various economic and political measures. In addition, the individual seeks freedom from want and insecurity. At times he may decide to sacrifice a bit of his freedom in exchange for a certain amount of security. Such is the case when he gives up complete freedom to spend all his income because he must pay Social Security taxes. It must be remembered also that individual freedom must be restricted to a certain degree in order to protect the freedom of all.

CHANGING ECONOMIC GOALS AND EMERGING PROBLEMS

As emphasized in this chapter, during the past few decades considerable emphasis has been placed on the achievement of our primary domestic economic goals of full employment, stable prices, and a healthy rate of economic growth. Coming out of the prolonged depression of the 1930s, with its chronic unemployment, followed by World War II, which caused severe shortages of consumer goods and services, it was appropriate to stress such economic goals as maximum production, maximum employment, and maximum purchasing power. The desire for steady jobs, good wages, economic security, stable prices, and an abundance of goods and services was quite natural. By and large, during the 1950s and the 1960s, the economy proved capable of attaining these goals. Indeed, continuing efforts will be made to achieve and even surpass these goals in order to bring unemployment below the 4 percent level, accelerate the potential rate of economic growth, and perhaps adopt some form of an "incomes policy" as a means of assuring stable prices. Nevertheless, today these goals in large part are taken for granted. Consequently, citizens of our society, although not ignoring these primary goals, are now placing more emphasis on the supplementary goals of the economy. The elimination of poverty, a proper balance between private and social production, the rebuilding of our cities, the preservation of our natural environment, and improvement in the quality of life are taking on even more importance. In addition, many citizens are seeking fresh solutions to existing economic and social problems, learning how to handle new problems that are arising, and adopting policies to prevent the occurrence of others that may be destined for the future.

CHALLENGE OF THE FUTURE

Not long ago a nonpartisan, nongovernmental Commission on National Goals studied American needs and formulated national goals for the future. Although there were many differences among the committee members on various points, they arrived at a set of major goals for America and Americans. Of the 15 goals suggested, all but three were economic or socioeconomic in nature. The primary and supplementary goals mentioned heretofore were included, as well as a few others such as urban renewal, education, health and welfare, technological efficiency, free trade, and national defense.

The proposals of the Commission on National Goals were addressed to us as citizens, rather than to the President or to Congress. They took the form of a challenge in the hope that every American would take part in the implementation of our national goals on an individual and national basis. "Our enduring aim," according to the Commission, "is to build a nation and help build a world in which every human being shall be free to develop his capacities to the fullest." During the past several years, definite progress has been made toward the ultimate attainment of many of these goals.

SUMMARY

1. American capitalism implies the right of individuals and firms to own, to use, and to benefit from the use of capital, or producer, goods.
2. In a free enterprise competitive system decisions as to what to pro-

duce, how much to produce, whether to produce for the present or the future, and how to distribute production are determined primarily by individuals and business firms.
3. Profit acts as an incentive for

firms to undertake the production of goods and services for the satisfaction of consumer demand.

4. Incomes to the various factors of production in the form of wages, rent, interest, and profit are determined indirectly in large part by consumer demand.

5. In a socialistic or communistic economy the decisions of what and how much to produce are made in varying degrees by the government.

6. In addition to the major goals of the American economy, such as full employment, stable prices, and economic growth, there are a number of important supplementary goals.

NEW TERMS

Free enterprise system, *p. 19*
Capitalistic system, *p. 19*
Competition, *p. 21*
Factors of production, *p. 22*
Command economies, *p. 23*
Socialism, *p. 24*

Communism, *p. 24*
Frictional unemployment, *p. 26*
Full employment, *p. 26*
Unemployment, *p. 26*
Underemployment, *p. 26*

QUESTIONS FOR DISCUSSION AND ANALYSIS

1. Briefly, if you were asked by a foreigner to explain American capitalism, how would you do so?

2. How are decisions made in the American economy regarding what and how much to produce? How does the existence of a monopoly in business or the presence of a labor union affect this decision-making process?

3. If a proprietor tells you that he is in business "strictly for the profit," how would you explain the broader role of his firm in the economy?

4. Exactly how does consumer demand influence the determination of income for the various factors of production?

5. Explain the major difference between the American and Soviet economies. How are economic decisions made in the Soviet Union?

6. Do you think our American economy is "creeping" toward socialism? Why or why not?

7. Would you give preference to any of our three major economic goals? Why or why not?

8. What role do you think the government should take regarding the attainment of our economic goals?

9. What does equality of opportunity mean? Does it have any relation to economic security?

10. Is there a conflict between economic freedom and greater equality in the distribution of income? Why or why not?

SUGGESTED READINGS

Cole, Charles L. *The Economic Fabric of Society.* New York: Harcourt Brace Jovanovich, Inc., 1969.

Drucker, Peter F. *Technology, Management and Society.* New York: Harper & Row, Publishers, 1970.

Friedman, Milton. *Capitalism and Freedom.* Chicago: University of Chicago Press, 1962.

Goals for Americans, The Report of the President's Commission on National Goals. Englewood Cliffs, N.J.: Prentice-Hall, Inc., 1960.

Heilbroner, Robert L. *Between Capitalism and Socialism.* New York: Random House, Inc., 1970.

Kelso, Louis O., and Mortimer J. Adler. *Capitalist Manifesto.* New York: Random House, Inc., 1958.

Oxenfeldt, Alfred A. *Economic Systems in Action.* New York: Holt, Rinehart and Winston, Inc., 1957. Chapters 1 and 2.

Petit, Thomas A. *Freedom in the American Economy.* Homewood, Ill.: Richard D. Irwin, Inc., 1964.

Robinson, Marshall A., Herbert C. Morton, and James D. Calderwell. *An Introduction to Economic Reasoning*, 3d ed. Washington: The Brookings Institution, 1967. Chapter 1.

Stans, Maurice H. *To 1990—A Long Look Ahead.* Washington: Department of Commerce, 1970.

3

Inputs, Outputs, and Payoffs

PREVIEW   Households want goods and services to consume. Business firms are the intermediaries that organize resources (inputs) to produce these goods and services (output). Payments by firms to the owners of resources (payoffs) in the form of wages, interest, rents, and profits constitute household income. This income is used to purchase the output of goods and services. Thus, a circular flow is established and maintained.

Recently the giant computer in the Department of Commerce, which registers the ever-changing population in the United States, was on view for the television audience. Had they so wished, the viewers could have noted the exact second when the population of this country reached 212 million. One minute later, however, several more persons were added to the total. By the end of the year, the births in the United States alone were reported to be around 3.5 million. This is only a small part, however, of the population growth which is worldwide. In many other countries the growth rate is far greater than it is in the United States, and if these rates continue, the world's population will increase sixfold within a century!

What is the impact of population growth on economic development? An expanding population results in an ever-increasing demand for the raw materials of nature. This demand tends to impoverish the world and makes economic growth more difficult. Some economists contend that rapid population growth stimulates economic progress, but such studies as have been made in the underdeveloped countries do not support this claim. For economic growth to take place, an increase in the amount of *production per unit of human labor* must be achieved.

THE MACHINE ANALOGY

The economy can be viewed as a giant productive machine. Inputs of productive resources are fed into one end. The machine rattles and whirs as the various resources are combined and put to work. From the other end of the machine, a flow of final goods and services emerges. The process of production, stripped conceptually to its bare essentials, is a continuous flow of physical inputs generating a continuous flow of physical output.

The magnitude and quality of the output flow is determined in part by the magnitude and quality of the input flow. Meager inputs can hardly be expected to result in abundant output. However, the volume of output is also affected by the efficiency with which resources are combined and production carried on. One of the most important questions in economics is, "What determines the ratio of output to input?" This ratio is a measure of economic well-being. The greater the output that can be attained, the more goods and services are available for consumption by the population. In physical terms, the ratio of output to input can be conceived of as the payoff—the return or prize—for efficient economic organization.

In an exchange or market economy, as we have seen, resources are owned by individuals and sold to business firms. The prices received by resource owners and the quantities of input they supply determine the money income they receive. Since this money income is used to purchase the output generated by the productive machine, money income per person may be regarded as the payoff for effort measured in money terms. The higher the per capita income, or average income per person, the greater the economic well-being of society.

In the remainder of this chapter, we shall explore in greater detail the nature of production, the characteristics of productive inputs, and the relation of production to income.

THE NATURE OF PRODUCTION

It is possible to obtain the material things we want from only two sources. One of these sources is the storehouse of nature from which we can with little or no effort obtain a few things—air, sunshine, and possibly some minor items of food. The other source is the stock of goods that has been created by the application of labor to certain natural resources, such as the soil and mineral deposits. Nonmaterial goods or services—police protection and medical advice, for example—are also made available only by the expenditure of human effort.

The production of most kinds of goods involves the use of natural resources, physical and mental labor, and machines and tools—all of which exist in limited quantities. For this reason, there is need for economy in the utilization of these factors of production. If petroleum, coal, timber, and labor are wasted and if machines in factories are impaired by careless use, the supplies of certain kinds of goods will be smaller than they might be and prices will be higher. On the other hand, if goods are produced efficiently and without needless waste, almost everyone can have more of the things he wants.

Indeed, there is a direct relation between physical production and the incomes we receive in the form of money. Expenditures by households on goods and services are the sales receipts of business firms. Firms use the money from sales to carry on production. That is, these same funds provide money incomes to the owners of the resources engaged in production (in the form of wages, rent, interest, and profit). Money income earned in the productive process is then used to purchase the goods and services that resources help to produce.

Goods and Services

Chapter 1 emphasized the fact that goods and services are scarce relative to our wants. This scarcity is traceable in turn to the relative scarcity of resources or factors of production required to produce goods and services. If the productive process is to be fully understood, it will be helpful to dwell a while upon the meaning of goods and services and upon the meaning of production.

Sometimes economists use the term "goods" as a short expression intended to include both goods and services. Goods in the more specific sense include material objects such as eggs, clothes, false teeth, and perfume. No less important, however, both from the viewpoint of human wants and from the viewpoint that resources must be used to produce them, are intangible services. Examples are haircuts, transportation, symphony concerts, education, and legal counseling. When the shorter term "good" is used hereafter, it will be interpreted to mean both types of want-satisfying objects, whether material or intangible.

A *good* is anything that has the power to satisfy a want. Any useful thing that exists in quantities sufficient for all who desire it and that can be obtained practically without any effort is a *free good*. Under most conditions air and sunshine are free goods. On the other hand, any useful thing that is scarce or that can be obtained only by effort or expense is an *economic good*. Most of the things that we desire are economic goods. In some regions of the earth, such as the tropics, the variety and the quantity of free goods are sufficient to maintain life on a simple level. Once the wants of the people increase beyond mere subsistence even in these regions, however, labor becomes necessary to provide the desired goods.

Economic goods are also classified as consumer and producer goods. *Consumer goods*, or consumption goods, include those goods that satisfy wants directly. Such goods consist of nondurable items, such as bread and meat, and durable consumer goods, such as radios, furniture, and automobiles. *Producer goods*, or *capital goods*, include machinery, tools, and raw materials, which satisfy wants indirectly by aiding in the production of either producer or consumer goods. The huge ovens used in large bakeries are producer goods because they help to satisfy one of man's fundamental needs for a consumer good, namely, bread.

The Productive Process

One is accustomed to thinking of production as synonymous with manufacturing. In economics, however, the term *production* is used in a much broader sense. It refers to all activities involved in making goods available to the final consumer. Extraction of iron ore, its refinement into steel, assembly of a refrigerator, shipment to a wholesaler, storage of the shipment and its division into smaller lots, display by the retailer, and delivery to the consumer's door are all stages in the productive process. Marketing functions such as advertising are part of the productive process as well; so are arrangements for installment payments and the provision of repair services on the refrigerator.

In general, all activities that contribute to the supply of tangible goods or intangible services are part of production. Accordingly, anyone is a producer who changes the form of materials so that they become more useful; who moves a material thing to a place where it is needed; who lends, sells, or otherwise helps to make the thing available for use by placing it in the possession of the person who has a use for it; or who renders a want-satisfying service. Since merchants, bankers, truckers, and military officers meet this definition no less than farmers, riveters, or artists, all are engaged in production.

Likewise, nonhuman capital employed in generating any wanted output is engaged in production. Examples such as farm tractors and blast furnaces are obvious. Less obvious perhaps are retail store mannequins, electronic computers, mailmen's uniforms, psychiatrists' couches, and stage sets being used as capital items engaged in production. When these are combined with appropriate kinds of labor, some want-satisfying good or service emerges.

FACTORS OF PRODUCTION

In the production process, natural resources, labor, capital, risk-taking, management, the character and industry of workers, government, and the stability of society, as well as other material and nonmaterial elements, are involved. In the study of a free enterprise economy, however, economists usually recognize four essential factors or agents of production that combine to produce goods and services. These factors are:

1. Labor, including both physical and mental effort directed to the production of goods.

2. Land, or natural resources.

3. Capital, in the form of durable goods that are used in production.

4. The entrepreneur, or enterpriser, who initiates and directs production and assumes the risks of production.

Labor

Labor is human effort—physical or mental—directed to the creation of either material or nonmaterial goods. The effort of each person thus employed is therefore productive. In the production of manufactured articles, productive labor includes the services rendered by managers, mechanics, unskilled workers, stenographers, bookkeepers, cashiers, buyers of materials, salesmen, and others. Likewise, the services performed by lawyers, doctors, actors, musicians, and teachers are productive. In any society the justification for the payment to, and the receipt of income by, individuals who provide physical or mental effort depends on the recognized relation of such effort to the production of goods and services wanted by consumers.

Noninstitutional Population. In the total population of a country, there are many persons who cannot be classified as capable of economic effort. They are too young or too old, or they suffer from deficiencies, mental or physical, that make them unfit for work. Although the laws of particular states may set the age limits below which minors cannot be gainfully employed, it is nevertheless true that children below these ages may be engaged in economic activity within the home or home industry, such as the farm, with beneficial effects both to themselves and all others concerned. The age at which minors may become economically productive, even if not gainfully employed, is thus subject to considerable variation, depending upon the customs and degree of affluence of the family and community.

It is equally open to question at what age a worker becomes superannuated and incapable of further economic effort. The manual laborer is likely to reach such an age somewhat earlier than the individual whose work has been largely mental. Some of the finest products of human genius have come from those who by any ordinary standard would be classified as aged. Although common ages of retirement in industrial occupations range from 60 to 68 years of age, these age limits are only industry's pronouncement that by that time the efficiency of the individual is likely to decline.

Those who are capable of economic effort thus constitute but a part of the total population. They represent what may be called the *noninstitutional population*. It is difficult, if not impossible, to determine the exact number of those who can be counted in the noninstitutional population, since that classification includes both those who are productively engaged although not gainfully employed and those not so engaged yet who are able to work.

The housewife is engaged in very necessary productive activities, but she is not classified as a member of the civilian labor force. Those whose means permit the enjoyment of leisure must be classified nevertheless as part of the noninstitutional population, although their effort may not be forthcoming except under unusual circumstances such as occur in time of war. As of 1973, the noninstitutional population 16 years of age and over was estimated to be 148.3 million out of a total population of 210 million.

Civilian Labor Force. Not all of the individuals in the noninstitutional population engage in productive work, and many of those who do are not remunerated with wages or salaries. To determine the effective productive manpower of our nation, we must look at the *total labor force*, which is made up of all those who are working or seeking work. In addition to laborers, the labor force includes proprietors, the self-employed, and members of the armed forces. It excludes, however, all persons engaged in incidental unpaid family work and all persons engaged exclusively in housework in their own homes or attending school full time.

By definition the *civilian labor force* is comprised of "all persons in the total labor force except members of the armed services." In 1973 the civilian labor force numbered 88.7 million.

The number employed was 84.4 million, and of the total employed, 81.0 million were engaged in nonagricultural employment, while the remaining 3.4 million were in agricultural work. Unemployment amounted to 4.3 million or 4.9 percent of the civilian labor force.

There were 57.3 million persons in the noninstitutional population who were not in the labor force. Of this total, 35.3 million were keeping house, and since they receive no remuneration for such service, they are not included in the labor force. Another 9.2 million were in school—high school, college, or otherwise. The remaining 12.8 million included those who are retired, those who do not want to work, and those who do not have to work.

In 1973 the largest single portion of the labor force (19.8 million) was engaged in manufacturing. The second largest employment category was trade with 16.3 million, and the government was the third largest employer with 13.7 million workers.

According to the Census Bureau, we may expect the labor force to grow at an accelerated rate. The average yearly increase from 1950 to 1960 was close to 800,000. But the yearly increase from 1960 to 1965 was approximately 1,200,000, and from the mid-sixties to the mid-seventies the labor force has been growing at a rate of 1,500,000 annually.

Changes in the size of the labor force have been accompanied by important changes in the composition of occupational groups. From 1940 to the present, there has been a decline in the percentage of the male population in the civilian labor force, from 83.7 percent to 76.2 percent. On the other hand, the percentage of the female population employed increased from 33.9 percent to 45.5 percent during the same years.

Labor Force Participation Rate. The continuous growth in the size of the labor force is explained primarily by the increase in total population rather than by a substantial change in labor force participation. The *labor force participation rate* is the ratio of the labor force to the total population.

With the exception of the years during World War II, the labor force participation rate has been remarkably stable during the past several decades—between 39.5 and 43.5 percent of the total population. The fact that it did increase to 46.5 percent during World War II indicates that the labor force has some degree of elasticity.

Quality and the Utilization of Labor. Production, of course, is affected not only by the size of the labor force and the number of persons employed but also by the quality and the effective utilization of the members of the labor force. Workers may or may not be working at their optimum capacity, and many persons in the labor force may fail to reach their full potential because of the lack of education and training. Furthermore, the utilization of labor will be affected by the stage of technological development in any economy and the degree of automation in highly developed economies. These factors are considered more fully under the discussion of capital on pages 45-49.

Land

About the middle of the eighteenth century, the Physiocrats—a group of French intellectuals—gave a prominent place in their economic theories to land, because agriculture was the principal industry and a large proportion of the goods that people used came directly from farms. Tools and machines were few and crude, and most of the power used in production was supplied by human beings. It was natural, therefore, that nature, represented by the soil, and human labor were regarded as primary factors in production. Since the Industrial Revolution, however, economists have placed increased emphasis on the importance of capital as a factor of production.

Land means more than fertility of the soil and standing room. It is synonymous with nature. As a factor in production, land includes the solid portion of the earth, the streams and other water areas, natural forests, minerals, sunshine, temperature, rainfall, wild fruits, and wildlife in the form of fish and animals. In other words, *land* denotes all the resources and conditions that have been freely supplied by nature and which aid man in producing the things that he needs. The production of all material goods is dependent upon nature's bounty. Land, however, is not a free good because it is limited as to quantity, and most of it in this country is owned as private property.

Our Natural Resources. Obviously our ability to produce the kinds and quantities of material goods we need is limited largely by the availability of natural resources. One of the most important of the natural resources is that of a favorable climate. The United States is very fortunate in that the geographic location and the extensive area of the country make possible a varied climate. As a result many kinds of agricultural crops and fruits may be grown here.

That the supplies of natural resources are limited has long been recognized. Some raw materials, such as cotton, wool, several kinds of fibers, and foodstuffs, are readily replenishable. On the other hand, timber of most kinds can be replaced only over a long period of time. Still other materials—coal, petroleum, iron ore, copper, and natural gas, for example—cannot be replaced. Given the present rates at which nonrenewable resources are being used up in production and given projected increases in these rates, it is expected that the majority of important mineral resources will be extremely scarce and therefore very costly 100 years from now.

Table 3-1 summarizes the effects of estimated future consumption rates for selected raw materials. The first column records the number of years that presently known world reserves would last if these materials continued to be used in production at a constant rate equal to the present rate. In fact, however, consumption of each resource has been increasing over time at a faster and faster pace. If this increasing rate is projected into the future, the number of years remaining until known world reserves are exhausted appear in the second column. The United States alone absorbs in its industrial processes 42 percent of the world consumption of aluminum, 33 percent of all copper consumption, 58 percent of natural gas, and 33 percent of petroleum. Consequently, it can be seen that the U.S., as the world's foremost industrial nation, contributes heavily to the world depletion rates, as reflected in Table 3-1.

Quantities of platinum, gold, zinc, and lead were not sufficient in 1973 to meet demand. Some experts predict that as demand continues to increase, silver, tin, and uranium may well be in short supply by the turn of the century. By the year 2050 several more minerals may have been exhausted even if the rate of consumption were not to increase.

The Conservation of Natural Resources. Under these circumstances the nation should pursue a policy of economizing in the use of our natural resources. The need for a policy of conservation does not mean that we

TABLE 3-1

PROJECTED
YEARS TO
EXHAUSTION
OF SELECTED
NONRENEWABLE
RESOURCES

	Constant Rate of World Consumption	Increasing Rate of World Consumption
Aluminum	100	31
Coal	2300	111
Cobalt	110	60
Copper	36	21
Iron	240	93
Natural Gas	38	22
Nickel	150	53
Petroleum	31	20

SOURCE: Donella H. Meadows, *et al., The Limits to Growth* (New York: Universe Books, 1972), Table 4, p. 56.

should refrain from using natural resources, but rather it means that we should conserve the supplies that we have. It is only reasonable to expect that each generation will make use of existing resources to satisfy its needs. At the same time, in the current utilization of raw materials, there is a social obligation to future generations not to waste these materials.

The adoption of an effective policy of conservation of natural resources requires an understanding of what measures are appropriate for particular resources. The acquisition of this knowledge and the establishment of objectives must be based upon information concerning existing supplies, methods of utilization, and the possibilities for economizing in the retrieval and use of raw materials.

Conservation of Land and Water Resources. The first problem encountered in establishing a policy for the conservation of farmland and waterpower is how to replenish what we have used. The fertility of much of our farmlands has been lost by erosion. Fortunately, however, the federal government has adopted a policy of trying to conserve the farmland resources that are left.

The reclamation of considerable areas of farmland has been made possible by means of irrigation. Still more land in some of the western states can be reclaimed in this way. It has been suggested that the federal government might well spend more money on irrigation projects in connection with power and conservation programs.

In an attempt to conserve timber resources, various measures are being pursued, although not with the vigor that many would like to see. Forest management to promote conservation involves the protection of forests from fire, disease, and insects, and the utilization of cutting practices that will achieve natural reforestation. In cases where suitable areas are not stocked, reforestation can be promoted by planting seeds and young trees. Many states are assisting in this program by furnishing young trees at very moderate cost in order to combat the tremendous annual loss from forest fires.

Considerable progress has been made in river valley development, but much remains to be done. Unfortunately efforts to solve the problem of river valley development create issues that become political. As a result, the economic problem may persist for years while the political issues are being debated.

A comprehensive policy for river valley development and conservation usually includes five objectives: (1) the control of floods, (2) improvements in sanitation, (3) the extension of water transportation, (4) an increase in recreational opportunities, and (5) the conservation of wildlife. In certain cases some of these objectives are emphasized much more than are others.

The Tennessee Valley Authority was created by the federal government for the principal purpose of developing the water resources in the Tennessee River Valley. The TVA is chiefly responsible for carrying out the plan, but it works in cooperation with certain state and private undertakings that are designed to develop waterpower. The Missouri River project is a plan for the conservation, control, and use of water resources in the Missouri River Basin through the cooperative efforts of federal, state, and local governments. The Hoover Dam on the Colorado River was completed in 1936 at a cost of $160 million. It can supply the domestic needs of 7.5 million persons for electric power.

Another spectacular conservation job is that of the St. Lawrence Seaway project, which is the result of a joint American-Canadian effort. A 27-foot deep waterway from Duluth, Minnesota, to the Atlantic Ocean allows ocean-going vessels to penetrate to inland ports. Installation of hydroelectric-power facilities was also part of the project.

Another project involving cooperation between nations was the joint undertaking by scientists from the United States and Russia to consider the problem of desalting seawater. Although a number of plants have been established in various parts of the world, including the United States, and are functioning successfully, the cost is still considered too high for most communities.

Conservation of Mineral and Metal Resources. Existing supplies of non-replenishable natural resources may be conserved in several ways. One way is the use of less wasteful methods of recovery. Fortunately we have made progress in this respect. For example, at one time a large portion of our coal was lost due to an eagerness to mine only the richer and thicker veins. As a result, mines were often abandoned before all the obtainable coal was removed. These mines were left to cave in and fill with water. Formerly a great deal of natural gas was lost by fire or evaporation. Now more efficient methods for the recovery of these fuels make it possible to avoid much waste and to utilize lower grades of deposits.

Petroleum and coal may be conserved by improved methods of utilization. Improvements in the efficiency of internal combustion engines are being made, and further improvements are no doubt possible. This may also be true of steam engines and heating devices that use coal. The extent to which we harness waterpower in our river systems enables us to save coal and petroleum. There seems to be little doubt that we shall soon witness even greater progress in the practical peacetime use of atomic energy derived from uranium or less expensive materials. Some scientists are studying the possibilities of utilizing solar energy. Whether the cost will be prohibitive remains to be seen. The utilization of the new sources of energy may produce rapid changes that will affect our own economy and that of people everywhere.

We can also import certain materials, such as petroleum and iron ore, and in this way avoid being entirely dependent upon our own diminishing supplies. America learned in World War II how far from self-sufficiency she was in supplies of essential minerals, metals, and other resources. By importing critical materials we may stockpile resources that are essential in time of war. But there is likely to be an increasing degree of competition among nations for natural resources wherever they are to be found.

Capital

According to Adam Smith, a person's capital is "that part of his stock from which he expects to derive an income." The accountant considers the capital of a concern as the money value of all assets of the business minus the debts that are owed. In business *fixed capital* is the amount invested in plant and equipment. *Working capital* is the amount by which the value of current assets—inventories, accounts receivable, cash, and the like—exceeds the total of short-term debts. In economics, however, *capital* consists of all tangible goods that have been produced by man and that may be used for the production of other goods, including services that have a social value. When thus used, capital refers to capital goods or producer goods and not to the money value of such goods.

The amount of capital invested per worker in 1972 has been estimated at nearly $20,000. In that year, the amount ranged from $123,000 in the petroleum industry—excluding pipelines and transportation—to $4,600 in the leather industry.

Function of Capital. The function of capital is to assist labor in production. The use of capital is not in itself satisfying, except to the extent that it may incidentally contribute to relieving the irksomeness of labor. Years ago the farmer used a hoe or a plow because it enabled him to produce a crop with less labor. Today he uses a tractor and other modern farm equipment that increase his productivity still more. The manufacturer uses presses, drills, and lathes, not to satisfy some personal craving, but to produce better goods with less effort and at lower costs than would be required if labor unassisted by capital were employed.

Savings and the Accumulation of Capital. The first capital that man used was probably a crude stick or stone. The long process of discovery and experimentation that must have gone on before even the simplest tools came into general use can only be imagined. But it is clear that, in the production of all but the very crudest things, considerable labor was necessary. Moreover, in the production of capital, the labor involved was diverted from the direct production of consumer goods.

When it became apparent that a weapon would aid man in his quest for food, he used part of his energy in fashioning a spear or a bow and in devising an arrow that would be effective for his purpose. Before that time all his productive effort was direct; but the labor he expended upon making the weapon was indirect. It was roundabout. First, he would make the weapon and then hunt and kill the animal he wanted for food. And he found that by diverting part of his efforts to the preparation for the hunt, he greatly increased the effectiveness of his efforts in direct production.

The creation of capital requires both saving and diversion of labor. Primitive man saved or withheld part of his effort and diverted it to the production of capital. Each successful invention made it possible for him to find time for improving the laborsaving devices he already had discovered or to discover and to devise others. This cumulative process has continued. Today society possesses so much laborsaving capital that only a portion of the working population is engaged in direct production. Now about 4 percent of those in civilian employment are in agricultural pursuits. The others are engaged in producing various kinds of consumer and capital goods and in commercial and professional occupations.

To most persons, saving implies abstinence and inconvenience. In the case of those who first produced capital goods, it was not always convenient to divert labor from direct production to the production of capital goods or to goods the use of which was not immediately satisfying. Even today, for the majority of those persons who establish small savings accounts and life insurance and annuity policies, saving involves the postponement of pleasure that might be derived in the present from the immediate purchase and use of goods.

On the other hand, some people have incomes so large that it is easier to save than it would be to find some reasonable way of spending all of their income. These individuals need not forego present pleasures in order to save.

If they buy the bonds of a manufacturing company that is engaged in the production of farm tractors or machine tools, they do not have to stint themselves in the satisfaction of their personal wants at the time. But the fact remains that even the rich man who lends a part of his money to a concern that makes capital goods thus makes possible the diversion of a part of the labor of the nation, which might otherwise be used for direct production, to the production of goods that will aid in future production. Therefore, in the consideration of the origin and replacement of capital, it is both the saving and diversion of labor from direct production that are important.

Our Technological Progress. The presence of people and the existence of rich supplies of material resources are not sufficient to bring about increasing production by economical methods. A workable technology and "know-how" are needed also.

For decades, technological progress in the United States has been the wonder of the world. To our people it has been the cause of far-reaching and tremendous changes affecting the social conditions and general welfare of the people. For one thing, it has promoted democracy. At one time, class distinction and occupational status were easily recognizable by the clothes people wore, by the methods of transportation they used, and by the houses in which they lived. In some cases we can still recognize these material evidences of economic position and social rank. But the availability of many commodities of good quality at prices that a majority of the people can afford has done much to obliterate the external evidences of economic status that once were so obvious.

For another thing, our technological achievement has made possible the emergence of America as a world power. Advances in industrial and manufacturing technology have made mass production methods possible and, hence, the great increase in goods both military and civilian. Half a century ago, for example, the usual method of cooking or of heating a house was by the use of wood or coal stoves. Most houses today are equipped with gas or electric stoves and central furnaces. In addition, refrigerators, home freezers, automatic washers, and other types of equipment make homes more comfortable and housework easier and more interesting. Progress in methods of production in the automobile industry has made it possible for most adults who want a car to have one.

Advances in engineering technology have helped to span a vast continent with excellent roads and bridges to facilitate the problem of transportation of goods and people. In the factories and in the mines, mechanical equipment reduces or entirely eliminates the drudgery and heavy, physical work formerly required. Air conditioning has greatly improved the efficiency of workers in offices, factories, and industrial plants.

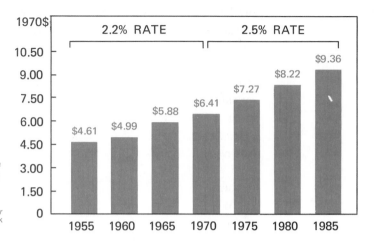

FIGURE 3-1

CHANGES IN OUTPUT PER MAN-HOUR

1955-1985

By 1985 the average worker will be producing more than twice as much per man-hour as he did in 1955.

SOURCE: *The American Economy: Prospects for Growth to 1985* (New York: McGraw-Hill Book Company, 1972), p. 6.

Advances in agricultural technology have been responsible for remarkable expansions of both food and fiber outputs over the years. Our developing technology is related to the problem of agriculture and conservation in more ways than that of increased farm production. We are no longer entirely dependent on the farm for cotton, wool, and vegetable fibers for materials from which to make our clothing. The development of dacron, orlon, nylon, rayon, and the like now makes it possible to produce articles of clothing from synthetic materials. Still other articles use both synthetic products and natural fibers in such a way as to combine the best features of each. Likewise, the invention and perfection of plastics are making possible innumerable substitutions for lumber and certain metal products.

Jet transportation now enables one to cross oceans or continents at tremendous speeds. Before long the small helicopter may be more widely used for individual and family transportation. Automobiles are air-conditioned; color television is here; and medical science continues to make progress in the conquest of human diseases.

All technological advancement is dependent upon advances in science, and it seems likely that the present rate of technological progress will continue. Present facts support the belief that changes in the methods of production and the tendency for the total national output of goods and services to increase will go on. Such advances, however, will require continuing research and the expenditure of huge sums of money for new kinds of capital goods. Yet upon such advances depends our continued recognition as a great economic and military power.

Automation. The Industrial Revolution was the result of improvements in certain methods of production. Now we are faced with other changes in production that may have another revolutionary effect on the economy. The reason is the tendency for an increasing number of industries to adopt automation as the method of controlling and directing production.

Automation implies the automatic control of machine production by other machines, so that a part of a productive process is completed without direct human aid or control. For example, most of the involved processes necessary to the refinement of petroleum have been, or may be, coordinated and carried on by machines and chemical processes with little or no human effort. Moreover, computers that almost seem to have the ability to think compute almost instantly the significance of great quantities of data needed for managerial purposes.

What will be the effects of automation on the demand for labor and on the economy in general? Many labor union leaders and others feel that the growing use of automation will increase unemployment. On the other hand, some employers and economists feel that adjustments of labor to the new methods of production can be made rather easily and without too much inconvenience and suffering. What does seem certain is that there will be a continuing decrease in the demand for unskilled labor and a corresponding increase in the demand for technicians of various kinds.

Nuclear Energy. Another matter, which may have important effects in the field of production, is the development of nuclear energy released by the fission of splitting of atoms that compose uranium and thorium. The energy thus released can be used to generate electricity, just as can be done by burning coal. Although the amount of potential energy in a pound of uranium is 3 million times that of a pound of coal, the process of releasing atomic energy is very expensive. At present it is still more economical for industry to obtain energy from coal or petroleum. A rapid switch from the use of coal to nuclear energy has not as yet taken place, but it is reassuring to know that atomic energy will be available when the supplies of coal and petroleum become depleted. In 1958, at Shippingport, Pennsylvania, the nation's first commercial atomic power station was officially inaugurated. Several others have been developed since then.

The Entrepreneur

The existence of supplies of natural resources, labor, and capital does not necessarily result in the production of goods. Before production can take place, these factors must be brought together, organized, and directed. Some individual or group must decide what is to be produced, when, where, and how. Until these decisions have been made and action has been taken to carry them into execution, the other factors of production are only potentially important.

Just who shall organize and direct the factors of production depends upon the nature of the economic society. In this and similar democratic countries the private entrepreneur occupies the strategic position of organizer and director of business and industry. In some countries the state may be the entrepreneur.

Essentially, the *entrepreneur* is the risk taker. Since nearly all production is for future use, risk is inevitable. From the time production is begun on a farm or in a factory, there are many possibilities of financial loss. Physical disaster by means of fire, flood, freezing, and other hazards affecting the plant or merchandise may occur; goods may be stolen; mismanagement may result in an excess of costs over revenue; and demand and prices may decline. Even the most efficient management cannot eliminate the possibilities of loss from some or all of these hazards. In a society that is largely capitalistic, the hope of realizing a profit is the motive for undertaking production.

Management is considered to be a prerogative of the entrepreneur. It is, however, a form of labor, and any compensation that may be imputed to the owner-manager of a business is a form of wages. In the case of corporations, the stockholders are in reality the entrepreneurs in the sense that they are the risk takers. The officers, although their salaries may amount to hundreds of thousands of dollars annually, are nevertheless hired employees. They do, of course, manage the finances and direct the operations of the corporation, which are delegated prerogatives of the entrepreneurial owners.

The entrepreneur is the most important of the factors in directing the structure of production in this country. In spite of the fact that in the course of time some controls and restrictions have been imposed upon freedom of enterprise in the United States, the quest for profits by means of the production and distribution of goods and services remains the motivating and directing power for undertaking production. It is the entrepreneur who in the largest measure creates the demand for investment funds. The anticipated demand of consumers is translated into a demand for natural resources and the services of workers. Since workers do not own the goods they produce, they cannot sell the goods to those who will use them. Hence, the workers are dependent upon the entrepreneurs for advances in the form of wages, which the employer hopes to recover when the goods are sold.

THE RELATION OF PRODUCTION TO INCOME

The payments received by the owners of the factors of production represent expenditures or costs of production to the business firm. At the same time, these expenditures by firms are incomes to those who receive them. Thus, production is the original source of income. The total amount of

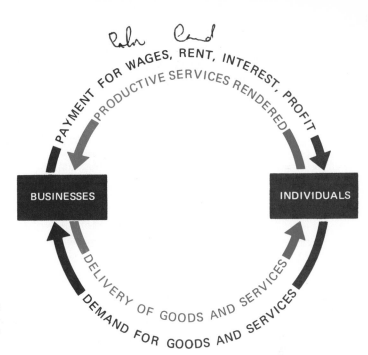

FIGURE 3-2

CIRCULAR FLOW—INCOME AND GOODS AND SERVICES

Household expenditures on goods and services generate income to resource owners for further expenditure.

payments to the owners of the factors of production constitutes the *national income*, which will be discussed at length in Part Two.

The fundamental relationship between money expenditures for production and incomes is shown graphically in Figure 3-2.

For the sake of simplicity in the construction of the chart, it is assumed that there are only two groups—producers and consumers. The consumers (individuals and families) provide productive services by supplying labor, land, capital, and entrepreneurship. In return, they receive income in the form of wages, rent, interest, or profits. Incomes thus received are spent for goods and services provided by the firms, and the money is then again paid out by the firms for productive services. Therefore, the income-expenditure flow goes on as long as the production and the consumption of goods continue. Expenditure and income are merely two aspects of what may be termed "the circular flow of income." This circular flow will be analyzed in greater detail in Chapter 5.

SUMMARY

1. Things that are useful—whether material or nonmaterial—are goods, although the term "services" is often used to distinguish nonmaterial goods from those that are material.

2. Production is the process of creating finished goods by using factors of production.

3. The four factors of production are: labor, land, capital, and entrepreneurship. Entrepreneurship includes the management and allocation of the other three factors within the business firm, as well as the assumption of risk.

4. There is urgent need for the practice of economy in the utilization of our natural resources. A national conservation policy should take into consideration certain economic conditions and developments in other countries.

5. Considering the economy as a whole, there is a circular flow of income to individuals and firms because expenditures for production are the original sources of incomes, which, in turn, become expenditures.

6. The circular flow of income is central to the operation of the economic system. A flow of resource inputs, or factors of production, generates the flow of output. A countermoving flow of money payments constitutes the "payoffs"— money wages, rent, interest, and profits that are the source of expenditures.

NEW TERMS

Good, *p. 37*
Free good, *p. 37*
Economic good, *p. 37*
Consumer goods, *p. 37*
Producer goods, *p. 37*
Production, *p. 38*
Labor, *p. 39*
Noninstitutional population, *p. 39*
Total labor force, *p. 40*

Civilian labor force, *p. 40*
Labor force participation rate, *p. 41*
Land, *p. 41*
Capital, *p. 45*
Fixed capital, *p. 45*
Working capital, *p. 45*
Automation, *p. 49*
Entrepreneur, *p. 50*
National income, *p. 51*

QUESTIONS FOR DISCUSSION AND ANALYSIS

1. How may goods be classified? Give examples of each class.

2. Who, if any, of the following are not producers: a coal miner; a physician; an entertainer; a merchant; a banker; a social worker; a United States Senator? Explain and justify your answer.

3. What is the main function of each of the factors of production?

4. What is the relation between saving and capital accumulation?

5. Are our human and material resources sufficient for the production of the goods we need?

6. Technology may be defined as "systematic knowledge of the industrial arts." What is the meaning of the expression? Give a number of examples of technology in American industry.

7. What are likely to be the effects of (a) automation? (b) the use of nuclear energy?

8. What more should be done than is being done to conserve our natural material resources? What part should the government play in a natural resources conservation program? Why?

9. Explain what is meant by the circular flow of income.

10. Can you see any relation between production and the value of money? If so, what is it?

SUGGESTED READINGS

The Suggested Readings for this chapter are included in Chapter 4, page 78.

4

The Role of Consumers, Business, and Government

PREVIEW Three institutions are central to the economy: households, business firms, and government. Consumption patterns of households dictate the types of goods produced and define the standard of living in society. Business firms are structured to facilitate the supply of these goods. Some are organized as one-owner establishments, some as partnerships, and some as corporations. Finally, the government performs essential economic functions by means of legislation, taxation, and public expenditures. These functions include protection of property rights, promotion of competition, and stabilization of business conditions.

The activities of consumers stand at the core of macroeconomic and microeconomic theory. The same is true of the activities of business firms. Together consumers and business firms form the private sector of the economy. For this reason, additional descriptions of each are warranted. So far we have ignored the public sector. To complete our sketch of the American economy, therefore, it is necessary that the functions of government be included, for these functions are critical to the operation of the economy.

THE VOICE OF CONSUMERS

Consumption refers to the act of utilizing a good or a service. This morning, for example, you may have consumed pancakes and syrup for breakfast. If you drove to school or work, your car consumed gasoline. It is not necessary to absorb a good completely in order to have consumption. In fact, a good may be consumed little by little and day by day, as are your automobile tires, the soles of your shoes, or the bristles of your toothbrush. The usefulness of some goods, such as a painting or a book, may last for a long time and may even increase with continued use, while the usefulness of other goods, such as a cold beer, is quickly exhausted.

Consumer Sovereignty

Few of us have the means necessary to satisfy all our individual wants. Consequently, we buy first those goods and services that provide the greatest amount of satisfaction per dollar spent, then those that render less satisfaction, and we do without others. We are forced to economize daily. Perhaps you deliberated whether to attend college or to buy a new car, or you decided to bring your lunch rather than to buy it in the cafeteria, or you debated with yourself whether to go on a date during the weekend or purchase a book for your personal library. Even if you are fortunate enough that you do not have to make choices between such alternatives, you are generally forced to economize your time. An individual often finds that he must give up a remunerative job in order to attend college. If he tries both, something may have to give. Frequently he will have to budget his time among his studies, his work, his recreation, his social life, and his sleep.

Not only do individuals economize but nations also. Typically the total wants to be satisfied are greater than the capacity of the nation to produce. Therefore, decisions must be made about what will be produced and who will receive the goods and services produced. In a free enterprise system consumers in the aggregate are the primary decision makers on these questions. Their voices come through loud and clear.

In order to understand this decision-making process, we must realize that there is a difference between a consumer want and a consumer demand. Consumers have innumerable wants, but these wants have no direct influence on the economy unless individuals are able and willing to offer money or other goods in exchange for the satisfaction of their wants. *Consumer demand refers to wants backed up by, or expressed in terms of, purchasing power.* For example, your desire for a new sports car will not induce the foreman to put another chassis on the assembly line. But if you appear at your local auto dealer and offer to buy it with cash or credit, your want becomes a demand. This demand will induce the automobile manufacturer to produce more sports cars. It is demand that motivates the economy and determines the use of manpower and resources.

Many times, however, the initiating force for the determination of production does not come directly from consumers. In our modern complex economy, the producer often takes it upon himself to offer certain goods and services in the hope of selling them to consumers. He may be assisted greatly by advertising that can acquaint the public with new and useful products. Through advertising, latent wants may become active.

This initiating action by the producer can bring about good or bad results. Certainly this method has brought about the production of many useful items that might never have been produced if the producer had waited for a manifestation of consumer demand before starting production. On the other hand, sometimes by employing certain tactics in order to sell his merchandise, the seller may implant or create a demand in the mind of the consumer for some item that may be of little use to him or that may even be detrimental to him. Nevertheless, the consumer is still king in our economy. Although he may not always exercise his prerogatives and powers, his acceptance is necessary if particular goods and services are going to continue to be produced and consumed.

Standards of Living

A *standard of living* consists of those goods and services that the individual or family strives to attain for the satisfaction of its wants. The emphasis is on a pattern of wants that may be only partly satisfied but the satisfaction of which constitutes a goal that the consumer seeks to attain. The wants that form such a goal are those which offer prospects of realization through efforts within the capacity of the individual or the family. We cannot all have palatial homes with heated swimming pools, drive Cadillacs, dine at the Waldorf, and belong to the best country clubs. But we can strive for a better home, a later model car, more frequent entertainment, and dinner out occasionally. Thus, our standard of living is that level of living which we not only strive for but which we have a reasonable chance to attain. It can thus differ from the actual level of living.

This standard of living will be higher for some than it will be for others. It will differ, depending on the individual, his immediate family, and his background, education, environment, capabilities, and good fortune. Although we frequntly hear about "the American standard of living," there is no way of determining exactly what this level is. Certainly it is not the country estate, chauffeur-driven limousine, and maid-and-butler status of high society. Perhaps it comes close to the ranch-type home, late-model car (or even two cars), automatic appliances, and occasional vacation trips characteristic of the middle income groups.

In spite of our large national income, however, the actual level of living of many individuals and families in the United States still leaves much to be desired. Often it falls short of the needs of the family. It certainly falls short of "the American dream." The "disadvantaged," the "underprivileged," and "war on poverty" are phrases used to suggest, among other things, that there are those who do not possess enough of this world's goods.

Consumption Patterns

Certain wants, such as food, clothing, and shelter, are common to all consumption patterns, but they may vary as to quantity and quality. Other wants will differ to a considerable degree depending upon the background and characteristics of the consuming unit.

Conspicuous Consumption and the Status Seekers. The great majority of families possess insufficient means to satisfy all their wants completely. The young and enterprising, those who wish to marry and set up house-keeping, realize the great gap between what they can afford and what they want. At this stage, great efforts will be made to advance the level of living until it comes closer to the desired standard of living. Here the problem of "keeping up with the Joneses" is the most pressing, for imitation and emulation are potent factors in advancing standards and stimulating efforts to realize them. An ideal situation is to be found when the gap between the desired and the attainable standard is not so great as to discourage efforts and ambition.

On the other hand, there are a number of individuals and families who consume to some degree merely for the "show" or prestige involved. Thorstein Veblen in his famous book of another generation, *The Theory of the Leisure Class*, coined the phrase "conspicuous consumption" by which he referred to that consumption engaged in for the purpose of attracting attention of neighbors or fellow citizens. Along the same lines, in his book, *The Status Seekers*, Vance Packard devoted considerable attention to that group of people who engage in particular types of spending and consumption primarily for the sake of obtaining a certain status or acceptance in the community.

The Affluent Society. Although it is generally stated that production is for the purpose of consumption and the satisfaction of wants, John Kenneth Galbraith in his best seller, *The Affluent Society*, challenged the basis of this concept. On the premise that we in America have overcome economic scarcity, he contends that we no longer produce solely because we need the goods and services but that we produce in large part to provide economic security.

According to Galbraith, because we are convinced that full and steady employment is a good thing, we produce to provide steady jobs and paychecks even though we may not need many of the goods and services. He holds further that, since we have an excess of consumer goods and services, many of which are mere frivolities, we need a better balance between private and social production. As an example, we have flashy automobiles but drive them frequently on second- and third-rate highways. We have color TV and abundant toys for our children, but we lack proper facilities and enough teachers necessary for the education of our children. We often fish with the best and fanciest gear but in polluted streams and rivers. What the exact balance between private and social production should be Galbraith does not say, but he does recommend some measures to bring about a different balance than now exists.

Saving and the Standard of Living

Paradoxical as it may seem, both spending and saving are parts of consumption, for saving is merely deferred spending. It is the degree of futurity in a want that determines whether the provision for it shall be called spending or saving. Some persons focus on the immediate future, and the need for making provisions for the satisfaction of extended future wants is not considered a matter of great urgency. In other cases there may be a strong concern for the future, and the wants that it expresses may call forth a large amount of saving, even on low income. Thus, it is through the effect of the decision to save or to spend on consumer items that individuals help choose whether we are going to produce for current or future consumption.

As a general tendency, when income increases and it is possible to satisfy wants of lesser intensity, greater wants for goods in the more distant future are likely to appear and the volume of saving will expand. Those who receive only small incomes are not likely to save much, for their income makes possible only the satisfaction of immediate pressing wants. The wealthy, on the other hand, are likely to save relatively large amounts, which represent a large percentage of their income, even though their level of living may be far higher than that of other individuals. Thus, as income increases, the tendency to consume will also increase but not at the same rate. Savings will grow and at a faster rate than income.

Changes in the Level of Living

Changes in the level of living may be either qualitative or quantitative. That is, changes may occur in the kinds of goods consumed or in the amount. Age and change of location or occupation or social position, as well as education, advertising, and new fads and fashions, are constantly influencing and modifying standards. Thus, new tastes develop, and old wants gradually disappear. In spite of the stabilizing influence of habit and custom, changes are brought about in consumption for all but the very old, and even old persons may change their manner of living.

Several major forces are working to raise the American level of living: rising real incomes; more education, both formal and informal; research and development by business firms and others that result in new and better products; and the typical consumer's desire to improve his level of living.

Price Changes and Real Income. Quantitative changes in the standard of living may be due to changes in incomes or in prices, or in both. *Real income, or the specific goods and services that one may purchase with the amount of money he receives during a period of time,* is determined by the size of money income and the prevailing level of prices. Quantitative changes may occur when income remains constant and prices change or when income changes while prices remain essentially the same; or both income and prices may change with favorable or unfavorable results. When both income and prices change, the following four relations are possible: (1) income may fall when prices are rising; (2) income may rise when prices are falling; (3) both income and prices may rise; or (4) both income and prices may fall.

The first condition is most unfavorable to the individual's level of living, for it means a definite reduction in real income. The second condition is most favorable, for both rising money income and falling prices contribute to an expansion of real income. Whether the third and fourth conditions will be favorable or unfavorable to levels of living obviously depends on rates of change in income and prices. If income rises faster than prices or falls more slowly than prices, an expanding level of living is possible, while the opposite relations will lead to a reduction in the level of living.

The Advancing Level of Consumption. During the past decade the population in the United States increased from 181 million in 1960 to 205 million in 1970. This was an increase of about 13 percent for the decade or an average increase of 1.3 percent annually. During this time income, expenditures, and the economic well-being of the population increased at an even greater rate. During the same period, for example, the median family's personal income before taxes increased from $5,620 to about $10,000 per year in 1970. This was an increase of 78 percent. Real income during the period increased by 44 percent.

Individuals and families not only earned more but they also spent more in the decade. Personal consumption expenditures, in terms of real dollars, increased more than 30 percent. By 1970, 80 percent of the population owned automobiles compared to only 60 percent in 1950. In fact, the percentage of families owning two or more automobiles rose from 7 percent of the population in 1950 to 29 percent by 1970. In the same period home ownership for city dwellers became more prevalent, increasing from 53 percent to nearly 65 percent of the families.

In regard to household appliances, the percentage of homes with television sets during the period 1950-1970 increased from less than 15 percent to 98 percent, refrigerators moved from 38 percent to 99.6 percent, and those households with mixers jumped from 12 percent to 77 percent. Housework was made easier as the percentage of homes with vacuum cleaners increased from 25 percent to 91 percent, electric washers moved from 32 percent to 70 percent, and the families using automatic dryers increased from less than 2 percent to more than 41 percent. Furthermore, housework was performed in greater comfort as 20 percent of our homes had air conditioners in 1970 compared to less than one percent in 1950.

In the matter of care of our population, the percentage of youngsters in the 14-15 year age bracket in school increased from 83 percent to 95 percent between 1950 and 1970. At the other end of the age range, the percentage of the population covered by old-age survivors, disability, and health insurance increased from 64 percent to 90 percent. At the same time a greater percentage of the total population was covered by life insurance, and there was a notable increase in the amount of insurance for hospital, surgical, and various other medical expenses.

Not only did individuals and families enjoy substantially increased economic well-being in the form of higher income and greater personal expenditures during the period, but also they had more time in which to enjoy it, since the amount of vacation time per worker increased by more than 10 percent during the period, and many workers obtained an increase in the number of paid holidays they received.

Facts such as these indicate that the level of living in general is distinctly improving. Nevertheless, there is always room for more improvement, especially since there are many families whose incomes and expenditures are still far below what might be accepted as the American standard of living. Fortunately personal incomes and expenditures during the next decade will probably show further improvement in the United States and elsewhere throughout the world.

THE STRUCTURE OF BUSINESS

Production involves more than the application of labor to material things or the performance of a service. In any economy production also requires the performance of four general functions: (1) deciding what, where, when, and how much to produce; (2) providing and assembling the factors of production; (3) managing productive processes; and (4) assuming inevitable risks.

Production may be organized by private individuals or groups on their own initiative. It may also be done by the people as a whole through the instrumentality of government, as in the cases of the post office system, the public schools, or the public highway system. Characteristically in our economic system, however, production is for profit and is carried on under one of three types of private business ownership and control: the single proprietorship, the partnership, or the business corporation. In addition, there are cooperative enterprises.

Single Proprietorships

The simplest type of business enterprise is the *single proprietorship*, a business with one owner. From the standpoint of numbers, single proprietorships predominate in all the fields of production, except manufacturing, as listed in Table 4-1. The total value of goods produced and sold by factories and stores owned by individuals, however, is small compared with that sold or produced by corporations. For example, about 16 percent of all retail establishments are owned by corporations; but these establishments sell more than 70 percent of all the goods sold by retail stores.

TABLE 4-1

SINGLE PROPRIETORSHIPS, PARTNERSHIPS, AND CORPORATIONS

1970

	Single Proprietorships (Thousands)	Partnerships (Thousands)	Corporations (Thousands)
Agriculture, Forestry, and Fisheries	3,018	124	37
Mining	51	14	14
Construction	685	51	139
Manufacturing	183	28	198
Transportation, Communication, Electric Gas, Sanitary Services	296	17	67
Wholesale and Retail Trade	1,992	201	518
Finance, Insurance, and Real Estate	566	320	406
Services	2,507	176	281
All Industries	9,400	936	1,665

SOURCE: *Statistical Abstract of the United States*, 1973, p. 471.

Ordinarily it is easy for one person to organize a small business enterprise if he has enough capital or the ability to borrow money for the purpose. Likewise, it is a simple matter to discontinue the business. The single owner exercises sole control, and his decisions are not subject to debate or veto by another. Any profits that may be realized belong to the single owner.

The definite advantages of a single proprietorship are offset by certain disadvantages. Since his ability to raise capital is limited to that which he owns or can borrow on his own credit, the owner may find it impossible to enlarge the business. Furthermore, if the owner fails to meet his financial obligations, the creditors not only can have the property used in the business sold, but they may look to any other property he owns for the satisfaction of their claims. The single proprietor must rely largely upon his own ability and skill. Of course, he may hire others to help in the management of the enterprise, but employees usually do not possess the interest and incentives of the owner.

Partnerships

A *partnership* is a business association resulting from a contract between two or more persons who agree to combine their capital and/or efforts for gain. The reason for the formation of a partnership is the fact that one or more of the disadvantages that attend the single proprietorship make it desirable for the owner to combine his capital or ability with that of one or more other persons.

Most partnerships are *general partnerships*, that is, each partner is liable for the payment of the debts of the firm. Profits and losses are shared equally or according to some agreed-upon ratio. For example, if partner Smith contributed more capital or spends more time at work in the business than does partner Jones, Smith might receive 60 percent of any profits and Jones, 40 percent. Usually the ratio for the distribution of profits and losses bears some relation to the capital contribution of the partners. If an agreement for the distribution of profits and losses has not been made and a lawsuit ensues, the court will usually rule that the profits and losses will be shared equally.

The partnership may have at least two important advantages over the single proprietorship. In the first place, two individuals are likely to possess more capital than does either alone. Moreover, the borrowing ability of two or more individuals is greater than that of one, provided their business reputations are good. In the second place, a partnership may combine abilities and skills that make it possible to conduct a business more efficiently than if one person undertook the enterprise alone or hired another to assist him. A skilled bookkeeper and a successful salesman, for example, might find it advantageous to form a partnership for the purpose of selling a line of merchandise. Thus, the advantage of combining capital and talent is an important incentive for the formation of partnerships.

The greatest disadvantage of a partnership is that of *unlimited liability*. This characteristic places a contingent claim against all the property of each partner, both business and personal, for the debts of the partnership. Another disadvantage of the partnership is the difficulty of transferring ownership. No partner can sell his interest in the firm except by the consent of all the other members, nor can an heir succeed to the membership in a partnership until he has been accepted by all the other members.

Business Corporations

With few exceptions, the two simpler forms of ownership served the needs of society very well prior to the Industrial Revolution. With the ever-increasing need for machinery, power, tools, and other equipment, and for large amounts of capital to be used in manufacturing and marketing greater quantities of goods, however, these methods of business financing and management proved inadequate to the requirements of the new order in production and exchange. It was to provide a financing device that did not have the weaknesses of the single proprietorship and the partnership that the corporation came into existence. Just as technological advance and specialization made large-scale production in industry possible, so the corporate form of business organization made possible the amassing of immense amounts of capital needed for mass production.

Nature of the Corporation. According to the classic definition given by Chief Justice John Marshall in the celebrated Dartmouth College case in 1819, "a corporation is an artificial being, invisible, intangible, and existing only in contemplation of law." This definition is based on the "entity theory" of the corporation, which holds that the *corporation*, by virtue of the legal power that creates it, is endowed with legal existence distinct and separate from the natural persons who organize it; and that it is a legal person, which, while being intangible, is real nevertheless. Accordingly, the corporation possesses the power to own property, to enter into contracts not prohibited by law, to sue in the courts, and to be sued. Thus, it enjoys some of the prerogatives of a natural person.

The courts have traditionally held to the entity theory, and as a result they have sometimes stated that individuals should be immune from punishment for many of the violations of law that have been committed by corporations. Within recent years, however, there has been a growing tendency for the courts to look upon a corporation as a voluntary association of persons and to hold the directors and officers of corporations personally liable for the illegal acts of the companies whose affairs they manage.

Management of Corporations. Stockholders own the corporation, but, as owners, they do not manage it directly. Rather, the stockholders elect a *board of directors*, usually composed of stockholders, which has delegated authority to determine the policies of the corporation and to appoint appropriate officers or agents to put the policies into operation. Thus, in effect, directors have the power to manage the corporate fund almost as exclusively as though the entire assets of the business belonged to them, as long as by their actions they do not obviously misuse the powers conferred upon them by law and by the corporate charter.

Directors are not legally liable for mistakes of judgment or for their acts that are within the law, but they may be prosecuted for actions not authorized by the charter. Also, they are personally liable for failures to make reports required by government and for incurring debts that are obviously unreasonable. Directors are not allowed to obtain a secret profit by the use of the property of the corporation or to use the funds of the business for their own personal gain.

Corporation Capital and Debt. *Corporation capital* consists of all the property or wealth held by the corporation. It includes the value of cash and other assets that have been acquired from funds provided by the stockholders or borrowed from other persons or firms. *Capital stock* designates that part of the capital invested in the corporation by the stockholders.

Value of Capital Stock. Frequently a definite value, or *par value*, is placed upon stock, which is printed or written on the stock certificate that is given to the stockholder. This par value may be practically any amount, such as $1, $10, or $100. As a rule, stock of original issue is not sold for less than par value, but it is often sold for more.

It has increasingly become the practice to issue *no-par-value stock* or stock that has no stated value. No-par-value stock is sold for whatever it will bring. Contrary to the opinion that might be held by some, the real value of a share of stock does not depend upon whether it is of par or of no-par value. From the standpoint of its value as an investment, the desirability of any stock depends upon the amount of income, present or prospective, to which the owner is or may be entitled.

The *book value* of stock is obtained by adding together the stated value of the capital stock held by stockholders and the amount of accumulated profit (surplus) held by the corporation, then dividing this sum by the number of the shares of outstanding stock. Thus, if the value of the outstanding stock is $1,000,000, as shown by the capital stock accounts in the company's records, and that of the surplus is $500,000, and there are 10,000 shares of stock outstanding, the book value of a share of stock is $150. The book value may not be the price at which the stock was sold when it was issued.

The *market value* of a share of stock is the price at which the stock is selling at a given time. The price may depend upon a number of things, but in general the factors that affect the market price of corporation stock are the present and the prospective earning capacity of the business and the policy of the directors in paying dividends to the stockholders or of plowing back the profits into the business.

Rights of Stockholders. Corporations, broadly speaking, may issue two kinds of stock, common and preferred. The term *common stock* originated a long time ago, when the earlier types of corporations issued only one kind of stock and the contributions of the stockholders were considered as constituting a common fund. As the term suggests, *preferred stock* carries with it certain preferential rights or privileges not permitted to holders of common stock. These preferences usually relate to the payment of dividends or to the distribution of the assets of the company in case of liquidation.

The holders of corporate common stock have the right to attend meetings of stockholders. They usually have the right to vote for members of the board of directors and on all questions that are submitted for action by the stockholders. Ordinarily the number of votes that a stockholder can cast depends upon the number of shares that he holds. A stockholder who does not plan to attend a stockholders' meeting may vote by proxy. That is, he may authorize some other stockholder—usually a member of the board of directors—to vote for him. Most of the small stockholders in the large corporations vote by proxy, if they vote at all.

The method of distributing the profits coming into possession of the corporation is left to the discretion of the board of directors; but, if profits are distributed to the holders of common stock, the amounts must be in proportion to the number of shares held. In the event of liquidation of the corporation, the holders of common stock have the right to share proportionally in the distribution of the assets of the company. No stockholder is entitled to a share of the assets, except in payment of dividends, unless the assets of the business are sold and the enterprise terminated, in which case stockholders are residual claimants in that they are entitled to take only what is left after the debts to all creditors have been satisfied.

Most preferred stock entitles the holder to a portion of the profits before anything is paid to the holders of common stock. The amount of the payment is designated as a percent of the par value of the stock, as 6 percent; or, if the stock has no par value, as a stated amount, as $6. In either case, the amount indicated must be paid before dividends are paid to the common stockholders.

The charter may specify that, in case of liquidation of the corporation, the holders of preferred stock shall have first claim upon the assets to be distributed. Such a provision as to preference is seldom of much value, however. If liquidation becomes necessary, there is usually little, if anything, left after the creditors have been paid. As this fact is generally known, stock that is preferential only with respect to the distribution of assets enjoys little more esteem than does the common stock of the same company.

Corporation Bonds. Corporations usually rely upon borrowing for a portion of their funds. Expansion of the buildings or the purchase of heavy equipment often calls for the expenditure of millions of dollars. Repayment of such amounts can be made out of profits only over a period of many years. For that reason funds for these purposes are frequently obtained by long-term loans represented by bonds. Essentially a *bond* is a formal written promise to pay a stipulated obligation at the date of maturity and to pay the holder an agreed amount of interest at stated intervals. A bond confers upon the lender the right to institute foreclosure proceedings if the borrower defaults in the payment of interest or principal.

Legally, a stockholder is the primary risk taker in a corporate enterprise. He risks his own money in the venture; and, if the enterprise fails, he is not entitled by law to look to another for its return. The bondholder, on the other hand, is a creditor of the business.

The distinction between a stockholder and a bondholder with respect to the risks each assumes, however, is one of degree. While it is true that the corporation is under contract to return to the bondholder the amount of his investment, there is always some uncertainty as to whether the promise can be kept. For a variety of reasons, such as a lessening of profit or bankruptcy, among others, the business may be unable to redeem its bond at maturity.

Diversity in Corporate Finance. The business corporation is primarily a financing device. The object is to assemble capital and place it under the control of a limited number of persons. In the case of large businesses, it is necessary to draw upon the savings of a great number of investors, and, since people differ in their attitude toward risk, it is necessary that the opportunities for investment in corporations that are seeking funds should be such that they will appeal to different people. Accordingly, common stocks provide an opportunity for investment for those who are willing to assume the risk of loss or the possibility of gain that ownership of common stock confers on the owner. For those who are more conservative but who seek a return on their money that is higher than they could obtain on more secure investments, preferred stock may be suited to their desires. Finally, those who wish to obtain an income from their money but who wish to avoid the risk that ownership entails find that bonds are best suited to their requirements.

Cooperatives

The single proprietorship, the partnership, and the business corporation are forms of ownership that are in harmony with the idea of the right of the owner of property to control it and to utilize it for the purpose of making a profit. But the operation of a business for the purpose of making a profit directly from the business is not always the aim of the owners, even in a society that is predominantly capitalistic. An exception is found in the cooperative society or association.

There is a lack of uniformity in the terminology used in classifying cooperative societies. We may say, however, that *consumers' cooperatives* are associations of individuals organized for the purpose of purchasing consumer goods and services for their members. *Cooperative marketing* organizations, most frequently made up of farmers, are associations of producers for the purpose of selling the products of the members. The aim of the consumers' cooperative is to enable the members to obtain goods and services at a cost lower than they could secure from stores that are operated for profit. The purpose of marketing cooperatives is to sell directly to central markets or to manufacturers that use farm products; that is, the farmer members perform additional marketing functions themselves and thus eliminate the services of some middlemen. Any savings that can be realized in marketing costs go to the members.

A *credit union* is a cooperative financing agency, the funds of which are supplied by members who receive a reasonable rate of interest. The members usually consist of wage earners and salaried employees, and loans are relatively small in amount.

In the cooperative the capital needed is supplied by the members and by borrowing. As a rule, interest is paid on both invested and borrowed capital, although it is not always allowed on the former. Consumers' cooperatives sell goods to the members at market prices, and any savings are paid to the members in proportion to their purchases.

Public Ownership

Public ownership in this country is not undertaken as a rule except when it is unprofitable for private enterprise to supply an essential good or service at prices that the great majority of the people can afford to pay. An outstanding example of public ownership in the United States is the post office system. Some cities own and operate their own waterworks, gas and electric plants, bus services, and other public utilities, and, of course, streets and highways have long been publicly owned and maintained. Other examples are public school systems and hospitals. For some time the United States government has been engaged in the development of electric power and conservation projects, of which the Tennessee Valley Authority is the best-known example.

Governmental enterprises are financed from funds obtained from the citizens by means of borrowing, taxes, or rates charged for services. The initial investment is usually obtained from loans, and any deficit from operations is made up by means of taxes. These facts are important in comparing the relative efficiency of government-owned and privately owned enterprises. The management of government-owned enterprises is usually placed in the hands of managers or directors who receive their appointment from officials who have been elected to office by the people. It should not be necessary to stress the fact that those who are to direct publicly owned enterprises should be chosen because of their ability and honesty and not because of their allegiance and political value to the appointing authority.

THE ROLE OF GOVERNMENT

When our economic system was described in Chapter 2, our attention was directed primarily to the two private sectors of the economy. For the sake of simplicity, the functions of government were ignored. The model flows of output and income depicted in Chapter 3, for example, did not consider the economic impact of government.

Obviously the economic role of government in the modern world cannot be ignored. We may view the absence of government in our previous discussion, aside from incidental references, as a convenient expository device. The actual economy is extremely complex, and our minds secure a firmer grasp on its operation if we introduce the interacting components one at a time.

The Economy and the Polity

To gain perspective, it is useful to think of any human society as composed of an economy and a polity. That aspect of society having to do with the allocation of resources and products—the aspect covering production and consumption—can be viewed as the economy. The other aspect having to do with law, control, and ultimate leadership can be conceived as the polity, or political system. This is not to say that there are no other aspects of society, but these two areas of human order and organization are central to any society.

Much of human history can be described by the way in which interests or actions in the polity have blended with or conflicted with those in the economy. For instance, in medieval Europe political power was concentrated in the hands of the king and the nobles. The medieval economy was almost exclusively agricultural; nobles owned the land that was cultivated by peasants, who were virtually without property. Thus, the economy was dominated by the polity—as it is in some underdeveloped nations today.

The Industrial Revolution gave birth to the factory system, technological advance, and entrepreneurship. Often the interests of those who emerged as powerful forces in the economy conflicted with the interests of kings and nobles. A strong mercantile class could, in some instances, dictate national policy to the king. Economic growth and a rapidly expanding middle class contributed to a change in the form of government itself. Democratic governments, or quasi-democratic governments, were more consonant with developments in the economy.

During the nineteenth century, prevalent political doctrines espoused a clear separation between the economy and the polity. Governments in the Western world retreated from the economic scene. It was at this time that Karl Marx called upon the working classes to overthrow capitalism and to merge the polity and the economy under communism. Thus does the pendulum swing, and thus is the world faced with the same issue today.

This brief historical sketch is not meant to be an interpretation of the course of all history. The important point is the fact that historical events have been very strongly influenced by the balance between the polity and the economy in all known societies. The relationship between public and private control can be seen in most major social issues in the United States today. Should the federal government support private schools? If so, does this mean government control over their freedom to determine their own form, content, and style of education? Will assistance to poverty-stricken families destroy private initiative? Will the magnitude of defense-related contracts with private industry enable the central government to dictate policy to business firms and labor unions? Underlying these questions is the ancient issue of balance between the polity and the economy.

Economic Liberalism, Pure and Mixed

Free enterprise capitalism is an outgrowth of the philosophy of economic liberalism of the nineteenth century and the early part of the twentieth century. The major tenets of economic liberalism were free trade, self-interest, private property, laissez-faire, and competition.

The Liberal Doctrine. According to *economic liberalism*, individuals were free to seek their own occupations, to enter into businesses of their choice, and to act as they saw fit within the legal environment to improve their individual economic welfare. Economic society was knit together through mutual exchanges that were founded on the division of labor. Self-interest was the motivating force of the economy. In order to increase his economic welfare, for example, an individual might decide to produce hats and to sell them at a profit. But by doing so, he would automatically be supplying goods to the community and providing employment for his fellowmen.

Order in the system was maintained by competition. Businesses competing with one another for consumer trade would develop new and better products or attempt to sell existing products at lower prices. Likewise, competition would prevent any firm from charging an excessive price. Free entry into and exit from the market would assure that sufficient competition was always present, and prices were determined by the free forces of supply and demand. Competition would prevent the growth of monopoly and insure the satisfaction of consumer demand. Not only were competitive forces to be responsible for the determination of the prices of consumer goods and services, but they were also to determine wage rates for workers.

Since self-interest was the driving force behind the economy and since competition was to serve as a regulator for the economy, a policy of *laissez-faire*, or nongovernment intervention, prevailed. This was a policy of government "hands off" in the economic activities of individuals and businesses. From an economic point of view, the primary functions of the government were to protect private property, to enforce contracts, and to serve as an umpire in the event of economic disputes.

Although economic liberalism envisioned a minimum amount of government intervention in the economy, the policy of laissez-faire has been greatly modified in recent decades. Monopolies arose. Markets were often controlled and consumers were exploited. Control over local labor markets by giant firms kept wages down, often below the living wage required by the dignity of human labor.

As a result of these and other abuses and imperfections, increased government intervention became necessary. Antitrust laws were introduced to prevent the restraint of competition by monopolies and business combinations. Labor laws were passed to protect the rights of workers. Food and drug laws were designed to protect the health of our citizens. In more recent decades government action in the form of socio-economic legislation, such as minimum-wage laws, Social Security, and environmental protection, has been taken to promote the common good.

Our Mixed Economy. As a result of the large amount of imperfect competition and the growing role of the government in economic affairs, our economy is now a *mixed economy*. It is a composite of highly competitive businesses on the one hand and of monopolies on the other. Giant corporations stand side by side with small single proprietorships.

Strongly organized labor exists alongside unorganized labor. Labor unions have a restrictive influence on many areas of managerial decision making that once were considered prerogatives of management. Although only approximately one fourth of the American labor force is organized, unions exert such a powerful influence on our economy that some economists refer to our system as a "laboristic economy." Unions today are as highly organized and bureaucratic as many of our large corporations in the United States.

Our economy is mixed also in the sense that the government regulates some industries and not others. Furthermore, the government owns and operates some businesses directly through various government agencies, such as the Tennessee Valley Authority and the United States Government Printing Office. State and local governments regulate and sometimes operate public utilities, such as gas, water, electrical power, and transportation companies.

The Economic Functions of the Government

Whether the government should intervene in the economy and to what extent it should intervene are controversial questions. For a better understanding of the government's role in the economy, let us consider the functions exercised by government in a modern economy.

Protect Individual and Property Rights. We have never had complete laissez-faire in our American economy. In fact, it is often said that absolute free trade and complete laissez-faire are incompatible. If we have absolute freedom, some individuals may, in doing anything they desire, engage in economic activities that interfere with the rights and freedom of others. In order to protect the rights and freedom of all, therefore, it is necessary to have certain restrictions on the use of individual and property rights.

Property must be protected, contracts must be enforced, and individuals must not be exploited. The institution of private property, for example, gives us the right to use our property as we like. But this does not mean that we can discharge poisonous gases from a chemical factory; nor may a monopolist use unfair means to prevent other firms from entering the market. As a consequence of previous and possible future violations of rights, we have several laws enforced by the government for the purpose of protecting individual and property rights.

Prevent Abuses and Inequities. Inequities frequently develop as a result of incongruities in our economic system. Our present agricultural price-support program sponsored by the government is a major undertaking designed to help keep farm income on an equitable basis with industrial incomes. Income inequities often exist in connection with minority groups. Consequently, an employer with a contract to do work or to supply goods to the federal government cannot discriminate against any employee because of race, color, or creed.

A large number of our laws were passed in order to correct abusive practices and economic inequities only after such abuses and inequities became prevalent. Examples include the passage of securities regulation and the establishment of the Securities and Exchange Commission in the early thirties after the stock market irregularities uncovered in the 1920s, the passage of the antitrust laws after the development of exploitative practices arising from economic integration, and the enactment of the Landrum-Griffin Act in 1959 after the revelation of irregularities in handling union funds disclosed by the Senate labor racket investigation during 1959. More recently, we have seen a number of federal acts passed to give us cleaner air and purer water, as well as others to prevent the continued deterioration of the national environment. Requirements of these laws are enforced, in large part, through the recently federally appointed Environmental Protection Agency (EPA).

It appears, then, that government intervention often takes place when our economic groups demonstrate that they are unable to regulate themselves or lack the self-discipline necessary to do so. Observing this pattern, numerous economic units in recent years have endeavored to regulate themselves in order to prevent the need for initial or further government regulation.

Promote Competition. Because of the inherent advantages of a high degree of competition in the economy, as we will explain in later chapters, the government endeavors to promote competition and prevent the restraint of trade. Consequently, antitrust laws prohibit monopolies, trusts, and conspiracies that are in restraint of trade. Collusion between sellers and/or buyers is likewise outlawed.

Mergers, consolidations, and other forms of business integration are restricted if they will tend to lessen competition. Historically, a lessening of competition has been deemed to occur when control of an industry is concentrated in a few hands. A court order preventing the merger of Bethlehem Steel Company and Youngstown Sheet and Tube Company in 1959 was a famous case in point. In the early sixties the Justice Department filed an antitrust suit to stop General Telephone and Electronics Corporation from acquiring Western Utilities Corporation and three telephone operating subsidiaries. The Justice Department asserted that the acquisition would give GT & E three of the largest independent telephone companies in the United States and that the merger would "substantially lessen competition in the manufacture, distribution, and sale of telephone equipment." The same reasoning guided the Supreme Court decision which held that the merger of the Philadelphia National Bank and the Girard Trust Corn Exchange would violate antitrust laws. Because of its concern with concentration in the communications industry, in 1969 the Justice Department filed suit to break up the radio-television-newspaper interests of the Gannett Company on antitrust grounds, forcing the company to sell station WREX-TV. Three similar suits followed within two years.

More recently, antitrust laws have been applied to conglomerates. These are mergers of firms engaged in the production of dissimilar goods or services. Thus, the notion of concentration inimical to competition has now been extended to cover ownership of assets across industry lines. A Justice Department suit to prevent acquisition of Jones and Laughlin Steel Corporation by Ling-Temco-Vought, Inc., alleged that the two firms "specifically considered" entering each other's industries and so the merger reduced "potential competition." To force International Telephone and Telegraph Corporation to divest itself of the Canteen Corporation, the Justice Department contended that the combined firm would benefit by inducing suppliers of IT & T to become buyers from Canteen, thereby reducing competition in the conveyance industry.

Promote the General Welfare. Although each individual and firm must promote his or its own self-interest, sometimes the welfare of all can be better promoted through the common effort of all. Since it is extremely difficult for all individuals and groups to get together on a scale necessary for some types of economic activity, improvement in the general economic well-being can be accomplished through and under the auspices of the government— local, state, or federal.

Government projects are usually undertaken only if the job proves to be beyond the scope or ability of private enterprise. Examples are construction of dams to provide flood control and electrical power. The building of roads, highways, and bridges is undertaken by the government because these generally are not profitable ventures for private enterprise. Our present system of widespread education would not exist if it were not supported by government. Government control and regulation of atomic energy, which could be disastrous if it were not used in a proper manner, benefit all of us.

The government endeavors to promote the general economic well-being through the operation of the Social Security System, which in addition to old-age pensions and unemployment compensation provides aid to the needy aged, to the blind, to widowed mothers, to dependent children, and others. The minimum-wage-and-hour law endeavors to insure a minimum level of living. Pure food and drug laws protect the public against various practices that could be injurious to the health and the welfare of individuals.

Stabilize Business Conditions. Since it has proven difficult for individuals and firms to do much about widespread unemployment or serious inflation, the government in the past few decades has taken a more active part in an effort to stabilize the level of economic activity. In fact, according to the Employment Act of 1946, the federal government is committed to use the economic measures at its disposal to create conditions that are favorable to a high level of employment. The general responsibilities and policies of the government in this and other areas will be discussed in subsequent chapters.

The government, of course, must exercise its economic functions judiciously. It must be careful, for example, in protecting individual rights not to impinge too much upon property rights. It must restrict business collusion without weakening free enterprise. It must promote the general welfare without stifling initiative.

Thus, it would seem that the best course of action for the government would be to let individuals and private enterprise do what they can for themselves, with the government intervening only when it is necessary to perform activities which individuals and private enterprise cannot perform for themselves or which they cannot perform adequately. Under such a situation, it is not surprising that issues frequently arise as to what individuals should be expected to do for themselves.

The Economic Tools of Government

In carrying out programs intended to have an impact on the economy, the government has recourse to two basic tools of economic policy. These are its power to tax and its authorization to spend.

The Power to Tax. In our mixed economy public enterprise exists side by side with private enterprise. The federal government maintains defense establishments, constructs public work projects such as dams, operates public utilities such as nuclear accelerators, and maintains national parks. In addition, the government finances educational programs such as scholarships, fellowships and loans, special training for the underprivileged, and vocational education. Agricultural assistance and highway construction are also important government activities. To carry out these projects and enterprises, of course, funds are needed. The primary source of funds is derived from the government's power to tax.

Both individuals and business firms are subject to taxation. At the federal level the single most important source of government revenue is the income tax. By means of variations in the tax rate, the government is able to control the flow of revenue obtained from the private sector of the economy. Several of the states have also imposed an income tax in recent years, but traditionally the states have relied primarily upon sales taxes. At the local level of government, property taxes and licensing fees have generated the bulk of expendable funds.

The Mandate to Spend. When the public approves of a government program, in effect the citizens confirm a mandate to engage in spending. Governmental efforts to promote technological advancement, to enforce civil rights legislation, to reduce poverty, to build interstate highways, or to fight a war all entail costs. Government activities are no exception to the laws of economics. Public approval of a government enterprise or program is tantamount to agreement by the private sector to submit to the additional tax burden necessary to make it a reality—unless some other government program is eliminated or diminished.

The larger is government and the more prominent is its role in society, the larger are the expenditures entailed by its activities. By the same token, tax payments by the private sectors to the government will rise along with the scale of government activities.

The Impact of Government

Government expenditures and tax revenues reflect the size of government. However, it is important to distinguish between two types of changes in expenditures and taxes.

Stabilization Policies. The government can be viewed as draining off potential demand—the source of income—from the private sectors by means of its tax receipts. The government bolsters or adds to demand—and thus income—when it injects greater expenditures into the production and income flow than it takes out in the form of taxes. Therefore, one economic impact of government is determined by the relationship between tax receipts and government expenditures. Without too great an oversimplification, we can say the government acts to increase output and income when expenditures exceed taxes, for the two need not be equal during any given time interval such as a year. Conversely, the government acts to repress income or the price level when taxes exceed expenditures.

By means of variations in tax revenues and expenditures, the government can counteract movements in the private sectors. When the economy dips into a recession and unemployment rises, the government can replace private spending and/or reduce taxes to encourage greater demand in the private sector. When there is pressure on the price level and inflation threatens, the government can drain off more purchasing power through taxes than it puts back through expenditures. It is by this device of varying expenditures *relative to* tax receipts that the government lends stability to the economy.

The Long Pull. These relatively short-run variations in taxes and expenditures are primarily a matter of the relation between the two, not a matter of the absolute size of each. The question relevant to stability is whether taxes are greater than, less than, or equal to expenditures during a given period. Both taxes and expenditures may be small and still permit *relative* variations, so long as both are not so miniscule that the impact of variations is trivial.

A different question is the absolute size of taxes and expenditures. As a practical matter (and subject to certain reservations) inequality between taxes and expenditures cannot be maintained indefinitely. Over very long periods they must be approximately equal. Changes in the absolute magnitudes of taxes and expenditures over the long run, compared to the level of income generated in the business sector, can be taken as a measure of the size of government. If government expenditures constitute a larger and larger percentage of all income payments, then the size and impact of government is growing.

Fears of a threat to individual freedoms that may accompany big government (just like fears of big business or big labor unions) should hinge upon the long-run trend of taxes and expenditures rather than upon year-to-year variations designed to induce stability. The political issue is whether the size of government exceeds the limits that are judged to be consonant with individual liberty. Short-run stability can be achieved by a government that is not so big as to exercise undesirable control over private decision making. The ultimate political issue revolves around the size of government that is best. Needless to say, the "best" size will vary with time and circumstances, and it is difficult to determine what size is most desirable at a given time and under given circumstances.

The Limits of Power

It seems we have come full circle in this discussion of the role of government in a private enterprise economy. We began by identifying possible conflicts of interests between the polity and the economy. These conflicts, and issues of checks and balances, are as old as human society itself. At times in the past, the political organization has dominated the economic organization. At other times the economic sector of society has operated with little interference from government. Nevertheless, the issue is a perennial one. In the present American society, with an advanced state of technology and a complex economic organization, the issue is still alive.

The size and impact of government has grown in response to social and economic problems that have been judged too large in scope or too serious in nature to be resolved by individuals or groups in the private sectors. If the problems are such as to demand more government activity and thus bigger government, it may be that the solution of social and economic problems is attained at the sacrifice of freedom in the private sectors. A higher level of economic welfare and a more widespread distribution of the fruits of production could bring greater government control over the allocation of resources and the efficiency of the economy.

Economics cannot, of course, provide final answers to questions about the most desirable size of government. The issues extend beyond the boundaries of economics proper and include considerations of political philosophy and social justice as well as economics. In a democratic society consensus among citizens ultimately determines the size, the form, and the functions of government.

SUMMARY

1. Consumption, although no less important to the welfare of a nation than is production, has only recently been subject to extensive analysis.
2. Economizing, or the process of applying scarce means in an effort to satisfy unlimited wants, is a major problem in any economy, both on an individual and a national basis.
3. Consumers are sovereign in the determination of what and how much is to be produced in our economy and partly in determining who will receive the fruits of production.
4. Consumption patterns change with many things, such as changes in income, education, and price levels. But a general pattern will show that as income increases a smaller percentage of income will be spent on basic necessities and a larger percentage will be spent on conveniences and luxuries.
5. The level of living in the United

States has definitely improved in the past decade, as well as over many previous decades, and will increase even more in the future.

6. In any economy production necessitates the making of certain decisions and the performance of certain functions, among which are the following: deciding what, where, when, and how much to produce; providing and organizing the essential factors of production; managing productive processes; and assuming financial risks.

7. In our economy these functions are ordinarily undertaken by private individuals and groups whose incentive is the making of profits and who set up a type of business organization that is considered appropriate. The important kinds of business organization are the single proprietorship, the partnership, and the business corporation. True cooperatives—either consumers' or marketing—are not operated for the purpose of earning profit but rather for the purpose of providing a service to the members.

8. A business corporation is a legal person that owns the assets and owes the liabilities of the concern. The stockholders own the corporation and manage it indirectly by delegating their managerial prerogatives to a board of directors.

Corporations obtain funds either from the sale of stock or by borrowing. Shares of stock represent equity interests, while bonds are evidences of creditor interests.

9. As a rule, cooperatives and public industries are designed to supply services and not to earn profits.

10. In free enterprise capitalism the doctrine of economic liberalism guided the balance between the political and economic spheres of influence during the nineteenth and early twentieth centuries, and a mixed economy has since emerged.

11. In our mixed economy the economic functions of government include protection of individual and property rights, prevention of abuses and inequities, promotion of competition and the general welfare, and stabilization of business conditions.

12. Government exerts its impact on the economy through taxation and spending. Short-run stabilization is a question of the relationship between tax receipts and expenditures. This relationship should be distinguished from the absolute size of taxes and expenditures.

13. Expansion in the size of government can create a threat to individual freedoms, but the issue entails philosophical and moral considerations as well as economic ones.

NEW TERMS

Consumption, *p. 53*
Consumer demand, *p. 54*
Standard of living, *p. 55*
Real income, *p. 57*
Single proprietorship, *p. 59*
Partnership, *p. 60*
General partnerships, *p. 61*
Corporation, *p. 62*
Board of directors, *p. 62*

Corporation capital, *p. 62*
Capital stock, *p. 63*
Par value, *p. 63*
No-par-value stock, *p. 63*
Book value, *p. 63*
Market value, *p. 63*
Common stock, *p. 63*
Preferred stock, *p. 63*
Bond, *p. 64*

QUESTIONS FOR DISCUSSION AND ANALYSIS

1. Do you think that consumers are really sovereign and that they have the ability to determine the type and amount of production that takes place in our economy?

2. How do you reconcile the concept of the affluent society label given to the U.S. economy with the government's "war on poverty"?

3. Exactly why is it that the percentage of income spent on basic necessities declines as income increases? Does this mean that the actual amount of money spent on foodstuffs is going to decrease in the next few decades as incomes rise? Why or why not?

4. Should anything other than economic values be taken into consideration when showing the improvement in our level of living? If so, what values?

5. What are the characteristics of each of the four major types of business organizations existing in our economy?

6. (a) What was Marshall's definition of a corporation? Explain in your own words what the definition means.

(b) Is the Marshall definition and the "entity theory" the same? Explain.

7. Many American corporations have from several thousand to several hundreds of thousands of stockholders.

(a) What difficulties would arise if all these stockholders were partners in their respective businesses?

(b) Would it be possible in most cases to get together the hundreds of millions of dollars that are needed to organize railroad, manu- facturing, and other big businesses if the partnership were the only kind of business organization available? Why?

8. (a) Distinguish carefully between stocks and bonds of a corporation.

(b) What determines the value of each?

(c) Which kind of corporation securities would you say is the better investment? Why?

9. "Stockholders have no say in the management of the corporation. The officers run the business as they please and they have no legal responsibility if they mismanage the funds of the business." Evaluate the statement.

10. (a) Why do corporations sometimes issue both stocks and bonds?

(b) Why do they issue different kinds of stocks and bonds?

(c) When are stocks preferable to bonds as a type of investment?

(d) When are common stocks more desirable than preferred stocks?

11. Is the doctrine of economic liberalism a major determinant of the role of government in today's American society?

12. In what areas do you observe a potential conflict of interests between private industry and government?

13. What are the economic functions of government in a private enterprise economy? Do you think there is a trend toward additional functions being assumed by government? Explain your answer.

14. How would you attempt to determine the most desirable size of government in the United States?

SUGGESTED READINGS

Aaker, D. A., and G. S. Day. *Consumerism: Search for the Consumer Interest.* New York: The Macmillan Company, 1971.

Blair, John M. *Economic Concentration: Structure, Behavior, and Public Policy.* New York: Harcourt Brace Jovanovich, Inc., 1972.

Bok, Derek C., and John T. Dunlop. *Labor and the American Community.* New York: Simon & Schuster, Inc., 1970.

Boulding, Kenneth E. *Principles of Economic Policy.* Englewood Cliffs, N.J.: Prentice-Hall, Inc., 1958.

Buchanan, James N., and Robert D. Tollison. *Theory of Public Choice: Political Applications of Economics.* Ann Arbor: The University of Michigan Press, 1972.

Cox, Edward F., *et al. Nader Report on the Federal Trade Commission.* New York: Richard W. Baron Publishing Co., Inc., 1969.

Department of Commerce, Bureau of the Census. *Annual Report on the Labor Force.* Washington: U.S. Government Printing Office, 1973.

Dougall, Herbert E. *Capital Markets and Institutions*, 2d ed. Englewood Cliffs, N.J.: Prentice-Hall, Inc., 1970.

Eyestowe, Robert. *Political Economy: Politics and Policy Analysis.* Chicago: Markham Publishing Company, 1972.

Galbraith, John K. *The Affluent Society*, rev. ed. New York: The New American Library Inc., 1970.

Hayek, Friedrich A. *Individualism and Economic Order.* Chicago: Henry Regnery Company, 1972.

Herfindahl, Orris C. *Natural Resource Information for Economic Development.* Baltimore: The Johns Hopkins University Press, 1969.

Katona, George. *The Powerful Consumer.* New York: McGraw-Hill Book Company, Inc., 1960.

Lyons, Barrow. *Tomorrow's Birthright—A Political and Economic Interpretation of Our Natural Resources.* New York: Funk and Wagnalls Publishing Company, 1955.

Mason, Edward S. (ed.). *The Corporation in Modern Society.* New York: Atheneum Publishers, 1966.

Meadows, Donella H., *et al. The Limits to Growth, A Report for the Club of Rome Project on the Predicament of Mankind.* New York: Universe Books, 1972.

Myrdal, Gunnar. *The Challenge of Affluence.* New York: Random House, Inc., 1963.

Schumpeter, Joseph A. *Capitalism, Socialism and Democracy*, 3d ed. New York: Harper & Row Publishers, 1950.

Zimmermann, Erich W. *Introduction to World Resources.* New York: Harper & Row, Publishers, 1964.

5

The Circular Flow of Economic Activity

PREVIEW The circular flow of economic activity and the price level are affected by the spending of the three basic sectors of the economy: consumers, businesses, and the government. At certain times, production, employment, and income will rise resulting in full employment and prosperity. Under other circumstances inflation will occur. At other times, when the total spending by the three sectors declines, a decrease in production, employment, and income will result. Perhaps, too, prices will fall. In this chapter we endeavor to analyze the basic causes of these changes in economic activity and the price level, and we attempt to account for our recent experiences with inflation and unemployment.

In Chapter 3 we learned that business firms and other economic units—such as government agencies and hospitals or nonprofit organizations—must utilize factors of production: land, labor, capital, and entrepreneurship. Since the first three of these factors are generally owned by someone other than the entrepreneur, he must remunerate the owners of these factors for the services they render. The payments by business firms for the productive factors naturally become income to the owners of these factors. This income in turn is used as purchasing power by the owners of the factors of production to buy goods and services. Likewise, the profits of the entrepreneurs, or businesses, become purchasing power with which they can buy consumer goods and services or secure additional factors of production.

The demand for goods and services by income recipients thereby leads to more production. In turn the productive process brings about additional payments of income to the owners of the factors of production. This continuous operation of demand, production, income, and new demand sets up a _circular flow_ of economic activity in our economy. This circular flow is the mechanism by which land, labor, capital, and entrepreneurial resources are allocated among alternative employments. It is sometimes referred to as the "wheel of fortune" because it is also the process by which we determine the remuneration to the factors of production and by which we distribute income to various individuals and firms in our economy.

CIRCULAR FLOW MODEL

Since we will be referring constantly to this concept, let us demonstrate it graphically by use of a model. Although there are many other economic units involved at this point, we will divide the model of the economy into two simple segments: business firms and individuals. Government will be added at a later point. In our modern-day economy, most individuals work for business firms or are in business for themselves. Individuals offer their productive services to firms in exchange for remuneration in the form of wages, rent, and interest. Owners of the firms receive a profit for their contribution.

These income recipients buy the goods and services produced by businesses. If all the produced goods and services are sold—and they should be if people spend all the income they receive for the goods and the services that are available—firms will be induced to produce a second round of goods and services, and the process will start over again. Continuation of this process keeps our economy producing, paying incomes, spending, and allocating goods and services to the individuals according to their demands. The process is demonstrated in Figure 5-1.

In this model it can be seen that all income finds its way into the hands of the individuals represented at the right in Figure 5-1. Since the profit of a

FIGURE 5-1

**CIRCULAR FLOW—
SIMPLE MODEL**

The outer circle represents money flows, while the inner circle denotes flows of real productive services and final produced goods and services. At point *A* the monetary flow is viewed by firms as the cost of production (including profit). At point *B* this same flow is viewed as income by individuals who own factors of production. The expenditures by individuals at point *C* constitute the sales receipts of business firms at point *D*.

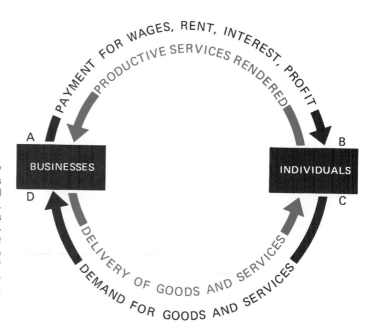

business becomes income to its owner, the individuals in the model include the owners of business firms as well as the owners of the other factors of production. The value of the goods and services produced is determined by the cost of production—that is, by the payments for manpower, resources, and capital in the form of wages, rent, and interest, plus the profits for the entrepreneurs. We can say, therefore, that the total payment of income in the economy is equal to the value or cost (including profit) of the production. Individuals, including business owners who receive income in the form of profits, will thus have sufficient income to buy the goods and the services produced by the economy.

A Stable Economy

If all income is spent, either on consumer or capital goods, business firms will move all the goods off the market and will be induced to produce the same amount again. We know from experience, however, that individuals do not spend their entire income. People save. What happens to the circular flow in this case? Unless there is additional spending from some source to make up for the amount of saving in the economy, saving may have an adverse effect on the level of economic activity. Let us assume that 500,000 units are produced and $500,000 is distributed in income. If individuals spend the $500,000 to buy 500,000 units of consumer and capital goods, all production will be sold at an average price level of $1 per unit. However, if people spend only $400,000 on consumer goods and save $100,000, not all goods will be sold unless the savings are used directly to purchase capital goods or are borrowed by individuals other than savers to buy consumer or capital goods. Thus, we can maintain a given level of economic activity only if we have an amount of borrowing and/or nonconsumer spending in the economy equal to the amount of savings. This is shown in Figure 5-2.

Since spending on capital goods is referred to as *investment* in current economic analysis, we can conclude by saying that as long as investment equals savings, we will have a stable flow of economic activity. Since total spending is nothing other than total demand and since income is equivalent to current production (supply), current demand for goods and services will equal current supply.

A Contracting Economy (investment less than saving)

Whenever investment does not equal savings, however, there will be a disruption in the circular flow of economic activity. For example, suppose that out of the $500,000 received by individuals, $400,000 is spent on consumption and $100,000 is saved. Moreover, suppose that out of the $100,000 saved only $75,000 is invested directly by the savers or indirectly

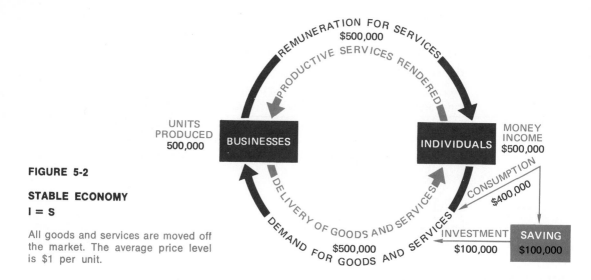

REMUNERATION FOR SERVICES
$500,000

PRODUCTIVE SERVICES RENDERED

UNITS
PRODUCED
500,000

BUSINESSES

INDIVIDUALS

MONEY
INCOME
$500,000

CONSUMPTION
$400,000

DELIVERY OF GOODS AND SERVICES

DEMAND FOR GOODS AND SERVICES
$500,000

INVESTMENT
$100,000

SAVING
$100,000

FIGURE 5-2

STABLE ECONOMY

I = S

All goods and services are moved off the market. The average price level is $1 per unit.

by the borrowers. In such a case, after producing 500,000 units valued at $500,000, producers would see only $475,000 returning to buy the goods produced. The level of economic activity would drop because one of two things or a combination of both would happen: (1) an accumulation of unsold goods would occur, or (2) a reduction in the prices of the goods would take place.

Inventory Accumulation. If the price level is maintained at $1 per unit, the $475,000 that flows back will purchase only 475,000 units. This leaves 25,000 units unsold in inventories, as shown in Figure 5-3. If the producers of 500,000 units sold only 475,000 units in one period, they might adjust their anticipated sales to 475,000 units for the subsequent period. Then production of 450,000 units in the subsequent period plus an inventory stock of 25,000 units remaining from the previous period would yield the desired supply of 475,000 units. This move would cut back current production, and the producers would use less manpower and fewer productive resources. As a result, there would be less income paid and spending would fall accordingly. The net result would be a decrease in economic activity in the subsequent period. In short, production, employment, and income would fall. This could lead to further declines in business activity resulting in more inventory accumulation.

Decline in Prices. Under certain circumstances, when $500,000 of income is paid out but only $475,000 returns to buy the goods produced, the market could be cleared; that is, all the goods could be sold by a reduction in the price level to 95 cents per unit. In such event, $475,000 could buy 500,000

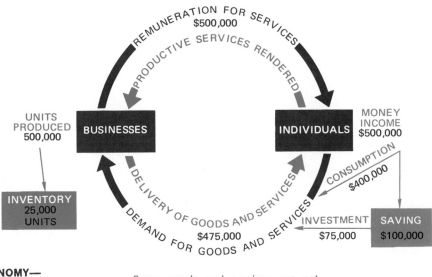

FIGURE 5-3

CONTRACTING ECONOMY—
INVENTORY ACCUMULATION
I < S

Some goods and services are not
moved off the market. The average
price level remains at $1 per unit.

units. In fact, that is what frequently happens: competition forces the prices
down when total supply exceeds total demand. If prices begin to fall, however, certain high-cost producers may not be able to make a profit by selling
at this lower price, and other producers will make less profit per unit.
Consequently, the incentive to produce will be weakened, many firms will
cut back production or go out of business, and total output in the subsequent period will be less. This means that fewer units of the factors of
production will be utilized, less income will be received, and total demand
will fall. See Figure 5-4.

Whenever investment is less than savings, total spending will be less than
total income and demand will be less than supply. The shortage of demand
will lead to a decrease in production in subsequent periods because of
inventory accumulation (goods not sold) or because of falling prices or a
combination of both. As production is cut, employment will decline and
income will fall. Hence, we will have a decrease in the level of economic
activity, which might precipitate a business depression. In fact, inventory
accumulation was in large part responsible for the decline of economic
activity in 1953-1954 and the recession in 1958. A less vigorous inventory
buildup in the 1959-1960 recovery, on the other hand, contributed toward
the mildness of the 1960-1961 decline. Inventory depletion of more than
$10 billion was largely responsible for the slowdown in the economy early
in 1967, and it was an important factor in the recession of 1970.

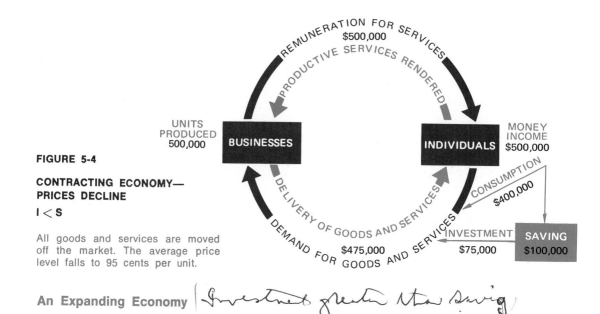

FIGURE 5-4

**CONTRACTING ECONOMY—
PRICES DECLINE**

I < S

All goods and services are moved
off the market. The average price
level falls to 95 cents per unit.

An Expanding Economy | *Investment greater than Saving* |

If total investment were to exceed total savings, businesses and individuals
would borrow more than they saved. This would cause spending to exceed
total income and demand to exceed total production. Assume 500,000 units
were produced and $500,000 was distributed in income. Assume also that
individuals spent $400,000 on consumption and saved $100,000 that found
its way directly or indirectly into investment. If business firms were to
borrow from some source (such as a bank that can create money) an additional $25,000 for the purchase of machinery and equipment, total investment
would be $125,000, which when added to the $400,000 in consumer spending would make total spending $525,000. Such action might cause an
increase in the level of economic activity or an increase in the price level,
depending on the circumstances. See Figure 5-5.

More Goods and Services. Naturally businessmen will endeavor to increase
production in order to satisfy the additional demand for goods and services.
If the economy is in a state of less than full employment—that is, if labor,
capital, and capacity to increase production are available—additional goods
and services will be forthcoming to satisfy the higher demand. Certainly if
there is an additional $25,000 available to buy goods, some enterprising
businessmen are going to produce the goods demanded. When they do, total
production will be increased to 525,000 units. In addition, the price level will
remain at $1 per unit since the $525,000 in spending is exchanged for the
525,000 units produced. Business firms that must pay for additional productive agents will pay $525,000 instead of the former $500,000, and income

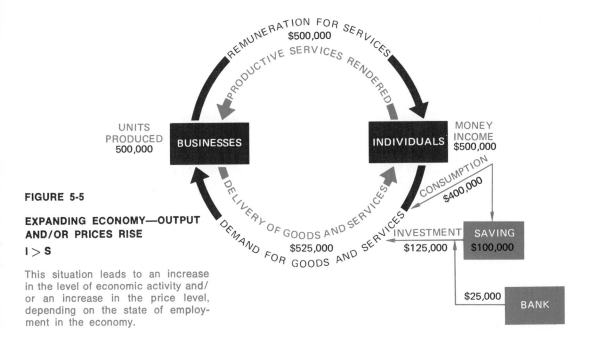

UNITS
PRODUCED
500,000

BUSINESSES

REMUNERATION FOR SERVICES
$500,000

PRODUCTIVE SERVICES RENDERED

INDIVIDUALS

MONEY
INCOME
$500,000

CONSUMPTION
$400,000

DELIVERY OF GOODS AND SERVICES

DEMAND FOR GOODS AND SERVICES
$525,000

INVESTMENT
$125,000

SAVING
$100,000

$25,000

BANK

FIGURE 5-5

**EXPANDING ECONOMY—OUTPUT
AND/OR PRICES RISE**

I > S

This situation leads to an increase
in the level of economic activity and/
or an increase in the price level,
depending on the state of employment in the economy.

will increase accordingly. This in turn will increase spending and bring about more production. As a result, the economy will be operating at a higher level of production and employment. Therefore, whenever investment exceeds savings, total spending will exceed total income, demand will be greater than supply, and there will be an increase in the level of economic activity provided that we are at less than full employment. This increase in economic activity will be necessary to meet and to satisfy demand.

Higher Prices. If the same situation occurs in a period of full employment, the immediate result will be higher prices (inflation) rather than an increase in economic activity. With full employment, businessmen will be unable to obtain the necessary manpower, resources, capital, and capacity needed to produce additional goods. It is true that some businessmen will endeavor to increase production in order to satisfy the demand for the additional 25,000 units. But the only way they will be able to obtain the necessary factors of production in the short run will be to bid them away from other producers. Resource prices will be forced upward as entrepreneurs bid against each other for the relatively scarce factors of production. Furthermore, instead of realizing expanded output, the product price level will rise to $1.05 per unit, and the $525,000 of spending will be used to buy 500,000 units of output as individuals bid against each other for the limited goods available. Although the composition of production (the amount of capital goods compared to consumer goods) may be changed, the total amount of production will not be changed. These circumstances caused the serious inflation in the post-World War II period, 1946-1948, and caused prices to rise noticeably from 1966 through 1970 after more than eight years of relative price stability in the economy. Other factors caused inflation to continue beyond 1970 and into 1974. If subsequent productivity can be increased through more efficient use of manpower, better utilization of resources, and expanded capacity, any inflationary pressures will tend to be alleviated.

Thus, we can say that at any time investment is greater than savings, an increase in the level of economic activity will result provided the economy is in a state of less than full employment. If we are at full employment, however, this situation will merely cause prices to rise.

Summary of the Circular Flow Model

In summarizing the foregoing presentation of the relationship of investment (I) to saving (S) and its effect on the economy, it is well to keep in mind that those who do the saving are not necessarily the same persons or economic units that do the investing. Consequently, there may be a divergence between the amount that investors are planning to invest and the amount that savers are planning to save. We will see later that this disequilibrium between planned investment and planned saving causes an expansion or contraction in economic activity until the economy reaches a level at which actual saving comes into balance with actual investment. But for the time being, we can sum up our demonstrations of the relationship of planned investment to planned saving as follows:

1. Whenever investment *is equal to* saving (I = S), the result will be equilibrium or a stable flow of economic activity. Prices will tend to remain stable.
2. Whenever investment *is less than* saving (I < S), the level of economic activity and/or the price level will decline.
3. Whenever investment *is greater than* saving (I > S), the level of economic activity will tend to increase if the economy is in a state of less than full employment. If the economy is at full employment, however, there will be no increase in the level of economic activity and prices will tend to rise.

GOVERNMENT AND THE CIRCULAR FLOW

Until about 40 years ago the primary objective of federal financing was to raise sufficient funds through taxation to cover the cost of performing the necessary services expected of the federal government. Therefore, great emphasis was placed on balancing the budget, even though budget experts were not always able to balance revenues and expenditures. In recent years, with the move away from laissez-faire, the government has at times purposely attempted to generate a surplus or a deficit as a means of stabilizing the level of economic activity.

A Balanced Budget

Since government spending can affect the circular flow of economic activity and the price level, a closer inspection is in order. A *balanced budget* means in effect that the government spends the same amount as it collects in taxes. What individuals and business firms do not spend in order to pay taxes will be spent by the government, and as a result, total spending in the economy will remain the same. Thus, a balanced budget tends to have a neutral effect on the economy. For example, as shown in Figure 5-6, if $50,000 were taxed out of $500,000 in total income, individuals would have only $450,000 for spending on consumption and investment. The adverse effect of the government tax, however, would be offset if the government in turn spent the $50,000 it received in taxes. Under such circumstances, total spending would remain at $500,000, and the total production would be moved off the market. There might be a change, however, in the composition of the goods and the services produced insofar as government

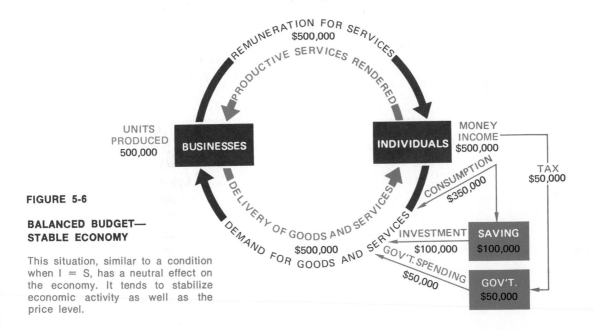

FIGURE 5-6

BALANCED BUDGET— STABLE ECONOMY

This situation, similar to a condition when I = S, has a neutral effect on the economy. It tends to stabilize economic activity as well as the price level.

spending would be substituted for private spending on consumption and investment.

A Surplus Budget

A *surplus budget,* that is, tax receipts in excess of government spending, will tend to decrease the level of economic activity or cause a decline in prices. During a period when strong inflationary forces exist, a surplus budget is occasionally used as an anti-inflationary measure. When the government spends less than it collects in taxes, total spending in the economy shrinks, which in turn has a depressing or deflationary effect on the economy. Assume in our circular flow that the government were to tax $50,000 but spend only $25,000. This would mean that total spending by consumers and investors would be reduced from $500,000 to $450,000 as a result of the tax payments. The reduction would be offset, however, only to the extent of $25,000 by government spending. In effect, total spending on consumption and investment plus government would be reduced to $475,000 for the economy as a whole. Consequently, spending would be less than income, demand would be less than supply, and there would be a decrease in the level of business activity or a decline in the price level, as shown in Figure 5-7.

A Deficit Budget

A *deficit budget*, expenditures in excess of what the government collects in taxes, will tend to bring about an increase in economic activity or to raise

(more Speeding then Coming)

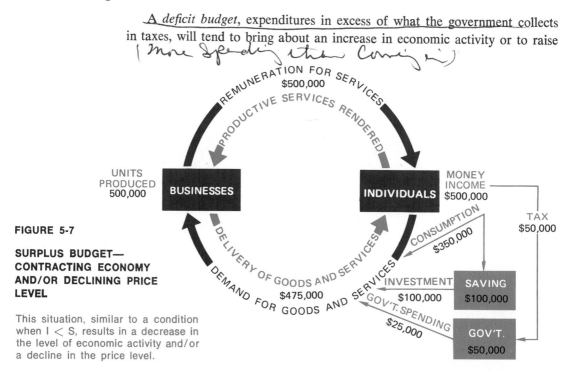

FIGURE 5-7

**SURPLUS BUDGET—
CONTRACTING ECONOMY
AND/OR DECLINING PRICE
LEVEL**

This situation, similar to a condition when I < S, results in a decrease in the level of economic activity and/or a decline in the price level.

prices, depending upon the circumstances. Since the government contributes more spending than it drains off the private sector in taxes, the expansionary effects of government spending will more than offset the contracting effects on consumption and investment. Referring once again to our circular flow concept, if individuals receive $500,000 in income for producing 500,000 units of goods and services and the government taxes $50,000, then total spending by consumers and investors will be reduced to $450,000. If the government spends not only the $50,000 it collects in taxes but also an additional $25,000 (which we will assume it borrows from the banks), total spending will rise to $525,000, as shown in Figure 5-8. Since total spending will exceed total income, demand will exceed the supply of goods and services available. Consequently, a deficit budget will tend to increase the level of economic activity if we are at less than full employment. If the economy is at a state of full employment, however, the budget deficit will merely cause a rise in the price level.

It must be realized that our examples were based on certain assumptions which may or may not prevail. For instance, we assumed that individuals pay taxes out of current incomes; we assumed that if individuals did not pay taxes, they would spend the money for consumption or investment; and we assumed

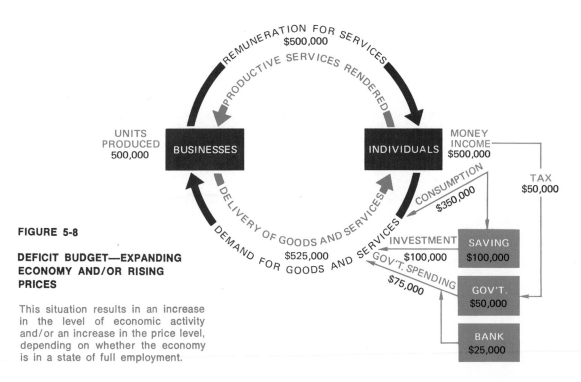

FIGURE 5-8

DEFICIT BUDGET—EXPANDING ECONOMY AND/OR RISING PRICES

This situation results in an increase in the level of economic activity and/or an increase in the price level, depending on whether the economy is in a state of full employment.

further that the government borrows from the banks instead of from the individuals and business firms in the economy. When these assumptions do not apply, our analysis will be modified—as we shall see later. The effects of government spending on the circular flow of economic activity can be summarized as follows:

1. A balanced budget tends to have a neutral effect on economic activity and the price level.
2. A surplus budget tends to decrease the level of economic activity and/or the price level. During a period of rising prices, however, a surplus budget can serve as an anti-inflationary measure without having any depressing effects on the economy.
3. A deficit budget, on the other hand, tends to increase the level of economic activity or the price level, depending on whether we are in a state of full employment.

CIRCULAR FLOW IN ACTION

In the past few decades we have had excellent examples of the various situations that have been described. In 1939 approximately 9.5 million persons were unemployed in the economy, and we were operating at 75-80 percent of our productive capacity while the price level was at 41.6 (1967 = 100). With the outbreak of World War II in Europe, the United States began producing defense goods for the Allies. The increased investment and government spending generated by the war brought about increased production, income, and employment. Although the increased investment and deficit spending increased the demand for goods and services, we were able to provide the additional supply required because we had the available manpower and resources with which to work. Total production in terms of constant (1958) dollars increased from $209 billion in 1939 to $298 billion in 1942. By 1942 the economy, for all practical purposes, was operating at near full employment, with unemployment of less than 3 million and capacity utilization of 90-95 percent.

Meanwhile, the price level rose from 41.6 to 48.8. Congress, realizing that further investment and deficit spending would lead to inflation, instituted price and wage controls which were in effect from 1942 to 1946. With the removal of economic controls in June, 1946 (at which time the price level was 55.0), spending continued at a high level as consumers, business firms, foreign nations, and the government demanded goods and services from the United States economy. From 1946 to 1948, the price level moved up briskly from 58.5 to 72.1, while production increased by a mere $11 billion because we did not have the available resources to increase output substantially. This is shown in Table 5-1.

TABLE 5-1

PRODUCTION, CAPACITY, PRICES, AND UNEMPLOYMENT

1939-1973

Year	Production [1] (Billions)	Capacity [2] Utilized %	Price [3] Level	Unemployment (Millions)	Unemployment as Percent of Civilian Labor Force
1939	$209	75–80	41.6	9.5	17.2
1942	298	90–95	48.8	2.7	4.7
1944	361	90–95	52.7	0.7	1.2
1946	313	90–95	58.5	2.3	3.8
1948	324	90–95	72.1	2.3	3.9
1949	324	80–85	71.4	3.6	5.9
1953	413	90–95	80.1	1.8	2.9
1954	407	80–85	80.5	3.5	5.5
1957	453	80–85	84.3	2.9	4.3
1958	447	75–80	86.6	4.6	6.8
1960	488	80–85	88.7	3.9	5.5
1961	497	75–80	89.6	4.7	6.7
1966	658	90–95	97.2	2.9	3.8
1967	675	85–90	100.0	3.0	3.8
1968	707	85–90	104.2	2.8	3.6
1969	726	85–90	109.8	2.8	3.5
1970	722	75–80	116.3	4.1	4.9
1971	745	75–80	121.3	5.0	5.9
1972	791	75–80	125.3	4.8	5.6
1973	837	80–85	133.1	4.3	4.9

SOURCE: *Economic Report of the President*, 1974.

[1] In 1958 constant dollars.
[2] Output as percent of capacity.
[3] 1967 = 100.

Notice that between 1939 and 1942 total production increased about 43 percent, for we put unemployed men to work and took up the slack of unused productive capacity. During this time the price level increased 17 percent. Most of the increase, however, occurred during the year prior to the enactment of price controls, at which time the U.S. economy was faced with shortages of material and manpower. In the war period, 1942-1945, we had practically no idle manpower to put to work, and the economy was operating at or near full capacity. In order to produce the additional goods needed for defense and war, we had to give up the production of some consumer goods and services.

In addition, total production was enlarged by working overtime, using marginal manpower, and operating multiple work shifts. In the period 1946-1948, production increased about 4 percent, while the price level rose 23 percent. Here again total demand exceeded total production, and the economy was operating at full capacity. Naturally, in the absence of price controls, the price level rose. In 1949 the total demand slackened. Although production remained about the same between 1948 and 1949, inventory depletion was noticeable, the price level dropped slightly, and unemployment rose by 1.3 million. Similar shifts in the relationship of investment to saving caused fluctuations of business activity and prices during the 1950s. We saw a rise in prices during the Korean conflict, a decrease of production and employment in 1954, increased economic activity and price rises in 1955-1957, the recession of 1958, a slow recovery in 1959, and the recession of 1960-1961. A major reason why we did not experience any substantial inflation in the 1958-1965 period, in spite of record-breaking production, employment, and income, was the fact that the economy was not operating at full employment of manpower or capacity, as observed in Table 5-1. But when we continued our high level of investment, large consumer outlays, and deficit spending after reaching full employment in January, 1966, the price level jumped 2.9 percent during that year, after having increased only 1.3 percent annually during the previous eight years. Within a few years prices were rising 5 percent or more annually.

INFLATION

In the foregoing analysis we assumed that inflation occurred only in a fully employed economy. Inflation may occur, however, in an economy at less than full employment.

Definition and Types of Inflation

There are many definitions of inflation. In the simplest sense—*inflation* is merely a persistent rise in the price level. But inflation may be one of four types: (1) demand-pull inflation, (2) cost-push inflation, (3) structural inflation, and (4) social inflation.

Demand-Pull Inflation. The type of inflation that we have discussed thus far is known as *demand-pull inflation.* Sometimes it is referred to as excess-demand inflation, and it occurs when the total demand for goods and services exceeds the available supply of goods and services in the short run. It is much more likely to occur in a fully employed economy because of the difficulty of producing additional goods and services to satisfy the demand. Competitive bidding for the relatively scarce goods and services forces prices upward. The excess demand, or excess spending, may result from several causes. Consumers may dishoard past savings, consumer credit may be liberalized, commercial and bank credit may be extended, or the money supply otherwise may be increased. Generally when the money supply or other forms of purchasing power increase faster than the productivity of our economy, demand-pull inflation results.

Cost-Push Inflation. The second type of inflation is known as *cost-push inflation.* The cost-push operation may occur in a fully employed economy or during periods of unemployment. Whether it starts with increased wages, higher material costs, or increased prices of consumer goods is difficult to say. If wages or material costs do increase for some reason, however, producers are likely to increase the prices of their finished goods and services in order to protect their profit margins. Rising prices in effect will decrease the purchasing power of wages. As a result wage earners, especially through their unions, may apply pressure for further wage increases. This in turn may lead to further increases in the price of materials and finished products, which in turn leads to further wage increases. Such a succession of events often develops into what we generally call the *wage-price spiral.*

Cost-push inflation has become more pronounced in the past few decades with the growth and strengthening of labor unions. It also has been aggrevated by the use of administered pricing by large and powerful producers. *Administered pricing* is simply a situation in which a seller can exert an undue influence on the price he charges for his product because of the absence of competition. Although usually referred to as cost-push, price-pull inflation, labor unions, in order to de-emphasize the influence of wage increases, will many times call it price-pull, cost-push inflation.

Structural Inflation. Another type of inflation that may occur with unemployment in the economy is *structural inflation.* This arises when there is a substantial shift in demand to the products of one industry away from other industries. It assumes that there is a certain amount of inflexibility and immobility among the factors of production and, specifically, that wages and prices tend to have downward rigidity and upward flexibility due to administered pricing and labor union pressures. If there is a heavy shift in demand to the products of Industry X and away from the products of Industry Y, for example, it could push production in Industry X to, or near, full capacity. Under these circumstances expanding demand could cause prices to rise in that industry as a result of demand-pull inflation. This will cause the general price level to rise, since it is assumed that prices in Industry Y will not decline because of inflexibility. In addition, because of the immobility of labor and other productive resources, Industry X may have to pay higher wage and material costs as it endeavors to attract more workers. This whole situation is aggravated when the inflationary effects spill over into other industries. The rise in wages and prices in Industry X may actually cause wages and prices to rise in Industry Y. The general increase in the price level could instigate wage increases and subsequently price increases in Industry Y. Although production and employment may be lessened as a result of demand shifts away from Industry Y, employers may be forced to pay higher wages to offset the higher living costs in an effort to hold on to experienced and skilled workers. In effect, structural inflation, which can occur at full employment or with unemployment, contains elements of both demand-pull and cost-push inflation. In our most serious bouts with inflation, some element of each type of inflation is generally present.

Social Inflation. In recent years economists have observed the growing occurrence of a fourth type of inflation known as *social inflation*. It results from the increasing demand for more government services in the form of Social Security payments, improved unemployment benefits, the distribution of more welfare, wider health care coverage, better rent subsidies, and a host of other social services. Social inflation is encouraged by the rising cost to private enterprise originating from greater fringe benefits, such as longer vacations, more paid holidays, shorter hours, better pensions, and broader hospital and insurance coverage for employees. Moreover, the cost of helping to preserve the natural environment through the use of expensive anti-pollution and depollution equipment, either by the government or by private enterprise, exerts increased pressure on the price level. Social inflation may occur at full employment, adding to demand-pull inflationary pressures, or at other times it may augment cost-push inflationary pressures.

One answer to each type of inflation is increased productivity. In demand-pull inflation, if productivity can be increased to provide the additional goods and services demanded, the inflationary pressure will be removed. On the other hand, the demand for goods and services can be reduced by reducing the money supply or by reducing spendable income. Cost-push and structural inflation can be modified if wage increases are kept in line with increases in productivity. If wage increases would accelerate in proportion to the increase in productivity, incomes would stay in balance with the amount of goods produced. Goods and services would be available when wage earners spent their higher incomes. Social inflation can be held in check, of course, by limiting government and private outlays for social services or by giving up spendable funds, through taxation and redirected expenditures, to cover their costs.

Recent Experience with Inflation

In the past few decades we have experienced all types of inflation. The highly inflationary period of post-World War II, 1946-1948, was characterized by a combination of all. We had not only excess demand for goods and services in a fully employed economy but also labor union pressure for substantial wage increases, which in turn were preceded and/or followed by price increases. Of course, businessmen maintained that the price increases were necessary because of wage increases. On the other hand, labor unions maintained that the wage increases were necessary because of the decrease in purchasing power of wages due to previous price increases.

During the period 1957-1959, we experienced some cost-push and structural inflation. In this period the economy was operating at less than full employment, but prices and wages continued to rise. In fact, during the recession of 1958, prices continued to rise in spite of increased unemployment and the existence of idle capacity. For example, steel wages and prices were raised at a time when the steel mills were operating at less than 60 percent of capacity and hundreds of thousands of steelworkers were laid off.

The slow but persistent rise in the price level of 1 to 3 percent annually, such as we had in the period 1958-1965, is often referred to as *creeping inflation*. Regardless of its cause, inflation is one of the major problems in the economy. Although it abated to some degree in the period 1958-1965, during which the economy operated at less than maximum employment and capacity, inflation became an important issue again during the full employment years of 1966 to 1969, when price increases varied from 2.9 to 5.4 percent annually. Furthermore, because of the presence of cost-push price pressures, inflation continued to be a major economic issue in 1970 and 1971, even though the economy had slowed down and was operating at less than full capacity and with considerable unemployment. This led President Nixon to impose wage and price controls in 1971. Among other measures Phase I of the controls program consisted of a 90-day freeze on prices and wages. Phase II followed, which involved a formula for limiting price increases to 2.5 percent annually and yearly wage increases to 5.5 percent.

Despite the compulsory controls of Phase II, the price level rose approximately 3.4 percent in 1972. With the abandonment of Phase II in January, 1973, and its replacement by voluntary price and wage controls contained in Phase III, it was anticipated that the price level would rise somewhere between 3.0 and 3.5 percent in 1973. However, when the price level began rising at an intolerable rate of more than 6 percent annually during the spring of 1973, the President again imposed a compulsory 60-day freeze on prices, but not wages, in June, 1973, under the auspices of Phase IV. More specific controls followed. The controls proved ineffective, however, and prices rose 8.8 percent in 1973.

Many business organizations, economic research agencies, and Senate investigation committees have spent considerable time in the past decade seeking an answer to the inflationary problem in our economy. Although we have many techniques for measuring and alleviating unemployment, complexities make it more difficult to measure the impact of inflation. Furthermore, it is more difficult to impose anti-inflationary measures, such as higher taxes, because of their political unpopularity.

THE THREE SECTORS

From what has been said it is apparent that there are three basic sectors in the economy. Each sector can have a substantial effect on the circular flow of economic activity and the price level. The largest and most stable is the *consumer sector*, which accounts for about two thirds of the total demand for goods and services in the economy. The most dynamic and volatile is the *business investment sector*. Although it accounts for only about 15 percent of total spending in the economy, business decisions to invest or not to invest are constantly changing because of the volatile outlook for profit expectations. The third sector, *government*, is today often used as a balance wheel in the operation of the economy. The federal government may increase spending and even engage in deficit financing to bolster the economy when there is an insufficient amount of private consumption and investment to maintain a high level of income and employment. At other times it may utilize a surplus budget as an anti-inflationary device.

Since all three sectors, especially the investment and government sectors, borrow from the banks, these institutions play a crucial role in the economic welfare of the nation. Banks can create money! This means that the banking system has a marked influence on the level of economic activity and the price level. If the banks open the horn of plenty to make credit readily available for business investment and government borrowing, it could lead to an increase in the level of economic activity or the price level, depending on the state of employment in the economy. Conversely, if the banking system tightens the screws on credit, a dampening or anti-inflationary effect on the economy could follow. Since the Federal Reserve System can regulate the amount and flow of bank credit in the economy, we will see in the ensuing chapters how it uses its regulatory measures in an effort to stabilize the level of economic activity and the price level.

SUMMARY

1. A circular flow of economic activity is generated in our economy as consumers express their demands and entrepreneurs hire the factors of production to produce the desired goods and services. Incomes are spent either for consumer goods and services or are invested in capital goods. When any saving takes place in the economy, it disrupts the circular flow unless the saving is offset by an equivalent amount of borrowing and investment.

2. Whenever investment is equal to savings, total spending is equal to income, demand is equal to supply, and all the goods and services are moved off the market. If investment is less than savings, however, a decrease in the level of economic activity and/or a decline in the price level results. On the other hand, if investment is greater than savings, an increase in the level of economic activity results if the economy is in a state of less than full employment. Otherwise it leads to higher prices.

3. A balanced government budget tends to have a neutral effect on economic activity and prices, whereas a surplus budget can lead to a decrease in business activity and/or lower prices. On the other hand, a deficit budget can lead to an increase in the level of economic activity or higher prices, depending on the employment status in the economy.

4. Higher prices, or inflation, result from four causes. Demand-pull inflation arises when the total demand for goods and services is greater than the available supply of goods and services. It usually occurs during periods of full employment when we are unable to increase the output of goods and services in the short run.

5. Cost-push inflation results when business firms increase their prices in order to offset an increase in the cost of labor and materials or for some other reason. Price increases lead to further increases in wages and materials, which bring about further increases in prices.

6. Structural inflation is a combination of demand-pull and cost-push inflation. Cost-push and structural inflation may occur in a fully employed or an underemployed economy. Likewise, social inflation may occur at any time.

NEW TERMS
Circular flow, *p. 79*
Stable economy, *p. 81*
Investment, *p. 81*
Contracting economy, *p. 81*
Expanding economy, *p. 84*
Balanced budget, *p. 87*
Surplus budget, *p. 88*
Deficit budget, *p. 88*

Inflation, *p. 92*
Demand-pull inflation, *p. 92*
Cost-push inflation, *p. 93*
Wage-price spiral, *p. 93*
Administered pricing, *p. 93*
Structural inflation, *p. 93*
Social inflation, *p. 94*
Creeping inflation, *p. 95*

QUESTIONS FOR DISCUSSION AND ANALYSIS

1. Explain the relationship of investment to saving and the effect of that relationship on the circular flow of economic activity.

2. How can the accumulation of large inventories have an adverse effect on the circular flow of economic activity?

3. Why does increased investment sometimes increase output and at other times merely affect prices?

4. Why is it necessary to consider the government sector of the economy as part of the circular flow?

5. What effect will a surplus budget have on the circular flow of economic activity?

6. Will a deficit budget always increase the level of inflation? Why or why not?

7. Do you think that government spending should be used to stabilize the level of production and employment? Explain.

8. Distinguish among the four types of inflation: demand-pull, cost-push, structural, and social.

9. Do you think the Administration in June, 1973, should have reinstituted compulsory price controls without wage controls? Why?

10. How much did the price level rise in 1974?

SUGGESTED READINGS

Economic Report of the President. Washington: U.S. Government Printing Office, 1972, 1973, and 1974.

Galbraith, John Kenneth. *The Affluent Society.* Boston: Houghton Mifflin Company, 1960. Chapters 8-10.

Haberler, Gottfried. "Incomes Policies and Inflation." *Special Analysis.* Washington: American Enterprise Institute, 1971.

Heilbroner, Robert L. *Making of an Economic Society.* Englewood Cliffs, N.J.: Prentice-Hall, Inc., 1962.

Heller, Walter W. *New Dimensions of Political Economy.* Cambridge, Mass.: Harvard University Press, 1966.

Kruse, Thomas M. "Inflation: An Examination of Its Causes, Its Consequences and Alternative Ways to Combat It." *Pittsburgh Business Review* (June, 1970).

Okun, Arthur M. *The Political Economy of Prosperity.* New York: W. W. Norton & Company, Inc., 1969.

Oxenfeldt, Alfred A. *Economic Systems in Action.* New York: Holt, Rinehart and Winston, Inc., 1957. Chapters 1 and 2.

"Price Stability: What Does It Mean? What Does It Cost?" *Monthly Review.* Kansas City: Federal Reserve Bank of Kansas City (March, 1971).

Rostow, W. W. *Stages of Economic Growth.* New York: Cambridge University Press, 1960. Chapters 1 and 2.

Schultze, Charles L., *et al. Setting National Priorities: The 1975 Budget.* Washington: The Brookings Institution, 1974.

Wallich, Henry C. *The Cost of Freedom.* New York: Harper & Row, Publishers, 1960.

PART TWO

National Production, Employment, and Income

6

Gross National Product and National Income

PREVIEW The dollar value of the total output of goods and services produced by the nation's economy is measured in terms of the gross national product. This GNP figure is refined further into measurements of total and per capita income. These concepts can serve as measures of economic progress and reflections of the changes in our level of living. Certain reservations, such as adjustments for inflation and increasing population, must be kept in mind, however, when using production and income figures for this purpose. GNP data also shows the allocation of the total output and the distribution of income resulting from that output.

In addition to the GNP and related data, other tools of economic analysis include the flow of funds, the input-output tables, and the measurement of total wealth.

Instead of using hypothetical figures when discussing the circular flow of economic activity as we did in previous chapters, we can use actual dollar measurements. Fortunately in the United States the Department of Commerce keeps a running tab on the dollar value of the goods and the services produced in our economy. This dollar value is broken down by various components, which makes analysis easier.

GROSS NATIONAL PRODUCT

Now that we have some idea of how total production is measured, we can consider the basic concept of production and its modifications. The basic concept is the *gross national product*, which by definition is the current market value of the total goods and services produced by our nation's economy over a given period of time. The GNP is stated on a yearly basis. For 1973 the GNP was $1,288.2 billion.

Components of the Gross National Product

In measuring the value of total production, it is necessary to make a distinction between intermediate and *end products*. Since a total that does not duplicate any items is desired, only the value of end products should be counted. *Intermediate products*, which are those products consumed in making other products, should not be counted; otherwise some products would be counted more than once. To use the classic example of the Department of Commerce:

> If the productive process during the year involves the production of wheat, its milling into flour, and the baking of bread which is sold to consumers, then the value of national output should equal the full value of the bread and should not count also the separate values of wheat and flour which have been used in the course of producing the bread.

This is illustrated in Table 6-1. If the value of the products at each stage of production were added, the total value of a loaf of bread would amount to 60 cents. This obviously overstated value results from double counting. Included in the value of the processed grain, for example, is the cost or value of the wheat sold at the farm. Likewise, the 18-cent value of bread as it leaves the bakery includes the value of flour from the mill. Since one loaf of bread is worth only 20 cents, not 60 cents, any double counting must be eliminated.

TABLE 6-1

VALUE ADDED

Stage of Production	Sale Value of Product	Value Added	
Wheat Sold at Farm	3¢	3¢	
Grain Processor	7¢	4¢	Represents Payments for:
Flour from Mill	12¢	5¢	Wages
Bread from Bakery	18¢	6¢	Rent
Bread at Retail Grocer	20¢	2¢	Interest Profit
	60¢		
Total Value Added		20¢	

Double counting, of course, could be eliminated by counting the value of the end products only. But here again it is difficult at times to tell whether some goods when produced are going to be end products or intermediate products. Will a new tire, for example, be an end product to be used as a replacement on an old car, or will it be an intermediate product to be placed on a newly manufactured car and included in the price of the automobile? Is coal an end product to produce heat for the home or an intermediate product used in the development and generation of electricity?

The other method of avoiding double counting is simply to count only the value added by each producer, instead of the value of his finished product. In this case we can see from our example that the farmer adds 3 cents in total value, the grain processor 4 cents, and so on down the line. The value added by each producer represents the amount he must pay for wages, rent, and interest, plus the profit he will receive. The value added by all producers totals 20 cents, the same as the value of the end product. Thus, summation of the value added by the various producers plus the value of services rendered by others will equal the total production of the economy. You can notice here, too, that the value added represents the total factor cost of production.

Our total production is not actually measured by the value-added method. It is measured from two principal points of view: as the summation of end products produced by the economy and as the summation of costs incurred in producing those products.

Net National Product. In putting out our total production each year we use up a certain amount of capital goods. Machinery, equipment, buildings, and tools depreciate with use. Some become obsolete and lose their value. Thus, GNP must be reduced by the amount of depreciation and obsolescence, generally called *capital consumption allowances*. Since capital consumption allowances totaled $109.6 billion in 1973, the *net national product*, or NNP, amounted to $1,178.6 billion. In general, capital consumption allowances are less than 10 percent of total production in the United States.

National Income. The NNP can be reduced to another meaningful concept called national income. The national income has a two-fold definition. First, it is considered as the total factor costs of the goods and the services produced by the nation's economy. In this sense it is equivalent to the amount that was paid for the use of land, labor, capital, and entrepreneurship in order to obtain a given GNP. Second, the national income also represents the aggregate earnings arising from the production of the GNP. In this sense it is equivalent to the earnings or income of the owners of the factors of production, which were used in producing the GNP. Thus, "total factor cost" and "aggregate earnings" are merely two sides of the same coin. The value of the national income can be obtained by adding all the earnings of labor and property in a given period. It can also be obtained by subtracting capital consumption allowances and indirect business taxes, such as sales taxes, from the GNP and making a few other minor allowances. After making such adjustments, in 1973 the value of the NI was $1,054.2 billion.

Personal Income. The national income figure can be reduced to a concept that is of more direct concern to individuals. By definition *personal income* is the current income received by persons from all sources. In addition to earnings from producing the GNP, it includes transfer payments from government and business. It excludes transfer payments among persons, however. A *transfer payment* occurs when a payment of money is made for which no current goods or services are produced. For example, an ex-serviceman attending college on the GI Bill may receive $220 per month.

This is truly a part of his personal income, but he produces no current goods or services in exchange for the money. It is true that he may have earned it, but it is payment for service in a previous period. In contrast, a factory worker or a government clerk receives income in exchange for his current production. Retired persons on business or government pensions are also receiving transfer payments.

Not only individuals but also nonprofit institutions are classified as "persons" for this purpose. Personal income is measured on a before-tax basis. It includes such things as wages, salaries, proprietor's income, rental income, interest, dividends, and transfer payments. National income can be reduced to personal income by subtracting from the national income that portion of corporation income that is taxed, plus undistributed profits, because neither of these segments of corporate income is passed on to individuals. This will leave only corporate dividends to be counted as part of personal income. In addition, we must subtract Social Security payments.

We must then add government and business transfer payments and make a few other minor adjustments. After doing this for 1973, we find that the personal income was $1,035.5 billion. The biggest factor accounting for the difference between national income and personal income is corporation taxes. For example, in 1973 corporations paid $56.2 billion in taxes.

Disposable Personal Income. Every breadwinner knows that we cannot spend every dollar we earn. There is quite a gap between our earnings and our take-home pay. The main cause for this difference is the fact that we pay federal and, in some cases, state and local income taxes. What remains of personal income after these deductions have been made is known as *disposable personal income*. Since income recipients can make the decision on whether to spend it and the direction in which it will be spent, this income is often called discretionary income. In 1973, income remaining to persons after deductions of personal tax and nontax payments to government, the disposable personal income, was $882.6 billion. Of this total amount we as individuals spent $828.7 billion for personal outlays and saved $53.8 billion. These and other GNP figures for 1973 are shown in Table 6-2.

Allocation of Gross National Product

The GNP is allocated to three major sectors of our economy: consumers, business, and government. Usually the largest bulk of goods and services is for the consumer. That part of total production in the form of machinery, equipment, buildings, inventories, and so on, is known as *private investment*. In this category are both domestic investment and net foreign exports, the latter representing the difference between exports from and imports to the United States. Government, the third sector, must, of course, buy goods and

TABLE 6-2	Gross National Product		$1,288.2
RELATION OF GROSS NATIONAL PRODUCT, NATIONAL INCOME, PERSONAL INCOME, AND SAVINGS	**Less:**	Capital Consumption Allowances	109.6
		Indirect Business Tax and Nontax Liability	117.8
		Business Transfer Payments	4.9
		Statistical Discrepancy	2.3
	Plus:	Subsidies Less Current Surplus of Government Enterprises	.7
	Equals:	**National Income**	**1,054.2**
1973	**Less:**	Corporate Profits and Inventory Valuation Adjustment	109.2
Department of Commerce Estimates		Contributions for Social Insurance	92.0
	Plus:	Government Transfer Payments	112.5
(Billions of Dollars)		Net Interest Paid by Government and Consumers	37.1
		Dividends	27.8
		Business Transfer Payments	4.9
	Equals:	**Personal Income**	**1,035.5**
	Less:	Personal Tax and Nontax Payments	152.9
	Equals:	**Disposable Personal Income**	**882.6**
	Less:	Personal Outlays	828.7
		Personal Consumption Expenditures	805.0
		Interest Paid by Consumers	22.5
		Personal Transfer Payments to Foreigners	1.2
	Equals:	**Personal Saving**	**53.8**

SOURCE: *Survey of Current Business* (January, 1974).

services to perform its necessary functions. The allocation of GNP to the three sectors (or four if you wish to count exports separately) of the economy for 1973 is shown in Table 6-3.

It can be observed from Table 6-3 that approximately 62 percent of the total production of our nation was in the form of consumer goods and services. About 16 percent was in the form of private investment, and the remaining 22 percent went to government and net exports. It is interesting to observe also that $74.2 billion, or 69 percent, of federal government purchases were used for national defense purposes. The federal government used another $32.7 billion in goods and services, while $170.3 billion, or 61 percent of total government purchases, were made by state and local governments. This is shown in Table 6-3.

Source of the GNP

When the three sectors of the economy—consumer, business, and government—purchase goods and services, they must pay for them. These

TABLE 6-3	Gross National Product	$1,288.2
GROSS NATIONAL PRODUCT OR EXPENDITURE	Personal Consumption Expenditures	805.0
	Durable Goods	131.1
	Nondurable Goods	336.3
1973	Services	337.6
Department of Commerce Estimates	Gross Private Domestic Investment	201.5
	Fixed Investment	194.0
(Billions of Dollars)	Nonresidential	136.0
	Structures	48.3
	Producers' Durable Equipment	87.7
	Residential Structures	58.0
	Change in Business Inventories	7.4
	Nonfarm Only	6.7
	Net Exports of Goods and Services	4.6
	Exports	101.3
	Imports	96.7
	Government Purchases of Goods and Services	277.2
	Federal	106.9
	National Defense	74.2
	Other	32.7
	State and Local	170.3

SOURCE: *Survey of Current Business* (January, 1974).

payments to the sellers of goods and services are in turn used to compensate the factors involved in the production of GNP. As was pointed out in our circular flow charts in Chapter 5, these factors are remunerated in the form of wages, rent, interest, and profit. Since these productive agents produce the goods and the services, they are considered as the source of the GNP. Listed in Table 6-4 is a breakdown of the remuneration to the various factors of production.

The following facts can be observed from Table 6-4:

1. Approximately 74 percent of the national income is paid out to employees in the form of wages and salaries and supplements to wages and salaries.
2. Farmers constitute about 4 percent of the labor force, and they receive just over 2 percent of national income.
3. Corporate profits comprise about 10 percent of the total income, but 44 percent of corporate income is paid out in taxes. The corporate tax liability in 1973 amounted to $56.2 billion. This left corporate profits after taxes of $70.2 billion. Of this amount corporations paid

TABLE 6-4	National Income	$1,054.2
	Compensation of Employees	785.3
NATIONAL INCOME,	Wages and Salaries	691.5
BY DISTRIBUTIVE SHARES	Private	546.1
	Military	20.8
1973	Government Civilian	124.6
Department of Commerce Estimates	Supplements to Wages and Salaries	93.9
	Employer Contributions for Social Insurance	49.0
	Other Labor Income	44.9
(Billions of Dollars)	Proprietors Income	84.3
	Business and Professional	57.5
	Farm	26.8
	Rental Income of Persons	25.1
	Corporate Profits and Inventory Valuation Adjustment	109.2
	Profits before Tax	126.5
	Profits Tax Liability	56.2
	Profits after Tax	70.2
	Dividends	27.8
	Undistributed Profits	42.4
	Inventory Valuation Adjustment	−17.3
	Net Interest	50.4

SOURCE: *Survey of Current Business* (January, 1974).

out $27.8 billion in dividends and held $42.4 billion in undistributed profits which, for the most part, were plowed back into industrial expansion.

The allocation and distribution of the gross national product and the national income can be seen in Figure 6-1.

Quarterly Reports on the GNP

To keep businessmen, public officials, and others informed—and to have figures available as a guide for the implementation of national economic policies—the Department of Commerce publishes quarterly reports on the GNP and related figures. These quarterly reports are expressed in annual rates. Actual production in any given quarter is adjusted for seasonal fluctuation. Then the seasonally adjusted figure is multiplied by 4 to convert it into an annual rate. For example, actual production for a given quarter may be $415 billion. The seasonally adjusted output may be $425 billion, which multiplied by 4 equals a seasonally adjusted quarterly total at an annual rate of $1,700 billion.

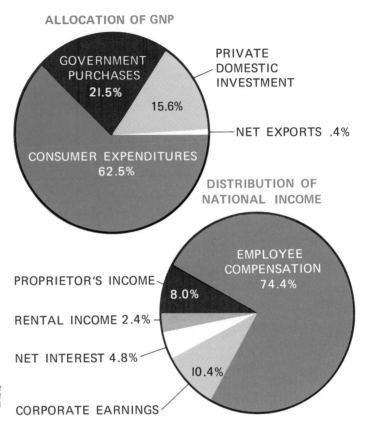

ALLOCATION OF GNP

GOVERNMENT PURCHASES 21.5%

PRIVATE DOMESTIC INVESTMENT

15.6%

NET EXPORTS .4%

CONSUMER EXPENDITURES 62.5%

DISTRIBUTION OF NATIONAL INCOME

EMPLOYEE COMPENSATION 74.4%

PROPRIETOR'S INCOME 8.0%

RENTAL INCOME 2.4%

NET INTEREST 4.8%

10.4%

CORPORATE EARNINGS

FIGURE 6-1

ALLOCATION OF GNP AND DISTRIBUTION OF NATIONAL INCOME

1973

Consumers absorb nearly two thirds of the GNP, and the government utilizes over one fifth of the total output. On the other hand, three fourths of the national income is paid out in wages and salaries.

SOURCE: Adapted from *U. S. Income and Output* (Washington: Department of Commerce, Office of Business Economics, November, 1958), and *Survey of Current Business* (January, 1974).

The system of quarterly reporting makes it easier to analyze movements in the GNP. Any quarter can be compared against another or can be measured against the annual total. This permits easier scrutiny of fluctuations in the level of business activity. With this method it is easy to spot the high and the low quarters of business fluctuations. Downswings and upswings in the economy can be recognized at an earlier date than they would be if the GNP were published on a yearly basis only. Observe the rate of change, for example, in Table 6-5.

Not only is the GNP given in quarterly figures, but also it is frequently revised. A preliminary estimate for a given year usually appears during February of the following year. A more accurate figure is released later in the spring and a final revision is made available during the summer. For example, the GNP for 1972, first estimated at $1,152.1 billion, was revised upward to $1,155.2 billion. For this reason, various references may quote different figures for the GNP for any given period.

		GNP	GNP
Year	Quarter	(Billions)	(1958 Prices)
1971 III		$1,056.9	$742.5
	IV	1,078.1	754.5
1972 I		1,112.5	768.0
	II	1,142.4	785.6
	III	1,166.5	796.7
	IV	1,199.2	812.3
1973 I		1,242.5	829.3
	II	1,272.0	834.3
	III	1,304.5	841.3
	IV	1,334.0	844.1

TABLE 6-5

GROSS NATIONAL PRODUCT, SEASONALLY ADJUSTED QUARTERLY TOTALS AT ANNUAL RATES

1971-1973

SOURCE: *Economic Indicators* (June, 1973) and (January, 1974).

Because information is collected from different sources, the various GNP accounts frequently will not balance when checked against each other. These differences are usually adjusted by writing the difference off to a statistical discrepancy. Notice in Table 6-2 on page 105 the statistical discrepancy of $2.3 billion. This may seem like a huge amount—and it is— but it represents an error equal to a small fraction of 1 percent. In dealing with the GNP and related figures, it should be remembered that the data are approximations rather than precise figures.

GNP and the Circular Flow

The GNP is allocated to households, business firms, and the government, who indirectly make payments to the owners of the various factors of production in the form of wages, rent, interest, and profits for their respective contributions to the GNP. Incomes received are used, in turn, to purchase goods and services. This sets up a circular flow of goods and services and money incomes such as that explained in Chapter 5 and demonstrated in Figure 6-2.

It can be seen from this figure that whenever there is a strong demand for goods and services by the three major sectors of the economy—consumers, investors, and the government—there will be a high level of production, employment, and income. A net increase or decrease in the demand by the various sectors will, of course, cause a change in the level of economic activity or the price level.

GNP AS A MEASURE OF ECONOMIC PROGRESS

Since the GNP is a measure of the total production of goods and services, it is frequently used as a measure of economic progress. By comparing

PRODUCT FLOWS
(IN BILLIONS)

GNP	$ 1,288.2
CONSUMERS	$ 805.0
BUSINESS	
INVESTMENT	$ 206.1
a) DOMESTIC	201.5
b) FOREIGN	4.6
GOVERNMENT	
PURCHASES	$ 277.2

GNP	$1,288.2
NI	$1,054.2
COMP. TO	
EMPLOYEES	$ 785.3
PROPRIETORS'	
INCOME	$ 84.3
RENTAL	
INCOME	$ 25.1
NET INTEREST	$ 50.4
CORPORATE	
PROFITS	$ 109.2

INCOME FLOWS
(IN BILLIONS)

FIGURE 6-2

Consumers, investors, and the government receive respective shares of the GNP. When they pay for their allocation of goods and services, it sets up an income flow of wages, rent, interest, and profits.

the GNP for various years, we can observe whether total output is increasing or decreasing. A change in total output entails a change in total income, and a change in income affects our level of living. Consequently, many people like to measure the level of living by the size of GNP. Furthermore, the size and rate of growth of GNP (along with the price level and the level of unemployment) is used as a major guide in determining the use of monetary and fiscal measures to stabilize our economy. However, whenever we use the GNP as a measure of economic progress, as a method of determining the level of living, or as a guide for the use of stabilization measures, we must keep certain modifications in mind.

Price Level

We know that GNP is the current market value of the total goods and services produced by our nation's economy. Actually the GNP can be increased merely by raising the prices of goods and services produced. Therefore, comparison of one year with another can be very misleading unless we make corrections for changes in the price level. For example, a Ford sedan with extras produced in 1939 entered the GNP at a value of approximately $1,100. Today, a comparable Ford sedan may be valued at \$4,500 or more. It is obvious that there has been no quadrupling in the physical production. Although it is true that the quality of the automobile is better today, most of the increase in value represents a higher price for material, labor, and profits. Thus, if we want to measure the actual change in the physical output of goods and services, we must adjust for price changes. In effect, we have to remove the element of price increases from the current GNP. This is true not only for automobiles but also for hundreds of thousands of other commodities that constitute the GNP. Instead of adjusting each item individually, we adjust them all simultaneously by

TABLE 6-6

GNP 1929-1973 CONVERTED TO CONSTANT DOLLARS (1958)

(1) Year	(2) Total Current GNP (Billions)	(3) Implicit Price Deflators 1958 = 100	(4) Constant GNP, 1958 (Billions)
1929	\$ 103	51	\$204
1933	56	39	142
1939	91	43	208
1942	158	53	298
1945	212	60	355
1946	209	67	313
1947	231	75	310
1948	258	80	324
1949	257	79	324
1950	285	80	355
1951	328	86	383
1952	346	87	395
1953	365	88	413
1954	365	90	407
1955	398	91	438
1956	419	94	446
1957	441	97	453
1958	447	100	447
1959	484	102	476
1960	504	103	488
1961	520	105	497
1962	560	106	530
1963	591	107	551
1964	632	109	581
1965	685	111	618
1966	750	114	658
1967	794	118	675
1968	864	122	707
1969	930	128	726
1970	977	135	723
1971	1,056	142	745
1972	1,155	146	791
1973	1,288	154	837

SOURCE: *Economic Indicators* (January, 1974).

using the *implicit price deflators*. This is an index that takes into account not only the price changes for all types of goods and services entering the GNP but also some change in the quality of various products. Thus, by dividing the total GNP for any year by the value of the implicit price deflator for that particular year, we can adjust the current GNP to a GNP in constant dollars (1958 dollars, for example). GNP in constant dollars is often called the *real* GNP, as shown in Table 6-6.

If we were to use the current GNP (column 2) as a measure of economic progress, we would be misled into believing that the GNP increased thirteen-fold between 1939 and 1973. If we look at the GNP in constant dollars, however, or the adjusted GNP (column 4), we can readily observe that the physical output of goods and services increased by only 300 percent during this period. The constant dollar GNP tells us much better than the GNP in current dollars what we want to know.

Looking at the GNP of 1933 as compared to that of 1929 in current dollars, we would be led to believe that production fell off about 46 percent whereas it actually declined only 30 percent. Then, too, we might erroneously consider that production increased approximately 23 percent from 1946 to 1948 by looking at the current figures. However, since it was a period of full employment in which increased spending merely led to higher prices, and the implicit price index increased from 67 to 80 during the period, we can get a true picture of increased productivity only by looking at the real GNP. This reveals that there was a mere 4 percent increase in output and not a 23 increase. The constant-dollar GNP also shows better the declines in 1946, 1954, and 1958, as well as the slowdown in the economy in 1960-1961 and the recession of 1970.

A similar effect can be observed in the quarterly GNP figures in Table 6-5 on page 109. Notice that the GNP in current dollars increased from $1,304.5 billion in the third quarter of 1973 to $1,334.0 in the fourth quarter of 1973, a nearly $30 billion increase. The constant-dollar figures for those same periods, however, show that the GNP actually increased by only $2.8 billion in the last quarter of 1973. Price increases, therefore, accounted for most of the increase in GNP in the fourth quarter of 1973.

Population

Another modification needed in order to use GNP as a measure of economic progress is an adjustment for population. It is true that the physical output of goods and services in 1973 was nearly four times as much as we produced in 1939. We must keep in mind, however, that more people produced this higher GNP. There were also more people sharing the goods and services we produced. It is necessary, then, to correct real GNP further by taking into account the increase in population. This can be done simply by dividing the real GNP in any year by the total population in that year.

We can, however, obtain a better measure of the average amount of goods and services received per person by first reducing GNP to disposable income, which is the spendable income or income after taxes. If we divide total disposable income by the total population, we will obtain the per capita disposable income. If we then adjust this figure for changes in prices, we will get a per capita income in constant dollars, or the *real per capita disposable income*. Other things remaining the same, a comparison of real per capita disposable income for any two years will give us a fair indication of what is happening to our level of living. We must remember, however, that per capita income is the average income per person. Many people make less than, and others more than, the average. At any rate, let us look at Table 6-7.

TABLE 6-7

TOTAL AND CURRENT AND CONSTANT DOLLAR (1958) PER CAPITA DISPOSABLE INCOME

1940-1973

(1) Year	(2) Current Total Disposable Income (Billons)	(3) Current Population (Millions)	(4) Current Per Capita Disposable Income	(5) Constant Dollar Per Capita Disposable Income (1958 Dollars)
1940	$ 76	132	$ 573	$1,259
1945	150	140	1,074	1,642
1950	207	152	1,364	1,646
1955	275	166	1,666	1,795
1960	350	181	1,937	1,883
1962	385	187	2,064	1,968
1963	405	189	2,136	2,013
1964	438	192	2,280	2,123
1965	473	194	2,436	2,239
1966	512	197	2,604	2,335
1967	546	199	2,749	2,403
1968	591	201	2,945	2,486
1969	634	203	3,130	2,534
1970	692	205	3,376	2,610
1971	746	207	3,603	2,680
1972	797	209	3,816	2,767
1973	883	210	4,195	2,890

SOURCE: *Economic Indicators* (January, 1974).

According to the table, the total disposable income indicated in column 2 increased over ten times between 1940 and 1973. When we divide this total by the population, however, it shows that the per capita disposable income, column 4, rose over sixfold during the period. Finally, after adjusting the current per capita incomes for price changes, we see that the real per capita disposable income (column 5) increased by approximately 130 percent. This is the best measure we have of progress in our level of living. While not perfect, it is more accurate to say that our level of living has increased 130 percent since 1940 than it would be to say that it increased tenfold. Even so, there are other reservations that we should make in utilizing GNP figures as a yardstick for our level of living and our economic progress.

Monetary Transactions

The GNP for the most part takes into account only goods and services for which there have been monetary transactions. If you buy a new desk, it is entered in the GNP; but if you make it yourself out of old lumber, it does not become a part of the GNP. If you hire a gardener to mow your lawn, the value of the service is entered in the GNP. If you mow your own lawn, however, it does not go into the GNP. If a housewife sends out the laundry, it is part of the GNP; but if she does it herself, it is not. There are many goods and services that, because they do not involve monetary transactions, never enter the GNP. Nevertheless, they are just as important to our level of living as most of the items that are counted in the GNP. This is a substantial defect when we want to use GNP as an indicator of our level of living. Think of all the items produced by means of do-it-yourself projects, or consider the services of housewives that add so much joy and comfort to our level of living. If we put an arbitrary minimum wage value of $90 per week on the housewife's service, for example, it would add about $160 billion annually to our gross national product.

Type of Goods and Services Produced

We usually think that the more we produce, the higher will be our level of living. However, there are exceptions. Sometimes the nature of the goods and services are such that we cannot raise our level of living through their consumption. For example, as a nation we produced 70 percent more goods and services in 1944 than we did in 1939. Out of the total output of $210 billion in 1944, however, almost 40 percent was in the form of military production. While it is true that tanks, guns, ships, airplanes, grenades, and missiles protect our level of living, they do not add to our enjoyment or level of living as do new homes, autos, clothing, and numerous other consumer commodities. Even today about 6 to 7 percent of our total production is for national defense.

Thus, in comparing the GNP of various years to get an indication of our change in living conditions, we may be misled if we neglect to consider the type of goods and services produced in each of those years. Likewise, it is difficult to compare the level of living in two different countries by comparing the respective value of their GNPs, for if one is highly militarized while the other is not, it can make a substantial difference.

Handling of Durable Goods

Except for houses, durable goods are added to GNP in the year in which they are purchased. When we purchase an automobile, a refrigerator, a set of golf clubs, or a bicycle, there is a value added into the GNP for that commodity. Although we receive services from the commodity in subsequent years, national income accounting handles it as though it were consumed in the year in which it was purchased. Normally as our incomes increase during prosperity periods, we tend to buy more of these durable items; but we cannot get full utilization out of them in one year. This tends to exaggerate the value of our income. On the other hand, in depression years we have an inclination to decrease our purchases of durable goods, but we still get service out of the items we previously purchased. This service is a form of real income. Since there is no accounting in the GNP for the length of service of durable goods bought in previous years, GNP frequently underestimates our level of living, especially during periods of declining business activity.

Leisure

Lastly, the GNP makes no allowance for leisure time. Even if we wanted to take it into account, how would we value it? It means more to some people than it does to others. Nevertheless, it should be considered when using the GNP as a measure of economic progress. It is true that we had more production and income in 1973 than we had in 1970, but to some extent we worked longer hours to obtain it. Likewise, the increased output during the period of World War II came at the expense of a reduction in leisure. Certainly the fact that we can now produce more during an eight-hour day than we formerly did in a ten-hour day must be considered as a substantial improvement in our level of living. This does not, however, show up anywhere in our GNP figures. Presently there is some move toward a 35-hour week. As this comes, it will raise our economic level of living, providing we maintain the same output of goods and services.

External or Social Costs

Another reservation that must be kept in mind when utilizing GNP data is the absence of *social costs*. When a firm produces goods and services, such internal factors as machine depreciation and obsolescence are considered as costs of production. Consequently, in GNP accounting these costs are subtracted from total production (GNP) in order to obtain net national product and national income. In addition to internal cost, however, external or social costs are involved in the production of goods and services. Effluence from a chemical plant into a stream or river, for example, may pollute the water, making it unsuitable for drinking, swimming, or even fishing. This in effect is a social cost to the community. Smoke from a factory may pollute the surrounding air, creating offensive odors or contributing to lung diseases. Aircraft noise from a jetport may create a sound hazard and decrease property values in the area. Since these external costs are not borne by the individual firm, they are not included in its total cost or the value added that enters the GNP. They are, however, real economic costs that must be borne by society in the form of deterioration of the environment. As the GNP increases in size, the external or social costs become larger and larger. Consequently, the net national product and the national income are overstated by several billions of dollars annually through the exclusion of these costs.

In summary, GNP figures are a fairly good indication of the total production of goods and services by our nation's economy. They can be used as a measure of economic progress, as an indicator of our level of living, if we use them in the right way. We must not be gullible when we hear the politician boast that our total production of goods and services increased some fabulous amount during his party's administration, or when his opponent charges that price increases obliterated all the advantages of higher incomes and wages. We must get the facts straight and use them properly. This is important because it will become more evident as we go along that the growth rate of the GNP, along with the price level and the level of unemployment, serves as a guide to the use of governmental action in an endeavor to stabilize the circular flow of economic activity.

FLOW OF FUNDS

The GNP records transactions only of those goods and services that are currently produced. It does not measure the financial transactions of goods sold during the current period that were produced at a previous time. For example, suppose Smith purchased a new auto for $4,000 in March, 1974. When he bought it, there would be an entry in the GNP for $4,000. However, if he sold the automobile through a used car dealer for $3,200 in October, 1974, this later transaction would not be entered in the GNP. Only the profit or commission of the used car dealer would enter the GNP as a payment for services rendered. Nevertheless, total monetary transactions as a result of the two separate sales of the same auto totaled $7,200.

Furthermore, since GNP measures only the value added by producers, double accounting is eliminated. The financial transactions required to get a good produced, however, are much greater than the total value added. This frequently happens in intercorporate sales. For instance, in our example on page 102 we eliminate double accounting by entering only the value added into the GNP. The value added was equal to the value of the end product, in this case the loaf of bread worth 20 cents. In order to get the 20-cent loaf produced, however, total financial transactions of 60 cents spread over various stages of production were necessary.

When one considers the resale of homes, automobiles, commercial property, and millions of other commodities that take place each year, it is easy to see why the GNP, although it does a good job of measuring current production, does not begin to measure the total financial transactions taking place within the economy in a given period. In 1973, for example, we had a GNP of $1,288 billion, but the total flow of funds for that year was probably four times as great. This typical relationship between the size of the flow of funds and the GNP is somewhat indicative of the indirect means of production referred to in Chapter 3.

Meaning of Flow of Funds

After studying for several years the problems of how to measure total financial transactions in the economy, the Federal Reserve first published its Flow-of-Funds System of National Accounts in December, 1955. At that time, calculations of total transactions for the years 1939-1953 were released. The Federal Reserve has since published data for subsequent years.

The initial *flow-of-funds system of national accounts* encompassed all transactions in the economy that occurred as a result of cash payments or extensions of credit. The system was broader than the GNP account, since the flow of funds arises from the transfer of existing assets as well as the sale and purchase of currently produced goods and services. It records the sale of old as well as new homes and the purchase of used as well as new autos. Purely financial transactions, such as a transfer of securities, are also included.

Sector Accounts

The flow-of-funds system made a major contribution to our knowledge of actual transactions in the economy. All monetary and credit flows are recorded in detailed statements of sources and uses for several sectors of the economy. The major sectors are:

1. Households
2. Business
3. State and local governments
4. U.S. government
5. Sponsored credit agencies

6. Monetary authority
7. Commercial banks
8. Private nonbank finance
9. Rest of the world

The original flow-of-funds sector accounts were a set of interlocking balance-of-payment statements. Each sector account recorded the purchases and sales of goods and services, the credit and capital inflows and outflows, and the changes in monetary balances for that sector. A typical transaction required four entries, two nonfinancial and two financial. For example, the sale of a refrigerator would be entered as a purchase for the buyer, a sale for the seller, a reduction in cash for the buyer, and an increase in cash for the seller. The first two entries are considered nonfinancial, while the last two are considered as financial transactions. If the refrigerator was purchased on credit, more than four entries were required since the borrowing and lending of money also had to be entered. Some transactions are purely financial in character, such as the sale of securities or the repayment of a loan.

Many times the buyer will be in one sector and the seller in another. In our example above, the buyer would be in the consumer sector and the seller, perhaps, in the corporate business sector. Thus, it was possible to trace the transactions between sectors.

Time Factor and Net Transactions

The flow of funds is still a relatively new tool of economic analysis and is continuously being improved and refined. One of the major handicaps in its early use was its dilatoriness. Publication of figures was several months behind. The data for one year would not be available, or released, until late in the subsequent year. On the other hand, GNP data usually had been readily available. For this reason, in 1959 the Federal Reserve began publishing flow-of-funds data on a quarterly basis and has made many revisions in the accounts since then to improve their usefulness for analytical purposes.

In making the change in the quarterly system, however, much of the detailed information available in earlier reports had to be sacrificed. For example, for the consumer sector earlier reports showed separately the incomes from payrolls, insurance, sales of commodities, tax refunds, dividends, and interest. In the current quarterly reports the income from payrolls, interest, and dividends is lumped together under income receipts. The only other source given is transfer payments.

Another important difference is in the fact that in the earlier form most flows were shown on a gross basis for a number of transactions, with consistent classification for all sectors. Consequently, the total flow of funds could be readily estimated. In the present quarterly version, however, the amount of detail shown for current nonfinancial flows varies from sector to sector, with less detail and more netting than formerly. As a result, the basic data for estimating many elements of the total flow of funds are not available. The Federal Reserve does hope to return to a more detailed account in a form consistent with the new quarterly system sometime in the future, however.

Sources and Uses

A very important contribution of the flow-of-funds system is the *statement of sources and uses of funds* for each sector. It is important from the viewpoint of economic analysis to know the source of consumer funds and the manner in which they are disposed. Likewise, it is important to know these facts for business, government, and the other sectors of the economy. Each sector's source of funds should be equal to its uses. These are shown for the household sector in Table 6-8.

The table shows only that consumers had personal income of $939.2 billion in 1972. After subtracting taxes and other deductions, consumers made personal outlays of $747.2 billion. Included in this was gross investments of $206.4 billion. They invested $157.8 billion in physical assets, such as residential construction, durable goods, and nonprofit plant and equipment. The remaining $48.6 billion was used to acquire financial assets, such as savings accounts, U.S. government securities, corporate stocks, and mortgages. These annual figures are obtained by averaging the half-year figures, also shown in the table.

Flow of savings is also recorded in the flow-of-funds accounts. It shows the gross and net savings for all sectors and indicates the uses to which these savings were allocated.

INPUT-OUTPUT ANALYSIS

For years economists and forecasters have relied on gross national product and related data to interpret changes and developments in our economy. Through the GNP it is easy to trace the allocation of total production to the major sectors of the economy—consumer, private investment, and government. Through the related national income and personal income, one can see how much income was distributed in the form of wages, rent, interest, and profit.

In 1964, however, the Department of Commerce published an updated version of the *input-output tables*, which provided a more detailed breakdown and permitted a closer analysis of production in our complex economy.[1] The input-output analysis is not new, having been originated by Professor Wassily Leontief a few decades ago. Until recently the necessary data for

[1] Morris R. Goldman, Martin L. Marimont, and Beatrice N. Vaccara, "The Interindustry Structure of the United States, A Report on the 1958 Input-Output Study," *Survey of Current Business* (Washington: Department of Commerce, Office of Business Economics, November, 1964).

TABLE 6-8

SECTOR
STATEMENTS
OF SOURCES
AND USES
OF FUNDS

1972-1973

(Billions of Dollars)

Category	1972	1972 H1	1972 H2	1973 p H1
		Households, Personal Trusts, and Nonprofit Organizations		
1 Personal Income	939.2	918.4	959.9	1007.9
2 Less: Personal Taxes & Nontaxes	142.2	139.3	145.1	146.9
3 Equals: Disposable Personal Income	797.0	779.1	814.8	861.0
4 Less: Personal Outlays	747.2	729.7	764.7	809.8
5 Equals: Personal Saving, NIA Basis	49.7	49.4	50.1	51.2
6 Plus: Credits from Govt. Insur.[1]	10.5	10.3	10.7	10.4
7 Capital Gains Dividends[2]	1.4	1.2	1.7	1.5
8 Net Durables in Consumpt.	23.6	21.4	25.9	32.1
9 Equals: Net Saving	85.3	82.2	88.3	95.3
10 Plus: Capital Consumption	105.9	104.1	107.7	112.9
11 Equals: Gross Saving	191.2	186.3	196.0	208.2
12 Gross Investment	206.4	200.5	212.1	223.7
13 Capital Expend. (Net of Sales)	157.8	152.6	163.0	178.3
14 Residential Construction	34.3	33.3	35.3	39.4
15 Consumer Durable Goods	117.4	113.3	121.5	132.7
16 Plant and Equip. (Nonprofit)	6.1	6.0	6.1	6.2
17 Net Finan. Investment	48.6	47.9	49.1	45.4
18 Net Acquis. of Financial Assets	117.5	112.0	122.8	112.4
19 Deposits and Credit Market Instr.[3] ..	97.5	94.5	100.4	91.6
20 Demand Deposits and Currency ..	12.8	12.5	12.9	4.5
21 Time and Savings Accounts	75.8	78.3	73.4	82.2
22 At Commercial Banks	29.8	30.5	29.2	44.5
23 At Savings Institutions	46.0	47.8	44.1	37.7
24 Credit Market Instruments	8.9	3.7	14.1	4.9
25 U.S. Govt. Securities	4.4	1.5	7.1	1.5
26 State and Local Oblig.	1.3	.2	2.4	4.8
27 Corporate and Foreign Bonds ..	4.9	4.5	5.2	.2
28 Commercial Paper	.4	−.8	1.6	.2
29 Mortgages	−2.0	−1.8	−2.3	−1.9
30 Investment Company Shares	−.6	−.8	−.4	−2.2
31 Other Corporate Shares	−5.2	−6.0	−4.4	−5.2
32 Life Insurance Reserves	7.3	6.8	7.9	7.8
33 Pension Fund Reserves	20.7	19.8	21.6	23.4
34 Net Investment in Noncorp. Bus. ...	−5.0	−4.9	−5.0	−4.8
35 Security Credit	.1	.1	.1	−.9
36 Miscellaneous	2.7	2.6	2.7	2.8
37 Net Increase in Liabilities	68.9	64.1	73.7	67.0
38 Credit Market Instruments	63.2	55.6	70.8	71.2
39 Home Mortgages	38.4	34.7	42.1	40.9
40 Other Mortgages	1.4	1.4	1.4	1.4
41 Instalment Cons. Credit	16.0	14.2	17.9	22.0
42 Other Consumer Credit	3.1	1.6	4.6	2.7
43 Bank Loans N.E.C.	2.9	2.4	3.4	2.4
44 Other Loans[4]	1.3	1.4	1.3	1.9
45 Security Credit	4.7	7.5	1.8	−5.2
46 Trade Debt	.5	.5	.5	.5
47 Miscellaneous	.5	.5	.6	.5
48 Discrepancy (11-12)	−15.2	−14.2	−16.1	−15.5

SOURCE: *Federal Reserve Bulletin* (September, 1973).

[1] Imputed saving associated with growth of government life insurance and retirement reserves.
[2] From open-end investment companies.
[3] Excludes corporate equities.
[4] Policy loans, hypothecated deposits, and U.S. Govt. loans to nonprofit organizations.
Note. Data revised for all periods: 1973 H1 based on preliminary and incomplete information.

this type of analysis have been rather scarce. The Department of Commerce study, however, provided a major breakthrough in the utilization of this powerful tool of economic analysis. In 1969 the input-output tables were expanded and undated to 1963.[2]

The revised input-output studies divide the total into 86 basic industries and about 300 subgroups. Through the construction of matrix tables, much like the mileage grid on a highway map, is shown the various inputs used by each industry in producing its final product. One table shows how the output of each industry is distributed to other industries or to final users. Consequently, one can trace the flow of output from one industry as it becomes input to another and finally ends up as consumer or producer goods.

Table 6-9 on page 122 shows, for example, that for every dollar of output the automobile industry uses 8.6 cents worth of steel and 2.2 cents in rubber products. It spends 1 cent for glass, 3 cents for screws and bolts, and so forth. Included in the $1 value of its auto product is a value-added item of 30 cents, which includes compensation of employees, corporate profits, and capital consumption allowance. These values are encircled in the table for your inspection.

This means that for every $1 billion in auto sales the industry uses $86 million in steel products. Further analysis shows that in order to produce this $86 million worth of steel, the steel industry in turn spends $1.6 million for coal (.019 $\times$ $1.00 $\times$ 86 million = $1.6 million), $4.0 million for iron ore, $2.2 million for electricity, and $1.5 million for chemicals. It pays out $36.6 million for value added. Thus, it is possible to determine the likely impact on 86 different industries that would result from a $1 or $2 billion increase in the demand for automobiles. Conversely, the adverse effect on other industries from an automobile strike or shutdown can be estimated in advance.

Still another table shows how much of an industry's products goes to each of the other 86 industries. Table 6-10 on page 123 shows that about 14 percent of the steel industry's $24.6 billion output, for example, is sold to the auto industry for its input. Nearly 9 percent, or $2.1 billion, of total steel output becomes input for new construction, and a similar amount is used by heating and plumbing industries. Less than 2 percent of steel production is used in the manufacture of farm equipment, but 4 percent is used by the metal container industry, as shown by the encircled items in the table. From this table a firm in the steel industry, for example, can see whether or not it is keeping up with its industry in the sale of products to various other industries. Furthermore, it can be observed in the last column

[2] Department of Commerce, Office of Business Economics, *Survey of Current Business* (Washington: U.S. Government Printing Office, November, 1969).

TABLE 6-9 INTERINDUSTRY STRUCTURE OF THE UNITED STATES, INPUT-OUTPUT DIRECT REQUIREMENTS PER DOLLAR OF GROSS OUTPUT, 1963

For the Composition of Inputs to an Industry, Read the Column for That Industry.

Industry No. / Input	29	30	31	32	33	34	35	36	37	38	39	58	59	60	61	62
1 Livestock & Livestock Products	0.00027				.05895			.00073								0.00092
2 Other Agricultural Products	.00088															
3 Forestry & Fishery Products	.00014															
4 Agricultural, Forestry & Fishery Services																
5 Iron & Ferroalloy Ores Mining							.00003	.00176	.04746	.00106	.00013					.00003
6 Nonferrous Metal Ores Mining		0.00013		.00093				.00003	.00606	.06242		.00025	.00038			.00007
7 Coal Mining	.00039		.00043	.00096	.00214	.00012		.00863	.01908	.00093			.00038	.00011		
8 Crude Petroleum & Natural Gas			.44937													
9 Stone and Clay Mining and Quarrying	.00036	.00202	.00364	.00099			.01251	.08347	.00284	.00128			.00005			.00004
10 Chemical & Fertilizer Mineral Mining	.00024	.00014		.00002 .00018	.00034 .00006	.00033	.00046 .00014	.00256 .00007	.00048 .00007	(*) .00007	.03620	.00012	.00004	.00029	.00011	.00035
26 Printing & Publishing	.00351		.02659	.03876	.03263	.00010	.04446	.01800	.01040	.01040	.00341	.02070	.00105	.00247	.00093	.00393
27 Chemicals & Selected Chemical Products	.10665	.20252	.02659	.18099	.00044	.00245		.00744	.00899	.00899	.00104	.00429	.00028	.00126	.00270	.00220
28 Plastics & Synthetic Materials	.00294	.09250		.00047	.04041	.00200	.00029	.00259	.00007	.00005	.00072	.00008	.00005	.00014	.00012	.00557
29 Drugs, Cleaning & Toilet Preparations	.05701	.00859	.00304	.00106	(*)	(*)	.00180	.00016	(*)	.00009	.03181	.00015	.00486	.00108	.00470	.00115
30 Paints & Allied Products	.00126	.00021	.00090													
31 Petroleum Refining & Related Industries	.06638	.04261	.07430	.00213	.00362	.00092	.00285	.01173	.00639	.00577	.00158	.00143	.00174	.00340	.00255	.00208
32 Rubber & Miscellaneous Plastics Products	.03193	.00419	.00008	.04502	.00840	.09180	.02128	.01048	.00061	.00112	.00293	.04025	.00233	.00663	.01310	.02671
33 Leather Tanning & Industrial Leather Products	.00003	.00004	.00010	.00054	.18555	.17718	.00008	.00035	.00021	.00012	.00004	.00003	.00003	.00004	.00007	.00023
34 Footwear & Other Leather Products	(*)	.00021		.00134	.00235	.02931	(*)	.00001	.00001	(*)	(*)	.00059	.00918	.00008	(*)	.00062
35 Glass & Glass Products	.01799	.00442	.00252	.00244	.00027	.00027	.06466	.00017	.00185	.00007	.00204	.00650	.00198	.00252	.00402	.00382
36 Stone & Clay Products	.00211	.00243	.00005	.00749	.00109	(*)	.02650	.11150	.19890	.00246	.40606	.02717	.00862	.02204	.00401	.00242
37 Primary Iron & Steel Manufacturing	.00002	.00950	.00230	.00507	.00188	.00188	.00237	.01159	.00001	.00950		.11206	.01366	.04046	.12569	.02754
38 Primary Nonferrous Metal Manufacturing		.06022	.00612	.00244		.00041	.00529	.00241	.02145	.34217	.01437		.00001	.04046	.02549	.03775
39 Metal Containers				.00021				.00171	.00003	.00027	.00029	.00015	.00058	.00038	.03857	.00265
40 Heating, Plumbing & Structural Metal Products	.00008	.00008	.00019	.00015		(*)	.00361		.00031		.00133					.00025
41 Stampings, Screw Machine Products & Bolts					.00009	.00011	.00055	.00017	.00606	.00298	.01950	.01002	.03423	.01356	.00589	.01647
42 Other Fabricated Metal Products		.00010	(*)	.00628	.00129	.00912	.00043	.01054	.01722	.00469	.00222	.01169	.02824	.01465	.02529	.01982
43 Engines & Turbines		.00056	.00030	.00668				.00015	.00010	.00077		.00008	.00437	.00257	.02639	.00008
44 Farm Machinery & Equipment				.00001		.00002		.00001	.00129	.00950			.00054	.00002	.00522	.00019
45 Construction, Mining & Oil Field Machinery				.00004				.00482	.00080	.00002	.00005	.00002	.00088	.00064	.00164	.00012
66 Communications; Except Radio & TV Broadcasting	.01991	.06022		.00332	.00219	.00427	.00328	.00495	.00417	.00315	.00149	.00321	.00167	.00793	.00286	.00791
67 Radio & TV Broadcasting																
68 Electric, Gas, Water & Sanitary Services	.00350	.00010		.00628	.00922	.00385	.03853	.03224	.02537	.02279	.00693	.00857	.00412	.00612	.00593	.00506
69 Wholesale & Retail Trade	.00892	.00455	.01787	.01071	.03628	.03260	.03686	.02555	.02994	.02977	.02984	.03985	.02304	.02015	.03141	.03529
70 Finance & Insurance	.00397	.04896	.01823	.03020	.00593	.00655	.00729	.00810	.00870	.00502	.00717	.00332	.00297	.00364	.00467	.00625
81 Business Travel, Entertainment & Gifts	.03363	.00645	.00980	.00496	.00263	.00635	.00680	.00735	.00339	.00327	.00501	.00899	.00280	.01112	.00841	.01518
82 Office Supplies	.00626	.01845	.00156	.00817	.00263	.00151	.00101	.00085	.00063	.00042	.00031	.00064	.00038	.00120	.00078	.00173
83 Scrap, Used and Secondhand Goods	.01211	.00123	.00040	.00088	.00058		.00466	.00025	.02684	.04274	.00108	.00321	.00108		.00015	
V.A. Value Added	.41076	.36189	.23357	.44618	.25933	.43906	.54793	.48121	.42459	.27884	.34135	.43229	.29709	.46130	.38490	.43435
T. Total	1.00000	1.00000	1.00000	1.00000	1.00000	1.00000	1.00000	1.00000	1.00000	1.00000	1.00000	1.00000	1.00000	1.00000	1.00000	1.00000

Column headings:
29 Drugs, Cleaning, and Toilet Preparations · 30 Paints and Allied Products · 31 Petroleum Refining and Related Industries · 32 Rubber and Miscellaneous Plastics Products · 33 Leather Tanning and Industrial Leather Products · 34 Footwear and Other Leather Products · 35 Glass and Glass Products · 36 Stone and Clay Products · 37 Primary Iron and Steel Manufacturing · 38 Primary Nonferrous Metal Manufacturing · 39 Metal Containers · 58 Miscellaneous Electrical Machinery, Equipment and Supplies · 59 Motor Vehicles and Equipment · 60 Aircraft and Parts · 61 Other Transportation Equipment · 62 Scientific and Controlling Instruments

SOURCE: *Survey of Current Business* (November, 1969).

TABLE 6-10 INTERINDUSTRY TRANSACTIONS, 1963 (Millions of Dollars at Producers' Prices)

For the Distribution of Output of an Industry, Read the Row for That Industry.

For the Composition of Inputs to an Industry, Read the Column for That Industry.

Industry No.	Industry	11 New Construction	36 Stone and Clay Products	37 Primary Iron and Steel Mfg.	38 Primary Nonferrous Metal Mfg.	39 Metal Containers	40 Heating, Plumbing, and Structural Metal Products	41 Stampings, Screw Machine Products, and Bolts	42 Other Fabricated Metal Products	43 Engines and Turbines	44 Farm Machinery and Equipment	45 Construction, Mining, and Oil Field Machinery	58 Miscellaneous Electrical Machinery, Equipment and Supplies	59 Motor Vehicles and Equipment	60 Aircraft and Parts	61 Other Transportation Equipment	62 Scientific and Controlling Instruments	Total
1	Livestock & Livestock Products	323																26,684
2	Other Agricultural Products		7														4	27,266
3	Forestry & Fishery Products																	1,751
4	Agricultural, Forestry & Fishery Services	3																1,772
5	Iron & Ferroalloy Ores Mining		17	1,168	15													1,429
6	Nonferrous Metal Ores Mining		(*)	1	891													1,519
7	Coal Mining		82	470	13						2	2	1		2		(*)	2,637
8	Crude Petroleum & Natural Gas																	12,265
9	Stone and Clay Mining and Quarrying	478	797	70	18		1	1	2			1	(*)	2		1	(*)	2,024
10	Chemical & Fertilizer Mineral Mining		24	12	(*)				4						4		2	696
26	Printing & Publishing	2	1	2	1								(*)	2				16,283
27	Chemicals & Selected Chemical Products	201	172	411	148	88	38	36	123	4	8	6	47	42	4	2	17	16,893
28	Plastics & Synthetic Materials		71	(*)	128	8		24	(*)				10	11	35	5		6,341
29	Drugs, Cleaning & Toilet Preparations		25	2	1				5	(*)	1	1	(*)	2	2	1	24	9,053
30	Paints & Allied Products	2	2		(*)	3	6	3	66	1	16	12	(*)	194	15	23	5	2,462
31	Petroleum Refining & Related Industries	308				78	90	27						69				21,837
32	Rubber & Miscellaneous Plastics Products	1,119	112	157	82	4	26	18	32	10	7	10	3	893	49	12	9	9,891
33	Leather Tanning & Industrial Leather Products	437	100	15	16	7	13	65	124	5	58	80	91	(*)	95	64	114	967
34	Footwear & Other Leather Products	(*)	(*)	(*)	(*)	(*)	(*)	(*)	(*)	(*)	14		(*)		(*)	(*)	3	3,427
35	Glass & Glass Products	1		45	35	5	74	19	10	18	(*)	14	1	366	1	1	16	2,932
36	Stone & Clay Products	81	1,065	45	136		21	1	72		9	639	15	79	36	20	10	9,548
37	Primary Iron & Steel Manufacturing	5,813	111	4,897	4,883	993	2,154	1,047	1,543	235	424	639	61	3,453	315	615	118	24,618
38	Primary Nonferrous Metal Manufacturing	⟨2,125⟩	23	1		35	671	287	742	92	22	46	253	547	579	125	162	14,272
39	Metal Containers	1,244	16	528	4	⟨993⟩	11	18	1				(*)	(*)	5		11	2,445
40	Heating, Plumbing & Structural Metal Products	6,159	(*)	8	43	3	⟨2,154⟩	30	68	4	6	40		23		189	1	8,996
41	Stampings, Screw Machine Products & Bolts	112	325	149	67	48	165	100	141	57	87	47	23	1,370	194	20	70	4,955
42	Other Fabricated Metal Products	975	425	424	(*)	5	339	71	338	25	51	91	26	1,130	210	124	85	8,963
43	Engines & Turbines	26	72		11		15	16	4	195	139	121	(*)	175	37	129	(*)	2,398
44	Farm Machinery & Equipment	2		32			2	20	24	25	147	88		21	(*)	26	1	3,080
45	Construction, Mining & Oil Field Machinery		46	20		(*)	38	(*)	35	23	20	164	(*)	35	9		(*)	4,062
66	Communications; Except Radio & TV Broadcasting	238	47	103	45	4	55	25	12	10	11	16	7	67	114	14	34	13,495
67	Radio & TV Broadcasting	180																2,308
68	Electric, Gas, Water & Sanitary Services	205	308	624	325	17	165	44	82	13	18	27	15	165	88	29	22	29,660
69	Wholesale & Retail Trade	5,453	244	737	425	73	230	112	251	74	118	132	88	922	288	154	151	120,613
70	Finance & Insurance	401	77	214	72	18	54	35	59	8	24	39	7	119	52	23	27	33,700
81	Business Travel, Entertainment & Gifts	359	70	83	47	12	82	31	78	17	21	29	20	112	159	41	65	7,793
82	Office Supplies	17	8	15	6	1	9	4	8	2	3	4		15	17		7	2,106
83	Scrap, Used & Secondhand Goods	38	2	661	610		14		12		9	9		43				1,518
I.	Intermediate Inputs, Total	39,629	4,594	14,166	10,292	1,610	5,625	2,718	5,220	1,467	2,068	2,455	1,281	28,139	7,711	3,109	2,421	
V.A.	Value Added	25,890	4,953	10,453	3,980	835	3,371	2,237	3,743	931	1,013	1,697	975	11,892	6,604	1,786	1,859	590,389
T.	Total	65,519	9,548	24,618	14,272	2,445	8,996	4,955	8,963	2,398	3,080	4,062	2,256	40,031	14,317	4,894	4,280	

SOURCE: *Survey of Current Business* (November, 1969).

of this table that the value added, $590 billion, was equivalent to the GNP for that year (1963).

It is easy to visualize that input-output data can become very complex when one is trying to analyze the flow of inputs and outputs among 86 industries in the economy. Anytime the input-output relationship of one industry to another changes, the matrix, or set of tables, has to be modified. Thus, the use of computers is essential to keep track of perplexing changes. Although the Department of Commerce study updates the input-output tables to 1963 only, it plans further updating and frequent revision. Consequently, this new tool of analysis will permit economists, businessmen, and government policymakers to interpret better the total effect of output changes at the industry and national levels. Furthermore, input-output data are compatible with the national income accounts so that the two can be used interchangeably in analysis.

NATIONAL WEALTH

Another concept of importance in the study of economics is that of wealth. It is important to emphasize that wealth is a stock rather than a flow concept. A stock is measured simply as the quantity at a given time, such as a dollar value of land or equipment. A flow, on the other hand, is measured as quantity *per period of time*, such as a dollar value of income per year or per month. Since wealth is composed of such things as machinery, equipment, buildings, land, and other economic goods, it is obvious that by applying labor and knowledge to the processing of this wealth we can produce additional goods and services, or income. Of course, the greater the base of wealth with which a nation has to work, the greater will be the flow of goods and services it can produce.

Consequently, it behooves any nation to add continually to its stock of wealth as a means of improving its economic welfare. Although there are various estimates of wealth, that shown in Table 6-11 indicates that total

TABLE 6-11

NATIONAL WEALTH IN CURRENT DOLLARS

1900-1968

(Billions of Dollars)

Year	National Wealth	Year	National Wealth
1900	$ 88	1950	$1,055
1910	152	1955	1,384
1920	374	1960	1,851
1930	410	1965	2,475
1940	424	1968	3,079
1945	570		

SOURCE: *Statistical Abstract of the United States*, 1973, and previous editions.

TABLE 6-12

**NATIONAL
WEALTH
OF THE
UNITED STATES**

1968

(Billions of Dollars)

Total National Wealth			$3,079
Reproducible Tangible Assets			$2,364
Structures		$1,537	
Residential (nonfarm)	$683		
Public Nonresidential	460		
Farm	50		
Institutional	55		
Other Private Nonresidential	289		
Equipment		611	
Producer Durables	377		
Consumer Durables	234		
Inventories		216	
Private Farm	30		
Private Nonfarm	172		
Public	14		
Land			715
Private		571	
Farm	153		
Nonfarm	418		
Public		144	

SOURCE: *Statistical Abstract of the United States,* 1973.

wealth exceeded $3.0 trillion in 1968. As can be seen in Table 6-12, the largest portion of our wealth is in the form of buildings. Next in importance is land. The next largest single category of wealth is in the form of producer's durable equipment. One notable omission from Table 6-12 is the pool or stock of manpower in the economy. Like the stocks of buildings, equipment, and land, the manpower stock yields a flow of productive services that generate income. However, a direct monetary value is difficult to put on human beings. We shall have more to say about this in Chapter 36.

Our national wealth and our productive capacity have been increasing continuously during the present decade, as seen in Table 6-11. In terms of constant dollars our real wealth has increased nearly sixfold since the beginning of this century. Since World War II it has been increasing at an annual average rate of 4 to 5 percent.

SUMMARY

1. The GNP is defined as the current market value of the total goods and services produced by the nation's economy over a period of time.

2. National income is a measure of the aggregate earnings arising from the production of the GNP.

3. Personal income and disposable income also can be derived from the basic GNP.

4. The GNP is distributed to three major sectors in our economy: consumers, private investors including net exports, and the government.

5. Factor payments for the GNP give rise to incomes in the form of wages and salaries, rental income, proprietors' income, net interest, and corporation profits.

6. When using the GNP as a measure of economic progress, it should be corrected for price changes and increases in the population. Other reservations, such as type of goods,

leisure time, nonmonetary transactions, and external or social costs, should be taken into consideration.

7. The flow of funds, a broader concept than the GNP, measures the total monetary transactions that take place in the economy.

8. Input-output tables permit an analysis of the flow of production from one industry to others and eventually to the final users.

9. Total wealth in the United States exceeds $3 trillion, with large amounts in the form of buildings, land, and equipment.

NEW TERMS

Gross national product, *p. 101*
End products, *p. 101*
Intermediate products, *p. 101*
Capital consumption allowances, *p. 103*
Net national product, *p. 103*
Personal income, *p. 103*
Transfer payment, *p. 103*
Disposable personal income, *p. 104*
Private investment, *p. 104*
Implicit price deflators, *p. 112*

Real GNP, *p. 112*
Real per capita disposable income, *p. 113*
Social costs, *p. 115*
Flow of funds system of national accounts, *p. 117*
Statement of sources and uses of funds, *p. 119*
Input-output tables, *p. 119*
National wealth, *p. 124*

QUESTIONS FOR DISCUSSION AND ANALYSIS

1. Explain how the gross national product gives rise to our total personal income.

2. Does the share of the national income that is in the form of compensation to employees seem excessive? Why or why not?

3. Has the government share of the GNP been increasing or decreasing in the past 10-15 years?

4. Why is it important to reduce the GNP or national income to constant dollar values when using them as measures of economic progress?

5. Should the services of housewives and other nonmonetary services be included in the gross national product? Why?

6. In future years would you prefer to have a 25 percent increase in income or a 30-hour workweek? Is it possible to have both?

7. How much more does it cost American consumers to purchase goods and services whenever the price index rises one percent?

8. Distinguish between the gross national product and the flow of funds.

9. Is it true that as we produce more and more goods and services we deplete our wealth? Why or why not?

10. How can the input-output tables be used to measure the impact on the total economy of a strike in a major industry, such as the steel or auto industry?

SUGGESTED READINGS

Board of Governors of the Federal Reserve System. *Flow of Funds, 1939-1953.* Washington: U.S. Government Printing Office, 1955.

——————. "Quarterly Presentation of Flow of Funds and Savings." *Federal Reserve Bulletin.* Washington: U.S. Government Printing Office, July, 1959.

Bober, Stanley. *The Economics of Cycles and Growth.* New York: John Wiley & Sons, Inc., 1968.

Burns, Arthur F. *The Frontiers of Economic Knowledge.* New York: John Wiley & Sons, Inc., 1965.

Butler, William F., and Robert A. Kavesh. *How Business Economists Forecast.* Englewood Cliffs, N.J.: Prentice-Hall, Inc., 1966.

Clark, John J., and Morris Cohen (eds.). *Business Fluctuations, Growth, and Economic Stabilization.* New York: Random House, Inc., 1963.

Clower, Robert W., and John F. Due. *Microeconomics.* Homewood, Ill.: Richard D. Irwin, Inc., 1972.

Committee for Economic Development. *High Employment Without Inflation: A Positive Program for Economic Stabilization* (July, 1972).

Dauten, C.A., and Lloyd M. Valentine. *Business Cycles and Forecasting*, 4th ed. Cincinnati: South-Western Publishing Co., 1974.

Department of Commerce. "Input-Output Structure of the U.S. Economy: 1963." *Survey of Current Business.* Washington: U.S. Government Printing Office, November, 1969.

——————. *U.S. Income and Output.* Washington: U.S. Government Printing Office, 1958.

Economic Report of the President. Washington: U.S. Government Printing Office, 1956-1974.

Goldman, Morris R., Martin L. Marimont, and Beatrice N. Vaccara. "The Interindustry Structure of the United States, a Report on the 1958 Input-Output Study." *Survey of Current Business.* Washington: Department of Commerce, Office of Business Economics, November, 1964.

Goldsmith, Raymond, and Christopher Saunders (eds.). *The Measurement of National Wealth.* International Association for Research in Income and Wealth, Series VIII. Chicago: Quadrangle Books, Inc., 1959.

Haberler, Gottfried. *Prosperity and Depression*, 3d ed. New York: Columbia University Press, 1941.

Harwood, E.C. *Causes and Control of the Business Cycle*. Great Barrington, Mass.: American Institute of Economic Research, 1947.

Katona, George. *Psychological Analysis of Economic Behavior*. New York: McGraw-Hill Book Company, 1951.

Lee, Maurice W. *Macroeconomics: Fluctuations, Growth and Stability*. Homewood, Ill.: Richard D. Irwin, Inc., 1971.

Lewis, John P., and Robert C. Turner. *Business Conditions Analysis*. New York: McGraw-Hill Book Company, 1967.

Manpower Report of the President. Washington: U.S. Government Printing Office, 1966-1974.

Moore, Geoffrey H. *Statistical Indicators of Cyclical Revivals and Regressions*. New York: National Bureau of Economic Research, Inc., 1950.

"New Applications of Input-Output." *Business Economics* (January, 1971).

Powelson, John P. *National Income and Flow-of-Funds Analysis.* New York: McGraw-Hill Book Company, 1960.

"Welfare Measurement and the GNP." *Survey of Current Business* (January, 1971).

7

Determinants of GNP

PREVIEW The level of economic activity (production, employment, and income) is determined by the amount of consumption, investment, and government spending in the economy. However, the GNP is not only affected directly by these factors but indirectly by means of the multiplier and accelerator effects. Knowledge of the multiplier and accelerator is essential for determining the actual amount of investment and/or government spending required to reach and maintain a given level of GNP and employment.

Whenever planned investment is greater than planned saving, it will cause the economy to expand, provided the economy is in a state of less than full employment. Conversely, when planned investment is less than planned saving, the economy will contract until saving is reduced to the level of investment.

What determines the size of GNP? Why is it larger in some years than it is in others? When is the GNP sufficient to maintain a state of full employment? Will GNP continue to grow in the next few decades? The answers to these questions are crucial to the status of our economy and the welfare of our people; consequently, they have important social and political overtones.

In the previous chapter it was noted that GNP is allocated among three basic sectors of the economy: consumers, investors (including net exports), and government. Naturally if these sectors are to receive goods and services, they must pay for them. The payments eventually become income to the owners of the four factors of production: labor, land, capital, and entrepreneurship. It is the demand for goods and services by the three sectors of the economy, therefore, that determines the total amount of goods and services that will be produced, or the size of GNP. Furthermore, these payments for goods and services determine the total income for the economy. Total demand by these sectors, therefore, determines the level of production, employment, and income. This process can be seen in Table 7-1, which shows the product and monetary flows in our economy. Products flow to the three sectors, and money flows from the sectors to the various factors of production, as demonstrated in Chapter 6.

It stands to reason, then, that anytime the total demand by the three sectors of the economy is the same in one year as it was in a previous year, the GNP should remain the same. Even if one sector should increase its

	Income Flow	Product Flow
NATIONAL PRODUCT AND INCOME ACCOUNT	GNP $1,288.2	GNP $1,288.2
	Less: Capital Consumption,	
	Indirect Business	Consumer Purchases .... $ 805.0
	Taxes, etc. .... $ 234.0	Business Investment .... $ 206.1
1973	National Income $1,054.2	A) Domestic $201.5
		B) Foreign 4.6
(Billions)	Compensation to Employees .. $ 785.3	Government Purchases ...... $ 277.2
	Proprietors Income .... $ 84.3	
	Rental Income .... $ 25.1	
	Net Interest .... $ 50.4	
	Corporate Profits .... $ 109.2	

SOURCE: *Survey of Current Business* (January, 1974).

demand, there would be no change in GNP if a corresponding decrease occurred in another sector. What happens, however, if there is a net increase in the total demand by the three sectors? Will the GNP increase by an equal amount, by a lesser amount, or by a greater amount?

MULTIPLIER EFFECT

Actually the GNP will increase by some multiple of the initial increase in spending by the three sectors. If domestic investment were increased by $15 billion, for example, the GNP might increase by $15 billion or $30 billion or more, depending upon what we call the *multiplier effect*. The multiplier is based on the simple phenomenon of responding of income. When a person receives income, he spends at least a part of it. His spending generates income for others, who in turn spend their incomes. As a result, the total income that arises from this continuous spending and responding of money will be larger than the original amount of spending on investment. The only limiting factor to this process would be the failure of someone along the line to respend his income in full or in part. In short, anytime money is withdrawn from the income stream, it will no longer generate additional income.

The size of the multiplier, then, will depend on the amount and the rapidity of responding additional income in the economy. The more the spending, the larger the multiplier, and vice versa. It is essential, therefore, to know something about the characteristics of consumption and savings in order to determine the size of the multiplier.

The Propensity to Consume

Anyone whose income rises may spend all the additional income, may save all of it, or may spend some of it and save some. Some persons, of course, will spend all their income immediately and then ask for more and borrow from their friends in the meantime. An individual may spend more than his current income at a given time by using up previous savings. However, we are concerned here principally with attitudes toward increases in income.

There are those who will save all of their additional income for some future use. These persons are on one end of the savings scale, while fast spenders are on the other end. The majority of persons belong to the middle group that will spend most of the additional income but save some of it. The more income this group receives, the smaller is the proportion of the additional income spent and the larger the proportion of the additional income saved. This characteristic is demonstrated by the conditions assumed in the hypothetical example utilized in Table 7-2.

TABLE 7-2

HOW MR. X DISPOSED OF INCREASES IN HIS INCOME

Income	Amount Spent	Amount Saved	Percent Spent	Percent Saved	Marginal Propensity to Consume (Percent)	Marginal Propensity to Save (Percent)
$ 6,000	$5,700	$ 300	95	5		
7,000	6,530	470	93	7	83	17
8,000	7,350	650	92	8	82	18
9,000	7,950	1,050	88	12	60	40
10,000	8,450	1,550	84	16	50	50

To start, assume that our hypothetical Mr. X had an income (after taxes) of $6,000, that his level of living was such that he spent $5,700, and that he was able to save only $300. Consequently, his *average propensity to consume* (*APC*) is 95 percent ($5,700 ÷ $6,000), and his *average propensity to save* (*APS*) is 5 percent ($300 ÷ $6,000). In effect he would be spending 95 percent of his income and saving only 5 percent. When his real income increases to $7,000, he will spend $6,530 and save $470. In short, his *APC* declines to 93 percent, and his *APS* rises to 7 percent. Of the $1,000 increase in income, he will spend $830 and save $170. If we consider the $1,000 increase as marginal because it was the last addition to his income (up to that time), his *marginal propensity to consume* (*MPC*) is $830 or 83 percent of the $1,000, and his *marginal propensity to save* (*MPS*) is $170 or 17 percent of the additional $1,000 total.

When Mr. X's income increases by another $1,000 to a total of $8,000, he will spend $7,350, or 92 percent, and save $650, or 8 percent, and his *MPC* is 82 percent while his *MPS* is 18 percent of the total increment. By the time his income reaches $10,000, his marginal consumption (*MPC*) is only 50 percent or half of the last $1,000, and his marginal saving is also

50 percent. With rising income the *APC* and the *MPC* fall, while the *APS* and the *MPS* rise.

A logical question is whether the behavior of Mr. *X* is typical of the millions of consumers in the United States. With rising income will the percentage of additional income spent, or the *MPC*, fall, and will the percentage saved, or the *MPS*, rise? In the earlier years of consumption analysis, the answer was that such behavior was typical of most individuals and families. There were good reasons for this conclusion, and statistics pointed in the same direction.[1] It was held that an individual with a small income would probably be forced to spend all of it for immediate needs and would be able to save little or nothing. As his income grew and his immediate wants were more fully met, he would give more consideration to future wants and would prepare to meet them through deferred spending, that is, through saving. As his income continued to grow, he could then provide more fully for future wants by more and more extensive saving.

Changes in Total Consumption

If the behavior of Mr. *X* is typical of the majority of income receivers, what can be said about consumption and saving as parts of total national income? Some indication of the relationship between income and saving is illustrated in Table 7-3.

TABLE 7-3

DISPOSABLE PERSONAL INCOME AND PERSONAL NET SAVINGS IN CURRENT PRICES

1929-1973 (Billions)

	1929	1933	1940	1950	1955	1960	1965	1970	1973
Disposable Personal Income ..	$83.3	$45.5	$75.7	$206.9	$275.3	$350.0	$473.2	$689.5	$882.6
Personal Outlays ..	79.1	46.5	71.8	193.9	259.5	330.0	444.8	634.7	828.7
Personal Net Saving	4.2	−.9	3.8	13.1	15.8	17.0	28.4	54.9	53.8
Saving as a Percent of Disposable Income	5.0%	−2.0%	5.1%	6.3%	5.7%	4.9%	6.0%	8.0%	6.1%

SOURCE: *Economic Report of the President,* 1974.

An inspection of the table shows that during the past few decades the average propensity to consume has been declining gradually and the average propensity to save, rising. In order to bring this about, of course, the marginal propensity to consume must be lower than the *APC*, and it must be constant or declining with the rise in income. The marginal propensity

[1] *Family Income, Expenditures, and Savings,* BLS Bulletin No. 1097 (Washington: U.S. Government Printing Office, 1950).

to consume for the period 1965-1970, for example, was 88 percent compared to 90 percent for the 1960-1965 period and more than 94 percent for the previous five-year period, 1955-1960. A similar gradual decrease in the marginal propensity to consume can be observed in comparing total consumption and savings to national income or by comparing the change in personal savings to the increase in per capita disposable income.

More recently some economists have suggested that the *MPC* may be more constant than was originally anticipated, especially when comparing annual total disposable income and aggregate consumption.

Nevertheless, whether the *MPC* remains constant or declines, we can generalize that, as a nation becomes wealthier, there is a tendency for consumption to increase by less than the increase in income and for savings to grow faster than does income. This was also true of Mr. *X* and his consumption and saving in relation to his total income. In fact, if individuals and families are likely to consume and save in the manner of Mr. *X*, total consumption will fluctuate less than will total income, and total savings will vary to a greater degree than will total income.

Savings may be invested directly by the saver or may be turned over to some agency that does the investing, as happens when the individual deposits his savings in a savings and loan association, leaving to the association the task of deciding what housing developments or projects are to receive loans. On the other hand, a large borrower with an established name and rating can turn to an investment banker for a large long-term loan in order to expand its plant, and its securities will be bought by savers in many parts of the country. Thus, there are established ways of investing savings.

The Multiplier

Whenever an investment is made in a new venture and the money is paid out, it becomes income to those who have provided services or materials. Some of this income will be spent for consumption, and some will be saved and invested. These portions will give rise to new income, which will be partly consumed and partly saved, with further increases in income, consumption, and saving until the impulse of the original investment is entirely exhausted. This multiplying effect of an original investment is most important. The ratio of the increase in the total income to an increase in investment is called the *investment multiplier*. Each dollar of investment will create additional income, but just how much income will be created depends upon the relation between consumption and saving.

An Example. Let us assume a marginal increase (indicated by Δ) of $10 billion in investment, and a ratio of 3 to 1 between consumption and saving. The result is shown in Table 7-4.

TABLE 7-4	ΔI Increase in Investment	ΔY Resulting Increase in Income	ΔC Additions to Consumption 75%	ΔS Additions to Saving 25%
INCREASES IN INCOME, CONSUMPTION, AND SArVING AS A RESULT OF INCREASED INVESTMENT	$10	$10.0	$ 7.5	$ 2.5
		7.5	5.6	1.9
	Multiplier	5.6	4.2	1.4
	Effect	4.2	3.2	1.0
		etc.	etc.	etc.
(Billions)	Total	$40	$30	$10

This marginal increase in investment becomes income to workers and others, in the form of wages, rent, interest, and profits. This expenditure of $10 billion will therefore increase incomes by a total of $10 billion. Of this income, three fourths ($7.5 billion) will be used for consumption, and one fourth ($2.5 billion) will be saved. As the $7.5 billion is spent for consumption goods, it creates new incomes to a total of $7.5 billion. Of this amount, three fourths will be used for consumption (three fourths of $7.5 billion is $5.6 billion) and one fourth, or $1.9 billion, will be saved. As the $5.6 billion is spent for consumption, it creates further incomes to that amount, of which three fourths ($4.2 billion) will represent an addition to consumption, and one fourth ($1.4 billion) will be saved. How rapidly these successive increases in income, consumption, and saving will occur depends largely on the speed with which individuals and families spend the incomes they receive.

The limit to the multiplying effect of the original investment will be reached when the total increase in income is $40 billion. The expansion of income is distributed in the form of additional consumption of $30 billion and additional saving of $10 billion. When the original impulse is completed, the ratio of the marginal propensity to consume to the marginal propensity to save is 3 to 1, or 75 percent to 25 percent, and saving has increased until it equals the original increment of investment. In this way total investment and total saving tend to become equal.

If the marginal propensity to consume were 80 percent, or $\frac{4}{5}$, instead of $\frac{3}{4}$, as shown in the example, the multiplier effect would be greater. If the initial increase of investment was $10 billion and the marginal propensity to consume $\frac{4}{5}$, the first income recipient would spend $8 billion and save only $2 billion. Those receiving the $8 billion would spend $6.4 billion and save $1.6 billion, and so forth down the line. The net increase in income resulting from the additional $10 billion investment would be $50 billion, of which $40 billion would be spent on consumption and $10 billion saved.

On the other hand, if the marginal propensity to consume were only 50 percent or ½, the multiplier effect would be less. With an initial investment of $10 billion, each income recipient would spend only one half of the income received and save the other one half. This would mean that the net increase in income resulting from an additional investment of $10 billion would be $20 billion, of which $10 billion would be spent on consumption and $10 billion saved. It becomes obvious, therefore, that the size of the multiplier is related directly to the marginal propensity to consume and inversely to the marginal propensity to save.

The Multiplier Formula. This being the case, we can now put into the language of a formula the relationship between the multiplier and the marginal propensity to consume as follows:

$$k = \frac{1}{1 - \dfrac{\Delta C}{\Delta Y}}$$

in which k is the multiplier, ΔC is the change in consumption, and ΔY is the change in income.[2] Since the 1 in the denominator of the formula is equivalent to or represents the total increase in income, when the marginal propensity to consume, $\dfrac{\Delta C}{\Delta Y}$, is subtracted from 1, the residual equals the marginal propensity to save, $\dfrac{\Delta S}{\Delta Y}$. Dividing the marginal propensity to save, $1 - \dfrac{\Delta C}{\Delta Y}$, or $\dfrac{\Delta S}{\Delta Y}$, into the 1 in the numerator of the formula gives us the multiplier, which is equal to the reciprocal of the marginal propensity to save. Although the formula emphasizes the marginal propensity to consume as being the active

[2] We can also write the formula as:

$$k = \frac{1}{\dfrac{\Delta S}{\Delta Y}}$$

where ΔS is the change in saving. When the marginal propensity to consume, $\dfrac{\Delta C}{\Delta Y}$, is subtracted from 1, the residual equals the marginal propensity to save, $\dfrac{\Delta S}{\Delta Y}$. We know that an addition to income must be spent or saved:

$$\Delta C + \Delta S = \Delta Y.$$

Dividing both sides of the equation by ΔY gives:

$$\frac{\Delta C}{\Delta Y} + \frac{\Delta S}{\Delta Y} = \frac{\Delta Y}{\Delta Y} = 1.$$

Thus, $\dfrac{\Delta S}{\Delta Y} = 1 - \dfrac{\Delta C}{\Delta Y}$.

factor in the determination of the multiplier, we can see, in short, that the multiplier is equal to the reciprocal of the marginal propensity to save.

To demonstrate a hypothetical application of the formula, assume that in period or year 1 the total income of an economy was $1,200 billion of which $900 billion was used for consumption and the remaining $300 billion saved. Assume further that in year 2 total income increased to $1,260 billion, of which $940 billion was spent on consumption and $320 billion saved. This would mean that of the $60 billion added to income, $40 billion was used for consumption and $20 billion held for savings. Inserting our figures into the formula, we can calculate the multiplier as follows:

$$k = \cfrac{1}{1 - \cfrac{\Delta C}{\Delta Y}} \qquad k = \cfrac{1}{1 - \cfrac{40}{60}} \qquad k = \cfrac{1}{\frac{1}{3}} \qquad k = 3.$$

The multiplier based on the marginal propensity to consume is 3, or we can say that it is equal to the reciprocal of the marginal propensity to save ($\frac{1}{3}$). Notice that the multiplier would have been approximately 4 if it had been calculated on the basis of the average propensity to save (that is, on the basis of $\frac{C}{Y}$ instead of $\frac{\Delta C}{\Delta Y}$). Why? The average propensity to consume in year 2 was close to 75 percent ($940 \div $1,260 = 74.6\%$) and the average propensity to save was 25.4 percent or about one fourth. It is evident then that the marginal propensity to consume serves as a more accurate basis on which to calculate the multiplier than does the average propensity to consume.

Although the multiplier can be calculated for any given propensity to consume, the schedule shown in Table 7-5 indicates the size of the multiplier for selected marginal propensities to consume.

Usually the multiplier is based on the spending or saving of disposable income, since it is that portion of income over which individuals have the freedom to make a decision to spend or not to spend. Various estimates of the multiplier for the American economy indicate that it is somewhere between 2 and 3, depending on the level of employment and the degree of business activity.

TABLE 7-5

MARGINAL PROPENSITY TO CONSUME, MARGINAL PROPENSITY TO SAVE, AND THE MULTIPLIER

MPC	MPS	Multiplier
1/3	2/3	1 1/2
1/2	1/2	2
2/3	1/3	3
3/4	1/4	4
4/5	1/5	5
5/6	1/6	6

The Acceleration Principle

Granting that we have a multiplier and can estimate its size, we can see that an increase in investment (or consumption or government spending) will bring about an increase in income by some multiple of the original increase. However, that is not all. As the increased income resulting from the multiplier effect is being respent, the demand for consumer goods and services will increase. This increased consumer demand may lead businessmen to increase their demand for machinery, equipment, and buildings to produce the additional consumer goods and services being demanded. They will, in turn, increase their investment to obtain the capital equipment needed to increase production. The relationship between this secondary, or induced, investment brought about by the spending of the increased income resulting from the multiplier is known as the *accelerator effect*.

Going back to our example in Table 7-4, remember that $10 billion of original or *autonomous investment* brought about a $40 billion increase in income via the multiplier effect. Of this $40 billion, three fourths, or $30 billion, was spent for consumption and the residual was saved. Now suppose that as a result of their optimism about an increase of $30 billion in additional sales, business merchants increase their orders for goods and services. This will cause the producers to increase output. In order to do this, the manufacturers may have to purchase additional machinery, equipment, and buildings. This means that secondary, or *induced investment*, will take place. It is often called "induced investment" because it is brought about or induced by the increased demand for consumer goods and services. For the purpose of illustration, assume that the induced investment is $7 billion, as shown in line 2 in Table 7-6. Of course, the value or size of the accelerator is difficult, if not impossible, to ascertain in actual situations, since it is extremely difficult to distinguish between autonomous and induced investment. To what extent firms invest in additional machinery, equipment, and buildings as a result of autonomous decisions and to what extent they are influenced to invest by the current level of expanding business activity because of the multiplier effect is difficult to say. Regardless of our inability to find an accurate measure, it can readily be understood that accelerator effects do operate in our economy and that they do influence the level of economic activity.

Interaction of the Multiplier and Accelerator

Not only will a multiplier effect result from autonomous investment, but a similar multiplier effect will also result from the induced investment. Thus, the multiplier effect on original investment brings about larger incomes, the spending of which induces secondary investment. The multiplier effect on the secondary investment in turn increases incomes still further. The second round of expanded consumer demand may bring about tertiary or *third order investment*. This in turn means more income and investment. In this manner the multiplier and the accelerator tend to augment the effects of each other and to boost income, investment, and employment in the economy. Interaction between the multiplier and the accelerator is demonstrated in Table 7-6. Keep in mind, however, that the process does not work in one direction only. A decrease in investment will have a negative multiplier effect on the economy.

TABLE 7-6

INCREASED INCOME AS A RESULT OF THE INTERACTION OF THE MULTIPLIER AND THE ACCELERATOR

(Billions)

Autonomous Investment	Induced Investment via Accelerator	Increase in Income via Multiplier	Increase in Consumption	Increase in Saving
$10	—	$40	$30	$10
—	$ 7	28	21	7
—	3	12	9	3
$10	$10	$80	$60	$20

If we measure the original investment, $10 billion, against the original increase in income shown on line 1 in Table 7-6, $40 billion, the multiplier is 4. If we measure the total autonomous and induced investment combined, $20 billion, against the total increase in income, $80 billion, we still have a multiplier of 4. This is known as the *simple multiplier*. On the other hand, if we measure the autonomous investment only, $10 billion, against the total increase in income, $80 billion, resulting from the interaction of the multiplier and the accelerator, the multiplier is 8. This is known as the *supermultiplier*. It is sometimes referred to as the *compound multiplier*. Since the supermultiplier is difficult to measure due to the inability of distinguishing between autonomous and induced investment, we usually deal in terms of the simple multiplier.

Of course, in this whole matter we must keep in mind that the accelerator effect may begin to take effect before the multiplier effect has run its full course. Table 7-6 shows that an induced investment of $7 billion results from the income expansion of $40 billion brought about by the multiplier on the autonomous investment. It is quite possible that some of this induced investment occurs before respending of income has reached the $40 billion level. Some may occur by the time respending of the autonomous investment has reached only $2 billion or $5 billion. In fact, tertiary investment may also begin to take place before the full effect of the multiplier on the autonomous investment is completed. Consequently, in any period after that in which the autonomous investment takes place, there may occur increased income as a result of the combined effect of autonomous and induced investment.

The compounding of investment and income can be seen in Figure 7-1. Increments of income resulting from the respending of the original investment are shown as A_1, A_2, A_3, and so on. Note that the marginal effects of the original investment decrease with each respending until it is exhausted, as indicated by the broken line. If induced investment should commence in period 2, however, as designated by B_1, B_2, B_3, and so forth, it will augment the increase in income in that and subsequent periods. Income from the spending and respending of tertiary investment, as shown by C_1, C_2, C_3, and so on, further augments income. The net result is that total income will increase more and reach a higher level than it would with the original investment only. On the other hand, such interaction of the multiplier and the accelerator causes a greater fluctuation in income, output, and employment than would otherwise take place. This can be observed by comparing the solid line with the broken line in Figure 7-1. In subsequent chapters, especially those dealing with business fluctuations and our efforts to stabilize the economy, the importance of the multiplier-accelerator effect will become more dramatic.

In the previous discussion we have kept the multiplier on both the original investment and the induced investment equal. It is quite possible, however, that as income increases from the interaction of the multiplier and the accelerator, the size of the multiplier may decrease. This could occur because as income increases there is a tendency for the marginal propensity to consume to decline. Consequently, as the *MPC* declines, the size of the multiplier

FIGURE 7-1

The combined effect of the multiplier and accelerator augments income but to some extent aggravates business fluctuations.

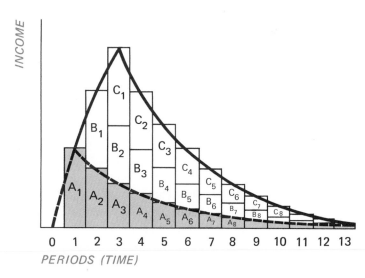

will decrease. If so, this would modify to some degree the effects of the action described above.

RELATIONSHIP OF INVESTMENT TO SAVING

It can be noted in our various examples, such as that in Table 7-4 on page 134, that changes in total investment and total saving tend to become equal. This is no mere coincidence. In fact, total saving and total investment are equal once the system reaches an equilibrium. Let us take a closer look at this phenomenon. Investment is defined as production that is not currently consumed. It may be in the form of machinery, equipment, buildings, or even increased inventories of consumer goods that are not immediately consumed. *Saving*, on the other hand, is the amount of current income not spent on consumer goods. Saving by the individual may take the form of spending for nonconsumer goods or hoarding of cash. For the nation as a whole, income is equal to total production. Since the income is equivalent in value to the goods produced, if income recipients do not spend money either for consumer or nonconsumer goods, the unsold goods will become increased inventories in the hands of the producers. Thus, any hoarding theoretically will be offset by investment in the form of an involuntary increase in business inventories. If this is the case, investment (goods produced but not consumed) will equal saving (income spent on nonconsumer goods plus hoarding). In Chapter 5 we indicated that the relationship between investment and saving determined movement in the economy. Here we will learn the distinction between and the importance of planned investment and realized investment.

Investment Equal to Saving

To look at it from another point of view, we can say that in a two-sector economy, excluding government, the national income, designated by Y, is equal to consumption, the value of goods produced and consumed, designated by C, and investment, the amount of goods produced but not currently consumed, designated by I. In short, national income equals consumption plus investment. This is written in equation form as: $Y = C + I$. On the other hand, the national income, designated by Y, is equal to total spending on consumer goods, designated by C, and the amount of saving, that amount of income not spent on consumer goods, designated by S. Consequently, national income equals consumption plus saving. This may be written in equation form as follows: $Y = C + S$. If this is true, then a simple syllogism indicates that investment equals saving, as shown at the top of page 141.

$$Y = C + I$$
$$Y = C + S$$
$$\text{Therefore, } I = S.$$

Planned vs. Realized Saving

Are the business firms and households that do the saving the same firms and households that do the investing? No, not always, and herein lies a source of difficulty. Because savers and investors may be different persons, *planned investment* may differ from *planned saving*. Investors may plan to invest more or less than the savers intend to save. What happens then? The answer to this question gives an important key to the determination of economic activity, that is, whether the economy is going to expand or contract. Anytime planned investment is greater than planned saving, forces will come into play to expand the level of economic activity. When planned investment is less than planned saving, the economy will contract; and when planned investment and saving are equal, the level of economic activity will be stable.

This can be illustrated as follows: Assume total production of $1,300 billion, with $1,100 billion in consumer goods and $200 billion in investment goods. If we produce $1,300 billion in goods, money income will equal $1,300 billion. Assume further that $1,100 billion of this income is spent for consumer goods and the remaining $200 billion is saved (spent on non-consumer items or hoarded). In such case the total demand for goods and services will be equal to the total supply. Investors plan to purchase an amount of machinery, equipment, buildings, and inventories to make up for the difference between consumer spending and total production. It should be remembered that even if hoarding does take place, its adverse effect on the level of business activity can be offset by investors obtaining a like amount of credit for investment purposes. What funds hoarders take out of the circular flow of income, investors replace with borrowed funds. When this occurs, total spending will equal total income, total demand will equal total supply, and all production will be cleared off the market. In terms of our symbolic notation:

$$Y \quad = \quad C \quad + \quad I$$
$$\$1,300 = \$1,100 + \$200 \rightarrow \text{Planned investment}$$

$$Y \quad = \quad C \quad + \quad S$$
$$\$1,300 = \$1,100 + \$200 \rightarrow \text{Planned saving}$$

Therefore, Planned I = Planned S.

Investment Greater than Savings

What happens now if planned investment is greater than planned saving? What forces come into play to expand the economy? When does the expansion come to an end? Let us assume a situation similar to that shown above with the exception that investors plan to invest $250 billion in machinery, equipment, and buildings, while savers plan to save $200 billion. Our formula then appears as follows:

$$Y = C + I$$
$$\$1,350 = \$1,100 + \$250 \rightarrow \text{Planned investment}$$

$$Y = C + S$$
$$\$1,300 = \$1,100 + \$200 \rightarrow \text{Planned saving}$$

Therefore, Planned I > Planned S.

If the investors follow through on their plans to invest $250 billion, economic activity will expand. Total production of goods and services will increase to $1,350 billion, $1,100 billion in consumer goods and $250 billion in investment goods. When production rises to $1,350 billion, incomes will increase accordingly. If income recipients intended to spend $1,100 billion on consumption and save the remaining $200 billion out of the original income of $1,300 billion, it stands to reason that they can buy more or save more out of $1,350 billion in income. Assuming that they originally intended to spend only $1,100 billion, we can assume, for simplicity, that they will save the additional $50 billion in income which they receive. Even if they do not save all of it, they will save a portion of it. But, so long as planned investment is greater than planned savings, the economy will continue to expand; and as income increases, the marginal propensity to save of the income recipients will increase. The economy will expand until income is high enough so that the saving out of such income will equal investment. Thus, whenever planned investment is greater than planned savings, the economy will expand. This expansion will come to an end and a new position of equilibrium will be reached at an income level where planned saving equals investment. At that point *realized investment* and *realized saving* will equal the original planned investment.

Notice in our example that originally planned saving was $200 billion. This meant that the average propensity to consume out of the $1,300 billion income was 85 percent, and the average propensity to save was 15 percent. As income increases to $1,350 billion, and assume that income recipients will spend $1,100 billion for consumption and save $250 billion, the average propensity to consume declines to 81.5 percent ($1,100 ÷ $1,350 = 81.5%), and the average propensity to save increases to 18.5 percent

($250 ÷ $1,350 = 18.5%). Thus, when planned investment is greater than planned saving, production will expand, income will increase, and the average propensity to save will continually rise until a point is reached at which actual savings equals the original planned investment. The situation at this point will appear as follows:

$$Y = C + I$$
$$\$1,350 = \$1,100 + \$250 \rightarrow \text{Realized investment}$$
$$Y = C + S$$
$$\$1,350 = \$1,100 + \$250 \rightarrow \text{Realized saving}$$

Therefore, Realized I = Realized S.

Even if we adopt a more practical point of view and assume that income recipients do not save all of their marginal income, the forces that come into play will be the same, but the total effect will be different. Assuming a marginal propensity of 50 percent, for example, when income rises to $1,350 billion, income recipients will spend $25 billion more on consumer goods and save only $25 billion. At this point planned investment, $250 billion, would still exceed planned saving of $225 billion. Then production and income would increase still further because $1,125 billion would be produced in the form of consumer goods and $250 billion in investment goods. This would further increase income to $1,375 billion. If the marginal propensity to consume were still ½, it would mean that $1,137.5 billion would be spent on consumption and $237.5 billion saved. Production and income would then rise to $1,387.5 billion, consumption to $1,143.75 billion, and saving would be $243.75 billion. Production, income, and saving would continue to increase by this process until income had reached a level where the realized savings equaled the planned investment of $250 billion. At that point, the equilibrium figures would be approximately:

$$Y = C + I$$
$$\$1,400 = \$1,150 + \$250 \rightarrow \text{Realized investment}$$
$$Y = C + S$$
$$\$1,400 = \$1,150 + \$250 \rightarrow \text{Realized saving}$$

Therefore, Realized I = Realized S.

In any given situation in which the planned investment is greater than planned savings, expansionary forces will set in and raise production and income until a point is reached at which planned saving out of the new, higher income will equal planned investment. The greater the marginal propensity to consume, or the less the marginal propensity to save, the longer and more intense the expansionary force. For example, in our recent example, if the propensity to consume had been $\frac{2}{3}$ instead of $\frac{1}{2}$, income recipients would have spent $33.4 billion of the original increase in income and saved only $16.6 billion. This would have increased production to $1,383.4 billion instead of $1,375 billion. If this process were continued, the savings would not come into balance with investment until the economy reached an income level of $1,450 billion instead of $1,400 billion. If the marginal propensity to consume were $\frac{3}{4}$, equilibrium would occur at the $1,500 billion level.

Investment Less than Savings

If for some reason businessmen are pessimistic and plan to invest only $150 billion, whereas income recipients plan to save $200 billion, the opposite reaction will occur. Assume that the economy had been operating smoothly at a production and income level of $1,300 billion with investment and savings in balance at $200 billion. If businessmen decide to invest only $150 billion in machinery and equipment, we will have the following situation:

$$Y = C + I$$
$$\$1,250 = \$1,100 + \$150 \rightarrow \text{Planned investment}$$

$$Y = C + S$$
$$\$1,300 = \$1,100 + \$200 \rightarrow \text{Planned saving}$$

Therefore, Planned $I <$ Planned S.

Total production will fall to $1,250 billion, $1,100 billion in consumer goods and $150 billion in investment goods, which in turn will reduce income to $1,250 billion. If consumers follow through on their plans to spend $1,100 billion on consumption, then saving will be reduced to $150 billion. At this point saving will come into balance with investment and equilibrium will again exist. It is evident, therefore, that anytime planned investment is less than planned savings, a contraction in the economy will result. As production decreases, income will fall; and as income falls, the marginal propensity to save will decline. The process will continue until a point is reached at which saving out of lower income equals the amount of the original planned investment. Under these circumstances, the equilibrium figures will appear as shown below:

$$Y = C + I$$
$$\$1,250 = \$1,100 + \$150 \rightarrow \text{Realized investment}$$

$$Y = C + S$$
$$\$1,250 = \$1,100 + \$150 \rightarrow \text{Realized saving}$$

Therefore, Realized $I =$ Realized S.

Of course, income recipients will not cut their saving by $50 billion in one swoop. They may decide that they want to save at least $175 billion and consequently cut consumption to $1,075 billion. In such case the contractionary effect on production and income would be intensified. Total production would then be cut to $1,225 billion, $1,075 billion in the form of consumer goods and $150 billion in investment goods. This process of reduced production, income, and saving will continue to a point where the total saving equals the original planned investment. If the marginal propensity to save were $\frac{1}{2}$, the new equilibrium figures would be approximately $1,200 billion for production and income, consumption would be at $1,050 billion, and investment and saving would be in balance at $150 billion. If the marginal propensity to consume were $\frac{2}{3}$, income would drop to $1,150 billion.

In summarizing this discussion, we may say that planned investment may be more than, equal to, or less than planned saving. If it is more or less, however, forces will come into play to make realized investment equal to realized saving. Another way to put it is to say that at the beginning of the period, *ex ante investment* may be greater than, equal to, or less than savings; but at the end of the period in which the adjusting forces take place, *ex post investment* equals savings. In short, *ex ante* $I \gtreqless S$, but *ex post* $I = S$.

PRACTICAL ASPECTS OF THE MULTIPLIER

Looking at it from another point of view, the multiplier is important in determining what amount of additional investment may be necessary to raise the economy from one level of economic activity to another. If we are at less than full employment, we can determine what increase in investment is necessary to obtain full employment. Suppose that after checking various sources—such as the McGraw-Hill Survey of Business Investment, the University of Michigan Survey of Consumer Finances, and the proposed government budgets—the following information is obtained. Business investment in a forthcoming year is to be approximately $200 billion, government spending $250 billion, and consumption $800 billion. Given these data, the estimated GNP will be $1,250 billion.

On the other hand, suppose it is estimated that the GNP necessary for a fully employed economy is $1,300 billion. This can be determined by multiplying the labor force times hours per worker per year times the output per man-hour. For example, if we assume the labor force in a given year to be 85 million (exclusive of the frictionally unemployed), our full employment GNP estimate would be as follows:

Labor Force	×	Hours per Worker per Year	×	Output per Man-Hour	=	Potential GNP
85,000,000		2,080		$7.35		$1,300,000,000,000.

If the GNP required for full employment is $1,300 billion but the estimated GNP will be only $1,250 billion, there will be some unemployment in the economy. A reasonable estimate of unemployment would be 4 percent or about 3.5 million. If full employment is desired, how much additional investment will be required? The answer depends in large part on the size of the multiplier. The gap between the estimated and potential full employment GNP is $50 billion. It is not necessary, however, to increase investment or initial spending by this amount. If the multiplier at this level of income were 2, as indicated by figures in Table 7-7, an increased investment of $25 billion would raise the GNP to a level of $1,300 billion. Out of the $50 billion increase in income, one half, or $25 billion, would be spent for consumer goods and the other half would be saved, provided the multiplier were 2. This would make consumption $825 billion, investment $225 billion, and government spending $250 billion for a total GNP of $1,300 billion, as shown in Table 7-7. If the size of the multiplier were 3, it would require an increase of $16.7 billion in investment to raise the GNP to the full employment level. Similar increases in the GNP may result with an initial increase in either consumer purchases or government spending.

TABLE 7-7

INCREASED INVESTMENT AND REALIZED GNP

(Billions)

	GNP	Consumer Purchases	Private Investment	Government
Estimated GNP	$1,250	$800	$200	$250
Increased Investment			+25	
Realized GNP	$1,300	$825	$225	$250

Such a procedure was followed in calculating the size of the historic income tax cuts of 1964. Knowing that we had excess unemployment of nearly one million and that the economy was operating about $30 billion under its potential capacity, the President's Council of Economic Advisers estimated that a $10 to $12 billion personal and corporate income tax reduction would close the *production gap* and move the economy toward full employment. Although it was anticipated that taxpayers would spend 93 percent of their tax reduction, it was calculated that, with a multiplier of 2 plus an accelerator effect, total income would rise by $30 billion or more. Whether it was due to the tax cuts primarily or to the accompanying complementary forces, such as a high level of investment, heavy federal outlay for the escalation of the war in Vietnam, substantial expansion of the money supply, and sizable deficit budgets, the economy did return to full employment within two years. During that time employment increased by about 2.7 million, the

GNP in constant dollars rose at an annual rate of 5 percent, and unemployment declined from 5.2 to 3.8 percent of the labor force. More recently, in the early 1970s, it was calculated that the economy was operating at $40 to $50 billion under its potential, and various measures were recommended to increase investment to plug the production gap between actual and potential production.

SUMMARY

1. The level of production, employment, and income in the economy is determined by the total spending by the four sectors of the economy: consumer purchases, domestic investment, net exports, and government purchases.

2. A net increase in investment will increase total income by some multiple of the original increase in investment.

3. The size of the multiplier is directly related to the marginal propensity to consume. The greater the marginal propensity to consume, the larger the multiplier.

4. Interaction of the multiplier and accelerator tends to augment business upswings and downswings.

5. Anytime investment is greater than saving, it will lead to an increase in the level of economic activity or an increase in the price level, depending on the state of employment existing in the economy.

6. Whenever planned investment differs from planned saving, forces will come into play to bring the economy into equilibrium at a point where realized investment and realized saving are equal.

7. From a practical point of view, the multiplier is useful for determining the amount of increased investment necessary to raise the GNP from one level to another.

NEW TERMS

Multiplier effect, *p. 130*
Average propensity to consume (APC), *p. 131*
Average propensity to save (APS), *p. 131*
Marginal propensity to consume (MPC), *p. 131*
Marginal propensity to save (MPS), *p. 131*
Investment multiplier, *p. 133*
Multiplier formula, *p. 135*
Accelerator effect, *p. 137*
Autonomous investment, *p. 137*

Induced investment, *p. 137*
Supermultiplier or compound multiplier, *p. 138*
Simple multiplier, *p. 138*
Third order investment, *p. 138*
Saving, *p. 140*
Planned investment, *p. 141*
Planned saving, *p. 141*
Realized investment, *p. 142*
Realized saving, *p. 142*
Ex ante investment, *p. 145*
Ex post investment, *p. 145*
Production gap, *p. 146*

1. When calculating the multiplier, is it better to base it on the average propensity to consume or the marginal propensity to consume? Why?
2. Why does the marginal propensity to consume decrease as income increases?
3. If individuals in the aggregate spent $24 billion of their last $40 billion increment of income, what would be the value of the multiplier?
4. If investment increased by $18 billion and the marginal propensity to save were $\frac{1}{3}$, by what amount would total income increase?
5. Give the formula for the multiplier. What is the estimated size of the multiplier for the United States?
6. What is the accelerator principle? How does it differ from the multiplier principle?
7. Demonstrate how the interaction of the multiplier and accelerator tends to augment income.
8. Explain what forces cause the economy to expand whenever planned investment is greater than planned saving.
9. Explain how $I < S$ ex ante, but $I = S$ ex post.
10. Check appropriate sources and ascertain whether a GNP production gap currently exists. If so, what is the size of the gap in dollar and percentage values? Considering the multiplier effect, what additional amount of investment (or government spending) is required to eliminate the production gap?

SUGGESTED READINGS

Burck, Gilbert, and Sanford S. Parker. "The Mighty Multiplier." *Fortune* (October, 1954), pp. 108-113.

Dernburg, Thomas F., and Duncan M. McDougall. *Macroeconomics*, 4th ed. New York: McGraw-Hill Book Company, 1972.

Dillard, Dudley. *The Economics of John Maynard Keynes.* Englewood Cliffs, N.J.: Prentice-Hall, Inc., 1948.

Economic Report of the President. Washington: U.S. Government Printing Office, 1962-1974.

Keynes, John Maynard. *The General Theory of Employment, Interest, and Money.* London: The Macmillan Company, 1951.

Leijonhufvud, Axel. *On Keynesian Economics and the Economics of Keynes.* New York: Oxford University Press, Inc., 1968.

Lindauer, John. *Macroeconomics,* 2d ed. New York: John Wiley & Sons, Inc., 1971.

Marshall, Natalie. *Keynes: Updated or Outdated?* Lexington, Mass.: D. C. Heath & Company, 1970.

McKenna, Joseph P. *Aggregate Economic Analysis.* Hinsdale, Ill.: The Dryden Press, 1972.

Samuelson, Paul A. "Interaction Between the Multiplier Analysis and the Principle of Acceleration." *Review of Economic Statistics* (May, 1939).

Shapiro, Edward. *Macroeconomics Analysis*, 2d ed. New York: Harcourt Brace Jovanovich, Inc., 1970.

8

A Further Analysis of the Determinants of GNP

PREVIEW The relationship of investment to saving is an important aspect in the size and growth of the GNP. If saving is greater than investment, or vice versa, the economy may reach a disequilibrium position and, as a consequence, move toward either contraction or expansion. However, economic measures may be taken to influence the variables that control consumption, investment, saving, and government spending. In so doing, the level of production, employment, and income within the economy can be changed.

Since the amount and rate of change in the GNP serve as measures of economic progress, help determine employment and income, and affect our economic standard of living, a closer inspection and deeper analysis of the determinants of the GNP is essential. The GNP, or the level of production, employment, and income, is determined by the total effective demand in the economy. This effective demand is composed of three basic elements: consumption, private investment, and government spending. Important in this modern income-expenditure analysis are the relationships between consumption and total output and between savings and investment.[1]

EFFECTIVE DEMAND

In seeking an explanation of what determines the GNP and the level of employment at any given time, analysis centers around the concept of effective demand. *Effective demand* is defined as the actual demand for goods and services by consumers, businesses, investors, and government.

[1] John Maynard Keynes, a British economist, was primarily responsible for the initiation and early development of the income-expenditure analysis of the economy, frequently called the "new economics." Subsequently others improved on the original Keynesian presentation. It is an approach to which many have contributed, and it has developed into an excellent tool of economic analysis. Modern monetary, fiscal, and psychological policies are difficult to understand without a knowledge of the principles of the income-expenditure analysis. Although the principles have been widely accepted, controversy still arises concerning economic policies based on these principles. Keep in mind that it is possible to accept the Keynesian tools of analysis without agreeing with the economic policies of Keynes, other leading economists, or political figures. It is possible, for example, to accept the income-expenditure analysis of why we have unemployment without agreeing with Keynes or the President's Council of Economic Advisers in regard to what we should do about unemployment.

If effective demand is sufficient, there will be a high level of economic activity. When effective demand for goods and services is less than current production or less than the amount of goods and services that the economy is capable of producing at full employment, difficulties arise. Under the first circumstance, the market will not clear all the goods and services produced. Consequently, GNP, employment, and income may decline. In the second circumstance, all goods and services may be cleared off the market, but there will be a production gap between potential and actual GNP and some unemployment will exist.

Furthermore, the greater the productive capacity of the economy, the more difficult it is to obtain and maintain full employment. This stems from the fact that total consumption is generally less than total output or income. Therefore, in order to have full employment, investment and/or government spending is necessary to fill the gap between what is produced and what is consumed. Furthermore, as output and income increase, the average propensity to consume declines. This means that the greater the total output, the larger the amount of private investment and/or government spending required to maintain a particular level of employment. Moreover, because the *consumption function* (which is a measure of the actual consumption at alternative levels of income) is relatively stable in the short run, effective demand will fluctuate primarily with changes in investment and/or government spending.

Since normal government spending at any given level of income probably is more stable than is the amount of private investment, the latter is definitely the most dynamic force in the determination of the level of business activity.

The relationship between income and output on the one hand and the consumption function on the other is an important key to the understanding of income-expenditure analysis. Given a particular amount of government spending, it is the relationship between income and consumption that determines the amount of investment required for any particular level of employment. In addition, because the average propensity to consume declines as income increases, a larger amount of investment is necessary to increase the level of output and employment. It must be remembered, however, that with any given amount of private investment, employment can vary with changes in government spending or consumption.

EQUILIBRIUM OUTPUT

In order to understand how the GNP and employment are determined by the income-expenditure relationship, it must be remembered that the total real output of the economy is equal to the total real income. When expenditures for output increase, income will increase by an identical amount, as shown by the *income-output line* in Figure 8-1. Notice that at any point on this line the output measured on the Y axis is equal to the income on the X axis. Furthermore, it must be remembered that it is a fundamental principle that as income increases consumption will increase but by less than the increase in income. In short, as income increases, the average propensity to consume declines. The consumption function, therefore, shown in Figure 8-1 is represented by line C, which moves in the same direction as income, upward to the right, but at a lesser slope.

At very low levels of income, the total consumption may actually exceed income. This can occur especially during a depression period as a result of inventory depletion. This is a period in which total orders and consumption of goods are greater than output, and business firms satisfy part of the demand by supplying goods out of their inventories. Such a situation is short-lived because the effective demand for consumer goods alone is greater than total output, and when inventories are diminished to the desired level, production will increase to take care of that portion of the demand formerly satisfied by inventory reduction.

Since a given amount of regular government spending will occur at varying levels of income, the combined consumption plus government spending

FIGURE 8-1

OUTPUT, INCOME, SPENDING AND SAVINGS

(Billions)

As income increases, consumption increases but by less than the increase in income. Consequently, this causes savings to increase as the economy expands.

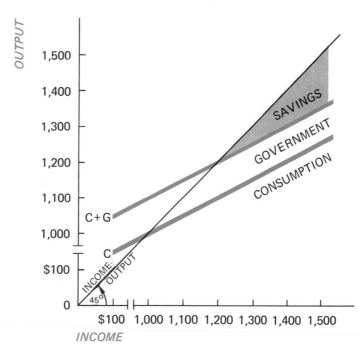

can be shown by line $C + G$. The amount of government spending is represented by the difference between the lines C and $C + G$. For simplicity, it is assumed that government spending will remain constant in the short run at all levels of income. Actually, however, government expenditures probably will increase with rising levels of income, since the government not only will be receiving greater tax revenues but also will be required to provide more services for its citizens.

RELATIONSHIP OF INVESTMENT TO SAVINGS

Since income is represented by the 45° income-output line and the line $C + G$ represents total consumer spending plus taxation (assuming a balanced budget), the residual between income and the spending on consumer goods plus taxation must represent saving. This saving at any level of income is represented by the difference between the income line and the $C + G$ line, as shown on Figure 8-1. It must be kept in mind that saving is defined as income after taxes not spent on consumer goods. It does not imply that savings are all in the form of cash, since some income may be spent on nonconsumer items. In fact, a considerable amount of the savings in the economy at any given time is channeled directly into investment. Nevertheless, the point to be made at this time is that the total amount of consumer spending plus taxation is not always equal to the total income or output of the economy. In such cases total demand is less than total output because the average propensity to consume is less than 100 percent of income.

Role of Investment

Total effective demand in the economy is made up not only of consumer demand and government spending, but it also includes investment. It is here that the key role of investment in our economy can be seen. If investment is sufficient to fill the gap between output and spending, created through savings, the total effective demand in the economy will equal the total output of goods and services, as measured by the GNP, and stability will prevail in the level of economic activity. If investment more than offsets the savings, however, effective demand will be greater than total output and the GNP, employment, and income will rise, provided manpower, resources, and capacity are available to increase total production. Otherwise prices will begin to rise and inflation will occur. On the other hand, a situation may exist in which investment is less than savings. In such a case, investment spending will be insufficient to offset the adverse effects of savings on the total economy, total spending will be less than total income, effective demand will be less than total output, and the economy will contract and/or prices will decline.

Expansion

Moving to Figure 8-2, note that at point *a* investment is greater than savings, the difference between the income line and the *C* + *G* line. As a result, total spending is greater than total income, and effective demand is greater than total output. Consequently, business firms will produce additional goods and services in order to satisfy the greater demand. As they do so, the economy expands and GNP and income increase. As income increases, note that the average propensity to consume declines and the average propensity to save increases. The economy will expand to a position where investment and savings are equal, at which level total effective demand will equal total output. In Figure 8-2, this is at point *b* where investment is just sufficient to fill the gap between income and the *C* + *G* line. Here investment equals savings, total spending equals total income, effective demand equals total output, and all goods and services will be moved off the market. According to the income-expenditure analysis, this is the point of equilibrium for the economy. At any position less than the $1,400 billion income-output level shown in Figure 8-2, forces will come into play to bring about an expansion in the economy. On the other hand, with the given amount of investment the economy will not expand beyond this position.

FIGURE 8-2

EFFECTIVE DEMAND GREATER THAN, EQUAL TO, AND LESS THAN TOTAL OUTPUT

(Billions)

Total effective demand is measured by the combination of consumption, investment, and government spending. Sometimes investment will be greater than savings, while at other times it may be less. This causes the economy to either expand or contract, respectively.

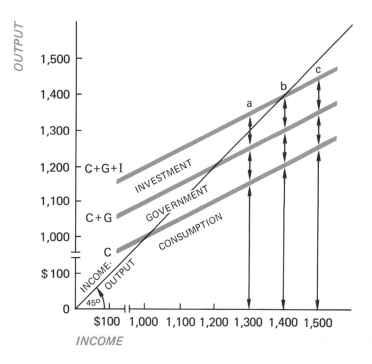

Contraction

Suppose that the economy moved out to an income-output level of $1,500 billion. Notice that at this level, total investment in the economy is insufficient to fill the gap in effective demand created by savings. At point c investment is smaller than savings, represented by the difference between the 45° income line and the C + G line. As a result, total spending is less than total income, effective demand is less than total output, and all goods and services produced will not be moved off the market. This means excessive inventories will appear, and business will cut production in the subsequent period or periods. As production declines, employment and income will fall. But, as income falls, remember that the average propensity to save will decline. Contraction will continue until a position is again reached at which savings come into balance with the lower amount of investment. This, of course, will be at point b in Figure 8-2, which shows income of $1,400 billion and a corresponding level of output.

Assuming a certain stability of consumer and government spending, according to the income-expenditure approach there is only one point of equilibrium for the economy for any given level of investment. If the economy is at any other level, forces come into play to bring about either an expansion or contraction in the economy. The direction in which the economy moves will depend on the relationship between investment and savings. Whenever investment is greater than savings, the economy will experience an increase in production, employment, and income, provided the economy is capable of expanding. Whenever investment is equal to savings, there will be a stable flow of economic activity. If investment is less than savings, however, there will be a contraction in the level of business activity and/or a decline in the price level, until the economy comes into balance at a lower level of GNP, at which investment and savings are equal.

UNEMPLOYMENT EQUILIBRIUM

The fact that investment and savings are equal and that a stable level of economic activity prevails is not necessarily good for the economy if such a situation should exist with a certain degree of unemployment present. For example, according to Figure 8-2, equilibrium will exist at point b at which consumption is equal to $1,200 billion, government spending $100 billion, and savings $100 billion. However, the amount of spending on investment, $100 billion, offsets the adverse effects of savings so that the total effective demand of $1,400 billion is equal to the total output of the economy. Thus, the economy is at an equilibrium point from which there is no incentive to expand or contract. This is fine if the GNP is at or near the full-employment level. But an important problem arises if the economy is in balance at a low level of employment, since there may be insufficient automatic adjusters to move the economy to higher levels of GNP and employment.

More Investment Required to Increase Employment

When the economy is in equilibrium at less than full employment, a higher level of employment can be attained by raising effective demand. This can be accomplished in several ways. According to the income-expenditure analysis, however, it is held that the consumption function is relatively stable in the short run; that is, the C curve does not shift significantly in the short run. Since this is true and we have assumed the amount of regular government spending to be constant at various levels of income, increased investment is necessary to move the economy to a higher level of income and employment. This is true because the gap between income and consumption plus government spending is greater at higher levels of output. In Figure 8-2, for example, it can be seen that the difference between the income line and the $C + G$ line is greater at point c than it is at point b. This indicates that savings will be greater at higher levels of output and income. Consequently, a greater amount of investment is necessary to reach and maintain the economy at point c than that required at point b. Since the average propensity to consume declines with higher incomes, there will be a larger gap between income and the $C + G$ line that must be filled with investment.

If the other forces, the consumption function and government, are assumed to be relatively stable in the short run, the level of production, employment, and income will be determined by the amount of investment taking place in the economy at any given time. Higher investment means greater employment and income, and a decrease in investment means lower income and employment. Therefore, according to the income-expenditure analysis, investment is the primary and most dynamic determinant of the GNP, or the level of economic activity.

Greater Consumption Helps

While income-expenditure analysis holds that the consumption function is stable in the short run, this does not mean that the absolute amount of consumption or the marginal propensity or average propensity to consume is constant. What is meant is that the line representing the various amounts that will be spent on consumption at different levels of income is relatively fixed. In the short run people have certain consumption patterns that will vary with changes in income. A close inspection of the consumption function, the C line of Figure 8-2, reveals that the absolute amount of consumption at varying levels of income differs and that the average propensity to consume decreases as incomes increase. Although the straight line C function implies a constant marginal propensity to consume, the MPC may actually decline, along with the APC, as income increases. But under given conditions the amount and percentage of consumption at different levels of income will remain as shown on line C in the short run. Although the consumption function may be relatively stable in the short run, in the long run individuals may actually change their consumption patterns and spend more or less of a given level of income.

An increase in the average propensity to consume at various levels of income would help move the economy toward a higher level of employment because it would decrease the gap between output and consumption. As a result, less investment would be required to maintain any given level of GNP, and it would make it easier to reach and maintain full employment. This is shown in Figure 8-3, where it can be seen that the same investment which results in equilibrium at point b could result in equilibrium at point c, if the consumption function were to increase sufficiently.

The amount of investment shown at point b fills the gap between output and consumption plus government spending as measured by the $C + G$ line. Although this amount of investment is insufficient to fill the gap between the

FIGURE 8-3

HIGHER CONSUMPTION RESULTS IN A HIGHER LEVEL OF OUTPUT AND INCOME

(Billions)

Total effective demand can be increased through an increase in consumption. This, in turn, will raise output, employment, and income.

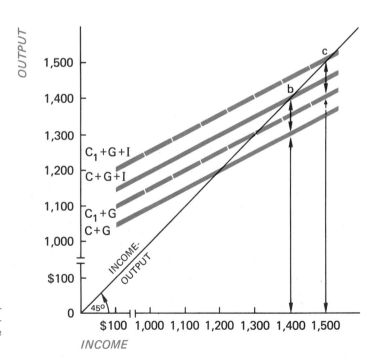

income line and the $C + G$ line at point c, if consumption is raised investment will adequately fill the gap between output and consumption at point c, as measured on the new consumption plus government line, $C_1 + G$, shown in Figure 8-3, which is higher because of an assumed increase in consumption. The upward shift of the consumption line makes it possible to reach a higher level of GNP, income, and employment without increasing the amount of investment in the economy.

Government Spending

The increased effective demand necessary to increase the GNP and raise the level of employment may come from an increase in either private investment or in the consumption function, or from a combination of the two. If the economy were in equilibrium at less than full employment and if it were desirable to raise the level of employment, every attempt should be made to increase the GNP by encouraging investment and raising the consumption function. A third force, government spending, can be used to bolster the level of economic activity when the necessary effective demand for a high level of employment is not forthcoming from consumption and private investment. According to the income-expenditure analysis, emergency government spending can be used to absorb the difference between output and the amount of effective demand as determined by consumption, regular government spending, and private investment. Therefore, total effective demand would be composed of three forces, with government spending acting as a stabilizer of the level of economic activity.

The use of government spending as a means of bolstering the GNP is shown in Figure 8-4, where it can be seen that the total effective demand is sufficient to maintain equilibrium at point b but not at point c. If the economy were to move up to an assumed full employment GNP level at point c without increasing either consumption, investment, or regular government spending, it could not stay at that level because of a production gap. In short, total effective demand would be less than total output. Investment would be less than savings, and the economy would contract until it returned to equilibrium at point b. If emergency government spending were injected to fill the gap between total output and effective demand resulting from consumption, investment, and regular government spending, however, total spending would equal total income, and total effective demand, including the emergency government spending, would equal the total output. In such a situation the production gap would be eliminated, all the goods and services produced would be moved off the market, and equilibrium would exist at the new higher level of employment, income, and output. Once in this new GNP position, of course, the removal of emergency government spending could

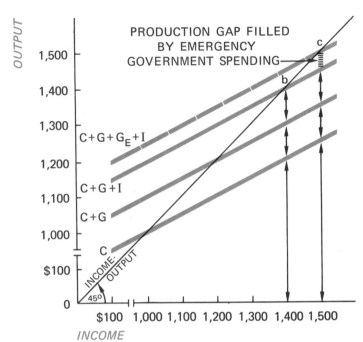

FIGURE 8-4

GOVERNMENT SPENDING RESULTS IN A HIGHER LEVEL OF OUTPUT AND INCOME

(Billions)

The production gap can be filled by the use of government spending. This, likewise, will increase production, employment, and income.

have an adverse effect on the level of economic activity, unless it were offset by an increase in either consumption, investment, or regular government spending.

Since there is no assurance that income and consumption will continue at their higher levels when emergency government spending is removed, it may be necessary to continue such government spending for a considerable period of time before the economy can make the proper adjustment to maintain the higher level of GNP without the assistance of emergency government spending, especially during a serious depression. This process of sustained government spending is part of what is known as *compensatory spending.* In other words, emergency government spending must be ample to make up or compensate for the lack of adequate consumption, investment, and regular government spending during periods of unemployment. Compensatory spending should be distinguished from what is known as *pump priming.* Pump priming implies that all that it takes to increase and to maintain the flow of goods and services at a higher level GNP is an original dose of emergency government spending.

Regardless of the method employed, compensatory spending or pump priming, the government must be cautious when securing funds to spend for the purpose of bolstering the economy. First, the government should not raise funds in a manner that will reduce private investment or consumption.

Invariably it will need to resort to deficit spending if the spending is to be effective as a means of raising the level of economic activity. If the government increases its spending by raising taxes, it will decrease the spendable income of consumers and investors. The consequent reduction in consumption and investment will decrease effective demand accordingly. Any advantage of government spending in this case will be offset in large part by the decrease in private consumption and investment. This offsetting effect could be minimized to some degree if the government were to tax primarily those incomes that were not going to be used for either consumption or investment. To design and impose such a tax, however, would be rather difficult. On the other hand, if the government borrows the funds, especially if it borrows from the banks, instead of obtaining them from taxation, private consumption and investment probably will not decrease. In this case government spending will be more effective in raising the level of economic activity.

Second, government spending should take place in a manner and direction that will not discourage private investment. The government should not compete with or discourage private spending. It should spend on those functions not generally performed by private enterprise. Furthermore, every effort should be made to raise effective demand or the GNP by encouraging consumption and investment before resorting to government spending as a means of bolstering the economy.

The income-expenditure analysis leads to the conclusion that government spending can be used as a means of stabilization. Increased government spending can be used to bolster a sagging economy, and decreased government spending can help prevent inflation. In short, government spending can be used to offset undesirable levels of consumption and/or investment.

As we will see later, many measures, such as area redevelopment programs, manpower development and training, extended unemployment benefits, emergency public works, tax credits on investments, personal and corporate income tax reductions, excise tax cuts, the poverty program, substantial increases in the money supply, and sizable federal deficits, were used in the first half of the 1960s and in the early 1970s in an effort to raise consumption and investment in order to bolster the level of economic activity in our economy.

THE PROBLEM OF INFLATION

If effective demand continues to increase once the economy has reached a state of full employment, inflation will result. Appropriate measures must be adopted to discourage further consumption, investment, and/or government spending if inflation is to be prevented or modified. In such case an increase in effective demand from any source will lead to still higher prices as consumers bid against each other for the relatively scarce amount of goods and services available, and investors compete against one another for the use of the limited manpower, resources, and productive capacity. In order to combat inflationary pressures, government spending can be reduced, taxes raised, interest rates increased, credit restricted, and other measures undertaken.

Since strong inflationary pressures seldom occur in the absence of huge government outlays, the first step to combat inflation would seem to be a reduction in government spending. Large government outlays, however, usually occur during wartime or during various emergency periods. Under such conditions, it would be rather unwise to win the battle against inflation by reducing government expenditures but to lose the military fight against the enemy because of the lack of war materiel. During wartime, therefore, when large government outlays for armaments are necessary, inflation has to be combated primarily by reducing consumption and investment for nonwar production.

This general wartime situation is illustrated in Figure 8-5, where it can be seen that total effective demand at point c is greater than total output. Although effective demand is greater than output and investment is greater than savings, it will be difficult to increase the level of economic activity or

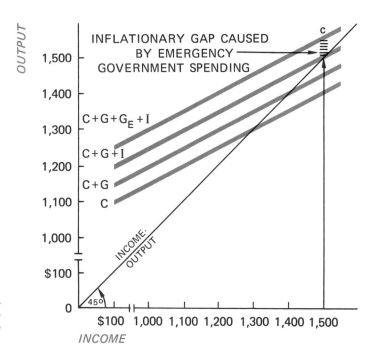

FIGURE 8-5

INFLATIONARY GAP
(Billions)

Excess effective demand at full employment causes inflation, since the economy cannot expand to fulfill the increased demand.

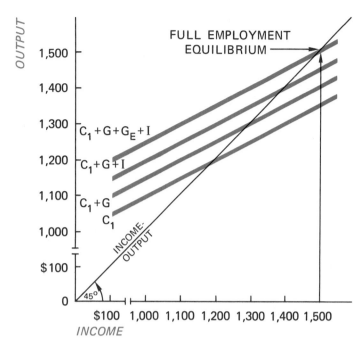

FIGURE 8-6

FULL EMPLOYMENT EQUILIBRIUM

(Billions)

Full employment exists when $I = S$ and total effective demand equals total output at the full employment level.

the real GNP if the economy is in a state of full employment. Under such conditions, if effective demand remains greater than output, prices are sure to rise. The task then is to reduce private consumption and/or investment to allow a sufficient gap between output on the one hand and total consumption, investment, and regular government spending on the other hand. This will permit the necessary amount of government wartime or emergency spending to take place without having total effective demand, including emergency government spending, exceed total production, as demonstrated in Figure 8-5.

In Figure 8-5, it can be seen that at point c investment plus emergency government spending more than fills the gap between output and the $C + G$ line, thus creating an *inflationary gap*. If consumption is reduced, however, to C_1, as shown in Figure 8-6, investment plus emergency government spending will fit in the larger gap between output and the line $C_1 + G$. Total effective demand will then equal total output at the full employment level, and the inflationary gap will be eliminated. A similar effect could be obtained through a reduction in investment or regular government spending.

In line with this analysis, we will see later that when the economy reached full employment in the latter half of the 1960s, such measures as tighter money, elimination of special investment incentives, reduction of non-military spending by the government, and substantial increases in personal and corporate taxes were used in an effort to reduce consumption, investment, and regular government spending as a means of combating inflation.

INCOME-EXPENDITURE ANALYSIS RECAPITULATED

According to the income-expenditure analysis, income increases as output increases. As income increases, consumption likewise increases but at a lesser rate than the increase in income. Since the average propensity to consume declines as income increases, savings will increase. Consequently, it will require a greater amount of investment to fill the gap between output and total consumption plus government spending at higher levels of income. To put it another way, more investment will be required to offset the greater savings at higher levels of income if all the goods and services are to be cleared off the market. If investment is greater than savings or vice versa, the economy will expand or contract. The economy will expand or contract until it comes into equilibrium at a position where investment equals savings. This position will not necessarily correspond with that of full employment.

Production, employment, and income fluctuate with fluctuations in investment. The real GNP may oscillate between a low level of economic activity and the full-employment level. Investment, according to the income-expenditure analysis, is a prime determinant of the level of economic activity. Since the consumption function is relatively stable in the short run, and assuming government spending to be constant, the level of employment cannot be increased except with an increase in investment. The greater the consumption function, however, the less investment required to maintain any given level of income and employment. Although economic activity fluctuates as investment increases or decreases, it will not fall below the point at which consumption plus government spending is equal to total output, except in the short run, because at that level the effective demand is greater than total output. Since production is less than effective demand at this point, it means that goods are probably being supplied out of inventories in order to satisfy the total demand. Consequently, the GNP will increase not only to satisfy current demand but to replenish inventories. On the other hand, economic activity cannot increase beyond the full-employment level regardless of the amount of investment. Increased investment, consumption, or government spending beyond this point can lead only to higher prices, since the economy will be incapable of producing additional goods and services in the short run. The economy, therefore, fluctuates between the point where consumption plus regular government spending is equal to total output and the full employment level. Economic activity, however, may very well fluctuate between various intermediate points without reaching either extreme.

Thus, business cycles occur primarily from changes in private investment. It is possible, however, that some fluctuation could be brought about by changes in consumption and/or government spending. On the other hand, government spending may be used to stabilize the level of economic activity by offsetting undesirable fluctuations in investment and consumption.

If the economy becomes stabilized at an undesirable level of employment because of insufficient investment, various economic measures can be utilized for the purpose of encouraging consumption and investment in order to raise total effective demand and the GNP. If such measures are unsuccessful, government further spending may be used to raise the level of economic activity.

DETERMINANTS OF INVESTMENT

Since investment is the key determinant of the level of production, employment, and income, it is important to know what determines the amount of investment in the economy at any given time. According to the income-expenditure approach, investment is determined by the relationship between the marginal efficiency of capital and the rate of interest.

Marginal Efficiency of Capital

The *marginal efficiency of capital* is the rate of return on an additional, or marginal, unit of investment over all costs except the rate of interest. It is often referred to as the rate of profit or the expected rate of profit. Since the marginal efficiency of capital is based on the expectation of profit, it is to some degree a psychological phenomenon and is dependent on the attitude and outlook of businessmen. It is based on anticipated sales and revenue, rather than on actual sales and revenue. Expected increases in productivity, sales, or prices, and cost reductions will enhance the marginal efficiency of capital. If anticipated revenues are not forthcoming, however, this may change the economic outlook, and the attitude of businessmen may change from optimism to that of pessimism, which, in turn, will decrease the marginal efficiency of capital. It is easy to see, therefore, that the marginal efficiency of capital is dynamic and subject to noticeable fluctuations arising primarily from changes in prices and sales. Changes in the marginal efficiency of capital account for variations in investment, which, in turn, cause changes in production, employment, and income.

Rate of Interest

The rate of interest, on the other hand, is the rate at which businessmen can borrow funds for investment purposes. It is determined, as explained more fully in Chapter 35, by the quantity of money in the economy and the liquidity preference, the latter being the desire of the community to hold assets in the form of cash. Sometimes liquidity is referred to as the propensity to hoard. The rate of interest, then, is simply the price that must be paid to induce savers to give up their liquidity. The stronger their liquidity preference, the higher the interest rate that must be paid to savers to induce them to part with their funds. Consequently, the rate of interest varies directly with liquidity preference. Liquidity may be desired for future transactions, for precautionary purposes, or for speculative motives. The rate of interest will likewise vary with changes in the quantity of money. Given a certain liquidity preference, the rate of interest will decrease if the money supply is increased, and it will increase if the money supply is decreased. Thus, the rate of interest varies inversely with changes in the quantity of money. To look at it in another way, if members of the community desire to hold a certain amount of liquid funds and the money supply is increased, this will automatically reduce the relative liquidity preference of the community and lower the rate of interest. Conversely, if the quantity of money is decreased, relative liquidity preference will be greater and the rate of interest will rise. The money supply may vary as a result of changes in currency or bank credit. Since bank credit is the more voluminous and dynamic of the two, it has the greater effect on the rate of interest.

Relationship of MEC to RI

Investment is determined by the relationship between the marginal efficiency of capital and the rate of interest. The greater the gap between the two, the more the inducement to borrow and invest. If the marginal efficiency of capital (*MEC*) is greater than the rate of interest (*RI*), businessmen will find it to their advantage to borrow funds for investment in machinery, equipment and buildings. If the *MEC* is 12 percent, for example, and the *RI* is 5 percent, businessmen could borrow and invest, and after paying the 5 percent on their borrowed funds, they would have a net return of 7 percent. As expansion of the economy proceeds, however, the marginal efficiency of capital eventually declines as sales begin to slacken, costs of production rise, and the prices that must be paid for capital goods begin to climb. At the same time as the economy expands, the rate of interest will rise because of the continued demand for more funds to finance business investment. Eventually a position is reached at which the *MEC* and the *RI* come into balance, let us say, for example, at 7 percent. At this point there is no further incentive for businessmen to borrow and invest, since the return from their investment will be just sufficient to cover their interest cost for borrowing the funds. Consequently, their net profit will be zero.

If the marginal efficiency of capital should become less than the rate of interest, the economy would contract. Businessmen would not borrow and invest in productive facilities simply to lose money, which would be the situation if the *MEC* were 3 percent, for example, and the *RI* were 5 percent. Not only would there be a lack of incentive to borrow and to invest in new productive facilities, but also many of those who had borrowed to invest would not be inclined to renew their loans in the absence of profit expectations. Furthermore, banks would be inclined to become more cautious about making loans and might actually recall some of the loans outstanding. As a result of the decrease in investment, the level of production, employment, and income in the economy would fall. As the contraction proceeded, the rate of interest would decline and eventually the marginal efficiency of capital would pick up. The economy would come into equilibrium again when the *MEC* and the *RI* came into balance. In fact, a slowdown in the economy may occur, according to the income-expenditure analysis, in any period in which the marginal efficiency of capital is near or less than the rate of interest.

It can be said then that whenever *MEC* exceeds *RI*, the real GNP will rise unless the economy is in a state of full employment, in which case prices will rise. As expansion takes place, forces come into play to bring them into balance. Whenever *MEC* equals *RI*, there will be a stable level of economic activity in the economy. If *MEC* is less than *RI*, however, the economy will experience a contraction. In this relationship the marginal efficiency of capital is the more important and dynamic of the two factors. It fluctuates more sharply than does the rate of interest, and it has a greater influence on the level of investment. To bolster the level of economic activity, however, it is usually easier to make artificial adjustments in the rate of interest than it is to influence the marginal efficiency of capital.

A Graphic Approach to Investment and Saving

The relationship of investment to saving can be tied into the consumption function and to the multiplier through graphic analysis. As you will recall, we have shown graphically that on a consumption function chart the marginal and average propensities to consume decrease as income increases and the marginal and average propensities to save increase as income rises. For a two-sector economy, excluding government, this is depicted in Figure 8-7.

Extracting savings from the picture, saving can be shown separately as indicated in Figure 8-8. Here it can be seen that saving may be negative at very low levels of income. However, saving generally will increase with an increase in income.

It can be demonstrated further that an increase in saving, S_1, other things being equal, will cause the GNP to decrease. Conversely, a decrease in saving, S_2, will cause the GNP to rise, since consumers will be spending more and saving less, as indicated in Figure 8-9.

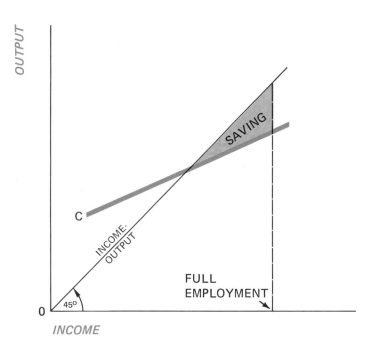

FIGURE 8-7

Saving is represented by the gap between income and consumption. Saving increases as income increases.

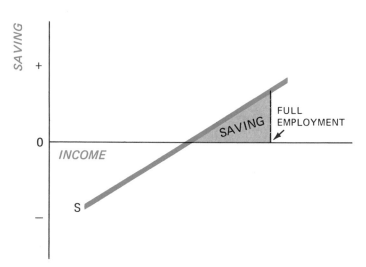

FIGURE 8-8

Savings will rise as incomes expand.

Now we will relate saving to investment and the multiplier. Assuming a given level of investment, there will be an equilibrium output and income where planned investment equals planned saving, $I = S$. This is shown as point *b* in Figure 8-10, where the GNP is $1,300 billion. At any less GNP, point *a* for example, planned investment is greater than planned saving, $I > S$. Consequently, the economy will expand. At a higher level of GNP,

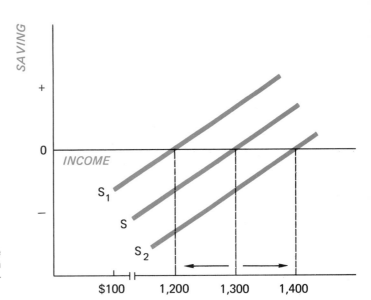

FIGURE 8-9

(Billions)

A decrease in saving will cause the GNP to rise, while an increase in saving will cause a decline in economic activity.

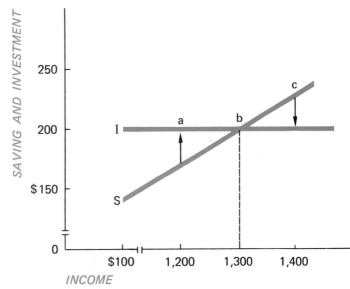

FIGURE 8-10

(Billions)

Equilibrium will exist at the GNP level where planned investment and planned saving are equal.

such as point *c*, planned investment is less than planned saving, $I < S$, and the economy will contract.

If investment increases to I_1, it will cause the GNP to rise, as shown in Figure 8-11. Notice, however, that a $50 billion increase of investment causes the GNP to rise by $100 billion, reflecting a multiplier effect of 2.

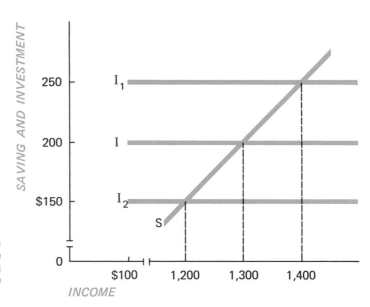

FIGURE 8-11

(Billions)

A rise in investment will cause an increase in economic activity, while a reduction of investment will bring about a dampening effect on the economy.

On the other hand, a decrease in investment of $50 billion to I_2 causes a $100 billion drop in the GNP, unless offset by some other factor.

THE THREE STRATEGIC VARIABLES

Assuming for the moment that government spending has a neutral effect, it can be said that the level of economic activity will be determined by consumption and investment. Consumption will vary with income and the actual amount of consumption will depend on the average propensity to consume at any given level of income. On the other hand, investment is determined by the marginal efficiency of capital and the rate of interest. Therefore, the determinants of the general level of economic activity can be reduced to three strategic variables: (1) the average propensity to consume; (2) the marginal efficiency of capital; and (3) the rate of interest. A change in any one of these will affect either consumption or investment, which, in turn, will change effective demand and the GNP. In the event that the three strategic variables are related in such a way that the economy is in a condition of less than full employment, economic policies may be employed that will change the variables in such a manner that the economy will expand. Reduced taxes, more liberal credit, lower interest rates, tax credits, accelerated depreciation measures, and other measures designed to increase consumption and investment may be utilized. If indirect measures do not effectively bring about the desired increase in real GNP, then direct government spending may be resorted to in an effort to bolster the level of economic activity. Before engaging in such spending, however, consideration should be given to its disadvantages as well as its merits. Opposite measures can be used to combat inflation.

RESERVATIONS

Although, according to the income-expenditure analysis, the level of economic activity will vary with investment and it is held that employment cannot increase without an increase in investment, certain reservations must be kept in mind regarding such statements. First, GNP and employment will not increase with an increase of investment if consumption or government spending decrease by an equivalent or a greater amount. Conversely, a decrease in investment does not necessarily lower output and employment if offsetting changes take place. Second, an increase in GNP could occur in the absence of increased investment, provided either consumption or government spending increased. In fact, certain anticyclical measures may be adopted to raise the consumption function in the short run as a means of reducing the gap between output and consumption that must be filled by investment. Furthermore, the fact that the income-expenditure analysis holds that the consumption function is relatively stable in the short run does not preclude the possibility of raising the consumption function in the long run.

INCOME-EXPENDITURE ANALYSIS IN REVIEW

The relationships of the various steps of the income-expenditure analysis can be summarized as follows:

1. Production (GNP), employment, income, and prices depend on effective demand.
2. Effective demand is measured by the total of consumption, investment, and government spending.
3. Consumption depends on the size of income and the average propensity to consume at that level of income.
4. Since the consumption function is relatively stable, and assuming government spending to have a neutral effect, changes in employment and income will result primarily from changes in investment.
5. Investment is determined by the marginal efficiency of capital and the rate of interest.
6. Marginal efficiency of capital is dependent upon profit expectations compared to the cost of capital assets.
7. The rate of interest depends largely upon liquidity preference compared to the quantity of money.
8. Liquidity preference is dependent on the strength of the precautionary, transactions, and speculative motives for savings.

TABLE 8-1   OUTLINE OF THE INCOME-EXPENDITURE ANALYSIS

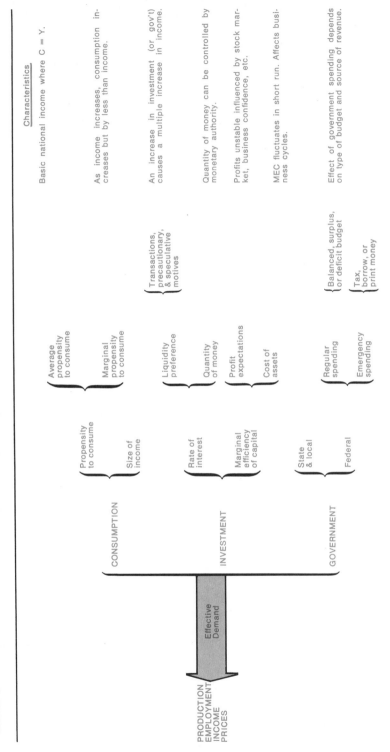

				Characteristics
				Basic national income where C = Y.
CONSUMPTION	Propensity to consume	Average propensity to consume		As income increases, consumption increases but by less than income.
	Size of income	Marginal propensity to consume		
INVESTMENT	Rate of interest	Liquidity preference	Transactions, precautionary, & speculative motives	An increase in investment (or gov't) causes a multiple increase in income.
		Quantity of money		Quantity of money can be controlled by monetary authority.
	Marginal efficiency of capital	Profit expectations		Profits unstable influenced by stock market, business confidence, etc.
		Cost of assets		MEC fluctuates in short run. Affects business cycles.
GOVERNMENT	State & local	Regular spending	Balanced, surplus, or deficit budget	Effect of government spending depends on type of budget and source of revenue.
	Federal	Emergency spending	Tax, borrow, or print money	

PRODUCTION EMPLOYMENT INCOME PRICES ← Effective Demand

SOURCE: Adapted from *The Economics of John Maynard Keynes* by Dudley Dillard, 1948, by permission of Prentice-Hall, Inc., Englewood Cliffs, N.J.

9. Government spending is the total of federal, state, and local expenditures. Federal spending may be either regular or emergency spending.
10. If consumption, investment, and regular government spending are insufficient to provide a high level of economic activity, emergency government spending may be used to raise the level of GNP, income, and employment.

These relationships are outlined in Table 8-1. From this outline it is possible to trace easily what effect a change in any of the determining factors will have on the level of economic activity. Other things remaining the same, for example, an increase in the size of income will bring about higher consumption, increase effective demand, and raise the level of production, employment, and income. If the economy is in a state of full employment, however, such a change will result in higher prices. A strengthening of liquidity preference will raise the rate of interest, decrease investment, lower effective demand, and result in a decrease of production, employment, and income. A lowering of the interest rate will have the opposite effect. It can be seen, further, that deficit government financing will raise effective demand, while a surplus budget will have a dampening effect on the economy unless used to combat inflation.

This schematic outline of the income-expenditure analysis can be used as a handy reference when analyzing and evaluating the effect of governmental economic measures designed to influence the level of economic activity.

SUMMARY

1. According to the income-expenditure analysis, the level of economic activity in the economy is determined by effective demand, which is composed of consumption, investment, and government spending.

2. As the GNP and income increase correspondingly, consumption will increase but by less than the increase in income. Thus, as output and income expand there is a wider and wider gap between output and consumption.

3. Provided government expenditures remain constant, a greater amount of investment is required to fill the gap between output and the total of consumption plus government spending as output is increased.

4. If investment is greater than savings at any given level of employment, it will be more than sufficient to fill the gap between the income-output line and the $C + G$ line. In such a situation effective demand will be greater than total output, and the economy will expand until investment and savings come into balance at a higher level of income.

5. If investment is less than savings at a desired level of employment, total effective demand is insufficient to move all the goods off the market at that level, and the economy will remain at, or contract to, a lower level.

6. If it is desired to raise the level of economic activity, the effective demand must be increased. This may be done by increasing

investment or consumption. In the absence of an adequate increase in investment and/or consumption, however, total effective demand may be raised by increasing government spending.

7. On the other hand, if investment is greater than savings at the full-employment level, inflation will result. In such event, it is desirable to lower the total effective demand. This can be done by lowering government spending, private investment, and/or consumer spending.

8. In a wartime economy, when it is not feasible to reduce government spending, strong measures must be taken to reduce consump-

tion and investment sufficiently in order that total effective demand will not exceed total output.

9. In general, it can be said that total employment will vary with private investment, but changes can also come about from variations in consumption and government spending.

10. Private investment, the most important determinant of the level of economic activity, is dependent upon the marginal efficiency of capital and the rate of interest.

11. Graphically, it can shown that the relationship between investment and saving affects the level of economic activity.

NEW TERMS

Effective demand, *p. 149*
Consumption function, *p. 150*
Equilibrium output, *p. 150*
Income-output line, *p. 151*

Compensatory spending, *p. 158*
Pump priming, *p. 158*
Inflationary gap, *p. 161*
Marginal efficiency of capital, *p. 163*

QUESTIONS FOR DISCUSSION AND ANALYSIS

1. Compare the gross national product of last year and the previous year. In terms of consumption, investment, and government spending, what was the basic cause(s) for the change in the GNP?

2. Do you agree that the consumption function is relatively stable in the short run? Why or why not?

3. If the average propensity to consume did not decline as income increased, would such a fact invalidate the income-expenditure analysis? Why or why not?

4. If investment is greater than savings, explain the forces that come into play to bring them into equilibrium.

5. If the consumption function and government spending remain stable,

what will be the relationship between changes in investment and employment? Why?

6. In your opinion should deficit government spending be utilized to raise the level of economic activity during periods of serious unemployment?

7. According to the income-expenditure analysis, how can inflation be prevented or remedied?

8. What are the determinants of investment? Explain how the relationship between these two determinants encourages or discourages investment.

9. Is it always necessary to have an increase in investment in order to increase employment in the economy? Explain.

SUGGESTED READINGS The Suggested Readings for this chapter are included in Chapter 7, page 148.

Short-Run Fluctuations

PREVIEW Business fluctuations are inherent in a capitalistic system. At times, because of confidence and exuberance on the part of consumers and investors, the economy will accelerate to a high level of employment and perhaps inflation. At other times when there is less optimism, the economy may slow down, causing a loss of jobs. Business fluctuations, especially pronounced periods of depression or inflation, can also have severe social and political consequences.

Since business cycles, in all probability, will affect the industry in which a person earns a livelihood and thus his own personal welfare, it behooves an individual to learn something about the nature, measurement, and causes of business fluctuations. Furthermore, if one can anticipate the occurrence of changes in economic and business activity, it will help him render more prudent economic decisions.

One of the striking features of our national income is its dynamism. It does not grow at a steady rate. Sometimes it expands rapidly. At other times it shows only a modest increase or decrease. In spite of its healthy growth in recent years, it has in the past declined at a rate that was disastrous to the welfare of the country. Fluctuations have been characteristic of the national economy since the early days of our nation.

Why does the economy not continuously produce income at full capacity, with jobs for all who want to work? What is implied by balance, or equilibrium, in the national income, especially with full employment? What are the characteristic features of the so-called business cycle? Can these fluctuations be eliminated by the concerted action of business and the government?

Most of us would agree that it would be great to have a national income as large as possible, one that continued to grow as the population increased, without serious fluctuations or adverse side effects, and with jobs for all. As stated by the late President Johnson in one of his last *Economic Reports*:

> We seek a free and growing economy which offers productive employment to all who are willing and able to work, generates steady and rapid growth in productivity—the ultimate source of higher living standards—while providing the new skills and jobs needed for displaced workers, and permits every American to produce and to earn to the full measure of his basic capacities.

The importance of maximizing income and output is best realized when the losses from depression or even operations at less than full capacity in prosperous periods are considered. Production losses were staggering during the great depression of the thirties; but even in the relative prosperity of the past few decades, much has been lost in the way of production and employment through minor depressions or recessions and the failure of the economy to maintain operations at full capacity. Figure 9-1 shows not only a sizable drop in production during the recessions of 1954, 1958, 1960-1961, and 1970, but substantial underproduction during the 10-year period, 1955-1965, and then again during 1969-1973. In fact, a rough estimate places the loss of production during the earlier period, as a result of our failure to maintain maximum operations, in the vicinity of $700 billion, an amount equivalent to one full year's production of goods and services. It has been estimated that the loss in the later period will approximate $150 billion.

FIGURE 9-1

ACTUAL AND POTENTIAL GROSS NATIONAL PRODUCT

The larger the gap between actual and potential GNP, the greater the unemployment in the economy.

SOURCE: *Business Conditions Digest* (February, 1974).

[1] Trend line of 3.5 percent per year (intersecting actual line in middle of 1955) from 1st quarter 1952 to 4th quarter 1962, 3.75 percent from 4th quarter 1962 to 4th quarter 1965, and 4 percent from 4th quarter 1965 to 4th quarter 1973.

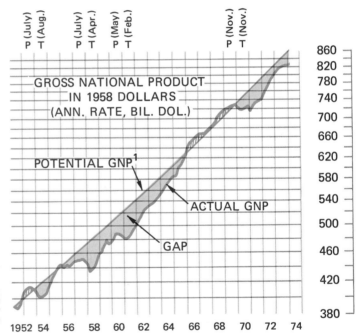

THE BUSINESS CYCLE

National income is subject to various types of disturbance, but the most pronounced is the business cycle. What is called a *business cycle* may be considered a process of cumulative change over a time span longer than a year. During the cycle all parts of the economy display marked changes in activity as they move through periods usually called prosperity, recession, depression, and recovery. Production, prices, incomes, and employment activities all show characteristic changes during the cycle; in fact, there is no part of the economy that is not affected in some way. Extensive studies have shown that these cyclical fluctuations are found in economies throughout the world. Because of the pervasive character of business cycles and their persistence during many years, it has been assumed that they inevitably accompany all complex modern economies, although they appear most clearly in those economies where free markets and private enterprise prevail.

Types and Length of Cycles

A study of past economic data reveals that there have been many and varied business fluctuations in our economy. Some cycles have been long, others short. Some have been severe while others have been mild. An analysis of the historical data reveals that business fluctuations may be classified as (1) minor cycles or (2) major cycles.

Minor cycles are those of relatively mild intensity in which the fluctuations are noticeable but not severe. They are shorter but more numerous than major cycles. Evidence seems to indicate that minor cycles occur every three to four years. In fact, some specific measurements show the average length of the minor cycle in the United States to be 47.6 months, with 26.2 months spent in the expansion stage of the cycle and 21.4 months in the contraction phase of the cycle. Since the end of World War II, we have experienced six minor downswings in the economy, in 1949, 1953-1954, 1958, 1960-1961, 1970, and 1974. It would be seven minor downswings if we desired to count the so-called mini-recession of early 1967.

Major cycles are those which show a wide fluctuation in business activity. They are usually characterized by serious depressions. This means widespread unemployment, lower income, and low profits or losses in many cases. Business cycle data indicate that major cycles occur about every ten years. Since World War II, however, we have experienced no major cycle. This may be due to our use of modern monetary, fiscal, and other measures and our built-in economic stimulus in the form of large-scale defense outlays.

Other types of cycles or fluctuations, such as long-wave building cycles, commodity price fluctuations, and stock market price fluctuations, have been revealed by research and economic analysis. In fact, cycles have a certain degree of ubiquity in the study of all aspects of economic activity.

Today business cycles are considered to have four distinct phases: prosperity, recession, depression, and recovery. *Prosperity* exists whenever there is an overall high level of economic activity. A *recession* occurs whenever there is a noticeable drop in the level of business activity. *Depression* is the period in which the level of business activity has dropped as far as it is going to drop in a particular cycle. *Recovery* occurs when the level of business activity begins to rise. The four phases of the cycle are shown in Figure 9-2.

Although we have more or less definite measurements of the length of the total cycle and even the length of the expansion and contraction periods of the average cycle, it is difficult to obtain a conclusive measurement of the average length of each of the four phases of the cycle. The main difficulty to such a measurement stems from the fact that there is no agreement as to exactly when we leave one phase and go into another.

It is a bit easier to measure the amplitude of a business fluctuation. In measuring the business cycle, however, it is necessary to make allowances for any forces affecting business fluctuations other than those that are inherent in the business cycle. The level of business activity at any time is affected by four forces or types of economic change: (1) the trend, (2) seasonal, (3) irregular, and (4) cyclical.

The *trend* is the directional movement of the economy over an extended period of time such as 30 to 50 years. It represents the long-run average change (growth or decline) in the economy. *Seasonal variations* are recurring fluctuations in business activity during a given period, usually one year. The cause of this fluctuation may be natural or artificial. We produce more farm commodities, for example, in the summer than we do in the winter

FIGURE 9-2

PHASES OF THE BUSINESS CYCLE

Economic activity—production, employment, and income—fluctuates with various phases of the business cycle.

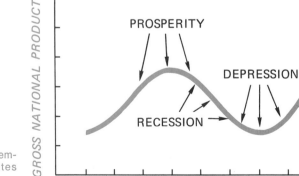

because of a natural cause, the weather. On the other hand, department stores sales increase very substantially during November and December, due to our custom of giving Christmas presents.

Irregular or *random fluctuations* in business activity result from some unexpected or unusual event. Such factors as serious flood, plague, pestilence, or drought can affect the economy as a whole or certain areas in the economy. *Cyclical fluctuations* are changes in the level of business activity that come about regardless of the trend, seasonal, or irregular forces. Business cycles may occur because of inherent forces in the economy. They may be influenced, however, to a considerable degree by external forces, such as wars, changes in the monetary system, and changes in population.

The intensity of the cycle may be determined by measuring the movement of the seasonally adjusted business activity above and below the trend line. If the actual business data are corrected for seasonal fluctuations and for any possible irregular forces, the actual data can then be compared to the trend line simply by measuring the difference between the actual data and the trend line values. In Figure 9-3, for example, the seasonally adjusted business activity is shown by the fluctuating line. The trend, which is the average level of business activity over a period of time, is shown by the straight line. The magnitude of the cycle at any point is measured by the difference between the value of the actual data and the trend line value. The value can be calculated also in percentage terms, as shown along with the rate of unemployment in the lower half of the graph.

FIGURE 9-3

MEASUREMENT OF BUSINESS ACTIVITY 1955-1973

Business cycles can be shown as fluctuations around a trend line, as shown in the top part of the figure, or they can be depicted as deviations from a norm, as indicated on the bottom half of the figure.

SOURCE: *The Morgan Guaranty Survey* (December, 1972).

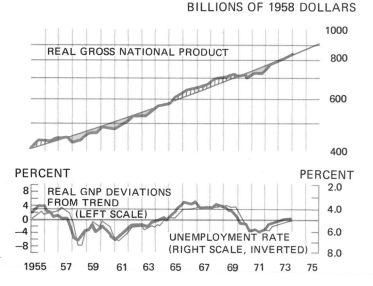

Pattern of the Cycle

Although some business cycles are short and others long, some fluctuations intense and others mild, and although there are considerable differences among economists as to the exact causes of the fluctuations, a definite pattern of the cycle appears to exist. Once a downturn has started, there is a cumulative action among several elements in the economy that tends to augment the downswing. During this downswing, however, forces eventually will come into play to arrest the depression and to start an upward movement. Once this upward motion begins, the reaction of individuals and businesses will be such that the upswing will be augmented. During prosperity, however, a force will build up that eventually will effect a downturn.

The elements or forces operating to bring about business cycles are of two kinds—internal and external. The internal forces, or *endogenous forces* as they are often called, are those elements within the very sphere of business activity itself. They include such items as production, income, demand, credit, and inventories. The external, or *exogenous forces*, are those elements usually considered as being outside the normal scope of business activity. They include such elements as population growth, wars, basic changes in the nation's currency, floods, drought, and other catastrophes that have a pronounced effect on business activity. We will first analyze the endogenous forces.

In order to see how the relationships among the various elements change and to see how these changes bring about oscillation of business activity, let us look at each phase of the cycle. We shall start with the depression phase and then move on to the others.

DEPRESSION

In addition to an adverse economic effect, depression may have serious social and political consequences. There is naturally more public concern about a serious depression than there is about a mild depression, but unemployed individuals and bankrupt firms are involved regardless of whether the depression is serious or mild.

Production, Employment, and Income

During a depression, production, employment, and income are at a low ebb compared with their respective status during prosperity. If income is low, the demand for consumer goods will be low; and a low demand in a period of ample supply generally will force prices down. Cost, too, will be relatively low because unemployed manpower, resources, and capacity will be bidding against each other for jobs, sales, and rent, respectively. Because sales are off and prices generally are down, profits will be low during a depression. This means low investments, for businessmen do not invest in new ventures or add to existing capacity unless they anticipate profits.

Inventories and Borrowing

Although in the early phases of a depression inventories may be rather high because of a previous inventory build-up, they will dwindle to a low position as businesses supply goods out of inventory and cut orders from the producers. Since production will be at a low level, businesses will have little need for borrowing for capital expansion. There may be some borrowing for refinancing, but this will usually be at a minimum. With the fall in commercial loans, bank reserves should be relatively high. Thus, we have a situation in which the banks have the ability to expand credit, but businesses are reluctant to borrow because profit expectations are dim. In addition, many firms that would like to borrow for refinancing will be poor risks; and the banks will not be too anxious to accommodate them, since banks tend to become more selective during depressions. In total, business loans will fall off substantially. This will tend to make excess reserves relatively high; and with the excess reserve high and demand for loans low, the normal reaction will be to force interest rates down.

Liquidity Preference and Saving

During the contraction phase of the cycle when prices are declining, the value of money rises. Individuals and businesses, if possible, will have a tendency to convert their idle assets into money. Therefore, we have a strong *liquidity preference* during depressions.

As incomes are lowered, on the other hand, the average worker will generally be required to spend a larger portion, if not all, of his income to provide the basic necessities and conveniences of life. Thus, our propensity to consume will increase while our propensity to save will decrease accordingly. Keep in mind, however, that although we are spending a larger percent of our income, the total amount of spending on consumption will be lower than it was during the previous prosperity period.

Replacement of Durables

When we are not producing at full capacity, there is less effort to replace worn-out machinery and equipment. Instead of replacing depreciated machinery, a firm can merely use other machinery that has not been in use. Only when it is really necessary, or when production starts picking up, will the average firm replace its machinery and equipment as quickly as they depreciate. Although some individuals and firms claim that a depression is the ideal time to replace their machinery and equipment because of the low prices, relatively few firms follow this policy. The lack of capital funds, the uncertainty of the future, and the fear of obsolescence discourage firms from following such a policy. Thus, the tendency of firms not to replace their worn machinery and equipment during a depression brings about sizable reductions in the production of such items.

Consumers, too, will have a tendency to repair and to patch up their durable goods instead of replacing them. People will be inclined to get a new set of tires and a tune-up job and to keep the old car instead of trading it in for a new one. We are more inclined to get our shoes resoled rather than buy new ones. We patch our worn overcoats, darn our socks, repair our appliances, put off buying a new home, and, in general, postpone our purchases of durable goods and other items that we can do without during a depression period.

Psychological Forces

All this, of course, has a tendency to keep the demand for capital goods and durable consumer goods low. Total production will be low and will result in idle capacity throughout the economy. With production, employment, income, prices, and profits low, a pessimistic attitude will undoubtedly prevail. Businessmen will not invest under such conditions, and their reluctance to invest will have a deflationary or contracting effect on the economy. Only when the businessman thinks that conditions are going to improve will he invest. Thus, his pessimistic outlook will have an adverse effect on the economy. Likewise, the consumer will decrease his spending. When his employment slackens and he is no longer receiving overtime pay, when some of his fellow workers are put on a short workweek, or when layoffs begin to appear in the plant, he will be more cautious about the way he spends his money and will cut down on installment buying. Thus, the action of business and individuals during a depression has a tendency to hold down the total demand for goods and services and make the climb to prosperity a little more difficult.

RECOVERY

Although corrective and expanding forces may be at work, their effect may be a bit slow as far as the unemployed individual and the unprofitable firm are concerned. Nevertheless, recovery always comes sooner or later. When it does, it may lead to a high level of business activity or something less than full employment.

What leads us from the road of depression to that of prosperity? It may be some exogenous force such as population increase, war, or the use of monetary or fiscal policy. Even without such external factors, however, the relationship of certain of the basic elements of the business cycle may shift eventually to a more favorable position and initiate an upward movement in the economy. Five changes that frequently occur may start the recovery.

Cost-Price Relationship. After a depression has existed for a period of time, a better cost-price relationship will develop. Statistical evidence shows that costs generally lag behind prices in their movements during the cycle. On a downturn, prices fall first and at a more rapid rate than costs. They also reach their low point before costs do. It is quite possible for prices to reach their minimum point while costs are still dropping. Eventually costs will dip lower than prices, and it will again become profitable for businesses to produce certain goods that may not have been yielding a profit. Prices frequently begin to rise sooner and faster than costs. Thus, on the upward swing of the cycle the margin between price and cost is widened, resulting in increased profits and more investments.

In a free competitive economy, during a depression unemployed men will bid against each other for jobs; firms with decreasing profits will compete against each other for sales; and landholders will compete against each other for rents. The total effect will reduce the costs of products and will gradually bring costs sufficiently below prices so that firms will find it profitable to operate. Firms will also be looking for new techniques and cost-saving devices in order to meet costs and make profits. Therefore, after we have been in a depression for some period of time, a more favorable price-cost relationship develops, which tends to increase productivity.

Inventory Changes. A second factor that tends to spur production is the method of handling inventories. After we remain in a depression for a period of time, inventories become depleted. Sales demand will be filled out of inventories for several months, and companies will finally come to the point where inventories will get so low that they will have to be replaced. When inventories stabilize at lower levels, all current sales will have to be satisfied indirectly by ordering goods from the producer. This may result in production increases sufficient to stimulate the economy.

Interest Rates. The accumulation of excess reserves and the downward pressure on interest rates may encourage some borrowing by businesses. A businessman who can make an 8 percent return by investing money in machinery, equipment, and buildings necessary to produce goods or services may defer doing so if he has to pay 6 percent interest on the money he borrows for investing. However, if the interest rate were to fall to 5 percent, 4 percent, or even less, he might be encouraged to invest his own or borrowed money. Such investment would increase production and employment.

Replacement Demand. Another stimulant to production may come in the capital goods area. Although firms and individuals have a tendency to postpone replacement of capital goods and durable consumer goods during a depression, they cannot do so forever. The old machinery can take only a certain amount of repair. Likewise, equipment wears out. Furthermore, improvements in new machinery that increase productivity may make it more economical for the businessman to replace old machinery. So it is also with the consumer. The old shoes can be resoled only so often before the uppers start falling apart. The family car may reach such a condition that it needs more than new tires. It may be more economical to get a new car than to make major repairs. Spending by businesses and individuals for replacement of capital goods and durable consumer goods will increase demand in those areas. This will lead to increased production and will give a boost to the economy.

Psychological Outlook. The general outlook may change. While it is true that businessmen and consumers tend to be pessimistic during a depression, most individuals realize that depressions do not last forever. Thus, after being in a period of low business activity for a number of months, people will begin to look for an upturn. In fact, many individuals may decide to spend on the presumption that an upswing is just around the corner. Businessmen also figure that they should get ready for better things, or they may figure that it is about time to look at the long-run view of the economy. In either case, a decision to invest in anticipation of future improvements may occur. Such action could start or help start the economy upward.

Incipient Stage of Recovery

A favorable change in any of these five areas—cost-price relationship, inventories, interest rates, replacement of capital assets and durable consumer goods, and the psychological outlook—may lead to an increase in employment. Sometimes the increase will be insufficient to bring the economy out of the depression. In fact, we may have a short spurt in business activity only to be followed by a slackening. The pickup may be substantial, however, especially if there is a concerted move of several of the forces.

Production, Employment, and Income

Regardless of what causes it, the force that leads us out of depression is the increase in production. If production increases, employment and income will naturally increase. With higher incomes, people will increase their demand. Prices will remain fairly constant during the early part of the recovery since the increase in demand will be met by an increase in the supply of goods and services. However, when demand increases sufficiently, prices will begin to rise. Cost, too, will remain relatively low, especially during the early part of the recovery, since competitive bidding for idle materials and manpower will be limited because of their abundance. Profits will increase as sales increase. Larger inventories will be held in the expectation of higher sales. Increased profits will bring about increased investment, which in turn will lead to greater demand for bank loans, and excess reserves theoretically will decrease. Higher bank deposits, however, often forestall the decrease of excess reserves until late in the recovery period or well into the prosperity period. As a result, interest rates will rise slowly.

As incomes increase, people will spend more and there will be a weakening of liquidity preferences. People will be inclined to spend their increased incomes because they were probably forced to do without many things during the depression period. Idle capacity will tend to diminish as output increases, and if the economy picks up to any extent, the general outlook will become more favorable. If the businessman is optimistic and thinks that business conditions are going to improve, he will be inclined to invest in machinery, equipment, buildings, and materials. As he does this, production, employment, income, and demand will increase. Likewise, the consumer will increase his spending. In fact, with a rosy outlook he will probably go into debt to obtain the goods and the services he desires. Thus, the economy will get an added boost and the recovery will be on its way.

PROSPERITY

Prosperity generally has favorable social and political consequences as well as a good economic effect on society, especially if it is high-level prosperity with full employment. Prosperity, however, is not all milk and honey. Certain ill effects, such as inflation, shortages of goods, and reckless spending, may develop.

Cost-Price Relationship

As production, employment, and incomes begin to rise, the interactions of the endogenous forces are such that they work congruously to augment the upswing. Although prices, for example, remain steady in the early part of the recovery, they will rise if the upswing continues. With increased production the economy eventually reaches the "bottleneck" stage, a period in which some goods are relatively scarce and marginal, higher cost facilities are pressed into service. This brings about an upward price movement. Such increases often trigger a general rise in prices. As explained previously, prices increase faster than do costs. During an upswing, this relationship results in higher profits since, in addition to greater sales, large profit margins will exist. This brings about further incentives for investment. This investment is increased by the multiplier-and-accelerator effect, and it can further activate the upswing.

Inventory Accumulation

The build-up of inventories also plays an important role in this phase of the business cycle. Most producers or merchants keep inventories at a certain ratio to sales. Therefore, when sales increase, the size of inventories increases. This means that production must increase not only to satisfy the greater demand by consumers but also must increase to build up inventories.

In addition to the normal build-up to keep the inventory in proper ratio to sales, a second force, namely the price factor, accelerates inventory accumulation. Many businessmen are very astute. They know how to make profits and that, if they build up inventories at low costs, profits will be magnified as prices increase. Therefore, whenever price increases are anticipated, there is a normal reaction that induces the average merchant to build up his inventory to the extent of increasing the ratio of inventory to sales.

When this action is multiplied by the hundreds of thousands of producers, wholesalers, and retailers who keep inventories, it can be seen how production would increase considerably beyond the actual consumer demand. This inventory build-up leads to a further increase in employment, income, and profits.

Replacement and Interest Rates

In addition to the inventory accumulation that augments the upswing, there is also a tendency to replace worn-out assets at an accelerated pace and to add new assets to meet the expected expansion of business, especially as the economy begins to approach the stage of full capacity. This replacement becomes all the more feasible when interest rates are still low. Since the interest rates are "sticky," there is an inclination to borrow before interest rates begin to rise. This increased investment, through the multiplier and the accelerator effects, adds to total income, and the cumulative action of the endogenous factors can push the economy up to a level of full employment.

Approach to Full Employment

During prosperity the levels of production, employment, and income are high, and high income means a large demand. As demand continues to increase, prices will rise, especially when we reach the stage of full employment where we can no longer increase supply fast enough to satisfy the demand. Cost will continue upward because of the competitive bidding for manpower, resources, and capacity. Inventories, investments, and the demand for loans will reach new levels. The decrease in excess reserves and the shortage of loanable funds will force the interest rates upward. Liquidity preference will decrease as prices begin to rise, giving a further impetus to the upswing. As prices rise, the value of money begins to decrease. Thus, many individuals and firms will endeavor to convert their money assets into property and other real goods. This, in turn, increases the total demand for goods and services and adds to the inflationary pressures of the economy.

An increase in the marginal propensity to save (decrease in the marginal propensity to consume) will appear, but it is usually not sufficient to stem the tide of the upswing in the economy. When the general outlook is optimistic, as it usually is during the prosperity period, further encouragement is given to consumption and investment in the economy. The level of economic activity may increase until we reach the stage of full employment. At that time further increases in demand, investment, loans, and such, can only lead to inflation.

RECESSION

Prosperity does not last forever. Downswings are certain to occur. Exactly when or to what extent is not easy to predict. Nevertheless, individuals and firms can prepare for such emergencies. Once a recession has commenced, it may lead to a mild or a serious depression depending on the circumstances existing in the economy at that particular time.

Cost-Price Relationship

During prosperity periods, the relationships between the endogenous factors eventually change in such a manner that they bring about a downturn in the economy. While production, employment, and income are at their peak, some tapering off in consumer demand may appear. Sometimes the mere fact that demand begins to increase at a decreasing rate can cause difficulty. One element bringing about a slackening of demand is the fact that the marginal propensity to consume declines as incomes increase. Consumer resistance eventually will bring about a halt to price increases, and the price level will stabilize at some point. Costs will continue to rise, however, even during prosperity as businesses attempt to increase output by bidding against each other for the relatively scarce manpower, resources, and capacity. The rising cost gradually squeezes out some of the profits, which tends to make businessmen a bit more cautious about investment.

Inventory Adjustment

When demand slackens and prices stabilize, producers, wholesalers, and retailers begin to get rid of excess inventory. Just as we have an inventory build-up adding to the recovery, we can have the reverse situation during a recession.

Furthermore, if prices stabilize or begin to fall, the wholesaler will endeavor to get rid of any excess inventory he is carrying. Therefore, he will supply goods out of his inventory rather than order goods from the producer. In fact, if the price level is dropping, he will not only get rid of his excess stock but will undoubtedly reduce the ratio of inventory to sales. As merchants fill more and more of the demand out of inventory, an adverse effect on production takes place. This in turn decreases employment and income and can precipitate a downswing in our economy.

According to some economists, inventory accumulation and depletion play a major role in the cause of business cycles. Frequently, cycles are characterized by this phenomenon. Inventory depletion, for example, contributed heavily to the slowdown in the economy in early 1967 and to the recession of 1970. It likewise was having some influence on the slowdown in the economy that was taking place early in 1974.

Replacement Demand

Reduced employment and income during a recession bring about a further reduction in demand. Profits diminish and investment falls off, especially with the high interest rates. Business finds it unnecessary to replace capital assets that wear out if there is no use for such machinery and equipment. Idle capacity begins to appear as production schedules are cut back. Consumers, likewise, begin postponing the purchase of durable goods. Instead of buying that new car, they will put new tires or retreads on the old one. They will make other durable goods last as long as possible. The more difficult it becomes to repay, the more reluctant individuals will be to extend or renew credit. Prices eventually will begin to fall. This will cause further postponement of purchases as buyers hold off in anticipation of further price cuts. Price declines will bring a further reduction in profits, which means less investment. This, in turn, will cut down production, employment, and income.

Liquidity Preference and Saving

Falling prices strengthen the liquidity preference as the value of money increases. The attempt to convert goods into money increases the supply of assets offered at a time when demand is low. This will have a deflationary effect. The propensity to save, however, will decline with the decrease in incomes. Although individuals and families may desire to save even more than they had in the past, they may be unable to do so because of reduced income or unemployment.

Reverse Multiplier

In general, the declining production, employment, income, profits, demand, and prices become cumulative. This results in a reduction in investment. The reduction in investment and consumer spending will be accompanied by a reverse multiplier effect and the accelerator may approach zero. Under such conditions, the general outlook may become pessimistic, which has an adverse psychological effect on both investors and consumers.

Status of the Endogenous Elements During a Recession

As the recession gets under way, the changing relationships of the endogenous elements are such that it tends to perpetuate the downswing.

The recession continues until it reaches bottom. Somewhere along the way the stage of depression is reached. Whether the depression is severe or mild, the business cycle will have been completed. The economy will have moved through the four phases of the cycle: depression, recovery, prosperity, and recession. Once in the depression, it will again require a change in the relationships of the endogenous elements to bring about an upswing in business activity. The economy will then move through another cycle, maybe of greater or less intensity, maybe of shorter or longer duration. The pattern is similar in each cycle, although the characteristics of each may differ somewhat in regard to cause, amplitude, and duration.

Modifying Factors

The duration and the intensity of these fluctuations can be modified by the use of monetary, fiscal, and psychological measures, as we shall see later. In fact, it is because we know the pattern so well that action can be taken to avoid the two extremes of the cycle: widespread unemployment at one extreme and run-away inflation at the other.

External forces also affect the level of economic activity and often generate business fluctuations. For example, a war has a profound effect on the level of economic activity. The requirements for war and defense materiel necessitate increased production and employment. Additional attempts to increase production may lead to inflation unless definite measures such as material and wage and price controls are utilized to combat rising prices.

Similar impetus may come to the economy from population growth, changes in the money supply, or government deficit spending. On the other hand, the termination of a war can have a depressing effect on the economy as production is cut back, unless there is a substantial increase in consumer demand and private investment to offset the decrease in defense spending. Adverse effects can also result from serious catastrophes that force a reduction in production and income.

The typical pattern of the business cycle also is modified to the extent that we do not have perfect competition in the economy. For example, labor unions may be forceful enough to prevent wages from declining during a recessionary period. Oligopolies may push prices up sooner than expected or prevent them from falling in a recession. Government regulations may alter the normal movement of the interest rates.

The fact that all endogenous elements may not move or act in precisely the fashion described heretofore is no indication that the pattern is invalid. In any particular cycle one or more of the elements may act contrary to its usual movement. But generally a sufficient number of them will react in the prescribed manner and with ample strength to overcome any countervailing force of a few maverick elements. Such was the case in the recessions of 1958 and 1970 when, because of institutional factors, the general price level actually rose somewhat instead of declining.

Some economists and government officials suggest that today business cycles are obsolete. They claim that through the use of various monetary, fiscal, and other economic measures we are able to prevent wide oscillations in production, employment, and income. It is true that our measures and power to stabilize the level of economic activity, and keep it growing at a good rate of expansion, have improved over the years. The underlying need for the use of these stabilizing measures, however, is the fact that in a free economy fluctuations do occur. Stabilization measures do not eliminate the business cycle but merely modify its impact or effects. Furthermore, the occurrence of recessions, nagging unemployment, full employment, inflation, and sluggishness in the economy, all in the past 15 years, certainly indicate that business cycles are still with us.

BUSINESS CYCLE INDICATORS

As business activity changes, these changes are reflected in different areas or sectors of the economy. In many cases we have statistics and indexes indicating the changes that are taking place. Although some of these indexes measure changes in particular activities, they are representative in that what is happening to one particular type of economic activity may be characteristic of the economy as a whole. In other cases we do have some measures of composite types of economic activity that pervade the economy. Therefore, they give a good reflection of the general status of the economy. Some business cycle analysts have combined a number of different indicators in an effort to develop a general indicator for the entire economy. For purposes of analyzing business cycles, statistical indicators are usually divided into three types: representative indicators, composite indicators, and general business indicators.

Representative Indicators

Although representative indicators are usually indexes that measure changes in a particular area of business activity, those that measure an essential area of business activity will reflect to some degree what is happening to the economy as a whole. These include the following.

Index of Iron and Steel Production. Since iron and steel are primary metals used in the widespread production of numerous durable goods, changes in the general level of business activity are readily reflected in the fluctuation of the index of iron and steel production. In 1970, when the nation's economy not only failed to achieve its potential 4 to 5 percent annual growth, but the real GNP actually declined less than one percent, steel mills were operating at less than 75 percent of capacity.

Bank Clearings or Bank Debits. Since 85 to 90 percent of our business activity is carried on by means of credit and checking accounts, it is obvious that any substantial changes in the general level of business activity will be reflected in bank clearings and bank checking deposits.

Railway Carloadings. Increased business activity calls for more transportation of goods, both raw materials and finished products. Since railroads are still an important means of transporting industrial commodities, the number of carloadings will fluctuate with changes in business activity. Although other means of transportation are important, the large decline of carloadings in 1958, 1960-1961, 1970, and 1974 corresponded to the drop in general business activity for each of these periods.

Electric Power Output. Electricity is our chief means of industrial power. Naturally there is a close correlation between electrical output and the overall level of business activity.

Other Indexes. Other representative indicators include paperboard production, which is important in industrial packaging; bituminous coal production; and the index of employment want ads. Many others have been used or suggested at various times, such as automobile production, agricultural output, and stock market prices, but these frequently tend to be erratic.

Composite Indicators

Composite indicators are usually indexes that measure some type of activity that is widespread throughout the economy. Therefore they are sure to give a good indication of the general level of business activity. Composite indicators include the following.

Index of Factory Employment. Although factory employment usually fluctuates more widely than does nonfactory employment or total employment, it is still a good indicator of economic change. In 1970, and again in 1974, for example, factory employment dropped relatively more than total employment in the economy.

Index of Payrolls. This index has some advantages over the factory employment index insofar as it reflects any changes in production due to overtime work or changes in the productivity per man-hour. On the other hand, its major weakness is that payrolls may change without any change in business activity, simply as a result of higher wages. Furthermore, premium pay for overtime work may distort the index to some degree.

Federal Reserve Board Index of Industrial Production. This is a commonly used indicator of business activity and is fairly accurate. A decline of 8 percent appeared in the index during the 1960-1961 recession, and it fell 2.2 percent in the spring of 1967. It also dropped from a peak of 110 (1967 = 100) in 1969 to a low of 102 in the recession of 1970. It started to decline late in 1973 and early 1974, forewarning the 1974 economic slump. Since the index measures industrial production only, which fluctuates more markedly than nonindustrial production and total production, it tends to exaggerate to some extent business cycle changes.

Gross National Product. Since the GNP covers all facets of production in the economy, it is the best indicator we have of the general level of business activity. When changes in the GNP are measured in constant dollars, they give a fairly accurate measure of the amplitude of business fluctuations, such as occurred in the 1970 recession, when the real GNP declined by $3.5 billion for the year. A decline in real GNP was likewise expected in the first half of 1974.

General Business Indicators

Most general business indicators combine a series of different indexes into one general index of business activity. Typical of these indexes are the following.

Index of American Business Activity. This index, published by the Cleveland Trust Company, compiles several different indexes and measurements to cover the period from 1790 to the present. The data are expressed in deviations from the norm or trend line.

Business Week Index. This index is compiled and published weekly in graphic and tabular form in *Business Week*. It reflects the combined movements of several individual series including raw steel production, automobiles, electric power, crude oil, paperboard, machinery, other transportation equipment, construction, and railroad carloadings. The movements of the *Business Week* Index are shown in Figure 9-4. From the figure the recession in the economy in 1970 is readily apparent. A slowdown was also readily observable from the data preceding 1974.

FIGURE 9-4

INDEX OF BUSINESS ACTIVITY

The movements of the business cycle and the 1970 recession in particular are readily apparent from an observation of this index.

SOURCE: *Business Week* (December 23, 1972).

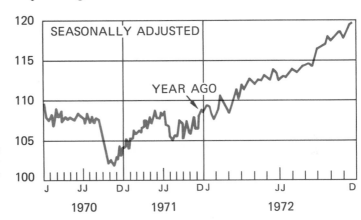

Statistical Indicators of Business-Cycle Changes. These indicators, published by the Statistical Indicator Associates, North Egremont, Massachusetts, comprise a total of 26 indicators. They include 3 separate groups: the *leading indicators*, which are composed of 12 indexes whose upward and downward turning points generally precede the peaks and troughs of general business activity; the *roughly coincident indicators*, a group of 8 other indexes whose turning points usually correspond with the peaks and troughs of general business activity; and the *lagging indicators*, made up of 6 indexes whose turning points occur after the turning points for the general level of business activity have been reached.

Data for each of the 26 indicators are shown in tables and graphs released weekly and/or monthly. One particular chart shows the percentage of each group of indicators that is expanding. The relationship of the leaders to the coincident and lagging indicators can be observed in Figure 9-5. Note that the leaders turned downward before the coincident and lagging indicators in the recession of 1970. The leading indicators, as well as the coincident indicators, also gave an early warning of the slowdown that occurred in early 1974. The current status of these indicators along with their interpretation

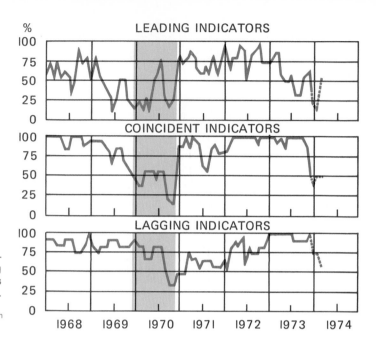

FIGURE 9-5

STATISTICAL INDICATORS

The relationship of the leading indicators to the coincident and lagging indicators from 1968 through 1974 is readily apparent from this summary.

SOURCE: *Statistical Indicator Associates*, North Egremont, Massachusetts (April 17, 1974).

and forecast of business conditions is maintained and published by the Statistical Indicator Associates.

Business Conditions Digest. This set of indicators published by the Department of Commerce contains graphs, charts, and tables for more than 100 National Bureau of Economic Research (NBER) business cycle indicator series, which are the source of those used by the Statistical Indicator Associates. The government publication plots 34 NBER Leading Indicators, 25 NBER Roughly Coincident Indicators, 11 NBER Lagging Indicators, numerous other U.S. Series with Business Cycle Significance, and 22 International Comparisons of industrial production. The series are presented in convenient form for analysis and interpretation by specialists in business cycle analysis. The Department of Commerce, however, makes no attempt to interpret them or to make business forecasts.

By following the business cycle indicators closely the business cycle analyst or the astute business executive may be able to anticipate pending changes in the level of business activity and try to make proper adjustments in the way of production schedules, employment, inventories, and financing to compensate for expected changes in business activity.

CAUSES OF THE BUSINESS CYCLE

Business cycles are rather complex phenomena, and a multiplicity of forces are active in the changing level of business activity. Although the study of business cycles is relatively new, a product of the past 50 years, there have been numerous theories offered for the explanation of business fluctuations. To date there is a lack of unanimity among the various theories regarding the exact cause of the cycle. At the same time, no one theory completely and satisfactorily explains the cause of business cycles. Nevertheless, a study of the various theories permits a better understanding of the possible causes of the cycles and a clearer understanding of the complexities involved in their analysis. Although there are disagreements among the theories, these are not always real differences. Frequently they are differences in emphasis. At other times it is obvious that one theory may be more applicable to a particular situation than is some other theory. At times a cycle may reflect some elements of several theories. For this reason it is worthwhile to be acquainted with the major theories. For the sake of simplicity we can classify these theories into four major categories: (1) real or physical causes; (2) psychological causes; (3) monetary causes; and (4) spending and saving causes.

Real or Physical Causes

A traditional explanation of the cause of the cycle is the *innovation theory*. According to this theory, business cycles are caused by innovations in the form of new products, new methods, new machines, or new techniques.

Innovation leads to increased production, employment, and income in the economy. As businessmen borrow to finance innovations, they set up new factories, buy raw materials, and hire workers. The increased income resulting from their spending, of course, increases the total demand in the economy. If their ventures are profitable, other investors will seek to imitate them. But as additional firms begin and continue to produce, a point of overexpansion eventually is reached. The reaction to this overexpansion brings about a contraction in the form of declining production, employment, and income. It is contended that the decline will be less than the expansion, and thus there will be a net gain in activity in the economy as a result of the innovation.

The intensity and duration of the cycle depends on the nature of the innovation. A simple innovation will result in a short, mild cycle. A series of innovations may occur in such an integrated manner, however, that the cycle could be more pronounced and continue over a longer period. Major innovations, such as the rise of the corporate form of business enterprise, the development of the steamboat, the perfection and use of electric power, the automobile, the radio, and the development of electrical appliances produce increased business activity on a larger scale.

Fifty years or so ago, *agricultural theories* of the business cycle were very popular. Early theories endeavored to relate the general level of business activity to such things as sun spots, under the assumption that these affected the weather, which in turn affected the volume of agricultural output, which had a definite effect on the level of business activity. Even though the proportion of agricultural production in the gross national product has declined dramatically, the volume of farm output today can influence to some extent the level of business activity. In short, a larger volume of agricultural output will require more manpower and equipment to harvest and handle the crop, more transportation facilities, increased storage facilities, and an increased amount of credit to finance these operations. Such activity should give an impetus to the total economy.

On the other hand, a change in the volume of agricultural output may change the income received by the farmer, the prices paid by industrial producers using agricultural raw material, and the prices paid by the consumer for foodstuffs. Such financial changes also can affect the level of business activity in general.

A third important real cause of the business cycle is manifest in the *accelerator theory.* According to this theory, an increase in the demand for consumer goods may lead to a greater than proportional increase in the demand for capital goods. For example, if consumer demand increases by 20 percent, it may require more than a 20 percent increase in capital goods to produce the additional consumer goods desired. Assume, for example, that 200 machines are used to produce 100,000 consumer units and that 20 machines, or 10 percent, must be replaced each year due to depreciation. This means that each machine turns out 500 consumer units per year. Assume further that consumer demand increases by 20 percent, from 100,000 to 120,000 units. In order to produce the additional 20,000 consumer units, it will require an additional 40 machines. Since the company will now order 60 new machines (20 for replacement plus the 40 additional machines), its demand for machines will increase 200 percent compared with the 20 percent increase in the demand for consumer units. On the other hand, as consumer demand stabilizes or slackens, the firm will not require any additional machines. In such case, its demand for machines will decrease in greater proportion than the change in consumer demand.

A similar phenomenon exists in the durable consumer goods industries and the handling of business inventories. It is for this reason that fluctuations in the production of capital and durable consumer goods are of greater intensity than are the fluctuations for the economy as a whole.

Psychological Causes

Although the psychological theory is seldom offered as a complete or independent explanation of the cause of business cycles, it is incorporated in some way in nearly every other theory suggested. In brief, the psychological theory holds that when investors and consumers react according to some belief as to future conditions, their actions tend to cause such a psychological outlook to become a reality. If investors think that conditions in the immediate future are going to be good, for example, they will increase their investment in machinery, equipment, and buildings in an effort to increase their total output and make more profit. Likewise, the consumer who foresees good times ahead will spend money more readily and perhaps seek additional credit to increase his spending power. Such actions will tend to give a boost to the level of business activity. If the investors, on the other hand, expect sales and prices to be lower in the future, they will slacken their investments, and businessmen will allow their inventories to dwindle and will be cautious about hiring additional workers. Likewise, if the consumer observes that jobs are difficult to obtain, that he is not getting any overtime, and that some men in the plant are being laid off or are on a short workweek, he may be a bit pessimistic about the immediate future. In such case he may limit his spending, may be cautious about taking on new debt, and may even try to save for a possible layoff. In such a case the actions of both the investors and the consumers will tend to bring about a slowdown in the economy.

Furthermore, the psychological theory holds that the actions of some of the business leaders can influence other businessmen and consumers to feel the same way. If our business leaders exude optimism and back it up with actual investments, this may influence the thinking of smaller businessmen about the prospects of the economy. If they follow suit with increased investment, this will add a fillip to the economy. Also, competition exerts a potent force on the economy in a psychological manner. Several firms competing for trade in a given area may misjudge their respective shares of the market. If they are optimistic, they may overestimate their individual shares. If several firms do this, it will tend to bring forth more production than is actually needed for the market. For a time there will be a substantial increase in business activity, but as the grim realities of the marketplace unfold, some or all firms may have to retrench on production. This, in turn, means a cutback in the demand for materials, labor, credit, and capital. Current production, employment, and income will fall as sales orders are filled by drawing on inventories instead of scheduling new production orders. In such a case a decline in the general level of business activity will set in.

Monetary Causes

Most monetary theories are based on the premise that the modern banking system in a typical industrial economy provides an elastic money supply through the use of bank credit. According to the monetary theory, the free and easy expansion of bank credit permits an overexpansion of investment in the economy from which there must be a contraction. If the investors had to rely on savings to finance their investments, the amount of investment would be limited naturally by a rise in interest rates as the demand for savings exceeded the supply. With the use of bank credit, however, the forces exerting pressure on the interest rates are modified. As a result, interest rates do not rise quickly, and frequently more investment takes place than would take place in the absence of bank credit. Eventually a position is reached in which the economy has excess productive capacity and abundant inventories. Further extension of credit at such a time only aggravates the situation. Readjustment comes about as businessmen slacken their investment, prices begin to fall, production schedules are cut back, unemployment increases, and a recession commences. Retraction of credit by the banks during this period further augments the downswing.

Monetary theorists maintain that in order to eliminate the business cycle it is necessary to eliminate bank credit. The banks, on the other hand, maintain that they do not cause business cycles, since they do not force credit upon anyone, and that they merely service the business community when it needs money. Furthermore, complete elimination of bank credit might eliminate the cycle, but it would also eliminate some of the healthy expansion and growth in the economy brought on by the use of bank credit. Some economists say that what is needed is a limitation on bank credit, especially during periods of full employment when inflationary pressures exist, rather than its complete elimination.

Spending and Saving Causes

The spending and saving theories are of two broad categories. The first are the *underconsumption theories*. Some underconsumption theories hold that the economy does not distribute a sufficient amount of income among the factors of production to permit the purchase of the total goods and services produced by the economy. The more widely accepted theory, however, is that the economy does distribute a sufficient amount of purchasing power to buy the total goods and services produced but that all the income or purchasing power is not utilized. Hence, some goods will be produced and not sold. As a consequence total production will be reduced which in turn reduces employment and income. One of the leading underconsumption theorists maintains that the basic cause of the difficulty is the unequal distribution of income in modern society. Individuals in higher income groups do not spend all their income for consumer goods but seek an outlet for their funds in the form of investments. For a while this investment spending leads to more production but eventually a point is reached at which those who would buy more consumer goods do not have sufficient income to do so, and others with sufficient income to buy more do not need additional consumed goods. The remedy suggested by underconsumptionists for the elimination or modifications of the business cycles is the lessening of inequality in the distribution of income. This they say can be accomplished to some degree by the use of steeply progressive income taxes, strengthening of labor unions, regulation of monopolistic pricing, and an increase of social ownership of certain industries. It is interesting to note that the first three of these suggestions are to some extent present in our economy today.

The other important spending and saving theory is that of underinvestment. The *underinvestment theory* holds that income in the economy is equal to total production and that, in order to clear all goods off the market, spending equivalent to current income must take place. Since spending on consumption is less than the total income, however, the difference must be made up in the form of investment, or spending on machinery, equipment, and buildings. Whenever investment spending is equal to the gap between income and consumer spending, the economy will be in a stable position. But whenever investment spending is insufficient to fill the gap between consumer spending and total income, total spending will be less than the value of the total output of goods and services, and surpluses will exist in the markets. This will initiate a downswing in the economy. If for some reason investment spending is more than sufficient to fill the gap between consumer spending and total income, the total demand for goods and services will be greater than the total output and it will tend to increase the level of business activity. Thus, business cycles are caused by variations in investment. The cycle can be modified or eliminated, therefore, by maintaining an adequate amount of investment. This is essentially the crux of the modern income-expenditure approach.

SUMMARY

1. Many disturbing forces prevent full-employment equilibrium, but the greatest of these in time of peace is the business cycle.

2. Business cycles may be classified as either minor or major. The minor cycles occur every three to four years; the major, approximately every ten years.

3. The average length of the minor cycles is 47.6 months, with 26.2 months spent in expansion and 21.4 spent in contraction.

4. Business cycles are measured as fluctuations above and below the trend line. Each cycle is made up of four phases—depression, recovery, prosperity, and recession.

5. The business cycle is the result of a complex series of interrelated, cumulative changes in business activity that sometimes lead to prosperity and sometimes to depression. Depressions mean a loss of billions of dollars in the nation's income.

6. Business cycles have a pattern, but the pattern is not uniform because of many disturbing forces within and without the cycle, and forecasting becomes correspondingly difficult.

7. Numerous indicators of business cycles exist. These can be categorized as representative indicators, composite indicators, and general business indicators.

8. No individual business cycle theory completely explains the cause of the cycle. Each theory, however, adds to the total understanding of business cycles. Business cycles may occur due to real, psychological, monetary, and spending and saving causes, or some combination of these.

<table>
<tr><td>NEW TERMS</td><td>

Business cycle, *p. 174*
Minor cycles, *p. 175*
Major cycles, *p. 175*
Prosperity, *p. 176*
Recession, *p. 176*
Depression, *p. 176*
Recovery, *p. 176*
Trend, *p. 176*
Seasonal variations, *p. 176*
Irregular fluctuations, *p. 177*
Cyclical fluctuations, *p. 177*
Endogenous forces, *p. 178*
Exogenous forces, *p. 178*
Liquidity preference, *p. 179*
Representaitve business indicators, *p. 189*
Composite business indicators, *p. 190*

</td><td>

General business indicators, *p. 190*
Leading indicators, *p. 191*
Roughly coincident indicators, *p. 191*
Lagging indicators, *p. 191*
Real or physical causes of the cycle, *p. 193*
Innovation theory, *p. 193*
Agricultural theories, *p. 193*
Accelerator theory, *p. 194*
Psychological causes of the cycle, *p. 194*
Monetary causes of the cycle, *p. 195*
Spending and saving causes of the cycle, *p. 196*
Underconsumption theories, *p. 196*
Underinvestment theory, *p. 197*

</td></tr>
</table>

QUESTIONS FOR DISCUSSION AND ANALYSIS

1. Distinguish between a cyclical fluctuation and a trend.
2. What are the four phases of the business cycle? How can you determine in which phase of the cycle the economy is at present?
3. What internal and external forces influence the level of business activity?
4. During recovery and prosperity, what forces are building up that eventually will help bring about a downturn in the economy?
5. Differentiate between a representative and a composite business cycle indicator.
6. Why should the Federal Reserve Board Index of Industrial Production tend to exaggerate changes that are taking place in the level of business activity?
7. Distinguish between the leading, roughly coincident, and lagging indicators of the Statistical Indicators of Business-Cycle Changes.
8. What indications of the innovation theory of the business cycle have you observed in recent years?
9. Do you think there is much validity to the underconsumption theory of the business cycle? Why or why not?
10. Which do you think is the most realistic of the theories? Why?

SUGGESTED READINGS

The Suggested Readings for this chapter are included in Chapter 6, pages 127 and 128.

The Goal of Full Employment

PREVIEW We usually consider the economy to be in a state of full employment when 96 percent of the civilian labor force is employed. This allows 4 percent frictional unemployment. The measure of employment and unemployment is taken through a survey method each month. It not only yields information on the total size and composition of the labor force but reveals much about the characteristics of both the employed and the unemployed.

The Employment Act of 1946 makes it the responsibility of the federal administration in office to use measures at its disposal to bring about conditions of maximum employment, maximum production, and maximum purchasing power. The Act provides for a Council of Economic Advisers to the President of the United States, and it requires the President each year to give an *Economic Report*. In this *Report*, the President usually outlines those measures he would like to see adopted to bring about or maintain full employment.

A definite relationship exists between the level of employment and the size of the GNP. When the real GNP decreases, unemployment usually increases. In fact, as we shall see, unemployment may develop even when the GNP remains constant or increases moderately over any extended period of time. Unemployment is detrimental to the economy because it reduces incomes. Falling income in turn causes consumer spending to decline, which further decreases demand and eventually the GNP.

Previously in referring to full employment, we were considering full employment of manpower, resources, and productive capacity. In this chapter, however, we are concerned primarily with employed and unemployed manpower. Unemployment of labor causes hardship to the worker and his family. From Table 10-1 on page 200, it can be seen that we have had periods of relatively full employment and periods of widespread unemployment. As the years pass, the size of the population will increase and the labor force will grow. We add to the labor force approximately 1.5 million new workers annually. Moreover, more than 2 million members of the labor force are displaced each year as a result of technological development and automation. Consequently, GNP must grow at a real rate of at least 4 percent annually if technological unemployment is to be prevented and ample jobs for new entrants into the labor force are to be provided. This makes the problem of maintaining full employment more complex.

THE LABOR FORCE

Customarily, between 40 and 45 percent of our total population are members of the labor force. This seems to be the norm for industrial nations throughout the world. However, the labor force is limited by definition. Many, such as housewives, who work just as much as do those in the labor force are excluded because of the nature of their work or because they receive no remuneration for it.

Size and Composition of the Labor Force

In order to understand the problem of maintaining full employment, let us look more closely at our labor force and our population. In 1973, we had a total population of 210.4 million. Of this total, 148.3 million were in the category of the noninstitutional population, that is, all persons 16 years of age or older including members of the armed forces but excluding persons in institutions.

TABLE 10-1

POPULATION, TOTAL LABOR FORCE, AND UNEMPLOYMENT

1930-1973

(Millions)

(1) Year	(2) Total Population	(3) Total Labor Force	(4) Unemployment	(5) Percent Unemployed [1]
1930	123.1	50.1	4.3	8.7
1940	132.6	56.2	8.1	14.6
1950	152.3	63.9	3.3	5.3
1960	180.7	72.1	3.9	5.5
1965	194.3	77.2	3.4	4.5
1970	204.9	85.9	4.1	4.9
1973	210.4	91.0	4.3	4.9

SOURCE: *Economic Indicators* (January, 1974), and *Statistical Abstract of the United States*, 1973.

[1] Of civilian labor force.

Total Labor Force. Of the noninstitutional population, 91.0 million were in the total labor force in 1973. The total labor force is made up of all those in the noninstitutional population who are working or are seeking work. Thus, it includes the unemployed as well as the employed. Furthermore, it includes proprietors, the self-employed, and members of the armed forces. However, the labor force excludes all persons engaged in incidental unpaid family work (less than 15 hours), those attending school, and all persons engaged exclusively in housework in their homes.

Civilian Labor Force. If we subtract the number of persons in the armed forces from the total labor force, the remainder is the civilian labor force.

By definition the civilian labor force consists of "all persons in the total labor force except members of the armed services." Since 2.3 million persons were in the armed services in 1973, the civilian labor force was 88.7 million, and of this total, 4.3 million or 4.9 percent were unemployed. The *unemployed labor force* includes all persons in the labor force seeking work, including those who are currently engaged in emergency relief work.

The *employed civilian labor force* is the difference between the civilian labor force and the unemployed. Technically, it includes all employed workers—including persons who did not work at all during the census week because of illness, bad weather, vacation, or labor disputes, but who had a job or business. Part-time as well as full-time employment is included. In 1973, the number employed was 84.4 million and, of this total, 3.4 million were engaged in agricultural work while 81.0 million were in nonagricultural employment.

There were 57.3 million persons in the noninstitutional population who were not in the total labor force. It is interesting to keep in mind that 35.3 million of this group were keeping house. Although a housewife may put in a harder day than the man of the house, she is not included in the labor force. Another 9.2 million of those not in the labor force were in school. The remainder, 12.8 million, was composed of those who are retired, individuals who do not want to work, and those who do not have to work.

A breakdown of the population and the labor force is shown in Table 10-2.

TABLE 10-2

POPULATION AND LABOR FORCE

1973

Category		Millions
1. Total Population		210.4
2. Noninstitutional Population		148.3
3. Total Labor Force		91.0
4. Armed Forces		2.3
5. Total Civilian Labor Force		88.7
6. Unemployed Labor Force		4.3
7. Employed Civilian Labor Force		84.4
8. Agricultural Employment		3.4
9. Nonagricultural Employment		81.0
10. Persons Not in the Labor Force		57.3
Keeping House	35.3	
In School	9.2	
Others	12.8	

SOURCE: *Economic Report of the President*, 1974, and *Statistical Abstract of the United States*, 1973.

Source of Employment. The bulk of the labor force is engaged in nonagricultural employment. The largest portion, 19.8 million, is engaged in manufacturing. The second largest category, which is wholesale and retail trade, has 16.3 million, and government employment is third with 13.6 million workers.

Trends in the Labor Force

The American labor force has definite characteristics, but these characteristics change with the passage of time. Some of the most pronounced trends are described in the following sections.

Teen-Age Employment. The percentage of teen-age employment has decreased. At present more than 51.2 percent of all males in the 18-19 age group are in school compared with 35 percent in 1950. Some of the decline in teen-age employment is the result of federal and state legislation that restricts the use of child labor. Larger influences, however, are probably the growth of compulsory school regulations, the expansion of educational facilities, and the increased demand for education in almost all areas of employment. Since more children are in school, there is less chance that they will also be a part of the labor force. Projections indicate that the labor force participation rate of males in the 18-19 age group, presently about 71 percent, will not increase in the next few decades, and in fact will fall to around 65 percent. Table 10-3 shows the increased percentage in school attendance.

TABLE 10-3

PERCENTAGE OF 18-19 AGE GROUP ATTENDING SCHOOL

Year	Percent of Total Age Group	Percent of Male Age Group
1950	29.4	35.2
1960	38.4	47.8
1965	46.3	55.6
1970	47.7	54.4
1972	46.3	51.2
1980 (estimate) [1]	60.0	72.0

SOURCE: *Statistical Abstract of the United States*, 1972 and 1973.

[1] Based on estimate of author.

Older Workers. The percentage of older male workers in the labor force has decreased. This has been partly the result of the introduction of federal old-age and survivor's insurance and the advent of industrial pensions. In 1973, only 23 percent of the men 65 years of age or over were in the labor force compared with 58 percent in 1930 and 60 percent in 1920. It is anticipated that by 1980 less than one fifth of those over 65 years of age will be in the labor force.

Female Workers. The number and the percentage of women in the labor force have increased. The increased amount of clerical and retail sales work, the increased need for stenographers, and the development of light manufacturing (those occupations in which women historically have been employed) have increased the demand for female labor throughout the United States. In addition, the opening of many other occupations as a result of recent equal employment opportunity laws has increased and will continue to increase the demand for women at the managerial and professional levels. Currently 38 percent of the labor force is composed of women. It is also interesting to note that more than one half (63 percent) of these are married women. Thus, it appears that the old saying, "a woman's place is in the home," belongs to a past era. Table 10-4 shows the number and the percentage of women in the labor force in the past few decades.

TABLE 10-4

EMPLOYMENT OF WOMEN IN THE CIVILIAN LABOR FORCE

1930-1973

(1) Year	(2) Total Employment (Millions)	(3) Female Employment (Millions)	(4) Female Employment as Percent of Total
1930	45.5	10.7	23.5
1940	47.5	12.0	25.3
1950	58.9	17.3	29.4
1960	65.8	21.9	33.3
1965	71.1	24.7	34.7
1970	78.6	29.7	37.8
1973	84.4	32.4	38.4

SOURCE: *Economic Report of the President*, 1974, and *Statistical Abstract of the United States*, 1973.

Skilled and Unskilled Workers. The percentage of unskilled workers in the labor force has decreased. With widespread use of complex machinery and equipment, it has become necessary for workers to learn how to operate such machinery and equipment. Consequently, the percentage of semiskilled workers in the labor force has increased while the percentage of skilled workers has remained relatively constant. The occupational breakdown of the labor force shown in Table 10-5 reveals this movement away from the unskilled categories. There has been a decrease in the percentage of both farm and industrial laborers. Note, however, the substantial increase in the percentage of professional, technical, and kindred workers. There has also been an increase in the percentages of craftsmen, clerical, and service workers.

Agricultural Employment. There has been a definite move away from agricultural occupations. In 1930, we had 10.3 million workers in agriculture. By 1940, there were only 9.5 million. In 1950 the number of farmers was down to 7.2 million. A decade later, 1960, it had dwindled to 5.5 million. For 1973, the figure was at 3.4 million. As a result of increased productivity, we produce more and more agricultural commodities with fewer and fewer farmers. This decrease in agricultural employment can be observed also in Table 10-5 by noting the two categories, Farmers and Farm Managers and Farm Laborers.

TABLE 10-5

MAJOR
OCCUPATION
GROUPS OF
EMPLOYED
PERSONS

1940 and 1973

Occupation	Percent of Total (1940)	Percent of Total (1973)
Professional, Technical, and Kindred Workers	8.0	14.2
Farmers and Farm Managers	11.6	1.9
Managers and Proprietors (except farm)	8.0	10.3
Clerical and Kindred Workers	9.8	17.1
Sales Workers	7.0	6.3
Craftsmen, Foremen, and Kindred Workers	11.7	13.2
Operatives and Kindred Workers	18.0	17.1
Private Household Workers	4.7	1.6
Service Workers (except household)	7.1	11.5
Farm Laborers	7.1	1.7
Laborers (except farm and mine)	7.0	5.1
Total	100.0	100.0

SOURCE: *Statistical Abstract of the United States*, 1973.

Organized Workers. Statistical evidence indicates that there was a substantial increase in the number and the percentage of organized workers in the labor force between 1935 and 1973. In the past several years, however, labor union membership has remained fairly stable in the vicinity of 20 million, or a little less than one fourth of the total civilian labor force. This stabilizing effect has resulted in large part because the labor force has not been growing as fast in those types of occupations and skills in which workers traditionally have been organized, such as the unskilled, semiskilled, and craft occupations. A considerable amount and proportion of the increase in the labor force has been in professional, technical, sales, clerical, and other white-collar occupations not traditionally organized by labor unions.

Size of the Labor Force. The size of the total labor force has been increasing continually. This increase in the labor force has come primarily from the growth in population. We have been adding nearly 1.5 million persons per year to our labor force during the present decade. The average annual increment in the 1950s was approximately 820,000 per year. In the 1960s the labor force increased at an average rate of 1,380,000 per annum. Continuous growth in the labor force can be observed in Table 10-6.

Even greater growth of the labor force is predicted for the next several years. Projections indicate that in the decade of the seventies the labor force will grow by 18.3 percent compared to 18 percent for the decade of the sixties.[1] By 1980, the labor force is expected to reach the 100 million level.

[1] These and other projections are contained in Department of Labor, *U.S. Manpower in the 1970's* (Washington: U.S. Government Printing Office, 1970).

TABLE 10-6

LABOR FORCE
AS A PERCENT
OF TOTAL
POPULATION

1930-1973

(1) Year	(2) Total Population (Millions)	(3) Total Labor Force (Millions)	(4) Total Labor Force Participation	(5) Total Civilian Labor Force (Millions)	(6) Civilian Labor Force Participation
1930	123	50	40.8%	49	40.0%
1940	133	56	42.1	55	41.4
1950	152	64	42.1	62	40.8
1960	181	72	39.9	70	38.7
1965	195	77	39.5	74	38.0
1970	205	86	42.0	83	40.5
1973	210	91	43.3	89	42.4

SOURCE: *Statistical Abstract of the United States,* 1959 and 1973.

During the 1970s the number of workers in the 25-31 age group will increase by a dramatic 49 percent, while there will be a decline in the percentage of 16-24 year old workers. During the sixties the increase in the percentage of youth 16-19 in the labor force grew by 43 percent. In the 1970s it will grow by only 11 percent. This should help reduce unemployment among the youth of the nation, which, at an average rate of 12 percent in the 1960s, was 3 to 5 times more than the adult unemployment rate in the sixties. But there will continue to be a rapid increase, 43 percent, in the number of young blacks entering the labor force during the decade. Unemployment rates among young blacks are usually double what they are among white teen-agers.

As shown in Figure 10-1, page 206, there will be substantial increases in the number of white-collar and service workers in the decade. Note the 50 percent increase in professional and technical workers and the 45 percent rise in service workers. On the other hand, blue-collar workers will grow at a much slower rate, and the number of farm workers will decline.

Labor Force Participation. Although the labor force has grown in size, the labor force participation rate has remained relatively stable. The labor force participation rate is the percentage of the population in the labor force. From Table 10-6 it can be observed that, with the exception of the war years, labor force participation has been between 39.5 and 43.3 percent for the total population. The fact that it did increase to 46.5 percent during World War II reveals that the rate of participation had some elasticity. Had it not been for this elasticity, war production would have been hampered severely. In spite of the fact that we had about 11 million persons in the armed services, the civilian labor force participation rate declined only three percentage points, or less than 1.5 million persons, during World War II.

As the young men and women left the civilian labor force to enter the armed services, their places were taken by the entry of new people into

OCCUPATIONAL GROUP   PERCENT CHANGE

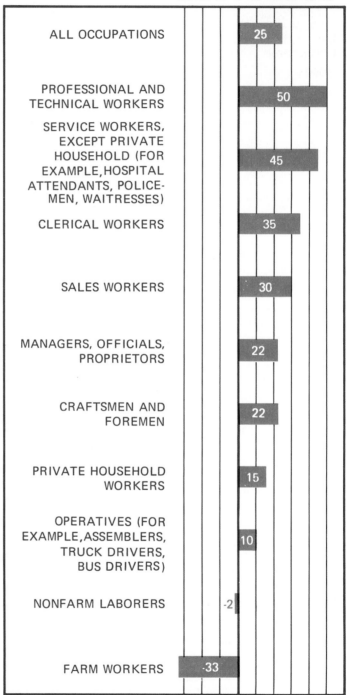

FIGURE 10-1

**LABOR FORCE GROWTH
BY SELECT CATEGORIES
1968-1980**

In the decade of the 1970s, the demand for some types of workers, such as professional, technical, service, clerical, and sales personnel, will increase at a faster pace than other categories of workers.

SOURCE: *U.S. Manpower in the 1970's*, Department of Labor, 1970.

the labor force. In fact, the total labor force increased 9 million between 1940 and 1945, whereas it increased only 3 million in the previous five years, 1935-1940. This rapid increase came from three major sources: (1) Many housewives entered the labor force to do what they could for the war effort; (2) a large number of school-age youngsters took jobs after school hours or left school to take full-time jobs; (3) about 2 million men formerly not in the labor force entered it during the war. Many retired workers were drawn back into the labor force. Many others formerly considered unemployable because of any number of minor physical, mental, or other handicaps found suitable jobs in our expanding economy.

EMPLOYMENT ACT OF 1946

Although expansion of the labor force helped to fill the gap during World War II, trouble was expected after the war when veterans returned looking for jobs. It was thought that many of the wartime entrants into the labor force would hesitate to leave. As the veterans returned, a surplus labor force might emerge, especially with the decline of war production. Many housewives, however, were content to leave the factories and offices to return to their homes. The youngsters reluctantly returned to school, and the oldsters went back to their fishing. Nevertheless, the civilian labor force did expand by 6.5 million within two years after World War II.

Some economists and government officials anticipated that we might have between 6 and 8 million unemployed in 1946, mainly because of the termination of wartime industries. But the economy made a quick transition from wartime to peacetime production. In spite of the fact that government defense spending decreased more than $50 billion from 1945 to 1946, the slack was taken up by large consumer spending, expanded business investments, and strong foreign demand for our products. As a result, the GNP fell only moderately in 1946. Unemployment averaged 2.3 million for the year and never exceeded 4 million in any one month.

Nevertheless, the fear that widespread depression and unemployment might occur with the cessation of war production led, in part at least, to the passage of the Employment Act of 1946. With the long depression of the 1930s still in mind, many private citizens, organizations, and public officials supported the Act, which was introduced shortly after the end of World War II.

Purpose of the Act

The original suggestion, known as the Full Employment Bill, would have made the government directly responsible for maintaining full employment.

The Bill called for a planned federal budget designed to take up any employment slack in the economy. However, this proposal was not enacted. The Employment Act passed by the Congress merely declared that it was the government's policy to use measures at its disposal to promote maximum employment, production, and purchasing power. Section Two of the Act reads as follows:

> The Congress hereby declares that it is the continuing policy and responsibility of the Federal Government to use all practicable means consistent with its needs and obligations and other essential considerations of national policy, with assistance and cooperation of industry, agriculture, labor and State and local governments, to coordinate and utilize all its plans, functions, and resources for the purpose of creating and maintaining, in a manner calculated to foster and promote free competitive enterprise and the general welfare, conditions under which there will be afforded useful employment opportunities, including self-employment, for those able, willing, and seeking work, and to promote maximum employment, production, and purchasing power.

Council of Economic Advisers

The Employment Act set up a Council of Economic Advisers (CEA) appointed by the President with the advice and consent of the Senate. Each appointee must be a person who is exceptionally qualified to analyze and interpret economic developments and to appraise programs and activities of the government in the light of the provisions and objectives of the Act. The Council reports to the President on current and foreseeable trends. He in turn makes recommendations to the Congress for a program to promote a high level of employment.

Specifically, it is the function of the Council "to develop and recommend to the President national economic policies to foster and promote free competitive enterprise, to avoid economic fluctuations or to diminish the effects thereof, and to maintain employment, production, and purchasing power." The Council has the further function to analyze existing programs and activities of the federal government for the purpose of determining whether they are consistent with the express purpose of the Act to maintain maximum employment.

The Act also requires the President to transmit to Congress an annual *Economic Report* within sixty days after the beginning of each regular Congressional session. The President customarily delivers this report in January of each year.

Joint Committee on the Economic Report

The *Economic Report* and all supplementary reports, when transmitted to Congress, are referred to the Joint Committee on the Economic Report.

This Committee, established by the Employment Act of 1946, is composed of seven members of the Senate appointed by the President of the Senate and seven members of the House of Representatives appointed by the Speaker of the House. The functions of the Joint Committee are: (1) to make a continuing study on matters relating to the *Economic Report*; (2) to study means of coordinating programs in order to further the policy of the Employment Act; and (3) to file a report with the Senate and the House containing its findings and recommendations with respect to each of the main recommendations made by the President in his *Economic Report.*

Meaning of Full Employment

The Act says nothing about a guarantee of jobs, but it does oblige the government to take steps designed to maintain a high level of employment. Nowhere does the Act define what is meant by maximum or full employment. The 1953 *Economic Report* of the President, however, did state specifically that "Under the Employment Act, full employment means more than jobs. It means full utilization of our natural resources, our technology and science, our farms and factories, our business brains, and our trade skills."

It is expected that we will have some unemployment in the economy at all times because of quits, discharges, relocation, and other causes. This type of unemployment has come to be known as frictional unemployment. Included in the frictionally unemployed are a number of people who are chronically unemployed because of certain mental, physical, or psychological handicaps. Over the past several years a number of committees and government agencies studying the problem have come to the conclusion that the amount of frictional unemployment should be about 4 percent of the civilian labor force. Thus, in 1946 full employment would have been construed as a condition in which 2 million or less in the labor force were unemployed. Today, however, with a civilian labor force approaching 90 million, normal frictional unemployment can be expected to be in the vicinity of 3.6 million. This 4 percent unemployment, or 96 percent employment figure, is cited frequently as a major goal for our economy.

The 4 percent unemployment figure has to be observed with certain reservations, however. Even when unemployment is higher than our national goal, some categories of workers will still be experiencing minimum unemployment. Notice in Table 10-7 that in October, 1973, when total unemployment was 4.5 percent, unemployment among white workers and among married men was 3.7 percent and 3.3 percent, respectively. On the other hand, when we reach the full employment level we should not become complacent. At that level there are still sore spots of unemployment in the economy. In January, 1966, for example, when the economy was in a state

TABLE 10-7	Category	Unemployment Rates	
		1973	1966
UNEMPLOYMENT RATES FOR VARIOUS CATEGORIES OF WORKERS IN THE LABOR FORCE	Married Men	3.3%	2.0%
	White Workers	3.7	3.5
	Males	3.9	3.4
(October, 1973, and January, 1966)	Total Labor Force	4.5	4.0
	Females	5.6	5.0
	Nonwhite Workers	7.7	7.2
	Male Teen-agers (16-19)	12.6	12.0
	Nonwhite Teen-agers	26.6	24.7

SOURCE: *Employment and Earnings*, November, 1973, and February, 1966.

of full employment with unemployment averaging 4.0 percent, unemployment among females was slightly higher at 5.0 percent. Notice also the much higher rates of unemployment among nonwhite workers, 7.2 percent, male teen-agers, 12 percent, and nonwhite teen-agers at 24.7 percent.

In the early 1970s it was suggested by various authorities that perhaps our full employment standard of 96 percent employment and 4 percent unemployment was outmoded. It was proposed that the structure of the labor force was shifting and that a new unemployment figure might be more appropriate as a measure of full employment. There are currently in the labor force a larger number of youngsters, women, and minority workers than existed in the late 1950s when we came to accept the 4 percent figure. These groups usually have higher rates of unemployment than the labor force as a whole. Consequently, it is argued that if more weight were given to these categories in establishing a normal unemployment figure today, it would be a figure in excess of 4 percent, perhaps 4.5 to 5 percent. A 4.6 percent figure, for example, was suggested in the 1974 *Economic Report of the President*.

Administering the Act

In the first 27 years of operation under the Act, the government had several challenges in maintaining full employment as a result of depressions or recessions in the economy. The first came in 1949, the second in 1953-1954, the third in 1958, the fourth in 1960-1961, and the fifth in the recession of 1970. Then, too, there was the problem of "nagging unemployment" in otherwise prosperous years from 1961 to 1965, as well as the economic slowdown in late 1973 and continuing into 1974.

In the first two depression periods, unemployment approached the 6 percent mark. In 1958, it exceeded 7 percent. In each case, the use of monetary, fiscal, and psychological measures by the federal government helped to send the economy back toward a high level of employment. In all instances, organized labor urged the government to take more drastic action to alleviate what the unions considered critical unemployment. On the other hand, many business organizations and a few labor leaders felt that the degree of unemployment was not too severe.

In the 1960-1961 recession unemployment again exceeded 5 million or 7 percent of the labor force. In fact, in the seven-year period 1958-1965 unemployment averaged nearly 6 percent of the labor force and was below 5 percent in only three months during that time. The problem of maintaining full employment in the early 1960s was aggravated by record annual additions to the labor force and the occurrence of a high rate of job displacement resulting from rapid technological advancements. Consequently, President Kennedy in his 1962 and 1963 *Economic Reports* called for strong measures to move the economy back toward maximum employment. Subsequently, several bills were passed in Congress, such as the Area Redevelopment Act, the Manpower Development and Training Act, the Emergency Public Works Act, the Economic Opportunity Act, the Appalachian Regional Development Act, and a tax credit bill to stimulate new investment. A record income tax reduction of $11 billion, $5 billion in excise tax cuts, and deficit federal budgets of more than $10 billion annually were also used as a means of attaining maximum production, employment, and income under the Employment Act of 1946.[2]

Another challenging period arose in the recession of 1970 when the economy was characterized by unemployment between 5 and 6 percent with inflation of more than 5 percent annually. Caution had to be exercised in order that measures designed to expand employment would add only minimal inflationary pressures to the economy. A similar situation was developing with the slowdown in the economy early in 1974.

Although in recent years there has been growing agreement as to the meaning of full employment, considerable disagreement still arises over the degree of government action that should be taken to prevent either moderate or widespread unemployment from developing. Should government action, including deficit spending, be used to maintain employment for all those in the labor force, including the suburban farmers who are working in the cities on industrial jobs, students who are working after school, the sons and daughters who are living at home, and the 20 million married women with husbands present who are holding down jobs?

[2] For more details on these measures see pages 329-338.

These are difficult questions. The Employment Act does not give us the answers. Let us hope that unemployment never reaches such a critical state that we are forced to make decisions on them. In the meantime certain supporters of the Act would like the role of the government to be spelled out more definitely. They would like to see concrete procedures set up by the Act for automatic action whenever unemployment reaches a certain level as specified by the Council of Economic Advisers. It has also been recommended by several noted economists, including a former chairman of the CEA, that the Act should be amended to include stabilization of the price level as a major part of its policy.

The President each year in his *Economic Report* gives a review of economic developments of the past year, the economic outlook for the forthcoming year, and an outline of the measures he would like to see adopted in order to obtain or maintain the objectives of maximum production, employment, and income. The President's message is then followed by a more detailed analysis of the current economic situation by the Council of Economic Advisers.

In its first 27 years of operation, the Council of Economic Advisers proved to be a worthwhile and successful organization. It has performed its task well and has greatly enlightened congressmen, administrators, businessmen, and many others on economic matters involved in the operation of the economy. The Employment Act of 1946 plays an important role in the operation of our economy. Both parties, Democrat and Republican, support the main objectives of the Act.

Regardless of which party happens to be in office in the future, it appears that the Employment Act is here to stay. Regardless of the makeup of its membership, provided they are competent economists, the recommendations of the CEA will not change drastically. We seem to be destined to use monetary, fiscal, and psychological policies in an endeavor to stabilize the economy and to maintain a high level of employment.

UNEMPLOYMENT RATES IN THE UNITED STATES AND ELSEWHERE

Before concluding our chapter on employment, it may be enlightening to compare unemployment rates in the United States with those elsewhere in the world. The faster economic growth rates of several other nations, such as West Germany, Japan, and France, often have been compared to the slower rate of economic growth in the United States. Likewise, critics have called attention to the fact that unemployment in many other countries is lower than it is in the United States. Studies in the early 1960s revealed that after making adjustments for differences in counting procedures among the various nations, unemployment rates in the United States were still considerably higher. Recent figures for the early 1970s indicate that this is still true, as shown in Table 10-8.

TABLE 10-8

INTERNATIONAL COMPARISONS OF UNEMPLOYMENT RATES FOR SELECT YEARS

(Adjusted to United States Definition)

Country	1960	1967	1970	1972
United States	5.5%	3.8%	4.9%	5.6%
Canada	7.0	4.1	5.9	6.3
France	2.2	3.0	2.2	2.9
West Germany	0.7	1.0	0.6	0.9
Great Britain	2.4	3.1	3.9	6.3
Italy	4.3	3.8	3.5	4.0
Japan	1.4	1.4	1.1	1.4
Sweden	—	2.2	1.5	2.7
Australia	—	1.4	1.4	2.2

SOURCE: *Statistical Abstract of the United States,* 1970 and 1973.

SUMMARY

1. There are over 210 million people in our nation today of whom about 90 million are in the labor force, working or seeking work.

2. The following trends in the labor force are observable: (1) a decrease in teen-age employment; (2) a decrease in the percentage of older workers; (3) a decline in agricultural employment; (4) an increase in the number and percentage of women in the labor force; (5) a decrease in the percentage of unskilled workers; (6) a fairly stable percentage of the labor force engaged in organized labor activities over the past few decades; (7) an overall increase in the size of the labor force; and (8) a relatively stable labor force participation rate.

3. For all practical purposes the economy is considered to be in a state of full employment when unemployment is 4 percent or less.

4. The Employment Act of 1946 requires the administration in office to use measures to promote maximum production, maximum employment, and maximum income.

5. The Employment Act provided for the establishment of the President's Council of Economic Advisers and requires the President to transmit to Congress an annual *Economic Report.*

6. Unemployment rates are generally higher in the United States than they are in most other major industrial nations.

NEW TERMS

Unemployed labor force, *p. 201*
Employed civilian labor force, *p. 201*
Employment Act of 1946, *p. 207*

Council of Economic Advisers, *p. 208*
Joint Committee on the Economic Report, *p. 208*

1. On what basis can we justify the membership of the armed services as a part of the total labor force?

2. Do you think that everyone who is seeking work should be classified as an unemployed member of the labor force? Why or why not?

3. Do you see any family social problems arising in connection with the increasing number and percentage of married women entering the labor force? Explain.

4. Do you think there should be a nationwide compulsory retirement age in order to make more opportunity for youngsters coming into the labor force?

5. Do you think that unemployed wives, whose husbands are still working, should be counted as unemployed in our national employment figures?

6. Technological development and automation displace approximately 2 million workers annually. Does this mean they all become unemployed? Explain.

7. Do you agree with the general objective of the Employment Act of 1946? Why or why not?

8. In calculating unemployment do you think an adjustment should be made in the unemployment figure to reflect the element of underemployment (short workweek) for the labor force as a whole? Why or why not?

9. Should price stabilization be made a dual objective of the Employment Act? Why or why not?

10. Do you agree that an economy with 4 percent or less unemployment is for all practical purposes a full-employment economy? Why or why not?

**SUGGESTED
READINGS**

"At Last, a National Manpower Policy." *Business Week* (August 7, 1971).

Chandler, Lester V. *America's Greatest Depression, 1929-1941.* New York: Harper & Row, Publishers, 1970.

Department of Labor. *U.S. Manpower in the 1970's.* Washington: U.S. Government Printing Office, 1970.

Flash, Edward S., Jr. *Economic Advice and Presidential Leadership.* New York: Columbia University Press, 1965.

Hailstones, Thomas J., Bernard L. Martin, and Frank V. Mastrianna. *Contemporary Economic Problems and Issues.* Cincinnati: South-Western Publishing Co., 1973. Chapter 2.

"High Employment Without Inflation." *Review.* St. Louis: Federal Reserve Bank of St. Louis (September, 1971).

Humphrey, Hubert H. *War on Poverty.* New York: McGraw-Hill Book Company, 1964.

"Jobs for All: Any Time Soon?" *U.S. News and World Report* (August 2, 1971).

Moore, Geoffrey H. *How Full Is Full Employment?* Washington: American Enterprise Institute for Public Policy Research, Study No. 14 (July, 1973).

"Nixon's New Economic Policy: Impact on Wages." *Business Week* (August 30, 1971).

"The U.S. Labor Force Projections to 1985." *Monthly Labor Review* (August, 1970).

PART THREE

Economic Activity
and Monetary Policy

11

Money and Economic Activity

PREVIEW Changes in the money supply significantly affect the level of economic activity and the price level. Indeed, an increase in the money supply can lead to an increase in production, employment, and income if the economy is in a state of less than full employment, while at full employment such an increase can cause inflation. On the other hand, a decrease in the money supply will lead to a decrease in the level of economic activity and/or a decline in the price level.

The Consumer Price Index (CPI) is used to measure such price changes in the United States economy. However, certain reservations must be kept in mind when using the CPI for this purpose. Generally, price changes in the United States as measured by the CPI have increased at a rate comparable to the average price change in the other major nations of the world.

Among other functions, money serves as a standard of value and a medium of exchange. Certainly it is the lubricant of the economic system. Money not only facilitates trade and exchange, but also affects the GNP, employment, and the price level.

THE SUPPLY OF MONEY AND ECONOMIC ACTIVITY

For many years economists held that money was passive and that it had no substantial effect on the economy. The Classical economists, for example, maintained that one had to remove the veil of money in order to understand how the economy really operated. For this reason they frequently gave explanations of the economic system in terms of a barter economy. The Classical economists' conception of money as passive can be demonstrated by the following type of explanation. Assuming full employment, they asked what would happen to the economy if everyone woke up one morning to find double the amount of money in their pockets, cash registers, and vaults. Since people could not buy any more goods and services because of the full-employment conditions, they held that the value of goods in terms of money would double but the total real purchasing power of each individual would remain the same. Although this is a simplified version of their concept, Classical economists truly underemphasized the role of money in the economy.

On the other hand, certain economists today reverse the situation, for they visualize money as a panacea for a wide variety of economic ills. Thus, they advocate manipulation of the money supply to remedy many undesirable economic conditions.

What is the effect of money on the economy? Perhaps a synthesis of the two extremes is in order. From observation and analysis it is evident that money is not a completely passive element. Nevertheless, it is also quite true that money cannot cure all or even most of the weaknesses of a particular economy. Empirical data suggest that changes in the volume of money can have a definite effect on the circular flow of economic activity and on the price level, depending on conditions existing in the economy.

The Monetary Equation

One way to explain the effects of money on the economic system is in terms of its quantity. The *quantity theory of money* attempts to explain the relationship between the quantity of money and the price level. It assumes that any money received will be spent directly or indirectly to buy goods and services. This is known as the *transactions approach*.[1] The theory is expressed by a simple formula:

$$MV = PT.$$

The various elements in the formula represent the following:

M = total money supply. For our purpose this includes all types of money and credit.

V = velocity of circulation or the number of times that the money supply turns over in a given period of time, such as a year. Velocity can be determined by dividing total spending in the economy by the money supply.

P = price level or the average price per transaction. We should keep in mind that P has no practical value and that this formula is merely a tool of analysis to determine the relationship between the four elements, M, V, P, and T, rather than a formula to determine the actual price level.

T = total transactions in the economy. For our purpose we will

---

[1] Another approach is known as the *cash balance approach*. It puts more emphasis on what individuals and firms do with their money—that is, spend it or save it—and the length of time they may hold on to their money. According to the cash balance approach $M = KTP$, or $P = \dfrac{M}{KT}$, where M = the money supply, T = total transactions, P = the price level, and K = that fraction of a year's transactions over which the community desires to hold cash. In this formula K is the reciprocal of V in the transaction formula.

consider it as the total physical units of goods and services produced and sold in the economy over a given period of time.[2]

The formula merely states that money times velocity (which equals the total spending in the economy) is equal to the average price times the total units produced or sold. In short, the formula states that total spending in the economy is equal to the cost of goods and services produced and sold. The formula $MV = PT$, then, is a simple truism, with either side roughly equivalent to the GNP.

Stable Money Supply. We can do more with the formula in a different form, especially if we isolate the element of price. This can be done by simple conversion. It follows mathematically that if $MV = PT$, then:

$$P = \frac{MV}{T}.$$

With this formula in mind, let us assume for a very simple example that the total money supply in the economy is \$10, that this amount of money is spent 8 times, and that 8 transactions takes place. If $M = \$10$, $V = 8$, and $T = 8$, then $P = \$10$, the average price per transaction. When these values are used in the formula, they appear as follows:

$$P = \frac{MV}{T}$$

$$P = \frac{\$10 \times 8}{8}$$

$$P = \frac{\$80}{8} = \$10.$$

Other things remaining unchanged, if the money supply remains constant, there will be no change in either the level of economic activity or the price level. In short, the level of economic activity will remain stable.

Increase in Money Supply. Now let us see what effect a change in the money supply can have on the level of economic activity and the price level. Since the effect of a change in the money supply will depend to some degree on the status of employment, let us assume a full-employment economy.

---

[2] In this formula, $MV = PT$, it is possible to let T represent either (1) the sale of goods and services currently produced over a given period of time, or (2) the sale of all goods and services whether currently or previously produced. Since the latter concept includes the resale of all commodities previously produced, such as used cars, old homes, and second-hand furniture, it is a much broader concept. The first concept is used here because the level of production and employment, and therefore the circular flow, is affected primarily by the sale of goods and services currently being produced rather than by the resale of old commodities.

This implies full employment of resources and productive capacity as well as manpower. Under such conditions if we increase the money supply, higher prices will result. When we are at full employment, it is almost impossible to increase the total output of goods and services quickly, that is, in the short run. Therefore, the additional money available can be used by individuals and firms only to bid against each other for existing goods and services. This situation will cause prices to rise, which means that inflation will result. Suppose the money supply increases from $10 to $20. In terms of our formula:

$$P = \frac{M \times V}{T} = \frac{\$20 \times 8}{8}$$

$$P = \frac{\$160}{8} = \$20.$$

Since total spending will now increase to $160, provided the velocity remains the same, and since our transactions cannot increase, the price level will rise to $20 per unit. An exception may occur if individuals for some reason decide to save the additional money they receive rather than to spend it. In such a case the velocity would decrease. For example, if the money supply were increased to $20 but $10 of it were hoarded and not used, the value of transactions, PT, would remain at $80. The hoarding constitutes a reduction in velocity. In calculating the formula under such conditions, the velocity would be equal to 4($80 ÷ $20 = 4) instead of 8. However, this is a rare occurrence. Usually an increase in the money supply in a full-employment period leads to higher prices, and rising prices usually induce people to spend their incomes faster in order to beat the price increases, which in turn increases V, the velocity. For this reason sizable increases in the money supply in a full-employment economy are likely to result in serious inflation.

If we make the same change under different circumstances, we will obtain different results. Suppose the money supply expands while the economy is operating at less than full employment. A larger money supply will lead to an increase in the level of economic activity instead of a rise in prices. For example, if the money supply were increased to $20, the additional money could be used to purchase additional goods and services that could be produced by the unemployed manpower, unused resources, and idle capacity existing in the economy. If the GNP were increased in proportion to the increase in the money supply, the price level would remain unchanged. Thus, the formula would have new values (M and T would be doubled), but the same price level would result:

$$P = \frac{M \times V}{T} = \frac{\$20 \times 8}{16}$$

$$P = \frac{\$160}{16} = \$10.$$

If we continued to enlarge the money supply, the economy might eventually reach full employment. Then any further increases in the money supply would again bring on higher prices. For example, if we push the money supply to $25 while V and T remain at 8 and 16 respectively, the price level will move up to $12.50 per unit, as shown:

$$P = \frac{M \times V}{T} = \frac{\$25 \times 8}{16}$$

$$P = \frac{\$200}{16} = \$12.50.$$

Fluctuations in the velocity of money can have an effect similar to changes in the money supply. In fact, the two frequently go hand in hand to compound the effect on the price level. Individuals and firms could negate any influence of the money supply upon prices and/or economic activity if they were to hoard so as to compensate for expansions in the money supply.

Decrease in Money Supply. A decrease in the amount of money can bring about a reduction in the level of economic activity and/or a decline in the price level. For example, if we were to reduce the money supply to $7 while V remained at 8 and T at 8, the price level would fall to $7, as can be seen from the formula:

$$P = \frac{M \times V}{T} = \frac{\$7 \times 8}{8}$$

$$P = \frac{\$56}{8} = \$7.$$

This situation assumes, of course, that the goods would be sold at lower prices rather than piled up as inventories.

Such a movement in the price level could be offset by an increase in velocity. This will often occur in a full-employment economy when individuals are in a frame of mind to buy goods and services. They will increase velocity to compensate for a relative scarcity of money. Many times, however, a decrease in the money supply and in the velocity work hand in hand to aggravate a price decline, especially during a recession period.

Changes in Money Supply and Velocity. In general, we can say that an increase in the money supply will lead to an increase in the GNP if we are in a state of less than full employment. This will mean more production, employment, and income to those in the economy. If we are at full employment, however, an increase in the money supply will merely lead to inflation. On the other hand, a decrease in the money supply will lead to a decrease in the level of economic activity and/or a decline in prices.

Similar effects can be brought about by variations in the *velocity of money*. If individuals spend their incomes faster, the turnover of the money supply will be greater and total spending will be increased. This could lead to an increase in the GNP and/or a price increase, depending upon the circumstances existing in the economy. A decrease in velocity, which results from spending at a slower rate, will lead to a decrease in production and/or a decline in prices. Thus, it would appear that the amount and flow of the money supply can affect business activity in the economy. This was demonstrated in the circular flow as we saw in Chapter 5.

As was stated previously, whenever investment is greater than savings, an increase in economic activity or a rise in prices follows. In the absence of a change in velocity, however, an increase in the money supply may be required to give businessmen the means by which they can increase their investment. Such an increase of investment may come about from an increase in the amount of currency or through an increase in bank credit. Likewise, government deficit spending is frequently financed by means of an increase in the money supply generated by bank credit. On the other hand, a decrease in investment or the accumulation of a government surplus could result in a diminution of bank credit, which would reduce the money supply.

From all indications, then, there is some relationship between investment-saving decisions and the status of the government budget on the one hand and changes in the money supply on the other. Furthermore, a change in any of these may affect the GNP and the price level. These relationships are shown in summary form below.

Conditions Tending Toward a Stable Flow of Economic Activity and a Stable Price Level:	Conditions Tending Toward a Decrease in the Level of Economic Activity and/or a Decline in the Price Level:	Conditions Tending Toward an Increase in the Level of Economic Activity and/or an Increase in the Price Level:
$I = S$	$I < S$	$I > S$
Balanced Budget	Surplus Budget	Deficit Budget
Stable Money Supply	Decrease in Money Supply	Increase in Money Supply

Effect of Changes in Money Supply in the United States

Whatever the source of money, a definite correlation can be found among the level of production, the price level, and the money supply. Table 11-1 shows the relationships that have existed for the past few decades. From the table it can be observed that during the period 1939 to 1942 the money supply increased approximately 50 percent. During that time the GNP in constant (1958) dollars increased from $209 to $298 billion, an increase of 43 percent. Thus, expansion in the money supply was accompanied by greater economic activity. It should be remembered that this was possible because we had more than 9.5 million men unemployed, we had ample unused resources, and we were utilizing less than 75 percent of our productive capacity early in 1939.

TABLE 11-1

MONEY SUPPLY, GNP, AND THE PRICE LEVEL

1939-1973

(Selected Years)

(1) Year	(2) Money Supply (Billions)	(3) Total Production (Current Dollars)	(4) Consumer Price Index [1]	(5) GNP (Constant 1958 Dollars)
1939	$ 36	$ 91	41.6	$209
1942	54	158	48.8	298
1946	110	209	58.5	313
1948	112	258	72.1	324
1952	127	345	79.5	395
1956	137	419	81.4	446
1960	142	504	88.7	488
1965	168	685	94.5	618
1967	183	794	100.0	675
1970	221	976	116.3	722
1972	256	1,152	125.3	790
1973	269	1,288	133.1	837

SOURCE: *Federal Reserve Bulletin* and *Survey of Current Business*, 1943-1974.

[1] 1967 = 100.

Therefore, when the increased money supply was used to increase consumer spending and investment, business firms put the unemployed men to work, utilizing surplus resources and absorbing idle capacity to produce the additional goods and services demanded by individuals and firms in the economy. In the meantime the price level increased moderately. Serious inflation threatened only when we nearly reached the full-employment stage in mid-1942. However, the inauguration of material controls, price and wage controls, and other measures in that year prevented the price level from increasing as much as it otherwise would have in the subsequent war years.

The table also shows that during World War II, or the period between 1942 and 1946, the money supply doubled. However, there was very little increase in the amount of goods and services produced by the nation's economy during that time. In terms of real GNP, production increased from $298 billion to $313 billion, an increase of only 5 percent. From the full-employment stage we had reached in mid-1942, it was difficult to increase production because of the relative shortage of manpower, resources, and productive capacity existing in the economy during that period. The economy would have experienced severe price increases had it not been for economic controls, including price ceilings.

When Congress finally decontrolled prices in June of 1946, inflationary pressures pushed prices up rapidly. As a result of pent-up consumer demand, the large holding of liquid assets (cash, bonds, and other assets easily converted into cash), high incomes, the need for business expansion, and the large foreign demand for American products, the price level skyrocketed 35 percent in a 24-month period. Since the economy was still in a state of full employment, we were unable to produce additional goods and services demanded by individuals and firms. Naturally consumers and firms were bidding against each other for the limited amount of goods and services available. This in turn forced prices upward. Much of the increased spending that caused the rise in prices was delayed action resulting from additions to the money supply which had occurred in previous years.

Between 1952 and 1956 increased productivity resulting primarily from technological development and managerial efficiency tended to hold prices relatively stable. But the price level rose again during the mid-1950s. It was relatively stable, however, from 1958 to 1965, a period of "nagging unemployment," with the price level increasing about 1.3 percent annually and real production increasing on an average of 4 to 5 percent. During this period increases in the money supply showed a closer relationship with the level of business activity than they did with the price level, because the economy had been operating at less than full employment.

But prices did begin to rise in 1966 when we reached full employment. Between 1965 and 1973 the money supply increased at an average annual rate of 7.6 percent and the price level increased 5.1 percent annually. In some of these years, prices increased as much as 8.8 percent. Prices during this period, which will be examined in more detail in Chapter 16, rose due to a combination of demand-pull and cost-push inflationary pressures. The data indicate once again that sizable increments to the money supply during periods of full employment tend to be inflationary.

MONEY SUPPLY AND ECONOMIC ACTIVITY—A GRAPHIC ANALYSIS

We have emphasized on a number of occasions that changes in the money supply can affect the level of economic activity and the price level. These changes can now be related to the determination of economic activity discussed in Chapters 7 and 8. Suppose the Fed, through various measures, brought about an increase in the money supply. This would lower the rate of interest, induce more investment, and, in turn, increase the level of economic activity. The rise in production, employment, and income would be beneficial to the economy. If the economy were at full employment, however, an increase in the money supply would merely bring about a rise in the price level. The various steps involved can be traced through in the schematic outline of the income-expenditure analysis shown on page 170 of Chapter 8. A decrease in the money supply, of course, would have the opposite effect.

The effect of a change in the money supply can also be related graphically through the investment-saving approach. We saw in Chapter 8 that liquidity preference was the desire to hold assets in the form of cash, as opposed to interest-bearing bonds or stocks. Furthermore, liquidity preference is related to both the quantity of money and the rate of interest. Since liquidity preference is a relative concept, generally the larger the quantity of money the less the liquidity preference; and the smaller the quantity of money the stronger the liquidity preference. The rate of interest, on the other hand, is the price that must be paid to induce the saver to part with liquidity. Consequently, the stronger the liquidity preference the higher the interest rate; and the weaker the liquidity preference the lower the interest rate that must be paid to induce the saver to give up his funds. Thus, a liquidity preference schedule can be drawn as shown in Figure 11-1(a).

As the quantity of money is increased, as shown in Figure 11-1(a), liquidity preference will be lower and interest rates will fall. A decline in interest rates, as shown in Figure 11-1(b), will generate an increase in investment to I_1. Finally, as indicated in Figure 11-1(c), the increase in investment brings about a higher GNP with a corresponding increase in employment. If the economy is at full employment, however, inflation will result. A decrease in the money supply will have the opposite effect.

MEASURING THE PRICE LEVEL

Among the goals or objectives of our economy stated previously are full employment, stable prices, a healthy rate of economic growth, and

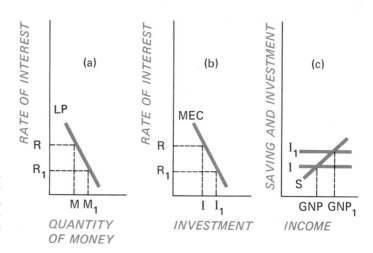

FIGURE 11-1

MONEY, INTEREST RATES, AND ECONOMIC ACTIVITY

An increase in the money supply lowers the rate of interest. A lower interest rate generates higher levels of investment. Higher levels of investment bring about an increase in economic activity (GNP).

equilibrium in our international balance of payments. In order to attain these goals we follow certain economic policies. In turn there are guides we use in determining what fiscal, monetary, and psychological measures should be implemented to attain our economic objectives. Three major guides are: (1) the size and growth of the GNP; (2) the level of employment or the rate of unemployment; and (3) movements of the price level. Not only should we understand the nature and structure of each of these indicators, we should be aware of any reservations that should be kept in mind when using them as guides to the implementation of monetary and fiscal measures. The GNP and the rate of unemployment we analyzed earlier. The price level, which we shall examine directly, is measured by a number of different price indexes.

Price Indexes

Prices are constantly in a state of flux, moving up or down depending on the state of business conditions. In some instances almost all prices may be moving in the same direction, while at other times some may be rising while others decline and still others remain stable. It would be nearly impossible to remember all these individual movements. Even if one could remember all the individual price changes, it would be of no great consequence. It is interesting to know that shoe prices are going up, that rents are coming down, and that potato prices are moving sideways; but such details may cause one to lose sight of what is happening to prices generally in the economy. It is convenient, therefore, to have some device by which the general or average movement of all prices in the economy is measured. For this reason, we construct price indexes.

Whether we observe the wholesale price index, the consumer price index, the spot market price index, or one of the numerous other price indexes calculated by various government agencies, it is worthwhile to know something about the makeup of such an index. A *price index* compares the average of a group of prices in one period of time with the average of the prices of the same group of commodities or services in another period. Prices are determined for a base period, and the prices in all subsequent periods are measured in relation to the base period prices. The Bureau of Labor Statistics, which calculates the Consumer Price Index, uses the *Laspeyres' formula.*[3]

Consumer Price Index. The most common and widely used index is the CPI or consumer price index. This index measures the price of a group of approximately 400 basic commodities and services out of the more than 1,400 required by an average family of four in a moderate-sized industrial community. These items are weighted according to the percent of total spending applied to each of several categories, such as food, rent, apparel, transportation, and medical care. A separate index is calculated for each of the categories as well as a composite for all commodities. Indexes are calculated for each of 37 metropolitan areas and 17 nonmetropolitan urban areas as well as for the United States as a whole.

Hypothetical Index. In calculating price indexes it is essential to hold the items, the prices of which are to be measured, constant both in quantity and quality. Only in this way can an accurate price index be obtained. Table 11-2 includes a hypothetical set of figures that show the general principle by which an index is calculated.

TABLE 11-2

HYPOTHETICAL PRICE INDEX

1939-1973

Year	Commodities	Price or Cost	Price Index 1939 Base Year	Price Index 1967 Base Year
1939	a b c d e	$200	100	42
1942	a b c d e	234	117	49
1946	a b c d e	280	140	59
1948	a b c d e	342	171	72
1952	a b c d e	382	191	80
1958	a b c d e	414	207	87
1960	a b c d e	424	212	89
1967	a b c d e	476	238	100
1973	a b c d e	634	317	133

[3] In its simplest form, the formula reads: $Ri = \dfrac{\Sigma qo\ pi}{\Sigma qo\ po}$, where the qo's are the average quantities of each item used by families in the wage-earner group in the base period, the po's are the prices for these items in the base period, and the pi's are the prices in the current period.

Assume that in 1939 it cost $200 per month to buy the commodities in the five basic categories represented by the letters *a*, *b*, *c*, *d*, and *e*. The price index in the fourth column represents the comparison of the cost of the basic commodities in any year to their cost in the base year of 1939. The index for 1939 must be 100 since the cost of the commodities in 1939 was 100 percent of their cost in that year. By 1942, however, these same commodities were costing $234. This meant that the price of these commodities, in general, increased 17 percent. Therefore, the index for 1942 was 117, that is, the prices were 117 percent of what they were in 1939 ($234 ÷ $200 = 1.17 = 117%). By 1948 the various commodities cost $342 and prices were 171 percent of what they were in 1939. In 1967 the price index reached 238, and was at 317 in 1973, which meant that prices had more than trebled in the period 1939-1973.

As you can see, the index gives us a means of comparing the prices at any time with the level that existed in the base year. The index for any given year can be obtained simply by dividing the cost in the given year by the cost in the base year. Any one year can also be compared with another simply by noting the change in the index.

Changing Base Year. For various reasons it is necessary to change the base year occasionally: our spending habits change over the years, new products enter the market, the proportions (weights) we spend on various categories change, and the comparison of current prices with prices in some period in the remote past may be meaningless to many individuals and businessmen. Actually the CPI was at one time based on the 1910-1914 period. In the late 1920s it was changed to a 1926 base, later on it utilized a 1935-1939 base, early in the 1950s it shifted to a 1947-1949 base, and later a 1957-1959 base was used. The Bureau of Labor Statistics is currently using a 1967 base period.

A change in the base year does not change the actual prices but merely changes the year to which current prices are compared. For example, if the base year for the index in Table 11-2 were changed to 1967, the cost of buying the commodities in 1967 would still be approximately the same,[4] but the index would read 100 instead of 238 as it did when the index was based on 1939 prices. The 1973 price index may read either 317 or 133, depending on the base period used.

The base year can be changed readily by dividing the series of data whose base is to be changed by the value for the year of the new base period. Although the cost figures in the price index, as shown in Table 11-2, are

---

[4] Some adjustment in the cost of the market basket will occur, however, if the weights given to different categories of spending change.

hypothetical, the index figures approximate the CPI data for those years. These figures could be converted into a new base year, such as 1973, simply by dividing the 1973 figure of 634 into each of the other figures in column 3. The same thing can be accomplished by dividing the 1973 index figure of 133 into the index figure for each of the preceding years (and eventually subsequent years) in column 5. Such a process, however, should not be used as a permanent substitute. For a periodic revision of current index numbers, the construction of a new index is not that simple. With changes in the basic commodities and with changes in the weights of the various commodities, the absolute cost of buying the "market basket" of goods and services may be more or less than the absolute cost of buying the former package of goods and services.

Components of the CPI. As mentioned earlier, the CPI market basket is made up of various components. These include such categories as all items, all commodities, durable goods, nondurable goods, food, apparel, all services, rent, transportation, and health and recreation. These in turn have subindexes. Since the prices of some goods and services rise faster than others, it is essential to use appropriate geographic areas and item categories when utilizing the index for specific purposes. Figure 11-2 on page 230, for example, gives some indication of how prices of services have been rising faster than the prices of commodities.

Limitations of CPI. The consumer price index merely measures the relative *change* in the cost of living, not the actual cost of living. A higher index in one city may not necessarily indicate that prices are higher in that city than they are elsewhere. It may simply mean that the cost of living has increased more rapidly in one city than it has in other cities since the base period. For example, assume that the actual cost of living for a family in City *A* for 1967 was $6,000 and the cost of living in City *B* was $7,200. Both of these costs would represent 100 for the respective cities in the base period 1967. If the actual cost of living in both cities increased by the same amount, say, $2,400, in some subsequent period such as 1974, the actual cost of living in City *A* would be $8,400 and that in City *B* would be $9,600. The cost-of-living index, or consumer price index, however, for City *A* would be 140, while that for City *B* would read 133.3. Thus, it is possible for a city with an actual lower cost of living to have a higher cost-of-living index number. The actual cost of living for a family of four in Dallas in 1972 was $10,422, while in San Francisco it was $12,324. The consumer price index in 1972 for Dallas, however, was 124.9 while that for San Francisco was 121.4 (1967 base year). Some idea of the actual cost of living can be

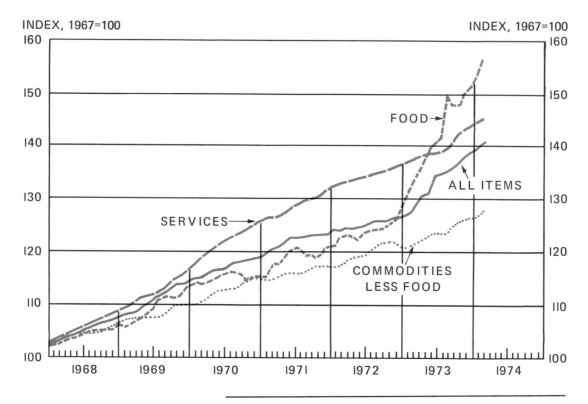

INDEX, 1967=100

INDEX, 1967=100

FIGURE 11-2

**CONSUMER PRICE INDEX
1968-1974**

Prices in some categories, especially services, in the consumer price index have risen faster than other categories of prices.

SOURCE: Department of Labor, Council of Economic Advisers.

		Commodities					Services		
					Commodities Less Food				
Period	All Items	All Commodities	Food	All	Durable	Nondurable	All Services	Rent	Services Less Rent
1963	91.7	93.6	91.2	94.8	97.9	92.7	88.5	95.0	87.3
1964	92.9	94.6	92.4	95.6	98.8	93.5	90.2	95.9	89.2
1965	94.5	95.7	94.4	96.2	98.4	94.8	92.2	96.9	91.5
1966	97.2	98.2	99.1	97.5	98.5	97.0	95.8	98.2	95.3
1967	100.0	100.0	100.0	100.0	100.0	100.0	100.0	100.0	100.0
1968	104.2	103.7	103.6	103.7	103.1	104.1	105.2	102.4	105.7
1969	109.8	108.4	108.9	108.1	107.0	108.8	112.5	105.7	113.8
1970	116.3	113.5	114.9	112.5	111.8	113.1	121.6	110.1	123.7
1971	121.3	117.4	118.4	116.8	116.5	117.0	128.4	115.2	130.8
1972	125.3	120.9	123.5	119.4	118.9	119.8	133.3	119.2	135.9
1973	133.1	129.9	141.4	123.5	121.9	124.8	139.1	124.2	141.8

obtained by checking the City Worker's Family Budget maintained by the Bureau of Labor Statistics for several major cities.[5]

A second limitation of the CPI has to do with quality, or improvement, of the products in the market basket. Although the BLS endeavors to construct a pure price index, economists responsible for the index are ready to

[5] See page 817 of Chapter 37.

admit that it is not always possible to ferret out all of the quality increases that creep into the market basket. As styles, models, material composition, design, and even flavor of products improve over the years, the survey takers may not be able to find a particular product identical with that used in the original market basket. To what extent the increase in the price of a standard product may be due to improvement in the product or to a pure price increase is difficult at times to ascertain. This distinction becomes all the more nebulous when annual increases in the price index are small.

Another limitation is the possibility of some built-in upward bias in the CPI. Changes in the price level are based primarily on changes in list prices. It is probable, however, that during periods of slack demand "transaction prices," prices at which goods are actually sold, are lower than the list prices. Various studies indicate that the size of the upward bias in the index approximates one to two percentage points annually.

Finally, it should be remembered that the CPI endeavors to measure changes in the prices of consumer goods and services only. Since these account for only about two thirds of the total spending in the economy, the CPI does not give a full account of what is happening to prices. It does not take into consideration changes in the prices of machinery, equipment, buildings, raw materials, or even houses. A broader price measure is the "GNP implicit deflators price," which endeavors to take into account changes in the prices of all goods and services produced by our nation's economy.

Value of Money

In addition to measuring changes in the price level, price indexes are also useful for determining the purchasing power of money. The value of money is based upon the amount of goods and services that a given amount of money will buy. If prices rise, a given amount of money will buy less and the value of money decreases. If prices fall, the value of money increases since a given amount of money will buy more. Today we usually talk in terms of changing price levels rather than in terms of changes in the value of money. You have often heard it said, however, that the value of the dollar is only 32 cents. Just what does this mean? It simply means that because of higher prices a dollar today will buy what 32 cents would have bought in the 1935-1939 period. Although the inherent value of the money is the same, its value relative to goods and services has changed.

The value of the dollar can be determined at any given time by dividing the dollar by the price index. Thus, the value of the dollar in 1939, using the then current price index, was $1.00 ($1.00 ÷ 1.00 = $1.00). In 1960 the dollar was valued at 47 cents ($1.00 ÷ 2.12 = $.47). In 1973 it was valued at 32 cents ($1.00 ÷ 3.17 = $.32). We should keep in mind, however, that the value of the dollar is only a relative comparison. There is nothing inviolable about this value. In fact, it can easily be shown that the dollar in 1973 was worth about 75 cents instead of 32 cents simply by using the base period of the current index, 1967 = 100 ($1.00 ÷ 133 = $0.75). It is possible also to make the dollar worth a dollar at any time by making the current year the base year for the price index.

Although the purchasing power of the dollar has declined since 1939, today we have many more dollars in income than we had in 1939. As a result the total purchasing power of the average individual has increased noticeably in the past 30 to 35 years. It is true that total purchasing power would be even greater if the price level had remained constant; but if it had remained stable, money incomes might not have increased so rapidly. The increases in the money incomes brought about in part the increases in prices and a decline in the value of the dollar. Unfortunately prices frequently go up as incomes rise.

We can obtain some idea of the total increase in purchasing power for the average individual from Table 11-3. In this table, the *money wage* (column 2) represents the average weekly earnings in all manufacturing industries. Column 4 is the real wage (the purchasing power of the money wage) in constant 1967 dollars. Column 5 is the percent increase in real wages over the base year, 1939. The *real wage* is determined by dividing the money wage by the cost-of-living index, that is, the consumer price index (1967 = 100). For example, the real wage for 1970 is $114.99 ($133.73 ÷ 1.163 = $114.99). This calculation in effect deflates the money wage to offset the effects of higher prices on the purchasing power of the subsequent money wage. The money wage for 1973, $165.24, was divided by the price index of 133.1% or 1.331, which deflated the money wage to $124.15 in terms of 1967 dollars.

Some interesting observations can be made from Table 11-3. Notice that the money wage nearly doubled between 1939 and 1945, but because of price increases the real wage increased by only 40 percent. The effect of price increases on the purchasing power of money is even more pronounced during the 1945-1950 period. During that time money wages **increased** almost 33 percent, whereas the real wages actually decreased by $1.11, a drop of almost 2 percent. In effect, price increases obliterated the advantages of higher wages during that period. It should be remembered that this was a period of full employment, during which it was difficult to

TABLE 11-3	(1)	(2)	(3) Percent Increase in Money Wage over Base Period (1939)	(4) Real Wage 1967 Prices	(5) Percent Increase in Real Wage over Base Period (1939)
MONEY WAGE VS. REAL WAGE 1939-1973	Year	Weekly Money Wage			
Average Weekly Earnings in Manufacturing Industries	1939	$ 23.64	—	$ 58.63	—
	1945	44.20	87	82.00	40
(1967 = 100)	1950	58.32	147	80.89	38
	1955	75.70	220	94.39	61
	1960	89.72	280	101.15	73
	1965	107.53	355	113.79	94
	1966	112.34	375	115.58	97
	1967	114.90	398	114.90	96
	1968	122.51	418	117.57	101
	1969	129.51	448	117.95	101
	1970	133.73	466	114.99	96
	1971	142.04	501	117.10	100
	1972	154.69	554	123.46	111
	1973	165.24	599	124.15	112

SOURCE: *Economic Indicators* (January, 1974), and previous issues.

increase productivity in response to the increased demand for goods and services that resulted from higher wages. Consequently, prices rose as consumers bid against each other for the scarce goods and services available.

The period 1950-1966 showed a sizable gain in real wages as the price level increased moderately. Weekly money wages increased by $54.02, or 90 percent, while the real wage increased by about 42 percent.

In 1967, however, price increases obliterated wage increases. The money wage rose by $2.56 per week, but the worker's real wage declined by 68 cents. In another year, 1969, a $7.00 weekly rise in money wages netted an increase of only 38 cents in real wages. In 1970 real wages declined $2.96 in spite of a money wage increase of $4.22 per week.

From 1939 to 1973, money wages increased nearly six times, from $23.64 to $165.24 per week. In the meantime, real wages increased about 112 percent. Although the worker's real wage did not increase as rapidly as did his money wage, there was some gain in real income despite the increase in price level. In terms of 1967 prices, the worker's money wage of $165.24 per week in 1973 would buy the same amount of goods and services that $124.15 would have purchased back in 1939, again showing a 112 percent increase in the real wage. In terms of 1939 prices, the worker's real wage during the 1939-1973 period increased from $23.64 to $50.12.

Effects of Price Changes

The economy in general has profited by the faster growth of wages over prices in the last few decades. Those whose incomes rise faster than prices actually can buy more goods and services than they could before the rise in wages and prices occurred. Some individuals, however, have been hurt by rising prices. Price increases usually bring about a redistribution of income insofar as those with fixed money incomes cannot buy as much when prices rise. This is one of the evils of inflation.

Inflation benefits those whose incomes rise with increases in business activity and prices. For example, business profits, wages of industrial workers, and salesmen's commissions are very susceptible to change. They change with increases or decreases in business activity and prices. It may be to their advantage when prices are on the rise. But since their incomes usually decline faster than do prices, they are at a disadvantage when prices are decreasing. Others are at a disadvantage during periods of rising prices. Civil service employees, bankers, some executives, schoolteachers, and pensioners are among those whose incomes tend to remain fixed or relatively stable in spite of changes in business conditions and prices. These individuals suffer from inflation but gain during a period of deflation, provided they maintain their incomes and their jobs. It seems, then, that whenever prices move substantially in either direction, inequities develop.

Changes in the price level also affect creditors and debtors, each in a different manner. Inflation is beneficial to debtors but detrimental to creditors. While deflation works a hardship on debtors, it enhances the value of the creditors' dollars. To illustrate, suppose you had borrowed $30,000 to build a home in 1960 with the stipulation that you repay the entire amount in one lump sum in 1975. In 1960 the creditor would give up $30,000 or the equivalent of a good three-bedroom home. When repaid by you in 1975, however, the $30,000 that the creditor would receive would purchase only about two thirds of the same type of home, since the cost of such homes would have risen to almost $45,000. Thus, the money with which the creditor would be repaid would have less total purchasing power than that which he gave up in 1960. On the other hand, you would be making repayment with dollars that had three fourths the purchasing power of those which you borrowed. Increased income that accompanied rising prices would have made it easier for you to repay the loan. If prices had fallen, the situation would have been reversed. You would have been repaying with dollars of greater value than those which you initially borrowed.

Inflation Here and Elsewhere

Although money income has increased faster than prices, causing purchasing power to increase, higher prices do have a considerable impact on the economy. A one percent increase in the price level, for example, means that American consumers pay over $8 billion more for the goods and services they buy during the year. This same one percent increase in prices means that businessmen expend over $2 billion more for machinery, equipment, and buildings, and, of course, things purchased by government expenditures cost over $3 billion more. Not only does a change in the price level affect current purchasing power, it also affects the value of our assets. A one percent increase in the price level depreciates the value of our accumulated savings by $5.0 billion, reduces the purchasing power of bonds held by the public by $1.0 billion, and reduces the protection of our life insurance by $15 billion. Consequently, it can be seen that any substantial changes in the price level can have far-reaching effects on the economy.

Nevertheless, price level increases in the United States have been moderate compared to those of many other nations throughout the world. Table 11-4 shows that in the years 1963-1971 the United States experienced less of an increase in its price level than did a number of other major nations. Figure 11-3 indicates that U.S. export prices during the period 1960-1972 increased at an average rate comparable to those of other major nations.

TABLE 11-4

INDEXES OF CONSUMER PRICES

1971

(Selected Countries)

(1963 = 100)

United States	132	Italy	134
Argentina	512	Japan	153
Brazil	1,268	Switzerland	135
Canada	130	United Kingdom	148
Denmark	154	Venezuela	115
France	138	Mexico	130
West Germany	127	Egypt	115
Belgium	134	Israel	155
Bolivia	156	Pakistan	144
China (Taiwan)	124	Sweden	145
Ireland	158	Uruguay	2,876
Chile	718	Indonesia	71,797

SOURCE: *Statistical Abstract of the United States*, 1973, pp. 817-818.

With some notable exceptions, most of the price increases shown in Table 11-4 have been moderate. Closer inspection of Table 11-4, however, will show that a number of nations have had serious inflationary problems in the past few decades. In the years 1963-1971 alone, for example, the

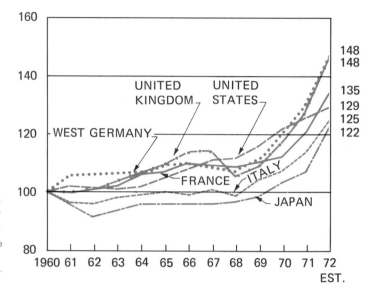

FIGURE 11-3

EXPORT PRICE INDEX
(1960 = 100)

Export prices for the United States have risen on an average with those in other major nations of the world.

SOURCE: *International Economic Report of the President,* March, 1973.

General Note: Based on export prices in U.S. dollars.

price levels in Brazil and Chile increased substantially. Chile's prices multiplied sevenfold, and in Uruguay the price index was 2,876 in 1971 compared to 100 in 1963. In the eight-year period Indonesia's rate of inflation was an astounding 71,797 percent, currently the highest in the world.

Although these rates of inflation are very serious, they by no means match the runaway inflation that occurred in post-World War I Germany. Just before the war the amount of currency in circulation in Germany was less than 3 billion paper marks. By 1924 the money supply, principally in the form of marks issued by the Reichsbank, was 1,520,510,653,710,000,000,000. (If you have trouble reading that figure, it amounts to 1.5 sextrillion.) By that time the German wholesale price level was more than a trillion times greater than it was in 1913.

SUMMARY

1. The effects of money on the level of economic activity and the price level can be analyzed by the use of the monetary equation $P = \dfrac{MV}{T}$.

2. An increase in the money supply will tend to bring about an increase in the level of economic activity during periods of less-than-full employment. During full-employment periods, however, increases in the money supply lead to inflation.

3. A decrease in the money supply can cause a decline of economic activity and/or a decrease in prices.

4. The actual price level is measured through a price index. The most widely used is the Consumer Price Index calculated by the Department of Labor on a 1967 base period.

5. The CPI can be used to determine

the value of the dollar and determine the real income of workers and families.

6. Changing price levels cause a redistribution of income. Those whose money incomes increase faster than prices experience a gain in real income. When money income increases slower than prices, real income decreases.

7. Rising prices, or inflation, tend to favor debtors more so than creditors.

8. In many countries prices have risen faster than they have in the United States economy.

NEW TERMS

Quantity theory of money, *p. 218*
Transactions approach, *p. 218*
Cash balance approach, *p. 218*
Velocity of money, *p. 222*
Price index, *p. 227*
Laspeyres' formula, *p. 227*

Consumer price index, *p. 227*
Hypothetical price index, *p. 227*
Base year, *p. 228*
Value of money, *p. 231*
Money wage, *p. 232*
Real wage, *p. 232*

QUESTIONS FOR DISCUSSION AND ANALYSIS

1. Under what conditions will an increase in the money supply have more influence on the price level than it will on the level of economic activity?

2. Distinguish between velocity and transactions in the monetary formula.

3. Is it possible for changes in the money supply and changes in velocity to move in opposite directions? Explain why or why not.

4. Do you think the money supply should be increased a specific amount each year for the purpose of financing normal increases in business activity?

5. The monetary formula serves as a tool of analysis rather than a device for constructing a consumer price index. Explain.

6. Do you think it is wise occasionally to change the base year in the consumer price index? Why or why not?

7. Assume the following: $M = \$2,000$; $V = 10$; and $T = 1,000$. Using the monetary formula, what will be the value of P? If the amount of money doubles, the velocity remains unchanged, and the transactions increase by 50 percent, what will be the new value of the price level?

8. In judging the cost of living for a particular city, can an individual rely on the consumer price index as a specific indication of how much it will cost to live in that particular city? Why?

9. As a salary or wage earner, would you prefer to have higher income or lower prices? Why?

10. If you were certain that the price level would gradually increase in the future, would you put your savings in a savings account or buy stock or property? Why?

SUGGESTED READINGS

Board of Governors of the Federal Reserve System. *Money: Master or Servant?* Washington: U.S. Government Printing Office, 1955.

Bureau of Labor Statistics. *Techniques of Preparing BLS Statistical Series*, Bulletin #993, Part I. Washington: U.S. Government Printing Office.

Gavett, Thomas W. "Quality and a Pure Price Index." *Monthly Labor Review* (March, 1967).

"New Economic Gauge (CPI) Will Affect Workers, Retirees and Business." *Commerce Today* (December 27, 1971).

"Price Stability: What Does It Mean? What Does It Cost?" *Monthly Review*. Kansas City: Federal Reserve Bank of Kansas City (March, 1971).

Rose, Peter S., and Lacy H. Hunt II. "Policy Variables, Unemployment and Price Level Changes." *Federal Reserve Bulletin*. Washington: U.S. Government Printing Office (January, 1972).

Spurr, William A., and Charles P. Bonini. *Statistical Analysis for Business Decisions*. Homewood, Ill.: Richard D. Irwin, Inc., 1967.

12

Money: Its Nature and Functions

PREVIEW The United States money supply, amounting to more than $269 billion, consists of currency plus demand deposits. Various kinds of money, such as metallic, paper, credit, and representative money, serve as currency. In order to perform its functions as a standard of value, a medium of exchange, a store of value, and a standard of deferred payment, a money must possess characteristics which give it stability and general acceptability. The largest portion of U.S. currency is in the form of Federal Reserve notes.

A nation generally adopts some type of standard for its monetary system, such as bimetallism, gold, or inconvertible paper. The United States has used various standards during its history and is currently on a modified gold bullion standard. As an international currency, the U.S. dollar in the past few years has been subject to some serious buffeting in the tempestuous seas of international finance.

Most of us use money every day. We see it, touch it, and spend it. But how many of us can define it adequately? Generally money is defined too narrowly. Some define it as the currency of a nation; others think in terms of legal tender. It is often referred to as the medium of exchange. However, such definitions automatically exclude the largest portion of our money supply—credit. In order that all segments of our money supply may be included, a broad definition is essential. Thus, we can say that *money* is anything which is commonly accepted in exchange for other goods and services.

TYPES OF MONEY

Commodity money, which was probably the first ever used, is that type in which some commodity actually serves as money. Many commodities, such as stones, cotton, shells, beads, various crops, metal, and paper, have served as money in different countries of the world over the past several hundred years. In various periods of American history, tobacco, corn, wampum, warehouse receipts, and bank notes, in addition to metal coin and paper currency, have served as money. In fact, many of these moneys were given legal tender status, which means that they were acceptable in payment of debts, both public and private.

There are two basic types of modern money, each of considerable importance: metallic money and paper money. *Metallic money* is a special type of commodity money in which some metal such as gold, silver, or copper is used. *Paper money* may or may not be backed up by gold or silver. If it is backed up by metal, paper money may be convertible—that is, the issuing agent (government) agrees to convert it into gold or silver or into other forms of money. Paper money, however, may be inconvertible. Although we have had various types of commodity money in the United States, all our currency today is in the form of coins and bills (paper money).

Each of these three types of money also may be classified according to its inherent value as (1) full-bodied money, (2) credit money, (3) representative money, and (4) demand deposits.

Full-Bodied Money

Full-bodied money is money in which the intrinsic value of the material content is equal to the monetary value (face value). For example, the inherent value of a $10 gold piece was equal to its monetary value of $10. Not only could you use the $10 gold coin to buy $10 worth of groceries, but also if the gold coin were melted down, its gold content could be sold for $10 in cash in the gold market.

Credit Money

Credit money is money in which the intrinsic value of the material content is less than the monetary value. For example, a silver dollar will purchase a $1 admission ticket to the theater, but for many years the actual value of the metal contained in the dollar was approximately 75 cents. Because of the growing demand for silver for monetary and industrial uses, in the past several years its price has risen. Consequently, the amount of silver in a silver dollar will now sell for more than 100 cents in most markets of the world. Credit money may be made of either metal or paper, or it may be in the form of checking deposits. Frequently it is referred to as *token money*. Sometimes money that is not backed 100 percent by reserves of coin or bullion is also referred to as credit money.

Representative Money

Representative money is money, usually paper, that serves in place of metallic money. It may be representative full-bodied or representative credit money, depending on which kind of money it is representing. Gold certificates that circulated in the United States prior to 1933 were a good example of the former. The silver certificate was an example of representative token money. Instead of coining all silver, the government held some in the form of bullion and issued silver certificates for circulation in the economy. Until a few years ago all of our one-dollar bills and five-dollar bills were silver certificates, but even these are now being retired. One of the advantages of representative money is that it is more portable than metallic money. At one time anyone who visited Las Vegas or Reno soon became aware of this fact. In these resort towns many business establishments, whether motel, restaurant, gas station, drugstore, or gambling casino, would give silver dollars in change when a customer paid his bills. It was very cumbersome to carry pockets full of this kind of money around. Silver certificates were much more convenient.

The government also issues credit money in the form of bills or circulating promissory notes. Sometimes it is referred to as *fiat money*, which is money backed up only by the promise of the government to redeem it or to exchange it for other types of money. United States notes, for example, are representative credit money. These were originally issued by the government during the 1860s when it was in need of money to finance the Civil War. Anticipating a short war, $150 million in greenbacks was issued. With the prolongation of the war, however, there were two additional issues of $150 million each. Thus, a total of $450 million in United States notes was printed. Since they had no gold or silver backing, the value of the greenbacks fluctuated with the fortunes of the war. At times when the Union armies were doing well in the battlefield, the greenbacks were accepted at face value. When the outcome of the war was uncertain, however, many were reluctant to accept greenbacks for fear that the Union might be defeated and might be unable to redeem the notes. Other persons, because of the risk involved, would accept the greenbacks only at a reduced value. At one point during the war, the value of the greenback fell to 35 cents. Some individuals made considerable capital gains by buying United States notes at low prices during the war and then exchanging them at their full face value after the war.

The Confederacy also issued representative credit money. Unfortunately the issuing agents, both the Confederacy and the states in the Confederacy, were unable to redeem their money after the war because of the lack of funds. As a result it became worthless. This has happened in many eras when nations have expanded the money supply with little regard to its backing.

Banks issue representative credit money in the form of notes and demand deposits. In fact, most of our currency is in the form of Federal Reserve notes, which are issued by the Federal Reserve Banks with the approval of the United States Treasury. Until a few years ago the gold reserve required for these notes was 25 percent. The other 75 percent of the backing was in the form of gold certificates, government securities, or note assets of the bank. Today there is no gold reserve requirement behind these notes.

Demand Deposits

The largest portion of our money supply is in the form of bank checking deposits, which are, for the most part, credit money. For the time being it will suffice to say that checks written against these deposits serve as money. Since the monetary value of a check is greater than the intrinsic value of the paper on which it is written, it is, of course, credit money. Furthermore, the money reserve behind checking deposits is less than 100 percent.

FUNCTIONS OF MONEY

In our complex economy money performs four important functions: (1) standard of value, (2) medium of exchange, (3) store of value, and (4) standard of deferred payment. The first two are said to be the major functions; the last two are often called secondary functions.

Standard of Value

Money serves as a standard of value or as a unit of account. This means that we can measure the value of all other commodities in terms of money. Without money it would be extremely difficult to compare the values of different commodities. How much would one horse be worth? We might say that it would be worth 6 pigs, 12 bushels of wheat, 8 pairs of shoes, or one half of a cow. Without money we would have to compare the value of the horse in terms of each article or commodity for which we might trade it. With money as a standard of value, however, we can express the value of the horse in terms of money. Since the values of all other commodities are likewise expressed in money, it is an easy matter to compare the value of the horse with any other commodity. We simply look at their respective dollar values. If the horse is valued at $150, it is equivalent in value to any other commodity or combination of commodities whose value is also equal to $150.

Medium of Exchange

In a barter economy the exchange of goods and services is extremely cumbersome. If an individual has a pig that he would like to trade for a pair of shoes, he must find someone who has a pair of shoes and wants to trade them for a pig. Thus, he has a problem of double coincidence of wants. Frequently he will have to engage in multiple exchanges in order to obtain what he wants. He may be forced to exchange his pig for two bushels of wheat, the wheat for a set of books, and the books for the shoes.

In a monetary economy the individual can simply sell the pig for cash and then spend the cash for the shoes. Thus, money serves as a medium of exchange. It is an economic catalyst. Money initiates action between buyer and seller, and it is the means by which an individual exchanges his labor indirectly for goods and services. Besides eliminating the need for a double coincidence of wants, money also facilitates the exchange of goods and services.

Store of Value

Money serves as a store of value insofar as excess goods can be converted into money and retained in that form. It may be difficult to accumulate and to hold wealth in the form of commodities, for some commodities are too bulky to store, others are perishable, and for some the cost of storing may be prohibitive. Think how inconvenient it would be if the apple grower or the automobile producer had to store his wealth in the form of surplus apples or cars instead of money. If such persons convert these goods into money, however, they can easily store their wealth. It is evident that if money is to be a good store of wealth, it must possess stability. A person would be reluctant to store his wealth in the form of money if he knew the purchasing power of the money would decline during the period in which the money was to be held.

When a nation has an unstable currency, its citizens may store their wealth in the form of some foreign currency or in gold or silver. If the value of money declines, perhaps they will be prompted to spend their wealth if it is in the form of money. Furthermore, if the price level of a nation is subject to severe fluctuations, its money will not serve as a good store of value.

Standard of Deferred Payment

In our economy, a great many purchases are made for which we do not pay cash. Instead the buyer agrees to pay the purchase price over a period of time. Usually he agrees to pay in cash and not commodities. Thus, money becomes a standard of deferred payment. A family may take 20 years to pay for a home. As the years go by and payments are made, the creditor is trusting that the money he receives will be usable and that its purchasing power will not decline to any serious extent. Therefore, in its capacity as a standard of deferred payment as well as a store of value, it is important that money be stable.

Sound money must be able to perform all four functions, and the American dollar does well in this respect. Some moneys do only a partial job. For example, the currencies of Germany after World War I, and the currency of China at one time, although serving as a unit of account and as a medium of exchange, were not used as a store of value or as a standard of deferred payment to any great extent because of their great instability and rapid depreciation. Similarly, in American colonial days it was common to keep accounts in terms of British pounds, shillings, and pence. Nevertheless, French and Spanish money circulated as a medium of exchange along with the British money. All of them were serving as a store of value and as a standard of deferred payment, but only one served as a unit of account. And in Brazil, where the price level has risen drastically in recent years, currency has been hard pressed to fulfill its functions because of the serious inflation.

MONETARY STANDARDS

A *monetary system* refers to all the kinds of money used in a nation. An essential feature of every monetary system is the monetary unit that is recognized as the basic standard of value or unit of account. In the United States the monetary unit is the dollar; in England it is the pound; in France, the franc; in Russia, the ruble; in the Philippines, the peso; and so on.

In one way or another the selection and continued use of a monetary standard has always been a problem for the nations of the world. Even after the selection of a standard, difficulties and problems arise which make it hard to maintain that standard. Let us consider, then, some of the theories and practices that relate to monetary standards.

Metallic Standards

Frequently we hear of *standard money*. If the basic monetary unit of a nation is defined in terms of gold and kept constant in terms of gold, that nation is said to be on the gold standard. If the nation's standard money is not kept constant in relation to gold or some other metal, that nation is usually considered to be on an inconvertible paper standard.

The Bimetallic Standard. A *bimetallic standard* of value exists when the unit of value, for example the dollar, is expressed in terms of either gold or silver (or any other two metals that may be selected). At one time the dollar was defined as 23.22 grains of gold or 371.25 grains of silver. The weight of the dollar in terms of each of the metals was fixed by the government. The relative values of the two metals when used for money, as indicated by their weights, is the *mint ratio*. Thus, in the above example, the mint ratio was about 1 (gold) to 16 (silver). The rate at which gold and silver exchange for each other in the market is the *market ratio*. For example, if 23.22 grains of gold would buy 348.3 grains of silver, the market ratio would be 1 to 15, respectively.

Advocates of bimetallism argue that the double standard results in more stable prices. The theory assumes that both metals will be used simultaneously as the standard of value. It recognizes that a change in the quantity of money in use will affect prices. And it holds that a greater change in the amount of money is likely to take place when there is a monometallic standard than when the standard consists of two metals linked together by an established mint ratio.

The bimetallic standard can be adopted by: (1) defining the monetary unit in terms of each of the two metals and fixing the mint ratio between the units; (2) allowing free and unlimited coinage of both metals; and (3) declaring both kinds of money to be legal tender. Under such an arrangement, both metals supposedly continue to circulate and the relative values remain the same.

In the event of an increase in the supply of one money metal, the exchange value of that metal in terms of the other would, of course, fall. But, it is argued, the cheaper metal would now be in greater demand for money uses than before. Individuals could buy up supplies of the metal at a price less than that set at the mint, have the metal coined into money, and make a profit equal to the difference between the mint and the market ratios. The increase in the demand for the cheaper metal would operate to restore the former market ratio. The assumption that demand and supply would thus automatically keep the mint and the market ratios equal is based upon what is known as the *compensatory principle of bimetallism*.

It must be conceded that the case of the bimetallists has the appearance of rationality. The compensatory principle is an adaptation of the well-recognized rule known as *Gresham's Law*. Popularly stated, the law says that an inferior or overvalued money will drive better or undervalued money out of circulation. More precisely, when two kinds of money, equal in nominal value but not equal in terms of demand, are in circulation, the less desirable will drive the better money out of circulation. The expression "Gresham's Law" is derived from the name of Sir Thomas Gresham who served for some years as financial adviser to the English Crown. In 1558 he was credited with having explained the principle of currency commonly summarized as "bad money drives out good," when he explained to the queen why newly minted coins containing more metal than old coins (which had been sweated and chipped) tended to disappear from circulation.

Gold Standards. The question often arises: Why gold? Could our money supply not be backed by something else? Yes, it could and at times it has been. But gold has a peculiar attractiveness to mankind. Not only does it glitter, but it has many artistic, decorative, and industrial uses. Since men of most nations seem ready to accept gold in exchange for other commodities, it can be used for the settlement of international balances of payments. The greatest attraction of gold as money, however, is its limited supply throughout the world and the fact that a minimum amount of 2 to 2.5 percent is added to the total world gold supply annually. If money is tied to the supply of gold, some degree of stability is imparted to the supply and the value of money. Furthermore, when several nations are on gold standards, it is easy to relate the value of different moneys to each other. Gold standards are not all identical, however. At various times three different types of gold standards have been used by nations throughout the world.

The Gold-Coin Standard. Under any type of gold standard, the monetary unit is defined in terms of gold. In the United States, for example, it was at one time defined as 23.22 grains of fine gold, or 25.8 grains of gold, nine tenths fine. Because of the pliability and softness of pure gold, gold coins usually contain an alloy to give them hardness and durability. Under a gold-coin standard gold coins circulate as currency. There is free and unlimited coinage of gold bullion. Gold coin serves as legal tender, and all money in the monetary system is convertible, directly or indirectly, into gold. Lastly, there is no restriction on the use of gold. It may be used either as money or for industrial and artistic purposes. Generally it may be converted freely from one use to the other, and there are no limitations upon the import and export of gold.

The Gold-Bullion Standard. If a government wishes to discourage the circulation of gold, it may establish a *gold-bullion standard.* In such a case money is defined in terms of gold, but gold is not coined; it is held by the government in bullion form. Money may be converted into gold under certain circumstances, however. When England entered World War I, it abandoned the gold-coin standard. When it resumed the gold standard in 1925, the law provided that gold was not to be coined and that other kinds of money in the system could be redeemed in gold bars of not less than 400 ounces, which were to be worth £3-17s.-10½d. an ounce. At the time, such a bar of gold was worth about $8,268. This limitation on the redemption privilege tended to discourage individuals from asking for gold.

The Gold-Exchange Standard. Before World War II, a nation with little gold could in effect go on a gold standard by tying its currency to that of some other nation which was on the gold standard. An arrangement was made whereby the nation not on the gold standard would convert its money into the money of a nation that was on the gold standard at a certain rate of exchange.

To illustrate the principle involved in such a *gold-exchange standard,* we can use the case of the Philippines and the United States. The Central

Bank of the Philippines made deposits in American banks, which by prior agreement would buy or sell Philippine pesos at a fixed exchange rate. The Philippine government then stabilized the peso-dollar exchange rate and consequently the peso-gold ratio by buying and selling pesos and dollars, depending on market conditions. This tie-in with gold, although indirectly, made the Philippine peso generally acceptable in international trade.

At times certain nations have found it expedient to arrange a gold-exchange standard, but the disadvantages of such a standard have eventually offset its advantages. For example, in a period of international strain and uncertainty, the government of the country on the gold-exchange standard might shift its deposits from one country to another. This might precipitate an international loss of faith in the monetary system of the country from which the deposit had been shifted.

The workability of any monetary standard or system is affected by payments made for goods imported from other countries and income received from payments for exports. At one time most economically advanced nations maintained some form of a gold-coin or a gold-bullion standard. But wars and unsettled international economic and political conditions brought about the demise of the gold standard.

Silver and Other Commodity Standards. By using silver in the same manner as indicated under the gold standards, it is possible to adopt a silver-coin, a silver-bullion, or a silver-exchange standard. The silver-coin standard, for example, has at times been widely used in Oriental countries. Silver, however, is not as stable in value as gold, and it is less convenient and less economical to handle when shipping large quantities of the metal. Other commodities besides gold and silver have at times served as money. Such items as tobacco, grain, copper, stone, and wampum have served as commodity money.

Inconvertible Paper Standards

Unlike the metallic standards, an inconvertible paper standard does not attempt to keep the value of the monetary unit constant in terms of a metal, such as gold or silver. Under an inconvertible standard the government may purchase and accumulate gold or silver at a fixed price, but it will not sell at a fixed price. Thus, it will not convert its money into a metal for the holders of the money. In some cases the government also may refuse to buy gold or silver.

Most inconvertible paper standards arose as a result of a breakdown in a nation's metallic standard. Frequently during times of war, depression, or other times of great disturbance and stress, it became difficult for a nation to meet its obligations to sell gold or silver at a fixed price because of the shortage of reserves. Such was the case with the currency of the Continental Congress, the assignats of the French Revolution, and the greenbacks of the Civil War. Likewise, during World Wars I and II practically all nations went off the gold standard, temporarily at least, and adopted an inconvertible paper standard in order to preserve their reserves, to prevent their gold from falling indirectly into the hands of the enemy, and to give the government more flexibility in expanding the money supply. In many cases when nations have used an inconvertible paper standard, eventual redemption in specie or a return to a metallic standard was taken for granted. Such was the case of the greenback period of the Civil War. In other cases, however, the currency eventually became worthless, such as the Continental currency (hence the expression "not worth a Continental") of the American Revolution, the assignats of the French Revolution, and the Confederate currency of the Civil War. After World War I, the British pound was restored to its prewar value. On the other hand, the German mark became nearly worthless, while other nations resumed payment in specie at greatly reduced parity from prewar days.

Generally nations prefer some type of metallic standard, but they seek refuge in an inconvertible paper standard when a metallic standard is unworkable or impractical for them. This is not to say that inconvertible paper standards are not good. In fact, they might be the best standards under particular circumstances. There are advantages and disadvantages to each type of standard. A key distinction between metallic and inconvertible standards is that in the former a nation's money supply is tied, directly or indirectly, to its gold or silver reserves. This establishes some definite perimeter on the amount of money that may be issued. Since this is not the case with inconvertible currencies, it is much easier to expand the money supply at the will of the government. From another point of view, the value of money and the price level are likely to be more stable with a metallic standard than they are with some inconvertible paper standard.

AMERICAN MONETARY STANDARDS

Since its inception the United States has utilized several types of monetary standards, including bimetallism, temporary inconvertible paper, and variations of the gold standard.

A Bimetallic Standard, 1792-1900

When the United States adopted the bimetallic standard in 1792, the weight of the silver dollar was fixed at 371.25 grains. It was estimated that the ratio of the market values of silver and gold—the market ratio—was

15 to 1. That is, 15 ounces of silver was worth 1 ounce of gold. Therefore, a mint ratio of 15 to 1 was adopted, which meant that the weight of the gold dollar was fixed at one fifteenth of that of the silver dollar, or 24.75 grains. There was considerable delay, however, in getting the mint into operation. In the meantime, the market ratio changed to about 15½ to 1. According to the mint ratio, silver became overvalued, and Gresham's Law began to take effect. When coined, 15 ounces of silver were equal to the value of 1 ounce of gold. The market, however, required 15½ ounces of silver to equal the value of 1 ounce of gold. As a consequence, gold, the under-valued currency, eventually disappeared from circulation. This happened because a holder of gold bullion or gold dollars could buy 15½ ounces of silver for 1 ounce of gold, have 15 ounces of the silver coined into dollars, and thus make a profit of ½ ounce of silver.

In an effort to bring the mint ratio into agreement with that of the market, Congress in the 1830s changed the weight of the gold dollar to 23.22 grains of fine gold, without making any change in the weight of the silver dollar. Subsequent events, including discoveries of rich deposits of gold and of silver, the Civil War, and changes in the monetary systems of other nations, produced changes in the market prices of gold and silver that were too drastic to be overcome by the operation of the compensatory principle.

During one period, for example, gold was overvalued at the mint compared to the market ratio and to some foreign mint ratios. In fact, silver coins were frequently exported or melted, and the silver bullion was exchanged for gold in the market. True to Gresham's Law, the overvalued gold was then brought to the mint for coinage. The inadequate flow of silver to the mint and the melting of silver coins caused a shortage of fractional silver coins. Consequently, Congress in 1853 reduced the silver content of silver coins in an attempt to eliminate the profitability of exporting or melting the coins.

During the Civil War the United States for very practical reasons went on an inconvertible paper standard when it ceased to redeem its paper money in specie. It stayed on an inconvertible paper standard until 1879. Although legally it returned to a bimetallic standard, for all practical purposes it went on a gold standard at that time by making all its money redeemable in gold. Furthermore, previous demonetization of silver had occurred when the Coinage Act of 1873 practically eliminated the coinage of silver dollars. Finally, after several decades of controversy regarding the merits of bimetallism and the efforts of the "silver interests" to maintain bimetallism, the United States officially adopted the gold standard when Congress enacted the Gold Standard Act in 1900.

The Gold Standard, 1900-Present

Although for a few decades we had been on a *de facto* (in fact) *gold standard*, it was not until the passage of the Gold Standard Act of 1900 that we went on a *de jure* (by law) *gold standard*. This ushered in the so-called golden age of the gold standard, which lasted until the outbreak of World War I. During this period not only the United States but most major nations were on the gold standard. The most important of these nations were on the gold-coin standard, while others were on a gold-bullion or a gold-exchange standard. The heyday of the gold standard, however, was interrupted by the outbreak of World War I. As the war commenced, all belligerent nations abandoned the gold standard by refusing to redeem their currencies in gold and by prohibiting gold exports. In many cases, gold coin and bullion were called in by the government or the central bank. This was done in order to prevent the nation's gold supply from falling into the hands of the enemy, to conserve the gold supply for the purchase of essential war materiel, to continue operations in the foreign exchange markets, and to maintain enough gold reserve to preserve confidence in the nation's money supply.

In spite of various problems involved, most nations returned to some form of gold standard during the 1920s, with the United States leading the way in 1919 by establishing the prewar gold content of the dollar. Britain, Switzerland, France, Germany, and other nations followed some years later. Gold coin, however, virtually disappeared except in the United States as most countries adopted gold-bullion or gold-exchange standards. In general, these postwar standards were managed to a greater extent than were the prewar gold standards. High tariffs and other restrictions initiated for various reasons, heavy war debts, an unstable flow of international lending, and other disturbances made the operation of the gold standard more difficult, especially in serving its function in settling the international balance of payments.

With the coming of the Great Depression in the early thirties, countries abandoned the gold standard in great numbers. The United States and France were the only major nations left on the gold standard at the beginning of 1933, and the United States went off it later that year. The general abandonment of the gold standard was precipitated in large measure by an international financial panic that was caused by foreign creditor demands for repayment in gold of short-term liabilities such as bank deposits and short-term government and commercial obligations. In most cases, the total credit demands exceeded the gold stock held by individual nations. Since they did not have the ability to redeem these obligations in gold, many nations were naturally forced to go off the gold standard.

Devaluation. With a 50 percent drop in the GNP between 1929 and 1932, an increase of unemployment from 1.5 million to more than 12 million, widespread bank failures, and a rash of commercial bankruptcies taking place, foreigners began large-scale withdrawal of short-term liabilities from the United States. Although our gold supply, then about 40 percent of the world total, remained above $4 billion, we lost over $270 million of gold in February and March of 1933. Under these conditions, we joined the parade and abandoned the gold standard on March 6, 1933, when the President placed an embargo on gold exports. Subsequently we returned to a gold standard, but it was feared that reestablishment of the dollar at the old gold content and full convertibility would lead to such an extensive gold drain that it would seriously affect the abilities of the banks to issue credit and would jeopardize our opportunity for domestic economic recovery.

After calling in practically all of the nation's gold held by citizens, businesses, banks, and other organizations, the United States returned to the gold standard on January 30, 1934. The new gold standard, however, differed substantially from that in operation prior to March, 1933.

1. According to the Gold Reserve Act of 1934, the value of the dollar in terms of gold was reduced. The gold content of the new dollar was 13.71 grains compared to the previous content of 23.22 grains, a reduction of approximately 40 percent. Consequently, the price of gold was increased from $20.67 to $35 per ounce. This meant that the gold supply, then worth nearly $4.2 billion, increased in dollar value by $2.8 billion to $7 billion.
2. Gold was, in effect, nationalized with some minor exceptions, and no currency in the United States was to be redeemed in gold.
3. The coinage of gold ceased, and all existing gold coins in the hands of the Treasury were converted into bullion.
4. Individuals and firms were prohibited from holding, transporting, exporting, or otherwise dealing with gold except under regulations specified by the Secretary of the Treasury.

Although a number of other nations, such as France, Belgium, Holland, and Switzerland, subsequently returned to the gold standard, each had devalued its currency and introduced considerable management into its monetary system. By the outbreak of World War II, gold had lost much of its appeal, and most of the gold standards were of a gold-bullion or a gold-exchange type. No major nation had returned to a gold-coin standard, and most nations of the world were on an inconvertible paper standard. Of course, during World War II the entire world went off the gold standard.

Many nations after World War II returned to a form of the gold standard under the auspices of the International Monetary Fund, but most of these gold standards were limited, and with the exception of the United States, the redeemability of currency for gold, even for international or industrial purposes, was severely limited in most nations throughout the world.

The Gold Avalanche. Although gold-economizing measures, such as the use of gold-bullion and gold-exchange standards, were prevalent in the early and mid-1930s, a wave of gold hit the world, especially the United States, in the latter part of the decade. The causes for this increase in the gold supply are multifold. First, a higher price of gold encouraged its production. During the 1930s the annual physical output of gold more than doubled, and the value of the newly mined gold more than doubled the world's supply of gold. A second cause of the increased gold supply was trade expansion with the Orient, which paid for its imports in large part with gold. The gold supply was further increased by the melting of scrap gold, which now brought a greater monetary reward to the seller.

While the world was experiencing a substantial increase in the gold supply, the United States was enjoying an even greater influx of the precious metal. The amount of gold held in the United States rose from approximately $7 billion immediately after devaluation of the dollar in 1934 to $22 billion at the end of the decade. It continued to increase in the 1940s, peaking at $24.5 billion in 1949. Although our economy did obtain some of its newly acquired gold from increased production and the melting process, the bulk of its increase, more than $16 billion, resulted from gold imports. This was due not only to a favorable balance of trade, but more so to the flight of capital that took place in Europe because of unsettled economic and political conditions preceding World War II. By 1949 the United States held 69 percent of the world's gold supply. Due to the scarcity of goods and services in many nations throughout the world after World War II, especially in the war-damaged nations, there was a great demand for American dollars as foreigners sought them in order to buy American products. In fact, during this time of dollar shortage there was a greater demand for American dollars than there was for gold. Consequently, there was a limited amount of gold drain from the United States.

Decline in U.S. Gold Stock. Circumstances favorable to the gold influx changed, however, in the decade of the 1950s. War-torn nations rebuilt their economies and increased their production of goods and services. American prices rose, making our products more expensive to foreigners. We encountered more competition in world trade markets. Because of these events, our favorable international balance of trade was made less favorable.

As the U.S. spent more money to maintain military installations overseas, granted more foreign aid, and Americans increased their investments abroad, the dollar shortage shrunk. Our international balance of payments became negative, in spite of a continued favorable balance of trade. The dollar shortage was eased and many foreigners began converting American dollars into gold. This caused a gold outflow from our nation that continued until 1972. By the late 1950s, our deficit balance of payments exceeded more than $3 billion annually. In fact, in the period 1958-1960 our adverse balance of payments exceeded $11 billion, and during that time we lost about $5 billion in gold and financed the rest of the deficit by increasing foreign holdings of short-term dollar assets. By July of 1968, our total gold reserve had dwindled from its peak of $24.5 billion in 1949 to $10.7 billion. This change in our gold holdings and those of the rest of the world are shown in Table 12-1 and Figure 12-1.

TABLE 12-1

GOLD RESERVES OF CENTRAL BANKS AND GOVERNMENTS

1949-1973

Year	Estimated World Total [1] (Millions)	United States (Millions)	International Monetary Fund (Millions)	Rest of World (Millions)	United States of Total (Percent)
1949	$35,410	$24,563	$1,451	$ 9,396	69
1950	35,820	22,820	1,495	11,505	64
1951	35,970	22,873	1,530	11,567	64
1952	36,000	23,250	1,692	11,055	65
1953	36,425	22,091	1,702	12,630	61
1954	37,075	21,793	1,740	13,540	59
1955	37,730	21,753	1,808	14,170	58
1956	38,235	22,058	1,692	14,485	58
1957	38,960	22,857	1,180	14,925	59
1958	39,860	20,582	1,332	17,945	52
1959	40,185	19,507	2,407	18,270	49
1960	40,525	17,804	2,439	20,280	44
1961	41,150	16,947	2,077	22,125	41
1962	41,275	16,527	2,110	22,640	40
1963	42,310	15,596	2,312	24,400	37
1964	43,060	15,471	2,179	25,410	36
1965	43,225	13,806	1,869	27,285	32
1966	43,185	13,235	2,652	27,300	31
1967	41,600	12,065	2,682	26,855	29
1968	40,905	10,892	2,288	27,725	26
1969	41,015	11,859	2,310	24,845	29
1970	41,275	11,072	4,339	25,865	27
1971	41,160	10,206	4,732	26,220	25
1972 (Dec.)	44,890	10,487	5,830	28,575	23
1973 (Sept.)	44,880	10,487	5,826	28,565	23

SOURCE: *Federal Reserve Bulletin* (February, 1974), and previous issues.

[1] Excludes U.S.S.R., other Eastern European countries, and Mainland China.

General Note: Represents reported gold holdings of central banks and governments and international institutions, unpublished holdings of various central banks and governments, estimated holdings of British Exchange Equalization Account based on figures shown for United Kingdom, and estimated official holdings of countries from which no reports are received.

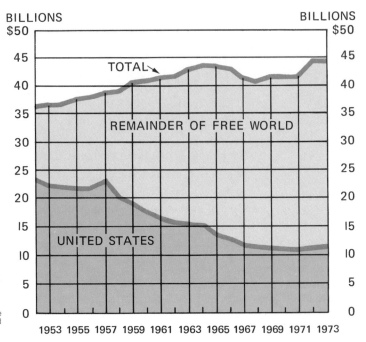

BILLIONS $50

45

40

35

30

25

20

15

10

5

0

TOTAL

REMAINDER OF FREE WORLD

UNITED STATES

BILLIONS $50

45

40

35

30

25

20

15

10

5

0

1953 1955 1957 1959 1961 1963 1965 1967 1969 1971 1973

FIGURE 12-1

OFFICIAL UNITED STATES AND WORLD GOLD HOLDINGS

The gold reserves of the United States have declined from 59 per-cent of the Free World total at the end of 1957 to 29 percent at the close of 1967. Currently the figure is 26 percent. Total official Free World holdings declined in 1966, 1967, and 1968 for the first time since 1935. These losses were due mainly to the purchases of gold by private speculators and hoarders through the London gold pool, most of which was supplied by the U.S.

SOURCE: *Gold and the Balance of Payments*, The First National Bank of Chicago, July, 1968, and *Federal Reserve Bulletin* (February, 1974).

Table 12-1 indicates that the world's gold supply increased from $35.4 billion to $43.2 billion during the period 1949-1965. During that time, however, the gold holdings of the United States dwindled by approximately 50 percent, and the percent of the world's gold supply we held decreased from 69 to 32 percent. Increased production and shifts in gold holdings resulted in sizable amounts of gold flowing into such nations as Belgium, France, West Germany, Italy, the Netherlands, Switzerland, and even the United Kingdom.

Some authorities viewed the gold drain with alarm. As a means of arresting the gold outflow from the United States, numerous measures were suggested: reduction of overseas military spending, decreases in foreign aid, adoption of more tying clauses to our aid, accelerated export promotion, buy American plans, and taxes on American investments abroad. In fact, a number of such measures were invoked by the federal government in an effort to ease the outflow of gold in the 1960s. Some monetary authorities suggested devaluation of the dollar as a means of correcting our deficit balance of payments position and reversing the drain of gold. In 1965 our 25 percent gold reserve requirement behind Federal Reserve Bank deposits was eliminated in order to free more gold for use for the international support of the dollar and the settlement of deficits in the balance of pay-ments. In 1967 a further proposal, to reduce or eliminate the 25 percent gold cover (reserve) behind Federal Reserve notes, was discussed in Congress. At that time about $11 billion of our $12 billion gold supply was serving as reserve behind our money supply. This left about $1 billion as free reserve that could be used for the settlement of dollar claims. Early in 1968 this measure was passed. Although it was not felt that we would need all $11 billion to make gold payments in exchange for dollars, it was suggested that there would be a great psychological advantage in letting the rest of the world know that we stood ready to use all our gold to support the dollar. The extent of these foreign dollar claims vis-à-vis the U.S. gold stock is shown in Figure 12-2. Furthermore, it was becoming evident that with continued increases in our money supply over the next few years our current gold holdings would be inadequate to maintain the 25 percent reserve ratio.

On the other hand, some monetary authorities looked upon the gold drain from the United States simply as a normal reaction in international

FIGURE 12-2

U.S. GOLD STOCK, AND FOREIGN DOLLAR AND SHORT-TERM INVESTMENT HOLDINGS

Foreign dollar holdings—deposits in U.S. banks and short-term investments—climbed from less than one half of the U.S. gold stock at the end of 1951 to nearly three times the stock at the close of 1967. A further gold outflow in early 1968, before the London gold pool was closed, raised the multiple to over three times. Even though U.S. gold holdings since that time have remained fairly steady, dollar holdings have risen to over six times the U.S. gold stock.

SOURCE: *Gold and the Balance of Payments*, The First National Bank of Chicago, July, 1968, and *Federal Reserve Bulletin* (February, 1974).

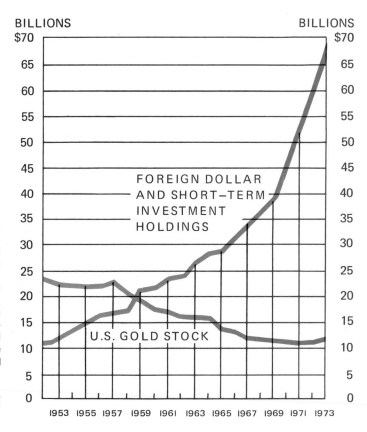

economics. They suggested that any nation is sure to gain and lose gold at various times and under certain conditions. They held that the better distribution of gold and the improved convertibility of several of the foreign currencies resulting from our gold drain would promote and facilitate world trade.

Since many other nations were having difficulties with deficit balances of payments and gold flows, it was frequently suggested that our gold outflow problem in the United States was merely symptomatic of a more basic and widespread problem—a shortage of *international liquidity*. At that time the primary means of settling international balances of payments was through the flow of American dollars, British pounds, and gold. Since world trade had increased at a much faster pace than the increase in dollars, pounds, and gold, it had become more difficult for nations and banks to obtain these forms of international liquidity.

To ease the gold drain from the United States, several interested nations of the world agreed in 1968 to the adoption of a two-tier gold price, one price for monetary purposes and one price for the free gold market. In short, instead of trying to keep both prices at $35 per ounce, it was decided to let the free market price of gold fluctuate. At the same time, these ten nations agreed not to supply the free market with gold. Prior to this the central banks of some of these nations had supplied gold to the free markets and, in turn, used dollars to buy gold from the United States in order to replenish their gold reserves. The Gold Pool nations also agreed to stop purchasing gold for monetary purposes in an effort to divert gold into the free market. By increasing the supply relative to demand, they hoped this would keep the *free price of gold* in line with the *monetary price* of $35 per ounce.

In 1969 the shortage of international liquidity was eased when the major financial nations of the world, through the International Monetary Fund, agreed to the creation of $9.5 billion in *Special Drawing Rights*, otherwise known as "paper gold." Since SDRs can be used for the settlement of international payments, this move took much of the pressure off the demand for dollars and gold. This, along with the two-tier gold price and other measures, helped to reduce the speculation in gold and bring the free market price of gold, which had reached $42.50 per ounce, down to the monetary price of $35 per ounce by December, 1969.

Continued large deficits in the U.S. balance of payments, the probability in 1971 of a deficit balance of trade for the first time in this century, and a weakening of the value of the dollar vis-à-vis the German mark led to renewed speculation about the devaluation of the dollar. This caused the free price of gold to rise above $42 per ounce by the summer of 1971. Finally, in August, 1971, President Nixon announced, among other sweeping changes in domestic and foreign economic measures, that the United

States Treasury would no longer sell gold for dollars. Furthermore, he imposed a 10 percent import surcharge on most dutiable items entering the United States.

In early 1972, the U.S. import surcharge was modified and the U.S. dollar was devalued by 8.57 percent when Congress officially raised the price of gold to $38 per ounce. As a part of the international accord, the Japanese agreed to revalue the yen, and the mark and the guilder were to continue to float (seek their own levels through market forces) before new exchange values were to be set for them. The French franc and the British pound were to hold their previous par values.

The United States balance of payments failed to improve to any substantial degree in 1972. Moreover, the international monetary authority failed to come up with any further solutions to the world monetary problems, and the position of the American dollar vis-à-vis foreign currency, especially the mark and the yen, continued to deteriorate. Consequently, in February, 1973, the United States again devalued. This time the value of the dollar was decreased by 10 percent and the monetary price of gold raised to $42.22 per ounce. Although it was anticipated that this second devaluation would eventually bring more stability to the international monetary scene, it failed to do so. Thus, the Committee of Twenty (C-20), representing the 20 leading financial nations of the world, sought a solution to the world monetary problems. Among other things, it was interested in a new parity system between world currencies, and some members sought the return of U.S. dollar convertibility into gold, SDRs, or other reserve currencies. In spite of several meetings it failed to find a solution in 1973. Furthermore, the decision of Arabian oil-producing nations to limit oil shipments abroad and to raise prices further disrupted world monetary stability. Japan, especially hard hit by the oil embargo, in effect devalued the yen early in 1974. France, a strong opponent of devaluation, finally decided in January, 1974, to permit the franc to float for six months. There was speculation that other nations might devalue or go to the float. By March, 1974, speculators had driven the free price of gold above $175 per ounce.

HOW GOLD IS MONETIZED

Naturally gold is important to our money supply. Although we are no longer on a gold-coin standard, our dollar is defined in terms of gold and we operate on a modified gold-bullion standard. Under the Gold Reserve Act of 1934, private persons are not permitted to hold any gold in monetary form;

but until 1965 gold was a required reserve for Federal Reserve Bank deposits, and until 1968 gold served as a reserve for our *Federal Reserve notes.*

Gold produced in the United States or sold to us by foreigners enters our money supply indirectly through the Federal Reserve System. When the Treasury buys gold, it pays for it by drawing on its deposit account at the Federal Reserve Bank. In doing so, the Treasury credits an equivalent amount to the gold certificate account of the Bank in order to provide a basis for restoring its deposit account at the Bank. Prior to 1968 the Federal Reserve had to hold a stipulated amount of gold behind its notes. But instead of holding gold, it could hold gold certificates. Thus, when the Treasury bought gold, it provided the gold certificate reserve for the Banks, and this reserve became the basis for Federal Reserve notes. These notes constitute the bulk of our nation's currency. It must be pointed out, however, that currency is only a fraction of our total money supply.

On the other hand, increased holdings of gold certificates by the Reserve Banks were required as a basis of expanding member bank credit, which added to the potential money supply of the nation. Since the gold certificate reserve that had to be held against Federal Reserve notes and deposits was only 25 percent prior to 1965, it is easy to see that a $1 billion increase in the gold supply could readily result in a $4 billion increase in bank reserves. An outflow of gold had the opposite effect unless offset by some other measure, such as a decrease in member bank reserve requirements, Federal Reserve purchases of securities in the open market, or a decrease in the gold reserve required behind Federal Reserve notes and deposits. The effect of a gold outflow was minimized also when the Federal Reserve was holding gold certificates in excess of that required by law. In such case, an outflow merely resulted in a decrease of the Federal Reserve's so-called *free gold reserves.*

AMOUNTS OF MONEY

Today all the money in the United States is credit money. The total amount of money in the economy is approximately $269 billion including the currency and coin held by the banks. Of this about one fourth, or $70 billion, is in the form of currency, that is, coins and bills. The remainder, $199 billion, is in the form of demand deposits. These deposits are considered as money because checks written on them can be used to purchase goods and services.

Of the total currency, $62 billion, or about 88 percent, is in the form of Federal Reserve notes. These notes are issued by the 12 Federal Reserve Banks. Formerly each note was secured by 25 percent gold. Today they are still backed to some extent by gold certificates with most of the remainder secured by government securities.

Silver certificates for decades were the second most important type of currency in the economy. Perhaps they are the most familiar to us since practically all the $1 bills and nearly one third of the $5 bills were of this type. Silver certificates had made up about 5 percent of the total currency. These certificates were issued by the Treasury against silver it purchased in the market, and they were backed up by either silver dollars or silver bullion. In 1963, however, the Treasury started to replace silver certificates with Federal Reserve notes. The silver bullion released in the process is used for striking silver coins at the mints.

The $321 million in United States notes, often called *greenbacks*, is mostly in the form of $2, $5, and $10 bills. Although when they were originally issued they were secured only by the promise of the government to pay, they are now secured by $156 million in gold bullion.

There is also a small quantity of other types of bills in circulation. These include *National Bank notes*, which were issued by the various national banks and secured by government bonds deposited with the Comptroller of the Currency. In this category also are *Federal Reserve Bank notes*, which are like the National Bank notes except that they were issued by the Federal Reserve District Banks. In addition, there is about $1 million in *Treasury notes* of 1890 still outstanding. All three are now obligations of the United States Treasury and are secured 100 percent by other types of money. They are, however, in the process of being retired, along with silver certificates.

The remainder of the currency is composed of silver and minor coins, which include dollars, half dollars, quarters, dimes, nickels, and pennies. In spite of our $7.0 billion in coins, business establishments have been experiencing some coin shortages in the past several years.

Our currency, all of which is legal tender, can be classified as shown in Table 12-2. This is the currency that we use in the everyday transactions of

TABLE 12-2

UNITED STATES CURRENCY IN CIRCULATION

November, 1973

(Millions)

Total	$70,296
Federal Reserve Notes	$61,991
United States Notes	321
Standard Silver Dollars	727
Fractional Coins	6,969
Federal Reserve Bank Notes	⎫
National Bank Notes	⎬ 288
Silver Certificates	⎭

SOURCE: *Federal Reserve Bulletin* (February, 1974).

the economy. It is the type of money used to buy groceries, pay the rent, purchase clothing, cover medical expenses, pay taxes, and deposit in the bank.

In addition to counting currency and demand deposits as money, some monetary authorities have suggested that savings (time) deposits should be included in our money supply. This suggestion has some merit insofar as savings can be withdrawn and spent. Others, however, contend that savings are put in a bank or savings institution to avoid spending and, therefore, should not be counted as a portion of the money supply. Furthermore, savings deposits are not created, such as demand deposits can be, and therefore do not add to the total money supply. Nevertheless, for analytical purposes the money supply is now classified as: M_1, composed of currency and demand deposits; M_2, which includes M_1 plus time deposits at commercial banks other than large time certificates of deposit (CDs); and M_3, which includes M_2 plus deposits at nonbank thrift institutions. Shown in Table 12-3 are the various categories of our money supply.

TABLE 12-3

MEASURES OF THE MONEY STOCK

January, 1974

(Billions)

M_1	$269	(currency plus demand deposits)
M_2	574	(M_1 plus time deposits at commercial banks other than large time CDs)
M_3	898	(M_2 plus deposits at nonbank thrift institutions)

SOURCE: *Federal Reserve Bulletin* (February, 1974).

SUMMARY

1. There are various types of money, such as commodity money, metallic money, and paper money.

2. Money has four basic functions: it serves as a standard of value, as a medium of exchange, as a store of value, and as a standard of deferred payment.

3. The major types of monetary standards are the bimetallic standard, the gold standard, and the inconvertible paper standard.

4. There are three variations of the gold standard: gold-coin, gold-bullion, and gold-exchange.

5. The United States originally adopted a bimetallic standard, but eventually changed over to a gold standard. It now uses a modified gold-bullion standard.

6. There has been a substantial drain of U.S. gold reserves in recent years as foreigners have converted dollar claims into gold holdings.

7. In an attempt to correct its deficit international balance of payments and arrest the gold outflow, the U.S. devalued the dollar in 1972 and again in 1973.

8. At the present time the money supply in the United States amounts to approximately $269 billion, of which $70 billion is in currency and the remainder in the form of demand deposits at commercial banks.

QUESTIONS FOR DISCUSSION AND ANALYSIS

1. Distinguish between full-bodied money and credit money.

2. What is the major advantage of representative money?

3. During a period of serious inflation, which two of the functions of money are least likely to be served? Why?

4. Under a bimetallic system, if the mint ratio of silver to gold were 16 to 1 and the market ratio were 17 to 1, what effect would this have on the coinage of the two metals?

5. Give an application of Gresham's Law in a modern economy.

6. Distinguish between a gold-coin and a gold-bullion standard.

7. What is the primary distinction between a metallic standard and an inconvertible paper standard?

8. What arguments can you give for the adoption of a bimetallic monetary standard?

9. What are some of the major advantages of the gold standard?

10. Why did the U.S. gold stock decline in the decade of the sixties?

11. How much gold is behind our money supply at the present time?

12. The estimated world gold supply increased from $41.2 billion in 1971 to $44.9 billion in 1972 and 1973. What accounted for this jump in the gold supply?

13. Has the U.S. resumed the gold convertibility of its dollar?

SUGGESTED READINGS

Commission on Money and Credit. *Money and Credit: Their Influence on Jobs, Prices and Growth*. Englewood Cliffs, N.J.: Prentice-Hall, Inc., 1961.

Dusenberry, James S. *Money and Credit: Impact and Control*. Englewood Cliffs, N.J.: Prentice-Hall, Inc., 1964. Chapters 3-4.

Federal Reserve Bank of Chicago. *Modern Money Mechanics*. Chicago: Federal Reserve Bank of Chicago, 1968.

Fellner, William. *The Dollar's Place in the International System*. Washington: American Enterprise Institute, 1972.

Friedman, Milton. *Dollars and Deficits*. Englewood Cliffs, N.J.: Prentice-Hall, Inc., 1968.

Klise, Eugene S. *Money and Banking*. Cincinnati: South-Western Publishing Co., 1972. Chapters 7 and 21.

"Money Stock." *Business Review*. Dallas: Federal Reserve Bank of Dallas (September, 1972).

Robertson, D. H. *Money*. New York: Pitman Publishing Corporation, 1948.

13

The Banking System and the Creation of Credit

PREVIEW   The largest and most volatile portion of the U.S. money supply is in the form of demand deposits. Demand deposits arise when someone deposits money into a checking account or when they are created through bank loans. Granting loans in the form of demand deposits adds to the nation's money supply. The ability of the banks to create demand deposits is affected by the money reserve that banks are required to hold in support of their deposits. The higher this money reserve requirement, the less credit the bank can extend in the form of demand deposits. This reserve requirement and other regulatory measures are under the control of the Federal Reserve System.

The United States experienced several different banking eras prior to the establishment of the Federal Reserve System. The Fed, as the Federal Reserve System is known, is an autonomous government agency consisting of 12 Federal Reserve Banks, about 5,700 member banks, an Open Market Committee, a Board of Governors, and several other minor organizational structures. Through various measures the Fed can control the amount and flow of money. Consequently, it can have a definite effect on the level of economic activity and the price level.

In the last chapter we learned about the currency component of the money supply. But individuals and firms do not always use currency to make purchases and pay their bills. More often than not a bill is paid by writing a check. Since checks serve as money, the total checking or demand deposits in our banks must be counted as a part of the money supply. Not all checking accounts, however, arise as a result of a deposit of currency by the check writer. Some checking deposits are created through bank credit.

CREATION OF CREDIT

In spite of the fact that demand deposits comprise the largest part of our money supply, they are the most mystifying part of it. Demand deposits are credit money. There are two types of demand deposits. A *primary deposit* is one that arises when an individual puts currency or checks into his checking account. Such deposits are considered as part of the money supply.

An increase in total deposits is offset, however, by any decrease in the currency outside banks that is also counted as part of the money supply.

A *derivative deposit* arises, on the other hand, when a person borrows money from the bank. It is so called because the deposit derives from the loan. Instead of giving the borrower cash, the bank may open a checking account for the individual. The checks he writes against this account serve as money. The bank honors the checks even though the individual puts no cash of his own into the bank. Nor does the bank necessarily put any cash into his account. Thus, there has been an increase in the money supply to the extent of the checks written. Because of the complexity of the monetary aspect of demand deposits, let us build up its explanation gradually, moving from personal IOUs, through bank notes, and finally to demand deposits.

Personal IOUs

Assume that Farmer Jim Smith needs $5,000 to buy foodstuffs, seed, and fertilizer, and to pay the help that he must hire to run his farm. Suppose that Jim requests his grocer to accept an IOU with the promise that he will pay when the crops are harvested. If the merchant does not know Jim or if he doubts his ability to repay the IOU, he will refuse Jim's offer. Jim may encounter the same difficulty when he tries to buy seed and fertilizer from the supplier. When he attempts to hire workers, he may endeavor to pay them in IOUs, with the promise to redeem the IOUs when the crops are harvested. The workers, however, may protest that they will be unable to buy food, clothing, shelter, and family necessities with Jim's IOUs. What Jim is really trying to do is to obtain credit, but because he is unknown, there may be uncertainties about his ability to repay. Since his personal IOUs are not negotiable, he will find it extremely difficult to operate on credit. But if Jim could get his IOUs accepted in exchange for groceries, feed, fertilizer, labor, and other necessary goods and services, his IOUs would be serving as a form of money.

Bank Notes

Since in our example Farmer Smith is unable to use his own credit, let us assume that he goes to the only bank in the community to borrow funds. In discussing his problems with the bank official, he will be told that if he wants a loan, he will have to put up collateral. Jim has a farm and equipment valued at $10,000, which he pledges as collateral for a $5,000 loan. For safety purposes, collateral in excess of the amount borrowed is generally required. If the loan is for one year, Jim will be asked to sign a note payable to the bank stating that he will repay the $5,000 plus 6 percent interest ($300) at the end of the year.

If the bank gave Jim $5,000 in legal tender currency, he could easily buy the commodities needed. People would certainly accept the currency without question. If the bank would lend cash, however, its ability to make loans and thus to make profit in the form of interest income would be limited. Suppose that the bank has $200,000 in cash reserves. If the bank were to lend all the money at 6 percent, it would make only $12,000 a year in interest. It was this limitation which led banks to search for a more profitable method of lending money. They found it in the use of bank notes, which were common during the last century.

Instead of giving Jim currency from its cash reserves, the bank might give him its IOU in the form of a bank note. In such a case the bank merely issued a note printed on fancy paper which stated that the bank would pay to the bearer, on or after a certain date, the particular sum of money stated thereon. Such notes, which were exchangeable for United States currency, were generally accepted as money by individuals and organizations in the community. Because the notes were negotiable, they were accepted in exchange for currency or commodities. Members of the community generally were willing to accept a bank note (the bank's IOU in effect) whereas they probably would reject Jim's IOU. Furthermore, whether they realized it or not, those who accepted the notes were protected by the fact that if Jim failed to pay his loan, the bank could sell his collateral in order to obtain the money to pay off the notes.

Since the notes served as money, any increase in the issuance of bank notes as a result of bank loans increased the money supply. Furthermore, since the bank could easily print notes, it was not limited in the amount of the loans that it could make. Instead of having $200,000 in cash to lend, the bank could lend $500,000, $1,000,000, or more in the form of bank notes. The more it lent, the more it made in interest charges. Thus, there was a strong incentive for the banks to make loans. From the bank's point of view, $1,000,000 in loans of this kind at 6 percent, yielding $60,000 a year in interest, was more profitable than lending $200,000 in cash at 6 percent, which yielded only $12,000 per year. In addition, the bank could hold its $200,000 in cash reserves. This process is demonstrated in Figure 13-1 on page 266.

After the notes had circulated for one year, the bearers could present them at the bank for redemption in Treasury currency. But who actually paid the notes? The bank? Not quite. If the notes were to be redeemed on Tuesday, March 2, Jim was scheduled to make repayment of his loan prior to that time, let us say on Monday, March 1. The funds for repayment of the loan were provided from the sale of Jim Smith's crop. Thus, when Smith paid the $5,300 ($5,000 principal plus interest of $300), the bank simply

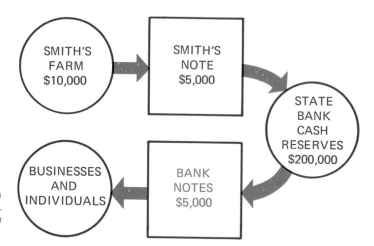

FIGURE 13-1

**LOAN MADE THROUGH
PROCESS OF BANK NOTES**

The bank notes are used by Smith
in payment for goods and services.
They circulate as money in the
community.

took the $5,000 and paid the note holders. The remaining $300 became income for the bank. This whole process could be accomplished without the bank's using one cent of its own money. It would merely be lending its credit or good name to the process.

Of course, if the notes were redeemable prior to the date on which Jim had to repay his loan, the bank would have to use some of its reserve funds in order to pay the notes. The bank would then return the money to the reserve fund when Jim paid his loan. Or, if some individual wanted to exchange the bank note for currency prior to its maturity date, the bank would pay from its own funds. However, the more often such practices occurred, the fewer notes the bank could afford to issue.

Demand Deposits

Although a bank should not let its note issues become excessive in relation to its cash reserves, the strong desire for profits led some banks to ignore this safety measure. As a result of the overissue of bank notes during the last century, many states began to restrict the banks' ability to issue notes. The federal government also discouraged the issuing of notes by certain banks. Eventually the bank note was supplanted by a new method of creating credit—the demand deposit, which is prevalent today.

If Smith were to come to the bank today to borrow $5,000, the bank, instead of giving him the loan in the form of bank notes, would grant the loan by creating for him a derivative demand deposit, as shown in Figure 13-2. Jim would put no money into the bank, but he would write checks against this demand deposit. These checks, which are drafts against the bank to pay the bearer a stipulated amount, serve as money, and people usually accept them in good faith in exchange for goods and services.

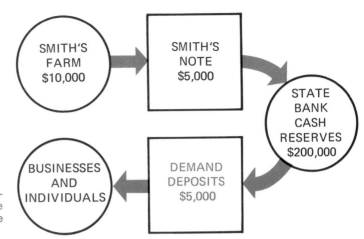

FIGURE 13-2

LOAN MADE THROUGH PROCESS OF CREATING BANK CREDIT

Checks are written by Smith in payment for goods and services. These checks circulate as money in the community.

Consequently, there is an increase in the money supply to the extent that checks are written against the demand deposits created. Since the bank does not lend currency, it might seem that there is no limit to the amount of loans which it can make in the form of demand deposits. The bank will, however, need to keep sufficient cash on hand to provide for those who want to redeem the checks.

Assume again that Smith receives a loan for one year that is repayable on March 2, 1976. For simplicity, let us say that he dates all his checks on March 2, 1976. In this case, at the time of redemption, who actually pays the checks? Once again it will be Jim. When he repays his loan, the bank will have the means of redeeming the checks. Just as with the notes, the whole process can be accomplished without having the bank lend any of its cash reserve. It may lend only its credit or good name to the process. Usually, however, the bank will have to provide funds to redeem some checks before Smith repays his loan.

If everyone who received a check cashed it and if the money were kept out of the bank permanently, the bank would need a reserve equal to the amount of checks written, or to the amount loaned in this case. If the bank had $200,000 in reserves to start with, it could lend only $200,000 because when checks equal to this amount were written and cashed, the reserve would become depleted. If the bank gave additional loans in the form of demand deposits, it could not honor the checks written against such loans.

In actual practice, however, this will not happen for three reasons: (1) Not all people cash checks immediately. Some of the checks may be endorsed and continue to circulate in the community before being cashed. (2) Some people, instead of cashing checks, will deposit them in the bank where they will be credited to the depositors' accounts. In this case no money leaves the bank. A bookkeeping entry merely transfers the value of the check from the account of the man who wrote the check to the account of the depositor of the check. There is no decrease in the cash reserve of the bank. (3) Even if someone cashes a check and takes the money out of the bank, the chances are very good that when he spends the money, it will eventually come into the hands of another person who will deposit the cash in the bank. In this event, the decrease in cash reserves resulting from redemption of the check will be offset by the return of cash by the person making the deposit.

As a result of these three factors, the bank can keep less money on hand than the value of its checks outstanding. The possibility of all check holders coming to the bank to redeem their checks at the same time is very remote. Thus, the amount of checks that can be written and the extent of loans that can be made in the form of demand deposits is limited only by the bank's ability to take care of those who want to cash their checks immediately. Since banks are interested in making a profit, they are encouraged to make as many loans as is reasonably safe. However, because some banks in the past overextended loans in relation to reserves, they were caught short. In order to prevent such abuses of the credit system, the states and the bank regulators placed restrictions on the amount of loans that could be made by a bank. For example, banks are now generally required to keep 7 to 22 percent cash reserves behind demand deposits, depending on their size. The amount of this reserve will limit the bank's ability to make loans.

If the bank is required to keep a 10 percent cash reserve behind its demand deposits (loans) and $200,000 is deposited in the bank, two lending alternatives are available to the bank:

1. The bank can hold $20,000 in cash as reserve against the $200,000 deposit and lend the remaining $180,000 in cash to those who request loans. If it does so, the bank's income will be limited to $10,800 ($180,000 $\times$ .06) if it charges 6 percent interest on the loans.
2. The bank can hold the entire $200,000 as cash reserves. In this case the $200,000 cash reserve can be used to back $2,000,000 in the form of demand deposits ($200,000 is 10 percent of $2,000,000).

Since the bank already has $200,000 on deposit as a result of the original primary deposit, it can extend its credit another $1,800,000 in the form of derivative demand deposits. If the bank followed this second alternative, its interest income on loans would be $108,000 ($1,800,000 $\times$ .06). The bank, however, would go to this extreme only if it were sure that it could retain its reserve intact. This is highly unlikely. It could under the three conditions

FIGURE 13-3

The bank holds the primary deposit as a reserve against the primary deposit and the newly created derivative deposits.

ORIGINAL DEPOSIT $200,000

STATE BANK CASH RESERVES $200,000

LOANS IN THE FORM OF DEMAND DEPOSITS $1,800,000

TOTAL DEMAND DEPOSITS..... $2,000,000
CASH RESERVES 200,000

stated on pages 267-268. In order for these conditions to prevail, however, there would have to be only one bank in the community. All individuals who received checks written by the borrower would pass them on to others or deposit them with that same bank. Any cash received from the redemption of checks also would be redeposited in that bank.

The biggest difficulty involved in following the second alternative would be in maintaining proper reserves: $200,000, with $2,000,000 in demand deposits outstanding. If the bank on any one day had more checks drawn against it than it had new deposits, there would be a net withdrawal of funds from the bank. Technically, this is known as an *adverse clearing balance*. Such an event would decrease the bank's total reserves. Indeed, it is conceivable that the entire $200,000 in reserves could be depleted. Worse still, in principle if not in practice, claims against the bank could amount to more than $200,000, so the bank would not be able to meet its obligations. Therefore, unless the bank had excess reserves, that is, unless the bank had reserves over and above that which it was required to maintain, it might easily get into difficulty. As a consequence, banks will follow the first alternative rather than the second. They will tend to hold $20,000 in reserve against the original primary deposit of $200,000 and to make loans to the extent of $180,000 in cash.

Multiple Expansion of Bank Credit

Even if the bank holds $20,000 in cash reserves against the original deposit of $200,000 and lends $180,000 in cash, there will be an expansion of credit. This will come about because what an individual bank may fear to do—that is, hold the entire $200,000 in reserve and lend $1,800,000 in the form of demand deposits—because of the possibility of an adverse clearing balance, the banking system as a whole can do through multiple expansion of bank credit. This can be shown in the following manner:

(1) If an individual bank were to extend credit to the full extent, the situation would appear as in Figure 13-3 above.

(2) The individual bank, however, will hold a 10 percent reserve against the original deposit and will lend the remainder, as demonstrated in Figure 13-4.

ORIGINAL DEPOSIT $200,000 → STATE BANK CASH RESERVES $20,000 → LOANS IN THE FORM OF CASH $180,000

FIGURE 13-4

The bank holds part of the primary deposit as a reserve against that deposit and lends the remainder in cash.

TOTAL DEMAND DEPOSITS.. $200,000
CASH RESERVES 20,000
CASH LOANS 180,000

In this case, the bank has less fear of adverse clearing balances because the loans were made in cash. There will be an increase in the money supply since there will exist $200,000 in demand deposits in addition to the continued circulation of $180,000 in cash as a result of the loans.

(3) Although the individual bank in the above situation increases the money supply to a limited degree, the cumulative action of all banks will increase the money supply nine times. This is brought about because the $180,000 in cash that is loaned will find its way into other banks as borrowers spend money and income recipients therefore deposit receipts in their own banks. These banks in turn will hold a portion of this money in reserve and will lend the remainder, which will eventually flow into other banks. For example, when the borrower of the $180,000 cash spends the money, it will come into the hands of others, and eventually the $180,000 will be deposited in other banks, which will hold $18,000 in cash reserves against the $180,000 deposits. These banks in turn will have $162,000 to lend. This process can continue until the total loans outstanding will be equal to $1,800,000 and the original $200,000 will be held in reserves in various banks. At that time the banks can lend no more money. This process, known as the *multiple expansion of bank credit*, is demonstrated in Figure 13-5.

Effect of Changes in Reserve Requirement

Another way of looking at this process is in tabular form, as shown in Table 13-1 on page 272, which shows how $2,000 deposited in one bank (Bank *A*) can be expanded into $20,000 in demand deposits and loans of $18,000.

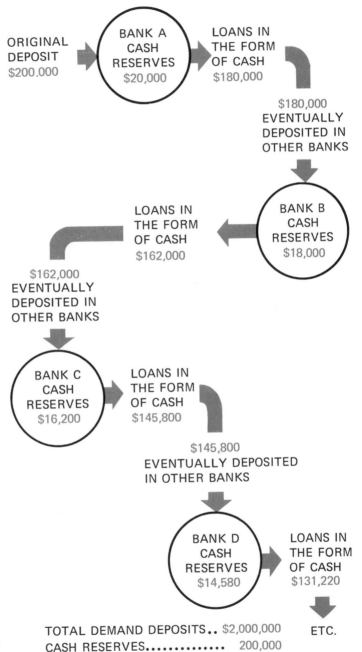

ORIGINAL DEPOSIT $200.000 → BANK A CASH RESERVES $20,000 → LOANS IN THE FORM OF CASH $180,000

$180,000 EVENTUALLY DEPOSITED IN OTHER BANKS

BANK B CASH RESERVES $18,000 → LOANS IN THE FORM OF CASH $162,000

$162,000 EVENTUALLY DEPOSITED IN OTHER BANKS

BANK C CASH RESERVES $16,200 → LOANS IN THE FORM OF CASH $145,800

$145,800 EVENTUALLY DEPOSITED IN OTHER BANKS

BANK D CASH RESERVES $14,580 → LOANS IN THE FORM OF CASH $131,220

ETC.

TOTAL DEMAND DEPOSITS.. $2,000,000
CASH RESERVES............. 200,000
CASH LOANS................ 1,800,000

FIGURE 13-5

MULTIPLE EXPANSION OF BANK CREDIT

Through the multiple expansion of bank credit, the total money supply can be magnified. Assuming a 10 percent reserve requirement, note how a $200,000 initial deposit leads to a ten-fold increase in total demand deposits.

TABLE 13-1

EXPANSION OF BANK CREDIT: 10% RESERVE REQUIREMENT

(1) Bank	(2) Deposit	(3) Reserve	(4) Loan
A	$ 2,000	$ 200	$ 1,800
B	1,800	180	1,620
C	1,620	162	1,458
D	1,458	146	1,312
E	1,312	132	1,180
F	1,180	118	1,062
G	1,062	106	956
H	956	96	860
I	860	86	774
J	774	78	696
Etc.	Etc.	Etc.	Etc.
	$20,000	$2,000	$18,000

If there is a 10 percent reserve requirement, it is assumed that Bank *A* will hold $200 against the original deposit of $2,000. Thus, it will have $1,800 in cash that it can lend. People who borrow this money spend it and circulate it in the community until it finally ends up in other banks, as people make deposits there. If all of these deposits were made in Bank *B*, that bank would hold a $180 reserve against its deposits of $1,800 and lend the remaining $1,620. This process continues until all the money is tied up in reserves in various banks. At such time the total deposits will equal $20,000, the reserves, $2,000, and the total loans outstanding, $18,000.

It should be kept in mind that the expansion of credit which increases the money supply results when the banks make loans in the form of demand deposits. Actually depositors can write checks equivalent to $20,000, and these checks serve as money. Thus, in place of a mere $2,000 in cash, we now have $20,000 in checks buying goods and services.

If the banks were required to keep a larger amount of reserves, their ability to expand credit would be reduced. If we assume the reserve requirement to be 20 percent, which is closer to the national average, instead of the 10 percent used in our previous examples, the bank would need to hold twice as much in reserves. This would reduce the bank's ability to extend credit, as shown in Table 13-2.

TABLE 13-2

EXPANSION OF BANK CREDIT: 20% RESERVE REQUIREMENT

(1) Bank	(2) Deposit	(3) Reserve	(4) Loan
A	$ 2,000	$ 400	$1,600
B	1,600	320	1,280
C	1,280	256	1,024
D	1,024	204	820
E	820	164	656
Etc.	Etc.	Etc.	Etc.
	$10,000	$2,000	$8,000

On the other hand, if the reserve requirement were only 5 percent instead of 10 percent, the bank's ability to extend credit would more than double.

Keep in mind also that just as we can have a multiple expansion of bank credit whenever there is a net increase in deposits at the bank, we can also have a multiple contraction of credit whenever there is a net withdrawal of deposits.

Recalling the relationship between the money supply and the level of economic activity, we can relate expansions and contractions of credit to the circular flow. First, changing the reserve requirement on demand deposits can alter the bank's ability to extend credit. In turn, changes in the money supply can alter the circular flow. It follows that we can influence the circular flow and encourage its acceleration or deceleration by changing the reserve requirement. This is exactly what happens in our economy. We use the reserve requirement along with several other monetary measures as tools to stabilize the level of economic activity.

Consequently, it might be beneficial to look at the institutional framework in which these principles operate. Let us take a look at the structure of our banking system.

DEVELOPMENT OF BANKING IN THE UNITED STATES

Rather than delve immediately into modern banking with its Federal Reserve System, we shall take a brief look at what preceded it. A historical background of our banking business should give us a better understanding of the need for our current system, the reason for its structure, and the basis of its authority and control.

First Bank of the United States, 1791-1811

When we became the United States of America in 1789, we set up a monetary system with the dollar as the basic unit of money. In addition, the Constitution gave Congress the "right to coin money and regulate the value thereof." Although there were a few state-chartered banks at this time, the first bank to receive a federal charter was the First Bank of the United States, established in 1791. It was chartered for a 20-year period with capital stock of $10 million, of which $2 million was purchased by the federal government and the remainder by businesses and individuals, including foreigners. The bank served all parts of the country at that time with branch offices in several major cities. The main office was located in the nation's capital, which was then Philadelphia.

Functions of the Bank. The bank performed four main functions:

1. It served as a regular commercial bank for individuals and business firms by accepting deposits and making loans through the issue of bank notes.
2. It served as a banker's bank or central bank. A central bank is one through which other banks can transfer funds and in which they can deposit excess funds.
3. The First Bank of the United States served also as a fiscal agent for the federal government. It acted as a government depository, transferred government funds around the country, and at times lent the government money.
4. The bank served as a regulating body for the state banks. In the main it endeavored to prevent the overissuance of bank notes by collecting notes of various banks and periodically presenting them for redemption.

Reasons for Opposition to the First Bank. Although the bank functioned well, there arose considerable opposition to it. The basis of this opposition was multifold.

1. Some opposed the bank because they had an aversion to anything that tended to enhance the powers of a centralized government. Since the bank was dominated by Federalists who were in favor of a strong central government, opponents saw it as a threat to states' rights.
2. Others claimed that the bank was unconstitutional since there was no provision in the Constitution expressly providing the federal government with the authority to establish a bank.
3. Because much of the bank's capital stock had been purchased by foreigners, some feared that our money supply would eventually be drained from the country and that foreigners would dominate finances in America.
4. Many people were opposed to paper money on the premise that the only good money was "hard money." Naturally they objected to the bank's policy of issuing notes.
5. Many of the state banks opposed the First Bank because they disliked its regulatory practice.

State Banking, 1811-1816

As a result of these and other objections, the bank's charter was not renewed in 1811, at which time its original charter expired. The demise of the First Bank of the United States left a gap in our banking system. In the absence of restrictive policies against them, the number of state banks increased threefold within five years, and note issues more than doubled. Poor bank management became prevalent, and abuses crept into the banking system. In addition, the federal government encountered difficulty in financing the War of 1812 without a centralized fiscal agent. As a result of disorder, depreciation of the currency, overexpansion of bank notes, and difficulty of government fiscal operations, a strong movement arose for a new federal bank.

Second Bank of the United States, 1816-1836

The Second Bank of the United States was given a 20-year charter in 1816. Its capital stock was set at $35 million, three and one-half times that of the First Bank. Once again the federal government purchased one fifth of the capital stock. The remainder was bought by individuals, businesses, and states in amounts of $300,000 or less. One fourth of the capital stock had to be paid for in gold or silver. The bank was governed by a board of directors, and one fifth of the board members were appointed by the President of the United States.

Functions of the Second Bank. The Second Bank of the United States, like its predecessor, performed the same basic functions.

Although the bank got off to a slow start, it prospered under the leadership of Langdon Cheves, who was elected president in 1819, and Nicholas Biddle, who became its president in 1823. The Second Bank stabilized the money system and exercised a restrictive influence on loose banking practices.

Opposition to the Second Bank. In spite of its prosperity and good influence, the bank at times had a hectic existence. Hostility to the bank arose, especially during the financial crisis of 1819. At that time an unsuccessful attempt was made to have Congress revoke the bank charter. Several states opposed the bank and tried to impair its operation by imposing taxes upon it. The action of Maryland in this regard led to a legal battle that reached the Supreme Court of the United States.

Maryland had levied a tax against the bank notes issued by the Baltimore branch of the Second Bank of the United States. McCulloch, the branch manager, protested the tax, but the Maryland courts upheld the authority of the state to impose the tax. The decision was appealed and finally went to the United States Supreme Court in the case of *McCulloch* v. *Maryland* (1819). The Court settled the argument not only about the tax but also about the constitutionality of the bank.

Chief Justice Marshall pointed out that according to the law of the land, Congress has the right to "coin money and regulate the value thereof."

He held that if Congress deemed it advisable to establish a bank in order to assist in the regulation of the value of money, such authority could be implied from the authority to regulate the value of money. After explaining that the power to tax could be used, in effect, to destroy, he declared the Maryland state tax on the notes of the Second Bank of the United States to be unconstitutional.

Political Issue of the Bank. In addition to the problem of opposition by the "hard money" enthusiasts, the state banks, the easy-money advocates, and those who disliked the element of central control, the bank also became a political issue. A running controversy concerning the functions and the merit of the bank developed between Nicholas Biddle, President of the Second Bank, and Andrew Jackson, President of the United States from 1829 through 1837.

Biddle and his followers made the recharter of the bank an issue in the 1832 presidential campaign. Formerly, he had applied to Congress for a recharter of the bank to take effect in 1836, and the measure passed both the House and the Senate. Although Jackson's opponents thought a veto of the recharter bill would result in his defeat in the 1832 election, Jackson vetoed the bill and returned it to Congress with one of his frequent biting messages. He attacked the bank on several matters and pointed out that Congress should look closely at the alleged evils of the bank's existence. The reelection of Jackson and many pro-Jackson Congressmen presaged an end to the bank's charter.

Wildcat Banking Period, 1836-1863

With the decline and expiration of the Second Bank of the United States, state banks began to grow rapidly. There were more than 1,600 in existence by 1863, compared to less than 400 in 1830. As a result of the diversity in state banking regulations, banking practices were anything but uniform.

Although some states developed sound banking regulations, many others were extremely lax. As a result, many malpractices occurred and banking in the United States was bordering on the brink of chaos. The amount of money in the form of bank notes and demand deposits fluctuated widely. The bank-chartering process of many states was abused in return for political favors. Many banks were established with inadequate capital. Hundreds of them failed to retain adequate reserves.

Many banks made risky loans on very shabby collateral. Officers frequently borrowed large sums of money from their own banks for speculative purposes. Several of the banks were poorly managed, and state supervision was often inadequate. One of the most prevalent evils was the overissue of bank notes. Some banks would not accept the notes of other banks or would accept them only at a discount. In fact, many banks were reluctant to redeem their own notes because of inadequate reserves. Counterfeiting became a big business, especially since many banks did a poor job of printing and used an inferior grade of paper for their bank notes.

The term *wildcat banking* supposedly came from a rather common practice. A bank, not wanting to be annoyed by people redeeming its notes, established its main office in a remote area. The bank issued notes from the branch banks located in major towns. It was not until the acceptors of such notes were informed that they must take the notes to the main office in order to redeem them that they realized they had been taken in. Some claimed that the main office was located in wildcat country. Thus, the name "wildcat banking" arose. Later the term was applied to other malpractices.

National Banking System, 1863-1913

The prevalence of abuses led many states to tighten their banking regulations. With the passage of time, however, it became evident that something more had to be done about the banking conditions in the United States. Not only were banks looked upon with suspicion by Americans, but foreigners also were becoming more aware of our ill-reputed banking practices. The need for a centralized banking system and for the regulation of state banks, a desire to stabilize the money supply, and the government's need for a fiscal agent led to the enactment of the National Currency Act of 1863. This Act was revised by the National Bank Act of 1864, which set up a new banking system. It sought to bring order to our banking system and to eliminate abuses that had run rampant during the previous decades.

National Bank Requirements. To insure bank safety, rigid capital requirements were established for the banks. The amount of capital required varied with the size of the city in which the bank was to be located.

At least 50 percent of the capital had to be paid in before the bank could commence operations. Originally all stock was subject to double liability, but this provision was subsequently dropped.

All banks in the system had to insert the word "national" in their names, and each national bank had to accept the notes of all other national banks at par. In order to assure the value and safety of these notes, they had to be backed up by government bonds. The bank had to deposit the bonds with the Comptroller of the Currency. Then the bank could issue bank notes up to 90 percent of the value of the bonds. This protected the noteholders because, if a bank failed to redeem its notes, the Comptroller of the Currency could sell the pledged bonds and use the funds to pay the noteholders.

Growth of National Banks. The federal government requested all banks to join the system. Many shied away from membership, however, because of the restrictive regulations, high capital requirements, and rigid supervision. When the banks did not join the system as quickly as anticipated, Congress decided to encourage membership by levying a 10 percent tax against the issue of state bank notes. Although more of them did join, several banks instead began making loans in the form of checking deposits against which no tax had been levied. The demand deposit soon became the prevalent method of making loans. It was not only more convenient but it also provided a way of avoiding the tax.

In the half century subsequent to the passage of the National Banking Act, membership in the system did grow but not so rapidly as did the number of state banks.

Weaknesses in the National Banking System. Although the National Banking System did much to improve the caliber of American banking, with the growth and development of the economy certain weaknesses in the System became apparent. To begin, banks were not permitted to make loans on real estate. This was especially detrimental to farmers since real estate was the main form of collateral possessed by farmers.

Another difficulty was that the National Banking System brought about a concentration of reserve funds to the financial centers. Country and small-town banks held their reserves in correspondent banks in larger towns. The banks in large towns tended to hold their reserves, which often included the deposits of the small-town banks, in the big cities, especially New York. Although the reserve funds gravitated very easily toward the money centers, money was slow in returning to the small-town and country banks when they requested return of their reserves. This problem was aggravated whenever there was a widespread demand by depositors for their money.

The major weakness of the National Banking System, however, was the "perverse elasticity" it brought about in the money supply. A prime function of a banking system is to supply the business community with money when it is needed during periods of increased business activity and to contract the money supply when it is not demanded. Under the National Banking System, however, the money supply did not expand and contract readily with the needs of business; rather, it tended to fluctuate in the opposite direction. This phenomenon occurred because government bonds were necessary backing for bank notes. During periods of prosperity, when an increased money supply was required to carry on a higher level of business activity, the banks had an inadequate supply of bonds to make the necessary loans in the form of bank notes. Since the interest on government bonds was a relatively low investment return during prosperity, the banks did not buy bonds in great quantities. During depression periods, however, when the yield on government bonds was a relatively good investment, the banks made heavy purchases of bonds. Thus, during prosperity they were unable to expand credit when it was necessary. On the other hand, they had all kinds of ability to expand the money supply during depressionary periods when businessmen were in no mood to borrow it.

By the turn of the century it became evident that the National Banking System, although a substantial improvement over the heterogeneous, poorly regulated, and inefficiently operated banking institutions of the "wildcat banking" period, was becoming outmoded and in serious need of revision. Along with the inelasticity of the money supply, the drain of reserves to the money centers, the banks' inability to lend on real estate, and the lack of coordination between state and national banks, the National Banking System left the government without a fiscal agent. Eventually a new system that would remedy these weaknesses was sought. With the expansion in our economy and the need for more money and credit, it was essential to revise our banking system.

Federal Reserve System, 1913-Present

Before establishing a new system, the government set up a commission to study banking in European countries as well as in America. Five years of investigation and analysis by the Aldrich Committee were carried on before Congress established the Federal Reserve System. This System incorporated the best from American and European banking practices and eliminated the weaknesses of the National Banking System. The Federal Reserve Banking Act of 1913 provided for a central banking system. Unlike many of the European nations that have one *central bank* (such as the Bank of Sweden, the Bank of England, and the Bank of France) the United States set up a system with 12 central banks. Probably the main reasons for not following the European idea of one central bank was the feeling in this country against strong central control and the fact that geographically we are a much larger country than any of the European nations. Today, although each Reserve Bank has a considerable amount of autonomy, the general policies for the entire System are determined by the Board of Governors in Washington, D.C.

STRUCTURE OF THE FEDERAL RESERVE SYSTEM

The Federal Reserve System is a complex and intricate system composed of a Board of Governors, 12 Federal Reserve Banks, branch banks, member banks, a Federal Advisory Council, an Open Market Committee, and several minor organizations. The "Fed" is a government instrumentality, yet it is not owned by the government. Member banks own the System, but its most important officials are appointed by the government. Each body within the Federal Reserve System has its individual function, but the functions of each are interrelated. Decentralization is an important characteristic of the Federal Reserve System.

The Board of Governors of the Federal Reserve System

The Board of Governors consists of seven members who are appointed by the President of the United States with the consent of the United States Senate. Board membership is a full-time position and carries a salary of $40,000 a year. Each member is appointed for 14 years and is ineligible for reappointment. Appointments are staggered in such a manner that a new appointee is assigned every two years. Each member must be selected from a different Federal Reserve district. The President of the United States selects the Chairman and the Vice-Chairman of the Board.

The Board has numerous powers including supervision of the Federal Reserve Banks. It approves and has the right to suspend or to remove officers of the Federal Reserve Banks. The Board must authorize Federal Reserve Bank loans to each other and review discount rates established by the Reserve Banks. It establishes reserve requirements within legal limits, regulates loans on securities, and at times regulates conditions of installment sales in addition to many other functions.

Federal Advisory Council

The Board of Governors may call upon the Federal Advisory Council for assistance. This is a committee of 12 members selected annually by the board of directors of each Federal Reserve Bank. They are men of prestige and banking acumen who meet at least four times a year with the Board of Governors. The FAC serves primarily in an advisory capacity to the Board of Governors. It confers with the Board on business conditions and other matters pertinent to the System.

In addition to the Federal Advisory Council, a number of other committees and conferences assist the Board of Governors on various problems. One of the most important of these is the Conference of Presidents of the Federal Reserve Banks, which meets occasionally of its own accord and meets with the Board of Governors at least three times a year.

Federal Open Market Committee

The Federal Open Market Committee is also composed of 12 members, including the 7 members of the Board of Governors. The other 5 members of the Committee are elected by the boards of directors of the various Federal Reserve Banks. Since there are 12 Banks but only 5 positions to be filled, the Banks are grouped into 5 units. Each unit elects one member for the Committee. The member selected must be either a President or a Vice-President of a Federal Reserve Bank. One member is elected from each of the following groups: New York; Boston, Philadelphia, and Richmond; Chicago and Cleveland; Atlanta, Dallas, and St. Louis; and Minneapolis, Kansas City, and San Francisco. Because of its importance and size, the Federal Reserve Bank of New York is grouped by itself. The New York Bank holds more than one fourth of the total assets of all the Federal Reserve Banks, it is located in the financial center of the world as well as the United States, and it is in the principal market for government securities. As we shall see later, the Federal Open Market Committee engages in the buying and selling of securities in the open market for the express purpose of influencing the flow of credit and money. Its actions also help in stabilizing the level of prices and economic activity.

Federal Reserve Banks

The Federal Reserve System divides the United States into 12 geographic districts. Each district has a Federal Reserve Bank named after the city in which it is located, and each district is given a number starting from the East Coast and moving to the West Coast. The districts are organized on the basis of the concentration of financial activity, not on the basis of geographic area. As a result, the St. Louis district geographically is about one half the size of the Kansas City district, but it does as much financial business as the latter. Several of the districts have branch banks. The Federal Reserve Bank of Cleveland, District 4, has branches in Pittsburgh and Cincinnati, for example. Because of its wide geographic area, San Francisco has four branches. The state of Alaska is served by the Seattle branch of the San Francisco district, and Hawaii is part of the head office territory of the San Francisco district. See Table 13-3 on page 282 or Figure 13-6 on page 283 for a complete list of the districts, banks, and branches.

Each Federal Reserve Bank is controlled by a board of directors consisting of nine members who are divided into three classes, with three members in each class. Class A directors are bankers elected by the member banks to represent them on the board. The member banks of the district are divided into three groups according to size, and each group elects one of the Class A directors. The Class B directors are elected in the same manner; but they cannot be bankers, for they are supposed to represent industry, commerce, and agriculture and should be engaged in such occupations at the time of their selection. The Class C directors must not be officers,

TABLE 13-3

FEDERAL
RESERVE
DISTRICTS
AND BANKS

District	Federal Reserve Bank	Branches
1	Boston	None
2	New York	Buffalo
3	Philadelphia	None
4	Cleveland	Cincinnati, Pittsburgh
5	Richmond	Baltimore, Charlotte
6	Atlanta	Birmingham, Jacksonville, Nashville, New Orleans
7	Chicago	Detroit
8	St. Louis	Little Rock, Louisville, Memphis
9	Minneapolis	Helena
10	Kansas City	Denver, Oklahoma City, Omaha
11	Dallas	El Paso, Houston, San Antonio
12	San Francisco	Los Angeles, Portland, Salt Lake City, Seattle

SOURCE: *Federal Reserve Bulletin* (February, 1974).

directors, employees, or stockholders of any bank. They are appointed by the Board of Governors of the System. One of the Class C directors is appointed by the Board of Governors as chairman of the board of directors of the Reserve Bank. A deputy chairman is also appointed by the Board of Governors. The chairman serves also as Federal Reserve agent. In this capacity he is responsible for the issuance of Federal Reserve notes.

The public nature of the Federal Reserve System is attested to by the fact that nonbankers constitute a majority of the board of directors of each Federal Reserve Bank. The board of directors of each Federal Reserve Bank appoints a President and a Vice-President who must be approved by the Board of Governors in Washington. These officers attend to the day-to-day operation of the Bank.

Federal Reserve Banks supervise member banks and conduct periodic examinations of the latter's operation. In the event that any member bank chronically engages in unsound banking practices, the Board of Directors has the authority to remove its officers and directors. Although such authority is seldom exercised, its presence helps to keep the member banks in line. The Federal Reserve Bank also has the power to set the maximum interest that may be paid by member banks on both savings and time deposits.

In addition to serving as central banks, or bankers' banks, the Federal Reserve Banks also serve as fiscal agents for the federal government. They handle the detailed work of issuing and redeeming government bonds, they hold deposits and disburse funds for the Treasury, and they perform many other fiscal duties. They supply money for the business communities in the form of Federal Reserve notes and regulate the member banks' ability to create credit.

FIGURE 13-6

THE FEDERAL RESERVE SYSTEM

The Federal Reserve System is composed of 12 districts, each with its own Federal Reserve Bank. Some large geographic districts, such as San Francisco, have branch banks in other cities within the district.

SOURCE: *Federal Reserve Bulletin.*

LEGEND

⚌ BOUNDARIES OF FEDERAL RESERVE DISTRICTS

★ BOARD OF GOVERNORS OF THE FEDERAL RESERVE SYSTEM

── BOUNDARIES OF FEDERAL RESERVE BRANCH TERRITORIES

■ FEDERAL RESERVE BANK CITIES

● FEDERAL RESERVE BRANCH CITIES

Federal Reserve Member Banks

There are approximately 14,160 commercial banks in the United States. Approximately forty percent (5,734) belong to the Federal Reserve System, and they are known as *member banks.* About 4,650 of these are national banks. When the Federal Reserve System was established, each national bank was required to join or to forfeit its charter. Membership is also open to state banks that can qualify. Many of them cannot qualify because of the high minimum capital requirement, and some do not like the System's restrictions and regulations. Others are reluctant to join because as nonmembers they are permitted to use certain major facilities of the System anyway. On rare occasions a member bank has withdrawn from the System. Although only about forty percent of the banks belong to the System, these banks do 75 to 80 percent of the total commercial banking business in the United States.

Each member bank is required to buy stock of the Federal Reserve Bank of its district. The original stock subscription called for an amount equal to 6 percent of the member bank's own paid-up capital and surplus. The Federal Reserve Act provided that stock would be sold to the public if the member banks did not buy sufficient amounts. It further provided that the federal government would buy stock if it was not all purchased by the banks and the public. To date, no stock has been sold to either the public or to the federal government. The member banks have purchased all the stock in the Federal Reserve Banks and have paid in over one half of their subscribed stock. As a result, we have a unique system in which the member banks completely own the Federal Reserve Banks, but most of the regulation or control of these Banks resides with the Board of Governors.

Although the member banks are operated for profit, the Federal Reserve Banks are operated strictly in the public interest. The Federal Reserve System pays a 6 percent dividend on its stock. Any profits over this amount are used to build up certain reserve surpluses or are turned over to the United States Treasury. Member banks are required to maintain most of their legal reserves with the Federal Reserve Banks. Vault cash, however, may be counted as legal reserve. In addition, member banks are subject to examinations and regulations by the Federal Reserve Banks. All member banks must insure their deposits with the Federal Deposit Insurance Corporation.

SUMMARY

1. At one time banks created money through the use of bank notes. Today they do it through the use of demand deposits.

2. For security purposes and to limit their ability to create credit, banks are required to keep a certain amount of reserves behind their demand deposits.

3. In general, the amount of credit created through the establishment of demand deposits will be some multiple of the actual cash reserves of the banks.

4. Changes in the reserve requirement can affect the bank's ability to create credit and therefore can affect the money supply and have an influence on the level of economic activity and the price level.

5. The United States has passed through several banking eras including that of the First Bank of the United States, the Second Bank of the United States, the wildcat banking period, the National Banking System, and the Federal Reserve System.

6. The Federal Reserve System, in operation today, is a complex system composed of several bodies, organizations, and committees.

7. Although only about forty percent of the banks in the United States belong to the Federal Reserve System, these banks do 75 to 80 percent of the commercial banking business in the nation.

8. The Federal Reserve System can affect the level of economic activity and the price level through the controls it exercises over bank credit and the money supply.

NEW TERMS

Primary deposit, *p. 263*
Derivative deposit, *p. 264*
Bank notes, *p. 264*
Adverse clearing balance, *p. 269*
Multiple expansion of bank credit, *p. 270*
First Bank of the United States, *p. 273*
Second Bank of the United States, *p. 275*
McCulloch v. Maryland, *p. 275*

Wildcat banking, *p. 277*
National Banking System, *p. 277*
Federal Reserve System, *p. 279*
Central bank, *p. 279*
Board of Governors, *p. 280*
Federal Advisory Council, *p. 280*
Federal Open Market Committee, *p. 280*
Federal Reserve Banks, p. 281
Member banks, *p. 283*

QUESTIONS FOR DISCUSSION AND ANALYSIS

1. Explain why a derivative bank deposit increases the money supply whereas a primary demand deposit does not.

2. What would happen to the money supply if we were to establish, as some have advocated, a 100 percent reserve requirement for demand deposits?

3. In your opinion, should banks be permitted to create credit? Why or why not?

4. Do you see any relationship between the multiple expansion of bank credit and the velocity of money?

5. Do you think that banks should be regulated by the states or by the federal government? Why?

6. Should foreigners be permitted to hold stock in our banks? Why?

7. Do you think that the requirement of the national banks to secure their notes with government bonds was a sound and wise policy? Why?

8. In what way did the Federal Reserve System improve the elasticity of the money supply?

9. Should all commercial banks be required to become members of the Federal Reserve System?

10. Do you agree with the policy of electing nonbankers to the board of directors of each Federal Reserve Bank? Why or why not?

11. Should banks operate as private businesses or as instrumentalities of the federal government? Why?

12. What are the merits of having the Federal Reserve Banks operate on a nonprofit basis?

13. Since the federal government owns no stock in the Federal Reserve Banks, why should it appoint the Federal Reserve Board of Governors?

SUGGESTED READINGS

Board of Governors of the Federal Reserve System. *Federal Reserve System: Purposes and Functions.* Westport, Conn.: Greenwood Press, Inc., 1968. Chapters 5, 11, and 12.

Eastburn, David P. *Money and Men and Policy.* Philadelphia: Federal Reserve Bank of Philadelphia, 1970.

Meek, Paul. *Open Market Operations.* New York: Federal Reserve Bank of New York, 1963.

Morgan Guaranty Trust Company of New York. "Will the Real Money Supply Please Stand Up." *Morgan Guaranty Survey* (April, 1971).

Samuelson, Paul. "Reflections on Central Banking." *The National Banking Review* (September, 1963).

Schultz, William J., and M. R. Caine. *Financial Development of the United States.* Englewood Cliffs, N.J.: Prentice-Hall, Inc., 1937. Chapters 5-20.

Soule, George, and Vincent P. Carosso. *American Economic History.* New York: The Dryden Press, Inc., 1957. Chapters 10, 18, and 23.

Taylor, George R. (ed.). *Jackson vs. Biddle: The Struggle Over the Second Bank of the United States.* Lexington, Mass.: D. C. Heath & Company, 1949.

14

Federal Reserve and the Money Supply

PREVIEW Through measures both general and selective the Federal Reserve can affect the amount and flow of money in the economy and, consequently, economic activity and the price level. General measures at the disposal of the Fed include authority to change reserve requirements that banks must hold against their deposits, manipulation of the discount rate at which member banks borrow from the Fed, and the buying and selling of government securities in open-market operations by which the Fed affects member bank reserves. At times the Federal Reserve has had control over specific uses of money and credit, such as margin requirements which affect the use of credit in stock market purchases, regulation of the conditions of installment sales, and regulation of housing credit.

Although the Fed has endeavored to use its various measures prudently in an effort to stabilize the level of economic activity and the price level, there are critics who suggest that its policies, measures, and timing could be improved.

Through its control over bank credit, the Federal Reserve System can affect the money supply. Thus, its actions have an effect on the level of economic activity and/or the price level. The Federal Reserve has many instruments or measures through which it can control bank credit: (1) member bank reserve requirements, (2) the discount rate, (3) open-market operations, (4) moral suasion, (5) control over installment sales, (6) control over credit in the purchase of new homes, and (7) stock market margin requirements.

The first four are referred to as *general controls* because they affect the overall supply of money. The remainder are referred to as *selective controls* because they affect the use of money for specific purposes in our economy. Let us see exactly how these controls are utilized in an attempt to stabilize the flow of economic activity or the price level. These controls may be used individually or collectively.

GENERAL CONTROLS

In using general controls, the Federal Reserve can influence the total amount and flow of credit and money; but these controls do little to encourage or restrict the use of money for specific purposes. There are occasions, however, when the Federal Reserve, by tightening credit as a hedge against inflation for example, may cause a shortage of money for many specific uses in the economy. In fact, it may cause a shortage of money for some specific activity that the Federal Reserve has no desire to restrict. If offsetting measures are not available in such situations, the advantages of a generally tight money supply must be weighed against the adverse effects of a money shortage for specific uses. Such was the case in 1966 when the money crunch severely affected the housing market. Again in 1968 and 1969 tight money and high interest rates designed to limit investment as an anti-inflationary measure resulted in an influx of Eurodollars for U.S. investments.

Member Bank Reserve Requirements

In the discussion of bank credit in Chapter 13, we learned that a bank's ability to extend credit is affected by the amount of reserves it must hold against demand deposits. We found that an increase in the reserve requirement would reduce the bank's ability to expand the money supply, and vice versa. From Chapter 13 we learned also that member banks are required to keep most of their reserves at the Federal Reserve Banks. Now we can add the fact that the Board of Governors has the authority to determine, within limits, the amount of reserves which the member banks must hold against demand deposits. Such reserve requirements as designated by the Board are referred to as the *legal reserve requirements*. Any reserve over and above this amount that a bank may have is an *excess reserve*. Both are important to the determination of the money supply. Member bank *legal reserves* must be in the form of deposits at the Federal Reserve Bank or vault cash.

Many times we read in the *Wall Street Journal* and elsewhere about net free reserves. Since the *net free reserves* are equal to the excess reserves minus member banks' borrowings from the Federal Reserve Banks, they will give a better indication of the member banks' ability to extend credit.

Legal Reserve Requirements. For purposes of setting reserve requirements, member banks originally were divided into three categories by the Federal Reserve: (1) central reserve city banks: those in the large financial cities, principally New York and Chicago; (2) reserve city banks: those in more than 50 moderate-size and larger towns; and (3) country banks: those not in the first and second categories. The Federal Reserve Act as originally passed in 1913 set the reserve requirement for demand deposits rigidly at 13, 10, and 7 percent for banks in each category respectively. The reserve required for time deposits (savings accounts) for all three categories was 3 percent. The Banking Act of 1935, however, provided that the reserve requirements could be doubled. Moreover, the Act empowered the Board of Governors to set the actual requirements somewhere between the old level and the new maximum. These limits were again modified in 1959. At that time an act of Congress provided for the termination of the classification "central reserve cities." At present the Board of Governors may alter reserve requirements of the member banks between the minimum and the maximum amounts as shown in Table 14-1.

TABLE 14-1

RESERVE REQUIREMENTS FOR MEMBER BANKS

	Demand Deposits		Time Deposits
	Reserve City Banks	Other Banks	All Banks
Minimum	10%	7%	3%
Maximum	22%	14%	10%

SOURCE: *Federal Reserve Bulletin*, monthly.

Currently a bank having net demand deposits of more than $400 million is considered a reserve city bank, and the city in which its head office is located is designated as a reserve city. Cities in which Federal Reserve Banks or branches are located are also reserve cities. Any banks having net demand deposits of $400 million or less are designated as banks outside of reserve cities and as such are permitted to maintain lower reserves.

Although the Board may alter the reserve requirements, it must stay within the legal limits. There have been times, however, when special legislation of Congress gave the Board authority to go beyond the normal maximums, such as during the post-World War II period and the Korean conflict.

Effect of Lower Reserve Requirements. The Board uses its power judiciously. During periods of low production, income, and employment, the Board may decrease requirements in the hope of increasing the money supply and bringing about an expansion of business activity. To show how this is accomplished, let us use a hypothetical example in which the banking system as a whole has no excess reserves on which to expand credit. Assuming a 10 percent reserve requirement, a picture of the situation at the beginning might appear as shown in Figure 14-1 on page 290.

FIGURE 14-1

**10 PERCENT RESERVE
REQUIREMENT**

With a 10 percent reserve requirement, the banking system can expand the money supply to ten times
the original demand deposit.

ORIGINAL
DEMAND
DEPOSITS
$200,000

ALL BANKS

TOTAL LEGAL
RESERVES
$200,000

LOANS IN
FORM OF
DEMAND
DEPOSITS
$1,800,000

According to Figure 14-1, all banks together are holding $200,000 cash reserves (10 percent) against total deposits of $2,000,000 ($200,000 in primary deposits and $1,800,000 in derivative deposits or loans). The banks in this situation cannot create any more credit. If the reserve requirement were decreased to 5 percent, however, the banks would have to hold only $100,000 in legal reserves against the $2,000,000 in demand deposits. This would free $100,000 of the existing reserve. If the $100,000 were left on deposit with the Federal Reserve Banks, it would become excess reserve. The banks could then extend another $2,000,000 in demand deposits by the process of multiple credit expansion described in Chapter 13. This is shown in Figure 14-2.

Thus, a decrease in the reserve requirement can increase the banks' ability to extend credit, and this in effect provides for an increase in the money supply. *Notice that reduction of the reserve requirement does not necessarily increase credit or the money supply* but merely the banks' ability to increase credit. Actually there will not be an increase in credit or in the money supply until businessmen or others actually borrow the money in the form of demand deposits and begin issuing checks against these deposits. Frequently in a depression period, the Federal Reserve will lower the reserve requirement; but businessmen will be reluctant to borrow and spend money

FIGURE 14-2

**5 PERCENT RESERVE
REQUIREMENT**

A 5 percent reserve requirement
permits an expansion of the money
supply to 20 times the original demand deposit.

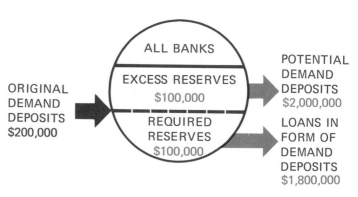

ORIGINAL
DEMAND
DEPOSITS
$200,000

ALL BANKS

EXCESS RESERVES
$100,000

REQUIRED
RESERVES
$100,000

POTENTIAL
DEMAND
DEPOSITS
$2,000,000

LOANS IN
FORM OF
DEMAND
DEPOSITS
$1,800,000

because of the poor return on capital investment. There are situations, therefore, in which the lowering of the reserve requirement may not result in an increase in the money supply.

Effect of Higher Reserve Requirements. The Board of Governors can decrease the banks' ability to expand the money supply by raising the reserve requirement. Assume once again a situation such as we had in Figure 14-1, in which the banks were "loaned up to the hilt." If the Board of Governors raised the reserve requirements from 10 percent to 20 percent, the banks would actually be short of required reserves. In such a case they would have to increase their reserve or recall some of the loans outstanding. See Figure 14-3.

FIGURE 14-3

20 PERCENT RESERVE REQUIREMENT

A 20 percent reserve requirement allows an expansion of the money supply to only five times the original demand deposit.

ORIGINAL DEMAND DEPOSITS $200,000 → ALL BANKS / TOTAL LEGAL RESERVES $200,000 → LOANS IN FORM OF DEMAND DEPOSITS $800,000

The action of the banks in recalling loans would reduce the demand deposits by a total of $1,000,000. Thus, it would in effect decrease the money supply by $1,000,000. Actually the Board of Governors would not do this, for it would greatly disturb and disrupt business activity. The Board is more inclined to use its power to prevent undesirable conditions from developing. For example, it tries to ease the money supply by lowering reserve requirements when the economy enters a period of declining business activity in the hope that it will help arrest the downward action. On the other hand, the Board endeavors to tighten up on the money supply by raising reserve requirements and by using other methods when the economy begins to reach the full-employment stage of business activity or when it otherwise shows signs of inflationary pressures. The decision is made from knowledge that further increases in the money supply through the extension of demand deposits will lead only to high prices. Let us demonstrate this point by setting up a new hypothetical case. Assume that there is a 10 percent reserve requirement and that the banks have excess reserves. The situation might appear as shown in Figure 14-4 on page 292.

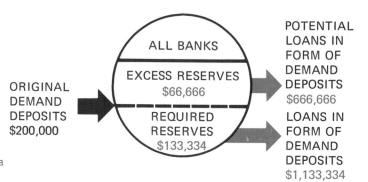

FIGURE 14-4

10 PERCENT RESERVE REQUIREMENT

Excess reserves can be used as a basis to expand demand deposits.

ORIGINAL DEMAND DEPOSITS $200,000

ALL BANKS

EXCESS RESERVES $66,666

REQUIRED RESERVES $133,334

POTENTIAL LOANS IN FORM OF DEMAND DEPOSITS $666,666

LOANS IN FORM OF DEMAND DEPOSITS $1,133,334

With $66,666 in excess reserves and a 10 percent reserve requirement, the banks can increase demand deposits by $666,666. If business activity is good, businessmen will borrow and there will be an increase in the money supply. If the economy is at full employment, however, the increased money supply will merely lead to higher prices. Under these circumstances, the Board of Governors could absorb the excess reserves by raising the reserve requirement. This would reduce the banks' ability to extend credit and thus would act as a deterrent to inflation. In our case in Figure 14-4, if the Board increased the reserve requirement to 15 percent, the banks would need $200,000 in required reserves against the $1,333,334 total deposits outstanding. The excess reserves of $66,666 would then become a part of the required reserve. Consequently, the banks would have no excess reserves and would lose their ability to extend credit. After such a change the status of the banks' reserves in relation to demand deposits would be as shown in Figure 14-5.

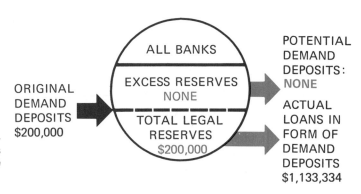

FIGURE 14-5

15 PERCENT RESERVE REQUIREMENT

An increase in the reserve requirements can be used to absorb excess reserves in order to reduce the banks' ability to extend credit.

ORIGINAL DEMAND DEPOSITS $200,000

ALL BANKS

EXCESS RESERVES NONE

TOTAL LEGAL RESERVES $200,000

POTENTIAL DEMAND DEPOSITS: NONE

ACTUAL LOANS IN FORM OF DEMAND DEPOSITS $1,133,334

Since the status of reserves in the individual banks will vary, some banks will be more affected than others by changes in the reserve requirements. For this reason, the Federal Reserve is somewhat cautious in the use of reserve requirements to control credit. When it does make changes in reserve requirements, generally it is by small amounts, such as one half of one percentage point at a time.

Principle to Remember. Regarding the Federal Reserve's control over the money supply through the use of reserve requirements, we may summarize by saying: An increase in the reserve requirements will decrease the banks' ability to extend credit. Conversely, a decrease in the reserve requirements will increase the banks' ability to extend credit.

Discount Rate

The *discount rate*, sometimes referred to as the rediscount rate, is the interest rate at which member banks may borrow funds from the Federal Reserve Banks. As you know, if you wished to borrow $100 at 8 percent from the bank for one year, you would have to sign a note payable to the bank (which becomes a note receivable for the bank). The bank would then discount your note for you. Instead of giving you the face value of the note, the bank would deduct the interest and pay you $92. However, you would repay the bank $100. The difference represents the interest, or discount.

A member bank may borrow from the Federal Reserve by rediscounting notes of its customers or by borrowing on its own promissory notes secured by its customers' notes, government securities, or by other satisfactory collateral. Borrowings by the first method are called *discounts* and by the second method, *advances*. The latter is the more popular method. But in either case the discount rate governs the cost of borrowing. Federal Reserve Banks, however, are not obliged to discount member banks' eligible paper. Discount facilities are a privilege of the member bank rather than a right. Furthermore, credit through this process is extended primarily on a short-term basis in order to enable a member bank to adjust its reserve position when necessary because of such developments as a sudden withdrawal of deposits or an unusually large seasonal demand for credit.

Discounting Process. Every commercial bank in the United States has among its assets a considerable number of notes receivable that it discounted in exchange for loans in the form of cash and demand deposits. If a member bank is low on reserves, it may rediscount these notes (called commercial paper) at its Federal Reserve Bank. As an alternative, member banks may borrow from the Federal Reserve Banks by using these notes or government securities as collateral. If the notes are used, the bank can obtain money on the notes at any time instead of waiting until payments on the notes are due. However, if the Federal Reserve Bank were to charge the member bank 8 percent interest for borrowing funds, the member bank would have to pay interest to the Reserve Bank in an amount equal to that which it would secure on its notes receivable. In effect, the member bank would make nothing on its own loans to individuals and business firms. Thus, when the discount rate is high compared to the commercial loan rate, the banks will be reluctant to use this rediscounting process to build up their reserves. If the discount rate is low, however, they will be more inclined to build up their reserves by discounting. Since reserves increase their ability to extend credit, a decrease in the discount rate may increase the money supply.

This process can be demonstrated graphically, but to see how it operates we must look at an individual bank instead of all banks. Assume that an individual bank has no excess reserve as indicated in Figure 14-6. Keep in mind that the individual bank does not necessarily lend demand deposits to some multiple of its reserve. It holds the proper fractional reserve against its primary deposits. The remainder becomes excess reserve that it can hold or lend. Thus, in our example the individual bank will hold $20,000 in legal reserve against the original $200,000 deposit and lend the remaining $180,000 in cash. As the $180,000 filters through the multiple expansion of bank credit, however, total demand deposits will be enlarged by some multiple of the original deposit.

According to the situation in Figure 14-6, the Acme National Bank will be unable to make further loans without excess reserves. The bank can build up its reserves through the discounting process. If the Acme Bank has made loans up to $180,000, it no doubt holds assets of $180,000 in notes receivable. Suppose that the bank is receiving 8 percent interest on these notes and that it can rediscount them at 6 percent. If the bank discounted $100,000 worth of the notes, it could still net 2 percent on them. This would mean annual income of $2,000. However, when the bank receives the $100,000 cash (or, as usually happens, a $100,000 credit is made to its reserve account in the reserve bank), it can lend this cash or $100,000 in demand deposits and make 8 percent on these new loans. Thus, by discounting and lending the bank will actually be making 10 percent on the $100,000: 2 percent net on the discounted notes plus 8 percent on the new notes. Interest income will amount to $10,000 (2 percent on $100,000 in old loans plus 8 percent on the $100,000 in new loans) compared to $8,000 (8 percent of $100,000) if no discounting had been carried out. In such circumstances it is profitable for the bank to discount its commercial paper, to build up its excess reserves, and to make additional loans. See Figure 14-7.

FIGURE 14-6

10 PERCENT RESERVE REQUIREMENT

A lack of excess reserves stifles a bank's ability to extend credit.

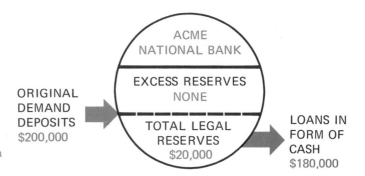

If the Federal Reserve Bank were to lower the discount rate, member banks would have an even greater incentive to discount. On the other hand, if the Federal Reserve Bank raised the discount rate to 7 percent, it would be less profitable for the Acme Bank to discount. If it were raised to 8 percent, it would not profit the bank to engage in the discounting process. Thus, banks can be encouraged to expand or contract credit by manipulation of the discount rate. Just as with changes in the reserve requirements, however, changes in the discount rates do not automatically lead to changes in the money supply. Businessmen and household members must increase their loans to make changes in the money supply effective.

In this regard, changing the discount rate has a secondary effect. The commercial loan rate is influenced greatly by the bank discount rate. For example, the *prime loan rate*, that is, that rate at which individuals and firms with the best collateral can borrow, is usually 1 to 1.5 percentage points above the discount rate. Thus, if the discount rate in Cleveland is 6 percent, the prime loan rate may be 7 to 7.5 percent. Usually when the discount rate

FIGURE 14-7

10 PERCENT RESERVE REQUIREMENT

A bank can add to its excess reserves, and thus its ability to extend credit, through the discounting process. In effect it borrows to add to its reserves.

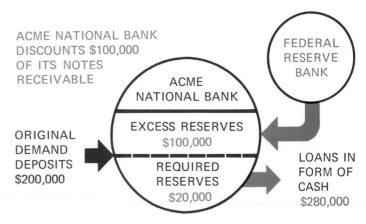

is lowered, the commercial loan rates are lowered. This may encourage businessmen to borrow. On the other hand, if the discount rate is raised, the commercial loan rates may be increased. This, in turn, may discourage businessmen from borrowing. The Federal Reserve Banks are aware of this fact and use the discount rate accordingly. It should be remembered, however, that the funds will still be available but at a higher cost.

When business activity is declining, the Federal Reserve Banks lower the discount rate to encourage member banks to discount and thereby to increase their ability to expand credit. The member banks in turn encourage businessmen to borrow by lowering the commercial loan rate. During full-employment inflationary periods, the Federal Reserve Banks raise the discount rate to discourage discounting, which in turn has a restrictive effect on the expansion of credit. Commercial banks discourage individuals and businessmen from borrowing by raising the commercial loan rates.

Of course, the Federal Reserve endeavors to use sound judgment in the use of the tools for control. The discount rate is changed by very moderate amounts, usually one quarter or one half of one percentage point at a time so that the change will not cause a serious disruption in business activity. This action is primarily preventive rather than remedial. In fact, the Fed maintains that frequently the discount rates are raised after a rise in commercial loan rates. In such cases the Fed's action in raising the discount rate serves to reduce the spread or gap between the discount rate and the commercial loan rate, thereby discouraging member bank borrowing.

The discount rate for each district is determined by the Federal Reserve Bank with the approval of the Board of Governors. Although the Reserve Banks initiate changes in the discount rate, the Board of Governors still has authority "to review and determine" discount rates. The discount rate often varies slightly for short periods between districts because of differences in the money markets. Usually when a district changes its rate, most of the others follow suit, since factors of national scope generally cause the change.

Advances to Member Banks. Instead of discounting customers' notes, however, member banks usually find it more convenient to borrow from the Federal Reserve Bank by discounting their own promissory notes at the Federal Reserve Bank, using government securities as collateral. This method of borrowing, known as an advance, differs from the previous method in form but not in substance. It is, however, a more popular method of borrowing. Such loans increase the member banks' reserves and enable them to expand credit. The members may request loans of their own initiative. For example, if a member bank's reserve should fall below the legal requirement, rather than attempt to recall loans in order to keep its demand deposits in line with its reserves, the bank may borrow funds from the Federal Reserve Bank to bring its reserves up to the legal reserve requirement. At other times when a bank is short of reserves, it may borrow from the Federal Reserve Bank in order to build up its reserves for credit expansion.

The Federal Reserve Banks may encourage member banks to borrow by lending money freely and at lower interest rates during periods of declining or slack business activity. At other times, especially during inflationary periods, the Federal Reserve Banks will discourage member-bank borrowing in order to tighten credit and put pressure on banks to increase commercial loan rates. Whatever its objective, the Federal Reserve can utilize the discount rate accordingly.

In addition to borrowing from the Reserve Bank, a commercial bank can adjust its reserve position by borrowing from other banks that have surplus reserves. This interbank borrowing takes place in a fairly well organized market, known as the *Federal Funds Market.*

Principle to Remember. Because of the intricacy of financial markets, a summary of our discussion on discount rates will help to establish our bearings at this point. A reduction in the discount rate will encourage banks to extend credit, encourage businessmen to borrow, and thus tend to increase the money supply. An increase in the discount rate will discourage banks from borrowing to expand credit, restrain businessmen from borrowing, and tend to limit expansion in the money supply.

Open-Market Operations

One of the most important instruments of monetary management is the Federal Reserve *open-market operation.* The Federal Open Market Committee (FOMC) has at its disposal the control over a portfolio of government securities including bonds, bills, certificates, and notes. If the FOMC wants to encourage the expansion of credit, it can direct the Federal Reserve Banks to buy bonds from member banks and individuals. This increases member bank reserves and enables the banks to make more loans. All member banks hold government obligations, and the Federal Reserve can induce member banks to sell government bonds and other securities by offering a premium price for them.

Purchase of Bonds. When the Federal Reserve buys bonds (usually in slack business periods), the excess reserves of the member banks are enlarged, thereby permitting them to expand credit. Let us demonstrate this graphically. Suppose that member banks have no excess reserves and therefore cannot extend any additional credit, as depicted in Figure 14-8 on page 298.

FIGURE 14-8

10 PERCENT RESERVE REQUIREMENT

A bank with no excess reserves cannot expand its credit.

ORIGINAL DEMAND DEPOSITS $200,000

ALL BANKS

EXCESS RESERVES
NONE

TOTAL LEGAL RESERVES
$200,000

LOANS IN FORM OF DEMAND DEPOSITS
$1,800,000

Under such conditions, if the Federal Reserve buys $100,000 of government bonds from member banks, it puts the money directly into the banks or credits their reserve accounts. This increases excess reserves and expands the banks' ability to make loans by $1,000,000 through the multiple expansion of bank credit. This situation is shown in Figure 14-9.

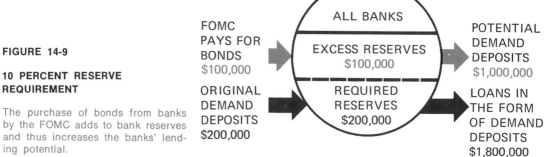

FIGURE 14-9

10 PERCENT RESERVE REQUIREMENT

The purchase of bonds from banks by the FOMC adds to bank reserves and thus increases the banks' lending potential.

FOMC PAYS FOR BONDS $100,000

ORIGINAL DEMAND DEPOSITS $200,000

ALL BANKS

EXCESS RESERVES
$100,000

REQUIRED RESERVES
$200,000

POTENTIAL DEMAND DEPOSITS
$1,000,000

LOANS IN THE FORM OF DEMAND DEPOSITS
$1,800,000

The same result can be accomplished by purchasing bonds from the individuals and businesses since these sellers will usually deposit in banks the money received from the sale of bonds. These deposits in turn increase bank reserves and may result in a potential increase in the money supply. This process is shown in Figure 14-10.

In this case, the potential expansion of credit is less than it is when the Federal Reserve buys government obligations directly from the member banks because the bank must hold $10,000 in reserve against the new deposits of $100,000 made by the individuals and businesses that sold the bonds. But the total effect on the money supply will be the same since demand deposits will rise by $1,000,000 in either case.

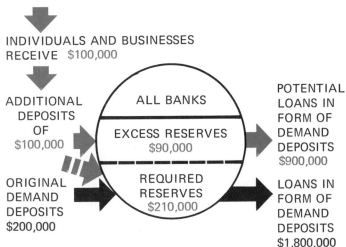

FOMC PAYS FOR BONDS $100,000

INDIVIDUALS AND BUSINESSES RECEIVE $100,000

ADDITIONAL DEPOSITS OF $100,000

ORIGINAL DEMAND DEPOSITS $200,000

ALL BANKS

EXCESS RESERVES $90,000

REQUIRED RESERVES $210,000

POTENTIAL LOANS IN FORM OF DEMAND DEPOSITS $900,000

LOANS IN FORM OF DEMAND DEPOSITS $1,800,000

FIGURE 14-10

10 PERCENT RESERVE REQUIREMENT

The purchase of bonds from individuals by the FOMC can also add to excess reserves, provided the sellers of the bonds deposit the receipts in their banks.

Sale of Bonds. During times of inflation or near inflation, the Federal Reserve may wish to absorb some of the excess reserves in existence. It can do so by selling government bonds to the member banks. The Federal Reserve can encourage the purchase of bonds and other government securities by offering them at a lower price. In order to buy bonds, member banks in all probability will have to give up some excess reserves, which in turn will decrease their ability to extend credit. If the Federal Reserve sells bonds to individuals or businesses, it is assumed that they will withdraw funds from member banks in order to pay for the bonds. This will reduce excess reserves and decrease the banks' ability to extend credit.

Principle to Remember. We must remember that the Federal Reserve's ability to affect the money supply through its open-market operation is restricted. Although the purchase of bonds from the banks will increase bank reserves, it does not mean that businessmen will borrow. On the other hand, selling bonds will not prevent expansion of credit unless a sufficient amount is sold to absorb all the excess reserves. The effectiveness of the Federal Reserve's endeavor to limit expansion of the money supply will depend on the status of excess reserves compared to the sale of bonds by the Federal Reserve.

Nevertheless, we can say in summary: Purchase of bonds in the open market by the Federal Reserve will increase the member banks' ability to expand credit, whereas the sale of bonds will decrease the member banks' ability to expand credit. Thus, the supply and the cost of credit can be affected by the actions of the Federal Open Market Committee. Frequently the Federal Reserve will combine measures for effective control. It may use open-market operations and/or higher reserve requirements to absorb excess reserves (moving banks to a minus net free reserve position) and then discourage member bank borrowing by raising the interest rate at the discount window.

Moral Suasion

Moral suasion is the term applied to a host of measures that the Federal Reserve uses to influence the activities of member banks. In addition to altering reserve requirements and discount rates and engaging in open-market operations to liberalize and tighten credit, the Federal Reserve may employ various measures to encourage banks to act one way or another. It does this by sending to member banks letters in which it encourages or discourages the expansion of credit. At other times, the Federal Reserve points out to businessmen and bankers in public statements the status of the economic situation and endeavors to persuade businesses and banks to use or to restrain credit. Loan examiners may be directed to become more selective in making loans; or, during personal interviews, the Federal Reserve officers may warn against speculative loans or suggest that banks become more liberal with their loans. The Federal Reserve may ration credit and suspend the borrowing privileges of member banks if necessary. In general, moral suasion will affect the money supply only to the extent that banks and businessmen are willing to cooperate.

SELECTIVE CONTROLS

All the controls that have been mentioned thus far are general controls because they affect the money supply in total, regardless of the use to which the money may be put. If commercial loan rates are forced upward through an increase in the discount rate, for example, people or businesses who desire to borrow for a multitude of purposes are affected. The Federal Reserve, however, does have certain discretionary controls that affect the use of money in the economy.

At times the Federal Reserve has been given authority to restrict credit for specific uses such as installment sales, home buying, and stock market purchases. The general purpose of these selective controls is to limit the use of credit in order to combat inflationary tendencies. These controls will be discussed in order to show how they operate to restrict the use of funds in each of the specific areas.

Control over Installment Sales

Control of consumer credit, instituted in 1941 under *Regulation W*, was in effect until 1947. Because of the postwar inflation, it was reinstituted in September, 1948; but it was withdrawn again in June, 1949. Regulation W was put back into effect in the fall of 1950 as a result of the Korean incident and then removed in 1952. The Regulation sought to limit the use of credit in retail sales by establishing the minimum down payment required for the purchase of certain types of commodities and by designating the length of time permitted for repayment of installment loans. Each of these measures individually restricts the use of credit, and when used jointly, the limitation on credit can be very pronounced.

Down Payment. Installment buying has the effect of increasing demand over and above what it would be if all sales were on a cash basis. Under certain conditions this can have a detrimental effect on the economy. For example, if large-scale installment buying takes place during periods of full employment, it can be very inflationary.

Prior to Regulation W, the only restriction on the use of credit in installment purchases was the voluntary limitation by the sellers or the finance companies. In most cases this was very little. An individual with $240 to spend could buy $2,400 worth of commodities by putting 10 percent down on each of several items. He could purchase, theoretically, one dozen $200 appliances by putting a down payment of $20 on each item.

Regulation W served to cut back some of this excess demand of the war and postwar periods by establishing a minimum down payment on numerous commodities. On automobiles the down payment was 33.33 percent, and on major appliances it was 15 percent. Under such regulations the individual with $240 to spend could buy only a fraction of the items that he could purchase prior to Regulation W.

According to our example, if a down payment of 15 percent were required, the demand would be limited to 8 items at a total value of $1,600 under the regulation, whereas previously the individual could have purchased 12 items at a total value of $2,400. In effect the Regulation would lower the amount of installment sales by $800 and reduce demand, which, in turn, would help to prevent inflation.

Length of Loans. That part of the Regulation which limited the period of time in which the loan had to be repaid also had an adverse effect on installment purchases. In most cases the repayment period was limited to 18 months. This forced the buyers to make larger monthly payments, which, it was hoped, would reduce the number of purchases of commodities on time. Table 14-2 gives some idea of the effect of changes in the amounts of down payments and monthly payments. It shows that a $200 commodity purchased with a 10 percent down payment and a 36-month loan requires a monthly repayment of $5 plus interest; but an 18-month loan with 15 percent down requires $9.44 plus interest.

Exactly how effective these controls were is difficult to say, but they did deter a considerable number of installment sales and thereby helped to hold down the total demand for goods and services.

TABLE 14-2		Cost	Down Payment	Length of Loan	Monthly Payments
REGULATION W AND CONSUMER CREDIT	Before Reg. W	$200	$20	36 mo.	$5.00 plus Interest
	After Reg. W	$200	$30	18 mo.	$9.44 plus Interest

Control over Mortgage Credit

Regulation X was the same in principle as Regulation W because it required a minimum down payment and limited the length of loans to prevent overextension of credit in the housing field. Regulation X was initiated in 1950 following the outbreak of hostility in Korea. It was suspended in 1952 as a result of the Korean truce and the decline in construction demand. Terms were not uniform for all loans, since higher down payments and shorter term loans were applied to higher cost homes and nonveteran purchases. One can see quite easily, according to Table 14-3, how a higher down payment and a shorter repayment period could discourage a family from buying a home. A $20,000 home purchased for $2,000 down and a $50 monthly payment, even though the period of the loan is for 30 years, is easier to finance than one with a $3,000 down payment and a $70.83 monthly payment for 20 years.

TABLE 14-3	Down Payment	Length of Loan	Monthly Payments
HOME INSTALLMENT PURCHASE	$2,000 (10%)	30 years	$50.00 + Interest
	$3,000 (15%)	20 years	$70.83 + Interest

Stock Market Margin Requirement

As a result of national experience with the use of credit in stock market speculation during the late 1920s, Congress in 1934 gave the Federal Reserve the authority to restrict the use of credit in the purchase of stocks.

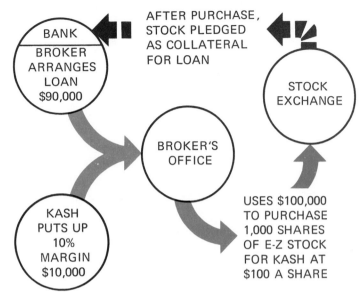

FIGURE 14-11

STOCK PURCHASED ON MARGIN

Stock can be purchased with a down payment. The remainder of the purchase price can be obtained by borrowing and using the acquired stock as collateral for the loan.

By this authority the Fed can now determine the minimum down payment that must be made on the purchase of stocks. The amount of money that can be borrowed against securities is always less than the current market value of the securities. The difference between the two is called the *stock market margin*. The higher the margin, the less the amount of stock that can be purchased with any given amount of funds.

During the 1920s, when there was no margin requirement, it was easy to buy stocks by making a down payment of 10 percent. Under such circumstances anyone with a decent credit rating could purchase $100,000 worth of stock with $10,000. For example, assuming a 10 percent margin, if Kevin Kash had $10,000 and a "hot tip" on a particular stock, he could arrange with his broker to buy $100,000 worth of E-Z Company stock, or 1,000 shares at $100 per share. The broker would take his $10,000, and, after arranging a loan of $90,000 through a bank or elsewhere, he would then purchase the 1,000 shares of stock. Kash then would pledge the stock just purchased as collateral for the loan, and the bank would have $100,000 collateral to cover a $90,000 loan. This procedure is illustrated in Figure 14-11.

Assume that the "inside" tip offered to Kash proved to be correct and the price of the stock rose to $110 per share in about three months. He could then sell the stock for $110,000, and with this money he would repay the bank loan of $90,000 plus $1,000 interest. He could pay the broker

$1,000 for his services, put back his original $10,000 investment, and pocket the remaining $8,000.

Suppose, on the other hand, that the tip proved to be a "dud" and the price of the E-Z stock started to fall. If the stock value declined, Kash's collateral would be reduced. The bank would then call upon him to keep his margin up. For instance, if the price of the stock fell to $95, the bank would require $5,000 more collateral to bring it up to $100,000 in value. Otherwise he might be asked to pay off some of the loan. If Kash were unable to do so and the price of the stock continued to fall, the bank would sell the stock before it fell below $90 because at that point the value of the collateral would be equal to the loan. If the bank were to sell at $92, it would get $92,000. After repayment of the loan ($90,000 plus $1,000 interest), Kash would have $1,000 remaining. After paying the broker his fee, Kash would be out $10,000 as a result of his little adventure in the stock market.

By control of the stock margins through *Regulation T*, the Federal Reserve can limit the purchase of stock on loans. In our example, $100,000 worth of stock was purchased with $10,000 under a 10 percent margin. If the margin were changed to 50 percent, only $20,000 worth of stock could be purchased with $10,000 cash. This would cut down speculation and would help to prevent price increases on the market. Margin requirements have varied considerably in the past, especially since 1935. At times they have been as low as 25 percent, and during postwar inflation they were raised to 100 percent.

In addition, the Federal Reserve controls the credit condition of short sales in the stock market. A *short sale* takes place when an individual sells stock he does not own by having the broker borrow the shares of stock to be sold. The individual, however, must deposit a certain percentage of good faith money. Although the individual is obligated to replace the stock at a later date, he hopes to buy it back at a lower price in order to make a profit. If he borrowed and sold 1,000 shares at $100 per share and then bought them back at a later date at $75, he could net $25,000 less commission and cost of borrowing.

POLICY OF FEDERAL RESERVE

The Federal Reserve is an independent organization and, as such, exercises a considerable amount of autonomy. Although the members of the Board of Governors are appointed by the President with the consent of the Senate, the Board is responsible only to Congress. As a result, it may or may not go along with the monetary policies of the administration. However, since both have the same objective, that is, to stabilize money flows and maintain a high level of business activity, their actions usually complement each other.

World War II

The Federal Reserve keeps a close watch on production, employment, and prices. If it observes or foresees an adverse swing in either direction, up or down, it uses its monetary controls accordingly. For example, during World War II when inflation threatened, reserve requirements on both demand and time deposits were increased toward the maximum, discount rates were increased, the Federal Reserve tightened up on loans to member banks, and moral suasion was used to discourage loans. In addition, the Federal Reserve was given authority to determine the conditions of installment sales, and the stock market margin requirement was pushed upward in an effort to prevent undue speculation in the stock market.

Unfortunately the Federal Reserve was hindered at this time from using its open-market operations as a weapon to combat inflation. Instead of selling bonds, which would have been an anti-inflationary measure, the Federal Reserve was obligated to buy bonds. In order to support the price of government bonds, the Federal Reserve consented to buy all bonds offered to it at an agreed-upon price. Since the agency stood ready to buy at all times at a stipulated price, the market price of the bonds could not fall below this price. This action made the sale of government bonds by the United States Treasury much easier than it otherwise would have been. Without the Federal Reserve as an ever-ready buyer, the prices on bonds would have fallen as individuals and businesses endeavored to resell the bonds they had purchased and as the government put new bonds on the market. If the market price had fallen, it would have cost the United States more to finance the war. For example, if the price of a $100 bond (face value) paying 2.5 percent interest fell to $95, the government would be forced to use one of two alternatives in selling new bonds: (1) The government could sell new bonds with a face value of $100 at a price of $95, a discount of 5 percent. This would mean that the government would have to pay $100 plus $2.50 interest per year for every $95 it borrowed. (2) The government could sell new bonds at $100 but pay at least 2.63 percent interest. Higher interest rates would be necessary because very few banks or businessmen would buy new bonds yielding 2.5 percent when old bonds selling at $95 would yield 2.63 percent interest ($2.50 ÷ $95 = 2.63 percent current yield). Furthermore, when yield to maturity (which includes the $5 capital gain on the discounted bond) is taken into account, still higher interest rates are necessary to sell new bonds.

Postwar Inflation

Although controls were somewhat liberalized immediately after World War II, they were raised to a new high during the postwar inflationary period, 1946-1948. Special legislation of Congress permitted the Federal Reserve to raise the reserve requirements four points over the normal maximums if it were deemed necessary. Although it did not take the full measure, in 1948 the reserve requirements for demand deposits were raised above their old maximums. In this period, discount rates were increased again, loans to member banks were restricted, and the banks were warned not to give speculative loans. Since the Federal Reserve was still supporting bond prices, it could not use its open-market operations as an anti-inflationary measure. Regulation W was restored to limit installment sales, and stock market margin requirements were raised to 100 percent.

Recession of 1949 and the Korean Conflict

The economy took a slight dip in 1949. Production fell, unemployment rose to nearly 4 million, and the price level declined five points. In an endeavor to offset the decrease in economic activity, the Federal Reserve lowered the reserve requirements, liberalized the loans to member banks, withdrew the regulation on installment sales, and decreased the stock market margin requirements.

With the outbreak of hostilities in Korea, the reserve requirements and the discount rates were increased, and member banks found it harder to get loans from the Federal Reserve. Regulation W on installment sales was reinstituted, and Regulation T on stock margin requirements was increased. Regulation X on home purchases was also added. These were all tapered off during the 1953-1954 decline in business activity that followed the Korean conflict.

Post-Korean Period

With the threatening inflation of 1955-1957, discount rates were raised seven times within a two-year period, increasing from 1.75 percent to 3.5 percent. The stock market margin was raised from 60 to 70 percent, and the Federal Reserve began to sell bonds in the open market since it no longer had to support bond prices. In addition, there was some discussion among government authorities about the feasibility of restoring the Federal Reserve's power to restrict installment sales, and a study was made concerning the possibility of restoring credit regulations.

With the decline in the economy that took place in the late 1957 and 1958 period, the discount rates were lowered four times between October 31,

1957, and May 1, 1958, bringing them down from 3.5 percent to 1.75 percent. During the same period the member bank reserve requirements were reduced by small decrements for all categories of banks. Likewise, the stock market margin requirements were lowered from 70 to 50 percent. All during the recession, the Federal Open Market Committee was buying securities in order to increase bank reserves. In addition, the Federal Reserve publicly announced that it had shifted away from the tight-money policy it had been following for the previous few years and that it intended to take proper action in an endeavor to ease credit and the money supply in the hope of helping to arrest the downswing in the economy.

When the economy began recovery after its low ebb in the spring of 1958, the Federal Reserve ceased liberalizing the money supply and gradually shifted toward tighter money. In a series of changes the discount rates were pushed from 1.75 percent up to 4 percent by the fall of 1959. The Open Market Committee was busy selling bonds to absorb excess reserves, and the Board of Governors began to warn against the dangers of renewed pressures on the price level. The net result was a general tightening of the money supply. But during the mild depression of 1960-1961, credit was again eased.

The 1960s and Vietnam

After the 1960-1961 recession, the Federal Reserve continued easy money measures, since the economy was still in a state of less than full employment. Monetary policy, along with several administration fiscal measures, contributed to the seven-year expansion in the economy from 1961 to 1968. As the economy approached full employment in late 1965, however, the Federal Reserve took steps to combat possible inflation resulting from record investment, high-level consumption, large government outlays for Great Society programs, and the escalation of the war in Vietnam. In December, 1965, the discount rate was raised from 4 to 4.5 percent and open-market operations were designed to tighten credit. During 1966, in fact, the Fed was able to swing member banks from a sizable plus net free reserve position to a minus net free reserve position. This did help bring a so-called money crunch in 1966, which caused a shortage of funds in the home mortgage market and adversely affected the housing industry. Although some government officials and others were critical of the Federal Reserve's action, the foresight of the Federal Reserve was instrumental in limiting the rise in the consumer price index in 1966.

By the end of 1966 and in early 1967, when the strongest inflationary impact had passed, at least temporarily, the Federal Reserve switched to less-tight open-market measures. But in order to help correct a deficit balance of international payments and ease the gold outflow on the international scene, and in order to alleviate renewed domestic inflationary pressures, the discount rate in March, 1968, was raised to 5 percent. This was the highest level in 30 years. It was pushed to 5.5 percent in April, 1968, and reached a peak of 6 percent in the spring of 1969.

The 1970s

Interest rates tumbled quickly, however, with the recession of 1970. The discount rate began dropping from its peak of 6 percent in mid-1970 and, by a series of .25 percentage point reductions, declined to 4.5 percent toward the end of 1971. The discount rate held firm for about one year, but started to rise in December, 1972. With the intensification of inflationary pressures in the economy following the removal of Phase II price and wage controls, the prime interest rate rebounded quickly and the discount rate was pushed up briskly to 5.75 percent by April, 1973. In April, when the prime rate reached 6.75 percent, a two-tier system was effectuated. The rate applying to large borrowers was set at 6.75 percent, but the rate to small borrowers was maintained at 6.5 percent. In May, 1973, the extension of the prime rate of large borrowers to 7 percent initiated much speculation about another upward movement of the discount rate. By August, 1973, the discount rate was at an all time high of 8 percent and the prime interest rate subsequently reached a record peak of over 10 percent.

Critics of Federal Reserve Measures

Not everyone, of course, is enamored with, or confident in, the Fed's ability to contribute toward the stability of economic activity and the price level. For years some of its most severe critics have claimed that the Fed lacks timing and that its shifts from liberal to tight money have been too drastic. These critics maintain that there is a substantial lag between the time that the Fed takes action and the impact of that action. Thus, they point out that when the Fed decides to tighten money during a period of prosperity and inflation, the impact of its actions may come several months later when the economy is actually in a downswing. Consequently, the initial action will, so they say, aggravate the downswing. Conversely, it is suggested that the major impact of liberalizing the money supply during a recession may not be felt until several months later when an upswing is taking place in the economy, thus augmenting inflationary pressures. Still others maintain that the Fed's discount policy has an adverse effect. Whereas the Fed raises the discount rate during inflationary periods to discourage member bank borrowing and relending to businesses, opponents of the Fed charge that such action, at least in the short run, causes commercial loan rates to rise. This in turn adds to the cost of production and contributes toward inflation.

In general these critics see the Fed's policy measures as contributing to fluctuations in the economy instead of bringing about stability. As a substitute for Federal Reserve stabilization measures, they recommend a continuous increase in the money supply of 3 to 4 percent annually, which would match the long-run average increase in the production of goods and services. In the absence of any conclusive evidence in either direction, however, the Federal Reserve seems willing to go along with its present measures, but with an attempt to sharpen their implementation.

RECOMMENDED CHANGES IN STRUCTURES AND POLICIES

After 50 years of operating under the National Bank Act, our banking system was changed with the inauguration of the Federal Reserve Banking Act in 1913. Approximately 50 years later a number of different committees and commissions were established to again analyze our system of money and credit.

After several months of study one such group, the Commission on Money and Credit established by the Committee for Economic Development, published its report in 1961. Among other things it recommended certain changes in the structure and policies of the Federal Reserve System. These recommendations included the following: that the discount rate be determined by the Board instead of the Reserve Banks; that open-market operations be vested in the Board; that the Board consist of five members only, eligible for reappointment after a ten-year term; that, although the autonomy of the Federal Reserve should be maintained, the term of office of the Chairman of the Board of Governors should be made coterminous with that of the President of the United States; that all insured commercial banks be required to join the System; that the reserve requirement for all classes of banks be identical; and that reserve-requirement limitations be changed. Although President Kennedy in his 1962 *Economic Report* made certain recommendations based upon the Commission's findings, no substantial organizational or policy changes were made.

Another source of recommendations has been Congressman Wright Patman, Chairman of the House Banking Committee and longtime critic of Federal Reserve autonomy. On several occasions in recent years Congressman Patman has suggested that the term of office of Board members be reduced from 14 to 4 years, that 12 members instead of 7 be appointed by the President, that the System be forced to obtain its operating funds annually from Congress, and that the Secretary of the Treasury be made Chairman of the Board of Governors as a means of curbing its independence. More recently, in 1973, because approximately 700 member banks left the Federal Reserve System in the 1960s and only 100 of the 1,500 new commercial banks formed during that period joined the System, Dr. Arthur Burns, Chairman of the Board of Governors, recommended that the Federal Reserve requirements be extended to nonmember banks in order to enlarge the Fed's control over the money supply.

SUMMARY

1. The Federal Reserve System has a certain degree of control over the nation's money supply, primarily through its ability to affect the volume and cost of bank credit.

2. The Federal Reserve controls over the money supply are of two types: general and selective.

3. An increase in bank reserve requirements will decrease the ability of banks to extend credit, and vice versa.

4. Lowering the discount rates can have a positive effect on the economy by encouraging bank borrowing and stimulating commercial borrowing.

5. The Federal Open Market Committee of the Federal Reserve can increase member bank reserves and therefore affect their ability to extend credit through the purchase of securities from the banks.

6. The Fed has the authority to set stock market margin requirements. At one time it also established the conditions of installment sales and the credit arrangements for the purchase of new homes.

7. The general policy of the Fed has been to use its controls to help stabilize the level of economic activity and the price level.

8. Not all economists agree with the effectiveness of the Fed's stabilization measures.

NEW TERMS

General controls, *p. 287*
Selective controls, *p. 287*
Legal reserve requirements, *p. 288*
Excess reserve, *p. 288*
Legal reserves, *p. 288*
Net free reserves, *p. 288*
Discount rate, *p. 293*
Discounts, *p. 293*
Advances, *p. 293*

Prime loan rate, *p. 295*
Federal Funds Market, *p. 297*
Open-market operations, *p. 297*
Moral suasion, *p. 300*
Regulation W, *p. 301*
Regulation X, *p. 302*
Stock market margin, *p. 303*
Regulation T, *p. 304*
Short sale, *p. 304*

1. Explain the difference between general controls and selective controls over bank credit. Which do you think has the greater force in regulating the money supply? Why?

2. Does the lowering of reserve requirements automatically increase the money supply? Why?

3. Do you agree that stabilizing measures of the Federal Reserve should be preventive rather than remedial? Why?

4. In what way can a change in the discount rate affect commercial loan rates?

5. What is the difference in the effect on the money supply between a member bank rediscounting its customers' notes and a member bank discounting its own notes?

6. What will be the effect of the purchase of bonds from individuals by the Federal Open Market Committee compared to the purchase of bonds from the commercial banks as far as expanding the money supply is concerned?

7. Do you think the Federal Reserve should support government bond prices by standing ready to buy all government bonds at par or face value? Why?

8. With the return to full employment in the mid-1960s, there was considerable discussion of the merits of reinstituting consumer credit controls. Do you think it would have been wise to do so? Why or why not?

9. Do you think that it is proper to permit the use of credit for stock market purchasing? Why?

10. Since the federal administration is usually held responsible for the state of the economy, do you think that it should have more control over the Federal Reserve in order to have more influence over monetary policy? Why or why not?

11. Evaluate the proposal to have a 3 to 4 percent annual increase in the money supply.

12. Do you think that the present autonomy of the Federal Reserve System should be maintained, or should it be modified as has been suggested?

SUGGESTED READINGS

Anderson, Clay J. *Monetary Policy-Decision Making*. Philadelphia: Federal Reserve Bank of Philadelphia (April, 1962).

Board of Governors of the Federal Reserve System. *Federal Reserve System: Purposes and Functions*. Westport, Conn.: Greenwood Press, Inc., 1968. Chapters 3 and 4.

Eastburn, David P. "The Federal Reserve as a Living Institution: A Prescription for the Future." *Business Review*. Philadelphia: Federal Reserve Bank of Philadelphia (March, 1970).

Federal Reserve Bank of New York. *Monthly Review* (January-December, 1964). (Anniversary issue with series of historical articles on the Federal Reserve System.)

Federal Reserve Bank of Philadelphia. "Discount Policy and Discount Rates." *Business Review* (January, 1959).

Federal Reserve Bank of Richmond. "The Discount Window." *Monthly Review* (April, 1965).

Federal Reserve Bank of St. Louis. "Two Critiques of Monetarism." *Review* (January, 1972).

Fishman, Leo. "The White House and the Fed." *Challenge* (July-August, 1966).

Meek, Paul. *Open Market Operations.* New York: Federal Reserve Bank of New York, 1963.

Money and Credit: Their Influence on Jobs, Prices, and Growth, Report of the Commission on Money and Credit. Englewood Cliffs, N.J.: Prentice-Hall, Inc., 1961.

Roosa, Robert V. *Federal Reserve Operations in the Money and Government Securities Markets*. New York: Federal Reserve Bank of New York (July, 1956).

Yeager, Leland B. *Monetary Policy and Economic Performance*, Special Analysis. Washington: American Enterprise Institute, 1972.

PART FOUR

Economic Activity
and Fiscal Policy

15

Stabilization Policies: Unemployment and Depression

PREVIEW It has been the economic policy of the federal government to use measures at its disposal to stabilize the level of economic activity and the price level. Consequently, when there is slack in the economy or a recession is in progress, various monetary, fiscal, and psychological measures are used to bolster the level of economic activity and bring about increased production, employment, and income. Monetary measures may be employed to expand the money supply, lower interest rates, and induce more investment. At other times, the federal government reduces taxes, increases spending, and incurs a deficit in the interest of stimulating the economy. Measures such as these were employed in the recession of 1958, in the period of nagging unemployment of the early 1960s, in the recession of 1970, and during the slowdown of 1974.

In preceding chapters it has been shown that the economy is susceptible to business fluctuations and that these fluctuations are due to changes in consumption, investment, and government spending. Since both unemployment and inflation are detrimental to the total economy, they should be avoided when possible. During periods of widespread unemployment various measures may be utilized to bolster the level of economic activity. On the other hand, serious inflationary problems may occur, especially during a war or a defense period, that require the imposition of economic controls. In total, short-run economic stability at a high level of employment and long-run economic growth are desirable objectives or goals for the economy. Slowdowns, depressions, and inflation are economic conditions to be avoided.

POLICIES TO ALLEVIATE UNEMPLOYMENT

The cost of a severe depression can be measured in billions of dollars. Important also, however, are the hardships that accompany unemployment, such as bankruptcies, waste of productive resources, plant idleness, and the resulting social deterioration.

When financial losses and social dislocations of serious dimensions occur, economic policies and measures may be developed and implemented in an effort to raise the level of economic activity. Even in the absence of a recession, economic measures may be used to stimulate the rate of growth in the economy to provide a higher level of production, employment, and income. These policies and measures should be consistent with the ideals of a democratic society; that is, in helping to create a greater degree of stability or to raise the level of business activity, they should not weaken the spirit of free enterprise. As stated by the Commission on National Goals, "Democracy must be preserved and not curtailed in the endeavor to find quick solutions to our many political, economic, and social problems."

Three general policies can be developed to promote maximum income with full employment: (1) consumption may be stimulated in such a fashion that the propensity to consume is increased; (2) conditions favorable to a high level of investment may be developed; and (3) government spending may be used in an effort to bolster the level of business activity.

Built-In Stabilizers

Over the past few decades we have developed a number of economic institutions, or practices, that tend to serve as built-in stabilizers for the economy. An outstanding example is the Social Security System, devised to insure greater continuity of income to the unemployed and to elderly persons. Unemployment compensation and old-age pension payments help to maintain consumption, even when recession occurs; they are shock absorbers that cushion the downward pressure of recession. The many supplementary unemployment benefit plans and guaranteed annual income plans developed by businesses or through labor-management negotiations are also helpful in this regard. In addition, economic stabilization features are cited as a major argument for a federally sponsored income maintenance plan. A stable tax structure can serve as a further built-in stabilizer. When prosperity occurs, higher returns from a given tax rate can result in a budget surplus and thus exert a *fiscal drag* on the economy to help ward off inflation. On the other hand, during a recession the smaller revenue from taxes causes a deficit and leads to the necessity of government borrowing. This creates what economists refer to as a *fiscal stimulus* for the economy.

Although not so noticeable, other government welfare programs have a similar effect. In addition, corporate retained earnings and family savings also can serve as built-in stabilizers.

Monetary Policy

It can be recalled from Chapter 14 that the Federal Reserve can and does influence the amount of money and credit in the economy, and that a liberalization of the money supply can raise the level of economic activity during periods of unemployment.

Whenever a recession occurs, it is important that bank credit be made easier, but only with proper safeguards. The Fed can help in making easier credit available by purchasing government bonds in the open market and paying for them by checks drawn against its own credit, which in turn will put the Federal Reserve member banks in a position to expand their reserves. A reduction of the reserve requirements will give the same result, for in either case the member banks are better able to make loans. A lowering of the discount rate serves as an additional inducement to member banks to borrow from the Federal Reserve Banks. Furthermore, liberalizing the money supply will lower interest rates. This should increase the gap between the marginal efficiency of capital and the rate of interest and encourage private investment. This, of course, raises effective demand and tends to eliminate the production gap.

Whether one or more of these methods will be used by the monetary authorities will depend on their judgment concerning the seriousness of the business recession or the need for expansion and the best way by which more liberal credit measures can be employed to stimulate the economy. Credit can be made more easily obtainable, but there is no certainty that business firms will increase their borrowings. If a recession has become serious and there is little prospect for improvement in business conditions, businessmen may hesitate to borrow freely, even if credit is readily available at a low interest rate.

Economic stability and growth has become a primary objective of monetary policy. In general, the Federal Reserve aims to expand the money supply and to ease the reserve position of the banks in times of falling production and prices. On the other hand, it restricts the money supply and tightens bank reserves in a time of overexpansion of business activity. A monetary policy, therefore, must be flexible and the Federal Reserve authorities must adjust their position quickly when economic conditions change. Because of its limitations, however, regulation of the money supply can only serve as a partial corrective to instability. The fiscal powers of the government are probably more effective for the task of raising the level of economic activity, especially during a period of serious unemployment.

Fiscal Policy

In addition to the efforts of forces in the private sector of the economy, the operation of the built-in stabilizers, and the utilization of monetary measures by the Fed and the Treasury to offset depressions and inflation, the federal government has a powerful tool of stabilization in its fiscal policies and measures. Government revenues and expenditures may be adjusted in a manner that will bolster the economy during a recession, combat inflation when the economy is overheating, and promote economic growth in the long run. In order to understand the role of fiscal policy in maintaining economic stability, let us first look at the government's sources of revenue and the direction of its spending. Three methods for financing government spending are available: (1) taxation, (2) borrowing, and (3) printing money.

Taxation. If taxation is used to finance government spending, caution must be exercised not to tax funds that otherwise would be used for consumption or investment. It would be of very little use to have the government spend more at the expense of consumption and private investment. The total effective demand would remain constant, and no increase of employment would result. On the other hand, if only idle funds were taxed, government taxation and spending would lead to an increase in total effective demand. In fact, if the government could design a tax to absorb all those funds that would not be spent on consumption or investment, government spending would always be sufficient to have total effective demand, including government spending, equal to total output. However, the practicality of designing and enforcing such a tax is rather remote. Any tax structure that is utilized generally will absorb consumer and investment funds to some significant degree. Furthermore, the equitableness of such a tax is questionable.

Borrowing. Borrowing is a more desirable method of raising funds for government spending when the purpose of spending the funds is to bolster the level of economic activity. The source of borrowing, however, will have a direct bearing on the effect. The government may borrow from individuals, businesses, or banks. In any case, the total effect will depend on whether or not it borrows idle funds. If it borrows funds through the sale of bonds, for example, to individuals and businesses who otherwise would use the funds for consumption and investment, the effect of government spending will be negated because the total effective demand will show no net increase. But if the individuals and businesses use idle funds—those not intended for consumption and investment—to buy the bonds, there will be a net increase in effective demand when the government spends the funds. This will bring about the desired effect of increasing production, employment, and income.

Since some individuals and businesses, especially for patriotic reasons, may give up otherwise spendable funds to buy government bonds, bank borrowing is usually recognized as the most feasible method of financing deficit spending in order to bring about an increase in the level of economic activity. It is not likely to have an adverse effect on the spending by individuals and firms out of their current income. It is true that banks may lend money that has been put into the bank by depositors. To this extent there would be merely a transfer of funds from the depositors to the government. However, since bank savings deposits are usually considered as idle funds by the depositors, that is, they do not intend to use them for consumption or investment immediately, government borrowing from the banks will have a positive effect toward increasing the level of employment. Furthermore, the government can borrow funds in excess of the actual savings without hampering consumption or investment spending. This is accomplished through the creation of bank credit. Usually when the government borrows by selling large amounts of bonds to the banks, the banks pay for the bonds by creating demand deposits for the government against which the Treasury can write checks. To this extent, there is an increase in the money supply as well as an increase in the total effective demand in the economy.

Printing Money. Similar results can be accomplished by using printed money to increase government spending. This method has an additional advantage insofar as it eliminates the necessity of having the government go into debt. Increasing government spending by increasing the amount of currency, however, is often difficult unless the government can increase the basis of the money supply, such as gold. Even with an inconvertible paper standard there is the possibility of overissue and depreciation of the currency. Printing and engraving presses cannot be run at will without some regard to the valuation of the currency. To print money without regard to its backing can be disastrous. Furthermore, although Americans accept the creation of credit by the commercial banks, we seem to have an aversion to the printing of money by the government without proper backing. As a result, printing money for the purpose of government spending has not been a very acceptable method of bolstering the economy.

Some economists, on the other hand, suggest that the government use printed money. They reason that printed money is just as substantial as bank credit. Since the government has the right to coin money and to regulate its value, they think that it would be wise to bypass the bank and print the money directly when needed for federal government expenditures to bolster the economy. These advocates cannot see why the bank should be paid an interest rate for providing a service that is primarily a function of the government. If the government prints the money instead of relying on the sale of bonds to the banks, which pay for the bonds by the creation of credit, it can avoid the cost of paying interest. Therefore, they suggest the use of interest-free financing. With this method, the Treasury would sell non-interest-bearing notes to the Federal Reserve Banks, which in turn would create deposits for the government. Otherwise the government could just print money. This group, including Congressman Patman, rationalizes this concept of interest-free financing by pointing out that since the bank created the money to buy bonds, no one is giving up anything or making any sacrifice of purchasing power. Furthermore, since there is practically no risk involved in government bonds, there is no need to make any interest charge for assumption of risk.

Methods of Increasing Government Spending

Once it has been decided to use government spending as a means of raising effective demand in order to increase the level of employment, there remains the question of the exact method of accomplishing the objective. Three methods are suggested: (1) increase spending and hold taxes, (2) hold spending and decrease taxes, and (3) increase both spending and taxes.

Increase Government Spending and Hold Taxes. In this method, there is a positive increase in the amount of money spent by the government. For example, if the government has been spending $300 billion annually and taxing the same amount, it has a balanced budget. Now suppose that it is decided to increase government spending to $320 billion annually. If taxes are held constant, the government will be forced to borrow $20 billion for its additional expenditures. If the government borrows from the banks, individuals and business firms will not be forced to give up spendable funds through higher taxation. As a result, the total spending (and therefore total effective demand) should increase for the economy as a whole. Incomes will increase not only by $20 billion but also by some multiple thereof, depending on the size of the multiplier. This method is beneficial insofar as the government can easily maintain close control over the direction of the additional government spending.

Hold Government Spending and Decrease Taxes. This is often referred to as the "tax remission" plan. It also results in a deficit budget. For example, assume that the government was running a balanced budget of $300 billion annually, as stated in our first case. If the government decides to decrease taxes $20 billion annually, it will be $20 billion short of needed revenue. As a result, the government will be forced to borrow $20 billion. If it borrows from the banks or borrows otherwise idle funds, it will increase the total spending in the economy by $20 billion plus the multiplier effect. Although the government will not be spending any more, it is assumed that the recipients of the tax remission will spend the money either for consumption or investment. To the extent that they may not, the effect of using this method to increase employment would be lessened. The direction of their spending may also be less effective. This method is politically popular because both individuals and firms are usually happy about reduced taxes.

It is also possible to use a combination of the two methods mentioned above by increasing government spending and decreasing taxes.

Increase Government Spending and Increase Taxes Proportionately. In this method, a balanced budget is maintained. The effectiveness of the method is limited by the fact that, while raising taxes, the government may absorb funds that otherwise would be spent for consumption and investment. Therefore, the whole success of the program depends on the ability of tax measures to collect idle funds and thus increase the total effective demand in the economy. Since most tax measures force consumers and investors to give up their spendable funds to some degree, it usually requires a larger amount of government spending to raise the level of employment a given amount by this method than it does by the first two methods mentioned. By the previous methods, the government can raise total effective demand by $20 billion, exclusive of the multiplier effect, through borrowing. If it desires to raise effective demand by $20 billion through government spending financed strictly by taxation, however, more than $20 billion will have to be spent.

For example, if the marginal propensity to save were one half, the government would have to tax and spend approximately $40 billion in order to raise effective demand $20 billion, exclusive of the multiplier. The first $20 billion of government expenditure would merely offset the decrease in consumption and private investment resulting from the tax. The second $20 billion would add to the total effective demand, since it in effect would come from savings that otherwise would not be spent. If the propensity to save were one third for the economy as a whole, government taxation and spending would have to be $60 billion to effectuate a $20 billion net increase in effective demand, exclusive of the multiplier and accelerator effect. If the propensity to save were one fourth, government spending would have to be $80 billion. Thus, it is easy to recognize the limitations of this method as a means of raising effective demand to increase the level of employment. It would be practicable only for spending of small amounts or if the tax could be designed to tap primarily idle funds.

Direction of Government Spending

If a decision is made to utilize deficit spending as a means of raising the level of employment, a question naturally arises regarding the direction of government spending. Should the government increase its everyday services? Should it provide extragovernmental services? Should the spending be for consumption or investment purposes? Should spending be concentrated or diversified? How much should it be and how long should it last? It is easy to see that once a decision is made to use deficit financing, it is only the beginning of the issue.

It was Keynes' philosophy that it was better to have a man produce something than to remain involuntarily idle. He further believed that it was the government's responsibility to do everything within its means to provide employment for those unemployed because of fortuitous circumstances beyond the control of individuals or firms. Therefore, he logically had no qualms about the use of deficit spending to raise the level of employment. To Keynes it was better to provide goods and services for the economy even if it required going into debt than it was to permit large numbers of men to remain idle, as was the case during the Great Depression. Not all people, however, agree. Keynes was inclined to favor public spending, especially on public works, as a means of raising the level of employment. Producing something rather than nothing results in a net gain to the economy as a whole. For example, it is much more beneficial to have workers building houses, dams, bridges, roads, and the like, than to have the workers idle.

It is possible to alleviate the effects of unemployment by the use of direct monetary payments to the unemployed, or by spending for public works.

Direct Payments. While this method makes certain that those suffering most from the evils of unemployment will receive direct aid, its total effect will be less than public investment in the form of public works. If the worker is given a direct handout, he will spend the bulk of the money on consumption, which will increase the level of economic activity to some degree, provided the funds he received did not come at the expense of consumption and investment elsewhere in the economy. Even if the worker is employed on a simple project such as leaf raking for the sake of respectability, the total effect will not be much greater. The capital needed to put a group of workers on such a job is limited to rakes, shovels, wheelbarrows, and perhaps a few trucks. Furthermore, the spending or direct income payment primarily for consumer goods may have no greater effect than drawing down excess inventories of consumer goods.

Public Works. On the other hand, a large public work, such as a bridge, a dam, a highway, or a building, will necessitate the use of a large number of capital goods and the production of a large amount of supplies, such as iron, cement, lumber, electric wiring, and glass plate. Furthermore, transportation will be stimulated to some extent by the movement of goods. Not only are payments made to contractors, but contractors must pay subcontractors, suppliers, and transportation companies in addition to the workers directly on the job. These men, in turn, spend on consumption. Consequently, workers will be employed in the production of consumer goods that are purchased by these workers. All this tends to build up the multiplier effect and may even stimulate the accelerator principle. Thus, more secondary and tertiary employment is generated through public works than by a leaf-raking project or by direct handouts.

Since an endeavor is being made to alleviate unemployment, public works would appear to serve the purpose better than other means. Not only is there a greater multiplier effect, but also there is always something to show for the spending and production efforts involved. Although it is wise to select practical and useful projects, Keynes suggests that it is preferable to spend money on useless projects rather than not to spend it at all. Even though the project may be of no value, the benefits obtained through the multiplier effect, according to Keynes, will be a net gain to the community. At least workers will have jobs and be able to purchase the consumer items they require.

The income-expenditure approach makes use of the employment multiplier, in addition to the investment multiplier, to show the net result of an increase in employment. The *employment multiplier, k'*, is the ratio of the total increase in employment, N, to the original increase of employment, N_2. Therefore, $k' = \dfrac{N}{N_2}$ or $N = k' \times N_2$. This formula is used to measure the change in total employment compared to a primary increase of employment in the investment industries. The employment multiplier may or may not be equal to the investment multiplier.

Once the employment multiplier is known, it can be determined rather easily what amount of employment on public works will be necessary to raise the level of employment by a desired amount. For example, assume an employment multiplier of 4 and a current level of 80 million employed. If it is desired to raise the level of employment to 90 million, it will require the hiring of only 2.5 million workers in the investment industries or in public works in order to increase total employment by 10 million (4 $\times$ 2.5 million). If the employment multiplier were 5, it would require the hiring of only 2 million workers to raise employment by a total of 10 million (5 $\times$ 2 million). Thus, the higher the employment multiplier, the easier it is to bring about a desired level of employment through public works.

Since both the investment and the employment multipliers decrease as income increases, as a result of the decrease in the marginal propensity to consume, the net effect of spending on public works will be greater in times of widespread unemployment than it will be as we approach the full-employment stage. Based upon the available statistics, it has been calculated that the multiplier for the United States is less than 3 and that it is fairly stable in the neighborhood of 2.5. However, the size of the multiplier fluctuates with changes in the business cycle.

It is true that public investment can be used to fill the gap between output and effective demand whenever consumption and private investment are insufficient to bring about a high level of employment. But it may require a sizable amount of spending or extended periods of time. In the United States we did attempt to alleviate the serious unemployment of the 1930s through deficit spending on public works. In spite of the fact that government spending at the time seemed very high to most Americans, Keynes implied that government spending would have to be increased still more if we hoped to reach the full-employment stage in the United States. Although we engaged in public investment for nearly a decade, we were still a considerable distance away from full employment. After World War II broke out, however, and we began to spend billions for defense and war purposes, we moved from a position of nearly 9 million unemployed in 1939 to full employment by 1942. Keynes felt that it was unfortunate that statesmen and economists did not realize that the same results could have been obtained through nonwar expenditures or that, if they did realize it, they were inhibited from admitting it by predilections of the Classical school. By the 1960s, however, these inhibitions seemed to have disappeared.

ANTIDEPRESSIONARY POLICIES OF THE THIRTIES

The economic, social, and political evils of unemployment emphasize the need for problem solving. In serious depressions, unemployment not only works a hardship on the individual employee and his family but also on the economy as a whole. Widespread and prolonged unemployment results in a loss of individual income and frequently brings about a deterioration of working skills. Furthermore, the loss of goods and services is tremendous. Labor is perishable. Labor time lost today through idleness is gone forever. It is true that the worker can work double time tomorrow to make up lost time today, but he could work the double time without having lost the original time.

Since many of our present-day expansionary policies and specific measures to bolster economic activity are based on lessons learned from previous decades, a capsule look at the beginnings, the 1930s, is in order.

Setting in 1930s

Some idea of the gigantic loss of goods and services resulting from unemployment in the 1930s was given by Henry Wallace, former Secretary of Agriculture. He estimated that in the 11-year depression period between 1929 and 1940 we lost 88 million man-years of work due to involuntary unemployment. At the then current productivity per man-hour rate, this represented a loss of nearly $350 billion. This amount of income would have built 70 million new moderate-priced homes, which would have been three times the number required to completely replace all of the slum areas in the United States at that time. Furthermore, the economic loss through idleness amounted to more than double the value of the capital stock in our private corporations. It was enough to build 350 public projects the size of TVA.[1]

The GNP in the 1930s ranged from a high of $103 billion in 1929 to a low of $56 billion in 1933 and averaged about $80 billion per year for the 11-year period. Since the GNP potential, as measured by 1929, was a little over $100 billion per year, a further comparison reveals that the loss of production due to layoffs during this period was equivalent to a shutdown of the entire economy for a period of more than three years. Thus, it is easy to see that the loss through unemployment during a serious depression can be staggering. Such a situation certainly lends support to the adoption of at least certain income-expenditure policies for raising the level of employment. Therefore, it should come as no surprise to learn that our economic policies of the 1930s and subsequently have paralleled, if not followed, the income-expenditure analysis in a great many respects.

Under the laissez-faire policy and the self-adjusting mechanisms of Classical economic doctrine, there is nothing to do during a depression except to wait for full employment to return. However, with millions of men unemployed, people going hungry, mortgages being foreclosed, values dropping, factories closing down, and Congressmen being plagued with complaints, it is difficult to stand by and wait for the economy to adjust itself back to a high level of employment. Furthermore, many people, especially voters, have a tendency to blame adverse economic conditions on the party in power. Therefore, besides the humanitarian motive (the promotion of social welfare) and economic justifications, political considerations usually enter the picture when a decision is being made about the use of antidepressionary measures.

New Deal Policies and Programs

Although the Administration of President Herbert Hoover to a certain extent moved away from its laissez-faire banner in an effort to improve economic conditions, at the time of the Presidential elections in 1932, according to the Bureau of Labor Statistics nearly 12 million persons were unemployed in the United States, not including millions more who were only partially employed or workers on short workweeks. In short, one out of every four workers was idle, and many of the others were working only part time. There seemed to be little doubt that the landslide vote for Franklin D.

[1] Henry A. Wallace, *Sixty Million Jobs* (New York: Simon & Schuster, Inc., 1945), Part I, Sec. III.

Roosevelt, who promised a New Deal for the people, manifested a minor political revolt brought on by adverse economic conditions and in particular by the excessive amount of unemployment in the economy.

Upon taking office, President Roosevelt pinpointed the primary objective of the Administration to halt the downward spiral of production, employment, income, and prices by bringing about an upward expansion of the economy through the use of monetary and fiscal policies. Like Keynes, he thought that it was the government's responsibility to take action which would help to bolster the economy. The money supply was liberalized, even to the extent of devaluing the dollar, and fiscal policy became a tool to bolster the level of employment. Public works and deficit spending became the order of the day. In addition, many programs were established to improve the purchasing power of the consumer.

Roosevelt's objective was to improve the purchasing power of the masses, which would bring about increased demand and with it increased profits, production, and employment. Unlike the previous Administration, which tried to work from the top down, that is, by extending aid to businesses in order to keep them operational, Roosevelt concentrated on working from the bottom up. Not only does this approach take advantage of the large propensity to consume among the lower income groups, but it usually is wise politically to take this approach since people vote and business firms do not. Measures that provided financial aid to farmers, refinanced home mortgages, set up unemployment compensation and old-age insurance, and established minimum wage laws were all acceptable to and very popular with the people.

In addition, several billion dollars were expended on public works in order to provide employment for millions of workers. The Civilian Conservation Corps was established to give work and educational opportunities to millions of young men, and the National Youth Administration provided needed work to those in college.

Rate of Deficit Spending

During the time these various public works and other public-investment programs were being tried, the federal budget was running a deficit. After 11 years of surplus financing and of reducing the large debt incurred in World War I, the government went into debt each year from 1931 to 1940. Although tax revenues increased during the depression years, expenditures moved up at a faster rate and the federal government went deeper into debt as a result of federal deficits averaging over $3 billion annually. During this time the national debt increased from $16 billion to $48 billion. In addition, state and local government debts were increased.

Lesson of the 1930s

Prior to the Depression, governmental units did their spending and building when everyone else did, that is, during prosperity. In the 1930s, however, public officials and others began to realize the value of public spending during depressions as a means of alleviating unemployment. They also became aware of the fact that much more could be accomplished through public works than through mere handouts for relief. Although the Administration and Congress may not have been influenced by Keynes, certainly they had adopted policies that paralleled those of the income-expenditure analysis. Our experience in the United States between 1933 and 1945 with the public-spending program indicates the following: (1) our early attempts to alleviate unemployment repudiated the pump-priming theory; (2) it verified the multiplier theory; (3) although large, our spending during the 1930s was insufficient and indicated the need for a very large outlay of government spending during depression periods; (4) the war proved that a sufficiently large outlay of government spending could return an economy from a position of a considerable degree of unemployment to a full-employment stage within a relatively short period; and (5) better results are obtained through spending on public works than could be obtained through direct relief payments.

Appraisal of Antidepressionary Measures

The actual success of our experiments to raise the level of employment with public investment is difficult to measure. Certainly we did not come even near reaching the full-employment stage, and the expansion that set in after the winter of 1933-1934, usually considered as the depth of the depression, was stopped far short of full employment with the downturn of 1937-1938. From a high of more than 12 million unemployed in 1933, conditions improved and unemployment dropped to 7.7 million in 1937. With the so-called recession of late 1937 and 1938, however, unemployment jumped over the 11 million mark in the first part of 1938 and averaged 10.4 million for the year. At the time we began producing defense materials for the Allies in 1939, unemployment was still approximately 9 million and as high as 10 million early in 1940. With the expansion of defense and war production it dropped to 2.7 million in 1942 and less than 1 million at the height of the war in 1944. Unemployment figures for the period 1929 to 1944 are given in Table 15-1.

It is evident from data in the table that there was some improvement in the level of employment as a result of the New Deal efforts. On the other hand, the results left much to be desired. Critics of public investment, especially the advocates of laissez-faire and the balanced budget, point to the

TABLE 15-1

UNEMPLOYED
IN THE
UNITED STATES

1929-1944

Year	Unemployed (Thousands)	Unemployed (Percentage of Civilian Labor Force)
1929	1,550	3.2
1930	4,340	8.7
1931	8,020	15.9
1932	12,060	23.6
1933	12,830	24.9
1934	11,340	21.7
1935	10,610	20.1
1936	9,030	16.9
1937	7,700	14.3
1938	10,390	19.0
1939	9,480	17.2
1940	8,120	14.6
1941	5,560	9.9
1942	2,660	4.7
1943	1,070	1.9
1944	670	1.2

SOURCE: *Statistical Abstract of the United States*, 1973.

figures to demonstrate the lack of success of the spending program. How can a program be called successful when after eight years of spending we still had over 9 million unemployed? Unemployment, according to the critics, may have been much lower if the government had stayed out of the picture and let automatic economic forces return us to full employment. On the other hand, we do not know what it might have been if the public-investment programs had not been in effect. It might have been much higher. As a result of not knowing, or of not being able to determine, what might have happened in the absence of our grand experiment, it is impossible to determine the success of the public-spending program.

We do know, however, that millions of unemployed workers were given jobs on public works and other government projects. Production, employment, and income were increased accordingly. Not only were people put to work directly on government projects, but also others were employed as a result of the multiplier effect. For example, it was estimated that for every person directly employed on a public works project another 2.5 persons were employed indirectly in producing and transporting supplies for the projects. Extending this to take into account the increased production of consumer goods required by the expending of income received by those workers, total employment increased fivefold for every person at the site of a public works project.[2] This would be equivalent to an employment multiplier of 5.

[2] Florence Peterson, *Survey of Labor Economics* (New York: Harper & Row, Publishers, 1947), p. 176.

While it is true that there was a considerable amount of waste and disorganization in early public works projects, many improvements came with experience. Hastily organized projects were replaced with those of a more permanent nature and greater social benefit. Management of the projects became more efficient. Early critics of the low wage scales saw wages rise. In addition to manual and clerical labor, later projects made use of writers, teachers, statisticians, actors, artists, and the like, who contributed services from which we are still receiving benefits.

Our experience of the 1930s leaves little doubt that our New Deal policies were similar to those advocated by the income-expenditure analysis, especially the idea of deficit spending and public works. Further evidence that we have accepted much of the income-expenditure theory can be found by analyzing the Employment Act of 1946. Here it is definitely stated that the Administration should use measures at its disposal, including monetary and fiscal policies, to create conditions favorable to a high level of production, employment, and income. The Act, as we learned in Chapter 10, established the President's Council of Economic Advisers and requires the President to render an economic report on the state of the economy each year. The experience of the 1930s also served as a basis for developing subsequent programs for dealing with unemployment in later years, including the 1960s and 1970s.

THE NEW ECONOMICS

Although the Eisenhower Administration, in addition to its strong reliance on monetary policies, did engage in some direct measures, such as modest tax cuts, federal extension of state unemployment benefits, accelerated spending on federal highways, and even an unplanned $12.9 billion federal deficit, in an effort to alleviate unemployment in the recessions of 1953-1954 and 1958, much more positive action in this direction was undertaken by the Kennedy and Johnson Administrations. On the basis that unemployment exceeded 5 percent or more of the labor force in every month except one during the five-year period 1957-1962 and the fact that the economy was operating at less than 90 percent of its capacity, President Kennedy in his 1962 *Economic Report* suggested the following depression-proof measures as a means of bolstering the economy and stimulating economic expansion:

1. Establish a Manpower Development and Training Program for the retraining of unemployed workers.
2. Provide a tax credit system for business firms that show a net increase in investment.
3. Grant the President standby authority to reduce taxes by as much as $10 billion as unemployment increased.

4. Grant the President standby authority to increase government spending on public works by as much as $2 billion in the event of a recession.

5. Enact a Youth Employment Opportunity Bill to set up a program for training, and to some extent to provide jobs, for youths entering the labor force.

6. Increase state unemployment compensation benefits and extend coverage to millions of additional workers.

Area Redevelopment Act, 1961

During his first year in office, President Kennedy was instrumental in bringing about passage of the Area Redevelopment Act of 1961, which endeavored to bring industry to depressed areas and jobs to displaced workers. The main features of this Act were the financial aids that were provided for distressed areas and for areas with labor surpluses. These financial aids took the forms of loans and grants for the construction of community projects and loans for private industrial undertakings of various types that would help to lessen unemployment in the affected areas. Included in the program was training to prepare workers for jobs in new and expanded local industries. In its first five years of operation, before it was incorporated into other programs, over 1,000 projects involving 65,000 trainees in 250 redevelopment areas had been approved.

Tax Credits to Stimulate New Investment, 1962

As a result of the request in the 1962 *Economic Report*, Congress did subsequently enact a bill providing a 7 percent tax credit allowance for new investment. It also permitted acceleration of depreciation cost as a means of encouraging new investment. The provisions of the Act were widely used by businesses and no doubt contributed to record levels of investment in the economy that followed, especially during the mid-1960s. At one time it was estimated that the government's loss of revenue resulting from the tax credits was approximately $2 billion annually.

Manpower Development and Training Act, 1962

In 1962 Congress also enacted the Manpower Development and Training Act. The primary purpose of this Act was to provide training for the unemployed and the underemployed in order to qualify them for reemployment or full employment. For this purpose the Act initially provided $435 million to be spent in three years. Unlike the ARA, the MDTA did not seek to allocate funds or benefits particularly to distressed areas of chronic unemployment or substandard levels of income. The Act allocated funds among states on the basis of each state's proportion of the total labor force, its total unemployment, and its average weekly unemployment payment.

The Act established training courses in those skills or occupations where there was a demand for workers, and the trainees had a reasonable chance of securing employment upon completion of the training program. Such programs were set up through the local state employment service utilizing state and local vocational education institutions, although private schools and other training institutions could be used. On-the-job training offered by an employer and jointly by employer and local school authorities was also eligible for federal support under the Act. Courses and programs established usually ranged in length from two weeks to one year. Trainees with work experience and heads of households were given a subsistence allowance while retraining or received an allowance equal to the average weekly unemployment benefits for the state.

It was anticipated that between 750,000 and 1 million persons would receive some sort of instruction or retraining during the three-year life of the program, and that more would receive the benefits of counseling, testing, and placement services provided by the Act. These figures were subsequently lowered to a total of 430,000 for the three-year program.

Although the MDTA program did get off to a slow start because of difficulties and complications involved in such a huge program, it began to pick up momentum toward the end of fiscal 1963. The Department of Labor reported that for the period of August, 1962, to December, 1966, nearly 10,000 programs involving 598,700 trainees had been approved under the Manpower Development and Training Act. During this period records indicate that nearly three fourths of the MDTA graduates were placed on jobs, most of them in occupations relating to their training. By 1965 the idea of having the states absorb one third of the cost of MDTA programs was abandoned, and the whole program was renewed with the federal government continuing to carry 90 percent of the total cost of the program. President Johnson stated that the Act need no longer be considered temporary, and asked that it be put on a continuing basis. By 1974 over 2 million enrollees had received training under MDTA programs.

Public Works, 1962

Although President Kennedy was not given standby authority either to reduce taxes or to increase federal spending on public works as requested in his 1962 *Economic Report*, Congress did in 1962 pass the Emergency Public Works Act, and subsequently appropriated $900 million to be spent on various projects to help reduce unemployment and stimulate economic growth.

The Historic Income Tax Cuts, 1964

In his 1963 *Economic Report*, President Kennedy pointed with pride to the economic accomplishments under his Administration. But he stressed that in spite of the gains we still did not have maximum production, maximum employment, and maximum income as called for under the Employment Act of 1946. He indicated further that the economy was growing at only 3 percent annually compared to a potential growth rate of 4.5 percent. Consequently, as a means of bolstering the economy and accelerating economic growth, he presented a budget of $98.8 billion and simultaneously requested a net tax reduction on personal and corporate incomes, which would result in a $11.8 billion deficit in the fiscal 1964 budget. This, of course, was a change in economic policy. Here, instead of antidepression deficit spending, we had introduced the idea that deficit spending should be used even during prosperity when the economy was not performing at its maximum potential. After 13 months of intermittent hearings and debate on the merits of the tax cuts, Congress finally, after President Kennedy's death, enacted a two-stage $11.5 billion personal and corporate income tax reduction bill in February, 1964. President Johnson immediately signed the bill into law with a word of encouragement to the general public to go out and spend the increase in their monthly incomes that would result from the tax reductions.

Excise Tax Cuts, 1965

In addition to the historic income tax reductions spread over a two-year period in 1964 and 1965, Congress added to this stimulant by providing for excise tax reductions of $5 to $6 billion on a broad array of goods and services from automobiles to entertainment. These tax cuts were to serve as a means of increasing the total demand for goods and services and to contribute to the improvement of production, employment, and income.

Appalachian Regional Development Act, 1965

As a result of the findings of President Kennedy's Appalachia Commission, Congress in 1965 enacted the Appalachia Bill, which provided for various types of aid for a 13-state area extending along the Appalachian Mountains from northern Pennsylvania to eastern Mississippi. The program for this depressed area was aimed at developing an economic base to encourage subsequent private investment as a means of improving its economy. In the early stages, major emphasis was to be placed on road construction, health facilities, land improvement and erosion control, timber development, mining restoration, and water resource surveys. The Act provided nearly $1 billion to improve the economic condition of the area in the hope of raising the production, employment, and income of its inhabitants.

The Economic Opportunity Act, 1964

Additional aid in bolstering the economy has come through various poverty programs. After President Johnson delivered a special message to Congress early in 1964 on the state of poverty in the economy and following considerable debate, the Economic Opportunity Act, frequently known as the antipoverty bill, was passed in August, 1964. Initially the Act provided $962 million to launch the *war on poverty*. Since then, it has been continued with annual appropriations of $1.5 to $2.0 billion. A look at some of the provisions of the Act, carried out through the Office of Economic Opportunity (OEO), will provide an insight into various aspects of the war on poverty.

Poverty Programs. The Act provided a number of programs for the youth of the nation, including a Job Corps, work-training programs, and work-study programs. In addition, the Economic Opportunity Act sought to provide stimulation and incentive for urban and rural communities to mobilize their resources in order to combat poverty through community action programs. Typical programs that fall within this part of the Act include those which provide employment, job training and counseling, health, vocational rehabilitation, housing, home management, welfare, and special remedial and other noncurricular educational assistance for the benefit of low-income families. Particular programs may include dental care for children, legal aid for the poor, rehabilitation houses for prison parolees, and social and recreation services by nonprofit agencies. The Act was also designed to meet some of the special problems related to rural areas in an effort to raise and maintain the income and living standards of low-income families and migrant workers in rural areas.

In an effort to bring about the establishment, preservation, and strengthening of small business enterprises and to improve the managerial skills of business operators, the Act provided for loans to such businesses. Guaranteed loans up to $25,000 are available for the establishment and strengthening of small business enterprises that will have the effect of preserving or raising employment in a given community.

Among other programs, the Act also provided for the recruitment and training of Volunteers in Service to America (VISTA). The VISTA program is very much like the Peace Corps but on a domestic basis. Subsequently the two programs were combined under one director.

Progress of War on Poverty. After a relatively slow start, activity on the poverty front picked up in 1965. One of the first programs developed was the Job Corps. By 1972 more than a quarter of a million young men and women had learned the basic educational skills at the Corps' 120 centers. The Job Corps had an enrollment of 49,000 for 1972.

In 1972 over one million young people were enrolled in work-training programs as members of the Neighborhood Youth Corps in more than 400 community operated projects throughout the nation. In 1972 approximately 100,000 students were receiving aid under the work-study programs established in 1,100 colleges and universities.

In 1972 more than 3,500 VISTA members were busy working with the disadvantaged in the city and rural slum areas, on Indian reservations, in mental hospitals, in migrant worker camps, and at Job Corps centers.

By 1972 more than 2 million persons had received special literacy instruction in various programs provided under the Adult Basic Education Programs, and more than 250,000 unemployed parents had received vocational and literacy instruction under the Work Experience Programs.

In the summer of 1965 the Office of Economic Opportunity, through Project Head Start, put more than one-half million youngsters of poor families through a preschool program to prepare them to receive maximum benefits when they embarked on their school careers. This project was duplicated in subsequent years. By 1972 more than 3 million young people had participated in this program.

In regard to Community Action Programs, which are providing a major thrust in the war on poverty, by the spring of 1972 several hundred grants totaling $4.0 billion had been made to 700 communities in all 50 states of the nation.

Although in the beginning there were some delays, duplications, and even abuses in the war on poverty, by and large it has made some progress in its effort to reduce poverty. Congress, at least, was sufficiently impressed with the accomplishments of the program that it continued to vote appropriations for the war on poverty. Through 1973 nearly $10 billion had been spent directly for war-on-poverty programs. In the early 1970s, however, the Nixon Administration began shifting some of the programs away from the OEO and into other federal agencies, such as the Departments of Labor, HEW, and Agriculture. Still, in 1972 Congress approved funding for the OEO through 1976. President Nixon, however, in early 1973, through the appointment of a new OEO Director, began dismantling that office by eliminating some of the poverty programs, reducing others, and transferring still more programs to other federal agencies. In April, 1973, a federal court issued an injunction against the dismantling of OEO and its programs, declaring that the President had no constitutional authority to undo what Congress had voted.

JOBS Program, 1968

In 1968 a Job Opportunities in the Business Sector (JOBS) program was launched by the Department of Labor and the National Alliance of

Businessmen. The program was built on a commitment by groups of businessmen in 50 metropolitan areas to hire thousands of seriously disadvantaged people and give them on-the-job training, counseling, health care, and other supportive services needed to make these individuals productive workers. The program was built on the premise that immediate placement on a job at regular wages, followed by training and supportive services, rather than training first in an effort to qualify for the job, would provide superior motivation for these disadvantaged workers. Although the program experienced many start-up problems, the most serious of which was worker turnover, or quits, by 1974 more than 400,000 disadvantaged workers had been given jobs by individual company efforts and through Department of Labor contracts. Six of every eight workers hired on federally financed programs were blacks and one in eight was Spanish American. The average JOBS worker had 10.3 years of schooling, had been unemployed more than 20 weeks during the year prior to his enrollment in JOBS, and had an annual income of $2,400. About half of the hirees were under 22 years old.

Deficit Spending in the Sixties

All these current measures were accompanied by continuous deficit spending throughout the 1960s. In fact, President Kennedy knowingly used deficit spending as a means of bolstering the level of economic activity. To his critics who claimed that the deficits resulting from increased spending and decreased taxes would be inflationary, he pointed out on a nationally televised program that his proposal would not be inflationary but would result in an increase in production, employment, and income because at that time the economy was operating at less than full employment of manpower, resources, and capacity. To President Kennedy and his Council of Economic Advisers, the deficits were to be down payments on future surpluses. The proposed deficit was labeled as a "fiscal stimulus." In short, the stimulus (deficit) would lead to a higher level of employment and income. At full employment the greater tax revenues would result in a surplus. Supposedly, when we reached the stage of full employment and budget surpluses, we could then declare a "fiscal dividend" in the form of increased government services or a further reduction in taxes. The payment of this fiscal dividend would then help avoid a "fiscal drag" on the economy that results from a surplus budget. Although we had a number of fiscal stimulants in the economy during the first half of the 1960s and eventually reached full employment by 1966, we never quite reached the surplus-budget stage. One part of the problem may have been that we were declaring fiscal dividends before reaching the full-employment and budget-surplus stage. Another major difficulty of determining how well this policy of fiscal stimulants, fiscal dividends, and the avoidance of fiscal drags would work stemmed from the unforeseeable acceleration of spending that resulted from the escalation of the war in Vietnam. The deficits for the period involved are shown in Table 15-2.

TABLE 15-2

REVENUES,
EXPENDITURES,
AND DEBT OF
THE FEDERAL
GOVERNMENT

1960-1975

(Billions)

Fiscal Year	Revenue	Expenditure	Surplus or Deficit	Total Debt [1]
1960	92.5	92.2	+ .3	290.8
1961	94.4	97.8	− 3.4	292.9
1962	99.7	106.8	− 7.1	303.3
1963	106.6	111.3	− 4.8	310.8
1964	112.7	118.6	− 5.9	316.8
1965	116.8	118.4	− 1.6	323.2
1966	130.9	134.7	− 3.8	329.5
1967	149.6	158.3	− 8.7	341.3
1968	153.7	178.8	− 25.2	369.8
1969	187.8	184.5	+ 3.2	367.1
1970	193.7	196.6	− 2.9	382.6
1971	188.4	211.4	− 23.0	409.5
1972	208.7	231.9	− 23.2	437.3
1973	232.2	246.5	− 14.3	468.4
1974 (est.)	270.0	274.7	−. 4.7	486.4
1975 (est.)	295.0	304.4	− 9.4	508.0

SOURCE: *Economic Report of the President*, 1974, and *Economic Indicators* (January, 1974).

[1] The change in public debt from year to year reflects not only the budget surplus or deficit but also changes in the government's cash on hand, and the use of corporate debt and investment transactions by certain government enterprises.

It was also suggested by a number of government agencies and private studies that some form of guaranteed annual income be established via a negative income tax or otherwise. President Johnson in December, 1966, established a national committee to examine the merits and disadvantages of such proposals. The committee in 1968 recommended that some form of income maintenance be adopted. Such a proposal was contained in the Nixon Welfare Reform Bill introduced into Congress in the early 1970s.

Return to Full Employment

During the early 1960s other socioeconomic measures, such as the introduction of the Medicare provisions of the Social Security Act, the increase in Social Security payments, and the hike in the minimum wage rate, were invoked in part with the idea that they would help reduce "nagging unemployment" and help stimulate economic growth. During this period, 1961-1965, the economy was continually establishing new records of production, employment, and income; and our real economic growth rate was exceeding 5 percent annually. In spite of all this, however, the economy had not reached full employment by early 1966. Unemployment, which had been near 7 percent of the labor force when the Kennedy Administration took office, averaged 6.7 percent for 1961, 5.5 percent for 1962, 5.7 percent for 1963, and 5.2 percent for 1964. Unemployment as late as June, 1965, totaled 4.3 million, or 5.5 percent of the labor force. During this time, moreover, the labor force was experiencing its most rapid growth in the history of the economy.

There was some discussion in the executive and legislative branches of the government about declaring another fiscal dividend in the form of a further income tax or excise tax reduction. By late 1965, however, the economy was approaching the stage of full employment. With record investment, high level consumption, large outlays for Great Society programs, and especially accelerated spending resulting from the escalation of the war in Vietnam, we were at full employment by 1966 and beginning to experience noticeable upward pressures on the price level. Discussions then shifted to enactment of anti-inflationary measures, such as tighter money, reductions in government spending, and tax hikes.

The Recession of 1970

During the period 1966-1970, the economy was at full employment, and we were concerned primarily with measures to combat inflation. As late as 1969 unemployment averaged 3.5 percent. With the recession of 1970, in which the real GNP actually declined (but less than one percent), the rate of unemployment rose to 4.9 percent for the year and in some months reached 5.5 and 6 percent. Although there were still some inflationary pressures in the economy, primarily of a cost-push nature, the Nixon Administration by late 1970 shifted its emphasis from anti-inflationary policies to expansionary policies in order to reduce unemployment and generate an increase in production. Included among the measures to bolster the level of economic activity were accelerated depreciation to encourage business investment, the enactment of a bill providing federal financing of 150,000 to 200,000 jobs in the state and local governments for unemployed workers, Federal Reserve actions to liberalize the money supply and bring about reductions in discount rates, the toleration of a $23 billion federal deficit for fiscal 1971 instead of the originally planned $1.3 billion surplus, the presentation of a federal budget for fiscal 1972 containing a planned $11.6 billion deficit (which finalized with a $23.2 billion deficit), a recommendation for a national health insurance plan, and a proposed program of federal-state revenue sharing.

While stressing the need for expansionary measures, President Nixon and his Council of Economic Advisers did not abandon anti-inflationary measures. The Administration did engage in more "jawboning" in an effort to hold the price line, and much more discussion arose regarding the reinstitution of wage-price guideposts or an incomes policy. President Nixon hoped that the rate of inflation would be reduced to 3.5 percent by the end of 1971 and that the unemployment rate would be down to 4.5 percent by that time. His economic game plan called for a return to full employment and stable prices by mid-1972.

It was evident by mid-1971, however, that progress toward his economic goals was minimal. Unemployment proved to be more stubborn and prices more sticky than anticipated. Sizable wage and price increases were prevalent in spite of an unemployment rate of 5 to 6 percent in the summer of 1971. Consequently, in August, 1971, President Nixon made sweeping and drastic changes in the game plan. Among other domestic and international measures, he imposed a 90-day freeze on all wages and prices, requested reinstitution of the tax credit to stimulate new investment, and asked Congress to reduce personal and corporate income taxes as a means of combating inflation, reducing unemployment, and expanding the economy.

In spite of continued expansion throughout the economy in the next two years, however, unemployment still averaged 5.6 percent in 1972 and 4.9 percent in 1973. In addition, over 200,000 people were employed in the public employment program. Early in 1973 the strict wage and price controls of Phase II of President Nixon's New Economic Policy were replaced by the more liberal measures of Phase III, and the economy found itself at the peak of a business boom. By mid-1973 the President had reimposed price controls through the Phase IV program, and by the end of the year the economy had begun to experience the early stages of a slowdown. The slowdown, coupled with the energy and fuel shortages, as well as with the very real threat of additional shortages cropping up throughout the economy, caused many forecasters to predict a recession for 1974. By January of 1974, unemployment was back up to 5.2 percent, with every indication that it would go even higher in the next few months. Therefore, early in 1974 measures were being formulated to avoid a recession.

SUMMARY

1. According to the income-expenditure analysis, various economic measures can be used to alleviate widespread unemployment or boost a sagging economy.

2. There are three sources of funds available to the government if it decides to increase total spending: taxation, borrowing, and printing money.

3. If the government decides to use fiscal policy to bolster the economy, better results toward that end usually can be attained with a deficit budget compared to a balanced budget.

4. In order to evolve a deficit budget, the government can follow either of the following two procedures: increase spending and hold taxes constant, or hold spending constant and lower taxes.

5. The direction of emergency government spending is also important since it can be influenced by the multiplier and accelerator effects.

6. Numerous stabilization measures were tried during the serious depression of the 1930s, the results of which are still debatable.

7. Federal government spending efforts during the 1930s depression caused the national debt to more than double.

8. In the early 1960s several economic stabilization measures were utilized in an effort to reduce the production gap, eliminate "nagging unemployment," and increase our rate of economic growth.

9. Expansionary measures were again used during the recession of 1970 and subsequently.

NEW TERMS

Built-in stabilizers, *p. 316*
Fiscal drag, *p. 316*
Fiscal stimulus, *p. 316*
Fiscal policy, *p. 317*
Employment multiplier, *p. 323*

New Deal, *p. 326*
Tax credits, *p. 330*
War on poverty, *p. 333*
Job Corps, *p. 333*
JOBS program, *p. 334*

QUESTIONS FOR DISCUSSION AND ANALYSIS

1. How does unemployment compensation act as a built-in stabilizer for the economy?

2. If the government decides to utilize deficit spending as a means of bolstering the economy, is it better to borrow from the banks or from the general public? Why?

3. What are the merits of increased government spending versus a tax reduction provided either is financed through borrowing?

4. What do you think of the idea of "interest-free financing" for government borrowing?

5. Is it true that government spending in any direction during a depression will have the same effect? Why or why not?

6. What are the advantages of government spending on public works compared to direct handouts as a means of alleviating a depression? Are there any disadvantages?

7. Evaluate the effects of the tax reduction program of 1964 and 1965.

8. On emergency public works do you think that employment should be limited only to those who are currently unemployed? Why?

9. In mid-1971 President Nixon vetoed a Congressional bill providing $2 billion for public works, in favor of a bill that provided for federal financing of up to 200,000 jobs in state and local governments. Comment.

10. What do you think of a federally guaranteed annual income as an antidepression measure?

SUGGESTED READINGS

Beveridge, W. H. *Full Employment in a Free Society*. New York: W. W. Norton & Company, Inc., 1951.

Chandler, Lester V. *America's Greatest Depression, 1929-1941*. New York: Harper & Row, Publishers, 1970.

Clague, Ewan. *Unemployment—Past, Present and Future*, Special Analysis No. 12. Washington: American Enterprise Institute (June, 1969).

Economic Report of the President, 1960-1974. Washington: U.S. Government Printing Office.

Galbraith, John Kenneth. *The Great Crash, 1929*. Boston: Houghton Mifflin Company, 1961.

Ginsburg, Helen. *Poverty, Economics, and Society*. Boston: Little, Brown and Company, 1972.

Hall, Robert E. "Why Is the Unemployment Rate So High at Full Employment?" *Brookings Papers on Economic Activity* (1970).

Hansen, Alvin H. *Monetary Theory and Fiscal Policy*. New York: McGraw-Hill Book Company, 1949.

——————. *Economic Policy and Full Employment*. New York: McGraw-Hill Book Company, 1947.

Heilbroner, Robert L. *Understanding Macro Economics*. Englewood Cliffs, N.J.: Prentice-Hall, Inc., 1965.

Manpower Report of the President. Washington: U.S. Government Printing Office, 1973.

Nickson, Jack W., Jr. *Economics and Social Choice*. New York: McGraw-Hill Book Company, 1971.

North, Douglass, and Roger L. Miller. *The Economics of Public Issues*. New York: Holt, Rinehart and Winston, Inc., 1971.

Stein, Herbert. *The Fiscal Revolution in America*. Chicago: University of Chicago Press, 1969.

16

Stabilization Policies: Inflation and War

PREVIEW Just as the federal government has at times used measures to expand the economy, so too has it employed various monetary, fiscal, and psychological measures to prevent or combat inflation. The Fed, for example, by tightening the money supply, raising interest rates, and engaging in open-market operations, endeavors to limit consumption and investment. The government may raise taxes, decrease its spending, reduce deficits, and even on occasion balance the budget in an effort to lessen inflationary pressures. At other times it has adopted wage-price guideposts and even imposed compulsory wage-price controls in an effort to stem the inflationary tide. Measures such as these were utilized with some success during the inflationary periods associated with World War II, the Korean conflict, the latter part of the 1960s, and the early years of the 1970s.

The *income-expenditure analysis* is often referred to as "depression economics." This stems from the fact that it originated, or at least crystallized, during the 1930s and consequently placed primary emphasis on the problem of unemployment. Concentrated efforts of its early advocates to determine the causes of and the remedies for equilibrium at unemployment levels caused people to think of the theory only in terms of depression policies. As a result, many people are inclined to lose sight of the fact that the income-expenditure analysis also treats inflation and suggests anti-inflationary policies. In addition, in recent years much emphasis has been placed on the analysis and use of expansionary measures to stimulate the economy to higher levels of activity, even though the economy may not be in a depressed state. Such measures are designed to move the economy from near full employment to full employment without causing inflation.

PROBLEM OF INFLATION

During periods of changing prices, some income recipients gain and others lose. The main hardships of inflation are the redistribution of income caused by rising prices and the deterioration of past savings. On the other hand, during depression there is not only a redistribution of income but also considerable unemployment. Probably due to the circumstances of the times in which the income-expenditure analysis was introduced, the inflationary problem did not appear as urgent as the problem of unemployment.

According to the income-expenditure approach, inflation will occur at the full-employment level if the effective demand exceeds total output. This will result when private investment and government spending are more than sufficient to fill the gap between consumption and total output. In short, investment will exceed savings. In such a case, current demand will exceed the value of the goods and services currently produced. Competitive bidding by spenders will force prices upward.

The effective demand may be high due to an easy money situation, high levels of investment and consumption, and large government outlays and/or deficit spending. Since the effective demand is greater than the output of goods and services, two alternatives exist to combat the inflationary situation. The first and best is to increase the total output of goods and services to satisfy the excess demand. But since this is not feasible in a full-employment economy in the short run, at least not on a scale large enough to alleviate a serious inflationary situation, we must rely on the second alternative—reduce the total spending.

MEASURES TO REDUCE TOTAL SPENDING

There are a number of methods available for reducing total spending in the economy. The reduction can be made in government spending, in private investment, and/or consumption. In any case both the economic and the political effects of such action must be considered. The method selected depends frequently on circumstances in the economy. Wartime inflation, for example, requires special measures.

Built-In Stabilizers

Our built-in or automatic stabilizers may not be sufficiently forceful during the upswing of the economy. Nevertheless, they are still there. With employment at a high level and unemployment at a low ebb, for example, payroll taxes will be maximized and disbursements from the Social Security System minimized. This will help rake off excess spendable funds from the economy. In a similar fashion the flow into and out of private supplementary unemployment funds will have an anti-inflationary effect. Insofar as our personal and corporate income tax structure is concerned, the given tax rates may yield a full employment surplus, which by its presence will be anti-inflationary if not cause a fiscal drag on the economy. With rising incomes there will be a decrease in the marginal propensity to consume, and the rising rate of personal and corporate savings will act as a deterrent to inflation.

Monetary Policy

The government may also use monetary policy to combat inflation. Measures designed to tighten the money supply and/or increase the rate of interest tend to discourage investment. This, of course, lowers the total effective demand and tends to bring investment into line with savings. Investment could be reduced to a point where it just fills the gap between the combined effective demand of consumption plus government spending and total production at full employment. This will eliminate the inflationary gap, as shown in Figure 8-5 on page 160. Here there is an advantage in having a central monetary authority that easily can raise, as well as lower, the interest rates for the purpose of raising or lowering the effective demand. The anti-inflationary effects of a rise in the interest rate, however, can be offset by a rise in the marginal efficiency of capital. Businessmen will not hesitate to borrow and invest even at a higher interest rate if profits are rising. This frequently occurs when prices, and consequently profits, rise quickly during an inflationary period. According to the income-expenditure analysis there is little that can be done directly under our existing economic structure about controlling the marginal efficiency of capital. For this reason the government must rely heavily on the manipulation of interest rates in combating inflation through its monetary policy.

Other Measures

The government may discourage investment and consumption by other means. It may impose credit restraint on both commercial and consumer loans. For example, it may limit borrowing for stock market purchases, it may tighten restrictions on housing credit, and it may restrain consumer credit. The government may also rely on patriotic spirit to encourage individuals and firms to save instead of spend and, if absolutely necessary, it may impose price and wage controls.

Government Surplus

Total spending may be reduced in the economy during an inflationary period by using policies opposite to those for increasing spending when expansion is desired. First of all, the government can limit its spending to essentials. Furthermore, it can operate with a surplus budget to reduce consumption and investment. If the government taxes more than it spends, it will tend to reduce the total effective demand in the economy. In this case, unlike the expansionary policies, the government should endeavor to tax spendable funds—those that are going to be spent on consumption and investment—rather than idle funds.

The government can combat inflation by building up a surplus in two ways: hold taxes and decrease spending or increase taxes and hold or decrease spending. It may combat inflation also to some extent by decreasing taxes and spending simultaneously.

Hold Taxes and Decrease Spending. If taxes are held constant and government spending is decreased for the purpose of combating inflation, it is more effective to decrease spending in those areas that tend to have the greatest multiplier effect. This method also has an advantage in that it is more palatable to the public than an increase in taxes. On the other hand, a reduction in government service necessitated by the decrease in spending may meet with some public resistance.

Increase Taxes and Hold or Decrease Spending. If higher taxes are to be used to combat inflation, taxes should be increased in such a manner that they absorb funds that otherwise would be spent on consumption or invest-ment. Here again public sentiment may have to be weighed. If taxes are already high, as they are likely to be during an inflationary period, consumers and investors may not be receptive to the idea of higher taxes. If this method is used to combat inflation, however, it is easy to see that a decrease in spend-ing along with higher taxes gives a double effect.

Decrease Taxes and Decrease Government Spending. The combination of lower taxes and lower government spending can be deflationary if taxes are decreased in those areas where the money would otherwise be held idle. This will reduce total spending by the amount of the government spending, provided those who receive the tax reduction save more as a result. A major problem with this last procedure is the difficulty involved in designing a tax remission that will not release spendable funds. Furthermore, even if such a plan could be designed, it would be difficult politically to rationalize a tax remission that is beneficial primarily to the higher income groups or to savers.

Regardless of the method used, the essential thing is to reduce effective demand. Thus, it is beneficial for the government to build up a surplus. In this way, it can absorb excessive spendable funds in the economy. Through taxation the government can reduce the total effective demand to a point where it will equal total output, and thus remove or lessen the inflationary pressure. A reduction in government spending can be used to bring total investment plus government spending into equality with savings. It can reduce government spending to a point where the combination of government spend-ing and investment will just equal the gap between consumption and output at full employment. On the other hand, an increase in taxes can be used to reduce the amount of consumption and investment to such a degree that government spending will fit into the gap between total private effective demand and total output, thus eliminating the inflationary gap.

If the government does use a surplus budget for the purpose of combating inflation, it is essential that the government maintain rather than spend the surplus. If it chooses to spend the surplus during the inflationary period, the desired anti-inflationary effects will be obliterated. In such an event, government spending merely replaces the decreased spending on consumption and private investment and thus inflationary pressures would remain. The desired anti-inflationary effect of the surplus could be negated also if the government were to use the surplus to reduce the national debt. In such case the recipients of debt repayment may use the funds for other purposes.

Borrowing

Another method suggested to reduce the excessive spendable funds in the economy is government bond drives. This can be an effective method of reducing total effective demand, provided firms and individuals buy bonds with money they would otherwise spend on investment and consumption. Unlike bond drives during a depression when an attempt should be made to tap idle funds, the greatest anti-inflationary effect in this case will come from tapping spendable funds. A bond drive can be used in conjunction with or in lieu of an increase in taxes. Frequently it is easier to induce firms and individuals to give up spendable funds through bond drives than it is to force them to give up funds through taxation.

WARTIME INFLATION

Some of our strongest inflationary pressures occur during wartime periods. These are also times, however, when care must be exercised in utilizing anti-inflationary measures in order that they will not hamper the war effort. Some of the methods suitable in peacetime would not be prudent in a war period.

Causes of Wartime Inflation

The causes of wartime inflation are basically the same as the causes of inflation in peacetime. In either case, the inflation is caused primarily by an effective demand in excess of the productive capacity of a full-employment economy. This may or may not be augmented by cost-push or structural inflation. The total demand for consumption, investment, and government spending is greater than total output. In a peacetime economy, the high effective demand usually results from high consumption and high investment. In a wartime economy, the effective demand exceeds the total output primarily because of the demand of the government for war materials. Since it is impossible to increase total output and since it would be folly to combat the inflation in wartime by reducing government spending, it is essential to tackle the problem in a different manner than in a peacetime economy.

Need for Reducing Consumption and Investment

In effect, it is necessary to reduce the effective demand for consumption and investment by an amount sufficient to permit government expenditure to fit into the gap between total output and the effective demand for consumption plus investment, as indicated in Figure 8-6 on page 161. Since much of the private investment will be converted into wartime production, a primary task is to reduce the demand for consumption. It becomes necessary to reduce not only the marginal propensity to consume but also the absolute amount of consumption. This is difficult to do because incomes rise substantially during a wartime economy. Thus, strong governmental measures may be required to adjust consumption to a proper level in a wartime economy.

Taxation. The ideal measure to combat wartime inflation is heavy taxation. Through taxation, purchasing power can be transferred from individuals and firms to the government. This reduces the effective demand of the private sector of the economy and makes room for the necessary increase in government spending on military goods and services. At the same time, it gives the government the means to make its purchases without going into debt. The most effective taxes are those that reduce consumption primarily, since a considerable amount of the private investment will still be essential. This means that taxes should hit hard at the middle and lower income groups whose propensity to consume is large. For example, very stiff income and sales taxes are beneficial. However, there may be considerable political opposition to such taxes. On the other hand, heavy taxes in the higher groups may do little more than tax away funds that would otherwise remain idle. Although such taxes would not have a powerful anti-inflationary effect, they would help pay for the war.

Voluntary Savings. A second method of combating wartime inflation is a program of voluntary savings, especially on the part of the consumer. Naturally the best method of accomplishing this is to encourage consumers to buy government bonds. In this way, they will not only give up the purchase of consumer goods but also will transfer purchasing power to the government, which it can utilize to buy war materials.

Even though an appeal is made to the patriotism of consumers, however, the success of such a measure in reducing consumption on a large scale is questionable. Frequently lower income groups will not readily reduce their consumption, especially since their incomes are increasing and they desire to buy goods and services that they were unable to purchase previously. Available evidence does not indicate that voluntary savings ever have been sufficient to arrest wartime inflation.

Compulsory Savings. Since voluntary savings are inadequate, it is sometimes advocated that more positive measures be exercised by the government. One of these is a scheme of compulsory savings. Compulsory saving is often justified on the basis of need and the common good. The government needs the money to finance the war, and it is in conformity with the common good to hold the price level. No one individual or group of individuals can restrain the upward movement of prices. If all individuals are forced to save, however, the result can be a very serious restraining effect on inflationary pressures. A compulsory-savings plan would require a deduction, in addition to income taxes, to be made from each individual's paycheck. This money would be credited to a special savings account which would remain blocked, except for emergencies. Interest would be paid on these savings by the government at an appropriate rate. The savings would be unblocked at, or sometime after, the end of the war, depending on the extent of inflationary pressures in the economy. In total such a plan could prove beneficial to consumers in the long run.

If compulsory savings are to be used (and they may be the answer if taxation and voluntary savings are inadequate to combat inflation), it is only equitable for the government to hold the price level. It would be unfair to force individuals to save in order to reduce consumer demand and then let the value of their savings deteriorate by permitting prices to rise. Thus, if necessary to hold the price level, price and wage controls may be used.

In the absence of compulsory savings or some other method of holding the price line, a steeply progressive income tax and a stiff *excess profits tax* will limit the opportunity of profiteers to gain at the expense of consumers in a wartime economy. There is the possibility that the profiteers may lend their newly acquired income to the government through the purchase of bonds if this income is not taxed. It may be more justifiable, however, to tax away any unearned increment of the profiteers rather than to permit them to hold claims against future resources by lending excess profits to the government.

POSTWAR INFLATION

Inflation occurs in the postwar period if effective demand remains higher than the total output of goods and services and full employment still exists.

This is very likely to occur since the decrease in military spending at the termination of the war is usually more than offset by the increase in private investment and consumption. Therefore, effective demand will exceed total production and thus cause postwar inflation, primarily because of the rapid rise in investment and consumption. The logical means, then, of combating the postwar inflation is to reduce or hold down private spending.

The same means that were used to combat wartime inflation may be used to fight postwar inflation, including heavy taxation, voluntary savings, and even compulsory savings and wage and price controls. It is more difficult, however, to apply these measures in a peacetime economy. Political and individual temperaments may not be conducive to the retention or imposition of heavy taxation and rigid control. Politicians, businessmen, and labor leaders will be anxious to rid themselves and the economy as a whole of burdening taxes and restrictive controls. Many self-sacrificing measures imposed during the war are warmly accepted in the spirit of patriotism. But, when the war ceases, an appeal to patriotism for the extension of such a measure often falls on deaf ears.

Anti-inflationary measures of wartime will work just as well in peacetime if given a chance. The longer and more severe the war, however, the greater the severity of restrictive controls necessary to combat the postwar inflation. At the same time, the longer the war lasts the more savings or liquid assets the individuals and firms in the economy will have which can be converted into spending at the termination of the war. This combination may present an explosive inflationary situation. Firms and individuals poised with large amounts of spendable funds will be anxious to get rid of controls. In addition, with the termination of wage controls, laborers, through their unions and otherwise, will seek wage increases which augment cost-push inflationary pressures. With government expenditures at a reduced level, it becomes essential to concentrate on the reduction of private investment and consumption spending at a time when business and the public are not psychologically disposed to the continued use of controls. For these reasons, it is generally more difficult to combat postwar inflation than wartime inflation.

INFLATIONARY EXPERIENCE IN THE UNITED STATES

The past few decades provide a suitable period for a study, analysis, and evaluation of our attempts to use anti-inflationary measures since they include peacetime, wartime, and postwar conditions. The strong and weak points of our various measures are to some extent evident during this period. During this span of time we experienced varying degrees of price stability, moderately rising prices, and strong inflationary pressures. To combat inflation, higher taxes, voluntary savings, budget surpluses, material allocations, wage and price controls, credit controls, and *rationing* were used.

World War II

Prior to World War II, we were still in a condition of unemployment. As indicated previously, in 1939 unemployment was in excess of 9 million. As we began to produce war materials for the Allies, employment picked up. When government spending on military production increased with our entry into the war, we soon reached full employment.

As we began to approach the bottleneck and full-employment stage in late 1941 and early 1942, it became evident that continued increases in government expenditures would result in higher prices. Government expenditures would have to be increased to execute the war properly, and total effective demand would exceed total output and inflation would occur unless steps were taken to prevent it. Not desiring to let the price level get out of hand, we did take steps to combat inflation, and many of these steps paralleled policies based on the income-expenditure analysis.

We increased taxes substantially, both at the personal and corporate levels, levied a heavy excess profits tax on businesses, and conducted large-scale bond drives in an effort to borrow funds, especially from individuals and businesses. In addition to these monetary and fiscal measures, we imposed many other controls. Included were a *controlled materials plan*, wage and price controls, a system of consumer rationing, regulation of consumer credit controls, and the use of manpower restrictions.

The total endeavor to reduce effective demand through these measures during World War II proved to be rather successful. The consumer price index (1967 = 100), which had increased from 42 in 1939 to 49 by 1942, increased only moderately during the war. It moved from 49 to 54.4 during the period of control, which lasted until June, 1946. This amounted to a price increase of 11 percent for the four-year control period compared to an increase of 17 percent for the three-year period immediately preceding the control period. Since some price increases must be permitted due to the exigencies of war production and since not all items are controlled, the price level should be expected to increase somewhat during a control period. Thus, to a certain extent our effort to suppress inflation and hold prices was successful.

Postwar Period

At the end of World War II, firms and individuals had the largest holdings of liquid assets—cash savings, bonds, and other assets easily convertible into cash—in the history of our nation up to that time. Since demand continued to rise, we still had a potentially inflationary situation. As a result, controls were not removed upon the termination of the war in August, 1945. In the early part of 1946, shortages still prevailed, some rationing existed, and people were still standing in queues to buy certain consumer goods. Many individuals were discouraged by the lack of available goods. Manufacturers felt hampered by the price controls. Various business associations and many individual manufacturers sought an end to price controls.

Finally, in June, 1946, Congress decontrolled prices. This unleashed a flood of spending that pushed total effective demand beyond our ability to produce. Not only were incomes at a record level, but individuals and firms had large holdings of liquid assets that they were eager to spend. In addition to the removal of price and wage controls, total tax revenues were decreased and the sale of government bonds decreased while bond redemptions increased. Fortunately we did keep the excess profits tax and rent controls, tightened up on the money supply, and reinstituted credit controls, and the government operated at a surplus in 1947 and 1948. Otherwise the inflationary effects would have been greater.

In the immediate postwar period we failed to adopt policies as stringent as we did during the wartime period. In addition, *excess-demand inflation* was supplemented by cost-push inflationary pressures manifest in the first, second, and third annual rounds of wage increases following World War II. The net result was that we did not combat the postwar inflation as well as we did the wartime inflation. The price level rose 30 percent in the two-year postwar period, 1946-1948, compared to 11 percent during the four-year period, 1942-June, 1946, during which we maintained rather rigid controls.

Finally, by 1949, total effective demand leveled off and our productive capacity caught up with it. Output remained stable, and unemployment reached a postwar high of nearly 4 million. By 1949 we had an ample supply of most types of consumer goods, the demand for business expansion had tapered off, and there was a sizable decrease in foreign demand, all of which mollified inflationary pressures and reduced the CPI for the first time in a decade.

Korean Conflict

In June, 1950, we were enjoying peace and economic prosperity. We were producing at nearly full capacity, and long-awaited consumer goods were readily available. Incomes were at a high level and consumers were spending generously. In addition, many were taking advantage of available credit to increase their purchases of commodities. The price level, which reached a peak in 1948, had stabilized and was beginning to decline slightly—a break for consumers.

With the outbreak of hostilities in Korea on June 25, 1950, the price situation changed rapidly. Prices increased more rapidly after the beginning of the Korean conflict than they did at the beginning of World War II because the former came at a time when we were near the full-employment level. Furthermore, purchases were accelerated as memories of shortages in World War II caused many people to buy and hoard nonperishable goods. The cause of this inflationary movement should be axiomatic to us by now. A nation using all its resources to provide consumer goods, services, and private investment cannot undertake a greatly expanded defense program without curtailing production of civilian goods. With the outbreak in Korea, it was well known that inflationary pressures would increase as our defense program expanded. As the total effective demand increased and consumer production gave way to military production, there was a growing gap between the demand for consumer goods and the available supply.

In order to combat the pending inflation, we eventually increased taxes, encouraged savings through bond drives, and used excess profits taxes to raise funds for the military effort and to combat inflation. We also used bank credit controls, reinstituted Regulation W on consumer credit, and established Regulation X to limit the purchase of new homes. A controlled materials plan was set up almost immediately.

Although we reinstituted price and wage controls, we were a bit tardy in doing so. This was unfortunate since we should have learned from our experience with World War II. Instead, in the early months of the Korean conflict indirect and voluntary measures were suggested to keep prices down. In an attempt to reduce the level of effective demand, businessmen, laborers, farmers, and consumers were admonished to exercise restraint. It was hoped that with increased production we could eventually strike a balance which would give adequate support to our military program and still fulfill consumer needs.

Price and Wage Controls. Recognizing the dangers that lay ahead, Congress approved on September 8, 1950, the Defense Production Act, which among other things authorized price and wage controls. The Act authorized the President to issue regulations and orders establishing ceilings on the prices of various materials and services.

However, in the months immediately following the passage of the Act, the government sought to stabilize prices by general measures and voluntary action. It increased taxes, imposed selective credit restrictions, and established control over the flow of scarce materials. Prices continued to increase, however, especially following the Chinese intervention in Korea in the fall of 1950.

As a result, on December 19, 1950, the Economic Stabilization Agency (ESA) published a set of Voluntary Pricing Standards as a guide to aid sellers who desired to cooperate in a program of voluntary price stabilization. In addition, hundreds of large firms were requested to give advance notice of any intended price increases, and discussions were held among producers of basic commodities to analyze methods of stabilizing prices. Although some sellers and manufacturers, motivated by patriotism, did attempt to comply with the objectives of the voluntary stabilization program, many prices continued to soar. In fact, during the following month the prices of basic commodities and foods advanced at a greater rate than they had during any of the previous six months. By the end of January, 1951, the CPI had increased over 7 percent. It became imperative that forceful action be taken since voluntary, partial, and indirect measures had failed to meet the challenge of inflation.

The first major step in the direct fight against inflation was the issuance of the General Ceiling Price Regulation (GCPR) on January 26, 1951. This was essentially a stopgap measure designed as a broad, sweeping action to halt the upward spiral of prices. Its purpose was to hold prices over the entire economy until more adequate regulations could be issued. This emergency measure froze prices for all covered commodities and services at the highest level at which they were sold, or offered for sale, during the base period, December 19, 1950, to January 25, 1951.

Shortly after GCPR was issued, other ceiling price regulations began to appear. In general, these regulations superseded GCPR. Their purpose was to remove certain commodities and services from pricing under GCPR and bring them under regulations specifically tailored to the market structure of the respective commodity. This proved to be a satisfactory and equitable approach to control. For example, Ceiling Price Regulation 7 established a markup type control, which was applied to certain branches of retail trade. CPR 22 was designed to return manufactures to the pre-Korean price level, but it permitted adjustments for certain subsequent material and labor-cost increases.

During a relatively short period, the Office of Price Stabilization (OPS), which had been established upon the creation of the Economic Stabilization Agency on September 9, 1950, grew from a skeleton crew to a force of more than 12,000 employees. Within six months after a Director of Price Stabilization was appointed, 13 regional and 84 district offices were established. Once started, OPS did a commendable job of holding prices. During

1951 there was a general leveling off of prices due in large part to price regulations.

Removal of Controls. In the latter part of 1951 and the first half of 1952, there was considerable softening in our economy. Price declines were in evidence in certain sectors. The defense program, which was running behind schedule, was extended over a longer period. However, the heavy inflationary pressures expected in late 1951 and 1952 did not materialize. Shortages predicted did not occur. Strengthening of consumer resistance to high prices, obliteration of scare buying, and accelerated debt repayment mitigated consumer demand. Businesses that had scheduled production of consumer goods at high levels in anticipation of increased demand accumulated large, high-priced inventories. Consequently, widespread sales and curtailment of production pervaded the economy in an attempt to improve inventory positions.

In 1952 government monetary measures were mollified or eliminated as the need for them disappeared. When the private demand for bank credit lessened in the early part of the year, both Regulation W, governing consumer installment credit, and the Voluntary Credit Restraint Program were suspended. Regulation X was also amended to permit lower down payments on the purchase of homes. Finally, the Defense Production Act of 1952 totally discontinued authority for Regulation W and for the Voluntary Credit Restraint Program.

Subsequently it became possible for OPS to begin suspending controls where they were no longer required. For emergency purposes, however, each suspension order included a specific "recontrol point." Fortunately the inflationary pressures were not too great thereafter, and OPS followed an orderly process of *decontrol*. Stronger indirect controls, through monetary and fiscal policies, were substituted in many cases for the direct controls. Complete decontrol was accomplished prior to the Korean truce in June, 1953.

Decontrol was more successful after Korea than it was after World War II. This may have been due in part to the fact that a more orderly decontrol process on a gradual basis was utilized, but the big factor was the state of the economy at the end of the Korean conflict compared to what it was after World War II. After Korea there was no large pent-up demand for consumer goods since we did not have to resort to rationing under OPS. Secondly, there was an absence of the large foreign demand, since production in other countries of the world had not been interrupted during the Korean conflict as it had been during World War II. Thirdly, businesses generally were not in need of expansion as they were after World War II, since they were able to obtain materials for private investment during the Korean episode. As a result, the price level did not take a jump at the time OPS decontrolled.

Wage and Price Guideposts

After several years of relative price stability during the 1950s, some price unrest was becoming apparent in the economy in the latter half of 1961. In seeking the continuation of price stability, President Kennedy in his 1962 *Economic Report* established a set of voluntary wage and price guideposts. If accepted by the major firms in the economy and in the collective bargaining power centers, it would do much, according to the President, to restrain upward pressures on the price level. As a guide for noninflationary wage behavior, the rate of increase in wage rates (including fringe benefits) in each industry was to be equated with the national trend in overall productivity increase. Based upon the fact that the average productivity per worker in our economy increased about 3 percent annually, the guideposts initially recommended that wage increases be held to 3 percent each year. This would allow the increase in wage costs to be absorbed out of rising productivity without necessitating a price increase. The guideposts did have some flexibility insofar as they suggested that any firm whose gain in productivity per man-hour was more than the guidepost figure should hold its wage increase to 3 percent and give consumers some benefit by reducing prices. On the other hand, it recommended that any firm whose increase in productivity was less than the guidepost figure could grant a 3 percent wage increase but offset this with an increase in prices. Subsequently using a five-year average, the guidepost figure was raised to 3.2 percent.

The guideposts, of course, stirred up considerable controversy in both wage and price circles. In many firms and industries where the rate of productivity was less than the national average, the guideposts were used by labor unions as a basis for a wage increase higher than the productivity rate increase within the firm or industry. In other firms or industries where the productivity rate exceeded the national average productivity increase, the firms often used the guidepost in an effort to limit the amount of a wage increase to 3.2 percent, even though they might have been able to afford higher wage increases. Another complaint was the fact that the guideposts tended to freeze labor's share of the national income.

Although the concept of price and wage guideposts seemed to be pushed out of the limelight by the emphasis on the tax cut in the 1963 *Economic Report* of the President and by the poverty package in the 1964 *Report*, the guideposts were emphasized again by President Johnson and his Economic Advisers in the spring and summer of 1964. The President's personal representative discussed with industry members the importance of noninflationary wage agreements between labor and management, especially in the automobile and other basic industries. Subsequently, however, the AFL-CIO stated officially and publicly that it did not intend to be limited by the wage guidepost in seeking wage increases during that year, and the President of the United Auto Workers stated that since the productivity increase in the automobile industry was much above the national average, the union was not going to limit its wage demands to the average of 3.2 percent. About the same time, steel companies were talking about the need for a price increase in order to offset some of their increasing costs. At that time President Johnson publicly warned that any increase in steel prices "would strongly conflict with our national interest in price stability."

With the return of stronger inflationary pressures in 1966, some delicate situations and open confrontations regarding the voluntary acceptance of the guideposts developed between the White House and/or the President's Council of Economic Advisers on the one hand and large industries and powerful unions on the other. Consequently, in 1967 the use of a specific guidepost figure was deemphasized, although the guidepost concept was still retained. By 1968, however, the guideposts were pretty well shattered as both labor unions and business firms posted wage and price increases substantially beyond the guidepost figures.

The War in Vietnam

After seven years of *nagging unemployment* and relatively stable prices following the 1958 recession, the economy in mid-1965 began approaching full employment. For seven years, 1958-1965, we had been dealing with the problem of a "production gap," with the economy operating at 8 to 10 percent under its potential capacity. During this time unemployment averaged 5.7 percent. We used many measures to bolster the economy and to accelerate our rate of economic growth during this time, as we saw in the previous chapter.

Economy in Transition. In the winter of 1965-1966, the economy entered a transition phase. By the middle of 1965, unemployment had fallen below 5 percent and by the end of the year it had dropped to 4.1 percent, approaching the full-employment level for the first time in seven years. With the record rate of private investment, exuberant consumer spending, continued expenses for "Great Society" programs, large federal deficits, and heavy outlays for the escalation of the war in Vietnam, it was obvious that there were likely to be considerable upward pressures on the price level. It appeared that we were moving from an economy of nagging unemployment and undercapacity with emphasis on poverty, to an economy of full employment, full capacity, shortages of skilled labor, scarcities of certain materials, and inflationary pressures.

Early in December, 1965, the Federal Reserve, by raising the discount rate, took what it considered an appropriate step to combat the clouds of inflation it foresaw on the horizon. Its action was both praised and criticized. During 1966 the Federal Reserve was successful to some extent in its attempt to apply some brake against inflation by tightening the money supply through the discount rate and open-market operations. This action contributed to the "money crunch" of 1966, which had a substantial impact on the construction industry. These effects can be observed in Figures 16-1 and 16-2.

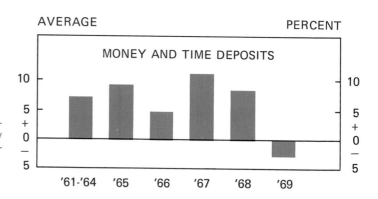

FIGURE 16-1

MONEY SUPPLY

The Federal Reserve, through various measures, tightened the money supply in an effort to combat inflation in 1966 and in 1969.

SOURCE: *Federal Reserve Bulletin* (June, 1969).

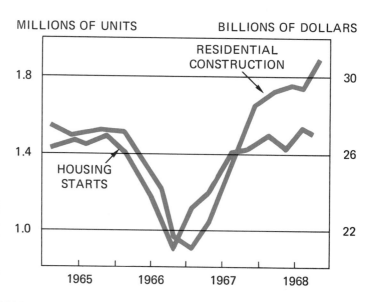

FIGURE 16-2

CONSTRUCTION ACTIVITY

The money crunch of 1966, caused by a tightening of the money supply, had an adverse effect on the construction industry.

SOURCE: *Federal Reserve Bulletin* (December, 1968).

By January, 1966, unemployment fell to 4.0 percent and in February it was down to 3.9 percent, the first time the full-employment level had been reached in more than seven years. The Administration, which only a few months earlier had been studying the possibility of declaring a fiscal dividend in the form of an additional tax cut in order to prevent a fiscal drag on the economy, faced a serious problem of deciding whether it should continue its expansionary fiscal measures or whether it should shift to anti-inflationary measures.

It was concerned, of course, that anti-inflationary devices could slow down the economy. Some contended that the proposed measures might cause the economy to reverse its upward trend of five years and even precipitate a recession. The Administration, and for that matter Congress also, clearly had the following choices of what to do about the inflationary pressures building up in the economy:

1. Do nothing and hope that prices would not increase by any more than the 2 percent predicted earlier.
2. Reduce government spending for domestic programs to offset the increased spending for defense in Vietnam.
3. Raise taxes to cover the cost of increased government spending.
4. Encourage the Federal Reserve to further tighten the money supply.
5. Impose wage and price controls.
6. Rely on *jawbone tactics* and implementation of the voluntary wage-price guideposts.

Inflation—1966. After much discussion and analysis the Johnson Administration took only limited precautionary measures against inflation. In large part, it rejected the idea of increasing taxes or reducing federal spending. Wage and price controls appeared to be an extreme. It did little to encourage or supplement the Federal Reserve's tighter money policy. On the other hand, the Administration did not sit by idly and do nothing. Early in 1966 it rescinded the excise tax cuts on automobile sales and telephone service. It also provided for an accelerated method of corporate tax collection and other minor measures to help avert inflation. But the Administration put its primary emphasis on jawbone tactics through its get-tougher policy in regard to implementation of the voluntary wage-price guideposts. Sometimes successful and at other times not, it endeavored to hold wage increases to the 3.2 percent guidepost figure, and it used persuasion of various types to influence major industries and labor unions to hold the price and wage line. Not until it became apparent that the price level was increasing at a 4 percent annual rate did the Administration take further action by suspending in

September, 1966, the 7 percent tax credit on new investment and the accelerated depreciation measures.

Although the price increases slowed down a bit toward the end of the year, the CPI showed an annual increase of 3.3 percent. In December, 1966, unemployment measured 3.8 percent of the civilian labor force compared to 4.0 percent 12 months earlier. Employment increased during the year by approximately 1.5 million workers on a seasonally adjusted basis and 3.4 million on a nonseasonally adjusted basis.

Mini-Recession—Early 1967. The price level (CPI) did stabilize in the latter part of 1966 and the first quarter of 1967, increasing by no more than .2 percentage points in any one month. It was evident that the economy was slowing down. In terms of constant dollars, figures for the GNP in the first quarter of 1967 actually declined by $400 million. This mini-recession of 1967, as it has frequently been labelled, was caused primarily by a decline in the rate of private investment of $15.5 billion. No doubt the suspension of tax credit on new investment had a pronounced effect on the rate of decline in new investment.

Although the President in his 1967 *Economic Report* mentioned the need for a 6 percent surcharge on personal and corporate income taxes to combat the inflationary tendency in the economy, the measure was not pushed to any degree in Congress in the early part of 1967. Many government officials, economists, and others naturally felt that inflation had been beaten and cited the fact that it was accomplished without any sizable tax increase, without any drastic cut in government spending, or without the imposition of wage and price controls. In fact, by the end of 1966 the Federal Reserve had ceased its tight money policy and in the first quarter of 1967 it was again displaying a more liberal attitude toward the creation of credit. The discount rate, for example, was decreased from 4.5 percent to 4 percent in April, 1967. As a stimulant to the sluggish economy, the 7 percent tax credit on new investment was restored in June, 1967, six months ahead of schedule.

Inflation Resumes—Mid-1967. The joys of the stable-price advocates, however, were short-lived, because by the second quarter of 1967 the consumer price index resumed its upward movement. By the end of 1967, the CPI had risen 3 percent for the year. Although unemployment again averaged 3.8 percent of the civilian labor force for 1967, by the end of the year it was down to 3.5 percent. As a result, members of the Administration and others were again talking about the need for restraint. Some government officials were even suggesting that direct controls of various kinds might be needed to cool the economy if management and labor did not hold wages and prices in check. By the end of 1967 and early 1968, the Federal Reserve moved toward a tighter money position by raising reserve requirements and moving the discount rate back to 4.5 percent.

The Income-Tax Surcharge—1968. In his *Economic Report* of 1968 delivered in January, President Johnson called for the imposition of a 10 percent surcharge on personal and corporate income taxes as a means of combating inflation. The size of the proposed surcharge was increased from 6 percent to 10 percent because signs of an overheated economy were more in evidence, including the pending size of the federal deficit in excess of $25 billion for fiscal 1968. The proposed bill to effectuate the tax became embroiled in a Congressional hassle as to whether it was better to increase taxes or reduce federal spending. As a result of prolonged hearings and debate in Congress, final action on the tax bill was delayed until June, 1968. At that time Congress imposed a 10 percent surcharge on personal and corporate income, making the tax retroactive to April 1 for individual income and January 1, 1968, on corporate income, effective until June, 1969.

The impact of the surtax fell more heavily on savings than expected, however, as consumers continued their outlays for goods and services, especially for new cars, and the rate of savings fell sharply. Fixed investment for plant equipment, which increased moderately in the first half of 1968, accelerated in the second half. Capital spending was no doubt spurred by the prognostication of investors that the 7 percent investment credit might again be suspended as an anti-inflationary measure. In spite of limited funds available for mortgages, there was no reduction in residential construction during the last half of 1968. There was some dampening in federal expenditures during this time and the federal deficit was reduced from a rate of $9 billion in the first half of the year to $3 billion in the second half.

By mid-1968 a number of hefty national wage negotiations had taken place within the economy, adding to the cost-push inflationary element. The shortage of skilled labor and even unskilled labor was evident in the economy. Average hourly wage gains of 7 percent in manufacturing industries during the year plus a reduction in savings offset the impact of the income surcharge. Consequently, labor unit costs rose sharply.

All this, of course, caused prices to continue their upward move through 1968. The cost of services, such as personal care, medical care, home ownership, and auto repair and maintenance increased rapidly. By the end of 1968, the consumer price index had risen 4.7 percent. Thus, in spite of the addition of a strong fiscal measure to accompany somewhat restrictive monetary measures, little success was achieved in arresting the upward movement of prices in 1968.

With prices and wages continuing to rise in 1969 the Federal Reserve, which had reduced the discount rate in August, 1968, in anticipation of strong anti-inflationary reaction to the tax increase, adopted a more restrictive policy. As a result of various monetary measures, the rates of growth of the money stock declined to about 2.5 percent in the first quarter of 1969, compared to an annual increase of 6 percent in 1967 and 7 percent in 1968. The Federal Reserve, through a series of changes, moved the discount rate from 5.5 percent in December, 1968, to 6 percent in April, 1969. By the summer of 1969 the prime rate for commercial loans offered by banks had reached 8.5 percent. Government bonds were yielding between 7 and 8 percent, high grade commercial bonds over 7 percent, and the interest rate on federal funds had approached the 10 percent level. These increases in interest rates, along with their subsequent declines, are shown in Figure 16-3.

FIGURE 16-3

INTEREST RATES

The discount rate was raised several times by the Fed in the late 1960s and again in the early 1970s in an effort to reduce inflation. Other interest rates were affected by changes in the discount rate.

SOURCE: *Federal Reserve Bulletin* (April, 1973).

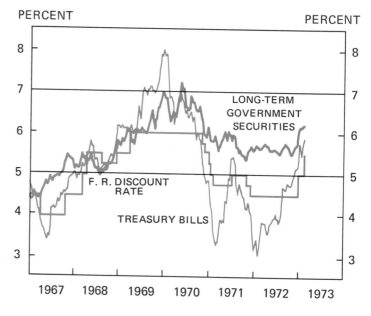

By the middle of 1969 prices were still rising, with the CPI at an annual rate of 6.3 percent in the first half of 1969. Price increases were especially noticeable in food costs, up at the rate of 9 percent annually, and services, which rose at a 7.5 percent annual rate in the first six months of the year.

Gradualism. With the inauguration of the Nixon Administration, inflation was cited as the nation's number one domestic issue. President Nixon adopted a policy of *gradualism* to bring inflation under control. In this regard, he wanted to return the economy to stable prices without seriously disrupting the growth in economic activity. Among other measures, he asked Congress to retain the 10 percent tax surcharge that was due to expire in June of 1969. The budget was balanced and, in fact, ran a slight surplus in fiscal 1969. Defense and other government spending was cut and the Fed tightened the money supply. Although there was some discussion about the need for wage and price restrictions of some type, President Nixon shied away from either formal or informal wage and price measures. By the end of 1969, it was apparent that the measures employed to "cool off" the economy were effective in slowing down production. But they were not effective in slowing down the rate of inflation. Although the real GNP declined in the fourth quarter of 1969, the price level was increasing at a rate of 6 percent.

With certain reservations, the forecasts for the year 1970 were favorable. Most analysts suggested that there would be some slack in the first half of the year, followed by a rebound in economic activity in the second half. It was the hope of the President's Council of Economic Advisers that the inflationary rate, which had been in the vicinity of 6 percent, would recede to 3 to 3.5 percent by the end of the year. Economic measures designed to cool the economy and bring about a reduction in inflation were expected to result in a slightly higher level of unemployment, up from 3.5 percent to, perhaps, 4.5 percent of the civilian labor force.

The economy did cool off in the first half of the year for a number of reasons, including a decline in business investment, a cutback in defense spending, a tightness of money, and a slow-down in housing starts. The two-quarter decline in the real GNP (fourth quarter, 1969, and first quarter, 1970) was followed by a sidewise movement in the second quarter of 1970. The price level, however, continued to rise at an undesirable rate of more than 5 percent annually. Measures designed primarily to arrest demand-pull inflation failed to contain cost-push price pressures. Unemployment increased more than anticipated and reached a rate of 5.5 percent by midyear. This left the Administration in the delicate position of deciding whether to continue anti-inflationary measures and risk the possibility of higher unemployment or shift to expansionary measures and risk the resurgence of inflationary pressures, an especially delicate decision in an election year.

Unfortunately the economy did not rebound in the second half of the year. Unemployment for the year averaged 4.9 percent and by the end of the year it had reached 6 percent. Although 1970 was officially labelled as a recession year, the CPI still managed to increase by 5.9 percent.

In the late months of 1970, the Administration shifted its emphasis to expansionary measures. A number of steps were taken to increase effective demand. Earlier in the year, the personal and corporate income tax surcharge was allowed to lapse. The Federal Reserve liberalized the money supply and adopted an accelerated depreciation schedule to spur business investment. Discount rates were lowered several times moving down to 4.75 percent within three months, and the Administration announced that the federal deficit for fiscal 1971 would be in excess of $18 billion and that the projected federal budget for fiscal 1972 showed an $11.6 billion deficit. The Administration was trusting that any resulting increase in effective demand would not evoke demand-pull inflationary pressures, since the economy was in a state of less than full employment. The Administration, however, was concerned about cost-push price pressures. Consequently, in early 1971 it began "jawboning" as a means of holding the price line and more was heard about the possibility of wage and price guideposts and an incomes policy.

The Game Plan. Economic forecasts for 1971 were good, but nothing spectacular. Most forecasts expected the GNP to be in the range of $1,045 billion to $1,055 billion for the year. It was anticipated that about half of the projected 6 to 7 percent increase would be in real production and the other half in higher prices. The President's Council of Economic Advisers set year-end goals of 4.5 percent unemployment and a 3.5 percent rate of inflation. The Nixon economic *game plan* was to restore full employment and stable prices by mid-1972. Measures designed to attain that growth rate, remove the production gap, and eliminate nagging unemployment, however, could very well add to price pressures and cause the rate of inflation to accelerate. The task of reaching stable prices was aggravated, too, by the fact that wage increases of 30 percent or more spread over a three-year period had been negotiated in the construction, auto, railroad, and tin can industries. Similar wage concessions in the steel industry in the summer of 1971 led to an immediate 8 percent average increase in steel prices. Some Congressmen, who in early 1971 recommended that President Nixon utilize the authority given to him in 1970 to impose wage and price restrictions on the economy, renewed their efforts after the steel settlement.

At the midyear Congressional hearings on the state of the economy, an Administrative spokesman indicated that the Administration was not going to reach its year-end goals of disinflation and reduction of unemployment. It was stated that price increases and unemployment were much more stubborn than anticipated. A month later, in response to an inquiry of what the Administration was going to do about inflation and unemployment, Secretary of the Treasury Connally stated that the Administration was not going to impose wage and price controls, it was not going to adopt wage-price guide-posts, it was not going to increase government spending, and it was not going to reduce taxes.

The New Economic Policy

Economic pressures regarding prices, wages, and the balance of payments brought about a change of attitude on the part of the White House by mid-1971.

Phase I: The 90-Day Freeze. With the knowledge that progress on his economic game plan was being stifled by substantial wage and price increases, President Nixon in August, 1971, made drastic and sweeping changes of domestic and international economic policies. Among other measures, he declared a 90-day freeze on all prices, wages, and rents, temporarily suspended convertibility of dollars into gold, imposed a 10 percent surcharge on imports, froze a scheduled pay increase for government employees, sought to reinstitute tax credits as a means of stimulating investment and jobs, asked Congress to reduce personal income taxes, and requested Congress to repeal the 7 percent excise tax on automobiles.

The President established a Cost of Living Council to work out details for restoring free markets without inflation during a transition period following the freeze. Congress did oblige the President by repealing the excise tax on automobiles and reducing personal income taxes by advancing the scheduled date for an increase in personal income tax exemptions.

Phase II. The 90-day freeze was followed by a Phase II control period. For the implementation of this phase the President established a Pay Board and a Price Commission. Each was to work out what it considered permissible noninflationary wage and price increases, respectively. The Commissions were composed of representatives of labor, management, and the general public. The Pay Board subsequently established a 5.5 percent annual wage increase as a maximum. It did allow that certain exceptions may be made to the 5.5 percent figure. The Pay Board, too, did allow scheduled raises that were to have taken effect during the freeze period to take effect during Phase II.

The Price Commission, on the other hand, indicated that it was going to attempt to hold overall price increases in the CPI to 2.5 percent annually. Since the President did not desire to set up an elaborate formal structure of wage and price controls, such as existed during World War II and during the Korean conflict, much of the stabilization program had to depend on voluntary compliance. The Cost of Living Council exempted most of the small business firms and their workers from any reporting requirements. Intermediate and larger size firms, however, were required to report changes in prices and wages. Larger firms, moreover, had to give prenotification of changes to the Price Commission and/or the Pay Board.

The immediate effectiveness of the New Economic Policy in combating inflation can be gauged somewhat by the fact that during the six months prior to the freeze, prices increased at an annual rate of 4.5 percent; but in the five months subsequent to the freeze, they increased at an annual rate of 2.2 percent. The price level for 1972, during which price controls existed for the entire year, increased 3.3 percent, as shown in Table 16-1.

The stability of prices in the first half of the 1960s compared to the inflationary period starting in 1966 can be seen in Table 16-1. From 1960 to 1965, for example, prices rose at an average annual rate of 1.3 percent. From 1965 to August, 1971, prices rose at an average annual rate of more than 4.5 percent.

Although employment increased substantially during this period, the amount and rate of unemployment, after dwindling early in the decade, has risen in the past few years. Note the net increase of over 1.5 million in unemployment since 1969 in Table 16-1.

Phase III. In January, 1973, after commenting favorably on the results of Phase II in stabilizing prices and wages, the President announced Phase III of his New Economic Policy, which in effect reestablished voluntary guideposts for price and wage increases. The guidepost figures used at that time were 2.5 percent and 5.5 percent annually for prices and wages, respectively.

Phase IV. The removal of compulsory Phase II controls proved to be premature, however. During the first five months after decontrol, the CPI rose at an annual rate of nearly 9 percent. Consequently, on June 13, 1973, President Nixon declared a 60-day freeze on prices. Wages were not affected at this time. Instead of ending the freeze on all goods at the end of the 60-day period, prices were unfrozen selectively, and Phase IV controls were imposed on various categories of goods and services at different times before and after the 60-day period.

Again large firms were required to give a 30-day prenotification of price increases. Unlike Phase II, however, firms did not have to wait for approval by the Cost of Living Council before putting such increases into effect. But the Council had authority to delay any price increases indefinitely, and it reserved the right to reexamine prices at any time. The new base period established was the fiscal quarter prior to January 12, 1973, the date of

TABLE 16-1

EMPLOYMENT,
UNEMPLOYMENT,
AND PRICES

1960-1973

Year	Total Employ- ment	Unem- ploy- ment	Rate of Unem- ployment	CPI (1967 = 100)	Rate of In- flation
1960	65,778	3,852	5.5	88.7	—
1961	65,746	4,714	6.7	89.6	1.0
1962	66,702	3,911	5.5	90.6	1.1
1963	67,762	4,070	5.7	91.7	1.0
1964	69,305	3,786	5.2	92.9	1.3
1965	71,088	3,366	4.5	94.5	1.7
1966	72,895	2,875	3.8	97.2	2.9
1967	74,372	2,775	3.8	100.0	2.9
1968	75,920	2,817	3.6	104.2	4.2
1969	77,902	2,813	3.5	109.8	5.4
1970	78,627	4,088	4.9	116.3	5.9
1971	79,120	4,993	5.9	121.3	4.2
1972	81,702	4,840	5.6	125.3	3.3
1973	84,409	4,304	4.9	133.1	6.2

SOURCE: *Economic Indicators* (January, 1974).

decontrol of Phase II. Price increases equal to dollar cost increases subsequent to the base period were to be permitted by Phase IV. No allowance was to be made for a profit mark-up on these cost increases. Controls were imposed on an industry-by-industry basis, thus providing more flexibility than was available under Phase II. At the time of the imposition of Phase IV, several high Administration officials indicated that they hoped controls could be removed by the end of 1973. Most of the controls were removed by early 1974. Unfortunately, the CPI rose 6.2 percent in 1973. (If the CPI were measured from December, 1972, to December, 1973, instead of by yearly averages, the price increase would be 8.8 percent for 1973.)

After a study of our experience with the use of anti-inflationary measures during World War II, the postwar inflationary period, the Korean conflict, the war in Vietnam, and the early 1970s, it becomes very evident that our anti-inflationary policies are based on the income-expenditure approach of economic analysis. Our reliance on heavy taxation, the encouragement of saving, the use of an excess profits tax, a controlled materials plan, and the imposition of price and wage controls are all within the scope of the income-expenditure analysis. On the other hand, we did not go so far as to institute a system of compulsory savings. Also, we were reluctant to impose sufficient restriction during the postwar (World War II) period to combat inflation successfully. Furthermore, we did remove Phase II controls a bit prematurely. Perhaps this stems from our general dislike for government intervention in a peacetime economy.

SUMMARY

1. Inflation can occur when the total monetary demand for goods and services is in excess of the value of currently produced goods and services.

2. Inflation can be offset by increasing production and/or reducing the demand for goods and services.

3. In a wartime economy it is difficult to reduce government spending as a means of combating inflation; therefore, measures must be used that tend to reduce consumption and private investment.

4. In addition to monetary measures, heavy taxation, voluntary savings, and wage and price controls, credit restrictions and manpower controls were used to combat inflation in World War II and during the Korean conflict. In addition, consumer rationing was used during World War II.

5. Economic controls were responsible for holding prices in check to some degree in both World War II and the Korean conflict.

6. Prices increased substantially after decontrol of prices at the end of World War II, but increases were very moderate after the Korean conflict.

7. Some anti-inflationary measures were imposed with the return of inflation with the escalation of the war in Vietnam after the mid-1960s.

8. The President's voluntary wage-price guideposts implemented in the early part of the 1960s disintegrated with the heavy inflationary pressures of the mid- and late 1960s.

9. With the continuation of inflation, compulsory wage and price controls were imposed in August, 1971.

10. Phase I and Phase II compulsory controls did help in holding inflation in check. But we reverted to voluntary controls in January, 1973, with the implementation of Phase III controls. This action proved to be a bit premature, however, and compulsory controls were reinstituted with Phase IV controls.

NEW TERMS

Income-expenditure analysis, *p. 341*
Voluntary savings, *p. 346*
Compulsory savings, *p. 347*
Excess profits tax, *p. 347*
Rationing, *p. 349*
Controlled materials plan, *p. 349*
Excess-demand inflation, *p. 350*
Price and wage controls, *p. 351*
Decontrol, *p. 353*

Wage-price guideposts, *p. 354*
Nagging unemployment, *p. 355*
Jawbone tactics, *p. 357*
Income-tax surcharge, *p. 359*
Nixonomics, *p. 360*
Gradualism, *p. 361*
Game plan, *p. 362*
Phases I, II, III, and IV, *pp. 363-365*

QUESTIONS FOR DISCUSSION AND ANALYSIS

1. Which would you favor, nagging unemployment and stable prices or full employment and creeping inflation? Why?

2. In order to combat inflation, do you think it is better to decrease government spending and hold taxes constant or to hold government spending constant and increase taxes? Why?

3. Should we tax sufficiently to pay the full cost of a war instead of borrowing and going into debt? Why?

4. Do you agree with the idea of compulsory savings during a wartime economy? Why?

5. In terms of the current GNP, how much more must consumers pay for the goods and services they buy for every one percent increase in the price level?

6. Do you think that voluntary pricing regulations such as those suggested in the President's wage-price guideposts will ever work in our economy? Why?

7. What action(s), if any, do you think the Administration should have taken in 1966 to combat inflationary pressures in the economy?

8. Should wage and price controls to combat inflation be utilized during a peacetime economy? Why?

9. Do you think Phase II controls should have been removed when they were, in January, 1973?

10. Check the current level of the CPI, and discuss what has happened to the price level since January, 1974.

SUGGESTED READINGS

Ackley, Gardner. *Macroeconomic Theory*. New York: The Macmillan Company, 1961.

American Institute for Economic Research. "Dr. McCracken on Price-Wage Controls." *Economic Education Bulletin* (January, 1972).

Boulding, Kenneth, and Emile Bendit. *Disarmament and the Economy*. New York: Harper & Row, Publishers, 1963.

Burns, Arthur F. *Prosperity Without Inflation*. Garden City, N. Y.: Doubleday & Company, Inc., 1958.

Economic Report of the President. Chapter 7, "The Employment Act: Twenty Years of Policy Experience." Washington: U.S. Government Printing Office, 1966.

"Federal Fiscal Policies of the 1960s." *Federal Reserve Bulletin*. Washington: U.S. Government Printing Office (September, 1968).

Feige, Edgar L., and Douglas K. Pearce. "The Wage-Price Control Experiment—Did It Work?" *Challenge* (July/August, 1973).

Harris, Seymour E. *Inflation and the American Economy*. New York: McGraw-Hill Book Company, 1945.

——————. *The New Economics*. New York: Alfred A. Knopf, Inc., 1952.

Hazlitt, Henry. *The Critics of Keynesian Economics*. New York: Van Nostrand Reinhold Company, 1960.

——————. *The Failure of the New Economics*. New York: Van Nostrand Reinhold Company, 1957.

Heller, Walter W. *New Dimensions of Political Economy*. Cambridge: Harvard University Press, 1966.

Hitch, Charles J., and Roland N. McKean. *The Economics of Defense in the Nuclear Age*. New York: Atheneum Publishers, 1965.

Miller, Roger L., and Raburn M. Williams. *The New Economics of Richard Nixon*. New York: Canfield Press, 1972.

Moore, Thomas Gale. *U.S. Incomes Policy, Its Rationale and Development*, Special Analysis, No. 18. Washington: American Enterprise Institute (December, 1971).

Morley, Samuel A. *The Economics of Inflation*. Hinsdale, Ill.: The Dryden Press, 1971.

Ozaki, Robert S. *Inflation, Recession . . . and All That*. New York: Holt, Rinehart and Winston, Inc., 1972.

"The Employment-Inflation Dilemma." *Business and Economic Review*. Chicago: First National Bank of Chicago (April, 1971).

17

Fiscal Policy and the Debt

PREVIEW   Sometimes federal deficits result from accidental circumstances. At other times they are planned. In either case a deficit enlarges the total size of our national debt. In the past few decades the federal budget has been used as a tool for stabilizing the level of economic activity. Deficits have been used to boost economic activity during sluggish periods, and surpluses, especially during periods of full employment, have helped prevent or combat inflation.

The largest annual increases in the federal debt occurred during World War II, and the national debt has risen from $285 billion at the end of the war to $485 billion today. There are numerous myths and problems associated with the national debt, including the fear of bankruptcy, the effect of debt on the money supply, repayment and the redistribution of income, passing the debt on to future generations, the burden to taxpayers, and the growing interest cost of maintaining the debt.

Over the past forty years or so, we have accepted and established a policy of economic stabilization and developed a set of anticyclical measures that can be utilized to combat depressions and inflation and to accelerate the rate of economic growth. We seek to bring about a more stable economy with the use of monetary, fiscal, and psychological policies. It is easy to observe those monetary measures that change the amount and flow of money. Changes in taxation and spending also are readily noticeable. It is sometimes difficult, however, to determine whether such measures are for stabilization purposes or otherwise. Although we do not have a crystallized psychological policy, there has been a strong tendency in recent years to encourage consumption and investment spending during some periods and to encourage thrift and savings at other times. Furthermore, attempts have been made to ward off undesirable movements in economic activity by creating a proper frame of mind among individuals and businessmen.

PATTERN OF ANTICYCLICAL MEASURES

In an endeavor to modify sluggish as well as inflationary tendencies in the economy, mild indirect measures are usually employed at first. If the adverse movement persists, however, stronger indirect and then direct anticyclical measures are generally utilized. We can summarize the stabilization measures at our disposal by referring to hypothetical, yet practical, situations. For example, when the economy is in a state of unemployment, we will generally use monetary policy to encourage consumption and private investment. There will be a general liberalization of the money supply, initially through the use of open-market operations and by decreasing the discount rates. Existing selective controls, especially credit restrictions, are modified or eliminated. Moral suasion is also employed to encourage bank lending, and the Federal Reserve Banks are less restrictive on loans to member banks. Although it is not always noticeable, the Open Market Committee usually begins to buy bonds in the early stages of a recessionary period. From past indications, the reserve requirements are the last monetary measure to be put into play.

Fiscal measures may be invoked simultaneously with the stronger monetary measures or may follow shortly after them. Reducing taxes while maintaining or increasing government expenditures is a popular method of converting to deficit government spending as a means of stimulating economic activity. However, increasing government expenditures while holding taxes constant or reducing them also may be used in an effort to expand production and employment. Higher government spending coupled with higher taxes is the least likely measure to be used to bolster the economy during a recessionary period.

During the time when monetary and fiscal measures are being used, the Administration and various other government agencies, including the Department of Commerce, the Council of Economic Advisers, the Treasury Department, the Office of Management and the Budget, the Federal Reserve Board, and others will be issuing persuasive statements in an endeavor to encourage consumption and private investment. The exact bundle of stabilization measures to be used and the pattern of their implementation will, of course, vary with circumstances and with different political administrations.

BUDGETARY POLICY

The use of fiscal measures obviously involves the federal budget. The size, growth, and nature of the budget, whether it is balanced or unbalanced, affects our national debt. Interrelated are monetary measures that may be involved in financing any deficit. Monetary measures likewise can have an influence on the structure and maturity of the national debt. In turn the management of the national debt itself can have a stabilizing or destabilizing effect on the level of economic activity and the price level. Consequently, we now turn to an analysis of budgetary policy and the many problems associated with the national debt.

Types of Budgets

The type of budget we have will affect the level of economic activity to some degree. There are three types: (1) a balanced budget, (2) a deficit budget, and (3) a surplus budget.

Balanced Budget. In general, a balanced budget has a neutral effect on the economy. Since government expenditures equal taxation with a balanced budget, total spending in the economy remains unchanged. What individuals and business firms give up in spendable funds to pay their taxes is counterbalanced by the government spending of the tax receipts. At times, however, it is possible for a balanced budget to bring about an expansionary effect in the economy. This occurs if the government taxes to some extent idle funds that would not otherwise be spent by individuals and businesses. Effective demand would then increase in relation to the taxation of otherwise idle funds.

Deficit Budget. A deficit budget will increase the level of economic activity or be inflationary, depending upon the status of employment in the economy. Remember that with a deficit budget the government spends more than it taxes. In order to take care of this excess of spending over taxation, the government is required to borrow funds. If it borrows idle funds or funds from the banks, which create money, the total effective demand of the economy will be increased. This occurs because the total spending by the government is greater than the amount of spendable funds given up by firms and individuals through taxation. Therefore, the level of economic activity will increase if the economy is at less than full employment, and inflation will occur if the economy is at full employment. It is for this reason that a deficit budget is frequently referred to as a fiscal stimulus by economic advisers in Washington. The tendency for a deficit budget to bring about expansion or inflation in the economy, however, will be offset to some extent if in borrowing the government obtains funds from individuals and firms that might otherwise be spent on consumption and investment.

Surplus Budget. A surplus budget tends to have a deflationary effect on the economy. In order to have such a budget, government taxation must exceed government spending. This means that government spending is insufficient to offset the decline in spendable funds given up by individuals and businesses in the form of taxes. As a result, there is a net decrease in effective demand. Consequently, a surplus budget is often considered by some economic policy makers as a fiscal drag on the economy. This drag effect, of course, would be modified to the extent that the government might tax idle funds that would not be spent otherwise. It could also be offset if the government were to use the surplus to retire the debt.

If used properly, fiscal policy can help to stabilize the economy and modify business cycles. A surplus budget can help prevent inflation during a prosperity period, and a deficit budget can help to offset the tendency of widespread unemployment during a recessionary period. Such use of budgetary policy is shown in Figure 17-1.

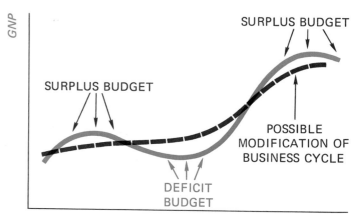

FIGURE 17-1

BUDGET USED AS AN ANTICYCLICAL DEVICE

A surplus budget reduces inflationary pressures during the peak of a business cycle, while a deficit budget lessens the adverse effects of recession and depression.

When the budget is used as a *tool for economic stabilization*, it is desirable to balance the budget over the period of the cycle instead of trying to do it on an annual basis. In order to accomplish this, it is necessary for the surplus of prosperity to equal the deficit of the recession. However, this is difficult to accomplish. A question might arise as to whether we should start such a practice by building up a surplus during prosperity and then spending it during the next recession, or whether we should incur the deficit during the recession and then repay the debt with the surplus obtained during the subsequent prosperity.

Assuming that the first method were utilized, a second problem would arise: How much surplus would need to be accumulated during the prosperity period? This would depend not only upon the inflationary pressures of prosperity but also upon the estimated need, or deficit, during the subsequent recession in the economy. It is practically impossible to determine what the duration and the intensity of the prosperity will be, let alone the duration and the intensity of the subsequent recession. Therefore, it is usually suggested that it is more feasible to run the deficit first. This also has its weaknesses. How can we be assured that the subsequent prosperity will be long enough or strong enough to permit an accumulation of a surplus sufficient to pay off the deficit incurred in the previous recessionary period?

Another weakness of the second method is that most administrators and legislators are willing to use deficit spending during a recessionary period to help alleviate unemployment, but many of them are reluctant to build up the necessary surplus during prosperity years. This was very evident from their actions in the first half of the 1960s and in the early 1970s, and especially in their slowness to take action to combat the inflation of 1966-1968 and in the mid-1970s. From a political point of view, the emphasis is often on tax reduction rather than higher taxes during a prosperity period, especially when there is a surplus in the federal budget. In short, deficit spending insofar as it can be used to bolster the level of economic activity can be very popular with the public during a recession, but increased taxes and/or a reduction in federal spending to combat inflation during a prosperity period is seldom popular.

It should be remembered also that a surplus acquired during a prosperity period should be held in cash reserve for best results. It can be used to pay off the debt subsequently but not until the level of economic activity begins to decline. If the surplus obtained during prosperity is used immediately to pay off the debt incurred by the deficit spending of the recession, it will merely result in putting back into the economy an amount of money equivalent to the surplus. Thus, the reduction of spendable income through taxation will be offset by government expenditures plus debt repayment. This means that the total spending of the economy will remain the same, provided the recipients of debt repayment spend or invest the money received from the government. In such a case, the surplus budget will have a neutral effect instead of being anti-inflationary. The better practice would be to hold the surplus funds until economic activity begins to decline. Repayment of the debt at such a time could give a boost to the economy if the recipient were to spend or invest these funds.

In recent years there has been a tendency to look at the so-called *full-employment budget* instead of the actual budget for the purpose of analyzing the fiscal effects of the budget. Regardless of the state of the actual budget, the full-employment budget is a measure of the potential revenue and expenditure that would result if full employment existed. It is said by some that the actual budget may be misleading. Let us say, for example, that the existing budget showed a deficit (or fiscal stimulus) of $15 billion and that the rate of unemployment was 6 percent. Projection may indicate that if the economy were at full employment (4 percent unemployment or less), the budget would show a surplus of $5 billion. Thus, if the economy expands toward the full employment level, it will encounter a fiscal drag, which would impede the attainment of a full employment objective.

Proponents of "functional finance," who look at the budget as a tool of stabilization and growth rather than as something to be balanced annually or even periodically, would contend that the inherent drag of the full-employment surplus should be eliminated if the economy is going to attain its goal of full employment. This, of course, could be accomplished by increasing the size of the current fiscal stimulus (deficit) through reducing taxes or by increasing government spending.

Carrying the analysis one step further, proponents of this theory claim that once full employment and a balanced budget have been reached care must be taken to prevent the development of a subsequent drag on the economy. It is pointed out that with a given tax rate, total revenues will increase by $10 to $12 billion annually as a result of the normal forces of growth in our economy. In order to prevent this from occurring, it is suggested that a fiscal dividend be declared either in the form of a tax reduction or an increase in federal spending. They place little emphasis on the notion that surpluses should be accumulated during prosperity to offset the deficits of previous periods.

PROBLEMS OF THE DEBT

Our experience with budgetary policy as a means of stabilizing business activity is rather limited. It is difficult, therefore, to determine whether we can time our deficits and surpluses accurately and have them of proper size to act as stabilizers of the economy. Furthermore, we have not had sufficient experience in the past 40 years to determine whether, in the absence of emergencies, the deficits and the surpluses can offset each other sufficiently to prevent a growing debt. We incurred a sizable debt during the depression of the 1930s as a result of our deficit-spending program. Without having had a chance to diminish this debt, we entered World War II, which pushed the debt up to about $285 billion. Our opportunity to reduce the debt was further hampered by the outbreak of the Korean conflict in 1950. The escalation of the war in Vietnam in the mid-1960s interfered with our experiments to use fiscal stimuli, fiscal dividends, and avoid fiscal drags on the economy. In the interim years, however, we made very little headway in reducing the debt. In fact, the federal debt, now at $485 billion, has grown to such proportions that it presents several problems. A few of these problems, including bankruptcy, redistribution of income, debt burden, effect on the money supply, size, refunding, and productivity are treated below.

Bankruptcy

It is often thought by the lay person that the debt may become so large that it will bankrupt the nation. It is commonly believed that the government may get into a situation where it will be unable to pay off the debt. This misunderstanding arises from the failure to distinguish clearly the true nature of government financing compared to the normal method of business financing. When the government borrows and repays funds, it is more like the financial transactions taking place within a family than the type of financing practiced by private enterprises.

Comparison to Business Debt. In accounting we learn that whenever a business has total current liabilities in excess of current assets, it lacks solvency. In short, it does not have sufficient cash to pay its current debts in the immediate future. In such a case, when debtors press for payment the company may voluntarily and legally have itself declared bankrupt, or the debtors may force the company into bankruptcy. In either case, the court will decide whether the business should continue under receivership, that is, under a court-appointed manager, or whether the assets of the company should be liquidated to pay off the creditors.

This basic difficulty arises in connection with a business debt because, whenever the firm pays off its debt, it decreases the total assets of the company. Money paid out actually leaves the firm, thereby reducing the assets. If debt payments are so large that the company is forced to suspend payment, the creditors may force liquidation of the firm through bankruptcy proceedings in order to recover payment on the debt.

Comparison to Family Debt. The national debt is more like an internal family debt than a business debt. Consider the family as a spending unit and suppose that a son borrows $125 from his dad for such things as dates, ball games, and school supplies over the period of the school year and that he intends to repay it from the money he earns from summer employment. When he borrows, he does so within the family unit. Likewise, when he repays the $125 in the summer, the money remains within the family.

When the son pays his debt, his individual assets are decreased by $125 while his father's assets are increased by $125. Therefore, the net assets of the family remain the same. Unlike the debt repayment of the firm, in the family situation no money leaves the family as a result of the debt repayment. There is merely a transfer of cash from one member of the family to another, or a transfer of assets from one member of the family to another. Therefore, there is no net reduction of assets nor is there any money leaving the family.

The Federal Debt. When the government borrows money, it generally borrows from individuals, businesses, and banks within the economy. When it makes repayment on the debt, the money stays within the economy. There is no reduction in total assets when the government makes repayment on the debt. Furthermore, the government's ability to repay is limited only by the total assets of the economy or, more immediately, by the total income of the economy and the government's ability to tax. For example, the national debt in 1973 was nearly $475 billion. Considering that the GNP for 1973 was in the vicinity of $1,288 billion and the total personal income was around $1,035 billion, it is easy to see that the total income of the nation was sufficient to take care of debt repayment if the government decided to raise taxes sufficiently to obtain funds required to pay it off. Theoretically, but unrealistically, the government could tax a sufficient amount to pay the debt off in the course of one year. If the government were to do this, it would not in any way reduce the total income or assets of the nation as a whole. The taxation and repayment of the debt would merely cause a redistribution of income, or cash assets, inside the economy. The income given up by individuals and firms in the form of taxes would be offset by payment to those holding the debt. Thus, the total income or assets of the economy would be the same after payment of the debt as before. The major difference is that income and cash assets held by various individuals and firms would be changed.

It is possible, but not probable, that some individuals and firms would have exactly the same holdings of assets after repayment of the debt as they did before. This would occur if an individual or a firm was taxed an amount equal to his or its holding of the debt. For example, a firm holding $10,000 in government bonds might be taxed $10,000 in order to help pay off the debt. Since it would receive a payment of $10,000 on its bonds when the debt was repaid, its total assets would remain the same.

Although a tax rate sufficient to pay off the debt in one year would be prohibitive, certainly over a relatively short period, say 30 or 50 years, the government could operate at a surplus sufficient to pay off the debt. Surpluses obtained during periods of inflation could be used to pay the debt during periods of contraction in the economy.

Effect of Redistribution of Income

The question arises: Why, then, does the government not take more positive steps to pay off the debt? Reluctance to reduce the debt by sizable amounts stems not only from the fact that the large tax burden necessary to do so would be politically unpopular, but also from the fact that it would cause disruptive economic repercussions. One important problem would be the redistribution of income brought about by repayment of the debt.

If the debt were to be paid off on a large-scale basis, heavy taxes would reduce total effective demand, especially among the lower income groups. Whether or not such reduction in effective demand would be offset when the government used tax money to pay off the debt would depend on what the recipients of debt repayments would do with the money they received. Since it is quite possible that the total propensity to consume or to invest of the debt holders who receive repayment would be less than that of the taxpayers in total, the net effective demand of the economy could easily be reduced by repayment of the debt. The possibility of this occurring becomes evident when we look at the ownership of the debt. It is generally agreed that the lower income groups do not hold much of the federal debt. It is held primarily by banks, businesses, government agencies, and individuals in the higher income groups. This is shown in Table 17-1.

Of course, if the debt holders would spend the income they received at the time the debts were repaid, there would be no adverse effect on the economy. This would tend to be the case if the debt were repaid during a full-employment period. It would be best, however, to pay off the debt during periods of less than full employment with money obtained through taxation during a prosperous or inflationary period. In this way, the debt could be used as a tool for economic stabilization.

TABLE 17-1		
OWNERSHIP OF UNITED STATES GOVERNMENT DEBT	Federal Reserve Banks	15.7
	Commercial Banks	14.9
	Mutual Savings Banks	.6
	Insurance Companies	1.3
	Other Corporations	2.6
1973	Individuals	16.5
	State and Local Governments	6.3
(Percent)	United States Government Agencies	26.0
	Foreign and International	12.3
	Miscellaneous Investors	3.8
	Total	100.0

SOURCE: *Federal Reserve Bulletin* (February, 1974).

Burden of the Debt

It is often thought that when the debt is not paid during the period in which it is incurred the burden of paying the debt is passed on to future generations. The extent to which this is true depends upon whether we are considering the effect on the total economy or on individuals and firms.

Effect on Total Economy. If we are considering the total economy, it is impossible to pass the real cost of the debt on to future generations. The real cost of the debt to the total economy can only be measured by the cost of goods and services that individuals and firms must forego when they give up their purchasing power to buy government bonds. When consumers and investors purchase such bonds they give the government revenue to make its purchases. For example, during World War II, citizens and firms gave up the purchase of automobiles, homes, food, clothing, machinery, raw materials, and the like. In the meantime, the government, with its borrowed purchasing power, bought tanks, planes, ships, ammunition, and other necessary war materials. The decrease in consumer production was in effect the real cost of the debt. The people in the economy at the time the debt was incurred shouldered the real burden of the debt through the loss of goods and services.

For the economy as a whole the debt repayment, whether repaid immediately or postponed to the future, will not cost anything in terms of goods and services. As a result of the redistribution of income that takes place at the time the debt is repaid, some individuals and firms may suffer a loss of purchasing power; but this will be offset by gains to others, and no net decrease in purchasing power in the economy will take place. For example, if the total debt were to be paid in a period of one year, the total tax necessary to pay off the current (1974) debt would be approximately $485 billion. This would have a tendency to decrease the purchasing power of the economy. It would reduce effective demand and result in decreased production. When the government paid out the $485 billion to debt holders, however, it would tend to offset the adverse effect of the tax. Total purchasing power in the economy would remain the same. The effective demand, and therefore production, would remain the same, provided the propensity to consume and to invest of the debt holders was the same as that of the general taxpayers. There would be no loss of total goods and services at the time the debt was repaid. Thus, since there is no cost for the economy as a whole when the debt is repaid, it is impossible to pass the cost of the debt on to future generations.

Effect on Individuals. Although the cost of the debt cannot be passed on to future generations from the viewpoint of the total economy, the burden for individuals and firms can be passed on to future generations. If the government were to pay off the debt in a relatively short period, say within the generation in which the debt occurred, the particular individuals taxed in order to pay the debt would have to give up purchasing power. Thus, they would be burdened with an individual cost of the debt to the extent that each is taxed. If payment on the debt is postponed for a generation or two, however, the tax will fall to a large extent on the descendants of those individuals and businesses in the economy at the time the debt was incurred. Thus, even though the net cost or burden of the debt cannot be passed on to future generations, the individual burden can be passed on to them.

For example, during World War II we incurred an enormous debt. If the debt had been paid off within the generation in which it was incurred, Mr. Smith, a taxpayer of the period, might have had to pay $1,000 in taxes in order to give the government the money to pay Mr. Jones, who, we will assume, was a holder of bonds and therefore an owner of the debt. This payment would have decreased the purchasing power of Mr. Smith, and it would have increased the purchasing power of Mr. Jones. If debt payment were postponed until 1980, however, Mr. Smith's grandson, a recent immigrant, or someone else in the economy would have to pay the taxes, especially if Mr. Smith had died in the meantime. Therefore, the individual burden of the debt would have been passed on from Mr. Smith to someone in a subsequent generation. Mr. Jones, who made a personal sacrifice to loan the government money through the purchase of bonds, would be deprived of repayment until a later date. In fact, if he passed away, his descendants would receive the individual gain at the time repayment was made instead of Mr. Jones. In actual practice, however, Mr. Jones could eliminate this difficulty by transferring his ownership of the debt to someone else through the sale of his bonds.

Effect on the Money Supply

Another problem involved in the repayment of the debt, which tends to strengthen our reluctance to pay it off, is the effect of the repayment on the money supply. We know that when an individual or a business loans the government money, there is no increase in the money supply. For example, if Mr. Smith buys a bond for $1,000, he generally will pay cash for it. Therefore, there is merely a transfer of cash from the individual to the government with no change in the total money supply. If a bank loans the government money, however, it can pay for the bonds in cash or through the creation of a demand deposit against which the government writes checks. In Chapter 13 we learned that the demand deposits brought about by the creation of credit increased the money supply. Therefore, if a bank were to buy $100,000 worth of bonds and pay for them with a demand deposit, it would increase the money supply accordingly. This process is referred to as *monetizing the debt.*

In Chapter 12 we learned that changes in the money supply could affect the level of economic activity and/or the price level. Therefore, when the government goes into debt by borrowing from the banks it increases the money supply and thus increases the level of economic activity, as it did from 1958 to 1965, or it adds inflationary pressures to the economy, as it did from 1966 to 1974.

During the period 1960 to 1974, the money supply increased from $142 billion to $269 billion. Of this $269 billion, $199 billion was in the form of demand deposits. Of the $199 billion, approximately $65 billion came into existence as a result of the sale of government bonds to the commercial banks. Therefore, the national debt today is supporting a sizable part of the total money supply.

We know that a decrease in the money supply will have a tendency to decrease our level of economic activity and/or decrease the price level, unless offset by some other force such as an increase in the velocity of money. Just as the debt was monetized when the government borrowed from the banks, the money supply will be decreased when the debt is paid off. This is known as *demonetizing the debt*. For example, if the government redeemed the $100,000 in bonds held by the bank, it would reduce demand deposits by that amount and reduce the money supply accordingly. Thus, if the government were to reduce the federal debt by sizable amounts over a relatively short period of time, it could reduce the money supply to such an extent as to have an adverse effect on the level of economic activity. Payment of the debt supported by bank credit would be beneficial during a period of full employment insofar as it could reduce inflationary pressures. During periods of less than full employment, however, such debt repayment could be inimical to the economy as a whole.

Size of the Debt

The mammoth size of the current debt, $485 billion, is in itself sufficient to discourage many people regarding its repayment. It might be pointed out that, although we have not reduced the debt absolutely, increased productivity and higher income have reduced the size of the debt relative to our annual income. For example, in 1946 the national debt was $285 billion. Our total income (GNP) for that year was $209 billion. Since the debt was considerably larger than our total income, it could not have been paid out of current income within a period of one year even if we chose to do so. In fact, to pay it off at the rate of $10 billion per year would have exerted quite a hardship.

Although the federal debt was a considerably larger amount in 1973, the total production of the nation had increased to $1,288 billion. Since the annual income of the nation exceeded the national debt, it would have been possible to pay off the debt within a period of one year. Although possible, of course, it would not have been feasible to do so. With a total national income exceeding $1,050 billion, however, if we were to decide to pay the debt off at the rate of $10 billion annually, not so much of a hardship would be created on the economy today as it would have been when the GNP was approximately $209 billion per year.

In effect, through our increased productivity and higher price level, the monetary income of the nation increased more than fivefold in the period 1946 to 1973. Since the absolute amount of the debt increased about 63 percent during this period, the burden of the debt relative to national income was reduced by two thirds. The debt in 1973 was about 38 percent of our GNP compared to about 135 percent in 1946. For this reason, those who were worried about the size of the national debt 20 to 25 years ago have less cause to worry about it today. It should be remembered, however, that decreasing income resulting either from a falling price level or from a drop in production or employment would increase the size of the national debt in relation to income and would make repayment more burdensome.

The suggestion has occasionally been made that we should postpone payment on the debt, since it becomes less burdensome as the years go on. To the extent that we increase income as a result of increased productivity, this suggestion has some merit. But if the higher GNP and therefore the greater income is brought about primarily by higher prices, the suggestion is a poor one, since greater problems than that of debt retirement will result from rising prices. Furthermore, if, due to continuous inflation, the purchasing power of a $100 savings bond at the maturity date is of less value than the $75 price of the bond at the purchase date, the purchase of bonds by individuals and firms could be discouraged at a time when the government needed money.

Refunding the Debt

When government debt obligations reach maturity at a time when the United States Treasury does not have the money to pay them, the problem of refunding the debt arises. At such a time, the federal government generally will issue and sell new bonds to raise money to pay off the matured obligations. This, however, may not be accomplished easily, especially when billions of dollars worth of bonds may be maturing within a short period of time. Furthermore, the government may be forced to pay a higher interest rate when it borrows funds for this purpose.

In the late 1960s and early 1970s the federal Treasury was paying interest rates of 7 to 8 percent for money it borrowed in the short-term market. With a 4.25 percent ceiling, it was almost impossible to compete for funds in the long-term market against high-grade corporate securities yielding 7 to 8 percent interest. For example, in 1971 billions of dollars worth of bonds paying 4.25 percent interest became due. At that time there was a 4.25 percent ceiling on the interest rate that the Treasury could pay on long-term government securities (those maturing in five years or more) that had been imposed by Congress. There was, however, no interest rate ceiling on short-term government obligations. In 1971 it was possible for an investor to buy many existing long-term government bonds at discounts that were yielding over 6 percent. In addition, many high-grade corporate bonds were yielding more than 7 to 8 percent.

Under these circumstances it would have been difficult for the United States Treasury to sell new long-term bonds at 4.25 percent when existing government bonds yielding more than 6 percent could be purchased in the open market. On a number of previous occasions the Treasury Department requested that the interest rate ceiling on long-term government bonds be removed in order to permit them to sell bonds at a higher interest rate. Since these requests had been denied the Treasury was forced to sell short-term government obligations on which there was no interest rate ceiling. Consequently, the United States Treasury offered several billion dollars of short-term bonds (those maturing in five years or less) at 7 percent interest. Although the Treasury did raise funds to pay off the matured obligations, the total cost of the debt increased because the interest rate on the new obligations (7 percent) was higher than that on the refunded portion of the debt (4.25 percent). Furthermore, it put itself in a position where it would have to pay off or refund again this portion of the debt in another five years. Had the Treasury Department been able to issue long-term securities at a competitive interest rate, it could have prolonged the payment or refunding date for 15, 20, or even 30 years. On a few occasions Congress has permitted the Treasury to extend to more than five years the maturity dates of certain short-term notes paying interest rates of more than 4.25 percent. This in effect was a foot in the door in the campaign to raise or eliminate the interest-rate ceiling on the national debt. More relief came in March, 1971, when Congress authorized the Treasury to issue bonds in amounts up to a total of $10 billion at rates of interest exceeding 4.25 percent per annum. Refunding the debt is quite a problem when one stops to consider that nearly $90 billion of the national debt, primarily short-term securities, becomes due and payable annually.

Burden of Interest Payments

Included each year in our national budget is more than $20 billion for payment of interest on the debt. Although taxation for the payment of this interest does not impose a net burden or cost on the economy as a whole, it does cause an annual redistribution of income and, therefore, a specific burden to individuals and firms in the economy. If the government had originally increased taxes instead of going into debt or if the government had paid off the debt shortly after it had been incurred, it would have imposed a smaller total burden on the individuals than it does when the debt repayment is postponed. With postponement of the debt the total redistribution of income necessary to retire the debt is not only the $485 billion, the principal amount, but also $22 billion or more annually for interest on the debt. It is a matter of judgment whether the individuals and firms would prefer the hardship of paying off the debt in a relatively short period of time or of giving up more of total income but spreading the hardship or inconvenience in smaller doses over a longer period of time. In spite of the higher amount of interest paid, in relation to income the interest payments were equal to 2.1 percent of national income in 1973 as compared to 2.8 percent in 1946.

Productivity of the Debt

If an individual or a business firm borrows money to put up a new building, to buy machinery and material, or to hire manpower to produce goods, it can increase its total productivity. The loan it receives is said to be productive, since it can increase the total output of the company and since it may enhance its profits. In fact, firms borrow billions of dollars annually for this very purpose.

Individuals may also borrow to enhance their purchasing power. They may be prompted to do this especially if the purchase of certain commodities has greater utility to them at the time of borrowing than the purchase of these commodities would have in the future. The major decision to be made before borrowing is whether the utility resulting from the current use of the goods purchased with the borrowed funds will be greater than the disutility involved in repaying the loan plus the interest at a later date. Evidently, we do prefer present utility in many cases since consumers borrow billions of dollars each year to buy automobiles, appliances, homes, consumer goods, and the like.

Government borrowing and the subsequent debt may be productive, or it may increase the total utility of the economy, in much the same manner as do business and consumer loans. By going into debt, the government is able to obtain the military goods necessary to win a war. Most of us agree that it would be a mistake to lose a war for lack of materials because of any inhibitions about going into debt. Financing government dams, reforestation projects, highways and roads, aircraft developments, educational facilities, manpower retraining programs, the elimination of poverty, medical research, space explorations, agricultural experiments, pollution control, and urban renewal through debt can be very productive. In some cases consumers' satisfaction may actually be increased as a result of the improvement of roads, the production of electricity, the development of recreation facilities, and the like. Similar to the individual or the firm, the nation or its administrators must decide whether increased productivity and the utilization of current consumption is of greater value than the disutility of paying off the debt.

DEBT CEILING

The statutory limit or ceiling on the national debt was first established in 1917 when Congress passed the Second Liberty Bond Act. Prior to World War II, Congress set individual ceilings on the various types of government indebtedness, but in 1941 it did away with the individual debt ceilings and created one ceiling on the total debt outstanding. Since the debt ceiling has been raised more than a dozen times in the past 20 years, increasing from

$275 billion in 1954 to $495 billion in 1974, the statutory limit on the national debt has been a topic of controversy in recent years.

A federal deficit accompanied by a rise in the debt ceiling will generally provoke more opposition than a deficit that does not involve a hike in the debt ceiling. Furthermore, the cause of the debt plays an important role in its acceptance. Large debt ceiling increases involved as a result of emergency situations have incurred less Congressional opposition than the smaller increases related with nonemergency periods.

Many arguments can be marshalled for and against the debt ceiling. Opponents of the ceiling maintain that it may at times limit needed expenditures on important government programs, such as defense or recession spending, whenever tax revenues are not up to expectations or the government has failed to increase taxes sufficiently to take care of its spending obligations. It is claimed also that a debt ceiling results in fiscal subterfuge by the Treasury. The statutory limit is on a defined portion of the total federal debt that is usually associated with the annual federal budget. The federal government, however, has many nonbudgetary financial obligations. Many federal agencies which normally borrow funds from the Treasury may be empowered to sell their own securities to private financial institutions and investors if they desire. Frequently when the Treasury is pinched for funds and is approaching the debt limit, it will request a particular agency to sell its own securities in the market rather than to borrow from the Treasury. Critics of the debt ceiling contend further that it restricts the freedom of the Treasury to manage the debt efficiently, especially when the debt is close to the ceiling. In such a circumstance, the Treasury may have to wait until old securities mature before issuing new ones for fear of going over the debt ceiling. Critics of the ceiling argue that it would be better for the Treasury to experiment with new issues sometime before the expiration of the old in order to try out the rate and to have time to make any necessary adjustment in order to obtain the best price. Otherwise the Treasury will be at the mercy of the market if it must wait until the time various issues expire before issuing new securities to replace them. President Nixon in 1969 endeavored to get around the debt ceiling by proposing a restructuring of the federal debt in such a manner that it would have excluded $100 billion of the current debt from the statutory limitation. This would have permitted the Administration to add to the debt without requesting an increase in the ceiling. His proposal, however, did not receive favorable treatment by Congress.

Proponents of the statutory limit stress the fact that the debt ceiling is needed to restrain government spending and that it prevents the national debt from getting dangerously high. Congress passes legislation and appropriates money for various bills. Once these are turned over to the Administration, Congress may review the spending bills individually and make adjustments in them. During this time, however, it does not have the opportunity to see the budget in total again. As a result of individual adjustments, total spending might be higher than the original budget approval. In such cases the debt ceiling would prevent the Treasury from borrowing amounts over the ceiling limit in order to finance such federal bills. Although the debt ceiling has been raised liberally by Congress in the past several years, its presence does tend to make Congress look a bit closer at the budget and decide whether they really want to approve of any appropriations that will necessitate borrowing and raising the debt ceiling. It might also be argued that insofar as the ceiling limits deficits in the annual budget, it makes the taxpayers more conscious of the total cost of government services. Many taxpayers may not balk at expenditures of $325 billion with a tax bill scheduled to be only $310 billion. But if they were taxed $325 billion in order to cover the total cost of federal spending, they might very well decide to do without some of the government services. In short, deficits and a rising national debt can deceive the taxpayers about the true cost of government services.

In 1972 Congress, at the request of the Administration and the Treasury, pushed the debt ceiling up to $465 billion in order to accommodate a $20 to $22 billion debt incorporated into the fiscal 1973 budget. The ceiling was raised to $485 billion in mid-1973, and in mid-1974 Congress raised it again to $495 billion.

SUMMARY

1. The federal budget can be used as a means of helping to stabilize the level of economic activity.

2. Deficits incurred to bolster the economy in recessions can be offset by surpluses accumulated to combat inflation during prosperity periods.

3. As a result of our inability to balance the budget, either annually or over the period of the business cycle, we have incurred considerable debt in the past few decades. The present national debt is in the vicinity of $485 billion.

4. Contrary to common belief, it would be exceedingly difficult to bankrupt the nation as a result of our large debt, since most of the debt is held domestically.

5. Repayment of the debt involves a problem of redistribution of income or assets.

6. The burden of the debt for the total economy cannot be passed on to future generations. It is possible, however, to pass the burden of the debt on to particular individuals and business firms in the future.

7. The federal debt can be monetized as it is incurred.

8. Annual interest payments on the federal debt exceed $22 billion.

9. Although the amounts of the national debt and the interest payments are increasing, their sizes relative to our total national income are declining.

QUESTIONS FOR DISCUSSION AND ANALYSIS

1. Distinguish between monetary policy and fiscal policy. Which do you think has the greater impact for stabilizing the economy?

2. Do you think that it is feasible to balance the budget over the period of a cycle? Give reasons.

3. Discuss the merits and weaknesses of a full-employment balanced budget.

4. What is the per capita value of the national debt today? What is the per family share of the national debt today?

5. If you owned a $5,000 government bond, would you be willing to relieve the government of its obligation to redeem that bond in order to help in eliminating our national debt? Why or why not?

6. Would the fear of national bankruptcy be more realistic if the federal debt were held primarily by foreigners? Why?

7. Explain the "monetization and demonetization of the debt" and its effect on the level of business activity.

8. It is said that the national debt is increasing absolutely but decreasing relatively. Explain.

9. How would the idea of interest-free financing alleviate the interest burden of the federal debt?

10. Do you think the ceiling on the national debt should be removed? Why or why not?

SUGGESTED READINGS

Backman, Jules, *et al. War and Defense Economics.* New York: Rinehart & Company, Inc., 1952. Chapters 1-14.

Buchanan, James M., and Richard E. Wagner. *Public Debt in a Democratic Society.* Washington: American Enterprise Institute, January, 1967.

Clark, John J. *The New Economics of National Defense.* New York: Random House, Inc., 1966.

Enke, Stephen. *Defense Management.* Englewood Cliffs, N. J.: Prentice-Hall, Inc., 1967.

Miller, Glenn H., Jr. *The Federal Budget and Economic Activity.* Kansas City: Federal Reserve Bank of Kansas City, June, 1969.

Schultze, Charles L., *et al. Setting National Priorities: The 1975 Budget.* Washington: The Brookings Institution, 1974.

The Budget and Economic Growth. New York: Committee for Economic Development, 1959.

The Federal Budget in Brief, Fiscal Year 1975. Washington: U.S. Government Printing Office, 1974.

The National Debt Ceiling Proposal, Legislative Analysis No. 4. Washington: American Enterprise Institute, 1969.

PART FIVE

The Public Sector

18

The Public Budget: Income and Outlay

PREVIEW We expect the government to provide us with certain goods and services that are not generally available through the private sector of the economy. Taxation provides the finances needed by government for such an undertaking. Although taxes are by far the main source of government revenue, funds are generated also from fees and fines, from special assessments, and from government-owned lands and enterprises. By and large we are requiring more and more services from the government at all levels—federal, state, and local. This has occurred because of the increase in population, the expansion of current government services, the development of new government services, higher levels of income, and the rise in prices. From time to time, consequently, the composition of government functions changes as the needs of our citizens change. Although our taxes seem high, the tax rate in the U.S. is a bit less than the tax rates in most other major industrial nations.

Most of the goods and services we use are produced and made available to us by the private sector of our economy. But a number of other things, many of which are taken for granted, are provided by the public sector, that is, by government. As a rule, the goods and services that are produced in the private sector can be obtained and used only if we have the money or the credit with which to obtain them. Most of the goods and services provided by government are "free" goods—including public schools and police protection—in the sense that we do not pay for them directly as we use them.

Does this mean that the goods and services provided by government do not have to be paid for? Of course not. We know that government at some level—local, state, or federal—pays the cost of the armed forces, highways, streets, police forces, welfare facilities, and public schools. As individuals, we do not necessarily pay the costs of these services according to the amount of the services we use. Rather the total amount of the services provided is paid for by general taxation.

What goods and services will be provided by government and how they will be paid for depends in large measure upon the philosophy of the government and the fiscal policies pursued by that government. If those who control and direct the government believe that the private sector of the economy does not provide certain needed goods and services, they will be inclined to enlist the aid of government in an effort to provide such goods and services. Consequently, in addition to the usual activities of government, such as road construction, public health services, education, parks and recreation, automobile licensing, and national defense, the public sector in recent years has been financing manpower development and training programs, business and mortgage loans, urban redevelopment, pollution control measures, medicare, model cities programs, rent subsidies, and other activities considered now as public service.

Not only has the public sector been compelled to provide new and additional services for society because they were not forthcoming through the private sector, but the federal government has often been compelled to take on various public functions because they were not being provided through state and local governments. This has been the case, for example, with education, mass transit, urban redevelopment, health care, and pollution control.

PUBLIC FINANCE

Public finance deals with the income and expenditures of government. For some purposes public finance is regarded as a subject distinct from that of private finance. Basically, however, the two are related. The results of taxation upon the incomes of individuals and businesses and the benefits of constructive governmental services affect private finance. On the other hand, the incomes of private individuals and businesses influence to a very real extent the nature and scope of the tax structure and the amount of revenues that governmental units can obtain.

In 1973 our national income amounted to $1,054 billion. In the same year the amount of payments to the federal government in personal, corporate, and other taxes and payments amounted to about $232 billion. In other words, the federal government, not counting state and local governments, had receipts from the people equal to about 22 percent of the national income. Was the amount of taxes too much? On what can we base our answers?

Although many people are opposed to increased government spending, some economists, as we noted earlier, contend that services of the public sector are inadequate today and that we have an imbalance between private and social production. Professor Galbraith, for example, suggests that today we produce through the private sector too many frivolous goods and services. He suggests more social production in the form of better schools, improved hospital facilities, more parks and recreational provisions, development of antipollution measures, and more basic scientific and medical research. These services, of course, would be financed through taxation, which by reducing private production would tend to improve the balance between private and social production. Galbraith, incidentally, opposed the historic 1964 tax reductions in favor of an increase in federal spending on social production, and he recommended increased federal spending in the 1970 recession.

What is the nature of the things that government provides in exchange for our money? Are the goods and services we receive through the government worth what they cost? Should taxes be increased, decreased, or remain as they are? Is our tax structure equitable?

These and many other questions pertaining to public finance are of interest to every citizen who is alert to matters that affect his own economic and social welfare and who is concerned about the welfare of others. An attempt to find satisfactory answers to such questions will suggest reasons for studying public finance.

FUNCTIONS OF GOVERNMENT

Our government system is based upon the national and state constitutions and statutory laws. The federal government was originally conceived as a confederacy of sovereign states, whose functions were to be those of providing military protection and of engaging in a limited number of activities considered desirable for the promotion of the general welfare in the nation as a whole. The appropriate functions of the state governments are assumed to relate to the needs of the people within the boundaries of each state. These functions now include the building of highways, support of the state-owned universities, aid to local public schools, and financing state hospitals. Finally, there are several units of local government, including cities, towns, counties, and various kinds of lesser governmental districts. The primary functions of these governments include the building and maintenance of streets, roads, public schools, health and welfare facilities and the provision of police protection.

As a general rule, those governmental activities which seem to pertain to the immediate and individual needs of the people tend to be performed by the smaller or local unit of government. The more widespread the need for a particular service, the more likely it is to be provided by the higher levels of government.

Government expenditures have generally shown a tendency to increase, as indicated in Figure 18-1 and Table 18-1. The origin of this phenomenon of increasing costs of government is not recent. If we study the expenditure curve for government in the United States for a century and a half, we find that the general tendency is upward. From 1946 to 1973, the total expenditures of government of all kinds increased, with federal expenditure showing by far the largest increase.

CAUSE OF RISING GOVERNMENT EXPENDITURES

What causes the rise in government spending? Truly there is a multiplicity of reasons. These include the expansion of existing functions, the development of new functions, higher price levels, population growth, higher incomes, and national emergencies.

Expansion of Existing Functions

There are no definite limits to the amount that should be spent by government for any activity which it performs. Therefore, even when it is decided that government will undertake the performance of a particular service, there is no absolute criterion by which the total expenditure for the service shall be determined. For example, the principle of public education has long been accepted in this country. Just how much will be spent for the education of the nation's youth during the next ten years is difficult to foresee. In recent decades the total amount of expenditures for public education has increased greatly, though not as much as that for certain other purposes. In 1950 state and local government expenditures for education amounted to $7.2 billion. By 1972 they amounted to $64.9 billion, and per capita expenditures on education had increased by more than 150 percent.

Consider, as another example, the cost of road construction by units of government. Before the advent of the automobile, expenditures for highway and street construction were small. Now these expenditures constitute one of the largest items in the budgets of state and city governments. Again, state

FIGURE 18-1

FEDERAL BUDGET RECEIPTS AND OUTLAYS

1961-1973

(For Years Ending June 30)

The federal budget continues to increase, with most years showing budget deficits.

SOURCE: *Statistical Abstract of the United States,* 1973.

¹ Estimated.

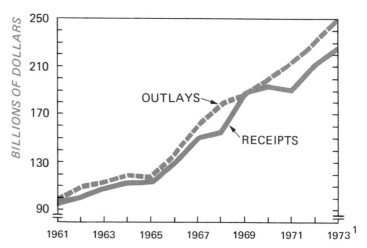

Fiscal Year	Receipts	Outlays	Surplus or Deficit (−)
Administrative Budget:			
1929	3,862	3,127	734
1933	1,997	4,598	−2,602
1939	4,979	8,841	−3,862
Consolidated Cash Statement:			
1940	6,879	9,589	−2,710
1941	9,202	13,980	−4,778
1942	15,104	34,500	−19,396
1943	25,097	78,909	−53,812
1944	47,818	93,956	−46,138
1945	50,162	95,184	−45,022
1946	43,537	61,738	−18,201
1947	43,531	36,931	6,600
1948	45,357	36,493	8,864
1949	41,576	40,570	1,006
1950	40,940	43,147	−2,207
1951	53,390	45,797	7,593
1952	68,011	67,962	49
1953	71,495	76,769	−5,274
Unified Budget:			
1954	69,719	70,890	−1,170
1955	65,469	68,509	−3,041
1956	74,547	70,460	4,087
1957	79,990	76,741	3,249
1958	79,636	82,575	−2,939
1959	79,249	92,104	−12,855
1960	92,492	92,223	269
1961	94,389	97,795	−3,406
1962	99,676	106,813	−7,137
1963	106,560	111,311	−4,751
1964	112,662	118,584	−5,922
1965	116,833	118,430	−1,596
1966	130,856	134,652	−3,796
1967	149,552	158,254	−8,702
1968	153,671	178,833	−25,161
1969	187,784	184,548	3,236
1970	193,743	196,588	−2,845
1971	188,392	211,425	−23,033
1972	208,649	231,876	−23,227
1973	232,225	246,526	−14,301
1974 [1]	270,000	274,660	−4,660
1975 [1]	295,000	304,445	−9,445

SOURCE: *Economic Report of the President,* 1974.

[1] Estimate.

General Note: Certain interfund transactions are excluded from receipts and outlays starting in 1932. For years prior to 1932, the amounts of such transactions are not significant. Refunds of receipts are excluded from receipts and outlays.

and local expenditures alone for roads and highways increased from $3.8 billion in 1950 to $19.0 billion in 1973, a 400 percent increase.

Development of New Functions

In addition to the expansion of activities that have long been recognized as proper functions of the government, new activities are added from time to time. One of the features of President Johnson's budget for fiscal 1964 was the recommendation for an "all out attack on poverty" in the United States. The program initially called for nearly $1 billion to be spent annually for the eradication of poverty. Subsequently the figure was raised to about $2 billion annually. In 1960 the federal government was spending less than $2 billion on health care. Today the figure exceeds $20 billion. Housing aid to moderate and low income families rose from $37 million to more than $2 billion within a decade. Beginning in the mid-1960s, the people and the governments of our nation became aware of the deterioration of our natural environment. Consequently, federal expenditures on pollution control and abatement rose quickly to more than $3 billion annually in the early 1970s. What it will be in five to ten years from now is difficult to foresee.

Changing Price Levels

As in the case of the private economy, changing price levels affect the amount of expenditures that are made by government. If prices rise, more money is needed for the performance of the usual functions of government. Hence, additional appropriations are necessary, unless it is decided to curtail or to discontinue certain activities. To provide the same government services in 1974 that were provided in 1960 cost 50 percent more because of higher prices. On the other hand, a declining price level does not result as a rule in a curtailment in the amount of funds spent by government. Even when funds become more than adequate and a surplus accumulates, taxation rates are usually reduced slowly, if at all, and new needs for governmental services, which quickly absorb the treasury surplus, are discovered.

Population Growth

One of the main causes for the expansion of governmental activities is that of population growth. Not only is more government service required because of sheer numbers, but increasing numbers magnify old problems and create new ones. As population increases and becomes more mobile, for example, improvements in transportation are needed. More schools, colleges, and teachers are essential. Increased urbanization aggravates social problems and highlights the need to find solutions for them. Crime and delinquency unfortunately seem to increase at a more rapid rate, or at least they attract more attention. Increasing the GNP to provide additional goods and services creates more pollution problems. Contracts between individuals and groups become more frequent, and questions as to individual rights become more complex.

Improvements in the means of transportation and communications have tended in many cases to raise the question as to just what is the major responsibility of each level of government for the performance of a particular function. For example, at one time public education was generally considered almost wholly the function of local government. Then state governments began to assume an increasingly larger part of this responsibility. Now there is a growing feeling that the federal government should provide a greater part of the funds needed for schools and colleges. In like manner, one may ask who should enforce and finance pollution abatement measures—the federal, state, or local government?

Higher Income

It is interesting to note that even in those capitalistic countries where individual and national wealth both have increased, there is an evident tendency for government to increase the scope and number of its activities. In the United States, for example, as average wealth has increased, the ability and the inclination of the population to finance better schools, better equipped hospitals, and electric power projects have increased, as has the inclination to undertake more socioeconomic measures.

National Emergencies

Wars always increase the amount of expenditures by the federal government, although they may not affect greatly the expenditures of local and state governments. For example, during the American Civil War federal expenditures rose twentyfold. During World War I, in the period from 1916 to 1919, the increase in the expenditures of the federal government was from $713 million to $18.5 billion. In 1940, the year before we entered World War II, federal expenditures amounted to $9.6 billion, while in 1945 they exceeded $95 billion. After the end of the war, federal expenditures declined somewhat. The Korean conflict in the early fifties caused another surge in federal spending, and in the 1960s the war in Vietnam added $20-$25 billion annually to our $50 billion plus defense budget.

War is not the only kind of emergency that calls for increased governmental expenditures. When widespread suffering or unusual privation occurs, governments more and more are inclined to try to extend financial aid to the people involved. During the 1930s the people demanded that the federal government especially concern itself to an unprecedented degree with the problem of unemployment. As a result federal spending, in an effort to overcome the great business depression, increased the national debt by more than $26 billion during the decade from 1930 to 1940. Prior to the business depression that prevailed during this time, it was the generally accepted belief that businesses and individuals should rely on their own efforts to extricate themselves from the effects of business depressions. But the acceptance of the New Deal philosophy caused the federal government to engage in various efforts to remedy the situation. Billions of dollars were spent to aid business and to create employment.

After World War II, and to some extent after the Korean conflict, billions of American dollars were poured into Europe and Asia to help reconstruct the wartorn economies of not only our allies but also our former enemies. In the fifties there were, in addition, large-scale programs of aid to underdeveloped nations to assist them with their economic progress. In the late fifties, after Sputnik, the United States government escalated its spending on its space programs. In the 1960s, not only were there large government domestic outlays to eliminate "nagging unemployment," but also there was great emphasis on government-sponsored measures, such as the war on poverty, medicare, manpower development and training, urban redevelopment, mass transportation, and antipollution. Many of these measures, as well as some additional new ones, are being continued in the 1970s.

SOURCES AND USES OF GOVERNMENT REVENUES

The study of governmental revenue and expenditures is complicated by reason of the fact that there are several classes of political units in this country. Specifically, there are the federal government, the 50 states, the District of Columbia, many insular possessions, and more than 90,000 municipal and local units consisting of cities, counties, townships, school districts, drainage districts, and other tax-collecting divisions. To some extent each of these units performs certain functions that are different from those of the others.

Composition of Federal Expenditures

During most of the decade following 1920, by far the larger part of federal spending was for the purpose of defense, the care of war veterans, and the payment of interest on the debts of World War I. During this time, payments for the purposes of supplying other services to civilians usually amounted to less than three quarters of a billion dollars annually.

After 1932, however, and up to World War II, the total amount of expenditures for agricultural aid, public works, relief work and relief payments, Social Security, old-age pensions, and other civil payments constituted the larger portion of federal government expenditures. In 1940 two thirds of all the funds expended by the government were used for such payments. Shortly thereafter, however, a change occurred in the relative size of various expenditures. In 1941 total expenditures incidental to the rearmament program amounted to more than $6 billion, and in 1944 the President called for an appropriation by Congress of about $100 billion, most of which was to be spent in the prosecution of the war. Since then the largest segment of the federal budget has been used for defense purposes, as shown in Table 18-2 and Figure 18-2. In the late 1960s and early 1970s another important shift took place in the character of federal spending as outlays for human resource programs took a striking upturn, as shown in Figure 18-3 on page 400.

Structure of State Expenditures

During the earlier decades of our young republic, state governments undertook the construction of canals and roads, gave aid in the establishment of banks, and in some instances encouraged the development of agriculture. Largely because the apparent need for most of such services diminished, the enthusiasm that at first accompanied these undertakings eventually waned. By the latter part of the nineteenth century, expenditures of state governments were for the most part limited to those that were necessary to carry on the essential functions of government. These included the maintenance of a relatively small executive force, the courts, and a legislative body. In a few states small appropriations were made for hospitals. But little responsibility was felt for supplying most of the social services which it is now customary for state governments to provide. Provisions for public education, recreation, public roads, and police protection were considered the proper responsibility of local government.

After 1900 the proportion of state expenditures expanded in relation to the expenditures of local governments. The factors that were primarily responsible for this change were the rapid growth in the use of automobiles and an increased recognition of the fact that the states had easier access to certain sources of revenues than did the local governments. For example, the states could levy taxes on gasoline and income more easily than could the local governments. It was logical, then, for the state governments to assume a larger part of the burden of the expenditures of local governments.

During the past half century the expenditures for all the functions performed by state governments have increased in absolute amounts. The

TABLE 18-2

BUDGET RECEIPTS
BY SOURCE AND
OUTLAYS BY
FUNCTION

1971-1974

(Millions of Dollars)

Description	Actual 1971	Actual 1972	Estimate 1973	Estimate 1974
Receipts by Source				
Individual Income Taxes	86,230	94,737	99,400	111,600
Corporation Income Taxes	26,785	32,166	33,500	37,000
Social Insurance Taxes and Contributions (trust funds):				
Employment Taxes and Contributions	41,699	46,120	55,610	67,866
Unemployment Insurance	3,674	4,357	5,262	6,267
Contributions for Other Insurance and Retirement	3,205	3,437	3,667	4,029
Total Social Insurance Taxes and Contributions	48,578	53,914	64,540	78,162
Excise Taxes:				
Federal Funds	10,510	9,506	9,683	10,198
Trust Funds	6,104	5,971	6,287	6,600
Total Excise Taxes	16,614	15,477	15,970	16,798
Estate and Gift Taxes	3,735	5,436	4,600	5,000
Customs Duties	2,591	3,287	3,000	3,300
Miscellaneous Receipts:				
Deposit of Earnings by the Federal Reserve System	3,533	3,252	3,350	3,700
Other Miscellaneous Receipts [1]	325	381	625	422
Total Miscellaneous Receipts	3,858	3,633	3,975	4,122
Total Receipts	188,392	208,649	224,984	255,982
Outlays by Function [1]				
National Defense	77,661	78,336	76,435	81,074
International Affairs and Finance	3,095	3,726	3,341	3,811
Space Research and Technology	3,381	3,422	3,061	3,135
Agriculture and Rural Development	5,096	7,063	6,064	5,572
Natural Resources and Environment	2,716	3,761	876	3,663
Commerce and Transportation	11,310	11,201	12,543	11,580
Community Development and Housing	3,357	4,282	3,957	4,931
Education and Manpower	8,226	9,751	10,500	10,110
Health	14,463	17,112	17,991	21,730
Income Security	56,140	64,876	75,889	81,976
Veterans Benefits and Services	9,776	10,731	11,795	11,732
Interest	19,609	20,582	22,808	24,672
General Government	3,970	4,891	5,631	6,025
General Revenue Sharing	......	......	6,786	6,035
Allowances for Contingencies and Civilian Agency Pay Raises	......	......	500	1,750
Undistributed Intragovernmental Transactions .	−7,376	−7,858	−8,381	−9,130
Total Outlays	211,425	231,876	249,796	268,665

SOURCE: *The U.S. Budget in Brief for Fiscal Year 1974.*

[1] Includes both federal funds and trust funds.

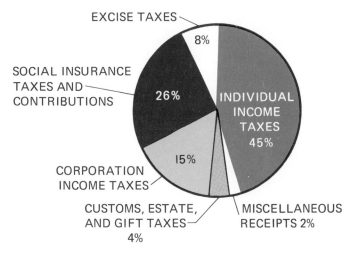

RECEIPTS

EXCISE TAXES

8%

SOCIAL INSURANCE TAXES AND CONTRIBUTIONS

26%

INDIVIDUAL INCOME TAXES 45%

15%

CORPORATION INCOME TAXES

CUSTOMS, ESTATE, AND GIFT TAXES 4%

MISCELLANEOUS RECEIPTS 2%

OUTLAYS (EXPENDITURES AND NET LENDING)

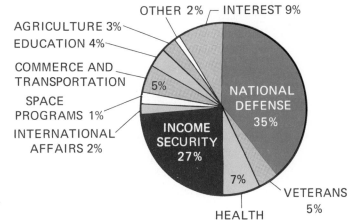

OTHER 2% — INTEREST 9%

AGRICULTURE 3%
EDUCATION 4%
COMMERCE AND TRANSPORTATION
SPACE PROGRAMS 1%
INTERNATIONAL AFFAIRS 2%

5%

NATIONAL DEFENSE 35%

INCOME SECURITY 27%

7%

HEALTH

VETERANS 5%

FIGURE 18-2

THE ANNUAL FEDERAL BUDGET 1970-1973
(Average Annual Percent Distribution, by Function. For Fiscal Years Ending June 30.)

The largest segment of federal receipts comes from personal income taxes, while the largest expenditure is for national defense.

SOURCE: *Statistical Abstract of the United States,* 1973.

relative amounts expended for general control and for public safety have tended to decrease. On the other hand, relative expenditures for social welfare greatly increased. Expenditures for the construction and operation of highways rose from negligible amounts in 1900 to a point where they now constitute 11% of all state and local expenditures. In 1973 education claimed the largest portion, more than one third, of state funds and close to one half of local government expenditures.

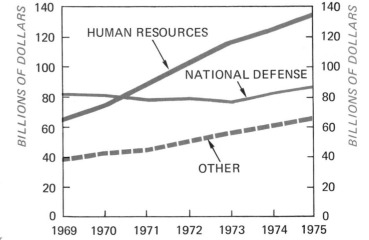

FIGURE 18-3

BUDGET TRENDS

In recent years there has been a trend toward more spending on human resource programs through the federal budget.

SOURCE: *The U.S. Budget in Brief for Fiscal Year 1974* (Washington: U.S. Government Printing Office, 1973).

Character of Local Government Expenditures

Although federal and state governments, through their increased expenditures, probably influence our lives more than local governments, it is the local governments that the average citizen "sees" daily. In everyday affairs the protective function of government is manifested by the policeman, the sheriff, the constable, and the fire department; the developmental and cultural functions, by the local school; health services, by public clinics and public health nurses; and the general productive function, by roads, public utilities, and public waste-disposal systems.

During the past few decades expenditures for the performance of most functions formerly undertaken by local government have grown. But in only a few instances have the relative expenditures increased. Unfortunately data for expenditures by local governments are not complete in many cases. In the smaller cities the relative amounts of funds used to promote public safety decreased; but they increased in cities having a population of 100,000 or more. Relative expenditures for streets and recreational facilities in the smaller cities decreased, while the relative amounts spent for education increased.

At one time total expenditures of local governments exceeded those of the federal government. Today, however, federal expenditures are more than three times greater than those of local governments. Relative state and local government revenues and expenditures are shown in Table 18-3 and Figure 18-4.

TABLE 18-3

STATE AND
LOCAL
GOVERNMENT
REVENUES AND
EXPENDITURES

Selected Fiscal
Years 1927-1972

(Millions of Dollars)

Fiscal Year [1]	General Revenues by Source [2]							General Expenditures by Function [2]				
	Total	Property Taxes	Sales and Gross Receipts Taxes	Individual Income Taxes	Corporation Net Income Taxes	Revenue from Federal Government	All Other Revenues [3]	Total	Education	Highways	Public Welfare	All Other [4]
1927	7,271	4,730	470	70	92	116	1,793	7,210	2,235	1,809	151	3,015
1932	7,267	4,487	752	74	79	232	1,643	7,765	2,311	1,741	444	3,269
1934	7,678	4,076	1,008	80	49	1,016	1,449	7,181	1,831	1,509	889	2,952
1936	8,395	4,093	1,484	153	113	948	1,604	7,644	2,177	1,425	827	3,215
1938	9,228	4,440	1,794	218	165	800	1,811	8,757	2,491	1,650	1,069	3,547
1940	9,609	4,430	1,982	224	156	945	1,872	9,229	2,638	1,573	1,156	3,862
1942	10,418	4,537	2,351	276	272	858	2,123	9,190	2,586	1,490	1,225	3,889
1944	10,908	4,604	2,289	342	451	954	2,269	8,863	2,793	1,200	1,133	3,737
1946	12,356	4,986	2,986	422	447	855	2,661	11,028	3,356	1,672	1,409	4,591
1948	17,250	6,126	4,442	543	592	1,861	3,685	17,684	5,379	3,036	2,099	7,170
1950	20,911	7,349	5,154	788	593	2,486	4,541	22,787	7,177	3,803	2,940	8,867
1952	25,181	8,652	6,357	998	846	2,566	5,763	26,098	8,318	4,650	2,788	10,342
1953	27,307	9,375	6,927	1,065	817	2,870	6,252	27,910	9,390	4,987	2,914	10,619
1954	29,012	9,967	7,276	1,127	778	2,966	6,897	30,701	10,557	5,527	3,060	11,557
1955	31,073	10,735	7,643	1,237	744	3,131	7,584	33,724	11,907	6,452	3,168	12,197
1956	34,667	11,749	8,691	1,538	890	3,335	8,465	36,711	13,220	6,953	3,139	13,399
1957	38,164	12,864	9,467	1,754	984	3,843	9,250	40,375	14,134	7,816	3,485	14,940
1958	41,219	14,047	9,829	1,759	1,018	4,865	9,699	44,851	15,919	8,567	3,818	16,547
1959	45,306	14,983	10,437	1,994	1,001	6,377	10,516	48,887	17,283	9,592	4,136	17,876
1960	50,505	16,405	11,849	2,463	1,180	6,974	11,634	51,876	18,719	9,428	4,404	19,325
1961	54,037	18,002	12,463	2,613	1,266	7,131	12,563	56,201	20,574	9,844	4,720	21,063
1962	58,252	19,054	13,494	3,037	1,308	7,871	13,489	60,206	22,216	10,357	5,084	22,549
1963	62,890	20,089	14,456	3,269	1,505	8,722	14,850	64,816	23,776	11,136	5,481	24,423
1962-63 [5] .	62,269	19,833	14,446	3,267	1,505	8,663	14,556	63,977	23,729	11,150	5,420	23,678
1963-64 [5] .	68,443	21,241	15,762	3,791	1,695	10,002	15,951	69,302	26,286	11,664	5,766	25,586
1964-65 [5] .	74,000	22,583	17,118	4,090	1,929	11,029	17,250	74,546	28,563	12,221	6,315	27,447
1965-66 [5] .	83,036	24,670	19,085	4,760	2,038	13,214	19,269	82,843	33,287	12,770	6,757	30,029
1966-67 [5] .	91,197	26,047	20,530	5,826	2,227	15,370	21,197	93,350	37,919	13,932	8,218	33,281
1967-68 [5] .	101,264	27,747	22,911	7,308	2,518	17,181	23,598	102,411	41,158	14,481	9,857	36,915
1968-69 [5] .	114,550	30,673	26,519	8,908	3,180	19,153	26,118	116,728	47,238	15,417	12,110	41,963
1969-70 [5] .	130,756	34,054	30,322	10,812	3,738	21,857	29,971	131,332	52,718	16,427	14,679	47,508
1970-71 [5] .	144,927	37,852	33,233	11,900	3,424	26,146	32,374	150,674	59,413	18,095	18,226	54,940
1971-72 [5] .	166,352	42,133	37,488	15,237	4,416	31,253	35,825	166,873	64,886	19,010	21,070	61,907

SOURCE: *Economic Report of the President*, 1974.

[1] Fiscal years not the same for all governments. See footnote 5.
[2] Excludes revenues or expenditures of publicly owned utilities and liquor stores, and of insurance-trust activities. Intergovernmental receipts and payments between state and local governments are also excluded.
[3] Includes licenses and other taxes and miscellaneous revenues.
[4] Includes expenditures for health, hospitals, police, local fire protection, natural resources, sanitation, housing and urban renewal, local parks and recreation, general control, financial administration, interest on general debt, and unallocable expenditures.
[5] Data for fiscal year ending in the 12-month period through June 30. Data for 1963 and earlier years include local government amounts grouped in terms of fiscal years ended during the particular calendar year.
General Note: Data are not available for intervening years.

TAX DUPLICATION

With an increasing need for more revenues, there is naturally much duplication of tax sources by the various levels of government. In many respects there has been a mad scramble by the different levels of government to find new and fruitful sources of additional revenue. Thus, governments

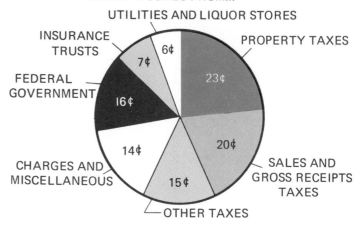

WHERE IT COMES FROM...

UTILITIES AND LIQUOR STORES

INSURANCE TRUSTS

6¢

7¢

PROPERTY TAXES

23¢

FEDERAL GOVERNMENT

16¢

20¢

14¢

SALES AND GROSS RECEIPTS TAXES

CHARGES AND MISCELLANEOUS

15¢

OTHER TAXES

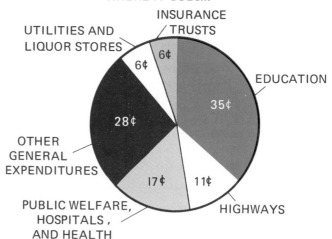

WHERE IT GOES...

FIGURE 18-4

STATE AND LOCAL GOVERNMENT REVENUE AND EXPENDITURE 1971

(State and Local Government Dollar: 1971)

State and local governments receive a large share of their revenues from property and sales taxes, while the largest expenditure is for education.

SOURCE: *Statistical Abstract of the United States,* 1973.

INSURANCE TRUSTS

UTILITIES AND LIQUOR STORES

6¢

6¢

EDUCATION

35¢

OTHER GENERAL EXPENDITURES

28¢

17¢

11¢

PUBLIC WELFARE, HOSPITALS, AND HEALTH

HIGHWAYS

have been breaking away from their traditional sources of revenue and in many cases encroaching on what had been considered the tax preserve of other forms of government. For years local governments have relied primarily on property taxes as a source of income. The states used the sales and motor taxes as heavy income contributors, and the federal government relied predominately on personal and corporate income taxes. In recent years, however, state income taxes have become prevalent, and now many cities are levying an income or earnings tax. In fact, in some cities the wage earner is paying a city, a state, and a federal income tax. Cities are also adopting sales taxes of their own. It has been proposed, too, that the federal government establish a national sales tax as a source of revenue.

In many cases federal tax funds obtained at the state and local level find their way back in the form of *grants-in-aid* to state and local governments. In fact, this source today constitutes one sixth of state and local revenues. Often, however, the amount of taxes collected from a particular state or local area is more than that returned by the aid program, which means that some state and some local governments are subsidizing grant-in-aid programs in other states or localities.

All this highlights the need for more analysis, revision, and clarity in our tax structure. In recent years one interesting suggestion has been that of the joint collection of federal and state income taxes. Another has been the concept of federal tax sharing by state governments. This is helpful to those states that now have difficulty imposing a state income tax and those states that do not have a large income base to tax. Professor Walter W. Heller, formerly Chairman of the President's Council of Economic Advisers, for example, recommends tax sharing in the form of a fiscal dividend as federal tax revenues rise with increasing income. This method would be helpful in avoiding a fiscal drag at the federal level as the economy expands. The federal-state revenue sharing program inaugurated by the State and Local Fiscal Assistance Act of 1972 will be examined in Chapter 20.

GOVERNMENT REVENUE AND INCOME

Government has five sources of revenue: government-owned land and enterprises, taxes, fees and fines, special assessments, and miscellaneous nontax revenues. Government may also secure funds for disbursement by borrowing. However, borrowing is not considered here as a source of revenue because funds secured in that manner create a liability or obligation that can be discharged only by the collection and disbursement of revenues.

Government-Owned Land and Enterprises

It may be possible for a unit of government to obtain income by means of the ownership of economic wealth. The wealth so owned may be classified as (1) the public domain and (2) public enterprises.

The Public Domain. All lands of whatever kind owned by government constitute a part of the public domain. Thus, parks, streets, highways, and reservations of timber, waste, and mineral lands are parts of the public domain. Ownership of land by the public is justified on the ground that the land involved can, in this way, better serve the public interest than it could if it were privately owned. When it becomes apparent that private ownership would result in uses of the land that would be of more social value than public ownership, the public domain may be disposed of by sale to private individuals or groups.

The revenues actually derived from the ownership of lands by government in the United States are relatively insignificant. How much income in the form of imputed rent might be ascribed to the ownership of building sites by governments is difficult to estimate. The amount, however, is probably much larger than is usually realized.

In the early days of the federal government, the sale of public lands was relied on to some extent to provide revenues for general purposes. Between 1781 and 1867 the government acquired by purchase or cession by the states nearly 2,300,000 square miles of territory, which constitutes more than two thirds of the current land area of our nation. Much of this vast domain was given to private companies to encourage the rapid building of railroads; a large portion of it was disposed of by sale or grant to speculators and farmers. The land still owned by the government, which is one third of the 3.2 million square mile total land area in the continental United States, consists of timber and mineral lands, parks, and wasteland. Sales from the products of this land, mostly lumber and minerals, are minimal in value. The public domains of state and local governments consist mostly of parks, highways, and streets, most of which yield little revenue.

Public Enterprises. Public enterprises include all those undertakings that are owned and operated by government for the purpose of supplying goods and services to consumers at established prices, which also provide a source of nontax revenue. Such enterprises are distinguished from public utilities that may be similar in nature but that are owned by private corporations, as are most of the railroads and power companies in the United States. Examples of public enterprises are some barge operations, street railways, water and sewage systems, electric power systems, gas facilities, and airports that are owned by units of government.

Enterprises of Federal Government. Industrial or commercial enterprises owned and operated by the federal government include the post office, the Panama Canal, the Tennessee Valley Authority and similar projects in the Colorado and the Columbia river valleys, the Alaska Railroad, and a host of corporations designed to aid business and to promote employment. The latter include corporations engaged in aiding housing construction, agriculture, and international trade. Some of these corporations are intended to be self-supporting; in other cases no immediate returns are expected.

Enterprises of State Governments. At present state-owned enterprises include docks and wharves, ferries, canals, mills and elevators, electric railways, and liquor stores. Aside from the income from the state-owned liquor stores, which totalled over $2 billion in 1973, the aggregate income of all state-owned enterprises is not comparatively large. Recent data show that about one third of the states have statewide monopolies of the distribution of liquors. Although they are very profitable, the primary reason for the establishment of a monopoly over the sale of liquor is that certain social problems incident to the use of liquor can best be handled if the state maintains such a monopoly.

Enterprises of Local Governments. In the field of municipally owned enterprises, the following are of the greatest importance: water supply, sewage and drainage, street railway, gas and electric facilities, and transportation service.

The reasons given to justify municipal enterprise are that there are certain kinds of undertakings that have an inherent tendency toward monopoly; that in many cases public ownership is more economical than private ownership; and that sometimes the operation of an industry below cost is desirable in order to provide the lower income groups with services which they could not otherwise enjoy. On the other hand, there are a number of criticisms in general of municipal public enterprises.

Taxes

A *tax* is a compulsory charge on wealth or income exacted by government for public use. It may be levied without specific reference to the value of the services that the government makes available to particular taxpayers. In contrast with the rates or prices charged by public industries, taxes are predicated upon the assumption that the services for which a tax is levied are more or less uniformly used by taxpayers. The power to levy taxes is inherent in sovereign government. In the case of the federal government, the power to levy taxes is conferred on Congress by the Constitution, which was the creation of the people who are themselves sovereign. Similarly, the state governments have the power to levy taxes. Local governments are empowered by the state government to levy taxes of certain kinds.

Taxes provide by far most government revenues. On the whole, receipts from other sources are relatively unimportant. At the present time units of government make use of various kinds of taxes. Broadly speaking, the following kinds of taxes are employed in the United States: income taxes, property taxes, commodity taxes, taxes on acts and privileges, sales taxes, and inheritance and estate taxes.

Fees and Fines

A *fee* is an amount paid by the recipient in exchange for a particular service rendered by government, such as the recording of a deed or mortgage, the issuance of a marriage license, copyright, passport, or other service. A *fine* is a charge imposed as a penalty for the violation of a law and is payable in money. Violation of traffic laws at the state and local level and violation of antitrust statutes at the federal level, for example, are punishable by fines. Fees and fines usually do not constitute an important source of revenue, although in the case of some local units of government they are important.

Special Assessments

A *special assessment* is a compulsory levy on private property for services rendered by government that result in an increase in the value of the property. Among the more frequent types of assessments are those made for grading, paving, sidewalks, the building of sewers, ornamental street lighting, and sidewalk snow removal. Assessments are levied against those who benefit directly from such a specific government service.

Miscellaneous Nontax Revenues

For the sake of completeness, it is perhaps desirable to note some other relatively unimportant sources of government revenue. In a number of states, it is possible for the state or local government, under the *right of eminent domain* (the right of the government to take private property for public use) to acquire land in excess of public needs for special purposes. For example, land along a highway might be condemned and bought by the state to be landscaped or to prevent it from being put to a socially objectionable use by the private owner. Later the land might be sold at a profit by the government. If the owner of property dies without legal heirs and without having willed his property, the intangible personal property goes to the state government in which the owner was domiciled, while his tangible personal property and real estate go to the state in which they are located at the time of his death. Occasionally all three types of government receive gifts and bequests from persons and organizations. Also, the federal government makes a profit, called *seigniorage*, by buying money metal and making it into coins worth more than the bullion cost.

Traditionally local and state authorities have been charged with the responsibility for performing some of the most important functions of government demanded by the American people. At the same time, great inequalities exist in the ability of many of the comparatively smaller units to finance these functions. For example, a poor unit of government cannot provide schools or roads of the same quality that is possible for the larger and more prosperous communities. Central units—federal or state—have a comparative advantage in the collection of most kinds of taxes. Therefore, the practice of grants-in-aid by the federal and the state governments by appropriations from the central treasury and of *shared taxes* has developed. Tax sharing occurs when the state government collects a tax, such as a tax on income or a tax on the sale of alcoholic beverages, and distributes to the smaller units of government a part of the funds thus obtained on the basis of the yield of the tax from these units. Among the objectives of grants-in-aid are the stimulation of effort by the smaller unit, the equalization of costs, the equalization of opportunity (as in the case of education), and benefit maximization of local expenditures by setting a standard for efficiency in the performance of a function.

THE BURDEN OF TAXATION IN THE UNITED STATES AND ABROAD

It is common practice for people to complain because taxes take so much of their incomes. It is true that the annual amount of taxes paid to the

FIGURE 18-5

TAX COLLECTIONS AS A PERCENTAGE OF GNP FOR U.S. AND OTHER NATIONS 1968-1970

When overall contributions are considered in terms of the total tax picture, taxes in the United States take a smaller bite of the GNP than in most of its industrialized counterparts.

SOURCE: Robert Ritchie, "The Tax Bite: How the U.S. Stacks Up," *Business Review*, Federal Reserve Bank of Philadelphia (April, 1973), p. 16.

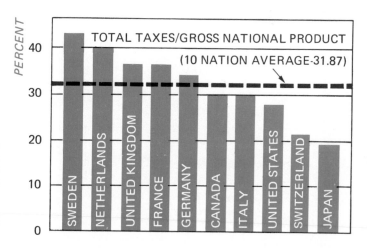

federal, state, and local governments exceeds one fourth of the value of all the goods and services produced in the nation during the year. But comparatively speaking, it is not as much as is paid by the people in many European countries. This fact is revealed in the data shown in Figure 18-5.

Other than Sweden, all of the nations indicated rely more heavily than does the United States on sales and property taxes. We spend a much larger percentage of our gross national product for defense than do the other nations listed.

SUMMARY

1. The subject of public finance is concerned with governmental expenditures, revenues and income, public debts, and the administration of public funds.

2. Broadly speaking, the functions of government in the United States are to provide for national security, production, regulation, public services, and promotion of economic growth and stability of the economy.

3. People spend most of their money for goods and services supplied by two classes of producers: private business and government. In a democracy, the nature of governmental activities and the extent to which people rely upon government to supply goods and services depends in large part upon the will of the citizens.

4. The noticeable tendency for governmental expenditures to increase may be traced to a number of causes, including rising prices, the expansion of functions already being performed, the undertaking of new functions, population growth, higher income, and emergencies.

5. The composition of federal expenditures changes over time. Prior to 1940 very little was spent for defense. However, defense spending absorbed the largest single share of the budget during the next three decades. With the 1970s, a shift in spending for human resource programs was in evidence.

6. The expenditures of state and local governments are for the performance of functions that more directly affect the people in smaller geographical regions. On the whole, there is a tendency for some of the functions formerly considered as belonging to local or state governments to be taken over by government on the next higher level.

7. The sources of government revenue are: government-owned land and enterprises, taxes, fees and fines, special assessments, and miscellaneous nontax revenues.

8. The amount of taxes collected by government in the United States relative to total production of goods and services is less than it is in most European countries.

NEW TERMS

Public finance, *p. 390*
Grants-in-aid, *p. 403*
Tax, *p. 405*
Fee, *p. 406*
Fine, *p. 406*

Special assessment, *p. 406*
Nontax revenues, *p. 406*
Right of eminent domain, *p. 406*
Seigniorage, *p. 407*
Shared taxes, *p. 407*

QUESTIONS FOR DISCUSSION AND ANALYSIS

1. What various functions are performed by government in the United States? Do you agree that government should be performing all these functions? Why or why not?

2. Indicate as definitely as possible the functions performed by the following units of government in the United States: (a) the federal government; (b) state governments; (c) local governments.

3. What productive functions does government in the United States perform? Why does government undertake these functions?

4. How do you explain the trends in governmental expenditures in the United States?

5. How do changes in the price level affect public expenditures?

6. How does an increase in the population affect public expenditures? Why?

7. Do local and national emergencies involving financial loss, such as a drought or flood, affect public expenditures? Do you think they should?

8. What are the four major sources of federal government receipts from the public? What are the two major categories of federal spending?

9. What are the two major sources of state and local government revenue? What are the two major categories of state and local government spending?

10. What sources of federal revenue have shown the largest increases in the past five years? Why?

11. What are the reasons for grants-in-aid?

12. Why is there a tendency for larger units of government to take over certain functions performed by smaller units?

13. Evaluate the following statement: "We are just as well off whether our income is in the form of public services or private income."

SUGGESTED READINGS

Anderson, William H. *Financing Modern Government*. Boston: Houghton Mifflin Company, 1973.

Buchanan, James M. *The Public Finances*. Homewood, Ill.: Richard D. Irwin, Inc., 1970.

Bureau of the Budget. *Federal Budget in Brief*. Washington: U.S. Government Printing Office. Current edition.

Burkhead, J. *Government Budgeting*. New York: John Wiley & Sons, Inc., 1956.

Colm, G. *Essays in Public Finance and Fiscal Policy*. New York: Oxford University Press, Inc., 1955.

Due, John F., and Ann F. Friedlaender. *Government Finance*. Homewood, Ill.: Richard D. Irwin, Inc., 1973.

Groves, Harold M., and Robert L. Bish. *Financing Government*. New York: Holt, Rinehart and Winston, Inc., 1973.

Levy, Michael. *The Federal Budget: Its Impact on the Economy*. New York: The Conference Board, 1973.

Pechman, Joseph A. *Federal Tax Policy*. New York: W. W. Norton & Company, Inc., 1971.

Poole, Kenyon E. *Public Finance and Economic Welfare*. Englewood Cliffs, N.J.: Prentice-Hall, Inc., 1956.

Ritchie, Robert. "The Tax Bite: How Well the U.S. Stands Up." *Business Review*. Philadelphia: Federal Reserve Bank of Philadelphia (April, 1973).

Schultz, William J., and Clement L. Harriss. *American Public Finance*. Englewood Cliffs, N.J.: Prentice-Hall, Inc., 1959.

Schultze, Charles L., *et al. Setting National Priorities: The 1975 Budget*. Washington: The Brookings Institution, 1974.

19

Taxation: Principles and Types

PREVIEW To generate sufficient tax revenues to cover the cost of providing the goods and services demanded by the public, the government must design and implement a tax system. In doing so it should follow certain well established criteria of taxation, such as equity, certainty, convenience, and economy. Numerous viewpoints exist, however, on the determination of equity, or fairness, in taxation. There is also much controversy about rates of taxation. Tax rates may be proportional or otherwise depending on the base to be taxed. Although taxes are paid by the person or organization against whom they are levied, the incidence of a tax in many cases can be shifted to others. Various kinds of taxes, such as those on general property, income, business operations, sales, and payrolls, are imposed by various units of government. There is an old saying that "the only certain things in life are death and taxes." Ironically even in death a person cannot escape taxes. There is always the inevitable estate and inheritance tax.

Many of us take the services of government for granted. Of course, we know that these services are not free and that they must be paid for. But it should be remembered that the more we expect of the government, the more we must pay in taxes. Who specifically pays? Does everyone contribute? Do some people pay less and others pay more than their fair share of the cost of government? These are only a few of the questions that arise in connection with a study of public finance.

The power to tax is a right of the sovereign. Originally in an absolute monarchy, the right, of course, belonged solely to the individual who was head of the state. In a democracy the right resides in the people. In their capacity as rulers, the people delegate the power to chosen representatives. As a result, the task of formulating tax laws is placed in the hands of legislative officials who, by the very nature of the situation, must always give thought to the political effects of such laws. Well-organized groups who can afford efficient lobbyists are able to present arguments to lawmakers concerning tax measures that an unorganized general public cannot do. As a consequence, tax laws may be designed to "pluck as many feathers with as little squawking as possible." Frequently it is expediency and not justice that is the guiding principle in the formulation of tax laws.

Taxes absorb a sizable portion of business and personal income. The ability of governments to perform their many political, economic, and social functions depends largely on our willingness to pay taxes. On the other hand, the payment of taxes has an influence on the economic decisions of the firm and the individual. A knowledge of taxes and our tax structure, therefore, is essential if we are to understand the extent and limitations of government services and the reaction of individuals and businesses to proposed tax legislation.

TAXATION: SYSTEMS AND EQUITY

A *tax system* is composed of all the taxes that a unit of government imposes in its effort to obtain the funds needed to carry out its various functions. How much the government should attempt to collect in total or through any one kind of tax depends partly upon the fiscal policy being pursued and to some extent upon the ideas of lawmakers as to what constitutes justice in taxation.

If it were the policy of the government to let the economy run itself, customary taxes would probably be utilized and the rates not changed too often. But with a government policy of economic stabilization, new taxes may be introduced and rates on current taxes altered to bring about the desired stabilization results. As we saw earlier, taxes may be decreased in order to give the economy a boost or to spur economic growth. At other times, tax rates may be increased to reduce effective demand in the hope of stabilizing the price level or preventing inflation. Excise taxes may be added or suspended, depending on economic circumstances. Depreciation rates that affect government tax revenues may be liberalized or tightened to bring about expansion of economic activity or to put a damper on the economy.

Basically the tax system should be adequate to yield the funds necessary for the government to provide the functions expected of it. In setting up or evolving such a tax system, certain guidelines are evident. The tax system, for example, should be easy to administer, it should be elastic so that it will yield necessary revenue in spite of changing economic conditions, and the burden of taxation should be distributed in accordance with standards of justice and equity.

Principles of Taxation

A *principle of taxation* is a general rule for the formulation of particular tax laws. For example, in levying taxes the government may try to follow a rule that taxpayers should be required to support the government according to their respective abilities to pay taxes.

From past history there are numerous instances where the tax-levying authority was a tyrant indifferent to the effects or equity of taxes on his subjects. Today taxing authorities are generally concerned with the effects of taxes upon those who must pay them and with the effects of taxes on the economic system. Even a little thought on the matter suggests that there are probably several principles that framers of tax laws should observe. An understanding of these principles helps to evaluate existing tax laws and tax proposals.

In his *Wealth of Nations*,[1] Adam Smith laid down the following tax maxims, which have become classic:

I. The subjects of every state ought to contribute towards the support of the government, as nearly as possible, in proportion to their respective abilities; that is, in proportion to the revenue which they respectively enjoy under the protection of the state.

II. The tax which each individual is bound to pay ought to be certain, and not arbitrary. The time of payment, the manner of payment, the quantity to be paid, ought all to be clear and plain to the contributor, and to every other person.

III. Every tax ought to be levied at the time, or in the manner, in which it is most likely to be convenient for the contributor to pay it.

IV. Every tax ought to be so contrived as both to take out and keep out of the pockets of the people as little as possible, over and above what it brings into the public treasury of the state.

These maxims of (I) equity or justice, (II) certainty, (III) convenience, and (IV) economy are still used as guideposts in the design of good taxes. Although Smith believed that equity in taxation suggested a tax rate which remained the same for all amounts of income, our tax rates are progressive, that is, the rates are higher for large incomes than for small incomes. More recently, tax analysts have stressed the importance of adequacy and simplicity in levying specific taxes and in building a tax system. Taxes should be sufficient in amount for the purpose for which they are levied, and they should not be more complicated to calculate and administer than is absolutely necessary.

Equity or Fairness in Taxation

What is a fair tax? Is it one the rate of which remains the same for all amounts of property or income? Does it apportion the burden on taxpayers in accordance with the cost of rendering a service by government? Does it impose the burden of payment according to the benefit received by an individual or a special group? Is it one that is apportioned directly according

[1]Book V, Chapter II, Part I.

to ability to pay? Does it follow the political-expediency principle, that is, the tax which works best is the best?

Various attempts have been made to establish principles that would be of practical value in apportioning the tax burden. Among the theories that have been advanced are the theories of (1) cost of service, (2) benefit received, and (3) ability to pay.

Cost of Service. Some experts suggest that individuals should contribute toward the cost of general government in proportion to the cost of the governmental services which they receive. The services implied here include those general services for protection to person, health, sanitation, and all others performed for the individual specifically. For the most part, such services are rendered to rich and poor alike. Other kinds of services, such as the building and maintenance of highways and schools, should, it is argued, be paid for by user fees.

Except for a few minor services of government, the cost-of-service theory is untenable. In the first place, it would be impossible to calculate the costs of the services to each individual. How, for example, would the costs of protection of persons and of property be allocated among individuals? If the protective services of government could be obtained only on a commercial basis, by purchase at a price that would cover the cost of performing the service, some would be able to obtain much greater protection than others. To argue that a wealthy homeowner should be entitled to more protection from fire by the city fire department than a less well-to-do owner, for example, or that one might obtain more protection than another from the police force, would be to adopt a philosophy radically opposed to that which is accepted in most democratic nations. In the second place, the adoption of such a principle would mean the denial of any responsibility of the state for those not financially able to pay for public services.

Benefit Received. The benefit theory in taxation holds that individuals should contribute in proportion to the benefits received from the services of government. It is related to the cost-of-service theory; in fact, it might be said that the two theories are merely different aspects of the same general idea. It is asserted that one's obligation to support his government varies in proportion to the benefits he enjoys by living under that government. One implication of this idea is that taxes should be proportional. For example, a man with $100,000 worth of real estate should pay ten times as much in taxes as a person with only $10,000 worth. This is the principle that is followed in levying taxes on real estate. This argument implies that the more property one owns or the more income he has, the more protection he receives from government and likewise the more it costs government to render these protective services to such an individual.

While the benefit theory contains a modicum of validity, an attempt to apply it to all taxes would result in the cessation of practically all government activities as they are now supplied. To begin with, how could the value of a service be calculated? If we concede that government has an obligation to provide sanitary and health services for the poor, are not these services more valuable to the recipients than they are to those who are more able to pay for them? Again, how should the costs of public education be allocated? Certainly the value of public schools is greater for the children of the poor than those of the rich, for the latter could be provided with private teachers. Although the benefit theory is not practicable as a guide for the formulation of taxes in general, it is in operation in certain cases. In such cases the similarity of the benefit and the cost-of-service theories is apparent. Nearly all taxes that are classified as fees, such as those for marriage or automobile licenses, are based somewhat upon the benefit theory.

Ability to Pay. The theory of taxation most often accepted without argument is that of ability to pay. How shall ability-to-pay taxes be determined? Shall we have recourse to objective standards by basing the tax on an objective thing, such as real estate or income? Or shall the tax be designed to produce an equality of sacrifice on the part of those who are taxed?

Objective Standards. It is sometimes held that all taxes should be proportional. If the tax base is real estate, then the total amount of the taxes to be paid by owners of property should vary with the assessed valuations of their property; if the tax base is income, the amount of the tax should be proportional to the amount of income received. Of course, most of those who hold this proportional idea probably have never given serious thought to the relative sacrifices involved in the payment of taxes by individuals with varying amounts of income. However, the fact that the proportional idea is widely accepted makes it a matter of importance.

Equality of Sacrifice. Many years ago John Stuart Mill [2] called attention to the fact that objective measurements of taxpaying ability alone are inadequate. He propounded a "subjective sacrifice doctrine." Mill, in effect, argued that, in trying to determine the ability to pay a tax, the effect of the tax on the scale of living and the degree of inconvenience to the individual are matters that should not be neglected.

The *equality-of-sacrifice doctrine* is based upon the law of diminishing marginal utility of income: when income is small, the marginal satisfaction of a dollar is much higher than when the income is large. A family with an income of $5,000 is much less "able" to pay $500 in taxes than a family with an income of $50,000 is able to pay $5,000.

[2] John Stuart Mill, *Political Economy* (London: 1848), Book V, Chapter 2, Sec. 2.

Perhaps a majority of persons would agree that a proportional tax of 10 percent on incomes would "hurt" the family with the smaller income much more than the one with the larger income. Since the former would already be living more nearly at the level of subsistence, payment of the tax would call for giving up the use of goods that are needed to sustain life or at least to maintain health. The payment of the larger amount of money by the wealthy family certainly would not make it necessary for them to forego actual necessities in the way of food, shelter, and clothing.

On the other hand, there are some who contend that a 10 percent tax would call for equal sacrifice by both families. They argue that people adjust their scale of living to their incomes, whether their incomes are large or small. Living is more than mere existence. Therefore, families and individuals with large incomes develop levels of living in accordance with their abilities to maintain them. A family with an income of $50,000 tends to acquire wants that can be satisfied only by certain comforts, conveniences, and surroundings. Having adapted itself to these things, so it is said, a decrease in ability to enjoy them entails proportionally as much sacrifice as does a proportional loss by a family on a lower level of living. For example, it is sometimes asserted that, if as a result of the payment of a tax a wealthy man is forced to give up his membership in an exclusive club, the feeling of sacrifice which he experiences may be as great as would be the sacrifice of a workingman who is compelled to forego attendance at ball games as a result of the payment of a tax. Such is the argument of those who advocate proportional taxes. As we shall see, progressive income taxes are based partly on the equality-of-sacrifice theory.

THE TAX-RATE STRUCTURE

The attitude of lawmakers with respect to the proper allocation of the tax burden is expressed in the tax-rate structure, which determines the amounts that individual taxpayers are called upon to pay.

The amount of a tax is determined by applying the tax rate to the tax base. The *tax rate* is a percentage; the *tax base* is the value of the object upon which the tax is levied. For example, if the rate is 20 percent of a net income, the percentage indicated is the rate, and the net income stated in terms of dollars is the base. In the case of taxes on real estate, the rate is usually given as so many mills or cents per dollar, or a percentage of the assessed valuation. Thus, the rate might be stated as 5 cents per dollar or 5 percent of the assessed value of the property.

The relations of rates to changes in the base are indicated by the terms proportional, progressive, degressive, and regressive.

Proportional Rates

A *proportional tax rate* is one that remains the same, regardless of the size of the base. For example, a 5 percent proportional tax on an income of $10,000 would amount to $500, and on $100,000, to $5,000. The most telling argument in favor of a tax-rate structure of this kind is that, after payment, the taxpayers are left in the same relative positions as they were before. Many who advocate proportional taxes admit that the application of the rate structure may not result in imposing equal sacrifice upon taxpayers; they defend their position, however, by denying that any satisfactory criterion for sacrifice has yet been demonstrated. Moreover, it is sometimes argued that reliance should be placed chiefly upon proportional taxes because they are simple to administer.

Progressive Rates

Because of a rather general acceptance of the idea that ability-to-pay taxes should increase more than proportionately to increases in the tax base, the rate for some taxes keeps pace with the rate of increase in the base. This is called a *progressive tax rate.* Thus, a tax of one percent on the first $1,000 of taxable income, 2 percent on the second $1,000 and so on, is a progressive tax. Of course, if this rate of progression were continued, the tax would absorb all income beyond $100,000 or more. Because of this fact, federal and state income taxes are progressive only up to certain amounts of income.

It is sometimes argued that progressive rates are unfair because they penalize the possession of wealth, the earning of income, and the exercise of superior talents. Carried to logical conclusions suggested by this argument, however, rates should be less than proportional, for by such an arrangement a premium would then be placed upon ability to accumulate wealth and to earn large incomes.

The possession of great wealth is not always an indication that the owner accumulated his wealth through frugality and hard work. In fact, most great private fortunes in existence today were not earned by the present owners. Many of the great American and English fortunes, as well as most others in the world, were inherited. Then, too, ability to earn a large income may be due to the possession of a rare talent or to some unusual skill or personal characteristic; it is not always attributable to unusual industry. As a result of these tendencies and perhaps because there are relatively few persons with exceptionally high incomes, there is a general tendency on the part of the American public and legislators to sanction steeply progressive income taxes.

It is sometimes said that progressive taxes lead to tax avoidance. Those who have large incomes or who own a great deal of wealth may find it worthwhile to employ experts to discover technical devices, or legal loopholes, for the avoidance of taxes. A counterargument is that the possibility of collecting the larger amounts justifies redoubled diligence on the part of tax administrators in making collections.

Another argument against progressive taxes is that they tend to relieve the poor from the payment of direct taxes, a fact which, it is claimed, causes a diminution of their sense of responsibility to support the government. It has been asserted that, if the poor are not taxed at rates as high as those for the rich, they will enjoy the services of government at the expense of others and will demand more and more, since the services may apparently be made available at little or no cost to themselves.

If the rate of increase is not too rapid, progressive tax rates are not likely to discourage initiative and industry. Moreover, with governmental expenditures at the level they now are, only progressive taxes can provide the revenue needed. What constitutes a reasonable progressive rate, however, is a debatable question.

Degressive Rates

Critics of progressive taxation point out that the determination of progressive rates rests upon the judgment of the individuals who establish them. Therefore, since there is no objective guide as to the steepness of the rates that should be adopted, what assurance is there, ask the critics, that the rates that may be proposed are fair and just? Moreover, it is argued, once a progressive rate structure is adopted, the logical stopping place tends to approach 100 percent, which, practically speaking, would mean confiscation of the value of the base (property or income) at that point.

In order to avoid confiscation, which the adoption of truly progressive rates would eventually achieve, progressive tax rates are usually progressive only up to a certain point. After that, they advance more slowly as the size of the base increases, and they finally reach a maximum. After the rate ceases to change when the base changes, the tax becomes proportional. Thus, income taxes are usually progressive up to a certain level of income, then degressive for an additional level of income, after which they remain proportional. A *degressive tax rate* calls for the payment of a larger amount of tax as the amount of the base increases, but the payments are not progressively larger. In other words, a degressive tax is a progressive tax the rate for which increases at a decreasing rate. For example, a tax of one percent on a $1,000 base, 2.5 percent on $10,000, and 3.5 percent on $100,000 would be degressive.

Regressive Rates

A *regressive tax rate* is one that decreases as the size of the base increases. For example, assume that the rate on an income of $1,000 is 5 percent;

that on an income of $2,000, 4 percent; $3,000, 3 percent; $4,000, 2 percent; and $5,000, one percent. In such a case the rate decreases as the base increases.

Opponents of the retail sales tax take delight in pointing out that, in effect, a retail sales tax is regressive. The basis for their argument is that the proportion of smaller incomes spent for taxable goods is higher than that of larger incomes. With a 4 percent sales tax, for example, a family with an $8,000 annual income may purchase $5,000 worth of taxable commodities and pay sales taxes of $200. On the other hand, a family with a $20,000 income may purchase $10,000 worth of taxable commodities. It will pay sales taxes of $400. Consequently, it is argued that the lower income family is paying a higher tax rate of 2.5 percent on the basis of its income ($200 ÷ $8,000 = 2.5%), whereas the higher income family is paying a tax rate of only 2 percent of its income ($400 ÷ $20,000 = 2%). It is incorrect to call the sales tax regressive, however, since the base of the tax is sales (purchases), not income. Both families are paying a proportional tax rate of 4 percent per dollar of purchases. This is truly a proportional tax rate compared to its proper base. If opponents of the sales tax are going to claim that it is regressive, they should be careful to emphasize that it is regressive in relation to income, not in relation to the true base of the tax. Furthermore, if they are going to talk about regressivity in regard to income, perhaps they should consider along with the sales taxes all the other taxes on income—federal, state, and local—that are steeply progressive.

To recapitulate, a proportional tax is one in which the rate remains the same as the base increases; a progressive tax is one in which the rate increase keeps pace with the rate of increase in the base; a degressive tax is one in which the rate increases as the base increases, but the rate increases at a decreasing rate; and a regressive tax is one in which the rate decreases as the base increases. Some taxes have elements of one or more different rates in their structure.

SHIFTING AND INCIDENCE OF THE TAX BURDEN

The burden of a tax does not always rest on the person or the concern paying the tax. For example, taxes on cigarettes, wines, liquors, and other consumer goods are paid by the manufacturer or distributor, who usually adds the amount of the tax to the selling price of the commodity and passes the burden of the tax along to the final consumer. Many taxes can be shifted, but it is not possible to shift the burden of a tax on personal income. The fact that it is possible to shift the burden of some taxes more easily than that of others is one reason for the continuing debate over what taxes should be levied.

Shifting of Taxes—Impact, Incidence, and Effect

In the study of the subject of the *shifting of taxes*, three stages or aspects of passing the burden on from one person to another are recognizable. The *impact of a tax* (stage 1) is the initial money burden entailed by the payment of the tax. For example, when an importer of British woolen goods pays the import duty, the impact of the tax is on the importer. But he adds the amount of the tax to the price of the materials. A tailor who buys the woolens from the importer reimburses the importer for the amount of the duty paid to the government and adds the amount to the prices of the suits he makes for his customers. Therefore, the burden of the duty is on the final users of the woolens and not on the person who paid the tax to the government. The same thing is true of sales taxes on certain commodities when the amount of the sales tax is added to the selling price of the commodity and in this way is passed on to the final purchaser of the commodity.

The *incidence of a tax* (stage 2) is the point at which the burden of the tax ultimately rests. For example, the incidence of a cigarette tax is on the consumer. The *effect of a tax* (stage 3) is an economic consequence of the payment of the tax. For example, the increase in the price of a good resulting from the payment of a tax on it is an effect. Also, if the increase in price results in a decrease in the quantity of the good that can be sold, this result is also an effect of the tax.

The burden of taxes on business firms of all kinds tends to be shifted forward to the ultimate purchaser. To some extent and in some cases, the effect is shifted backward, as when an increase in price by the amount of the tax results in a reduction in sales and consequently a decrease in the demand for materials and labor for the production of the good. In such a case, part of the effect of the tax would be shifted backward to the suppliers of the materials and to the labor forces involved.

The subject is so involved that it is difficult in most cases to trace the cause-and-effect relationships that arise in the process of shifting. We may, however, state some generalizations as to the possibilities and direction of the shifting of certain kinds of taxes. These generalizations are valid in most cases.

The following taxes are usually shifted forward, in whole or in part: sales taxes, excise taxes (such as taxes on alcoholic beverages, tobacco, and cosmetics), customs duties, and business taxes. The extent to which each of these taxes can be shifted to the final consumer depends largely on the effect that the tax has on demand and costs of production. If the demand for the product taxed is highly inelastic, most of the tax can be shifted forward. If the demand for the product is elastic, it is probable that a part of the tax burden will be shifted forward, part will be borne by the payer, and part will be shifted backward in the form of a decrease in the demand for the factors that produce the goods on which the tax is levied.

Taxes on net personal income, monopoly profits, and inheritances cannot be shifted; neither can a poll tax, a tax on most kinds of consumer goods in the hands of consumers, and taxes on land (not including taxes on houses). In the case of taxes on land, by and large, the tax cannot be shifted because the value of land depends on the capitalized value of the economic rent (net return) of the land, and a tax reduces the amount of the net return from the land. Subsequent purchasers of the land will tend to value it according to its capitalized income less the amount of taxes. The same is true only to a limited extent of the effect of taxes on rental houses. Houses are reproducible, and the supply is more elastic than that of land. Since a tax decreases the amount of net income from houses built for rental purposes, a tax tends to keep the supply of such houses from expanding. Therefore, it is usually possible for landlords to raise their rents by an amount equal to only a part of the tax. In cases where real estate values in a community are decreasing, it is more difficult to shift the tax burden to tenants.

Direct and Indirect Taxes

By definition a *direct tax* is one that cannot be shifted; an *indirect tax* is one that can be shifted. The distinction between the two is clear, according to definition. However, when individual taxes are considered, it is not always certain as to whether they are direct or indirect. For example, it is ordinarily thought that a tax on a mortgage on real estate is a direct tax. If the mortgagee is compelled to pay a tax on his claim against the mortgagor's property, however, will he not demand a higher rate of interest for his loan and, in this way, shift the burden of the tax to the mortgagor? Therefore, if lenders know that they will have to pay a tax on the mortgages they receive as security for loans, they will pass along at least part of the burden of the tax to borrowers in the form of increased interest rates. Likewise, most commodity taxes, such as federal and state taxes on cigarettes, are included in the selling price of the commodity and in this way become "hidden taxes."

Trends in the Use of Direct and Indirect Taxes

Indirect taxes—commodity taxes and others—have been characteristic of aristocratic forms of government. It is also true that for many years after the adoption of the Constitution, by far the greater part of the revenues of the national treasury was obtained from indirect taxes, such as customs duties on imported commodities and excises on domestic products. During the past 50 years or so, however, there has been a noticeable tendency in the United States to make greater use of direct taxes in the form of personal income taxes. In fact, during the first few decades of its operation, the federal government obtained a sufficient amount of revenue from tariff and custom duties alone to finance nearly 90 percent of its customary functions. Today a small percentage of federal revenue comes from such sources. In 1973, for example, 45 percent of federal receipts came from personal income taxes and about 15 percent from corporation income taxes.

Property taxes provide about 23 percent of combined state and local government revenues. In 1973 property taxes provided over $42 billion. At the same time, sales taxes accounted for more than 20 percent of state and local revenues.

In recent years the rapid increase in expenditures by the federal and the state governments has resulted in an eager and constant search for new bases upon which taxes may be laid. As a consequence the number of business and commodity taxes has increased, and some of the preexisting taxes of these types have become heavier.

TAX EVASION AND TAX AVOIDANCE

Using the modern system of budgeting, taxes are imposed for the purpose of obtaining approximately predictable amounts of revenue. It is expected that individuals and business concerns will pay the taxes which they owe the government. To the extent they do, they will bear their equitable shares of the total tax burden as conceived by the government. If they fail to make payments as was anticipated in the law, an increased burden will be placed upon those who are unable to avoid or evade payment.

Tax Evasion

By *tax evasion* we mean the deliberate failure to pay a tax for which one is legally liable. In tax evasion no attempt is made to conform to the letter of the law. Tax evasion is illegal. The methods employed by those who seek to evade taxes include failure to list with the assessor items subject to tax, smuggling into the country goods upon which duties are imposed, and failure to report correctly the amount of income.

Tax Avoidance

Tax avoidance is accomplished by taking advantage of a technicality in the tax law. As long as the individual conforms to the letter of the law, he may possibly avoid payment, although it may be clearly evident that he has deliberately arranged his affairs for the purpose of escaping payment of taxes which otherwise he would have to pay. The more recent tax laws have reduced the number of so-called loopholes by which taxes may be avoided.

Roundabout ways have been devised for raising the pay of corporate executives and other employees without incurring the same amount of taxes that otherwise would have to be paid. For example, a corporation may provide an executive such services as cars, club memberships, or trips to vacation resorts; these may be deductible expenses for the business without being considered as personal income for the recipient. Payment of an "installment bonus" to an executive may be extended over several years, the idea being to hold a part of the bonus money until the executive has retired from his position. At that time his total income will be less, and he will be in a lower income tax bracket.

Payments by corporations to pension funds for the benefit of employees when they retire are not immediately taxable to the employees, and the income so applied by the corporation is not taxable. Rather, it is considered a cost. An executive may be given the right of a stock option whereby he can buy stock in his corporation at a price less than that at which the stock is selling in the market. A company may guarantee that an employee's family will be paid a lump sum or a monthly income in case of his death. These and other methods have been devised to enable the payment of increased remuneration to executives of certain corporations without rendering the increased compensation subject to the full impact of the income tax. An individual, by investing in tax-exempt municipal securities instead of putting his money into federal government bonds, the stock market, or a savings and loan association, will not have to pay income tax on the interest earned. Of course, in all probability he will earn a smaller return than he would from the other types of investments. Such tax-avoidance methods are not legally evasion, but their successful use does enable the recipients to avoid taxes that would be inevitable if the value of the increased compensation were paid directly.

KINDS OF TAXES

In light of the above discussion, we shall analyze in turn the following kinds of taxes that are commonly used: the general property tax; income taxes; business taxes; sales taxes; death and gift taxes; and Social Security taxes.

The General Property Tax

Ordinarily it is assumed that there is a positive relation between the value of the economic goods that an individual owns and his ability-to-pay taxes. Moreover, property owners are beneficiaries of the protective services of government, in addition to other services. It is not surprising, therefore, that property has been the object of taxation in all countries. By the time of the

Civil War, the general property tax in the United States had come to be accepted as the basic means of raising state and local revenues. According to judicial interpretation, the Constitution prohibits the use of property taxes by the federal government.

Definition of the General Property Tax. Although in principle the *general property tax* is a tax upon all wealth that has exchange value, in practice it is customary to classify property according to legal categories:

1. Real property (land, buildings, and other permanent fixtures).
2. Personal property (movable things of exchange value, such as livestock, motor vehicles, business fixtures, household furniture, machinery, tools, corporation stocks and bonds, bank deposits, and accounts receivable).

Most state governments make little or no use of the general property tax, but it is the source of a great deal of local tax revenue.

Exemptions of Property. A considerable portion of the property values, both real and personal, in the United States is exempt from taxation. Property owned by the federal government is not subject to taxation by state and local governments. State and local governments, of course, do not tax their own property. As a rule the property of nonprofit enterprises is exempt from taxation. Examples of such nonprofit enterprises include educational, charitable, and religious institutions. Farmers, likewise are frequently beneficiaries of liberal exemptions. Many states permit local governments to utilize tax exemptions as a lure to new enterprises. For example, in order to induce a new manufacturing enterprise to start in the locality, a municipality may grant the firm immunity from taxes for a number of years.

Assessment of Property. Assessment for taxation purposes means the listing and appraisal of all property subject to taxation. The assessment of real, personal, and business property is made by local assessors. Real property in rural districts is assessed annually in many of the states. In the others, as many as ten years may elapse between assessments. In the case of urban realty, assessment is undertaken more seriously than in the rural areas. In some of the larger cities, tax officials are attempting to place the assessment procedure on a scientific basis. Unfortunately inefficiency is not the only defect attendant upon assessment. Favoritism in the form of underassessment and even the outright omission of property from the assessment rolls have sometimes been revealed.

Defects of the General Property Tax. It is sometimes stated facetiously that there are only two things wrong with the general property tax. One of these is that it is indefensible in theory; and the other, that it does not work in practice. Although it would seem that this is too sweeping an indictment, it is true that the general property tax is characterized by a number of defects.

One of the chief defects of the general property tax is the inequitable tax burden that it places on the owners of real estate, especially land. A great part of the national income is produced by the rendition of services or by businesses that have little apparent connection with land. In normal times income from manufacturing alone is several times that of agriculture. The total amount of personal income received by proprietors for business and professional services in 1973 was about three times as large as the total amount received by individual farm proprietors.[3] Furthermore, income from real estate is often irregular and sometimes long deferred. Idle lots and residential and business properties are often not utilized for long periods of time. In the meantime the owner must pay his taxes.

In many areas the general property tax treats all property as a homogeneous whole. Yet property varies widely as to income-producing possibilities. The economic rent of rural and urban land is a source of income when the land is being utilized. But household furniture, appliances, jewelry, and most automobiles do not yield net income.

Variation in assessment rates is one of the chief defects in land taxes. Some of these variations are due to the lack of assessment standards and to lack of time and ability on the part of assessment officers. Too frequently, perhaps, they are due to design or carelessness. A number of states have recently passed legislation affecting the value assessments of real and personal property.

Assuming diligence and honesty on the part of assessors, it is comparatively easy to locate and list real estate. Land and houses cannot be concealed beyond the detection of the listing officer, if he really wishes to find them. On the other hand, it is extremely difficult without the cooperation of the owner to locate such personal property as notes receivable, money, and jewelry.

Most fiscal experts accept the theory that ability-to-pay taxes increase faster than the amount of income. Then, if only progressive rates are just, property taxes are inequitable because they are proportional.

Finally, the general property tax often results in double taxation. For example, where there is a mortgage on real estate, the owner pays a tax on the assessed value and the holder of the mortgage pays a tax on his lien.

Why the General Property Tax Is Retained. In view of the glaring defects of the general property tax, it is reasonable to ask why the tax is retained.

---

[3] Council of Economic Advisers, *Economic Indicators* (Washington: U.S. Government Printing Office, February, 1974).

For a long time some state and all local governments have depended upon property taxes to provide a large part of needed revenue. Force of habit, therefore, is a factor in the retention of the tax. In addition, the sudden elimination of property taxes would give present owners the benefit of a windfall of values, because such action would increase the selling value of real estate. Taxes on real estate are a dependable source of revenue. Since the property on the tax lists is known, the amount of revenue obtainable can be predicted with approximate certainty. If the tax is not paid by the owner, the property may be sold by the government. Finally, it is possible to refine and improve the general property tax so that many of its most objectionable defects can be minimized. This hope for improvement causes even severe critics to refrain from calling for its outright abolition.

Income Taxes

An *income tax* is based upon income that may be measured in terms of money over a given period of time. As a rule, taxes are imposed only upon net taxable income and not on total receipts. In theory the income tax rests upon a sound foundation. In the first place, unless taxes are confiscatory, net income is the primary source from which taxes can be paid. In the second place, the use of net income as the tax base makes it possible to adopt progressive rates which are designed to impose burdens according to ability to pay.

In calculating taxable income, certain deductions are made from gross income. These include expenses incurred in connection with the creation of the income. Examples of such expenses are professional expenses, wages and salaries paid for the operation and maintenance of the business, depreciation of business property, taxes, and rent. They do not include living expenses or expenses not connected with the pursuit of a profession or the operation of the business enterprise from which the income is derived.[4]

In addition, it is the practice to permit the subtraction of certain amounts for personal exemptions—$750 in the case of the federal tax. These exemptions are fixed for single persons, for a man and his wife living together, and for dependents who must rely upon the taxpayer for financial support.

---

[4] What constitutes net or taxable income is a problem that must be solved arbitrarily by those in authority. For example, in calculating the amount of their federal income tax for 1973, individuals were allowed to deduct $750 from their total incomes before figuring their tax. State and municipal income taxes allow individuals various exemptions. Exemptions for the support of members of a family and for charitable organizations are provided in both federal and state income tax laws. Also, the federal law permits the taxpayer to deduct the amount of his state and local taxes before calculating his federal income tax liability. The justification for various proposed methods of figuring taxable income is often a matter for heated disputes.

State Income Tax Laws. By 1973, at least 44 states and the District of Columbia had personal income tax laws. The laws vary as to the type of tax rates. Usually, however, the tax rate is progressive up to a maximum, usually ranging from one percent on the first $1,000 or $2,000 of taxable income up to 5 or 6 percent.

Municipal Income Tax Laws. Philadelphia in 1939 was the first American city to adopt an "earnings" or income tax law. At present a number of the larger cities have similar laws, including Cincinnati, Columbus (Ohio), Springfield (Ohio), St. Louis, Scranton, Toledo, Dayton, Detroit, and Louisville. Also, several hundred municipalities have some form of income tax. The relative amount of total revenues of local governments from this source varies considerably.

Is the Income Tax a "Good" Tax? The income tax is levied on the major source of taxpaying ability—income; and this tax cannot be shifted. Is it possible to adjust rates to taxpaying ability? It has been said that state and local income tax rates are regressive as to the burden they impose on large incomes because the progressive rates apply only to middle-class incomes. The range of federal income tax rates, however, is extensive.

There are those who feel that the federal government relies too much on individual and corporate income taxes with which to finance the government. It is asserted that the government could speed up the rate of growth of the economy by reducing income taxes. Further, it is argued that our balance of payments with other countries could be handled better by reducing, as they do in many foreign countries, the corporate income tax and imposing a value-added tax on goods produced for domestic consumption. The value-added tax, which will be explained more fully in the next chapter, is imposed on the difference between the amount of sales and the amount of purchases by a company on goods produced for domestic use. Then, too, because of circumstances affecting the source and amount of income, the calculation of personal or business income is often not an easy problem.

There are those, including some economists, who feel that income taxes impede the growth of the economy in two ways: (a) highly progressive income taxes reduce the incentive of persons in high levels of income to work, and (b) such taxes hold both savings and consumption below the level that they would attain if only consumption were taxed by means of the right kind of a sales tax.

Although these and other criticisms of income taxes attract considerable attention at times, it does not appear that the taxes on personal and corporate incomes are likely to be abandoned.

Business Taxes

Business taxes are levies upon certain business enterprises simply because of their nature and the services they perform. According to this definition business taxes include taxes on the following bases: capital stock, incomes of corporations, excess profits of corporations, payrolls of employers, the quantity or the value of natural resources sold, and permits to operate certain types of business. Within recent decades taxes on business have become increasingly important as a source of revenue, both to the federal government and to state and local governments. The reasons are that such taxes meet with the approval of the general public because it is considered that business enterprises are special beneficiaries of the services of government. And, too, it is not always recognized that many, if not most, taxes of this kind are indirect and therefore may be shifted.

The practice of taxing business corporations has developed largely during this century. At the present time only a few states levy taxes on corporate stock, while more than half tax corporate income. The federal government also taxes the income of corporations. There are two objectives in levying taxes on corporations. One of these is the aim to impose a business tax, and the other is to collect taxes from the stockholder "at the source," that is, before income is paid to the recipient.

It is not always possible to say where the incidence of business taxes rests. Some of these taxes can be shifted easily from the payer to others. Some of them are not so easily passed on. For example, it is probable that parts of payroll taxes are shifted, some of them forward in the form of increased prices and some of them backward in the form of lower wages. In the final analysis, it is probable that the real justification for the use of business taxes is to be found in the fact that they are expedient. They are easy to apply, and they are productive. In a great many cases they meet with popular approval.

Sales Taxes

The most important sales taxes are excise taxes and general sales taxes. An *excise tax* is levied upon the sale of a particular commodity or service, whereas a *general sales tax* covers the sale of most or all commodities. The general sales tax is the most important of the taxes that are levied by the states on commodities that are bought by consumers from retail stores. Ninety percent of the states levy general sales taxes that range from 2 to 6 percent on retail sales of consumer goods.

In most cases states have adopted the sales tax since 1945. The reason for this is that expenditures for education, road building, and other services by state governments have increased rapidly since the end of World War II, which has made it imperative for the states to find new sources of revenue.

Is the general sales tax a good tax? That depends upon what we mean by a good tax. The sales tax is easy to calculate. It is productive of revenue. Perhaps we might add, in most cases there appears to be no better alternative, at least in the thinking of many people.

There is in some cases considerable interstate avoidance of the sales tax by those who live near the boundary of another state in which there is no sales tax law. Such people can do much of their shopping and marketing out of state without having to pay a sales tax.

As we have remarked before, the sales tax is erroneously considered by some to be, in effect, regressive as to the burden it imposes upon consumers. It is true, of course, that a 4 percent rate on purchases of groceries would be the same for a higher or lower income family. But it can be admitted that the sales tax is regressive in relation to income. On the basis of ability to pay, the family with an income of $10,000 a year may be less able to pay a tax of 4 percent on its purchases of groceries than is a family with an income of $20,000.

There are those, however, who feel that a general sales tax on consumer goods is desirable because the tax is regressive relative to income. They point out that both federal and state—and particularly the federal—income tax rates are steeply progressive, at least up to a certain point. Therefore, so it is said, there is need to counterbalance these progressive rates on personal and corporate incomes with a tax on consumer goods and services, the rate of which is the same for all purchasers.

Death and Gift Taxes

The term *death taxes* is used to refer to taxes imposed upon property, the title of which passes from a decedent to his heirs or beneficiaries. These taxes are of two kinds. One is an *estate tax*, which is levied upon the entire estate of the decedent. The other is an *inheritance tax*, which is levied upon the individual shares of a total estate that are transferred to heirs and beneficiaries. A *gift tax* is one that is levied upon *inter vivos* gifts, or gifts between living persons. The government levies a gift tax equal to three fourths of the estate tax to discourage avoidance of the estate tax by the making of gifts. The federal government levies an estate tax, and all the states except Nevada levy death taxes of one kind or another.

Theoretically, an estate tax is a tax levied on "the right to transmit property," while an inheritance tax is one that is levied on "the right to receive property." In either case, the amount of the tax is determined by the application of a certain rate to the net value of the property involved. The federal estate tax is 3 percent of the first $5,000 above $60,000 (which is not taxed by the federal government) to 77 percent on the net value of estates above $10 million. The state death tax rates on estates and inheritances vary a great deal, and these taxes generally account for a minimal amount of state revenue.

Are death taxes desirable? According to those who favor such taxes, the payment of death taxes does not impose any burden on persons, past or present. In addition, it is contended that such taxes are needed to prevent the perpetuation and increase of great fortunes, which may result in too great a degree of social, economic, and political inequality. On the other hand, there are those who are convinced that high death tax rates are undesirable for two reasons. For one thing, the payment of death taxes may result in great inconvenience to certain business firms, the ownership of whose property may be affected by the death of the owner. Secondly, the payment of taxes such as these absorbs funds that would otherwise be available for consumption and for much-needed private investment.

Whatever the merits of these or other arguments that may be offered for and against death taxes, it seems that people in general are in favor of taxes on estates and inheritances. It should be recognized, however, that there is a limit to which these taxes can be used without bringing about a change in the form of the economic system. Since the ownership of private property changes with each generation, if the amount of property exempted from taxation is too small and the maximum rates are too high, it will be only a matter of time until the ownership of most of the wealth of the nation will pass into or at least through the hands of government because of the payment of these taxes.

Social Security Taxes

The Social Security Act, which became law in 1935, is, as the title implies, designed to provide a certain minimum amount of economic security for individuals and families. Broadly speaking, the law makes provisions for unemployment compensation; old-age, survivors, disability, and health insurance benefits; medicare; and grants-in-aid to states for the purpose of helping the states to provide economic aid to those persons who are not entitled to aid under other provisions of the law. The provisions of the Social Security Act and Social Security taxes will be discussed in Chapter 40, along with other measures to provide economic security and to reduce poverty among various groups in our economy.

SUMMARY
1. The right of taxation is a prerogative of political rulers, hence the evident appropriateness of the study for citizens who are themselves their own rulers. Moreover, as we tend to look more and more to government to provide broad functions in the economy, the subject of public finance and fiscal policy becomes increasingly urgent.

2. The fundamental principles that should be observed in devising taxes are equity or justice, certainty, convenience, and economy. What constitutes equity in taxation depends in large measure upon one's social philosophy. The theories that have been advanced as proposed guides in framing tax laws are the cost-of-service, benefit, and ability-to-pay theories.

3. The tax rate structure is composed of individual tax rates that may be proportional, progressive, degressive, or regressive as to their rates. It is generally conceded that progressive rates, at least to a certain extent, are more in accordance with the idea of justice than is any other type of rate that has practical applicability.

4. The shiftability of the burden of a tax depends upon the vendibility of the object taxed and upon the elasticity of the demand for and the supply of the object. Where the demand for the object is inelastic, the burden of the tax can be shifted; where the demand is elastic, less of the burden may be shifted, depending in large part upon the actual degree of elasticity.

5. Tax evasion is illegal and considered reprehensible; tax avoidance is legal and usually considered respectable.

6. Unless we are willing to confiscate private property, net income is the major source of tax-paying ability; hence, other things being equal, it is desirable to use taxable income as the chief basis for raising government revenue. Advocates of progressive income taxes justify such rates on the basis of ability to pay. Practical considerations, however, at least partly account for the continuing use of taxes on property, commodities, and business. Death taxes are justified on the grounds that there is a social need for the partial redistribution of property owned by certain decedents and that the payment of the tax imposes no burden upon the payer. Even if the validity of the conclusion from this argument is conceded, however, the question remains as to how progressive the tax rate should be. Both ethical and economic considerations are involved in any serious attempt to answer this question.

NEW TERMS

Tax system, *p. 412*

Principle of taxation, *p. 412*

Equality-of-sacrifice doctrine, *p. 415*

Tax rate, *p. 416*

Tax base, *p. 416*

Proportional tax rate, *p. 417*

Progressive tax rate, *p. 417*

Degressive tax rate, *p. 418*

Regressive tax rate, *p. 418*

Shifting of taxes, *p. 420*

Impact of a tax, *p. 420*

Incidence of a tax, *p. 420*

Effect of a tax, *p. 420*

Direct tax, *p. 421*

Indirect tax, *p. 421*

Tax evasion, *p. 422*

Tax avoidance, *p. 422*

General property tax, *p. 424*

Income tax, *p. 426*

Business taxes, *p. 428*

Excise tax, *p. 428*

General sales tax, *p. 428*

Death taxes, *p. 429*

Estate tax, *p. 429*

Inheritance tax, *p. 429*

Gift tax, *p. 429*

1. What are the characteristics of a desirable system of taxation?

2. (a) Do you think that Adam Smith's maxims of taxation are adequate criteria for a "good" tax?

(b) Are they easy to follow in formulating a tax law? Why or why not?

3. Would it be practical to finance aid for the needy aged on a benefit-received tax theory? Why or why not?

4. (a) What would be the results if an equalitarian theory of taxation were adopted?

(b) Is it possible for a tax to be equal but still not equitable?

5. (a) Are taxes for nonfiscal purposes justifiable? Why or why not?

(b) Are taxes ever used for non-fiscal purposes? If so, give an example.

6. Distinguish between a tax rate and a tax base. Give an example of each.

7. Illustrate income tax rates that would constitute (a) a proportional tax, (b) a progressive tax, (c) a regressive tax, and (d) a degressive tax.

8. With regard to tax-rate structure, how would you classify each of the following: personal income tax; corporate tax; sales tax; property tax; excise taxes?

9. Should it be possible to shift a tax? Why or why not?

10. (a) What are the advantages and disadvantages of a direct tax?

(b) Why is it not always easy to distinguish between a direct and an indirect tax?

11. (a) Distinguish between tax evasion and tax avoidance.

(b) Is it easier to evade some taxes than others?

(c) Is it easier to avoid some taxes than others? Give examples.

12. What are the arguments for and against the following taxes: (a) gift taxes; (b) inheritance taxes?

13. Did the federal tax cuts of 1964 on personal and corporate income and the surcharge of 1968 involve a change in our tax structure? Explain why or why not.

SUGGESTED READINGS

Groves, Harold M., and Robert L. Bish. *Financing Government*. New York: Holt, Rinehart and Winston, Inc., 1973.

Gutkin, Sydney A., and D. Beck. *Tax Avoidance vs. Tax Evasion*. New York: The Ronald Press Company, 1959.

Hatzman, Robert S. *Federal Income Taxation*. New York: The Ronald Press Company, 1960.

Isard, W., and R. Coughlin. *Municipal Costs and Revenues Resulting from Community Growth*. Boston: Federal Reserve Bank, 1957.

Raiff, Donald D., and Richard M. Young. "Budget Surpluses for State and Local Governments: Undercutting Uncle Sam's Fiscal Stance?" *Business Review*. Philadelphia: Federal Reserve Bank of Philadelphia (March, 1973).

Strayer, P. J. *Fiscal Policy and Politics*. New York: Harper & Row, Publishers, 1958.

20

New Concepts In Government Revenue

PREVIEW At all levels of government, particularly at the state and local levels, there has been a search in the past decade or more for additional revenues to match growing public expenditures. This has led to higher tax rates on existing tax bases, as well as explorations for new sources of revenue. In some respects this has led to a duplication of taxes. More and more state and local governments, for example, have been levying income or earnings taxes, a source of revenue at one time tapped almost exclusively by the federal government. New taxes have been proposed, such as the value added tax (VAT), for the purpose of raising additional income or as a substitute for some existing taxes. Likewise, a national sales tax has been proposed for the same purposes. Federal-state revenue sharing was inaugurated in 1972 as a means of adding to state and local revenues. In a somewhat desperate effort some states have turned to the lottery and other forms of gambling to enhance their revenues.

At the federal, state, and local levels, the need for additional revenues has led in the past few years to some new developments in the fields of taxation and revenue funding. Among the concepts being discussed, explored, and implemented are the value added tax, a national sales tax, federal-state revenue sharing, and the lottery.

VALUE ADDED TAX

The *value added tax* (VAT), which is widespread in Europe, has been proposed frequently for adoption in the United States. In fact, enough consideration has been given to a VAT in the United States that the Nixon Administration drafted a Congressional bill for its adoption in 1972, although it subsequently abandoned the plan to introduce the bill into Congress until a more appropriate time. Although in many respects the VAT is similar to a sales tax, VAT is not a sales tax. Neither is it an excise tax. It is, however, a tax on the production of all goods and services imposed at each stage of production. Each producer pays a tax at a specific rate on the value added by his productive process. Consequently, in actuality it is a tax on the GNP, which as we know is the current market value of the total goods and services produced by the nation's economy in a given year. The producer (taxpayer) receives a credit or refund for any VAT tax included in the price of the goods he purchases, or he pays taxes only on the value added by his productive process. In this manner VAT is different from a *cascade tax*, in which the producer pays a tax on the full value or price, including taxes, of the goods he purchases. As we shall see, VAT avoids the practice of paying a tax on a tax.

How VAT Works

There are several versions or methods of computing VAT. The simplest is the subtraction method. Take Commodity X, for example, which retails at $8,500. Assume that the processor of the raw material required to produce Commodity X started from scratch but sold the raw materials to the manufacturer for $800. If the VAT rate were 5 percent, the processor of the raw material would pay a tax of $40, as shown in Table 20-1. The manufacturer who purchases the raw materials then fabricates them into finished goods and sells them for $1,800. Through his fabrication he has added a value of $1,000 to the product. Consequently, he would be required to pay a tax of $50 ($1,000 $\times$ .05 = $50). Notice that if the tax were on the sale value of the product instead of the value added the manufacturer would pay a tax of $90 ($1,800 $\times$ .05 = $90). In similar fashion the wholesaler who adds value of $600 would be taxed $30, and the retailer would pay a tax of $55 on his value added of $1,100. This, of course, he can pass on to the consumer, as can the earlier processors, by incorporating the tax into the sale price of their product.

Notice, too, that the total VAT paid is $175 on a total value added of $3,500 ($3,500 $\times$ .05 = $175). On the other hand, a 5 percent sales tax would yield $425 ($8,500 $\times$ .05 = $425).

An alternative method of collecting VAT is through the credit method. With this approach each producer would pay a tax on the sale of his product instead of the value added. But he would receive a tax credit for any VAT included in the price of the materials he purchases. In this method, for example, the raw materials processor would pay a $40 tax on the goods sold ($800 $\times$ .05 = $40). The VAT on the manufacturer's sales would be $90 ($1,800 $\times$ .05 = $90). He would, however, be given a tax credit of $40 against the $90 tax to offset the probable inclusion of the $40 VAT paid by the raw material processor included in the price of the goods he sold to the manufacturer. This method would also result in a total VAT of $175. Each producer would pay a 5 percent tax on goods sold which would yield a total revenue of $425 ($8,500 $\times$ .05 = $425), but offset tax credits of

$250 ($5,000 $\times$ .05 = $250) would result in a net tax of $175 ($425 — $250 = $175).

TABLE 20-1

COMPUTATION OF VAT

Category	Cost of Materials	Sale of Product	Value Added	VAT Tax (5% Rate)
Raw Material Processor	$ —	$ 800	$ 800	$ 40
Manufacturer	800	1,800	1,000	50
Wholesaler	1,800	2,400	600	30
Retailer	2,400	3,500	1,100	55
Totals	$5,000	$8,500	$3,500	$175

Another method of computing VAT is by the addition method in which the producer would pay a tax on payments to each of the factors of production. The manufacturer, for example, who added value of $1,000 may have had payments for wages of $500, rent of $200, interest of $100, and profits of $200. In such case he would pay the 5 percent VAT as he reimburses each of the owners of the factors of production used in his production process and in addition pay a 5 percent tax on his profits.

There are, of course, advantages and disadvantages of each method of computing and collecting VAT. Although the subtraction method is simpler, one advantage of the credit method is that it is more difficult to evade the tax. To obtain a tax credit the taxpayer has to present receipts of his purchases and give receipts for his sales. In this way it is easy for the tax collector to determine the value added and the proper tax to levy.

The Pros and Cons of VAT

Many facts have been gathered and arguments generated about the merits of VAT. Included among its many advantages are:

1. It provides a means of raising additional revenue.
2. It is more equitable than a retail sales tax.
3. It is easy to administer.
4. It can be readily substituted for other forms of taxes.
5. The rates can be flexible.
6. Since the tax base (GNP) is continually increasing, it will yield additional revenue over the years.
7. It will help improve our balance of payments.

Opponents of VAT cite the following disadvantages:

1. American taxpayers, both individuals and firms, are already overtaxed.

2. Although VAT is proportional in reference to its base, it is regressive in regard to income.
3. VAT is nothing more than a gigantic sales tax.
4. The burden of the tax will fall on the consumers.
5. It would impose an identical tax rate on all goods and services; therefore, it lacks the flexibility of some other taxes.
6. What VAT proponents desire is primarily a substitute for corporate income taxes.
7. VAT is merely a foot in the door to a much larger VAT rate later.

VAT Elsewhere

Although not a new tax, VAT has only recently come into common usage. It was initially introduced in France in the mid-1950s, and it is now an integral part of the tax system of many European countries, especially since it was recommended for adoption by the nations of the European Economic Community. Those European nations presently using VAT include France, Germany, Belgium, Denmark, Ireland, Luxembourg, the Netherlands, Norway, and Sweden. VAT went into effect in Italy, Austria, and the United Kingdom in 1973 and will probably be adopted soon in Switzerland.

In addition to its other advantages, VAT has benefits in international trade. Most VAT nations exercise the privilege granted under the General Agreement on Tariffs and Trade (GATT) that permits a nation using VAT to rebate to businesses the tax on commodities that are to be exported. In addition, GATT permits nations using VAT to levy a *border tax* on commodities being imported from nations that do not utilize a VAT system. Under these rules producers and exporters in the United States operate at a disadvantage for two reasons: first, there is no rebating of corporate income tax on commodities that are exported; and second, the United States has no border tax on any goods coming from other nations, particularly VAT nations. Consequently, many U.S. businesses, especially exporters, find the idea of VAT to be more equitable than the income tax.

A form of VAT was tried in the state of Michigan when it adopted its Business Activities Tax in 1953. Due to strong opposition it was replaced, in spite of its efficiency, in 1967 with a state income tax. During the 14 years that it was in effect, revenues from this source increased fivefold.

How Much and for What?

VAT rates in most foreign nations are high, since VAT is generally a major source of government revenue. In most cases VAT was adopted as a replacement for the sales tax. Furthermore, many of the European nations have multirate structures, with lower rates on foodstuffs and necessities and the highest rates on luxuries. In France, there are four different VAT rates. The general rate is 23 percent; farm and food products are taxed at 7.5 percent; fuel and electricity, at 17.6 percent; and luxuries, at 33.3 percent. In Germany the general rate is 12 percent. In European countries VAT usually applies to both goods and services. There are certain exceptions where it does not apply, however, such as doctor or lawyer fees; and in some places, rents.

It has been estimated that a 10 percent VAT rate applied to the United States economy would generate about $70 billion annually in tax revenues. If adopted in the United States, however, in all probability it would be at a lower rate until taxpayers became accustomed to the tax and until the Internal Revenue Service worked any bugs out of the system.

As stated earlier, VAT has been proposed as a means of raising additional revenue, as an alternative to other new forms of taxation, such as a national sales tax, and as a substitute in whole or in part for existing forms of taxation, such as the corporate income tax and the property tax. In particular VAT has been suggested as an alternative to a national retail sales tax. Although it is similar in many respects to a sales tax, there are a number of differences between the two. One such difference is the fact that the retail sales tax makes little or no attempt to differentiate between the sale of goods and services for final consumption and the sale of goods and services to be used as intermediary products in the production of other commodities. Thus, much more tax revenue would be collected through a retail sales tax, unless several types of exemptions were provided.

The VAT has frequently been mentioned as a substitute for the federal personal income tax, in whole or in part. One weakness of the present income tax is that not all income is subject to the tax because of exemptions or loopholes. It is suggested that VAT would eliminate the exemptions and plug the loopholes.

Among other recommendations it is often suggested that VAT be used as a substitute, in whole or in part, for the corporate income tax. Numerous reasons are given in support of this proposal, such as the fact that VAT is more equitable, replacement of the corporate income tax will stimulate investment, and VAT will improve our international balance of payments. Opposite viewpoints, however, sound just as convincing, and much is made of the fact that a progressive income tax would be replaced by a tax that is regressive in nature in regard to income. There still is a considerable amount of uncertainty, however, regarding the ability to shift the VAT and uncertainty as to whether corporate income taxes can be shifted either backward to suppliers or forward to consumers.

President Nixon has expressed favor of VAT as a substitute, at least in part, for the property tax. In particular, it has been suggested that the proceeds from VAT could replace that portion of the property tax being used to finance public education. Those who favor this proposal cite the numerous reasons why the property tax is an inefficient means of raising funds for educational purposes, such as the current overburden of the property tax base, the difference in the tax base (property values) among communities, and the wide variances in the quantity and quality of educational facilities and resources in different communities throughout the United States. The use of VAT funds would eliminate a number of these inconsistencies and provide for improvement and more uniformity of public educational facilities throughout the nation. Of course, there are a number of objections to the use of VAT as a means of financing public education. The principal objection is the fear that it would lead to a diminution of control of education by local government.

NATIONAL RETAIL SALES TAX

As the debate goes on of whether new forms of taxation should be instituted for some of the existing tax forms or of whether new forms should be devised for the purpose of adding to total revenue, other controversies abound regarding the new types of tax forms to employ. In either case there are a number of supporters who favor the inauguration of a *national retail sales tax*. Some proponents argue that VAT is in effect a tax on consumption. Since the incidence of the tax is passed on to consumers, why not tax consumers directly through a federal retail sales tax and avoid all the complexity and bookkeeping involved with VAT? It can be argued that a federal retail sales tax is more economical and effective in regard to the collection of revenues but that VAT is more equitable. In the United States, however, the problem of tax evasion is not as widespread as it is in many European countries, where a major advantage of VAT is that it makes widespread tax evasion difficult. Furthermore, in the United States the mechanism for collecting the retail sales tax is well established, since most of our states have such a tax. But that too may create a problem, since a federal retail sales tax imposed along with the current state retail sales taxes would add to the tax bite at the retail level and may generate antagonism toward the tax, particularly if it is used as a source of new revenue rather than as a substitute for an existing tax form.

Since the total tax base of retail sales is greater than the VAT base, a 5 percent federal retail sales tax would yield greater revenue. That, of course, is a definite advantage of a national retail sales tax, since the same amount of revenue could be raised with a smaller tax rate than required through VAT.

REVENUE SHARING

Revenues are needed particularly at the state and local government levels, which are subject to severe financial pressures. These pressures result from two forces: (1) an increasing and expanding demand for city and state public services; and (2) a limited number of tax sources available to the state and local governments.

During the past two decades, state and local expenditures have increased considerably for a number of reasons, including:

1. A larger percentage of the population in the school age brackets;
2. A movement of rural families into the cities where more public service is given; and
3. A continuation of many outdated programs which are difficult to terminate because of social and political pressures.

Inflation, too, has added its burden, just as it has with federal expenditures. Table 20-2 gives some indication of the rate of increase of state and local government spending compared to the rise in federal government spending. Observe that, during each five-year period in the last 15 years, state and local government expenditures have increased at greater rates than federal expenditures. Moreover, during the past 21 years, state and local expenditures as a percentage of all government expenditures have increased over 6 percentage points, from 40.0 percent to 46.3 percent, an increase of about 16 percent.

Fortunately the federal government relies heavily for its revenue on personal and corporate income taxes, which have a continuously rising tax base, and Social Security taxes, which are likewise affected. Personal income taxes account for 45 percent of federal revenues; corporate income taxes, 15 percent; and Social Security taxes, 26 percent. Moreover, the progressive income tax rates produce tax revenues in greater proportion than the increase in the national economy. It has been calculated that a one percent increase in the GNP will result in a 1.5 percent increase in federal revenues.

TABLE 20-2

GOVERNMENT EXPENDITURES

1950-1971

(Billions)

Year	All Governments	Federal	Percent of All Governments	Percent Increase (Federal)	Total	State	Local	Percent of All Governments	Percent Increase (State and Local)
1950 ..	$ 70	$ 42	60.0	—	$ 28	$11	$17	40.0	—
1955 ..	110	70	63.6	66.7	40	14	26	36.4	42.9
1960 ..	151	90	59.6	28.6	61	22	39	40.4	52.5
1965 ..	206	119	57.8	32.2	87	31	55	42.2	42.6
1970 ..	333	185	55.5	55.5	148	56	92	44.5	70.1
1971 ..	369	199	53.8	7.6	171	66	105	46.3	15.5

SOURCE: *Statistical Abstract of the United States,* 1973, p. 410.

Consequently, increased federal expenditures can be financed in large part from the increase in federal revenues resulting from the progressivity of our present federal tax structure without resorting to higher tax rates or other sources of taxation.

State and local governments, however, are not in so favorable a financial position. They rely heavily on property, sales, gross receipts, and customs taxes for the largest share of their revenue. These taxes in large measure are proportional (and, in fact, regressive in relation to income) and respond or change slowly with economic growth. On the other hand, state and local expenditures have been increasing 30 percent faster than the GNP growth rate. Consequently, in recent years state and local governments have found it necessary to increase rates on existing taxes and levy new taxes. This has put an undue burden on some of the old tax bases, such as property and sales. It, too, has caused state and local governments to invade the area of earnings and income taxes, where the federal government has traditionally predominated. In many cases, the state and local governments have been looking more and more toward the federal government for aid. Although federal grants to states have been used for decades, they have been increasing in amount in recent years and now account for 16 percent of state and local revenues.

Most of this aid has been for specific purposes. In 1973, for example, aid was given for items such as national defense ($67 million), agriculture ($1.2 billion), natural environment ($1.3 billion), commerce and transportation ($5.9 billion), community development and housing ($3.6 billion), education and manpower ($6.6 billion), health ($5.8 billion), and income security ($12.7 billion). Federal grants-in-aid to the states increased from $10.9 billion in 1965 to $45.0 billion in 1973. Although the states and local governments have sometimes had a little leeway in the use of these funds, generally the federal grants have been earmarked to be used for a specific purpose and under stated conditions. The state and local governments have not been empowered to use these funds to finance other governmental needs. Thus, it eventually became evident that state and local governments were in need of federal assistance but of a different kind. All this led to the idea of federal-state revenue sharing, crystallized in the 1960s as a means of helping states raise revenues.

The concept of general revenue sharing as it developed involved two general characteristics: (1) a specific amount or percentage of federal revenues was to be distributed to state and local governments; and (2) there was to be little or no restriction on the use of these funds. The major difference between federal grants-in-aid and general revenue sharing is the unrestricted nature of the revenue sharing funds. Consequently, revenue sharing was an innovation and a marked departure from the usual grant-in-aid.

Some of the Pros and Cons

In the late 1960s and early 1970s a number of federal-state revenue sharing proposals were discussed and debated in Congressional committees. Proponents generally maintained that federal assistance was needed to help relieve state and local governments of financial hardships caused by inadequate revenues and lack of tax sources. Opponents of revenue sharing, however, argued that the plight of state and local governments was exaggerated and that the projected growth of state and local revenues was underestimated. They also maintained that if citizens in a community or state wanted more or better services they should be willing to pay for them through local taxes.

Those in favor of revenue sharing pointed out that, in the years ahead, as the GNP rises federal revenues will rise and result in federal surpluses. Such surpluses, they maintained, could cause fiscal drags on the economy. A sensible way of removing this fiscal drag is through revenue sharing, which also will relieve the fiscal burden of state and local governments. Opponents contested the notion, based on our budget record of the past several decades, that surpluses and drags would arise. Moreover, they pointed out that if they did occur they might be needed as an anti-inflationary measure if the economy was in a boom period.

Advocates of revenue sharing indicated that such a program might block the encroachment of federal influence into what are traditionally considered areas of state and local government activities. Opponents, of course, argued that the granting of federal funds, although unrestricted, may increase the influence of the federal government in many areas of state and local government activity.

Proponents of revenue sharing claimed that it would permit more efficient use of tax resources, since state and local governments could direct the funds where they were most needed. They also claimed that it would eliminate some duplication in the use of tax funds. Critics maintained that state and local governments may not be any more efficient, if as much so, as the federal government in using tax funds.

Advocates of revenue sharing contend that it is more equitable than the present grant-in-aid procedure. They contend that the wealthier and more populated states contribute more in federal taxes on a per capita basis than the less populated states. Yet these heavy contributors receive lower per capita grant funds. Revenue sharing diminishes this effect by allowing those states with a heavier tax burden to share more generously in revenue sharing.

Opponents of revenue sharing object to this contention by pointing out that states per se are not rich or poor, but rather the people in the states are rich or poor. These opponents hold that the current tax methods redistribute income from states with a high per capita income to states with lower per capita incomes. Moreover, the revenue sharing method could result in transferring funds from low per capita income states to higher per capita income states, if the latter had a higher tax effort. Furthermore, both rich and poor people live in both high and low per capita income states.

The State and Local Fiscal Assistance Act of 1972

After months of debate and hearings, Congress inaugurated federal-state revenue sharing with the enactment of the State and Local Fiscal Assistance Act of 1972. The Act allocated over $30 billion to be shared by the 50 states and about 38,000 state and local government units during a five-year period. During the first year, 1972, $5.3 billion was to be distributed to the various governments, with one third going to the states and two thirds to the local governments (cities, counties, villages, and townships). Revenue sharing funds were in addition to existing federal funds, since no reductions were made in regular federal programs.

Distribution of Funds. Revenue sharing funds are allocated to state and local governments according to a somewhat complicated formula. A local government's share, for example, is calculated by multiplying its population by its local tax effort and then by a relative income factor. The resulting product is then compared to the total of products for all other local governments within the state, and funds are distributed accordingly.

A state's share of the revenue can be determined by using either of two methods. The first is similar to that above in determining revenue sharing for the local governments. It involves the total population of the state, its general tax effort, and its income factor. When the product of these is obtained, it is compared with the sums of the products of other states. Funds are then allocated accordingly. The second method involves a formula that takes into consideration five factors: total state population, urbanized population, per capita income, income tax collections, and the state's general tax effort. The state may select the one method of the two that gives it the most revenue.

Table 20-3 shows the revenue distributed to the states in the calendar year 1972. Notice that for the nation as a whole the federal government allocated on average $25.47 per capita. Southern states and those which are sparsely populated did better than the average distribution. Ten states received over $30 per capita: Mississippi, $40.08; South Dakota, $36.98; Alabama, $33.09; New York, $32.20; Vermont, $32.13; North Dakota, $31.23; New

TABLE 20-3

REVENUE
SHARING
AMONG THE
STATES

State	Total for 1972 (Millions)	Per Person in State's Population
Alabama	$116.1	$33.09
Alaska	6.3	19.42
Arizona	50.2	25.80
Arkansas	55.0	27.81
California	556.1	27.17
Colorado	54.6	23.18
Connecticut	66.2	21.47
Delaware	15.8	27.95
Florida	146.0	20.11
Georgia	109.9	23.29
Hawaii	23.8	29.43
Idaho	19.9	26.26
Illinois	274.7	24.42
Indiana	104.3	19.71
Iowa	77.0	26.72
Kansas	52.8	23.40
Kentucky	87.3	26.47
Louisiana	113.6	30.54
Maine	31.1	30.26
Maryland	107.0	26.38
Massachusetts	163.0	28.16
Michigan	221.9	24.43
Minnesota	103.9	26.67
Mississippi	90.7	40.08
Missouri	98.8	20.78
Montana	20.6	28.63
Nebraska	42.9	28.11
Nevada	11.1	21.13
New Hampshire	15.2	19.74
New Jersey	163.6	22.21
New Mexico	33.2	31.22
New York	591.4	32.20
North Carolina	135.5	25.99
North Dakota	19.7	31.23
Ohio	207.0	19.20
Oklahoma	59.4	22.56
Oregon	56.2	25.77
Pennsylvania	274.0	22.97
Rhode Island	23.6	24.35
South Carolina	81.5	30.59
South Dakota	25.1	36.98
Tennessee	98.4	24.41
Texas	244.5	20.99
Utah	31.4	27.88
Vermont	14.8	32.13
Virginia	105.2	22.09
Washington	84.1	24.42
West Virginia	52.3	29.36
Wisconsin	133.9	29.63
Wyoming	9.7	28.11
Average for United States		25.47

SOURCE: "It's Official: Who Gets What from Revenue Sharing," *U.S. News & Report* (October 9, 1972), p. 94.

Mexico, $31.22; South Carolina, $30.59; Louisiana, $30.54; and Maine, $30.26. At the other end of the spectrum, each of four states received less than one half the per capita allocation to the highest state, Mississippi. These were: New Hampshire, $19.74; Indiana, $19.71; Alaska, $19.42; and Ohio, $19.20.

Table 20-4 shows the revenue shared among the 130 largest cities in the nation. Three cities, New York, Washington, and Baton Rouge, received shares amounting to $30 or more per capita. At the other extreme, eight cities received less than $8 per capita in revenue sharing. In general, prosperous suburban communities drew smaller amounts than larger cities, since the distribution formula favors localities with lower average incomes. New York City, for example, drew a $31.90 per capita share while nearby Westchester County received only $9.29 per capita.

Administration and Use of Funds. Revenue sharing funds are administered through a newly established trust fund for that specific purpose. Each state and local government established a trust fund to receive revenue sharing deposits. The federal government's obligation is rendered through the Office of Revenue Sharing within the U.S. Treasury Department. State and local governments must file annual reports regarding revenue sharing transactions with the Secretary of the Treasury.

Once they receive funds, state governments are at liberty to use their portion of the funds as they see fit. But local governments are somewhat restricted in their uses of shared revenue. They may use these funds only for priority expenditures. Included under priority expenditures are two categories:

1. Ordinary and necessary maintenance and operating expenses for the following:
   a. public safety, including law enforcement, fire protection, and building code enforcement;
   b. environmental protection, including sewage disposal, sanitation, and pollution abatement;
   c. public transportation, including mass transit systems and streets and roads;
   d. health;
   e. recreation;
   f. libraries;
   g. social services for the poor or aged; and
   h. financial administration.

2. Ordinary and necessary capital expenditures authorized by law.

TABLE 20-4 REVENUE SHARING AMONG 130 LARGEST CITIES [1]

City	Total for 1972 (Millions)	Per Person in State's Population	City	Total for 1972 (Millions)	Per Person in State's Population	City	Total for 1972 (Millions)	Per Person in State's Population
New York	$247.5	$31.90	Honolulu	$12.5	$19.89	Columbus, Ga.	$2.2	$14.20
Chicago	69.5	20.62	El Paso	5.5	16.99	Tacoma	3.7	23.84
Los Angeles	35.4	12.61	St. Paul	4.5	14.36	Jackson, Miss.	4.3	28.23
Philadelphia	43.8	22.44	Norfolk	6.7	21.89	Lincoln	1.8	11.79
Detroit	36.5	24.13	Birmingham	7.1	23.59	Lubbock	1.9	12.96
Houston	14.0	11.38	Rochester	2.3	7.74	Rockford, Ill.	2.0	13.73
Baltimore	23.9	26.37	Tampa	5.6	20.31	Paterson	2.6	18.25
Dallas	9.7	11.49	Wichita	2.1	7.73	Greensboro	2.8	19.16
Washington, D.C.	23.6	31.26	Akron	4.1	14.90	Youngstown	2.4	17.32
Cleveland	14.1	18.79	Tucson	4.3	16.48	Riverside, Calif.	1.2	8.82
Indianapolis	7.0	9.38	Jersey City	4.9	18.65	Fort Lauderdale	1.3	9.21
Milwaukee	11.2	15.64	Sacramento	3.3	12.79	Evansville	1.9	13.43
San Francisco	19.3	26.94	Austin	2.1	8.43	Newport News	2.4	17.22
San Diego	6.5	9.36	Richmond, Va.	5.5	21.90	Huntsville, Ala.	2.9	20.84
San Antonio	7.8	11.90	Albuquerque	6.4	26.39	New Haven	2.9	21.10
Boston	17.8	27.69	Dayton	4.6	18.79	Colorado Springs	1.2	8.61
Memphis	9.8	15.76	Charlotte	4.5	18.50	Winston-Salem	2.5	18.78
St. Louis	12.7	20.41	St. Petersburg	3.5	16.37	Torrance, Calif.	1.0	7.54
New Orleans	14.7	24.84	Corpus Christi	2.9	14.09	Montgomery	3.3	24.94
Phoenix	9.3	15.96	Yonkers	1.8	8.64	Glendale, Calif.	0.8	6.19
Columbus, Ohio	5.7	10.55	Des Moines	2.2	10.93	Little Rock	2.4	18.06
Seattle	9.9	18.58	Grand Rapids	2.7	13.57	Lansing	2.0	14.96
Jacksonville	4.0	7.51	Syracuse	3.3	16.62	Erie	2.8	21.40
Pittsburgh	11.7	22.46	Flint	4.5	23.20	Amarillo	2.1	16.17
Denver	12.2	23.68	Mobile	5.7	29.83	Peoria	1.7	13.03
Kansas City, Mo.	10.2	20.15	Shreveport, La.	3.3	18.19	Las Vegas	1.0	8.31
Atlanta	4.6	9.21	Warren, Mich.	2.1	11.79	South Bend	1.8	14.73
Buffalo	7.3	15.84	Providence	4.3	24.03	Topeka	1.2	9.92
Cincinnati	8.5	18.79	Fort Wayne	2.1	12.01	Raleigh	1.7	13.85
Nashville	6.4	14.24	Worcester	4.5	25.70	Macon	2.0	16.05
San Jose	4.0	9.05	Salt Lake City	3.9	22.07	Garden Grove, Calif.	0.7	5.63
Minneapolis	4.8	11.08	Gary	3.1	17.50	Hampton, Va.	2.2	18.62
Fort Worth	4.2	10.69	Knoxville	3.7	21.43	Springfield, Mo.	1.5	12.80
Toledo	4.5	11.64	Virginia Beach	2.4	14.15	Chattanooga	2.4	20.07
Newark	8.4	22.07	Madison, Wis.	1.9	11.25	Savannah	2.1	17.65
Portland, Oreg.	8.6	22.55	Spokane	3.3	19.45	Beaumont	1.8	15.13
Oklahoma City	6.8	18.39	Kansas City, Kans.	1.6	9.79	Berkeley	1.2	10.04
Louisville	9.5	26.19	Anaheim	1.2	7.03	Huntington Beach	0.6	5.30
Oakland	5.8	15.97	Fresno	3.1	18.84	Albany, N.Y.	1.3	11.23
Long Beach	3.7	10.45	Baton Rouge	5.1	31.03	Columbia, S.C.	2.3	19.83
Omaha	3.6	10.49	Springfield, Mass.	4.4	27.11	Pasadena	1.1	9.63
Miami	7.0	20.78	Hartford	3.3	21.10	Elizabeth, N.J.	1.6	14.26
Tulsa	3.0	9.12	Santa Ana	1.5	9.67	Independence, Mo.	1.1	9.71
			Bridgeport	2.6	16.74			

SOURCE: "It's Official: Who Gets What from Revenue Sharing," *U.S. News & World Report* (October 9, 1972), pp. 94–95.

[1] State figures include funds allocated to local governments within each state. Per capita state figures are based on U.S. Census Bureau estimates of population on July 1, 1972; city figures are based on 1970 census.

According to the Act, state and local governments may not use revenue sharing funds for educational or welfare purposes, since they receive billions of dollars from the federal government for such purposes. Nor can revenue sharing funds be used as matching funds by state and local governments to obtain federal grants for special projects requiring matching funds.

As a means of avoiding duplication, the State and Local Fiscal Assistance Act contains a provision which permits the federal government to provide an income tax collection service for the states beginning in 1974. This is a voluntary service and will be provided only to those states requesting such service. Under such an arrangement state income taxes would be collected along with federal income taxes and the state proceeds turned over to the respective states.

It is still a bit early to pass final judgment on the merits of revenue sharing. Soon after the Act was implemented, however, its proponents and critics were issuing complimentary and derogatory statements, respectively, about the program. One major objection, even from some of its proponents, is the manner in which funds are distributed. There is concern that the distribution formula tends to favor sparsely populated states and does not give as much aid as anticipated to heavily populated urban areas which are wrought with social and economic ills. There is concern, too, about the restriction on the use of funds for educational and welfare purposes. Some feel that this restriction diminishes the true spirit of revenue sharing. On the other hand, critics object to the lack of restrictions on the use of funds for public works. They point out that there is nothing in the Act that would prevent communities from using revenue sharing funds for new sports stadiums or racetracks.

By 1977, when the current Act is permitted to expire or be renewed, many arguments both pro and con will have been debated. At that time, however, there is a good probability that weaknesses in the current Act will have been eliminated, improvements added, provisions amended, dollar amounts increased, and the Act renewed, thus perpetuating revenue sharing.

Alternatives to Revenue Sharing

A number of measures have been proposed as alternatives to revenue sharing or as supplementary means of helping states and local governments raise revenue. Three of those which have received considerable attention are tax credits, tax reductions, and federalization of the present system of welfare payments.

It has been recommended that tax credits toward the payment of federal income taxes be given for those who pay state and local income taxes.

Such a practice, it is suggested, would soften taxpayer resistance to state and local government income taxes. It would encourage many state and local governments, not currently imposing an income tax, to adopt income-tax plans. Other states could increase their rates in order to meet current revenue needs.

A second proposal is the outright reduction of federal income taxes. This would not only be popular as both an economic and political move, but it would provide leeway for state and local governments to increase taxes, be they income taxes or other taxes. There still would be the task of convincing the taxpayers of the need for higher state and local taxes. Taxpayers, with their newly attained disposable income, may be reluctant to yield it to another tax collector. In fact, taxpayer resistance may induce some state and local communities to forego higher taxes. A problem also exists regarding the type of tax increases meted out by the state and local governments. An increase in state and local income taxes could offset the income gained by the reduction in federal taxes. Moreover, those hit by a rise in state and local income taxes would be the same individuals and corporations gaining from the reduction in federal taxes. But if taxes other than income taxes were raised, such as property and sales taxes, different individuals would be affected. Furthermore, the total revenue raised may be less than the loss of tax revenue from the decrease in federal income taxes.

A third alternative that received some attention during the Congressional hearings on revenue sharing is the proposal to federalize welfare payments. Currently welfare payments are a heavy burden on state and local government budgets. Consequently, it has been suggested that the federal government assume all welfare programs, which would relieve the state and local governments of this great financial drain. Cited as an advantage of this is the opportunity to standardize welfare payments throughout the nation. In this manner welfare recipients in poor states would receive benefits similar to those in the more prosperous states. Resultantly, standardized welfare payments would reduce much of the current migration of poor families to urban centers in wealthier states where such families can at present take advantage of higher welfare payments.

LOTTERIES

In the past decade the pressures for additional state funds and the growth of taxpayer resistance to new or higher taxes has led to something new in the way of raising revenue—the *lottery*. This has been supplemented in the past few years by the outright sanction of gambling as a means of raising state funds.

In 1964 New Hampshire became the first state to use a lottery as a method of raising revenue for the state. Lottery tickets were sold to the general public, prizes were awarded, and after subtracting the prize and administrative costs the state retained the net proceeds for its treasury. Although a small operation, the success of the New Hampshire lottery encouraged other states to adopt this device. New York entered the business in 1967 and became the largest producer of lottery revenue by a state. Table 20-5 shows a number of states inaugurating lotteries in the early 1970s, including New Jersey, Connecticut, Pennsylvania, Massachusetts, Michigan, and Maryland. Ohio was scheduled to adopt a lottery, and did, before the end of 1974. Similar fund raising lotteries are under consideration in California, Illinois, Iowa, Maine, Louisiana, Vermont, and the District of Columbia.

Prizes in the eight states currently using the lottery range up to $50,000 weekly, with periodic jackpots of $1,000,000 or more. Massachusetts, for example, has a $1 million jackpot every five weeks. Tickets, like the Irish Sweepstakes, can be purchased for a few dollars.

How successful are the lotteries? Although the success of legalized gambling in driving the underworld element out of gambling is doubtful, there is some evidence that lotteries have added funds to the state coffers. But even on this score they have not generated as much revenue as originally anticipated. Again, Table 20-5 shows that in the eight states operating lotteries, ticket sales have totalled nearly $1.2 billion over several years. However, after subtracting $636 million in prizes and operating costs, a net of $550 million has been added to state revenues. Although all revenues help when money is needed, lottery revenue produces a very small percentage of total state revenues. In 1970 alone, state and local government revenues amounted to $148 billion. In one year, 1970, New York had $16 billion in general revenue compared to its receipt of $202 million in three years from the lottery.

The arguments for and against the lottery as a means of raising revenue are numerous. In addition to the economic issues, there is one of morality for many taxpayers and legislators. Proponents like to point out that the lottery is a good source of revenue, that it is equivalent to a voluntary tax, that people are going to gamble anyway and the state might as well get its cut, that it saves the average taxpayer money, and that the revenues for the lottery are put to good use, especially in the states where the funds are used directly for education and welfare. Opponents, of course, can muster many arguments. They contend that the tax is uneconomical (high collection costs compared to receipts), that the revenue is uncertain, that it does not provide sufficient revenue, that the taxpayers should not be encouraged to gamble,

TABLE 20-5

THE TAKE
FROM STATE
LOTTERIES:
HOW MUCH
AND WHERE
IT GOES

State and Starting Date	Total Ticket Sales (Millions)	Prizes and Operating Costs (Millions)	Left for State (Millions)
New Hampshire ...... (March, 1964)	$ 36	$ 20	$ 16 for education
New York .... (June, 1967)	417	215	202 for general purposes
New Jersey .... (January, 1971)	325	165	160 for education, maintaining state institutions
Connecticut .... (February, 1972)	52	28	24 for general purposes
Pennsylvania .... (March, 1972)	178	103	75 for old-age assistance
Massachusetts .... (March, 1972)	93	56	37 to cities and towns for general use
Michigan .... (November, 1972)	81	46	35 for general use
Maryland .... (May, 1973)	5	3	2 for general use
Total	$1,187	$636	$551

SOURCE: "Now, an Epidemic of Legalized Gambling." *U.S. News & World Report* (July 23, 1973).

that it reduces taxpayers' direct responsibility, that the state has no right to get into the gambling business, and that gambling is immoral even if the funds are used for a worthy purpose. Regardless of which way the arguments tip the scales in individual states, it appears that the use of the lottery will be extended as more and more states take it under consideration.

In addition to the lottery, some states have recently been legalizing other types of gambling as a means of raising revenues. More than one half of the states now permit pari-mutuel betting at horse racing and dog racing tracks. Total state revenues from this source exceed $500 million annually. New York City, through its Off-Track Betting Corporation, generates over $12 million annually in funds for the state and local governments. Bills are now pending in Michigan and Massachusetts to permit off-track betting (OTB) in those states. Legalized OTB is under consideration in a half dozen other states. In some states gambling commissions are studying the feasibility of sports pools and numbers games. It is contended that these would be the source of much revenue since they appeal to many small betters who are willing to risk a few cents a day in the hope of hitting it big. But as the plans to raise more revenue from gambling grows, so does the resistance from various groups. Consequently, gambling as a source of revenue for state and local governments is developing into a hot controversy, with good odds that it will not be settled solely on economic grounds.

SUMMARY

1. In seeking new sources of revenue, various governmental units have tried or discussed a number of innovations in the past decade.

2. Recently at the federal level strong consideration was given to the concept of a value added tax (VAT). As the name implies, this would be a federal tax on the value added by various producers. Although there are several versions of VAT, in the final analysis the consumers would end up with the brunt of the tax.

3. It has been suggested that VAT could be used as a substitute for the corporate income tax, that the revenue derived therefrom could be used to support education and permit a reduction in local property taxes, or it simply could be used as a means of raising additional revenue. Although many pros and cons have been raised concerning VAT, it has been used successfully in several other nations.

4. Since the burden of VAT is by and large shifted to the consumer, it is sometimes suggested that it would be simpler to adopt a national sales tax. A big advantage of the latter is that it would be easier to raise a given amount of revenue through a national sales tax than it would be via VAT.

5. Another innovation much discussed and finally adopted through enactment of the State and Local Fiscal Assistance Act of 1972 is federal-state revenue sharing. Unlike federal grants-in-aid to the states, which carry specific restrictions, shared revenues tend to have far fewer restrictions. The present Act calls for a total of $30 billion of federally collected funds to be turned over during a five-year period to the state and local governments according to a designated formula. One third of the funds is directed to the states and the other two thirds to local governments. Distribution of funds to governments varies according to population, income, and the tax effort of the recipient government. Funds may be used for a variety of purposes other than education and welfare activities.

6. Alternatives to revenue sharing include federal tax credits for the payment of state and local income taxes, federal income tax reductions to allow more leeway for increases in state and local income tax or other tax rates, and the federalization of welfare payments to relieve the state and local governments of this financially burdensome requirement.

7. In a desperate effort to raise funds, a number of states in the past decade have adopted a gambling lottery. Initiated in 1964 by New Hampshire, there are now nine states using lotteries as a source of revenue. Although a lottery produces a minimal amount of total state revenue, many other states now have it under consideration.

8. In addition, a number of states

are now legalizing other forms of gambling, such as pari-mutuel and off-track betting, as a means of raising revenues. Consideration has been given by some states to the feasibility of utilizing sports pools and the numbers game.

9. Although there are many arguments for and against the use of gambling for raising government revenues, a serious objection is raised from several quarters concerning the morality of such a practice.

NEW TERMS

Value added tax (VAT), *p. 433*
Cascade tax, *p. 434*
Border tax, *p. 436*
National retail sales tax, *p. 438*

Revenue sharing, *p. 439*
State and Local Fiscal Assistance Act of 1972, *p. 442*
Lottery, *p. 447*

QUESTIONS FOR DISCUSSION AND ANALYSIS

1. Do you think the United States should adopt a value added tax? Why or why not?

2. Indicate how a value added tax can be shifted to the consumer.

3. Would you recommend that VAT, if adopted, be used as a substitute for either the corporate income tax or local property taxes? Explain.

4. For an exporter, what advantage does VAT have over the corporate income tax?

5. Compared to VAT, could the same revenue be obtained more efficiently with a national sales tax?

6. Explain the principle of revenue sharing.

7. Distinguish between a federal grant-in-aid and federal-state revenue sharing.

8. On what basis are funds distributed to the state and local governments under the State and Local Fiscal Assistance Act of 1972?

9. Do you think federal restrictions should be placed on the use of shared revenue by the states? If so, what restrictions?

10. Do you think revenue sharing should be increased or expanded? Why or why not?

11. What share of state revenues can be attributed to lottery income?

12. Economically, do you think the lottery, or other forms of gambling activity, is a good source of revenue for governments?

SUGGESTED READINGS

Floyd, Robert H. "The Very Controversial Tax on Value Added." *Monthly Review*. Atlanta: Federal Reserve Bank of Atlanta (July, 1972).

Heller, Walter, *et al. Revenue Sharing and the City*. Baltimore: The Johns Hopkins University Press, 1968.

"How Value Added Works in Europe." *Business Week* (February 26, 1972).

Lindholm, Richard W. "Toward a New Philosophy of Taxation." *The Morgan Guaranty Survey*. New York: Morgan Guaranty Trust Company (January, 1972).

McLure, Charles E., Jr., and Norman B. True. *Value Added Tax: Two Views*, Domestic Affairs Study 7. Washington: American Enterprise Institute for Public Policy Research, November, 1972.

Musken, Selma J., and John F. Cotton. *Sharing Federal Funds for State and Local Needs*. New York: Praeger Publishers, Inc., 1969.

"Now an Epidemic of Legalized Gambling." *U.S. News & World Report* (July 23, 1973).

Reuss, Henry S. *Revenue Sharing: Crutch or Catalyst for State and Local Governments?* New York: Praeger Publishers, Inc., 1970.

"The Fiscal Squeeze on States and Municipalities." *Monthly Economic Letter*. New York: First National City Bank of New York (October, 1969).

PART SIX

Economic Growth and
the American Experience

21

Long-Run Economic Growth

PREVIEW Because of our growing population and our rising productivity per man-hour, it is essential to attain a certain economic growth rate if we are to keep unemployment and recession from occurring. In order to absorb annually 1.5 million new entrants into the labor force plus the reabsorption of the 2 million or more workers displaced each year because of technological development and automation, we need an annual real growth rate of 4 percent.

Economic growth can be measured in many ways, but the most popular is in terms of the GNP. A number of projections forecast a GNP in the vicinity of $1.7 to $2.0 trillion by 1985 in terms of 1970 dollars. There are several techniques for increasing our economic growth if desired, but growth brings problems as well as benefits.

Although the level of economic activity may fluctuate in the short run, generally there is a tendency for the economy to grow in the long run. This long-run trend of national output and income is no less important to the welfare of a nation than short-run stability.

The rate of economic growth has become a topic of considerable analysis and discussion. Here and elsewhere throughout the world, the rate of economic growth is closely related to numerous social problems, such as poverty, unemployment, housing, pollution, population increase, political stability, and foreign aid. It is indeed startling in this day of technological advancement to learn that more than one half of the world's 4 billion people go to bed hungry every night and that these and many more have inadequate clothing, shelter, and medical care. The answer to many social problems is a higher rate of economic growth along with a proper system of distribution.

The economic growth rate is a crucial issue in many underdeveloped nations, as we will see in Chapter 44, "Economic Development," and in Chapter 45, "The Emerging Nations." Even in the United States, whose total production is greater than the combined output of any six nations in the world, the economic growth rate is a major issue. When our growth rate is too slow, unemployment and loss of income results. When the economy attempts to grow too rapidly, inflation occurs. Thus, many questions arise concerning the uses of economic growth. Should the benefits of economic growth be channeled into a higher level of living via direct consumer spending on goods and services in the private sector of the economy? Or should the benefits of economic growth be directed to the citizens of the economy through conventional public spending on such things as roads and highways, education, parks, recreational facilities, hospitals, and medical research? Some have suggested that the benefits of growth be utilized through the public sector primarily on programs dealing with poverty, national health insurance, income maintenance, Social Security, urban renewal, mass transit, rent subsidies, pollution controls, and other newly explored socioeconomic measures.

THE NEED FOR ECONOMIC GROWTH

As has been pointed out previously, our economy must grow continuously just to maintain our existing level of living. The reason is two-fold. First, since we add more than 1.5 million workers to the labor force each year, we must produce more if we are going to have jobs for these new workers. Secondly, because the productivity of the labor force tends to increase more than 2 percent annually as a result of technological development and improved labor efficiency, we can produce the same level of output with fewer and fewer workers as time progresses.

Thus, output must grow if we are to absorb the 1.5 million new entrants into the labor force plus the 2 million or more workers who are displaced annually because of technological development and automation. If we merely produce the same level of output each year instead of increasing it, we will have fewer jobs, growing unemployment, and a decline in the per capita income of the nation. In order to maintain, or improve, existing levels of living, it is necessary to increase output continuously, unless, of course, workers are content to take the benefits of higher productivity in the form of shorter working hours instead of goods and services. If not, the economy must grow at some particular rate merely to remain at a standstill relative to per capita output and income. Experience indicates, for example, that with a real growth rate of less than 4 percent the American economy suffers from nagging unemployment and limited per capita gains in output and income. It takes a 4 percent growth rate just to stabilize the level of unemployment. Full employment and substantial per capita gains, however, seem to occur when the economic growth rate exceeds 4 percent. Each additional 3 percentage point increase above the 4 percent figure results in a decrease in unemployment of roughly one percent. The potential annual growth rate of the American economy is currently 5 percent, reflecting a 1.75 percent increase in available man-hours and a 2.5 to 3.5 percent rise in output per man-hour.

Unemployment at the end of 1969 was 2.8 million, or 3.5 percent of the civilian labor force; but by the end of 1970, unemployment was 4.9 million, or 6.0 percent of the civilian labor force. Why? Simply because the real output of goods and services, instead of growing, declined by a fraction of a percent in 1970. Consequently, we failed to absorb all the new entrants into the labor force plus some of those who were displaced because of technological development and automation. Furthermore, a sizable number of workers withdrew from the labor force because they were unable to find work. At the end of 1971, total unemployment was no better, still reading about 6 percent; in that year the real growth rate was only 3 percent. Since the real growth rate for the economy in 1972 was 6.4 percent, unemployment decreased from 5.9 percent in January, 1972, to 5.1 percent in January, 1973. However, after falling to 4.5 percent in mid-1973, unemployment rose back to 5.2 percent in January, 1974.

In many underdeveloped nations it is a major task to keep the economy growing at the same rate as the population. When the economy grows at a lesser rate, the per capita output and income and the level of living of a nation decline. This occurs in several nations where production is limited and most of it must be used to satisfy current consumption needs. These nations have little opportunity, in the absence of outside aid, to devote a sufficient portion of their production to capital formation. In such case it is difficult to improve the nation's production potential, which is necessary for a healthy rate of economic growth.

ECONOMIC GROWTH AS A NATIONAL GOAL

Although the need for a healthy rate of economic growth had received increasing emphasis in the 1950s, President Kennedy gave a certain definiteness to the goal of economic growth in his *Economic Report* of 1962 when he stated:

> While we move toward full and sustained use of today's productive capacity, we must expand our potential for tomorrow. Our postwar economic growth—though a step ahead of our record for the last half century—has been slowing down. We have not in recent years maintained the 4 to 4.5 percent growth rate which characterized the early postwar period. We should not settle for less than the achievement of a long-term growth rate matching the early postwar record. Increasing our growth rate to 4.5 percent a year lies within the range of our capabilities during the 1960s.

So important is the growth problem to the future of our economy that President Kennedy in August, 1962, established a Cabinet Committee on Economic Growth to coordinate federal activities in this field and to advise the President on steps to accelerate the growth of our economy. It was the task of the committee to report to the President periodically on the following:

1. Ways to utilize the interest, energy, initiative, and experience of private industry, agriculture, and labor for national economic growth;
2. The impact of existing government programs and private economic trends on current and foreseeable rates of growth;
3. Additional administrative measures and legislative proposals that might be desirable, together with their budgetary implications; and
4. Ways to organize the federal government more effectively to promote economic growth.

The work of the Cabinet Committee was supplemented by that of another committee studying the growth problem, the Interagency Growth Study Committee, which had the responsibility for developing and supervising an integrated program of studies of United States economic growth.

In his annual manpower report to Congress, President Johnson in 1965 cited the need for a sustained economic growth rate of 4.75 percent annually for the next six years in order to reduce unemployment to acceptable levels. In the report the Department of Labor indicated that the "acceptable" unemployment rate was 3 percent, as compared to the customary 4 percent.

Since economic growth has become such a definite goal for our economy, a large number of questions naturally arise concerning its attainment. What exactly do we mean by economic growth? How is it measured? Why is it so necessary or important? What are the alternatives to economic growth? How do we attain or accelerate economic growth? What is the proper rate of economic growth for our economy? We will seek to explore these and other questions in the following pages.

HOW GROWTH IS MEASURED

The rate of economic growth is related to many other economic problems in our economy. Certainly it is basic to the problem of persistent or nagging unemployment that plagued the economy from 1958 to 1966. It was the immediate cause of the 1970 recession. Since total output of goods and services affects our per capita income and level of living, economic growth is an important factor in analyzing the effects of the so-called population explosion. The rate of economic growth is seriously affected by automation, a problem in itself, and surely any proposal for a shorter workweek will have to reckon with the effect of such a move on our economic growth.

Economic growth is a broad concept with many ramifications and meanings. Regarding growth, one might talk in terms of the total number of jobs for the economy by a given year, such as 1985. Economic growth may be determined in terms of our productive capacity or by the increase in productivity per man-hour. One favorite way of measuring economic growth, for example, is in terms of the potential increase in the index of industrial production. Other persons like to measure economic growth by the increase in per capita disposable income, which has a direct effect on our level of living. The most common and perhaps best measure of economic growth, however, is the gross national product. When used, of course, it should be in terms of constant dollars. Furthermore, it is well to compare the GNP to the growth in population, since per capita growth gives a better measure of the improvement in our level of living. Economic growth as measured by the GNP also should be calculated in terms of the *actual growth rate* vs. the *potential growth rate*, as shown earlier in Figure 9-1 on page 174, in order to yield additional meaningful comparisons.

ECONOMIC GROWTH IN THE UNITED STATES

In an effort to determine what the rate of economic growth has been in the past several years, whether in terms of GNP, total employment, or productive capacity, much will depend upon the period of time taken into consideration. Growth does not proceed at a uniform rate; sometimes it accelerates and at other times it lags. If the growth is measured during a period of acceleration, the rate obtained will be greater than the average for a longer period. It is a well-established fact that our real or constant dollar economic growth rate since 1900 has been about 3 percent per year. It also is pointed out frequently that the growth rate since 1929 has been 3.1 percent in terms of the total output of goods and services. It can be shown, however, that the constant dollar GNP grew by 3.7 percent annually for the period 1950-1972, and 4.0 percent or more during various years in the 1960s.

During World War II, under the state of national emergency, the growth rate in some years exceeded 10 percent. For more recent years, Table 21-1 shows that the economic growth rate in constant dollars was 5.1 percent in the early 1960s (1960-1966) in contrast to a 3.6 percent growth rate in the period 1965-1972. This latter period, however, included the recession of 1970, in which the GNP growth rate was negative.

Sources of Growth

Economic growth results from three major sources: first, from the increase in productivity per man-hour, which is estimated to be increasing about 3 percent per year since World War II; second, from the increase in the size of the labor force, which has been increasing at a rate of 1.75

TABLE 21-1

RATES OF
ECONOMIC
GROWTH
FOR THE U.S.

1910-1972

Terminal Year	Initial Year													
	1910	1915	1920	1925	1929	1935	1940	1945	1950	1955	1960	1965	1970	1971
1911	2.6	(x)	(x)	(x)	(x)	(x)	(x)	(x)	(x)	(x)	(x)	(x)	(x)	(x)
1916	1.9	7.9	(x)	(x)	(x)	(x)	(x)	(x)	(x)	(x)	(x)	(x)	(x)	(x)
1921	0.6	0.4	−8.6	(x)	(x)	(x)	(x)	(x)	(x)	(x)	(x)	(x)	(x)	(x)
1926	2.9	3.9	5.2	5.9	(x)	(x)	(x)	(x)	(x)	(x)	(x)	(x)	(x)	(x)
1931	1.6	1.9	1.7	−1.0	−8.8	(x)	(x)	(x)	(x)	(x)	(x)	(x)	(x)	(x)
1936	1.8	2.1	2.0	0.7	−0.8	13.9	(x)	(x)	(x)	(x)	(x)	(x)	(x)	(x)
1941	2.6	2.9	3.1	2.4	2.2	7.6	16.1	(x)	(x)	(x)	(x)	(x)	(x)	(x)
1946	2.7	3.0	3.1	2.7	2.6	5.7	5.5	−12.0	(x)	(x)	(x)	(x)	(x)	(x)
1951	2.9	3.2	3.3	3.0	2.9	5.2	4.9	1.3	7.9	(x)	(x)	(x)	(x)	(x)
1956	2.9	3.2	3.3	3.0	2.9	4.7	4.3	2.1	3.9	1.8	(x)	(x)	(x)	(x)
1961	2.8	3.1	3.1	2.9	2.8	4.2	3.8	2.1	3.1	2.1	1.9	(x)	(x)	(x)
1965	3.0	3.3	3.4	3.1	3.1	4.4	4.1	2.8	3.8	3.5	4.8	(x)	(x)	(x)
1966	3.1	3.3	3.4	3.2	3.2	4.5	4.2	3.0	3.9	3.8	5.1	6.5	(x)	(x)
1967	3.1	3.3	3.4	3.2	3.2	4.4	4.1	3.0	3.8	3.7	4.8	4.5	(x)	(x)
1968	3.1	3.3	3.4	3.2	3.2	4.4	4.1	3.0	3.9	3.7	4.7	4.6	(x)	(x)
1969	3.1	3.3	3.4	3.2	3.2	4.4	4.1	3.0	3.8	3.7	4.5	4.1	(x)	(x)
1970	3.0	3.2	3.3	3.1	3.1	4.2	3.9	2.9	3.6	3.4	4.0	3.2	(x)	(x)
1971	3.0	3.2	3.3	3.1	3.1	4.2	3.9	2.9	3.6	3.3	3.9	3.1	2.7	(x)
1972	3.1	3.3	3.4	3.2	3.2	4.2	4.0	3.0	3.7	3.5	4.1	3.6	4.6	6.4

SOURCE: *Statistical Abstract of the United States,* 1973, p. 321.

(X) Not applicable.
General Note: Percent. Figures represent average annual compounded rates of change in gross national product, based on estimates by Department of Commerce of real gross national product (expressed in constant dollars). Minus sign (−) denotes decline. To obtain annual rate of change between any two years shown, find column for initial year at top of table and read figure in that column opposite terminal year shown at left.

percent annually in the same period; and third, from a change in the total number of hours worked by the labor force, or average length of the workweek per worker. Although the rate of economic growth during the 1960s from the first two sources, productivity per man-hour and number of workers, should have yielded a potential 4.7 percent annual increase in the GNP for the period of the 1960s, it was less (4.0 percent) than that because the average workweek declined somewhat for the period due to unemployment and other causes.

U. S. Growth Rate vs. Other Nations

Although the U.S. economy has been increasing at a fairly brisk clip, it has been lagging in comparison with economic growth in several other leading industrial nations. In the 1960s, for example, Japan's economy, which has an exceptionally high rate of investment, as shown in Figure 21-1, grew by 11.1 percent annually. The rate of economic growth in France, as shown in Table 21-2, for the same period was 5.8 percent, Italy 5.7 percent, and Canada 5.2 percent. Very high rates were also attained in other nations, such as the Republic of Korea, Thailand, Mexico, and Iran. The United Kingdom had one of the lowest growth rates, 2.7 percent, compared with 4.0 percent for the United States. The growth rate in Soviet Russia was about 6 to 7 percent. The original Common Market nations (West Germany, France, Italy, Belgium, the Netherlands, and Luxemburg) as a whole showed a substantially greater growth rate than the United States, Canada,

TABLE 21-2 GROWTH RATES OF GNP—INTERNATIONAL COMPARISONS, Selected Periods, 1913-1970

Period	United States		Canada		France		Germany, Fed. Rep.		Italy		United Kingdom		Japan	
	Total	Per Capita	Total	Per Capita	Total	Per Capita	Total	Per Capita	Total	Per Capita	Total	Per Capita	Total	Per Capita
1913-1929 ...	3.1	1.7	2.4	0.7	1.7	1.8	0.4	−0.1	1.8	1.2	0.8	0.3	3.9	(NA)
1929-1950 ...	2.9	1.8	3.2	1.8	−	−0.1	1.9	0.7	1.0	0.3	1.6	1.2	0.6	(NA)
1929-1970 ...	3.2	1.9	3.9	2.1	2.6	2.0	4.2	3.0	3.3	2.5	2.2	1.7	5.1	(NA)
1950-1960 ...	3.2	1.4	4.0	1.3	4.9	3.9	8.6	7.1	5.6	4.8	2.7	2.3	8.2	7.0
1950-1970 ...	3.6	2.1	4.6	2.3	5.3	4.3	6.7	5.5	5.6	4.8	2.7	2.2	9.8	8.6
1960-1970 ...	4.0	2.7	5.2	3.4	5.8	4.7	4.8	3.9	5.7	4.8	2.7	2.1	11.1	9.9

SOURCE: Adapted from *Statistical Abstract of the United States*, 1973, p. 320.

− Represents zero. NA not available.

General Note: Percent. Rates derived from data adjusted for price changes and represent average annual compounded changes in real output from initial to terminal year of period. For details concerning methodology, see source.

or the United Kingdom. Economic growth in many of the European nations has not only been higher, but it has been steadier and more stable than the growth experience in the postwar United States.

In comparing the growth rate of the United States with other nations, it should be remembered that their larger growth rates result in part from the fact that their current levels of economic activity are relatively low by comparison with that of the United States. Therefore, any substantial absolute increase in total production appears as a relatively large percentage increase. In the United States where the absolute level of production is two to three times greater than that in other leading industrial nations throughout the world, a given absolute increase in production will naturally be a smaller percentage increase than it would be in a less advanced economy.

FIGURE 21-1

Japan's good growth record is related to a strong investment effort, made possible by a relatively low level of consumer and government expenditures and a low tax rate.

SOURCE: *World Business*, Economic Research Division of the Chase Manhattan Bank (October, 1968).

General Note: Data relate to 1964-1966 at constant dollars.

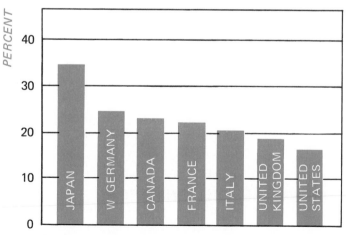

Whether the other nations can continue their high rates of economic growth after they reach higher levels of total and per capita output remains to be seen.

ECONOMIC GROWTH, THE PRODUCTION GAP, AND UNEMPLOYMENT

The problem of sufficient economic growth in effect parallels the problems of the production gap in terms of persistent or nagging unemployment. The President's Council of Economic Advisers first pointed to this issue in the 1962 *Economic Report.* At that time the economy was operating at 8 to 10 percent under potential capacity, and total production was $30 to $35 billion below our potential. This was due, according to the Council, primarily to an insufficient effective demand for goods and services in our economy. Although the Council indicated that problems of structural unemployment did exist, they contended that the primary source of high unemployment was lack of markets for goods and services and that the lag in economic growth brought into better focus the problems of structural unemployment.

Since then we have had some years of full or nearly full employment associated with solid real growth rates. On the other hand, production gaps and unemployment have been associated with slow economic growth rates. Referring back to Figure 9-1, page 174, observe the production gaps during the period of 1958 to 1965, contrasted to low levels of unemployment and no production gaps during the period 1966-1969, when growth rates were substantial. Observe too the recession of 1970 when the GNP growth rate was actually negative. A production gap still existed in 1973 and 1974 in spite of real growth rates of 6 percent in 1972 and 1973. In these cases the economic growth rate was good but not sufficient to eliminate the production gap and all of the excessive unemployment. As mentioned earlier, it takes a 4 percent annual increase in the GNP just to stabilize the level of unemployment. It requires an additional three percentage points in economic growth to reduce unemployment one percent. In 1972, with a real growth rate of 6.4 percent, unemployment declined from 5.9 in January, 1972, to 5.1 in January, 1973. Although unemployment declined further to 4.5 percent in mid-1973, a production gap of approximately $40 billion still existed in late 1973 and early 1974, and unemployment was still above the full employment level.

FORECASTING THE GNP THROUGH ECONOMIC GROWTH

There are several methods of projecting economic growth or of estimating the future GNP, but it should be remembered that they are estimates and not precise measurements. Projected growth can be based on past experience, or new data can be constructed regarding the future.

Extrapolating the Trend Line

One fairly simple and often used method of showing future economic growth and estimating the GNP at a future date is by extrapolating the trend line of a time series of the GNP. This method has certain weaknesses and must be used with definite reservations. The estimated GNP will be fairly accurate provided that economic variables, such as population changes, technological development, productivity, hours of work, and the rate of unemployment, remain constant. Of course, the actual growth may deviate from the trend line because of cyclical fluctuations. Furthermore, the actual growth rate may be greater or less than the trend line if the economy expands at a slower or faster pace than the extrapolated line.

Another difficulty with this method is that it is possible to have different trend lines depending on the dates used in calculating the trend line. In fact, quite a controversy has developed among some of our leading national economists regarding the size of the gap between potential employment and output and actual employment and output.

An example of a trend line extrapolation is shown in Figure 21-2. Note that the GNP for 1985, using an annual 4.2 percent real growth rate factor, is expected to be in the vicinity of $2.0 trillion in terms of 1971 dollars and rise to $2.5 trillion by 1990. If a 3 percent inflation rate factor is added to this forecast, the 1985 projection would read well over $3 trillion in current

FIGURE 21-2

The GNP, which was $1,288 billion in 1973, will rise to nearly $2 trillion by 1985 in terms of 1971 dollars. In the meantime, GNP per worker will grow from about $13,000 to nearly $20,000 per worker.

SOURCE: *A Look at Business in 1990.* A summary of the White House Conference on the Industrial World Ahead (Washington: U.S. Government Printing Office, 1972).

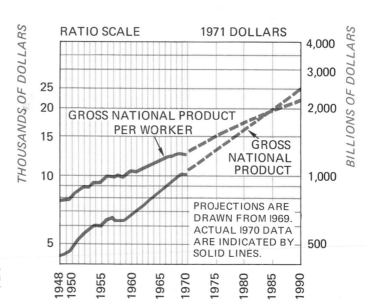

1985 dollars. Observe, too, that the GNP per worker will rise from about $13,000 per worker in 1971 to nearly $20,000 per worker in 1985 in terms of 1971 dollars.

Growth-Rate Formula

The future trend line of the GNP may also be projected by using the following steps: (1) Calculate the average annual increase in GNP for the past few decades or some similar time period; (2) make adjustments necessary in this average to account for any factor that will cause the economy to expand at a faster rate or slower rate in the future; (3) apply this growth rate cumulatively for the number of years in the period between the present and the year for which it is desired to estimate the GNP. This, of course, is merely a variation of the compound interest rate formula and can be stated as follows: $GNP_n = GNP_o (1 + r)^n$, where GNP_n is the future gross national product, GNP_o is the current GNP, r is the annual rate of economic growth, and n is the number of years between the current and desired future date for which the GNP is estimated.

This method suffers from some of the same weaknesses as the first method, extrapolating the trend line. First, the rate of economic growth based on past periods may differ depending on the years observed. Second, the rate of growth may change for some unforeseeable reason in the future. Third, the actual GNP may deviate from the projected GNP in any given year because of business fluctuations. Nevertheless, certain estimates of the GNP made on this basis are possible. If a growth rate of 3.5 percent is used, the estimated GNP for 1985 in constant 1970 dollars is $1,635 billion. Using the same formula, but applying an average growth rate of 4 percent, would yield a GNP for 1985 in the vicinity of $1.76 trillion. Various estimates of the GNP for 1985 based on selected growth rates are shown in Table 21-3.

TABLE 21-3

ESTIMATED GNP FOR 1985 BY GROWTH RATES

GNP 1970 (Billions of Dollars)	Growth Rate (Percent)	Estimated GNP 1985 [1] (Billions of Dollars)
	3.5	$1,635
	4.0	1,758
$976	4.5	1,888
	5.0	2,029

[1] In constant 1970 dollars.

Labor Force Formula

Another popular method of projecting the GNP into the future is by use of a formula that employs labor force and productivity projections. This method also can be used in any current period to calculate the GNP needed to maintain full employment and to measure the gap between potential and actual GNP. The potential output of goods and services can be calculated by multiplying the size of the labor force times hours per worker per year times output per man-hour. This may be stated as follows: GNP = Labor Force × Hours per Worker × Output per Man-hour. A number of forecasts using this method have indicated a GNP of more than $1.7 trillion for 1985 in terms of constant 1970 dollars. One such estimate is shown in the series of Figures 21-3 through 21-6.

Figure 21-3 shows the estimated GNP for 1985 at $1,738 billion using the formula mentioned above, or a 77 percent increase in the 15-year period. Figure 21-4 indicates that the estimate will approach $2.8 trillion if a 3 percent annual price inflation factor is incorporated into the calculation. For numerous reasons not all industries will grow at the same rate. Figure 21-5 shows some categories growing at a much faster rate and others at slower rates. Although average industrial growth for the 15-year period will be 93.0 percent, some industries will grow by 150 to 250 percent while many others will grow less than 50 percent, and a few will actually decline. As a result of this 3.9 percent annual growth, average family income will rise to well above $10,000 by 1985. Furthermore, as shown in Figure 21-6, the growth will result in a considerable impact on income distribution with many more families moving into the higher income brackets, and the existence of poverty, as we know it today, reduced to a minimum.

YEAR	EMPLOYMENT (MILLIONS)		HOURS PER YEAR		MAN-HOURS OF WORK		OUTPUT PER MAN-HOUR		GNP
1970 =	78.6	×	1,934	=	152.0 BILLION	×	$6.41	=	$974 BILLION
1985 =	100.6	×	1,846	=	185.7 BILLION	×	$9.36	=	$1,738 BILLION
	UP 28%		DOWN 4.6%		UP 22%		UP 46%		UP 77%

FIGURE 21-3

**GROSS NATIONAL PRODUCT
1970 and 1985***

SOURCE: Adapted from *The American Economy—Prospects for Growth to 1985*. McGraw-Hill Economics Department, 1972.

* In 1970 dollars.

Using a 3.9 percent annual growth rate, employment times output per man-hour will yield a GNP of $1.7 trillion by 1985, as measured in constant 1970 dollars.

MEASURES TO ACCELERATE ECONOMIC GROWTH

A number of steps or measures have been suggested that will increase our rate of economic growth. Some of these are designed to bring actual production closer to our potential capacity. Others will not only increase actual output but also will increase total capacity to produce. A number of the measures are quantitative in nature, while others are qualitative. Some measures will increase total output by increasing the input of labor, resources, and capital; others will increase total output by increasing the output per unit of input. No attempt is made here to analyze the merits of each of the measures suggested below, but it should be remembered that each involves a cost, and some cost more than others. Nor is any attempt made at this point to evaluate the total effectiveness of each measure, since this will vary as a result of circumstances and changes in other factors. The measures to promote economic growth are classified into three broad categories: the *labor factor*, the *investment factor*, and the *consumption factor*.

The Labor Factor

Since labor is essential to all forms of production, some gain in total production and capacity can be obtained from an increase in the total labor input or from an increase in the productivity of labor by a variety of measures.

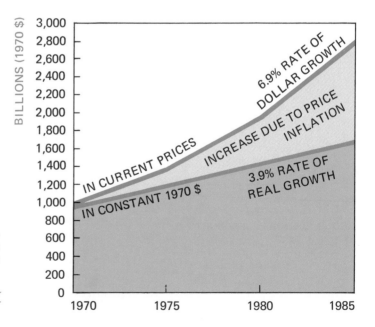

FIGURE 21-4

**GNP
1970-1985**

If an inflationary factor of 3 percent is added to the real growth rate, the GNP in 1985 will approach $2.8 trillion.

SOURCE: *The American Economy—Prospects for Growth to 1985*. McGraw-Hill Eonomics Department, 1972.

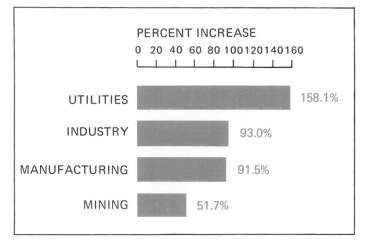

FIGURE 21-5

INDUSTRIAL GROWTH PROJECTIONS 1970-1985

Some industries will grow at a faster rate than others in the next decade or more.

SOURCE: *The American Economy—Prospects for Growth to 1985.* McGraw-Hill Economics Department, 1972.

PERCENT INCREASE

0 20 40 60 80 100 120 140 160

UTILITIES — 158.1%
INDUSTRY — 93.0%
MANUFACTURING — 91.5%
MINING — 51.7%

Increases in the Size of the Labor Force. Such increases could come from an increase in the population or an increase in the labor force participation rate. Although little could be expected from changes in the birthrate, especially in the short-run period, the size of the labor force could be increased substantially through immigration. The total impact this would have on economic growth, of course, would depend on the percentage increase in the immigration rate and on the vocational, educational, and professional level of the immigrants.

The size of the labor force also can be increased through an increase in the labor force participation rate. In recent years the rate has been about 40 to 42 percent of the total population. In past decades it was a few percentage points higher, and during the emergency of World War II it was as high as 46 percent. An increase in the labor force participation rate of one percent would add 2.1 million persons to the labor force. This would yield an increase of approximately 2.7 percent, or $35 billion, to the GNP. Such an increase easily could be attained in the labor force, since there are many nonmembers who would gladly enter the labor force if they thought that jobs were available. Many retirees would be delighted to return to active employment, youngsters would accept part-time jobs after school, and many housewives, especially those with grown families, could be encouraged to take jobs.

Increase in the Quality of the Labor Force. Formal education has been instrumental in raising the productivity of our labor force over the past several decades. Since nearly 23 percent of our population over 25 years of age has not completed high school and another 14.4 percent has not finished grade school, it is readily apparent that there is room for improvement, particularly among minority groups, in the educational standards of our labor

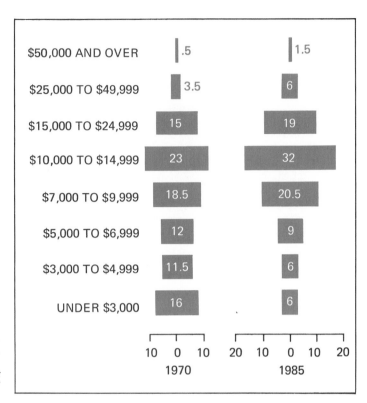

FIGURE 21-6

REDISTRIBUTION OF INCOME
Percent of Households in Income Class (1970 Dollars)

More than one half of American families will have incomes exceeding $10,000 per annum by 1985, as measured in constant 1970 dollars.

SOURCE: *The American Economy—Prospects for Growth to 1985.* McGraw-Hill Economics Department, 1972.

	1970	1985
$50,000 AND OVER	.5	1.5
$25,000 TO $49,999	3.5	6
$15,000 TO $24,999	15	19
$10,000 TO $14,999	23	32
$7,000 TO $9,999	18.5	20.5
$5,000 TO $6,999	12	9
$3,000 TO $4,999	11.5	6
UNDER $3,000	16	6

force. The median school years completed was 12.2 years as of 1972. Not only should youngsters be encouraged to remain in high school, but more should be encouraged to go beyond the high school level. In the matter of formal education, it has been estimated that an additional year of schooling would add about 10 percent to the productivity of the average worker. It has been estimated, however, that adding one year to the educational level of the labor force could within a few decades raise total productivity by 5 to 7 percent. This objective of raising the educational level by one year could be attained without the loss of the youngster to the labor force simply by accelerating the educational program in order to permit students to complete their education in a shorter period of time or by giving them more education in a given period of time.

In addition to raising the level of formal education, the quality of the labor force can be improved through training programs. Whether they be company and/or union sponsored training programs, adult education courses, vocational education programs in the high school, or training and retraining projects sponsored by local civic and charitable organizations, each can have an effect on worker productivity and result in upgrading the worker and his contribution to economic growth. The merits of development and training are manifest by the Area Redevelopment Act, the Manpower Development and Training Act, many state worker-training programs, and even by the Economic Opportunity Act. The combined effect of retraining under these various acts has resulted in improving the productivity of millions of workers in the past several years.

Longer Hours. Economic growth can be accelerated also by adjusting standard hours of work per week or per day. Although it is conceivable that due to the law of diminishing marginal productivity an increase in hours could actually result in a decrease in total productivity, in all probability the marginal product of the worker per additional hour is still a positive figure. Consequently, total productivity and economic growth could be raised by an increase in the number of hours worked. An expansion of the average workweek, however, would seem to be a move against the trend of shorter hours.

More Efficient Use of Labor. It is possible to obtain greater output from more efficient use of labor in many ways. For instance, the elimination of featherbedding on various types of jobs would enhance productivity per worker and free displaced workers for production elsewhere. In many cases, this would require union-management cooperation. In addition, worker mobility, both occupational and geographic, should be improved in an effort to increase economic growth. Workers should learn that in a growing and dynamic economy they may at sometime in their life be forced to learn a new trade or skill. The need for some skills lessens or becomes nonexistent, and the demand for many new skills arises. And, being realistic, workers cannot expect to remain in a particular geographical area all their lives. At the present time, over one fifth of our nation's population changes residence by moving across state boundaries each year.

Economic growth could also be improved by the removal of racial and sexual barriers in the labor market. Frequently qualified, skilled, and professional workers are denied access to jobs with greater productivity because of discrimination. Thus, discrimination prevents the maximum utilization of a large segment of our labor force. The elimination of discrimination could add noticeably to the national product.

It is also quite possible that economic growth could be affected by the promotion of greater safety among workers. It is estimated that the potential GNP is reduced by approximately 4 percent as a result of labor time lost through sickness and accidents. It is also estimated that about $7 billion in total production is lost as a result of excess labor in the agricultural industry. In still another area approximately $2.6 billion in production is lost annually because potential workers are in prison or engaged in criminal activities instead of productive labor. Auto accident fatalities cause the death of over 50,000 persons each year, of which approximately 20,000 are members of the labor force. The resultant loss of production from this cause is approximately $250 million annually. Some mention, too, should be made about the loss of work due to death and injuries resulting from wars and accidents other than those in autos. The annual loss in production in any particular year as a result of the cumulative number of deaths over the previous years amounts to billions of dollars.

The Investment Factor

Since there is a high correlation between capital investment and total productivity in the American economy, any measures that will increase the total capital outlay or improve the productivity of the capital outlay per dollar of investment will help to accelerate the growth of economic activity in our economy.

Private Sector. At the present time, total assets of corporations alone exceed $1,000 billion. Total national expenditures on plant and equipment have been between $100 to $125 billion annually for the past several years. The amount of assets at the disposal of the average factory worker is in the vicinity of $26,000. Investment per worker in machinery and equipment ranges all the way from $113,500 in the petroleum industry to $4,500 in the leather industry. Obviously the productivity of a worker is increased by the use of additional capital at his disposal. In fact, it has been estimated that an increase of $10 billion, or less than .5 percent, in total private investment in the economy will increase the GNP by approximately $1 billion per year indefinitely.

Another source indicates that we should step up the proportion of total national output going into private investment. Currently the proportion is about 15 percent, which includes expenditures on both commercial and residential construction, as well as producers' durable goods. It should be advanced to a higher percentage in order to set in motion a slow but progressive reduction in the average age of America's stock of plant and equipment.

On this matter, a number of economic organizations early in the 1960s, including the Committee for Economic Development, made a strong point that among the many reasons for the current low rate of private investment, one of the most important was the high rate of taxation on corporate profits. Consequently, in addition to a reduction in personal income taxes, they suggested a program for reducing corporate taxes.

Such measures as the 7 percent tax credit allowance for new investment, larger and faster depreciation allowances, and corporate tax cuts stimulate the rate of investment. By means of comparison, the major reason for the 10 to 11 percent annual GNP increase in the Japanese economy in recent years is their over 30 percent investment/GNP ratio.

Public Sector. In addition to private investment in the economy, there are large outlays of public investment made each year. Capital expenditures for roads, dams, waterways, scientific research, and educational facilities have a definite effect on the productivity of the nation.

Savings. Since savings are a prime source of funds for investment, it is essential to increase the supply of savings if it is desired to accelerate the growth of the economy via the investment route. Perhaps even more important, since bank credit is usually available when savings are inadequate, is the job of assuring that any additional savings will be invested. Businessmen and others do not borrow and invest unless they foresee profits. Consequently, steps would have to be taken to stimulate investment in the economy. In addition to the reductions in corporation profit taxes, accelerated depreciation allowances for tax purposes, and tax credits for new investments mentioned previously, liberalized monetary policies and reduced interest rates also can serve to induce businesses to borrow and invest.

Research and Development. Since a tremendous amount of new investment results from the implementation of ideas and the commercialization of new products discovered through research, investment in the economy can be increased through the stimulation of research. New ideas, new methods, and new products generate production and require capital outlays, which in turn accelerate economic growth. Therefore, the devotion of more resources, both manpower and capital, to research would prove profitable to the nation. Since similar benefits flow from public investment in research, the channeling of more tax receipts into government research activities can enhance economic growth. In addition, government subsidies for nonpublic research also can prove to be helpful. At the present time $30 billion annually is being spent on R & D by businesses, government, and universities in the United States. This is forecast to double by 1985.

Automation. In the areas of both private and public investment, total productivity can be increased by acceleration of technological development and automation. For maximum economic growth, measures should be undertaken to stimulate research and development of new types of machinery and equipment. Restrictions and barriers by employers, employees, and unions to the implementation of automated methods should be limited if a higher growth rate is desired. Although certain problems arise in connection with automation, especially temporary displacement of workers and unemployment, efforts should be made to alleviate the probelms connected with automation rather than endeavoring to restrict or prevent automation itself.

It is apparent that we often produce at less than capacity and that we could accelerate our rate of economic growth, but an important factor restraining the maximization of economic growth is the lack of a continuous demand for goods and services sufficient to clear our maximum potential GNP off the market. There is no doubt that if ample demand for goods and services were always present, we would maintain a full employment level and spend our efforts seeking ways and means of rapidly increasing our total output. Obviously, then, an important stimulus for accelerating economic growth lies in the realm of maintaining the demand for goods and services.

Fiscal Policy. The presence of insufficient demand at various times in the past few decades has influenced much of the fiscal policy of the federal government. Convinced that the slack in our economy and the failure to attain a higher rate of economic growth were due to an insufficiency of effective demand, various administrations have used government expenditures financed through deficit spending in order to bolster inadequate demand. In this regard tax reductions, designed to stimulate both consumption and investment, have been applied to both corporations and individuals. Without endeavoring to argue the merits of such a tax reduction program, it can be said that tax cuts have had some effect in raising the level of effective demand in the economy and have aided in stimulating economic growth, especially when one considers the multiplier and accelerator effects of the increased spending.

In addition, spending for emergency public works has been used as a method of increasing effective demand in the economy. Various international trade measures have been used to encourage exports and, consequently, have had a stimulating effect on business activity for the economy. The implementation of manpower development and training programs and anti-poverty programs, although designed to deal primarily with the retraining of workers and the reduction of poverty, gave an impetus to the economy through their effect on total demand.

Monetary Policy. Measures designed to liberalize the money supply and to reduce rates of interest can have some influence on the level of effective demand. Readily available funds at low interest rates can encourage borrowing for investment purposes. Thus, the whole gamut of Federal Reserve and Treasury controls may be used in this direction, unless, of course, inflationary pressures begin to appear in the economy. In fact, there are those who believe that a more active and aggressive monetary policy, especially in regard to continuous increases in the money supply, could do much to stimulate economic growth in our economy. It has often been suggested that changes in the money supply are responsible for changes in investment, which in turn have a dominant influence on the level of economic activity and the rate of economic growth.

Such international monetary measures as floating exchange rates, SDRs, and devaluation, which are actually designed to encourage exports, also can have a positive effect on investment and economic growth. Likewise, monetary policy can be utilized in such a manner that it will increase consumption. Since the production of consumers' goods and services is such a sizable portion, approximately 63 percent, of our national income, even a small boost in consumer demand can have a noticeable effect on the GNP and the rate of economic growth. Consequently, readily available money and liberal financing conditions, which facilitate the purchase of housing, automobiles, and other big ticket items, make the attainment of a higher rate of economic growth less burdensome.

Business Promotion of Consumption. Producers and retailers can do more to stimulate consumption with new and better products, more effective advertising, and improved customer service. New methods of distribution, new marketing techniques, and lower prices can also help stimulate consumer buying.

RELATED PROBLEMS OF ECONOMIC GROWTH

A great many other suggestions of a minor nature could be made regarding the acceleration of economic growth. The larger measures we have been discussing suggest that there is little doubt of our capability of attaining a greater rate of economic growth if we desire it. However, a number of complications arise in this regard.

First, it is apparent that many of the measures that would accelerate economic growth would aggravate old problems or bring new ones to the economy. For example, we could hasten automation to spur economic growth, but this would add to the problem of structural unemployment. We could easily increase the size of the labor force to produce more goods and services, but would we have sufficient demand for the additional production? We could encourage more savings in the economy, but there may not be sufficient investment opportunities to absorb the additional amount of savings. Additions to our total productive capacity, while increasing our production base and growth rate potential, may not be utilized because of an insufficient demand for goods and services. If we really want growth, the workweek could be lengthened. But this would bring forth some opposition, especially by those who are seeking a reduced workweek without a reduction in total take-home pay.

Increased public spending in many directions is suggested for accelerating economic growth. However, if the spending is financed through taxation, consumers and investors will be forced to give up some of their demand for goods and services. If deficit financing is used instead, it will increase the size of an already growing national debt. The same might be said for deficit financed tax reductions as a measure of attaining a higher growth rate. In this case, where do the burdens of the debt begin to outweigh the advantages of a higher growth rate? Furthermore, in seeking a faster growth rate, the economy might be pushed into an inflationary situation. If so, how do we measure the adverse effects of inflation against the benefits of greater growth?

Since it is a primary task of the economy to choose among the alternative uses of resources and manpower, to what extent will a higher growth rate facilitate this task? To what extent will the consumers have the final say in how our resources are to be utilized? In line with this thinking, there is no assurance that what we need is the attainment of a certain overall or general growth rate. Perhaps what is needed more is the establishment of discriminatory growth rates, seeking greater expansion in some sectors of the economy compared to other sectors. In such a case, the task of aggregate economic growth would be a little more difficult to accomplish.

Who Makes the Decisions?

It is certain that many of the measures suggested to achieve a higher rate of economic growth would involve government intervention in and government direction of the economy. This, of course, means some loss of economic freedom. Therefore, we may have to face the problem of how much of our existing economic freedom we desire to sacrifice in the interest of a higher rate of economic growth. In this connection, who would set the goals? The Employment Act, for example, could be amended easily to refer to a specific rate of growth instead of the general goal of maximum production. If the specific rate of economic growth were not attained over a particular period of time, whose responsibility would it be to see that it was achieved and how much control would be exercised in seeking the specific rate of growth?

Cost of Economic Growth

It is obvious that we cannot think in terms of economic growth by itself. Growth for the sake of growth is not a worthy objective. Even the idea of growth for the purpose of staying ahead of competitor nations has a shallow ring. Growth does have a function in terms of providing adequate production, employment, and income. It is also important in terms of raising the standard of living and providing for national defense. But growth has a cost, in terms of leisure, freedom, and government intervention, which in many respects is still unmeasured. It is also probable that many of the purposes, objectives, or functions served by economic growth could be attained by other means, such as disarmament, more emphasis on noneconomic values, or limitations on the official size of our labor force.

SUMMARY

1. Economic growth is a social and political issue as well as an economic issue.

2. It is essential for our economy to grow at 4 percent annually in order to avoid the development of unemployment and a deterioration of our level of living.

3. Economic growth has been one of our major economic goals for the past 15 years or more.

4. Economic growth can be measured in several ways, but generally the most useful is in terms of GNP.

5. The economic growth rate for decades averaged about 3 percent annually for the U.S. economy, but in the past several years it has grown at 4 to 6 percent annually. Several foreign nations, however, have had higher growth rates than the United States.

6. There appears to be an inverse relationship between the growth rate and the level of unemployment in the U.S. economy.

7. Three methods of forecasting economic growth through the GNP are: extrapolation of the trend, the growth rate formula, and the labor force formula.

8. Several forecasts place the GNP in the vicinity of $1.7 to $2.0 trillion by 1985 (in terms of 1970 or 1971 dollars), with some sectors of the economy growing at a more rapid rate than others.

9. There are numerous methods of accelerating the economic growth rate. These include improving the size, quality, and uses of the labor force; increasing private and public investment; and raising the level of consumption.

10. Economic growth has a price in terms of problems related to that growth.

NEW TERMS

Economic growth, *p. 457*
Actual growth rate, *p. 459*
Potential growth rate, *p. 459*
Growth rate formula, *p. 464*

Labor force formula, *p. 464*
Labor factor, *p. 466*
Investment factor, *p. 470*
Consumption factor, *p. 472*

QUESTIONS FOR DISCUSSION AND ANALYSIS

1. Should a specific growth rate be set for the American economy? If so, what should it be?

2. Does it matter what our growth rate is so long as we have a high level of employment?

3. In what channels should the benefits of economic growth be directed: more consumer goods and services; more conventional public service; more socioeconomic measures; or more leisure

for members of the labor force?

4. What alternatives to economic growth can you suggest for the purpose of attaining some of the objectives sought through economic growth?

5. Should the fact that some foreign economies are growing at a faster rate than the United States economy be a cause of concern? Why or why not?

6. To what extent is our present

defense budget, in the vicinity of $75 to $80 billion annually, serving as a stimulus to economic growth?

7. How does investment affect the growth rate of an economy?

8. Should the growth rate of the U.S. economy, along with the level of unemployment, be made a political issue in presidential elections? Give your reasons.

9. Of what value are forecasts of economic growth and GNP to economists, government officials, and businessmen?

10. Do you see any dangers in the loss of economic freedom that might be entailed wih the measures to promote a higher rate of economic growth?

SUGGESTED READINGS

A Look at Business in 1990, A Summary of the White House Conference on the Industrial World Ahead. Washington: U.S. Government Printing Office, November, 1972.

"A Look at the Great Economy of 1985." *Business Week* (December 18, 1971).

Campbell, Walter J. "Is There Still Time to Save U.S. Industry?" *Industry Week* (October 4, 1971).

Deming, F. L. *The Numbers Game—A Sudy of Economic Growth.* Minneapolis: Macalester College, 1960.

Department of Labor. *U.S. Manpower in the 1970's.* Washington: U.S. Government Printing Office, 1970.

Eitman, Wilford J. "Investment in the Decade of the Seventies." *Michigan Business Review* (January, 1971).

Goals for Americans, The Report of the President's Commission on National Goals. Englewood Cliffs, N.J.: Prentice-Hall, Inc., 1960, pp. 163-190.

Knowles, J. W. "The Potential Economic Growth in the United States," Study Paper No. 20, prepared for the Joint Economic Committee, 86th Congress, 2d Session. *Employment, Growth, and Price Levels.* Washington: U.S. Government Printing Office, 1960.

Landsberg, Hans H. *Natural Resources for U.S. Growth.* Baltimore: The Johns Hopkins University Press, 1964.

The American Economy: Prospects for Growth to 1985. New York: McGraw-Hill Book Company, 1972.

The Seventies—A Look Ahead at the New Decade. Princeton, N.J.: Dow Jones Books, 1970.

"The U.S. Labor Force Projections to 1985." *Monthly Labor Review* (August, 1970).

Wallich, Henry C. *The Cost of Freedom.* New York: Harper & Row, Publishers, 1960.

"White House Conferees Seek Answers to 1990 Business Problems." *Commerce Today* (February 7, 1972).

22

Growth, Problems, and Priorities

PREVIEW   Most analysts are pleased with the long-run outlook for our economy. But as the economy grows, so will the related problems of pollution, congestion, energy shortages, and the depletion of resources. The annual growth dividend, in the form of additional productive capacity, can be used to provide additional consumer goods and services, or it can be used to alleviate some of the existing and growing problems of the economy. Worldwide disarmament would provide an additional dividend insofar as it would release manpower and resources to be devoted to uses other than defense and war production. In addition to preserving the natural environment, other long-run problems or goals of the economy deal with the elimination of poverty, the guaranteed annual income, national health insurance, urban redevelopment, mass transit, consumerism, improvements in the quality of life, and energy, food, and fuel shortages.

Economic growth is not all milk and honey. It is true that growth will provide more jobs, higher incomes, shorter working hours, and additional goods and services, but there is a price to pay. As the population and the gross national product grow, related problems develop. Congested cities, crowded highways, urban blight, foul air, polluted water, higher noise levels, energy shortages, and resource depletions are but a few of the present side effects, or external effects, of growth which become more acute as the economy expands. In fact, some critics of growth, more seriously than not, have referred to the GNP as the gross national pollution.

SIDE EFFECTS OF GROWTH

In earlier decades there was little concern over the *external effects of economic growth.* In fact, in the 1930s, 1940s, and 1950s the billowing of smoke from factory chimneys was a welcome sight because it meant jobs, income, food, and shelter for families. At other times it was an indication of active defense production essential to winning a war. The external effects of such production were minimal and were considered as something to be tolerated in order to obtain the advantages of high level production, employment, and income. With continued economic growth, however, the cumulative side effects became a concern. When streams and rivers were unable to absorb and cleanse burgeoning effluents of pollutants, when the air in many areas became saturated with gaseous and particulate matter, when the noises from large jet airports became unbearable, when energy blackouts occurred, when cities became too congested, when highways and roads became overcrowded, and when resource shortages became more frequent, the people of the nation became concerned about the adverse external effects of economic growth.

Consequently, in the 1960s individuals, business firms, civic organizations, naturalists, and government agencies and legislators, among others, began to call for action to remedy the situation. Antipollution laws were passed, federal funds appropriated, and business resources allocated for cleaning up and preserving the environment. Although we still have a long way to go, there is much more being done in this direction today than there was a decade ago. Consumers still want jobs, income, and goods and services, but they also desire clean air, pure water, noise abatement, decent housing, safe roads, spacious cities, reliable sources of energy, and a general improvement in the quality of life. Only when we are ready to make a national commitment and consumers are willing to pay the cost, whether in higher prices or a reduction in consumer goods production, will we optimize the blending between output and its external effects.

Looking ahead into the next 30 years, the demand for some materials, such as copper, iron, zinc, lumber, petroleum, and coal, will double. The demand for nuclear energy will be 100 times as great as it is today. It will take nearly twice as much food to feed the growing population, and the economy will use 2.5 times more electricity by 1990. Such demands will put heavy strains on the economy. In fact, there are some forecasters who are predicting dire shortages by that time.[1] Consequently, there is need for much exploration to find and exploit new sources of resources, as well as an increasing need for large scale R & D to develop substitute materials.

Although we produce many goods and services and our output and consumption will continue to grow, our productive capacity is not infinite. In the future, even more than in the past, selections will have to be made and choices determined by consumers, businesses, and the government. National priorities will have to be established. We can, for example, have more goods and services and tolerate additional pollution. On the other hand, we may devote more resources and manpower to preserving the natural environment and be satisfied with a slower growth rate in the production of consumer goods and services. We can produce more autos and further clog our roads and highways, restrict the output and use of autos, or devote more resources and manpower to building more and better roadways. We can have faster

---

[1] Dennis L. Meadows, *Limits to Growth* (New York: Universe Books, 1972).

jets along with more noise and pollution, or we can choose slower travel, less noise, and less air pollution. We can use more electrical conveniences and risk energy blackouts, get by with fewer conveniences, or devote more financing to develop additional sources of energy.

Economic decisions are generally made through the market mechanism. Consumers are not always fully informed, however, regarding the true price of their choices, especially when it comes to external costs of producing goods and services. As the external effects become more acute, however, perhaps consumers will become more aware of these costs in making their choices.

THE GROWTH DIVIDEND

One way of looking at where we are going and the resources and manpower we have to devote to additional output is through the *growth dividend*. Assuming that we obtain a projected real economic growth rate of 4 percent or more annually during the 1970s, this means an approximate annual gain of $50 billion in the next few years, rising to a real gain of approximately $60 billion annually by the end of the decade. Some analysts refer to this in a broad sense as the growth dividend. Thus, a major question arises. How will we use this additional output of goods and services? Traditionally the decisions of what and how much to produce have been decided primarily in the marketplace. We no doubt will continue to use this mechanism in the future for deciding the kinds of goods and services to produce. Consequently, a sizable portion of our future increases in productivity will be in the form of consumer goods and services and private investment.

There is a specific amount of our productivity gain, however, that readily can be shifted in one direction or another by forces other than those of the marketplace. The initial influence or control of this segment of goods and services comes in the form of higher taxes. If existing federal tax rates are maintained in a growing economy, they tend to produce increasing tax revenues. It is estimated that at current tax rates, for example, a $50 billion increase in the GNP will produce an additional $18.5 billion in federal revenue. Approximately one half of this increment is absorbed in providing existing services, referred to as baseline expenditures, for the additional population. This leaves a residual of $9 to $10 billion which, in a narrow sense, is more often referred to as the growth dividend.

One estimate of the growth dividend is that projected by the President's Council of Economic Advisers. According to its estimate, Table 22-1 shows the constant dollar (1969 = 100) GNP rising from $931 billion in 1969 to

TABLE 22-1

REAL GROSS NATIONAL PRODUCT, 1955, 1966, AND 1969, AND PROJECTIONS FOR 1975-1976

(Billions of Dollars, 1969 Prices)

Claim	Actuals			Projections	
	1955	1966	1969	1975	1976
Gross National Product Available	569.0	845.5	931.4	1,199	1,251
Claims on Available GNP	569.0	845.5	931.4	1,188	1,232
Federal Government Purchases	69.8	88.3	101.3	83	83
State and Local Government Purchases	53.8	94.4	110.8	140	144
Personal Consumption Expenditures .	344.3	519.2	577.5	768	802
Gross Private Domestic Investment ..	96.9	137.5	139.8	192	198
Business Fixed Investment	55.1	92.0	99.3	128	134
Residential Structures	34.5	29.4	32.0	52	52
Change in Business Inventories ...	7.3	16.1	8.5	12	13
Net Exports of Goods and Services ..	4.2	6.1	1.9	5	5
Unallocated Resources	.0	.0	.0	11	19
Addendum: Federal Surplus or Deficit (−), National Income Accounts Basis	5.6	−.2	9.3	25	32
Per Capita Personal Consumption Expenditures	2,083	2,637	2,842	3,529	3,641

SOURCE: *Economic Report of the President,* 1971.

$1,199 billion in 1975 and $1,251 billion by 1976. Since the normal claims against the GNP by the government, consumers, and private investors will equal $1,188 billion in 1975 and $1,232 in 1976, this leaves unallocated resources of $11 billion for 1975 and $19 billion for 1976. This unallocated portion of the growth dividend will be equivalent to 1 to 2 percent of the GNP by the mid-1970s. In analyzing the table one must remember that federal purchases represent outlays for goods and services only. They do not include transfer payments or grants-in-aid. Total federal spending, including these latter items, was projected to rise from about $185 billion in 1969 to $216 billion in 1975 in terms of constant 1969 dollars. This included a $4 billion rise in baseline expenditures along with a $15 billion increase for new initiatives. This, of course, would absorb much of the scheduled unallocated 1 to 2 percent increase in our GNP for 1975 and 1976.

THE PEACE AND DISARMAMENT DIVIDENDS

We will see subsequently that production increments from our average annual growth rate in the economy are available for various uses, whether in the form of additional private production or social production. At the height of America's involvement in the war in Vietnam, there was much discussion about the probability that another sizable portion of our total production could be redistributed when peace came in Vietnam. It was suggested that the so-called *peace dividend* would be available for increasing the production of consumer goods and services, for increasing savings, for private investment, or for the provision of additional government and social services. In order to obtain some idea of the potential size of the peace dividend, it is necessary for us to look at the defense sector of the economy.

Potential Size of the Peace Dividend

Although there was some uncertainty about the exact amount, the Department of Defense estimated that at the height of American involvement in Vietnam about $27 billion of the $80 billion 1969 defense budget was allocated to spending for the war in Vietnam. With peace talks going on in Paris, the U.S. troop withdrawal already in progress, and the attempts to Vietnamize the war by having South Vietnam take over a greater share of the military action, questions naturally arose regarding the effect on our domestic economy of a U.S. withdrawal from Vietnam. Would it cause a recession? If not, how would the decline of $27 billion in defense spending be offset? Would it be through government spending elsewhere in the economy? Would we cut taxes and rely on the private sector of the economy to increase spending as an offset to the decrease in defense spending?

Many special interest groups had an eye on the peace dividend, hoping for a share when it was redistributed. In fact, some were hoping that the peace dividend would be used to finance many socioeconomic projects; but, for a number of reasons, the size of the peace dividend was not to be as large as it first appeared. First, it could not be expected that there would be an absolute moratorium for spending in Vietnam once peace was established. Troop withdrawal was to be gradual. Furthermore, it was anticipated that many of our military men, instead of being discharged, would be redeployed to other troubled spots throughout the world. Second, it would be necessary to police the peace. Consequently, some troops were to be left in Indo-China. Third, some form of aid probably would be extended for reconstruction and development in Vietnam. Finally, some of the spending in Vietnam would be transferred to the normal growth and development in the general defense program.

What Happened to the Peace Dividend?

Although the number of U.S. troops in Vietnam was reduced from 550,000 at the height of the war to a few thousand by the fall of 1972, spending on national defense did not decrease proportionally. The defense outlays in years 1968 to 1970 ran at approximately $80 billion annually. They were reduced to $76 billion in 1973. But they appeared to bottom out at that level. In spite of the reduction of U.S. troops in Vietnam, defense spending was scheduled to rise to $81 billion in 1974 and to nearly $88 billion in 1975. What happened to the expected peace dividend? For one thing, much of the spending for Vietnam was transferred to the regular defense budget, which had suffered during our peak involvement in Vietnam. Second, another large portion of the supposed savings was obliterated as a result of the inflationary effects on the regular defense budget. Moreover, the number of persons in the armed services were not reduced in proportion to the pull-out of troops from Vietnam. Troops in some cases were redeployed elsewhere. Also, some military personnel were left in Indo-China for emergency purposes. Thus, the peace dividend did not materialize to any sizable degree.

New Hope—The Disarmament Dividend

Currently the major powers of the world are engaged in Strategic Arms Limitation Talks (SALT). As these serious, albeit sporadic, meetings bear fruit, they hopefully will result in substantial disarmament in the future that should produce a sizable *disarmament dividend* for the United States and others.

ALTERNATIVE USES OF THE DIVIDEND

Somewhere along the line a decision will have to be made in regard to the use or uses of the potential growth dividend. Basically, it can be allocated in several directions—in the form of lower taxes, for the accumulation of a budget surplus, or for increased government spending.

More specifically, the benefits of the growth dividend can be used to:

1. Expand existing federal services and programs, especially those not now fully funded;
2. Inaugurate new federally sponsored socioeconomic programs;
3. Share revenue with states to alleviate their pressing financial needs;
4. Reduce taxes and let the private sector decide what use should be made of the growth dividend;
5. Accumulate a surplus for the purpose of retiring the federal debt.

Increase Government Services

The growth dividend may be used in whole or in part to add to total government spending via the extension of existing government services and the establishment of new programs. In addition to the extension of existing education, health, crime prevention, foreign aid, space exploration, and transportation programs, several new programs have been proposed. A number of these (such as the establishment of a guaranteed annual income, the eradication of air pollution, the rebuilding of our cities, the implementation of a national health insurance system, the elimination of poverty in America, and a federal revenue sharing program) are discussed elsewhere in this chapter.

A recent selection of some of the growth dividend programs, proposed by economists, labor leaders, businessmen, legislators, and others, compiled by the Council of Economic Advisers, added up to $40 billion per year.

Increased government spending on economic and social programs would certainly offset any adverse impact resulting from the decrease in defense spending. In this case, there would be no doubt that decreases in defense spending would be matched dollar for dollar with offsetting expenditures elsewhere in the economy. Consequently, the extension of existing governmental programs and additions of new social and economic programs have been given prime consideration, along with selective tax reductions, as a means of apportioning the disarmament-and-growth dividends. Care will have to be exercised in distributing any dividend to insure that it is used, at least in part, to reduce any inflationary pressures that exist in the economy at the time.

Federal-State Revenue Sharing

Not many people realize that state and local expenditures for goods and services exceed federal expenditures, including federal outlays for defense. In 1973, for example, the federal government's share of the GNP was $106.9 billion, while state and local expenditure amounted to $170.3 billion. Furthermore, as we saw in Chapter 20, in the next decade federal spending is going to increase moderately, while there will be a very substantial increase in the size of state and local expenditures. We are putting more and more demands on state and local governments for services of all kinds. But many municipal and state governments are hard pressed for funds to carry out their current programs. Their sources of tax revenues are limited. Property is already overtaxed; taxes on businesses often drive them to out-of-state locations; consumers resist higher sales taxes; and city and state income taxes add to the already heavy burden of the taxpayer.

With the projections of higher expenditures and limited tax sources, more and more interest is being generated in federal-state revenue sharing programs. The State and Local Fiscal Assistance Act of 1972 returns a minimal amount of federal income tax revenue to the state and local governments in order to alleviate the need for raising taxes at the state and local levels. Much praise and opposition has been aimed at this program. Various improvements have been offered, many of which involve the use of the growth dividend.

Reduce Taxes

All or a portion of the growth dividend may be used to lower taxes in order to increase consumption of goods and services. This could come in the form of lower personal income taxes or in the form of the elimination of some excise taxes. In either case, the real disposable income of consumers would increase. This would, in effect, give consumers the final decision on the use of the dividend through their decisions to spend or not to spend and by the direction of their spending. This would increase the demand for goods and services and/or savings. The total impact on the economy would depend on whether consumers were inclined to increase their demands for goods and services. Since consumers have a high rate of spending, however, it can be assumed that tax reductions would have salutary social, economic, and political effects.

Some or all of the dividend could be used to encourage investment directly by lowering business and corporate taxes, by allowing larger tax credits to stimulate investments, or by other means. The impact here is a little more uncertain. A reduction in government spending, for example, without a corresponding increase in spending elsewhere could cause some slack in the economy. Under such circumstances businessmen may be reluctant to increase investment in spite of lower taxes. On the other hand, a tax reduction that increased consumption could generate an increase in investment, even though business taxes were not decreased. Consequently, it would appear to be less desirable to use the dividend wholly for business tax reductions. Some combination of business tax reductions and other measures could prove to be more beneficial.

Accumulate a Budget Surplus

Instead of lowering taxes or increasing government spending, the growth dividend could be used in whole or in part to accumulate a budget surplus with the hope of eventually paying off some of the national debt. If the entire dividend were used for this purpose, however, it would no doubt precipitate a serious recession that could develop into a full-blown depression. To rake off $8 to $22 billion in potential purchasing power from the economy without any offsetting spending measures would cause a sizable decrease in production, employment, and income. Even if the debt were repaid, thus putting the money back into the economy, it would cause a redistribution of income toward higher income groups (the debt holders). Since it is generally assumed that these groups have a lower propensity to consume than the average for the economy, it could cause an adverse effect on production, employment, and income. Therefore, this would appear to be a less desirable choice for the use of the dividend.

It is quite reasonable, however, to assume that a portion of the dividend could be channeled in the direction of a budget surplus and subsequent reduction of the national debt. The size of the surplus accumulation would have to be watched closely, however, to make sure that it was not causing an adverse effect on the economy.

CHANGING ECONOMIC GOALS AND EMERGING PROBLEMS

During the past few decades considerable emphasis has been placed on the achievement of our primary domestic economic goals of full employment, stable prices, and a healthy rate of economic growth. Coming out of the prolonged depression of the 1930s, with its chronic unemployment, followed by World War II, which caused severe shortages of consumer goods and services, it was appropriate to stress domestic economic goals, such as maximum production, maximum employment, and maximum purchasing power. The desire for steady jobs, good wages, economic security, stable prices, and an abundance of goods and services was quite natural. By and large, during the 1950s and the 1960s the economy proved capable of attaining these goals. Indeed, continuing efforts will be made to achieve these goals and even raise our sights on them to bring unemployment below the 4 percent level, accelerate the potential rate of economic growth, and perhaps, adopt some form of a permanent "incomes policy" as a means of assuring stable prices. Nevertheless, today these goals in large part are taken for granted. Citizens of our society, although not ignoring these primary goals, are now placing more emphasis on new or supplementary goals for the economy. In addition, they are seeking fresh solutions to existing economic and social problems, learning how to handle new problems that are arising, and adopting policies to prevent the occurrence of others that may be destined for the future.

Insights into some of these goals, along with related economic problems, are given below. Several of these are analyzed in detail in other chapters of this text. With just the brief treatment given here, however, it becomes obvious that all of these goals and the solutions of contemporary economic problems cannot be attained immediately or in the short run. Thus, in the true sense of economizing, selections will have to be made and national priorities established, by the economic marketplace or otherwise, for orderly growth and progress in our economy.

Elimination of Poverty

Although we have a per capita GNP of more than $6,000 and a per capita personal income of nearly $5,000—much higher than those of any other nation—there is great concern on the part of many citizens that a large number of workers and families are still living at poverty levels. In the early 1960s one fifth of our families were living in poverty with an income of $3,000 or less per annum. From Chapter 40 we will learn that, even though the percentage of poor families had been reduced to less than 12 percent by 1973, there is still much concern about the degree of poverty in America. With continued economic growth plus help through poverty and manpower development and training programs, it is hoped that we can bring most of the poor families into the mainstream of economic life by raising their income above the poverty level by 1980.

Guaranteed Annual Income

Another proposal designed to quickly reduce poverty is the *guaranteed annual income*. This would provide a minimum income for every family regardless of whether the breadwinner worked. An early proposal of this nature was made by the Office of Economic Opportunity in the mid-1960s. Since then, the concept has been proposed by a number of other governmental agencies, labor unions, Presidential commissions, and business leaders. There have been in the last five to six years a dozen or more definite proposals, including a negative income tax plan, a family allowance plan, and a social dividend plan, some of which are detailed in Chapter 40.

One variation of the negative income tax plan is based on a current poverty level income of $4,000 per annum for a family of four. Families receiving more than $4,000 annually would pay income tax as usual. But four-person families with less than a $4,000 income would not only pay no income tax, they actually would receive a refund in the form of a negative income tax. It is estimated that the cost of this plan would be about $12 billion annually. The cost of other plans range from $12 billion to $40 billion annually. The beginnings of a guaranteed annual income plan are contained in the Nixon welfare reform bill which became stalled in the Senate after being passed by the House of Representatives in 1971. The bill provides for a basic income maintenance of $2,400 annually for all families in America. In 1972 Senator Ribicoff, a strong advocate of income maintenance, backed away from his goal of pushing an income maintenance bill through Congress, with the recommendation that more time for research and experimentation be taken before adopting such an awesome measure as income maintenance. A new approach to income maintenance, however, was being prepared by the Administration for presentation to Congress in early 1974.

A related proposal for eliminating poverty and providing income for families has been recommended by a number of study groups, both private and governmental. It would establish the federal government as an "employer of last resort." Under this concept, whenever a worker is unable to find a job, the federal government would provide employment for him. Some semblance of this concept was contained in the Congressional action of 1971 (Emergency Employment Act), which provided for federal funding of more than $1 billion annually for 150,000 to 200,000 jobs for the unemployed. These jobs were created at state and local government levels during fiscal 1972 and 1973.

There are some sociologists and others, however, who believe that we will not conquer poverty until we accept the notion that income should be divorced from work or employment. One such recommendation is that a maintenance income from the government should be given to each family or individual as an absolute constitutional right.

National Health Insurance

With the success of the medicare programs for the aged and the rising cost of medical care in general, attention is now being turned to the feasibility of medical care coverage for persons of all ages. Here again a number of bills have been formulated for introduction into Congress. Senators Kennedy and Javits, among others, have introduced national health insurance bills into Congress. United States Representatives Griffiths and Burleson have drafted national health insurance bills. A proposal has been submitted by the American Hospital Association. At the same time, the American Medical Association is supporting "Medicredit," otherwise known as the Health Insurance Assistance Act, introduced by Senator Hansen. Objectives and coverages of the bills vary. Costs vary, ranging anywhere from $8 billion to $75 billion annually. President Nixon, in an attempt to stem the tide of suggested federally financed plans, recommended in 1971 a national health plan that would be financed in large part by the private sector of the economy. In 1972 and 1973 Congress held hearings on various national health insurance plans incorporated into a number of proposed Congressional bills. Then, in early 1974, President Nixon presented a revised plan to Congress. Some of these plans will be analyzed in more detail in Chapter 40.

Preserving Our Natural Environment

People today not only want more goods and services, but they also want clean air, pure water, and noise abatement. There is a growing awareness that as production of more goods and services increases at an accelerated pace, it is taking its toll on our natural environment through air, water, and noise pollution. In the past few years there has been more and more emphasis placed on ecology measures. Federal and state laws along with city ordinances have been passed in an effort to slow down, if not prevent, the deterioration of our environment. In many cases, fines have been levied and court orders issued against violators. But much remains to be done. One big issue, of course, is who should pay the cost involved: the polluter, who deteriorates the atmosphere or water with his unclean discharge; the depolluter, who must clean the air or water before he can use it in his production process or for consumption purposes; or the government, by paying directly to clean up the environment or by paying indirectly, through tax credits, for example, to encourage businesses to install antipollution and depollution devices? Or, should charges be levied against the consumers who use the products that contribute to pollution? Should the cost be borne out of profits? Or, should payment come through higher prices for products in order to provide the means for the manufacturers and fabricators to install antipollution or depollution devices? In almost any case the consumer is going to have to bear the largest share of the cost, directly or indirectly, in the form of higher prices, fewer products, or higher taxes.

As a nation, we can either take more goods and services and not worry about the deterioration of the environment, or we can take fewer goods and services than we are capable of producing and channel some of our money, men, and resources into preserving the environment. Once we as a nation have made an economic commitment to do the latter, technology can go a long way toward solving the pollution problems of our economy. Costs involved in eliminating water, air, and noise pollution range upward toward $100 billion, plus an annual outlay of several billion dollars thereafter as a means of preserving the environment. In 1973 it was estimated that $274 billion would be spent on environmental improvements in the United States economy during the next 10 years.

Enforcement of antipollution measures is another problem. Should it be at the local, state, or federal level? It would do New York little good to pass stringent antipollution laws if New Jersey did not. Polluted air could easily blow across the Hudson from Newark into Manhattan. How fair would it be competitively for the city of Cincinnati to pass stringent antipollution laws that might require a soap producer, such as Procter & Gamble, to raise prices or reduce profits, if Lever Brothers were not subject to the same or similar antipollution costs in operating its plant in Illinois? In similar fashion, the effectiveness of Ohio to prevent its manufacturers from polluting the Ohio River could be easily negated if states such as Pennsylvania, up the river, and Kentucky, across the river, did not restrict river pollution. Some antipollution measures may be effective at the local level, but others have to be carried out on a regional or national scale.

Several federal clean air acts, to be described in Chapter 23, represent a systematic effort to deal with air pollution problems on a regional basis.

Additional local and state programs place a greater emphasis on control and abatement activities. Although a Federal Water Pollution Control Act was passed in 1956, thus far its enforcement has been somewhat lax. In 1971, Ralph Nader's Task Force on Water Pollution accused the federal government of contributing to the declining purity of water by failing to act vigorously against polluters. Even so, a 1972 report issued by the federal Environmental Protection Agency indicated that there had been some improvement in the purity of water in the previous decade.

Many city, state, and federally operated facilities are as guilty as private enterprise of contributing to air and water pollution. With a national awareness of the adverse effects of pollution, however, new efforts are being made to reverse the trend of environmental deterioration. Private industry, for example, is spending billions of dollars annually on ecological measures and pollution controls. New laws are being passed and government agencies are becoming more active in the enforcement of current controls.

Urban Economics

Since World War II, there has been a mass movement of city dwellers and businesses to the suburbs. With the abandonment of the central city by many higher income families and prosperous businesses, this has in large part left the inner city to lower income groups and marginal businesses. Due to inadequate maintenance and repair, many buildings have depreciated and property values have declined. All this, too, has played havoc with city finances by reducing its tax base. The problems of the urban economies have been magnified by the continuous migration of families from rural into urban areas. In many respects the rural poor become a part of the urban poor and end up in slum areas. Although some efforts have been made in the past few decades toward urban renewal, much more needs to be done to prevent urban blight and the evolution of slums. At issue here is the cost of rebuilding the cities. Who shall bear this cost—the private sector of the economy or the government sector? If the government sector, shall it be the local government? If local, shall the cost be shared by the suburban cities as well as the central city? Should part of the cost be financed by the federal government?

Housing. As this move to the cities continues during the 1970s, housing needs will be accentuated. Not only will there be a need for new housing, homes, and apartments in the suburban areas, but there will be a pressing need for urban renewal in the inner cities. This is necessary to provide housing for lower income groups and as a means of attracting some of the suburbanites back into the cities. Housing starts were in the vicinity of 1.5 million annually during the 1960s. But national goals of 2 million or more annually have been set by a national commission. With the rapidly rising cost of construction in recent years, many families are going to find it difficult to finance adequate housing. Private industry will certainly do its share by providing housing to meet economic demand. But more and more pressure will be put on the government to help provide housing for low-income families.

An alternative to government housing projects being experimented with at the present time is the rent subsidy. Accordingly, a poor family is permitted to live in a higher level economic neighborhood by receiving a rent subsidy from the government to make up the difference between the actual rent and what the family can afford to pay. Proponents of rent subsidies suggest that they are preferable to government-sponsored housing projects.

Mass Transportation. The move into the cities from rural areas and the movement from the inner city to the suburb have accentuated the transportation problems of the cities. The suburbanite must get into the city; once there he, along with the city dweller, must move around within the city. On occasion it is necessary to travel to other cities. With the decline in the use of buses and the demise of passenger rail traffic, more reliability has been placed on the automobile. Along with widespread auto ownership, including millions of two- and three-car families living near the cities, jammed expressways and clogged thoroughfares are the order of the day. Commuter trains and rapid transit systems are being used beyond their optimum capacities, and most airports are crowded. Travel between cities within a megalopolis is becoming more burdensome.

To alleviate crowded conditions, some cities have installed subways, constructed overhead monorails, banned autos from downtown areas, and even experimented with walking-malls and moving sidewalks in downtown areas. As the movement into the cities increases in the next few decades, the problems of traffic control and the mass movement of people will become more acute. In many cases cities will not be able to solve their mass transportation problems without help. It will require intercity cooperation and planning, state assistance, and aid from the federal government. Perhaps more emphasis will be placed on President Nixon's proposal to alleviate the problems by reversing the flow of businesses and people back to the smaller towns and rural areas.

The whole problem of urban transportation, of course, was aggravated by the gasoline shortages that occurred in late 1973 and into 1974. That situation spurred a renewed interest in mass transit.

Ghetto Economics. In the past decade and a half, more light than ever before has been focused on the economic problems of minority groups, especially blacks. Because of past inequities and injustices, such as inadequate educational facilities, lack of job opportunities, discrimination in housing, and in some cases racial prejudice, blacks as a group are in the lower income brackets. Consequently, measures were started in the 1960s to alleviate their plight. Improved educational facilities, aid through many federal and local employment programs, and more opportunities for jobs through the private sector of the economy have all contributed toward this improvement. Although there are more poor whites than there are poor blacks, there is still a much higher percentage of blacks living in poverty.

Currently unemployment among the nonwhites, including blacks, Puerto Ricans, Mexicans, and the American Indian, is nearly double the unemployment rate of the labor force as a whole. Unemployment among nonwhite teenagers usually runs 20 to 25 percent, double that for all teenagers in the labor force. With the census and BLS projections that the nonwhite population will grow about 75 percent faster than the white population in the decade of the seventies, the problem will not melt away. In fact, it may become more acute.

Industry is faced with the issue of whether it should recruit workers from the ghetto, train them for employment in its suburban plants, and orient them to suburban living, or whether it should locate its plants in a ghetto area to provide jobs for the labor force there and, in so doing, give economic aid to the ghetto area.

Black Capitalism. Another goal of minority groups, particularly blacks, is to have more of their members become business entrepreneurs. They want a piece of the economic action which they help create by their labor and their spending. Often, however, the blacks lack the professional training, experience, and financial support necessary for success in business. Recently, increased emphasis has been placed on the development of *black capitalism* through programs that will provide the training, skills, knowledge, experience, and money for blacks to become successful entrepreneurs. Again an economic cost is involved. The question arises, what should be the source of this capital? Should the capital originate from savings, equity capital, loans from the private sector of the economy, or grants from the government? In many respects, just like the underdeveloped nations, the black community needs an infusion of capital from outside sources if it is going to meet its objectives.

The Cost of Crime. Related to our urban problems is the rising cost of crime. Poverty, slums, lack of educational and recreational facilities, and unemployment often breed delinquency and crime. The suburbs, however, are not without their problems in this respect. Drug addiction aggravates the crime problem. Not only is growing crime a terrible social problem, but it is a serious economic problem. The economic loss to individuals and businesses resulting from theft and property damage is enormous, the cost of insurance is rising at a quickening pace, and the financial outlays of individuals, institutions, and businesses for security and protection have skyrocketed. Governmental units have substantially increased their outlays for the prevention and detection of crime and the protection of their citizens. The cost of this crime naturally diverts money, resources, and manpower away from legitimate economic activity which could enhance our level of living.

Consumerism

For decades, through economic growth, we have demonstrated our ability to annually produce the world's greatest quantity of goods and services. Today, however, consumers are becoming more and more concerned about the quality of the goods and services we are producing. Our governmental agencies are becoming more active in the enforcement of pure food and drug laws, auto safety regulations, medical standards, and environmental protection. The Office of the Special Assistant for Consumer Affairs is taking a more active role in promoting the welfare of consumers in America. The National Commission on Product Safety has made numerous suggestions for new laws to protect consumers in various ways. Businesses now are more liberal in their return sales allowances and in exchanging or repairing faulty merchandise. The enactment of the Truth in Lending Act, along with the proposal for "truth in packaging," has added emphasis to the growing role of consumers. The crackdown on misrepresentative advertising, the ban on cigarette TV commercials, the withdrawal of polluting soaps and detergents from the market, the recall of millions of faulty automobiles by manufacturers, and the spread of information about mercury poisoning in fish are all part of the new consumer movement.

The involvement of many young adults and other groups adds to the momentum of the consumer movement. The findings of Ralph Nader sparked the interest of the public in consumerism. The continuing work of Nader's Raiders will no doubt add to the emphasis of this movement. To be sure, the days of *caveat emptor* (let the buyer beware) have long passed. Today, in many respects it appears that we are shifting toward the concept of *caveat venditor* (let the seller beware).

Quality of Life

Although still interested in having an abundance of goods and services, it is apparent that Americans today are shifting to an emphasis on the quality of goods and services and on the quality of life. They are interested in eliminating injustices and inequities, and they seek to improve the economic and social conditions of their fellowman. Some of them are more interested in making a contribution to society than they are in promoting their own economic well-being. Leading corporations have moved away from a prime emphasis on profit maximization toward a desire to provide quality goods and services and better working conditions for their employees. Consumers, businesses, and government are working together to improve economic and social conditions. New goals, such as the elimination of poverty, income maintenance (guaranteed annual income), and a system of national health insurance are indicative of this change. Our interest in preserving our national environment indicates a willingness to sacrifice goods and services in order to prevent a deterioration of the gifts of nature. The problems of urban economics are in large part social in nature, and the many proposals to improve the economic and social welfare of minority groups indicate a strong desire to cooperate in finding solutions to problems of our fellowman.

Parents seek better education for their children. Workers desire more leisure in the form of longer vacations, more holidays, and shorter hours. Meaningful employment is desired over routine jobs, and early retirement with adequate pensions are lifelong goals. In short, now that we do have affluence in our output of goods and services, America can afford a better quality of life and can even sacrifice some of its economic gains in order to achieve that quality.

Energy, Food, and Fuel Shortages

A number of studies and reports in the past decade, including that sponsored by the Club of Rome and conducted by Dennis L. Meadows of M.I.T., warned of pending scarcities of natural resources vis á vis the growth of world population. Limited attention was given to pending shortages, however, until a few years ago.

A first real indication that shortages could occur in the United States economy was the electrical power black-out in New York City and the subsequent brown-out periods that resulted from an insufficiency of electrical power. In the early 1970s, poor harvests, inclement weather, and a rise in the price of feed grains and chemicals, along with a growing demand for meat, caused a scarcity of beef in 1972 and 1973. Consequently, the price of beef rose substantially, and in some markets there was a shortage of beef. The large-scale purchase of grains from the United States by the Soviet Union in 1972 highlighted a scarcity of wheat that sent the price of wheat skyrocketing from $1.50 per bushel in 1972 to more than $5.00 per bushel within a year.

The presence of shortages was further dramatized in 1973 when the oil embargo by the Arabian states reduced petroleum supplies for the United States. Although imports account for only 6 percent of the United States oil supply, the loss of imports was sufficient to cause a shortage of fuel oil for homes and factories and gasoline for motor vehicles. As a result, fuel oil was rationed in several Eastern states, and gasoline for autos and trucks was supplied in limited quantities. A number of states rationed gasoline by various methods, many service stations went out of business because of lack of supplies, and truckers demonstrated and struck in protest of limited supplies and high prices. In response, the Administration appointed a Federal Energy Director ("Czar") to coordinate the production, allocation, and pricing of scarce petroleum products. As a result of the shortages, however, the price of gasoline rose from an average of 35¢ per gallon to more than 50¢ per gallon, and in some places sold for $1.00 per gallon. The Federal Energy Office also had rationing coupons preprinted in the event that it became necessary to resort to coupon rationing to allocate scarce gasoline supplies.

The fuel and energy shortages, of course, were instrumental in hastening Congressional approval of the Alaskan pipeline to eventually bring oil from the North Slope into the United States mainland markets. The bill had been stalled in Congress for environmental considerations. The shortages also accelerated the experimentation and processing of shale oil, a process that had been considered too costly beforehand.

The energy, fuel, and gasoline shortages were in part responsible for the GNP slipping from a limited growth outlook to a no-growth, or recession, period in 1974. Hundreds of thousands of layoffs in 1973 and 1974 were directly attributable to these shortages. In the auto industry the gasoline shortages led to such a dramatic shift in demand away from larger size cars to smaller cars that the industry was forced to make a mass conversion of its facilities to small car production.

Much of the consternation in the economy in the form of scarcities, shortages, layoffs, shifting of resources and manpower, and higher prices was a normal market reaction. There were, however, certain charges of monopolistic restrictions and oligopolistic pricing. Nevertheless, the shortages did confirm previous suggestions that resources could be pinching against an increasing demand, which could affect the growth pattern and even the standard of living of American consumers. Although the shortages may be somewhat short-lived as new sources of energy, food, and fuels are produced or developed, no longer can the American producer or consumer take for granted that supplies will readily be forthcoming even though he may have money to pay for them. More and more the American producer and consumer will have to engage more consciously in the process of economizing—how best to apply scarce means to satisfy unlimited wants.

International Issues

In addition to domestic goals and priorities, as a nation we are interested also in cooperating with other nations in seeking solutions to multinational issues and problems. Stabilizing our international balance of payments and arresting the gold outflow, promoting trade among nations, providing foodstuffs to help alleviate world hunger, and contributing toward the support of international organizations all require time, resources, and financing. Should the United States, for example, follow the recommendation of the World Bank that each developed nation contribute an amount of aid equivalent to seven tenths of one percent (0.7%) of its GNP in the form of aid to underdeveloped nations? This would increase our foreign aid bill from $3 billion annually to more than $9 billion. If we did so, we obviously would be able to do less in other directions. Consequently, in the order of national priorities, this and other multinational demands have to be balanced with our domestic goals.

SUMMARY

1. As the economy grows it will create many related problems, such as pollution, congestion, and the depletion of resources.

2. In order to preserve or improve our natural environment, more and more resources and manpower in the future will have to be devoted to that task.

3. There is a need for consumers to become more aware of the external effects of production if they are to make wise selections of goods and services.

4. A growth dividend of $50 to $60 billion annually will result from the normal forces of growth in the economy during the next decade.

5. A $50 billion annual growth dividend produces a $9 to $10 billion annual increase in federal revenues.

6. The government can use this dividend (revenue) to expand existing government services, estab-

lish new government services, reduce taxes, reduce the national debt, or share it with the states.

7. There is also the possibility of a "disarmament dividend" if most nations ever reach agreement on the reduction of armaments.

8. As the economy grows, existing goals of full employment, stable prices, and a healthy rate of economic growth will be taken for granted.

9. With growth, however, new goals will be established and new problems created.

10. Major issues or problems of the future include the elimination of poverty, guaranteed annual income, national health insurance, preservation of the environment, urban issues, consumerism, improvement in the quality of life, and the elimination of energy, food, and fuel shortages.

NEW TERMS

External effects of growth, *p. 477*
Growth dividend, *p. 479*

Peace dividend, *p. 480*
Disarmament dividend, *p. 482*

QUESTIONS FOR DISCUSSION AND ANALYSIS

1. Why is there a different attitude today about the deterioration of the natural environment as compared to a few decades ago?

2. Explain the economic choice between additional goods and services and the preservation of the environment?

3. Is it necessary to reduce our output of goods and services in order to improve the natural environment?

4. Explain the growth dividend and the disarmament dividend.

5. Should the growth dividend be used primarily for tax reductions or for the implementation of various social and economic programs?

6. If the growth dividend were to be used primarily for social and economic programs, would it be better to put all resources into a few major programs or divide them among several programs?

7. If disarmament talks should result in a 50 percent reduction in the U.S. defense budget, what do you suggest be done with such a disarmament dividend?

8. What mechanism do you think should be utilized for establishing priorities for the use of the growth dividend?

9. Should the government, private enterprise, or consumers bear the cost of antipollution devices?

10. Would you personally prefer to have more economic goods and services or an improvement in the quality of life?

11. During periods of shortages, do you think it best to ration gasoline through the pricing mechanism by allowing the price to rise, or to use coupon rationing of some type? Explain.

SUGGESTED READINGS

Bolton, Roger E. *Defense and Disarmament: The Economics of Transition.* Englewood Cliffs, N.J.: Prentice-Hall, Inc., 1966.

Building a National Health-Care System. New York: Committee for Economic Development, 1973.

Burch, Gilbert. "How Big a Peace Dividend?" *Fortune* (June 1, 1968).

Crocker, Thomas D., and A. J. Rogers III. *Environmental Economics.* Hinsdale, Ill.: The Dryden Press, 1971.

Lecht, Leonard A. *Goals, Priorities and Dollars.* New York: The Free Press, 1966.

Meadows, Dennis L. *Limits to Growth.* New York: Universe Books, 1972.

Schultze, Charles L., *et al. Setting National Priorities: The 1975 Budget.* Washington: The Brookings Institution, 1974.

23

Environmental Economics and Pollution

PREVIEW Traditionally economic theory has been treated as a closed system of analysis. The system is closed in the sense that economic theory seeks to explain output, income, and prices—to the exclusion of the effects of economic activity on nature and the quality of life. These external effects of economic activity include environmental pollution, depletion of natural resources, and urban blight. While injurious spillover effects have been discounted in the past, growing concern for the environment has aroused new applications of economic theory. Since harm to the environment is related to economic growth, public policies must strive for a balance between growth and protection of the environment.

In the preceding two chapters, we have stressed the process by which national output grows and the uses to which greater output can be put. An assessment of American economic growth would hardly be complete, however, without a deeper analysis of the escalating environmental problems created by expanding production. Industrialization, we know, leads to long-run growth and has been interpreted to mean progress. Yet statistical measures of growth, such as the rise in GNP, take no account of damage to the environment. To the extent that environmental abuse is not reflected in growth statistics, actual economic progress is less than economic growth.

Harm to the environment is a by-product of both production and consumption. The process by which national production and consumption are pushed ever higher generates detrimental side effects. We shall see now, more specifically, how these side effects take the form of social costs not borne directly by individual producers or by individual consumers. For convenience, we shall group these social costs under three headings: pollution, depletion of natural resources, and urban blight.

FORMS OF POLLUTION

The air of our nation is befouled by more than 260 million tons of toxic substances issuing yearly from automobiles, power plants, factories, and many other sources. Lake Erie receives 1,600 million gallons per day of waste waters from 120 municipalities. The phosphates, nitrates, and other plant nutrients settling into the lake have caused an estimated growth of one billion pounds of algae. Today Lake Erie cannot sustain many forms of indigenous marine life. Jet engines scream over suburban homes, while those who live in the country must contend with litter and rubbish along their rural highways and their hiking trails. These are all different but related forms of environmental pollution and deterioration.

Fouling the Air

Today there are well over 300,000 manufacturing establishments in the United States. Practically every one is a contributor to air pollution. The worst offenders include petroleum refineries, steel mills, chemical plants, and rubber manufacturers—pumping sulphur dioxide, carbon monoxide, fluorides, metallic oxides, and fumes of arsenic lead into the atmosphere. At the same time, electric generating stations, by burning coal and oil as fuel, emit tons of sulphur dioxide each year. Manufacturers are not the only offenders, however. One hundred and seventeen million motor vehicles in the United States are the chief sources of carbon monoxide and smog-forming hydro-carbons. In addition, the average American discards about 2,000 pounds of solid wastes yearly, leading to 4.5 million tons of air pollutants from refuse disposal by burning. Just to heat our homes we consumers exude almost 10 million tons of air pollutants per year.

The source distribution of air pollutants for 1970 is shown in Table 23-1. Of the 264 million tons, nearly 55 percent comes from transportation (primarily motor vehicles). Another 17 percent is traceable to stationary fuel combustion: power plants, home heating, and so on. Slightly less than 14 percent finds its way into the atmosphere from industrial smokestacks; 7 percent from agricultural burning; 4 percent from refuse disposal; and 3 percent from other sources.

TABLE 23-1

AIR POLLUTANT EMISSIONS

1970

Source of Pollution	Millions of Tons					Percent Share by Source
	Carbon Mon-oxide	Sulphur Oxides	Hydro-carbons	Particu-lates	Nitrogen Oxides	
Transportation	111.0	1.0	19.5	0.7	11.7	54.5
Fuel Combustion (stationary)	0.8	26.5	0.6	6.9	10.0	17.0
Industrial Processes .	11.4	6.0	5.5	13.3	0.2	13.8
Agricultural Burning .	13.8	—	2.8	2.4	0.3	7.3
Solid Waste Disposal	7.2	0.1	2.0	1.4	0.4	4.2
Miscellaneous	2.8	0.3	4.3	0.9	0.1	3.2
Share by Type of Pollutant (percent) .	55.7	12.8	13.1	9.7	8.6	

SOURCE: *Statistical Abstract of the United States,* 1973, p. 178.

The bottom row in Table 23-1 gives the percentage of total emissions contributed by each type of pollutant. It can readily be seen that carbon monoxide is the principal offender, with other types yielding roughly equal shares.

Of course, reference to United States statistics does not imply that air pollution is unique to this country. Air pollution is an offshoot of industrialization rather than any particular politico-economic system. In Japan and the Soviet Union, to cite only two examples, contamination of the atmosphere has kept pace with the speed of industrialization. The degree of contamination approaches crisis proportions as economic growth is stimulated. The Public Health Service estimates that over 44 million people in the United States live in areas having critical air pollution problems. Carbon monoxide, sulphur oxides, and nitrogen oxides (77 percent of all emissions) are all potentially lethal. Worse still, they cannot be effectively eliminated from the atmosphere with present technology.

Removal of air pollutants is often not as easy as it might at first appear. Man has not yet discovered a pollution-free source of energy. Electricity, which seems so free of pollution effects, is today generated primarily by burning oil, a source of sulphur oxides. Conversion, as a consequence of the recent petroleum shortage, would probably entail the burning of coal, also a source of sulphur oxides. Substantial air pollution could be avoided by substituting nuclear-powered generators, but cooling by water creates another serious problem of thermal pollution.

Since the automobile is a primary polluter, substitution of an electric automobile for a gasoline-burning automobile might seem attractive. If vehicles were connected to overhead power sources, more electricity would have to be generated, which would change, rather than avoid, the pollution threat. Battery driven cars, as an alternative, are inefficient and prohibitively expensive. Greater hope for cleaner driving is offered by the Wankel or rotary engine. Invented by Felix Wankel in West Germany and later improved by a Japanese manufacturer, who began shipping Wankel-powered cars to the United States in 1971, the Wankel engine, like the internal combustion engine, emits carbon monoxide, unburned hydrocarbons, and oxides of nitrogen. Because pistons are replaced by a rotor, the Wankel engine is much smaller and lighter in weight. It has fewer than half the moving parts of a V-8 internal combustion engine and takes less than one fourth the space. Consequently, there is more room under the hood for anti-emission devices. Also, the engine's venting system makes emissions easier to handle. General Motors Corporation purchased the patent rights to the Wankel engine in 1970, and GM engineers predict that small cars powered by these engines will be available by the mid-1970s. One must recognize, however, that emission-control devices themselves are far from perfect. Experiments conducted from 1972 through 1974 demonstrated that these devices lead to greater gasoline consumption per mile, stalling, and other inefficiencies or expenses.

It is obvious that the effort in finding technological remedies to pollution is great, but it is necessary in order that we may lessen the actual menace to human survival posed by pollution. Many biologists, warning against the continuation of present trends, predict much more for the future than dirty cities, corrosion of all kinds of materials, and an increase in pulmonary diseases, such as lung cancer and emphysema. The shortage of the oxygen supply of our planet may soon be critical. North America already obtains oxygen from the sea (the continent consumes more oxygen than its trees and plants create). However, the oxygen produced by the sea—by green plant life in ocean waters—is threatened by thermal pollution and by oil content in the water.

Spoiling the Water

In the language of economics, air is a "free" good. Air is a resource provided by nature and is available in abundance to everyone. As a matter of fact, we do not even stop to think that we are using air. Since air is a free good, the negative social consequences caused by its misuse are not directly allocated to the costs of producing goods and services. Because there is no assigned cost to its use (thus, no assigned cost to its misuse), air can often be misused without penalty to the guilty person or firm.

There are parallels between the use and misuse of air and the use and misuse of many bodies of water. There is little need to repeat such comparable illustrations. However, for the purpose of emphasizing environmental abuse arising from the conception of nature as a "free" good, two examples are in order. One is the example of almost any business firm located on the shores of a river or lake. The other is the example of a household located on the same or similar body of water. To begin, both are inclined to use the water as a means of dispensing with waste.

Of course, each must dispose of its waste in some manner, and a nearby river or lake offers a "free" dumping area. An alternative for the firm would be to use other means of refuse disposal, such as hauling its refuse to another land site for incineration. The firm recognizes, naturally, the cost of doing so. Given the choice, the firm can minimize its cost by taking advantage of the water.

Similarly, alternative methods for disposing of household refuse may appear to be more costly or to require more effort. Even though the household may not have to pay such a cost through direct outlay by hiring a garbage disposal firm to transport and dispose of its waste, the household, nevertheless, would probably have to bear the cost through higher property taxes needed to support a refuse-disposal facility. Thus, the incentive to pollute the water body is intensified. The town elders find it more expedient to pipe effluents into the river or lake than to raise taxes. By choosing to dump untreated sewage and solid wastes into water bodies construed as free disposal areas, communities have in effect decided to misuse natural resources in order to avoid more costly alternatives.

After years of many companies and households following this practice, the extent of water pollution is already critical. A map of polluted waters in the United States shows that every region is affected. In 1973 one survey revealed that virtually all of its water samples showed traces of pesticides. Almost 40 percent of the samples recorded safety levels below federal standards. A small percentage displayed the presence of poisons, such as mercury and arsenic, in dangerous quantities. Unfortunately, even many of those categorized as potable actually stunk!

Some problems of inland water bodies are not the result of deliberate misuse. Many are the consequence of poor foresight. Dams provide hydro-electric power and flood control. But what of the disadvantages created by such dams? Construction of the Aswan Dam in Egypt threatens to destroy more farmland than it brings into production; in controlling the floodwaters, the dam eliminates the dispersion of the rich soil that such waters leave after they recede. Engineers have made possible the building of great dams on the Colorado River, but each dam produces a lake in the desert. Behind Hoover Dam is Lake Mead. Almost a billion gallons of water are lost daily from this lake through evaporation, leaving a residual of salt. The cumulative effect of this and similar situations at other dams on the Colorado River is a safe-water yield of only 13 million acre-feet per year, with 2 million acre-feet (13 percent of the flow) lost by evaporation. This causes one to wonder about the long-run consequences of constructing such dams and even whether this is a necessary and/or socially approved cost.

The oceans, like most inland bodies of water, are not exempt from serious levels of pollutants. Some pollution is the result of accidents: an oil tanker breaks up off New Jersey beaches or an oil well in the Santa Barbara channel develops a leak. Other pollution is a cumulative and unforeseen result of production for private gain to the neglect of nature; it is said that penguins as far away as the Antarctic have DDT in their blood. Although accidents and unanticipated side effects are not insignificant, most ocean pollution is the result of calculated decision. Sewage, industrial wastes, oil, unusable auto parts, garbage, bombs, and even deadly nerve gases are dumped into our oceans—under the auspices of both public and private agencies.

Newsweek magazine, in reporting on the Thor Heyerdahl raft voyage across the Atlantic, said:

> The RA II took 57 days to complete her 3,270 mile voyage—a journey marred by the amount of pollution in the sea. For weeks at a stretch, said Norman Baker, Heyerdahl's American navigator, "we saw no sign of man—except his garbage, and we saw that all the time."

Generating Noise Pollution

We shall devote less space to noise pollution for two reasons. First, unlike air and water pollution, noise pollution does not actually threaten human survival. Second, people other than those directly and immediately exposed to it are rarely conscious of the potential dangers of noise pollution. In fact, more research is needed to identify and measure the effects of noise on humans. Only time will tell whether the physiological, psychological, and cultural results of excessive or constant noise have lasting consequences on our social organization.

Noise pollution, though less dangerous than other pollutants to humans and animals, has become an irritant destructive to the quality of life. The most commonly cited illustration is the giant jet plane taking off or landing. At least of equal importance is the incessant rumble, created by automobile motors, horns, and construction machinery, found in almost any city. Medical studies have demonstrated a higher incidence of defective hearing among city dwellers than among occupants of rural areas. Even in the absence of physical consequences, however, some preliminary evidence suggests that exposure to excessive and/or constant noise tends to produce irritability which, among other things, impairs human relations.

As with air and water pollution, much noise pollution results from cost minimization by both producers and consumers. It is possible but expensive to muffle the sound of jet engines. Higher costs would be transformed into higher air fares, so consumers would have to be willing to bear part of the cost. The same applies to other forms of disturbing noise. Basically, solutions to noise pollution are costly to individual producers and consumers, whereas the negative effects of uncontrolled noise generally are borne silently by the population.

The Garbage of Man

In his popular book, *Future Shock*,[1] Alvin Toffler characterized modern industrial society as "The Throw-Away Society." Napkins, towels, diapers, nonreturnable bottles, curtains, cans, toys, plastic sacks, pastry tins, T.V.

[1] Alvin Toffler, *Future Shock* (New York: Bantam Books, Inc., 1971).

dinner containers—all are used quickly and thrown away. Disposable tooth-brushes are on the market, precoated with toothpaste for one-time use. We now may buy paper clothing. Perhaps we may ultimately see an age of something close to transient buildings. The average "life expectancy" of dwellings has steadily declined from about 100 years for houses built in the Colonial period to less than 40 years today. Whole cities are torn down and rebuilt at astonishing rates.

In the past, permanence was an ideal and reuse a necessity. The ideal of permanence was reflected in man's creative and productive energy. Man built to last, whether what he built was a cathedral, a house, or a pair of boots. The necessity of reuse was dictated by an economy of scarcity. Use of a product only once, or for a brief time, was foreign to current middle-aged Americans during their early years. This idea is also foreign to societies less advanced industrially.

There is no doubt that "The Throw-Away Society" is an outgrowth of economic prosperity. The advantages to any one household in such a society are clear. Housekeepers need not be bothered by washing and ironing; the chore of cleaning and returning bottles is avoided; preliminaries to baking and cooking are done industrially at much saving of time and effort in the household. But what of the problems of disposing of "the disposables"? Highway litter is a national scandal. Cans, paper, and bottles are found in the most unlikely provinces of nature, including virgin forests, moors, and remote ponds and streams.

Defacement of the natural environment, through litter and spoliation, is less critical than another side effect of using these household conveniences. While nonsolid wastes are mixed with our air and water, nearly 2,000 pounds of solid wastes per American are buried annually. As the throw-away process accelerates, burial space for waste becomes more scarce. Today, a year's refuse of 10,000 people is enough to cover an acre of land to a depth of seven feet. As more land coverage is allocated to solid waste burial, the equilibrium of nature (so far as plant nutrients are concerned) is distorted. Many towns, comfortable in their assessment of disposal space for human refuse a decade ago, now are overwhelmed by the number of abandoned autos, discarded refrigerators, and other junk that somehow must be removed from sight. To summarize, disposal of waste materials from past production has become an important economic activity in itself, competing for resources that could otherwise be used for current production.

DEPLETION OF NATURAL RESOURCES

Pollution is a by-product of current production and consumption. Our present polluted environment may assume crisis proportions with the additional pollution from future economic growth. In like manner, we now suffer the cumulative effects inherited from past production. In addition to the delayed consequences of earlier pollution, irreplaceable natural resources are now threatened by past failures to adopt strong conservation policies.

If yesterday's production has left us today with depleted natural resources, then today's production will further deplete these dwindling resources. When virgin forests are cut down, coal fields are exhausted, oil wells are pumped dry, and the Mesabi Range is mined out, we will be forced to resort to the use of second-growth timber, oil shale, and taconite. These represent inferior resources which can be developed only at increasing cost. Assuming we as a nation are willing to bear these costs, it still must be recognized that these low-grade natural resources are not inexhaustible.

There is more to the natural resource issue than simply the conservation of productive inputs; that is to say, we must be concerned with the time it will take before we exhaust one source and turn to inferior grades of inputs. There is also the question of whether certain natural resources should be subjected to the productive process at all. Should lumber companies be permitted to fell giant redwoods that have taken centuries to grow? By implication, should consumers be deprived of the use of redwood in dwelling construction? Should strip miners be allowed to uproot virgin forests and literally level small mountains in order to get at the minerals so useful ultimately to consumers? [2] Should some restraints be placed on the spread of housing developments in order to preserve some of the remaining American wilderness?

The history of private enterprise in the United States is one in which natural resources, existing in great abundance, have provided a cheap and ready source of raw material inputs for the productive process. Thus, little thought was given to conservation, and decade by decade natural resources have become more scarce. With the diminution of irreplaceable resources has come an awareness that continued resource exploitation will deprive the populace of benefits for which there are no real substitutes.

Some natural resources have dual uses. They can be used up in production and thereby offer consumer satisfaction through the resulting final product, or they can be consumed (enjoyed) directly without their disappearance or transformation. Forests, for instance, can be cut down to build houses; on the other hand, in their natural state forests offer recreational areas, natural beauty, and refuge for wildlife. Whenever such irreplaceable

---

[2] Strip mining, used primarily for coal and copper but also for other minerals, is the cutting away of layers of earth to expose mineral resources in giant open pits. As deposits have become more scarce, firms have found strip mining to be more economical than tunneling.

resources of nature are used as inputs in the productive process, they are lost forever as a direct source of human enjoyment.

To an increasing extent the pleasure derived from nature is being lost as nature is subjected to production for salable output, not only in the United States but in all industrialized countries. This, coupled with crowded living conditions, the asphalt and concrete, and the hustle and bustle of modern existence, makes nature an increasingly precious "commodity." Along with the various forms of pollution of the environment, deprivation of the joys of nature must be counted among the forms of environmental abuse.

URBAN BLIGHT

Urban economics has many aspects—the economics of transportation, housing, recreation, and minority groups, to name but a few. Later in the book, in Chapter 39, urban economics will be studied more comprehensively. In the present chapter we are concerned with only one aspect of urban economics, namely, *urban blight* as a form of environmental decay.

Over the course of the past century, America has changed from a predominantly rural society to a predominantly urban society. Not only in the United States but in other industrial nations, and even in some underdeveloped countries, there has been a mass exodus from farms and small towns to the cities. Today, for most Americans the city is our immediate environment. Urban living has provided more abundant and varied employment opportunities. Urban living also offers conveniences not available in the country. But, as we are now so painfully aware, the process of urban and suburban growth has spawned the problem of urban blight.

City Development

Of the two principal geographic theories of city development, the concentric ring theory and the sector theory, a combination of the two seems most often to describe the pattern of growth that produced modern cities around the world. Essentially, the *concentric ring theory* indicates that cities grow outward, forming larger and larger circular configurations—like ripples created when a rock is tossed into a lake. However, these circles are not perfect in shape. They may be distorted by expansion of population along local transportation routes, pressing the city outward in a configuration resembling a many-pointed star. A lakefront, river, or mountain may truncate these forms to half-circles, as in Chicago. Manhattan, Los Angeles, and certain European capitals are other exceptions. Nevertheless, a fundamental circular pattern of city growth can be discerned here and abroad.

The *sector theory* stresses that a city's growth pattern is formed because certain areas are best suited to facilitate various social or economic functions. A sector will encompass those activities—such as predominantly commercial or predominantly residential activities—dictated by conditions most conducive to the effective performance of the activities. For example, railroads were built where land is relatively flat, factories in turn located along railroads, trade centers grew along local transportation routes, and residential areas emerged where people could take advantage of a view or enjoy pleasant surroundings. Thus, we see that city growth in reality can be described as superimposing upon the concentric ring concept the socio-economic functions performed within each ring. As these functions have changed over time and as circular urban growth has continued, the contemporary city has emerged.

At the center of the city is a downtown business district containing office buildings, travel depots, hotels, banks, theaters, and a central shopping area. Surrounding this nucleus is another circle of larger diameter. Here one finds warehouses, small factories, and railroad yards. Housing in this second circle is decayed and neighborhoods are typically no more than slums. Farther out on another circle are the dwellings of blue-collar workers, and farther still are the homes and apartments of the upper-middle class, such as the professional people and middle business management. Farthest from the inner city are to be found the mansions and estates of the very wealthy.

A dynamic process creates this concentric structure. At first, when the city is young, middle-income and wealthy people live relatively close to the center. Then, as the city prospers these income groups move farther out in order to occupy newer or better homes, and their former neighborhoods undergo change. Homes are broken up into rooming houses or tenements for occupancy by recent immigrants, the poor, and unskilled migrants from rural areas. Maintenance is kept to a bare minimum, and thus slum conditions begin.

In the United States the concentric development of cities turns slums into racial or ethnic ghettos. At one time, most residents of blighted sections were blacks, recent European immigrants, or migrants from rural areas. Today, with the flight to the suburbs, the inner city is populated to an increasing extent by blacks, Puerto Ricans, and Mexican-Americans.

The Economics of Slum Housing

Rents for dwellings in slum areas are not necessarily lower than rents in middle-class neighborhoods. The supply of housing space in slums is fixed, or nearly fixed. As poor immigrants, rural migrants, and minority groups enter the city, they create a demand for this low-quality housing. With control over a scarce supply, landlords can often command more rent per room (or per square foot) in slum areas than can be asked in well-maintained neighborhoods. As a consequence, slum dwellers are forced to occupy fewer rooms per family because of the high rent per room.

To elaborate, consider first the case in which a family located in a slum has the same housing needs as another family located in a middle-class neighborhood. This could be a case, for example, in which the two families have the same number of members, identical incomes, and the same willingness to spend on housing space, but the slum family is subjected to ethnic or racial discrimination. This family is not permitted to rent in the better neighborhood. Given equal demand by the two families, suppose further that the supply of housing is greater in the middle-class neighborhood. For reasons described in the preceding section (the breaking up of space as middle-income families move out), assume the supply of housing *per family*, that is, the number of rooms per family, is less in the slum area. Since supply relative to demand is greater in the middle-class neighborhood, the rent *per room* will tend to be less.

Consider next the case in which the slum resident has a lower income and thus a lower demand for housing. Slum rents per room may still be greater than rents per room in well-maintained areas, however, for it is a question of supply relative to demand. Though a slum family's demand may be less, the supply of rooms per family may also be less. Only if demand is so weak that it more than compensates for limited supply will rents per room be lower in slum housing.

This theoretical exposition helps to explain why slumlords buy up and subdivide homes when families move out of the inner city. Such "block busting" tends to raise property values and rental incomes after property has been sold and subdivided. Efforts by the federal government to redevelop the inner city have to some extent aided the middle class at the expense of the poor. When old tenements are torn down and new housing developments put in their place, the previous tenants often cannot find housing as good as that which they were forced to vacate. Tenants who move into the development can afford the rent, while evicted poor families seek decayed housing elsewhere, intensifying the pressure for conversion of marginal areas into new slums.

Blight as Environmental Defacement

The direct victims of urban blight are those who suffer from substandard housing, the accompanying poor schools, a higher incidence of disease springing from unsanitary living conditions, greater subjection to crime, and lack of decent recreational areas. Yet in a real sense the entire society suffers.

Some critics have spoken of "sight pollution," including the ugliness of inner cities allowed to run to ruin. One who has traveled widely needs only to compare the inner core of some cities of the world—Copenhagen, Zurich, Paris, Amsterdam—with Harlem, Watts, or South Chicago to realize the extent to which urban blight affects the overall quality of urban living. Every city has its poor section, but not all such sections have been changed by neglect into slums.

Few can escape the social consequences arising from the decay of major portions of our cities. The stereotyped well-to-do businessman with a substantial home in the suburbs, removed from the cruel realities of slum living, still has to drive through these slum areas on his way to a downtown office, albeit on a super highway. Man is a communal being. If a citizen can take pride in the beauty of his city, who can argue that he does not feel depressed in viewing its ugly side? As with pollution and a disregard for nature, negligence toward urban blight results in environmental damage.

PRIVATE VS. SOCIAL COSTS

A theme has been running through our discussion of environmental economics. The theme is this: business firms and households make decisions based upon the direct costs to them. Yet their decisions impose indirect costs upon others. These costs or side effects are what constitute the environmental crises we face today. Side effects reveal themselves in pollution, excessive exploitation of natural resources, and urban blight.

Costs and Alternative Resource Uses

Costs, ultimately, mean the value of resources used up in the productive process. In the context of environmental economics, two definitions are important. *Private cost* is the cost to a single business firm or to a household. Thus, a firm considers its direct outlay on labor, land use, and capital equipment in bringing its final product to the market for sale. Private cost is measured by the price paid for these resource services. As such, private cost reflects the value of the best alternative uses of productive inputs under the firm's control, as evaluated by the firm itself.

In contrast, *social cost* is the cost to the community as a whole. Sometimes social costs are not identifiable in terms of quoted market prices; they are nevertheless real. Whereas private cost reflects the value of best alternative resource uses as far as a private firm or household is concerned, social cost reflects the value of the best alternative uses of resources available to the whole society, as evaluated by society.

Environmental problems are created by a discrepancy between private and social costs. A firm that contributes to air or water pollution does not include the cost of pollution in computing its costs of production. The fallout effects—such as deprived fisheries, dirty beaches, or unhealthy air—are borne by others. A body of water may be considered by a firm as a free means of waste disposal. The water has no alternative use *to the firm as such*. That same body of water, however, may have a valued alternative use, such as a source of seafood or recreation, to the rest of society. In a word, private efficiency economizes the uses of only those resources the individual producer must pay for. Social efficiency economizes the uses of all of society's resources.

In a private enterprise economy, the success of a business firm is measured by its profitability. Therefore, the profit motive, while it rewards efficiency, promotes private efficiency only. This does not mean that environmental injury is restricted to capitalistic economies. It is a matter of record that socialistic economies, likewise, have abused the environment. The Russians, Japanese, and Norwegians are no less responsible than North Americans for overfishing the oceans. Government owned and operated enterprises—whether these be governmental agencies in our "mixed economy" or arms of the state in socialistic economies—have been no less guilty than strictly private establishments in ignoring social costs. Discrepancy between private and social cost is an inheritance of industrialization, coupled with deficient public policies, rather than a necessary result of either capitalism or socialism.

Frequently both firms and society at large use an identical standard for calculating the costs of production, namely, the prices of factor services set by the market. Social cost and private cost often differ, but occasionally they are identical. The more they tend to be equated, the more satisfied citizens are likely to be with allowing a market mechanism to allocate resources among alternative uses. The more private and social cost valuations differ, the more inclined are citizens to seek interference with the market mechanism by means of governmental regulation.

Externalities

Divergence between private and social cost is an example of what economists call *externalities*. Externalities are of two kinds: externalities in production and externalities in consumption. Externalities are sometimes labeled third-party effects or spillover effects because parties other than those participating in a contract or bargain are affected.

In general, externalities can be beneficial or harmful. Consider first external effects in production. Suppose a complex of manufacturing firms in a community undertakes long-run expansion. Aside from direct gains in employment and wages and aside from direct economic benefits to suppliers and customers, indirect windfalls typically accrue to others. For instance, new roads built primarily for access to the firms are available for use by all. Likewise, the increase in the numbers of workers in these firms leads to the establishment of new recreational facilities, such as golf courses and theaters. On the other hand, traffic congestion on the roads would be a negative external effect. Water-discharged effluents that harm the local fishing industry (or sport fishing), greater amounts of dirt that settle on homes, and smog that affects community health adversely are all examples of harmful externalities.

The classic example of externalities in consumption is the "neighbor and me" phenomenon. If I paint my house or keep my lawn beautiful, I improve my neighbor's view. I also enhance the value of his property. Conversely, when I allow my property to run down, he suffers both esthetically and monetarily. In spite of our usual simplification in economics, it is true that "no man is an island unto himself." Our theory assumes that I gain satisfaction only from what I consume. In actuality I may also derive satisfaction from what my neighbor consumes—and he, from what and how I consume.

The central question, then, is one of balance between external diseconomies (harmful spillover effects) and external economies (beneficial spillover effects). As we shall see, most external benefits tend to be reflected in market phenomena, and thereby enter the computation of gross national product. That is, the majority are accounted for by national income and product statistics. Most harmful externalities, however, escape accounting by being "buried" in so-called free resources or collective consumption.

Collective Consumption

Air, water bodies, forests, and mountains all have the double feature of being both resource inputs and goods consumed. Ocean waters cool nuclear power plants and help to produce electricity; ocean waters are also utilized for swimming, boating, and clamming. We exhaust pollutants into the atmosphere as an offshoot of production, and at the same time we also consume the atmosphere to live. We build houses from trees, and often we simply rest in the shade provided by trees.

The peculiar feature of all these earth resources is that they are, to a greater or lesser extent, collectively consumed. By *collective consumption* we mean consumption that cannot be assigned so much to one and so much to another household. The entire body of consumers shares, on a non-assigned basis, some available mass of the thing consumed. Examples include city parks, mountain wilderness, lakes, and police protection. Collective consumption is contrasted with individually consumed goods or services that can be assigned on a unit rate to individual users, such as gallons of city water per year, pounds of dry detergent per month, auto mileage per year, and hours per month of maid service.

We emphasize collective consumption because most environmental problems involve natural resources which on the one hand are consumed directly but collectively and at the same time are used as productive inputs for privately evaluated output. Because consumers do not purchase these goods and services the way they do fruit juices or homes, organized consumer resistance to the depletion or spoliation of natural resources is very difficult.

ECONOMIC GROWTH AND ECOLOGY

Ecology is not an idea conceived in the social sciences. Originally, in the biological sciences where it had its beginning, ecology was simply the study of interrelationships between organisms and their environment. Recently, however, the term ecology has been adopted by the social sciences and has since come to mean the study of interaction between organized human behavior and the environment.

Organized human behavior in the economic realm has generated remarkable growth in output as measured by GNP. Yet the process by which we push GNP ever higher causes environmental side effects that detract from our well-being. Despite the sustained growth of GNP, an increasing number of people have come to suspect that a threat to our high standard of living awaits us in the not too distant future. The word ecology is used more and more with a sense of foreboding.

Both industrialized nations and those less advanced industrially take pride in their gross national product as a measure of national welfare. No doubt a greater abundance of material goods and services does add to our well-being, other things remaining unchanged. But are the Nepalese, with a GNP of about $50 per capita, really less happy than Americans with a GNP of $6,000 per capita? Economists have never advanced such a claim. Still, there is widespread belief in what one critic has called "GNP fetishism." Preoccupation with boasting about GNP, in the expectation that continued growth will raise human welfare, has dulled our sensitivity to the welfare-reducing environmental effects of faster growth.

Computing GNP

As we saw in Chapter 6, gross national product is a statistic emerging from our national income and product accounting system. GNP is nothing more than the sum total of the value added in production by each producing unit. Moreover, value added is derived by deducting from the value of a firm's output (total revenue) those costs incurred in purchasing the output of other firms.

Firm *A*, for example, sells its yearly output to consumers and has annual sales receipts of $100,000. All raw materials used in its productive process have a value of $60,000. The difference of $40,000—value added in production—is a measure of the firm's contribution to national output. This sum is available to the firm for distribution to resource owners as income in the form of wages, interest, rent, and profit.

Suppose, for the sake of simplicity, that all of Firm *A*'s raw materials are purchased from Firm *B*. Suppose also that Firm *B* sells its entire output to Firm *A*. Then Firm *B* has a total revenue of $60,000. If in turn Firm *B*'s raw material inputs are valued at $35,000, the value added by Firm *B* equals $25,000. Firm *A*'s $40,000 plus Firm *B*'s $25,000 plus the value added by each of the other producing units in the economy constitutes gross national product.

Now in the context of environmental economics, what must be emphasized is the fact that the *salable* output of each firm is used to compute GNP. It is as if each firm were a giant sausage machine. Raw material inputs are poured into one end, and human labor turns the crank. On the output end of the machine are two openings. Out of one comes the finished and packaged sausage. Out of the other comes a flow of wastes and environmental pollutants. Then a government statistician proceeds to count as value added the output of one opening (the value of packaged sausage) minus the cost of raw material inputs. Effluents coming from the other opening are ignored. That is, "good outputs" are counted while "bad outputs" are treated as if they do not exist.

Another way of stating the same thing is to say that only private costs are considered in the calculation of GNP. Social costs are not. From the salable output of a firm is deducted the cost of material inputs *to the firm*. If the cost imposed on society but not borne by the firm, the cost effects of polluting output, were to be deducted from sales revenues, the resulting measure of the firm's contribution to national production would be significantly less.

Deducting Social Costs

Some social costs are easily measured; others are very difficult to measure. Nevertheless, even if rough estimates are used, these could be built into a new social accounting system. From GNP would be deducted the cash value of all damage done by spillages, effluents, and emissions. Statistical measures of net production (net of environmental damage) could thereby be developed.

To illustrate, let us suppose that total ecological harm has been an increasing percentage of real GNP (GNP in constant dollars). These hypothetical percentages are assumed to be the following:

1957 through 1961:	10.0% of real GNP
1962 through 1965:	12.5% of real GNP
1966 through 1969:	15.0% of real GNP
1970 through 1973:	17.5% of real GNP

The results are summarized in Figure 23-1, where the top curve is a plot of GNP in constant 1958 dollars from 1957 to 1973. From GNP in each year is deducted the appropriate percentage as specified above in order to derive the hypothetical lower curve.

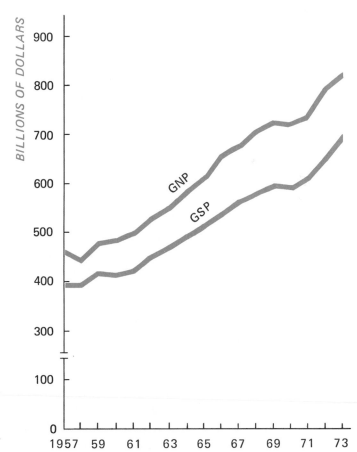

FIGURE 23-1

Losses from environmental effects cause net production (net of social costs) to be less than GNP.

SOURCE: *Economic Report of the President,* 1974.

The vertical distance between the two curves is an estimate of the dollar value of all social costs generated by negative externalities. The lower curve itself can be taken to measure national output after these deductions from GNP have been made. Let us call this concept *gross social product* in contrast to gross national product. The national income and product accounts begin with GNP to derive net national product, national income, and so on. Alternatively, or together with the product series, GSP could be used as a base to derive net social product, social income, and so on.

GNP in Figure 23-1 shows an annual average growth rate of about 5 percent per year from 1957 through 1973. However, the annual average growth rate shown by our hypothetical GSP over the same time interval is less than 4 percent per year. If we focus upon the growth of GNP as a measure of our material well-being, we shall delude ourselves into believing that our living standard is rising faster than it is in fact. Notice that neither concept measures our total well-being or happiness as a nation. But the growth rate of GNP, which takes no account of environmental effects, overestimates even the growth of our purely material well-being.

Measuring Material Welfare

As long as national economic goals are based on statistics that reflect value added rather than overall material welfare, governments will be guided by these numbers. As a consequence, economic policies will be formulated to raise value added instead of national economic well-being. As a nation, we could eventually find ourselves in a predicament born of policies that successfully enhance the growth of GNP but leave us worse off. One alternative is that described in the previous section, namely, to deduct from GNP the costs associated with destructive externalities.

A second method is to split the GNP figure into two components. The first would record that fraction of GNP which was produced with renewable resources and recyclable wastes. In a sense, this figure would be similar to net national product (GNP minus capital depreciation) in that it would subtract from output the "depreciation" of all natural and other resources regarded as free. The second component would record the total value of production based on the exhaustion of irreplaceable resources and the generation of indestructible wastes. If this distinction were made, it would be clear that the production of "clean" GNP—the first component—is a national gain in material welfare. In contrast, the production of "dirty" GNP—the second component—would be at best a temporary welfare gain at the expense of further harm to the environment.

The most important question is not whether one or another measure should be adopted. What is far more important is that the national income and product accounting system be modified to reflect environmental damage. With statistical measures from these accounts in hand, governmental authorities could mold public policies designed to maximize the first component of GNP described above (clean output) while minimizing the second component, rather than maximizing the sum of the two.

ISSUES OF PUBLIC POLICY

Ecological imbalance on the planet is definitely a most serious problem. Yet overindulgence in rhetoric can impair our ability to solve the problem. Behind many slogans concerned with ecology is a silent accusation against some supposedly greedy corporation intent upon spoiling the environment for its own gain. Such thoughtless sloganeering is reminiscent of the barbs cast at munitions manufacturers as war profiteers in the early part of this century. Since that time we have come to understand that war is a complex political, moral, and psychological event involving a population generally, and not the simple creation of munitions tycoons. However, most of us do not fully understand that ecological distortion is something in which the vast majority of mankind shares.

We mentioned earlier that heightened pollution is not a product of capitalism but of industralization. Consumers, that is to say, the population generally, also participate in pollution, share in the depletion of natural resources, and contribute directly or indirectly to urban blight. The fact that consumers are partially responsible does not excuse callous attitudes on the part of private firms. Rather, the responsibility of consumers, by condoning the harmful productive practices of firms, fosters the realization that environmental abuse is not limited to one sector of society. In general, whenever decision makers—be they firms, households, governments, or other public agencies—do not take account of the full social costs of their actions, the potential for destructive externalities is present. Unless ecological consciousness is raised, the wave of enthusiasm which perhaps peaked in the early 1970s will recede without lasting effect.

Public Control

Even if the usage of DDT were to be limited to its present level, the DDT intake of all the world's animals would go on rising. The reason is that animal intake in the coming years will show the cumulative effect of past practices. Likewise, the carbon dioxide content of the atmosphere, up 14 percent since 1900, would go right on rising if our consumption of fossil fuels were to remain constant.

Esthetic and economic damage to the environment does not occur by a single means. Neither will it be corrected by a single remedy. Some forms of ecological imbalance have been present for many decades, but these can be controlled when we are willing to devote the resources and the time and energy necessary for their control. Litter, excessive noise, sewage, and urban blight are examples. Other ecological problems, which have suddenly become critical, seem to be curable in time. These include pollution of the air and water. By allocating more resources to research and experimentation, there is reason to believe that new technologies capable of reducing these pollutants can be developed. Unfortunately other ecological problems were not even suspected until it was too late. The peregrine falcon is now extinct and the American eagle is threatened by widespread use of DDT. Because we do not even know all the consequences of common industrial practices, it is difficult to arrive at effective solutions.

Environmental abuse may be remedied in three ways. One way is to repair the damage after it has been done. A second way is to modify production and consumption so as to decrease environmental damage. The third way is to prohibit certain economic activities.

In some instances, repair is least costly. To provide trash collection in resort areas is clearly cheaper than prohibition of access to these areas. Some persons would say it is more economical to restore land and to plant new vegetation than to abandon mineral reserves now exploited by strip miners. An example of altered use, rather than complete prohibition, is provided by the automobile. As a practical matter, legal prohibition of the motor vehicle would be drastic if not unattainable. Yet with present technology, nothing short of prohibition will stop automobile pollution. Therefore, short of needed inventions, and allowing for the fact that society simply will not give up the automobile, the best practical course would seem to lie in a combination of measures: emission control devices, innovative power plants such as the Wankel engine, and greater use of alternative means of transportation. It must be recognized, however, that these measures will not completely solve the problems created by dangerous carbon dioxide pollutants.

Complete prohibition may be the only recourse when all else fails. Of course, prohibition of an economic activity is easier when some substitute activity is feasible, as in London when coal burning was banned in 1953. Gas and electricity were more expensive but less toxic. In general, no one means of correcting environmental abuse is always best, and the decision depends on relative costliness and effectiveness.

Who Pays the Cost?

Economics alone does not decide for public officials what actions should be taken to restore a healthy environment. As a general rule, a given corrective action is warranted if the benefits exceed the costs. Economics can help to evaluate benefits and to identify and evaluate costs. Since corrective action short of complete prohibition requires the use of resources, there is a question of who should bear these costs.

If all costs of production, including social costs, are fully internalized, a firm's product will sell at a higher price. By means of the market mechanism, consumers will pay, at least in part, for measures that reduce environmental harm. It might be argued that the firm is at fault and should bear the full cost. However, some sharing by consumers appears unavoidable. If costs of production are raised but firms are not allowed to raise prices to cover these cost increases, profits will decline and firms will have an incentive to reduce output and employment. As output reduction becomes widespread, total supply on the market will decline. Consumers competing for a scarcer supply will bid up the price. Thus, indirectly market forces still will act to raise the price.

Fines for pollution could be introduced, and such fines would discourage firms from taking certain risks. Taxes could also be levied. However, fines and taxes, once levied on producers, are treated as costs. Then market forces operate to raise prices. In general, a community committed to restoration of a clean environment must be prepared to assume the cost of doing so through foregone output, higher prices, or increased taxes.

PROMISING SIGNS?

Neither industry nor government has been quick to develop pollution control measures. Even in the face of an impending environmental crisis, public pressure has not been sufficient to stir the government until recently. It was not until 1955 that the first public law was passed—seven years after 20 people died and nearly 6,000 became ill in Donora, Pennsylvania, from four days of thermal inversion and pollutants, accompanied by fog.

Law and the Environment

The earliest governmental efforts dealt with air pollution. Public Law 84-159, passed in 1955, authorized the U.S. Public Health Service to prepare research proposals, disseminate information, and conduct studies on air pollution. However, the appropriation was only $5 million yearly for five years, a tiny fraction of government expenditures. The Clean Air Act of

1963 went much further. In addition to sanctioning research, this Clean Air Act authorized the Public Health Service to take corrective action where air pollution was an interstate problem and to grant money to local agencies to initiate or expand control programs. Authorized funding amounted to $25 million for 1965, $30 million for 1966, and $35 million for 1967.

The Clean Air Act was amended in 1965, establishing control standards for motor vehicle emissions. Other amendments raised funding levels from $46 million in 1967 to $74 million in 1969.

While this law was being amended, Congress in 1967 passed the Air Quality Act, which proposed a systematic method of coping with air pollution through regional action. The Act called for states to set air pollution standards, which were to be enforced locally if possible. It also gave muscle to local, state, and federal authorities in their fight against pollution. This Act appropriated funds of $74 million for 1968, $95 million for 1969, and $134 million for 1970.

By 1970 both the legislative and the executive branches of government had come to realize that the situation required even more drastic action. The Clean Air Act of 1970 was addressed principally to motor-vehicle emissions. It called for a 90 percent reduction in existing levels of hydrocarbons and carbon monoxide by 1975 and a 90 percent reduction of nitrogen oxides by 1976. But the law went further to set national emission standards for all "significant new pollution sources." The Clean Air Act of 1970 authorized $1.1 billion through 1973, with $350 million designated for research on low-emission fuels or standards and over $650 million for grants to state and local authorities. However, its primary impact was felt in the specification and enforcement of national pollution standards.

Responsibility for enforcement of the law was vested in the Environmental Protection Agency. Formed in the same year, the Agency assumed all authority formerly delegated to the Water Quality Administration, National Air Control Administration, and other bureaus concerned with pesticide regulation, radiation safety standards, and solid waste management. The Clean Air Act of 1970 requires EPA to publish standards designed to protect public health and authorizes citizens to take civil court action against private or governmental officials failing to carry out provisions of the law. Activities of the Environmental Protection Agency have been vigorous. In the first 11 months following its charge by Congress, the Agency initiated 159 criminal indictments. Although the Agency was also used to obtain injunctions to stop discharges of harmful wastes into water bodies, its primary efforts in the first two years were directed toward air pollution, especially motor-vehicle emissions.

A comprehensive piece of legislation dealing with water pollution came in the form of the Federal Water Pollution Control Act Amendments of 1972. Commonly referred to as "The Clean Water Act," this legislation aims at ending pollution of American waterways by 1985. To do so, the bill authorized the spending of $24.6 billion over the first three years. Most of this, $18 billion, is to be spent on sewage treatment plants. Yet every sort of water pollutant, from heavy metals like mercury and cadmium to overheated water from electrical power plants, is defined and limited.

During 1972 the United States Congress passed two other laws addressed to the state of the environment. The Environmental Pesticide Control Act gave intrastate as well as interstate jurisdiction over pesticide sales to the EPA, and the Act streamlined cancellation procedures when products are found to be harmful. Congress also passed a strong noise control bill that empowered the EPA to set decibel standards for all noise sources.

International cooperation was stressed in the United Nations Conference on the Human Environment held in Stockholm in June of 1972. Out of this conference emerged a resolution to establish a new U.N. Environmental Agency to control ocean dumping, monitor atmospheric and terrestrial health hazards, safeguard animal life, exchange information, and emphasize population control. Because of national disagreements, principally between industrialized nations and underdeveloped nations, the United Nations General Assembly has not to date acted on the proposed resolution.

Energy and Ecology

What assessment can one make of these legislative efforts? Something is being done to combat pollution, but prospects for the future are far from certain. Toward the end of 1973, political and economic events produced antagonism between energy developers and environmentalists. When the Arab oil embargo and shortages in domestic petroleum supply relative to American demand created what came to be known as an energy crisis, lobbyists for several private interests intensified their efforts to ease antipollution laws, citing the need to exploit additional sources of energy. President Nixon's special energy message to Congress late in January of 1974 called for relaxation of air quality standards. The Emergency Energy Act passed by Congress in March, 1974, allowed greater latitude in burning "dirty" fuels, restricted the enforcement powers of the EPA, and permitted delays in the deadlines for compliance with emission standards. Although the President vetoed the Act (primarily because of its provisions for gasoline rationing and oil-price rollbacks) and his veto was sustained by Congress, the Administration's counterproposal also contained provisions which set back the environmental movement.

During the first quarter of 1974, administrative actions in the public sector raised further tension points between ecology and the search for additional energy sources. The Department of the Interior ruled that energy needs took precedence over ecological interests and opened federally protected oil shale lands for development. The federal government and the state of California lifted a ban on drilling in the oil-rich but geologically unstable area of the Santa Barbara channel. Several large cities temporarily eased their own clean-air regulations.

Energy shortages in the short run are obvious and pressing. However, in the longer run the important issue is that of a balance between adequate sources of relatively clean energy on the one hand and conservation of the environment on the other. With increasing population, urbanization, and industrialization, the environmental crises will worsen unless the goal of a healthy environment receives even higher priority in the decade ahead. The fight against environmental abuse is going to be costly. Nevertheless, we are better able to pay these immediate costs than we will be to meet the incredible costs that will be brought to us in the future because of our present hesitancy to act against environmental abuse.

SUMMARY

1. Damage to the environment includes pollution, depletion of natural resources, and urban blight. Pollution takes the form of air and water pollution, sound pollution, and defacement of the environment through litter and waste disposal.

2. Environmental harm is one critical form of what in economics has long been called externalities. Negative externalities are, in effect, social costs.

3. Computation of GNP allows for private costs only. If social costs were taken into account, it would become apparent that gains in our general welfare are less than the growth of GNP.

4. Corrective action toward environmental abuse falls into three categories. These include repair to existing damage, modification of economic activities to reduce environmental spillover effects, and complete prohibition of some activities.

5. There are no uniform solutions to the environmental crisis. Benefits vary, and all actions entail costs. The general rule is that action is warranted when expected benefits exceed costs.

6. There are some signs that American society is responding at last to environmental problems through government intervention. Yet corrective actions appear to be overly cautious.

QUESTIONS FOR DISCUSSION AND ANALYSIS

1. What are the different forms of environmental damage? Which are most critical today?

2. In what ways have rapid advances in technology influenced the air pollution problem?

3. Distinguish between private and social costs. What is the relationship between social costs and pollution?

4. What is meant by externalities in economics? Give some examples of beneficial externalities and harmful externalities.

5. What does economic growth have to do with environmental problems?

6. Do you believe we overestimate our nation's productive greatness when we ignore environmental effects in computing GNP?

7. Is growth in GNP a precise indicator of national economic welfare? Why or why not?

8. What, in your opinion, are the major policy issues having to do with the environment?

9. Why has it taken so long for our country to recognize pollution for the hazard that it is?

SUGGESTED READINGS

Bohm, Peter. *The Economics of Environment.* New York: St. Martin's Press, Inc., 1971.

Campbell, Rex R., and Jerry L. Wade. *Society and Environment.* Boston: Allyn & Bacon, Inc., 1972.

Commoner, Barry. *The Closing Circle; Nature, Man and Technology.* New York: Alfred A. Knopf, Inc., 1971.

Edel, Matthew. *Economics and the Environment.* Englewood Cliffs, N.J.: Prentice-Hall, Inc., 1973.

Falk, Richard A. *This Endangered Planet.* New York: Random House, Inc., 1971.

Grad, Frank P., George W. Rathjens, and Albert J. Rosenthal. *Environmental Control.* New York: Columbia University Press, 1971.

Heber, Lewis. *Crisis in Our Cities*. Englewood Cliffs, N.J.: Prentice-Hall, Inc., 1965.

Ridker, Ronald G. *Economic Costs of Air Pollution*. New York: Praeger Publishers, Inc., 1967.

Strotz, Robert H. *Economics of Urban Air Pollution*. Washington: Resources for the Future, 1966.

Zurhorst, Charles. *The Conservation Fraud*. New York: Cowles Book Co., Inc., 1970.

PART SEVEN

Prices and Competition

24

The Price Mechanism

PREVIEW In a free enterprise economy the pricing system plays the major role in determining the allocation of manpower and resources, the distribution of income, and the rationing of goods and services. Prices are usually determined by the free forces of supply and demand. On occasion, however, prices are influenced by other factors, such as social forces, monopoly, and public authority.

Thus far we have concentrated primarily on macroeconomics. We have looked at the economy in general through its three major sectors and have analyzed the determinants of total production, employment, and income. We have investigated both the primary and the supplementary goals of the economy, and we have studied the various economic policies and measures employed in an effort to attain these goals. Now we turn to the area of microeconomics, where we analyze the problems and the issues associated with the individual, the business firm, the markets for particular goods or services, and the allocation of resources among various uses. Since prices guide consumption, output, and employment decisions, our analysis will center upon the price mechanism.

VALUE AND PRICE

Price is simply the exchange value of a commodity or service in terms of money. That is easy enough to understand. What is not so easy to comprehend is why various goods and services sell at particular prices, why prices change in relation to each other, or why the entire price level may rise or fall.

In a frontier society trade is carried on by means of *barter*—the exchange of one commodity for another. A pair of skin shoes, for example, may be traded for a fur cap. Then the price of the cap is the pair of shoes, or vice versa. There is no need for money in a transaction of this kind. In a more highly developed society barter as a means of trade is cumbersome and impractical. The would-be buyer of a cap, for example, usually does not have what the seller wants, perhaps a pair of shoes. Therefore, in order to facilitate the exchange of a great variety of goods and services, it is convenient to adopt a common denominator of value—something that can be used to measure the exchange value of both tangible and intangible goods.

Such a common denominator or unit of value may be a dollar, which in the United States is equivalent to 11.37 grains of gold; a mark in Germany; a franc in France; a pound in England; a ruble in Russia; or a peso in the Philippines. The government can print paper certificates or strike coins to represent a certain number of these monetary units. As we have already shown in Chapters 12 and 13, checking accounts held in commercial banks also serve as a medium of exchange. By use of either currency or credit, therefore, a good or service can be exchanged for a definite amount of money. The money in turn can be used to buy other commodities or services that the holder of the money may want.

Value

The word "value" implies worth. In economics, value refers to the worth of goods and services. At one time, economists discussed at length two functional aspects of value. For example, Adam Smith, in his *Wealth of Nations*, observed, "The word 'value' has two different meanings, and sometimes expresses the utility of some particular object and sometimes the power of purchasing other goods which possession of that object conveys." The first meaning indicated refers to *value in use*; the second, to *value in exchange*, which emerges from value in use.

Although we consume both economic goods and free goods, only economic goods and services have value. An economic good is one that is material, useful, scarce, and transferable. Other things being equal, the greater the usefulness of an item, the greater will be its value. It must also possess the characteristic of transferability, otherwise it will have value in use only and not value in exchange. Your typewriter, automobile, clothing, and numerous other items are economic goods.

On the other hand, ragweed and garbage, having no utility, are both noneconomic goods. A free good is one that possesses utility but has no price. Any good that is useful and transferable but exists in practically unlimited quantity will have no value in exchange. It may, however, have a very high value in use. Air in most cases is a free good. It cannot command a price, however, because all one has to do to obtain a sufficient quantity of it is to breathe. Of course, warm air in the wintertime and cool air in the summertime are relatively scarce. Consequently, when we pay to heat and air-condition our homes and offices for comfort or purify the air for other reasons, the air takes on characteristics of an economic good and has economic value.

Services, likewise, have economic value if they are useful, scarce, and transferable. Consequently, we pay for medical aid from a doctor, the advice of a lawyer, service by a waitress, and entertainment by a comedian.

Price

Exchange value is the capacity of a good to induce someone to consider giving something of value in trade for the good. Price is the expression of exchange value in terms of money. That exchange value precedes an expression of price is indicated by the fact that exchanges of goods and services sometimes take place without the aid of money.

While in many cases it is possible to effect exchanges of goods and services directly by agreeing on the ratios of their values, the inconvenience of barter resulted in the adoption of money as a medium of exchange. With practice, it is comparatively easy for people to relate the value of an economic good to money, thus establishing a price. It is true that money, especially paper money, has little economic value aside from its possible use as a medium of exchange; but it acquires value because of the purposes for which it is customarily used. Besides, its exchange value in terms of goods and services in general is more nearly stable than any other one thing. The money used by a nation becomes the common denominator of all exchangeable values.

MARKETS

In any study and analysis of markets, it should be remembered that there are markets for both *products* and *resources*. We are familiar with the price and market conditions surrounding the sale of products like steel, automobiles, shoes, entertainment, or food service. These are usually final products or services. But there is a host of markets for intermediate products and resources, such as iron ore, labor, space, and capital. Prices in these intermediate markets—whether these prices are wages for labor, rent for space, or interest for the use of capital funds—can have an important influence on prices in the final product market.

As economists use the term, a *market* refers not so much to a particular place where things are bought and sold as it does to the whole area in which the forces of demand and supply operate. This concept of a market is somewhat different from that which is often implied. For example, one speaks of the local egg market, of the wheat market at the Chicago Board of Trade, or of the securities market at the New York Stock Exchange or the American Stock Exchange. Of course, when the term "market" is used in these connections, the meaning is clear and the use is entirely correct. In a study of the operation of demand and supply as determinants of market price, however, it is necessary to conceive of the market as being more extensive in area than that involved in the place where buyers and sellers meet face to face and exchange titles to goods. It is necessary to think in terms of the whole area in which individuals and groups engage in the activities related to the buying and selling of the commodity under consideration.

When the commodity is unique, such as works of art or handmade articles, the market may be small. In the case of most goods, however, the area over which the forces of demand and supply operate, either directly or indirectly, is extensive. The wheat market, for example, is almost worldwide. Wheat produced in the United States, Canada, Argentina, Australia, and in other countries may move to any point on the earth that is served by transportation and communication facilities. The supply of wheat is affected by weather conditions, methods of production, and the natural productivity of the soil in all the regions adapted to the growth of the grain. The demand for wheat products is largely conditioned by the purchasing power of people and by their eating habits. These are factors that directly affect the supply of and the demand for wheat and its products in all localities. In addition, the availability of other kinds of grain has indirect effects.

The wider the market and the more nearly competitive it is, the stronger is the tendency for the price of an article to become and to remain uniform over the whole market area. If the wheat market were entirely free, the price of wheat, except for differences in marketing costs, would tend to be the same all over the world. However, political barriers, such as import tariffs and regulatory programs, affect the supply and the price of commodities in individual nations.

DETERMINANTS OF PRICES

To understand how a particular market price is determined, two sets of factors must be considered. One set is that of demand and supply, or the prices which potential buyers are willing to pay and potential sellers are willing to take. The other set is comprised of several social determinants.

Demand and Supply

The underlying factors that determine the price of a commodity or a service are demand and supply. As we shall see in the next chapter, the operation of these factors may be modified or, in some cases, controlled indefinitely. Nevertheless, they remain basic and their influence persists. For practical purposes, however, actual money prices are often influenced in great measure by social conditions and forces other than those that relate directly to the demand for and the supply of commodities.

Social and Economic Institutions

Social forces affect or modify the demand for and the supply of practically every good. Social price determinants refer to certain organized or established social practices and recognized conditions that may be referred to as (1) custom and tradition, (2) competition, (3) monopoly, and (4) public authority.

Custom and Tradition. At one time custom played the predominant role in the determination of prices. Any departure from customary price carried with it the likelihood of moral condemnation by the public. Even now the influence of custom on prices cannot be entirely ignored. For example, the prices charged for candy bars, chewing gum, and certain professional services in a particular region are more or less customary prices. With generally rising prices, sometimes the size, the quantity, or the quality of particular goods will be altered in preference to changing their customary prices.

Competition. Market competition—competition in buying and selling—implies that buyers are bidding for units of a good at certain prices and that sellers are competing with each other by offering to sell units of that good at various prices. The buyers are competing for the goods, and the sellers are competing for the buyers' money. Competition assumes that, as a rule, the individual consumer will tend to act in a manner that will maximize his economic welfare. Under competitive conditions sellers and buyers are assumed to be actuated by motives of economic self-interest.

This assumption of self-interest is sometimes criticized on the ground that even in economic transactions human beings are not always guided by selfish motives. Considerations other than those of an economic nature sometimes do influence the parties to a transaction. For example, a seller, because of his sympathy for a needy buyer, may not exact the highest possible price he could obtain. Likewise, a sympathetic buyer may refrain from driving a hard bargain in dealing with a seller who is in financial straits. Such instances, however, are exceptions to the rule.

Where competition is truly effective, the individual can do little to influence market prices. The price at which wheat sells on the market, for example, is usually fixed by the offers and bids of millions of sellers and buyers, no one of whom is able to exert any appreciable influence on the market price. The daily prices on the large grain exchanges would not be measurably higher if any particular seller of wheat refused to sell at the prevailing price; nor would the price go down if he were to sell. Prices are not affected much by the buying or failure to buy of any one buyer. The reason why the transactions of individual buyers and sellers have little or no influence on prices in a competitive market is that the quantity exchanged in a single transaction is small in comparison with the total amount bought and sold.

Monopoly. By contrast, *monopoly* is a condition under which a single seller has control of the total supply. In such a situation the seller can, if he chooses, exact the highest possible price for his product. If the price offered is not satisfactory to him, he may refuse to sell; or he may sell part of his stock to that bidder who will pay the price he asks and sell the remainder at a lower price; or he can withhold it altogether. But if he is to sell his goods, he must be willing to agree to some price that buyers will pay. On the other hand, buyers may be forced to pay a higher price than they think the commodity is worth, especially if it is a necessity, because there are no alternative sources of supply available to them.

In most cases, both competitive elements and monopolistic elements are present in the marketing situation since these elements are major forces in determining prices.

Public Authority. Prices are sometimes determined by public authority. Where government has taken over the function of price determination, the declared objective has usually been the promotion of the public good or the protection of the public from exploitation. For example, the attempt of the federal government to influence farm prices continues after many years because the incomes of farmers are low in comparison with those of certain other economic groups. The remedy sought is to raise the prices of the items that the farmers sell. Likewise, in order to protect low-income wage earners, the Fair Labor Standards Act establishes minimum wages that employers must pay.

During World War II and the Korean conflict, the government intervened to control prices, either directly or indirectly. The justification of such controls, of course, was that under great emergency conditions the usual processes by which prices are determined are greatly distorted. Under such circumstances, price and wage controls are necessary to keep resources and manpower flowing in the proper productive and distributive channels in order to attain a balance of consumer, capital, and military goods and services essential to winning the war.

A policy of price fixing by governmental authority implies, at best, an assumption that the promotion or the preservation of some value other than economic value is important. At its worst, price fixing by public authority implies neglect of or disregard for the nature and importance of economic forces in price determination. Considerable opposition came from the business community and labor centers in the mid-1960s when the federal government attempted to more stringently enforce President Johnson's voluntary wage-price guideposts. But in the period 1971-1973, the government found much support when it imposed wage and price controls as a means of limiting the impact of inflationary forces in the economy.

THE FUNCTIONS OF PRICES

In our economy prices perform three basic functions:

1. Prices allocate factors of production to specific uses.
2. Prices determine distribution of the total output or the national income.
3. Prices serve as a mechanism for rationing goods and services.

The extent to which prices perform these functions satisfactorily depends upon the manner in which prices are determined.

Functions of Prices in a Free Enterprise Economy

Where free enterprise exists, market prices are relied upon to indicate the demand for goods and services of different kinds. A rise in the price of beef is interpreted by cattlemen to mean that more cattle is wanted by consumers. A decrease in the price of beef is likewise notice that demand is less than supply. Therefore, if the former price is to be restored, there must be either a decrease in the number of beef cattle offered on the market or an increase in the demand.

In the absence of authoritarian price fixing, price is the result of the relationship between the demand for and the supply of a commodity. For example, in most cases if the demand for a good remains constant while the supply diminishes, the price will rise. If the demand diminishes while the supply remains constant, the price will fall. On the other hand, as a rule, if demand and supply increase or decrease proportionally, the price will not be affected. Other possible combinations in the relationships between demand and supply tend to produce certain definite changes in the price of a good. The prices resulting from demand and supply are assumed to be determined automatically so long as producers and consumers are free to act according to their own inclinations.

In a free enterprise economy indications of a need for more or for less goods of a particular kind are made known by fluctuations in market prices. Under such a system, it is assumed that customers know what goods and services they want, how much they want, and what price they are willing to pay. Profit-seeking producers are depended upon to provide the quantity and quality of goods that are wanted. Existing or potential entrepreneurs are assumed to be ready and willing to provide the goods desired, as long as the price is such that there is an opportunity for making a profit.

The reliability of prices as a guide to production depends upon the extent to which competition prevails. Where monopoly exists, high prices (as we shall see later) cannot always be relied upon to bring about an increase in production.

Prices and the Allocation of the Factors of Production. When the desire for profits is assumed to be the incentive for production, prices are depended upon to allocate resources or factors of production among alternative uses. Other things being equal, business firms undertake to utilize land, labor, and capital for the production of those goods that seem to promise adequate profit.

The process by which the factors of production are directed to the production of goods according to profit prospects is not a simple one. Generally, before undertaking the production of a good, the entrepreneur estimates the number of units that he can sell at various prices. Although a number of methods are available for making such estimates, none of them is precise or foolproof. Consequently, there is always a certain element of error or risk involved. Nevertheless, the producer must arrive at some estimate of his probable income and expenses if he is to proceed with any degree of intelligence. First, he estimates the quantity he could sell at various prices. Then he estimates the cost of producing these quantities. If he decides that the undertaking would be worth the risk—that he could probably make a satisfactory profit—he sets about gathering the labor, capital, and materials needed for producing an approximate number of units. The amount of labor, capital, and natural resources he will employ in production will depend, in part, upon the price he has to pay for the units of each factor.

Obviously, then, price is the primary determining factor in decisions affecting the utilization of the factors of production. In the first place, estimates as to possible revenue can be arrived at only by a consideration of expected selling prices of finished goods. The volume of demand for each of the factors of production will, in turn, depend upon the price of each factor in relation to its productivity.

The demand for productive factors derives from the demand for finished goods. The prices of finished goods depend at least in part upon their scarcity. The scarcity of finished goods, however, may be conditioned largely by the scarcity of the factors of production. Consumer demand, reflected in the commodity price, tends to direct the relatively scarce land, labor, and capital into the production of those goods which will enable producers to pay the highest prices for the factors of production.

Whether the goods that are produced are those that are socially most beneficial is another matter. Under a system of free enterprise, however, it is assumed that the needs of society for goods and services of various kinds and quantities are indicated by prices. For example, it is taken for granted that a rise in the price of bread will cause more productive resources to be devoted to the production of wheat and bread. Notwithstanding efficient operation of the market, however, price is not an infallible guide to the production of those goods that are the most socially necessary or desirable for the general welfare of society. Although the composition of production is determined by a democratic process based upon prices and dollar votes as expressed by consumers, this situation can lead to inequities since those with the most dollars have the most votes. If certain individuals or groups acquire an excessive number of dollars and others have an extreme scarcity of dollars, the unbalanced distribution could operate to the detriment of the total economy. In fact, we might envision a situation in which an economy might produce an ample supply of luxury apartments, swimming pools, and high-priced automobiles while having an insufficient amount of bread, medical care, or low-cost housing essential for the best interest of society.

To abandon prices as a method of directing production, however, requires the substitution of political controls, such as those existing in the Soviet economy. Except in times of emergency or in the production of certain goods, such as school buildings or highways, Americans have preferred to rely as much as possible on free market prices rather than government edict to decide what use shall be made of the factors of production. In the American economy, when the powers of the government have been invoked to influence production, it has generally been in an indirect fashion, such as making more credit available for the construction and purchase of homes, favoring domestic producers with an import tariff, paying subsidies to farmers, or granting financial aid to the needy and the aged.

Prices and the Distribution of National Income. By our system of prices and the dollar votes, we do more than determine what is going to be produced. We also determine, at least in part, the income that is to be received by owners of the various factors of production. Since revenue from the sale of goods and services to consumers is the means by which businessmen purchase factors of production, the more we are willing to pay for these goods and services, the greater the means at the disposal of the producer to obtain the necessary factors of production. Although many other things— such as the productivity of labor, the stage of technological development, the supply of resources, and the presence of labor unions—have a direct bearing on the payment to the factors of production, revenue from consumer demand is the ultimate source of income payments. Our strong demand for automobiles and homes, for example, is in large part the reason why automobile and construction workers are among the highest paid in the nation. Our desire for entertainment affords large-scale salaries for Hollywood and TV talent. The demand for choice downtown office space provides high rental income to the landlord. The income received by the owners of these and other factors of production in the form of wages, rent, interest, and profits, of course, provides the purchasing power needed to obtain a certain share of the total goods and services produced by the nation's economy. Thus, our pricing system generally serves to distribute our national income and to divide the total output of goods and services among the owners of the factors of production according to their respective economic contributions as measured by the consumer demand.

Prices and the Rationing of Goods. The possibility of getting goods and services of any kind usually depends upon the amount of money buyers have to spend and the prices of the goods they wish to buy. When personal income is high in proportion to the prices of goods, people can afford to buy a wide range of commodities. On the other hand, in any economy when money incomes are small in proportion to the prices of goods, only a fortunate few are able to obtain more than the simple necessities of life. Since the total desire for goods and services is generally greater than the capacity of the economy to produce, the system of consumer demand and prices serves as a rationing mechanism to allocate the available goods and services. As prices rise, those with higher incomes and the willingness to pay will be able to obtain particular goods and services, while others who do not have the income or are unwilling to pay the high prices must go without those particular goods or services.

With a given amount of money to spend, one may select those articles that he can afford according to the intensity of his desire for them. In this way he gives priority to those wants of which he is most conscious at the time. By a process of balancing wants against money expenditure, he is able to derive the greatest total amount of satisfaction from the use of his money.

Functions of Prices in Command Economies

In a totalitarian society, most prices are fixed directly or indirectly by a central authority and not necessarily by the forces generated by the action of sellers and buyers. In Nazi Germany, for example, the central government determined what and how much should be produced. By one means or another, wages, rent, and interest were fixed, or at least controlled within narrow limits, by public authority. Maximum prices for consumer goods were established. Stiff penalties, including fine and imprisonment, were levied against violators. On the whole, however, the Nazis were able to control prices and production and to retain a semblance of the institution of private property and production for profit.

In Soviet Russia practically all land and capital are owned by the state. Rent, interest, and profits as forms of private income are generally prohibited, except that the government may pay interest on savings deposits. The savings thus acquired are used to promote production according to the plans of the government. Nearly everyone is an employee of the state. To some extent wages in the different industries may be manipulated in such a way as to attract labor into those lines of production that the authorities wish to expand. The prices of most goods are fixed by the state, and in many cases a system of rationing is employed in an effort to restrict the amounts that individuals may buy. Although retail prices as set by administrative order are intended broadly to reflect conditions of supply and demand, prices in the Soviet economy are primarily tools in the hands of planners. For decades the pricing system was used as the primary means of assuring the production and consumption of the items they had planned, rather than as a voluntary mechanism guiding the operation of the economy. In recent years there has been considerable analysis and discussion among the Soviet planners regarding the flexible pricing and profit system adopted as a means of eliminating waste and inefficiency in the Soviet economy. The Soviets have been experimenting with such a system in some consumer goods industries, such as shoes and clothing, for the past ten years. Profits are regarded as merely a measure of efficiency, and the use of profits is subject to control by the state.

In England a major attempt was made after World War II to set up a system of democratic socialism. Wartime price controls and rationing were continued on a wide scale. In some cases government influenced prices by direct action; in others, by indirect methods. More recently Britain in the mid-1960s established an incomes policy to influence prices and wages. When this did not prove to be as successful as anticipated, the government did for a time enforce direct price and wage controls. Although controls were subsequently removed, they were reinstituted in 1973.

Thus, we are able to grasp one of the essential differences between a system of free enterprise and an economy that is controlled by a central governmental authority. Under free enterprise capitalism, prices are relied upon to reflect the relative demand for particular goods and services; to direct the utilization of the factors of production; to allocate shares of the national income to the owners of the factors of production; and to enable individuals to derive the greatest possible satisfaction from the money they have to spend. Under a centrally controlled economy, prices are used mainly to allocate resources and to distribute shares of the national income *according to the judgment of policy-making officials* and to enable consumers to satisfy their wants by using goods that are made available for purchase. In a socialized economy, what should be produced and the allocation of the factors of production are matters that are decided by a planning authority.

SUMMARY

1. Price is exchange value stated in terms of money. Prices come into existence and function in the economy because of the necessity for exchanging goods and services.

2. A market may imply either a particular place or an extended area where the forces of supply and demand operate.

3. In a free enterprise capitalistic economy the underlying price factors are demand and supply. Actual prices, however, are influenced in any given case by the operation of the social institutions or practices that affect prices in the economy. These institutions include custom and tradition, competition, monopoly, and public authority. By contrast, prices in a highly centralized economy are generally fixed by a central governmental authority.

4. Prices perform three major functions: (a) they serve as a means for the allocation of the factors of production; (b) they provide a method for the distribution of the total output or national income; and (c) they serve as a device for the rationing of economic goods.

QUESTIONS FOR DISCUSSION AND ANALYSIS

1. Define price.

2. Explain two different concepts of a market.

3. Distinguish between "value in use" and "value in exchange." Which one has the greater influence on price? Why?

4. In the absence of money, how is price manifested?

5. Give an example of the price of a commodity or service that is determined, at least in part, by each of the following methods: (a) custom; (b) competition (c) monopoly; and (d) public authority.

6. What are the three major functions of prices in a free enterprise economic system?

7. How do prices help to determine incomes and distribute the national output among the factors of production?

8. "Price serves as a rationing mechanism." Explain.

9. Does the price system assure the best possible allocation of resources and production of goods and services? Explain.

10. How are the decisions regarding what and how much to produce made in the Soviet economy? Do they use a price system at all? If so, in what manner?

SUGGESTED READINGS

Mansfield, Edwin. *Microeconomics, Theory and Applications*. New York: W. W. Norton & Company, Inc., 1970.

Massel, Mark S. *Competition and Monopoly*. Garden City, N. Y.: Doubleday & Company, Inc., 1964.

Schumpeter, Joseph A. *The Nature and Necessity of a Price System*. New York: Columbia University Press, 1934.

25

Demand and Supply

PREVIEW   Market price is determined by demand and supply. In the absence of external forces, an equilibrium price is established at the point where the demand for and the supply of a particular good are equal. Prices fluctuate with changes in demand and supply. An increase in demand, for example, causes the price of a commodity to rise and the amount sold to increase, and vice versa. An increase in supply causes prices to fall and the amount sold to rise. Many factors cause changes in demand and supply. For instance, a change in demand may result from, among other things, a rise in income, an increase in population, or a change in the price of competing goods. The revenue of the seller is affected by the price. Sometimes it would benefit him to sell more of a commodity at a lower price. But this will depend on consumer responsiveness to a change in price. This responsiveness, measured by price elasticity of demand, along with other measures of elasticity, helps determine the market price.

In a free enterprise system, the forces of demand and supply are relied upon to determine prices. Consumers express their demand in the prices they are willing to pay for various products. Business firms seeking profit cater to consumer demand by offering goods and services at various prices. Consequently, a market is established in which the final price is determined on the basis of costs to the producer and usefulness to the buyer.

Changes in either demand or supply bring about adjustments in the amount of goods and services sold, or price changes, or both. If consumers throughout the nation, for example, begin buying more power lawn mowers, retail outlets will have to order inventory replacements and additional mowers from wholesalers. Manufacturers in turn begin to produce more power mowers. Depending on the available supply and the cost of resources, these additional mowers may be supplied at the same or at a different price. At any rate, consumer demand is made known to the producers through the marketing structure. At other times, suppliers will endeavor to anticipate the demands of consumers and supply the goods before there is a strong reflection of demand. The system does not work perfectly; at times there are lags and leads in the market, gluts and shortages occur, and prices fluctuate. But considering the billions of items produced and sold each year, the system somehow seems to do an excellent job of satisfying consumer demand.

The demand for goods of all kinds—producer goods as well as consumer goods—can be traced to the demand for goods and services that directly satisfy human wants. For example, the demand or desire of individuals for shelter gives rise to a demand for brick and lumber, which, in turn, gives rise to a demand for iron and steel with which to make tools and machines for the production of brick and lumber, and so on. Therefore, we may say that the demand for a commodity that grows out of the desire to satisfy the demand for some other commodity or service is *derived demand.*

UTILITY AND WANTS

Our study of demand begins by considering the nature of utility and value. We shall learn why goods are wanted, why some goods are wanted more than others, and what happens to our wants as we acquire or consume one or more units of a particular good. We shall then proceed to discover how the ratios by which goods are exchanged for each other are established. In this way we can acquire a clearer understanding of the nature and significance of prices.

Here it is important to remember that *utility* is the power of a good or service to satisfy a want. It is not a physical property; neither is it a constant quality or quantity. It is the capacity of a good or service to give satisfaction to particular individuals at a particular time or over a period of time. Since utility is measured by the satisfaction a consumer derives from a good or service, utility varies with different individuals at a given moment, and it may fluctuate from time to time, depending upon the needs and circumstances of individuals. Consumption is the act or process of using goods or services, which results in the absorption of utility.

Effect of Consumption on Utility

When you are extremely thirsty, you possibly would be willing to pay 25 cents or more for a cold drink, for which ordinarily you would be willing to pay only 10 cents. The reason is that the drink would have the capacity to give you great satisfaction at the time.

After drinking the contents of one container, however, you might not buy another. The reason is simple: you are not as thirsty as you were. You could have other identical containers for the payment of the same price as for the first one; but for you the utility of a bottle or can of cold liquid has decreased. It is entirely possible that you could enjoy drinking more, but the pleasure that could be derived from doing so may not be sufficient to induce you to buy another container at the same price that you paid for the first. This is but one example of the fact that one's craving or desire for a particular good becomes less as additional units of that good are consumed.

Actual consumption, however, is not essential in order that a decrease in utility occur at a particular time. Mere possession of a good may be sufficient to bring about a decrease in the utility of the good. For example, you may have no immediate use for a box of shotgun shells. If you expect to go hunting in the future, however, you would be willing to pay something for a box of shells. You might even buy two boxes. After having acquired one or more boxes, your inclination to buy an additional box would be less than before because for you it would not have as much present utility as the previous one purchased.

Marginal Utility

The utility to an individual of a single unit of a good at a given time is referred to as the marginal utility. More precisely, we may say that *marginal utility* is the utility differential that results from the consumption of one more or one less unit of a homogeneous good. Assume that you have two pencils that are exactly alike. You might not wish to part with one of them. At the same time, the loss of one of them would not mean as much to you as it would if you had only one. Now suppose that you had a dozen pencils, all alike. You would more readily part with one of them than if you had only two. The loss of one would not make a great deal of difference to you. Likewise, the amount you would be willing to pay for an additional pencil would depend upon how many you had. Since all the pencils are alike, the utility of one pencil more or one pencil less depends upon the number possessed. When the number possessed is large, the marginal utility of a pencil of that kind is less than if the supply were smaller.

The conclusion is that in the consumption or acquisition of additional identical units of a good, a point is reached where the consumption or the acquisition of an additional unit will yield less satisfaction than did the previous unit consumed or acquired. This relationship between the number of units and the utility derived therefrom is commonly referred to as the *law of diminishing marginal utility*, and it is demonstrated in Figure 25-1. While this general relationship is accepted as a matter of course and is readily demonstrable, its influence upon human conduct and business operations is complex.

Failure to distinguish between the marginal utility and total utility may lead to erroneous conclusions as to the relative social importance of goods and services of different kinds. To individuals and to society as a whole, a carat weight of diamond usually has a higher value than does a bushel of wheat because ordinarily the marginal utility of a diamond is higher than the marginal utility of a bushel of wheat. The utility of the total supply of wheat, however, may be greater than that of the total supply of diamonds.

Consumption Tends to Balance Marginal Utilities

When we purchase or consume a good, we do so because that good gives more utility than others that we might obtain for the same expenditure of money. Other things considered, we generally buy or consume quantities of those goods or services that have the highest marginal utility to us.

We seldom attempt to acquire or use a good to the extent that our desire for that good is completely satisfied. Rather, we attend to that want which at the time is most urgent; that is, we spend our dollars on units of those goods and services whose marginal utilities are highest, until a point is reached where the marginal utilities of other goods are as great or greater. Since wants are numerous, since they are recurrent, and since marginal utilities of goods fluctuate, the average consumer finds that spending is a constant process of trying to equalize the marginal utilities of goods and services in relation to dollars spent. The apparent improbability of equilibrating the marginal utilities of various goods and services in reality makes the decision-making process more interesting. But, if the consumer were to reach the equilibrium level, he would be at a point where he could spend a dollar in any direction and obtain the same amount of utility. In short, he would be at a point where $\dfrac{MU_x}{P_x} = \dfrac{MU_y}{P_y}$.

In many cases the decisions of what and how much to consume are made subconsciously. Especially does this occur when incomes are low and most spending has to be for basic food, clothing, shelter, and personal care. But as real income increases and our discretionary income becomes larger, more consideration and deliberation may be given to the spending process because of the larger number of possible choices available.

Utility is a prime motivation in the determination of wants. Exchange value is needed, however, to secure goods and services in order to satisfy wants. Thus, utility and exchange value actively affect prices.

From the standpoint of the desire for goods and services, utility is the cardinal factor. When we consider the problems that relate to the distribution of goods, however, exchange value is the matter of central importance. Since the emergence of utility and exchange value precedes prices, it is desirable that we examine the steps leading from utility and demand to price.

DEMAND

In studying the influence of demand on the price of any given commodity or service, we must recognize two levels of demand—individual or personal demand and market demand. Market demand is merely the aggregate of personal demand.

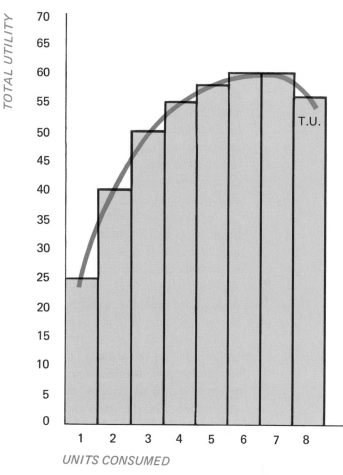

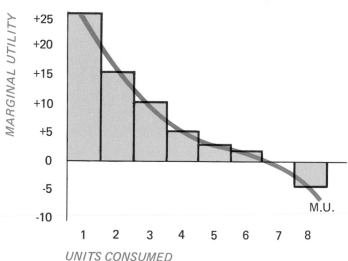

FIGURE 25-1

TOTAL UTILITY VS. MARGINAL UTILITY

As additional units of a good are consumed, total utility will increase up to a certain point, but the addition to total utility, marginal utility, resulting from each successive unit consumed will diminish. If a sufficient number of units are consumed, a point may be reached where marginal utility is negative, causing total utility to fall.

Individual Demand

Demand implies something more than need or desire. Of course, the individual must feel a need for the utility that a good or service can provide before he will consider ways and means of procuring the good or service. In addition, however, he must possess purchasing power if he is to satisfy his need. You may have a strong desire, for example, for a new model Corvette or Thunderbird, but unless you have the cash to pay for it or the ability to buy on credit, your desire will have no influence on the market. Individual demand therefore implies a desire plus some purchasing power. It signifies the quantity of a good that an individual stands ready to buy at each price at a particular time.

As stated above, the utility of a good to an individual at a particular time depends upon the number of units that he has recently consumed or that may be available for use when he wants them. If the number of units that have been consumed or that are available is large, the marginal utility of an additional unit is likely to be lower than it otherwise would be. Hence, the price of a commodity will usually affect the quantity that an individual will buy at a given time. For example, a housewife may buy one pound of butter at the grocery at a given price, but she would purchase less if the price is higher. On the other hand, she may buy two pounds if the price is low enough. Again, merchants are aware of the relationship of the subjective prices of potential buyers—the prices that buyers will pay—to quantities that will be bought when they conduct sales at reduced prices and give quantity discounts.

Market Demand

Market demand (or simply demand) consists of the total quantity of a good that would be bought in the aggregate by individuals and firms at each of several prices at a given time. *Demand*, therefore, is defined as a schedule of the total quantities that purchasers will buy at different prices at a given time. An accurate schedule of this kind for a specific commodity is difficult to construct in advance because it requires that we know just how many units people would actually buy at various prices. We do know, however, that at a given time people will tend to buy more units of a good at a low price than they will at a high price. The reasons, of course, are the three simple and general facts that (1) sooner or later the law of diminishing marginal utility operates in connection with the consumption of any kind of a good, (2) purchasing power is not equally distributed among possible buyers, and (3) the desire for a particular good varies with different individuals and groups. A lower price for an article, therefore, generally results in the sale of a larger amount of that product. Conversely, a higher price, other things remaining the same, usually tends to curtail the amount that can be sold. Thus, we are justified in concluding that the quantity of a good that people will buy tends to vary inversely with the price.

The expression "tends to vary inversely," as used here, does not imply that the variation in the amount sold is always proportionate to the change in price. Indeed, in many instances, a decrease of 50 percent in the price of a good probably would not result in a 50 percent rise in the number of units sold; nor would an increase of 100 percent in the price likely result in a corresponding decrease in the amount that would be purchased. In some cases the change in the quantity sold might be more than proportional to the change in price; in others, it might be less.

A Market Demand Schedule

Since the quantity of any good demanded ordinarily tends to vary inversely with its price, we can construct a hypothetical schedule of prices and quantities to illustrate this relationship. Let us assume that on Tuesday, at noon, the buyers on the Chicago Board of Trade would buy at different prices the amounts of wheat shown in the second column, D (demand), in Table 25-1. Notice that larger amounts of wheat would be bought at lower prices.

TABLE 25-1

DEMAND SCHEDULES FOR WHEAT

If the Price Is:	Thousands of Bushels That Will Be Bought		
	D	D$_1$	D$_2$
$2.50	2,000	3,000	1,000
2.45	2,300	3,400	1,300
2.40	2,800	4,300	1,610
2.35	3,500	4,800	2,100
2.30	4,200	5,600	2,700
2.25	5,100	6,625	3,425
2.20	6,075	7,650	4,400
2.15	7,250	9,000	5,410
2.10	8,500	10,400	6,700
2.05	10,000	12,000	8,000

The relation between price and the number of bushels that would be bought is represented graphically in Figure 25-2. The vertical line, OY, indicates at regular intervals the price per bushel; and the horizontal line, OX, shows the quantity in millions of bushels. Now we can locate points that lie at the intersection of a line drawn horizontally and to the right from each price shown on OY and a line drawn vertically and upward from each corresponding quantity as indicated on OX. Thus, to locate the point for the demand for 5,100,000 bushels at $2.25 a bushel, a horizontal line to the right is drawn from that price and a vertical line upward is drawn from

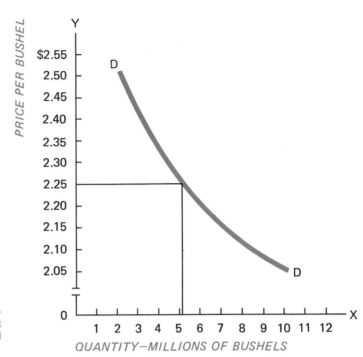

FIGURE 25-2

DEMAND CURVE FOR WHEAT

A typical demand curve slopes downward to the right, indicating that greater quantities will be purchased at lower prices.

that quantity. The point of intersection of two lines is thus determined by reference to the two coordinates, price and quantity.

When all the points have been located in this way, they specify a curve that slopes downward to the right. If the price and the quantity changes were infinitely small and if they varied according to the proportions indicated in the schedules, the result in the graph would really be such a curve. For our purposes, therefore, we may construct a curve to indicate demand. This curve is merely a graphic way of representing how in this case the quantity of wheat that would be bought varies inversely with price.

The demand schedule may be represented by a curve or by a straight line. The curve may have a slight or a steep slope, it may be continuous or discontinuous, or it may be smooth or jagged, depending on the nature of the demand for the particular product and the ability to obtain sufficient information to plot the demand schedule. Consequently, there are all kinds and shapes of demand curves.

Although the normal or typical demand curve moves downward to the right, it is not uncommon to find a product for which the demand curve will move downward to the right over a given range of prices, but then eventually it will curve backward to the left. This would indicate, of course, that in certain price ranges less of the product would be purchased at lower prices.

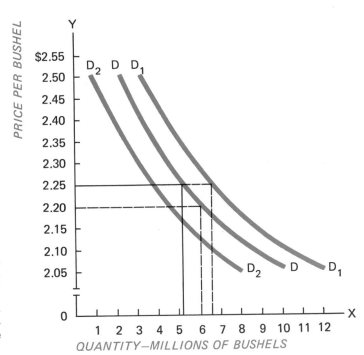

FIGURE 25-3

DEMAND CURVES FOR WHEAT

An increase in demand causes the demand curve to shift to the right, indicating that a greater quantity will be sold at each respective price. A decrease in demand causes a leftward shift of the demand curve, indicating that lesser quantities will be sold at respective prices.

Prestige items are sometimes in this category. Mink coats, for example, are a status symbol to many people. As the price is lowered, more people will buy mink coats. But, if the price became so low that almost anyone could afford to buy a mink coat, it would lose its prestige status and it is possible that few women would want to buy one.

Change or Shift in Demand

Remember that on a typical demand curve, more will be sold at lower prices. Notice on the demand curve in Figure 25-2 that at a price of $2.25 a little over 5 million bushels of wheat would be sold, but at a price of $2.20 more than 6 million would be sold. Consequently, if a price of $2.20 were charged instead of $2.25, does this mean that there is an increase in demand? Absolutely not. Remember that we defined demand as a schedule of amounts that would be purchased at various prices at a given instant of time. Even though we altered the price from $2.25 to $2.20 and sold more, this is not a change in demand. Nothing has happened to the demand schedule. We simply moved to a lower price to take advantage of larger sales at lower prices. This is known as a movement on the demand curve, or is sometimes referred to as a change in the quantity demanded, and should not be confused with a change in demand. In order to have a *change in demand*, or what is sometimes referred to as a shift in demand, a greater or lesser amount of the product would be purchased at given prices.

An increase in demand means that a greater quantity will be bought at the same price. Thus, in Table 25-1, D_1 is a schedule showing an increase in the amount that will be purchased at each of the prices as compared with that for D in the second column. If the demand curve for D_1 is plotted, it will lie to the right of that of D, as shown in Figure 25-3. It indicates, for example, that at a price of $2.25, 6.6 million bushels will be sold instead of the 5.1 million bushels as indicated on the original demand curve, D.

A decrease in demand means that a smaller quantity will be bought at the same price. In Table 25-1, D_2 is a schedule showing a decrease in demand as compared with that for D. The curve for D_2 would lie to the left of that for D, as shown in Figure 25-3. A change in demand may result from a number of different causes, such as a change in income, a change in population, new uses for a product, more advertising, and even a change in the price of competing products.

ELASTICITY OF DEMAND

Since demand is a schedule of amounts that will be purchased at various prices, the seller is often faced with a problem of determining at which price to offer his goods for sale. It is true that a greater amount of sales can be made at lower prices. But will greater revenue from the larger sales offset the reduced revenue from the lower price? Since the change in sales is not always proportional to the change in price, this can present a real problem not only to sellers but also to buyers. Fortunately there is a way to measure the change in the relationship between price and the amount sold. *Price elasticity of demand* is a measure of consumer responsiveness to a change in price. Whether a merchant will benefit by an increase or a decrease in price will depend on the degree of price elasticity.

Measuring Price Elasticity of Demand

Let us illustrate price elasticity of demand by constructing three demand curves and measuring their elasticities. In Figure 25-4, observe that for the demand schedule D, 1,600 units are sold at the price of $10; but if the sale price were only $8, the number of units sold would then be 2,000. Elasticity may be measured in either of two ways: (1) by the formula method, and (2) by the total revenue method.

Formula Method. The formula simply measures the relative change in amount sold to the relative change in price and may be stated thus:

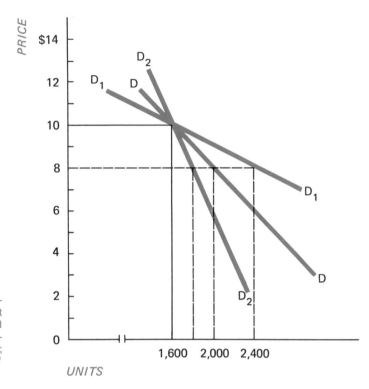

FIGURE 25-4

DEMAND CURVES SHOWING
DIFFERENT ELASTICITIES

On the graph each curve in a designated price range has a different
measure of price elasticity. Demand
curve D shows unit elasticity of demand; D_1 reveals an elastic demand;
and D_2 indicates inelasticity of
demand.

$$\text{Price Elasticity} = \frac{\%\ \text{change in quantity}}{\%\ \text{change in price}}$$

A few minor problems arise in applying the formula. The percentage
changes can be computed by using the original price and quantity as bases.
If this is done, however, the result will be a different measure of elasticity,
depending on whether the price is being decreased or increased. If the price
is decreased, notice that the $2 price change is a 20 percent change com-
pared to the original price base of $10. If this 20 percent change is divided
into the 25 percent change in quantity ($400 \div 1,600 = .25$), the measure
of elasticity would be 1.25 ($.25 \div .20 = 1.25$). On the other hand, if the
price has been moved from $8 up to $10 and the amount sold decreased
from 2,000 units to 1,600 units, the percentage change in price would be
25 percent ($2 \div \$8 = .25$) and the relative change in amount would be
20 percent ($400 \div 2,000 = .20$). In this case, elasticity of demand would
measure .8 ($.20 \div .25 = .8$). Obviously this would lead to much confusion.

This difficulty of conflicting measurements can be avoided by using a
constant base in calculating percentage changes in price and quantity. This
can be done by always using the lower (or upper) extremity of the change

as a base whether moving upward or downward. In the case above, if $8 and 1,600 units were used as the bases in computing the percentage changes, the measure of elasticity, whether lowering or raising prices, would be 1.0. Lowering the price from $10 to $8, for example, will result in a 25 percent change when the lower extremity is used as a base of the change ($2 ÷ $8 = .25). If the amount sold at the lower price, $8, is 2,000 units compared to the 1,600 units that would be sold at the higher price, $10, this also represents a 25 percent change (400 ÷ 1,600 = .25). This yields a measure of elasticity of 1.0 (.25 ÷ .25 = 1.0). Since the same price and quantity bases and the same absolute changes are involved when the price is raised from $8 to $10, the measure of elasticity is the same in either direction. Since the formula is designed to measure the effects of only small increments or decrements in price, any mathematical error will be minimal.

Another method often used is to calculate the percentage change by using an average base. Consequently, the percentage change will be identical whether moving up or down on the price axis. In our example above, the absolute change in price of $2 would be divided by $9 (the average price between $10 and $8) and equal to 22 percent. The relative change in amount sold would likewise be 22 percent (400 ÷ 1,800 = .22). Consequently, the measure of price elasticity of demand would be 1.0, or unit elasticity (.22 ÷ .22 = 1.0). This means that a given change in price will bring about a proportional change in the quantity sold. A 1 percent decrease in price results in a 1 percent increase in quantity sold. A 3 percent increase in price will result in a 3 percent decrease in quantity, and so forth. A coefficient of elasticity of 1.0 is known as *unit elasticity* and is the point of demarcation between an elastic and an inelastic demand. Any value greater than 1.0 is known as an *elastic demand*, and anything less than 1.0 is referred to as an *inelastic demand*.

Now let us measure the elasticity for the demand schedule D_1 in Figure 25-4. Observe that when price is changed from $10 to $8, a 22 percent change when using the average price as a base of the change, the quantity demanded increased from 1,600 to 2,400 units, an increase of 40 percent (800 ÷ 2,000 = .40). In this case the measure of elasticity is 1.8 (.40 ÷ .22 = 1.8). This means that a 2 percent change in price, for example, will result in a 3.6 percent change in the quantity demanded. In short, consumer demand is elastic and the quantity demanded will change in greater proportion than the change in price.

Demand schedule D_2 shows less consumer responsiveness to a change in price. Notice that a 22 percent decrease in price from $10 to $8 results in a mere 11 percent increase in quantity sold. This gives an elasticity of demand of .5, which indicates that the demand is inelastic and that a change in price will bring about a less than proportional change in the amount sold. A 1 percent change in price will result in a .5 percent change in the quantity sold. A 3 percent increase in price will result in a 1.5 percent decrease in sales.

Total Revenue Method. Of what importance is this information about elasticity, inelasticity, and measures of 1.8, .5, and 1.0? To the seller, it is extremely important, since it indicates what is going to happen to total revenue received from the sale of products as prices increase or decrease. Likewise, it is important to the consumer. After all, total revenue received by sellers from the sale of the product is nothing other than total expenditures on the product by buyers. From a given consumer income, more spent on one commodity, of course, means that there will be less to spend on other commodities.

The total revenue method of measuring elasticity is less exacting, but it tells more directly what happens to total revenue. Furthermore, it shows more clearly the important significance of a coefficient of elasticity. Let us take the three demand schedules from Figure 25-4 and put them in tabular form as shown in Table 25-2.

TABLE 25-2

Demand Schedule	$E = \dfrac{\%\ \text{Change in Quantity}}{\%\ \text{Change in Price}}$	Total Revenue Method $\$10 \times 1,600 = \$16,000$	Type of Elasticity
D	$\dfrac{.22}{.22} = 1.0$	$\$8 \times 2,000 = \$16,000$	Unit
D_1	$\dfrac{.40}{.22} = 1.8$	$\$8 \times 2,400 = \$19,200$	Elastic
D_2	$\dfrac{.11}{.22} = .5$	$\$8 \times 1,800 = \$14,400$	Inelastic

Column 2 in the table represents the measures of elasticity calculated by the formula method. The top figure in column 3 represents the total revenue, $16,000, from the sale of products when the price is $10. This is true for each of the demand schedules. But notice that when the price is lowered to $8 on demand schedule D, the total revenue remains the same. Since the coefficient of elasticity is 1.0, the change in quantity demanded is proportional to the change in price. As price is lowered, the decrease in revenue from the decrease in price is offset by the increase in revenue from the increase in sales. Consequently, total revenue, $16,000, remains the same. In this case the seller may be indifferent regarding his price.

In the case of demand schedule D_1, notice that total revenue increases as the price decreases. This again is because the elasticity is 1.8, or greater than 1.0. In the case of D_1, the decrease in revenue from the lower price is more than offset by the increase in revenue from the higher sales, and the net result is that total revenue increases from $16,000 to $19,200. In such a situation the seller may find it beneficial to increase his output and lower his price in order to gain more sales. Notice the fact that the existence of an elastic demand can be a disadvantage if one desires to raise the price. As shown here, if the producer with demand schedule D_1 were to raise his price from $8 to $10, his total revenue would decrease from $19,200 to $16,000.

In our third case, demand schedule D_2, we have an inelastic demand of .5 as measured by the formula method. In column 3 you can see that if price is lowered from $10 to $8, total revenue will fall from $16,000 to $14,400 because the change in quantity demanded is less than proportional to the change in price. In this case the increase in revenue from the increased sales is insufficient to make up for the decrease in revenue resulting from the decrease in price. The net result is that total revenue decreases as price decreases. In this case the producer would not find it beneficial to decrease his price. On the other hand, notice that as a result of the inelasticity of demand, a rise in the price will not engender a substantial decline in sales. Since consumer responsiveness is less than proportional to the change in price, the increase in revenue from the higher price will more than offset the decrease in revenue from the decrease in sales. In such case it could be beneficial for the seller to raise his price. In fact, it is very interesting to note, as we shall see later, that most of the government antitrust suits against price fixing occur in industries where there is a limited number of firms and a highly inelastic demand.

This presentation of the total revenue method of measuring elasticity can be summarized by remembering the following: If a change in price occurs and total revenue remains constant, the demand has unit elasticity. If total revenue moves in the opposite direction from the price change, the demand is elastic. When total revenue changes in the same direction as the price change, the demand is inelastic.

This can be related to the formula method, of course, by pointing out that if the coefficient of elasticity is 1.0, the total revenue will remain constant. If it is greater than 1.0, total revenue will move in the opposite direction as the price change; and if it is less than 1.0, total revenue will move in the same direction as the price change.

Characteristics That Affect Price Elasticity

It is not easy to construct an empirical demand curve, let alone calculate the elasticity of demand for a product. In the first place, it may be difficult to gather sufficient statistical information to determine how much of a good consumers will buy at each of a series of prices. But it can be done and is being done more and more for firms by business economists and market analysts. Secondly, if a price change is made in an effort to observe the change in quantity demanded, the analyst must be certain that no other changes are taking place, such as an increase in income or greater advertising expenditures, that also will have an influence on the demand for the product.

Nature of Product. Nevertheless, certain products or services by their very nature tend to have a demand that is either more or less elastic. Milk, for example, is a basic ingredient of the family diet, especially for children. Consequently, if the price of milk rose by 25 percent, sales probably would not fall by that amount, since parents would be reluctant to deprive their children of milk. On the other hand, since a mink coat is not generally considered a necessity, a 25 percent increase in its purchase price may readily deter many potential customers from making a purchase.

Size of Expenditure. In similar fashion, items that constitute a small expenditure in a total family budget tend to have an inelastic demand. The price of salt or a book of matches may be increased by 50 or 100 percent without substantially affecting the quantity demanded. But if you were going to purchase a sports car for $4,000, for example, and you were suddenly told that the price was $5,000 instead of $4,000, you might very well change your mind about the purchase. In short, a large percentage change on a small expenditure does not affect our total budget nearly as much as a large or moderate price change on a large budget item. Consequently, small expenditure items tend to have more inelasticity than large expenditure items.

Durability of the Product. Consumer responsiveness to a change in price is also influenced by the durability of a good. If a good is durable and can be patched up or repaired, the owner may prefer to continue using an old item, such as an overcoat, television set, or automobile, instead of purchasing a new one if the price is raised. On the other hand, a drop in the price of new television sets may induce the owner to purchase a new set instead of repairing the old one. Such a choice is not available with the utilization of perishable goods, however. If the wick or mantle of a camping lamp burns out, the only reasonable alternative is to purchase a new one. The same is true with such items as ink for a fountain pen, gasoline for your car, and food for the table. Obviously, then, perishable goods tend to have less elasticity than durable goods.

Complementary vs. Substitute Goods. The same holds true for *complementary goods* in comparison with *substitute goods*. If the price of airline transportation were to increase, for example, the traveler may go by rail, by bus, or drive his own car. If the admission price of a Broadway show were to rise, a young couple may decide to attend a movie instead. In the opposite case, a person does not stop driving his car that may have cost anywhere from $3,000 to $5,000 simply because the cost of new tires, which he may need, rises by 10 to 25 percent. Substitute goods or services tend to have greater consumer responsiveness or demand elasticity than complementary goods and services.

Number of Uses. Price elasticity of demand is also affected by the number of actual and potential uses that exist for a service or product. In this way it is related somewhat to the substitution effect. If there is only one, or relatively few, uses for a product, lowering the price may induce a limited increase in sales. If the product has multiple uses, however, and its price is lowered, it will have many more sources for increased sales from actual and potential users. Consider, for example, the effect of reducing the price of Christmas tree light bulbs compared to the effect of reducing the price of regular light bulbs, which have a wide variety of uses.

Dual Characteristics. No doubt you can think of many other commodities for which the demand tends to be elastic or inelastic. Sometimes it is difficult to ascertain in which direction the elasticity leans, if the good happens to have some characteristics of both elasticity and inelasticity. An automobile, for example, is a large expenditure; it is durable; and there are substitute means of transportation—all of which tend to make the demand for new cars elastic. But many Americans consider the auto a basic necessity. Furthermore, it can be purchased on the installment plan. These and other features tend to make the demand for automobiles less elastic. Various measures have placed the elasticity of demand for automobiles somewhere between .5 and 1.5.

Although the elastic characteristics of some goods and services may outweigh the inelastic characteristics, Table 25-3 will help you keep in mind the effect that the nature of various items have on elasticity.

TABLE 25-3

Tend Toward Elasticity	Tend Toward Inelasticity
Luxuries	Necessities
Large Expenditures	Small Expenditures
Durable Goods	Perishable Goods
Substitute Goods	Complementary Goods
Multiple Uses	Limited Uses

Range of Elasticity of Demand

Elasticity of demand may range from one extreme to the other, from perfect elasticity at one end to perfect inelasticity at the other. A product for which there is a perfectly elastic demand would be one for which there was an infinite quantity that could be sold at a given price. It would be possible for the producer to sell his entire supply at the present market price. As we shall see later, such a condition exists from the viewpoint of a single firm under perfect competition. A classic example of a perfectly elastic demand exists in agriculture. Once the price of wheat is established by supply and demand or by government parity, the individual farmer can sell all his available supply at that price. A perfectly elastic demand is depicted as a straight horizontal line as shown in the left-hand diagram of Figure 25-5.

FIGURE 25-5

**THREE DEMAND CURVES
SHOWING DIFFERENT
ELASTICITIES**

Perfect price elasticity of demand is shown by a straight horizontal line, indicating that an infinite amount can be sold at a given price. Perfect inelasticity is shown by a straight vertical line, indicating that the same amount will be purchased regardless of price. Unit elasticity is shown by the hyperbola, indicating that quantity changes are equal to price changes.

A perfectly inelastic demand indicates that the same quantity of a product will be bought regardless of the price. A change in price results in no change in the quantity demanded. Such a demand is represented by a straight vertical line as shown in the middle diagram in Figure 25-5. Very few, if any, commodities have a perfectly inelastic demand. Approaching it, however, may be the purchase of passenger automobile license plates. Whether the price is $30, $20, $10, or $5, no motorist will buy more than one set of license plates for his car. As the price is raised, he will not buy less than one set. There is, however, a price at which it may not be worthwhile to purchase license plates for some old jalopies or at which owning a second car may become too expensive. In such an event, a rise in the price will result in a decrease in the quantity demanded.

Although we tend to say that the more horizontal the demand curve, the more it tends to be elastic, this is not always true. Anytime you have a straight line demand schedule, there will no doubt be certain areas of the schedule that are elastic, others that are inelastic, and at some spot it may measure unit elasticity. Related to this is the notion, which sometimes exists, that a 45° line represents unit elasticity. This would not be true on a conventional type demand curve. Both of these fallacies can be clarified by referring to Figure 25-6. Notice on the demand line that a change in price from $9 to $8, a price change of less than 12 percent, brings about a change in quantity demanded from 10 to 20 units, an increase of 67 percent (using the midpoint as the base of the percentage change). At the lower end of the vertical axis a price change from $2 to $1, which represents a 67 percent change in price, results in an increase in quantity demanded from 80 to 90 units, or a quantity change of less than 12 percent. At one end of the scale we have a price elasticity of demand of more than 5.0; at the other end, a highly inelastic measure of less than .2. Observe further that, if price were changed from $5.50 to $4.50 and the quantity demanded moved from 45 units to 55 units, unit elasticity would prevail. Any change in price through the range of $10 to $5.50 is elastic, but any change in price between $4.50 and $1.00 is inelastic. In fact, on the given demand schedule the point of maximum revenue for the seller would be in the vicinity of $5 since a higher price would result in a decrease in revenue as would a lower price. Obviously on a straight line demand curve it is possible for a product to be elastic at some price ranges and inelastic at others. For a demand schedule to possess unit elasticity throughout, it would have to be represented by a hyperbola,

FIGURE 25-6

**DEMAND CURVE SHOWING
DIFFERING DEGREES
OF ELASTICITY**

Any straight line demand curve has varying measures of elasticity. This figure indicates that, in the upper reaches of the curve, demand is elastic, whereas the lower part is inelastic. Somewhere between the two extremes there will be unit elasticity of demand.

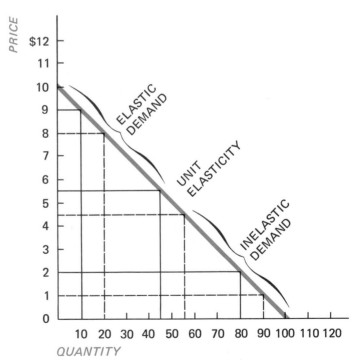

as shown in the right-hand diagram of Figure 25-5. On such a curve, changes in price and quantity are proportional throughout.

Cross Elasticity of Demand

The quantity demanded of a particular commodity or service is affected not only by changes in the price of that commodity but also by the changes in the price of other commodities. Suppose, for example, that two commodities are close substitutes and there is a decrease in the price of Commodity B while the price of Commodity A remains the same. Consumers will begin shifting from the purchase of Commodity A to Commodity B. This substitution effect will cause a decrease in the demand for Commodity A and an increase in the quantity demanded for product B. From a practical point of view, a rise in the price of meats may cause us to eat fewer steaks and more hamburger and poultry. A rise in the price of butter may result in greater consumption of margarine. Certainly a decrease of $100 or $200 in the price of a Chevrolet would lead to higher sales at the expense of Ford and Chrysler products, provided they did not lower their prices. Higher stock prices lead to an increase in bond sales. This phenomenon, a change in the demand for one commodity as a result of a change in the price of another, is known as *cross elasticity of demand*. It is an important concept in a competitive industry or between competitive products where the price actions of one competitor can have a strong reaction on the demand of another. The formula for cross elasticity can be written as follows:

$$\text{Cross Elasticity} = \frac{\% \text{ change in the quantity of } A}{\% \text{ change in the price of } B}.$$

Cross elasticity exists not only between substitutes but also between complementary products. In contrast to substitutes, which show a positive cross elasticity, complementary goods show a negative cross elasticity. With substitute goods, as the price of one goes up, the demand for the substitute increases. With complementary goods, when the price of a basic commodity goes up, the demand for the complementary good falls along with the demand for the basic commodity. The sale of records, for example, may very well fall if the price of record players increases and there are fewer record players purchased.

Since many firms are concerned not only with total sales but also with market penetration, the cross elasticity formula may be stated in terms of market share. The formula for *market share elasticity* relates the percentage change in the price of product B to the percentage change in the market share of product A.

Income Elasticity of Demand

A major factor affecting the demand for any commodity is the level of income of the buyers. Until now we have assumed that the level of income has remained unchanged. But the incomes of individuals, families, and business firms change; and such changes in income affect the demand for particular commodities and the demand for goods and services in general. In the case of most goods, an increase in the income of buyers tends to bring about an increase in the demand for particular goods, which causes the demand curve to shift to the right. As income rises, consumers purchase more at any given price. This can be very easily observed during a period of prosperity. In case of a decline in employment and income, however, the demand curve for many, if not most, goods and services falls and shifts downward to the left.

This relationship between changing income and changes in demand is known as *income elasticity of demand*. If the demand for a product increases in greater proportion than the increase in income, then income elasticity will be greater than 1.0, and the product will be income elastic. If, however, the increase in sales is less than the increase in income, income elasticity will be less than 1.0, and the product will be income inelastic. If the change in income and demand is proportional, the product will have unit income elasticity. The formula for measuring income elasticity of demand is shown below:

$$E_1 = \frac{\% \text{ change in quantity}}{\% \text{ change in disposable income}}.$$

Naturally income elasticity, or *income sensitivity* as it is often called, varies for different commodities. It is generally low for basic necessities since these are items we must purchase even when our incomes are low. Therefore, we do not have a great need to purchase more of them as our incomes increase. Many convenience items, luxuries, and services tend to have a high income elasticity since we can afford more of these things only as our incomes increase. In planning for future growth, it is important for firms and industries to know something about the income elasticity of their products. Will the demand for their products increase at the same, a slower, or a faster rate than the general level of income in the economy? Fortunately the United States Department of Commerce lists the income sensitivity for several hundred different types of products. Income sensitivity measures range from a high of 3.1 for boats and pleasure aircraft and 2.0 for new cars to lows of .5 for gasoline and .2 for electricity.

Quantity Sold as a Function of Price

Although we usually think of the quantity of a good sold as dependent upon, or as a function of, price and express it as $q = f(p)$, it should be readily apparent now that many other factors besides price affect the quantity of a good sold. The quantity sold is also influenced by the level of income, by the price of other goods, by advertising outlays, and by several other considerations. Thus, it is just as proper to write $q = f(DI)$, disposable income, or to combine all factors affecting quantity sold into one equation and express it as follows: $q = f(p, DI, p_x, a, \ldots)$ etc., where p is the price of the product itself, DI is the level of disposable income, p_x is the price of other commodities, and a is the advertising outlay.

SUPPLY

As in the case of the demand for goods, there are also two aspects of the supply of goods: individual supply and market supply.

Individual Supply

Individual supply of a good that is offered on a market signifies the quantities of the good that an individual stands ready to sell at various prices. To determine the total supply that any individual might offer to sell, it would be necessary to know exactly how much he would sell at each possible price. For example, if water were very scarce and one possessed a limited supply, he might be induced to sell a few gallons at a certain price. If the price offered were higher, he might sell a larger quantity; and at a still higher price, he might be willing to sell even more. But if his life depended upon his retaining a minimum supply for his own use, he would not part with all of the remainder at any price. This example illustrates the point that individual supply, which is contributed to the total market supply, consists only of that portion of an individual's stock that he can be induced to sell at various prices.

We customarily speak of "buying" goods with money or of "selling" goods for money. We scarcely ever think of buying money with goods. There is no good reason, however, why we should not regard the seller of goods as a buyer of money, except that money is the commonly accepted medium of exchange, that the exchange of goods is usually expressed as prices in terms of money, and that the word "buy" is derived from an Anglo-Saxon term that implies acquiring property by paying a price.

It might seem that, from the seller's standpoint, marginal utility is not so significant as it is from the buyer's position. In reality, however, the marginal utilities of both money and goods determine the subjective prices of both buyers and sellers. The conditions in each case differ, but the influence of marginal utility is equally important. It is the seller's desire for money, either to hold or to spend for other goods, that induces him to sell what he has to offer. Of course, other things being equal, he endeavors to recover the cost of his goods and in addition a margin of profit. But in the final analysis, the cost of acquiring his stock of goods is not the only determinant of his subjective price. If market price falls below his costs of production or of acquiring a new supply, the relative utilities of money and units of goods at the time will determine the price that he is willing to take. Of course, if he possesses sufficient withholding power—that is, if his demand for money is not too urgent—he may refuse to sell his goods at a loss. He may prefer to wait and see if the market price will rise. Otherwise in a competitive market he must sell at the prevailing market price. When he does sell, his act is conclusive evidence that the marginal utility of the money he receives is equal to or greater than that of the goods he gives up.

Market Supply

The *market supply* of a good consists of the total quantities of the good that sellers stand ready to sell at different prices at a given time. A schedule representing the market supply of a good would contain all the quantities of the good that all potential sellers would sell at various prices. As in the case of the demand for a good, it is essential to keep in mind that we are considering here the behavior of a great many individuals or firms. The market supply refers to the total quantities of a particular homogeneous article, one that is identical with all the sellers. Supply, like demand, is always specific. For example, there is no purpose in talking about the supply of automobiles in the market. To be meaningful as far as measurement is concerned, we must talk about the supply of Fords, Chevrolets, Plymouths, Cadillacs, Datsuns, and various other makes and models. It is obvious that the supply of and the demand for Cadillacs constitute a different market than the demand for Datsuns.

A Market Supply Schedule

As in the case of demand, it is possible and convenient for purposes of analysis to construct a market supply schedule. Therefore, let us set up a hypothetical market supply schedule for wheat on the Chicago Board of Trade at noon on Tuesday, as shown in the first and second columns of Table 25-4.

The same method used in plotting the demand curve for wheat can be used to plot the supply curve, which is shown by S in Figure 25-7. A supply curve is a line indicating the number of units of a good or service that will be offered for sale at different prices. The supply curve rises from left to right because, as the price rises, greater amounts will be offered for sale at higher prices and the intersections of lines drawn from prices and quantities climb higher to the right.

TABLE 25-4	If the Price Is:	Thousands of Bushels of Wheat That Will Be Offered		
		S	S$_1$	S$_2$
SUPPLY	$2.50	10,000	11,050	8,950
SCHEDULES	2.45	9,600	10,800	8,400
FOR WHEAT	2.40	9,200	10,400	7,800
	2.35	8,475	9,800	7,200
	2.30	7,800	9,050	6,250
	2.25	6,850	8,400	5,250
	2.20	5,900	7,250	4,250
	2.15	4,800	6,400	3,000
	2.10	3,600	5,250	1,600
	2.05	2,000	4,000	0

An increase in supply means that a greater quantity will be offered at a given price. Thus, in Table 25-4, S_1, the third column, shows that at $2.50 more wheat will be offered for sale than was indicated in the first schedule, S. And so for each price, a greater quantity will be offered for sale. A decrease in supply means that a smaller quantity will be offered for sale at a given price. If we plot the supply curve for S_1, the curve will lie below that for S; and the curve for S_2, showing a decrease in supply, will lie above that for S.

The Elasticity of Supply

Elasticity of supply refers to the relation between a given change in price and the resulting change in the quantity of a commodity or service that will be offered for sale. Market supply is the obverse or counterpart of market demand. In the case of reproducible goods, the quantity demanded *usually* tends to vary inversely with price. The supply offered, on the other hand, ordinarily tends to vary directly with price; that is, a higher price usually results in a greater amount offered for sale.[1] It should be noted, however, that, just as with demand, when price changes and a greater or lesser amount is offered for sale, this is not a change in supply. It is merely a movement along the supply curve. If a given percentage change in the price of a good results in a greater percentage change in the quantity supplied, the supply is elastic. If the percentage change in the price results

[1] In exceptional situations an increase in price may result in a decrease in the quantity of a particular good or service offered for sale. The failure of an increase in wages beyond a certain point to bring about an increase in the quantity of labor has been noted by industrialists in their attempt to industrialize underdeveloped regions in Africa, Asia, and elsewhere. As wages were increased beyond a certain point, workers found it unnecessary to work as many hours as before in order to maintain their accustomed levels of living. Likewise, in the industrially progressive nations, improvements in technology enable workers to produce more goods and to earn higher wages within a given time. As a result, a given increase in wages beyond a certain point will not result in anything like a corresponding increase in the quantity of labor; actually the quantity may decrease.

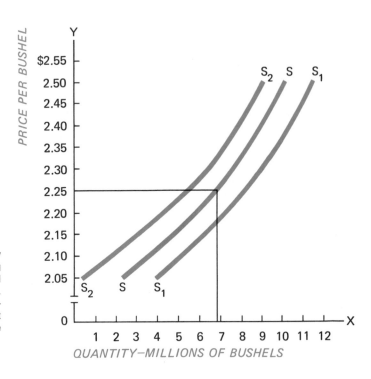

FIGURE 25-7

SUPPLY CURVES FOR WHEAT

When supply increases, the supply curve shifts to the right, indicating that greater quantities will be offered for sale at the respective prices. A decrease in supply shifts the supply curve to the left, indicating that less will be offered for sale at the respective prices.

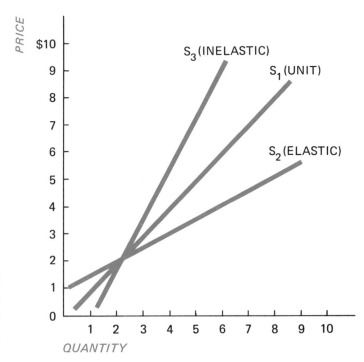

FIGURE 25-8

SUPPLY CURVES SHOWING DIFFERENT ELASTICITIES

Supply curve S_1 shows unit elasticity of supply, indicating that the amount offered for sale will change in proportion to price changes. S_2 shows an elastic supply in which the amount offered for sale changes in greater proportion than does price. S_3 indicates an inelastic supply.

in a lesser percentage change in the quantity offered, the supply is inelastic. And if the percentage change in price results in a proportionate change in the quantity offered for sale, elasticity is unitary.

A change in supply means that a different quantity will be offered for sale at each price. An increase in supply means that a larger amount will be offered, and a decrease in supply indicates that a smaller quantity will be offered at the same price. The implications of these statements are illustrated graphically in Figure 25-7, which represents the three supply schedules shown in Table 25-4.

The same formula used to measure the elasticity of demand can be applied to measure the elasticity of supply. Figure 25-8 shows supply curves representing differing degrees of elasticity.

The extreme limits of elasticity of supply range from that of perfect elasticity to that of perfect inelasticity. A perfectly elastic supply exists when an infinite quantity will be offered for sale at the same or a higher price; but, of course, nothing at all will be offered for sale at any lower price. A perfectly inelastic supply exists when a change in price results in no change in the quantity that will be offered for sale.

The total quantity that will be offered for sale and the elasticity of supply are limited both by the quantity in existence at the time and by estimates of prospective sellers as to probable costs of producing future supplies of the good. In the long run, however, the elasticity of the supply of reproducible goods is conditioned by the availability of the factors of production and by the costs of production.

HOW DEMAND AND SUPPLY DETERMINE PRICE

Now let us assume that at noon on Tuesday the demand for and the supply of wheat on the Chicago Board of Trade are as shown in the second columns of Tables 25-1 and 25-4, as reproduced in Table 25-5.

	Price per Bushel	Demand (Thousands of Bushels)	Supply (Thousands of Bushels)
TABLE 25-5 **DEMAND AND SUPPLY SCHEDULES FOR WHEAT**	$2.50	2,000	10,000
	2.45	2,300	9,600
	2.40	2,800	9,200
	2.35	3,500	8,475
	2.30	4,200	7,800
	2.25	5,100	6,850
	2.20	6,075	5,900
	2.15	7,250	4,800
	2.10	8,500	3,600
	2.05	10,000	2,000

At what price will wheat sell on the commodity exchange? The price will be determined by the interaction of demand and supply and will be at the point where "demand and supply are equal." More precisely, the price will be determined where the quantity demanded equals the quantity supplied. Since the market will be cleared at this price, it is known as the equilibrium price.

To show the interactive relationships of demand and supply, we can reconstruct the demand and supply curves for the schedules in Table 25-5, superimposing one on the other as in Figure 25-9. With reference to price and quantity, the curves intersect at a point that indicates a price of $2.21 and a quantity of 6 million bushels. What is the significance of this?

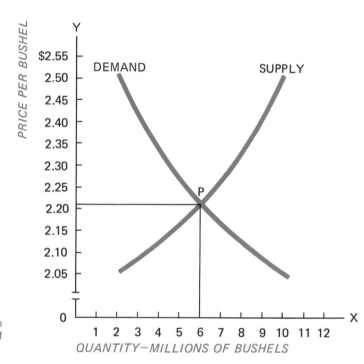

FIGURE 25-9

DEMAND, SUPPLY, AND MARKET PRICE

Equilibrium price is determined in the free market by the interaction of demand and supply.

It simply means that at a price of $2.21, 6 million bushels will be bought, and an equal amount will be offered for sale. According to our definition of competition, since no one transaction can affect the price, any buyer who wants to buy wheat at this price can buy all he wants. Likewise, any seller can sell at the same price. No buyer whose subjective price is higher than $2.21 needs to pay more because he can buy all he wants at that price. And no buyer unwilling to pay that much can buy.

On the other hand, sellers whose subjective prices are lower than $2.21 can sell at the higher price. And those who are unwilling to sell at that price will have to keep their wheat because buyers can obtain all they want at that price. Therefore, the price of $2.21 is the equilibrium price and cannot change until there is a change in the relationships between demand and supply. This explains what we mean when we say that the forces of demand and supply are impersonal and that under a condition of pure competition no one individual can influence the market price either by buying or refusing to buy, or by selling or refusing to sell.

Under these conditions of demand and supply, if the price were anything other than $2.21, the quantities consumers would be willing to buy and the amount of wheat offered for sale would be out of balance. In such a situation forces of the market would come into play to adjust the price to $2.21, or the equilibrium level. At a price of $2.25, for instance, the quantity of wheat sellers would be willing to supply would exceed by approximately 2 million bushels the quantity demanded by buyers. Consequently, not all the wheat would be sold. But notice that there are sellers who are willing to sell their wheat at lower prices of $2.23, $2.22, etc. Rather than hold their wheat they will offer to sell at the lower prices. As the price is lowered, notice that certain buyers would not pay $2.25 for wheat but will pay $2.24, $2.23, of less. Therefore, as the market conditions force the price of wheat downward, the number of sellers decreases and the number of buyers increases until the amount of wheat offered for sale and the quantity purchased come into balance at an equilibrium price of $2.21.

On the contrary, if a price of $2.15 exists in such a market, it cannot continue. At that price the quantity demanded exceeds the quantity supplied by more than 2 million bushels, and some buyers would have to go without. But observe that some of the buyers are willing to pay more than $2.15 for a bushel of wheat. Rather than go without they would offer higher prices of $2.17, $2.19, and upward. As they bid the price upward, a twofold action takes place in the market. The higher prices will deter some buyers from making purchases, and they will induce more sellers to offer their product for sale. The resulting increase in the amount offered for sale and the decrease in the amount that will be purchased finally bring supply and demand into balance at the equilibrium price of $2.21. In a freely competitive market no other price can prevail. At any other prices either surpluses or shortages of the good will exist in the short run, as shown in Figure 25-10.

If someone wants to set the price at other than the market price established by the free forces of supply and demand, the market will have to be rigged or the forces of supply and demand changed. This is exactly what happens when the government sets a parity price for certain agricultural commodities that is higher than the market price or when it establishes a ceiling price lower than the market price during a wartime period. Likewise, business firms charged with price fixing are often guilty of collusion with other firms in an effort to interfere with the free forces of demand and supply.

In agriculture, for example, if the free market price of wheat were $2.21 per bushel and Congress set a parity price for farmers at $2.30 per bushel, large gluts would develop on the market. As seen in Figure 25-10, at a price of $2.30 the amount supplied would be nearly 8 million bushels, but the quantity purchased would be less than 5 million bushels. The only way the government can maintain such a price is by offering to pay the farmer $2.30 per bushel. In such a case the government would be stuck with excessive stocks of wheat. In order to avoid this as much as possible, the guarantee of a parity price to the farmer is generally accompanied by a limitation of production designed to limit the supply of a commodity. For example, if the acreage limitation on the production of wheat was such that it limited the supply to S_1, the higher price could be sustained on the market without the occurrence of a surplus or the need for large government purchases.

On the other hand, suppose that the equilibrium price had been $2.10 per bushel but as a result of wartime demand the price level rose to $2.21 per bushel. If the government decided to establish a ceiling price of $2.10,

FIGURE 25-10

SURPLUS, SHORTAGE, AND EQUILIBRIUM

An artificial price higher than the equilibrium price will cause a surplus. The only way such a price can be maintained is by "rigging the market," such as by forcing a reduction in supply. A price lower than the market equilibrium will result in shortages.

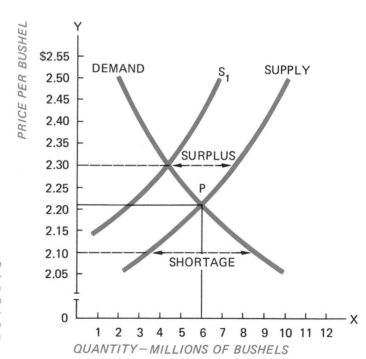

FIGURE 25-11

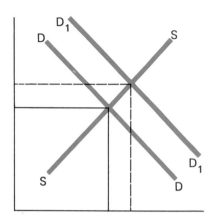

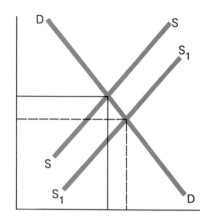

An increase in demand causes price to rise and the amount sold to increase. A decrease in demand causes price to fall and the quantity sold to diminish.

An increase in supply causes price to fall and the quantity sold to increase. A decrease in supply causes price to rise and quantity sold to decrease.

shortages would occur in the market as shown in Figure 25-10. The normal force in the market would tend to move the price level up to $2.21, the free market price. The only way, in the absence of an increase in supply or decrease in demand, that the government can enforce the $2.10 ceiling price is through strict regulation and penalizing violators, as it did during World War II, the Korean conflict, and in the 1971-1973 price control period. Nevertheless, the fact that shortages exist and some buyers are willing to pay a higher price usually leads to black-market operations.

Under competitive conditions the number of possible relationships between demand and supply is practically infinite. For instance, demand may increase while supply remains constant; or vice versa. Again, demand may increase while supply decreases; or vice versa. Or both demand and supply may increase, but demand may increase more than supply.

In any case, however, we can rely on this simple principle: In any new relationship between demand and supply, an increase in demand relative to supply is sure to result in a higher price; any decrease in demand relative to supply will result in a lower price. On the other hand, an increase in supply will lower the price and a decrease in supply will raise the price, other things remaining unchanged, as shown in Figure 25-11.

Tracing the effect of multiple changes in demand and supply becomes a bit more complex. Referring to Figure 25-12, notice that when both demand and supply change in the same direction, each tends to offset the effect of the other on price but to augment the effect of each other on the amount sold. When they change in the opposite direction (for example,

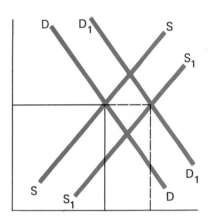

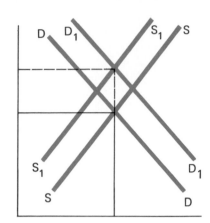

FIGURE 25-12

If both demand and supply increase by an equivalent amount, price will remain constant but the quantity sold will increase. If both supply and demand decrease by an equivalent amount, the price will remain the same but the quantity sold will decline.

If demand increases but supply decreases by the equivalent amount, the price will increase but the quantity sold will remain the same. If demand decreases but supply increases by an equivalent amount, price will decrease but the quantity sold will remain constant.

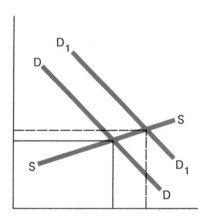

FIGURE 25-13

With a given increase in demand, the more elastic the supply, the greater the effect on quantity sold and the less the effect on price.

With a given increase in demand, the less the elasticity of supply, the greater the effect on price, and the less the effect on quantity sold.

when demand increases and supply decreases), they tend to augment the effect of each other in regard to price but to offset the effect of each other in the matter of amount sold.

When demand or supply changes, in either the same or the opposite direction as the other, but the degree of change in one is greater than in the other, this too, complicates the result. The slope of the demand and supply curves will likewise have an effect on how much price and quantity sold will be affected with given changes in supply and demand, as shown in Figure 25-13.

THE CONCEPT OF COMPETITIVE MARKET PRICE

Clearly the conditions of demand and supply and the determination of market price in the above discussion are hypothetical and very much simplified. It is difficult, if not impossible in many cases, to set up the actual demand and supply schedules for goods and services that are bought and sold daily on the markets. Yet we can be justified in reaching certain conclusions as to how such schedules would look in a purely competitive market if we could construct them.

By formulating a definition that conforms to the essentials of a purely competitive market, we can arrive at the only logical conclusion regarding the manner in which market price would be determined under ideal market conditions. The conclusion is this: Under given conditions of demand and supply, an equilibrium price results that will "clear the market."

In our treatment of market price up to now, we have been concerned only with the demand for and the supply of a good at a particular time. Over long periods of time both individual prices and prices in general rise and fall. Does this imply that there is a norm around which prices tend to fluctuate? We shall deal with this question in the following chapters.

SUMMARY

1. In a free enterprise system the forces of demand and supply are relied upon to determine prices.

2. Individual demand signifies the quantities of a good that an individual stands ready to buy at different prices. Due to the operation of the principle of diminishing utility and to limitations of purchasing power, an individual will usually buy more units of a commodity or a service at a lower price than at a higher price.

3. A market may imply either a particular place or an extended area where the forces of demand and supply operate.

4. Market demand is the total quantity of a commodity that will be bought in the market at a given time. It may be represented by a schedule indicating the quantities of a commodity that would be purchased at different prices. An increase in demand implies that more of a commodity will be purchased at given prices; a decrease in demand means that fewer units will be purchased at given prices.

5. Elasticity of demand refers to the ratio between the percentage change in price and the percentage change in the quantity of a good that will be purchased as a result of the change in price. There are various degrees of elasticity of demand. It is significant because of its relation to revenue.

6. Price elasticity of demand may be measured by either the formula method or the total revenue method. A coefficient of elasticity of 1.0 designates unit elasticity. Anything above 1.0 is said to be elastic, while any measure below 1.0 is inelastic. According to the total revenue method, if total revenue moves in the opposite direction from a price change, the demand is said to be elastic. If it moves in the same direction, it is inelastic; and if total revenue remains constant, unit elasticity exists.

7. Among the factors that affect price elasticity of demand are the nature of the product, its possible uses, its price in relation to total budget expenditures, the durability of the product, and the availability of substitutes.

8. It is also possible to calculate cross elasticity, market share elasticity, and income elasticity of demand. In many respects these are as important as price elasticity.

9. The supply of a good or service at a given time is the quantity that sellers will offer for sale at different prices. The term may refer to individual or market supply. Supply may be represented by a schedule of the quantities that will be offered at different prices at a given time. Like that of demand, the elasticity of supply for different products varies.

10. Under competitive conditions, price is fixed at that point where demand and supply are in equilibrium, and it cannot change unless there is a change in demand or supply or both.

NEW TERMS

Derived demand, *p. 538*
Utility, *p. 538*
Marginal utility, *p. 539*
Law of diminishing marginal utility, *p. 539*
Market demand, *p. 542*
Demand, *p. 542*
Demand schedule, *p. 543*
Change in demand, *p. 546*
Price elasticity of demand, *p. 546*
Formula method, *p. 546*
Unit elasticity, *p. 548*

Elastic demand, *p. 548*
Inelastic demand, *p. 548*
Total revenue method, *p. 549*
Complementary goods, *p. 551*
Substitute goods, *p. 551*
Cross elasticity of demand, *p. 555*
Market share elasticity, *p. 555*
Income elasticity of demand, *p. 556*
Income sensitivity, *p. 556*
Market supply, *p. 558*
Elasticity of supply, *p. 559*

QUESTIONS FOR DISCUSSION AND ANALYSIS

1. Define demand. What are the three basic elements contained in the definition?
2. Why does a normal demand curve slope downward to the right?
3. Distinguish between a movement on the demand curve and a change in demand.

4. Name several factors that could cause a change in demand.
5. Define price elasticity of demand.
6. If 50,000 units of a good could be sold at a price of $20, but 60,000 units could be sold at a price of $18, would the demand for the good be elastic or inelastic?

What would be the coefficient of elasticity?

7. Indicate whether the demand for the following tend to be elastic or inelastic and explain why: (a) shoelaces, (b) portable home air-conditioning units, (c) college textbooks, (d) professional entertainment, and (e) new homes.

8. Distinguish between perfect elasticity, perfect inelasticity, and unit elasticity of demand. Indicate what type of demand curve represents each of these types of elasticity.

9. Distinguish between cross elasticity and income elasticity of demand. Give the formula for measuring each.

10. Explain how the demand curve facing a particular firm can be of different elasticity from the demand curve for the entire industry.

11. Why does the supply curve slope upward to the right?

12. Explain why under competitive conditions market price cannot be higher or lower than that established by the free forces of demand and supply.

13. If both demand and supply decreased but demand decreased more than supply, what would happen to price?

14. If demand increased, would the effect on price tend to be greater if the supply curve were elastic or inelastic?

SUGGESTED READINGS

Kirzner, I. M. *Market Theory and the Price System.* New York: Van Nostrand Reinhold Company, 1963.

Lancaster, Kelvin. *Introduction to Modern Microeconomics.* Chicago: Rand, McNally & Company, 1969.

Levenson, Albert M., and Babette S. Solon. *Essential Price Theory.* New York: Holt, Rinehart and Winston, Inc., 1971.

Liebhafsky, H. H. *The Nature of Price Theory.* Homewood, Ill.: Dorsey Press, 1963.

Watson, Donald Stevenson. *Price Theory and Its Uses.* Boston: Houghton Mifflin Company, 1972.

26

Production, Cost, and Profit

PREVIEW The production function is performed by business firms that seek profits. Consequently, they will utilize natural resources, manpower, and capital in certain proportions, with the proportions depending on both the explicit and implicit costs and the productive contributions of the various factors of production. A firm will continue to use inputs to provide goods and services for the community so long as the cost of the additional inputs is less than the revenue derived from the sale of its additional output. Its equilibrium output, or maximum profit position, will be at the point where its marginal cost equals its marginal revenue.

The inducement for business firms to assume the risks of production is the hope of profit. *Profit* is the difference between revenue and cost. Cost per unit of input and the revenue per unit of output are determined primarily by the forces of demand and supply. Under perfectly competitive conditions there is nothing the firm can do to control the revenue it receives per unit of output, for revenue per unit of output is nothing other than the product price determined by aggregate market forces of demand and supply. There is nothing the firm can do either regarding its cost per unit of input because cost per unit of input is the price of a factor of production determined by supply and demand in the factor or resource market. Nevertheless, the firm can alter its cost per unit of output. A decrease in cost per unit of output can be accomplished by using better production techniques, by obtaining more efficient use of labor, by spreading its fixed cost over a greater range of output, and by other methods. Since a firm's cost of production largely determines the supply of goods that it offers on the market and affects its profit position, a further insight into cost concepts is in order at this point.

THE PRODUCTION FUNCTION

In providing a supply of goods or services, the quantity offered for sale will be affected by costs of production. Production cost, however, will in turn be affected by certain physical relationships between factor inputs and product output. The relationship between factor inputs and product output is called the *production function* of the firm. This production function exhibits certain properties that determine the way in which cost varies with output.

Law of Diminishing Returns

The essential function of management in providing a supply of goods is to organize land, capital, and many types of labor so that the best combination of these factors of production will be used. There should not be too much of one factor and too little of another. The farmer, for example, realizes that, with a given amount of land, he should employ a certain amount of labor and a specific number of machines. Likewise, the office manager knows that the most efficient operation of a certain number of machines requires a definite number of employees. In either case, if the factors engaged in production are not in the right proportion, the unit cost will be higher than it otherwise would be, and the manager will not realize the maximum returns from his efforts that his firm might be capable of achieving.

In every instance where goods are being produced, there is an optimum proportion of the factors of production. This optimum or "best" proportion of the factors is determined in part by the *law of diminishing returns*, or the law of diminishing productivity as it is sometimes called.

To illustrate the law of diminishing returns and its effects on cost of production, let us assume that an entrepreneur owns a tool shop with four machines, adequate space, and an ample supply of raw material. If he hires only one worker who attempts to operate all four machines, the net result will be a limited amount of production, since it will be difficult for one worker to attend to all of the machines, keep the supply of raw material flowing smoothly, remove and package the finished product, maintain the premises, and do other jobs connected directly or indirectly with the operation of the machines. In fact, some of the machines may be idle a good part of the time. If the entrepreneur were to hire a second laborer of equal ability, he would find that his total production would increase. It no doubt would more than double, since he would not only get direct benefits of the physical labor of the second worker, but also the machines would be operating more of the time. Consequently, his total output might rise from 10 units to 22 units.

A similar increase might take place when the entrepreneur hires a third worker if production rose to 36 units. In fact, upon hiring a fourth worker he could have one man attending each machine, and production might rise still further to 52 units. In each case the increase in production per additional worker exceeds that of the previous worker. This increase in output per additional worker is known as the marginal product of labor.

Marginal Product. The *marginal product* of any input is the increase in total output resulting from an additional unit of input. In this case our input is labor. But how long can this marginal product continue to increase? Provided all other factors—space, machines, materials—remain fixed, a point will soon be reached at which the fixed factors will become overtaxed or reach their maximum use compared to their underutilization in the early stages of production. Upon hiring a fifth man, for example, the entrepreneur may find that production still rises. The fifth man may run stock, package material, and do other jobs that permit the machine tenders to devote more time to their machines. But the increase in production may be less than it was with the addition of the fourth man. Let us say production expands by 15 units instead of 16, as shown in Table 26-1.

If additional workers are hired, the marginal product will diminish further. A sixth man may serve as a relief worker, and total production may rise to 78 units, an increase of only 11 units, as a result of the improved efficiency of all workers stemming from ample rest periods. As the hiring of additional workers continues, you can visualize a situation being reached in which the fixed factors are taxed to full capacity and there will be absolutely no increase in output. In fact, a stage might even be reached where workers begin getting in each other's way and a decrease in total production could result.

TABLE 26-1	Units of Input	Total Output	Marginal Product	Average Product
INPUT, OUTPUT, MARGINAL PRODUCT, AND AVERAGE PRODUCT	1	10		10
	2	22	12	11
	3	36	14	12
	4	52	16	13
	5	67	15	13.4
	6	78	11	13
	7	84	6	12
	8	88	4	11
	9	90	2	10
	10	90	0	9

Although it is possible to have increasing marginal productivity, especially in the early stages of production, and even constant marginal productivity over a certain range of output, diminishing marginal productivity is more prevalent. Consequently, we hear much about the *law of diminishing marginal productivity*, or *diminishing returns*. This law may be stated as follows: As additional units of a factor of production are combined with fixed quantities of other factors, a point will be reached where the increase in output resulting from the use of an additional unit of the variable factor will not be as large as was the increase in output due to the addition of the preceding unit. The operation of this law in general applies to the use of any factor of production, and it affects the supply of particular goods and services to be offered for sale.

Average Product. In dealing with the cost of production, not only are we interested in the marginal product but also in the average product because it too affects the per unit cost. *Average product* can be defined simply as the output per unit of input. Thus, in Table 26-1, where 3 units of labor input are utilized and the resulting total production is 36 units, the average product is 12 units ($36 \div 3 = 12$). But observe, too, that the average product, like the marginal product, increases, reaches a maximum, and then declines. This follows from the fact that additions to the total product—marginal product—influence the average product. Any time the marginal product is greater, it pulls up the average product. When the marginal product is less than the average, it reduces the average product. This relationship is shown in Figure 26-1. Notice that, even after the marginal curve reaches its peak and starts downward, the average product curve continues upward until the two values are equal.

This relationship between marginal and average product is very much like baseball batting averages. If in the early part of the season, for example, Johnny Bench has 40 hits out of 120 times at bat, his average will be .333,

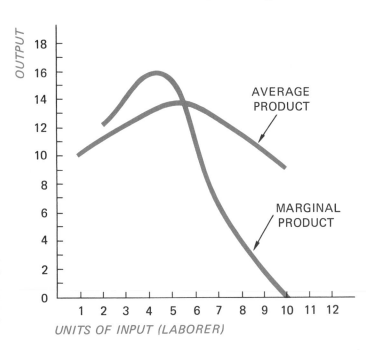

FIGURE 26-1

RELATIONSHIP OF MARGINAL PRODUCT TO AVERAGE PRODUCT

The marginal product will rise, reach a maximum, and then decline. So long as the marginal product is greater than the average product, the average product will rise. When the marginal product is less than the average product, the average product will fall.

not unusual for a slugger of his caliber. If he goes out the next day and slams 4 hits in 6 trips to the plate, his daily, or marginal, average is .667, and his seasonal average will rise to .349 (44 ÷ 126). On the other hand, if he had a bad day and got only 1 for 6, his marginal or daily batting average would be only .167, and it would pull his season average down to .325.

Remember that in order to pull the average product down, the marginal product must be less than the average product, not merely declining. Notice in Table 26-1 and Figure 26-1 that marginal product with the addition of the fifth unit of labor declined from 16 to 15 units, but the average product rose from 13 to 13.4 units. This is because the marginal product of 15, although diminishing, is still larger than the average product of 13. But, again, a point is actually reached where the average product, like the marginal product, begins to decline.

The law of diminishing returns is important for two reasons: First, it affects production costs. Because of its influence on costs, the problem of finding the optimum combination of productive inputs is one of the most important responsibilities of management. Second, the marginal productivity of a factor of production under competitive conditions is the most important determinant of the income that the owners of the factors can expect to earn. We shall pursue this matter further in the chapters dealing with wages, rent, and interest.

Returns to Scale

The law of diminishing returns applies when one or a few productive agents in the input mix are varied and the remainder are held constant. But what happens if all productive agents are varied proportionally? Suppose, for example, that all factors in the input mix were doubled. Would output double, increase by 50 percent, or perhaps even 150 percent?

If output changes in a given proportion to the change in inputs, constant returns to scale exist. A doubling of all inputs, for example, will double output. On the other hand, when output increases in smaller proportion than the expansion of inputs, it is an indication of decreasing returns to scale. That is, if the entrepreneur were to double all inputs, then output would not double. In contrast, increasing returns to scale imply that a doubling of all inputs would more than double output.

Increasing and constant returns to scale may take place, especially at smaller scales of operation, when an entrepreneur expands the total input mix without changing the proportion of the ingredients of the mix. If he continues to add to the scale of operation, however, he may run into the area of decreasing returns to scale as the operation becomes rather large, complex, and cumbersome. To a certain degree this may be attributed in part to the law of diminishing returns.

Frequently the entrepreneur expands his scale of operations by increasing the input mix by a given proportion without increasing proportionally the ingredient of management. As the scale of operation increases through the addition of men, machines, material, equipment, and the like, a heavier burden is placed upon management. In effect, all factors may be changing except top management. Thus, in addition to decreasing returns to scale, diminishing returns may be taking place as management becomes overtaxed. In any case it is quite possible that increasing and constant returns to scale may be found where the scale of operations is small, but at large scales of operations decreasing returns to scale may be prevalent. Furthermore, after the point of decreasing returns to scale has been reached, additional productive factors may be of less value to the entrepreneur. Consequently, this situation will influence the price he is willing to pay for them.

Principle of Proportionality

The entrepreneur combines labor, land, and capital in those proportions that will yield the best results, not only in quantity but also in quality. Within the limits set by the requirements of the technology employed, he can vary the amounts of the factors to secure that combination of factors that will prove to be the most economical with respect to production cost. Thus, for example, where labor is plentiful and capital scarce, it is usually more economical to use a larger amount of labor and a smaller amount of capital in the input mix. Again, where site values are high, a shoe factory may be built on a small area but with many floors and with a different arrangement of machinery and labor than would be the case where land is cheap and the factory building could be built over a larger area and with fewer floors. Therefore, within the limits set by the requirements of the technological process, the amounts of the factors in the input mix may be varied without a reduction in the volume of product. This is commonly known as the *principle of variable proportions*, but it is frequently called the principle of substitutability.

The laws of diminishing returns and returns to scale and the principle of proportionality are of great importance because they influence the demand of the entrepreneur for units of the factors of production. The producer will always strive to employ factors in that proportion which will mean least cost. Within the limits permitted by the technological requirements of his business, he will use cheap factors more freely and the costly factors more sparingly. Therefore, his demand for units of each of the factors is affected by their relative cost to him.

How far will the entrepreneur go in employing units of each factor within the limits of variable proportions? Granted that the technological process permits variation in amounts of factors used, he will want to find the least-cost combination, if possible. Where necessary, he will call to his aid the services of engineers, cost accountants, and other experts. He wants his cost dollars to go as far as possible, and he will achieve this aim when the last dollar spent on each factor yields the same amount of revenue. If by using capital he can get a higher production return for his dollar than by using additional labor, he will continue to add more capital than labor until the returns per dollar from both have attained the same proportions. This point of combination of labor, land, and capital is the *least-cost combination*. It is a point that depends on a great many variables, and it is constantly subject to change.

Any improvement in the technological process or any change in the quantity, quality, or price of the factors of production will inevitably lead to a new least-cost combination. If the price of a factor rises without a change in its quality, this factor will be used more sparingly and other factors more freely.

COSTS OF PRODUCTION

The real cost of a supply of goods consists essentially of real productive inputs—intellectual and physical effort and the sacrifices incident to saving. For all practical purposes, of course, the measure of production cost is money, and the amount of such production costs is figured in terms of payments for labor, capital, materials, and other items directly or indirectly related to production. In addition, in a capitalistic economy an imputed cost allowance is made for the services of the entrepreneur, since it is the opportunity for profit that induces the entrepreneur to assume the risks and to undertake the production. Once in operation, a certain minimum profit is essential if the entrepreneur is to continue his efforts in producing a good or serivce. This amount of profit, therefore, is considered as a cost of production. Any profit over and above this nominal amount, whatever it may be, is known as *economic profit* or *pure profit*.

Alternative Uses and Opportunity Costs

Under a system of private enterprise, a factor of production is usually employed for the production of a specific good only if it is worth more when used for the production of that good than it would be if used to produce something else. For example, if there is competition for labor, the automobile manufacturer bids for the labor of mechanics by offering to pay at least as much for their labor as do other employers of mechanics. Other employers likewise compete for the labor of workers of all types.

The same principle operates to determine the cost of materials used by a producer. The automobile manufacturer and all other users of steel must pay a price for steel that is at least equal to the value of that material if used for some other purpose. Likewise, the cost of capital goods and borrowed funds in the form of bank loans is largely determined by the value of such goods or funds if devoted to some other use.

The amount of payment necessary to attract a given factor of production away from a similar or the next best opportunity for employment is referred to as *opportunity cost*. This cost exists whether payment is made in the form of cash expenditures or not. For example, suppose that you are a self-employed farmer and that you have a farm on which corn would be the most profitable crop to produce and wheat would be the next most profitable. If you decide to grow corn, the opportunity cost of producing a corn crop will be the value of your land and labor if they were used to produce a wheat crop.

External Economies

As an industry grows and develops, *external economies*—those realizable outside of individual plants—sometimes increase. These economies result from a greater degree of specialization in the procurement of materials, processing, financing, and distribution. For example, in the production of automobiles external economies have become possible because of increased specialization in various steps in physical production (for example, the production of parts by specialized firms), credit facilities, transportation, and selling. These developments, together with the huge size of individual plants and of the industry as a whole, make low unit costs possible when the industry is operating at a rather high level of production.

Explicit and Imputed Costs

Expenditures for production that result from agreements or contracts are *explicit costs*. Such costs are always recognized because they are stated in objective terms, usually in terms of money, and are a matter of record. Expenditures that are attributable to the use of one's own factor of production, such as the use of one's own land, are *implicit* or *imputed costs*. In normal accounting procedure imputed costs are often ignored. For example, salary costs arising from one's own services in his business may not be deducted as a cost in arriving at the amount of his taxable income for his proprietorship. Nevertheless, in determining the true profit, imputed costs for the use of one's own land, labor, or capital must be recognized as a part of the real cost of production.[1]

Cost Tendencies

As we have seen, in some plants and industries the volume of production can be increased without changing the unit cost. In others—at least for a time—an increase in production results in a decrease in unit cost. In still others a point may soon be reached where an increase in production results in a rise in unit cost.

Plants and industries in which costs per unit do not change as the volume of production varies are rare if, in fact, they are to be found at all. Tailoring establishments, where the main costs are those for labor and materials, are examples of an industry where unit cost does not vary greatly with changes in the number of units produced. But even in tailoring establishments, certain fixed costs vary with the number of units of output.

Both in individual firms and in industries as a whole, unit cost of production usually varies with the volume of production. When a plant is not operating at full capacity, additional units can be produced, and the increase in production may result in a decrease in the cost per unit produced. For example, after a given number of workers have been employed, as a rule the employment of additional workers will result in more than a proportionate return for the additional labor cost. The increasing returns can be attributed to economies within the plant that are made possible by a greater division of labor, to a more nearly continuous use of equipment, to better terms in purchasing larger quantities of materials and equipment, and to other savings. In any plant the tendency toward increasing returns is likely to manifest itself for some time.

Certain industries are said to be "decreasing cost industries." Railroad transportation is frequently cited as an example of this kind. On the other hand, agriculture and other extractive industries are said to be characterized by increasing costs. Such a classification, however, is justified only on strictly practical grounds, for the truth of the matter is that, within certain ranges of production, practically all establishments and industries as a whole operate under a condition of decreasing costs; and, after a certain level of production has been reached, they can operate only at increasing unit cost.

In the case of railroads, the capacities of the roads have been planned to accommodate a certain potential volume of freight and passenger transportation. Therefore, from the start of service, unit cost decreases and continues to decline until the volume of transportation reaches the amount that can be

[1] For a further explanation and example of how imputed costs affect profits, see pages 588-590.

carried at minimum costs. This is why in earlier days, before government regulation of railroad rates, there was at times terrific competition among some railroads for freight and passengers. After the maximum volume has been reached, additional tonnage and passengers can be carried only at increasing operating costs. The same may be said in principle for agriculture and mining. Neither in individual plants nor in industries as a whole is productive effort immune to the operation of the law of diminishing returns or increasing costs. The utilization of potential plant and industrial capacity may make decreasing costs possible for a while. But if increased production results in pushing the combination of the factors of production farther and farther away from the ideal proportions for such factors, a tendency toward increasing costs will eventually develop.

The least-cost position of a firm is attained when with a given capacity certain proportional amounts of land, labor, capital, and management are utilized. When the firm is operating at this level, unit cost is at the lowest possible level in the existing firm. At the same time, a larger output may be produced by increasing one or more, but not all, of the productive factors. When this is done, unit cost will increase because the law of diminishing returns will affect costs adversely. In the long run individual firms and industries as a whole may overcome the tendency toward increasing cost by the employment of improved technology. If production is pushed beyond a certain point, however, the tendency will recur. For example, in the coal mining industry a producer may utilize modern methods of production and dig coal that is near the surface. But if increased demand calls for a larger supply that can be obtained only by recourse to deeper mining of coal of no better quality, the cost per ton will increase eventually.

Classifications of Costs

Now that we have seen how the physical factors of production can affect the supply of goods and the general cost of production, we can explain and analyze the various costs used by the economist in his study of the business firm.

The costs of production in an individual plant may be classified broadly into fixed costs and variable costs. *Fixed costs* are those costs that remain constant as output varies. Unless the plant capacity is changed, the total amount of fixed cost in a firm does not vary with the volume of production. The aggregate of the items of fixed cost is frequently referred to as *overhead*. Such items include bond or mortgage interest incurred for the construction or purchase of plant and equipment, certain depreciation and obsolescence costs, property taxes, and insurance. In addition, a portion of salaries and wages paid for executive and supervisory services may properly be regarded as fixed expenses, for a minimum managerial staff must be maintained even when the business is operating at a limited capacity.

Although the total fixed costs remain constant, fixed costs per unit of production decrease with an increase in output. For example, if the total fixed cost in a given plant is $1,000,000 and 100,000 units are produced, the amount of fixed costs incurred in producing any one unit is $10. If production is increased to 1,000,000 units, the fixed costs per unit, or the average fixed cost, is $1.

Average fixed cost is calculated by dividing the total fixed cost by the number of units produced. As we have indicated, average fixed cost continues to decrease as it is spread over a larger number of units, but it never disappears entirely. Column 8 of Table 26-2, for example, shows what happens to a $50 total fixed cost when it is converted to average fixed cost.

TABLE 26-2

(1) Input	(2) Total Output	(3) MP	(4) AP	(5) TFC $	(6) TVC $	(7) TC $	(8) AFC $	(9) AVC $	(10) ATC $	(11) MC $	(12) AR $	(13) TR $	(14) MR $	(15) Profit $
1 ...	10	—	10	50	10	60	5.00	1.00	6.00	—	2	20	2	(−40)
2 ...	22	12	11	50	20	70	2.27	.91	3.18	.83	2	44	2	(−26)
3 ...	36	14	12	50	30	80	1.39	.83	2.22	.71	2	72	2	(− 8)
4 ...	52	16	13	50	40	90	.96	.77	1.73	.63	2	104	2	+14
5 ...	67	15	13.4	50	50	100	.75	.75	1.49	.67	2	134	2	+34
6 ...	78	11	13	50	60	110	.64	.77	1.41	.91	2	156	2	+46
7 ...	84	6	12	50	70	120	.60	.83	1.43	1.67	2	168	2	+48
8 ...	88	4	11	50	80	130	.57	.91	1.48	2.50	2	176	2	+46
9 ...	90	2	10	50	90	140	.56	1.00	1.56	5.00	2	180	2	+40
10 ...	90	0	9	50	100	150	.56	1.11	1.67	—	2	180	2	+30

Variable costs are costs of production other than fixed cost, such as labor and materials. *Average variable cost* is the unit variable cost, which is found by dividing the total variable cost by the number of units produced. Until the point or condition of diminishing returns from the use of the variable factors of production is reached, average variable cost decreases as production increases, if, of course, the prices of the variable factors do not increase. Soon after the law of diminishing returns begins to operate, however, average variable cost increases as the number of units produced increases.

An Example. In Table 26-2, for example, it can be seen that if the cost of a variable unit of input is $10, the total variable cost will increase by $10 each time an additional unit of input is added. Consequently, total variable cost increases from $10 to $100 as the units of input increase from 1 to 10. This total variable cost can be converted to an average variable cost by dividing the total output shown in column 2 into the total variable cost shown in column 6. Notice that the average variable cost starting out at $1 per unit of output drops to $.75 per unit in line 5 and rises thereafter, reaching $1.11 with the tenth unit of output on line 10. Notice, also, that the point of the lowest average variable cost corresponds with the point of diminishing average productivity, or the point of highest average product.

Total cost is the sum of total fixed and total variable costs at a particular level of production. *Average total cost* is found by dividing total cost by the number of units produced or by adding the average fixed and average variable costs. Total cost increases as production increases but not proportionately. Average total cost decreases, as a rule, until a certain number of units has been produced—depending on the intercost relationships and the point where diminishing returns begins to operate. Soon after the point of diminishing returns is reached, the average total cost increases as production increases. This is shown in column 10 of Table 26-2, which indicates that the lowest average total cost is on line 6 at $1.41.

An exceptionally important concept to the economist is incremental or marginal cost. *Marginal cost* is the increase (decrease) in the total cost resulting from the production of one more (less) unit of output. Marginal cost is influenced strongly by the law of diminishing productivity, and the shape of any marginal cost curve will depend on the shape of the marginal product curve. Column 3 of Table 26-2 shows the marginal product schedule. Column 11 of Table 26-2 shows the marginal cost for our hypothetical firm. Notice that the values of marginal cost decrease, reach a minimum, and then rise thereafter. Observe further that as the marginal product rises, the marginal cost declines. Then, when the marginal product starts to decrease, the marginal cost begins to increase. The point of lowest marginal cost, $.63 as shown on line 4, corresponds with the point of highest marginal product, also shown on line 4. This reveals the close, but inverse, relationship between marginal product and marginal cost.

In computing the marginal cost, remember that it refers to the increase in total cost per additional unit of output, not input. Since the increase in total cost shown in column 7 is the increase per unit of input, this incremental cost must be converted to incremental cost per unit of output (marginal cost). Since the second unit of input cost $10 more but resulted in an increase in total output of 12 units, the marginal cost, or increased cost per unit of output, will be equal to $.83, as shown on line 2 of column 11. Similarly, if the successive increments of total cost are divided by the respective marginal products, the marginal cost for each line will be found.

The Example in Graphic Form. The relationship of these cost values can be seen much more clearly, of course, if they are presented in graphic form, as shown in Figure 26-2. In this case the average fixed cost, *AFC*, will be represented by a curve continuously decreasing in value as total fixed costs are spread over a wider and wider range of output. The average variable cost, *AVC*, will be a curve decreasing, reaching a minimum, and then rising in value because of the presence of the law of diminishing marginal productivity. The average total cost, *ATC*, which is a combination of the *AFC* and the *AVC*, likewise will drop and then rise again. Notice that as both the *AFC* and *AVC* are falling the *ATC* will be falling. A point is reached at which the *AVC* starts to rise while the *AFC* is still declining. What happens to the *ATC* at this point will depend on the relative strength of the two curves.

In Figure 26-2, notice that initially the downward pull of the *AFC* is stronger than the upward push of the *AVC* so that the *ATC* continues to drop for a while. But eventually the upward push of the *AVC* overcomes

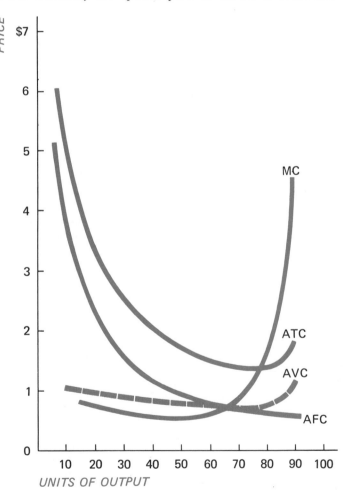

FIGURE 26-2

GRAPHIC RELATIONSHIP OF AVERAGE FIXED COST, AVERAGE VARIABLE COST, AVERAGE TOTAL COST, AND MARGINAL COST

Average fixed cost, *AFC*, will continue to decline as output increases. Average variable cost, *AVC*, will decrease, reach a minimum, and then rise, as will the average total cost, *ATC*. Marginal cost, *MC*, will decrease, reach a minimum, then rise. The *MC* will intersect the *AVC* and *ATC* at their lowest points.

the downward pull of the *AFC*, and the *ATC* rises thereafter. Graphically, the marginal cost curve, *MC*, will decrease, reach a minimum, and then rise due to its close relationship with the marginal product curve. Anytime marginal cost is less than average variable cost or average total cost, it will effect a reduction in the *AVC* and/or *ATC*, in much the same manner that the marginal product affects the average product. Whenever *MC* is greater than the *AVC* or *ATC*, it will cause them to increase. Furthermore, by its very nature *MC* will cross, or intersect, the *AVC* and the *ATC* lines at their lowest points.

REVENUE AND PROFIT

In the preceding chapter we saw that the demand schedule indicates the quantities of a commodity or service that will be purchased at various prices. It was pointed out, too, that under competitive conditions the price would be determined by the free forces of supply and demand. Although conditions are not always competitive and the forces of demand and supply are not always unencumbered, we will accept for the present the supposition that the market price becomes the price at which an individual firm can sell its product. This will permit us to look at some revenue concepts and relate them to the cost concepts in order to analyze the profit situation for an individual firm.

Revenues

Average revenue, as used by the economist, is the price per unit sold. It is the market price from the viewpoint of the seller, and it may be computed by dividing the total revenue by the number of units sold. *Total revenue*, of course, is the amount of revenue or income received from the sale of a given quantity of goods or services. It can be calculated readily by multiplying the average revenue, or price, by the number of units sold.

An extremely important and more complex concept used by the economist is marginal revenue, which parallels the marginal cost concept explained earlier. *Marginal revenue* is the increase (decrease) in total revenue that results from the sale of one more (less) unit of output. This can be calculated by dividing the increase in total revenue resulting from the use of an additional unit of input by the increase in total product.

In our example in Table 26-2, the values of the marginal revenue and the average revenue are identical. This will not always be the case. Anytime you are dealing with other than perfectly competitive conditions, the values of the marginal revenue and the average revenue will differ. With a constant price, however, whenever the firm sells an additional unit at the market price of $2, it will add $2 to its total revenue, and the marginal revenue has to equal the average revenue, or price.

Profit

Total profit is the difference between total revenue and total cost. Whether a firm makes a profit, and how much profit, depends on the relationship of its revenue to its costs. Even when a firm is not making a profit, the decision as to whether to continue to operate or shut down will depend, again, on its cost-revenue relationships. A firm can analyze its profit situation in many ways. For instance, it may compare its total revenue to its total cost by using a break-even chart, or it may engage in marginal analysis by dealing with its marginal revenue and marginal cost concepts.

Total Revenue vs. Total Cost

By comparing total revenue with total cost over a given range of output, a firm can determine at what levels it makes a profit and at what levels it suffers losses. Furthermore, by constructing a break-even chart, it can determine at what point its losses cease and profits begin. This, of course, is known as the *break-even point*. It may be given in terms of the total output needed to break even, or it may be analyzed in terms of total inputs. Other firms construct their break-even charts in terms of capacity to indicate at what level they must operate their plant in order to avoid losses and make profits. Naturally a firm will endeavor not only to reach the break-even output or capacity but also to go beyond it as far as is profitable. It must avoid the pitfall, however, of pushing too far beyond, as it may encounter rapidly rising marginal costs at, or near, capacity levels. In such an event, total profits may actually decline in spite of higher output. The maximum profit position will be that level of output, or capacity, where there is the greatest gap between total revenue and total cost, as shown in Figure 26-3.

Another advantage of a break-even chart is that the cost can be broken down into total fixed cost and total variable cost. In fact, if desirable, the variable cost can be segmented further into a variety of costs, including such items as direct and indirect manufacturing cost, material cost, labor cost, and selling costs.

Putting the values from our hypothetical firm into a break-even chart, as in Figure 26-3, shows the total fixed cost of $50 represented by a straight horizontal line. This indicates that the fixed costs remain constant at a given range of output. Total costs, which continually increase, are represented by a line moving upward to the right. The difference between total cost and total fixed cost represents the total variable cost. Since the price at which each unit sells is constant, the total revenue is shown by the line moving upward

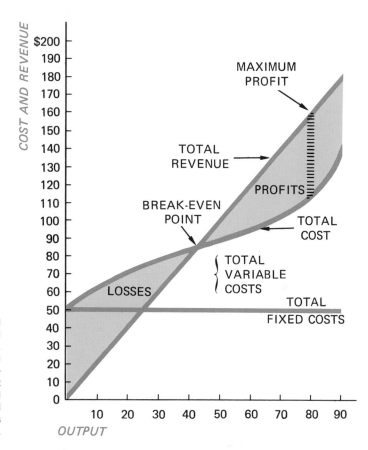

to the right at a constant slope. The break-even point is at 42 units of output. Although profits are made at all levels of production beyond this point, maximum profit is made when production is in the vicinity of 80 units.

The same information can be interpolated from Table 26-2, which indicates that the break-even point will come somewhere between the third and fourth units of input, or between 36 and 52 units of output. Likewise, the maximum profit position will be the seventh unit of input, which corresponds with production in the vicinity of 80 units.

Marginal Revenue vs. Marginal Cost

It is only reasonable to assume that anytime a firm can add to its total profit by producing more or fewer units, it will act accordingly. Consequently, the firm's profit picture is often analyzed in terms of what happens to cost and revenue with the addition of one more unit of input or output. Whenever the production and sale of an additional, or marginal, unit adds more to revenue than it does to cost, profits are sure to increase, or losses diminish, whatever the case may be. If the production of one more unit adds more to cost than it does to revenue, the opposite is true. We have available two such concepts that tell us how much is added to revenue and how much is added to cost with each additional unit of output. To determine the point of maximum profit for the firm, all we have to do is observe their relationship.

Marginal revenue, *MR*, measures the increase in total revenue per additional unit of output, and marginal cost, *MC*, measures the increase in total cost per additional unit of output. Therefore, anytime *MR* is greater than *MC*, profits will rise or losses will diminish. On the other hand, if *MR* is less than *MC*, profits will decrease, or losses will increase. A firm will profit by increasing its production so long as its $MR > MC$. It will pay to reduce production whenever $MR < MC$.

In most cases marginal revenue is a constant or decreasing value, and the marginal cost is a continuously increasing value. Therefore, as a firm adds units of output, it eventually reaches a point at which $MR = MC$. This is its maximum profit position, since at any less level of production $MR > MC$ and at any greater level of production $MR < MC$. In our hypothetical firm, for example, it can be observed that the *MR* has a constant value of $2, while the *MC*, after reaching a low of $.63, continuously increases to more than $5 as production reaches 90 units. Comparing the *MR* in column 14 with the *MC* in column 11, it can be seen that, at all levels of production up to and including that associated with the seventh unit of input, *MR* exceeds *MC*. Therefore, the firm will continue to produce up to that point. It will not add the eighth unit of input, however, since the *MR* is less than the *MC* for the output that will be forthcoming. Consequently, the firm will maximize profits, according to the marginal analysis, at a level of output in the vicinity of 80 units. This, of course, corresponds with the maximum profit position indicated on the break-even chart illustrated in Figure 26-3.

This method will be examined in greater depth in subsequent chapters. In the meantime, let us consider another aspect of the cost-revenue relationship.

Minimizing Losses in the Short Run

Thus far we have been dealing with the pleasant situation of a firm making a profit, but what happens if the firm is suffering a loss? Suppose, for example, in our problem the average revenue received by the firm was only $1, as determined by the forces of the market. Assuming that the costs remained the same, our firm would not be able to make a profit at any level of production. It would, however, minimize its losses with 7 units of input, or 80 units of output. What then should the firm do, continue to operate or shut down? The answer will depend on the relationship of cost to revenue and on whether we are talking about the short-run or the long-run period.

In economics the *short run* is a period of time in which some factors of production are fixed. The *long run* is a period of time in which all factors of production, including machinery, buildings, and other capital items, are variable. In the short run, for example, it may be possible for a firm to increase its output within a given range by adding more workers, putting on another shift, buying more raw materials, and manipulating other variable factors without increasing the capacity of its fixed plant and equipment. If given enough time, however, it could increase its output greatly in the long run by adding to its capacity with the construction or purchase of new plant and equipment. Consequently, in the long run even the fixed factors become variable. The actual length of this period is rather nebulous and varies with different industries. Obviously the calendar time involved in the long run for the steel industry, which requires construction of huge mills, is much longer than the long-run period in the garment industry, where a firm can purchase additional machines, floor space, and loft capacity within a matter of a few weeks.

If a firm is operating at a loss in the short run, and we will assume it is minimizing its losses, the question still remains whether it should continue to operate or shut down. The answer will depend very much on the relationship of its fixed to its variable cost and the relationship of the variable cost to its total revenue.

Assume that a firm has a total fixed cost of $60,000 and a total variable cost of $40,000 for a total cost of $100,000. At the same time suppose its total revenue is $50,000. It is obvious that the firm is suffering a loss of $50,000. Nevertheless, it is better for it to continue to operate in the short run rather than shut down. Notice that by operating, the loss is only $50,000; but if it were to shut down, its loss would be greater. It is true that if it were to close down, its total cost would drop by the amount of its variable cost, $40,000; but keep in mind that its revenue would drop to zero. Furthermore, it would still have its fixed cost of $60,000 to pay, and its loss would be $60,000 instead of $50,000. Although the firm would not be making a profit, by operating it would be recovering all of its variable cost and some of its fixed cost. This is often referred to as "making a contribution to overhead" and is a principle that guides many firms not only in the decision of whether to shut down in the short run, but also in deciding whether to continue certain lines of production that are not profitable.

Notice in our example that if the total revenue for the firm were only $30,000, it would be better to shut down in the short run. In such a case the increased cost of operating, the $40,000 variable cost, is more than the revenue from operating. Consequently, by operating, the total loss incurred would be $70,000. On the other hand, if the firm were to shut down, its total loss would be only $60,000, the amount of the total fixed cost.

In summation, it pays a firm to operate at a loss in the short run as long as it can recover its variable cost and make a contribution to overhead. If it cannot recover its variable cost, however, it is more profitable to shut down in the short run. One way of ascertaining quickly whether a firm is recovering its variable cost is to compare the average revenue with the average variable cost at the point of equilibrium, or the point of minimum losses. If the AR is equal to or greater than the AVC, it will pay the firm to continue its operation.

Whether under a loss condition the firm desires to continue operations in the long run will depend on a multitude of factors, such as the cost of new assets, its competition, the general outlook for its products, and the general status of the economy. But unless it can see some improvement in its profit picture, it would not be wise to pour additional capital into a nonprofitable enterprise.

ECONOMIC PROFIT VS. ACCOUNTING PROFIT

The concept of economic profit is often misunderstood, and it is frequently confused with the term *business* or *accounting profit*. The net income or net loss shown on the accountant's income statement is simply the difference between the total income of the business and its total expenses in a given period. The accountant lists only the explicit costs of doing business. These costs consist of the actual payments of cash or of bookkeeping entries for the expense accounts, such as wages, material, and depreciation. In order to find the true economic profit, the economist will consider any implicit cost that may be involved. These costs will consist of allowances for the use of the owner's own factors of production, such as labor, land, or capital, that are used in the input mix. He does this in order to reduce any income to a true economic profit.

As an example, let us assume that there are two gas stations with identical plant facilities located catercornered to each other, one selling Zip gasoline and the other Pep. Assume further that the entrepreneur of the Zip station, Mr. Zipper, rents his station, borrows the money to buy his inventory, and hires a manager to operate the station; and that the entrepreneur of the Pep station, Mr. Pepper, uses his own funds to buy his station and to finance his inventory, and manages the station himself. If their sales were identical for a given period, their respective income statements may appear as shown in Table 26-3.

TABLE 26-3

Zip Service Station Income Statement			Pep Service Station Income Statement		
Net sales		$120,000	Net sales		$120,000
Cost of goods sold		90,000	Cost of goods sold		90,000
Gross profit on sales		$ 30,000	Gross profit on sales		$ 30,000
Operating expenses:			Operating expenses:		
Rent	$4,800		Wages	$6,000	
Wages	6,000		Insurance	300	
Salary	7,500		Depreciation	800	
Insurance	300		Other	500	7,600
Interest	400				
Other	500	19,500			
Net income		$ 10,500	Net income		$ 22,400

At first glance it appears that the Pep Service Station is making more than double the profit that Zip is making. A closer look at the figures, however, reveals that the economic profit of the two firms may be identical. Notice that Mr. Zipper paid out a specific rent of $4,800, a manager's salary of $7,500, and interest of $400 on his loan. These, along with the others, are explicit costs of doing business, and the accounting profit of $10,500 in this case will correspond to the true economic profit from operating the business. In the case of the Pep Service Station, however, the business profit of $22,400 is not the true economic profit. Certain implicit costs must be computed.

Since Mr. Pepper is working as manager in his own service station, this use of his own services is a cost of doing business. The imputed value of his service can be determined by calculating what he could earn in a similar job working for someone else. As we learned earlier in this chapter, this is known as opportunity cost. Specifically, opportunity cost can be measured by determining what amount of income a factor of production could earn if used in a similar or the next best capacity elsewhere. In this case it is readily determinable that Mr. Pepper could probably have earned at least $7,500 per year managing another gas station, if the salary Mr. Zipper is paying to his manager indicates a reasonable salary for that type of work.

Likewise, assume that Mr. Pepper had borrowed $8,000, paying 5 percent interest in order to finance his inventory. This means that his money tied up in inventory could have been earning at least $400 per year invested elsewhere. Therefore, it is costing him $400 in opportunity interest to use his own money in the business. The opportunity rent can be determined by calculating the net rent that could be earned by renting the building to someone else. In this case assume he could rent the station for $4,800, the same rent Mr. Zipper was paying. However, since the depreciation cost of the building is $800 per year, the implicit net rental income from the station would be $4,000. Thus, implicit net rental income plus the depreciation charge is equal to the gross rental income of $4,800, which is equivalent to the rent paid by Mr. Zipper. Now if we were to add these imputed costs totaling $11,900 to the operating expenses of the Pep Service Station, the total operating expenses would increase from $7,600 to $19,500, and it would show the same economic profit as the Zip Service Station, $10,500.

Is this to say that the Pep Service Station did not earn $22,400? No, not at all. It is merely saying that of the $22,400 total earnings, only $10,500 can be attributed to profits. The remainder is earned from the use of other factors of production. Another way to look at the situation is to say that the Zip Service Station had a business income of $10,500, which was all economic profit. On the other hand, the Pep Service Station, or Mr. Pepper in particular, had a business income of $22,400, but it should be allocated as follows: $7,500 as salary income, $4,000 as net rental income, $400 as interest income, and $10,500 as economic profit.

This is a very important distinction in economic analysis. Many entrepreneurs, especially those operating small businesses, are misled because they lack an understanding of the true nature of economic profits. Suppose, for example, that the gross profit on sales of the Pep Service Station fell to $15,000. Deducting the operating expenses as shown in the preceding income statement, $7,600, would leave a business profit of $7,400. Mr. Pepper might think that his business is doing well since it shows a $7,400 business profit. Actually the business is operating at an economic loss. If he subtracts his imputed costs, he would have the following breakdown of his $7,400 business income: salary, $7,500; rental income, $4,000; interest income, $400; and an economic loss, $4,500. His business is not making a profit at all but is suffering a loss. If the situation continues, he would do better economically to sell his station, reinvest his money in bonds, and go to work for someone else.

PURE PROFIT

From an economic point of view, profit is a residual of income over and above all economic costs, both explicit and implicit, that results from the operation of a business. It is a return to the entrepreneur for risk taking. Profits are dynamic in that they are constantly changing in amount. New business firms are established in the hope of making a profit and other businesses fail because of lack of profit. During the 1960s, over 4 million new firms were established in the United States. But during that same period about 3 million firms went out of business. Thus, we had a net increase of 1,100,000 firms in the decade. In addition, another 4 million firms changed owners. Although in 1972 there were 317,000 new business incorporations, the net increase in the total number of corporations was only 6,000. Starting a business involves a risk, but the opportunity for profit induces hundreds of thousands of individuals annually to try to become successful entrepreneurs. More important than the success or failure of an individual business enterprise, however, is the freedom in our economic system that permits an individual to go into business for himself.

Profit Under Competitive Conditions

Pure profit is a return to the entrepreneur from the operation of the business. It may be either large or small. It excludes any return from the use of the other factors of production utilized in the input mix. If the profit is too small or if the firm suffers a loss, it may go out of business. That amount of profit that is neither excessive nor minimal but is the amount necessary to induce the entrepreneur to stay in business is called *nominal profit*. It is measured by the opportunity cost of the services of the entrepreneur. Usually nominal profit is considered as an economic cost of doing business. When it is, the nominal profit position becomes a no-profit position as far as the business operation is concerned. As pointed out earlier in this chapter, any amount over and above this can be called pure profit. Under conditions of pure competition, profit, in addition to being residual and dynamic, is a temporary phenomenon. The conditions of pure competition are such that anytime a pure profit exists, forces come into play to eliminate such pure profit. This is so because of the nature of pure competition, as we shall see subsequently.

Profit Under Imperfect Competition

Conversely, in a monopoly, for example, if a pure profit situation exists, the monopolist may be able by various means to effectively block the entry of new firms into the industry. Thus, profit becomes more than a temporary phenomenon. Furthermore, since the output of the monopoly becomes the total supply on the market, the monopolist can influence the market price by changing his output. In this way he can set the price where it will yield him the greatest profit. Under a condition of monopolistic or imperfect competition—which is usually the case—profits may be larger than they would be under pure competition.

The cost and revenue picture for an individual firm and what it may be able to do about it will depend to a considerable extent on the type of competition that prevails in its industry. Therefore, it is pricing and profits under various types of competition that we turn to in the next few chapters.

SUMMARY

1. In providing a supply of goods or services for the market, the cost of production is affected by physical factors, such as the law of diminishing marginal productivity, returns to scale, and the principle of proportionality.

2. The most widely recognized of these factors, the law of diminishing marginal productivity, means that as additional units of a factor of production are combined with a fixed quantity of other factors, a point will be reached where the output resulting from the use of an additional unit of the variable factor will not be as large as was the output due to the addition of the preceding unit.

3. In analyzing a firm's cost, the economist considers not only the explicit cost but also the imputed cost of using one's own factors of production, such as labor or land, in the productive process. Imputed costs are generally measured in terms of alternative uses to which the factor of production could be applied.

4. Costs may be classified as fixed or variable. Total cost is a combination of both. In addition to totals, costs may be broken down into unit cost, such as average fixed cost, average variable cost, average total cost, and marginal cost.

5. The price received per unit of output, as determined by the forces of demand and supply in the market, is known as average revenue to the firm. Marginal revenue is the increase in total revenue that results from the sale of an additional unit of output.

6. A firm can analyze its profit position by means of a break-even chart on which is plotted total revenue, total cost, total fixed cost, and total variable cost. In addition to ascertaining the break-even point, a firm can also determine its maximum profit level on such a chart.

7. The maximum profit position of a firm can also be determined by marginal analysis. A firm will maximize its profits or minimize its losses, whichever the case may be, by operating at the point where marginal revenue equals marginal cost.

8. Even if a firm is suffering a loss, it will benefit the firm to continue operating in the short run so long as it is recovering its variable cost and is making a contribution to overhead.

9. Economic profit differs from accounting profit in that the latter excludes imputed costs for the use of one's own factors of production.

10. Pure profit is the return to the entrepreneur or business firm from the operation of the business. It is an amount over and above the costs of production, both explicit and implicit. Imputed costs are measured by opportunity costs, which are determined by the income that could be obtained by putting a given factor of production to an alternative use.

NEW TERMS

Profit, *p. 570*
Production function, *p. 570*
Law of diminishing returns, *p. 571*
Marginal product, *p. 572*

Law of diminishing marginal productivity, *p. 572*
Average product, *p. 573*
Returns to scale, *p. 574*

QUESTIONS FOR DISCUSSION AND ANALYSIS

1. Distinguish between the concepts of diminishing marginal productivity and returns to scale.

2. What effect does the size of the marginal product have on the average product? Explain.

3. How can opportunity cost be used to measure the imputed value of a factor of production?

4. What is an increasing cost industry?

5. Explain why the average variable cost decreases, reaches a minimum, and then rises again, while the average fixed cost continues to decrease as output increases.

6. Is it true that, whenever marginal cost is rising, the average variable cost and the average total cost must also rise? Why?

7. Distinguish between average revenue and marginal revenue.

8. How is the maximum profit position determined on a break-even chart? What components are needed to construct a break-even chart?

9. Why is the point at which marginal revenue is equal to marginal cost the maximum profit position for a firm?

10. If a firm were suffering a loss, under what conditions would the firm find it beneficial to continue operations rather than to shut down?

11. A merchant owns his store and the lot on which it is situated. His investment in these items is $75,000, and the prevailing rate of interest is 5 percent. Assume that his net sales in one year amounted to $45,000; that the cost of goods he sold was $30,000; that he hired a clerk for $3,600; and that other expenses totaled $3,750. Did he realize any profit? If so, what kind of profit?

12. What is pure profit, and how is it measured?

SUGGESTED READINGS

Bain, Joe S. *Pricing, Distribution, and Employment*. New York: Holt, Rinehart, and Winston, Inc., 1953.

Becker, Barry S. *Economic Theory*. New York: Alfred A. Knopf, Inc., 1971.

Boulding, Kenneth E. *Economic Analysis*. New York: Harper & Row, Publishers, 1955.

Brennan, Michael J. *Theory of Economic Statistics*. Englewood Cliffs, N.J.: Prentice-Hall, Inc., 1970.

Cohen, Kalman J., and Richard M. Cyert. *The Theory of the Firm*. Englewood Cliffs, N.J.: Prentice-Hall, Inc., 1965.

Leftwich, Richard H. *The Price System and Resource Allocation*. New York: Holt, Rinehart and Winston, Inc., 1973.

Marshall, Alfred. *Principles of Economics*. New York: The Macmillan Company, 1948.

Nicholson, Walter. *Microeconomic Theory: Basic Principles and Extensions*. Hinsdale, Ill.: Dryden Press, 1972.

Stigler, George J. *The Theory of Price*. New York: The Macmillan Company, 1973.

27

Pure Competition

PREVIEW Price and output are determined in large part by the degree of competition in an industry. Pure competition is an ideal market structure in which there are numerous buyers and sellers of an identical product. All buyers and sellers are well informed about markets and prices, and there is free entry into and exit from the market. Under such conditions no individual buyer or seller can determine or influence price. Price will be determined by the aggregate actions of all buyers and sellers or by total supply and demand.

Each producer will have to accept the prices of inputs and outputs as determined by market forces and adjust his output to maximize his profit. If profits do exist in an industry, however, competition will induce additional firms into the industry. This will cause output to increase, price to fall, and economic profit to diminish and disappear. Firms will tend to operate at a no-profit, no-loss equilibrium position. They will recover all cost, including a nominal profit as a return to the entrepreneur. In the long run consumers will purchase the product at a price equal to its cost of production. This is one of the cardinal features of pure competition.

Many types of competition exist in the American economic system. Since there are over 8 million firms, exclusive of farms, doing business in hundreds of industries, it is possible to find various degrees of competition within each industry and numerous shades of competition between different markets. Market situations may range all the way from perfect or pure competition to pure monopoly. Although there are fundamental differences between types of competition, sometimes conditions in a firm or an industry will contain elements of more than one type. Furthermore, a firm may find itself in one type of competitive market in selling its products but in a different type of competitive market in buying its raw materials or hiring labor.

The basic types of market structure are pure competition, pure monopoly, monopolistic competition, and oligopoly. Among the distinguishing characteristics of different types of markets are the number of firms in an industry, the presence or absence of product differentiation, and the ability of any or all firms in an industry to influence the market price. Since pure competition affords a theoretical standard by which we measure the economic and social value of other forms of market structure, we shall first analyze the purely competitive industry.

CHARACTERISTICS OF PURE COMPETITION

Pure competition is an ideal set of market conditions that assumes the following characteristics: [1]

1. *There are numerous sellers in the market, all selling an identical product.* This means there are no quality differences, no brand names, no advertising, nor anything else that would differentiate between the products of various sellers.

2. *All buyers and sellers are informed about markets and prices.* If it is possible to buy the product at a lower price, customers would know about it. If one seller is putting his product on the market cheaper than others, all buyers are aware of this. Furthermore, if one producer can offer a good on the market at a lower price than competitors because of certain cost advantages, other producers will soon learn why and how it can be done.

3. *There is free entry into and exit from the market.* It is a condition of a competitive market that anyone who desires to produce and sell goods in a particular market may do so, without any undue encumbrances. This, of course, would exclude the protection of patent rights, the absence of excessive capital requirements, the availability of the necessary factors of production, freedom from government regulations, and other conditions that may hinder or deter a person or firm from going into the production of a particular type of good or service. Likewise, it assumes that the firm is free to sell its business, to dispose of its factors of production, and to go out of business, or to convert to the production of a different product at any time. Pure competition also assumes that there is perfect mobility on the part of the factors of production.

4. *No individual seller or buyer can influence price. Price is determined by the aggregate actions of all buyers and sellers or by market supply and market demand.* To fulfill this condition, there must be enough sellers in the market so that each one's contribution to the total supply is infinitesimal. Consequently, whether a firm produces more or less has no appreciable effect on the total supply. Under such circumstances each seller must accept the market price as determined by aggregate demand and supply. He will not be able to obtain a

---

[1] Although the phrase "pure competition" is sometimes used interchangeably with the phrase "perfect competition," there is a degree of difference in the meanings of the two. *Perfect competition* implies that there is perfect information about markets and prices on the part of all buyers and sellers, perfect mobility of the various factors of production, and perfectly free entry into and exit from an industry. In short, perfect competition is more idealistic and a higher degree of competition.

greater price for his product because all products of that kind are identical. Buyers have knowledge of this fact, and they know the prices at which goods are available. This does not preclude the possibility, however, that the market price could be changed by the actions of many, or all, firms. If an individual producer increased his output by 50 or 100 percent, for example, the change in total supply would be so insignificant that it would not affect the market price. On the other hand, if each of a large number of producers increased his output by 3, 5, or 10 percent, this could affect supply appreciably and result in a change in market price. It is assumed, however, that all firms would then be bound by the new market price.

A case in point is the production of wheat in America where there are more than one half million producers. Whether Farmer Smith increases his production from 100 to 1,000, or even to 10,000 bushels will have little, if any, effect on a market price of $5.50 per bushel when there is a total supply of more than 1.4 billion bushels on the U.S. market each year and 10.6 billion bushels on the world market. On the other hand, if each wheat farmer in America increased his output by a mere 3 percent, it would increase the total U.S. wheat supply by more than 42 million bushels and no doubt would tend to lower the market price. Similarly, 200,000 producers market 10.5 million 1,000-pound bales of cotton annually, approximately one half million or more farmers supply more than 113 billion pounds of milk yearly, and 48,000 growers produce over 2.5 billion pounds of peanuts each year.

PRICE AND PROFIT IN THE SHORT RUN

Under pure competition each producer faces a perfectly elastic demand curve; that is, he can sell his entire supply of the commodity at the market-determined price. His profit will depend upon the difference between the average total cost of production and the selling price, multiplied by the number of units sold. Since he is in business to make a profit, each producer will try to produce that number of units the sale of which will yield him the greatest profit.

Acting alone, a producer can do little or nothing to change the market price. As we learned earlier, it will make no appreciable difference on price if he sells much or nothing. This is not true, however, for the industry as a whole. If a great many or all producers increase or decrease production, the total market supply will be affected, which will result in a change in price, assuming that demand does not change.

Under a condition of pure competition in an industry that is producing a standardized commodity, how many units of the commodity will each producer undertake to produce? This question cannot be answered exactly, but we can acquire an understanding of the factors that help to determine the amount that each one will produce.

Let us assume a period of time that is just long enough to allow each of the producers to adjust his output to the most profitable level without enlarging or modernizing his plant. This is the short-run period, which is intermediate between the instant of time at which market price is determined by demand and supply and the long-run period. Under the assumed short-run conditions we shall see how each producer will attempt to set his output where his marginal cost becomes equal to his marginal revenue. For the sake of simplicity, we assume that no new factories will be built in the industry and that existing plants will not be enlarged. But it is assumed that each firm is free to vary its volume of production from zero to its maximum existing capacity.

Adjustment of Production to Price in the Short Run

Just how much will the single firm undertake to produce? In most real situations it would probably be impossible to say, for two reasons. First, it is not likely that the entrepreneur could predict exactly what his production cost would be at different levels of production. Second, he is likely to be satisfied with a "good" or "reasonable" amount of profit, which would cause him to refrain from attempting to squeeze out the last possible cent of profit from his business.

Nevertheless, it is realistic to assume that, other things being equal, the producer is motivated by the desire to make as much profit as possible. This assumption does not deny the fact that the producer probably has values and interests other than those that relate to money. But for the purpose of economic analysis, it is necessary to give attention here only to those matters that affect the profit possibilities of a productive enterprise operating under conditions of pure competition.

Therefore, in order to arrive at a logical determination of the firm's output, we proceed on the assumption that the entrepreneur will undertake to produce that amount which will maximize the firm's profit or minimize its loss. What that volume of production will be depends upon the firm's cost and revenue relationships.

Cost and Revenue Relationships: An Illustration. Let us assume that for a certain producer (1) total cost, (2) average total cost, (3) marginal cost, (4) average revenue and marginal revenue, and (5) total revenue are as shown in Table 27-1.

According to the assumed costs and revenues shown in the table, the market price (average revenue) is $1.80 per unit. At this price the producer can sell all that he might produce. How many units will he produce? He will produce the number that will be the most profitable, which is 12 or 13. Let us see why.

As shown in the previous chapter, profit or net gain is the difference between total cost and total revenue. Therefore, if average cost and average revenue remain unchanged and it is profitable to sell one unit, it is more profitable to sell a greater number.

But, as we see from the table, the average total cost varies as the number of units produced changes, while average revenue remains the same. If he produces and sells one unit, he will lose $8.28, the difference between the total cost, $10.08, and the total revenue, $1.80. If he produces and sells 5 units, he will lose only $4.44. And if he produces and sells 12 units, he will make a profit of $2.28. If he produces and sells 13 units, he will make the same amount of profit as he would if he sold 12 units, because the

TABLE 27-1

COST AND
REVENUE
SCHEDULE

Number of Units of Output	Total Cost (TC)	Average Total Cost (ATC)	Marginal Cost (MC)	Average Revenue and Marginal Revenue (AR-MR)	Total Revenue (TR)	Total Gain or Loss (TG or TL)
1	$10.08	$10.08		$1.80	$ 1.80	− $8.28
			$1.14			
2	11.22	5.61		1.80	3.60	− 7.62
			.90			
3	12.12	4.04		1.80	5.40	− 6.72
			.72			
4	12.84	3.21		1.80	7.20	− 5.64
			.60			
5	13.44	2.69		1.80	9.00	− 4.44
			.54			
6	13.98	2.33		1.80	10.80	− 3.18
			.54			
7	14.52	2.07		1.80	12.60	− 1.92
			.60			
8	15.12	1.89		1.80	14.40	− 0.72
			.72			
9	15.84	1.76		1.80	16.20	0.36
			.90			
10	16.74	1.67		1.80	18.00	1.26
			1.14			
11	17.88	1.63		1.80	19.80	1.92
			1.44			
12	19.32	1.61		1.80	21.60	2.28
			1.80			
13	21.12	1.62		1.80	23.40	2.28
			2.22			
14	23.34	1.67		1.80	25.20	1.86
			2.70			
15	26.04	1.74		1.80	27.00	0.96
			3.24			
16	29.28	1.83		1.80	28.80	− 0.48
			3.84			
17	33.12	1.95		1.80	30.60	− 2.52

marginal cost for producing the thirteenth unit is exactly equal to the marginal revenue that he would receive from the sale of the additional unit. And if he pushes production up to 14 units, his profit will decrease to $1.86, since the *MR* of the 14th unit is less than the *MC*. Should he produce and sell 17 units, he would lose $2.52, because after marginal cost and marginal revenue become equal, marginal cost continues to rise above marginal revenue. The principles involved here operate in any kind of business or industrial establishment.

We can illustrate graphically by means of Figure 27-1 what we have said with regard to cost and revenue relationships. Reference to the figures in the Cost and Revenue Schedule (Table 27-1) will enable the reader to locate points on the cost and revenue curves in Figure 27-1. Notice that the equilibrium output corresponds with the point of intersection between the marginal revenue curve and marginal cost curve at 13 units of output. The difference between average revenue (price) and average cost at this point represents profit per unit. The profit per unit multiplied by the equilibrium output measures total profit.

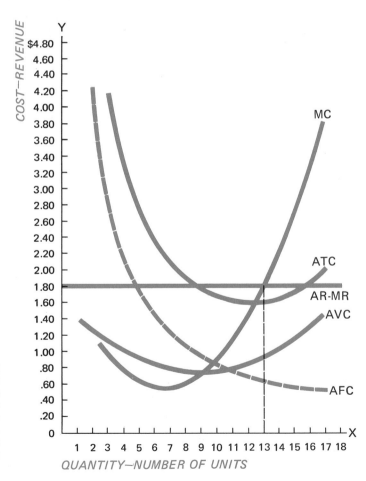

FIGURE 27-1

COST AND REVENUE CURVES

So long as *MR* > *MC*, output will expand until *MR* = *MC*. At that point profit will be maximized (or losses minimized). At the equilibrium output, profit per unit will be equal to the difference between *AR* and *ATC*. Total profit will be equal to the profit per unit multiplied by the equilibrium output.

The point of intersection of *MR* and *MC* is called the equilibrium point because, once the firm reaches that position, there is no incentive to move to any other level of output. If it is not operating at that point, the firm is motivated by the prospect of greater profit to either increase or decrease its output until the equilibrium position is attained. If *MC* is less than *MR*, an expansion of output will increase profit; if *MC* is greater than *MR*, a contraction of output will increase profit. When *MC* equals *MR*, total profit is at a maximum.

Cost and Revenue Relationships: Further Considerations. In addition to average, marginal, and total costs and revenues, other aspects of costs are of concern to management. These matters pertain to fixed and variable costs, which are illustrated in Table 27-2. An understanding of these two aspects of costs enables us to comprehend why average, total, and marginal costs in given situations exhibit the tendencies they do.

TABLE 27-2

COST SCHEDULES FOR A PERIOD OF TIME

(1) Output: No. of Units	(2) Total Fixed Cost (TFC)	(3) Average Fixed Cost (AFC)	(4) Total Variable Cost (TVC)	(5) Average Variable Cost (AVC)	(6) Total Costs (TC)	(7) Average Total Cost (ATC)	(8) Marginal Cost (MC)
1	$8.64	$8.64	$ 1.44	$1.44	$10.08	$10.08	
2	8.64	4.32	2.58	1.29	11.22	5.61	$1.14
3	8.64	2.88	3.48	1.16	12.12	4.04	.90
4	8.64	2.16	4.20	1.05	12.84	3.21	.72
5	8.64	1.73	4.80	.96	13.44	2.69	.60
6	8.64	1.44	5.34	.89	13.98	2.33	.54
7	8.64	1.23	5.88	.84	14.52	2.07	.54
8	8.64	1.08	6.48	.81	15.12	1.89	.60
9	8.64	.96	7.20	.80	15.84	1.76	.72
10	8.64	.86	8.10	.81	16.74	1.67	.90
11	8.64	.79	9.24	.84	17.88	1.63	1.14
12	8.64	.72	10.68	.89	19.32	1.61	1.44
13	8.64	.66	12.48	.96	21.12	1.62	1.80
14	8.64	.62	14.70	1.05	23.34	1.67	2.22
15	8.64	.58	17.40	1.16	26.04	1.74	2.70
16	8.64	.54	20.64	1.29	29.28	1.83	3.24
17	8.64	.51	24.48	1.44	33.12	1.95	3.84

In Table 27-2, total costs (6), average total cost (7), and marginal cost (8) are the same as those in Table 27-1 on page 599. In addition, this table shows fixed and variable costs—totals and averages.

Column 1 shows that 17 units can be produced by the business firm without enlarging its plant. Column 2 shows that the total fixed cost (*TFC*) for the period is $8.64. The average fixed cost (AFC), Column 3, varies inversely and proportionately with the number of units produced. Column 4 shows the total cost of the variable factors used in production (TVC), including materials and labor. The amount of the average variable cost (AVC), Column 5, is found by dividing the total variable cost, Column 4, by the number of units produced, Column 1. The average variable cost per unit decreases until 9 units are produced, and then it begins to rise because of the law of diminishing returns. Contrast this behavior with that of the average fixed cost, which decreases continuously.

The total cost (TC) at any of the possible levels of production is shown in Column 6. The amounts in this column are the sums of the amounts in Columns 2 (TFC) and 4 (TVC). The average total cost, shown in Column 7 (ATC) is calculated by dividing the amount of the total cost, Column 6 (TC), by the number of units at that level. Column 8, marginal cost (MC), shows the amount of extra cost that results from the production of an additional unit. Marginal cost results only from the use of additional units of the variable cost factors because average fixed costs decrease proportionately as the number of units produced increases. Therefore, the amount of marginal cost can be ascertained by subtracting the amount of total variable cost, Column 4 (TVC), from the next higher amount, or by using the figures in Column 6 (TC) in the same way.

The significant relationships between these costs are shown graphically in Figure 27-2. Costs in dollars and cents are measured along the OY axis, and the quantity of output, along the OX axis.

To review, if the price is $1.80 (see page 599) and if fewer than 9 units or more than 15 are produced, the producer will lose money, because it is only when he produces from 9 to 15 units that average revenue (price) is above average total cost. If he produces 9 units, his profit will be $0.36 (total revenue, $16.20, minus total cost, $15.84, equals $0.36). If he produces 10 units, his profit will be $1.26; if 11, $1.92; if 12, $2.28; if 13, $2.28; if 14, $1.86; if 15, $0.96; and if he produces 16 units he will lose $0.48.

Note that, after producing 13 units, marginal cost rises above marginal revenue. Although some profit or net revenue could be realized by producing and selling 15 units, maximum profit cannot be increased by producing more than 13 units, the number for which marginal cost and marginal revenue are exactly equal. If marginal cost and marginal revenue did not coincide exactly for the production and sale of a whole unit, then it would be most profitable to produce that number of units indicated by the point that is nearest the whole number where they are equal.

FIGURE 27-2

COST AND REVENUE CURVES

If profits exist under conditions of pure competition, as shown with the price and marginal revenue curve *AR-MR*, new firms will enter the market, causing a reduction in price to AR_1-MR_1. Under these conditions profit will disappear, as shown by the relationship between AR_1-MR_1 and *ATC* at the point of intersection between MR_1 and *MC*. If losses occur, as they would under conditions of AR_2-MR_2, the firm will drop out of the industry. This will reduce supply and cause a rise in price to AR_1-MR_1. Equilibrium will occur at a price of $1.61.

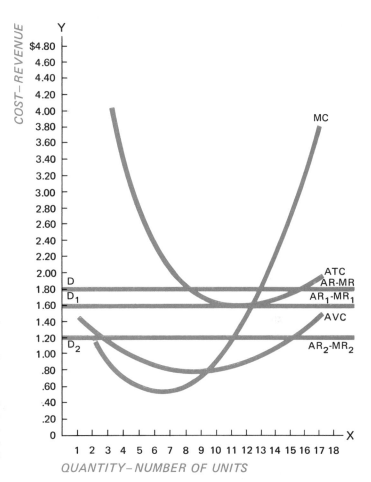

Now suppose that the price, instead of $1.80, is $1.61 as shown in Figure 27-2 above. Note that at this price *ATC*, *MC*, AR_1 and MR_1 are practically equal at the point of intersection of the MR_1 and *MC* curves. What does this signify? It means that the most the producer can hope for is to "break even." By producing 12 units, his average revenue will be just equal to his average cost. If he produces another unit, average total cost and marginal cost will rise above marginal revenue. If he insists on producing more, say 16 units, his average total cost will be $1.83, due to increasing average variable cost. This means that he would lose $3.52. If he stops short of 12 units, say 8, his average total cost will be $1.89, while average revenue will be only $1.61, and his total loss will amount to $2.24.

Again, assume that the price (AR_2, MR_2) is $1.20 as shown in Figure 27-2. How many units will he produce? We can see that regardless of how many he produces, he cannot hope to make a profit because, for any number of units, average total cost is above average revenue. But notice that by producing 11 units he will receive $13.20 revenue. This means that he will recover the amount of total variable cost ($9.24) and reduce the amount of fixed cost to $4.68 ($8.64 — $3.96). He will not produce more than 11 units, however, because beyond that point marginal cost rises above marginal revenue. Therefore, the point at which he can minimize his loss is by producing 11 units, the number that is nearest the intersection of marginal cost and marginal revenue.

In this case it will pay the firm to continue to operate in the short run rather than shut down. By operating, the net loss is only $4.68 compared to what it would be, $8.64 (the amount of the total fixed cost), if the firm were to close down. As mentioned in the previous chapter, it will pay the firm to continue to operate in the short run rather than to shut down so long as it can recover its variable cost. Whether it can do so may be ascertained by comparing the AVC to the AR at the equilibrium level. If the AR is equal to the AVC, it will recover its variable cost. If $AR > AVC$, it will also recover a part of its fixed cost; or, as we stated earlier, it will make a contribution to overhead. How much of a contribution it will make can be observed from the graph. Although the fixed cost is not drawn on the chart, remember that since $ATC = AFC + AVC$, the AFC will be represented by the difference between the ATC and AVC curves at the point of equilibrium.

On the other hand, visualize a situation in which the market price may be only $.60 for the firm in question. Not only would the firm suffer a loss at any level of output, but even at the equilibrium level, or point of minimum loss, the AR would be less than the AVC. In this situation, the firm would not recover its variable cost and would find it less costly to shut down rather than operate in the short run. In such a case AR would be less than AVC at the equilibrium point.

Individual and Market Supply in the Short Run. Of course, there are many variations of cost conditions in different business firms. Faced with the prospect of a given market price, each firm undertakes to produce that quantity of a good which will yield the greatest profit or which will keep losses at a minimum. Within the limits of the capacity of his plant, each entrepreneur will follow this principle in determining his output. The total market supply, then, for the short-run period will be the total production of all the firms in the industry operating at that level which is most advantageous to each one of them.

Short-Run Equilibrium Price

We may conclude, therefore, that competitive *short-run equilibrium price* is that price which results from the interaction of demand and supply over a short period of time. Market supply includes the total of all goods produced by the individual firms in the industry with existing facilities and operating as nearly as possible at the point where marginal cost equals marginal revenue. The part of the supply that is produced at this point constitutes the marginal part of the market supply. For this reason, normal price in the short run is that price that tends to equal the cost of producing the marginal portion of the supply during the period.

What might be called "short-run equilibrium price" is not a stable price, for at the given market prices prevailing during the short-run period, *submarginal producers*—those whose total cost is greater than their revenue—could not break even. These producers would eventually improve their efficiency or disappear. If they disappeared, the supply would decrease, which would cause the price to rise. If they improved their efficiency, the supply would increase, which would cause market price to decline. Moreover, the presence of *supramarginal producers*—those who are making profits—would attract newcomers to the industry, which would result in an increase in the supply of the good and a decrease in the market price.

PRICE AND PROFIT IN THE LONG RUN

Under conditions of pure competition economic profits are residual, dynamic, and ephemeral. Profit is residual insofar as it is revenue that remains after deducting both explicit and implicit costs, including a nominal profit as an imputed cost of the entrepreneur's service. Profits are dynamic insofar as they are constantly changing in amount and among firms. Under purely competitive conditions profits are ephemeral, or temporary, in that, if profits are being made, long-run forces will come into play that tend to reduce or eliminate economic or pure profit. On the other hand, if losses are generally being suffered, market forces tend to bring about adjustments that may cause profits to appear.

Profit Differentiation Among Firms

First of all, it should be remembered that all firms under conditions of pure competition pay an identical price for input factors, and all sell their finished goods, or output, at a uniform market price. It is still possible, however, for profits among firms to differ. One of the main reasons for this difference is that, even though all firms have the same unit cost for inputs, some firms use their inputs more efficiently. In the short run some of them may be using better production techniques, they may be spreading their fixed cost over a larger range of output, and they may be using other measures to lower per unit cost of output. At any given market price, therefore, it is possible to have some firms making a profit, others breaking even, and still others suffering a loss. This is demonstrated in Figure 27-3.

A change in the market price, as it moves up or down, can affect the profit status of each firm. A change in the per unit cost of inputs, likewise, can affect the profit of each firm by altering its average cost curve. In the long run it is assumed that the submarginal firms will reorganize their productive factors in order to make a profit or else will drop out of business. Remember that pure competition assumes that all sellers are informed about markets, prices, and costs. Therefore, if one firm for some reason is able to produce at a lower cost, others will know how it can be done. In the long run adoption of similar production techniques will enable the others to adjust their factors in order to reduce costs.

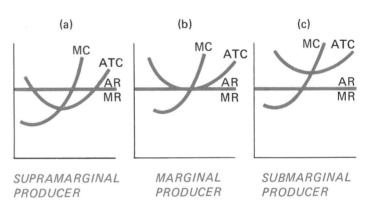

FIGURE 27-3

With any given price there will exist supramarginal firms that will enjoy profit because of their ability to keep cost below price. There also will be marginal firms that are breaking even and submarginal firms that are suffering losses because of their relatively high cost.

(a) *SUPRAMARGINAL PRODUCER*

(b) *MARGINAL PRODUCER*

(c) *SUBMARGINAL PRODUCER*

How Profits Disappear

Under conditions of pure competition, competitive forces tend to eliminate economic profit. This is due to the freedom of firms to enter into and exit from the industry. If a profit is being made by firms in the industry, outsiders can gather information on how to produce and share in the profits being made. Indeed, they have both the incentive and the freedom to do so.

It is true that no individual supplier can influence price under conditions of pure competition; but, if a number of new suppliers enter the market, the addition of their supplies to the total market supply could very well result in a decrease in market price. If profits still remain even at the lower price, firms would continue to enter the industry, continuously lowering prices until a point is reached at which the price will equal the average total cost and profit will be eliminated. On the other hand, if the price were below cost and firms in the industry were suffering losses, firms would drop out of business. In the long run the market supply would be reduced, causing price to rise and losses to disappear in the industry. This whole process can be demonstrated graphically, as in Figure 27-4.

FIGURE 27-4

LONG-RUN EQUILIBRIUM PRICE AND PROFIT

As firms enter an industry in which profits exist, it will cause an increase in supply, as shown in Figure 27-4a. This will cause prices to fall until a no-profit equilibrium position is reached, as shown in Figure 27-4b.

FIGURE 27-4a

INDUSTRY DEMAND AND SUPPLY AND MARKET PRICE

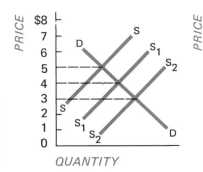

FIGURE 27-4b

INDIVIDUAL FIRM PRICE, COST, AND PROFIT

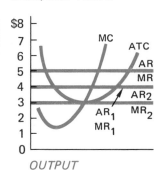

Assume that the intersection of demand (D) and supply (S) in Figure 27-4a establishes a market price of $5 per unit. This then will be the average revenue (AR) for each of the firms in the industry, as shown in Figure 27-4b. Assuming that these cost and revenue relationships are typical for the industry, individual firms will be making profits. These profits, however, will induce new firms to enter the industry. As they enter, total supply on the market will increase, and market price will be lowered to $4, as shown by the intersection of S_1 and D. This in turn will lower the AR and MR curves for each of the firms in the industry, thereby reducing profits. Since profits still exist even at this price, firms will continue to enter the industry, increasing the market supply to S_2 and reducing the price to $3 per unit. At an average revenue and marginal revenue of $3, there will be no economic, or pure, profit for the firms in the industry. At this point there is no further incentive for additional firms to enter the industry. Not only are the firms in equilibrium because they are operating at the point where $MR = MC$, but also equilibrium will exist in the industry because there is no incentive for firms to enter or leave the industry. There is no excess profit to attract new firms. On the other hand, since existing firms will be covering all explicit and imputed costs, including a nominal return to the entrepreneur, they will not necessarily be inclined to withdraw from the industry.

You can visualize what would happen if the initial market price were such that losses existed in the industry. As firms dropped out of the industry, the total supply on the market would decrease, raising the market price and the marginal and average revenue of the individual firms. This process would continue until the price was raised sufficiently to eliminate losses. At that point, no losses or no profit, there would be no further incentive for firms to leave the industry, and equilibrium would again be established.

Before leaving this topic, it should be remembered that we demonstrated the movement from a short-run profit position to a long-run, no-profit equilibrium by adjustments in the market price or average revenue. It is also possible, however, that the long-run profit squeeze may be accelerated by an upward pressure on the cost of inputs. Then the average total cost curve will shift upward. As new firms enter the industry, their combined demand for inputs may very well increase the total demand for raw material, labor, capital, and other inputs. This in turn could raise the market price of inputs and the average total cost curve for individual firms, causing a reduction in profits. Consequently, the competitive forces in the economy work from two angles—the downward pressure of prices and the upward pressure on cost—to eliminate economic profits in the long run.

The Long-Run Cost Curve

Under pure competition, or highly competitive conditions, the consumer obtains a good or service in the long run at a price that equals cost. Another advantage of competition is the fact that price in the long run is equal to *minimum* average cost, that is, the lowest point on the average cost curve. As we mentioned previously, there are various types and kinds of firms under competitive conditions. Although the typical firm may be in equilibrium at a no-profit position, as shown in Figure 27-4, there may be other firms operating at a larger scale that are making a profit with the given market price. Pure competition assumes that all firms are informed about any cost advantages that may arise due to larger scale operations. Consequently, the no-profit firms, observing the larger scale operators making a profit, will be inclined to enlarge their operations in order to enhance their profits. As they move toward the larger scale of operations, of course, the total supply in the market will increase, forcing market price downward. If industry equilibrium comes into existence at the larger scale of operations and the firms reach a no-profit position, competition may very well lead some aggressive innovators to try operating on a still larger scale in the hope of reducing cost in order to make profits.

If the firm is successful and does make profit at the larger scale of operations, existing producers will follow suit and others will enter the industry at this new, larger scale of operations. As they do so, the supply will increase once more, forcing the price down still further. Eventually a point of diminishing returns will be reached on the scale of operations. This will be known as the *optimum scale of operation*. At any larger scale there will be no further cost advantages arising from size. In fact, average total cost may increase due to inefficiencies arising from excessive bigness. By

FIGURE 27-5

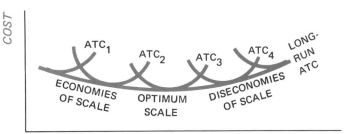

The long-run *ATC* curve will decrease as the scale of operations is
expanded up to a certain level, resulting in economies of scale. Beyond that level long-run *ATC* rises
because of diseconomies of scale.
The optimum scale is found where
the long-run *ATC* is lowest.

joining all the short-run average total cost curves, we can develop a long-run average total cost curve, as shown in Figure 27-5.

At any scale of operations up to the optimum scale, it is said that *economies of scale* exist because long-run *ATC* decreases as the size of the plant increases. Beyond the optimum scale, however, *diseconomies of scale* come into existence, causing the long-run *ATC* to bend upward.

We can demonstrate how price in the long run equates with the lowest point on the average cost curve at the optimum scale of operations. Figure 27-6 contains a series of short-run cost curves. Assume that the industry is in equilibrium and that the typical size firm in the industry is operating at Scale 1 and the price level is AR_1. Firms seeking profits will expand to Scale 2 at which level profits will be made with price AR_1. But as firms expand operations and new firms enter the industry at this more profitable size of operation, the total supply on the market will increase and price will fall to AR_2. At this price or any price below AR_1, firms operating at Scale 1 will suffer losses and must reconstruct or reorganize their plants and equipment in order to operate at the larger scale or go out of business.

When Scale 2 becomes typical for the industry and profits are no longer possible, someone in seeking to reduce cost further may move to Scale 3. At this scale profits will be made providing the market price is AR_1 or AR_2 or at least higher than AR_3. But again the profits will be short-lived. Since all producers are well informed, they will expand to the larger size, Scale 3, in order to take advantage of cost reductions. As they do so, supply increases and price will fall eventually to AR_3. The process may continue; but at Scale 4 costs rise instead of continuing to decrease, due to diminishing returns and the complexities of excessive bigness. The final result is that competitive forces under pure competition will drive the price to a point that is equal to the cost of production at the lowest point of the long-run *ATC* curve at the optimum scale of operation. What buyer or consumer could ask for a better deal than this?

FIGURE 27-6

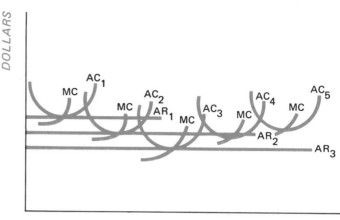

As the scale of operation is enlarged, price will fall. This can result in losses to those continuing to operate at the old, smaller scale of operations. The scale is enlarged, and price continues to fall until the point is reached where price is equal to the lowest point on the optimum scale of output.

THE SOCIAL IMPACT OF PURE COMPETITION

Theoretically there are two virtues of industry-wide and economy-wide pure competition: (1) competition stimulates initiative and productive energy, and (2) competition results in minimum prices to consumers. Under an assumed condition of pure competition throughout the economy, efficiency in all divisions of production would be promoted and only the most efficient entrepreneurial undertaking would survive. The existence of high profits in any field of production would induce most of the producers to increase their outputs and encourage additional entrepreneurs to enter the field, with the result that the supplies of goods or services would increase and prices would decline. The demand for the factors of production would be competitive, which would enable the owners of each of the factors to obtain fair and reasonable prices for what they had to sell. Potential entrepreneurs would be encouraged to discover and to produce new types of goods and services that would be desired by consumers.

As a consequence of economy-wide competition, profits would either disappear or would be reduced to the minimum necessary to induce only the most efficient entrepreneurs to undertake the risks of production. At the same time, the prices of goods and services would be at the lowest possible level consistent with the practice of personal freedom by individuals.

Pure competition would serve the consumer very well. It would result in greater production, the use of more resources and labor, lower prices, and less profits than would exist under noncompetitive conditions. However, competition is not without its disadvantages. It frequently results in an unnecessary duplication of plant and equipment; it often brings forth an endless and sometimes needless variety of models and fashions; and at other times it causes a waste of resources, especially in the extractive industries. Although competition benefits the economy as a whole, it can cause financial hardship for individual producers and displacement of workers as business firms are forced out of business by more efficient producers. It is also possible that in some industries, such as public utilities, many firms, each operating at a small scale, will not be able to provide a good or a service as cheaply as a few firms producing at a much larger scale.

THE CONCEPT OF COMPETITIVE PRICE

The concept of competitive price assumes conditions that are not easily found in the everyday business world. Moreover, it may be argued that, if we assume conditions of pure competition in all areas of production with no change in demand or in the techniques of production, the result would be a static economy.

That conditions of perfect or pure competition seldom, if ever, exist is readily admitted by economists. Nevertheless, the concepts of pure competition and normal competitive price serve as a model for comparing the social consequences of different forms of market structure. The abstract model of pure competition provides essential criteria for any serious analysis of pricing and profits under existing forms of imperfect competition. It is difficult to understand the disadvantages to consumers resulting from monopolistic pricing and restrictive practices unless one understands what the consumer would gain as a result of greater competition. It is difficult to understand the reason for antitrust laws that promote and protect competition until one understands what is being promoted and protected. Therefore, the study of pricing and profits under pure competition, instead of being a useless venture into the realm of mental gymnastics, provides a solid foundation for economic analysis in the world of reality.

SUMMARY

1. There are several types of models of economic competition, ranging from pure competition at one extreme to pure monopoly at the other.

2. Pure competition is an ideal set of market conditions in which there are numerous buyers and sellers of an identical type of product. These buyers and sellers are well informed about market conditions and prices. Although there is free entry into and exit from the market, no individual buyer or seller can influence the market price, which is determined by total supply and total demand.

3. Under conditions of pure competition, each firm will operate at its maximum profit, or equilibrium, position as determined by the intersection of its marginal cost and marginal revenue curves.

4. A firm that is suffering a loss may continue to operate, rather than shut down, in the short run so long as it is recovering its variable cost and making a contribution to overhead.

5. In the long run economic forces will come into play to reduce price and to eliminate economic or pure profit under conditions of pure competition. Consumers eventually will receive the product at a price that is equal to the cost of production.

6. A long-run cost curve can be constructed from a series of short-run cost curves for firms at different scales of operations. Competitive forces arising from economies of scale in the long run will result in a lower price to the consumers.

7. A knowledge of pricing and profits under idealistic conditions of pure competition serves as a basic foundation for analyzing the various forms of imperfect competition that exist in the economy today.

NEW TERMS

Pure competition, *p. 596*
Perfect competition, *p. 596*
Short-run equilibrium price, *p. 604*
Submarginal producers, *p. 605*

Supramarginal producers, *p. 605*
Optimum scale of operation, *p. 608*
Economies of scale, *p. 609*
Diseconomies of scale, *p. 609*

QUESTIONS FOR DISCUSSION AND ANALYSIS

1. What characteristics or conditions must be present for pure competition to exist?

2. Distinguish between perfect competition and pure competition.

3. Explain why the individual seller in pure competition can have no effect on the market price.

4. In terms of marginal revenue and marginal cost, how is the equilibrium level of output for the firm determined?

5. By examining a marginal revenue and marginal cost graph, how can you ascertain the following: (a) whether the firm is making a profit or suffering a loss; (b) if the firm is suffering a loss, whether it should shut down or continue to operate in the short run?

6. The average revenue and the marginal revenue curves are iden-

tical under conditions of pure competition. Why?

7. Explain how profits disappear in the long run under conditions of pure competition.

8. Distinguish between short-run equilibrium price and long-run equilibrium price.

9. Differentiate between a short-run cost curve and the long-run cost curve.

10. What is meant by economies and diseconomies of scale?

11. If a graph shows the average revenue, marginal revenue, average total cost, and average variable cost, can the average fixed cost be determined from such a graph? If so, how? Can the marginal cost be determined from such a graph? If so, how?

SUGGESTED READINGS

The Suggested Readings for this chapter are included in Chapter 26, pages 593-594.

PART EIGHT

Nonprice Competition

28

Monopoly and Monopolistic Competition

PREVIEW At the other end of the competitive scale from pure competition is monopoly, a market condition in which there is only one producer of a good or service. Unlike a firm engaged in pure competition, a monopolist, because he is the sole supplier, can have a considerable degree of influence on price. He can exert this influence by altering his output, which in effect is the total supply for the market. Consequently, instead of accepting the market price as determined by total supply and demand, the monopolist can adjust his output in an effort to seek the most favorable market price. Once a maximum profit position is reached, it can be maintained and continued for an extended period of time, provided the monopolist has the means, economic or otherwise, to prevent competitors from entering the market.

Somewhere between pure competition and monopoly is the market structure of monopolistic competition. In this type of market structure there are a large number of firms, each producing similar but differentiated products. Although the general market price is determined by total supply and demand, each seller has a limited degree of control over the market price of his commodity due primarily to the product differentiation of the good or service he is offering.

As a result of the supplier's ability to influence price in both monopoly and monopolistic competition, it can be expected that price will be somewhat higher under these market structures than under conditions of pure competition.

Under pure competition market price is the price that exists when demand and supply are in equilibrium. In the short-run period, price results from the relationship of demand and supply, the supply being the output of all the plants in the industry operating as nearly as possible at the point where marginal cost equals marginal revenue. In the long-run period, price results from the interaction of demand and supply, the supply being the output of all the plants in the industry after they have achieved optimum capacity and are operating at the level where marginal cost and marginal revenue, and average total cost and average revenue, are equal. In none of these situations can the individual buyer or seller exert any appreciable control over price.

MONOPOLY

At the other end of the competitive scale is *pure monopoly*. This is a market condition in which there is only one producer or seller of a commodity. Furthermore, it assumes that there are no close substitutes for the particular good or service. This latter assumption, of course, makes it difficult for a pure monopoly to exist. It may be, for example, that Ford Motor Company has a monopoly on the production and sale of Ford cars. But so long as car buyers can turn to Plymouths, Chevrolets, Gremlins, and numerous other makes of autos, Ford truly does not have a pure monopoly power.

In many cases a landlord will have a monopoly on the location of a certain rental property. After all, he is the only one who has that particular piece of property to rent. But since there may be several other choices of similar property near that location, it cannot be claimed that he is a monopolist. Like pure competition, pure monopoly is more of an abstraction than a reality. There are very few, if any, markets in which there is a sole supplier; and in most cases there are numerous substitute products available.

The Characteristics of Monopoly

The major characteristic of monopoly is the degree of control over price exercised by the seller. In any market, demand and supply set the market price. In pure competition the individual supplies of many sellers make up the aggregate or market supply. But with a monopoly the individual supply of the monopolist is identical with the market supply. On the other hand, since he is the only supplier, the total demand on the market becomes a demand for his individual product. Therefore, anytime the monopolist increases or decreases his individual supply, it will affect the market price. Instead of having to take the market price as given and adjust his output to the most profitable position, as the case may be under pure competition, the monopolist can adjust his output in order to attain the most favorable market price within limits. The monopolist does not have complete control over the market price, of course, because he cannot force customers to buy at prices they are not willing to pay.

Because of the complexity of our markets today, it is rather difficult to determine who is and who is not a monopolist. A firm may produce a multitude of commodities, many of which are sold in the market in competition with identical or similar products. But among its products there may be one item for which there is no competition. Is this company then a monopolist or not? Furthermore, even a pure monopolist can maintain that he is in competition with other firms, not for the sale of a particular good or service, but for the acquisition of the consumer's dollars. Although there are a number of near monopolies in the American economy today, pure monopoly is nonexistent except for government-regulated public utilities. Industries that have at one time approached monopoly include aluminum, prior to World War II, shoe machinery, nickel, and Pullman railroad cars.

Sources of Monopoly

Monopolies may develop or come into existence from a number of sources. But the essence of obtaining and maintaining a monopoly is the erection of barriers to the entry of other firms into the industry. The stronger such barriers, the easier it is to protect a monopoly position. As we saw in the previous chapter, if a firm is enjoying a profitable operation, the normal reaction under competitive conditions is to induce additional firms into the market, which will result in a profit squeeze. But if a monopoly can effectively block the entry of new firms into the business or industry, it can continue to enjoy its monopoly profits.

Economies of Scale. In some industries it is uneconomical for firms to operate competitively. The "heavy industries," such as steel and heavy machinery, that require the centralized control of vast amounts of capital in order to achieve the economies of large-scale production, tend to be monopolistic. In such industries pure competition is not feasible, for if many firms were to supply the market, none could produce enough to take advantage of the low per unit cost associated with economies of scale. Even though most of the largest industries are not pure monopolies, they tend to have monopolistic characteristics.

Theoretically in an economy that fosters and encourages free enterprise, individuals singly or in combination have a right to engage in any legal undertaking. In practice, however, ability to engage in the production of certain kinds of goods is limited to those who can command great sums of capital. For example, to set up an enterprise capable of realizing the usual economies in the production of steel or automobiles requires an investment of hundreds of millions of dollars. Obviously, therefore, we cannot expect to have a sufficient number of steel companies to provide the same degree of competition that is found in the textile industry. Even if it were possible to have hundreds of large automobile manufacturers, such a situation would be socially wasteful.

Natural Monopolies: Public Utilities. Some industries by their very nature tend to foster monopoly and repel competition. For example, confusion, waste, and inconvenience would result if several gas companies were to compete for the trade of consumers in an urban area.

In addition to waste through duplication of assets, just think of what the condition of our streets would be if three or four gas companies were tearing up streets for the purpose of repairing gas lines. Traffic would be in a constant state of disruption. Visualize the unsightliness of three strings of telephone wires and poles of competing companies traversing the streets and lawns in a new residential subdivision. What about the safety of passengers and pedestrians if buses from four different transit companies were to race each other from corner to corner to pick up passengers?

In such cases, where one or two firms can adequately supply all the service needed for a community, it is desirable to limit the number of firms within a given territory offering these services. Under these circumstances, it becomes imperative for the government to exercise its powers to regulate services and prices. This is done by granting a monopoly, or franchise, to one or a few firms subject to control by a public service commission.

Control of Raw Materials. Another effective barrier to entry is the ownership or control of essential raw materials. Here the right of private property can be exercised to prevent rivals from developing. Although it is difficult to gain complete control of raw materials, and in many cases there may be close substitutes for a particular raw material, this method of blocking competition was effective for years in the production of aluminum. The Aluminum Company of America retained its monopoly position for years through its control of nearly all sources of bauxite, the major ingredient of aluminum production. The International Nickel Company of Canada exercises near monopoly control through its control of nearly 90 percent of the known nickel reserves of the world. In Africa and elsewhere most of the diamond mines are owned by the DeBeers Company of South Africa, and a large portion of the world's molybdenum supplies are controlled by one company.

In a similar fashion ownership of any site or lot of land may give the owner a certain degree of economic advantage over others. Within its area a shop in a choice location in a small town, for example, enjoys an advantage that partakes of the nature of monopoly, although the results that may follow as a consequence are not considered of great social significance.

Patents and Copyrights. The Constitution confers on Congress the power to "promote the progress of science and the useful arts, by securing for limited times to authors and inventors the exclusive right to their respective writings and discoveries."

A patent gives the holder the exclusive right to use, to keep, or to sell an invention for a period of 17 years. The Patent Office was created in 1790 to provide for the registration of patents. At that time it was presumed that the inventor himself would make use of his discovery. In the 19th century, however, the growth of corporate enterprise gradually eclipsed the independent inventor. Most patents today result from well-financed, well-organized, and highly specialized research conducted by numerous skilled and technical workers in elaborate laboratories. Easy access to technological knowledge by the average person is becoming more and more difficult.

The original purpose of patent law was not to give the inventor a permanent monopoly of his invention. This is evident from the fact that patent grants were made for a limited number of years; that the applicant for a patent was required to disclose and specify what he had discovered, in order that the public might have the benefit of the invention after the expiration of the patent term; that a patent could be granted only for processes and devices of a technological nature; and that the invention be "sufficiently useful and important" to justify the grant of a monopoly for a period of years. In spite of these safeguards against an undesirable amount of monopoly arising from the grant of a temporary exclusive right, the control of patents is used as an important source of monopolistic power by some large corporations.

Possible procedures in using patents and the patent laws to stifle competition vary. The granting of patents for useless devices and processes increases the likelihood that inventors of worthwhile innovations will encounter lawsuits for infringement. By making slight changes or improvements in a patented device or process, the owner may file an amendment to his patent and thus prolong its life. Perhaps the most effective method for maintaining control that a patent gives a manufacturer is to scare away new rivals by threats of infringement suits.

Patent control and improvement has played an important role in the development of many of our well-known giant corporations of today, including International Business Machines, National Cash Register, General Electric Company, Radio Corporation of America, AT&T, General Motors, Westinghouse, and many others. At the present time nearly two thirds of all new patents are obtained by corporations. In the past few decades some large companies, such as General Electric and AT&T, have each obtained several hundred patents annually.

Competitive Tactics. A firm may eliminate its rivals or effectively block the entry of new firms into its field through the use of aggressive and sometimes unfair tactics. Past years have seen the use of temporary selling below cost to weed out or bankrupt smaller competitors, the vilification of competitors' products, pirating of administrative personnel, applying undue pressure on suppliers or financial sources, and sometimes outright blackmail. Although many of these tactics have since been declared illegal by antitrust laws, there is still much aggressive competition taking place in our economy that makes it difficult for new firms to enter some industries.

At other times in industries characterized by large-scale operations, the mere fact that some firms are established and have been doing business for years makes it difficult for newcomers to break into the inner circle. Witness the difficulties experienced by the otherwise dynamic Kaiser Corporation regarding its entry after World War II into the auto industry, from which it withdrew in a few short years, and even its entry into the steel industry, in which it finally succeeded.

PURE MONOPOLY PRICE

In our attempt to understand how monopoly price is determined, it is important to keep in mind the definite and clear concept of what is implied by "pure monopoly." The concept of pure monopoly implies a situation where there is a single seller of a good for which there is no available close substitute. Whether the monopolist exercises his power to fix the highest possible price for what he sells depends largely upon whether he is deterred by fear of possible government regulation or potential competition, or by the desire to achieve or to maintain the goodwill of the public which affects the sales of his product.

Pure monopoly occurs under one of two possible conditions: (1) the supply may consist of one unit of a unique good or it may consist of a limited number of *nonreproducible* units of a good for which there is no available close substitute; or (2) the supply may be *reproducible.*

Monopoly Price When the Supply Is Fixed

If the supply of a good is limited to one unit, the highest price possible, of course, is that which the most eager prospective buyer is willing to pay. Examples of this situation are to be found in the auction of a unique object of art, such as an antique, an Oriental rug, or a painting, and in the sale of a rare coin, a stamp, or a superior plot of land. In such a case the article can be sold to the person whose subjective price is highest.

If the seller has a number of units that are nonreproducible, the situation is considerably different. Assume that each prospective buyer would buy only one unit of the good. Since it is likely that the subjective prices of the prospective buyers are not identical, the seller may offer one unit for sale at a time at the highest price he can obtain, which will be the price that the most eager buyer is willing to pay. Except in some auction sales, examples of such a selling procedure are seldom found. There are cases, however, in which sellers possessing monopolistic powers use their opportunities to exact as high an average price as possible by "feeding" the supply to the market gradually or by making their goods available to different buyers at different prices. A modification of these methods is followed in the marketing of diamonds.

Monopoly Price When the Supply Is Reproducible

The supply of most goods is reproducible. Within limits a monopolist can produce and maintain the supply at whatever level he chooses. Under such a condition the price will be uniform for all buyers and can be established by the seller at that point which will yield him the greatest total profit. Where this point will be located depends upon the nature of the demand for the monopolist's product and his costs of production.

The Monopolist's Demand Curve. Under pure competition, demand for the output of a single firm can be represented by a straight horizontal line. The individual producer is unable to influence the market price either by increasing or decreasing his supply. He is able to sell any quantity that he may offer at the current market price. The situation of the monopolist, however, is different. He is the only supplier of the good, and the demand curve for his product slopes downward to the right *because it is the market demand curve of all buyers.* The less essential the product, the more elastic is the demand. The more essential it is, the less elastic is the demand. Hence, the first question to be considered by the monopolist is, "How many units of my good can I expect to sell at various prices?" The answer will enable him to determine the number of units he wishes to produce.[1]

The monopolist's position is reflected in Figure 28-1. Since there is only one producer, the demand curve for the product of the individual firm is also the demand curve for the entire industry. *D* is the demand curve. The demand curve is also the average revenue curve for the firm.

In Figure 28-1 the total revenue at 1,100 units is $8,800, at 1,000 units it is $10,000, while at 900 units it is $10,800. Thus, the monopolist can obtain a higher price and a larger revenue by limiting the supply. If he increased his sales from 1,000 to 1,100, his total revenue would decrease. Of course, if the demand were elastic, it would be more profitable for him to increase the supply.

The Monopolist's Cost Curves. As in the case of most other producers, the monopolist's cost per unit usually decreases for a while as the number of units produced increases. If he pushes production to the point where marginal cost increases, however, before long the average total cost will also

---

[1] The student may find it helpful to review the discussion of elasticity of demand in Chapter 25.

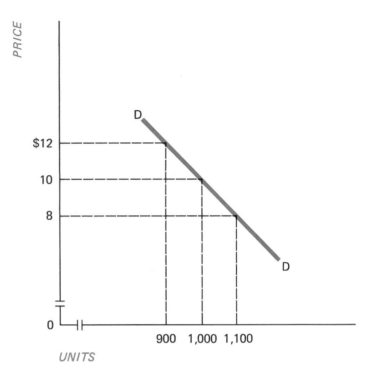

increase. The increase in the average total cost per unit does not manifest
itself until after an increase in marginal cost has taken place because the
increase is due to an increase in variable costs. The increase in variable
costs must become great enough to offset the decrease in average fixed costs
before there will be a rise in average total cost. How long the monopolist
will continue to increase production after marginal cost begins to rise will
depend upon the number of units that can be produced before the production
of the next unit will result in a marginal cost greater than the corresponding
marginal revenue.

Relations Between the Monopolist's Cost and Revenue Curves. Let us
assume that the monopolist's cost and revenue situation is as shown in
Table 28-1.

Inspection of this table reveals that the level of production at which profit
is maximized is reached when 8 units are produced. Since marginal cost
and marginal revenue become the same for 9 units, the same amount of
profit, $24.48, will be realized if 9 units are produced. But if more than
9 units are produced, profit will decrease because marginal cost rises and
continues to rise above marginal revenue. If 12 units are produced, there
will be a loss of $2.64.

TABLE 28-1

COSTS AND
REVENUES
FOR A
MONOPOLY

(1) Units of Output	(2) Average Total Cost	(3) Total Cost	(4) Marginal Cost	(5) Average Revenue	(6) Total Revenue	(7) Marginal Revenue	(8) Net Revenue or Loss
1	$20.00	$ 20.00		$16.48	$ 16.48		− $ 3.52
			$14.72			$15.00	
2	17.36	34.72		15.74	31.48		− 3.24
			10.40			13.52	
3	15.04	45.12		15.00	45.00		− 0.12
			7.04			12.04	
4	13.04	52.16		14.26	57.04		4.88
			4.64			10.56	
5	11.36	56.80		13.52	67.60		10.80
			3.20			9.08	
6	10.00	60.00		12.78	76.68		16.68
			2.72			7.60	
7	8.96	62.72		12.04	84.28		21.56
			3.20			6.12	
8	8.24	65.92		11.30	90.40		24.48
			4.64			4.64	
9	7.84	70.56		10.56	95.04		24.48
			7.04			3.16	
10	7.76	77.60		9.82	98.20		20.60
			10.40			1.68	
11	8.00	88.00		9.08	99.88		11.88
			14.72			0.20	
12	8.56	102.72		8.34	100.08		− 2.64

Since average total cost is less at 10 units than at 9 units, and since at 10 units average revenue is still greater than average total cost, it might appear at first glance that it would be profitable to produce the larger number. This conclusion, however, is not justified because, after 9 units have been produced, the cost of producing another unit would be greater than the amount of revenue received from the sale of the additional unit (marginal cost, $7.04; marginal revenue, $3.16). Thus, it is the relationship between marginal cost and marginal revenue that is significant in determining the point at which the producer limits his supply.

The relationships of the cost and revenue curves may be plotted as shown in Figure 28-2.

In Figure 28-2, *AR*, average revenue, is the monopolist's demand curve. This curve sloping downward to the right indicates that, as the selling price decreases, a larger number of units will be bought. *MR*, the marginal revenue curve, suggests that as the number of units sold increases, the amount of marginal revenue per unit decreases.

Because the monopolist is faced with a negatively sloped *AR* curve (demand), his marginal revenue will be less than the *AR* curve, and the *MR* curve will decline at a faster rate. Remember that in pure competition, where the seller has a horizontal or constant *AR* curve, every time an additional unit is sold at the market price, let us say $5, that amount is added to the total revenue. Consequently, the *AR* and the *MR* curves are equal. The monopolist, however, faces a situation where in order to sell a larger quantity price must be lowered. He may, for example, be able to sell 1 unit at $10 or 2 units at $9. Keep in mind that it is not a situation where he can sell 1 unit at $10 and 2 more at $9, because one of the two buyers who

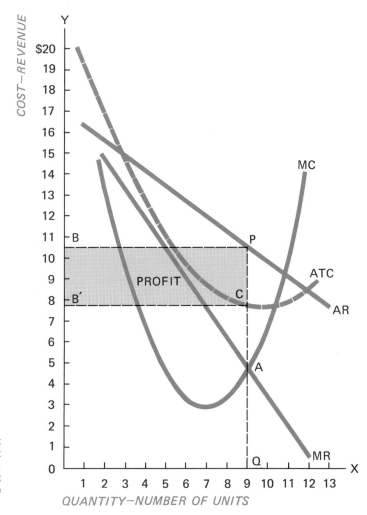

FIGURE 28-2

**COST AND REVENUE CURVES
FOR A MONOPOLY**

A monopoly will maximize its profit
at the point where *MR* = *MC*. At
that point, unlike pure competition,
the *AR* will be above the *MR*. Profit
per unit will be represented by the
difference between *AR* and *ATC*.

would pay $9 is the same one who is willing to pay $10. The monopolist's
choice then is to sell 1 unit only at $10 or both of them at $9 each. If he
chooses to do the latter, his *AR* will be $9 but his *MR* will be $8. This is
so because his total revenue from the sale of 1 unit would be $10, but the
total revenue from the sale of 2 units is $18, an increase of $8. If, instead
of selling 2 units at $9 each, he were to sell 3 units at $8, his *AR* would
fall to $8 and his *MR* would drop to $6. This can be seen from Table 28-2.

In short, *AR* of the monopolist will decline because he receives a lower
price on the additional goods that are sold. The *MR* will decline at a faster

TABLE 28-2

MARGINAL
REVENUE—
COMPETITION
VS. MONOPOLY

	Pure Competition				Monopoly		
Quantity Sold	Price	Total Revenue	Marginal Revenue	Quantity Sold	Price	Total Revenue	Revenue Marginal
1	$5	$ 5	—	1	$10	$10	—
2	5	10	$5	2	9	18	$8
3	5	15	5	3	8	24	6
4	5	20	5	4	7	28	4

rate than the AR because in selling a larger number of units the monopolist takes a lower price also on the units than he could have sold at a higher price had he selected to sell fewer units. Thus, if he decides to sell 2 units at $9 rather than 1 unit at $10, his total revenue will increase by $9 from the sale of the second unit, as such, minus the $1 less he takes on the sale of the original unit he could have sold for $10 had he sold it alone. Likewise, if he decides to sell 3 units at $8 instead of 2 units at $9, his total revenue will increase by $8 from the sale of the third unit, as such, minus $1 less on each of the 2 previous units he could have sold for $9 if he had sold only 2 units.

ATC, the average total cost curve, shows the behavior of average total cost as an increased number of units is produced. MC, the marginal cost curve, indicates the decreasing or increasing amount of cost that is incurred as additional units are produced by the monopolist. The shapes of these curves are the same as those of a competitive firm and are traceable to the law of diminishing returns.

Under the conditions represented in Figure 28-2, at a production level of 9 units marginal cost and marginal revenue are exactly equal. Beyond point (A) it would become less profitable to produce an additional unit. Beyond that point the marginal revenues of additional units would be less than the marginal costs. Demand being what it is, the price at which 9 units would sell is $10.56. This is shown by the lines PB and PQ, which indicate price and quantity, respectively. The total revenue from the sale of 9 units, then, would be 9 times $10.56, or $95.04. In the figure the total receipts from the sale of 9 units is represented geometrically by the area $OQPB$.

The cost of producing 9 units is 9 times the average total cost of $7.84, or $70.56. The total cost is represented by the area $OQCB'$, which is less than the area $OQPB$ by the size of the area embraced within $BPCB'$; this area represents the net profit of $24.48 ($95.04 − $70.56). (This area is greater than that of any other rectangle that has the distance from ATC to AR for a chosen number of units as its height and the length equal to the number of units as shown along the OX axis.)

It is not difficult to visualize what would happen if additional firms were to enter this industry. The increase in supply and decrease in market price that would result would soon eliminate profits. But if the monopolist can effectively block entry of new firms, he can maintain his price and profits. Consequently, it is often said that monopoly results in a higher price, the use of fewer resources, and greater profit than would be the case under pure competition.

Restraints on Monopoly Price

People often assume, however, that monopoly implies an exorbitant price. There may be some justification for the belief that goods produced by a firm which is a monopoly, or virtually so, will be sold at a price that will exploit the public. It would be a mistake, however, to think that monopoly always means an exorbitant price. In the first place, the monopolist cannot charge more for his product than the consumers are willing to pay. Referring to Figure 28-1 on page 622, it can be seen that the monopolist cannot sell all he desires at a given price. He can, for example, sell 1,000 units at $10 per unit, but notice that he cannot sell 1,100 or 1,200 units at that price. Consumers just will not buy that many. Furthermore, he cannot raise his price to $12 and still hope to sell as many units as he did at $10. Just because a firm has a monopoly, it cannot arbitrarily set a price and sell all it wants to sell at that price. It is true that it can alter its supply in order to attain the best possible price for itself. But it still must price within the limits of consumer demand. It may very well be, however, that the price which is most profitable to the monopolist, and within the reach of a limited number of consumers, would deprive a large number of consumers from enjoying the product.

There are several major economic considerations which may deter the monopolist from selling his goods at the highest possible price. These include the following:

Lack of Knowledge. Even if no other factors were involved, it is usually impossible for a monopolist to ascertain his probable demand and cost at different levels of production. This might prevent him from fixing his production schedule at exactly the point that would prove most profitable to him. Although he may be able to say with assurance that up to a certain point the demand for his good is inelastic, he cannot safely take it for granted that this would be true beyond the present price.

Desire to Discourage Competition. In many cases the fear of arousing competition serves as a deterrent to the usual inclination of the monopolist to adjust the supply of his product to the most profitable level, even if he knows what that level is. Although his exact profit may remain a secret, if the business is making high profits, others who may be interested in exploring the possibilities of setting up a competing business will suspect his secret. Therefore, the producer who enjoys a virtual monopoly may be content with a reasonable profit, rather than encourage the rise of competitors who would compel him to lower his price and to reduce his profit.

Of course, not all monopolists are restrained by the existence of potential competition. For example, the owner of a single hotel in a newly developed tourists' center may "cash in" on his opportunity and charge all he can; or the producer of a patented device may sell his product at the highest price possible. In such cases, however, it may be only a matter of time until competitors will arise and force a decrease in price. When the producer enjoys a natural monopoly or when he has control of great financial resources, the fear of competition may not be an important factor in the determination of monopoly price.

Customer Relations. Although we assume for the sake of marginal analysis that the firm will seek to maximize profit, this is not always the case in actual practice. Frequently firms, even monopolists, will be satisfied with a reasonable profit. Frequently a firm will take into consideration the goodwill of its customers and not try to antagonize them with exceptionally high or exorbitant prices. After all, the monopolist must depend on these customers for many years for his revenue. Squeezing out the maximum profit with the highest price in the short run may cause a loss of customers through public resentment and result in less than maximum profits in the long run. Again, a case in point is the auto industry, which in the immediate post-World War II years could have extracted much higher prices than it did under conditions of strong demand and limited supply. Some utility companies at times charge less than they are authorized for the sake of good customer relations.

Fear of Government Regulation. The price of a commodity that is widely used and popularly regarded as a necessity may become a matter of concern to the public. Therefore, the monopolist who attempts to control or limit production of such a commodity in order to yield the largest possible profit runs the risk of government intervention. Traditionally in the United States, government has been loath to compel producers to reduce profits. But when consumers become convinced that they are being charged an unreasonably high price for a commodity that is used by a large number of the people, political pressure may result in the enactment of antimonopoly laws or the setting up of a government-owned enterprise to compete with the monopolist.

Although not a monopolist, General Motors is in a precarious position because of its high profits. It was the first billion-dollar-annual-profit (before taxes, of course) manufacturing corporation in the United States, having reached the level in 1955 and having exceeded the two-billion-dollar mark in recent years. As a result of its high profits, the curiosity of the government antitrust division has been aroused at times as to why it makes such large profits. At the present time, if GM reduces the price of its cars substantially in order to lower profit, it will certainly increase its share of the automobile market at a time when the antitrust division is asking questions as to why GM controls such a large share of the market. Some of the less profitable producers in the auto industry, such as American Motors or Chrysler, might seek a government investigation on charges that GM is endeavoring to gain a larger share of the market by granting generous wage increases and fringe benefits to its union workers, which could not be duplicated by the smaller producers without running into financial difficulty. In the past few years the drug industry has been subject to damaging criticism for its limited output, high prices, and large profits.

MONOPOLISTIC COMPETITION

Between pure competition and pure monopoly is a wide range of market conditions, which include oligopoly and monopolistic competition. A market situation may border on pure competition at one extreme or monopoly at the other, or it may be somewhere in between. Oligopoly, which will be discussed in detail in the next chapter, is a market condition with relatively few firms. *Monopolistic competition* is a market condition in which there is a relatively large number of firms supplying a similar but differentiated product, with each firm having a limited degree of control over price. Regarding monopolistic competition, some idea of what is implied can be gathered from the very name itself. It implies a blending of both monopoly and competitive characteristics. Monopoly indicates some degree of control over market supply or price. On the other hand, competition of a purely competitive nature indicates that no individual supplier can influence price. Putting the two together indicates that there is some degree of control over price, but that it is limited.

The major characteristic of monopolistic competition is product differentiation. It is this product differentiation that permits the limited degree of control over price. The major difference between oligopoly and monopolistic competition is in the number of sellers. In oligopoly there must be few enough sellers that the actions of one on price and/or output noticeably affect the others. In monopolistic competition there must be a sufficiently large number of sellers that the actions of any one have no perceptible effect on the others. Some idea of the nature of monopolistic competition and its distinction with other forms of competition is apparent from the case of coffee. Assume that there were a large number of firms selling coffee of an identical quality, no brand names, no advertising claims, and all packaged in the same type of container. Assume further that a price of 95 cents per pound was established by the aggregate supply and demand on the market. Under such conditions of pure competition no seller could get more than the market price for his coffee. Why would a buyer purchase any one seller's coffee at a higher price when he could obtain identical coffee for 95 cents from several other sellers? On the other hand, if there were only one seller, he could change the market price by limiting or expanding his supply on the market.

Differentiated Products

More realistically, we have a relatively large number of coffee producers supplying a similar but differentiated product. It is different because some coffee is "good to the last drop," another is "mountain-grown," another is "decaffeinated," and one is "freeze-dried." There are many different blends with numerous tastes and packaged in a variety of containers. Although they may all be selling for about the same bulk line price as determined in the market by the aggregate demand and supply for coffee in general, it is the product differentiation, whether real or psychological, that permits an individual firm to have some degree of control over the price at which it will sell. On the other hand, it is the similarity among the coffees that limits this degree of control.

Consumers buy a particular brand of coffee because they like the taste, admire the package, or are swayed by an advertising jingle on TV. Consequently, if the maker of a particular brand, let us say Old Judge Coffee, decided to raise his price a little above the market level, he would not lose all his customers, as would be the case under pure competition. We can assume that most of the Old Judge buyers would be willing to pay a few cents, 3, 5, or perhaps 10, more than the general market price because of the difference in Old Judge. But the seller cannot raise his price too much above the market price. When the price differential becomes too great, buyers may still feel that Old Judge is different, but not that different! When the price reaches a certain level, they will shift to other brands of coffee.

On the other hand, if Old Judge were to lower its price by a few cents from the average market price of 95 cents, it would probably gain very few customers via the substitution effect. Housewives buy certain brands because they feel there is something different about them. If their feeling is strong, they are not going to leave their particular brand favorite and shift to Old Judge for the sake of a few cents. But if Old Judge reduces its price substantially, many of the housewives may feel that the quality difference is not great enough to deter them from making a switch to the lower-priced Old Judge coffee. In such a case, a point may be reached at a lower price where the sales of Old Judge coffee would increase substantially, provided other coffee producers did not react by lowering their prices. Nevertheless, product differentiation gives the individual supplier a certain price range within which he may raise or lower his prices without substantially affecting his sales or those of his competitors. This is the monopolistic aspect of monopolistic competition. But if Old Judge raises its price too high compared to other brands, it will lose customers; and if it lowers its price sufficiently, it can draw customers away from other brands. This is the competitive aspect of monopolistic competition.

As a result, we will usually find products at a variety of prices within a general market price range in monopolistic competition. With a large number of sellers, there is less concern about competitors' reaction to a firm's reduction in price. But instead of strong price competition, the firms may stress product differentiation, use heavy advertising, and emphasize packaging to sell customers. With a large number of firms in the market, however, there is less likelihood of firms engaging in collusive practices to fix price or to limit output.

Monopolistic competition is prevalent in the retail industry. First of all, the numerous outlets in each large city are differentiated as to location, sales personnel, store layout, service, and other aspects of retail selling. Secondly, they handle numerous commodities that are produced under monopolistically competitive conditions. In addition to grocery stores and department stores in large metropolitan areas, gasoline service stations, dry cleaners, and barber shops tend to approach conditions of monopolistic competition. The manufacture of costume jewelry, metal house furniture, and toys, plus the production of toothpaste and beer, generally fall within this category.

Short-Run Price and Profit

The demand curve faced by the monopolistic competitor is not a horizontal, perfectly elastic demand curve characteristic of pure competition. Nor is the firm's demand curve identical with the market demand as is the case of monopoly. Even though there are a large number of firms, remember there may not be so many as there are in pure competition, and their products are differentiated. Consequently, the firm will be able to sell more or less by lowering or raising its price. But since this degree of control is limited by the fact that the firm's supply is a small portion of the total supply on the market, that it has many competitors, and that its product is still similar though differentiated, its demand or average revenue curve will slope downward to the right. Furthermore, it will tend to be more elastic than the demand curve for the total industry. Of course, the closer monopolistic competition approaches pure competition, the closer to horizontal will be the demand or average revenue curve of the individual firm. The more market conditions move in the direction toward oligopoly or monopoly, the less elastic the individual firm's demand curve will be and the closer it will approach the industry demand curve.

Again, keep in mind that when the demand, or average revenue, curve slopes downward to the right, the marginal revenue curve will move in the same direction but at a steeper slope. Typical short-run cost and revenue curves for a firm engaged in monopolistic competition are shown in Figure 28-3. Figure 28-3a depicts the general range of prices established in the industry around the intersection of total supply and demand. Figure 28-3b shows a monopolistic competitor making a profit. Note that his price, although slightly higher than the average price established by supply and demand in the market, is still within the general price range at which most producers will sell their products. Figure 28-3b shows that with this price and the accompanying cost the firm will produce 30,000 units and enjoy profits as shown in the rectangle.

Long-Run Equilibrium

If short-run profits are generally available in the industry, however, they will be an invitation for new firms to enter. As these new firms enter the market with their similar but differentiated products, the total supply on the market will increase. This, in turn, will decrease the market price and lower the average revenue of each firm in the industry. So long as there are no severe restrictions to entry, the process will continue until supply and price are such that profits for the average firm will be eliminated, as shown in Figure 28-3c. Notice that at the point of equilibrium, 28,000 units of output, the firm will be making no economic or pure profit in the long run. Furthermore, its total sales will have dropped somewhat as a result of competition in spite of the total increase of sales in the market. Thus, in the long run under conditions of monopolistic competition consumers will receive a differentiated product at a price that is equal to the average total cost of production for the firm. Of course, if firms in the industry had been suffering losses in the short run, the opposite reaction on price would have occurred. As firms dropped out of business, the total supply on the market would have decreased, forcing market price upward. Average revenues for

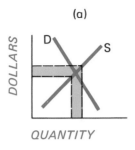

(a)

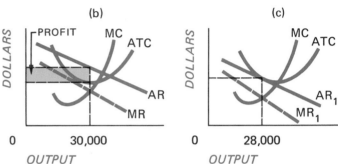

FIGURE 28-3

Figure 28-3a shows how demand and supply establish a general price area under conditions of monopolistic competition. Figure 28-3b shows a firm in monopolistic competition making a profit. Figure 28-3c indicates a no profit equilibrium position.

the firms in the industry would have risen until losses were eliminated and equilibrium was established at a no-profit, no-loss position in the long run.

Notice, however, that even though the consumer receives the product at a price that equals the cost of production in the long run, this price is not as low as it would be under conditions of pure competition. Because of the slope of the average revenue curve, it cannot become tangential to the average total cost curve at the lowest point on the *ATC* curve as does the horizontal average revenue curve characteristic of pure competition. Hence, the equilibrium price under monopolistic competition must be higher than the price under pure competition, assuming identical costs.

Pure Competition vs. Monopolistic Pricing

The weight of economic evidence indicates that a high degree of competition is beneficial for the consumer. As stated before, there is a tendency toward lower prices, the use of more resources, and less economic profits in the long run under competitive conditions. To the extent that competition exists in an industry, the amount of profit for each firm tends to decline to the point where average revenue is equal to average total cost. This means that the consumer will be able to purchase the good at a price equal to the lowest possible average total cost of production for a given scale of operation. Since the demand (the *AR* curve) for the output of a single firm under imperfect competition slopes downward to the right, the marginal revenue curve slopes downward also, but *below* the average revenue curve. There-fore, the two cost curves and the two revenue curves cannot coincide at the point where the average revenue and the average total cost curves coincide, as is the case under pure competition.

In most cases of monopolistic competition there is a tendency, in the long run, for monopoly profits to decline and for cost-revenue relationships to become adjusted as shown in Figure 28-4. But even at the point of no economic profit, where average revenue equals average total cost, the price cannot correspond to the lowest point on the *ATC* curve. As a result of the less than perfectly elastic demand, or the downward sloping nature of the *AR* curve, the long-run equilibrium price will be higher under any form of imperfect competition than it will be under pure competition for identical cost conditions.

In Figure 28-4, *ATC* and *AR* coincide at *P*, and *MC* and *MR* intersect at *P'*. Thus, *OA* units would be produced, price being at *S*. If either fewer or more units were produced, a loss would result because, for any other quantity, average revenue is less than average total cost—*AR* lies below *ATC*.

Since there is a tendency for production to be adjusted to the point where marginal revenue and marginal cost are equal, the result of monopolistic competition in the long run might appear to be the same as that of pure competition. Such a conclusion, however, would be erroneous because, under monopolistic competition, the point of equality of marginal revenue and marginal cost does not coincide with that for average revenue and average total cost.

In Figure 28-4, *DD'* represents the straight-line curves for marginal revenue *MR'* and average revenue *AR'*, which coincide under pure competi-tion (the demand to the individual seller being perfectly elastic). The point where marginal cost and marginal revenue are equal (point *Q*) is also the point at which average total cost and average revenue are equal. Thus, under a condition of pure competition the price would be at *D*, and *OB* units would be produced. Consequently, under pure competition (assuming that pure competition is feasible and possible), the price is lower and the supply greater than under monopolistic competition.

This assumes, however, that the scale of operation for the small firm in pure competition is the same as that for a larger firm in some form of imperfect competition, such as monopolistic competition, oligopoly, or monopoly. Although the scale of operation of firms in monopolistic competi-tion may be similar to those in pure competition and therefore their cost curves nearly identical, oligopolies and monopolies generally operate at much larger scales of operation. With the resulting lower average total cost curve of the oligopoly or monopoly, it is possible to have an equilibrium

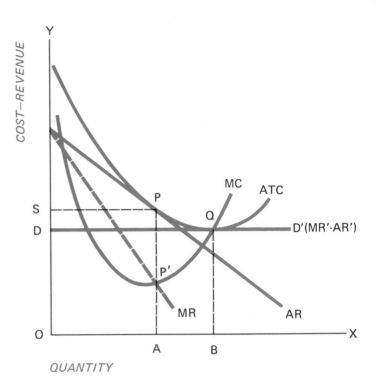

FIGURE 28-4

POSSIBLE LONG-RUN MONOPOLISTIC PRICE

Assuming identical cost curves, a firm operating at a no profit equilibrium position under conditions of pure competition will have a lower price, will supply more goods, and will use more resources than will a similar firm operating under monopolistic conditions. Here we show a price, *D*, and an amount supplied, *OB*, for the firm in pure competition, versus a higher price, *S*, and a smaller amount supplied, *OA*, for the monopolistic firm.

price lower than that possible under purely competitive conditions. Nevertheless, the monopolist's or the oligopolist's price is not equal to the lowest point on his average total cost curve. This can be seen in Figure 28-5.

FIGURE 28-5

In all likelihood a monopoly or oligopoly will not have an identical cost curve with that of a firm in pure competition. A monopolist or oligopolist will generally operate on a larger scale with a lower average total cost curve. Consequently, a monopolist or oligopolist, even though not pricing at the lowest point on his *ATC* curve, operating at a no profit position, can have a lower price than the firm in pure competition, which has a higher *ATC* curve.

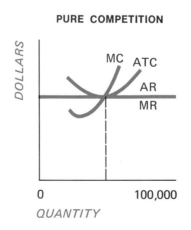

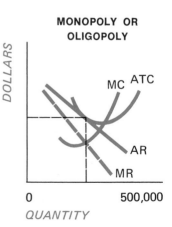

1. Pure monopoly is a market condition in which there is one seller. The fact that he is the only producer and the fact that there are no close substitutes for the product give the monopolist the ability to set the price by altering his total supply.

2. Monopolies may arise from a number of possible sources, such as economies of scale, the nature of the industry, control of raw materials, the granting of patents or copyrights, or because of the use of various types of competitive tactics.

3. A monopolist's ability to retain monopoly profits depends in large part on existing barriers to the entry of new firms into the industry. But monopolists do not always charge the maximum possible price because they may not know their true cost and revenue, they may desire to discourage competition, they may desire to promote better customer relations, or they may fear government regulation.

4. Monopolistic competition is a market condition in which a large number of firms each produces a similar, but differentiated, product. Product differentiation tends to give each firm a limited degree of control over the price of its product.

5. Just as with pure competition and monopoly, the firm in monopolistic competition will maximize its profits, or minimize its losses, at the point where marginal cost equals marginal revenue. Pricing under monopolistic competition, however, is likely to be higher than it would be under conditions of pure competition.

NEW TERMS

Pure monopoly, *p. 616*
Natural monopoly, *p. 617*
Patents, *p. 618*
Copyrights, *p. 618*

Nonreproducible goods, *p. 620*
Reproducible goods, *p. 628*
Monopolistic competition, *p. 628*
Differentiated products, *p. 629*

QUESTIONS FOR DISCUSSION AND ANALYSIS

1. Explain how a monopoly can exercise control over price. Is this control absolute? Explain why or why not.

2. What are some of the sources of monopoly?

3. What is the economic justification for granting a monopoly franchise to a public utility?

4. What is the relationship between the average revenue curve for a monopolist and the demand for the product of his industry?

5. Why do the average revenue curve and the marginal revenue curve of a monopolist diverge, whereas these curves are identical for a firm in pure competition?

6. Will a monopolist always endeavor to maximize profits? Why or why not?

7. Should unused patents be declared public property after a certain period of time and be made available to the general public? Why or why not?

8. Explain how product differentiation gives a firm engaged in monopolistic competition a certain degree of control over price.

9. Why will long-run equilibrium price be higher under monopolistic competition than it will under conditions of pure competition?

10. Is it possible for a monopoly or an oligopoly to make a profit and still have a lower price than a firm engaged in pure competition, which is selling its product at a price that is equal to its cost of production? Explain.

11. Would there tend to be more advertising in market conditions of pure competition than in monopolistic competition? Explain.

SUGGESTED READINGS

Adams, Walter. *The Structure of American Industry*. New York: The Macmillan Company, 1971.

Bain, Joe S. *Industrial Organization*. New York: John Wiley & Sons, Inc., 1968.

Clower, Robert W., and John F. Due. *Microeconomics*. Homewood, Ill.: Richard D. Irwin, Inc., 1972.

Kogiku, K. C. *Microeconomic Models*. New York: Harper & Row, Publishers, 1971.

Shows, E. Warren, and Robert H. Burton. *Microeconomics*. Lexington, Mass.: D. C. Heath & Company, 1972.

29

Oligopoly: Competition Among the Few

PREVIEW Oligopoly is a market condition in which relatively few firms produce identical or similar products. The firms are few enough that each, by altering its output, can have a substantial degree of control over the general market price established by total supply and demand. Any firm, however, that alters its output or reduces its price must consider the reaction, or retaliation, of its competitors. This is especially true when a competitor may have a lower cost structure and is able to undersell a firm that initiates a price cut. Although prices will vary somewhat around the general market price when product differentiation occurs, oligopoly is frequently characterized by a high degree of nonprice competition— product differentiation, advertising, packaging, and so on— as opposed to aggressive price competition.

Although there is little, if any, pure competition or pure monopoly in the American economy, it is replete with oligopoly and monopolistic competition. Under these forms of competition prices are usually higher and profits greater than they would be under conditions of pure competition.

The forms of competition found in the American economy are many and varied. In addition to pure competition there are several types of imperfect competition. Two of them, pure monopoly and monopolistic competition, were analyzed in the preceding chapter. Another market condition is that of *duopoly*, in which two firms supply the total product of a particular market. But probably the most intriguing of all market conditions from the point of view of economic analysis is that of oligopoly.

OLIGOPOLY

Oligopoly is a market condition in which relatively few firms produce identical or similar products. It might involve two or three firms or a dozen or more, depending on the nature of the industry. To be oligopolistic, however, there must be few enough firms that actions of any one on matters of price and output will have a noticeable effect on the others. The basic characteristics of oligopoly are (1) the ability of individual firms to influence price and (2) interdependence among firms in setting their pricing policies. If only three firms supply a particular good, any one of them could influence the market price by altering the amount it offers for sale. An increase in supply by any one firm would increase total supply and tend to depress the market price. If one firm cut its price, it would gain a larger share of the market at the expense of the other two firms. But the other firms might react by lowering their prices also. This retaliation would again affect all firms' market shares—and might wipe out the initial gain of the price-cutting firm. Whether or not the firms would gain from such price competition would depend on the elasticity of demand for the product.

An oligopolist may be reluctant to engage in price competition because of the possible reaction of his competitors. Consequently, many forms of nonprice competition, of which product differentiation is very prevalent, are found among oligopolists. Oligopolistic conditions sometimes lead to collusive practices, such as price leadership, pooling, and other techniques designed to fix prices or limit quantity.

In addition to the aluminum, steel, and copper industries, oligopolies exist today in the manufacture of automobiles, farm equipment, chemicals, tires, oil, cigarettes, electric motors, tin cans, and tractors, among others. A number of oligopolies also exist in nonmanufacturing industries. In some cases we have oligopoly with a standardized, or homogeneous, product, such as steel and chemicals. In other cases we have oligopoly with a differentiated product, such as the automobile and cigarette industries.

Price Determination

Pricing under oligopoly is more difficult than it is under other market conditions. The firm may be faced with a determinate or indeterminate price situation; that is, it may or may not be able to determine what amount can be sold at various prices. What will happen to sales when an oligopolist changes price will depend in large part on the reaction of competitors. In fact, an oligopoly is often described as a market situation in which the number of sellers is so few that each must take into consideration the reaction of its rivals. This, of course, is a different situation from that of monopolistic competition, where the number of competitors is so large that an individual seller can ignore the reactions of its competitors. Fear of retaliation by competing firms, as we shall see, can be a strong force limiting price competition under oligopolistic conditions.

Three reactions by rivals are possible when an oligopolist changes supply and/or price. First, competitors may choose to ignore the price change. In this event the demand and average revenue curve for the individual firm will be known with a reasonable degree of accuracy and may appear as D shown

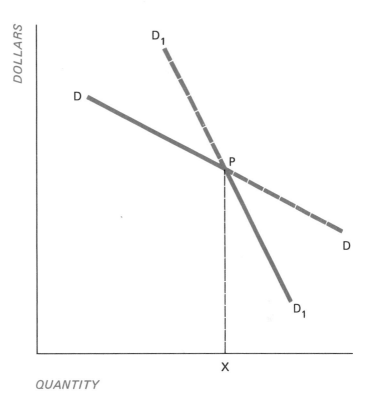

FIGURE 29-1

For an oligopoly, *D* represents the demand curve if other firms do not react to a price change. D_1 represents the demand if other firms match a price change. The greatest fear of the initiator of a price change is that competing firms will match a price reduction but not a price increase. This action by competitors would result in a "kinked" demand curve, DPD_1.

in Figure 29-1. Secondly, a change in price by an oligopolist may be met by a similar change by rivals. If they do follow suit, the demand or average revenue of an oligopolist may appear as D_1 shown in Figure 29-1. Notice that the demand curve D_1 will tend to be less elastic, since the gain in sales resulting from lower prices will be lessened if competitors lower their prices also. On the other hand, the firm initiating a rise in price will not lose as many sales as it otherwise would if rivals increase their prices also. In short, the substitution effect resulting from the price change will be lessened if other firms follow suit regarding the price change.

A third, and more likely situation, may arise. Rivals may follow suit for a decrease in price but ignore a rise in price. If one firm were to reduce price, its increase in quantity sold might be less than anticipated as rivals cut prices also. This would tend to eliminate any substitution effect, or increase in sales at the expense of other firms. The price cut initiator would experience some increase in sales, however, as total industry sales expand in response to the lower price charged by all firms. On the other hand, if a firm raised its price and its rivals did not, the decrease in sales might be greater than anticipated as a result of its loss of sales to rivals through the substitution effect. In this case the oligopolist's demand curve would be the same as that of D for any price above P, but identical with D_1 for any price below P. Such a demand curve would appear as DPD_1, as shown in Figure 29-1. This is referred to as a "kinked demand curve." Such a situation, of course, can lead to price stability, since the demand curve of the individual firm will tend to be inelastic if price is moved downward and elastic when its price is moved upward. Under these circumstances, price P may become the maximum revenue point for the firm, and X becomes the equilibrium output. Thus, there would be little incentive for the firm to change its price or output.

Another factor that causes a tendency toward a stable price in oligopoly is the discontinuous nature of the marginal revenue curve that results from a kinked demand curve. At the equilibrium level corresponding with the point of the kink, there will be a gap in the marginal revenue curve as shown in Figure 29-2, which includes the marginal revenue curves that would accompany the demand curves shown in Figure 29-1. Here it can be seen that for that portion of the oligopolist's demand or average revenue curve that accompanies line D, the marginal revenue will be MR up to the output at point X. Beyond that output, however, the marginal revenue curve for the firm will follow MR_1, which accompanies the lower part of the oligopolist's demand curve, D_1. Consequently, the firm's marginal revenue, a combination of MR and MR_1, will be discontinuous (or have a gap) at point X. As a result of this gap, whenever there is a change in the cost of production, there will be no incentive to change price or output so long as the marginal cost curve moves up or down within the gap. The vertical gap in the marginal revenue schedule is observable in Figure 29-3.

FIGURES 29-2 AND 29-3

The kinked demand curve will produce an unusual marginal revenue curve. From the point of equilibrium, X, if price is increased and other firms do not follow suit, MR will move to the left along the line MR. If price is lowered, however, MR will follow along MR_1 as shown in Figure 29-2. This will produce a gap in the MR curve, as is more clearly shown in Figure 29-3.

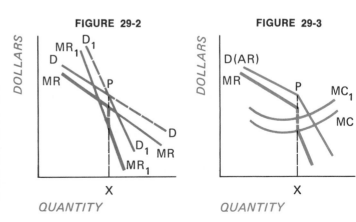

FIGURE 29-2

FIGURE 29-3

Price Rigidity

The tendency toward price rigidity in oligopoly contributes to nonprice competition, often referred to as nonaggressive competition. As a result, great emphasis is placed on product differentiation, and there is tremendous stress on advertising as part of the competition among sellers. Sellers are constantly offering a great variety of styles, models, promotional deals, guarantees, and the like. But they seldom engage in price competition. Witness, for example, the pattern of competition in the production and sale of automobiles, soaps, cigarettes, toothpaste, tires, coffee, and transportation, where the emphasis is on nonprice competition.

Questions often arise about both oligopoly and monopolistic competition regarding the merits of product differentiation and nonprice competition. On the one hand, it can be pointed out that there might be great duplication of facilities, especially among monopolistic competitors, that many of the product differences may be insignificant, that there is a great waste of resources and manpower associated with frivolous models and styles changes, that planned obsolescence is costly to the economy, and that advertising is often misinformative and results in nothing but an increase in the cost and the price of the product. On the other hand, it can be shown that research for product differentiation often results in improvement in the quality of a product, that models and styles afford the consumer a better choice in his purchase, that planned obsolescence motivates the consumer to make new purchases of better products, and that advertising performs a definite function of informing consumers about different products and their uses. It can be contended, also, that advertising helps finance numerous intermediary services, such as entertainment, newspapers, magazines, and community contributions. Advertising also provides numerous small utility products, such as ball-point pens, calendars, and other items used as customer advertisement gimmicks. In order to determine the socioeconomic value of nonprice competition, therefore, one would have to weigh advantages and disadvantages. This, of course, would involve a considerable number of value judgments.

The tendency of price stability associated with oligopoly, however, often leads to collusive practices. This occurs especially where there is a high degree of inelasticity for the product and relatively few firms in the industry. The highly inelastic demand, especially with a kinked demand curve, makes price competition unprofitable not only for the individual firm but also for the industry as a whole. The fewness of firms makes it easier for them to enter into an agreement, either tacit or formal, to limit output or to fix price. Court dockets in recent years have been replete with antitrust suits against such collusive practices in several industries. A few of these and other practices leading to price stability are explained below.

Price Stabilization by Agreement of Producers. Wherever it is possible for them to do so, the sellers of a commodity or a service tend to compete only "within limits" and to "live and let live." In other words, manufacturers, merchants, farmers, and wage earners sometimes come to an agreement—specific or tacit—that will restrict competition on the basis of price. This propensity of sellers to protect their own interests is not a recent development. The classic remark of Adam Smith in the *Wealth of Nations* refers to this fact:

> People of the same trade seldom meet together, even for merriment and diversion, but the conversation ends in a conspiracy against the public, or in some contrivance to raise prices. It is impossible to prevent such meetings, by any law which either could be executed, or would be consistent with liberty and justice.[1]

In West Germany, England, and other European countries, cartels and "institutes" composed of manufacturers have been accepted and taken for granted for a long time. Their purposes are to eliminate overproduction, to divide the market territory, to rationalize industrial and commercial practices, to control prices, to regulate output, and, when possible, to maintain profits. The result is the formalization of national or even international oligopolies.

In the United States, the cartelization of business and industry has usually been looked upon with suspicion or outright disapproval. In many cases the common-law doctrines of conspiracy and of restraint of trade have been invoked to prevent or to break up attempts to fix prices or to control production by common agreement. As we shall see in the following chapter, various statutes have been enacted to implement the application of these doctrines.

Nevertheless, price agreements—tacit or otherwise—are not exceptions to the general rule that sellers compete within limits. Probably one of the most common methods by which producers attempt to pursue a course of limited competition is by means of trade associations. Although most trade associations are not monopolistic as to either purpose or effect, certain association activities do enable members to adopt policies that modify the degree of competition that otherwise would prevail. Such activities include annual conventions for the discussion of common problems of production and marketing; the establishment of codes of ethics, which may, for example, prohibit sales below cost; dissemination of statistics as to inventories, sales, and other matters; the maintenance of research and advisory services and experimental laboratories, the benefits of which are made available to

---

[1] Cannan ed., 1904, Vol. I, p. 130.

members; the collection of data as to prices at which goods are sold; establishing collection services; and others, many of which are only remotely, if at all, related to the possibilities of controlling prices.

Price Leadership. In some cases one firm may be able to set the price for the whole industry. *Price leadership* occurs when one firm achieves such a predominant position in an industry that other firms follow the leadership of the dominant firm in setting their own prices. Of course, this does not mean that price leadership is practiced in any or all of the industries where one company produces a relatively large portion of the total market supply. But where price leadership does occur, one firm—or a few at most—is so large that it is likely to produce more than the combined total of the other firms.

There are many reasons why the smaller firms may be willing to set their prices in conformity with those set by the leader. For one thing, some smaller firms may be reluctant to compete with the big firm by lowering prices. They may realize that the larger firm, if it chooses to do so, could enter into a price-cutting war in which the smaller firms would suffer most. With its stronger financial resources, and probably a lower ATC curve resulting from a larger scale of operation, the large firm could lower prices to a level that would bankrupt the smaller firms within a short time. Again, the smaller firms may willingly accept the price established by the leader, since it is likely to be relatively stable and afford the smaller producer a comfortable or reasonable profit. The greater certainty of a continuation of prices at something approaching a certain level enables any firm to adjust production to the most profitable point.

Basing-Point Pricing. Years ago the practice of the steel and cement industries, especially, was to quote "delivered prices" of their commodities. In using this system of regulating prices, the freight charges are calculated by the seller from a basing point, which is designated as the point of delivery. To illustrate how the system works, suppose that Chicago is established as the basing point for steel manufactured in Pittsburgh and sold in Ohio and adjoining states. Then a buyer of steel in Cleveland, for instance, would be required to pay the factory price at Pittsburgh plus the freight *from Chicago*, although the steel was shipped directly from Pittsburgh. This is known as the *basing-point system*. Many manufacturers established single or multiple basing points for the quotation of prices.

Critics of the basing-point system argue that it constitutes an exercise of monopoly power. They contend that the development of competing establishments in different parts of the country is prevented. Proponents of the system as emphatically insist that it is a desirable way of stabilizing prices.

Stable prices, they maintain, are helpful to users of the products while final consumers are not exploited.

In 1948 the United States Supreme Court upheld an order by the Federal Trade Commission against 74 cement manufacturers to cease and desist from using the basing-point system. The Court agreed that the basing-point system is contrary to the spirit of competition and that it constitutes a form of price discrimination that is illegal.

Product Differentiation. Producers of commodities that are similar and which, therefore, may easily be substituted for the products of other producers, usually attempt to emphasize the peculiar superiority of the article they offer for sale. This practice is referred to as *product differentiation.*

The maker of a brand of toothpaste, for example, is not content merely to produce an article that is useful for cleaning teeth. He hopes that prospective buyers will become convinced that his product is really better than those of his competitors. Therefore, he attempts to achieve distinction for his toothpaste by putting it in a package that is noticeably different from that of other brands, by giving it a certain flavor, and by making emphatic and repeated claims to its superiority over other brands. He avails himself of any or all of the advertising media. Of course, his product may be superior to others of a similar nature; but whether it is or not, his aim is to convince the buying public that it is superior. To the extent that he succeeds, he reduces competition. Once he has built up a demand for his product, he is able to exercise more control over the price of his product. A major purpose of product differentiation is to make the demand curve for the product less price elastic and less cross elastic. Then price increases by the firm or price decreases by its competitors will bring a smaller loss of sales.

But the producer of a differentiated product must live in constant fear that he will lose his customers, for, as a rule, buyers' tastes and preferences are fickle. One person may smoke one brand of cigarettes for years and then suddenly switch to another brand. Or a housewife in search of variety may try another brand of coffee and thereafter continue to use it. In any case, the possibility of a shift from the use of one brand to another is enhanced if the price of the former is raised. Hence, the manufacturer endeavors to keep his product before the public by means of advertising. How much advertising costs actually add to the final cost of goods is uncertain. But as compared to final costs under a hypothetical condition of pure competition, we know that the total annual cost is increased by many hundreds of millions of dollars.

Administered Prices. An *administered price* is a predetermined price that is fixed by the seller. In arriving at a decision to set the price of his product, the manufacturer, merchant, or other producer calculates the total amount of his fixed and variable costs. Then he estimates his sales over a period of time at prices that would yield him an expected profit on the number of units sold. He then sets the price that he feels will yield him the greatest amount of profit for the period.

If it appears that the estimated sales will be realized, the administered price is likely to be maintained. If sales should be more rapid than had been anticipated, the price may be raised. On the other hand, if sales are very slow and there appears to be little reason to think that they will increase, the seller may lower the price.

It is evident, therefore, that administered prices are responsive to the influence of demand, although they do not fluctuate as frequently or as much as do purely competitive prices. Like most other sellers, those who administer prices may be inclined to "charge what the traffic will bear." But they are not likely to forget that over a period of time the possibilities for realizing a profit are conditioned by consumer demand for their product and that this demand may change.

Most product prices are administered prices. This is as it must be, and it would be impracticable to assume that producers would undertake to produce goods or that retail stores would stock merchandise if all prices were so flexible and unpredictable that they would change from day to day, or even from hour to hour! The conclusion, therefore, is that administered prices pose no threat to the welfare of the people so long as the prices of essential commodities and services are not fixed freely by those who possess monopoly power—power that is subject to neither an effective degree of competition nor a salutary vigilance by government.

At the same time, the varying degrees of price flexibility due to differences in the ability of sellers to administer prices sometimes create problems that give rise to political issues. This has been true of the "farm problem," as we shall learn in Chapter 38. The fixing of minimum prices for farm products was intended to assure the farmer a fair income. Most of these efforts, directly or indirectly, have been in the nature of government support of farm prices. These efforts have not been designed to give the farmer the power to administer the prices of products in the way a manufacturer does. That would be impossible because practically all farm products are homogeneous and standardized and are not identified with a particular producer. But to a certain extent these efforts are designed to overcome the disadvantage of the farmer who must sell in a market where the demand for his product is practically purely competitive and buy in markets where the prices of goods are largely administered by the sellers.

COMPETITION AMONG BUYERS

Just as there can be different types of competition among sellers, there can be varying degrees of competition among buyers. In a case where there are numerous buyers, purchasing a commodity under identical conditions, who are well informed about price and market conditions, and in which no individual buyer is large enough to change the total demand or influence the market price, it can be said that pure competition among buyers exists. The numerous housewives in a given locality certainly form a purely competitive buyers' market for the products of the local grocery store. The Avon lady and the Fuller Brush man likewise have numerous household outlets for their products.

To distinguish a monopoly in selling from a monopoly in buying, we use the term *monopsony* to refer to a condition in which there is only one buyer for a good or service. Although pure monopsony is difficult to find, such a market does exist in the government purchase of gold. Other monopsonies can be found in local areas where there may be only one granary to service the local farmers. Sometimes a near monopsony will exist when a large-scale employer moves into a predominately rural area. He may be the only major buyer of labor in the area.

Oligopsony exists when a few buyers dominate the market. In the tobacco market, for example, there are numerous producers but relatively few buyers. It is quite possible for any of the four major tobacco firms to influence the market demand and consequently the market price by their decisions to buy more or less tobacco. A similar situation exists in the purchase of commercial jet aircraft and the buying of original automobile equipment, such as headlights, horns, steering wheels, and pistons, for which there is a limited parts market, or automobile after-market, compared to the original purchases made by Ford, GM, Chrysler, and American Motors. The author of a college textbook faces an oligopsonistic market in the publication of his manuscript, as does a rookie professional baseball player in selling his athletic ability.

Monopsonistic competition, a condition in which there are many buyers but who offer differentiated conditions to sellers, is very prevalent in the American economy. In any large-sized community, for example, a large number of firms hire labor, offering a variety of working conditions and fringe benefits. The manufacturer of toys deals with a monopsonistically competitive market in the distribution of his product.

THE AMERICAN MARKET STRUCTURE

The variety and complexity of our markets certainly confirm the notion of a mixed economy, as referred to in Chapter 4. Not only is the economy in this sense mixed for the total economic system, it may be mixed for an individual firm. Quite often a firm dealing in a purely competitive market in buying its raw material, labor, and other units of input will have a monopoly or near monopoly in selling its finished product. At other times a *bilateral monopoly* may exist. This is a situation in which a monopsonist faces a monopolist. The monopsonist is the only buyer on one side of a market, and the monopolist is the only seller on the other. There are many times, too, when a multiproduct firm will sell some of its goods in a competitive market, others as an oligopolist, and perhaps have a monopoly in the sale of one product.

Of course, a seller's influence on supply or on price will depend on the nature of the market in which he is dealing. The type of market will also condition his initiating actions and his reactions to changes by others. Furthermore, as we have already seen, the type and degree of competition influences the price and output policies and the profit picture of individual firms and of industries in total.

Concentration Ratios

Although it is difficult to measure the degree of competition, monopoly, oligopoly, or monopolistic competition that exists on the seller's side of the market—or how much competition, monopsony, or oligopsony exists on the buyer's side—some indication of the concentration in production can be obtained from an inspection of Table 29-1 compiled from the *Census of Manufacturing*. The *concentration ratio* is the percentage of total shipments in a given industry that is produced by the four leading firms in that industry. It is certain that imperfect competition (which includes monopoly, oligopoly, and monopolistic competition) exists in a substantial portion of the American markets for goods and services.

Workable Competition

Economists for the past 30 years or more have been suggesting a concept referred to as *workable competition*. This implies that it is not necessary to have all the conditions of pure competition in order to serve the best interest of the consumer. It also implies that some forms of imperfect competition may be workable under suitable conditions. In order to have workable competition at least three basic conditions have been suggested: (1) there must be a reasonably large number of firms; (2) there must be no formal or

TABLE 29-1

CONCENTRATION
IN 25 SELECTED
INDUSTRIES

1970

Industry	Percent of Industry Shipments Accounted for by:	
	4 Companies	8 Companies
1. Telephone Apparatus	94	99
2. Motor Vehicles	91	97
3. Cigarettes	84	S
4. Tires and Tubes	72	89
5. Soap and Detergents	70	79
6. Aircraft	65	87
7. Photographic Equipment	75	86
8. Aircraft Engines	65	87
9. Blast Furnaces and Steel Mills	47	65
10. Radio and Television Sets	48	67
11. Motors and Generators	50	62
12. Farm Machinery	40	51
13. Shipbuilding	46	65
14. Construction Machinery	42	53
15. Malt Liquors	46	64
16. Metal Stampings	40	46
17. Toilet Preparations	39	52
18. Petroleum Refining	33	57
19. Refrigeration Machinery	31	48
20. Shoes, Except Rubber	28	36
21. Bread and Cake	29	39
22. Paints and Allied Products	22	34
23. Machinery Tools	24	37
24. Book Publishing	21	35
25. Women's Dresses	10	13

SOURCE: *Statistical Abstract of the United States*, 1973, pp. 706-709.

s Withheld because data did not meet publication standards.

tacit agreement regarding price and output; and (3) new firms should be able to enter without serious impediment or disadvantage. Others might add to this the fact that no firm should be large or powerful enough to coerce other firms. But even here, it is difficult to ascertain the exact meaning of workable competition. What is meant by a reasonably large number of firms? Is it 5, 10, or 25? Obviously it will depend on the type of industry. What is meant by "no serious impediment to entry"? Would an exceptionally large capital requirement qualify as a serious impediment?

It is easy to see that trying to decide on those industries in which workable competition does or does not exist depends largely upon the interpretation of the person making the judgment. Some economists, for example, would consider the automobile industry, with its relatively few major producers, an example of workable competition; but others would not. More would classify the steel industry as workable competition, but still some economists would disagree. Here again we face that perennial problem of implementing economic theory or knowledge. Nevertheless, many industries fitting the categories of oligopoly or monopolistic competition could readily qualify as cases of workable competition.

degree of efficiency in production. At the same time, they recognize that in the production of most goods and services pure competition is not possible or feasible. And they would also indicate that the advantages of a certain amount of industrial concentration, even without a high degree of public control, more than offset the disadvantages.

Monopolistic Competition and Public Policy

It is not an oversimplification of our complex economic system to say that the chief disadvantage of regulation is that of maintaining the essentials of a free enterprise system within a legal framework. The solution of problems relating to the maintenance of effective competition cannot be found by arbitrary and purely legalistic procedures. Of course, there must be statutes designed to protect competition and limit monopolies; but, if such statutes are to accomplish the purpose of promoting the general welfare, they must be based upon a recognition of the economic realities involved. The most important of these realities are: (1) the factors that condition the costs of production of specific products in the real world of industry and business, and (2) the need to maintain a business environment in which private enterprise cannot find a complete shelter from competition. Unfortunately, it is not possible to state quantitatively the amount of protection against competition that an industrial or business firm should enjoy. As a generalization, however, it can be said that no private enterprise should be permitted to find an overall shelter that would be impervious to that amount of competition—actual or potential—which is needed to encourage sufficient production at reasonable prices.

SUMMARY

1. Oligopoly is a market condition where there are relatively few firms producing identical or similar products. Because of the limited number of firms, each firm must consider the reaction of rivals in matters relating to output and price.

2. A peculiar characteristic of oligopoly is the kinked demand curve, which exists when rivals follow one firm's drop in price but do not follow if it raises price. This and other conditions of oligopoly tend to result in price stability in an oligopolistic industry. Price stability can be obtained through a number of devices, such as formal and tacit agreements, price leadership, basing-point systems, product differentiation, and administered pricing.

3. Competition among buyers also varies. In the buyers' market there exist pure competition, monopsony, monopsonistic competition, and oligopsony.

4. The economy is made up of a complex mixture of many types and degrees of competition among both buyers and sellers. It is generally agreed that a large amount of competition is beneficial to the total economy. There are, however, some merits, as well as disadvantages, to other forms of competition in certain industries.

5. Workable competition is described as a condition in which there is a reasonably large number of firms in an industry, there is no agreement among the firms regarding output or price, and new firms are free to enter the industry without serious impediment or disadvantage.

NEW TERMS

Duopoly, *p. 637*
Oligopoly, *p. 637*
Price leadership, *p. 643*
Basing-point pricing, *p. 643*
Product differentiation, *p. 644*
Administered price, *p. 644*

Monopsony, *p. 646*
Oligopsony, *p. 646*
Monopsonistic competition, *p. 646*
Bilateral monopoly, *p. 647*
Concentration ratio, *p. 647*
Workable competition, *p. 647*

QUESTIONS FOR DISCUSSION AND ANALYSIS

1. Why does an oligopolist have to be concerned about the actions or reactions of his rivals?

2. What conditions lead to price leadership in an industry?

3. Explain the "kinked demand curve" characteristic of oligopoly. How does it tend to lead toward price stability?

4. Explain the concept of "administered prices."

5. There appears to be a correlation between industry concentration ratios and the capital investment required for undertaking production in particular industries. Explain.

6. Distinguish between monopoly and monopsony, and between oligopoly and oligopsony.

7. What conditions are necessary for "workable competition" to exist?

8. Do you think that we have too little competition in the American economy today? Why or why not?

9. It has been proposed by a noted industrialist that whenever a company attains 25 percent or more of the business in a basic industry, it should be required to submit to a specific public agency a program for creating at least one new company out of the old as a means of maintaining competition. Comment.

SUGGESTED READINGS

Grayson, Henry. *Price Theory in a Changing Economy*. New York: The Macmillan Company, 1965.

Lloyd, Cliff. *Microeconomic Analysis*. Homewood, Ill.: Richard D. Irwin, Inc., 1967.

Maxwell, W. David. *Price Theory and Applications in Business Administration*. Pacific Palisades, Calif.: Goodyear Publishing Company, Inc., 1970.

Stigler, George J., and James K. Kindahl. *The Behavior of Industrial Prices*. New York: National Bureau of Economic Research, Inc., 1970.

Watson, Donald S. *Price Theory in Action*. Boston: Houghton Mifflin Company, 1972.

30

Large-Scale
Enterprise
and
Public Policy

PREVIEW   Some firms through their very large size have the ability to exert a considerable degree of control, or influence, over price. This gives them an economic advantage over their competitors, and they are many times able to obtain and retain higher prices and a larger profit than would be the case under more competitive conditions. Firms use several means and devices, including financial, marketing, and physical integration arrangements, to get into such a favorable position. The move toward bigness is legal so long as it does not tend to create a monopoly or restrain trade. Because of the advantages of competition to the consumer, the antitrust laws are designed and enforced to preserve, protect, and promote competition and to prevent monopoly and restraint of trade.

The sales of close to 80 American industrial corporations exceed $2 billion annually. Nearly 90 other firms have annual sales in excess of $1 billion. To many, these giants of production are symbolic of free enterprise. They represent the superiority of American technology and ability to do things in a big way. To others, however, their existence and continuing growth means a diminution of competition which poses a threat to the free enterprise system. Except in the case of large-scale industrial conflict, the public seldom seems to understand or appreciate the influence that big business may have on the social and economic life of the individual.

The corporate form of business enterprise makes large-scale operations possible. If only the sole proprietorship and the partnership were available, it would be extremely difficult to assemble enough capital to produce on the most economical and profitable scale. In addition to providing the device for operating simple, unitary business firms, the corporate form of organization has also made it easier for some firms to grow in size and strength by combining in one of several ways with other corporations.

In many major lines of production large-scale operators dominate the industry. In the fields of transportation, communication, and manufacturing, the chances for the newcomer to reach important proportions are small indeed. He is often hemmed in by giant companies that are frequently the result of mergers, amalgamations, or other types of corporate integration. There is nothing wrong or illegal about large-scale operations or business integration as long as they do not interfere with the rights and freedom of others to produce and compete. Any type of business organization or activity that limits competition, however, is contrary to American public policy. Since competition has so many advantages and is a salient feature of a free enterprise economy, much of our legal environment is designed to protect, preserve, and promote competition.

THE SIZE OF BUSINESS ENTERPRISE

Business firms range in size from one-man operations with capital investments of only a few dollars to corporations with hundreds of thousands of stockholders and billions of dollars' worth of assets. Therefore, it is difficult to draw a line between small business and big business. It may be helpful, however, to quote from the Small Business Act passed by Congress in 1953, which is intended to provide government help to small business concerns by means of advisory service, financial aid, and management and technical assistance.

Under authority of the Act, the Small Business Administration undertakes to aid small business along the following lines: product development, product marketing, development of new and improved products, "inventive" ideas, unpatentable ideas, government-owned patents, privately owned patents, product redesign, and new processes of production.

The Act states further that a small business is "one that is independently owned and operated and not dominant in its field of operation." The Small Business Administration has declared that any manufacturing firm employing fewer than 250 persons is classified as small. Those firms with 1,000 or more employees are classified as large. Firms with 250 to 1,000 employees may be classified as either small or large depending on the nature of the industry in which they operate. In the distribution trades, dollar volume is used as a measure of size.

On the other hand, we have some firms with billions of dollars in assets and sales plus employees numbering in the tens and hundreds of thousands. Among the largest industrial producers, whether in terms of sales, assets, profits, or number of employees, are such firms as General Motors Corporation, Exxon of New York, Ford Motor Company, General Electric Company, and United States Steel Corporation. A complete list of the 25 largest industrial corporations is shown in Table 30-1. Notice that all of these corporations, as well as the next 142 largest, have sales in excess of $1 billion annually. Furthermore, the 500 largest industrial corporations each has sales in excess of $100 million per year. It should be remembered also that not all large corporations are industrial in nature. A number of commercial banks, such as the Bank of America, Chase Manhattan, First National City Bank, the Cleveland Trust Company, National Bank of Detroit, Wells Fargo Bank, and three dozen more make loans ranging from $1 billion to $21 billion each year. Among the merchandising giants are such well-known names as Sears, Roebuck & Company with sales of $11.0 billion annually, Great Atlantic & Pacific Tea with $6.4 billion, Safeway Stores with $6.1 billion, and Kroger Company with $4.0 billion. Other multibillion dollar sales enterprises include J. C. Penney Company, S. S. Kresge, and Federated Department Stores. There are also giant operators in the insurance, transportation, and utilities industries. Intelligent citizenship requires an understanding of why and how giant business firms have come into existence and how they affect American economic society.

TABLE 30-1

THE 25 LARGEST INDUSTRIAL CORPORATIONS

1973

(Ranked by Sales)

Rank	Company	Sales ($000)	Assets ($000)	Net Income ($000)	Employees
1	General Motors	35,798,289	20,296,861	2,398,103	810,920
2	Exxon	25,724,319	25,079,494	2,443,286	137,000
3	Ford Motor	23,015,100	12,954,000	906,500	474,318
4	Chrysler	11,774,372	6,104,898	255,445	273,254
5	General Electric	11,575,300	8,324,200	585,100	388,000
6	Texaco	11,406,876	13,595,413	1,292,403	74,918
7	Mobil Oil	11,390,113	10,690,431	849,312	73,900
8	International Business Machines	10,993,242	12,289,489	1,575,467	274,108
9	International Tel. & Tel.	10,183,035	10,132,571	527,837	438,000
10	Gulf Oil	8,417,000	10,074,000	800,000	51,600
11	Standard Oil of California	7,761,835	9,082,248	843,577	39,269
12	Western Electric	7,037,290	4,828,143	315,305	206,608
13	U.S. Steel	6,951,905	6,918,535	325,758	184,794
14	Westinghouse Electric	5,702,310	4,407,665	161,928	194,100
15	Standard Oil (Ind.)	5,415,976	7,018,013	511,249	46,589
16	E. I. Du Pont de Nemours	5,275,600	4,832,200	585,600	118,423
17	General Telephone & Electronics	5,105,296	10,749,370	352,076	196,000
18	Shell Oil	4,883,808	5,381,164	332,694	32,080
19	Goodyear Tire & Rubber	4,675,265	3,871,043	184,756	152,929
20	RCA	4,246,800	3,300,800	183,700	126,000
21	Continental Oil	4,224,004	3,693,265	242,664	39,796
22	International Harvester	4,192,544	2,812,667	114,296	107,890
23	LTV	4,177,057	1,829,145	49,888	65,700
24	Bethlehem Steel	4,137,633	3,919,264	206,609	118,000
25	Eastman Kodak	4,035,520	4,302,081	653,475	120,700

SOURCE: *Fortune* (May, 1974).

ADVANTAGES OF LARGE-SCALE ENTERPRISES

There is no simple explanation for the growth of big business. The aim of those who have promoted and organized the great business concerns has been to make greater profits, provide better goods or services, reduce cost, and/or provide better stability of production and employment. The opportunities for accomplishing these objectives are not the same in all situations. In each case, one or more of the following factors has contributed to the formation or growth of large-scale American corporations: (1) economy in production by the use of more capital; (2) advantages of integration of control; (3) utilization of by-products; (4) diversification and stabilization of production; (5) research; (6) reduction of competition and the stabilization of prices; and (7) increased advertising possibilities.

Economy in Production by the Use of More Capital

Up to a certain point, the costs of production in most industries vary somewhat inversely with the amount of machinery and equipment used. In the modern cigarette factory, for example, where packages ready for the market move in endless streams, nearly all the work is done by machinery. The artistically packaged product costs only a few cents to manufacture, whereas if production were largely by hand, the cost and hence the selling price would be prohibitive. The same thing in general holds true wherever standardization of productive processes is possible. The necessity for more capital is often a reason why smaller concerns merge, consolidate, or form some other type of combination.

Integration of Control

The production of most goods involves the performance of a series of related processes. The number of processes depends upon the nature of the particular product produced. Under a system of division of labor, the steps in the productive process may be performed by separate establishments. The raiser of livestock, for example, grows beef cattle that are sold to the cattle buyer, who sells them to the packer, who sells the finished product to the retailer who, in turn, sells it to the consumer. Each producer is thus dependent upon the one next in order in the progress of the product toward the consumer.

The dependence of one producer on another has its disadvantages. The steel manufacturer, for example, desires a constant and dependable supply of iron from the blast furnace. And the blast furnace, in turn, should have a steady supply of iron ore. Anything that interferes with the flow of supplies disrupts production and results in increased costs. To bring about an integration of several or all the processes and activities connected with the manufacture or sale of a product, concentration of control of several kinds of establishments is often undertaken. Whether the result is lower costs than would be the case if the various processes of production were performed by independent establishments depends upon whether integrated control actually results in more efficient and stable production than would otherwise be the case. If savings do result and are passed along to the consumer, prices of the finished product will then be lower.

Utilization of By-Products

In many kinds of manufacturing, production of a product results in a number of by-products that can be converted into useful goods. For example, in the meat-packing plants the primary aim is to prepare meat of different kinds and cuts. But in the large plants a great many materials accumulate daily that in the aggregate possess much potential value. Bristles may be made into brushes; bone, into buttons, bone meal, and knife handles; blood and other waste, into fertilizers; hides, into leather; glands, into extracts for pharmaceutical products; and so on. The oil refining industry is perhaps a more spectacular example of the possibility of utilizing by-products when production is undertaken on a large scale. The processing and sale of by-products may reduce the cost of each of the products produced in the establishment. The result may be a reduction in price and higher profits.

Diversification and Stabilization of Production

Somewhat related to economies that result from the utilization of by-products is the diversification of products. Formerly an application on a small scale of the principle involved here was the practice of the same dealer to sell ice in the summer and coal in the fall and winter. By undertaking to supply both products, the dealer was able to utilize much of his equipment the year round.

Likewise, the large manufacturer may find it profitable to engage in the production of electric ranges, refrigerators, washing machines, and similar products, the manufacture of which calls for the use of facilities and skills that are common to the production of all these products. Frequently by dovetailing production of diversified products the firm can provide more stable employment and income for its employees and at the same time improve its profit position.

Research

Many of the machines that helped to spur the Industrial Revolution were the outcome of hit-and-miss experiments based on ideas that were little more than mere notions. Many of the ideas eventuated in machines and tools that increased the productivity of labor. But by comparison, those machines and tools were crude affairs when judged by their lineal descendants found in modern factories. The improvements in machines and equipment have resulted largely from advancements of knowledge in the fields of engineering, physics, and chemistry. In recent decades the branches of pure science taught in colleges and universities have been put to practical use by large manufacturing concerns. Many processes of manufacturing are largely the application of the principles of physics and chemistry and of the formulas evolved in laboratories.

Formerly products underwent relatively few changes from the original state of the materials from which they were made. There were only a few kinds of steel; now there are many. Woven fabrics were merely twisted threads made from cotton, wool, or flax; now they are frequently composite products, produced by combinations of many fibers that have undergone several chemical treatments. In the textile industries, revolutionary progress has been made by the discovery of methods of producing orlon, dacron, nylon, rayon, polyesters, and a vast array of other new materials. The modern automobile is a marvel of engineering that embodies devices for comfort and convenience which existed only in the dreams of inventors 50 years ago. And in the great manufacturing establishments, the scientists pursue their work, equipped with modern laboratories and facilities for discovering new products and for improving others that have already come into use.

In most lines of production, the smaller firms cannot provide the funds needed for research. Hence, they are handicapped in their efforts to compete with the large establishments. In other cases, however, a research and development organization may exist for the benefit of all members of the industry. Currently over $30 billion annually is being spent on research and development. Industries provide more than two thirds of these funds; the remainder comes from university and federal funds.

Reduction of Competition and the Stabilization of Prices

Next to acquiring a legal monopoly, the best way to achieve protection against competition is to acquire economic and financial strength through size. When a business is large enough to dominate the field, it can set prices that are likely to be adopted by smaller and economically weaker establishments. Although it may not succeed in acquiring a complete monopoly, its prospects for continued profits are more nearly certain. If big enough, it does not have to live in fear that its market will be ruined by others who resort to price-cutting tactics. The desire to "stabilize prices" has been an important motive behind movements to concentrate economic power and control.

Increased Advertising Possibilities

An efficient selling organization aided by advertising is necessary for the marketing of goods in large volume; quality alone, even superior quality, is not sufficient. Goods must be sold; it is not likely that they will be bought without selling effort. The cultivation of a wide market requires the expenditure of large sums of money. The little business, if it aspires to a position of leadership, is handicapped in its efforts to convince the people that they need and want its product. Many small concerns, therefore, have concluded that increased marketing possibilities could be realized by effecting a combination of some kind with one or more of their competitors. A few years ago, for example, one of our largest soap manufacturers was ordered by the court to divest its holding of a liquid bleach firm it had previously acquired. The court held that the advertising power of the parent company gave an undue advantage to the subsidiary firm in the bleach market.

TYPES OF CORPORATE COMBINATIONS

Business combinations may be classified in several ways. For most purposes, however, we can say that combinations of business functions and firms take one or more of four forms of integration: (1) vertical, (2) horizontal, (3) complementary, or (4) conglomerate.

A *vertical integration* is one that comprises companies that engage in the different steps in manufacturing or marketing a product. One of the best examples of this type of combination is that of the United States Steel Corporation. This company controls or operates ore mines, coke ovens, blast furnaces, barges, steel mills, rolling mills, and fabricating plants.

A *horizontal integration* results from bringing under single control a number of companies engaged in the sale or production of the same or similar products. Of the four types of combination, this is the oldest. The trusts that were characteristic of the latter part of the 1800s were frequently of the horizontal type. General Motors Corporation, which originally was a combination of automobile producers, is a classic example of horizontal integration. Many horizontal combinations are to be found in the transportation industry, retail merchandising, and manufacturing.

Complementary integration takes place when companies selling allied, but not competitive, products combine. For example, manufacturers of different kinds of building materials might reduce various selling expenses by forming a complementary combination.

Conglomerate integration, as the name implies, is a broad type of business combination. It may be neither horizontal nor vertical. In essence it integrates across industries. Technically it occurs where a large company that might have entered a new business through internal expansion instead enters by acquiring an important concern already in the business. Frequently the term refers to a corporation in a number of unrelated markets. Much has been heard about conglomerates in recent years. A number of reasons are given for their growth since World War II. Some dynamic business leaders, for example, feel that good management can operate successfully in most fields of business. Once they prove their efficiency in one industry, they are ready to take on firms in other industries. To them the conglomerate is a means to extend their efficiency to other areas and to improve corporate earnings. To others the conglomerate provides an outlet for funds that have been accumulated from operating successfully in the original business of the conglomerate. Sometimes conglomerates are developed as a defensive mechanism by diversifying operations and protecting earnings. In this way if the original industry in which the firm operates is not doing well, its earnings can be bolstered through higher earnings in other industries. Brunswick, for example, accelerated its move toward conglomeration when it began experiencing reduced sales and earnings in its original business, bowling equipment. Through acquisition it is now involved in a wide range of products including school furniture, boats, surgical instruments, and aircraft parts.

Although there has been much publicity and controversy in recent years about conglomerates, there are still exceptional cases. What makes a conglomerate? Does a corporation become a conglomerate when it operates in 5, 10, or 15 different industries? No one has laid down specific criteria on this matter as yet. A study by *Fortune* magazine of the 500 largest industrial corporations indicated that the bulk of them operated across a limited number of industries. This can be observed from Figure 30-1. One of the largest and best known conglomerates at that time was Litton Industries, which according to the study operated in 18 different industries. Today Litton has assets of over $2 billion, with annual sales of $2.6 billion, and is the forty-seventh largest industrial corporation in the United States. But it has since been surpassed in conglomerate activities by such stalwarts as IT&T and Gulf & Western. Other outstanding conglomerates include General Tire in 17 industries; General Electric Company in 14 industries; Armour & Company in 11 industries; Dow Chemical in 10 industries; and Ford Motor Company in 8 industries. These and other conglomerates are shown in Table 30-2 on page 662.

METHODS OF EFFECTING CORPORATE COMBINATIONS

Prior to the development of modern methods for the formal integration of two or more business firms, the less formal device of "gentlemen's agreements"

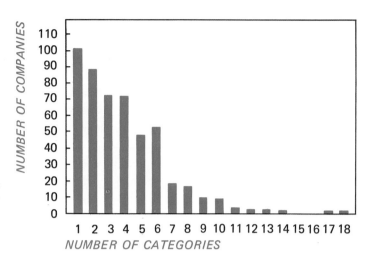

FIGURE 30-1

A considerable number of companies operate in several different categories of industry. Note the large number that operate in 3, 4, 5, 6 or more industries.

SOURCE: *Fortune* (June 15, 1967), p. 176.

was sometimes used as a means of lessening competition. Such agreements might be either overt or tacit, and they might be secret or openly arrived at. But in each case, they were designed to limit the degree of competition between the parties involved.

Corporate combinations may be accomplished in many ways. Some of the organizations formerly utilized to limit competition have been declared illegal. But sometimes the new methods of lessening competition that have evolved are as effective as those which have been prohibited by statute. Following are the more important of these methods: (1) pools, (2) trusts, (3) holding companies, (4) mergers and amalgamations, (5) community of interests, and (6) interlocking directorates.

Pools

An early method of controlling production and prices by means of corporate combination or concerted action was that of pooling. Essentially, a *pool* was a federation of independent units sometimes used to limit production, to control prices, or to accomplish both purposes. One device was an agreement to limit the output by each unit. Two or more producers would agree to accept a production quota in order to limit total output to a point that would not "spoil" the market. Under this plan it was not necessary to fix prices by common agreement; limitation of output was relied upon to maintain profitable prices.

Another method involved an agreement to limit the territory in which each producer would sell his product. Still another method, which was adapted to the use of railroad companies, called for an agreement to share net profits according to certain ratios. For example, two competing railroads might agree to pay, say, 40 percent of the earnings of each road to their respective stockholders, the remainder to be paid into a common fund that would be divided in the ratio of, say, 30-70. The stronger the company, the better pooling arrangement it might expect to make with its competitor.

The chief advantage of a pooling agreement lay in the fact that it could be easily formed or abandoned. In addition, the companies involved retained their identities, and with the cessation of the pooling agreement they

TABLE 30-2

CONGLOMERATE DIVERSIFICATION BY NUMBER OF INDUSTRY CATEGORIES

Company	Categories	Average Annual Growth in Earnings Per Share 1961-1966 (Percent)	Company	Categories	Average Annual Growth in Earnings Per Share 1961-1966 (Percent)
Allied Chemical	9	7.54	General Dynamics	10	—
American Cyanamid	9	12.92	General Electric	14	6.58
Amer. Mach. & Foundry	10	(5.50)	General Precision	8	9.23
Armour	11	—	General Tire	17	12.43
Armstrong Cork	8	10.98	Goodrich	8	9.31
Avco	9	13.67	Goodyear	8	8.51
Bendix	10	8.02	Grace (W. R.)	12	18.30
Borden	9	8.35	Gulf & Western	8	26.79
Borg-Warner	12	14.28	I.B.M.	8	19.22
Brunswick	11	(41.87)	I.T.T.	13	71.89
Castle & Cooke	8	—	Johnson & Johnson	8	16.91
Chrysler	9	68.99	Kaiser Industries	8	28.56
Consol. Electronics	8	14.35	Kidde (Walter)	11	—
Dow Chemical	10	13.72	Litton Industries	18	35.09
Du Pont	9	(1.50)	Lockheed Aircraft	10	15.76
Eagle-Picher	8	21.98	Minnesota Mining & Mfg.	8	12.15
Eltra	11	21.99	National Distillers	9	13.17
Evans Products	8	—	Ogden	9	29.36
FMC	10	20.34	Olin Mathieson	9	15.15
Fairchild Camera	8	15.47	Rexall	10	13.45
Farmland Industries	8	—	Texas Instruments	9	27.09
Firestone Tire & Rubber	10	9.76	Textron	13	27.93
Ford Motor	8	8.76	Universal American	8	3.47

SOURCE: *Fortune* (June, 1967).

regained their independence. On the other hand, there were two important disadvantages. In the first place, pools were of a temporary nature. They were usually made for a definite period of time, and there was always uncertainty as to the possibility of renewing the agreement to the satisfaction of all the parties concerned. In the second place, these agreements were not enforceable in the courts. In most cases such agreements were considered violations of the principles of common law. The Interstate Commerce Act in 1887 and the Sherman Antitrust Act in 1890 specifically were based on the assumption that most pools were intended to restrain trade and were therefore unlawful. But some kinds of pooling agreements are legal for certain types of foreign trade, agricultural, and marine insurance.

Trusts

In a *trust* the stockholders of the corporations involved deposited their stock certificates with one or more trustees and received in exchange trust certificates. The trustees thus acquired controlling interest of the corporations. As a consequence, they could select the members of the boards of directors of all the corporations whose stock they held. The holders of the trust certificates were entitled to receive whatever dividends might be declared by the directors of the respective concerns.

The most famous of the trusts was engineered by John D. Rockefeller and several of his associates. In 1870 Rockefeller and others had organized the Standard Oil Company, with capital of $1,000,000. Two years later the National Refiners Association, a pooling arrangement, was formed. This association controlled four fifths of the petroleum business. By 1879 it had acquired control of 90 percent of all the refineries and pipelines in the country. The instability of the organization, however, prompted the managers to seek a more nearly permanent form of association, which was done by placing the stock of the companies in the hands of a board of trustees consisting of nine members. The clamor of the public against the near-monopoly resulted in legal proceedings that finally, in 1892, culminated in an order by the Supreme Court to dissolve the trust. Companies were reorganized as constituent entities, but in the case of some of the companies involved it was frequently charged that control by the former officials was maintained by informal agreement.

Other great trusts that attracted attention at the time were the "Cotton Trust," the "Whiskey Trust," the "Lead Trust," and the "Sugar Trust."

Holding Companies

A *holding company* is a corporation whose function is to hold the common stock of other corporations. Most holding companies are not of the pure form since they are, in addition, operating companies. In its pure form, the holding company is the lineal descendant of the trust, and was evolved when the trust became unlawful.

A holder of 51 percent of the voting stock is able to control the corporation about as effectively as though he owned all the stock. The holding company, being accorded the recognition of a legal person, may be used for the purpose of acquiring a controlling interest in the stock of the companies whose policies and practices it is desired to control. Since the corporation has long enjoyed the status of a legal person, it was difficult for lawmakers to come to the conclusion that its prerogative of holding stocks of other corporations might be contrary to the public welfare. In cases where most of the stock is held by widely scattered stockholders or where only a small part of the stock has voting rights, ownership of less than 51 percent enables a person or a holding company to control the corporation.

In 1904 the Northern Securities Company, which held a controlling interest in the Northern Pacific and the Great Northern railways, was convicted of violating the Sherman Antitrust Act and ordered to dissolve. In 1911 the Standard Oil Company of New Jersey, which held a controlling interest in 37 subsidiaries, was convicted of violating the Sherman Antitrust Act. It was deemed guilty of the following practices:

> Rebates, preferences and other discriminatory practices in favor of the railroad companies, restraint and monopolization by control of pipelines, and unfair practices against competing pipelines; contracts with competitors in restraint of trade; unfair methods of competition, such as local price cutting at the points where necessary to suppress competition; espionage of the business of competitors, the operation of bogus independent companies, and payment of rebates on oil, with the like intent; the division of the United States into districts and the limiting of the operations of the various subsidiary corporations as to such districts so that competition in the sale of petroleum products between such corporations had been entirely destroyed. . . .[1]

The success of the federal government in these two notable antimonopoly cases did not mean that the holding company device ceased to be lawful or that it would become ineffective. It merely meant that the device must be used within the bounds of reason; what is unreasonable depends upon the judgment of the court in a given case. Many indictments of holding companies have been brought into court. Some have resulted in orders to dissolve, while others have been dismissed.

Mergers and Amalgamations

A *merger* is the absorption of one or more corporations by another. That is, one corporation acquires the stock of one or more other corporations and then dissolves these corporations. In an *amalgamation*, the corporations involved form a new corporation, exchange their stock for that of the new corporation, and all give up their individual charters. As far as results are concerned, there is no important distinction between a merger and an amalgamation.

In a holding company combination, the companies affected retain their corporate identities, and externally they may appear to be independent concerns. The different companies retain their organizations of directors and

[1] 221 U.S. 42-43 (1911).

officers; and, unless the entire stock of a subsidiary company is held by the holding company, some of the stock is retained by various stockholders.

The principal advantage of a merger or amalgamation as compared with a holding company is that these arrangements simplify organization and control. Control is direct, and it is not necessary to resort to the formality of utilizing the boards of directors of constituent companies, as is true in the case of the holding company. Another advantage is that it is more difficult to make a legal charge of monopoly against a merger or an amalgamation. Courts generally hold that a corporation cannot be convicted of violation of antitrust laws merely because it is big, nor are there any statutory limits as to the size of businesses. Moreover, when the assets of two or more companies are owned by one company, it is difficult to find a method by which they can be unscrambled without unduly burdening the companies involved.

If, however, it is possible to prove that a merger or an amalgamation is intended to monopolize production or trade, the move may be checked by the courts. According to the Clayton Act of 1914, and as amended in 1950, it is unlawful for one company to acquire the stock or assets of another where the purpose is to lessen competition and where the corporations are subject to regulation by the Federal Trade Commission.

In June, 1962, the Supreme Court's consideration of the acquisition of the G. R. Kinney Company by the Brown Shoe Company required a detailed analysis of the 1950 Amendment to the Clayton Act. The Amendment prohibits corporate acquisitions ". . . where in any line of commerce in any section of the country, the effect of such acquisition may be substantially to lessen competition, or to tend to create a monopoly." The Court's decision to prohibit the acquisition indicated a decided change in public policy toward the degree of centralized corporate control to be allowed. This decision was reinforced in the Von Grocery Company case, in 1965, when a merger between two supermarkets in California was blocked by the Court even though combined they did only 7.5 percent of the grocery business in the Los Angeles area.

Community of Interests

A *community of interests*, with respect to the control of corporations, exists when a small number of persons having other interests in common hold the stocks of two or more corporations. Examples of a community of interests are to be found where members of a family hold large blocks of stocks in the same companies. In a situation of this kind it is comparatively easy for the small group to control all the companies as effectively as though those companies were entirely owned by one group. A community of interests does not provide for a direct sharing of profits.

The cartel, which has long been employed in most European countries, is in some respects an application and an extension of the principle underlying communities of interests as a method of "coordinating" production by different firms. A *cartel* is a voluntary association of private business concerns for the purpose of coordinating marketing practices. It may engage in price fixing, limitation of production, the division of marketing territories, and the pooling of profits. Cartels have played an important part in international trade. But they are contrary to the letter and spirit of American antitrust laws. In 1961 a federal jury indicted 29 electric equipment firms for fixing prices and sent 7 corporate executives to jail. More recently, 8 major steel companies and 2 executives were indicted for conspiring to fix steel prices. In 1972 the Big Three auto firms were charged, but subsequently acquitted, with conspiring to set prices on fleet car purchases and leases. Also, the major oil companies have recently been charged with price fixing.

Interlocking Directorates

An *interlocking directorate* exists when two or more corporations have officials who serve on the board of directors of each company. Of course, it would not be fair to assume that such members would be disloyal to any one company on whose board they served. But in practice it is hardly conceivable that the similarity of interests would not result in a certain degree of cooperative action. The possibility for concerted action in the control of the companies involved is apparent. Because of charges that interlocking directorates were used as a means of restraining trade, the Clayton Act prohibits common directors of large national banks and of industrial corporations with a net worth of over $1 million when there is actual or potential competition. Railroad companies may have interlocking directorates with the approval of the Interstate Commerce Commission. With approval of the SEC, public-utility companies may have directors who also serve on the boards of banks.

CORPORATE SIZE, COSTS, AND PRICES

In the long run in a highly competitive market the price of a commodity tends to equal its per-unit production cost (including reasonable profits). Efficiency tends to lower production costs and hence the market prices of commodities. In most kinds of production the lowest unit cost can be achieved only if considerable quantities of the required factors of production are combined and directed by a central management. Even with efficient management, the lowest possible unit cost will not be realized if the scale of production is too small. On the other hand, if an attempt is made to produce on too large a scale, the quantity of the factors of production needed may be so large that dispersion of management and lack of coordinated effort may result in a higher unit cost than would be likely if the scale of production undertaken were smaller. (See pages 609-610 for a graphic analysis of this phenomenon.)

These considerations have given rise to the concept of optimum size of the business firm. *Optimum size* is that size which results in the lowest cost of production per unit. Hence, if all the firms in each industry are of optimum size and if competition in consumers' markets is effective, the market prices of products will be at the lowest possible level. This level will be just high enough to induce only the most efficient producers to provide the goods and services needed.

Whether some of our giant business firms are too large to achieve the utmost economy in production is a debatable question. Some economists and managers of business have expressed the opinion that certain firms may be too large and diverse in their operations; that is, production costs are higher than they would be if production were on a smaller scale or the range of products reduced.

ANTITRUST LAWS

The growing importance of big business in the life of the nation has led to the passage of both state and federal laws designed to regulate corporate combinations and practices. The most notable of these laws are five federal statutes; namely, the Sherman Antitrust Act (1890), the Clayton Act (1914), the Federal Trade Commission Act (1914), the Robinson-Patman Act (1936), and the Public Utility Holding Company Act (1935). In spite of these laws, however, a considerable degree of centralized corporate control of business in certain areas remains. Moreover, new corporate combinations can still be effected without incurring the disapproval of the courts. How to set legal limitations on the size of business organizations without impairing the right of free enterprise and hampering economical production is a continuing problem.

Sherman Antitrust Act

The first two sections of the Sherman Antitrust Act declare that (1) "every contract, combination . . . or conspiracy in restraint of trade or commerce among the several states is hereby declared to be illegal" and (2) "every person who shall monopolize, or . . . combine or conspire to monopolize any part of the trade or commerce among the several states . . . shall be deemed guilty of a misdemeanor. . . ." Section 7 provides for triple damages by making it possible for an injured party to "recover threefold the damages sustained by him and the costs of the suit" from a defendant who has been convicted of violating the law.

Although the statute condemns "every contract" intended to restrain trade by means of a monopoly, courts have generally held that the restraint must be "undue" and "unreasonable" before it is illegal. Of course, what is reasonable depends upon the judgment of the court. This "rule of reason" was emphatically enunciated by the United States Supreme Court in 1911 in the famous Standard Oil case.

In 1892 in the decision disposing of the suit by the government against the E. C. Knight Company, the Court held that a sugar trust composed of the companies that produced 98 percent of the sugar in the country was engaged in manufacturing and not commerce. Therefore it was decided that the sugar refiners were not guilty of violating the law. In the case against the United States Steel Corporation by the government in 1920, the Court held that mere bigness was not a proof of violation. This principle was also invoked in the International Harvester case of 1927. Subsequent cases, however, have held otherwise, beginning particularly with the Alcoa case in 1945, in which Judge Learned Hand indicated that the concentration of economic power is undesirable even in the absence of unfair practices.

Clayton Act

In spite of the Sherman Antitrust Act and of several convictions under the law, the tendency toward corporate combinations continued. In an attempt to "put teeth" into the Sherman Antitrust Act, the Clayton Act was passed in 1914. It prohibits (1) price discriminations that would result in lessening competition or tend to create monopoly; (2) tying clauses in contracts whereby buyers of goods are required to agree not to use the product of a competitor of the seller; (3) the acquisition of the stock of one corporation for the purpose of lessening "competition between the corporation whose stock is so acquired and the corporation making the acquisition"; and (4) interlocking directorates.

The Clayton Act exempted labor organizations from the application of the Sherman Act—at least, it seemed to. And it limited or restricted the issuance of labor injunctions for the purpose of breaking strikes. Consequently, the Act was often referred to as labor's *Magna Carta*, because it states that "the labor of human beings is not a commodity or article of commerce." Many labor leaders thought that under this law unions could not be considered as trusts or monopolies, hence subject to antitrust action. Unfortunately for their hopes, however, they were doomed to disappointment, for in 1921 in *Duplex Printing Press Company* v. *Deering*, the Court held that the Sherman Act applied to unions under certain conditions.

Section 7 of the Clayton Act was amended by the Anti-Merger Act, otherwise known as the Celler-Kefauver Amendment, in 1950 so that now it is illegal for one corporation to acquire the assets, as well as the stock, of another company where the acquisition of such assets might (1) "substantially lessen competition between them," (2) "restrain commerce," or (3) "tend to create a monopoly."

Federal Trade Commission Act

The Federal Trade Commission Act declares "that unfair methods of competition in commerce are hereby declared unlawful. The commission is hereby empowered and directed to prevent persons, partnerships, corporations, except banks, and common carriers subject to the acts which regulate commerce, from using unfair methods in commerce." [2]

Originally the functions of the Commission were to investigate reports of violations of the Sherman Antitrust Act and other antitrust laws and to recommend needed legislation for the control of monopolies. The Wheeler-Lea Act (1938) gave the Commission the power of initiative to restrain business practices that it considers detrimental to public interest, including false advertising and the adulteration of manufactured products.

Robinson-Patman Act

The Clayton Act was amended by the passage in 1936 of the Robinson-Patman Act, which was primarily designed to prevent "unfair" competition in trade by the giving or the receipt of discounts or services when such act would amount to discrimination and result in a substantial reduction of competition. Unfortunately, however, it is often very difficult to apply the law in particular cases.

The Public Utility Holding Company Act

The purposes of the Public Utility Holding Company Act (1935), the provisions of which are administered by the Securities and Exchange Commission (SEC), are: (1) to eliminate the issuance of securities on the basis of fictitious asset values; (2) to eliminate and prevent an unnecessary "pyramiding" of holding companies in the public utility industry; (3) to limit powers of holding companies over their subsidiaries; and (4) to prevent the development or extension of holding companies that have little or no worthwhile relation to operating companies. The law contains what has been called a "death sentence clause," which requires the dissolution or simplification of holding company structures that are considered unjustifiably complex.

[2] 36 U.S. Stat. 717.

Current Antitrust Merger Policy

With the large number of mergers and the high degree of business integration taking place in industry in recent years, the Justice Department in 1968 issued a 27-page set of "merger guidelines." There were, for example, over 12,500 mergers in manufacturing and mining alone during the 1960s. The purpose of the guidelines is to enlighten businessmen on the direction of antitrust enforcement. The guidelines indicated that the antitrust department will continue to challenge the following broad types of mergers:

1. Horizontal mergers involving direct competitors, where in highly concentrated markets the acquiring and the acquired firm each account for as little as 4 percent of their market.
2. Vertical mergers involving suppliers and their customers, such as shoe manufacturers and shoe retailers, where the supplier accounts for 10 percent or more of total market sales and the customer accounts for 6 percent or more of total market purchases.
3. Conglomerate mergers where the merger creates a danger of reciprocal buying, and where the acquiring company's promotional resources are so great as to enhance an acquired company's existing dominance in its field.

Because they are still relatively new, and because their problems are somewhat novel and in need of extensive analysis, the guidelines on the conglomerates are still a bit vague compared to the guidelines on the older types of horizontal and vertical types of integration.

FAIR-TRADE LAWS

In 1931 California passed a resale price-maintenance law that made it possible for manufacturers to set the retail prices of their products. Within a few years nearly all the states had similar laws, although the courts in several of the states had declared these laws invalid. Most of these fair-trade laws contain a "nonsigner" provision whereby a manufacturer may enter into a resale price agreement with only one retailer which makes the agreement binding on all other retailers in that state handling the manufacturer's product even though the others have not signed the agreement.

Since most of the merchandise affected by the state price-maintenance laws is bought and sold in interstate trade, such laws were contrary to the aims of the Sherman Act. In order to remove the evident conflict between the state laws and the federal statute, Congress passed the Miller-Tydings Act in 1937. This law exempted from prosecution firms that agreed to maintain prices in states having price-maintenance laws. From 1937 until

1951 price competition between retailers in the sale prices of many articles of merchandise practically disappeared in most of the states.

In 1951 the Supreme Court ruled that resale price agreements were not binding on nonsigners. As a result of this decision, keen competition and drastic price cuts by retailers of fair-trade merchandise followed; but not for long. The proponents of fair-trade practices quickly marshalled their influence and persuaded Congress to pass the McGuire Act in 1952. This Act amended the Federal Trade Commission Act by providing that fair-trade agreements are enforceable in states having fair-trade statutes and that such agreements may be binding on nonsigners as well as signers of such agreements. Thus, an agreement between a manufacturer and a single merchant in a state that legalizes fair-trade agreements becomes binding on all other merchants handling the same merchandise.

Some manufacturers contend that fair-trade practices enable them to stabilize the prices of their products which, in turn, makes it possible for them to plan production and sales, and thus to realize economies which can be passed on to consumers in the way of lower prices. Critics of these price-maintenance laws have pointed out that laws of this kind encourage monopolistic prices and discourage price competition. Nor by any means are all retailers in agreement that the so-called fair-trade laws are desirable or necessary. Moreover, some economists argue that, while such laws may make it possible for manufacturers of nationally advertised products to make more profits in the short run, it is likely that in the long run the practice of price-maintenance will stimulate increased competition and thus make it more difficult for the same manufacturers to maintain their positions in their respective industries.

DOES BIG BUSINESS THREATEN FREE ENTERPRISE?

Most serious-minded and capable students who have studied the economic and political significance of large-scale enterprise in our economy seem to agree that the existence of large business firms does not of itself pose a threat to the continuation of free enterprise. Of course, when there are only a few large firms in an industry, the competitive situation is different from what it is when there are hundreds of producers in an industry, as is the case in some industries and fields of commerce. This fact does not imply that large-scale management and production are less desirable than production by a large number of small producers. The main question here is: Is big business sufficiently competitive on the basis of prices and quality of products?

The prices of many of the products of large producers are "administered," that is, fixed in advance, which is not true of the prices of other goods, agricultural products especially. Administered prices are fixed on the basis of estimated costs, including profits. If such prices do not meet with acceptance in the market, however, the producer must readjust the prices of his products; otherwise he will suffer financial loss. He may, of course, suffer a loss even if he reduces prices.

In only a few instances must the buying public rely entirely on the product of any one manufacturer. The essential thing about a product is the service that the product can render. When we observe the situation in the marketplace, we almost always discover that there are two or more brands of a product, any one of which will provide the essential service needed. In a free society consumers have the opportunity of selecting and buying the brand of merchandise that appears to offer the best value for the money.

In setting their prices, the managers of large-scale enterprises in recent times have been influenced primarily by long-run profit prospects. Any producer who fails to be guided by long-run considerations only encourages competition. Of course, it is possible to give examples where even large-scale businesses have apparently been more concerned with making profits immediately than in the more remote future.

It is necessary for government to scrutinize continuously the practices of business management of all types and dimensions, for by means of collusive practices or by outright integration business firms can engage in monopolistic practices that are detrimental to public welfare and might even threaten the existence of free enterprise. Some monitoring by government should be utilized for constructive purposes. We have statutes that are definitely designed to prevent corporate practices that would endanger the continuation of free enterprise in particular industrial and business areas. In a dynamic society of the type in which we live, it should not be surprising that these laws need to be amended from time to time. It is highly important, of course, that the laws be honestly and intelligently enforced. This is especially true if we are to rectify economic abuses resulting from extensive economic integration and consolidation.

That economies can result from large-scale production is easily understood, and as long as there is effective competition the results of these economies will be passed on to consumers in the way of lower prices. But lacking effective competition, big business must be prepared to accept increasing government regulation—direct or indirect—of various types.

Apparently, the federal government is not opposed to big business. But it does appear to be the conviction of government that giant enterprises should grow from within, and not by absorbing other firms. This was the theory propounded by the Justice Department in the 1960s in attacking the proposed acquisition by the Humble Oil and Refining Company of the

Western marketing and refining facilities of the Tidewater Oil Company. Likewise, it was the rationale behind the court order requiring ITT to divest itself of Hawaiian Telephone Company in 1972.

In spite of continued integration, however, the total number of business firms in our economy is continually increasing. In the ten-year period 1961-1970 the total number of business enterprises in the United States increased by about one million. During 1972, 317,000 new businesses incorporated, but nearly 10,000 old corporations went out of business due to bankruptcy alone. Thousands of other firms quietly closed their doors for other reasons. Starting a business involves risk, but the opportunity for profit induces hundreds of thousands of individuals annually to try their hands as entrepreneurs. More important than the success or failure of an individual business, however, is the freedom in our economic system that permits an individual to own property or the means of production, to go into business for himself, or to work at any job or profession for which he is qualified.

SUMMARY

1. Much of the production in our economy is carried on by large-scale enterprises, which are made possible by the corporate device as a form of business organization.

2. The Small Business Act that was passed by Congress in 1953 is designed to help small business firms by providing advisory service, financial aid, and technical assistance.

3. There are several advantages that accrue from the growth of large-scale enterprise, including economy in production, integration of productive processes, utilization of by-products, diversification of production, increased possibilities for research, reduction of competition, and increased advertising possibilities.

4. Broadly speaking, business combinations are vertical, horizontal, or complementary combinations, although they frequently have two or all three of these characteristics. In recent years the conglomerate type of integration has been gaining considerable popularity.

5. Today, the usual method of effecting a combination of business firms is by the use of the holding-company device, merger, or amalgamation, although other methods may be employed to bring about a centralization of control.

6. The most important federal laws that relate to the control of business combinations and monopolistic practices are: the Sherman Antitrust Act (1890), the Clayton Antitrust Act (1914), the Federal Trade Commission Act (1914), the Public Utility Holding Company Act (1935), and the Robinson-Patman Act (1936). It is often charged that the federal fair-trade laws, the Miller-Tydings Act (1937), and the McGuire Act (1952), encourage the growth of centralized business control of prices.

7. The economies resulting from large-scale enterprise benefit consumers where the demand is elastic and as long as there is a workable and effective degree of competition.

NEW TERMS

Vertical integration, *p. 659*
Horizontal integration, *p. 659*
Complementary integration, *p. 659*
Conglomerate integration, *p. 659*
Pool, *p. 661*
Trust, *p. 663*
Holding company, *p. 663*
Merger, *p. 664*

Amalgamation, *p. 664*
Community of interests, *p. 665*
Cartel, *p. 666*
Interlocking directorates, *p. 666*
Optimum size, *p. 667*
Antitrust laws, *p. 667*
"Rule of reason," *p. 668*
Fair-trade laws, *p. 670*

QUESTIONS FOR DISCUSSION AND ANALYSIS

1. How does one distinguish a small business from a large business? Why should the government have a policy of aid to small businesses?

2. Income reports indicate corporate profits before taxes for some companies range from $250 million to more than $1 billion. In these corporations executive salaries range from $50,000 to more than $800,000. Do you think there should be any limitation on either corporate profit or executive salaries? Why or why not?

3. What reasons account for the growth of big business? Which one would you say is the most important?

4. Would car buyers obtain a better deal if automobiles were made under conditions of pure competition rather than under the present conditions of large-scale oligopoly? Explain.

5. In 1973 private industry employed more than 375,000 persons and spent $20.3 billion in research and development. What effect might this have on the growth of large-scale enterprise?

6. (a) What is the Sherman Antitrust Act? (b) When was it passed? (c) Has it done away with corporate combinations?

7. (a) Have mergers and amalgamations become more important than the other forms of corporate combinations? (b) How do you account for the trend?

8. The Northern Manufacturing Company, located in Pennsylvania, manufactures four kinds of plastic products. It owns several patents for the products that it produces. It has assets valued at $15,000,000 and has outstanding $8,000,000 of common stock and $2,000,000 of 6 percent noncumulative preferred stock. The bonded indebtedness is represented by $4,000,000 of 5 percent 20-year bonds.

The Southern Manufacturing Company, located in Tennessee, also manufactures a line of plastic products, some of which closely resemble in nature and use those produced by the Northern Manufacturing Company. It owns the patents for its products and also 75,000 acres of timberland which supplies a considerable amount of the materials that it uses. The assets of the company are valued at $20,000,000. The outstanding stock of the company amounts to $19,000,000, of which $9,000,000 is 6 percent cumulative preferred. There are no bonds.

The Mid-Western Company is located in Ohio. It manufactures most of the chemical products used by the Northern and the Southern companies. Its assets are valued at $12,000,000, and it has outstanding $10,000,000 in common stock.

Assuming the above facts:

(a) Would a combination of the three companies have any possible advantages to any or all of the companies? Why? Might there be any disadvantages? Explain.

(b) If the companies decided to combine, what methods of combination might be employed? What would be the advantages and disadvantages of each?

(c) If a combination occurred, what type would it be?

(d) If a holding company were formed to control the companies, what total amount of stock of the three companies would it be necessary for the holding company to obtain? What would be the total amount of assets that it would then control?

9. Do you think that fair-trade laws which permit "resale price maintenance" protect or prevent competition? Explain your position.

10. The Department of Justice has declared at times that a pending merger will create a monopoly or otherwise restrain trade. Such was the case in the proposed merger between Bethlehem Steel Company and Youngstown Sheet and Tube Company, the second and the fifth largest producers in the steel industry in 1959. Combined they would have produced more than one fifth of the nation's total steel output, still less than that of the U.S. Steel Corporation. In a similar, but smaller scale operation, the merger of two grocery store chains that comprised 7.5 percent of the Los Angeles market was blocked by the Justice Department in 1965. Do you think that such decisions, which prejudge the effects of a merger, are just? Why or why not?

SUGGESTED READINGS

Adams, Walter. *The Structure of American Industry*. New York: The Macmillan Company, 1971.

Adams, Walter, and Horace M. Gray. *Monopoly in America: The Government as Promoter*. New York: The Macmillan Company, 1955.

Andreano, Ralph L. *Superconcentration/Supercorporation*. Andover, Mass.: Warner Modular Publications, Inc., 1973.

Broude, Henry W. *Steel Decisions and the National Economy*. New Haven: Yale University Press, 1964.

Demsetz, Harold. *The Market Concentration Doctrine*. Washington, D.C.: American Enterprise Institute for Public Policy. AIE-Hoover Policy Study 7, August, 1973.

Fusilier, H. Lee, and Jerome C. Darnell. *Competition and Public Policy: Cases in Antitrust*. Englewood Cliffs, N.J.: Prentice-Hall, Inc., 1971.

Galbraith, J. Kenneth. *American Capitalism: The Concept of Countervailing Power*. Boston: Houghton Mifflin Company, 1952.

————————. *The New Industrial State*. Boston: Houghton Mifflin Company, 1967.

—————. *Economics and the Public Purpose*. Boston, Mass.: Houghton Mifflin Company, 1973.

Glover, J. D. *The Attack on Big Business*. Cambridge: Harvard University Press, Graduate School of Business Administration, 1954.

Kaplan, A. D. H. *Big Business in a Competitive System*. Washington, D.C.: The Brookings Institution, 1954.

Leonard, William N. *Business Size, Market Power and Public Policy*. New York: Thomas Y. Crowell Company, 1969.

Mueller, Willard F. *A Primer on Monopoly and Competition*. New York: Random House, Inc., 1970.

Nelson, Ralph L. *Concentration in the Manufacturing Industries in the United States*. New Haven: Yale University Press, 1963.

Sayles, Leonard R. *Individualism and Big Business.* New York: McGraw-Hill Book Company, 1963.

Scherer, F. M. *Industrial Market Structure and Economic Performance*. Chicago: Rand McNally & Company, 1970.

Shepard, William G. *Market Power and Economic Welfare*. New York: Random House, Inc., 1970.

31

Government
Regulation
of Prices

PREVIEW Not all prices are determined by the free forces of supply and demand or by administered pricing. The government has considerable influence on the prices of many goods and services. Federal, state, and local governments, for example, determine the prices charged by the many business enterprises which they operate directly. Public Service Commissions established by the government regulate the services offered and the rates charged by the many public utilities, such as gas, electricity, and telephone companies, throughout the country. The transportation industry is subject to traffic rates approved by appropriate government agencies. Tariffs on imports likewise have a bearing on the prices of domestic as well as imported products. Minimum wage laws affect the price of labor and indirectly the products of labor, and the Federal Reserve can influence the rates of interest charged by banks. Farm pricing, of course, has been a long-standing example of government regulation of prices.

In times of emergency the federal government has resorted to compulsory price controls on all goods and services. At other times wage-price guideposts have been established. Currently there is much discussion regarding the feasibility of a permanent incomes policy for the U.S. economy.

In the preceding chapters we analyzed the principles of price determination under conditions in which government played only a minor role. In reality the government—and especially the federal government—exercises considerable influence on the prices of many goods and services. Although certain direct methods are used by government to regulate prices, the methods usually employed are indirect, and for this reason are not so apparent to the public.

Public control over prices ranges from fixing the prices of goods and services the government sells (such as postal services and printed materials) to that of affecting interest rates through its borrowing. In its effort to control prices, government may use direct means, such as regulating public-utility rates, or it may use indirect methods, as it has in the past to successfully pressure the steel, copper, banking, and other major industries to rescind publicized price increases.

WHY THE GOVERNMENT INTERFERES WITH THE MARKET

The philosophy of laissez-faire capitalism that was generally accepted during most of the nineteenth century assumed that price fixing or control was not a major function of government. Public utilities at that time were few and relatively unimportant. For the most part, it was thought that the existence of free enterprise and the forces of competition were adequate to bring about fair and reasonable prices. The unrestricted operation of natural economic laws, it was assumed, would cause resources to be devoted to the production of those goods and services most desired by the people. Not only would prices be fair, it was argued, but the public welfare would be promoted much more effectively than could be the case if government directed production and controlled prices.

In the course of time, however, circumstances have created conditions that make it appear feasible for government to take a more active part in the determination of production and prices. Specifically, there are certain fields in which the people have demanded that government itself engage in production on a far wider scope than formerly was thought desirable. These include highway construction, the building of schools and the undertaking of other educational projects, the construction and maintenance of hospitals and general health facilities, electric power production, urban redevelopment, and enforcement of antipollution measures.

Also inducing government regulation of prices is unrestrained competition which, instead of promoting consumer welfare, has sometimes encouraged monopolies or near-monopolies that have not always been operated in the maximum interest of the public.

Furthermore, the social impact of the Great Depression in the 1930s, of two world wars, plus involvement in two limited wars, all occurring during the past 50 to 60 years, has brought some major adjustments to the capitalistic order in the United States. The disorganizing effects of the catastrophes required drastic and unusual measures to maintain certain economic activities.

As a result of protracted experience in dealing with emergency conditions in the economy, the attitudes of people concerning the relation of government to business and prices have undergone a change. Moreover, the nature of international relations is such as to constitute a continuing emergency. Partly in connection with our desire to win and to maintain international friendships during a period of world tension, the federal government has found it expedient and worthwhile to extend economic and military aid to nations in almost all parts of the world. From 1945 to 1973 the cost of this aid was more than $150 billion. Much of this aid came in the decade following World War II in the form of grants and loans to countries in Western Europe for the purpose of rebuilding their war-torn industries and restoring their military strength. Nearly all the rest of such aid has been extended to countries in the Far East, Middle East, Latin America, and Africa for development purposes, such as building modern factories and transportation facilities. Although the purpose of these grants and loans was not to influence prices of American-made goods, it is hardly conceivable that such huge expenditures could be made without affecting the prices of many commodities in the United States.

GOVERNMENT INDUSTRIES AND PRICE POLICIES

For a long time after the federal government was inaugurated in 1789, the post office was the only important commercial enterprise of the government. It was not until 1900 that Congress authorized the building of Alaskan railroads, and a few years later, the Panama Canal. Both the railroads and the canal were, by the standards of the time, costly projects. Since then, and especially during recent decades, the industrial enterprises owned and operated by the federal government have increased in number and variety. They include those conducted by the Tennessee Valley Authority, inland barge lines, a housing authority, several power facilities, financing corporations, and many others.

Before the repeal of the Eighteenth Amendment to the Constitution (the liquor prohibition amendment), state governments had not engaged in many important businesses. There were some instances, including the ownership and operation of docks and wharves, ferries, printing plants, irrigation projects, cement plants, mills, and warehouses, that were exceptions to the rule; but they were of comparatively little importance. With the repeal of the Eighteenth Amendment, however, many of the states decided to monopolize the sale of alcoholic beverages within their respective boundaries. At present about one third of the states exercise such a monopoly. On the whole, it appears that the experience of the states has been satisfactory. The amount of investment is relatively small, sales are made for cash, there is little or no fixed expense in the way of long-term debts, the number of employees is not large, and, as a result, the liquor stores are generally very profitable.

The ownership and operation of some types of industrial and commercial enterprises by municipalities is the rule and not an exception. The more important enterprises of this kind include waterworks, railways, asphalt plants, parking garages, electricity, and, in some cases, gas utilities and transportation facilities. In many cases, municipally owned enterprises are natural monopolies.

As a general rule, the policy of government in the United States has been not to engage in a business or industry in competition with private enterprise. At the same time, this policy cannot be strictly observed if government is to undertake the production of any good or service and thereby control its price. For example, government-owned schools, hospitals, roads, power dams, and the post office system compete to a certain extent with some types of private enterprise.

In any economy such as that of the United States, the justification for government ownership of an industry is usually partly economic and partly social. The policy of public ownership in this country is seldom justified on purely economic grounds. For example, one reason for the operation of state liquor stores is the desire of the people for the state government to maintain a limited control over the consumption of alcoholic beverages. In the case of the post office, it is claimed that the nature of mail service and the educational possibilities of mail communication make it desirable for the post office facilities to be owned and operated, or at least controlled, by the central government. In the case of multipurpose dams that develop electricity, among other things, it is contended that in most instances they are too costly for private enterprise to build.

In fixing prices for government enterprises, rates may be set without following full cost-pricing guidelines. Unlike a private enterprise, a government-owned enterprise does not have to earn a profit or even cover production costs in order to continue in existence. Deficits, if they occur, can be met out of tax revenues or by borrowing from the public.

In some cases certain government monopolies are justified on fiscal grounds. For example, the manufacture and sale of tobacco products by the state is a favorite monopoly in some countries. In the past the production of salt, matches, and camphor has been the object of government monopoly in certain nations. Since such articles have a rather inelastic demand, they may be easily produced and sold by government at a profit, even when production methods are uneconomical.

PUBLIC-UTILITY RATES

Those industries that are recognized by law as being "affected with a public interest" to an exceptional degree are operated under special franchises that shield them from unlimited direct competition. Usually these are industries in which the size of the market is relatively small compared to the optimum scale of operation. Consequently, in open competition the industry could not support many firms at this optimum size. Therefore a franchise is given to one or a few companies to provide the service to the public. In turn, the franchised firm must accept the regulatory provisions of the granting government, whether it be federal, state, or local. Examples of public utilities include railroads, gas, water, telephone, and electric-power companies. They provide services that are essential to all or, at least, to most of the people. They are expected to serve the public without discrimination and at uniform prices. Because of the traditional attitude of individualism and opposition to state control of industry in this country, the public-utility field has expanded slowly. Only when experience has demonstrated the impracticability of competition as the regulator of price has government in this country undertaken to regulate prices by means of franchises and utility commissions.

The Problems of Public-Utility Prices or Rates

When government is confronted with the necessity of fixing public-utility rates it faces a twofold problem: (1) the rate structure must be such that it will permit a fair return on capital invested in the enterprise, and (2) specific rates for particular kinds of services must be established.

The Rate Level. In controlling railroad and other public-utility rates, both the public and the investors in the enterprises must be considered. While the public is entitled to fair rates, bondholders, who have loaned funds to the utilities, are also entitled to receive the contract rate of interest on their loans. In addition, the stockholders are entitled to earn some profits. Otherwise the investors will be penalized, and funds for the replacement or expansion of the enterprises will not be forthcoming. Moreover, by setting rates so low that the earning of interest and profits is impossible, the government would in effect confiscate private property for public use, which is prohibited by the Constitution.

What, then, is a fair rate of return to the owners of public utilities, and how is it calculated? Should a public-utility company expect to earn the same rate on its investment that other well-managed concerns in competitive industry earn? In this connection we must not forget that the public-utility company operates under a franchise that gives it a high degree of monopoly. For that reason, its income is more certain and more stable than that of a firm operating under more competitive conditions. Most states and federal utility regulatory agencies indicate that public-utility companies should have an opportunity to earn 5 to 8 percent on the value of their investments.

Ordinarily the value of an investment is calculated on the basis of the expected yield in terms of income from the investment. In the case of a public-utility company, however, the yield depends upon the specific rates that the company is permitted to charge. The value of the investment, therefore, must be determined in some other manner. Regulatory commissions and courts tend to use one of two methods: (1) *original or historical cost, less depreciation, and* (2) *cost of reproduction, new, less depreciation.*

According to the first method, the actual cost of building and equipping the enterprise is determined and depreciation allowances are deducted, leaving the present value of the assets of the company.

In using the second method, an estimate is made of the cost of providing a similar plant and equipment at current prices. From this estimated cost, appropriate allowances for depreciation are deducted in order to arrive at the present value. Obviously, if present reproduction costs have increased. the result is to give a higher value to the investment of the company than would be shown by the use of the historical cost method.

Courts and public-utility commissions have also used the *prudent-investment concept* in arriving at the value of the assets owned by a public-utility company. In counting the expenditures made in acquiring its assets, a company is permitted to include only those expenditures that would be made by a prudent and honest management. The prudent-investment concept establishes the value of the investment at a figure that is consistent with the quality and the amount of the services provided by the company. A higher investment figure, resulting from the inclusion of unjustifiable expenditures, would cause the investment figure to be greater and would provide a basis for permitting the company to charge higher prices.

Having ascertained the value of the investment, it is simple to calculate the amount that would constitute a fair amount of income to the company. For example, assume that the value of the investment is determined to be $100 million and that a fair rate of return is 6 percent. The level of rates should be such as to permit the company to earn an annual net profit of $6 million (6 percent of $100 million).

Incidentally, in periods of inflation and rising prices, public-utility companies are inclined to favor the use of the reproduction-cost method in determining the value of their investments for rate-making purposes. On the other hand, in periods of deflation and falling prices they may be more favorable to the idea of basing rates on original production costs. Unfortunately the rulings of the courts have not been consistent as to which method should be followed.

Specific Rates. Some of the problems encountered in fixing specific utility rates or tariffs may be appreciated by considering railroad rates. Different ton-mile rates (the charge for hauling a ton of freight one mile) must be fixed for different classes of goods. Obviously the same charge should not be made for hauling a ton of coal as is made for hauling a ton of silk. Nor would it appear reasonable to charge as much per ton-mile for hauling a ton of live cattle as for a ton of dressed meat.

One method of computing a specific rate or tariff for a particular class of freight is to allocate to each class of commodities a proportional amount of the fixed costs of the railroad. After such an allocation has been made, the amount of the direct cost, such as the cost of handling and special services, can be added. A moment's reflection, however, reveals that this procedure is impracticable, for most costs—especially fixed costs—are joint in their nature; that is, they are costs that cannot be identified and charged to any one or more classes of goods or services. For example, money obtained from a bond issue may be used to build a roadbed over which both passengers and coal are hauled; and the interest payment on the bonds is an annual joint expense or cost. It is difficult to unscramble—except by arbitrary procedure—fixed costs and to isolate the proportional part of each fixed cost belonging to any one class of freight or passenger service. Moreover, certain bulky goods could not "stand" a charge that would cover their proportional cost of transportation. Certain goods, like hay, coal, and timber, can be transported to places where they are wanted only if the cost of transportation is partly subsidized by rates charged for commodities the value of which is more concentrated.

Before the passage of the Interstate Commerce Act (1887), it was common practice for railroads to deliberately and unhesitatingly follow the principle of "charging what the traffic will bear." Now with our various federal and state commissions for the regulation of railroads and other public utilities, arbitrary rate discrimination is not permitted. In the case of the railroads there are many rates, but each rate is set by the appropriate governmental authority and with the public interest, as well as that of the railroads, in mind.

Similar problems arise in the truck transportation industry, where thousands of rates, or tariffs, must be established for the multitude of commodities carried by both local and over-the-road haulers.

Just how can a utility commission determine whether the rates for a particular service are fair? For example, should households and industrial users of electricity be charged different rates? If so, what should be the differential? The commission must study the whole problem of the rate level and rate structure with reference to the nature and the amount of the investment by the utility company and attempt to arrive at a conclusion as to what are reasonable rates for each type of user. Determining just what is reasonable involves giving attention to the probable elasticity of the demand for electricity when used for household and industrial purposes, and to the costs occasioned by providing services to each type of user. If too high a rate is set, the amount of electricity sold will not be as high as it would be if the rate were lower. This implies that in fixing public-utility rates there may be discrimination in the sense that the charge for some classes of services may not be proportional to the total costs of the service. But rate discrimination in this sense, when scientifically and fairly imposed, is justifiable and conducive to the public welfare.

Changes in Public-Utility Rates

As a rule, public-utility rates lag behind changes in the general price level. Unlike competitive prices, they are not readily responsive to changes in demand and supply. In periods of falling prices, they are not reduced as rapidly as other prices. On the other hand, a rise in prices in general is not ordinarily accompanied by a corresponding rise in public-utility rates. One reason for the lag is the time it takes to prepare and process an application for a rate increase. Before permitting a change in rates, the regulatory agencies feel that they should have conclusive evidence which will justify a change.

Public-Utility Rates—Theory and Practice

The difficulties that are encountered in trying to fix public-utility rates in accordance with theoretical principles can be appreciated by reference to a few famous cases decided by the United States Supreme Court. The basis for public utility regulation was established in the case of *Munn* v. *Illinois* in 1877, when the Court ruled that the state could regulate any industry clothed with a public interest. In 1898 in a second important case, that of *Smyth* v. *Ames*, the Court ruled in effect that utility rates should be sufficient to permit a "fair return on a fair investment." In deciding whether the rates fixed for a railroad company would yield "a fair return on a fair value of the property," Justice Harlan stated:

> . . . in order to ascertain that value, the original cost of construction, the amount expended in permanent improvements, the amount and market value of its bonds and stock, the present as compared with the original cost of construction, the probable earning capacity of the property under particular rates prescribed by statute, and the sum required to meet operating expenses, are all matters for consideration, and are to be given such weight as may be just and right in each case.[1]

More recently, in 1944 in the case of the *Federal Power Commission* v. *Hope Natural Gas Company* the Court held that in fixing rates, public-utility commissions should be guided by what was a new concept: "the end-result doctrine." It was the opinion of the Court that the overall rate structure should provide the company with earnings sufficient to attract whatever

[1] 169 U.S. 466, pp. 546-547.

amount of new capital might be needed to supply the public with necessary services. This ruling gave public-utility commissions and companies more latitude in fixing rates.

At the same time, this ruling did not provide a simple criterion that is definite enough to enable public-utility commissions to fix rates that are unquestionably fair to both consumers and investors. For example, suppose the number of customers, including households and industries, of an electric-power company is increasing. And suppose further that the company has almost reached its capacity to supply light and power. How much more capital does the company need for an adequate expansion of its facilities? Is it likely that the demand for electricity in its territory will continue to increase? Or is it possible that the demand will level off, or even decrease? Is technology in the electric industry changing so that certain present-day methods of production and distribution will soon be out-of-date? What other factors should be considered? And, finally, what rate is adequate to enable the company to earn sufficient interest and profit to attract the capital it needs? These questions, as well as others that might be raised, enable us to appreciate some of the difficulties that are to be encountered in an attempt to apply "the end-result doctrine" in particular cases.

Thus, while it seems necessary for government to regulate the prices of certain natural monopolies, the problem of fixing the prices in each case is extremely difficult.

TARIFFS ON IMPORTED GOODS

Since early in our history the federal government has pursued a policy of "protecting" certain American industries by levying taxes on imported goods. Such tariffs, or taxes, have been designed to protect our home industries from foreign competition by enabling domestic producers to sell their goods at higher prices than would otherwise be possible. A number of specific arguments have been advanced to justify a protective-tariff policy. Broadly speaking, however, it appears that the general public has supported a protective-tariff policy because of the feeling that such a policy encourages national economic development and prosperity. Problems of tariffs will be discussed in Chapter 42.

GOVERNMENT CONTROL OF INTEREST RATES

The regulation of interest rates, the price of borrowing money, has long been regarded as a prerogative of government. In this country, the states have established legal and maximum contract rates of interest. *Legal rates of interest* apply to judgments, matured obligations, and contracts for loans in which no rate is specified. In such cases interest not in excess of the legal rate may be collected. Most states have comprehensive small-loan statutes that fix separate maximum rates for loans ranging up to several hundred dollars. It is not uncommon for rates on some of these loans to be as high as 3 percent monthly, or 36 percent annually.

The Federal Reserve through its monetary policies, especially through the establishment of discount rates, has a strong influence on the price of borrowed funds. The Treasury, too, as a result of its demand for borrowed funds can substantially influence interest rates in the money market. Moreover, the interest rate ceiling imposed on long-term securities is in a way a method of setting a price.

Federal government funds made available to borrowers at low interest rates also affect interest rates in general. Examples of federal agencies that help in this way to provide funds or to guarantee loans include the agencies under the Federal National Mortgage Association, loans by the Small Business Administration, loans to educational institutions, and the types of government-sponsored credit institutions that supply agricultural credit.

In addition, legislation enacted by Congress, such as the "Truth-in-Lending Bill," which requires all lenders to quote interest rates in terms of the average annual rate, has had some effect on interest rates in certain money markets.

MINIMUM-WAGE LAWS

Minimum-wage laws are a form of price regulation by government. Such laws are designed to put a floor under wages by fixing the least amount that employers may pay for certain kinds of work. The history of minimum-wage legislation in the United States is long and involved. In 1912 Massachusetts passed the first state law providing for a minimum-wage commission with the power to establish minimum wages in industries that appeared to be exploiting the labor of women and minors. Within a decade 14 other states had passed similar laws, most of which were invalidated by a ruling of the United States Supreme Court which held that such laws violated the property rights of employers.

Under the National Industrial Recovery Act of 1933, codes adopted under its provisions contained stipulations as to minimum wages. The general aim of these provisions was to increase the purchasing power in the hands of the public by increasing wages and thereby to cause an increased demand for goods and services. This, it was hoped, would increase employment and perhaps raise prices from their low level.

Other federal minimum-wage laws include the Davis-Bacon Act (1931) and the Walsh-Healey Act (1936), both of which relate to wages paid for work under federal government contracts, and the Civil Aeronautics Act (1938), which applies to the pay of pilots and copilots on airlines.

The federal Fair Labor Standards Act of 1938 requires that minimum wages be paid in most industries other than agriculture. The law also places "a ceiling" over hours by requiring that payment at a rate of time and one half must be made for more than 40 hours a week of work. The law applies only to industries engaged in interstate commerce, and provisions of the law have practically eliminated child labor in most industries. In addition to the federal laws, about half of the states have some kind of a minimum-wage law.

It is not always clear what the effects are when an attempt is made to raise wages by means of minimum-wage laws. In a majority of cases, however, the enactment of a minimum-wage law will result in some increase in unemployment. The reason is easily detected. In a low-wage industry some firms are probably not operating at a profit level. This means that some employees may be paid more than their labor is worth to the employer. If wage rates are raised still higher, the necessity for laying off some or all of the employees is apparent. In this respect the adverse effect of a raise in the minimum wage may have its greatest impact on those we most desire to help, the youth, the marginal worker, and the hard-core unemployable. The higher wage rate will make it more difficult for employers to profitably hire or retain these people.

On the other hand, an increase in minimum wages may stimulate efforts on the part of employers to find ways to improve managerial efficiency and to increase the productivity of workers. Furthermore, it is argued that the increased purchasing power in the hands of workers resulting from the higher minimum wage will increase consumer demand for goods and services. This, in turn, will increase production and employment. Although a number of studies have been made of the number of persons directly losing their jobs due to the imposition, or raising, of the minimum-wage rate, there are few studies to show the number who may have found employment as a result of higher consumer spending.

FAIR-TRADE PRICING

Some federal and state laws seem designed to promote a policy of widespread competition without interfering directly in the fixing of prices to consumers. This appears to be true in the case of the Robinson-Patman Act (1936), which prevents wholesalers from selling to large retailers at a greater discount than is allowed small merchants except as the larger discounts can be justified on the basis of quantity purchases. The law was designed partly to give a degree of protection to small dealers in their competition with the large chain stores.

On the other hand, the Miller-Tydings Act (1937) permitted agreements between manufacturers and retailers to maintain retail prices when approved by state fair-trade laws. Thus, the manufacturer could establish the retail price of his goods in spite of the Sherman (1890) and the Clayton (1914) Acts, which were designed to prevent combinations to control production and prices. Under most state fair-trade laws, all nonsigners of the contract were bound if the seller entered into an agreement with only one buyer in the state.

In 1951 the Supreme Court refused to enforce the nonsigner clause in the fair-trade laws. In 1952 the McGuire Act was passed, which declares that the fair-trade laws are enforceable in those states having a law that permits manufacturers by agreement with one retailer to fix the price of a good sold by all the other retailers in the state. In short, the McGuire Act legalized the nonsigner clause. With the advent and widespread development of the discount store and other new marketing techniques in the past few decades, the use of fair-trade pricing has diminished considerably.

GOVERNMENT REGULATION OF FARM PRICES

During World War I the unprecedented worldwide demand for the products of American agriculture caused farm production to expand. Additional land came into production. Power-driven machinery increased the productivity of farm workers so that by 1920, when agricultural exports fell, the domestic market could not absorb farm output at prices that would cover the cost of producing a large part of the supply. As a result, the prices of farm commodities relative to the prices of industrial products decreased for a number of years.

The growing disadvantage of the farmer finally resulted in the passage of the Agricultural Marketing Act in 1929, with an appropriation of $500 million to be used in "stabilizing" farm prices. The method to be employed to effect stabilization was simple: the government would undertake to buy surplus amounts of wheat and cotton that could not be sold in the market at satisfactory prices. The plan contemplated the subsequent sale of the government purchases when to do so would not depress market prices. The sponsors of the measure, however, were disappointed. The prospects of government aid in supporting prices served to encourage the production of more wheat and cotton. As production rose, prices declined still further.

The government found itself in possession of cotton and wheat that it could not dispose of without depressing an already low and declining market. Eventually the surpluses were either sold at a loss or were distributed to needy persons. The money loss resulting from the experiment in price control amounted to nearly $345 million, quite a large sum at that time.

The failure of the Agricultural Marketing Act, however, did not deter the federal government from trying to do something about the "farm problem." Since then a number of laws have been passed in an effort to regulate farm prices and farm incomes in a way that would be satisfactory to farmers and equitable to consumers. The nature of these laws and the success that has been achieved by the federal government in its attempt to regulate farm prices and incomes will be discussed at greater length in Chapter 38.

The government follows a policy that in effect guarantees minimum prices for certain farm products. The forces of demand and supply, which formerly were relied on to regulate the prices of cotton, wheat, tobacco, corn, rice, and more than a dozen other crops, are subject to intervention. In some cases, in spite of provisions in the law for the limitation of production, vast quantities of certain farm products are accumulated by the government. In fact, the "ever-normal granary," envisioned by the original sponsors of price-control measures, often overflows. Some of these supplies in the past have been disposed of as gifts to various institutions and foreign countries.

EMERGENCY PRICE CONTROLS

Great social emergencies often result in modifications of economic organization and procedures. A rapid change in economic organization and practices, in turn, usually calls for an extension of the powers of government over business.

Price Regulations Under the NRA

The National Recovery Administration, created under authority of the National Industrial Recovery Act of 1933, offered the various industries an opportunity to operate largely under rules that could be established by the trade associations representing them. The rules embodied in the "codes" adopted by the associations usually provided for minimum prices, as well as some form of control over the output of the industry. Frequently the codes stipulated that minimum prices should not be below the "cost of production."

At the time, the urgent need to provide employment for millions of unemployed workers and the eagerness of employers to see prices rise prevented a critical appraisal of the law in terms of its long-run effects on the economy. But in retrospect, it is evident that the Act contained contradictions. In the first place, it provided for the cartelization of industry under the protection of the government. The antitrust laws were in effect suspended. At the same time—according to the assertions of the sponsors of the law—the Act set up the machinery to "promote" competition and to "make capitalism work." In 1935 the Supreme Court declared the law unconstitutional on the ground that it was an illegal transfer of legislative power by Congress to the President.

Wartime Government Price Controls

In more recent history the United States has imposed wage-price controls on three different occasions: (1) during World War II; (2) during the Korean conflict; and (3) during various periods between August, 1971, to January, 1974, which was associated in large part with the war in Vietnam. In all three cases controls were initiated with a wage-price freeze, but eventually evolved into a formula of some type for regulating prices and wages. Economists generally agree that economic controls can suppress inflation by preventing overt wage and price increases from taking place. Nevertheless, the overall effectiveness of controls as a means of eliminating the causes of inflation is frequently debated by economists and others.

INCOMES POLICY

The United States has been flirting with an incomes policy for the past decade or more. During this time the concept has moved from obscurity to the forefront of economic debate. In the interim, a number of foreign nations have adopted incomes policies as a means of limiting inflation. An incomes policy is a broad set of voluntary, quantitative guidelines that apply to prices, wages, and other forms of income, such as rents and interest, and that may or may not carry some type of economic sanction for nonconformists.

Wage and Price Guideposts

After experiencing four to five years of relative price stability, some price unrest was becoming apparent in the economy in the latter half of 1961. In seeking the continuation of price stability, President Kennedy in his 1962 *Economic Report* established a set of voluntary wage and price guideposts. If accepted by the major firms in the economy and in the collective bargaining power centers, it would do much, according to the President, to restrain upward pressures on the price level. As a guide for noninflationary wage behavior, the rate of increase in wage rates (including fringe benefits) in each industry was to be equated with the national trend in overall productivity increase. Although general acceptance of the guideposts would maintain the stability of labor cost per unit of output for the economy as a whole, it would not stabilize labor cost per unit for individual firms or industries. Based upon the fact that the average productivity per worker in our economy increased about 3 percent annually, the guideposts initially recommended that wage increases be held to 3 percent each year. This would allow the increase in wage cost to be absorbed out of rising productivity without necessitating a price increase. The guideposts did have some flexibility insofar as they suggested that any firm whose gain in productivity per man-hour was more than the guidepost figure should hold its wage increase to 3 percent and give consumers some benefit by reducing prices. On the other hand, it recommended that any firm whose increase in productivity was less than the guidepost figure could grant a 3 percent wage increase but offset this with an increase in prices. Subsequently, using a five-year average, the guidepost figure was raised to 3.2 percent.

Naturally the guideposts stirred up considerable controversy in both wage and price circles. In many firms and industries where the rate of productivity was less than the national average, the guideposts were used by labor unions as a basis for a wage increase higher than the productivity rate increase within the firm or industry. In other firms or industries where the productivity rate exceeded the national average productivity increase, the firms often used the guidepost in an effort to limit the amount of a wage increase to 3.2 percent without decreasing prices, even though they might have been able to afford more. Another complaint was the fact that the guideposts tended to freeze labor's share of the national income.

Shortly after the guideposts were publicized in January, 1962, several large steel companies announced, in April, price increases for their products. A rather piqued President Kennedy publicly reprimanded the steel company executives, and the antitrust division threatened to investigate the companies' actions. After several hasty meetings in and out of the White House, the steel companies rescinded their price increases. At that time the use of presidential powers to directly influence the pricing practices in a given industry was met with strong but mixed reaction on the part of business, labor, and the general public.

Although the concept of price and wage guideposts seemed to be pushed out of the limelight by the emphasis on the tax cut in the 1963 *Economic Report of the President* and by the poverty package in the 1964 *Report*, the guideposts were emphasized again by President Johnson and his Economic Advisers in the mid-1960s. About the same time, steel companies were talking about the need for a price increase in order to offset some of their increasing costs. At that time, however, President Johnson publicly warned them that any increase in steel prices "would strongly conflict with our national interest in price stability." With the return of stronger inflationary pressures in 1966, some delicate situations and open confrontations regarding the voluntary acceptance of the guideposts developed between the White House and/or the President's Council of Economic Advisers on the one hand and large industries and powerful labor unions on the other. Consequently, in 1967 the use of a specific guidepost figure was deemphasized, although the guidepost concept was still retained. By 1968 the guideposts were pretty well shattered as both labor unions and business firms posted wage and price increases substantially beyond the guidepost figures.

Nevertheless, continually rising prices brought a renewed interest in the guidepost concept during 1969 and 1970. Although President Nixon avoided the use of guideposts as late as the spring of 1971, Congress did in 1970 give the President authority to impose wage and price controls. During the period 1970-1971, when the CPI was still rising 5 or more percent annually, several business groups, labor leaders, government officials, and Congressmen urged some type of formal restraint, such as the reinstitution of wage and price guideposts, the implementation of an incomes policy, or the adoption of absolute wage and price controls.

Phase I: The 90-Day Freeze

With the knowledge that progress on his economic game plan was being stifled by substantial wage and price increases, President Nixon in August, 1971, made drastic and sweeping changes in domestic and international economic policies. Among other measures, he declared a 90-day freeze on all prices, wages, and rents, temporarily suspended convertibility of dollars into gold, imposed a 10 percent surcharge on imports, froze a scheduled pay increase for government employees, sought to reinstitute tax credits as a means of stimulating investment and jobs, asked Congress to reduce personal income taxes, and requested Congress to repeal the 7 percent excise tax on automobiles.

The President established a Cost of Living Council to work out details for restoring free markets without inflation during a transition period following the freeze. Congress did oblige the President by repealing the excise tax on automobiles and by reducing personal income taxes by advancing the scheduled date for an increase in personal income tax exemptions.

Phase II: Wage-Price Formula

The 90-day freeze was followed by a Phase II control period. For the implementation of this phase the President established a Pay Board and a Price Commission. Each was to work out what it considered permissible noninflationary wage and price increases, respectively. The Commissions were composed of representatives of labor, management, and the general public. The Pay Board subsequently established a 5.5 percent annual wage increase as a maximum, although it did allow certain exemptions to be made to the 5.5 percent figure. Also, the Pay Board permitted most scheduled raises that were to have taken effect during the freeze period to take effect during Phase II.

The Price Commission, on the other hand, indicated that it was going to attempt to hold overall price increases in the CPI to 2.5 percent annually. Since the President did not desire to set up an elaborate formal structure of wage and price controls such as existed during World War II and during the Korean conflict, much of the stabilization program had to depend on voluntary compliance. The Cost of Living Council exempted most of the smaller business firms and most workers from any reporting requirements. Others, however, were required to report changes in prices and wages. Larger firms, moreover, had to give prenotification of changes to the Price Commission and/or the Pay Board.

The effectiveness of the price controls in combating inflation can be gauged somewhat by the fact that, during the six months prior to the freeze, prices increased at an annual rate of 4.5 percent. In the five months subsequent to the freeze, they increased at an annual rate of 2.2 percent.

Prices were much more stable in the first half of the 1960s compared to those of the inflationary period starting in 1966. From 1960 to 1965, for example, prices rose at an average annual rate of 1.3 percent. From 1965 to August, 1971, prices rose at an average annual rate of 4.9 percent. In the year following the price freeze the CPI rose at an annual rate of 3.0 percent.

Phase III: Return to the Guideposts

In January, 1973, after commenting favorably on the results of Phase II in stabilizing prices and wages, President Nixon announced Phase III of his New Economic Policy, which in effect reestablished voluntary guideposts for price and wage increases. The guidepost figures used at the time were 2.5 percent and 5.5 percent annually for prices and wages respectively.

Phase IV: Compulsory Controls Again

The removal of compulsory Phase II controls proved to be premature, however. During the first five months after decontrol, the CPI rose at an annual rate of nearly 9 percent. Consequently, on June 13, 1973, President Nixon declared a 60-day freeze on prices. Wages were not affected at this time. Instead of ending the freeze on all goods at the end of the 60-day period, prices were unfrozen selectively, and Phase IV controls were imposed on various categories of goods and services at different times before and after the 60-day period.

Again large firms were required to give a 30-day prenotification of price increases. Unlike Phase II however, firms did not have to wait for approval by the Cost of Living Council before putting such increases into effect. But the Council had authority to delay any price increases indefinitely, and it reserved the right to reexamine prices at any time. The new base period established was the fiscal quarter prior to January 12, 1973, the date of decontrol of Phase II. Price increases equal to dollar cost increases subsequent to the base period were to be permitted by Phase IV. No allowance was to be made for a profit mark-up on these cost increases. Controls were imposed on an industry-by-industry basis, thus providing more flexibility than was available under Phase II. At the time of the imposition of Phase IV, several high Administration officials indicated that they hoped controls could be removed by the end of 1973 or early in 1974.

CAN GOVERNMENT FIX EQUITABLE PRICES?

Nearly everyone agrees that it is sometimes necessary or desirable for government to fix certain prices. However, when specific prices are fixed, they are not likely to meet with the approval of all the people affected. This fact is illustrated by the experience of a number of states in their efforts to impose price controls on the sale and purchase of milk. Some of these states have laws which, by and large, prevent retailers from selling milk "below cost." Others fix minimum and maximum prices. In a great many metropolitan areas federal regulations prescribe the minimum prices that dealers must pay milk producers.

These efforts to control the price of milk are evidently satisfactory to some elements of the population—the milk producers especially. Other groups are less than satisfied. These are, as a rule, the consumers, who feel that they are forced to pay higher prices than would be the case if milk prices were not fixed by milk commissions. Government economists estimate that milk price laws and regulations add hundreds of millions of dollars to consumers' milk bills. Milk producers and others, however, contend that such control by government is necessary to the maintenance of an adequate supply of milk.

As organized economic groups acquire political power, they usually tend to seek consideration at the hands of legislative bodies. Right or wrong, they are likely to feel that they have problems which government should assist in solving. Frequently they feel that the prices of the goods or services they sell need protection which only government can provide. Since the economic system does not work perfectly, it is always possible that a plea for government aid or protection will be supported by plausible arguments to the effect that "this is an exception to the rule" and therefore something should be done about it.

Practically every group—whether labor, business, farm, or professional—seeks special legislation of one kind or another. Not all of the laws desired by particular groups affect or would affect prices directly. But most of them are directly or indirectly related to the prices of the products or services that the interested groups sell. Admitting the desirability for certain instances of government regulation of prices, we must not lose sight of the fact that, while the political control of any price may solve one problem, it often creates one or more other problems.

Each price in the fabric of the price system is related in one way or another to every other price. In some cases the relationship is more or less obvious. For example, it is evident that retail prices are related to the cost of living. Likewise, it is easily seen that the retail prices paid by consumers are based partly on the cost of raw materials. Therefore, if government, either by direct or indirect methods, extends effective control over the prices of such materials, the income of merchants and the expenditures of consumers may be affected. For example, if the government levies a tariff on petroleum imported into this country, such a tax may raise the price of gasoline although it may stimulate production and employment in the petroleum industry.

Perhaps most people understand to some extent the interrelationship of prices and would concede that the effects of controlling one price are bound to react throughout the whole price structure. Nevertheless, each pressure group, when it tries to enlist the help of government for the purpose of gaining a price advantage of some kind, appears to hope that somehow the final negative results—if any—to themselves will be less than the positive advantage to its members at the moment and in the future. To the extent that groups are motivated by this hope and act accordingly, we may expect to see an extension of government control over prices. And as the control of prices by government increases, dependence on politics and government for success in business will characterize American producers more than it once did.

That government may exert even more influence over prices in the future is not at all improbable. If it does, the result need not be the destruction of the principles and practices that underlie the American system of free enterprise. But to preserve the virtues of the present system, it is essential that no group or combination of groups be permitted to use government for the purpose of regulating prices for their own advantage and to the detriment of the public. This means that a balance of political power arising from and representing all economic groups must be maintained. What is even more important is that individuals in the various economic groups and their leaders be increasingly motivated by a real interest in the economic well-being of all.

SUMMARY

1. For some time there has been an increasing tendency for government to take an active part—directly or indirectly—in the determination of prices. Two reasons account for this tendency: first, nationwide emergencies; and second, growth of the belief that it is a proper function of government to protect consumer interest in prices.

2. Government fixes or influences prices in various ways. In the case of government-owned-and-operated industries and businesses, it fixes the prices of the services or goods that it produces and sells. As a rule, however, the object of government industries and businesses is not the making of a profit. On the other hand, public utilities are private industries offering services the prices of which are set with the approval or direction of a public service commission. The problem of determining public-utility rates calls for consideration of the value of the assets owned by the utility company, the nature and amount of operating costs, the establishment of a level of rates, and the designation of specific rates.

3. Most states specify legal and maximum interest rates. The Federal Reserve System controls certain interest rates directly and influences others through its regulatory powers over member banks. Through its lending agencies, such as those that help to provide agricultural credit and credit for home building and repairs, the federal government influences interest rates, and state governments fix maximum interest rates.

4. The federal minimum-wage law applies to wages of workers employed in interstate industries. The first minimum-wage law in the U.S., however, was passed by a state legislature. In addition, many states have enacted fair-trade laws.

5. Price regulations for agricultural products have not solved the farm problem, but they are still in operation. Government price controls during wartime, however, have proved to be fairly successful.

6. Some attempt was made to establish a set of voluntary wage-price guideposts during the early 1960s as a means of preventing inflation.

7. Our experience with inflation in the latter part of the 1960s and the early 1970s led to the imposition of wage-price controls, which lasted initially until January, 1973. After being removed, they were subsequently reinstated, however.

8. Phase III of President Nixon's New Economic Policy called for the elimination of price controls and the reinstitution of wage-price guideposts. Unfortunately, steep price increases necessitated the restoration of compulsory price controls under Phase IV.

9. The probability of an incomes policy for the economy in the future is uncertain. To whatever extent it may be adopted, it is a restriction on the market forces that determine prices and wages.

NEW TERMS	Public-utility rates, *p. 681*	Legal rates of interest, *p. 685*
	Original cost, less depreciation, *p. 682*	Minimum-wage laws, *p. 686*
		NRA codes, *p. 689*
	Cost of reproduction, new, less depreciation, *p. 682*	Incomes policy, *p .690*
	Prudent-investment concept, *p. 682*	Wage-price guideposts, *p. 690*
		Price freeze, *p. 692*
	Fair return on a fair investment, *p. 684*	Phases I, II, III, and IV, *p. 692*

QUESTIONS FOR DISCUSSION AND ANALYSIS

1. In a free enterprise system why is it necessary for a government to regulate, control, or influence some prices? Give illustrations of direct and indirect methods that government may employ in its attempt to influence prices.

2. Why should the government or the public service commission fix or regulate public-utility rates?

3. In connection with the regulation of public utilities, explain what is meant by "original" or "historical" costs; by "reproduction" costs; the "end-result doctrine."

4. Should interest rates be controlled by government? Why or why not?

5. If government fixes minimum wages in an industry at a level that employers cannot afford to pay, should the government have a responsibility to provide jobs for any workers who may thereby become unemployed? Give reasons for your answer.

6. Do you think that a manufacturer should be able to establish the price at which his product will be sold at the retail level? Why or why not?

7. Do you agree or disagree with the government farm price support program? Why?

8. What are the advantages of a price "freeze" during an emergency?

9. Do tariffs (taxes) on foreign-made watches and bicycles affect the prices of similar commodities made in this country? If so, how?

10. Do you agree with the concept of wage and price guideposts? If so, do you think that they should be made compulsory?

SUGGESTED READINGS

"Dr. McCracken on Price-Wage Controls." *Economic Education Bulletin*, American Institute for Economic Research (January, 1972).

Economic Report of the President. Washington: U.S. Government Printing Office, 1972, 1973, and 1974.

Feige, Edgar L., and Douglas K. Pearce. "The Wage-Price Control Experiment—Did It Work?" *Challenge* (July/August, 1973).

Floyd, Robert H. "Incomes Policy—A Quick Critique." *Monthly Review*. Atlanta: Federal Reserve Bank of Atlanta (December, 1971).

Friedlaender, Ann. *The Dilemma of Freight Transport Regulation*. Washington: The Brookings Institution, 1969.

Moore, Thomas Gale. *U.S. Incomes Policy: Its Rationale and Development*, Special Analysis No. 3. Washington: American Enterprise Institute (April, 1971).

Phillips, Charles F., Jr. *The Economics of Regulation*. Homewood, Ill.: Richard D. Irwin, Inc., 1969.

Richmond, Samuel B. *Regulation and Competition in Air Transportation*. New York: Columbia University Press, 1961.

Slesinger, Reuben E., and Asher Isaacs. *Business, Government, and Public Policy.* New York: Van Nostrand Reinhold Company, 1968.

Stahl, Sheldon W. "Incomes Policies—An Idea Whose Time Has Come." *Monthly Review*. Kansas City: Federal Reserve Bank of Kansas City (September-October, 1971).

"Wage-Price Curbs Through the Ages." *Wall Street Journal*, September 23, 1971, p. 20.

Wald, Haskell P. "The Third Economy." *Public Utility Fortnightly* (July 8, 1965).

PART NINE

Income Distribution

32

Wages:
Labor's
Share of
Income

PREVIEW There are two forms of income distribution—the distribution among individuals (personal distribution) and the distribution among factors of production (functional distribution). Wage income is the functional share of labor. Among the theories advanced to explain labor's share, the most important are the marginal productivity theory and, more recently but less developed, the bargaining theory of wages.

We began this book by stressing allocation decisions. In any economic system, regardless of particular economic or political institutions, resources must be allocated among alternative uses. Also, products must be allocated among users or consumers. In an exchange economy markets largely determine what goods and services are to be produced, how much of each is to be produced, and who shall get various shares of the produced goods and services. Parts Seven and Eight of this book dealt with questions of what and how much will be produced. Part Nine is addressed to the third question: how is output to be distributed?

INCOME DISTRIBUTION

In primitive societies, custom usually settles the distribution problem. The chief of the tribe, for example, gets special treatment and so does the medicine man. Even in a highly civilized society like that of the United States, custom operates to some degree in the division of wealth, as in the case of tipping and Christmas bonuses. In some economies the amount each person gets is decided by an omnipotent central government that plans payments and rewards according to a program of welfare acceptable to or imposed upon its people. In the United States the amounts received by people are determined largely by the markets for the factors of production. However, the government occasionally steps in to modify the result—witness veterans' benefits, Social Security, and minimum-wage laws.

Forms of Income

People get their incomes in a variety of forms. A very large number receive wages or salaries in return for their services. Some hold bonds and mortgages and receive income in the form of interest, while others own property from which they receive rent. Owners of business enterprises may get a return known as profits or dividends.

So numerous are the ways in which income is acquired that the question may well be asked whether there is any explanation for this variety other than the astuteness of a person and the degree of his good fortune. No doubt fortune plays a part. One's talents and skills also play a part. Nevertheless, systematic forces tend to determine the nature and the amount of income that individuals receive. These economic forces operate so as to apportion to each person an income proportional to the value of his contribution to national production.

Personal Distribution of Income

Chapter 6 demonstrated that the net volume of output in a nation during a given period of time constitutes the nation's real income for that period. The national income, moreover, is the combined result of all people working together. Efficiency in production dictates a division of labor and function. Some supply labor; others supply land, capital, or entrepreneurial services. Certain individuals supply more than one productive factor; for example, both labor and capital.

In a complex economic system, people do not take home as real income the actual goods or services they help to produce. With a division of labor, some indirect method of distributing national income is necessary. Output is measured in money value, and amounts of money equal to the value of goods produced are apportioned among individuals. If a man employed by a firm is paid $30 for a day's work, the value of the man's labor is presumed to be worth $30. If another man is paid $100 for the use of his capital, the dollar amount is taken as the value of his capital contribution toward the production of national income.

Our study of income distribution is divided into two parts: (1) functional distribution and (2) personal distribution. Analysis of income division among workers, owners of land, owners of capital, and operators of business is called the *functional distribution of income*. In short, income depends upon the productive contribution of each of the various factors of production. The question of functional distribution is a question of the shares going to wages, interest, rent, and profit.

The study of conditions that determine the division of income among individuals is called the *personal distribution of income*. Each phase of the study is important, for it helps to throw light on the economic and social conditions that determine the division of income among the millions of income recipients in the United States.

Chapter 37 is devoted to the personal distribution of income. In that chapter we shall investigate income differences by occupations, age, color, sex, and geographic location. In our immediate study in this chapter and the following three chapters, we will focus upon the shares of national income allocated to different factors of production.

Functional Distribution of Income

In economics the study of income distribution is largely concerned with the shares going to the factors of production. Functional income distribution (sometimes referred to as factorial distribution) in the form of wages, interest, rent, and profits is of significance (1) because it is based on general principles which have been explained in earlier chapters and (2) because it is only on the basis of such principles that a satisfactory public policy can be developed.

The problem of distribution is as old as the study of economics, and it becomes more perplexing as our economy becomes more complex. In the early days of the self-sufficient economy a family produced directly the goods and services it required. If there were surpluses, families would exchange goods. In this system an individual generally used his own labor effort or that of his family, his own land, his own tools, and he directed the production of the goods and services he needed. Using his own labor, land, and capital and assuming the institution of private property to exist, it was obvious that he was entitled to sole ownership of the fruits of his production.

In our modern industrial economy the problem of income distribution is more intricate. A producer must still use the basic factors of production. In bringing together these factors, however, the entrepreneur may use the labor of other persons, the land of some, and the capital of yet others. By combining these factors, a good or a service is produced that has a certain value. Now the big question arises: What should be the share of, or payment to, each of the factors for its particular contribution to the total product? In a barter economy remuneration could be made in kind; that is, each factor could be compensated with a certain share of the good produced. In our modern economy, however, remuneration for the factors of production—labor, land, capital, and entrepreneurship—is made in the form of monetary payments of wages, rent, interest, and profits, respectively, as shown in Figure 32-1.

The theory of distribution is not always presented as a single or as a completely integrated theory. It is often presented as a group of theories, each concerning one factor of production. Nevertheless, a theory about one factor cannot be studied without regard to the whole. If a particular theory allocates more income to one factor of production, it may mean that other factors receive less. On the other hand, each factor could increase its remuneration without detriment to the others if the total size of the economic pie were increased. Thus, any increase in productivity through better use of any or all factors can be beneficial to all.

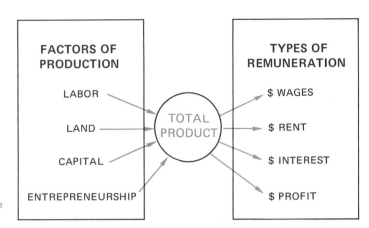

FIGURE 32-1

FUNCTIONAL DISTRIBUTION

Factors of production share in the proceeds of national output.

Prices as Income

In a capitalistic system with competitive markets for goods and services, there are also markets for factors of production. Supply of and demand for the factor in question sets a price in the same way it does for any good. This price is an expression of the exchange value of a unit of that particular grade of the factor; it has been set in the market as the result of the competitive judgments of buyers and sellers with respect to its use in production.

One who receives a price for a factor service receives at the same time an income in the form of wages, rent, or interest. The risk taker or entrepreneur is the recipient of the residual that remains after the owners of these factors have received their compensation. Thus, in a capitalistic system, markets are the agencies through which the national income is distributed to those who produce it. From this point of view, the capitalistic processes of production and distribution are like the two sides of a coin; one cannot exist without the other. They are really but two ways of looking at the same process, creating goods on the one hand and generating income on the other.

WAGES, LABOR'S SHARE

That part of the nation's income received by those who supply productive labor is called *wages*, although various other terms are employed—such as salary, bonus, honorarium, stipend, fee, and commission—to indicate payments for particular forms of service. What conditions set a price, called a wage rate, for the services of labor, and why is the price high, low, or average? Furthermore, what leads to a change in this price, making it higher or lower?

When a wage is expressed as a price, it is usually called a *money wage*. What the money wage will buy in the market at any particular time is called the *real wage*. The relation between these two different ways of expressing wages is complex, for the conditions determining money wages are not the same as those affecting real wages. You will recall from Chapter 4 the discussion of changes in levels of living that deal with this problem. In Chapter 11, "Money and Economic Activity," we discussed how prices, including wages, are affected by changes in the value of money. In the present chapter we shall be concerned with money wages because they are prices, but always with the understanding that real wages, discussed elsewhere, are of more importance.

What is labor's share of the total product? Labor receives most of the money value of the total goods and services produced through the combined effort of the factors of production. In 1973 labor received, in the form of wages and salaries, 74 percent of the national income. Labor's share of the total income apparently has been increasing somewhat in the past few decades, as shown in Table 32-1.

TABLE 32-1

WAGES AND SALARIES AS A PERCENT OF NATIONAL INCOME

1929-1973

Year	National Income (Billions)	Wages and Salaries (Billions)	Wages and Salaries as a Percent of National Income
1929	$ 86.8	$ 51.1	59
1933	40.3	29.5	73
1935	57.2	37.3	65
1940	81.1	52.1	64
1945	181.5	123.1	68
1950	241.1	154.6	64
1955	331.0	224.5	68
1960	414.5	294.2	71
1965	564.3	393.8	70
1970	800.5	603.9	75
1973	1,054.2	785.3	74

SOURCE: *Economic Report of the President*, 1974.

This rise in labor's share may be more appearance than reality since it is quite probable that the percentage of members in the labor force who are now working for others and receiving wages and salaries has increased to some extent in the past few decades. At any rate, the data give some indication of labor's share of the total product, so that we may later compare it to the shares accruing to the other factors of production.

HISTORICAL WAGE THEORIES

Economists have been attempting to solve the problem of economic distribution for 200 years, and during that time scholars of the subject have witnessed a whole parade of theories about distribution. Some of the most interesting of these theories have been about wages. For this reason and also to provide background for current wage theories, some of the outstanding earlier theories will be reviewed.

Subsistence Theory of Wages

The subsistence theory of wages, in vogue between 1775 and 1850, was promulgated by Adam Smith, David Ricardo, and Thomas Malthus. The theory held that wages would be equal to that amount which would permit the worker to subsist, neither getting too much above nor below this level.

The market wage was determined by the supply of and the demand for labor. On the other hand, the natural wage or *subsistence wage* was that wage which was needed to sustain the worker and to replace him when he passed away. Thus, if each worker were to replace himself with a son, he would have to provide for a family of four. Theoretically, his family would include a son and a daughter to replace himself and his wife.

If the market wage were equal to the natural wage, a stable population, or work force, would exist. On the other hand, since the theory held that there was a relatively fixed stock of foodstuffs and other basic necessities for living, the demand for workers was fairly stable. Since the productive yield of the earth was also the source of wage payments, the amount of goods or money available for wage payments was limited, which further added to the stability of the demand for workers.

According to the theory, if for some reason the market wage exceeded the natural wage, workers would have larger families. Wages above the subsistence level would provide better diets, better housing, better medical care, and the like. There would be lower infant mortality, less malnutrition, and greater longevity. Thus, a market wage above the subsistence level would cause an increase in the rate of population growth. As the supply of workers increased while demand remained fairly constant, the market wage would fall. It could not go far below the subsistence level, however, because, once it did, the supply of workers would decrease. Families would then have insufficient income for food, medical care, and adequate shelter. There would be higher infant mortality, more sickness, and earlier deaths. Workers, to curtail the size of their families, would act to decrease population growth. The supply of workers would decline, or at least increase at a decreasing rate. With a constant demand, the wage rate would drop until it again reached the subsistence level.

Consequently, the market wage would fluctuate around the natural wage in the short run, never going too far above or too far below. In the long run, however, wages could only be determined by the subsistence level of a worker. For this reason, the subsistence theory became known as the "iron law of wages."

The wages fund theory was popular during the nineteenth century. In fact, the theory was carried over into this century in some of our early textbooks. Its leading exponent was John Stuart Mill, who crystallized the theory in his *Principles of Political Economy* published in 1848. This theory was also based upon the relationship of population growth to a scarce economic yield from the earth. Hence, it overlaps the subsistence theory.

The wages fund theory held that employers set aside out of the revenues of previous years a certain amount to be used for the payment of wages. This sum was a fixed amount known as the *wages fund.* If the population was large compared to the size of the wages fund, it simply meant that each laborer had to take a lower wage. On the other hand, if the population was small compared to the size of the wages fund, each worker could have a higher wage. Furthermore, according to this theory, since the wages fund was fixed, it did one segment of workers no good to organize in order to obtain a higher wage. Anything that they gained came at the expense of their fellow workers. This theory naturally led to the conclusion that it was beneficial for workers to limit their numbers. Thus, Mill and others were advocates of measures to limit population expansion.

According to both the subsistence and the wages fund theories, the worker's prospects were rather hopeless. Stress upon the "niggardliness of nature," scarcity, the "iron law of wages," and the fixed wages fund gave him little hope for the future. It is no wonder that economics in those days came to be known as the "dismal science." It is also no wonder that this economic philosophy encouraged the socialistic doctrines of Karl Marx and others. Marx probably had in mind the "iron law of wages" when in the *Communist Manifesto* he called upon the workers of the world to unite and throw off their shackles.

The central fallacy in both theories is the unjustifiable assumption that the productivity of workers, the supply of foodstuffs, and other basic necessities were all fixed. As a result of increased productivity and a growing supply of goods and services from the yield of the earth, real wages have continuously increased in most parts of the world for several generations.

MARGINAL PRODUCTIVITY THEORY OF WAGES

Among current theories the most widely recognized is the marginal productivity theory of wages. Actually the *marginal productivity theory* is a theory of demand for labor. It postulates that the wage is determined by both the demand for and the supply of labor. When the market is in equilibrium, the wage will equal the value of the marginal product of labor.

In Chapter 26 the marginal product of any one productive factor was explained as the increase in total output resulting from an additional unit of input. Value of marginal product is defined as the increment of total output multiplied by the product price at which the additional output is sold. Therefore, when the market is in equilibrium, a daily wage will equal the dollar value of the addition to output contributed by a day's work.

Several crucial assumptions underlie this theory: (1) that the labor market is freely competitive in the same sense that a product market was described as competitive in Chapter 27; (2) that firms demanding labor maximize profit; (3) that both capital and labor are mobile among industries and regions; and (4) that workers in the same grade are interchangeable and are therefore paid the same wage in a given job. The first two assumptions clearly indicate that this marginal productivity theory of wages is simply an application of the theory of the competitive firm to the demand side of the labor market.

The Demand for Labor

Under conditions of pure competition, both the price of a finished product and the price of labor are determined by the forces of supply and demand. The demand for labor begins with an analysis of one firm in a competitive industry and builds up to the labor demand on the part of the entire industry.

Theory of the Firm. Assume an employer can hire all the labor he desires at a wage of $20 per day. This wage has been set in the market by the aggregate forces of supply and demand. How these forces determine the wage is a matter we put aside for the moment. We will return to it. Assume further that the employer can sell his finished product at $4 per unit and that his production effort is subject to the law of diminishing returns.

In Table 32-2, Column 1 shows the number of laborers used. Column 2 shows the total output from the use of a given number of workers. The marginal product of labor, the increase in total product per additional labor unit, is shown in Column 3. Note that the point of diminishing marginal productivity is reached after the employment of the fourth worker. Column 4 represents the total fixed cost with which you are already familiar. Column 5 shows the wage set in the market. This wage is also referred to as the *average outlay* because it is the amount of money that the employer must put out for each additional worker hired. Column 6 is the total cost, made up of both the variable and the fixed cost. Column 7 represents the *marginal outlay*. This is a new term, which may be defined as the increase in total cost per additional unit of *input* hired (worker). Keep in mind that it differs from the term marginal cost used in Chapter 26, which was defined as the

TABLE 32-2

(1) Units of Labor	(2) Total Units of Output	(3) Marginal Product	(4) Total Fixed Cost	(5) Average Outlay (Wage)	(6) Total Cost	(7) Marginal Outlay	(8) Average Revenue (Price)	(9) Total Revenue	(10) Marginal Revenue Product	(11) Total Profit
1 ...	10		$50	$20	$ 70		$4	$ 40		−$ 30
2 ...	22	12	50	20	90	$20	4	88	$48	− 2
3 ...	36	14	50	20	110	20	4	144	56	34
4 ...	52	16	50	20	130	20	4	208	64	78
5 ...	67	15	50	20	150	20	4	268	60	118
6 ...	80	13	50	20	170	20	4	320	52	150
7 ...	90	10	50	20	190	20	4	360	40	170
8 ...	98	8	50	20	210	20	4	392	32	182
9 ...	103	5	50	20	230	20	4	412	20	182
10 ...	106	3	50	20	250	20	4	424	12	174
11 ...	108	2	50	20	270	20	4	432	8	162
12 ...	108	0	50	20	290	20	4	432	0	142

increase in total cost per additional unit of *output* produced. Notice, too, that it is a constant amount because an employer will be able to hire any number of workers at the given market price determined by supply and demand.

From the revenue point of view, Column 8 represents the price received for the finished product, otherwise known as average revenue. Notice that, according to conditions of pure competition, an individual firm can sell any number of units at a given market price. Column 9, total revenue, is obtained simply by multiplying average revenue by total product. *Marginal revenue product*, shown in Column 10, is the increase in total revenue resulting from the use of an additional unit of *input* (labor). Observe again that it differs from the term marginal revenue, which is the increase in total revenue from the sale of an additional unit of *output*. Since each unit of labor added increases total product by a diminishing amount after a given number of units of labor are employed, which in this case is 4, marginal revenue product declines as output increases because of diminishing marginal productivity.

To maximize profits the firm will continue to add to production so long as total profit expands. If marginal revenue product is the increase in total revenue per additional unit of labor used and the marginal outlay is the increase in total cost per unit of labor used, anytime that marginal revenue product exceeds marginal outlay, total profits will increase (or losses will diminish). If marginal revenue product is less than marginal outlay, however, total profits will decrease. Since marginal revenue product (*MRP*) eventually declines as workers are added and marginal outlay (*MO*) remains constant, a point is reached at which the *MRP* equals *MO*. At this point the firm will have maximum profits and equilibrium output. In summary, a firm will hire workers so long as the *MRP* of their labor is greater than the *MO*, and it will not pay a worker more than the value of his *MRP*.

In Table 32-2 the firm will hire the first eight workers because in each case the *MRP* of each worker hired is greater than the *MO* required to hire him. Note also that in each case the total loss is decreased or the profit of the firm is increased by the size of the difference between *MRP* and *MO*. It is assumed that the firm will also hire the ninth worker because total profit will neither increase nor decrease as a result. No more workers will be hired, however, because the *MRP* of the tenth and subsequent workers is less than the *MO*. To hire the tenth or subsequent workers would reduce total profits. Maximum profits are made with the ninth worker. This becomes the equilibrium level of employment.

The relationship between productivity, wages, and employment is demonstrated in Figure 32-2. Assume first that the market wage is $20, as illustrated in Table 32-2. Because the wage is independent of the number of workers hired by the firm, marginal outlay is depicted as the horizontal line labeled *MO* (Wage). The *MRP* curve is a chart of the firm's marginal revenue product schedule. For any employment short of 9 workers the *MRP* curve lies above the *MO* curve, while for employment in excess of 9 workers the *MRP* curve lies below the *MO* curve. Intersection of the two curves represents equilibrium employment, that is, employment which maximizes the firm's profit.

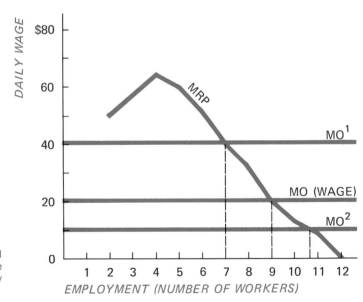

FIGURE 32-2

EQUILIBRIUM WAGES AND EMPLOYMENT

If the wage rate is $20, the firm will employ nine workers. If the wage rises to $40, the firm will employ seven.

Notice what happens if the wage is changed. Suppose the wage were to rise from $20 to $40. The new wage is shown by the horizontal line MO^1, which intersects the MRP curve at employment of 7 workers. On the other hand, a drop in the wage to $10 per day—denoted by the line MO^2—would result in an expansion of employment. Therefore, given the productivity of workers and the state of demand for the product (represented by a stationary MRP curve), the theory holds that a rise in wages will reduce employment of labor and a drop in wages will increase employment.

Labor productivity may change, however. By means of better training or improvement in the tools and equipment used by labor, the productivity of all workers may increase. Figure 32-3 depicts a rise in labor productivity, which causes the marginal revenue product curve to shift from its original position labeled MRP to its new position labeled MRP^1. At a wage of $20, employment will rise from 9 to 11 workers. Similarly, a decline in labor productivity will cause the marginal revenue product curve to shift downward, for example, from MRP to MRP^2 in Figure 32-3. At a wage of $20, employment will then decrease.

A change in demand for the final product will also affect employment. Suppose the product price, shown in Column 8 of Table 32-2, were to rise from $4 to $10 because of an increase in demand for the final product. Since marginal revenue product equals Column 3 multiplied by Column 8, it follows that marginal revenue product will be larger for each alternative level of employment. Therefore, the MRP curve will shift upward to MRP^1 in Figure 32-3, and employment will expand from 9 to 11 workers.

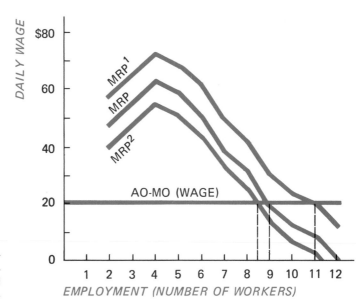

FIGURE 32-3

CHANGES IN THE MARGINAL REVENUE PRODUCT

When labor productivity increases or demand for the final product increases, the demand for labor will increase. The converse is also true.

Conversely, a drop in product price caused by a decrease in product demand will cause the *MRP* curve to shift downward—say from *MRP* to MRP^2—and employment will decrease at a given wage.

Industry Demand. For simplicity, let us suppose there are 1,000 identical firms in the competitive industry. Then any one of the firms can be analyzed with the help of Figures 32-2 and 32-3. Consider Figure 32-2. If the wage were to be $20, one firm would employ 9 workers, so the industry would employ 1,000 × 9 or 9,000 workers. Given the state of product demand and given the productivity of labor, at a wage of $40 the entire industry would employ 1,000 × 7 or 7,000 workers.

By following this procedure, we can determine the number of workers that the industry would hire at each alternative wage. But this is nothing other than the industry demand curve for labor. The industry demand curve is drawn as D_L in Figure 32-4. Before examining the labor market further, however, let us turn to the supply of labor.

The Supply of Labor

The analysis of labor demand referred to labor of a particular kind or grade. Likewise, labor supply will refer to a particular kind or grade within which individual workers are assumed to be interchangeable. There are many ways to define a grade of labor. Economists have sometimes used occupations, but some combination of categories is usually required. The *Dictionary of Occupational Titles* compiled by the United States Employment Service provides job descriptions for more than 22,000 different job titles. These can be classified into as few as 11 occupations, but accuracy of description is sacrificed in the process.

Another approach is to define labor type in terms of skill: unskilled, semi-skilled, skilled, white-collar, or professional workers. Unskilled workers, such as farmhands or hod carriers, usually perform heavy manual labor where strength rather than expertise is required. Semi-skilled work calls for relatively short periods of adjustment or apprenticeship characteristic of many factory jobs. Skilled workers, such as carpenters or bricklayers, require more intensive apprenticeship training and perform tasks that cannot be reduced to a series of mechanical operations or performed by machinery. White-collar workers—clerks, secretaries, supervisors, and so on—are engaged in a variety of office or retail jobs demanding different degrees of skill. Finally, professional workers are those who have had long and exacting training, such as lawyers, physicians, and business managers.

Regardless of the categories utilized, the supply of labor is interpreted to mean the supply of a particular kind or type of labor to a particular industry. Moreover, the market in which labor services are bought and sold is assumed to be a competitive market. The supply of labor is defined as the amount of labor that would be offered at each alternative possible price. As in other markets, only a limited quantity of labor will be forthcoming at a low price; at successively higher prices larger amounts of labor will be offered for hire. Graphically speaking, the supply curve of labor takes the shape of a typical market supply curve. The curve slopes upward to the right.

The shape of a product supply curve has as its foundation the theory of the firm's production and cost. Why is it assumed that the labor supply curve has a similar shape? This is where the third assumption of the marginal productivity theory comes into play. A labor supply curve is drawn under the condition that wages in other industries and regions are *conceptually* held constant. Since labor, like capital, is assumed to be mobile, workers will respond to wage differentials. If the wage paid by a certain industry were to rise, workers would be attracted from other industries and/or regions. Therefore, larger amounts of labor will be offered to the industry in question at higher wages.

Labor Market Equilibrium

The industry demand curve for labor and the supply curve of labor to the industry are brought together in Figure 32-4. Let D_L denote labor demand and S_L labor supply. Intersection of the two curves determines the market

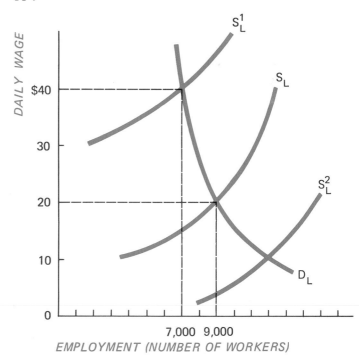

FIGURE 32-4

LABOR MARKET EQUILIBRIUM

The demand for and supply of labor determine the market wage rate and level of employment.

wage. At this equilibrium wage the labor market is cleared in the sense that all workers willing to accept employment at a wage of $20 can find employment in the industry.

To conform with previous diagrams depicting a single firm, the equilibrium wage is set at $20 and total employment is set at 9,000 workers by the market forces of demand and supply.

Now suppose labor supply were to change from S_L to S_L^1. This could mean a decrease in the number of workers offering their services in employment at any given wage (the curve moves to the left) because of a rise in wages paid in other labor markets. It could also mean that any given number of workers refuses to accept employment unless a higher wage is paid (the curve moves upward, which amounts to the same thing as a move to the left). Then the effect will be an increase of the market wage to $40. However, employment will decline to 7,000 workers. Conversely, an increase in labor supply, to S_L^2 for example, will reduce the wage but expand employment.

Figure 32-5 exhibits a situation under which both demand and supply are changing. The initial equilibrium is represented by point P_1. Let us compare this with point P_2. The supply of labor has decreased to S_L^1 (perhaps an insistence upon higher wages by labor). At the same time, however, labor demand has expanded to D_L^1. The net effect is an increase in both wages and employment. Higher wage demands by labor can be offset by

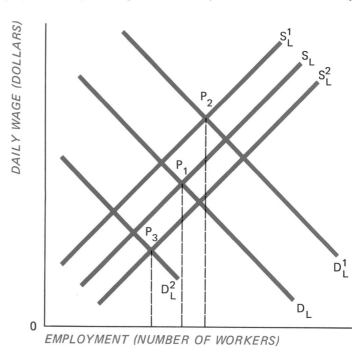

FIGURE 32-5

CHANGES IN MARKET EQUILIBRIA

Changes in the wage rate and employment are due to changes in labor demand, labor supply, or both.

greater labor productivity, by rising product prices due to expanding consumer demand for the product, or by both. Employment might have fallen in the early 1970s as we experienced a series of sizable wage increases. Instead, during that time the increase in wages was offset by a comparable or greater rise in product prices. As a consequence, there was no shrinkage of employment in the period 1971-1973.

Another possibility is displayed in the comparison of point P_1 with point P_3. An increase in labor supply to S_L^2—or acceptance of a lower wage by a given quantity of workers—would have led to an increase in employment if labor demand had remained constant. But the change in supply is accompanied by a reduction in demand from D_L to D_L^2. As a result, employment is reduced. Falling wages did not increase employment during the Great Depression of the 1930s. As wages fell, product demand and product prices fell at a faster rate because of declining household income. The net effect was a reduction in employment and product demand and yet a further decrease in demand for labor.

Reservations on the Theory

The marginal productivity theory of wages is a useful theoretical apparatus for interpreting actual variations in wages and employment in the economy. The assumptions of pure competition and complete mobility of productive factors do, however, call for some comments.

Marginal Productivity Theory Under Imperfect Competition. The marginal productivity theory becomes more complex under conditions of imperfect competition. Imperfect competition exists, for example, in the form of monopoly, or oligopoly, in the selling of the finished product. In such a case the price received from the sale of each additional unit produced will decline as output increases, as explained in Chapter 28. This condition, of course, will change the shape and the slope of the marginal revenue product curve.

On the other hand, if monopsony, oligopsony, or monopsonistic competition exists in the market for the purchase of labor, the individual employer will not be able to hire any quantity of labor at a given market wage. In fact, he will be forced, because of the nature of imperfect competition, to pay a higher wage as he hires additional units of labor. Then the wage, or average outlay, will no longer be equal to marginal outlay, as it is under conditions of pure competition. Since the wage of all workers will be the same, it means that when an additional worker is hired at a higher rate, total cost will increase not only by the amount of the additional wage but also by the fact that the wage of all other workers will be increased to this new higher level.

Graphically, for an individual firm the average outlay or wage will be represented by a line sloping upward to the right. Neither average nor marginal outlay is drawn as a horizontal line. Marginal outlay will be represented by a similar line at a higher position and sloping at a greater rate. In short, marginal outlay will increase at a faster rate than the average outlay. These relationships are shown in Figure 32-6. Consequently, at the equilibrium level of employment, or the point of maximum profits for the employer, marginal revenue product will equal marginal outlay; but the wage paid, average outlay, will be less than the marginal revenue product of labor. Thus, under conditions of imperfect competition, because marginal outlay and average outlay diverge, the wage will not tend to equal the marginal revenue product of the worker. In conclusion, the marginal productivity theory of wages applies differently under imperfect competition.

Other Complications. In addition to the fact that very little pure competition actually exists in our economy, it must also be remembered that the marginal productivity theory is based on a number of assumptions that may be somewhat idealistic. What happens, for example, if the employer is not interested in maximizing profits but in merely making reasonable profits?

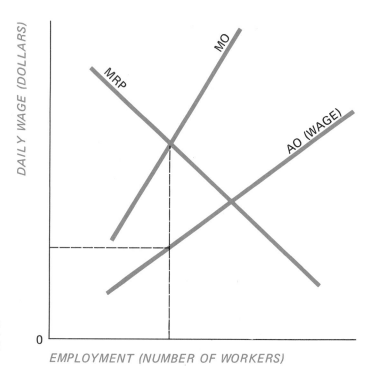

FIGURE 32-6

EQUILIBRIUM OF A FIRM: IMPERFECT COMPETITION

In the absence of competition among buyers of labor services, the equilibrium wage lies below the marginal revenue product of labor.

Are workers really as mobile as the theory assumes? Do monopsonists necessarily pay the lowest wage possible? To what extent do the worker and the employer know the value of the marginal revenue product of the worker? These and other complications have led practical businessmen and most labor-union leaders to reject the marginal productivity theory of wages.

Even though an employer may claim that the theory does not explain wage determination, generally he will admit that he will not hire additional workers unless they will increase his profit. Therefore, the businessman in his practical way is following the guiding principle established by the theory. Perhaps the future will bring a refinement of the theory to fit the data available from the employer, or vice versa, in order that there may be a more practical application of the theory.

BARGAINING THEORY OF WAGES

A popular theory of today is the *bargaining theory* of wages. This theory holds that wages are set somewhere between a maximum and a minimum depending on the relative bargaining strength of two parties, labor and management. Although labor's wage demand may be much higher than it expects to get, the union has a certain minimum—a floor below which it will not go. On the other hand, even though management's wage offer may be less than the firm can pay, there is a certain maximum above which it will not go. Thus, the union will not accept any wage below its minimum, and management will not settle for any wage above its maximum. Just where the wage rate will be set between these extremes depends on a number of local, national, and institutional factors.

The bargaining theory is more a description of how wage rates are arrived at than it is a theory of wages. In order to understand how wages are determined under the bargaining theory, we must learn what determines the minimum and the maximum between which wages will be set. For this we may have to return to some of the more conventional wage theories, especially the marginal productivity theory of wages. What determines the minimum wage that the union will accept? Certainly it will be nothing lower than the subsistence level, and probably in today's economy the subsistence level is more akin to that nebulous concept, "the American standard of living." What the union will regard as a minimum depends upon a multitude of factors. It may depend upon what workers are getting elsewhere; it will be influenced by the cost of living; and aggressiveness of the union will have its effect. Certainly, too, wage demands will be determined in large part by what the union thinks the value of the workers' productivity is to the company. Thus, the labor union will rely to a certain extent on the marginal productivity theory in setting wage demands for its members.

On the other hand, the maximum above which the company will not yield will be determined by the productivity of labor. In most cases, management will not grant a wage that is greater than the value of the product of labor. Otherwise the firm will suffer a loss of profits. Just how much below this maximum management's wage offer will be again depends on many factors. Among these factors are the firm's desire for maximum profits, its policy toward unionism, the cost of living, the strength of the union, the wage rate of its competitors, and so on.

In essence, the bargaining theory has to look elsewhere or incorporate other theories, especially the marginal productivity theory and some modernization of the subsistence theory, in order to explain how wages are determined. Furthermore, the bargaining theory cannot be a completely valid theory of wages, since it does not explain wage determination in all cases. Wages were determined, for example, for many years before we had labor unions. Even today many wage rates are determined by means other than collective bargaining, since only about one fourth of the labor force in America is organized into unions.

SUMMARY

1. Income distribution in our free enterprise system takes place through the markets for the services of labor, land, and capital. The prices for these services are wages, rent, and interest.

2. Wages, rent, and interest are income to the recipients; to the entrepreneur they are costs. The entrepreneur who employs the factors of production may receive a profit as a return for his willingness to undertake a risk.

3. Labor's share of the national income in 1973 was 74 percent, with the remainder going to the other factors of production.

4. A wage is fundamentally the price paid for a particular kind of labor service, which is determined in large part by the supply of that kind of service relative to the de-

mand for it. But wages are also considered in terms of what they will buy, and this is called the real wage.

5. None of the historical wage theories satisfactorily explains wage determination in today's labor markets. According to the current marginal productivity theory of wages, the wage of all workers of a particular grade will tend to equal the marginal revenue product of that grade of labor.

6. The bargaining theory of wages is more a description of wage-rate determination by the collective bargaining process than it is a true wage theory. It becomes more valid as a wage theory, however, if modified to incorporate elements of certain other theories, such as the marginal productivity theory.

QUESTIONS FOR DISCUSSION AND ANALYSIS

1. Distinguish between functional distribution and personal distribution of income.
2. Which is more important in contemporary American culture, functional or personal income distribution? Why?
3. Can you imagine a way in which wage income might be construed as a form of profit? Explain.
4. What do you see as the major weakness of the subsistence theory of wages?
5. In the marginal productivity theory of wages under conditions of pure competition, why will the wage tend to equal the marginal revenue product of labor?
6. Under the marginal productivity theory, explain how an increase in wages will cause a decrease in employment. Can there be offsetting changes?
7. Why is it that under conditions of imperfect competition the wage paid does not equal the marginal revenue product of labor?
8. Under the bargaining theory of wages, how would you explain the determination of wages in a non-organized industry?
9. How appropriate do you think the conventional wage theories are for explaining labor's share of the national income?

SUGGESTED READINGS

American Economic Association. *Readings in the Theory of Income Distribution*. Philadelphia: The Blakiston Co., 1946. Chapters 12-19.

Bloom, Gordon F., and Herbert L. Northrup. *Economics of Labor Relations*, 7th ed. Homewood, Ill.: Richard D. Irwin, Inc., 1973.

Burton, J. F., *et al. Readings in Labor Market Analysis*. New York: Holt, Rinehart, and Winston, Inc., 1971.

Finkel, Sidney R., and Vincent J. Tarascio. *Wage and Employment Theory*. New York: The Ronald Press Company, 1971.

Kuhn, Alfred. *Labor: Institutions and Economics*, rev. ed. New York: Harcourt Brace Jovanovich, Inc., 1967.

McConnell, Campbell R. *Perspectives on Wage Determination: A Book of Readings*. New York: McGraw-Hill Book Company, 1971.

McCormick, B. J. *Wages*. Baltimore: Penguin Books Inc., 1970.

Reynolds, Lloyd G. *Structure of Labor Markets: Wage and Labor Mobility in Theory and Practice*. Westport, Conn.: Greenwood Press, Inc., 1971.

Robinson, James W., and Roger W. Walker. *Labor Economics and Labor Relations*. New York: The Ronald Press Company, 1972.

Rowan, Richard L., and Herbert R. Northrup (eds.). *Readings in Labor Economics and Labor Relations*, rev. ed. Homewood, Ill.: Richard D. Irwin, Inc., 1972.

Williams, Clifford G. *Labor Economics*. New York: John Wiley & Sons, Inc., 1970.

Witney, Fred, and Benjamin Taylor. *Labor Relations*, 2d ed. Englewood Cliffs, N.J.: Prentice-Hall, Inc., 1972.

33

Labor-Management Relations

PREVIEW Labor unions have become an important establishment in American society. They are organized around the local and, upward, to the national or international office. Union objectives include wage increases, job security, control over working conditions, and control over the labor supply. Toward these ends, unions may utilize strikes and boycotts, and employers may counter with various means, including political techniques and propaganda. In the final analysis, these conflicts are generally resolved through collective bargaining or law.

The marginal productivity theory of wages, even when modified to allow for imperfect competition, fails to account for the activities of labor unions on the supply side of the labor market. The bargaining theory of wages, while recognizing the importance of unions, does not provide a theoretical analysis of union objectives. In order to comprehend more clearly the operation of the labor market, a deeper probe into the objectives and methods of both parties to wage negotiations will prove helpful.

In this chapter we will first outline the historical development of unionism in the United States. Following a description of different union types, the objectives and methods of both organized labor and business management will be explored. We conclude the chapter with a review of labor legislation and collective bargaining.

To begin, we must distinguish between craft or trade unions and industrial unions. In a *craft* or *trade union* the membership is comprised of workers in a single occupation or in closely related occupations. As the name suggests, an *industrial union* is composed of all classes of workers in a given industry.

A BRIEF HISTORY OF ORGANIZED LABOR

The first local trade union, an organization of carpenters, was founded in 1791 in Philadelphia. In 1794 two more unions were formed, and several came into being in the succeeding decades. For the most part, the goals of these unions were confined to gaining welfare benefits covering sickness and funeral expenses and the formulation of rules for apprentices. Some efforts were made to practice collective bargaining in the determination of wages.

Political Unions: 1860-1881

The Civil War created conditions that favored the development of union activity. Because of rising prices, expanding product demand, and a shortage of workers, unions grew in number and strength.

The momentum attained during the Civil War continued after the guns were silenced. It seemed to many employees and their leaders, however, that the time had come when working people must look to politics to solve some of their problems. Accordingly, many labor unions became identified with political movements and philosophies. One such organization, the National Labor Union, was chiefly concerned with securing laws that would restrict the working day to eight hours. A number of "industrial congresses" were held in an effort to unify the political aims and efforts of organized labor. The 1870s were characterized by several destructive strikes. During this decade, however, business depression caused the labor movement to wane.

During the 1880s, there was a notable increase in worker group consciousness. This sentiment found expression in the rapid growth of the Knights of Labor, formed in 1869 as a secret order. During the 1880s, it abandoned its secret rituals and began to enlist general membership. The Knights of Labor sought a cooperative society to replace the existing capitalistic and competitive order. Its slogan was, "An injury to one is the concern of all." Its immediate aim was to secure increased wages for workers, a reduction in the length of the working day, and the abolition of child and convict labor. For several years the increase in membership was phenomenal. By 1886 membership in the Knights of Labor was about 700,000. The rise of the more practical American Federation of Labor, however, and the disastrous outcome of a number of strikes caused the Knights of Labor to disappear almost as quickly as it had risen to prominence. Thus, a major movement toward labor unionism of an idealistic type subsided.

National Federations: 1881-1933

Contemporaneous with the rapid rise of the Knights of Labor was the organization and early growth of the American Federation of Labor. The latter organization dates from 1881, when the Federation of Organized Trades and Labor Unions was formed. The name of the federated union was changed in 1886 to the American Federation of Labor. In 1881 the membership of affiliated unions was 40,000.

The American Federation of Labor grew in numbers and strength until World War I, although the rate of growth was by no means regular. During the years of war prosperity from 1915 to 1920, membership in all kinds of trade unions rose rapidly from 2.5 million to 5.5 million. After the war, from 1920 to 1923, trade union membership decreased by 1.5 million. In the depression during the 1930s, total membership declined to 3 million.

AFL Philosophy During the Period. For half a century the underlying philosophy of the American Federation of Labor and that of the railroad brotherhoods (engineers, conductors, firemen, and trainmen) controlled the nature and aims of American unions. This philosophy assumed a continuation of the fundamental institutions of free enterprise and did not question the ethical foundations upon which these institutions rest. The Federation was composed of the "aristocracy of the laboring class" and sought to further the interests of skilled workers in certain specific occupations.

Ideological Unions. In 1905, an organization opposed to capitalism, called the Industrial Workers of the World, was formed in Chicago. It was made up of representatives of socialists, anarchists, and industrial unionists. Practically the only characteristic that members had in common was a bitter hatred and distrust of capitalism. The I.W.W. was never able to muster a strength of more than perhaps 68,000; this membership number was reached in· 1931.

The Trade-Union Educational League, later called the Trade Union Unity League, was another union with motives and aims similar to those of the I.W.W. It was organized in 1920, and by 1931 it claimed a membership of 100,000. In all its essentials it was communistic. During the depression of the 1930s, the league lost strength, and in 1938 it was disbanded.

Industrial Unionism: Since 1933

The last four decades, during which organized labor has experienced its greatest gains, have been characterized by the development of favorable labor legislation, the growth of industrial unionism, the split in the labor movement, and the merger of the AFL and the CIO.

National Labor Relations Act. In 1935, Congress passed the National Labor Relations Act, which guarantees the right of collective bargaining. The Act provides that, where a majority of the workers manifest a desire to bargain collectively, the employer has no alternative to dealing with the duly selected representatives of the group.

To carry out the intention of the Act, a National Labor Relations Board was established. The Board has power to supervise elections in situations where there is a dispute as to whether a majority of employees desire that a particular union should represent them in negotiating trade agreements with the employer. (A majority of the votes cast determines the issue.) It may investigate charges of unfair practices by an employer. It has the power to call upon employers to "cease and desist" from "unfair" labor practices.

If employers fail to obey, the Board may seek to enforce its order by securing a court injunction. The Act, of course, was a great boon to the unions, especially industrial unions, in their efforts to organize labor.

Formation of the CIO. For years there was divided opinion among leaders in the AFL over the question of promoting the growth of unions on an industry-wide basis. Some insisted that in the organization of unions the nature of an industry, and not workers with certain skills, should be the guiding consideration. For example, in the automotive industry, it was said that efforts should not be directed to forming separate unions of machinists, patternmakers, molders, chemists, toolmakers, and so on. Rather there should be a union made up of all workers in the automotive industry.

Failure to find agreement led to the formation of a self-appointed committee composed of the heads of eight international unions. This Committee on Industrial Organization—headed by John L. Lewis, president of the miners' union—began a determined campaign to organize the workers in several very important industries. Successful organization of the great automotive, steel, and other industries that had previously resisted the efforts of the Federation to organize them along craft lines confirmed the argument of Lewis and his co-workers. As a result of conflict regarding policies, the CIO leaders and their unions were expelled from the AFL in 1938. At this point the committee established an independent federation, which became known as the Congress of Industrial Organizations. Within a few years the CIO attained a membership of several million and reached its peak in the 1940s with nearly 7 million members.

Merger of AFL-CIO. The split in organized labor had several important effects, both on the labor movement and on the public. Some of the craft unions in the AFL liberalized requirements for admission. Rivalry between the AFL and the CIO caused the leaders of unions to compete with each other in winning concessions from their respective employers. On occasion, jurisdictional disputes between unions led to strikes, even though no issue between a union and an employer was involved. Disunity in the support of or opposition to candidates for public office weakened the political power of organized labor.

Both sides recognized that this division among labor unions was detrimental to the strength and progress of the organized labor movement. After a long period of negotiations, a merger of the American Federation of Labor and the Congress of Industrial Organizations was effected on December 5, 1955, creating a total membership of about 16 million. The constitution of the organization states that membership shall be chosen regardless of race, creed, color, or national origin. Furthermore, "raiding" of members from one union by another and jurisdictional disputes are to be discouraged. It is also a declared purpose of the AFL-CIO "to protect the labor movement" from corrupt influences and practices of all kinds, including the efforts of Communists to gain control of the constituent unions. The federation adopted six Codes of Ethical Practices which set forth principles that apply to the following matters: the issuance of charters to local unions; the handling of health and welfare funds; labor racketeers and Communists and Fascists in unions; investments and business interests of union officials; financial activities of unions; and the practice of democracy in union affairs.

With some minor exceptions, the philosophy and objectives of organized labor in the United States are, and always have been, conservative as compared with the ideas and aims of organized labor in most other nations. At present, union leaders are perhaps more inclined to favor government spending in order to relieve unemployment than are most managers in industry and business. But, on the whole, American unions rely on "business unionism," or collective bargaining with employers, to achieve their objectives. As to political party preferences, unions (perhaps like other organized groups) appear to follow the policy of "rewarding their friends and punishing their enemies."

Independent Unions

Not all national unions belong to the AFL-CIO. The railroad "brotherhoods," the Teamsters Union, the United Mine Workers, and since 1968 the United Auto Workers are the largest of those which do not belong.

In some cases there is a union in a plant that is not affiliated with a national organization of any kind. These are company unions. Usually company unions are formed as a result of the encouragement of the employer in his attempt to avert the formation of a union of the usual type. As a rule—so it is often argued—such a union can be largely controlled by the employer. Naturally the national unions and union federations are not in favor of company unions.

THE STRUCTURE OF LABOR UNIONS

Labor unions, whether they be industrial unions or craft unions, have as their primary purpose the promotion of the objectives of their members. To implement these objectives, organized labor has established a structure of local, national or international, and federated unions.

The Local Union

Individual workers belong to local unions and only indirectly to national and federated organizations. As a rule, locals in manufacturing establishments are confined to workers in a single plant, and officers of the locals are elected by secret ballot. Although it is not uncommon for the elected officers to receive some compensation, officers typically continue their trade and receive no regular salary as union officials. Many unions employ a full-time salaried business agent or business manager who keeps the records of the local, aids in adjusting grievances, and assists in collecting dues from delinquent members. Indeed, the largest locals maintain full-time clerical forces.

Shop stewards, who are not officers of the local union, are usually elected by the departments within a unionized establishment. The chief function of a shop steward is to see that working conditions prescribed by the union-employer contract are observed. As a consequence, he brings to the employer any grievances on the part of workers in his department.

National and International Unions

Most local unions are amalgamated in national or international unions. The main functions of the national unions are: (1) to promote and extend union organization by securing additional members for existing locals and to organize new locals; (2) to aid locals in their negotiations with employers; and (3) to take an active part in the conventions of the national federation with which they are affiliated. Some international unions include locals in the United States, Canada, Puerto Rico, and the Canal Zone.

The majority of national unions hold annual conventions. Some, however, hold their conventions only once every three, four, or even five years. All locals send delegates to their national conventions. Many national unions defray expenses and permit a daily allowance for delegates.

Between general conventions, the affairs of the national unions are entrusted to an executive board. To this body is committed the duty of executing the rules and instructions established by the convention. The general executive board may issue or withdraw charters of local unions, set aside the bylaws of local unions not in conformity with the national constitution, remove officers who are judged incompetent, fill vacancies in official positions, pass judgment on actions of national officers, direct the auditing of the union's records, and attend to a variety of other matters relating to the conduct of the national and local unions.

National Federations of Unions

The general aim of federated unions is to promote, protect, and encourage the labor movement among their local and national labor organizations. The functions of the federations include: promoting and protecting the interests of unions in regard to matters dealt with by the legislative, judicial, and executive branches of all the units of government; expanding union membership; determining the jurisdictional boundaries of unions; publishing

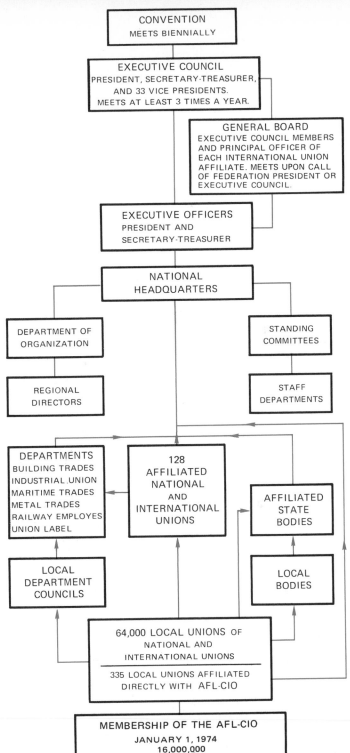

FIGURE 33-1

STRUCTURE OF THE AFL-CIO

The AFL-CIO, like any good organizational structure, has several levels of management with different line and staff functions.

SOURCE: Adapted from *Directory of National Unions and Employee Associations*, Department of Labor.

and supplying journals and printed information of various kinds to members and the public; conducting research on matters of interest and importance to union labor; and providing legal services to unions and their members.

UNION OBJECTIVES AND METHODS

To promote the interests of their members, labor unions follow rather uniform policies. Such policies may be interpreted as a set of objectives together with the means adopted to pursue these objectives. Although the general objective—to promote the economic welfare of the worker—generally prevails, immediate objectives vary with the social, political, and economic climate.

Union Objectives

The primary objectives of labor unions are security for the union itself, in order to preserve its role as representative of the workers, and working conditions that benefit the union membership. Other, more specific, goals are intended to serve these primary objectives.

Union Security. In order to deal effectively with employers, unions insist they must have sufficient power. Therefore, they seek to establish conditions of employment including the closed shop, the union shop, the preferential shop, and the agency shop.

As the term is most frequently used, a *closed shop* is an establishment that operates under a collective-bargaining agreement not to employ nonunion workers. Before nonunion workers are employed, they are required as a condition of employment to become and to remain members of the union with which the employer has an agreement. Practical distinctions between union-shop and closed-shop agreements are often vague.

A *union shop* closely resembles the closed shop in that a union-shop agreement requires any nonunion worker who secures employment in the establishment to become a member of the union at the end of a specified probationary period, say 30 days. Thus, a union-shop agreement provides for a type of closed shop with respect to the union status of employees.

A *preferential shop* exists when a union contract requires that the employer give special consideration to union employees. For example, the agreement may stipulate that, in hiring additional workers, preference be given to union members; or the agreement may provide that, in case of layoffs or promotions, union members shall be given preferential consideration.

Of growing importance in recent years, especially in states with right-to-work laws, is the agency shop. An *agency shop* is one in which the worker is not compelled to belong to the union, but a nonunion member is required to pay to the union a fee equivalent to the amount of the dues for a union member.

On the other hand, employers perhaps would prefer the *open shop*, which implies that the employer is free to hire employees without reference to any restrictions imposed by a union.

Although the Taft-Hartley Act (1947) prohibits the closed shop, some unions continue to insist that closed-shop agreements with employers are essential to the security that unionized employees should have. No other policy of labor unionism has aroused so much partisan discussion. Employers are, as a rule, convinced that the principle of the closed shop is entirely repugnant to the American concept of freedom. The unions are aware of the monopolistic nature of closed shops, but they contend that control of the supply of labor available to an employer is necessary to place the employee on an equal footing with the employer who, individually and in association with other employers, exercises great control over job opportunities.

Increasing and Maintaining Wages. Samuel Gompers, one of the founders of the AFL, said that it was "the object of trade unions to bring workers more and ever more of the product of their toil." He meant by this that as the productivity of labor increases because of improvements in organization and techniques of production, real wages should rise. This is the attitude of labor unions today. Moreover, the unions contend that wage rates should be adjusted to rises in the cost of living for two reasons: (1) wage increases should be sufficient to offset decreases in the value of money wages; and (2) only if consumer purchasing power is maintained can the goods turned out by the mass-production industries find a market.

In recent years unions have placed increasing emphasis on their demands for more and greater fringe benefits, such as larger pension benefits, earlier retirement, more holidays, and longer vacations. A recent estimate indicated that fringe benefits alone were costing employers over $78 billion a year, and they now account for over 12 percent of wage costs in manufacturing industries. According to figures of the Department of Labor, the amount of fringe benefits in a ten-year period rose 186 percent as compared with a rise of 111 percent in wages.

Hours of Work. Organized labor seeks to justify its advocacy of a gradual decrease in the workday and the workweek with several arguments: (1) It contends that the rapidly increasing productivity of industry makes possible the production of more goods with less work than formerly. (2) Individuals should have more time for their cultural improvement. (3) Increased leisure stimulates the demand for more and different goods. (4) The problems of the democratic way of life require that workers have time to study public problems and to participate intelligently in political efforts to solve these problems. (5) A reduction in the work period would result in an improvement in the health of the working population and create more jobs.

The Fair Labor Standards Act, passed by Congress in 1938 and since amended, provides time and one-half pay for overtime work beyond 40 hours a week. Now some union leaders are talking about a 35-hour week, and others are even suggesting 32 hours. An alternative approach to increased leisure time, introduced on an experimental basis in the early 1970s, is the four day–40 hour workweek. The normal workweek is condensed into four days, yielding a three-day weekend. This plan is growing in popularity. A recent study made by the American Management Association of the 4-40 plan indicated that more than 100,000 employees in 700 to 1,000 firms or organizations are using the plan. Most of the firms reported increased benefits, such as higher productivity and reduction in absenteeism, as a result of the 4-40 plan. A similar approach, stretched over a longer time period, is the extended vacation. In the steel industry, for example, workers are now eligible for four-week vacations. In addition to the regular four-week vacation, under certain circumstances senior employees may apply for extended vacations up to a total of 13 weeks.

From the employers' standpoint the validity of the argument for a shorter work period hinges on the question of productivity. Can workers produce enough goods in a shorter period to enable employers to maintain or to increase wages? As a rule, employers have tended to oppose any reduction in the work period without a corresponding reduction in wages or a corresponding increase in labor productivity.

Use of Laborsaving Machinery and Processes. Unions concede that in the long run new inventions and improved processes in production give rise to a greater demand for labor from a greater number of industries. Still, unions recognize the fact that loss of jobs and unemployment because of improvements in productive processes will result unless appropriate measures are taken to find work opportunities for displaced workers.

The unions insist that all new improvements in productive processes should be utilized immediately by employers but not at the expense of workers whose services in their present jobs will no longer be needed. They argue that every new machine should pay for itself. If certain jobs are abolished, it is the responsibility of the employer to provide work for displaced employees at no reduction in wages. Where such an adjustment is not possible, social security laws should provide against undue loss of income to the worker while he seeks other work.

Restriction and Regulation of Output. Restriction of output refers to the withholding of a reasonable amount of effort on the part of workers.

Featherbedding implies union rules that provide for the employment of more workers than are needed. To the employee and labor organizations restriction may be used legitimately for the protection of workers. To the employer the practice is indefensible and is utilized for the purpose of cheating him.

From the social standpoint it may be difficult to justify a policy of restricting output. But unions, like associations of employers, are compelled to give attention to immediate conditions. Unions decry the necessity for the policy of restricting work to an amount that they consider reasonable. Nevertheless, they insist that the protection of the welfare of their members requires that they be realistic.

Control of the Labor Supply. In the case of the craft unions, organized labor insists that new workers should meet the requirements established by the unions. The objectives of the unions in attempting to control the number of apprentices who may be trained and admitted to work are to insure that training has been adequate and to control the number of journeymen who prepare to enter a trade. Some of the craft unions undertake to prescribe the time apprentices shall serve, the qualifications of instructors, and the conditions under which training shall take place.

In some trades, where helpers work with the mechanics, it is found that the helpers become as proficient as journeymen. As a result, the well-trained helpers constitute an addition to the supply of journeymen, which increases competition for jobs in situations not controlled by union rules. For the purpose of limiting the number of helpers who may be employed, many of the unions have established rules as to the ratio of helpers to journeymen. In fact, some organizations of labor attempt to prevent the employment of helpers.

Some unions attempt to secure the enactment of ordinances requiring practitioners of a trade to secure a license. The unions that make the most use of this method include plumbers, electricians, barbers, motion-picture operators, and stationary engineers and firemen. Nearly all the states have laws requiring licenses for persons engaged in some or any of these callings.

Union Methods

Union demands upon employers may erupt because workers are worried about their employment and income. Most often labor leaders take the initiative; in order to achieve a position of worth in the minds of union members, they press for more advantages for the workers. Regardless of the source, unions have used a variety of methods to attain their objectives.

Collective Bargaining. *Collective bargaining* means that agreements on wages and working conditions are made with employers by representatives of the larger body of organized workers. Such agreements, if lawful, become binding to a certain extent upon all individuals.

Collective bargaining has become the central negotiating method of labor unions. Organized labor insists that only by collective agreements between employers and employees can workers enjoy equality of bargaining power with employers. Unions argue, in effect, that labor markets tend to be monopsonistic. That is, because the employer-employee relationship is a one-to-many relationship, the purchaser of labor services has disproportionate power to control wages. Under individual bargaining, where competition among workers prevails, the union alleges that wages are set for all workers at the level of those who will accept the lowest compensation. If monopsony is characteristic of the labor market, the wage will be less than the marginal revenue product of labor (see Figure 32-6).

Most of the time union-management problems are settled by peaceful negotiation. Sometimes, however, the inability of collective bargaining to reach a mutually agreeable settlement leads to the adoption of more drastic methods on the part of unions.

Strikes. A *strike* is a temporary concerted cessation from work by a group of employees for the purpose of compelling an employer to accede to their demands. Strikers feel that by stopping work they do not cease to occupy the status of employees and that they do not forfeit the right to return to their jobs when the dispute has been settled. Some employers, however, feel that when an employee leaves his job, he abandons the employment relationship. An attempt by employers to fill positions vacated by strikers, of course, is resented by the striking employees.

A *general strike* is one that involves the workers in all industries of a city, region, or other large area. General strikes are to be distinguished from strikes that are *industry-wide* in their scope. The former partake of the nature of sympathetic strikes to achieve the common aims of workers in different industries, while the latter occur for the purpose of achieving or of maintaining a system of collective bargaining on some issue in a given industry. General strikes always have been condemned by the courts.

Jurisdictional strikes arise because of a dispute between rival unions and not because of a demand upon the employer. For example, a dispute between metal workers and pipe fitters belonging to different unions may arise. Both groups may claim they are entitled to perform a certain kind of work involving the use of metal material. If the dispute cannot be settled, a strike by one or more unions may result, although none has a complaint against the employer.

Picketing. A union picket is a union member posted near the entrance of a place of employment by a labor organization during a dispute with the employer. The usual functions of pickets are to inform other employees, any prospective employees, and the public that a dispute exists; to persuade nonstrikers to join in the strike; and to discourage anyone from entering the place for the purpose of working. Mass picketing is the parading or assembling by a considerable number of strikers before the work establishment in order to dramatize the strike or to provide moral, and sometimes physical, opposition to workers who refuse to recognize the strike.

Mass picketing is generally held to be illegal. Other forms of picketing are generally considered legal if they are peaceful, but the courts do not agree on what constitutes peaceful picketing.

Picketing is a logical outgrowth of the attitude of union members who walk out on strike. The strikers take the position that leaving their places of work in concert does not constitute abandonment of their jobs. It is their intention to resume their places when the grievance has been adjusted. If some workers remain at their jobs, the strikers realize that the prospect of a successful strike is weakened to that extent. If workers not previously employed in the place of work take their jobs, the strike cannot succeed. This accounts for the emphasis of the union and the pickets on seeing to it that all employees and others observe the strike. As a rule, peaceful methods of persuasion are used. If, however, some workers persist in refusing to honor the strike or if new employees attempt to enter the place, more forceful methods are likely to be utilized. These often include the use of derisive or abusive language and threats of personal violence.

Boycotts. A *boycott* is defined as a "concerted effort to withdraw and to induce others to withdraw from economic or social relations with offending groups or individuals." [1] Sometimes a distinction is made between a primary and a secondary boycott. The *primary boycott* refers to a situation where the aggrieved workers resolve not to patronize a firm because of their own complaint against the management. The *secondary boycott* is an action by a labor union whereby the union prohibits its members from working for or having any dealings with a concern whose employees have struck.

The aim in establishing a boycott is to bring economic pressure to bear on a producer or seller of goods. Many boycotts have proved ineffective because it was impossible to persuade the public or other workers not to patronize the aggrieving party. Other attempts of labor groups to inflict financial injury on an employer, however, have been very effective.

As a rule, primary boycotts have been considered legal, but secondary boycotts have frequently been declared illegal. The Taft-Hartley Act prohibits secondary boycotts.

[1] *Encyclopedia of the Social Sciences*, Vol. II, p. 662.

Sabotage. The term sabotage has been commonly used to refer to actions by employees intended to restrict production or to inflict damage on an employer's property or his business. It is said that use of the term originated from the acts of French workers in the early days of the Industrial Revolution when they sometimes threw their *sabots*—wooden shoes—into the moving parts of machinery because of the fear that the increasing use of machinery would destroy their jobs.

No important labor group now advocates the use of sabotage in the sense that they encourage the destruction of property. But the resentment of dissatisfied workers has sometimes resulted in acts of destruction. Broken factory windows and other types of damage have occurred during strikes that were attended by strife between the strikers and officers of the law.

Propaganda and Political Pressure. In any contest between labor and management, public opinion weighs heavily in the determination of the outcome. Labor unions recognize this fact and make efforts to create favorable public sentiment. In attempting to influence public opinion, however, unions often encounter difficulties. First, people not directly affected by the issues have little more than a passing interest. Second, while newspapers and magazines may not be anti-union in attitude, they are seldom pro-union. Third, when a struck plant is surrounded with marching pickets, workers appear as the aggressors or the disturbers of industrial peace in the community.

Like other organized groups, unions attempt to secure passage of favorable legislation. For a long time common-law doctrines of conspiracy and restraint of trade served as powerful weapons used by employers to combat the growth of unionism. With the passage of the National Labor Relations Act in 1935, however, organized labor enjoyed protective legislation. Because many employers and other groups were opposed to the law, unions maintained active lobbyists in order to resist any unfavorable change in the law. In spite of their efforts, several state legislatures have passed laws limiting union activities, and union protectionism in the NLRA was modified in 1947 by the passage of the Labor Management Relations Act (Taft-Hartley).

EMPLOYERS' OBJECTIVES AND COUNTERMETHODS

The primary objective of an employer is the long-run profitability of the business firm. Since higher wages, greater fringe benefits, and certain working conditions act to raise the cost of production, employers naturally resist union demands. There is no doubt that some union activities result in mutual benefits for both employees and employers. Nevertheless, strikes, boycotts, and similar union methods have adverse effects upon the firm's profitability. Employers have tended to react against the initiative taken by organized workers.

For every method of strategy used by labor unions, employers have at one time or another made use of a counterstrategy. Some of these methods utilized in the past by employers have now been outlawed.

Injunctions

An *injunction* is an order from a court commanding that an individual or a group do or refrain from doing an act. When a court issues a labor injunction, it is expected that labor leaders will obey the order. If they do not obey, under the common law they become liable for a judgment of *contempt of court*. If they are found guilty of contempt, they are subject to fine or imprisonment, or both, at the discretion of the court. Of course, one who disobeys an injunction is also liable for prosecution for any damages to property that he may have caused.

The almost indiscriminate use of injunctions at one time caused labor leaders to charge that the courts were merely the tools which employers could invoke in their disputes with labor. Organized labor feared the law but often regarded the courts with scorn and contempt. In fact, there have been labor leaders who boasted of the number of times they had defied the courts and had served jail sentences for such defiance.

The Norris-LaGuardia Act limits the power of federal judges to issue injunctions in connection with disputes between employers and employees. The general purpose of this federal statute, enacted in 1932, is to exempt labor unions from injunctions issued by federal judges. It specifically accords to labor the right to strike, to belong to a union, and to engage in other practices, many of which rendered union members liable to prosecution under common law, as well as under the Clayton and the Sherman Antitrust Acts.

Later more than half of the states also enacted legislation that placed restrictions on the use of injunctions by state courts. Under the Taft-Hartley Act, however, the application of the Norris-LaGuardia Act has been narrowed. The newer law provides that, when in the opinion of the President of the United States a threatened or actual strike or lockout would "imperil the national health and safety," the Attorney General may be empowered to obtain an injunction to stop or to prevent the proposed or actual interruption of production. Such an injunction may run for 80 days.

Lockouts

A *lockout* is a temporary cessation of the operation of his business by an employer in an attempt to win a dispute with his employees. Logically it is the employer's equivalent of the strike. In terms of overt action and the number of occurrences, however, the lockout is a relatively unimportant device for use in conflict with employees. Employers seldom shut down their plants in order to coerce labor.

Blacklists

A *blacklist* is a list of the names of union members secretly kept and exchanged by employers or employers' associations for the purpose of preventing certain workers from obtaining other employment after having been discharged because of union affiliation or activity. Formerly there was no question as to the legal right of employers to maintain and to circulate lists of workers who were considered objectionable because of their connections with a labor union. The blacklist was considered nothing more than the employer's version of the boycott. The Taft-Hartley Act rules out blacklisting, along with a number of other "unfair" practices by employers.

Yellow-Dog Contracts

A *yellow-dog contract* is a "promise, made by a worker, as a condition of employment, not to belong to a union during the period of employment, or not to engage in certain specified activities, such as collective bargaining or striking." [2] The term was one of contempt, applied by employees to their fellow workers agreeing to such a contract. It implied that any man who agreed to give up his constitutional right of association was cowardly and that he possessed a "yellow streak." Yellow-dog contracts formerly were enforced by the lower courts with the approval of the United States Supreme Court in 1917. The Norris-LaGuardia Act (1932) made such contracts unenforceable.

Strikebreakers

A *strikebreaker* is an individual hired by an employer to replace a striking employee. The term is also applied to "strong-arm" men and spies employed to foment violence and confusion among strikers. Several of the states have laws that prescribe conditions under which employees may be recruited to take the places of striking workers. Two federal statutes now make illegal the transportation of strikebreakers across state boundaries.

Company Unions

A *company union*, as mentioned previously, is an organization of employees in a particular plant that is not affiliated with an outside labor group. Restriction of membership to workers in a single plant is in contrast to those unions which have a broad regional or national membership.

The passage of the National Industrial Recovery Act in 1933 gave impetus to the company union movement. One section of the Act guaranteed

---

[2] Joel I. Seidman, *The Yellow Dog Contract* (Baltimore: The Johns Hopkins University Press, 1932), p. 11.

to labor the right of collective bargaining. Some employers, fearing unionization by locals affiliated with national unions, encouraged their employees to form single-plant organizations. No doubt some employers sincerely believed that a company organization would make for more amicable relations between labor and management. Others, however, were willing to accept the company union only as the lesser of the two evils with which they seemed confronted. The National Labor Relations Act made it an "unfair labor practice" for an employer to encourage formation of a company union by offering financial aid. Under the Labor Management Relations Act employers are not permitted to dominate or attempt to control any labor union.

Propaganda and Political Pressure

Employers and employers' associations, like employees and labor unions, know the importance of public opinion in the settlement of industrial disputes. Moreover, they actively seek to secure the passage of laws that, in their opinion, will not discriminate against them in their relations with their employees. In the case of a strike that affects a whole community or interrupts business to a considerable extent, individual employers, as well as an association to which they may belong, are likely to place their case before the public in newspaper advertisements.

In their efforts to secure the enactment or retention of laws that will exercise a restraining influence on labor organizations, employer groups often distribute printed materials which set forth arguments for or against laws pertaining to labor relations in industry. Like the large labor organizations, industrial, commercial, and financial groups attempt to prevent the enactment of laws that are considered unfavorable to their own interests.

THE LAW AND INDUSTRIAL PEACE

There are two ways of attempting to maintain industrial peace. One way is by the passage and enforcement of laws that circumscribe the liberties of individuals; the other is by a spirit of employee-employer cooperation in particular situations. For the most part, peaceful relations in the United States are maintained, not by the constraints of law, but by a willingness on the part of people to concede that individuals possess rights in common. Moreover, certain rights are assigned to individuals and groups in their particular capacities. Having conceded the existence of these rights, most people ordinarily show a proper respect for them.

Frequently, in interpreting a written law or in applying a common-law doctrine, the court must determine whether the defendant had "just cause" for employing a particular means. In making the determination judges are sometimes confronted with situations in which they are likely to be influenced by their social philosophy and their attitudes toward economic issues. In this connection United States Justice Oliver Wendell Holmes observed years ago: "The ground for decision really comes down to a proposition of policy of rather delicate nature concerning the merit of the particular benefit to themselves intended by the defendants and suggests a doubt whether judges with different economic sympathies might not decide a case differently when brought face to face with the same issue." [3] Therefore, the common law, the statutory law, and the philosophy and attitude of the court all play a part in court decisions.

Common-Law Doctrines

English and American common law is predicated on a philosophy of individualism and the right of private property. As one authority has remarked, "What is peculiar to Anglo-American legal thinking is an ultra-individualism; an uncompromising insistence upon individual interests and individual property as the focal point of our jurisprudence." [4] Two common-law principles or doctrines have played a major role in judicial decisions affecting labor disputes. They are the doctrine of conspiracy and the doctrine of restraint of trade.

The Conspiracy Doctrine. The basic theory of the *conspiracy doctrine* is that a lawful act by an individual may be unlawful when it is the result of a concerted agreement. For example, it has been held that it was legal for an individual worker to ask for an increase in wages. When individuals acted jointly, however, for the purpose of demanding a wage increase, courts during the early history of trade unions often ruled that any united action of workers was in itself a violation of the law. For a long time courts tended to take the position of outlawing all union activity. Then, in 1842, the Supreme Court of Massachusetts ruled that a combination per se to raise wages was not illegal unless it resulted from "a combination of two or more persons, by some concerted action, to accomplish some criminal or unlawful purpose, or to accomplish some purpose not in itself criminal or unlawful by criminal means." [5] This ruling was a considerable departure from the traditional interpretation and application of the conspiracy doctrine.

In general, according to common law, courts tend to hold that a combined act by individuals is legal if the purpose is the benefit of the members of the

---

[3] "Privilege, Malice, and Intent," *Harvard Law Review*, Vol. VIII (1894), p. 114, as quoted in E. E. Witte, *The Government and Labor Disputes* (New York: McGraw-Hill Book Company, 1932), p. 52.

[4] Roscoe Pound, *The Spirit of the Common Law* (New York: Marshall Jones Company, 1921), p. 27.

[5] *Commonwealth* v. *Hunt*, 4 Metcalf 111 (1842).

group. If the purpose is the injury of the employer, the organization is illegal. Where the organization undertakes to accomplish a purpose that is legal by employing an illegal means, such act of the organization itself is declared illegal and individual members become liable for the actions of the group. In a given case the question to be settled is whether the act of a labor organization is for the purpose of gaining a benefit for the workers or of injuring the employer. Since a union may feel that it can gain its point only by inflicting financial loss on an employer, the court must decide whether the loss to the employer or the benefit to be gained by the workers is of the greater importance.

The Restraint-of-Trade Doctrine. According to the *restraint-of-trade doctrine*, any contract that restrains trade is against public policy and is unenforceable. Moreover, when persons combine to effect an agreement that will restrain trade, the combination may be regarded as a criminal conspiracy. At common law a combination for the purpose of peacefully persuading an employer to grant an increase in wages was usually allowed to be legal. If the purpose was to coerce him by using "unreasonable" means, such as a strike, picketing, or a boycott, the combination was held to be a conspiracy in restraint of trade. What was reasonable in any case, of course, depended upon the judgment of the court.

Laws and Agencies

Other than the Federal Anti-Injunction (Norris-LaGuardia) Act—which was discussed earlier—the more important statutes and agencies concerned with industrial peace have been the National Labor Relations Act, the Labor-Management Relations Act, the Federal Mediation and Conciliation Service, and the Labor-Management Reporting and Disclosure (Landrum-Griffin) Act.[6]

The National Labor Relations (Wagner) Act. This federal statute was enacted in 1935. Sections 7 and 8 contain the following provisions:

> Sec. 7. Employees shall have the right to self-organization, to form, join, or assist labor organizations, to bargain collectively through representatives of their own choosing, and to engage in concerted activities, for the purpose of collective bargaining or other mutual aid or protection.
> Sec. 8. It shall be an unfair labor practice for an employer—
> (1) To interfere with, restrain, or coerce employees in the exercise of the rights guaranteed in section 7.

[6] The Railway Labor Act (1926) endorsed unionism. Previously, between 1890 and 1914, 14 states had passed laws designed to prevent discrimination by railroads against unions. These laws were declared by the courts to be unconstitutional. The National Industrial Recovery Act (1933) gave statutory approval to collective bargaining. When the Supreme Court invalidated part of the Act, the whole Act became ineffective.

(2) To dominate or interfere with the formation or administration of any labor organization or contribute financial or other support to it.

(3) By discrimination in regard to hire or tenure of employment or any term or condition of employment to encourage or discourage membership in any labor organization.

(4) To discharge or otherwise discriminate against an employee because he has filed charges or given testimony under this Act.

(5) To refuse to bargain collectively with the representatives of his employees.

The law also provided for the creation of a National Labor Relations Board, which was to function as a quasi-judicial body for the carrying out of the provisions of the Act. The Board could order secret elections by employees or otherwise determine the bargaining agency of a union in case of a dispute as to who were the proper representatives for collective bargaining; decide what were unfair labor practices; issue "cease and desist" orders to employers adjudged guilty of unfair labor practices; and apply to the courts for aid in enforcing its decisions.

The Labor Management Relations (Taft-Hartley) Act. Opposition to the Wagner Act resulted in 1947 in the passage by Congress (over the President's veto) of the Labor Management Relations Act, popularly known as the Taft-Hartley Act. The Wagner Act was not repealed, but the Taft-Hartley Act nullified or modified many provisions which had been objectionable to employers.

The law was frankly intended to impose curbs on labor organizations. Businessmen and business organizations had long contended that such restrictions were necessary in order to place management on an equal basis with the unions. The measure was acclaimed by conservative management and just as emphatically denounced by labor unions. Management asserted that it placed both management and labor on an equal footing before the law. Labor spokesmen branded it as a "slave labor" law and predicted that its enforcement would reduce workers to a position of serfdom.

In general, the changes effected by the new law were: (1) management was given a new set of legal rights; (2) new rules were imposed on the scope and methods of collective bargaining; (3) provisions were made to prevent unions from coercing individual employees to join a labor organization; and (4) a substantial change was made in the organization and the authority of the National Labor Relations Board.

The law requires that both labor unions and management respect the right of individual workers to join or not to join a union. Unions cannot refuse to bargain with an employer if he meets the requirements of the law. Annually a union that has been recognized by an employer may be required to prove that it represents a majority of the workers in a given establishment, and an employer may request an election by the employees before he recognizes a union as their bargaining agent. He is not compelled to recognize a union of foremen. Striking employees who have been discharged by an employer may not participate in an election concerning collective bargaining.

A union may be sued by an employer, another union, or an employee for the acts of any one of its officials, including shop stewards. Featherbedding, that is, compelling employers to pay for unnecessary services, is prohibited. Officials of the unions are liable for their acts whether such acts are authorized by higher officials or not. The law prohibits secondary boycotts, jurisdictional strikes, and secondary strikes.

Regarding union security, the Taft-Hartley Act prohibits the closed and preferential shops. Although it permits the union shop, a provision of the Act, Section 14(b), provides a means or loophole by which a state may legislate against compulsory forms of union membership, such as the union shop. In short, the Taft-Hartley Act allows the union shop, provided the state does not have a law against it.

This section of the Taft-Hartley Act led to a wave of state right-to-work laws, which declare it illegal for an employer to require a worker to join a union as a condition of employment. The right-to-work laws have led to bitter controversy as the pros and cons have been debated back and forth. By 1974, 19 states had right-to-work laws. They have been voted upon but defeated in several other states, and 5 states passed but later repealed their right-to-work laws.

The Act contains a provision whereby the President, if he believes that an impending strike or a strike in progress might endanger the national health and safety, may appoint a board to study the facts in the case. The board does not have the power to recommend how the dispute shall be settled. After a report by the board, the President may ask the Attorney General to file a petition for a court injunction restraining the calling of the strike or the continuation of the strike.

Unions are required to report to the Secretary of Labor: (1) the amount of compensation of its three principal officers whose compensations are more than $5,000 a year; (2) the manner in which elections are conducted; (3) the amount of initiation fees and of annual dues; (4) the qualifications for admission to the union; and (5) the sources of its receipts and the amount of its assets. Furthermore, each union must supply each member with a statement of its annual receipts. According to the Act, each union official had to file a non-Communist affidavit before the union could use the services of the National Labor Relations Board. Although the affidavits are no longer required, an amendment to the Act absolutely bars a Communist, or anyone who had been a member of the Communist Party in the previous five years, from holding union office. Violation of this clause is a criminal offense punishable by a fine up to $10,000 and/or imprisonment up to one year.

As is the case with business corporations, unions are not permitted to contribute money directly to political party organizations for the purpose of influencing the election of federal officials. Unions, however, are able to circumvent this prohibition by setting up their own "political action" units composed of individuals favorable to the candidates who are approved by the unions.

The law gives the government the power to decide when there is a slowdown in an establishment which amounts to a strike. In practical terms, this means that it may become incumbent on the Board and the courts to establish levels of production or speed on an assembly line below which production may not fall without rendering the workers guilty of striking.

The Taft-Hartley Act provides for the creation of a position to be filled by an official who has sometimes been referred to as the "labor czar." This official is the General Counsel of the National Labor Relations Board; he is appointed by the President with the approval of the Senate. He acts in the name of the Board but is not responsible to that body. His decision is the final word with reference to investigations, complaints under the statute, and the cases that may or may not be presented to the Board. It is his responsibility in some cases to obtain an injunction to prevent unfair labor practices.

The Labor-Management Reporting and Disclosure (Landrum-Griffin) Act. The Landrum-Griffin Act, which was passed by Congress in 1959, is an important amendment to the Taft-Hartley Act. It imposes upon unions a number of requirements that the sponsors of the law contended were necessary in order to prevent unscrupulous union leaders from exploiting workers, employers, and the public.

Among other things, the law provides state courts and labor agencies with recognized jurisdiction over certain union-management cases; limits boycott practices by unions; with minor exceptions, outlaws all agreements between unions and employers whereby the employer agrees in advance not to do business with an "unfair" (to labor) business firm or a firm in which there is a strike in process; restricts picketing for the purpose of winning membership for a particular union; contains provisions designed to limit the power of union leaders in the union elections and management; requires annual detailed reports to the Secretary of Labor in regard to union finances; and bars Communists from union office.

Labor spokesmen were opposed to the enactment of the Landrum-Griffin Act and felt that it would retard the growth of unions, particularly in the

South. One of the provisions to which they objected especially was that which gives state courts more jurisdiction in dealing with labor disputes. Union leaders feared an increase in the use of court injunctions in the control of union activities.

The Federal Mediation and Conciliation Service. In 1915 the United States Labor Department inaugurated a conciliation service, which for 32 years was very successful in helping to settle industrial disputes. The United States Conciliation Service possessed no mandatory powers, and mediators were available only on the permission or invitation of the parties to a dispute. In 1947, however, Congress decided that the attitude of the Labor Department was not unbiased. Accordingly, the Taft-Hartley Act changed the name of the Service to that of the Federal Mediation and Conciliation Service (FMCS) and provided that the Service shall be an independent federal agency, the chief of which shall be appointed by the President and approved by the Senate and shall report annually to Congress. Under the law the FMCS is required to "proffer its services" whenever it decides that a dispute may "cause a substantial interruption of commerce." In case the director of the FMCS cannot bring the disputants together, he must urge both parties to submit the employer's last offer to a secret vote by the employees.

The National (Railroad) Mediation Board and the National Railroad Adjustment Board each has jurisdicition over the different classes of railroad employees, such as train and yard service and shop crafts. If either of the boards is unable to settle a dispute that threatens to tie up transportation, the President is notified. He may appoint an emergency board of a fact-finding nature, which is required to render a report within 30 days. Meanwhile a strike is illegal.

In recent years the parties to industrial disputes have in many cases agreed to a "fact-finding board" appointed by a government (federal or state) official. As the name implies, the function of the fact-finding board is to investigate, collect, and make known the facts in a labor dispute.

A THREAT TO FREE ENTERPRISE?

The results of work stoppages due to disagreements between employees and management affect many citizens and business firms other than those immediately involved. These results may not be measurable, but they are real nevertheless. Outstanding examples of what may be the effects of a work stoppage were the four-month strike in the steel industry that occurred in 1959 and the prolonged strike in the auto industry in 1967. In both cases, millions of dollars of wages and profits were lost by the striking workers and the steel companies. In addition, companies dependent upon steel lost profits and were compelled to lay off many of their employees. In 1973 the number of strikes and lockouts in the country totaled over 5,100 involving nearly 2 million workers who suffered a loss of over 25 million man-days of labor. The loss in production, wages, and profits is incapable of calculation.

Ordinarily the device relied upon to minimize work stoppages is that of voluntary agreement between employees, or their unions, and management. But suppose employees and management cannot come to an agreement? Suppose that the mediation and conciliation services provided by the federal government and some of the states are ineffective? Shall employees or management be permitted to go on strike or to close down places of employment? What then? Obviously where key industries are involved, government eventually would be forced to take over. To that extent at least the free enterprise system would not be working as it is supposed to work.

In order to prevent long, drawn-out work stoppages, should we enact compulsory arbitration laws that compel unions and managements to submit their disputes to an arbitrator whose decision would be final? The proposal for compulsory arbitration raises a number of important questions. If a government arbitrator fixes wages, will he not also have to fix the number of working hours and the working conditions? And if so, will not government eventually have to fix the prices of goods and services that are produced? Of course, if it should become the responsibility of government to do all these things, it would mean that the free enterprise system had ceased to operate. It is very important, therefore, that union leaders, management, and the general public recognize the seriousness of this problem.

SUMMARY

1. The history of organized labor in the United States is coextensive with the history of the nation. The labor movement, like that of collective practices used by some employers, was not in accord with the underlying theory of laissez-faire and pure competition.

2. Evolution of the labor movement is marked by periods that may be called early growth, development of national unions, rise of political unions, growth of national union federations, and the maturity of industrial unionism.

3. Formation of the CIO liberalized the requirements for union membership. Merger of the AFL and CIO in 1955 was designed to increase the strength of organized labor by removing causes of friction between trade unions and industrial unions; through united strength organized labor hoped to achieve greater political power.

4. Broadly speaking, the objectives of organized labor at present are to achieve union security, to increase wages, to regulate hours of work, to protect workers from detrimental effects of laborsaving devices, to limit output within what labor considers the bounds of reason, and to exert control over the labor supply.

5. The primary method used by unions to pursue their objectives is collective bargaining. When collective bargaining has failed or been denied to unions, more drastic devices, such as strikes and political pressure, have been employed.

6. The countermeasures of employers include injunctions, lockouts, blacklists, yellow-dog contracts, the use of strikebreakers, formation of company unions, and propaganda and political pressure.

7. Two ways of attempting to maintain industrial peace are by the passage and application of laws and by the practice of union-management cooperation.

8. The National Labor Relations Act provided an unprecedented amount of protection to unions, which greatly promoted the organized labor movement. The Labor Management Relations Act, which was strongly opposed by unions, nullified many of the provisions of the NLRA and restricted several other provisions. In general the LMRA increased the legal rights of employers, set up new rules for collective bargaining, attempted to limit the power of unions to induce workers to become members of unions, and reorganized the National Labor Relations Board. The Labor-Management Reporting and Disclosure Act of 1959 restricts further certain acts of unions and union leaders.

NEW TERMS

Craft or trade union, *p. 721*
Industrial union, *p. 721*
Closed shop, *p. 728*
Union shop, *p. 728*
Preferential shop, *p. 728*
Agency shop, *p. 728*
Open shop, *p. 729*
Featherbedding, *p. 731*
Collective bargaining, *p. 731*
Strike, *p. 732*
General strike, *p. 732*
Jurisdictional strikes, *p. 732*
Picketing, *p. 733*
Boycott, *p. 733*
Primary boycott, *p. 733*

Secondary boycott, *p. 733*
Injunction, *p. 735*
Lockout, *p. 735*
Blacklist, *p. 736*
Yellow-dog contract, *p. 736*
Strikebreaker, *p. 736*
Company union, *p. 736*
Conspiracy doctrine, *p. 738*
Restraint-of-trade doctrine, *p. 739*
Norris-LaGuardia Act, *p. 739*
Wagner Act, *p. 739*
Taft-Hartley Act, *p. 740*
Landrum-Griffin Act, *p. 742*
Federal Mediation and Conciliation Service, *p. 743*

QUESTIONS FOR DISCUSSION AND ANALYSIS

1. One company may have to negotiate with a half dozen or more craft unions within its plants. Another company may do all its bargaining with one industrial union representing all the workers within the company. Would it not be better for both the company and the union if all workers were represented by the same union? Explain.

2. Is the labor union a logical outgrowth of the development of an industrial society? Why or why not?

3. Why may it be said that labor-union philosophy in this country has, for the most part, been conservative?

4. (a) What are the functions of a federation of unions?

(b) Which of these functions do you consider the most important? Why?

5. (a) What are the arguments for collective bargaining as opposed to individual bargaining?

(b) What are the arguments against collective bargaining?

6. What is your attitude toward automation and technological development? Would it be the same if you were a union member?

7. Do you favor the organization of white-collar workers? Why or why not?

8. In your own mind, how would you justify the right of a group of workers to engage in a strike? Explain.

9. Do you think teachers in the public schools have a right to strike? Why or why not?

10. Assume that two unions are seeking to organize the workers in a particular plant. Each union threatens to strike the plant unless the company recognizes it as the bargaining agent for all the workers. Should such jurisdictional strikes be permitted? Why or why not?

11. (a) How do labor unions justify picketing?

(b) How do employers justify their opposition to picketing?

12. What methods are or have been employed by management in disputes with organized labor?

13. (a) What were the most significant provisions of the Wagner Act?

(b) Why was the law objectionable to management?

14. How does the Taft-Hartley Act differ from the National Labor Relations Act?

15. Is "big labor" a threat to free enterprise? Why or why not?

SUGGESTED READINGS

Bakke, E. W., Clark Kerr, and C. W. Anrod. *Unions, Management, and the Public*, 3d ed. New York: Harcourt Brace Jovanovich, Inc., 1967.

Bloom, Gordon F., and Herbert R. Northrup. *Economics of Labor Relations*, 7th ed. Homewood, Ill.: Richard D. Irwin, Inc., 1973.

Bull, George. *Industrial Relations: The Boardroom Viewpoint*. Levittown, N.Y.: Transatlantic Arts, Inc., 1972.

Chandler, Margaret K. *Management Rights and Union Interests*. New York: McGraw-Hill Book Company, 1964.

Derber, Milton. *The American Idea of Industrial Democracy, 1865-1965*. Urbana, Ill.: University of Illinois Press, 1970.

Gitlow, Abraham L. *Labor and Manpower Economics*, 3d ed. Homewood, Ill.: Richard D. Irwin, Inc., 1971.

Heneman, H. G., Jr., and Dale Yoder. *Labor Economics*, 2d ed. Cincinnati: South-Western Publishing Co., 1965.

Kassalow, Everett M. *Trade Unions and Industrial Relations*. New York: Random House, Inc., 1970.

Myers, A. Howard. *Labor Law and Legislation*, 4th ed. Cincinnati: South-Western Publishing Co., 1968.

Robinson, James W., and Roger W. Walker. *Labor Economics and Labor Relations*. New York: The Ronald Press Company, 1972.

Taft, Phillip. *Organized Labor in American History*. New York: Harper & Row, Publishers, 1964.

34

Rent:
Payments for
Quality
Differences

PREVIEW Land, as the term is used in economics, includes all natural resources. Rent, the income attributed to the use of land in production, arises from land fertility and location. The amount of rent is determined by the demand for land and its available supply. While demand is influenced primarily by national income and population growth, the accessible supply is in large part determined by transportation and advances in technology.

Rent is a familiar term. A payment arranged by contract for use of an apartment or a home is the most common usage of the term. Similarly, an automobile, a machine, or a set of tools can be rented. This form of rent payment may be called *contract rent*.

In economics the term "rent" is interpreted more broadly. *Economic rent* may be defined as payment for the use of land and other natural resources which are fixed in total supply when these resources are combined with others. Hereafter, when we use the term "land" we shall interpret the term to include not only land as such but also those natural resources which, like land, are fixed in total supply. Contract rent may or may not equal economic rent. But in the long run the two tend to coincide in value.

When a rent payment is made by the entrepreneur to another party (who owns the land), the payment is referred to as *explicit rent*. Frequently, however, the entrepreneur owns the land himself. Just as his take-home income might consist in part of wages for labor he contributes to the productive process of his own firm, so too a part of his personal income may consist of rent for the firm's use of his land. Such rent is called *implicit rent*. Suppose farmer Smith rents from Mr. Jones 100 acres adjoining his own farm of 100 acres. Payment to Jones for the use of his 100 acres is explicit rent, while the imputed payment to himself for the use of his own 100 acres is implicit rent. Unless otherwise indicated, the analysis of economic rent will include both implicit and explicit rent.

THE PRODUCTIVITY OF LAND

Sometimes the productive services of land are consumed directly. Rather than being combined with labor and capital to produce some other tangible good, the land yields immediate services. City parks, national parks, recreation grounds, and hunting and fishing preserves are examples of areas that have been set aside for purposes of amusement, recreation, or sport. The geographic area may have to be improved and maintained by the application of capital and labor. Roads, dams, or equipment may have to be built and repaired. Nevertheless, when combined with these means of improvement or access, the land itself yields services that are no less important than other goods or services consumed by households.

Fertility

If land is considered without respect to individual ownership, obviously some countries are fortunate in containing large expanses of fertile agricultural land and in holding liberal supplies of the other resources, such as easily accessible forests, minerals, and oil reserves. This is particularly true of the United States and the Soviet Union, but a similar situation is to be found as well in a few other countries. Some countries, like Tibet and Iceland, however, have only limited supplies of these vital resources. The people of these countries consequently are burdened with an economic disadvantage.

If land is considered from the point of view of individual units, it is obvious that some farms are more fertile than others. The rocky fields of New England cannot compare with the rich black soils of Illinois and Iowa. The rich lands of the Mississippi Valley are more conducive to plant growth than are the heavy clays of mountainous regions. Soil has a complex structure, including a silica base, humus, chemicals, and moisture, all of which can appear in various proportions. Furthermore, the climate, with its seasons, amount of precipitation, and temperature, is an equally important factor with respect to production. Mineral resources likewise vary in their desirability, since some supplies are richer and larger and are nearer the surface than others.

Location

Location is no less significant than fertility, and relative transportation costs operate like degrees of fertility to affect the yield of a natural resource. Improvements in transportation that lower costs make resources more accessible and, in effect, change their economic locations. So important is the factor of accessibility that land usage may be largely determined by the distance from the land to markets. For example, truck gardens are usually found near the great centers of population; mixed farming, at a greater distance; and cattle raising and lumbering, at more remote localities.

Scarcity

Of great significance is the fact that the total supply of land, as the term has been defined, is fixed. It is true that water can be brought to desert soils by irrigation systems, and thus large new tracts of land may be opened to productive use. In this way it might appear that new land is created. This increase in productive soil, however, is possible only through the addition of capital. The same is true of those areas that have been opened to cultivation through the drainage of swamplands. The discovery of new resources, such as new oil pools, might be considered as an addition to land; and this is indeed the case, since what was before unknown is now known, but actually no new resources have been created except through discovery. Thus, in its original state, land is a gift of nature rather than a man-made good; all that man can do is to discover new supplies or make the existing supplies more productive through effective capital expenditures.

The fact that land supply is essentially fixed is a matter of vital importance in many respects. When agricultural prices are favorable and farm income is increasing, for example, the farmer may quite naturally wish to add to his acres under cultivation. If all the available land is occupied, however, the fact that it is limited in amount means that he must bid for its use against others who have the same desire. Thus, the rent of land and its value are subject to marked fluctuations as the prospects of farm income improve or decline. In similar fashion, the desire of people to settle in large numbers in cities increases the demand for urban land, while the supply of these desirable locations remains fixed.

HOW RENT IS DETERMINED

Even if all land were of the same quality for a given use, rent would appear as soon as the land was no longer to be had merely by occupying it. As soon as land becomes scarce so that competition for its use appears, rent will arise. But the great differences in the rents of land are not to be explained merely by its scarcity. One of the most notable features of this factor of production, a feature that distinguishes it sharply from capital and labor, is the wide variation in its economic qualities. It is this variation in fertility or location, or both, that accounts for the great differences in rents for different parcels of land.

Rent Measured from the Extensive Margin

Because land varies greatly in fertility and location, the equal application of labor and capital to different parcels of equal areas will lead to larger returns on the better land. The relationship of rent to yield may be illustrated by the diagram in Figure 34-1.

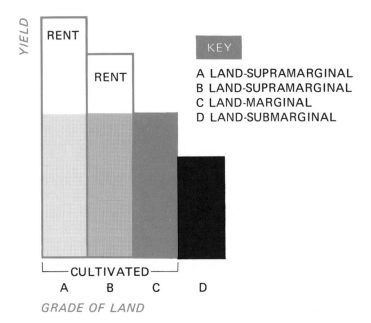

FIGURE 34-1

If equal amounts of capital and labor were applied to all grades of land, rent would accrue to the lands of superior quality.

The heights of the blocks represent the returns that may be obtained from lands of different grades of fertility with equal application of labor and capital. The lowest grade in use, *C* land, can be called no-rent land. It is land at the margin of cultivation. The land may be so poor in quality that the cultivator recovers in the yield only the wages of labor and the interest on capital employed. If these returns cannot be realized, the land is *submarginal*; that is, it is not worth cultivating with existing methods and costs. On the superior, or *supramarginal lands*, rent is the difference between output produced on the superior parcels and that produced on the marginal parcel. This differential in production is economic rent. Where land is held as private property, the owner can demand as contract rent on the land the value of the economic rent.

Among different lands of equal accessibility, those of better quality will be the first to come under cultivation. The grade of land labeled *A* will be the first to be used, since it will yield the largest volume of product for a given application of labor and capital. Only when this land has been entirely occupied will men turn to grade *B* land. When all the land of grade *B* has been occupied, an increasing population and growing demand justify the cultivation of grade *C* or *marginal land* because it provides the revenue necessary to cover its cost of cultivation. Grade *D* land will not be cultivated, since it is submarginal and will not return a yield sufficient to cover its cost of cultivation. Thus, rent has an extensive margin.

Such is the course of development in the use of land when economic factors are given full consideration. It is true, however, that in the course of historical development the best lands are not always the first to be used. For example, the first English colonists in what is now the United States cultivated the rocky New England soil, and only later did the rich lowlands of the Mississippi Valley come into use. But many New England farms have now reverted to forest or have been put to recreational use, because they are essentially submarginal, while the farmlands of the Midwest command high rent. Insofar as the qualities of land are known at any particular time and the parcels of land are conveniently located, they will be cultivated in the order of economic value indicated in the diagrams.

Rent Measured from the Intensive Margin

Thus far the assumption has been made that equal amounts of labor and capital have been applied to all grades of land, and rent has appeared in connection with the better lands because of their superior yields. Such equal application of labor and capital, however, is often not true in practice. It would not be economical to turn to grade *B* land if the application of an additional unit of labor and capital yielded more on grade *A* land than it would on grade *B* land. As a matter of fact, superior lands are cultivated more intensively than inferior lands. It is only the diminishing returns on better lands that lead to the extensive use of poorer land. Differing intensity of land use is illustrated in Figure 34-2.

Equal application of capital and labor in the production of wheat yields 20 bushels an acre on *A* land, 15 bushels on *B* land, 10 bushels on *C* land, and 5 bushels on *D* land. If the 10 bushels on *C* land are sufficient only to cover production cost, this land may be cultivated but it will be no-rent or marginal land. *D* land, being submarginal, will not be cultivated.

Additional applications of labor and capital on the better lands will yield additional returns but at a decreasing rate because of the operation of the law of diminishing returns. The first application of capital and labor will be applied to *A* land because *A* land is most productive. Inputs of capital and labor will be carried to the point at which *B* land becomes equally productive at the margin. Then other resources will be assigned back to *A*, then to *B*, and so on. This process tends to operate until land is cultivated to the marginal, or no-rent, point. That is, the yield on the better lands at the intensive margin from the last units of labor and capital will be no greater than the yield at the extensive margin from equal units of labor and capital.

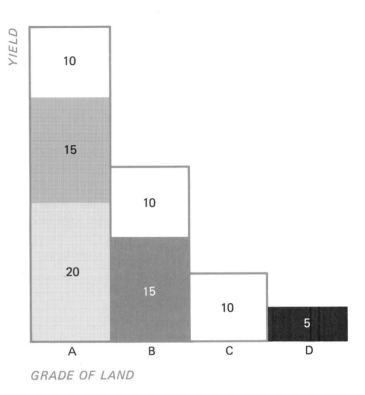

YIELD

| 10 |
| 15 |
| 20 |

| 10 |
| 15 |

| 10 |

| 5 |

A   B   C   D

GRADE OF LAND

FIGURE 34-2

Capital and labor are applied more intensively on superior land up to the point at which marginal yields are equalized among lands of different grades.

Location Rent

As mentioned previously, rent may also arise due to the location of land. In most cases economic rent, or economic surplus, depends upon the revenue received from the sale of goods produced on the land compared to the cost of such production. Assuming that the yields of two parcels of land are the same and that the costs of production are identical, location rent will depend on the cost of transportation.

Take, for example, two parcels of land of equal fertility and with identical costs of production. Assume that parcel *A* is located 100 miles from the nearest market for its products and that parcel *B* is located 200 miles away. Assume further that wheat is produced by both at a cost of 60 cents a bushel and can be sold in the market at $1 per bushel. If it costs the owner of parcel *A* 5 cents per bushel to ship his wheat to the market, he will net a return of 35 cents per bushel of wheat. If, on the other hand, it costs the owner of parcel *B* 10 cents per bushel to ship his wheat to the market, he will net a return of 30 cents per bushel of wheat. Since factors other than location are identical, this difference in net return of 5 cents per bushel is due to the superior location of parcel *A* over parcel *B* and is known as the *location value* or *location rent*. If a third parcel of land 300 miles away with a transportation cost of 15 cents per bushel were utilized, the location rent on parcel *A* would increase to 10 cents per bushel of wheat and parcel *B* would change from no-rent land to that yielding a location rent of 5 cents per bushel of wheat sold. Land will continue to be used at the extensive margin of location up to the point where the cost of transportation absorbs the difference between the selling price and the cost of producing the wheat. If a second dose of capital and labor applied on a closer location will yield a higher net return than a dose of capital and labor applied at the marginal location, land will be used more intensively at the closer location. Location rent, therefore, has both an extensive and an intensive margin.

Because of the differences in fertility and location characteristic of all natural resources, land will be cultivated or otherwise utilized with different degrees of intensity. In every case utilization will tend to be carried to the margin where the land yields no rent and only the costs of the factors are covered. Labor, capital, and business management will tend to be so distributed over all the land in use that the most effective utilization and maximum yields can be attained. The maximum effective use of all land is reached when no increase in output can be gained by shifting labor, capital, and enterprise from one piece or use of land to another. Although the perfection implied in this statement is hardly to be attained in actual practice, because of constantly changing conditions, it is nevertheless the object of economic calculation and a goal of organized business effort.

Urban-Site Rent

Thus far the discussion of rent and of the conditions that make it possible has been limited to use of land in agriculture with only passing reference to other uses. Examples of the agricultural use of land may easily be found to illustrate the origin and nature of rent, but the principles of rent determination for agricultural land hold equally true for other types of land. In the case of urban land, however, it may not be so clear at first glance that those principles are equally valid, since urban land does not always yield a tangible product by which differences in yield can be measured.

The use of land in cities depends almost entirely upon the site or location in relation to the varied human activities so characteristic of crowded population centers. Some land is wanted for residential purposes. It must be in or near the city with easy access to transportation and yet sufficiently far away to escape some of the bustle and confusion of city life. Preferably it should be in a "good neighborhood" and in a scenic setting. Some sites will afford all these and other advantages more than will others. The residence values indicated here are intangibles, but they are no less real, since they influence human choices and thus make some sites more valuable than others.

When sites are wanted for shops or business offices, other considerations come into play. A store located in the heart of the downtown business district where shopping traffic is heavy will yield a greater economic rent and command a larger contractual rent than will an identical store selling the same products at the same prices but located on the periphery of the downtown business district. Due to its better location the one store will draw more customers, make more sales, have a faster inventory turnover, and have a lower labor cost per unit of sales. Other things being equal, the difference in profits or net revenue of the two stores will be due to the difference in location and, therefore, it is referred to as location rent.

In large cities certain areas become associated with particular types of business activity, as the financial center, theater row, the downtown shopping district, or the urban shopping center. Insofar as such districts become so well known that people will frequent them because of their particular attractions or prestige, these sites will be preferred to others for certain business purposes. They are, in fact, fundamentally similar to agricultural land, in that the application of labor and capital to those areas will yield a larger return than elsewhere. The degree of intensive utilization of such areas is often indicated by the height of the buildings. Since the nucleus or central area is limited in extent, it can, in effect, be multiplied within limits by the addition of floors. The uneven skylines of American cities have become an indication of the relative rents of urban land as measured from the intensive margin. The heights of buildings rise as more desirable sites are utilized, because all land is subject to the law of diminishing returns. The higher the building, the less certain it is that the floors near the top will yield a return commensurate with their cost. Usually those at the very top will command better rents, however, because of their prestige value.

Other Land Income

In the case of mineral lands, such as coal resources, the return to the owners is not called a rent, but a *royalty*, since the net income is estimated on the basis of so much per ton of coal mined and not per unit of area per year. The reason for this distinction is found in the fact that, in the case of coal, an unrenewable resource is being taken from the land, and there is no certainty that after the exhaustion of the mineral deposits the land will be suitable for any other use. Some coal lands are richer than others because the coal seams are thicker and lie nearer the surface and the land is closer to the market for coal. The royalty is a differential return per ton, determined by reference to marginal costs of mining; it is thus essentially economic rent that accrues to the owner of the land. Since coal may be mined at various rates per unit of time because of the composition and structure of the mine, some coal lands will yield a much larger return than others.

Can the marginal productivity analysis, which was so prominent in the study of the demand for labor, also be applied in the study of the demand for land? The answer is in the affirmative, for land will be used in combination with labor and capital up to the point where the last unit of land contributes no more to the total product than the unit cost. Although the nature or quality of the unit may vary, as an acre of farmland or a square foot in a warehouse, the principle of marginal productivity holds for land as it does for the other factors. In any type of enterprise, the land that is required will be demanded up to the point where the last unit, so far as can be determined, will yield no more than its cost in terms of prevailing prices. The marginal productivity analysis, which has already been applied in relation to labor, is equally significant in the case of natural resources when they are called for in any given use up to the point where the last unit will only pay for itself under existing conditions of prices and costs.

In terms of geometry, the demand curve for land will be negatively sloped (slope downward to the right) primarily because of the law of diminishing returns. Three different states of demand are shown in Figure 34-3, namely D_1, D_2, and D_3. The supply curve of land is labeled S. Each horizontal segment designates the price per unit of land at which that grade of land would be marginal. Thus, the use of Grade A land would be such that the cultivator would recover from its use enough to cover the wages of labor and the interest on capital at a land price of only $10 per unit. Grade B land, however, would require a price of $20 to cover all costs, Grade C is marginal at a price of $27, and Grade D is marginal at a price of $33.

Suppose the demand for land is D_1. Then the equilibrium price of land will be $20. With this state of demand, Grades A and B will be employed. However, Grade B will be marginal because price will cover only cost. Owners of Grade A land receive a rent of $10, equal to the $20 price minus a cost of $10. Grades C and D are submarginal and will not be employed.

If demand should increase to D_2, Grade C land becomes marginal and is brought into productive use. At a market price of $27, the rent on Grade A land rises to $17, and the owners of Grade B land receive a rent of $7 per unit. Grade D land remains submarginal.

An expansion of demand to D_3, so that the land price rises to $33 per unit, brings all available land into productive employment. Rent on Grade A land rises to $23; that on Grade B increases from $7 to $13. For the first time a rent, amounting to $6 per unit, accrues to the owners of Grade C land. Any further expansion of demand would have the effect of raising the rent on all land without increasing the total quantity of land employed (under the assumption that the quantities of Grades A, B, C, and D together exhaust the total land supply).

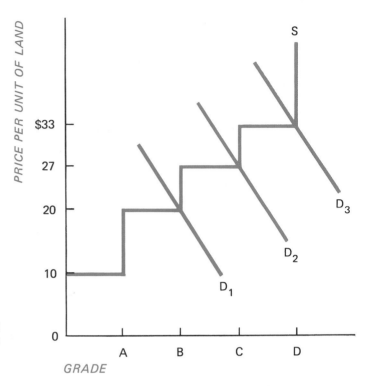

FIGURE 34-3

EMPLOYMENT OF LAND

Rent rises as the demand for land
expands with a fixed supply of each
grade of land.

Causes of Changes in Demand and Supply

Since rent is a return that the owners can demand for the use of their
land because of its superiority over marginal or no-rent land, any change in
economic conditions that leads to the use of more land will also lead to higher
rents on the better lands. If all land is in use up to the marginal point, an
increase in demand for the products of land because of a growing population
or improving levels of living will lead to the use of land that has heretofore
been submarginal. It has been submarginal, or not worth utilizing, because
its economic qualities of fertility, productivity, or location have been less
than those of lands in use. An increase in the supply of labor and capital
will thus cause the extensive margin to be pushed farther out, because the
increased demand makes it profitable to bring still poorer land into use.
When this occurs, rent will appear on what was formerly marginal land, and
rents will be higher on the better lands because of the greater difference in
yield from them in comparison with the new marginal land. Hence, so long
as conditions develop that make it necessary to turn to poorer land, rents
will rise on the better lands, and the total amount of that share of the
national income known as rent will increase.

This general tendency for rents to increase as population grows or as levels of living improve may be counteracted to some extent by any development in technology that leads to less use of land. The great irrigation developments of the West, which represent the application of capital in order to improve use of land, have brought fertile desert soils into use. Poorer soils in the East or South will consequently be forced out of cultivation unless the demand for their products increases. The development of better lands will have a tendency to keep rents down or even reduce them. Technological improvements may, in fact, become so extensive and important that resort must be had to government subsidies or crop limitation programs in order to reduce agricultural production and to prevent the decline in rents for farmland from becoming catastrophic in its effects.

In the long run the increase or decrease in rent as one of the shares of the national income will depend on whether the more effective use of land will counteract the tendency toward the use of more land as population increases and levels of living rise. The density of population may increase to such an extent that more and more labor and capital will be employed on land with increasing yields per acre but declining yields per unit of labor and capital. Such has been the situation in the densely populated lands of Europe and the Far East, particularly in China and India. This situation can be alleviated by improvements in agriculture, provided, of course, population does not increase proportionately. These improvements may take the form of better transportation, the opening up of new lands, and the improvement of old lands through irrigation, drainage, and the increased use of fertilizers and equipment. Improvements may also take the form of a more scientific cultivation which employs new methods, the use of better fertilizers, more productive seeds, and the breeding of higher quality animals. The application of more scientific methods will lead to a greater volume of production at the same or even lower costs. If the demand for the products is inelastic, a decline in their prices will force the poorer lands out of cultivation and rents on the better lands will decline. If, however, the increased volume of products can be disposed of abroad with advantage or can be absorbed at home without declining prices, there is no certainty that a decline in rent will accompany such improvements in techniques or productivity.

From the social viewpoint, rent is not a cost of production. Land is the free gift of nature. It is not man-made, and it has cost society nothing. As we saw in Chapter 27, long-run competitive price must be high enough to cover per-unit production costs. Essentially, costs of production are comprised of human exertion in the form of labor and of sacrificed or postponed consumption in the form of saving. Hence, since land costs society nothing, as a factor of production it cannot be a cost in the production of goods.

Rent is determined by productiveness of the superior lands over marginal land. So long as competition prevails, the owner of land is powerless to increase his rent merely because he may want to do so. How great his rent will be depends upon the superiority of his land as compared with no-rent land. If the price of the product that can be produced on his land rises, his rent will rise also; or if more rent can be realized from some other use of the land, eventually the land will be used for the best alternative purpose.

Of course, from the standpoint of the individual producer, rent, whether contractual or imputed, is a cost of production; but the payment of rent, or the receipt of rent by the owner-operator, does not have any permanent effect on the price of the product of land. If this were not true, the price of the product could be raised or lowered merely by increasing or decreasing rent. Since, however, rent is merely the differential in returns from the use of lands that vary in productiveness relative to marginal land, due to quality and location, the manipulation of rent to affect production costs is not possible for any great length of time.

Quasi Rent

The term "rent" is also employed by some economists to refer to any exceptional or unusual gains that accrue to any durable factor of production other than land or natural resources. Some durable capital goods resemble land in that their supply can be adjusted to demand only over a comparatively long period of time. Such goods cannot be duplicated quickly for reasons of cost and, therefore, command unusual returns with sudden changes in demand. Similarly, some persons of more than ordinary ability can command exceptional returns because they are few and competition with them is difficult. When units of a factor have a monopoly control through induced scarcity, they may also command unusual returns. Such unusual or exceptional returns to superior units of a factor are often called *quasi rents*, as contrasted to economic rent of land.

SINGLE-TAX THEORY

A reform movement that at one time received widespread attention is the single-tax program extensively publicized by the San Francisco newspaper publisher, Henry George, during the latter decades of the preceding century. It was the contention of George that, since landowners receive an income created by social and economic conditions rather than by their own efforts, the state could without injustice absorb all economic rents by means of a tax. The funds so collected would, he contended, be sufficient to finance all the functions of government. For that reason his proposal is often referred to as the *single-tax theory*.

In a communistic state, such as Soviet Russia, the differences in the yields of natural resources or land are claimed by the state, and rent does not exist as a return to private owners. Since it is the demand by society for the services and products of land that causes some land to be utilized intensively and different grades of land to be brought into use, thus causing rents to arise, it might appear logical that such rents should go to the society to be used by the government as it sees fit. But it is not probable that the funds from the tax would be sufficient to meet governmental needs. In today's economy, rental income comprises about 2.5 percent of our national income, whereas total government spending is an amount equivalent to approximately 25 percent of our national income. Furthermore, it is quite probable that the removal of all other taxes would serve as a pronounced stimulus to all forms of productive enterprise not vitally dependent on rents, but such gain would be accomplished only with loss to those who relied on rents as the basis for their incomes.

Windfall gains, corresponding to unearned increments in the value of land, occur in other phases of economic activity without any effort on the part of the lucky recipient. If gains not due to the efforts of the individual are to be taxed away, it would appear reasonable to appropriate all such gains and not merely some of them.

The author of the single-tax theory believed that poverty in the midst of abundant resources could be ascribed only to the fact that rents were appropriated by the few, while the many could not enjoy these gains because they could not acquire rent-yielding lands. With private property in land, the holders of rent-yielding lands had a monopoly, George believed, which had to be reduced or removed if capitalism and private property were to survive. He found the solution to the problem of poverty in a single tax, which would make the gains from superior resources the property of all, while serving as the means for promoting the general welfare. But his proposal appeared to undermine the institution of private property and was naturally opposed by all those who found their welfare dependent on existing property rights. The adoption of a single tax on rents would represent a profound change in social and economic relations. Because this theory proposes to bring about such extensive changes by one method only, it must be called utopian, that is, it is a less practicable means of increasing the general welfare than are those programs which are less spectacular because they seek the same objective through many gradual and piecemeal adjustments.

VALUE OF LAND

Assume that a farmer has paid $20,000 for 100 acres of good farmland. He wishes to realize a gross return of 10 percent on his investment, or

$2,000; that is, a rent of $20 an acre. Is there any certainty that he can secure a tenant who will pay him such a rent? This question can be put in more general terms. Is it the value of a parcel of land, such as this farm, that determines the rent that its owner will receive, or is it the rent of the land that determines the value? So far as the first question is concerned, if the tenant decides that he can cover all costs of operation, including his wages and interest on capital he may use, and clear $20 an acre in addition, he may decide to rent the farm. But there is no certainty that, because the farmer has paid $20,000 for the farm, he can obtain a net return of 10 percent on his investment, or a rent of $20 an acre. This will occur only if others are willing to accept his estimate of the superior productiveness or economic rent of the land. Falling prices of farm products may have so changed the estimates of prospective tenants concerning the rent of $20 an acre that the farm will remain without a tenant.

Rent and Land Value

This illustration is intended to point out the fact that fundamentally it is rent that determines the value of land rather than the cost of land that determines rent. Land is wanted for what it will yield. Even the glow of pleasure that may come to the owner because he is an owner would probably mean little to him if he felt the land was entirely useless. Land that is entirely useless yields nothing that can satisfy wants; no rent can be derived from it, and it has no value.

The present value of land is essentially the present value of all future returns, discounted to the present. Since land is usually considered the most durable of goods, these future returns can be considered as extending into the indefinite future. The sum of these returns can be determined by capitalizing the present return, or rent, at the rate at which all future returns are discounted. Thus, if it is expected that a plot of land will continue to command a rent of $50 annually and the rate of discount or capitalization is 5 percent, the capitalized value of the acre will be $50 ÷ .05, or $1,000; that is, $1,000 invested at 5 percent will yield $50 annually in perpetuity.

This is the case, however, only where it is assumed that future returns will in all probability continue to be equal to present returns. Where land yields a product that cannot be replaced, there is not the same certainty of continuous returns in the future. The problem of the capitalization of returns on coal land is of this nature. In order to ascertain the value of such land, it is necessary to know (1) the probable total volume of coal that can be extracted per acre, (2) the probable rate of extraction per year, and (3) the royalty per ton. When these facts are known, the value of the land will represent the capitalization of its returns per year for the number of years during which mining may continue. The same process of valuation occurs wherever land resources are of a nonreplaceable nature and the land is in all probability not fit for other uses. In this regard, however, much progress has been made in recent years in developing methods for restoring the usefulness of land destroyed by strip mining.

Reasons for Changes in Land Values

It is often apparent that land has been given a value which at its present rate of return, or rent, represents a very low rate of capitalization—in fact, a rate far below prevailing rates in other types of investment. The explanation is to be found in the fact that land, far more than the capital instruments created by man, is considered as particularly durable and, therefore, capable of yielding returns into the indefinite future. An even more important reason for the apparent low rate of capitalization is the fact that, in a country such as the United States where increasing yields are the result of technological improvements, probable increments in rent are also capitalized and added to the value of the land. The history of housing developments is a familiar story, and the increase in value of building lots in such developments often goes far beyond the cost of the capital improvements when added to the original value of the land.

If land is subject to increases in value because of the capitalization of prospective increases in its rent, it will also be true that land values may decline when it becomes evident that the rents are likely to decline. Desirable neighborhoods sometimes become less desirable to a class of tenants with high incomes because families with lower incomes move into the neighborhood. The course of traffic may be altered by reason of changes in transportation facilities, and the rents and values of some locations will be diminished as those of others are enhanced. Poor agricultural land may be driven below the margin of cultivation by improvements on better lands and a decline in rent which follows. In fact, such declines in value may be widespread when the prices of agricultural products and consequently the rents of farmlands fall to lower levels.

RENT AS A SHARE OF THE NATIONAL INCOME

Although our technical definition of the term "rent" differs to some extent from the common usage of the term, some idea of that portion of rent involved in the national income is shown in Table 34-1.

The figures shown for rental income are those accruing to persons only. This fact automatically excludes the rental income that may be going to corporations. It also excludes any implicit rent that may be earned by owners of land and other factors of production. It does include the imputed net rental returns to owner-occupants of nonfarm dwellings, patents, and copyrights. Nevertheless, the table gives us some idea of the actual rental income of persons compared to income from wages and salaries as presented in Chapter 32. The statistical evidence also indicates that rental income as

TABLE 34-1

RENTAL INCOME AS A PERCENT OF NATIONAL INCOME

1929-1973

Year	National Income (Billions)	Rental Income of Persons (Billions)	Rental Income as a Percent of National Income
1929	$ 86.8	$ 5.4	6.1
1933	40.3	2.0	5.0
1935	57.2	1.7	3.0
1940	81.1	2.9	3.6
1945	181.5	5.6	3.0
1950	241.1	9.4	3.9
1955	331.0	13.9	4.2
1960	414.5	15.8	3.8
1965	564.3	19.0	3.3
1970	800.5	23.9	3.0
1973	1,054.2	25.1	2.4

SOURCE: *Economic Report of the President*, 1974.

a portion of the national income has decreased compared to a few decades ago, while it has been rather stable in recent years. In fact, it constitutes roughly the same percentage of national income as does net interest payments, as we shall see in the next chapter.

SUMMARY

1. Land includes all natural resources that can be employed in the production of wealth. Units of land differ in fertility and location, and these differences are relatively permanent.

2. As soon as land becomes scarce and cannot be had by mere occupation, rent will arise and be determined by the marginal productivity of the units employed. Differences in rents arise from the relatively permanent differences in the fertility and the location of the units employed.

3. Rent can be measured from both the extensive and intensive margins of the land used.

4. The general level of rents is determined partly by conditions affecting the demand for land, such as the rate of growth of population and rising levels of living, and partly by conditions affecting the supply, such as better transportation and advances in technology.

5. The level of rents at any particular time is determined by the prices of the products of land, for rent is the result of a price situation, not its cause.

6. Differences in productivity of comparable physical units of labor and capital, if sufficiently permanent to affect their prices, may give rise to differences in returns that can be called "quasi rents." Differences in returns induced by scarcity created through monopoly control of any factor of production also take on this character of quasi rent. **7.** In the long run, land values are determined by the capitalization of prospective rents to be derived from the use of the land.

NEW TERMS

Contract rent, *p. 747*
Economic rent, *p. 747*
Explicit rent, *p. 747*
Implicit rent, *p. 747*
Extensive margin, *p. 749*
Submarginal land, *p. 750*
Supramarginal land, *p. 750*

Marginal land, *p. 750*
Intensive margin, *p. 751*
Location rent, *p. 752*
Urban-site rent, *p. 753*
Royalty, *p. 754*
Quasi rents, *p. 758*
Single-tax theory, *p. 758*

QUESTIONS FOR DISCUSSION AND ANALYSIS

1. How does economic rent differ from contract rent?

2. Distinguish between explicit and implicit rent.

3. How is it determined whether a parcel of land is rent yielding or no-rent land? Give examples of the intensive use of land and the extensive use of land.

4. Give illustrations to show how urban land areas differ in their economic qualities.

5. Why might rent be paid on one unit of land and not another even though the two units are of the same quality?

6. Does "land" in the economic sense include other natural resources? If so, which types of natural resources?

7. Where is no-rent land most likely to be found in the United States?

8. Does marginal productivity analysis apply to land and other natural resources whose supplies are fixed? Explain.

9. What effect does the establishment of a National Park tend to have on the value of surrounding land?

10. How do changing prices of the product lead to the shifting of land use and to changing rents?

11. If a parcel of land yields a rent of $5,000 per year, what will be the change in its capitalized value if the prevailing rate of return rises from 5 percent to 8 percent?

12. What is the relationship between rent and the value of land?

SUGGESTED READINGS

Barber, William J. *A History of Economic Thought*. Baltimore: Penguin Books Inc., 1967.

Becker, Gary. *Economic Theory*. New York: Random House, Inc., 1971.

Boulding, Kenneth. *Economic Analysis*, 4th ed. New York: Harper & Row, Publishers, 1966.

Brennan, Michael J. *Theory of Economic Statics*, 2d ed. Englewood Cliffs, N.J.: Prentice-Hall, Inc., 1970.

Clower, Robert W., and John F. Due. *Microeconomics*. Homewood, Ill.: Richard D. Irwin, Inc., 1972.

Ricardo, David. *Principles of Political Economy and Taxation*, edited by E. C. K. Gonner. London: G. Bell and Sons, Ltd., 1891.

Robinson, Joan. *Economic Heresies: Some Old-Fashioned Questions in Economic Theory*. New York: Basic Books, Inc., Publishers, 1971.

Whittaker, Edmund. *A History of Economic Ideas*. New York: Longmans, Green and Co., Inc., 1955. Chapter 13.

35

Interest
and Profit

PREVIEW Interest, the income payment to suppliers of capital, is determined by the demand for and supply of loanable funds. Demand originates with consumers, private producers, and government—all as borrowers. Supply emerges from savings and the expansion of credit (both bank credit and government credit). Unlike the demand-supply theory used to explain wages, rents, and interest, profit has been interpreted as a residual income explained by (1) innovation, (2) monopoly power, (3) risk taking, and (4) managerial efficiency. All four appear to play a part.

Interest is the return received by the owner of funds for their use, and the interest payment expressed as a percentage of funds loaned is the *interest rate*. Actually there is no such thing as "the" interest rate. Rather, there are several rates determined in different money markets. For example, the credit standing of the government is much higher than that of a person who is compelled to borrow from a loan shark. Therefore, the government can borrow at a lower interest rate.

All interest rates in the markets for loanable funds are contractual rates. Some loans are made for consumption purposes and are not used directly to create additional goods or services. Consumption loans can serve indirectly to stimulate business activity by permitting consumers to purchase goods immediately instead of later. Other than loans to government, the greater part of all loans, however, is directed toward the creation of new capital goods. Since capital is a factor of production, the value of its contribution to production is reflected in interest rates.

THEORIES OF INTEREST

Various theories have been advanced to explain the nature and cause of interest. Each of these theories attempts to give an explanation by emphasizing certain factors or elements that are evident in the interest situation. None of them assumes that the facts which are stressed in other theories are entirely unimportant. They differ, therefore, largely with respect to the emphasis that is placed on certain causal factors.

Marginal Productivity Theory of Interest

The *marginal productivity theory* holds that interest is a price paid for the use of capital and that the rate is determined by the net productivity of capital. For example, assume that, without increasing his other expenses and after allowing for depreciation, a manufacturer can increase the value of his output $10,600 by installing a machine costing $10,000. Since the increase in his total product attributable to the use of the machine would be $10,600, the amount of imputed interest would be $600, or 6 percent of $10,000. In other words, receipts from the sale of the additional product would be enough to repay a loan of $10,000 for the purchase of a machine costing that amount, and $600 besides. If he borrowed a second $10,000 and the total returns were $10,300, the imputed interest would be only $300, or 3 percent. This net return from the use of an additional unit of capital is sometimes called the *natural rate of interest*. Obviously it would be to the borrower's advantage to continue to borrow funds so long as his marginal revenue product, or natural rate of interest, remained greater than (or at least equal to) the cost or the *market rate of interest* of the last unit of capital (or funds) borrowed.

As long as the natural rate of interest exceeds the market rate, it will pay entrepreneurs to borrow money for investment in machinery, equipment, and buildings. As they continue to borrow and invest, however, the law of diminishing marginal productivity will force the natural rate of interest to decline. At the same time, the sacrifice of immediate access to funds on the part of lenders will force the market rate upward. This process continues until a point is reached at which the natural rate of interest will equal the market rate of interest. At this point, borrowing and investing will be stabilized and the rate of interest will have reached an *equilibrium rate*. This example would seem to explain the demand for capital by showing why the borrower could afford to pay for the use of capital. But it does not explain the source of capital or the cost to the lender.

Those who hold to the marginal productivity theory as being the most satisfactory explanation of interest usually recognize that it is not a complete explanation. They concede that the theory assumes that only a given amount of capital exists. In other words, the marginal productivity theory attempts to explain interest in terms of demand for capital without giving much attention to the supply of capital.

Time-Preference Theory of Interest

People usually place greater value upon goods in the present than goods in the future. That is to say, the satisfaction of immediate wants is more urgent than provision for the satisfaction of future wants. Accordingly, there is always a tendency to use money or goods for the satisfaction of present wants rather than to save them for use in the future.

The *abstinence* or *time-preference theory* of interest attempts to explain interest as a reward for foregoing present consumption. Therefore, if the individual is to be induced to save, he must be offered the prospect of greater consumption in the future in exchange for the sacrifice of present consumption. The difference between the amounts is interest.

In terms of money, ask yourself whether you would prefer to have $100 today or $100 one year from now. Most of us would prefer the $100 now because we have what is called a *positive time preference.*

Since $100 today is more valuable to us than $100 a year from now, what amount of money to be received one year from now is equivalent to having $100 today? Let us say that today you would consider $105 received a year from now as bringing you the equivalent satisfaction of $100 today. If so, you would part with your $100 by lending it to someone for a year only if you received $105 in return. This difference is the interest rate, in this case 5 percent. It is a payment for giving up the current use of purchasing power in return for a repayment later. Since various individuals have different time-preference values, interest rates may vary. Generally the current rate will be set to some extent by the marginal time preference of those with money who are willing to lend it and forego its immediate use.

The merit of the abstinence theory is that it sets forth the necessity for paying interest. However, it does not explain how it is possible for interest to be paid. It ignores the demand for the use of capital, which in the determination of interest is as important as the supply.

Liquidity Preference Theory

As the phrase "liquidity preference" suggests, people may prefer to hold wealth in the form of money rather than put it out in some form of investment. When money is invested, it is "tied up," oftentimes in ventures that cannot easily be turned back into money except perhaps at a loss. When wealth is held in the form of money, there is no return earned on it.

Wealth may be held in the form of money because of its necessary use as a medium of exchange or because it is a store of value. The motives that lead to the holding of money are three in number: (1) the transactions motive, (2) the precautionary motive, and (3) the speculative motive.

The *transactions motive* is an expression of the need to hold money to serve as a medium of exchange in the near future for ordinary transactions.

The *precautionary motive* refers to the withholding of money for the purpose of meeting various unknown but perhaps anticipated emergencies. In these two uses of money as a medium of exchange, the quantity needed may be relatively stable and even predictable.

The *speculative motive*, however, is more unpredictable in its effect on the use of money, since it is an expression of the judgment of people concerning the uncertainties of the future, both economic and political. People will hold money as a store of value if they anticipate that such holding will mean a better investment in the future or if they feel that the interest rate does not represent a rate of return in keeping with the risks involved. The lower the rate of interest, the more they will be inclined to hold their wealth in the form of money, especially if the uncertainties of the future are exceptionally great. Since the interest rate is the price that must be paid to induce the individual to part with his liquidity, when liquidity preference weakens, the interest rate will fall; and when liquidity preference becomes stronger, the interest rate will rise. Hence, the strength or weakness of liquidity preference becomes an important factor in the demand for and the supply of money and exercises a strong influence in the determination of interest rates.

Going a bit further, the theory holds that the market rate of interest will be determined by the quantity of money in the economy and the degree of liquidity preference. With a given liquidity preference, an increase in the quantity of money will lower the interest rate and a decrease in the quantity will force the interest rate upward. On the other hand, with a given quantity of money, a strengthening of liquidity preference will increase the rate of interest, while a weakening of liquidity preference will cause a decrease in the rate of interest, provided the quantity of money remains constant.

Interest as a Market Price

A comprehensive theory of interest is one that recognizes both the demand for and the supply of capital. Then the conclusion emerges that interest rates are market prices that result from the interaction of demand and supply, as in the case of wages. This is the interpretation of interest rates followed in this chapter: marginal productivity, time preference, and liquidity preference theories will find their appropriate places in the explanation. Interest rates may be considered merely as prices paid for the use of money, no matter whether the money is derived from private savings, from business surplus, or from the expansion of bank credit, and without regard to whether it will be used by a consumer to buy a car, in a business to expand equipment and increase production, or by government to meet its obligations. It is not the source of money, or its use, that is important, but only its amount. This emphasis on the money market for the explanation of interest rates considers both the supply of and the demand for capital.

DEMAND FOR CAPITAL AND LOANABLE FUNDS

The *demand for capital* may be defined as a schedule of the amounts of loanable funds that borrowers will take at alternative prices. In general, the higher the price that must be paid for the use of funds, the less will be the amount of funds that borrowers will be willing to take; the lower the price, the more they will take.

For convenience the demand for funds to purchase goods or services may be classified into three categories: (1) for personal or private consumption; (2) for productive uses; and (3) for governmental uses, some of which, of course, may be for productive and some for consumptive purposes.

Consumption Loans

Families frequently find themselves in need of consumer goods or services for which they are unable to pay immediately. Some buy on credit the year round. Part of this group is composed of those who live in poverty and who are unable to save any part of their earnings; once they are in debt, the best they can do is to pay a part of what they owe and thereby secure further credit. Others in this group are not content to live within their means. While the income they receive might be such as to permit them to buy essentials, their desire for a higher level of living causes them to be in debt constantly.

Aside from the habitually indebted, many families on occasion wish to buy on credit. Houses, automobiles, and household furniture are often purchased on credit with payment made in regular installments. Sometimes medical services and perishable consumer goods are unexpectedly needed and must be obtained on the basis of credit.

There are others who buy on credit even though they can afford to pay cash. Buying on credit may be more convenient; people may desire to maintain a good credit reference; or they may feel that they obtain better service on merchandise and appliances while the goods are still being paid for. Regardless of the motive, more and more families are using credit in this fashion. In fact, we may say that in large part the old adage "save first to buy later" is gradually being changed to "buy first and save later."

Production Loans

Production loans are made with the expectation that, by the time the borrower must pay the loan and interest, the use of the funds so borrowed will have increased his revenue by an amount sufficient to enable him to repay the principal and interest. In other words, production loans are undertaken on the assumption that they will be self-liquidating. This is the most important distinction between loans made for consumption purposes and those made for productive purposes.

The demand for production loans is conditioned by what investors think about the future of business. If it appears that the possibilities of making profits are good, the demand for funds is stronger than if the prospects are less promising. It is important to understand that it is the prospect of profits, and not necessarily the physical productivity of capital, that induces businessmen to borrow. Business managers are primarily concerned with an increase in output to the extent that such an increase will prove profitable.

When funds are wanted for the purposes of carrying on current operations, such as meeting payrolls and purchasing materials, the borrower seeks short-term loans. These loans are obtained by borrowing from commercial banks or by issuing a series of short-term notes, which are sold through commercial paper houses equipped to furnish such services to business concerns. Funds that are borrowed for the purpose of construction and the purchase of equipment are usually wanted for a longer period, varying from 5 to 75 or more years.

The amount of funds that a borrower-producer will seek, whether for fixed capital or for operating purposes, will depend upon his estimate of the marginal productivity of capital. To illustrate what is meant by this, assume that by borrowing $1,000,000 for a period of 20 years, a manufacturer believes he could increase the value of his output by at least $2,000,000 during the period. Then he might feel justified in borrowing $1,000,000 if he could obtain it at an interest rate of not more than 5 percent. If he should obtain the funds and if his expectations were realized, he could pay the annual interest charge of $50,000 for 20 years plus the principal and not lose anything. Any amount realized in excess of the total of the principal and the interest charges would be net gain.

Governmental Loans

The expenditures of government—local, state, and national—are mainly financed by taxation and borrowing. When the attitude of government is that of laissez-faire, the aim in normal times is to keep governmental expenditures down and to depend almost wholly upon taxation to obtain the funds needed. In the event of war or any emergency that disturbs the economic order, however, the government most often resorts to borrowing.

As governments assume more responsibility for the general welfare, especially if they attempt to accomplish their purposes quickly, the frequency and the amount of borrowing increase. For example, until about 1930 the aim of the federal government was to maintain a "balanced budget"; that is, it endeavored to finance expenditures by means of taxation so that borrowing, except for short-term periods, would be unnecessary. The business depression of the 1930s, with its attendant unemployment and hardships, caused the government to abandon its traditional hands-off policy with respect to matters affecting the well-being of individuals and businesses.

Money was spent by the government to relieve the consumption needs of citizens. Also, the government undertook directly the creation of capital by engaging in the construction of hydroelectrical projects, the construction of roads, various kinds of conservation undertakings, and other projects. In greater volume the government began to supply needed funds to industry, agriculture, and business through various agencies that it created. Such undertakings by the national government called for funds on a scale such as had never been thought possible before. To obtain the funds, the government resorted to borrowing on a large scale. During World War II, the Korean conflict, and the war in Vietnam, heavy military expenditures led to budget deficits financed by borrowing.

The expenditures of local and state governments, even in times of business depression and war, are usually financed by means of taxation. Sometimes, however, local and state governments find it desirable to raise funds by borrowing. The construction of highways, hospitals, school buildings, libraries, and recreational facilities frequently calls for expenditures that would impose a considerable increase in taxes if payment were made at the time.

SUPPLY OF CAPITAL AND LOANABLE FUNDS

Capital consists of tangible instruments of production, which are used for the purpose of producing either consumer or producer goods. Ultimately the source of the *supply of capital* is the savings of the people. The chief significance of savings is that they make possible the diversion of labor and material resources for the creation of capital goods. The production of these producer goods can take place only when it is possible to divert labor and other resources from the production of goods and services that would be consumed immediately to the production of these capital or producer goods that aid in future production.

We are now prepared to consider from the practical standpoint the supply side of the capital market. As we have seen, the savings of individuals are not ordinarily in the form of goods but in money or credit. The same is true of group savings, such as the surpluses of corporations. Therefore, ordinarily what is borrowed or what is loaned by investors is funds rather than goods.

Savings, the Source of Loanable Funds

Loanable funds consist of money and bank credit that are available to borrowers. It should be recognized, however, that the basis of the purchasing power that results from saving is accumulation of goods. For example, a farmer who saves 100 bushels of wheat or who utilizes materials and labor to construct a barn possesses things that have exchange value. He may retain these items of wealth and reckon their exchange value in terms of dollars. He may exchange them for money, or he may keep them and obtain purchasing power by pledging them in payment for a loan. In any case, the source of the increase in his purchasing power is the thing of value which he has managed to save. So it is with the economy as a whole. The source of purchasing power that may be given in exchange for goods or loaned to another is the savings of the people as a whole.

Time Preference Once More

Time preference plays an important part in the savings of individuals. A given quantity of money or goods has a greater value now than the same quantity in the future; and the more distant the future, the greater is the value of present money or goods in comparison with that of the future. Persons will save their money instead of spending it for present gratifications only when they feel that its use will bring them greater satisfaction in the future than at present.

Individuals often find themselves at the margin of time preference. They debate as to whether a given amount of money should be spent or saved. Whatever tips the scales in favor of the future results in the decision to save. If, while the debate is under way, a premium is offered for saving, the probability of saving becomes greater. This is the function performed by the interest rate; it offers an additional incentive for saving by increasing the possible satisfaction that might result from the use of a given amount of money in the future.

Liquidity Preference Once More

The difference between the potential supply of funds in the market and the amount actually offered at a given rate is due partly to the factor of liquidity preference. Money on hand is more liquid than money invested. As a precaution against unforeseen contingencies, potential investors may prefer to hold their financial resources partly in liquid form. Also, they may follow this policy because they are waiting for more promising investment prospects. If they are businessmen, they may hold varying amounts on hand in accordance with the varying need for cash in business transactions. These are some factors that account for differences between the volume of saving and the volume of investment funds available in the money market at particular rates of interest.

Corporate Savings

Sound corporate management requires that a part of the net earnings of an enterprise be retained in the business and not paid to stockholders in the form of dividends. After reserves have been set aside to replace old or obsolete machinery and equipment and to provide funds for the redemption of long-term debts, it is usually the policy of the board of directors of a corporation to keep a part of the profits for future use. In some cases, the particular use to which the funds are to be put may be determined in advance, as, for instance, the expansion of the plant. In other cases, the management may not have decided just how the surplus funds will be used. Whether the use of the funds has been predetermined or not, the amount withheld from the stockholders is a form of savings.

Savings Sponsored by Government

Some of the funds gathered by government are used for the purpose of capital formation. Roads, streets, power dams, power-generating equipment, and atomic power facilities are sometimes produced with the money obtained by government through taxation or borrowing. To this extent government aids in encouraging the accumulation of capital, for only through such action by government will some kinds of capital be created.

Expansion of Bank Credit

As we saw in Chapter 13, banks may extend credit by an amount several times that of the funds they actually have on hand. In this way the banks create a supply of loanable funds that does not result directly from the sacrifice and savings of individuals.

In general, the credit created by banks is loaned to individuals and concerns engaged in production. Bank loans are made to merchants, farmers, and manufacturers to be used for the current operations of their businesses; to entrepreneurs for the purposes of creating capital goods; and, in recent times, on a large scale to government (especially the federal government). As a rule, it is the policy of banks to lend to borrowers who expect to use the funds for productive purposes; this means that the use of the loans is likely to result in the further accumulation of savings and of capital goods in the community or nation. Of course, these expectations are not always realized. As to the amounts of funds loaned to government—particularly those made to the federal government during the Great Depression, during World War II, and during the Vietnam War—much of it was not intended for ordinary productive purposes.

Expansion of Government Credit

In times past the extension of credit by government was a minor function. As a rule, governments were borrowers instead of lenders. Sometimes government assumes the roles of both borrower and lender on a vast scale. During the great business depression of the thirties, the federal government became the largest lender in the world. Largely through the Reconstruction

Finance Corporation, established in 1932 and continued until 1953, the government loaned many billions of dollars to certain governmental departments and to private business enterprises, including banks and railroads. With the advent of World War II, the government extended credit to private concerns for the construction of armament factories and other facilities for the production of war materiel. The extent of these loans dwarfed all others made by banks and individuals.

Beginning in the late fifties and extending throughout the 1960s, the federal government enlarged the scope of its lending operations. Firms of modest size, especially those managed by minorities, were included through the Small Business Administration. Education was aided by a variety of loan programs, such as those for assisting college building construction and for making direct loans to students. Urban reconstruction and highway extensions were loan-financed through the newly created Department of Transportation and Department of Housing and Urban Development (HUD). In the early seventies, loans assumed an even greater role in government-sponsored activities. In line with this trend, commitments to programs of the past two decades were continued by substitution of loans for grants. For example, to an increasing extent, educational grants to college students have been replaced by loans. Local corrective measures for environmental damage, such as effective sewage treatment, are co-sponsored by the federal government through loans to states and municipalities rather than through outright subsidies.

From what source does government obtain the funds that it lends? It may be from tax revenues, from the savings of individuals and business concerns, or from banks and other credit institutions. The basis for the loans to government is the faith in the government's willingness to repay the loan with interest; and the basis for faith is the taxing power of the government. Thus, the only effective limit to the amount of loanable funds that can be created by government borrowing and lending is the faith of individuals and business concerns as to the ability of the government to redeem its promise to repay its debts. If confidence in the ability of government to redeem its promises deteriorates, borrowing by government becomes more difficult, and hence the supply of loans from this source will decrease. Of course, if it chose to do so, the government could resort to printing money or to creating credit on its own account and thus make available funds in unlimited amounts.

DETERMINATION OF THE MARKET RATE OF INTEREST

Interest rates are prices paid for the use of loanable funds. Hence, the same principles of demand and supply that influence prices of commodities also operate to set the prices for loanable funds. The demand and supply process of determining the rate of interest can easily be explained. What is more difficult is the explanation of the factors that underlie and affect the demand for and the supply of loanable funds.

The demand for loanable funds is a schedule of the amounts of funds that borrowers will take at various interest rates. As we have seen, the two most important factors that determine the size of the demand for loanable funds are the marginal utility of present goods to prospective borrowers and the marginal productivity of capital in particular establishments. These factors result in subjective prices of funds in the minds of individual consumer and producer borrowers.

The supply of loanable funds consists of the amounts of funds that are available for loans at a given time at various interest rates. The sources of the supply of loanable funds and the incentives that induce individuals, business concerns, and others to save or to make funds available for loans have already been discussed. As we recall, time preference is a significant consideration to many of these individuals whose savings are important in providing the supply of loanable funds.

The demand for and the supply of loanable funds in a given money market are shown in Figure 35-1.

As we have said, there would be some savings even if people had to pay banks or others to safeguard their funds. Therefore, we may begin the supply curve below the horizontal axis, which indicates that there would be some

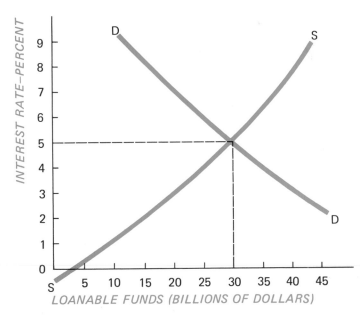

FIGURE 35-1

The equilibrium interest rate, determined by demand and supply, is such that lenders and borrowers have reached decisions that they regard as stable.

loanable funds available even if the interest rate were negative. Otherwise the demand and supply curves in the figure are characteristic of the usual demand and supply curves for commodities in a competitive market situation. Assuming that the facts as to demand and supply are as represented in the figure, we conclude that the interest rate would be 5 percent and that it would remain at that level until the relative positions of demand and supply changed. At any higher rate of interest, the supply of loanable funds would be greater than the demand, and at any lower rate the demand for funds would exceed the supply. In either case market forces would come into play to lower or raise the interest rate until it reached the equilibrium level of 5 percent.

ROLE OF PROFITS

Capitalism implies the use of capital or producers' goods for the production of additional goods and services. This capital may be in the form of machinery, buildings, and equipment; or it may be represented by money that can be used to purchase capital goods. Under the free enterprise, capitalistic system, such capital goods are owned and used primarily by the individuals and firms in the economy rather than by government bodies. In addition, the incentive for obtaining and using capital goods to produce additional goods, whether more capital goods or consumer goods, is profit.

Although the ultimate end of economic activity is consumption, the immediate end for most businessmen is profit. In an endeavor to make a profit, businesses cater to consumer demand. Through the prices we are willing to pay as consumers, we give businesses the means and the revenue necessary to purchase labor, land, and capital to produce the goods and services we demand. The stronger the demand, the greater the profit potential and the greater will be the incentive to produce. Thus, profits play a central role in the operation of our free enterprise system.

THEORIES OF PROFIT

Although profit is a return to the entrepreneur and is frequently looked upon as a remuneration for undertaking a risk, there are several theories of profit.

Innovation Theory

According to this theory, profits will arise because of innovations. The entrepreneur who comes up with a new product, a new process, or a more efficient method of producing a product may earn an *innovation profit*. Actually the innovation theory is tied in very closely with our explanation of profit under conditions of pure competition. Assuming an equilibrium, no-profit position, what can the producer do to achieve a profit position? Since the cost of productive agents and the market price of the finished goods are determined by the forces in the market, the only way he can increase his profits is to reduce cost with new and better machinery or more efficient production techniques, or to come out with a new and better product that will not be bound by the market price for the existing product. In short, he may come up with some innovation that will increase his profit by either decreasing his cost or increasing his revenue.

In our economy innovations are continually taking place, and innovation profits are very much in evidence. On a large scale such developments as electric power, the rise of the corporate form of business, the automobile, the airplane, invention of modern appliances, radio, and television—all have brought about innovation profits. Since we seldom have conditions of pure competition, we have not seen the elimination of profits from most of these innovations. The forces of competition, however, have brought about higher production and relatively lower prices for most of these goods in the past several decades.

The ball-point pen offers a classic example of innovation profits. When first put on the market by Reynolds Pen Company after World War II, these pens sold at a price of $12.50. In the first year or two, profits to Reynolds were phenomenal. Within a few years dozens of new firms had entered the market, and the prices fell to as low as 69 cents, which eliminated most of the innovation profit. In the 1950s William Frawley, however, substantially improved the operation of the ball-point pen by bringing out a new, improved type of ink. In effect he innovated the innovation. The subsequent formation and development of his Paper-Mate Company proved to be extremely profitable, which permitted him to sell out for a large capital gain. Other substantial innovations in recent years have been the Wankel engine, human conveyor belts in airline terminals, Winnebago motorized homes, credit cards in the finance industry, computer editing of novels, and pretaped electronic audio events that can be tuned into family TV units for closed-circuit viewing.

All profits cannot be attributed to innovation, however, since frequently profits exist without innovations, and profits often continue to exist long after the innovation has run its course. Therefore, a consideration of some of the other profit theories is necessary if we are properly to understand profit in all its ramifications.

Monopoly Profits

Profits may arise or be maintained because of the existence of a monopoly or some degree of monopolistic competition. Frequently an innovator will obtain sufficient control of the market to enable him to discourage competition and thus maintain his profit position. *Monopoly profits* arise through the ability of the producer to control the price in such a manner that it will not fall to a point where the average revenue and average cost are equal. This may be done through patents, by efficient management, or by devious methods of regulating output and discouraging other firms from entering the market. Profit that arises from such a situation is sometimes referred to as an "economic rent," since it is income from the use of factors of production that have an inelastic supply.

The monopolist may be successful in limiting the entry of other firms into the industry by the use of patent rights, by the exclusive ownership of the source of raw materials, or by the fact that the market is small compared to the optimum scale of operations of the monopolist so that it is unprofitable for other firms to enter the industry. Public-utility companies that operate under franchises are examples of producers that receive profits because they enjoy a degree of legal monopoly.

Monopoly profits also may arise in some industries where there are relatively few firms and collusive practices are used to limit the total output of the industry. In still other cases the capital expenditures necessary to enter a particular business may be large enough to deter many would-be producers from entering the market. Lastly, monopoly profits will occur when product differentiation exists. In such cases, which are prevalent in our economy, the differentiation permits some degree of control over price and, therefore, leads to monopolistic profits.

Since a considerable amount of imperfect competition exists in our economy, it is evident that monopoly or monopolistic profits are very prevalent. In many cases, however, it is the substantial innovation profits, or prospects of such profits, that lead to measures which promote imperfect competition.

Risk-Bearing Theory

It is often stated that profits are the prize for risk undertaken by the enterpreneur in the operation of the business enterprise. According to this theory, it is held that, since the other factors of production have a contractual agreement specifying a rate for their services in the form of wages, rent, and interest, profit is a residue that may exist after these factors have been compensated. Since there may be no profit at all and a loss may actually be incurred, a certain amount of risk is assumed by the entrepreneur. Thus, it is argued that, if all goes well, he is entitled to any and all return over costs. Furthermore, since the other factors take little or no risk, they are entitled to only the agreed-upon remuneration.

Because of the risk involved, the price of the product must be high enough to induce the entrepreneur to undertake the organization, development, and operation of the business. Usually the more risky the venture, the greater must be the promise of profits. Furthermore, the presence of risk discourages a number of would-be entrepreneurs from starting a business. This limits the number of producers, at least at the beginning, and, therefore, results in a higher profit for those venturesome enough to take the chance.

Although the risk-bearing theory may explain who should receive the profit and why, it does not necessarily explain the source of or the reason for profit. In many cases profits are not commensurate with the risk involved. In fact, the venture may be so risky that it is doomed to failure, and no profits will be realized. In other cases, such as a monopoly by patent rights or control of the source of raw materials or a monopoly through the grant of a public-utility franchise, good profits may exist with a minimum of risk.

The risk-bearing theory considers only the risks inherent in the operation of the business. Such risks include that of consumer acceptance or rejection of a product, a change in prices, or the risk that competitors will enter the market with a new and better product. Other risks, such as loss by fire and loss through liability suits, are external to the operation of the business. Since most of these external risks can be insured against, such risk can be reduced. Even here if the entrepreneur wants to assume such risk, he can increase his chances for greater profit or greater loss. On the other hand, loss from internal risks may be guarded against to some extent by wise and prudent management.

A substantial risk was undertaken by Henry Ford in using his own and borrowed funds to establish the largest single factory in the world for the production of automobiles. Walt Disney poured millions and millions of dollars into the development of Disneyland before he ever realized a penny of revenue from its operations. Numerous small businessmen risk their capital, time, and effort in business enterprises each year in an endeavor to make a profit. Some of them are successful and are rewarded with a profit, but many others are not so fortunate and become bankrupt.

Windfall Profit

Whether perfect or imperfect competition exists, profits often arise by mere chance. In the late 1930s, for example, many junk dealers were loaded with unwanted cars packed two and three high. With the advent of World

War II and the cessation of automobile production, however, these junk-car dealers found a lucrative market for spare parts and could sell their scrap to the steel mills at a good price. In the mid-1950s many fur dealers were caught with large inventories of inexpensive furs. The advent of the Davey Crockett fad, accompanied by the demand for coonskin caps and other fur-trimmed items, provided a profitable market for the sale of their products. Consider the owners of Batman or Captain Marvel comics in the early seventies; also, consider the owners of McGovern-Eagleton buttons and posters. Persons in possession of any of these can in many instances demand prices in excess of 1,000 percent of their original purchase price.

Frequently an unexpected increase or decrease in the market price of a commodity may result in a windfall profit or loss. Land values may change with shifts in population or changes in business and industrial centers. These and other such situations bring about profits that are due neither to innovation nor to monopoly. Such profits do not arise from the normal operations of the business but result from factors generally outside of and beyond the control of the business, such as changes in the weather or the occurrence of business depressions.

Managerial Efficiency

A good argument can be made for the fact that profits arise as a result of managerial efficiency. Numerous instances exist in which it can be shown that management, through more efficient operations, can reduce the cost of doing business, can anticipate and avoid changes that will adversely affect the company's income, can improve marketing techniques that will make the product more salable, and can add to its product line in order to increase its revenue.

Not all profits can be attributed to managerial efficiency. In fact, in some cases good profits exist in spite of poor management. There are other cases in which a top-notch manager may be in a position where a profit cannot be made regardless of the efficiency of his management. Frequently a talented business executive is transferred from one department or branch to another. Although he may exercise better judgment and display more efficiency in the new position than did his predecessor, his superior ability may not be identifiable in the income statement.

Sometimes a change in management can turn a losing situation into a profitable operation. Such was the situation in the late 1940s when Henry Ford II, with the able assistance of Ernest Breech, took over the management of the Ford Motor Company. The company had been losing millions of dollars annually and was in a relatively poor financial position compared to its former days of glory. The new policies, organization, techniques, and practices adopted by the new management returned the company to a leading position in the industry, and it has been making a healthy profit for many years.

Granted that profits may arise because of managerial efficiency, as they frequently do, the question arises as to the disposition of such profits. Last century and the early part of this century, when it was common for the owner to operate his own business, performing the functions of both entrepreneur and manager, this was less of a problem. In modern-day corporate practice, however, with its absentee ownership, it is customary to hire managers to operate the business. Should the owner receive all the profits for his risk-bearing function, or should management receive the profits because of its efficiency? One solution is the bonus system. In this way the owners, who are legally and economically entitled to the profits, share them with management. This permits management to participate in the enjoyment of profits if and when they reach certain predetermined levels. To a large extent, this is a recognition by the owners that profits may arise because of, and certainly are affected by, managerial efficiency.

The highest paid executive in the nation, a company president, for example, received a salary of $425,000 plus $513,000 in bonuses and other compensations for a total income of $938,000 for 1973. The second highest paid executive received $456,000 in bonuses in addition to his salary of $423,000. Publication of corporate executive salaries for 1973 reveals that more than 700 corporate officials earned over $100,000 annually. Of these about 295 earned between $200,000 and $400,000 per year. Most of the incomes were a combination of salaries and bonuses. At the other end of the management ladder, however, many junior executives or middle-management men receive only a few hundred dollars annually in bonuses.

Many firms have profit-sharing systems in which all employees who fulfill certain age or years-of-service requirements receive a share in the profits. Numerous advantages and disadvantages can be listed and analyzed for such profit-sharing systems. Some claim that profit sharing is "foreign" to the free enterprise system because the entrepreneurs take the risk and should receive all the profit. Furthermore, others claim that since labor takes no risk and does not share in the losses of the business, it is not entitled to any of the profit. But those advocating profit sharing, especially the hundreds of companies in the Council of Profit Sharing Industries, maintain that it is a means of recognizing the workers' contribution to greater productivity.

Conclusion

It appears that profit may arise from a multiplicity of causes, either individually or in combination. Numerous examples could be cited to show that profits have actually occurred from each individual cause. Others can be cited to show that a combination of causes, such as innovation and managerial efficiency, may be responsible for the existence of large profits. In fact, cases are known where the lack of good management resulted in substantial losses for firms with valuable innovations. It is the hope of gaining profits that usually induces individuals and companies to seek innovations, undertake risks, develop managerial efficiency, and endeavor to gain a monopoly. Speculation, likewise, is often undertaken in the hope that circumstances will change and bring about windfall profits, although endeavoring to plan such windfall gains may be put in the category of risk bearing or managerial efficiency.

Profits are the most dynamic, unstable, and uncertain of the various forms of income. They are temporary phenomena under conditions of pure competition and under some forms of imperfect competition. Although monopolistic practices may be used to protect and maintain profits, the rise of substitutes and imitations constitutes an ever-present threat to the continuation of monopolistic profits.

INTEREST AND PROFIT AS SHARES OF NATIONAL INCOME

We have seen that labor receives the great bulk of total national income—in the neighborhood of 74 percent. We have also seen that rental income constitutes only 2 to 3 percent of national income. The remainder, roughly 23 percent, is divided between recipients of interest income and profits.

Capital's Share of the National Income

Capital, like land, receives one of the smaller shares of the national income, as can be observed from Table 35-1. It can also be seen that interest as a percentage of the national income decreased considerably in the two decades prior to 1950. One reason for this phenomenon is the fact that interest, especially on long-term loans, provides a fixed income to the capitalist. Thus, when the general level of business activity declines and prices and incomes fall, interest income does not fall as fast as the total income of the economy. This can be observed for the year 1933 in which total interest income actually declined but became a relatively larger share of the national income. Conversely, when the general level of business activity increases and prices rise, fixed interest income or even a moderately rising interest income becomes a smaller share of the national income. This is reflected in the figures for the years 1940-1955. This was true especially in the period 1942 to 1951, during which time incomes and prices were rising

TABLE 35-1

NET INTEREST
AS A PERCENT
OF NATIONAL
INCOME

1929-1973

Year	National Income (Billions)	Net Interest (Billions)	Net Interest as a Percent of National Income
1929	$ 86.8	$ 4.7	5.4
1933	40.3	4.1	10.2
1935	57.2	4.1	7.2
1940	81.1	3.3	4.1
1945	181.5	2.2	1.1
1950	241.1	2.0	0.9
1955	331.0	4.1	1.1
1960	414.5	8.4	2.1
1965	564.3	18.2	3.2
1970	800.5	36.5	4.6
1973	1,054.2	50.4	4.8

SOURCE: *Economic Report of the President,* 1974.

but interest rates were maintained at abnormally low levels as a result of government action in supporting bond prices. Interest as a share of national income has risen moderately in the past 15 years and more markedly in the past 10 years due to higher interest rates and an increase in loanable funds.

The Entrepreneurs' Share of the National Income

Profit is the most dynamic and uncertain segment of our total income. Since it is a residual and a noncontractual income, there may be nothing left after taking care of other factor costs of doing business. It is almost certain to change from month to month and from year to year. This means that the entrepreneurs' share of the national income will vary from year to year and will fluctuate considerably between periods of prosperity and depression. Nevertheless, some idea of the entrepreneurs' share of the national income can be obtained from the figures given in Table 35-2.

From the table it can be observed that for the selected years profits varied from a low of 11.7 percent of the national income in 1933, a depression year, to a high of 31.1 percent in prosperous 1950. This fluctuation is greater than that for any of the other three factors of production. The suddenness with which profits can change is revealed somewhat by comparing the years 1929 through 1935, in which profits decreased from 29.5 percent of the national income in 1929 to 11.7 percent in 1933 and then increased to 24.8 percent of the national income by 1935. It is also interesting to note that in 1933 corporate profits were a negative $1.2 billion, which meant that corporations lost $1.2 billion that year. In recent years, profits as a share of national income fell from about 23 percent in the 1960s to a little over 18 percent in the early 1970s. By analyzing the figures it also

TABLE 35-2

PROFITS AS A PERCENT OF NATIONAL INCOME

1929-1973

Year	National Income (Billions)	Income of Unincorporated Enterprises (Billions)	Corporate Profits (Billions)	Total Entrepreneurial Income (Billions)	Total as a Percent of National Income
1929	$ 86.8	$15.2	$ 10.5	$ 25.7	29.5
1933	40.3	5.9	− 1.2	4.7	11.7
1935	57.2	10.8	3.4	14.2	24.8
1940	81.1	13.1	9.8	22.9	28.2
1945	181.5	31.4	19.2	50.6	27.9
1950	241.1	37.5	37.7	75.2	31.1
1955	331.0	41.7	46.9	88.6	26.7
1960	414.5	46.2	49.9	96.1	23.1
1965	564.3	57.2	76.1	133.3	23.6
1970	800.5	66.9	69.2	136.1	17.0
1973	1,054.2	84.3	109.2	193.5	18.4

SOURCE: *Economic Report of the President,* 1974.

becomes apparent that income of unincorporated enterprises tends to be a bit more stable than corporate profits. This stems from the fact that unincorporated enterprises consist in part of farmers, other self-employed persons, and many small service enterprises whose income sometimes is more a return for services rendered than a pure profit.

SUMMARY

1. Contractual interest is money paid for the use of borrowed money. It is usually stated as a percentage rate per unit of time. When an owner uses his own capital, an interest rate may be imputed.

2. When loans are employed for the creation of capital, interest is the return accruing to capital for its services in production.

3. Interest can be paid on capital for its services in production because of the productivity of capital in the process, and the marginal productivity of capital will determine the rate that can be paid.

4. Time preference is a psychological factor expressing an individual's attitude toward the future. It serves to explain the "abstinence" of the saver, as well as the utility of loans to the borrower.

5. The liquidity preference theory holds that the rate of interest is determined by the relationship between the quantity of money and the desire for liquidity.

6. The potential supply of funds in the money market is derived partly from savers directly and partly through the expansion of bank credit. The market rate of interest on loans of funds is determined by supply and demand in much the same way that product prices are determined by supply and demand.

7. Profits play an integral role in our economy. It is the hope for profit that induces entrepreneurs to undertake the operation of businesses that provide goods and services for members of the economy.

8. There are several theories of profit: innovation, monopoly, risk bearing, windfall, and managerial efficiency. Profits may arise from any one of these causes or some combination thereof.

9. Since profits can be affected by external as well as internal forces, the entrepreneur or manager must be ever alert to changing conditions that will decrease or increase his profits.

10. Profit, the entrepreneur's share of the national income, is the most dynamic and uncertain of all four shares. There is, however, a tendency for the rate of return on the property shares—rent, interest, and profits—to equalize in the long run.

NEW TERMS

Interest rate, *p. 765*
Marginal productivity theory of interest, *p. 765*
Natural rate of interest, *p. 766*
Market rate of interest, *p. 766*
Equilibrium rate of interest, *p. 766*
Time preference theory, *p. 766*
Transactions motive, *p. 767*
Precautionary motive, *p. 767*

Speculative motive, *p. 767*
Demand for capital, *p. 768*
Supply of capital, *p. 771*
Innovation profit, *p. 777*
Monopoly profits, *p. 778*
Risk-bearing theory of profit, *p. 778*
Windfall profit, *p. 779*
Managerial efficiency theory of profit, *p. 780*

QUESTIONS FOR DISCUSSION AND ANALYSIS

1. Interest is a price. Explain.

2. Entrepreneur John Smith borrows $10,000 at 5 percent for use in his business. He also uses $5,000 of his own funds in the business. What is his annual interest cost?

3. How does the marginal productivity theory of interest explain why the employer can afford to pay for the use of capital? Give an example.

4. (a) What are the main sources of demand for loanable funds?

(b) What important changes have occurred in the demand for loanable funds in recent years?

5. What factors determine the demand for loanable funds?

6. Explain how time preference plays an important part in the accumulation and the borrowing of savings by individuals.

7. How does bank credit add to the supply of loanable funds?

8. How are market rates of interest determined?

9. What is the role of profit in a free enterprise economy?

10. What do we mean by monopoly profits? Why are monopoly profits not so temporary as are the profits under conditions of pure competition?

11. Can you list certain items for which innovation or windfall profits have occurred in the past few years?

12. Why, according to the risk-bearing theory, should the entrepreneur be entitled to all of the profit?

13. Do you think that the concept of profit sharing is contrary to the capitalistic system? Why or why not?

SUGGESTED READINGS

Bohm-Bawerk, E. von. *Capital and Interest*, translated by William Smart. Clifton, N.J.: August M. Kelley, Publishers, 1970.

Cagan, Phillip. *Changes in the Cyclical Behavior of Interest Rates*. New York: Columbia University Press, 1966.

Cassel, Gustav. *The Nature and Necessity of Interest*. New York: The Macmillan Company, 1903.

Childs, John F. *Earnings Per Share and Management Decisions*. Englewood Cliffs, N.J.: Prentice-Hall, Inc., 1971.

Conrad, Joseph W. *An Introduction to the Theory of Interest*. Berkeley: University of California Press, 1959.

Dudick, Thomas F. *Profile for Profitability*. New York: John Wiley & Sons, Inc., 1972.

Glyn, Andrew, and Robert Sutcliffe. *Capitalism in Crisis*. New York: Pantheon Books, Inc., 1972.

Knight, Frank. *Risk, Uncertainty & Profit*. Chicago: University of Chicago Press, 1971.

Robinson, Claude E. *Understanding Profits*. Princeton, N.J.: Van Nostrand Reinhold Company, 1961.

Sherman, Howard J. *Profits in the United States*. Ithaca, N.Y.: Cornell University Press, 1968.

Van Horne, James C. *The Function and Analysis of Capital Market Rates*. Englewood Cliffs, N.J.: Prentice-Hall, Inc., 1970.

36

Human Capital

PREVIEW Factor prices are the prices of productive services. A wage, interest rate, or rent measures the market value of a flow of services per unit of time. The sources of these services—labor, capital, and land—also have an economic value. This is wealth, or the value of a stock in contrast to a flow. In general, present stock value is the discounted sum of expected future flow prices over the productive life of the stock. Thus, a laborer can be regarded as human capital. His future earnings are determined by his health, education, and mobility.

The previous four chapters were devoted to the analysis of markets for the factors of production. Wages, rent, and interest are prices determined in the markets for labor, land, and capital (or capital funds) respectively. Profits accrue to the entrepreneur after he deducts from sales receipts both the contractual and the imputed costs of production. These costs, from the viewpoint of the business firm, are income payments from the viewpoint of those who own the productive factors.

Resource or factor prices are the prices of services. A wage is the price paid for labor services, such as a day's work. It is worth emphasizing that a wage is not the price of a laborer per se, namely, the one who owns and supplies the labor services. Likewise, rent is the price per unit of the services of land used in the productive process for a specified period of time. Rent is not the price of land itself. Interest is the price paid for the use of funds, usually to purchase capital equipment and employ its services for a given time period. Men, land, and capital equipment are sources of a flow of services that are combined to generate a flow of final goods and services. Men, land, and capital equipment embody, so to speak, a potential flow of productive services over their employment lifetime.

If factor prices are the prices of flows, what then determines the prices or economic values of the sources of these flows? What determines the value of land as opposed to the rent for its use over a defined time period? What determines the value of the capital stock in contrast to the price (interest payment) for its use per period of time? By extension of this concept of the value of a source of productive services, we can ask another question. What determines the *economic* value of a laborer as distinguished from his wage, which is the price of his service per period of time?

From the earliest days of economics, the value of land and the value of capital were major concerns. Only in recent years have economists come to ask the final question posed in the preceding paragraph. Because of the conceptual similarity between men and capital—the embodiment of a flow of productive services that are priced in the market—economists have come to speak of *human capital.* In a meaningful sense one can view the economy as having at any given time a total capital stock, part of which is nonhuman capital and part of which is human capital. Economic growth is a function of the rate of increase of human and nonhuman capital, that is, investment in human or nonhuman capital. Economic growth is also a function of technological change applied to either type of capital, that is, improvements in the quality of human or nonhuman capital.

In this chapter we will take an overview of the four shares of national income allocated to labor, land, capital, and entrepreneurship. Capitalization of income will be used to relate the income flow (a factor price) to the value of the stock yielding the services that generate income. Special emphasis will then be placed upon the value of human capital and its determinants.

THE FOUR SHARES

Although no one theory explains completely the functional distribution of income, each theory adds to our knowledge of the complex process by which the economic system does in fact generate a distribution. Statistical data do not correspond precisely to the theoretical definitions we have used. Imputed wages, rent, and interest pose especially difficult problems. It is difficult to separate them from contractual payments. Nevertheless, it will be useful to combine the statistical evidence on shares of national income presented in Chapters 32, 34, and 35. The functional distribution of national income for 1973 is presented in Figure 36-1.

It is obvious from Figure 36-1 that the largest share of income by far goes to labor. Perhaps this is as it should be because there are so many individuals in this category. Whether labor's share should be more or less is difficult to say. The smallest shares are those received by land and capital. Nevertheless, they are important and necessary factors in the operation of our economy. Profit, of course, is the most dynamic and uncertain share of total income. The calculations of shares are at best estimates, however, since the entrepreneur's share (proprietor's income) includes a certain amount of undetermined imputed wages, rent, and interest, as well as pure profit.

Because of competitive market forces, there is a tendency for the rate of return of property income from land, capital, and entrepreneurship to equalize

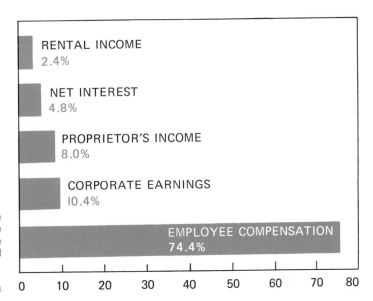

FIGURE 36-1

FUNCTIONAL DISTRIBUTION OF
NATIONAL INCOME

1973

RENTAL INCOME
2.4%

NET INTEREST
4.8%

PROPRIETOR'S INCOME
8.0%

CORPORATE EARNINGS
10.4%

EMPLOYEE COMPENSATION
74.4%

The largest share of national income
goes to labor. The next largest share
takes the form of profits, while the
smallest shares are received by land
and capital.

SOURCE: *Economic Report of the President,* 1974.

in the long run. This happens because of the mobility of capital and of the entrepreneurial function. The rate of return in the form of rent, interest, and dividends tends to come into balance as entrepreneurs and others shift investments from one factor to another. If interest rates are high, they may disinvest in stock in order to purchase bonds. The expanded demand for bonds will tend to lower the yield rate on the bonds as the prices of bonds are forced upward and increase the yield on stocks as their prices fall. At other times capital may flow into the purchase of rental property if it is returning more than either stocks or bonds. It is interesting to note that in 1973 the average interest rate, the average yield on stock, and the average rental yield were all between 3 to 7 percent.

CAPITALIZATION OF INCOME

If the owner of a productive resource leaves that resource in employment, the owner will continue to receive an income payment year after year. The periodic income payments in exchange for productive services can be related to the value of the source of these services by means of a process known as *capitalization of income.* In order to facilitate a clear understanding of capitalization, we shall carry out the discussion in this section in terms of interest payments on money assets deposited in a savings account in a bank. The concept of capitalization will then be extended to the value of land, nonhuman capital equipment, and human capital.

The Concept of Present Value

Suppose you were to deposit $100 in a savings account at a commercial bank. Suppose, further, that the bank pays an interest rate of 5 percent per year on savings accounts. What would be the value of your $100 one year hence? Obviously it would be $105: the original $100 plus $5 in interest credited to your account. Note that your $100 is an asset (a stock) which, when put to use by the bank, earned an income (a flow) of $5 per year.

We can turn the question around. At an interest rate of 5 percent, what is the value today of $105 in a savings account one year from today? The *present value* of $105 one year hence is $100. One simply reverses the process of adding to the asset the amount of earned interest. The reverse process is known as *discounting* the $105 at a 5 percent interest rate to obtain its present value. If $100 today is worth $105 a year later, then $105 a year later is worth $100 at present.

The time duration can be extended. Suppose you were to begin with $100 in a savings account and leave the account untouched for two years. At the end of the first year, the account would amount to $105. But during the second year interest would be earned on the $105 left in the account rather than on $100. At 5 percent the $105 would earn $5.25 during the second year. Therefore, the value of $100 today is $110.25 two years hence. Again, we can reverse the process. It follows that the present value of $110.25 two years hence is $100 if the interest rate is 5 percent per year.

Let us carry the example one step further. Suppose the funds are left untouched in the savings account for a third year. During the third year, the 5 percent interest would be paid on $110.25, the total accumulation at the end of the second year. Five percent of $110.25 amounts to $5.51. When this interest payment is added to the principal, the account has a value of $115.76. Thus, the value of $100 three years hence is $115.76, and a sum of $115.76 to be held three years in the future has a present value of $100.

Single-Period Discounting

These simple notions can be expressed by means of a formula. Let PV symbolize the present value; let i denote the interest rate; and let V_1 represent the value one year in the future. Then we can write

$$PV(1 + i) = V_1.$$

In our example given previously, it was stated that the value today, namely PV, is $100. Moreover, the interest rate was specified as .05, that is, 5 percent. By substitution in the formula above, the value of V_1 is obtained:

$$\$100(1 + .05) = \$100 + \$100(.05) = \$100 + \$5 = \$105.$$

Instead of assuming knowledge of PV and i, we can postulate that V_1 equals $105 and that i equals .05. Then we have

$$PV(1 + .05) = \$105.$$

We wish to find the present value of $105 one year hence. Both sides of the equation are multiplied by $\dfrac{1}{(1 + i)}$, so the formula is expressed as

$$PV = \frac{1}{(1 + i)} V_1.$$

Substitution of the known $V_1 = \$105$ and $i = .05$ yields

$$PV = \frac{1}{(1 + .05)} \quad \$105 = \frac{\$105}{1.05} = \$100.$$

Multiperiod Discounting

Using the single-period formula as a basis, discounting over a two-year duration can be derived. Let V_2 denote the value two years in the future. Then the formula is

$$PV(1 + i)(1 + i) = V_2.$$

Why is this so? Remember that $PV(1 + i) = V_1$. Therefore, the formula states

$$V_1(1 + i) = V_2.$$

That is, the value at the end of the first year has added to it the interest earned in the second year (based upon that value, not the original PV) to determine the value at the end of the second year. In the case of the illustration:

$$\$100(1 + .05)(1 + .05) =$$
$$\$105(1 + .05) = \$105 + \$5.25 = \$110.25.$$

Once more, let us reverse the process by discounting a value two years in the future. The formula is rewritten as

$$PV = \frac{V_2}{(1 + i)(1 + i)}.$$

Setting $V_2 = \$110.25$ and $i = .05$, we have

$$PV = \frac{\$110.25}{(1.05)(1.05)} = \frac{\$110.25}{1.1025} = \$100.$$

Whereas it takes only $105 one year hence to equal $100 at present, it takes $110.25 two years hence to equal an identical present value. We can state this same conclusion in a slightly different way. The more distant is the deferred payment or income, the lower is its present value. For example, $1,000 two years in the future has a smaller present value than $1,000 received one year in the future. Assuming an interest rate of 5 percent, Table 36-1 illustrates the principle.

TABLE 36-1

Future Payment	Time Received	Present Value
$1,000	One year in the future	$952
$1,000	Two years in the future	$907
$1,000	Three years in the future	$864
$1,000	Four years in the future	$823
—	—	—
—	—	—
$1,000	Twenty years in the future	$377

VALUE OF NONHUMAN CAPITAL

Our discussion thus far has been restricted to a savings account with a present value, predetermined interest payments, and the value of the account at different future dates. The concept and method of capitalization can be applied, however, to determine the value of land and capital equipment. Preceding chapters were concerned with the determination of prices of factors of production by market forces of demand and supply. In turn, these prices constitute income for owners of the factors. For our purposes in this chapter, we can assume that the market has determined rental and interest income per period of time (such as per day or per year) for each period that the services of land and capital are purchased for use in production. The problem is to determine the value of these sources of the flow of services.

Land Value

Let us assume a parcel of land of which each acre has been yielding an income of $200 a year and, as far as can be determined, will continue to do so. What is an acre of this land worth at present? One answer might be its cost to the present owner which, let us suppose, was $2,600. But the difficulty is only postponed because one can raise the question, why did the acre cost this amount?

The value of the acre is traceable to the fact that it yields a net return of $200 a year. This year's return is $200, but next year's return of $200 is not worth $200 now. It is the present worth of the acre that is wanted. If the rate at which the future is discounted by those interested in the market for land is 5 percent, the yield of $200 next year will be discounted by 5 percent to approximately $190. The present worth of $200 two years hence will be still less because of two years' discount. In short, the present worth of the acre is its capitalized value, which is the sum of all future incomes discounted to the present at some particular rate. In the present case, with an annual net yield of $200 an acre and a discount rate of 5 percent, the present worth of the acre is $200 divided by .05 or $4,000. From another point of view, $4,000 invested at the current rate of interest of 5 percent will yield an income of $200 annually. Thus, the parcel of land that yields $200 annually is also worth $4,000.

In the discounting formula, the value of land is what we have called PV. The V_1, V_2, and so on are the rental incomes of $200 per acre per year. Finally, the rate used to discount the future yields is the interest rate of 5 percent. The formula appears as

$$PV = \frac{V_1}{(1+i)} + \frac{V_2}{(1+i)^2} + \frac{V_3}{(1+i)^3} + \frac{V_4}{(1+i)^4} + \cdots$$

$$= \frac{200}{(1.05)} + \frac{200}{(1.05)^2} + \frac{200}{(1.05)^3} + \frac{200}{(1.05)^4} + \cdots$$

The number of V's to be inserted is equal to the number of years that the land will bring a rental income. It can be shown mathematically that if the land is to be employed indefinitely into the future at a rent of $200 and if the interest rate is 5 percent, then

$$PV = \frac{\$200}{.05} = \$4,000.$$

The mathematics of the argument is not of primary importance. The important point is this: If markets operate perfectly under conditions of competition, the present value of land will equal the sum of all future rental payments, each payment discounted back to the present. If markets do not operate perfectly, the value of land will still tend to equal the discounted sum of future income payments from the land.

Capital Value

These principles apply also to the capital stock of the economy or that stock owned by a single individual. Therefore, not much in addition needs to be said. The nature of stocks and flows can be emphasized by considering the alternatives open to an entrepreneur. He can purchase a machine with a relatively long, useful life. On the other hand, he has the option of renting the machine from someone else. What is the relationship between a market rental price per week or per year and the price he would have to pay for the machine itself?

The marginal productivity theory of factor pricing applies to the services of a machine. Marginal productivity together with supply conditions of the market determine a price that is similar to a rental price. Thus, these factor prices in each period assume the role of the V's in our formula. Given an interest rate, the present value of the machine itself can be determined as the sum of the discounted future prices or net incomes per period. If the quoted market price of a machine is less than its present value to entrepreneurs, it will pay business firms to purchase more machines—to invest or expand their capital stock. If the market price of a machine is greater than its present value, demand for machines will decrease.

The existence of such inequalities, however, will set in motion forces that will act to bring about equality of the machine price and its present value. In the former case, expanding demand will bid up the quoted market price, and market price will fall in the latter case. In long-run equilibrium under conditions of competition, the price of a capital stock item, such as a machine, will equal the sum of the discounted future income payments per period derived from its employment.

VALUE OF HUMAN CAPITAL

The evaluation of land and nonhuman capital, as stocks that embody flows of productive services, sets the stage for evolution of human capital. After all, if the concept of present value can be applied to land and capital equipment, there is no logical reason why it cannot also be applied to manpower. This is not to say that one can put a price tag on a human being. Only the *economic* value of a human being as a source of labor services over an extended time period is subject to evaluation. Every person possesses other characteristics that no economist would pretend to reduce to monetary terms.

The Age-Income Profile

Over his entire working lifetime an individual will earn income in each year of employment. Does this sequence of annual earnings exhibit some definite pattern common to all? Obviously the pattern will differ among individuals. Average lifetime labor earnings, as well as the rate of increase or decrease over time, differ among occupations, among industries of employment, and among regions of the country. Union membership may affect wages in a given occupation and industry. Earnings even differ among individuals in the same job classification because of personality factors. Nevertheless, it is possible to identify a "typical" *age-earnings pattern*, granting that no individual case can be precisely described by the "typical" pattern.

Figure 36-2 presents such a "typical" relationship between income and age. Age, starting at birth, is recorded in years on the horizontal axis. On the vertical axis is measured net annual earnings in dollars per year. Since net earnings may be negative in one or more years, the vertical axis extends below the origin in the diagram. Any one point on the curve represents net labor earnings for a given age, and the entire curve traces out the stream of lifetime earnings.

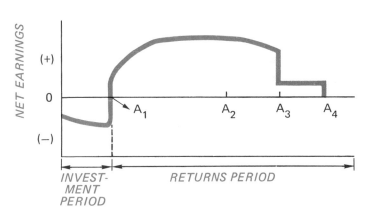

FIGURE 36-2

AGE-EARNINGS PATTERN

A typical age-earnings profile shows negative net earnings before one enters the labor market, positive earnings during employment, and a decline in income after retirement.

At first net earnings are negative, indicated by the earnings curve drawn below the horizontal axis. From birth up to age A_1 may be called the "investment period" or period of human capital formation. The expenses of bringing a potential laborer to the age at which he enters the labor force—provision of food, clothing, shelter, general education, and specific training—exceed his earned income if he has any earned income. Generally part if not all of this expense is borne by someone other than the laborer himself, such as his parents or other members of the family.

From age A_1 through age A_3 is the period of active employment. When the individual enters the labor force and finds employment, his net earnings (income minus expenses of earning that income) become positive. Positive net earnings rise as the worker gains experience and expertise in his occupation. Typically, earnings will plateau—or grow at a much smaller rate—for a considerable period of time. Thereafter, until retirement, there may well be a gradual loss of earning power as personal productivity declines with advancing age.

Age A_3 in the diagram denotes the age of retirement from active employment. At this age income drops to a level determined by the pension coverage available to the worker and the expenses related to age. Retirement income continues until the age of death, designated as A_4. During this period, normally higher medical costs must be deducted from gross pension income, generating a net income which is often less than that earned at the time the worker entered the labor force.

The span of years from age A_1 to age A_4 has been labeled as the "returns period." Whereas the primary expenditure occurs in the earliest years, in preparation for employment, the economic returns accrue in the form of income in subsequent years. During the "returns period" the worker may still incur expenses to keep abreast of developments in his occupation or to otherwise maintain his earning power. Nevertheless, the largest bulk of expenses arise prior to employment and are most often borne by someone other than the worker who enjoys the economic gains.

Figure 36-2 is drawn under the assumption that national income does not rise. If national income does increase, the earnings curve will shift upward after age A_1. However, the curve may shift downward to the left of age A_1 as the costs of investment in human capital rise. As mentioned earlier, the age-earnings profile will differ among occupations, industries, regions, and even among individuals. Still, an overall pattern similar to that described in the diagram appears to hold in practice.

Present Value of the Income Stream

The net earnings at age one could be designated as V_1, net earnings at age two as V_2, and so on through net earnings at age A_4. At any given age, by applying an appropriate discount rate to future expected income, the present value of the laborer at that age could be determined by applying the formula used to determine land value on page 793. It is simply a question of inserting the proper dollar value for each V, deciding upon the interest rate i, and doing the arithmetical calculation.

Assume retirement is expected at age 65 and death is expected (from mortality tables) at age 75. Then a worker of age 20 could sum 55 years of expected future annual earnings (75 minus 20), each discounted back to the present, in order to determine his own human capital value. Likewise, a worker of age 40, with the same assumptions, could sum 35 years of expected future annual earnings (75 minus 40), each discounted back to the present, to determine his capital value. A machine, as it is used, depreciates and has a smaller capital value. Similarly, a worker, once he has entered the labor force and other things being the same, finds that his capital value declines with greater age because he has fewer productive (income earning) years remaining.

We see and measure earnings and wealth of a nonhuman type much more easily because these inanimate goods are bought and sold. In contrast, a person sells only his current services as they are performed. Nevertheless, each employable person does represent—or contain within him so to speak— a future flow of services that have a market price. Although there are no markets for the sale of people (except in a slave society where slaves do carry an exchange price as the value of capital), there are indicators of the value of human capital. Occasionally people do sell some rights to their future labor services. Athletes are often paid bonuses for their future playing services. They sign with a ball team to play exclusively for that team. By doing so they are selling off part of their capital value in that their capital value consists of future services. Long-term contracts without advance bonuses, found especially in the field of entertainment, are essentially an exchange of human capital value for wealth *in other forms*. To the extent that contractual exchanges of wealth or capital value in one form are traded for wealth in another form, the notion of human capital is recognized socially.

DETERMINANTS OF HUMAN CAPITAL

A young adult in a modern exchange economy might well ask what determines his economic value as a person. Since human capital value is a function of lifetime earnings, the answer lies in those factors that determine future earnings per year. So we are back to the market forces of demand and supply once more—with one exception. The determination of present capital value is couched within the context of long-run planning by the individual. The market rewards the individual's talent if that talent is in demand. Of course, certain talents are peculiar to individuals and cannot be made part of systematic social planning. The star athlete or entertainer is a case in point. Yet over a lifetime of employment, an individual in a free society has great latitude in deciding upon courses of action that enhance or detract from his human capital value.

Diet and Health Care

Studies of economic growth have attributed from 30 percent to 60 percent of the causes of economic growth in the United States to the improving quality of the American labor force. Among the important reasons why the American labor force has the wherewithal to accelerate productivity are the diet and health care of the American population. With notable exceptions among the economically deprived, Americans are better fed, better housed, and better cared for than any other people in the world.

The extent to which diet and comfortable shelter lead to greater physical and mental dexterity and the extent to which greater dexterity contributes to economic productivity are difficult to document. Statisticians cannot quantify with accuracy the impact of diet upon performance in employment. Yet it is undeniable that strength, endurance, and mental alertness are dependent upon the intake of protein, vitamins, and fats in proper combinations. As the diet of the labor force has improved over time, the productivity and lifetime earnings of labor have likewise increased.

Perhaps of more importance are advances in medical science. Many illnesses and physical defects that formerly would have incapacitated a worker are no longer serious. Developments in hospital care have reduced job absenteeism. Discoveries in drugs and surgery have reduced mortality rates, increased labor-force participation, and lengthened productive life expectancy. Thus, compared to his counterpart at the turn of the century, a worker today is capable of remaining in the labor force for a longer period of time and of sustaining a higher level of productivity while he is an active member of the labor force.

Unfortunately, however, improved diet and medical care have also created some economic problems. Because of conventional retirement policies, an older worker may be required to leave the labor force as a full-time worker while he is still capable of many productive years in employment. Whereas better diet and medical care have extended the number of capable years, retirement policies and competition from younger workers have created employment problems for workers of advanced age. Involuntary nonparticipation in the labor force is greater and unemployment rates are higher for workers over 50 years of age as compared to those less than 50 years old. An employment problem for the older worker is beginning to emerge. The problem has already assumed such proportions that the federal government has undertaken studies which are intended to serve as guidelines for policies to ameliorate the income and employment difficulties of older or aged persons.

Education

The rapid expansion of education in the United States is probably the most important factor explaining the improving economic quality of the American labor force. Not only has a greater percentage of the population shared in formal education, the level of educational attainment (years of schooling) has also increased steadily over time.

Educational expansion since 1950 is reflected in Table 36-2. From 1950 to 1973, the number of high school pupils more than doubled. During the same period, the number of students enrolled in some form of higher education beyond high school nearly quadrupled. Studies on the economics of education have shown that this great expansion of college enrollments is traceable to a larger percentage of youngsters who actually complete four years of secondary school, rather than a substantial enlargement of the percentage of high school graduates who decide to attend college. In addition to rising absolute numbers, percentages of the relevant age-group in the population who are enrolled in school have increased as well. In 1950, about 83 percent of those of high school age were enrolled in school; by 1973 the figure had risen to over 93 percent. Only 32 percent of the college age population were enrolled in college in 1950, whereas 23 years later almost half were enrolled. The extreme right-hand column in Table 36-2 records the median number of years of school completed by persons 25 years of age or older. From 9.3 years in 1950, average educational attainment in the population rose to 12.3 years in 1973.

TABLE 36-2

MEASURES OF EDUCATIONAL ATTAINMENT

1950-1973

Year	Enrolled High School Students (Millions)	Enrolled College Students (Millions)	Median Years of School Completed, Persons 25 Years of Age and Over
1950	6.7	2.2	9.3
1955	8.0	2.4	10.2
1960	10.2	3.6	10.5
1965	13.0	5.7	11.3
1970	14.7	7.4	12.2
1973	15.5	8.7	12.3

SOURCE: *Statistical Abstract of the United States,* annually; U.S. Bureau of the Census, *Current Population Reports,* Series P-20.

Institutions of higher education perform two *economic* functions. First, they provide a consumer service. Education yields direct utility or satisfaction; it is consumed like any other good or service in the economy. Second, institutions of higher education provide a producer service in that they impart to students skills which increase labor productivity. These skills may emerge from formal professional training, such as medicine, law, business, or engineering. Vocational education contributes to the economy a vast array of technicians, mechanics in various specializations, and diverse types of administrative personnel. Skills may also result from general studies or liberal arts studies that train the mind to think abstractly, for analytical ability can be applied to a wide variety of problems. A modern economy to an ever-increasing extent utilizes a complex technology that relies upon a highly skilled and sophisticated labor force. Since World War II industry and government have expanded the employment of scientists, engineers, economists, statisticians, and psychologists in greater proportion than other types of labor. Within the past several years employment opportunities in industry have opened for sociologists, political scientists, and social workers. The demand for computer programmers and technicians has undergone a radical increase during the past ten years.

It has been said that the "education industry" is fast becoming one of the most important producer-good industries in the economy. Accordingly, economists have turned their attention to the economics of education. In terms of the formal analysis of human capital, expenditures on education can be regarded as an investment in human capital. General and professional education enlarges the number of highly skilled laborers, thereby increasing the overall productivity of the labor force and promoting a higher rate of economic growth.

Except for the cost of child care and rearing, expenditures on education constitute the largest component of expense during the "investment period" depicted in Figure 36-2. Outlays on education are expected to yield a return in the form of greater earnings during the years of employment. The return to *additional* education is the difference between two present values: the present value of the expected income stream associated with a higher level of education minus the present value of the expected income stream associated with a specified lower level of education. The difference between the two present values can be compared with the incremental outlay or cost of undertaking the additional education. If the differential in present values exceeds the cost, the return on the investment in human capital is positive.

To illustrate, suppose the investment is a four-year college education. The return to a college education can be construed as the earning potential of a college graduate as opposed to the earning potential of secondary school graduates. Let us assume the value of the sum of discounted annual earnings from age 22 to age 62 for a college graduate is $700,000. Assume the present value of annual earnings from age 18 to age 62 for one with 12 years of schooling is $500,000. Then the gross return to an investment in a college education is the differential of $200,000. What are the costs? There are three. First, there is the direct outlay for tuition, fees, and books. Second, if the individual were to attend a residential college, there is the cost of living on campus over and above what the cost would be to live at home. Third, there is the income foregone during the period of college attendance, for if a person were not to attend college, he could be earning in each of four years the income of a secondary school graduate. Let us suppose the total cost is $40,000. Then the net return on the investment is $200,000 minus $40,000 or $160,000 over his employment lifetime. This is an average of $4,000 per year. An investment of $40,000 in the present will yield a return of 10 percent per year in the future.

This approach to the economics of education is an application of marginal analysis. From a purely economic viewpoint, individuals have an incentive to make the investment in education if the present value of future returns exceeds cost. From a social viewpoint resources will be allocated more efficiently if the investment is undertaken, because individuals' contributions to national income in the future outweigh the present use of resources to execute the investment. As investment expands, the increased demand for education will act to raise the cost of education. Simultaneously, the greater supply of highly educated labor will operate to reduce the annual income paid to this type of labor. Therefore, as investment in human capital increases, the rate of return will decline—just as the rate of return declines with expanded investment in nonhuman capital. In the long run equilibrium investment will be stabilized at the margin where the marginal return is just equal to the marginal cost.

On-the-Job Training

On-the-job training is very similar to education in its economic consequences, except that the training is provided by the employer or in some instances by a labor union. As compared to formal education, the training is more specifically oriented to a particular job. It is also of shorter duration. Of course, the training raises future annual earnings of the trainee. Like education, job training is an investment in human capital. If the cost of training is to be paid for by the employer instead of by the worker, however, the decision of whether to undertake the investment differs somewhat. In this case the marginal productivity theory of the demand for labor can be used to examine the effects of on-the-job training.

Three types of training can be distinguished: general, specific, and mixed. General on-the-job training is most similar to formal education. The skills acquired by the individual can be used in alternative employments. Though the training is received while the worker is employed in one firm, he may carry the skills with him if he chooses to change his employment. Since benefits accrue to the worker in the form of greater productivity and future earnings and since the employer has no guarantee of his remaining in the firm's employ, the employer will be unlikely to assume any of the cost of training. In the absence of training, the worker would be paid a daily wage equal to the marginal revenue product of his grade of labor (see Chapter 32). If he does receive training on the job, his daily wage during the training period will equal this marginal revenue product minus the full training cost per day. Upon completion of the training, the employer would be willing to pay to the worker his full marginal revenue product. Note that his *MRP* is now greater than what it had originally been in the absence of training. Thus, the worker bears the cost of the investment and reaps benefits in the form of a higher annual or daily wage. So long as the worker remains with the firm—but only so long as he remains with the firm—the employer also benefits from increased labor productivity and lower costs of production.

Specific training may be defined as that type of training that cannot be applied to employment in another firm. The operations are peculiar to the firm's production technique or the product itself so that acquired skills cannot be used elsewhere. When skills are not transferable, the employer is usually willing to bear the full cost of training. The worker is paid a wage equal to the full marginal revenue product of unskilled labor during the training period. Upon completion of training, his *MRP* and wage are both raised. The worker benefits from greater productivity as long as he is employed by this same firm, and the employer benefits from greater labor efficiency and lower costs of production.

Finally, mixed training is a combination of general and specific training. Mixed training is most common. While some of the acquired skills are peculiar to the firm, others are transferable to other employments. In this case the worker and the employer are usually willing to share the cost of training. During the training period the worker is not paid the full marginal revenue product of unskilled labor, but neither is his actual wage reduced by the full cost of his training.

Labor Migration

The Classical economists assumed that workers would migrate in response to differentials in current wage rates. If the current wage was higher in one industry or region than another, it was assumed that labor would move from the lower to the higher paying industry or region. Even though it was recognized that labor is not completely mobile, this traditional thought prevailed until very recent times. With the new emphasis upon investments in human capital, the present value of an expected future income stream replaced the current wage as the variable providing the incentive for workers to migrate among occupations, industries, or regions. We shall focus upon regional migration.

Migration as Investment. Migration is another form that investment in human capital may take. Geographic relocation, perhaps over a very great distance, is a long-term commitment. The decision to uproot his family, abandon a familiar community, leave his friends, or relinquish seniority status in his job may be no less crucial for a person than his decision to undertake additional education. Like education, however, geographic movement may raise his human wealth, that is, his value as a source of future labor services.

Let us consider two regions called region *A* and region *B*. Suppose a worker is located in region *A*. If he looks forward to remaining in *A*, he can expect to earn a stream of annual earnings over his remaining lifetime. The sum of these annual earnings, each one discounted to the present, yields the present value of employment in region A. For short, we designate this by the symbol $PV(A)$. If region B has a different wage, or a different time pattern of earnings, the present value of employment in region B, $PV(B)$, will differ from that in region A.

The differential, $PV(B)$ minus $PV(A)$, constitutes a gross return from migration. If the difference is negative, there is no economic incentive to move. In order to determine whether the investment in relocation bears a positive return, the cost of movement must be deducted from a positive gross return. If the cost is represented by $C(AB)$, then the net return from migration, $N(AB)$, is given as

$$N(AB) = [PV(B) - PV(A)] - C(AB).$$

If $N(AB)$ is positive, there is an economic incentive to move from region A to region B. The prospective migrant can then expect to reap monetary benefits for the remainder of his working lifetime.

Americans on the Move. Americans are a mobile people. The average American will move some 14 times in his lifetime. In a single year, between 1972 and 1973, an estimated 8.0 million persons migrated from one county to another. Of these, about 3.0 million moved to a noncontiguous state. Over a three-year interval, between 1970 and 1973, almost 25 million persons five years of age or older migrated to a different county. This amounts to 13 percent of the total population five years of age or older, and approximately half of these moved to a different state.

Sociologists have seen in American mobility a change in the traditional structures of our society. One is a conversion from the "extended family" (consisting of parents, children, grandparents, and relatives living in close proximity) to the "nuclear family" (parents and children only, divorced geographically from other relatives). The effects on child rearing, concepts of community, and even cultural alienation are far-reaching.

Economists, too, have emphasized the importance of migration, for these geographic flows are intimately connected with structural unemployment in the United States. Migration patterns influence the conservation of resources, public policies of aid to depressed economic areas, programs of road building, and legislation designed to assist aged persons. Thus, identification and measurement of the major determinants of labor mobility will advance our knowledge of resource pricing and income determination.

Because there are certainly several nonmonetary considerations that influence the decision to relocate or not to relocate, this analysis does not provide a comprehensive theory of migration. Nevertheless, the analysis does help to explain the characteristics of migrants. Consider age. All other things being the same, the number of years over which greater earnings can be enjoyed as a result of migration decreases as age increases. Given higher earnings in region B, the gross return to migration $[PV(B) - PV(A)]$ will be smaller for an older worker than for a younger worker in region A. Why? Because the older worker can look forward to a shorter future working life over which he can increase his earnings by migration. Statistical evidence bears out this theoretical conclusion. For example, among workers 25-34 years of age, 8.2 percent migrated between 1970 and 1973, compared with 4.3 percent of the 35-44 age group and 2.2 percent of the 45-64 age group.

Educational attainment is another variable affecting mobility. Because income increases with education in all regions, the age-earnings profile, such as that depicted in Figure 36-2, is higher for a person of greater educational attainment, other things being the same. Consequently, for two workers of the same age but with different levels of educational attainment, the differential $[PV(B) - PV(A)]$ will be larger for the more highly educated worker. Therefore, the economic incentive to migrate is greater for the more highly educated. Again, this theoretical inference is supported by statistical evidence. Within each age group, the percentage of the age group migrating rises with the number of years of school completed. For example, within the 30-34 age group, 8.3 percent of those with less than 5 years of schooling migrated between 1970 and 1973, compared with 10.9 percent of those with 12 years of schooling and 18.2 percent of those with 16 or more years of schooling.

Once the characteristics of migrants are taken into account, labor mobility can act to widen the disparity of incomes among regions of the United States—contrary to the expectations of the Classical economists. In general, younger workers with more education and fewer dependents move more readily from low-income to high-income and high-growth areas, leaving behind older and less educated workers. Such migration patterns tend to widen regional income differentials, at least in the short run unless offset by capital movements.

SUMMARY

1. Prices of factors of production are income to the owners of the factors. This income from services rendered is distinguished from the value of the source of these services, which is a stock of wealth.
2. Capitalization of income is the method used to determine the value

of a source of services.

3. Just as land has a value different from the current rent for its services and capital equipment has a value different from the price of a unit of its service in production, so do human beings have an economic value distinct from wages as the price of current labor services.

4. We are used to measuring current earnings and the wealth of nonhuman capital because this capital can be bought and sold.

Although a person sells only his current services, each person does represent human wealth or capital.

5. The value of human capital is computed as the present value of the stream of future earnings from the sale of labor services.

6. The most important determinants of human capital value are diet and health, education, on-the-job training, and migration among regions, industries, and occupations.

NEW TERMS

Human capital, *p. 788*
Capitalization of income, *p. 789*
Present value, *p. 790*
Discounting, *p. 790*
Single-period discounting, *p. 790*

Multiperiod discounting, *p. 791*
Age-earnings pattern, *p. 795*
On-the-job training, *p. 801*
Labor migration, *p. 802*

QUESTIONS FOR DISCUSSION AND ANALYSIS

1. Why does employee compensation comprise the largest share of national income?

2. Explain the concept of present value and provide two numerical examples.

3. How might the national emphasis on wage rates contribute to a greater concentration of income?

4. What is the difference between a wage and the value of human capital?

5. What do you think is your own capital value? Explain.

6. How does geographic migration affect the migrant's capital value?

7. How would you go about choosing an occupation?

8. How does higher education serve the national economy?

9. How does higher education challenge the national economy?

SUGGESTED READINGS

Becker, G. S. *Human Capital, A Theoretical and Empirical Analysis*. Princeton, N.J.: Princeton University Press, 1964.

Benson, C. S. *The Economics of Public Education*, 2d ed. Boston: Houghton Mifflin Company, 1968.

Blaug, Mark. *Economics of Education: A Selected Annotated Bibliography*, 2d ed. Elmsford, N.Y.: Pergamon Press, Inc., 1970.

——————. *Economics of Education 1*. Baltimore: Penguin Books, Inc., 1968.

Brennan, M., M. Schupack, and P. Taft. *The Economics of Age*. New York: W. W. Norton & Company, Inc., 1966.

Kiker, Billy F. *Investment in Human Capital*. Columbia: University of South Carolina Press, 1971.

Schultz, Theodore W. *Investment in Human Capital, The Role of Education and of Research*. New York: The Free Press, 1971.

Wykstra, Ronald A. *Human Capital Formation and Manpower Development*. New York: The Free Press, 1971.

Personal Income Distribution

PREVIEW By how much do incomes vary among occupations? Are the earnings of men and women equal for comparable work? Who and where are the poor in our society? Is the disparity in incomes widening or narrowing? These are the inevitable questions raised when personal income distribution is considered. Available measures of income distribution suggest that the number of Americans categorized as middle class is increasing while the problem of disadvantaged low-income families persists.

The functional distribution of income and the capital value related to a stream of income over time go only part way toward explaining the incomes received by people. Many persons earn income from ownership of more than one factor of production. Although every employed person receives a wage or salary, many are the recipients of rent, interest, or dividends as well. Relatively few derive their total income by clipping interest coupons from bonds or receiving stock dividends.

Regardless of how much we may theorize about the distribution of income to the various factors of production, the average American citizen is more interested in how much income he, personally, is receiving. He is not only interested in his own income, but he is also curious about the income of his neighbors, co-workers, and fellow Americans. An analysis of personal income distribution highlights many of our current economic and social problems. These economic and social problems, in turn, serve as reasons for political action of one type or another.

WHAT IS PERSONAL INCOME?

Total personal income for a given year is the income received by individuals, by unincorporated businesses, and by nonprofit institutions from all sources. It includes transfer payments from government and business, such as Social Security benefits and military pensions. Disposable personal income is personal income minus taxes, including not only income taxes but also property and other taxes. Both definitions of income, personal and disposable personal, have been fully described in Chapter 6.

The aggregate figures for disposable personal income may be divided by the estimated population for a given year in order to determine the per capita distribution of income. Table 37-1 gives these forms of personal income for selected years to indicate the magnitudes involved and the changes that have occurred over a period of 33 years.

TABLE 37-1

TOTAL INCOME
AND PER CAPITA
INCOME FOR
SELECTED YEARS

1940-1973

(1) Year	(2) Total Personal Income (Billions)	(3) Disposable Personal Income (Billions)	(4) Per Capita Disposable Income	(5) Per Capita Disposable Income in Constant 1958 Dollars
1940	$ 78.3	$ 75.7	$ 573	$1,259
1945	171.1	150.2	1,074	1,642
1950	227.6	206.9	1,364	1,646
1955	310.9	275.3	1,666	1,795
1960	401.0	350.0	1,937	1,883
1965	538.9	473.2	2,436	2,239
1970	808.3	691.7	3,376	2,610
1973	1,035.5	882.6	4,195	2,890

SOURCE: *Economic Report of the President*, 1974.

Even from this limited amount of data, certain interesting conclusions can be drawn. There has been a great expansion of income, especially from 1945 on. The change in the consumer price index from 42.0 in 1940 to 133.1 in 1973 (on the basis of 1967 as 100) is a measure of the depreciation of the dollar, as well as of the rapid inflation in money income. No doubt a part of the increase in income, however, was due to a real expansion in incomes as a result of the profound changes in the economy during the war and post-war years.

Per capita disposable income (column 4) indicates that average income has increased faster than the population. Insofar as this increase was not due to inflation, the average level of welfare has shown a definite tendency toward improvement, particularly in the postwar years, as reflected by the increase in real per capita income or per capita income in constant dollars (column 5).

HOW PERSONAL INCOME IS DISTRIBUTED

These brief facts are revealing in themselves, but they must be supplemented by a more detailed analysis of the distribution of personal income. Such analysis will show the way in which income is distributed by families, by sex, by rural and urban location, by color, and by regions and states. The better our information, the more comprehensive will be our knowledge of the conditions of personal and family welfare in the United States.

In Table 37-2 we have a picture of the distribution of income by families for two years, 20 years apart. The figures represent actual income and not disposable income after taxes.

Some conclusions can be drawn from this survey. In 1950, 43 percent of all families were receiving less than $3,000 annual income; but two decades later only 9 percent were in this low income group. Related data show that in 1950 these same two income groups (up to $3,000) received 15.4 percent of the total income, but 20 years later, with personal income approximately $580 billion greater, they received 2 percent of the total.

We may look at these facts in another way. In 1950 the largest percentage of families, 25 percent, in any one income group was at the under $2,000 level; but in 1970 the largest percentage, 27 percent, was several income groups higher. Related data show that in 1950 the greatest amount of income was in the income group $3,000-$3,999; but in 1970 there was a progressively larger amount of income in each of the income levels above the $3,000-$3,999 category.

A further check of the facts will reveal a similar improvement in income status for the period. The conclusion might, therefore, be drawn that economic welfare, as indicated by personal income distribution, had shown a

TABLE 37-2

DISTRIBUTION OF INCOME BY FAMILIES

1950 and 1970

Family Personal Income Before Taxes	Percent of Families and Unattached Individuals	
	1950	1970
Under $2,000	25	5
$ 2,000 to 2,999	18	4
$ 3,000 to 3,999	20	5
$ 4,000 to 4,999	14	5
$ 5,000 to 5,999	9	6
$ 6,000 to 6,999	5	6
$ 7,000 to 9,999	6	20
$10,000 to 14,999	2	27
$15,000 and over	1	22

SOURCE: *Statistical Abstract of the United States*, 1973.

marked increase during this period. But the increase in the consumer price index from 72.1 in 1950 to 116.3 in 1970, an increase of 61 percent in 20 years, obliterates some of the apparent improvement in incomes.

Distribution of Personal Income by Sex and by Color

Although the number of occupations in which women engage has vastly increased as a result of World War II, the current Women's Liberation movement, and the passage of the Equal Employment Opportunities Act, there is still considerable disparity between the incomes of men and women in the same field of work. Even when it is acknowledged that women display greater dexterity than men in some lines of work, women do not usually command the same wages as men.

There are several reasons for this disparity. In spite of recent trends to the contrary, women are not so well organized or so willing to fight for better pay. A money-earning occupation remains for many women an interim activity before marriage or a part-time activity after marriage. Since over 60 percent of the women in the labor force are married, frequently they look upon their wages as supplementary income. Consequently, they may be less dissatisfied than men with lower wages. Whatever may be the reasons for disparity of income between men and women, these can only be determined by careful study of each occupation in which both sexes are employed.

Table 37-3 gives some facts that indicate the continuing disparity between the wage and salary incomes of men and women. In 1950, 37 percent of the

TABLE 37-3

MONEY INCOME— PERCENT DISTRIBUTION BY INCOME LEVEL AND BY SEX

1950 and 1970

Family Personal Income Before Taxes	1950		1970	
	Male	Female	Male	Female
Under $1,000	20.7	51.8	10.4	27.6
$1,000-1,999	16.4	23.6	8.3	19.2
$2,000-2,999	21.6	18.1	6.9	11.8
$3,000-3,999	20.9	4.5	6.8	10.3
$4,000-4,999	9.6	1.2	6.2	8.8
$5,000-5,999	4.6	0.3	6.7	6.9
$6,000-6,999	2.0	0.1	7.0	4.9
$7,000-9,999	2.0	0.2	21.0	7.5
$10,000-over	2.0	0.2	26.7	9.0
Median Income	$2,570	$953	$6,670	$2,237

SOURCE: *Statistical Abstract of the United States*, 1973.

men but over 75 percent of the women were in the two lowest income brackets; two decades later more than 46 percent of the women but less than 19 percent of the men were still in these brackets. By 1970 the percentages indicate that men had moved up the wage and salary scale much more rapidly than women. The medium wage or salary income indicates the same large differences, for in 1970 median wage or salary income for men was almost three times as great as that for women.[1] When so many women are engaged in so many occupations for at least part of their working lives, this great disparity in income is a matter of considerable economic and social significance.

A problem of even greater significance is the disparity of income between white and nonwhite families. Table 37-4 shows that even as recently as 1970, when only 3.8 percent of all white families were in the two lowest income categories, there were still 11.1 percent of all nonwhite families in those two

---

[1] The median is the value that divides the distribution into two equal parts, one half of the cases falling below this value and one half of the cases exceeding this value.

categories. At the other end of the income ladder, a small percentage of the nonwhites were in the higher income brackets. Furthermore, the median income of all white families was considerably greater than that of the nonwhite families.

Distribution of Personal Income, City and Farm

If income is derived from an occupation practiced in a city, the chances are that it will be greater than if it is derived from the same occupation practiced in the country. In 1970, nonfarm income receivers had a median income of $10,006. Income receivers classified as farm-operator families

TABLE 37-4

MONEY INCOME— PERCENT DISTRIBUTION OF FAMILIES BY INCOME LEVEL AND BY COLOR OF HEAD

1950 and 1970

Family Personal Income Before Taxes	1950		1970	
	White	Nonwhite	White	Nonwhite
Under $1,000	10.0	28.1	1.4	3.4
$ 1,000- 1,999	12.2	25.3	2.4	7.7
$ 2,000- 2,999	17.3	23.5	3.7	9.0
$ 3,000- 3,999	21.3	13.5	4.6	8.8
$ 4,000- 4,999	14.4	4.3	4.9	8.2
$ 5,000- 5,999	9.6	1.9	5.5	9.0
$ 6,000- 6,999	5.5	1.5	5.8	7.4
$ 7,000- 9,999	6.1	1.7	20.1	18.2
$10,000-14,999 ⎫	3.5	.3	27.9	17.3
$15,000-over ⎭			23.7	10.9
Median Income	$3,445	$1,869	$10,236	$6,516

SOURCE: *Statistical Abstract of the United States*, 1973.

had a strikingly lower median income of less than $6,773. It must not be forgotten that a median is a measure of the central tendency of a distribution that may include wide extremes.

Different circumstances may lessen the effects of income differentials. Living costs are usually higher in cities; but urban costs are by no means uniform. This circumstance is admitted by some large corporations, under stress of competition, by payment of higher wages for the same work in larger than in smaller cities. Such differential payments help to raise urban income averages. On the other hand, the farmer may live off his land directly, "from garden to table." It is not certain that income averages always make allowance for this fact. In spite of these considerations, income disparities help to explain the dissatisfaction of many farmers with their occupation and their constant agitation for parity prices or other means of increasing their income. In addition, differences in income between urban and rural families no doubt explain in large part the movement of farm families into the cities and suburbs.

Distribution of Personal Income by Regions and States

The map in Figure 37-1 shows per capita income averages for 1973 by states. A comparison can be made with the national average of $4,918 for that year. The areas of highest and lowest per capita income, as well as two intermediate levels, are shown. Of all states, 33 fall below the national average. The states above the average are the areas of exceptional industrial and commercial development, which are, consequently, the areas of densest population.

It can be seen from Figure 37-1 that the greatest flow of income per person originates in four regions. One is called the Middle Atlantic states (New York, New Jersey, and Pennsylvania). The second is the north-east Atlantic Seaboard. The third is classified by demographers as the East-North Central region, which is loosely the Midwest, particularly its northern section. The fourth major region lies on or near the West Coast. Regional differentials in per capita earnings no doubt reflect the location of high-growth industrial firms in the high per capita regions.

IS DISPARITY IN INCOMES DECREASING?

Are the rich very rich and the poor very poor? Are the rich getting richer and the poor getting poorer, or is income distribution moving toward equality?

Shares of National Income

The percentage of total money income received by each tenth of the total number of spending units for the years 1950 and 1970 is indicated in Table 37-5. In 1970, for example, the lowest 10 percent of the units received 2 percent of total money income; the next 10 percent received 3 percent of total income. These two tenths of the family units, when added together (cumulative), received a total of 5 percent of income. The fifth 10 percent of all spending units received 7 percent of income, and the lower 50 percent of the spending units received nearly one fourth of total money income. Here, then, is a measure of disparity in personal incomes for 1970, and the same distribution holds approximately today.

The data for 1970 may be compared with that two decades earlier in order to determine what differences have developed. In the earlier year the lower 50 percent of the spending units received 23 percent of total income, and in 1970 they still received 23 percent; therefore, the lower 50 percent was no better off in 1970 on a relative basis, although the absolute dollar value of incomes rose. The figures just quoted are for incomes before the federal income tax. If income after this tax is considered, we can conclude that the federal income tax has a tendency to reduce disparity in disposable incomes.

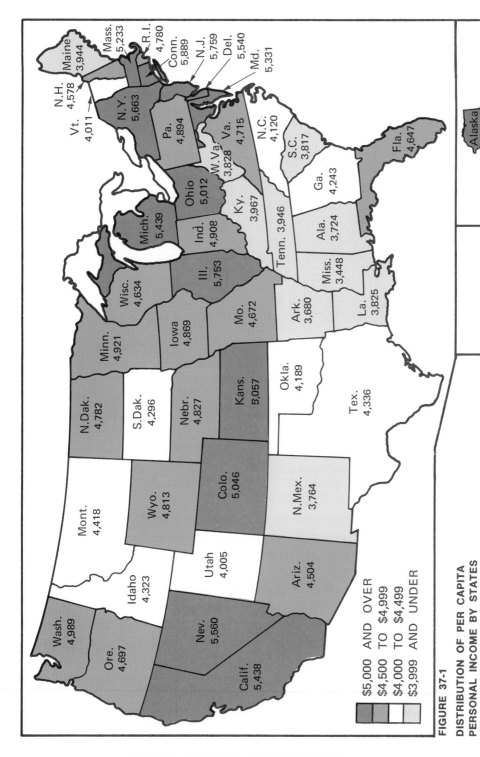

SOURCE: *Survey of Current Business* (April, 1974).

FIGURE 37-1

DISTRIBUTION OF PER CAPITA PERSONAL INCOME BY STATES

1973

Per capita income varies among states, ranging from a high of $5,889 in Connecticut to a low of $3,448 in Mississippi. With a mean of $4,918 for the U.S. as a whole, notice that some areas of the nation tend to have higher incomes than others.

$5,000 AND OVER
$4,500 TO $4,999
$4,000 TO $4,499
$3,999 AND UNDER

	Percent of Total Money Income Before Federal Income Tax			
			Cumulative	
Family Units	1950	1970	1950	1970
Lowest Tenth	1	2	1	2
Second Tenth	3	3	4	5
Third Tenth	5	5	9	10
Fourth Tenth	6	6	15	16
Fifth Tenth	8	7	23	23
Sixth Tenth	9	9	32	32
Seventh Tenth	11	11	43	43
Eighth Tenth	13	13	56	56
Ninth Tenth	15	17	71	73
Highest Tenth	29	27	100	100

TABLE 37-5

SHARE OF TOTAL MONEY INCOME RECEIVED BY EACH TENTH OF THE NATION'S FAMILY UNITS

1950 and 1970

SOURCE: *Statistical Abstract of the United States,* 1972.

Distribution of Income Levels

Table 37-5 shows that the shares of total money income going to the upper and lower ends of the distribution have not changed noticeably over the past two decades or more. One must recognize, nevertheless, that national income also rose during this period. As a consequence, the 23 percent in the lower half of the scale in 1970 are receiving larger money incomes than the 23 percent did in 1950. In 1950 over 42 percent of all spending units had incomes below $3,000; but 20 years later less than 9 percent had incomes this low. Nearly 70 percent of all families had money incomes in excess of $7,000 in 1970 as compared to about 9 percent in 1950.

There is a complication, however. As we all know, the cost of living has also increased. The consumer price index rose from 72.1 in 1950 to 116.3 in 1970. Since inflation affects money incomes as well as prices, this inflationary tendency may create the appearance of greater equality in the distribution of income.

In order to take both rising national money income and a rising cost of living into account, Figure 37-2 presents two distributions—one for 1950 and one for 1970—expressed in constant 1970 dollars (in dollars of 1970 purchasing power). Figure 37-2 refers to white families; Figure 37-3, referring to nonwhite families, is discussed below. On the horizontal axis of the diagram are recorded levels of income in dollars of constant purchasing power. The vertical axis records percentages of all families. Thus, a point on the curve denotes the percentage of white families with a specified income, and the entire curve depicts a distribution of real income. Since the smooth

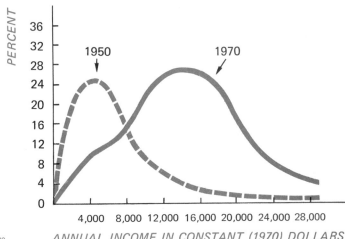

FIGURE 37-2

REAL INCOMES OF WHITE FAMILIES BEFORE TAXES 1950 and 1970

The percentage of white families in the middle-income range has increased significantly.

SOURCE: *Statistical Abstract of the United States*, 1973.

curve is drawn as an approximation to percentages of families recorded for specified income ranges in the published statistics, the diagram is intended to convey an overall impression of a real income distribution. Between 1950 and 1970 the peak segment of the curve moved to the right, indicating that a much larger percentage of families is in the middle-income groups today than was true two decades ago.

Figure 37-3 presents comparable data for nonwhite American families. Here again, we see a rightward movement of the curve between 1950 and 1970. There has been an increase in the percentage of nonwhite families in the middle-income range but proportionately fewer in this range than in

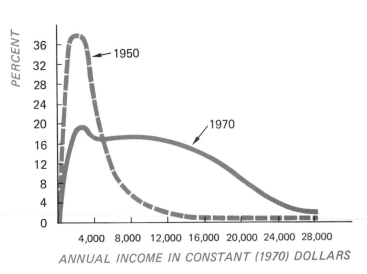

FIGURE 37-3

REAL INCOMES OF NONWHITE FAMILIES BEFORE TAXES 1950 and 1970

The percentage of nonwhite families in the middle-income range has increased, but the increase is proportionately less than that of white families.

SOURCE: *Statistical Abstract of the United States*, 1973.

the case of white families. Over these two decades there was a decided reduction in the percentage of nonwhite families with incomes below $4,000 per year. But the peak of the 1970 curve at an income below $4,000 indicates that a greater percentage of nonwhites falls into this income range than in any other.

We may conclude that both white and nonwhite Americans have shared in growing national prosperity, but whites have advanced to a greater extent than nonwhites. More of both groups, yet proportionately more of the white families, have moved into the middle-income range. Certainly this suggests an improvement in living conditions. Does it, however, suggest a strong tendency toward greater income equality? To an extent, yes. Almost complete equality would be depicted by a curve with a very high peak (close to 100 percent of families) at the average income and very little "spread" or dispersion in either the upper or lower direction. The fact that the 1970 curves exhibit wide dispersion in the leftward or low-income direction indicates, however, that income inequality related to poverty is still a serious national problem.

Family Liquid Assets

Liquid assets, that is, those readily convertible into cash, are an important supplement to current income, especially during periods of family emergency when additional spending power is needed. Unfortunately families with limited incomes also tend to have very few, if any, liquid assets. Since assets are accumulated out of past savings, a family with a history of low income has had little chance to save. Thus, low current income is most often associated with meager liquid assets as well.

In 1973 it was estimated that about 30 percent of all families had liquid assets below $500 in value. These assets include savings accounts, United States savings bonds, checking accounts, and other securities, but exclude currency. In fact, one out of every seven families reported no liquid assets whatsoever. Households with little or no assets to fall back on when emergencies arise are many times forced to rely on some form of public assistance.

INCOME AND FAMILY BUDGETS

Incomes of individuals and families differ for a multitude of reasons, some physical, some social, and others psychological. Skill, training, talent, education, ambition, fortitude, inheritance, and many other factors, including at times plain luck—good or bad—affect earning capacity and income. Whatever the cause, we do have considerable disparity in income among American families. This has led to some serious problems in our economy.

When we compare family personal income with the City Worker's Family Budget, some startling facts are evident. Since the 1971 Budgets for the various cities, one measure of the cost of living, range from $12,819 in the Boston area to a low of $9,408 in Austin, Texas, it can be seen by referring to Table 37-2 (even though Table 37-2 reflects 1970 data rather than 1971 data) that approximately one half of all family units have incomes insufficient to maintain even the intermediate BLS family budget. These budgets, computed for a four-person family, are shown for selected cities in Table 37-6. Even if we subtract the unattached individuals, who are included as family units, more than one half of all families in the United States have incomes inadequate to provide the moderate level of living suggested by the BLS budgets. Although a number of these families have less than four members and would not require the full amount contained in the budget, there are still many families living at a sub-CWFB income level.

TABLE 37-6

ANNUAL COSTS OF AN URBAN INTERMEDIATE BUDGET FOR A FOUR-PERSON FAMILY *

1971

	Budget Costs				
Area	Total	Food	Housing [1]	Transportation	Other [2]
Urban U.S.	10,971	2,532	2,638	964	4,837
Atlanta, Ga.	9,813	2,364	2,092	940	4,417
Austin, Tex.	9,408	2,274	1,971	931	4,232
Baltimore, Md.	11,013	2,482	2,372	977	5,182
Boston, Mass.	12,819	2,739	3,543	1,026	5,511
Chicago, Ill.	11,460	2,558	2,864	1,025	5,013
Cleveland, Ohio	11,330	2,489	2,970	991	4,880
Denver, Colo.	10,639	2,366	2,499	961	4,831
Detroit, Mich.	10,754	2,544	2,456	917	4,487
Los Angeles, Calif.	10,985	2,431	2,636	978	4,940
Nashville, Tenn.	9,976	2,269	2,349	963	4,395
New York, N.Y.	12,585	2,943	3,273	918	5,451
Philadelphia, Pa.	11,404	2,766	2,574	926	5,138
St. Louis, Mo.	10,944	2,593	2,524	1,052	4,775
San Francisco, Calif.	11,683	2,538	2,992	1,013	5,140
Seattle, Wash.	11,124	2,629	2,707	956	4,832

SOURCE: Adapted from *Statistical Abstract of the United States,* 1973.

* Includes a 38-year-old employed husband, wife not employed outside the home, 8-year-old girl, and 13-year-old boy.
[1] Includes the weighted average cost of renter and homeowner shelter, house furnishings, and household operations.
[2] Includes medical care, clothing and personal care, other family consumption, gifts and contributions, basic life insurance, occupational expenses, Social Security, and personal income taxes.

A more striking feature is the number of families considered in the poor, or poverty, category. Although the concept of the affluent society was highlighted in the late 1950s with the publication of John Kenneth Galbraith's book, *The Affluent Society* (see Chapter 4), President Kennedy showed concern about the amount of poverty in the United States in the early 1960s. After the untimely death of President Kennedy in 1963, President Johnson developed a program in 1964 for the war on poverty. Classifying any family with an income of less than $3,000 and an unattached individual with an income of less than $1,500 to be poverty-stricken, the President in his 1964 *Economic Report* pointed out that in 1962 approximately one fifth of the American families were poor. Over 9 million families comprising more than 30 million persons had money incomes below the $3,000 level. Moreover, it was pointed out that 5.4 million families, consisting of more than 17 million persons, had incomes of less than $2,000 per year. There were another 5 million unattached individuals with incomes of less than $1,500 per year.

On the basis of this and related data, President Johnson pushed through Congress in 1964 his so-called poverty package in the form of the Economic Opportunity Act, which carried an appropriation of $962 million to finance various measures designed to eliminate poverty in America. This act provided funds for various retraining and educational programs, a youth job corps, and aid to college students, as well as loan arrangements for both businesses and the poor.

The precise income level used to define poverty is arbitrary to some extent. The family income level of $3,000 used in 1964 is a matter of judgment. If the same criterion were used today, one would find that less than 9 percent of all families have incomes below $3,000, as compared to 16 percent in 1965; about a quarter of all unattached individuals have incomes under $1,500, as compared to a third in 1965. However, as we have seen, both money incomes and prices have increased over the past decade. For this reason many economists now use a figure of more than $4,000 for a family and over $2,000 for an unattached individual to denote poverty. On the basis of these revised income levels, roughly 14 percent of all families are poverty stricken, while slightly more than 33 percent of all unattached individuals fall into the poverty category. It can readily be seen that these percentages do not differ greatly from the 1965 figures or even the 1962 figures. Recent policies designed to cope with the persistence of poverty in our society will be discussed in Chapter 40.

WHERE DO WE GO FROM HERE?

Great disparity in the distribution of income is serious indeed. Not only an individual but the whole society may suffer. In an age of great technological advance, low scales of living are a tacit criticism of the effectiveness of our economic organization. Among those who are sensitive to the meaning of general welfare, economic deprivation stimulates activist movements to change the operations, if not the structure, of the system. Disparity also means great differences in educational opportunity, even in a country blessed with a public school system. Vocational training may not be available in sufficient amounts to improve the lot of the poor. Reduced output and unbalanced production are further ills that can be traced to disparity in personal incomes.

If the general welfare can best be promoted by the maximum effective operation of the economic system under conditions of full employment, inequality due to deprivation of opportunity must decrease the effectiveness of the system. When inequality leads to such results, it is necessary to seek ways and means for reducing the disparity of incomes in order to insure a more effective and stable economic order. Such an objective is consistent with the recommendation of the Commission on National Goals that inequalities based on race, color, creed, and sex must be reduced substantially if not eliminated completely.

Severe poverty can be eliminated without weakening or destroying the free enterprise system. Absolute equality in the distribution of income is undesirable. Distribution according to ability alone without regard to established laws of property is unattainable in a capitalistic system. Even when the social and legal institutions characteristic of free enterprise are accepted without question, attempts to reduce disparity of incomes run into twin dangers: reduction of incentive and enhanced power of the state and its bureaucracy. It is for this reason that the attack on inequality through the progressive income tax, retraining programs, educational grants, productive loans, and other remedial measures should be subject to constant review. Under these circumstances the steering of a course that will create more advantages than disadvantages is a task that falls for astute economic and political policy making.

SUMMARY

1. Any analysis of incomes as prices of factor services should be supplemented by a study of the actual distribution of personal incomes as disclosed by statistical studies.

2. The two kinds of analysis are not antithetical but complementary, and both are necessary if some understanding of the distribution of income is desired.

3. Statistical studies indicate generally lower levels of income for females than males, for rural residents than urban, for nonwhites than whites, and for some states and regions than others.

4. Knowledge of these disparities can have great practical impor-

tance, for such disparities indicate to sellers where the greatest purchasing power is located and to others where greater opportunity is probably to be found.

5. There is some evidence that disparity in income distribution is decreasing but the changes have been complicated by notable shifts in the price level and in the purchasing power of the dollar.

6. Statistics indicate that nearly one half of the families in the United States have incomes insufficient to meet the requirements of the intermediate BLS City Worker's Family Budget. Furthermore, according to some measures, roughly 14 percent of all American families are classified as poor.

7. Any attempts to reduce disparity in incomes should avoid reduction of incentive on the one hand and enlargement of government functions with bureaucratic dominance on the other.

NEW TERMS

Income distribution by families, *p. 808*

Income distribution by sex, *p. 809*

Income distribution by color, *p. 809*

Income distribution by region, *p. 812*

Shares of national income, *p. 812*

Liquid assets, *p. 816*

City Worker's Family Budget, *p. 817*

Poverty income level, *p. 818*

QUESTIONS FOR DISCUSSION AND ANALYSIS

1. Explain by example how some recent political action was related to the distribution of income.

2. Why is average farm income lower than average urban income?

3. Why is per capita income lower in some states than in others?

4. Do you think there should be a limitation on the amount of income that may be received by any individual? Why or why not?

5. It has been suggested by a certain high-ranking labor official and others that we should guarantee every American an income of $6,000 annually whether he works or not.

Comment.

6. What are the ill effects of great disparity in the distribution of personal incomes?

7. Under what conditions does an economic system promote welfare most effectively?

8. What is meant by the statement, "The problem of disparity in incomes is more successfully met through indirect attack than through a frontal charge"? Illustrate.

9. Do you agree that any family receiving less than $4,000 per year is living in poverty? Why or why not?

SUGGESTED READINGS

Baster, Nancy. *Distribution of Income and Economic Growth*. Geneva: United Nations Research Institute for Social Development, 1970.

Bronfenbrenner, Martin. *Income Distribution Theory*. Chicago: Aldine-Atherton, Inc., 1971.

Budd, Edward C. *Inequality and Poverty*. New York: W. W. Norton & Company, Inc., 1968.

Lydall, Harold F. *The Structure of Earnings*. Oxford: Clarendon Press, 1968.

Miller, H. P. *Income Distribution in the United States*. Washington: Department of Commerce, Bureau of the Census, 1966.

——————. *Rich Man, Poor Man*. New York: Thomas Y. Crowell Company, 1971.

Pen, Jan. *Income Distribution: Facts, Theories, and Policies*. New York: Praeger Publishers, Inc., 1971.

PART TEN

Current Domestic Problems

38

Competition and Pricing in Agriculture

PREVIEW Agriculture is one industry that in many respects approaches conditions of pure competition. In addition to a large number of commercial farms, the industry is composed of thousands of small independent farmers. There are so many farmers that no individual producer can influence price. Price is determined by the total supply and demand for particular products.

Substantial increases in productivity per farmer and productivity per acre have led to declines in agricultural prices over recent decades. Due to the presence of price inelasticity of demand for agricultural products, farm income declined in spite of the higher production. Farm income was further curbed by the income inelasticity of demand for agricultural products. Consequently, when family incomes rose with the general expansion of the economy, farm income did not increase proportionally.

Government efforts over the past half century had been used to limit farm output, maintain prices, and raise the income of farmers. This long-run trend, however, was interrupted in the early 1970s. Growing needs at home, plus severe food shortages elsewhere in the world, led to increased demand for American farm products. At the same time inclement weather, which interfered with the planting and harvesting of some crops, had an adverse effect on supplies. These changes in supply and demand resulted in greater sales at higher prices, substantially raising the income of the farm sector. This may be a temporary phenomenon, however. If so, there still will be a need in the future to channel some excess resources and manpower out of farming into more productive uses within the economy.

The agriculture sector of the American economy in its unregulated state is often cited as an industry approaching conditions of pure competition. The reasons for this are numerous. First, there is certainly a large number of buyers and sellers. One might say that there are 212 million or more consumers of American farm products. On the other hand, there are presently 2.8 million suppliers of various farm products. Two thirds of these suppliers are commercial farms. In particular there are over 580,000 farms producing wheat for cash grain, 200,000 suppliers of cotton, 102,000 vegetable growers, and over 500,000 farms raising livestock.

Second, most of these farms are producing and selling identical products insofar as most of the crops and meats are graded and labeled according to federal standards. Third, market prices are generally known to all buyers and sellers concerned. Fourth, until recent decades (before government regulations, that is) there was free entry into and exit from the farm industry, and any producer could readily increase his total output. Therefore, farmers or buyers individually could not affect prices on the farm market. Prices were determined by the free forces of aggregate supply and demand.

If competition is so good for the economy, what has happened in recent decades in farming? Why is it so heavily regulated today? As we will see, just as a lack of competition can be detrimental to the economy, especially to consumers, too much competition among sellers can be disastrous to producers. When the economic forces that would correct such a situation result in economic hardship to a large number of persons, then the economic problem becomes also a social problem and a political issue.

THE COMPETITIVE PROBLEM

The productivity of the American farmer has increased tremendously in the past several decades, but farm income, with the exception of the last few years, has not increased proportionally. Indeed, gains in farm income have lagged behind the growth of other incomes in the economy. The basic cause of the farm problem is that we have excessive resources devoted to agriculture compared to our demand for farm commodities. Consequently, farm income is relatively low compared to other sectors of the economy. The solution to this problem lies in the improvement of farmers' living conditions without creating other social problems either for the farmer or for others in the economy.

Although agriculture is one of our largest and most competitive industries, the percentage of persons engaged in agriculture has steadily declined. The population of the United States increased from 3.9 million persons in 1790 to 210 million in 1973, but the percentage of workers engaged in agriculture declined from 90 percent in 1790 to about 4 percent of the civilian labor force in 1973. Furthermore, farm population as a percentage of total population dropped from 23 percent in 1940 to 4.5 percent in 1973. This change in the relative size of the farm population is evidence not only of the great development in nonagricultural industries but also of the increasing productivity of agriculture. As a result of the shift of population from farms to urban centers, the United States is now characterized primarily as an urban industrial nation rather than an agricultural nation.

Changes of such a marked nature could not have come about without a revolution in methods of agricultural production. The causes of this revolution must first be considered if the present-day problems of agriculture in their relation to our total economy are to be understood.

THE AGRICULTURAL REVOLUTION

The great revolution in methods of production, often called the Industrial Revolution, which began in England in the latter half of the eighteenth century, was characterized by two fundamental changes: (1) the use of steam power with its productive advantages over the power of wind and water or the muscles of man and animals, and (2) the transformation of tools into machines. This revolution, which was to have such momentous consequences in other fields of industry, had little effect on agriculture. Perhaps one important reason is that steam power could not be effectively adapted to tillage of the soil, which required a mobile rather than a stationary source of power.

A revolution in agriculture, similar to the Industrial Revolution in manufacturing, occurred with the development of the tractor and subsequent inventions of farm machinery. As late as 1940, 1.5 million farm tractors were in use, but by 1973 the number of tractors on farms had increased to more than 4.5 million. During the same period the number of horses and mules in use decreased correspondingly. Much of this change occurred during and after World War II. The tractor enabled the farmer to increase his crop acreage, since the reduction in the number of horses and mules released for other uses millions of acres that had been devoted to the production of food for these animals. The results of this change in the source of power were a reduction in labor costs and an increase in production. The tractor and ancillary equipment, of course, permitted the farmer to cultivate more land and to harvest a greater volume of crops in a shorter period of time.

Farm Machinery

The second change in agricultural methods has been the widespread use of machines made possible by the tractor. The old tools of the husbandman, such as the hoe, sickle, and rake, have been transformed into power plows, cultivators, seeding machinery, manure spreaders, grain combines, corn pickers, haying machinery, cotton harvesters, and spraying machines, to mention only some of the machines. All of these are powered by the tractor or by electricity, which in recent decades has become a common adjunct of the farm.

On the 2.8 million farms in the United States in 1973, there were 4,469,000 tractors, 725,000 grain combines, and 593,000 mechanical corn pickers. Including about 3 million horses and mules, farmers in 1973 had more than double the farm power and machinery that they had at the beginning of 1940. By the transformation of tools into machines, the relative contribution of capital in turning out a given quantity of produce has increased, and the contribution of labor has decreased. Capital has been substituted for labor in producing a vastly expanded output. Greater use of machinery tends to make the farmer more independent of the weather, since critical operations can be speeded up. When farm machinery is used, however, increased capital investment is necessary; and farms must be of sufficient size to warrant the investment, unless cooperative use of machinery is practiced.

Other Changes in Production

The relatively recent revolution in the machine technology of agriculture had been preceded by other equally notable changes in methods of production. Ever since the establishment of the Department of Agriculture in 1862 and of the State Land Grant Institutions under the Morrill Act in the same year, the federal government has been committed to a program of improved production methods in agriculture. State and local agencies, private and public, have assisted as well. As a result, new varieties of crops, improved and cheaper fertilizers, new means of controlling insects and diseases, crop rotations, and better methods of culture have been developed. Not only have crops benefited, but livestock production has been improved also. Some notion of the increasing use of machinery and fertilizer can be observed in Figure 38-1.

FIGURE 38-1

SINCE 1950 THE USE OF FARM MACHINES ROSE 30 PERCENT, FERTILIZER TREBLED, BUT FARM LABOR WAS HALVED

The use of modern machines and more and better fertilizer has increased considerably, whereas the use of farm labor has declined markedly.

SOURCE: *Statistical Abstract of the United States,* 1973, p. 603.

General Note: FARM REAL ESTATE refers to land and farm buildings, with the exception of homes.

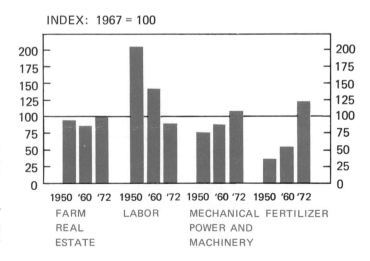

INDEX: 1967 = 100

PART TEN / CURRENT DOMESTIC PROBLEMS

Governmental Land Improvements

In addition to these revolutionary changes in the effectiveness of agricultural production, the federal government has been responsible for measures pertaining to conservation, irrigation, and reclamation. These measures have brought new and better lands into cultivation. In the 20-year period, 1950-1970, reclamation projects increased the amount of irrigated acreage under cultivation by 67 percent, while the gross crop value of irrigated lands increased 225 percent. Such a widely publicized change in method as contour plowing is contributing its share to the conservation of good arable land. Improvements of this type add one more contribution to the reduction of agricultural costs and the increased productivity of agricultural labor. Continued government promotion of such projects can be expected.

EFFECTS OF THE AGRICULTURAL REVOLUTION

For centuries agriculture was typically an industry of small farms and small-scale production, but in the past few decades the larger farm has become more common. It is worthy of note that in 1942 when the total number of farms was divided into two groups according to income, the upper 50 percent received 82 percent of the total net cash income of agriculture, while the lower 50 percent received only 18 percent. Today one million, or nearly 40 percent, of all American farms have annual sales of $2,500 or less. Sales average less than $1,000 per year for these farms. These farms possess less than 10 percent of the total farm acreage, and the value of their total sales constitutes less than 3 percent of total farm sales in the U.S. economy. These relatively unproductive farms constitute the problem area in agriculture. In 1973, for example, the average annual income of the rural family was about two thirds of the average annual urban family income. At that time it was still apparent that productive efficiency must continue to be increased or farm prices raised substantially if the level of living of farm families was to be improved; otherwise farmers must find their way into other occupations.

Although the issue of small-scale vs. large-scale farming has become commonplace, it has not yet attained the significance already reached by its counterpart of small vs. large business in other fields of economic activity. The total number of farms decreased from 5.6 million in 1950 to 2.8 million in 1973. Although the number of farms whose values of sales were below $10,000 annually (in 1959 constant dollars) decreased from 1.6 million in 1949 to less than one third of a million in 1970, the number of farms whose values of sales exceeded $10,000 increased from 484,000 in 1949 to 948,000 in 1970. Furthermore, the number of farms with 1,000 acres or more increased from 120,000 to 151,000 during the same period. At the same time the total acreage per farm has nearly doubled since 1950 while the total farm acreage actually decreased by 7 percent. This trend toward a decreasing farm population and a decreasing number of farms accompanied by an increase in the size of farms is shown in Figure 38-2.

FIGURE 38-2

FARM POPULATION, FARMS, AND FARM SIZE 1950-1972

Although the number of farms and the farm population has decreased, the size of farms has increased.

SOURCE: *Statistical Abstract of the United States,* 1973.

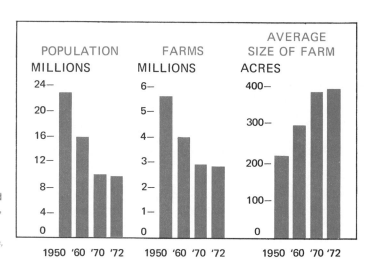

Increasing Yields Mean Lower Costs

One reason for this trend is increasing yields at lower costs. Although machine costs have increased, they have been more than offset by the resulting decline in labor costs. On the basis of 1967 as 100, the index of output per man-hour rose from 35 in 1950 to 127 in 1972; that is, farm output per man-hour increased about 250 percent during that period. On the same basis and for the same period, the index of man-hours of farm work fell by 56 percent; and the index of total farm output rose about 50 percent.

Increased agricultural productivity benefits the American consumer. In 1910 one farmworker produced enough to feed five people. By 1940 his output could feed 10.7 persons, and by 1960 he was providing sufficient foodstuffs to support 25.8 persons. By 1973 each farmworker produced enough food and fiber to take care of the needs of more than 47 persons.

Technological development in the agricultural industry permitted American farmers to produce 60 percent more wheat in 1973 than they did in 1950 in spite of the fact that they used 30 percent fewer acres for wheat production. In the same period 92 percent as much cotton was grown on one half fewer acres, and 22 percent more potatoes were harvested on 30 percent fewer acres. The yield of milk was about 3 percent more with 23 percent fewer cows. This trend toward greater productivity can be seen in Figure 38-3. In addition, there has been a greater disparity between high-cost and low-cost producers.

FIGURE 38-3

CROP PRODUCTION PER ACRE AND OUTPUT PER MAN-HOUR INCREASE AS MAN-HOURS OF LABOR DECLINE

Farm output per acre has increased and output per man-hour has risen even though fewer man-hours of labor are used in agriculture.

SOURCE: *Statistical Abstract of the United States,* 1973.

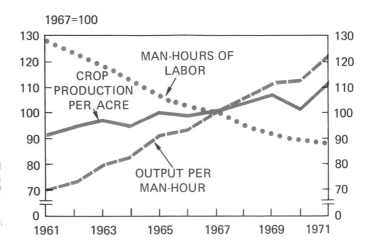

Falling Prices—Inelastic Demand

In the absence of an increased demand, improvements in agricultural productivity and the resulting increase in the supply of farm products leads to falling prices. The demand for agricultural products insofar as they represent foodstuffs is both price and income inelastic. Consider first the effect of a relatively price inelastic demand. When price falls, the quantity demanded does not increase proportionally.

Foodstuff is a basic essential; it is perishable; there are few, if any substitutes; and we have, until recent years, spent a smaller and smaller portion of our income each year on food. These factors make agricultural commodities highly price inelastic. Consequently, when supply increases and prices decrease, the total revenue of farmers will fall. This can be seen in Figure 38-4. If supply increases from S to S_1, for example, the price will fall in greater proportion than the increase in amount sold, causing total revenue to decrease (see pages 546-555 in Chapter 25).

A single farmer's reaction to such a drop in price might well be to increase his production in order to restore his income. If all farmers follow such a policy, however, it will only aggravate the situation. The secondary increase in supply will further depress price and cause income to fall again. Faced with an inelastic demand, the best action that farmers could take would be to reduce total production. This would cause prices to increase

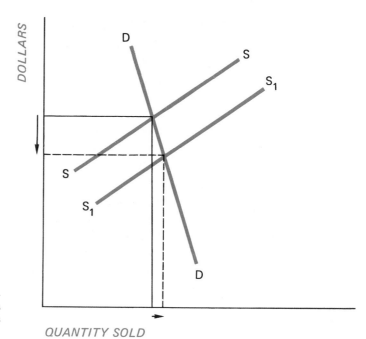

FIGURE 38-4

**SUPPLY INCREASE CAUSES
PRICE AND REVENUE DECREASE**

Because the demand for farm products tends to be price inelastic, as
supply increases and price declines
total revenue will fall.

QUANTITY SOLD

in greater proportion than purchases decline, thus increasing total revenue. This was in fact the case in 1973, when farmers destroyed baby chicks by the thousands. However, with millions of producers and free enterprise, it is generally difficult to obtain collective action to accomplish this end. In recent decades the federal government, however, through regulation has been limiting production and establishing minimum prices of farm products in order to improve the income of farmers.

The demand for food products, furthermore, is income inelastic. As national income has increased, there has not been a corresponding increase in demand for agricultural products. People prefer to buy more clothes, automobiles, household equipment, other manufactured products, and services rather than increase their food consumption greatly. At most, changes in food consumption represent shifts from one product to another rather than any large increase in the total quantity consumed. As levels of living improve, the per capita consumption of fruits, vegetables, dairy products, eggs, and meat increases at the expense of potatoes and cereals. With increasing production and an inelastic demand there is a downward pressure on farm prices. From 1950 to 1971, wheat fell from $2.01 per bushel to $1.32, corn from $1.56 to $1.06 per bushel, oats from 81 cents to 60 cents per bushel, and cotton from 32 cents per pound to 28 cents per pound. During this period of 21 years, the general price level, as measured by the

BLS Consumer Price Index, rose more than 68 percent, while farm prices increased only 10 percent. While it is true that farm prices and incomes have risen substantially since 1971, this may well be only a temporary phenomenon; depressed prices and incomes of the farming sector have certainly been the rule for the past several decades.

Certainly this indicates that farm products are generally income inelastic. The increase in demand for farm products resulting from an increase in disposable income has done little to offset the loss of income from falling prices. A demonstration of the double effect—price inelasticity and income inelasticity—can be seen in Figure 38-5. Notice that the expanded revenue from the increased demand D_1, still does not compensate for the loss of revenue resulting from falling prices. In Figure 38-5, total revenue under the original demand and supply conditions, D-S, was \$4,000 (\$2 $\times$ 2,000 = \$4,000). The total revenue under changing conditions, D_1-S_1, is \$3,125 (\$1.25 $\times$ 2,500 = \$3,125). In short, although total supply and demand for agricultural products have both increased, supply has increased at a greater rate than demand, so farmers are confronted by lower prices and lower income.

The continuing problem facing agriculture up until the early 1970s can now be summed up. As a result of the progressive revolution in agricultural methods, production had been greatly increased under the competitive conditions prevailing in agriculture, and prices had shown a pronounced tendency to decline. Where farms were of sufficient size and machinery was employed, the decline in prices was offset through reduced costs of production. Such

FIGURE 38-5

SUPPLY INCREASE IN EXCESS OF DEMAND INCREASE LOWERS PRICE

Because the demand for farm products tends also to be income inelastic, increases in demand are usually insufficient to offset the adverse effect on revenue resulting from an increase in supply.

farm families who were fortunately situated could not only survive but could even prosper. Where farms were small and improved methods were not effective in bringing about an adequate reduction in costs, farm incomes were reduced to low levels, and emigration to other employments was necessary. In fact, fewer people were needed in agriculture if the benefits of low-cost mechanized production were to be passed on to consumers without depressing the farm-family income. This adjustment to the conditions created by our technological revolution was the most fundamental long-run problem facing agriculture.

SHORT-RUN INSTABILITY IN FARM INCOME

Like other receivers of income, the farm family is interested largely in maintaining and increasing its income. Much of its effort is directed toward this end. But the income of the farmer is peculiarly subject to fluctuation. The conditions under which he develops his products are only partly subject to his control, and the markets in which he sells his products are likely to be highly competitive. Forces over which he has no control may lower or raise the prices of his products and the costs that enter into their production. Under these circumstances his yearly income may be subject to wide and often undesirable variations, which increase his insecurity.

The profits of the farmer, and therefore his money income, are determined by two major factors: (1) the profit per unit of product, which is determined by the relation between costs and selling price, and (2) the number of units, that is, the volume of production, which the farmer is able to produce and sell. The conditions that affect the farmer's costs, selling prices, and volume of production will at the same time determine his profits and, therefore, his money income. As in other types of industry, the conditions that affect these variables are numerous and changing; but in agriculture some of these conditions are so different as to merit particular consideration.

Relatively Pure Competition

The farmer is a producer of foodstuffs and raw materials, which cannot ordinarily be branded or identified as the product of a particular producer. He is not, therefore, in a position to build a clientele of consumers, who will show a preference for his particular product which will enable him as a result to escape the pressure of competition. Each farmer, in fact, is likely to produce only a very small fraction of a relatively uniform product, such as wheat, cotton, corn, or pork. He is consequently in competition with all producers of the same product; and since there are nearly 3 million farms in the United States and hundreds of thousands of producers of the individual products, the markets for agricultural commodities approach conditions of pure competition.

Slow Adjustments in Production

If the price of his product falls, the farmer will not be inclined to restrict production, since his contribution to the total volume is so small that individual limitations of production will probably not affect the price. In this respect his behavior is in contrast to that of the large industrialist, who can control his volume of production and whose contribution to the total is so large that any change in volume will have a distinct effect on the price. If the price of his product falls, the farmer, on the contrary, may increase his production for two reasons: (1) because he wants to maintain his income, and he may gain from greater volume what he has lost in profit per unit, and (2) because production costs in agriculture are largely fixed costs, which decrease per unit as the number of units produced on a given farm increase. Taxes, rent, capital, and availability of family labor are all essentially fixed costs; the only variable costs are hired labor, power, fertilizer, and seed, which in the aggregate form a rather small percentage of the total costs. Under these circumstances the determination of marginal cost in relation to price is difficult. Because of these special conditions affecting agricultural production, the volume of production does not rapidly adjust itself to changes in prices; and where adjustments in volume are slow to occur, prices will show a greater degree of variability.

Cyclical Influences

Agriculture is only one sector of the total national economy; and, because of the interdependence of the various parts of the economy, agricultural prices and incomes reflect the economic conditions prevailing in other parts of the economy. If the national income is high and the economy is in a state of expanded production, the demand for raw materials will increase in volume, and the demand for foodstuffs, inelastic as it is, will change in the quality of its requirements even more than in its quantity. Consumers, for example, may not eat greater quantities of food, but they may very well purchase more T-bone steak in preference to hamburger. On the contrary, when depression prevails, purchasing power is limited, and lower industrial demand reduces agricultural prices and incomes. Thus, the farmer is at the mercy of fluctuations in the economy over which he has little or no control but which bring about pronounced short-run changes in his welfare.

Agriculture and Foreign Trade

Another factor of great importance to the future of agriculture in this country is the relation of agriculture to our foreign trade. In spite of the fact that agricultural products have constituted a declining percentage of our total exports over the last three decades, large portions of some of our agricultural products continue to be exported. In 1971, exports of farm products accounted for 17 percent of the value of all farm products sold. One fourth of all cropland cultivated was used for growing export products. These agricultural exports constituted 18 percent of the total of all our exports. It is obvious that changes in agricultural exports, as occurred in 1972 and 1973, are of great importance in their effects on farmers' prices and incomes. The issues are complicated, however, for they are political in nature as well as economic; and in this respect the fortunes of agriculture are dependent on the foreign trade policy that is developed by this country.

A Case in Point: 1972-1973

The long-run trend in the decline of farm prices was interrupted in 1972. Growing needs at home as a result of a booming economy, plus severe food shortages elsewhere in the world, led to increased demand for America's farm products. Particularly pressing was the effect of the huge $750 million grain sales to the Soviet Union. At the same time inclement weather on the U.S. mainland, which interfered with the cultivation and harvesting of certain crops, caused some temporary food and commodity shortages, forcing prices upward. The price of wheat, for example, skyrocketed from $1.32 per bushel in 1971 to more than $5.00 per bushel in the spring of 1973, and corn prices rose sharply from $1.06 per bushel in 1971 to more than $3.00 in 1973. Prices of soybeans doubled, and prices of oats, cotton, and beef likewise rose sharply. In fact, the Agriculture Department for the first time in many years increased acreage allotments in an effort to bring about an increase in the supplies of farm commodities. All this, of course, resulted in greater sales at higher prices, substantially raising the income of the farm sector of the U.S. economy, as shown in Figure 38-6. By the fall of 1973, however, farm prices were beginning to drop as a record harvest came to market. Moreover, farmers were complaining that increases in production costs were obliterating some of their anticipated profits. Consequently, the surge in farm prices and income may turn out to be a temporary, or short-run, phenomenon. If so, there will still be a need in the future to work toward long-run adjustments in agriculture.

LONG-RUN ADJUSTMENTS IN AGRICULTURE

If American agriculture is to be adjusted effectively to the revolutionary changes that have been occurring in farming methods, policies of long-run adjustment will be necessary. Particularly important is the question of prices

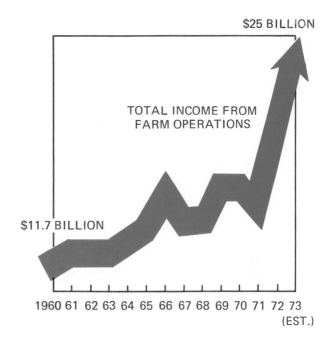

TOTAL INCOME FROM
FARM OPERATIONS

$25 BILLION

$11.7 BILLION

1960 61 62 63 64 65 66 67 68 69 70 71 72 73
(EST.)

FIGURE 38-6

**FARM INCOME: SOARING TO A
RECORD HIGH**

Farm income surged upward in the
early 1970s due to higher prices and
greater sales at home and abroad.

SOURCE: *U.S. News & World Report* (August 27,
1973).

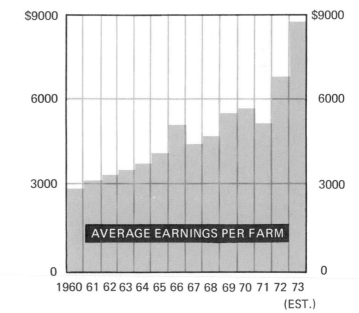

AVERAGE EARNINGS PER FARM

1960 61 62 63 64 65 66 67 68 69 70 71 72 73
(EST.)

for agricultural products. In this connection the economy is faced with two basic alternatives: either (1) the adjustments between agriculture and the rest of the economy must be made more fluid so that a better balance is established; or (2) agriculture will face a long period of depressed income, with prices maintained at minimal levels through some form of government assistance. From the point of view of the long-run welfare of the people as a whole, the first alternative seems preferable as the fundamental basis for development of policy.

An issue of equal importance with price policy is the matter of production adjustments, particularly in the size of the farm. If agriculture is to prosper in the long run, it is also necessary to develop policies that go beyond production and supply; it may be desirable to promote the expansion of demand at home and abroad for agricultural products, in order that surpluses may become less of a threat in the future. Equally important is a continued high level of economic activity in order to insure a better balance between agriculture and the remainder of the economy.

Increased Domestic Demand for Agricultural Products

As indicated earlier, the demand for agricultural products is both price inelastic and income inelastic. With bumper crops and surpluses, prices fall. As a result sales increase, but they increase less than prices decline. Thus, real farm income falls. On the other hand, because of the limitations of the human stomach, when incomes increase, there is not a corresponding increase in the purchase of farm products. Thus, as the economy expands and real incomes increase, there is not necessarily an increase in the welfare of the farmer. For example, during the prosperous 1950s the real income of workers in nonagricultural industries increased by 21 percent, but net farm income dropped by 2 percent during the same period. Farm conditions improved in the 1960s, however, when net income per farm increased 41 percent compared to an increase of 14 percent in the real income of nonagricultural workers.

The possibilities of alleviating farm surpluses by increasing consumption tend to be limited. Generally increased consumption of some foods is counterbalanced by decreases in others, and the total demand for foodstuffs especially tends to remain relatively stable. With increased incomes, however, there has been a move toward increased consumption of animal products and fruits and vegetables at the expense of wheat and potatoes. Some long-run improvement in the farm situation may occur if the trend continues, since the production of animal products requires more land, labor, and other resources than does the production of crops.

It might be expected that with the addition of 2.3 million consumers each year, the economy might eventually reach a position where the supply and demand for agricultural output would come into balance. If output were fixed, the increased demand from this source would soon take up the slack. Since increases in productivity, however, have been keeping pace with increases in the rate of population growth, prospects of help from this source are also limited.

It is sometimes suggested that the conversion of farmlands into highways and for urban and industrial uses will restrain increases in farm output. But, once again, such developments have had no appreciable effect on the total farm output.

Probably one of the most practical means of increasing domestic consumption is through an increasing use of farm products as raw materials or intermediate goods for industrial production. Thus, research and development that find new uses for agricultural products in industry should be fostered and encouraged because they will help in the long run with the solution of the farm problem.

Foreign Demand

Any policy of agricultural price fixing that attempts to maintain domestic prices above world prices will tend to curtail our exports and raise world prices, thus stimulating production in other countries. Such domestic prices can be maintained only by subsidizing exports to insure export of surpluses or by reducing production at home to the size of the domestic market. Subsidizing exports is likely to lead to economic warfare and reduced trade; reducing the volume of production reduces farm income, even when prices are fixed. If the domestic price is considerably higher than the world price, it might even be thought necessary to raise tariffs or set import quotas to prevent farm imports. If domestic production is reduced and import quotas are set on the basis of existing farm ownership, high-cost production is maintained and low-cost production is restricted.

These observations are relevant and appear to justify the abandonment of price-fixing programs; the only alternative is to accept world prices for our export commodities and then to attempt through international cooperation to enlarge the markets for farm products. In the domestic field this would mean that low-cost producers would thus be able to expand production for both domestic and foreign markets at the expense of high-cost producers.

But if price-fixing programs are to be continued, and if American agriculture is not to be entirely at the mercy of fluctuating world prices, cooperative action will have to be taken with foreign nations to bring about a greater degree of stabilization. Actions to stabilize world prices include: (1) an expansion of world trade on a permanent basis with a permanent reduction of trade barriers, (2) international cooperation in stabilizing exchange rates and capital movements, (3) special arrangements or agreements with respect to problem commodities, and (4) a growing reliance upon collective security and the settlement of disputes through peaceful means.

The government of the United States has been particularly prominent in its efforts to promote these four objectives. Its efforts to bring about lower tariffs on agricultural commodities during the Kennedy Round of GATT (General Agreement on Tariffs and Trade) negotiations culminated in substantial tariff reductions commencing in 1967. In addition, the large-scale grain deal with the Soviet Union, negotiated in 1972 and amounting to $750 million or more, opened up a whole new area of export for U.S. farmers that had an almost immediate impact on farm income. In fact, for the first time in many years, the Department of Agriculture in 1973 increased acreage allotments for the production of grain.

High-Level Economic Activity

The long-run solution to the problem of agricultural prices and income lies in part in maintaining a high level of national income and assisting farmers to shift production and reduce costs so that incomes will be increased or maintained at the prevailing level of market prices. The most essential feature in any long-run program of agricultural betterment is the need for continuous high-level prosperity with a growing national income and full employment, for this will mean a relatively high and stable demand for the farmers' products. It also makes it easier for farmers shifting out of agriculture into meaningful employment in other sectors of the economy. A large national income implies a high level of economic activity, and insofar as a high level of economic activity can be maintained and the fluctuations of the business cycle minimized, the agricultural sector will require less extensive government assistance.

Agricultural Price Policy

In the long run, any policy that attempts to hold agricultural prices in fixed relationships with each other or with other prices through a "parity" program is likely to raise as many problems as it solves. If new developments reduce the cost of production of one commodity relative to another, the prices of the two commodities should be free to reflect the changes in cost, for otherwise farmers cannot be expected to shift to those crops they can grow most efficiently. If a price is fixed above the natural market level that balances competitive supply and demand, excess production will tend to occur, as is shown in Figure 38-7.

Assume that, as a result of an increasing supply, the equilibrium price fell to $1.50 per bushel for a particular type of grain. If the government

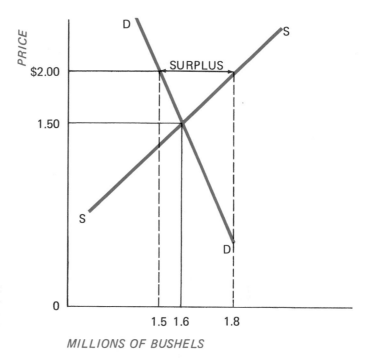

FIGURE 38-7

**PRICE HIGHER THAN MARKET
PRICE RESULTS IN SURPLUS**

Anytime a price is established that
is higher than the equilibrium market price, it will cause a surplus to
appear on the market unless some
method is used to restrict output.

established a guaranteed price of $2, excess production of 300,000 bushels
would occur. Although it would mean lower income to the farmer, the $1.50
price would clear the market of all supply. At a $2 price, however, total
production would rise to 1.8 million bushels while total purchases would
equal 1.5 million bushels, leaving a 300,000 bushel surplus. One way to
avoid such a surplus would be to reduce the supply through regulation
limiting output. The other alternative, in the absence of an increase in
demand, is to have the government purchase the surplus. This indicates once
again that in order to set a price, other than the equilibrium price brought
about by the free forces of supply and demand, it is necessary to rig
the market.

Under these circumstances either production and marketing quotas must
be set, or the surplus must be disposed of by selling abroad or by subsidized consumption at home. If an attempt is made to meet these difficulties
through control of production, high-cost production is likely to be maintained (particularly when acreage allotments are made on a historical basis)
and production in low-cost areas will be restricted. When this occurs, prices
to consumers will be maintained at a high level, and the nation as a whole
will be prevented from enjoying the lower costs resulting from improved
techniques of production.

In view of all these considerations, a government price-support program should be regarded as only temporary, while continued efforts are being made to bring about a better adjustment of farm production.

PRICE-SUPPORT PROGRAMS

During World War I and the period of demobilization that followed in 1919, the prices of agricultural products in the United States rose rapidly until the index of prices received by farmers (base 1910-1914) that had stood at 101 in 1914 was 215 in 1919, although total agricultural production had expanded only about 10 percent. The depression that began in 1920 started with a fall in agricultural prices, with the result that the index of prices received by farmers fell to 124 in 1921; and total agricultural income fell from $15 billion in 1919 to $8 billion in 1921. Total agricultural production, however, fell only about 5 percent during the same period. As has been pointed out in the preceding discussion, agricultural production is relatively stable, more so than is industrial production. Agricultural prices, and consequently agricultural incomes, are unstable.

Fear of a recurrence of these depressed conditions in American agriculture after the close of World War II in 1945 led to a strengthening of price-support programs which had been developed during the depressed 1930s. Although total agricultural production during World War II had increased by about 33 percent, a rapid decline in production was not to be expected; and another worldwide depression (which was generally predicted) would perhaps mean a disastrous collapse in agricultural prices and incomes. As a matter of fact, agricultural prices continued to rise in the years following the war until the index stood at 285 in 1948, and only in 1949 did a recession occur in agricultural prices, as well as elsewhere, when the agricultural price index fell to 249. In the meantime, however, the Agricultural Act of 1948 had been passed, with revision and extension of price supports, and this has been followed by further adjustments in price supports by subsequent acts. Thus, in spite of the desirability of a free price structure in order that long-run adjustments might be more effectively realized, short-run considerations of instability have proved more pressing and have led to increasing controls over agricultural prices.

The price-support programs are administered by the United States Department of Agriculture through the Commodity Credit Corporation (CCC) and the Commodity Stabilization Service (CSS). These operations include the price-support program of the Agricultural Acts, the International Wheat Agreement, Section 32 programs, the national school-lunch program, marketing agreements, the sugar program, and other programs. Each of these programs is intended to contribute to the maintenance of farm incomes.

Under the price-support programs, minimum prices are established for a number of commodities, basic and nonbasic, and these prices are supported through loans, purchases, or agreements to purchase by the CCC on the basis of parity prices and acreage allotments. Price support is required on such commodities as corn, cotton, wheat, tobacco, rice, peanuts, wool, mohair, tung nuts, honey, and milk and butter fat, and in the case of other commodities, at the discretion of the Secretary of Agriculture.

The national school-lunch program encourages the increased domestic consumption of agricultural commodities with the object of improving the nutritional status of children, as well as reducing surpluses. Federal funds have been made available for this purpose as well as many other programs to utilize our farm surpluses both here and abroad.

Marketing agreements and order programs enable farmers to establish and maintain orderly marketing conditions through control of quantity, quality, and rate of shipment from the producing area to all markets. Milk is the most important commodity in this connection, although fruits, nuts, and vegetables may also be involved. The sugar program is concerned with the stabilization of sugar prices through control of sugar imports and effective marketing of the domestic supply.

As this brief description indicates, these price support programs are extensive and have as their objects not merely remunerative prices for farmers but also effective disposal and use of surpluses and more orderly marketing, and hence increased stability in agricultural production, prices, and income.

The CCC and Related Organizations

The Commodity Credit Corporation was organized in 1933 under the laws of the State of Delaware as an agency of the United States, but in 1939 it was transferred to the Department of Agriculture, and in 1948 it received a permanent federal charter. The corporation is capitalized at $100 million, but its total obligations to purchase loans held by lending agencies may be extended to the sum of $10 billion. Early in the 1960s its investment in price support operations, that is, the value of inventories, reached $6 billion but subsequently declined to the vicinity of $1 to $2 billion in the early 1970s. During the decade 1960-1970, the CCC made loans totaling more than $20 billion.

In accordance with the terms of its charter, the functions of the CCC are: (1) to support the prices of agricultural commodities through loans, purchases, payments, and other operations; (2) to make available materials and facilities required in connection with the production and the marketing of agricultural commodities; (3) to procure agricultural commodities for sale to other government agencies, foreign governments, and domestic, foreign, or international relief and rehabilitation agencies; (4) to remove and to dispose of surplus agricultural commodities; (5) to increase domestic consumption of agricultural commodities and to promote new uses and new markets for them; and (6) to export agricultural commodities and to aid in the development of foreign markets for them.

The Commodity Stabilization Service, the Agricultural Research Service, and the Agricultural Marketing Service coordinate the various activities of the Department of Agriculture in production and marketing. Major activities are concerned with (1) price and supply programs and the agricultural conservation program, and (2) marketing services and regulatory and research programs. Thus, the Commodity Credit Corporation and related organizations serve as the agencies for putting into practical effect the provisions of the various agricultural acts and other legislation concerning agriculture.

Parity Prices

The *parity price* of a farm commodity is a standard for measuring the purchasing power of that commodity in relation to prices of other goods and services during a definite base period, that is, the price which will give the commodity the same purchasing power as it had during a given base period (usually 1910-1914). This price may be called a fictitious price, since it serves as a measuring device rather than as an actual price.

The formula for calculating parity prices, originally established by the Agricultural Act, has been amended many times. Parity prices are calculated each month by the Bureau of Agricultural Economics according to a formula that takes into consideration the Index of Prices Received by Farmers over a ten-year period and the Index of Prices Paid by Farmers. In this way the government attempts to tie farm prices to industrial prices.

The significance of the parity price of a commodity lies in the fact that it serves as a base from which government *support prices* may be calculated for the loans, the purchases, or the agreements to purchase of the CCC. According to the Agriculture Act of 1954, support prices for 1955 crops could not be more than 90 percent or less than 82.5 percent of parity. A greater price range was permitted for 1956 and subsequent years. These supports are mandatory in the case of all farmers who cooperate, that is, whose marketing quotas have not been disapproved and whose acreage allotments or marketing quotas are in effect.

Once the support, or parity, price is established for a commodity, it is guaranteed to the farmer through the Commodity Credit Corporation. If the market price is above the parity price, the farmer can sell his crop in the market. What happens if the market price is below parity? In such a case the CCC steps into the picture. Assume, for example, that a farmer harvested 1,000 bushels of wheat and that the parity price was $3.00 per bushel but the market price was only $2.65 per bushel. Instead of selling his wheat at the lower market price, the farmer can obtain a loan on his crop from the CCC at a value of $3.00 per bushel. Consequently, the farmer can borrow $3,000 and deliver his crop to the CCC for collateral. Theoretically as more and more farmers deliver their wheat crops to the CCC, instead of selling them on the depressed market, it should cause the market price to rise. If the market price rises to $3.00 per bushel or above, the farmer can withdraw his grain from the CCC warehouse, sell it in the market, and repay his $3,000 loan. What happens if the market price does not reach the parity level of $3.00 per bushel? In such a case, the farmer will let the CCC assume his crop in payment of the loan. This is not a dishonor of the loan but a conventional method of repayment. In effect, the CCC is giving the farmer a price of $3.00 per bushel for his wheat, which is the parity price.

The Effects of Price Supports

The government price-support program has included a variety of other measures designed to limit supply through acreage allotments or marketing quotas, or to expand demand for agricultural products either in the United States or abroad. The increasing need for certain types of raw materials for military defense also strengthens the demand. These efforts to bring about a more adequate adjustment of supply and demand to the levels set by the support prices are necessary if growing surpluses are not to become an increasingly serious problem. If, as a result of support prices, agricultural prices of commodities for export are higher than world prices, a part of the surplus may be disposed of abroad through dumping.

This procedure may be politically advantageous, but it adds to the burden of the American taxpayer. Nor is there any certainty that price supports will be of any greater advantage to the marginal farmer than to the farmer with low costs, for the marginal farmer is still exposed to the competition of the latter and to the danger of larger surpluses and lower prices. His relative position continues the same. In spite of the increasing productivity of agriculture, or perhaps because of it, the farm population of the United States declined between 1940 and 1973 from more than 30 million to less than 10 million. In the past 33 years the farm population has declined from 23 percent of the total U.S. population to less than 5 percent. This long-term trend may do more to bring about favorable adjustments in agriculture than a level of fixed prices under government control.

One major reason for the ineffectiveness of our present system of production control is the use of acreage allotments. An attempt is made to curtail production by limiting, or allotting, the number of acres that may be devoted to the production of particular crops. In exchange for his cooperation, the farmer is assured a support price for the sale of his commodities. Although acreage limitations restrict the number of acres that may be used for particular crops, it does not necessarily reduce, or even effectively limit, the total production of the crop. There is nothing that prevents the farmer from using better methods, better seeds, improved fertilizers, and the like to obtain a greater yield per acre. In most cases the farmers are now growing more on their limited acreage than they did on their full acreage of previous years. Furthermore, the farmers can use their nonallotted acreage to produce nonsupport commodities, and today more than one half of total farm sales are of nonsupport commodities. Although his acreage is limited, there is no limit to the amount a farmer can grow and market from these acres.

Furthermore, as seen earlier, even though the number of farms and the number of farmers are declining substantially, the total acreage cultivated is not declining noticeably. Evidently those leaving agriculture are selling out in large part to those who remain. Consequently, the total acreage cultivated continues to be about the same while the average-size farm is growing larger and larger. With better techniques, new methods, improved seed, and more fertilizers continuously applied to a larger and larger portion of total acreage, production is sure to rise.

As a result, at times huge surpluses accumulate in government warehouses as support prices are paid for these commodities. The federal government paid $46 billion in the 1933-1966 period in the form of crop loans for the purpose of supporting farm prices. As of 1970, it had $1.8 billion worth of commodities stored in warehouses and was paying about $200 million annually, or over $500,000 per day, to store these commodities.

Price supports and soil-bank payments may help the marginal farmer, but in addition they help many farmers who need no help. There are usually several farms that receive crop loans of more than $250,000. In the early 1960s, for example, each of a half dozen large commercial farms was receiving as much as $1 to $4 million annually, which it paid back with interest at later dates. At that time 25 farms were receiving payments in excess of $361,000 each, and 13,000 farms were receiving $20,000 or more annually in government payments. In addition, 2.5 million farmers received checks from the government for programs other than price-support loans.

ADDITIONAL AID TO FARM INCOME

Until the mid-1960s, the surplus of major farm commodities was still substantial in spite of unremitting efforts to dispose of them without depressing their prices. The decline in farm income led to further study to develop additional methods of adjusting agricultural production to demand and to a parity level of prices. According to the Agricultural Act of June, 1956, a *soil-bank program* was established that offered limited payments per acre to farmers who agreed to take crop lands out of production and place the acreage under soil-building cover crops or trees. Although farmers with especially promising crop prospects were reluctant to accept this program, in spite of a liberal schedule of payments, it was attractive to those farmers who were afflicted by adverse conditions, such as droughts or pests. The farmers whose incomes were likely to be reduced by losses from these sources benefited by the soil-bank program, and the danger of further increases in surplus crops was somewhat reduced. Land that had been retired from production of crops already in surplus was not shifted to production of other crops with the danger of further surpluses, but it was allowed to lie fallow or be planted with soil-enriching legumes or trees. The Agricultural Act of 1956 also provided for the disposal of existing surpluses, particularly cotton, through sale in foreign markets.

Unfortunately the soil-bank program had a limited effect on total agricultural output. It might have had a greater impact if it had been more effective in inducing farmers to take out of production some of their more productive lands. As it operated, the farmer taking certain acreage out of production was inclined to put his inferior land into the soil bank. On the other hand, there was nothing to prevent him from farming more intensively on his better lands. The net result was that farm output in some cases actually increased. Taking entire units or farms out of production instead of parcels on individual farms might have proved to be more effective.

Before any effective long-run agricultural policies can be formulated and implemented, a decision must be made regarding our objectives. One of the most important and basic questions is whether or not we desire to maintain family-sized, owner-operated farms that return a satisfactory family income or whether we desire to move toward more large-scale, corporate-owned commercial farms. If the latter is desired, perhaps one of the best ways to achieve such a goal is by the eventual removal of all government supports and controls. This, of course, would force the inefficient, high-cost producer from the market. It would mean that many small, marginal, family-operated farms eventually would be eliminated. Large-scale commercial farmers then could compete against each other in much the same manner as do our industrial firms. We have been reluctant to follow such a goal, however, for a number of reasons. In the first place, there are certain economic advantages to the family-sized farm. Secondly, to follow such a policy would be harsh if not ruthless from a short-run economic, social, and political point of view.

From an economic point of view, any measures designed to accomplish this objective would result in the displacement of hundreds of thousands of farmers and their families. Farmers would have to seek new trades or occupations, find new residences, and probably suffer a loss of income in making the transition. Social hardships from such a move would be very pronounced. When an industrial firm is forced out of business, the workers involved usually find other jobs in the same industrial environment. The family may stay in the same town, send their children to the same school, and even maintain the same circle of friends. Farming is more than an occupation, however. It is a way of life. If a farm is closed down, it may well mean that the family will have to change its whole economic and social environment. It will have to move to an industrial center where the father can seek employment of a different nature; it will have to become accustomed to urban living; the children will go to a different school; and the family will need to make new friends.

Although less than 5 percent of the population still live on farms, farmers constitute an important political force. Any measures that would cause either economic hardship or social hardship to the farmers could result in strong political repercussions. Frequently it is found that farm measures or farm legislation which would be wise economically may prove to be politically unfeasible for the legislator or the administrator who advocates or supports such measures.

If, as the Commission on National Goals stated in 1960, farmers must receive a more equitable income and the ultimate goal in agriculture is to bring about a better balance between the supply of and the demand for agricultural commodities, a number of alternatives present themselves. Each has certain merits and weaknesses:

1. In the light of current low levels of farm income, the government might maintain and even increase price supports and other income stabilization measures. In that case, however, stringent production controls would have to be imposed in order to prevent surpluses from glutting the markets. Restrictive controls would necessarily result in serious shifts in production. They might lead to the protection of less efficient farmers.

2. Government price supports and other farm programs could be discontinued, leaving the job of producing and disposing of farm products up to the free market. This would put heavy reliance on the competitive forces of the market to bring the supply of farm products into line with demand and eventually eliminate excess capacity. Under such circumstances, market chaos could be expected for a short time at least. In the long run it might prove to be effective. However, there is no assurance of this. Because of the strong economic, social, and political repercussions that would set in with the complete

removal of controls and price supports, it is doubtful that the farmers, the public, and the government are ready to accept this alternative as a solution to the farm problem. Furthermore, if controls were completely removed, the farmers of our nation could justifiably criticize and demand the removal of various types of subsidies we have on other commodities and services produced by the maritime, housing, aviation, health, and magazine industries, and by many small businesses. Also, they could legitimately protest welfare and income payments of all kinds to urban families, including our minimum-wage laws.

3. The government could continue its patchwork job of price supports, government loans, the soil bank, and other measures in the hope that the situation would improve. Adjustments in production and population growth might eventually bring about a better balance between supply and demand, ultimately relieving the government of the necessity of regulating prices and output. Such action, however, might merely prolong our present difficulties, and the so-called opportune time for the removal of government regulations might never arrive.

4. A more feasible alternative would be a gradual but definite removal of government regulations and price-support programs until such time as farm prices may be determined by demand and supply. If such a policy were adopted, it would have to be recognized that the basic problem in agriculture is one of excess production compared to demand. We . have more farmland and farmers than the economy needs at present. Production must be curtailed and demand increased. But an effective program will involve people. Rather than let the cold and harsh logic of the marketplace disrupt the lives of hundreds of thousands of farmers, however, as would be the case in the second alternative just mentioned, some effective program would have to be found to channel these hundreds of thousands of farmers out of farming and into more productive pursuits in an orderly fashion. Government-sponsored educational, training, and rehabilitation programs for the younger farmers and for the children of farmers would make the transition much easier.

A similar plan was recommended by the Research and Policy Committee of the Committee for Economic Development when it released its publication, "An Adaptive Program for Agriculture," in 1962. The committee rejected both the laissez-faire and the protectionist approaches to the agriculture program. Its adaptive approach outlines a program "to permit and induce a large, rapid movement of resources, notably labor, out of agriculture." Although this approach calls for government action, it suggested government measures that would operate within the framework of a free market, not against it. Its plan also allows for full production rather than calling for a limitation on production.

In 1967 the National Advisory Commission on Food and Fiber, established earlier by President Johnson, included in its report some long-run suggestions for a more rational farm policy. The Commission felt that the time was ripe for a major shift in the direction of U.S. food and fiber policy. It recommended unanimously "that the United States adapt its policies to accomplish a market-oriented agriculture." In this regard the Commission favored aid to the farmers in the form of direct payments. It recommended that price supports be set modestly below a survey average of world prices. The Commission rejected the concept of supply management. Lastly, it emphasized the need to channel labor and other resources out of the farm sector into more productive uses, and it proposed specific measures to accomplish this outflow.

As a result of increased domestic and foreign demand for U.S. farm products, coupled with limited supplies, the prices of many agricultural commodities rose substantially in the 1972 to 1974 period. This improved farm income and alleviated, at least in the short run, a number of farm problems. In fact, in response to shortages, acreage allotments on a number of farm products were increased to provide larger supplies. In addition, Congress passed the Agriculture and Consumer Protection Act in 1973, the principal innovation of which is to provide a system of target prices for basic crops such as wheat, feed grains, and cotton. When market prices are above the target prices, no government "deficiency payments" are made to farmers, and the government's influence is minimized. On the other hand, when market prices fall below the target prices, government payments to farmers make up the difference between target and market prices on base production.

SUMMARY

1. As a result of the technological revolution in agriculture, beginning with the development of farm machinery and culminating in the tractor as the source of power, productivity has increased so greatly as to make small farm methods relatively unprofitable.

2. The instability of farm prices and income has been due in part to short-run factors, such as business fluctuations, wide variations in foreign demand, natural hazards, and the pressure of pure competition on slow adjustments to changing market conditions.

3. Increased domestic and foreign demand, coupled with some commodity shortages in 1972 and 1973, led to much higher farm prices and increased farm income. This, however, may be a temporary phenomenon.

4. A basic cause of the relatively low income of farmers is the fact that the demand for farm products is both price and income inelastic.

5. Government can help the farmer by promoting domestic and foreign demand for farm products, particularly nonfood products, by research into new products and new and better uses of old products, by a program of land utilization aimed at retiring marginal land to less intensive uses, and by promoting a full-employment equilibrium that can absorb excess farm labor.

6. In the short run government can aid the farmer, particularly the marginal farmer, by programs designed to limit production and supply and by maintaining prices at more profitable levels through parity pricing and soil conservation. In the long run, however, more definite policies will have to be formulated and effectuated if the farm problem is to be solved.

7. Price fixing will in the long run fail in its objective, while creating serious burdens for the taxpayer and labor, if productivity continues to increase with or without the aid of government.

8. A number of long-range farm programs as a means of solving our farm problem have been suggested by various economic organizations.

9. As a result of increased demand, limited supplies, and higher prices, farm income improved substantially in 1973 and 1974.

NEW TERMS

Agricultural revolution, *p. 825*
Morrill Act, *p. 826*
Price-support programs, *p. 840*
Commodity Credit Corporation (CCC), *p. 840*

Parity price, *p. 842*
Support prices, *p. 842*
Soil-bank program, *p. 845*
National Advisory Commission on Food and Fiber, *p. 848*

QUESTIONS FOR DISCUSSION AND ANALYSIS

1. How does the farm problem in the U.S. differ from the farm problem in most underdeveloped nations where there is a shortage of foodstuffs?

2. How can the use of machinery and fertilizers, which contribute so greatly to farm productivity, possibly aggravate the farm problem?

3. There are two major alternatives to the solution of the farm problem: (1) to channel resources and manpower out of agriculture, and (2) to increase the demand for agricultural commodities. Which is the better approach? Why?

4. Do you visualize the price-support program as a long-run or short-run solution to the farm program? Why?

5. Although the number of farms has decreased substantially in the past decade or two, the amount of farm acreage has decreased very little. Explain this phenomenon.

6. Explain how price inelasticity of demand intensifies the income problem of the farmer.

7. Do you think that the move toward fewer but larger farms in the U.S. economy is beneficial to consumers?

8. Do you think that the U.S. should sell wheat and other grain to Communist nations? Why or why not?

9. Should the government continue to support farm prices and farm income or let supply and demand determine farm prices and farm income? Why?

10. Do you think the improvement in farm income in the early 1970s is indicative of a permanent recovery in the farm sector? Explain.

SUGGESTED READINGS

An Adaptive Program for Agriculture. New York: Committee for Economic Development, October, 1962.

Benedict, Murray R. *Can We Solve the Farm Problem?* New York: Twentieth Century Fund, 1955.

Department of Agriculture. *Agricultural Marketing Service, Agricultural Prices*. July 15, 1972.

Department of Agriculture. *Price Programs. Agriculture Information Bulletin*. Published annually.

Goals for Americans, The Report of the President's Commission on National Goals. Englewood Cliffs, N.J.: Prentice-Hall, Inc., 1960.

Hathaway, Dale E. *Problems of Progress in the Agricultural Economy*. Glenview, Ill.: Scott, Foresman and Company, 1964.

Heady, Earl O. *A Primer on Food, Agriculture, and Public Policy*. New York: Random House, Inc., 1967.

Owen, Wyn F. *American Agriculture: The Changing Structure*. Lexington, Mass.: D. C. Heath & Company, 1969.

"Plenty of Food on the Way—Report from U.S. Farm Belt." *U.S. News & World Report* (August 27, 1973).

Ruttan, Vernon W., *et al. Agricultural Policy in an Affluent Society*. New York: W. W. Norton & Company, Inc., 1969.

Schultz, T. W. *Production and Welfare of Agriculture*. New York: The Macmillan Company, 1949.

The Food and Agricultural Act of 1962. Washington: Department of Agriculture.

Toward a Realistic Farm Program. New York: Committee for Economic Development, December, 1957.

39

Urban Economics

PREVIEW Cities today are faced with a growing number of complex socioeconomic problems. Solutions to some of these problems are not being supplied through the private sector of the economy. Yet city governments, hard pressed for finances and resources, are ill prepared to handle these problems. Consequently, cities have been receiving more and more aid from the federal government. Three important aspects of this urban plight, not extensively covered elsewhere in this text, are considered in this chapter. They are housing and urban development, mass transit, and crime.

For decades, if not centuries, the study of economics was primarily micro in nature, dealing with the analysis of the individual, the firm, and the industry. A few decades ago a shift to macroeconomics, dealing with the aggregates of the total economy, occurred. Of more recent interest is the study of regional economics, which concerns the relationship of economic factors within a limited geographic area.

Historically, cities have been engaged in conventional economic issues of zoning, education, taxation, public services, and acquiring and holding industries. Today heavy emphasis is placed on the study of urban economics, centering around the many socioeconomic problems of the cities, such as unemployment, housing, slum clearance, urban renewal, transportation, congestion, mass transit, energy shortages, pollution, and crime.

THE URBAN POPULATION

These socioeconomic problems have been aggravated by the continued growth of our urban population, as well as by the difficulties created by major cities becoming larger in area and more congested. This urbanization movement is recognizable in the figures presented in Table 39-1.

TABLE 39-1

URBAN AND RURAL POPULATION

1910-1970 [1]

(Percent)

Place	Previous Urban Definition					Current Urban Definition		
	1910	1920	1930	1940	1950	1950	1960	1970
Urban ...	45.7	51.2	56.2	56.5	59.6	64.0	69.9	73.5
Rural ...	54.3	48.8	43.8	43.5	40.4	36.0	30.1	26.5

SOURCE: *Statistical Abstract of the United States*, 1973, p. 18.

[1] Prior to 1960 excludes Alaska and Hawaii. "Previous urban definition" used prior to 1950 when a number of large densely settled places were not included as urban because they were not incorporated. All the population residing in urban-fringe areas and in unincorporated places of 2,500 or more is classified as urban according to the "current" definition.

Today, fully three fourths of the United States population reside in an urban setting. Moreover, there are 65 large metropolitan areas with populations exceeding one half million, and 33 of these have populations in excess of one million. Not only have the problems of the cities been magnified by the migration of people into the cities, but since World War II there has been a mass movement of city dwellers and businesses to the suburbs. The abandonment of the *central city* by many higher income families and prosperous businesses has in large part left the inner city to lower income groups and marginal businesses. One aspect of this can be seen by the change in the percentage distribution of white vs. nonwhite population in the central cities, remembering that the nonwhite population is in a lower income stratum than the white population. Table 39-2 shows that, in 1950, 32.0 percent of the total population lived within the central cities, and by 1970, 31.5 percent were still so located. A closer inspection shows that, in 1950, 31.1 percent of the white population lived in the central cities. By 1970, however, only 27.9 percent of the total white population lived in the central cities. On the other hand, by 1970 more than half, 56.5 percent, of the black and other minority population lived in the central cities, compared with 39.2 percent in 1950. Notice that, in the move from rural to urban locations, there was a relatively greater movement of nonwhites than there was of the white population.

TABLE 39-2

POPULATION, URBAN AND RURAL, BY RACE

1950 and 1970

Year and Area	In Thousands			Percent Distribution		
	Total	White	Negro and Other	Total	White	Negro and Other
1950, Total Population	151,326	135,150	16,176	100.0	100.0	100.0
Urban	96,847	86,864	9,983	64.0	64.3	61.7
Inside Urbanized Areas ..	69,249	61,925	7,324	45.8	45.8	45.3
Central Cities	48,377	42,042	6,335	32.0	31.1	39.2
Urban Fringe	20,872	19,883	989	13.8	14.7	6.1
Outside Urbanized Areas	27,598	24,939	2,659	18.2	18.5	16.4
Rural	54,479	48,286	6,193	36.0	35.7	38.3
1970, Total Population	203,212	177,749	25,463	100.0	100.0	100.0
Urban	149,325	128,773	20,552	73.5	72.4	80.7
Inside Urbanized Areas ..	118,447	100,952	17,495	58.3	56.8	68.7
Central Cities	63,922	49,547	14,375	31.5	27.9	56.5
Urban Fringe	54,525	51,405	3,150	26.8	28.9	12.3
Outside Urbanized Areas	30,878	27,822	3,057	15.2	15.7	12.0
Rural	53,887	48,976	4,911	26.5	27.6	19.3

SOURCE: *Statistical Abstract of the United States*, 1973.

General Note: An urbanized area comprises at least one city of 50,000 inhabitants (central city) plus contiguous, closely settled areas (urban fringe). Data for 1950 according to urban definition used in the 1960 census; 1970 data according to the 1970 definition.

Accompanying the shift of higher income families and prosperous businesses out of the inner city has been a physical deterioration of property within the inner city. As a result of inadequate maintenance and repair, many buildings have depreciated and property values have declined. All this has played havoc with city finances by reducing the tax base.

Although some efforts have been made in the past few decades toward urban renewal, much more needs to be done to prevent urban blight and the evolution of slums. At issue here are the costs of rebuilding the cities. Who shall bear the cost—the private sector or the government sector? If the government sector, shall it be the local government? If local, shall the cost be shared by the suburban areas as well as the central city? Should part of the cost be financed by the federal government? We shall look at these and other issues in the next few pages.

HOUSING AND URBAN RENEWAL

As the move to the cities continues during the 1970s, housing needs will be accentuated. Not only will there be a need for new homes, apartments, schools, churches, and shops in the suburban areas, but there will be a pressing need for *urban renewal* in the inner cities. This is necessary to provide housing for low-income families and to attract some of the suburbanites back into the cities. Housing starts were in the vicinity of 1.5 million annually during the 1960s, but a national goal of 2 million or more had been set by a national commission. In the 1970s housing starts have accelerated to 2.4 to 2.5 million annually. With the rapidly rising cost of construction in recent years, however, many families are going to find it difficult to finance adequate housing. Private industry will certainly do its share in providing housing to meet economic demand. Nevertheless, more and more pressure will be put on government to help provide housing for low-income families.

Urban Renewal

Many cities in the past two decades have embarked on urban renewal programs. The general objectives of such programs are: (1) the elimination of urban blight and slum living conditions, and (2) enhancement of the central city's economic position within the metropolitan area.

Blight and slum areas are present in most American cities. A large number of substandard living units, if not dangerously dilapidated houses and apartments, are found in slum areas. To some extent, such living conditions are a manifestation of the impersonal forces of the market: the private sector of the economy, in terms of supply and demand, is providing low grade housing. Consequently, it is involved in the efficient allocation of resources, and there should be little need for public housing.

Although some landlords may desire to improve their properties, imperfections exist in the housing market as they do in some other economic markets. One or a few landlords alone, for instance, cannot improve a neighborhood to any substantial degree. All must participate in a dedicated endeavor to improve a neighborhood if the project is going to be successful. Unfortunately this is an infrequent occurrence because of the lack of cooperation from property owners.

This so-called *neighborhood effect* is abetted by current federal and local tax structures and credit restraints. Tax laws, for example, permit a flexible application of depreciation. Consequently, a profit-seeking landlord is encouraged to accelerate the depreciation on his property without necessarily spending money on the upkeep and repair of his buildings. Once his property is depreciated, the landlord can sell it. The new owner in turn can then begin anew to depreciate the property at an accelerated pace to maximize his profits, and perhaps then he will resell the property. As a result the property may receive a minimum of upkeep and repair, in which case buildings can soon become dilapidated and slums develop.

The structure of local property taxes also contributes toward the development of slum areas. Tax assessments and tax payments are based more on the market value of property than on the use value or profitability. This leads to crowded conditions and discourages outlays for renovations of property. Then, for two main reasons, it is often more difficult for landlords or resident owners to obtain credit for renovation and repair of housing in slum areas: first, because of the property values and the neighborhood, and secondly, because of the lack of strong credit ratings by these groups. Prejudice, too, has been a factor in perpetuating slums, since it restricts the mobility of minority groups and forces many low-income groups to live in deteriorating neighborhoods.

A third imperfection of the housing market results from the social cost generated by slum neighborhoods but borne by the city as a whole. Slum areas often become breeding grounds for disease, social unrest, crime, and other social ills. These external diseconomies are not reflected in the true cost of housing in the slum areas.

Problems caused by the migration of higher income families and business enterprises out of the central cities are aggravated by the continued immigration of poor and minority groups into the central city. Due to economic, racial, and other barriers, many of these families are unable to obtain adequate housing elsewhere and are compelled to accept shelter in deteriorating sections of the city. Many of these persons are in need of costly public services, particularly welfare, employment, and health services; cities may find it difficult to offer such services under present budget constraints. As a result of these and other imperfections in the housing market, especially in the slum areas, there is not a true reflection of supply and demand or an accurate measure of costs and benefits.

The economic forces pulling the more affluent families out of inner cities also have drawn many commercial and industrial establishments to the suburbs as well. This movement has been magnified by the increasing use of auto and truck transportation. As inner city commercial structures become depreciated or obsolete and need replacement or expansion, owners find zoning ordinances restrictive, large parcels of suitable land often unavailable, the cost of razing buildings expensive, the price of land acquisition intolerable, and traffic congestion irritating. These conditions are less than conducive to the further development of inner city locations. Consequently, enterprisers often opt for a suburban location where land and facilities are available, traffic is less congested, parking space is plentiful, and adequate housing for workers is nearby.

This movement of commercial enterprises out of the central cities further reduces the city's tax base and aggravates its financial problems. Moreover, it contributes to urban blight, particularly when abandoned buildings and stores are not rented or resold and thus remain empty.

The task of eradicating slums, eliminating substandard housing, and strengthening the economic position of the central city requires a comprehensive and lengthy effort. For a number of reasons, private enterprise thus far has not seen fit to do the job. Local governments in most cases do not possess the financial clout to undertake the task, and state governments have not responded well to the urban crisis. Thus, much has been left up to the federal government in providing both leadership and finances for urban renewal.

Federal Urban Renewal Legislation

The federal government has been involved with urban renewal in various ways since the days of the Great Depression of the 1930s. An extensive Congressional study of urban problems conducted during and after World War II led to acceleration of federal participation in the remedy of urban problems with the passage of the Housing Act of 1949. This Act proposed the elimination of substandard housing through the clearance of slums and blighted areas. It also called for the escalation of housing construction to relieve shortages and recommended decent housing and a suitable living environment for each American family. Although emphasis was placed on the need for private funds to attain these objectives, a revolving federal fund of $1 billion was established to provide loans to local communities to begin work on these goals.

In one way the passage of the Housing Act of 1949 was an admission that the private forces of the market had not provided adequate resources to cope with the problem of urban slum clearance and blight removal. Moreover, the Act was a recognition that urban slums, blight, and the lack of adequate housing had become a widespread national problem requiring federal help.

This Act was followed during the next two decades by others, amending, revising, and adding to the original Housing Act. In 1954 the concept of slum and blight clearance gave way to a more comprehensive approach to renewal including redevelopment, rehabilitation, and conservation activities. The 1954 Act broadened the power and authority of the Federal Housing Administration (FHA) and the Federal National Mortgage Association (Fannie Mae) in the housing area.

In 1956 Congress authorized financial assistance to households and enterprises forced to relocate because of urban renewal activities. The Housing Act of 1959 allocated federal funds to communities to help develop Community Renewal Programs (CRPs) and gave assistance to colleges undertaking urban renewal activities. In 1961 an amendment increased authorization of federal grants up to $4 billion. The amendment liberalized relocation payments for those displaced by urban renewal, increased grants for nonresidential purposes, and, among other things, provided for the physical expansion of hospitals located in blighted areas. In 1964 rehabilitation was encouraged by additional federal funds and 20-year loans at a nominal interest rate of 3 percent per annum for projects in renewal areas. In 1965 Congress, through the Housing and Urban Development Act, extended additional grants of $2.9 billion over a four-year period to communities for planning and implementing code enforcement in blighted areas. Thirty-five percent of these grants was made available for renewal in nonresidential areas.

During this period many new government agencies, such as the Urban Renewal Administration and the Renewal Assistance Administration, were formed to help with the solution of urban problems. Moreover, the Department of Housing and Urban Development was raised to Presidential Cabinet status, stressing the growing importance of housing and urban development. In 1966, through an act of Congress, the famed Model Cities Program was implemented to supplement and integrate many aspects of current antipoverty programs, slum clearance projects, and renewal efforts into single projects. In 1970 the Uniform Relocation Assistance and Land Acquisition Policies Act provided for additional personal and financial assistance of up to $15,000 for homeowners and $4,000 for tenants displaced by federal, or federally assisted, renewal projects.

Although most of the urban renewal slum clearance and other projects are initiated by local communities, financing has come in large part from the federal government. As a result, a close consortium has developed among local governments, city residents, private enterprises, and the federal government in an effort to rid the cities of slums and blight, improve housing conditions, and strengthen and renew the position of the central cities. Some idea of federal participation in this effort can be seen in Tables 39-3 and 39-4, which indicate that the federal government has committed a total of over $8 billion for over 2,000 urban renewal projects throughout the nation.

TABLE 39-3

GROWTH OF URBAN RENEWAL PROJECTS UTILIZING FEDERAL GRANTS

1950-1971

(Dollars in Thousands)

Year	Reservations Outstanding	Program Status at End of Year			
		Project Approvals Outstanding			
		Total	Completed	Execution	Planning
1950	$ 198,774	124	—	8	116
1951	282,724	201	—	9	192
1952	329,228	259	—	27	232
1953	348,540	260	—	61	199
1954	377,170	278	—	87	191
1955	553,665	340	—	110	230
1956	826,684	432	1	132	299
1957	1,019,294	494	4	180	301
1958	1,324,173	645	10	281	354
1959	1,388,647	689	26	365	298
1960	1,866,160	838	41	444	353
1961	2,467,631	1,012	65	518	429
1962	3,014,314	1,210	86	588	536
1963	3,680,603	1,402	118	671	613
1964	4,279,496	1,545	174	796	575
1965	4,940,269	1,699	227	894	578
1966	5,667,539	1,812	289	979	544
1967	6,253,871	1,947	338	1,037	572
1968	7,038,659	2,038	424	1,164	450
1969	7,313,997	2,030	477	1,161	392
1970	7,835,584	2,090	542	1,181	367
1971	8,180,768	2,071	622	1,230	219

SOURCE: U.S. Department of Housing and Urban Development, *Statistical Yearbook*, 1971.

The Controversy over Urban Renewal

Urban renewal is still a relatively new and controversial concept in our economy; especially debatable is the federal financing of urban renewal projects. Since the expenditures result in visible physical units, the results

TABLE 39-4

URBAN RENEWAL
PROJECTS WITH
FEDERAL
GRANTS, BY
STATE AS OF
DECEMBER 31,
1971

(Dollars in
Thousands)

State	Urban Renewal Projects		
	Location	Project	Grants Approved
Total	964	2,071	$8,180,768
Alabama	38	81	177,256
Alaska	9	15	46,268
Arizona	1	4	15,292
Arkansas	19	39	103,385
California	40	72	500,656
Colorado	5	13	70,447
Connecticut	38	85	486,263
Delaware	1	6	23,609
Dist. of Columbia	1	7	94,798
Florida	6	9	51,792
Georgia	45	83	162,784
Guam	2	2	13,130
Hawaii	2	10	58,590
Idaho	3	4	21,918
Illinois	21	64	228,799
Indiana	20	41	140,211
Iowa	14	22	101,497
Kansas	12	28	104,990
Kentucky	26	50	143,161
Louisiana	4	8	17,774
Maine	10	18	41,284
Maryland	11	36	202,688
Massachusetts	33	82	541,999
Michigan	53	106	336,402
Minnesota	18	38	151,992
Mississippi	18	24	51,666
Missouri	16	32	129,515
Montana	2	2	9,072
Nebraska	—	—	
Nevada	3	4	7,629
New Hampshire	10	18	38,470
New Jersey	55	125	471,183
New Mexico	7	7	45,786
New York	77	164	1,036,752
North Carolina	32	74	233,152
North Dakota	5	6	17,917
Ohio	35	80	423,946
Oklahoma	6	19	138,658
Oregon	6	12	49,401
Pennsylvania	113	257	704,169
Puerto Rico	34	59	70,224
Rhode Island	4	16	81,144
South Carolina	6	13	27,419
South Dakota	—	—	
Tennessee	36	75	263,270
Texas	22	55	181,262
Utah	—	—	
Vermont	1	1	2,391
Virginia	17	55	190,035
Virgin Islands	3	5	6,263
Washington	8	13	47,735
West Virginia	9	15	39,794
Wisconsin	6	16	75,324
Wyoming	1	1	1,606

SOURCE: U.S. Department of Housing and Urban Development, *Statistical Yearbook*, 1971.

are subject to scrutiny and comment by the general public as well as by parties directly concerned.

A major objective or goal of federal urban renewal programs is the erection of better housing for low-income families. Unfortunately urban renewal has provided housing primarily to middle and higher income groups. Relatively little housing has been provided for the poor and lower income families. In fact, in the two decades, 1950-1970, only 170,000 housing units were erected through urban renewal. This seems contrary to the intended goals of the program. Some urban renewal administrators, however, contend that there has been a shift in emphasis and that better housing is necessary to entice middle and upper income families back to the inner city. Housing for lower income families, they contend, can be provided directly by other federal programs.

There is also some question about the effectiveness of providing displaced families with suitable housing and moving expenses. Relocation adjustment payments have averaged about $400 per family. The Department of Housing and Urban Development (HUD) publicizes that 82 to 94 percent of all displaced families have relocated to standard housing. Critics, however, challenge HUD figures on the basis of bias, saying that HUD applies rigorous standards to justify the acquisition of property but rather loose standards to relocation property.

Critics point out also that urban renewal causes the demise of many small enterprises. Many of them, forced to close down, never open again for a number of reasons such as age, moving costs, and high rents in other areas. As of 1970, 75,000 firms had obtained financial relocation assistance totaling $218 million. Proponents of urban renewal, on the other hand, maintain that many of the businesses were marginal in nature and were on the brink of bankruptcy anyway. Urban renewal, they say, merely advanced the date of demise for them.

In promoting urban renewal many advocates state that renewal of the central city would increase the tax base and tax revenues, as new buildings and businesses enhance property values. Critics contend that this may not be true, especially when the loss of tax revenues during the interim period between demolition and reconstruction is considered. Unfortunately insufficient data are available to measure the effect of urban renewal on the tax revenues of the central cities.

Another aspect of urban renewal is the effect of the spending involved on the local economy. Proponents of urban renewal contend that every public dollar spent on renewal projects induces about $3.65 in investment by the private construction sector of the economy. Moreover, they say if federal dollars only are considered the ratio is $1 to $5.11. Strong rebuttals are offered by the opponents of urban renewal, who contend that when all federal spending on housing, including that by the FHA and FNMA, is taken into consideration, the ratio is closer to one to one. Evidence would seem to indicate that there is some multiplier effect, and therefore there exists a ratio somewhere between the two extremes.

It is charged by the critics that urban renewal in effect redistributes income in the wrong direction. The government taxes money from poor states, they say, and redistributes it through urban renewal to wealthier states. This is contrary to the stated goals of other welfare programs. This does happen, of course, since most urban renewal projects are located in the most populous and wealthy states where large cities are located. Proponents of urban renewal do not deny that this takes place to some extent. But they suggest that it is more than balanced by welfare programs that redistribute income in the other direction.

Lastly, there are critics of urban renewal who contend that the use of federal funds for urban renewal is unconstitutional, since there is no expressed authority for the federal government to commit funds for this purpose. Particularly is this true, they say, when the right of eminent domain is used to acquire property from individuals which is then eventually resold by the government to others for private use. Urban renewal proponents, however, cite the 1954 Supreme Court decision in the case of *Berman* v. *Parker*, which established the right of the federal government to engage in urban renewal activities.

In spite of the criticism or lack of progress, it appears that urban renewal is destined to continue for many years to come. Indeed, it could well be accelerated if states decide to spend some of their revenue sharing funds for this purpose.

An alternative to government housing projects being experimented with at the present time is the rent subsidy. Through such a subsidy, a poor family is enabled to live in a higher level economic neighborhood by receiving a rent subsidy from the government to make up the difference between the actual rent and what the family can afford to pay. Proponents of rent subsidies suggest that they are preferable to government-sponsored housing projects.

URBAN TRANSPORTATION

Another urban issue of great importance and complexity is the transportation problem. *Urban transportation* involves the movement of people into and out of the central city as well as within the city itself. The problems differ in various cities depending on a multitude of factors such as size, location, topography, age, and the allocation of resources to the problem. The urban transportation problem has in large part been caused by the growing dependence on the automobile and the lack of available and convenient mass transportation, as well as the refusal of people to use such facilities where they do exist. Attempts to alleviate the problem of traffic congestion by the construction of multilane expressways have, thus far, not solved the problem. In fact, in some respects these attempts have worsened the inner city traffic problem by dumping more cars into the inadequate streets of the inner cities. Endeavors to alleviate the situation through the use of mass transit facilities, toll gates, off-street parking facilities, walking malls, and car pools have not noticeably reduced traffic congestion.

History of Mass Transit

Mass transit is not something new. Many forms of it have been in existence since the growth of large cities. In the United States the omnibus became a major vehicle for urban transportation in the 1830s. The omnibus, a horsedrawn vehicle accommodating eight passengers, had its greatest popularity in the 1870s. It was replaced, in large part, by the horsecar. The horsecar differed from the omnibus insofar as it ran on a steel track instead of over cobblestone roads. It therefore provided a smoother, faster, and more comfortable ride than did the omnibus.

One of the first instances of mechanized transportation was the cable car, introduced in San Francisco in 1873. This vehicle could easily ascend hills and travel faster than the horsecar. The cable car was popular until the turn of the century. It was replaced by the electric streetcar, which could travel farther and faster. Consequently, the streetcar was in part responsible for pushing the city and its suburbs to broader limits. Electric streetcars still exist today in a few large cities such as Boston, Cleveland, Pittsburgh, New Orleans, and San Francisco.

The importance of the streetcar, nevertheless, faded with the introduction of the motor and trolley buses, the latter being powered with electricity supplied through overhead wires. The value of motor buses became obvious during the depression of the 1930s, when cities were endeavoring to reduce maintenance costs associated with the use of the streetcar and the trolley bus.

At an early stage in the period of growth of mechanized transportation, some of the larger cities adopted mass transit systems. New York constructed the first elevated rapid transit system in the United States in 1868. Subsequently elevated transportation facilities were erected in Boston, Philadelphia, and Chicago. Subways, too, became popular in most of these same large cities. But for most cities today, buses are the sole means of public transportation.

Unfortunately mass transit facilities have not kept pace with the needs of the burgeoning urban population. The problem has been intensified by the growing use of the automobile; individuals and families, holding tight to their near-sacred prerogative for personal mobility, have been reluctant to use mass transportation.

Impact of the Automobile

The mass production of automobiles in the second decade of this century initiated the radical change that was to occur in transportation and urban living in the next several decades. The automobile accelerated the movement of many middle and higher income families to the suburbs, leaving behind lower income and minority groups. Urban sprawl broke the tie between mass transit and many of its patrons, since mass transit operations were not equipped to provide adequate service to a scattered and mobile-minded population. In an effort to offset declining patronage and revenues, transit companies raised fares and cut services. Existing services in many areas deteriorated as transit companies found it more and more difficult to compete with the automobile. The continued growth of automobile usage and the inability of mass transit to adequately handle urban transportation needs led to acute traffic congestion.

The extent to which Americans rely on the automobile for transportation is manifest in motor vehicle ownership statistics. Today 82 percent of households own at least one auto, and approximately one third of the families own two or more autos. Figure 39-1 shows that the total number of auto registrations in the United States today is about 96 million compared to 27 million just 30 years ago. In addition, there are 21 million trucks and buses helping to crowd the highways. In some states, such as California, New York, and Ohio, automobile ownership is more prevalent than in others. Furthermore, there are more automobiles registered in California than in any country of the world except West Germany, France, Japan, and Great Britain.

Families and individuals use their autos for a variety of purposes, as shown in Figure 39-2. It is obvious from this figure that the use of the auto is not always a necessity. America's great love for automobiles has helped create traffic congestion of unprecedented magnitude. In addition to the sheer number of cars trying to move from place to place, the situation has been made more intolerable by diverse traffic patterns, inadequate streets, construction of new buildings in urban areas, and peak-hour usage of roads. In this last regard, for example, 56 percent of those going to and from work drive alone, 26 percent ride with others, 14 percent use public transportation, and 4 percent use some other means of commuting to and from work. Talking specifically of direct costs, such as the price of gasoline and wear and tear on individual cars, automobile transportation is quite

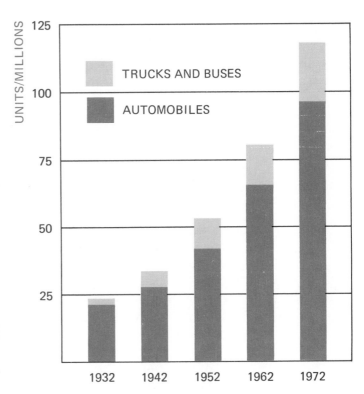

FIGURE 39-1

TOTAL MOTOR VEHICLES REGISTERED

At present there are nearly 120 million motor vehicles traveling United States roads and highways.

SOURCE: Automobile Manufacturers Association, *1972 Automobile Facts and Figures.*

FIGURE 39-2

PURPOSES OF AUTOMOBILE TRIPS

The average car is used for a variety of purposes. The most common usages are earning a living, family business, and social and recreational functions.

SOURCE: Automobile Manufacturers Association, *1972 Automobile Facts and Figures,* p. 35.

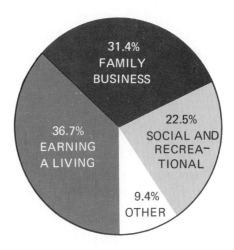

expensive compared to public transit. Other costs created by traffic congestion, such as air and noise pollution, are borne by both the individual motorist and society. In spite of these high costs, however, Americans for the most part prefer to use their automobiles. In the meantime mass transit systems continue to deteriorate.

The Decline of Public Transportation

In spite of the rise in total population in the United States in the past few decades, the increasing use of the automobile has brought about an absolute decrease in the number of passengers utilizing public transportation. This striking decline is shown in Figure 39-3, which indicates a drop from a peak of 19 billion passengers in 1945 to less than 9 billion in 1970. This, naturally, has had a substantial effect on the profit picture of public transit operations in the United States. Figure 39-4 reveals how losses continued to mount during the decade of the 1960s. As a result, a large number of mass transit companies are on the verge of bankruptcy. Last-ditch efforts to improve their financial status by raising fares and cutting services and costs have often failed to remedy the situation. Because of the bleak financial outlook, a number of private transit companies have been converted to public ownership. Fifteen years ago there were only seven publicly owned mass transit systems. These were in Boston, Chicago, Cleveland, Detroit,

FIGURE 39-3

AVERAGE FARE/REVENUE PASSENGER 1935-1970

In the past few decades there has been a drastic decrease in the number of passengers using public transportation while fares have increased dramatically.

SOURCE: American Transit Association, *1972 Transit Fact Book*, p. 4.

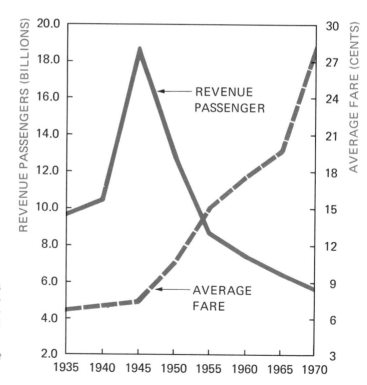

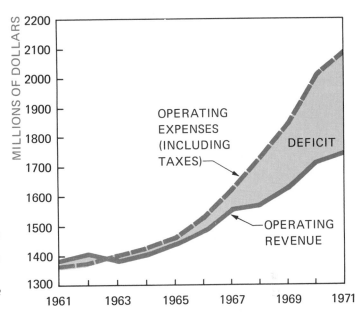

FIGURE 39-4

RESULTS OF TRANSIT OPERATIONS 1961-1971

In the past decade public transit operating expenses have risen much faster than revenues, resulting in larger and larger deficits.

SOURCE: American Transit Association, *1972 Transit Fact Book*, p. 5.

New York, Seattle, and San Francisco. Since that time private transit companies in 16 other major American cities have succumbed to public ownership, and presently there are a dozen more cities taking it under consideration. But public ownership does not solve the financial plight of mass transit companies. Deficits still occur, and in fact sometimes they are deepened if management decides to reduce fares and increase service. Instead of relying on fares to cover costs, however, public transit companies are subsidized with taxpayers' money. This highlights the controversy of whether the user or the general public should pay for public transportation.

Costs of Transportation

Although speed and convenience are essential factors in choosing a means of transportation, cost must also be considered. To many commuters the auto wins over mass transit in all respects. However, the motorist does not always take into account the full cost of his travel. In using a public means of travel the rider on a privately owned transit company bus, for example, has to bear the full user charge for his travel. But when he drives his automobile, some costs of automobile usage are hidden. There are *private costs* which are borne by the motorist himself, and they may be divided into two categories: (1) *Direct costs*, which are costs for such things as gasoline, oil, license fees, and excise taxes; and (2) *indirect costs*, which are costs such as insurance premiums, personal property taxes, and obsolescence. In most cases the motorist calculates the cost of his transportation only in terms of direct costs. He seldom takes into account his indirect costs. There is a considerable difference, however. The average direct cost, exclusive of parking fees, of a motorist traveling in a new or recent model car was estimated to be 3 to 4 cents per mile in 1972. But if all private costs, both direct and indirect, are considered, the average cost of transportation to the motorist was about 12 cents per mile. The cost per person is reduced, of course, if two or more commuters ride in the same automobile. On the other hand, this cost has increased noticeably with the substantial rise in gasoline prices in 1973 and 1974.

If the true cost of automobile travel is to be ascertained, however, one must factor in the *social costs*, which are borne by society as a whole and not directly by the individual motorist. A large number of costs resulting from automobile usage are due to congestion. These include the loss of business and leisure time, fatigue, the cost of accidents, injuries and death, noise and air pollution, solid waste pollution associated with junk autos, the cost of enforcing safety regulations, the cost of traffic direction by the police, and the cost of constructing new roads and highways. While these social costs are recognizable, they are difficult to allocate to individual motorists. If this were possible, however, it would be apparent to the average car owner that he was underestimating his cost of transportation. Even so, many motorists would still prefer the automobile over mass transit because of the speed and convenience of the automobile.

The Role of the Federal Government

Private mass transit companies have difficulty operating in the black without charging high fares and limiting services. In doing so, they are serving fewer and fewer patrons. This especially hurts the lower income groups that must rely on public transportation. On the other hand, when local governments take over a mass transit company, they generally lower fares, improve facilities, and provide more services, while going more into the red. The difference is made up through a subsidy out of tax funds or otherwise. This, of course, heightens the controversy over who should be paying for mass transit, the user or the general public or both. A number of cities in this dilemma have been looking to the federal government for financial assistance in providing mass transit service.

The role of the federal government in constructing highways goes back to 1916, and a number of federal highway acts have been passed since that time. The early acts in general provided federal funds out of general tax revenues to be allocated to the states for the construction, improvement, and repair of interstate, intrastate, and rural roads. The Federal Highway Act of 1956, however, established a highway trust fund. Federal gasoline taxes, taxes on vehicles and tires, and taxes on trucks and buses are deposited into the trust fund. These funds are then available for distribution to various highway projects. Little of these funds has been available, however, to relieve urban congestion and related traffic problems. In fact, it was not until 1964 that the federal government passed any substantial legislation regarding urban mass transportation.

Urban Mass Transportation Act of 1964. According to this Act, the federal government is empowered to finance two thirds of the cost of approved capital expenditures for qualified mass transit companies. Funds can be used for such outlays as land acquisition, parking facilities, buses and other moving equipment, and stations. State and local governments are required to provide the remainder of the funds. If a private mass transit company is on the verge of bankruptcy and the city is in danger of losing its transit services, the federal government may supply 50 percent of the funds necessary for the purchase of a transit company by the city government. Congress appropriated $375 million for implementation of the provisions of the Act.

Urban Mass Transportation Act of 1970. Under this Act Congress provided $3.1 billion to be distributed in loans and grants over a five-year period for mass transit purposes. Whereas the earlier Act provided funds for capital outlays only, a major feature of the 1970 Act was the approval of federal funds to be used to help defray the operating costs of urban mass transit. This dealt more directly with the current problem of many of the transit companies as to how to avoid or make up losses.

Some Pros and Cons. The controversy still exists over the federal government's role in mass transit. Part of the controversy in regard to urban transportation is the argument that has surfaced between those favoring highway development and those favoring the development of mass transit. The highway program has been amply and successfully funded through the highway trust fund. As taxes are paid, they automatically provide income to the trust fund, which can then be distributed for highway projects. On the other hand, there is no automatic source of federal funds for urban transportation. Funding depends on Congressional appropriations, which thus far have been comparatively meager. In 1971, for example, $4.8 billion in federal funds was spent on highway projects. In the same year only $215 million of federal funds was spent for mass transit.

Proponents of mass transit suggest that a more balanced distribution of funds between the highway and urban transportation programs is necessary. Moreover, critics of the present distribution process claim that the uncertainty of federal funds associated with urban transit aggravates the problem. Under such circumstances some local and state governments are reluctant to commit local funds and resources to improve existing systems or provide new mass transit facilities. Consequently, it is argued that a separate trust fund should be established, or a portion of the highway trust fund allocated, for urban transit usage. This argument has been receiving increasing support in the past few years, especially since the highway trust fund has been accumulating surpluses. These surpluses reached $5 billion in 1973. Some progress toward a better balance was made in 1972 when the U.S. Senate agreed that highway trust fund money could be used for rail commuter systems as well as for highways. In 1973 a Congressional bill provided for the distribution of funds out of the highway trust fund for urban transit use. A sum of $1 billion was to be available to purchase buses and to finance rail systems, including subways. In addition to trust fund money, the bill provides $3 billion out of federal general revenues for grants to urban mass transit projects.

Present and Future Progress

Future solutions to the problem of urban transportation will depend on the allocation of funds and resources to the various cities which have such a need. It will depend also on the success of some of the newly established rapid transit systems that have been put into operation in the past few years with the aid of federal funds. Included among these projects is the 11-mile rail rapid transit line connecting downtown Cleveland and intermediate spots with its airport. The 11-mile trip takes 22 minutes. Another project is the rapid transit system connecting downtown Philadelphia with some of its suburbs. This system, called the Lindenwold Line, was constructed in 1969. It is 14.4 miles long, cost $94 million, and so far is considered a successful project.

One of the most comprehensive rapid transit systems to go into operation in recent years is the Bay Area Rapid Transit System (BART). It services three counties in the San Francisco Bay area. The total cost of the project is estimated at $1.2 billion, $80 million of which came from the federal government. The largest part of the funds came from a $792 million bond issue launched by the three counties. It was the largest bond issue ever undertaken for an urban transportation system. The system consists of 75 miles of track, 16 miles of subway tunnels, and a 4-mile tunnel-tube under the San Francisco Bay. The system went into operation in 1972.

Another large-scale system, which commenced operations in 1973, was the Metropolitan Atlanta Regional Transit Authority (MARTA). This system is to cost an estimated $1.4 billion. The federal government is financing two thirds of the cost, while the remainder is coming from a one percentage point increase in the state sales tax. When completed this new rapid transit system, with trains arriving every 90 seconds, is expected to relieve urban traffic congestion in the booming city of Atlanta.

Unfortunately there are relatively few metropolitan areas in the United States that have recently constructed or are in the process of constructing new rapid transit systems, although there are a number in the planning stage. Whether these plans come to fruition will depend in large measure on financing. In this regard it appears that the cities are going to need help from the federal government or elsewhere if they are to get these projects underway and find real solutions to urban traffic congestion.

CRIME IN THE CITIES

An outgrowth of our urban problems is the rising cost of crime. Poverty, slums, lack of educational and recreational facilities, and unemployment

TABLE 39-5   CRIMES AND CRIME RATES BY TYPE, 1960-1972 (In Thousands, Except as Indicated)

Item and Year	Total	Violent Crime					Property Crime			
		Total	Murder and Non-negligent Man-slaughter	Forc-ible Rape	Rob-bery	Aggra-vated Assault	Total	Bur-glary	Larceny, $50 and Over	Auto Theft
Number of Offenses:										
1960	2,020	286	9	17	107	153	1,734	900	507	326
1965	2,937	384	10	23	138	213	2,553	1,266	794	493
1967	3,811	496	12	27	202	254	3,316	1,611	1,049	655
1968	4,477	590	14	31	262	283	3,887	1,835	1,274	778
1969	5,013	657	15	37	297	308	4,357	1,956	1,528	872
1970	5,581	733	16	38	348	331	4,848	2,177	1,750	922
1971	5,995	810	18	42	386	365	5,185	2,368	1,875	942
1972	5,892	828	19	46	375	389	5,064	2,345	1,838	881
1960-1970, percent increase	176	156	78	124	225	116	180	142	245	183
Average annual percent increase	11	10	6	8	13	8	11	9	13	11
1970-1972, percent increase	6	13	17	23	8	17	4	8	5	−4
Rate per 100,000 Inhabitants:										
1960	1,126	160	5	10	60	85	967	502	283	182
1965	1,516	198	5	12	71	110	1,317	653	410	255
1967	1,926	251	6	14	102	129	1,676	814	530	331
1968	2,240	295	7	16	131	142	1,945	918	637	389
1969	2,483	325	7	18	147	152	2,158	969	757	432
1970	2,747	361	8	19	171	163	2,386	1,071	861	454
1971	2,907	393	9	20	187	177	2,514	1,148	909	457
1972	2,830	398	9	22	180	187	2,432	1,126	883	423
1960-1970, percent increase	144	126	60	90	186	92	147	113	204	150
Average annual percent increase	9	9	5	7	11	7	10	8	12	10
1970-1972, percent increase	3	10	14	21	5	14	2	5	2	−7

SOURCE: *Statistical Abstract of the United States,* 1973.

General Note: Data refer to offenses known to police. Rates based on Bureau of the Census population data, excluding armed forces abroad.

often breed delinquency and crime. The suburbs, however, are not without their problems in this respect. Not only is growing crime in urban centers a terrible social problem, but it is a serious economic problem. The economic loss to individuals and businesses resulting from theft and property damage is enormous, the cost of insurance is rising at a quickening pace, and the financial outlays of individuals, institutions, and businesses for security and protection have skyrocketed. Governmental units have substantially increased their outlays for the protection of their citizens. The cost of this crime naturally diverts money, resources, and manpower away from legitimate economic activity which could enhance our level of living.

Rise in Crime

It may seem a bit incongruous, but crime increases with the growing affluence of our nation. Table 39-5 shows that the incidence of crime increased by 11 percent annually in the decade 1960-1970, while the crime rate incidence per 100,000 population increased at an annual rate of 9 percent. The figures are similar for both violent crime and crime against property. Although one would expect more crime to occur in urban areas, because that is where the people and property are, the urban areas have a

TABLE 39-6   CRIME RATES BY POPULATION GROUPS, 1971

Item	Total	Violent Crime					Property Crime			
		Total	Mur-der	Forc-ible Rape	Rob-bery	Aggra-vated Assault	Total	Bur-glary—Break-ing or Enter-ing	Lar-ceny—Theft [1] (Except Auto Theft)	Auto Theft
Population Group										
Total, 7,011 Agencies ..	[1] 4,433	422	8.8	21	209	183	4,006	1,229	2,277	500
Total, 4,958 Cities	[2] 5,394	539	10.3	25	284	220	4,852	1,432	2,776	644
57 Cities, 250,000 or More	7,188	1,047	19.2	44	633	351	6,135	2,026	3,010	1,099
98 Cities, 100,000-249,999	6,429	503	10.8	27	226	240	5,921	1,790	3,392	739
260 Cities, 50,000-99,999	5,001	300	5.9	17	126	151	4,699	1,243	2,956	499
509 Cities, 25,000-49,999	4,331	243	4.8	12	95	131	4,085	1,042	2,646	397
1,224 Cities, 10,000-24,999	3,687	188	3.9	10	51	123	3,497	880	2,366	251
2,810 Cities, Less Than 10,000	2,954	171	3.5	8	31	128	2,782	722	1,887	173
Suburbs, 2,795 Agencies [3]	3,492	206	4.2	14	70	117	3,283	975	2,003	306
Rural Areas, 1,667 Agencies ...	1,388	116	5.9	11	15	85	1,266	532	658	77

SOURCE: *Statistical Abstract of the United States*, 1973.

[1] Population group data include and selected city data exclude larceny under $50.
[2] Includes manslaughter by negligence, not shown separately.
[3] Agencies represented in surburban areas are also included in other city groups.
General Note: Data refer to offenses known to the police per 100,000 population.

much greater *rate of crime* than nonurban areas. In 1972, for example, the FBI Crime Index showed that in standard metropolitan statistical areas (SMSAs) the violent crime rate was 3.5 times as great as the crime rate in nonurban areas. Moreover, the crime rate in smaller cities was about half the rate in SMSAs. Furthermore, crime is more apt to occur in large congested urban areas, as indicated in Table 39-6, which shows a higher rate of crime associated with larger urban areas. Verifying this, Table 39-7 shows the rates of crime for selected cities. Note the high crime rates in such large cities as Detroit, San Francisco, Washington, New York, Los Angeles, and Cleveland.

TABLE 39-7

CRIME RATES BY SELECTED CITIES

1971

Selected Cities		Selected Cities	
Detroit	8,373	Houston	4,757
San Francisco	8,228	San Antonio	4,021
Washington	6,917	Chicago	3,779
New York	6,729	San Diego	3,606
Los Angeles	6,511	Indianapolis	3,053
Cleveland	6,232	Philadelphia	3,043
Baltimore	5,960	Milwaukee	3,031
Dallas	5,460		

SOURCE: *Statistical Abstract of the United States,* 1973.

General Note: Data refer to offenses known to police per 100,000 population.

Civil disorder, too, has disturbed the peace of those living in the cities more so than in rural areas. Civil disorder not only has caused the loss of life, but it has resulted in the destruction of property and the loss of income as stores and factories have closed and workers have stayed away from their jobs. As a sociological sidelight, there is more of a tendency for disturbances to take place in the warmer months of the year, although civil disturbances in general have tapered off in the past few years. A survey of 20 cities in which civil disorders took place in 1967 indicated that poor housing, unemployment, police practices, inadequate education, and poor recreational facilities were the most frequent causes of civil disorder. This is shown in Table 39-8.

Cost of Crime

Much of the cost of crime is hidden, but sufficient data are available to indicate some of its cost. Table 39-9 shows the known cost of crime in 1965 to be about $21 billion annually. Making allowances for higher prices only, the cost of crime today exceeds $30 billion annually. An additional

TABLE 39-8

Grievance Category	Cities [1]	Points	Grievance Category	Cities [1]	Points
Police Practices	14	45.5	Disrespectful White Attitudes	4	6.5
Unemployment, Underemployment	17	42.0	Discriminatory Admin. of Justice	3	4.5
Inadequate Housing	14	36.0	Inadequate Federal Programs	1	2.5
Inadequate Education ..	9	21.0	Inadequate Municipal Services	1	2.0
Poor Recreation Facilities	8	21.0	Discriminatory Consumer and Credit Practices .	2	2.0
Ineffective Political Structure and Grievance Mechanisms	5	14.0			

SOURCE: The National Advisory Commission on Civil Disorders, *Report* (March, 1968).

[1] Where grievances were mentioned as significant.
General Note: Data are based on surveys made in 20 cities where civil disorders occurred. Grievances evaluated as to significance in each city and rank and points assigned to the 4 most serious, as follows: 4 points for 1st place, 3 for 2d, 2 for 3d, and 1 for 4th. Total points for each grievance category represents number of cities in which it was ranked among the top 4 multiplied by the number of points. Thus, a 4-point grievance assigned to 2 cities amounted to 8 points. Judgments of severity based on frequency of mention of a particular grievance, relative intensity with which it was discussed, references to incidents exemplifying it, and estimates of severity.

TABLE 39-9

ECONOMIC COST
OF CRIME BY
COMPONENTS
OF COST

1965

(In Millions of
Dollars)

Component	Cost	Component	Cost
Total	20,980	Illegal Goods and Services	8,075
		Gambling	7,000
Crimes against Person [1]	815	Narcotics	350
Homicide	750	Loansharking	350
Assault and Other	65	Prostitution	225
Crimes against Property [2]	3,932	Alcohol	150
Commercial Theft Unreported .	1,400	Enforcement and Justice	4,212
Fraud	1,350	Police	2,792
Robbery, Burglary, Larceny,[3]		Corrections	1,034
Auto Theft	600	Courts	261
Embezzlement	200	Prosecution and Defense	125
Forgery and Other	82	Private Costs Related to Crime ..	1,910
Arson and Vandalism	300	Prevention Services	1,350
Other Crimes	2,036	Insurance	300
Driving While Intoxicated	1,816	Prevention Equipment	200
Abortion	120	Counsel, Bail, Witness Expenses	60
Tax Fraud	100		

SOURCE: Executive Office of the President, The President's Commission on Law Enforcement and Administration of Justice, *The Challenge of Crime in a Free Society*, 1967.

[1] Loss of earnings, etc.
[2] Transfers and losses.
[3] $50 and over.

cost has to be added due to the higher amount of crime. The cost of crime against persons is measured in loss of earnings, while crime against property is measured in actual losses by burglary, theft, embezzlement, and the like. The cost of illegal services is measured by gambling and other losses. The price of law enforcement and crime prevention is also included in the total cost of crime. Included, too, are the costs to individuals and businesses to secure themselves against crime. Table 39-10 shows losses to business due to crime.

TABLE 39-10

BUSINESS LOSSES DUE TO CRIME, BY TYPE OF CRIME

1967-1968

Type of Crime	Total (Millions of Dollars)	Percent
Total	3,049	100
Burglary	958	31
Robbery	77	3
Vandalism	813	27
Shoplifting	504	17
Employee Theft	381	12
Bad Checks	316	10

SOURCE: U.S. Small Business Administration, *Crime Against Small Business*, Senate Document 91-14, 1969.

General Note: Data are based on interviews with a sample of businesses filing business tax returns with Internal Revenue Service in 1966 for 1965. Interviews conducted during May-July, 1968, covering losses during preceding 12 months.

The cost of fighting crime, which is borne primarily by local governments, increased threefold between 1960 and 1971. Expenditures for police services, courts, and penal institutions rose from $3.5 billion to $10.1 billion during that period. That amounted to $49 per capita in 1971. Figure 39-5 shows that local governments paid nearly two thirds of this cost. Some help has come to state and local governments in recent years through the federal

FIGURE 39-5

EXPENDITURES FOR POLICE SERVICE, COURTS, AND PRISONS (Estimate for Year Ended June 30, 1971)

Local governments pay most of the bill for police and related services, but federal grants for these services have been getting larger.

SOURCE: *U.S. News & World Report* (June 5, 1972).

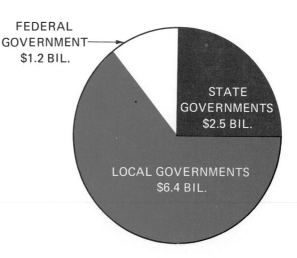

FEDERAL GOVERNMENT $1.2 BIL.

STATE GOVERNMENTS $2.5 BIL.

LOCAL GOVERNMENTS $6.4 BIL.

Law Enforcement Assistance Administration (LEAA). This aid was increased by a sizable amount in the late 1960s and early 1970s and now is approximately $700 million annually. The federal government, too, is spending about $2 billion annually for various crime reduction programs.

In spite of the application of more funds and resources to prevent and fight crime, it continues to grow and plague many citizens. In 1972 nearly 6 million people were victimized by crime of one type or another, while at the same time over 6.5 million individuals were arrested for committing crime. During that year about 19,000 people were murdered, 22,000 committed suicide, nearly 2.4 million homes and businesses were burglarized, about 2 million persons were victims of larceny, 881,000 owners lost their cars as a result of theft, 389,000 persons were assaulted, and 46,000 were forcibly raped.

In addition to the threat of organized crime, urban dwellers and businesses are menaced by nonorganized crime as well. In sections of some large cities, the crime rate is so high that people are afraid to walk the streets at night; they need special security for their homes and apartments; automobiles must be locked and protected; mugging has become commonplace; and even taxicabs hesitate to make pickups and deliveries there. In the cities, too, vandalism is rampant, shoplifting has reached a serious level, and burglary occurs frequently. Also, narcotics traffic has infiltrated not only the central city and the slum areas but posh suburbs as well.

As crime increases, the direct losses to individuals and businesses rise, and the cost of crime prevention and law enforcement likewise increases. At present 3 percent of total state and local direct expenditures are for police protection. This is money that could be spent for other goods and services if crime were not so prevalent.

FEDERAL AID TO URBAN AREAS

Housing and urban renewal, urban transportation, crime in the cities—these are only three of the several major problems faced by urban governments. Unfortunately these and other acute problems will likely get worse before they get better. Furthermore, the cities will become more directly involved in these and other issues in the future. State and local government spending on goods and services, exclusive of transfer payments, has been increasing at a faster rate than federal spending in the past few decades, as shown in Table 39-11.

In addition, it is estimated that in the 15-year period, 1970 to 1985, state and local spending will increase by 92 percent compared to a 28 percent increase in federal spending for goods and services. It is anticipated,

TABLE 39-11

STATE AND LOCAL VS. FEDERAL SPENDING

1950-1973

(In Billions of Dollars)

Year	Total	Federal	Percentage Increase (Federal)	State & Local	Percentage Increase (State & Local)
1950	$ 37.9	$ 18.4	—	$ 19.5	—
1955	74.2	44.1	140	30.1	54
1960	99.6	53.5	21	46.1	53
1965	137.0	66.9	25	70.1	52
1970	219.5	96.2	44	123.3	76
1973	277.2	106.9	11	170.3	38

SOURCE: *Economic Report of the President*, 1974.

FIGURE 39-6

FEDERAL AID TO URBAN AREAS

In 13 years the federal government will have spent more than $160 billion to help metropolitan areas and their residents. That figure does not include some federal programs that provide funds directly to people, such as federal pay, Social Security, and veterans' benefits.

SOURCE: "After $160 Billion to Rescue Cities—," *U.S. News & World Report* (April 10, 1972).

* Not available.

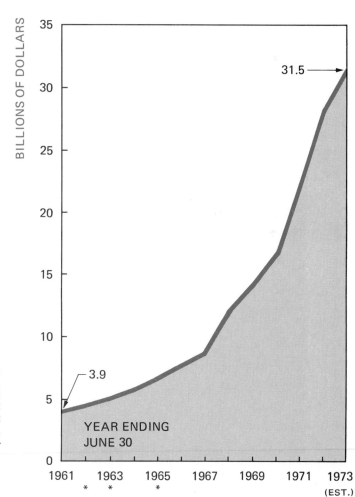

BILLIONS OF DOLLARS

31.5

3.9

YEAR ENDING JUNE 30

1961   1963   1965   1967   1969   1971   1973
       *   *   *   (EST.)

however, that a good portion of the funds for urban spending will come from the federal government in the form of grants, loans, and shared revenue. The trend in this direction is obvious from Figure 39-6, which shows a seven-fold increase in federal aid to urban areas during the period 1961-1973.

At one time some authorities questioned whether the federal government should be involved in local problems, such as housing, transportation, unemployment, crime, and pollution, but the controversy today has gone far beyond that stage. It appears that federal help in solving urban problems is an accepted practice. The controversy today is rather over how much help the federal government is going to render.

SUMMARY

1. Three major urban economic problems were considered in this chapter: housing and urban renewal, mass transit, and crime. These problems become more acute as people migrate from rural to urban areas, and these problems are increased by the movement of people from the central cities to the suburbs within the urban areas.

2. With housing and urban renewal there is a two-fold problem. The first is to provide adequate housing for the urban population, particularly for the middle and lower income groups. The second is to eliminate the slums and blighted areas and to restore or renew the economic health of the central cities, which are being abandoned in large measure by higher income groups and prosperous businesses. Since the private sector of the economy has been slow to resolve these problems, more reliance is being placed on the local governments to do so.

3. Local governments, as a result of limited revenues and resources, have in turn looked to the federal government for aid in this and other urban matters. Consequently, a series of housing and urban renewal acts have provided financial help for housing and urban renewal. There is still a controversy, however, regarding the extent to which the federal government should go in this matter.

4. The increasing reliance of urbanites on the automobile for transportation and the decline in the use of mass transit facilities have created a problem of congestion and have resulted in a decline of patronage and profits for mass transit companies.

5. In seeking a solution to the problem of congestion, a number of schemes have been adopted in various cities throughout the nation. But the problem has not been eradicated as yet. As a result of declining profits, more and more privately owned public transit companies are being converted to government ownership.

6. Although this does not solve the problem, fares are generally reduced and patronage increased when the local government takes over a transit company. However, losses are many times magnified and then subsidized out of general revenues. In recent years more federal funds have been made available for the improvement of mass transit in our cities. Advocates of mass

transit suggest, however, that a trust fund should be established, similar to the highway trust fund, for financing improvements in urban mass transit operations. Gasoline shortages in 1973 and 1974 accelerated public interest in mass transit.

7. A third urban problem is crime. Although crime is not limited to the cities, the amount of crime and the rate of crime in urban areas is substantially greater than that occurring in rural areas. Furthermore, the larger cities tend to have greater crime rates than middle-sized and smaller cities. The total known cost of crime has been increasing rapidly in the past decade or more, and it is now more than $30 billion annually. Approximately two thirds of the cost for law enforcement and the prevention of crime is borne by the cities.

8. Since the tax revenues and resources of the cities are limited compared to the funds needed to solve their many urban problems, the federal government has been responding by allocating more funds to the urban areas in order to help them solve some of their growing socioeconomic problems.

NEW TERMS

Central city, *p. 852*
Urban renewal, *p. 853*
Neighborhood effect, *p. 854*
Federal Housing Administration (FHA), *p. 856*
Federal National Mortgage Association (Fannie Mae), *p. 856*
Community Renewal Programs (CRPs), *p. 856*
Department of Housing and Urban Development (HUD), *p. 856*
Model Cities Program, *p. 856*
Uniform Relocation Assistance and Land Acquisition Policies Act, *p. 856*

Berman v. Parker, *p. 860*
Urban transportation, *p. 860*
Mass transit, *p. 861*
Private costs of transportation, *p. 865*
Direct costs of transportation, *p. 865*
Indirect costs of transportation, *p. 865*
Social costs of transportation, *p. 866*
Federal Highway Act of 1956, *p. 866*
Urban Mass Transportation Act of 1964, *p. 867*
Urban Mass Transportation Act of 1970, *p. 867*
Rate of crime, *p. 871*

QUESTIONS FOR DISCUSSION AND ANALYSIS

1. Do you think the federal government should be providing funds to cities for housing and urban renewal? Why or why not?

2. How does urban renewal affect the tax base and tax revenues of the central cities?

3. Should businesses forced to close down due to displacement by urban renewal be compensated for their losses by the government? If so, to what extent and for how long?

4. Should automobiles be banned from entering the downtown district, as they are in some cities? Why or why not?

5. Do you think that the public mass transit system should be privately owned or owned by the city government? Explain.

6. Whether privately or city owned,

should the public transit company be subsidized out of tax revenues?

7. Should the federal government set up a mass transit trust fund similar to the highway trust fund? Why or why not?

8. Should cities or other governmental units put a limit on the size of cars to be permitted in congested areas?

9. Do you prefer rent subsidies or public housing to provide housing for the poor? Explain.

10. What interdependent factors cause crime rates to be higher in urban areas compared to rural areas?

11. There is a bill pending in Congress that would compensate those that are victimized by crime. Do you favor the passage of such a bill? Why or why not?

SUGGESTED READINGS

"After $160 Billion to Rescue Cities—." *U. S. News & World Report* (April 10, 1972).

Alexander, D. G. "Livable Cities." *Current History*, Vol. LIX (August, 1970), pp. 85-90.

"Billions for Urban Renewal but Not Enough to Go Around." *U. S. News & World Report* (April 20, 1970), pp. 27 and 28.

"Hard Times for Public Housing." *U. S. News & World Report* (March 20, 1973).

Leinwand, Gerold. *The Traffic Jam.* New York: Washington Square Press, 1969.

Luna, Charles. *The Handbook of Transportation in America.* New York: Popular Library, 1972.

Rockefeller, David. "What It Will Take to Bring Cities Back to Life." *U. S. News & World Report* (June 7, 1971), pp. 50-52.

Smith, Fred. *Man and His Urban Environment.* New York: Man and His Urban Environment Project (November, 1972).

"Staving Off Auto Paralysis." *Business Week* (February 28, 1970), pp. 54-56.

U.S. Department of Housing and Urban Development. *Benefit-Cost Applications in Urban Renewal: Summary of the Feasibility Study.* Washington: U.S. Government Printing Office, 1968.

Walters, A. A. *The Economics of Road User Charges.* Baltimore: The Johns Hopkins University Press, 1968.

"When Traffic Jams Stall the Nation." *Business Week* (December 6, 1969), pp. 186 and 187.

Williams, Ernest W., Jr. *Future of American Transportation.* Englewood Cliffs, N.J.: Prentice-Hall, Inc., 1971.

"Winning the War Against Organized Crime." *U. S. News & World Report* (June 5, 1972).

Yandle, B. "Urban Renewal: The Precondition for Take-Off." *Land Economics*, Vol. XLVI (November, 1970), pp. 484-486.

40

The Struggle Against Poverty

PREVIEW Early efforts to alleviate the effects of poverty took the form of federal Social Security legislation, coupled with public assistance (welfare) programs by the various states. In recent years, Social Security benefits have been expanded, especially in the area of health care. Today, two major weapons against poverty are under consideration: national health security, in the form of a comprehensive government-sponsored health insurance plan, and a guaranteed annual income for every family in the nation.

In the spring of 1968, representatives of the Poor People's Campaign converged upon the nation's capital and built Resurrection City near the Washington Monument. Their purpose was to bring to the attention of Congress in a dramatic way the plight of the poor. The United States is the wealthiest nation in the world. Yet, as we have seen previously, between 12 and 21 percent of the population lives in poverty, depending upon the definition of a poverty-level income. Nine percent of American families have annual incomes below $3,000, while 14 percent of all families have incomes below $4,000 per year.

Over the years, a number of public programs have been devised to help reduce the incidence of poverty. Most attempt to supplement meager family incomes or to expand opportunities for the poor to increase their productivity and their earnings. Now pending are proposals for more comprehensive attacks on poverty. Before analyzing these proposals, however, it is necessary that the nature and incidence of poverty be understood.

ECONOMIC INSECURITY

Whatever may destroy or reduce one's wealth or income is a source of *economic insecurity*. Likewise, whatever may deprive one of opportunities to earn income and to accumulate wealth is a source of economic insecurity. For example, suppose you are employed and paid a certain monthly salary. You cannot be absolutely certain that your salary will not be cut or that you will not be discharged for one reason or another. Those who are accustomed to an income from investments in corporate stocks may find that their dividends shrink drastically or cease entirely. If you live long enough, you will eventually become too old to work, at which time your salary or wage payments will cease. These are but a few of the reasons why future income is highly uncertain.

In addition to the risk of losing what one has, there is insecurity arising from a possible denial of opportunities to earn an adequate income. Some young people have had benefits from childhood that prepare them well for earning a good livelihood. Others, for reasons beyond their personal control, have not enjoyed these benefits. A man entering the labor force with very little education and no acquired skills cannot usually find employment in other than low-paying jobs. In an economy of increasing technological complexity and more sophisticated labor requirements, jobs for which he can qualify may be declining on a relative basis. When jobs do arise, some employers may discriminate against certain applicants because of race, sex, religion, or age. For these reasons also, future income is highly uncertain.

Social Security

People can never be made completely secure in the sense that future income can be guaranteed. The world in which we live is a world of uncertainty; we cannot predict the future. Therefore, *social security* is not the removal of all economic insecurity. Social security is any means of *protection against* loss, reduction, or deprivation of wealth or income by methods that do not result in net monetary profits to any private firm or organization. One of the most important functions of an economic system is to provide opportunities for individuals to achieve a reasonable degree of economic security. The degree of security that is "reasonable" is debatable. But the same is true of many other things we take for granted, such as personal freedom.

In practice, efforts to achieve economic security through social policy are identical with efforts to insure continuity of a minimum income. Two aspects of policy are involved. The first is insurance against a permanent situation of a poverty level of living. The second is guarding against interruptions of income because of illness, layoffs, or old age. If even a smaller flow of income can be assured during periods when income would otherwise cease, some degree of security will be experienced.

Causes of Insecurity

What are the causes of economic insecurity? There are two causes: (1) unemployment and (2) weak earning power while employed. However, these are only symptoms in a sense, because there are a variety of reasons why a person finds himself unemployed or why he must accept low wages or chronic unemployment.

During a depression there is widespread unemployment, and one remedy is the vigorous pursuit of monetary and fiscal policies to promote stimulation of general business activity. Stabilization policies have already been discussed in Part Four. Sometimes unemployment is structural rather than cyclical. A particular industry or region may be declining relative to the rest of the economy. Consequently, localized pockets of unemployment appear.

Because they have been examined elsewhere in the book, we shall not discuss in this chapter either cyclical or structural unemployment. These types of unemployment affect all labor in the economy or a sector of the economy. Rather, emphasis will be placed upon unemployment and low income that arise from characteristics of the worker. These causes of economic insecurity will persist even when the economy (or a sector of the economy) is not depressed. The characteristics of workers can be classified in many ways: age, sex, color, educational attainment, geographic location, and so on. Age is probably the most useful point of departure because social policies and legislation have had at least an indirect focus upon different age groups.

INCOME AND AGE

The distribution of income by age shows that the lowest incomes are found among those in the full-time labor force 20 years of age or less and among those in the population 60 years of age and over. When classified by age, it is the oldest members of the population and the youngest members entering the full-time labor force who experience the most difficult income and employment problems. Moreover, a comparison of their incomes today relative to the average income in 1950, 1960, and 1970 shows that their incomes have declined. The income and employment problems of the very young and the very old are becoming more pronounced over time.

Low Incomes Among the Young

A *relatively* low income for the youngest members of the labor force is to be expected. Only after a worker has been in the labor force for some time does he acquire the experience to warrant wage increases, receive promotions, and gain seniority rights. In addition, new workers on a job are likely to be the first to be laid off when a slowdown in production occurs and the last to be rehired when activity picks up again. The layoff period contributes to relatively low annual earnings.

Nevertheless, those active in the full-time labor force at age 18 or less contribute most to the low-income figure for the 20-or-less age group. These are the elementary school or high school dropouts. When competing for jobs with those who have completed secondary school or further education, they are at a disadvantage. With less education or vocational training, they are forced to accept the lowest paying jobs.

The primary solution to the problem of poverty among the young appears to be in social programs that promote education and training. Recognition of the problem and efforts to combat the waste of manpower resources as well as the personal deprivation were incorporated in the Area Redevelopment Act (1961), the Manpower Development and Training Act (1962), and the Economic Opportunity Act of 1964. Operation Head Start and Operation Follow Thru, the Job Corps, and the Neighborhood Youth Corps seek to eliminate the causes of unemployment and low income. At the elementary school level, students with culturally and economically deprived backgrounds receive special tutoring. Study habits and the value of learning are stressed. The Job Corps attempts to develop skills, to promote steady work habits, and to instill respect for a job well done. Community Action agencies and neighborhood health centers promote hygiene, preventive medicine, and proper diet.

In the absence of programs to educate and train more of the young, their income and employment problems are carried through life and become even more severe in old age. To the extent that efforts to extend and improve education are successful, not only will the incidence of poverty among the young be reduced but the incidence of poverty among the aged of the future also will be reduced.

The Intermediate Age Group

Among those between 25 and 60 years of age, residence in a so-called depressed area appears to be an important factor in a person's receiving a low income. It was noted in Chapter 36 that geographic mobility declines with greater age. Workers between 40 and 60 years of age are much more reluctant than those below 40 to move out of depressed areas. They tend to remain even when they can earn only half the income they could earn elsewhere.

Aside from the immobility of those who reside in depressed areas, work interruption creates income and employment problems for the intermediate age group. However, in the aggregate this age group fares much better than the youngest members of the labor force. In turn, the young are in a better relative income and employment position than older and aged workers.

Problems of the Older Worker

The later years of life have been called the golden years. However, for many these years are filled with financial anxiety. Of all age groups, those 60 years of age and over exhibit the lowest incomes.

There is evidence that as a worker ages he becomes less productive. Experience may count to his advantage in competition with younger workers. Nevertheless, with some notable exceptions older workers are less adaptable to changing technology entailing new techniques of production. As a rule the older worker is less mobile across occupations as well as across geographic regions. When opportunities for higher income occur, he is less likely than his younger counterpart to take advantage of them.

These factors contribute somewhat to low income among older workers. The single most important factor, however, is nonparticipation in the labor force. A relatively high rate of nonparticipation begins around 50 years of age and grows progressively with age thereafter. If nonparticipation were voluntary retirement with sufficient income from a pension and savings, there would be no economic problem. The data indicate that this is not so. The highest rates of nonparticipation occur in the lowest paying occupations, and income from all sources for the nonparticipants is the lowest in the age group itself. This suggests that nonparticipation in the labor force is involuntary for a great many older workers. Due to the lack of employment opportunities that offer an adequate income, the older worker may decide to "retire" in discouragement.

Since for many decades the incidence of poverty has been greatest among the oldest members of the population, legislation and social security programs have been directed primarily toward this age group. Any economic insecurity to which the young and intermediate age groups are subject is carried forward into old age, where they are compounded by problems peculiar to old age itself.

THE NATURE AND EXTENT OF POVERTY

Before his death in 1963, President Kennedy became concerned about the number of families in our economy that were living on substandard incomes. As a result, he directed his Council of Economic Advisers to undertake a study of poverty in the United States. Although he did not live to see its fruition, the study served as a basis for designing the war-on-poverty program instituted by passage of the Economic Opportunity Act in August, 1964. The findings of the Council of Economic Advisers is contained in large part in the 1964 *Economic Report of the President.*

The Poverty Level

Realizing that the measurement of poverty is not simple, the *Economic Report* defined poor as "those who are not now maintaining a decent standard of living" or those whose basic needs exceed their means to satisfy them. Since the needs of various families differ and since there is no precise way of determining the number of families that have insufficient resources to meet their particular needs, the *Report* utilized what, by consensus, was thought to be a minimum acceptable level of living for an American family. It considered the "low-cost" budget publicized by the Social Security Administration for a nonfarm family of four that cost $3,955 in 1962, "the economy plan" of that budget, which was $3,165, and other studies. In the final analysis the *Report* established $3,000 (before taxes and expressed in 1962 prices) as the line of demarcation between poverty and nonpoverty.

This $3,000 annual or $60 weekly budget for a four-person family assumed expenditures of one third, or about $5 per person per week for food, $67 monthly for rent, and the remaining $25 a week for clothing, transportation, house furnishings, medical and personal care, insurance, recreation, and other items. Any person with no family who had an income of less than $1,500 per year was also considered in the poverty classification.

Incidence of Poverty

The President's *Report* indicated that of the 47 million families in the United States in 1962, one fifth of these families, comprising more than 30 million persons, had money incomes below $3,000 per year. Of these, 5.4 million families, containing more than 17 million persons, had incomes below $2,000 per year. Furthermore, more than one million children were being raised in very large families, 6 or more children, with incomes of less than $2,000 annually. In addition to these families, 5 million "unrelated individuals" (persons with no family) had incomes below the $1,500 level. Thus, nearly one fifth of our total 186.6 million population in 1962 was poverty-stricken.

Among other characteristics of the poor, the *Report* indicated the following:

1. Twenty-two percent of the poor are nonwhite, and nearly one half of all nonwhites live in poverty.
2. Over 60 percent of the heads of poor families have only a grade school education.
3. Of all nonwhite faciles headed by persons with eight years or less of education, 57 percent are poor. But this percentage falls to 30 percent for those with a high school education and to 18 percent for those with some college education.
4. When nonwhites are compared with whites at the same level of education, the nonwhites are poor twice as often.
5. One third of all poor families are headed by a person over 65 years of age, and almost one half of all families headed by a person 65 or over are poor.

6. Of the total families in poverty, 54 percent are urban dwellers, 16 percent live on farms, and 30 percent are rural nonfarm residents.

7. Over 40 percent of all farm families are poor, and more than 80 percent of nonwhite farmers live in poverty.

8. Although less than one half of the poor are in the South, a Southerner's chance of being poor is twice as great as that of a person living elsewhere in the country.

9. One quarter of the poor families are headed by a woman, and nearly one half of all families with a female head are poor.

10. A family headed by a young woman who is nonwhite and has less than an eighth grade education is poor in 94 out of 100 cases. Even if she is white, the chances are 85 percent that the family will be poor.

In summary the *Report* indicated a heavy concentration of poverty among the nonwhites, the poorly educated, the elderly, rural dwellers, Southerners, and families headed by women. Because of the seriousness of the poverty situation, Congress in August, 1964, passed the Economic Opportunity Act, frequently known as the antipoverty bill. This Act provided $962 million to launch the war on poverty, and from 1964 to 1973 a total of $15 billion had been expended under this program.

Developments in the Seventies

Of the $15 billion appropriated for antipoverty efforts from 1964 through 1973, nearly $12 billion has been dispensed by the Office of Economic Opportunity (OEO). Rather than specifying a single, centralized program, the antipoverty legislation encompassed a variety of projects coordinated through OEO. These have included the Job Corps, the Neighborhood Youth Corps, Community Action, Operation Head Start and Operation Follow Thru, Legal Services for the Poor, National Health Centers, programs for Indians and for migrant and seasonal workers, and VISTA. Each project or agency has attacked one or more causes of poverty or conditions associated with poverty, such as health standards, education, family planning, and community facilities.

Diminishing Incidence of Poverty. Since 1964 the number of those officially defined as poverty-stricken has declined considerably. Figure 40-1 traces the trend in numbers of people living in poverty as defined by a poverty-level income of $3,000 per year for a family and $1,500 per year for an unrelated individual. It can be seen at a glance that the number of Americans in poverty declined from about 36 million in 1964 (the year

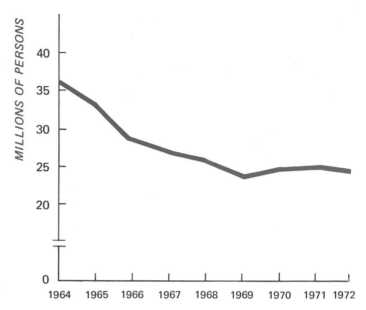

FIGURE 40-1

NUMBER OF PEOPLE LIVING IN POVERTY, AS DEFINED BY THE FEDERAL GOVERNMENT

The number of Americans defined by the federal government as living in poverty decreased from approximately 36 million in 1964 to less than 25 million in 1972.

SOURCE: U.S. Bureau of the Census, "Current Population Reports," Series P-23.

of the Economic Opportunity Act) to slightly more than 24 million in 1969. By 1971 the number had increased to 25.6 million, but dropped again in 1972 to 24.5 million, which is 32 percent less than the number in 1964.

However, as we know, the period 1964 to 1972 was marked by steady inflation. Even as money incomes rose, the purchasing power of each dollar of income diminished. As mentioned in Chapter 37, few economists believe that a $3,000 family income is adequate as a measure of poverty today. Also, absolute numbers do not tell us what proportion of the population lives under conditions of poverty.

Table 40-1, therefore, identifies the trend of low-income families and unrelated individuals in dollars of constant (1972) purchasing power. Moreover, those having low incomes are expressed as percentages of U.S. totals. The percentage of white families with real incomes below $3,000 has declined consistently from 18.5 percent in 1950 to 5.9 percent in 1972. Likewise, the fraction of nonwhite families with real incomes below $3,000 fell from almost half in 1950 to less than one fifth in 1972. Unrelated individuals with incomes below $1,500 show the same trend: poor whites were down from 41.8 percent to 16.6 percent, and poor nonwhites declined from 52 percent to about 27 percent.

If the poverty limit were to be changed to a real income of $5,000 for a family and $3,000 for an unattached individual, reduction in the incidence of poverty would still be evident. As Table 40-1 shows, the percentage of families and individuals living in poverty by this definition declined over the 22-year period 1950-1972. The percentage of poverty-stricken white families fell from 37.2 to 14.5, while the percentage of nonwhite families dropped from 74.1 to 35.2. Unrelated individuals living in poverty by this definition decreased from 61.4 percent to about 42 percent in the case of whites, and from more than 74 percent to less than 54 percent in the case of nonwhites.

TABLE 40-1

PERCENT OF HOUSEHOLD UNITS IN A LOW-INCOME CATEGORY, IN CONSTANT (1972) DOLLARS

Family Incomes Below $3,000 and Individual Incomes Below $1,500					
	1950	1955	1960	1965	1972
White					
Families	18.5	14.7	12.0	9.1	5.9
Unrelated Individuals	41.8	38.4	32.9	25.6	16.6
Nonwhite					
Families	46.2	38.3	33.7	24.8	17.7
Unrelated Individuals	52.0	51.2	49.8	35.2	26.9

Family Incomes Below $5,000 and Individual Incomes Below $3,000					
	1950	1955	1960	1965	1972
White					
Families	37.2	28.7	23.9	19.2	14.5
Unrelated Individuals	61.4	59.4	53.9	50.1	42.4
Nonwhite					
Families	74.1	61.4	54.5	47.0	35.2
Unrelated Individuals	74.4	74.6	68.3	61.0	53.7

SOURCE: U.S. Bureau of the Census, "Current Population Reports," Series P-60 (December, 1973).

Some have argued vigorously that antipoverty programs have been instrumental in reducing the incidence of poverty. Others have argued with equal vigor that the smaller number and percentage of Americans who live in poverty can be attributed principally to the growth of the economy and to rising general prosperity since World War II, especially during the 1960s. Critics representing the Nixon Administration go even further, however, in claiming that projects sponsored by the Economic Opportunity Act have been wasteful and inefficient and that the results are not worth the costs.

A New Strategy. In his budget for the 1974 year (July 1, 1973, to June 30, 1974), President Nixon requested from Congress a zero appropriation of money for the Office of Economic Opportunity. In effect, he proposed to dismantle the entire office. Many of OEO's projects would be transferred to other federal agencies and continued, some at higher funding levels but most at reduced funding. The Job Corps had already been spun off in 1969 to the Department of Labor, and then it had been trimmed down financially.

The Neighborhood Youth Corps had also been assigned to the Labor Department with only some projects continued. Operation Head Start and nutrition programs were reassigned to HEW in 1971, and in the same year VISTA was incorporated into ACTION (a new comprehensive agency for all voluntary services). As of 1974, President Nixon proposed, in effect, that all remaining functions of OEO be delegated to other agencies or be phased out.

The largest OEO program to be phased out is the network of Community Action agencies. In mid-1973 there were 907 local agencies employing more than 180,000 people, entailing a federal expenditure of $1.2 billion. Local and state governments, left to finance these efforts if they approve of them, might have fallen back on the new federal program of revenue sharing. However, in specifying the uses of federal funds derived from revenue sharing, Congress excluded education and welfare and put a ceiling of $2.5 billion on grants for social services. Therefore, local governments must either absorb the costs of phased-out programs or divert funds from other activities now supported by revenue sharing.

If the Nixon proposals are voted by Congress, or if funds are impounded by the Administration despite Congressional appropriations, then the direction and magnitude of antipoverty efforts will be changed. Whatever the immediate outcome, it appears that the project approach (other than social insurance) will give way to a more comprehensive approach stressing general income supplements rather than particular conditions associated with poverty. This approach will be discussed later in the chapter.

SOCIAL INSURANCE

As mentioned earlier, efforts to achieve economic security through social policy are identical with efforts to insure continuity of a minimum income. Insurance operates on the principle that a small payment (or premium) by a large number of people will cover even a substantial loss that may occur to a relative few. Thus, *social insurance* applies the principle to the continuity of a minimum income.

Continuity of income to the individual may be created entirely by aid received from relatives and the public. This method of ensuring economic security is not always available or desirable. Insurance of continued income may also be provided in some cases in the form of pensions for military service.

A continuous flow of income may be provided by means of private insurance. When the individual purchases life insurance, he is providing some continuity of income for his survivors or himself. He may insure himself against the risks of accident and against many other contingencies if he is in business or is employed. Since some continuity of income for large numbers of workers was first attempted through private insurance in cases of industrial accidents, the term "social insurance" distinguishes this form of economic security from that of private insurance.

The development of large-scale governmental measures to combat economic insecurity has proceeded more slowly in this country than in Europe. The tradition of independence and self-help has been more deeply rooted here than in the more densely populated nations of Western Europe. A state program for promoting greater economic security was first started in Germany in the 1880s, and it spread gradually to other countries. Compulsory unemployment insurance was established by Great Britain in 1911 and by many other countries on the continent of Europe within a short time. But not until 1935 was the federal Social Security Act passed in this country, although workmen's compensation was established as early as 1911 in a number of states; and one state, Wisconsin, had begun compulsory unemployment insurance shortly before 1935. Only with the general realization that a depression such as that of the 1930s is an economic disaster against which the tradition of self-help is of little avail was the way paved for a measure that could contribute in some degree to a heightened sense of security.

THE SOCIAL SECURITY ACT

As a result of widespread distress resulting from unemployment during the severe depression that began in 1929, the problem of social insurance received increasing attention during the early 1930s. The agitation for something better than haphazard treatment of unemployment and destitution resulted in President Roosevelt creating the Committee on Economic Security in June, 1934, to study the problem, and in the passage of the Social Security Act on August 14, 1935.

Although considered reasonably liberal at the time, provisions for *old age and survivors insurance* contained in the Social Security Act were never intended to do more than provide necessities for a minority of the workers. The increasing inadequacy of the benefits was emphasized by the growing demand on the part of the workers for some form of company retirement allowances of a more liberal character, a retirement allowance of $100 a month being a common figure in labor-management negotiations. As a result of increasing agitation, several Social Security amendments were passed. The purposes of these amendments were: (1) to extend the coverage and to liberalize the benefits of old-age and survivors insurance, (2) to broaden and to liberalize federal grants-in-aid to states for maternal and child-health and child-welfare services, and (3) to permit the receipt of other sources of retirement income without suffering the loss of Social Security benefits.

The Social Security Act covers a number of programs designed to prevent individuals and families from becoming destitute. One of the objectives of the Act is to keep families together and to enable children to grow up in health and security.

The methods by which this legislation has been put into effect are complex, and the law and its interpretations are so extensive as to call for the services of experts. Complexity necessarily results from the fact that millions of persons are involved. The extension of coverage by the amendments of 1950 added 10 million persons to those already insured, and subsequent amendments have added other millions; the total number of persons with taxable incomes under old-age, survivors, disability, and health insurance benefits in 1973 was 96 million. Numbers of this size are peculiar to the United States; they are greater than the total population of many European countries where social insurance has long been in force. Such large numbers give rise to difficult problems of organization and administration.

Because of this problem of numbers, various methods of administration have been devised to insure effective management with due regard to regional differences. The plan of old-age, survivors, disability, and health insurance benefits is administered entirely by the federal government, but unemployment insurance has been left to the states with federal encouragement of minimum standards. The welfare provisions of the Social Security Act represent an attempt to encourage adequate state programs through federal grants-in-aid. The burden of organization and administration is thus shifted in part to the states, while a fair degree of uniformity in state programs has been attained.

Unemployment Insurance

Despite generally prosperous conditions for nearly three decades, the United States did experience serious unemployment in four post-World War II recessions, modest unemployment in the period of nagging unemployment from 1958 to 1965, and a worrisome downturn in the early seventies. One of the purposes of the Social Security law is to relieve the burden of unemployment.

For the purpose of establishing an *unemployment insurance* fund, the Social Security Act required that each employer of four or more persons must pay a federal tax at the rate of 3 percent of the first $3,000 in wages received by the worker in a year. In 1961, this tax was increased to 3.1 percent, of which 0.4 percent went to the federal government to help administer the program. Effective in 1972, the tax was again raised, to 3.2 percent, and the tax base was extended to the first $4,200 in wages. Another slight increase to 3.28 percent took effect in 1973. If a state unemployment insurance law meets certain general conditions specified in the Social Security Act, employers may credit their state taxes against 90 percent of the federal tax, which lessens the cost of the tax. The state law may provide for additional taxation of payrolls for unemployment insurance, or it may remit a portion of its share of the tax to the employer on the basis of merit rating.

The most important of the general conditions that the state law must meet are: (1) All unemployment compensation must be paid through public employment offices or through such agencies as the Bureau of Employment Security may approve; and (2) no worker may be denied compensation if he refuses new work where a labor dispute is in progress or where the wages, hours, and working conditions are substantially less favorable than those to which he has been accustomed; likewise, he may not be denied compensation if, as a condition of employment, he is required to join a company union or to refrain from joining any bona fide labor organization.

As a result of these provisions of the Act, all states have passed unemployment insurance laws approved by the Bureau. The federal public employment offices have become important agencies (1) for determining the volume of unemployment, since each benefit claimant covered by the law and out of work must register with an employment office, and (2) for finding other work of equal grade within the capacity of the worker. Since state laws usually require a waiting period of one to three weeks before compensation payments begin, it is expected that this time will be utilized by the worker, with the assistance of the employment office, in seeking new employment.

Compensation to the Unemployed Worker. The compensation received by the worker in case of unemployment varies with the provisions of each state law, both in the dollar value of benefits per week and the number of weeks during which compensation is allowed. In 1973, the nationwide average was $57.42 per week collected for 14 weeks. Weekly payments ranged from $35.68 in Puerto Rico and $39.75 in Mississippi at the lower end of the scale to such highs as $67.61 in New Jersey and $76.18 in Washington, D.C.

As these facts indicate, the amount of compensation per worker is not large, especially when considered in relation to the cost of living. The compensation is, of course, not intended to equal the loss of earnings due to unemployment but to serve as a means of meeting most urgent needs while other employment is being sought. The payments of unemployment benefits through public employment offices are a highly effective arrangement, since such payments are supplemented by an organized search for productive and more remunerative employment. They are also an effective statistical measure of the volume of unemployment.

Merit Rating of Employers. An important feature of the unemployment compensation laws of the majority of states is the provision for reduction of contributions by employers to the state fund on the basis of each employer's unemployment record. The establishment of merit ratings and the consequent reduction in the percentage of contribution to the state fund are designed to serve as strong financial incentives to the employer to devise means of reducing unemployment in his business to a minimum. Undoubtedly the development of merit-rating systems has been valuable in emphasizing to the employer the necessity of devising ways and means of avoiding layoffs. While it may be possible for the employer to develop greater stability of employment at a time when business conditions are favorable, there is no certainty that this would be true in time of depression.

Old-Age, Survivors, Disability, and Health Insurance Benefits (OASDHI)

The most important provision of the Social Security Act is that which established a system of *old-age, survivors, disability, and health insurance.* As a result of several amendments, notable changes have been made in the original provisions of the Act, but only the major features of the Act and its amendments will be considered here.

Administration and Coverage. This portion of the Social Security Act is administered entirely by the federal government through the Social Security Administration. As the result of successive amendments to the Act, most types of employment have been brought under the law. Workers in commerce and industry, most farm and household workers, self-employed persons, employees of nonprofit organizations and of state and local governments, and those in active military service are now included. The only principal workers not covered are federal employees covered by some other federal retirement system. The law in effect now covers nine out of every ten persons who work for a living.

Sources of Funds. The tax by which funds are provided for payment of these benefits is collected at identical rates from both employer and employee. The employee's contribution is deducted from his paycheck by the employer, who sends both contributions to the Treasury Department. A person whose net earnings from covered self-employment is more than $400 annually pays his Social Security tax when he files his federal income tax. Rates and earnings subject to tax, beginning in 1937 and extending to the present, are shown in Table 40-2 on page 896. These tax rates have been designed with the expectation that the proceeds will pay the entire cost of old-age, survivors, disability, and health benefits and the cost of administering the program.

Use of Funds. All taxes from employers, employees, and the self-employed under the federal old-age and survivors insurance program are paid to District Directors of Internal Revenue and then are placed in one of the Social Security trust funds (Federal Old-Age and Survivors, Disability, Hospital, or Supplementary Medical trust funds). Such receipts as are not needed for current expenditures are invested in interest-bearing obligations of the United States, in accordance with the requirements of the law. The procedure in this respect is the same as that of private insurance companies, except that investment can be made only in securities of the federal government; the interest received makes possible a lower rate of contributions than would otherwise be necessary.

At the beginning of 1973, total assets of these funds were approximately $47.1 billion. During the year, income from contributions and interest on investments amounted to $60.8 billion. Benefit payments plus administrative costs were $58.5 billion, leading to an excess of income over outlays equal to $2.3 billion. Thus, assets at the beginning of 1974 were valued at $49.4 billion.

Social Security Benefits. The amount of monthly Social Security benefits is determined from average monthly or annual earnings. In 1973, over 29 million persons received Social Security benefits. For a worker and his wife the average benefit was $248 per month.

Prior to 1960 severely disabled workers over 50 years of age were entitled to disability insurance. Any disabled worker under 50 years of age had to wait until his 50th birthday in order to receive benefits. In the meantime, however, he could have his earnings record "frozen," that is, his account would not be subject to further additions that might represent very low earnings. An amendment to the Social Security Act in 1960, however, permitted disabled workers under 50 to receive disability benefits, providing they fulfill the other required conditions of eligibility.

Medicare (Health Insurance). About 20 million persons in the nation are 65 years of age or older. As Figure 40-2 demonstrates, the number of older Americans has been rising, and the estimated number by the year 2000 is 28 million, while the projection for 2025 is 42 million. Our older citizens are most subject to the very great expenses of medical and hospital care and at the same time have the least income among all age groups to meet these expenses. The United Hospital Fund has estimated that the average cost to a patient in the New York area rose from $15.55 per day in 1947 to $40.92

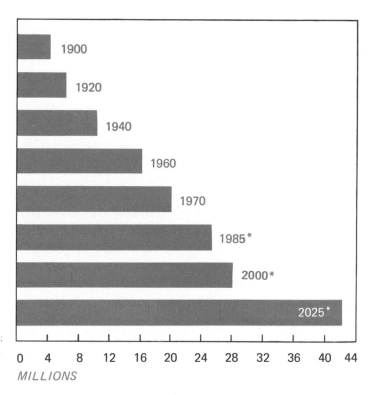

FIGURE 40-2

THE INCREASE IN OLDER AMERICANS, AGE 65 PLUS

The number of aged Americans has increased fourfold in the past 70 years. Their number is expected to double in the next 50 years.

SOURCE: 1900 through 1970, Census of Population; 1985 through 2025, U.S. Bureau of the Census, "Current Population Reports; Population Estimates and Projections," Series P-25, No. 480.

* Projected.

in 1962 and to more than $100 in 1974. To an elderly person living on Social Security benefits, these costs are staggering.

In 1966 Congress amended the Social Security Act to provide medical and hospital care for older citizens. *Medicare*, as it is called, provides two coordinated plans for nearly all people age 65 and over. A hospital plan covers hospital and related services, and a voluntary supplementary medical insurance plan covers physician's services and related medical services. While hospital insurance is financed by regular Social Security taxes, medical insurance is available to the retiree on a voluntary basis through the payment of a $5.80 per month premium payment. Those 65 years of age and over whose incomes do not exceed a variable maximum are eligible for benefits consisting of up to half the expenses of medical and hospital care after deduction of the first $60 in expenses.

Grants-in-Aid to States. Although the principal emphasis of the Social Security Program has been laid on unemployment compensation, old-age pensions, and more recently Medicare, the law makes provision also for grants-in-aid to the states for specific programs in the field of health and welfare. These programs have to do with (1) the needy aged, (2) dependent children, (3) the needy blind, (4) maternal and child welfare, and (5) the permanently and totally disabled. In order to obtain federal grants-in-aid, the states are required to establish their own programs for each of the above classifications.

The federal grant varies with each type of program established. Benefits to recipients likewise vary. In the case of old-age assistance, aid to the blind, and the permanently and totally disabled, the maximum in recent years has been $70 per month, while the maximum aid for dependent children has been $30 per month. The type of old-age assistance referred to here is not to be confused with old-age insurance. Old-age assistance is noncontributory; that is, it represents financial aid for the needy who do not come under the old-age, survivors, disability, and health insurance benefits. As old-age insurance comes to include more of the total working population, federal and state aid to the needy aged will decline in importance.

1972 SOCIAL SECURITY AMENDMENTS

From the date of its passage in 1935 until the end of World War II, the Social Security Act remained essentially unchanged. The period from the late 1940s through the mid-1960s saw several revisions, each extending benefits at the margin to the unemployed, the disabled, or the retired. Most notable and far-reaching were the amendments of 1966, establishing Medicare. Toward the end of the sixties and into the early seventies, growing concern about high rates of indigence among the aged and disabled led to agitation for an expanded attack on poverty via this established legislation.

Changes in Benefits

In 1972 Congress approved a massive Social Security package in the form of amendments to the Social Security Act. The first of two legislative steps, signed into law on July 1, 1972, raised benefits by 20 percent, effective in September of that year. As a consequence, the average retired couple received $269 a month as compared to $224 prior to passage of this amendment. In addition to a projected escalation of across-the-board benefits in future years, the new Act for the first time acknowledged the necessity of a "real income" concept, for the legislation provides that Social Security benefits will go up in every year that there is significant inflation.

On October 17, 1972, Congress passed the second stage—a bill that gives more than $5 billion a year in expanded benefits to widows, the disabled, those who do some work while in retirement, and many others. Pensions for widows and widowers were raised. For instance, a widow now receives at age 65 a pension equal to the one her husband would have received at age 65, whereas formerly she received 82.5 percent of that amount. Early retirees between 62 and 64 years of age are allowed modest gains, while late retirees get a bonus for the extra working years. Low-paid workers have been granted substantial gains. The minimum pension for a retired person at age 65 went from $84.50 a month to $170 a month if the retiree was in covered employment for 30 years. For a couple, the minimum pension is $255, compared with $127 formerly.

The disabled at any age were made eligible for health-care protection under Medicare. About 1.7 million people are thus being aided. Moreover, disabled widows and widowers are eligible now for Medicare at age 50 rather than age 65, disabled children of retired or deceased workers qualify for Medicare assistance if they became disabled before age 22, and Medicare generally was extended to cover ailments not previously covered.

Changes in Costs

Of course these enlarged benefits entail added costs, which are to be met in two ways. One is a rise in the percentage tax rate on earnings for all employed workers. The other is a rise in the ceiling on earnings subject to the Social Security tax.

TABLE 40-2

SOCIAL SECURITY CONTRIBUTIONS— CHANGES IN EFFECTIVE AND SCHEDULED CONTRIBUTIONS

Time Period	Increase in Taxable Earnings (Dollars per Year)	Increase in Tax Rate (Percent)
1937 to 1949	3,000 (no change)	1.00 (no change)
1949 to 1959	3,000 to 4,800	1.00 to 2.50
1959 to 1964	4,800 (no change)	2.50 to 3.62
1964 to 1968	4,800 to 7,800	3.62 to 4.40
1968 to 1972	7,800 to 9,000	4.40 to 5.20
1972 to 1973	9,000 to 10,800	5.20 to 5.85
1973 to 1974	10,800 to 13,200	5.85 (no change)
Future:		
1974 to 1986	13,200 (no change)	5.85 to 6.25
1986 to 2011	13,200 (no change)	6.25 to 7.30

SOURCE: *Statistical Abstract of the United States,* 1973; *U.S. News and World Report* (Dec. 18, 1972), p. 40, and (Oct. 30, 1972), pp. 16 and 17; and *Social Security Bulletin.*

Changes implemented in the past and projected changes in the future are summarized in Table 40-2. At the time the Social Security Act was made law, and for 12 years thereafter, maximum earnings subject to tax and the tax rate were both held constant. The rate was one percent on earnings up to $3,000 paid by the employee and an equal rate paid by the employer.

As benefits have been enlarged, so too has the cost—to $10,800 taxable earnings at a rate of 5.85 percent in 1973. The maximum base rose to $13,200 annually for each worker in 1974, and the rate will eventually rise to 7.3 percent levied on the employee, with the same rate imposed upon the employer.

In effect, both workers in general and their employers are expected to pay the added cost of providing greater benefits to those in the lowest income brackets. At the same time, relatively better paid employees can look forward to increased support after retirement. What orders of magnitude are involved? A worker subject to the maximum tax in 1973 (earning $10,800 or more) pays $632 annually matched by an equal payment by his employer. Similarly, a worker eligible for the maximum pension in 1973, retiring at age 65, can earn up to $2,100 annually while he receives a pension of $3,113 per annum. His pension declines according to a formula as earnings rise, so the benefit becomes zero at earnings of $8,326 yearly.

NATIONAL HEALTH INSURANCE

Amendments to the Social Security Act since 1966 have added and expanded medical-cost assistance (Medicare) to other benefits for retirees and their dependents or survivors. Federal grants to the states (*Medicaid*) have helped to defray the costs of health care for the indigent. Nevertheless, the last few years have witnessed growing agitation for some form of national health insurance program to cover citizens generally.

This upsurge of interest is traceable to two factors. One is the unprecedented rise in the cost of medical services, particularly those related to hospital care. Since 1960 the cost of health care has climbed by more than 50 percent, outdistancing the 31 percent rise in the consumer price index. Physicians' fees alone have increased by 58 percent. A second factor is heightened dissatisfaction with the Medicaid approach to health care, under which the federal government bears half or more of the cost of a variety of local programs. Many legislators decry the fact that the federal share may be a more than adequate portion of inadequate local efforts and that Congress has no control over the aggregate dollar amount of these federal contributions.

Comprehensive national health insurance is a form of social security extending well beyond public assistance found in earlier legislation, including the Social Security Act and all of its amendments. Most proposals cover the under-65 working individual as well as retirees and their dependents.

Basic health insurance proposals which have been submitted to Congress fall into four categories. The catastrophic illness approach is essentially a format to cover the costs of illness in excess of a deductible amount to be paid by the patient, where the deductible amount is related directly to the patient's income.

A second plan, the tax-credit approach, is a voluntary program, under which the federal government would pay insurance premiums for the poor and allow income tax credits for all others toward the purchase of private health insurance.

A third plan, sponsored by the Nixon Administration, is a mixed private-public system. This approach would establish a two-part national program to cover almost all of the population under age 65. The program would consist of: (1) employers' providing for employees and their families a private health insurance policy, with premium subsidies in some versions, and (2) a federally operated and subsidized plan for low-income families.

A proposal most attuned to the traditions of the Social Security Act is the Kennedy-Griffiths Bill. Standardized benefits for all people (regardless of age or income) would include physicians' services, hospital services, psychiatric services, dental care, medicines, and the costs of a variety of therapeutic devices. The program would be financed nationally, relying on the same methods as Social Security taxes to provide half the revenue. Since all ages and income levels would be eligible, tax revenues now used to support Medicare and Medicaid would be supplemented by federal contributions to cover the other half of estimated cost. These contributions would be financed out of general federal revenues.

At this writing, no definitive action on this issue has yet been taken by the legislative or executive branches of our government. There seems little doubt, however, that the Congress will vote, and the executive branch will approve, some form of national health insurance in addition to, and doubtless related to, the forms of public assistance now incorporated into the amended Social Security Act.

GUARANTEED ANNUAL INCOME

One cure for poverty is a guaranteed minimum income for all citizens. If a minimum income were to be insured by means of outright grants from the federal government financed out of tax revenues, other members of society would in effect be making gifts to those who earn less than the minimum. The transfer payments would be of very substantial magnitude, and it would be the middle-income families rather than the rich that would bear the primary financial burden. Outright grants would not in themselves increase the productivity of the poor. Moreover, they would likely discourage some incentives on the part of some of the poor to raise their own earned incomes.

Anyone with an income from work that is slightly in excess of the minimum would be tempted to work less and to let his income decline. The differential would be made up by transfer payments from others.

An alternative method is a negative income tax. At present the United States has a progressive income-tax structure. The tax rate (percentage of income paid in taxes) rises as income is higher. The same principle could be applied in the downward direction. The percentage of income taken in taxes would decrease with income to a tax of zero at a defined income level. Those with incomes below that level would be assigned a negative tax. That is, they would receive a payment from the Internal Revenue Service, and the amount of the payment would increase as income is lowered. This method, although it is less discouraging to incentives for self-betterment, tends to suffer from the same basic shortcomings as the outright federal grant.

In the past the United States has not chosen to eliminate poverty in either of these ways. Instead attempts have been made to attack the underlying causes of poverty. Some programs bring direct financial aid to the needy. Most of the programs, however, attempt to expand opportunities for the poor to increase their productivity and thus their earnings. Emphasis has been placed upon training and retraining programs, expanded educational opportunities, unemployment insurance, retirement income, and other means.

During the 1972 presidential election campaign, however, the issue of a guaranteed annual income came to the forefront. Both the Republicans and the Democrats advocated some form of guaranteed income, with the differences arising primarily in the levels recommended. The Democrats proposed a system of *personal tax credits*. For low-income taxpayers, personal tax credits would replace personal exemptions, standard deductions, and low-income allowances. With the objective of replacing most of the current cash welfare programs, which have been severely criticized for inefficiency and abuses, tax credits would offset income-tax liability and would be paid in cash to the extent that there is no tax liability to offset. In this way, the credits would serve as income guarantees.

The Negative Income Tax

In effect, a personal tax credit system is a way of implementing a *negative income tax*, first espoused by economist Milton Friedman in 1962. Some guaranteed income level is set, and a rate of reduction is specified. The rate of reduction is the percentage rate at which the negative-tax payments are reduced as the family's income rises. This rate is less than the rise in income, so for each additional dollar of earned income a family receives, the negative-tax payment is reduced by less than a dollar. By employing this method, the combined family income rises as earned income increases. If the guaranteed income were set at $4,000 per year and the rate of reduction set at 50 percent, a family with no income would receive a negative tax payment of $4,000. Suppose the following year the family earns $1,000. Then the negative tax payment is reduced by half of that amount, that is, by $500. Consequently, the negative-tax payment is $3,500 and earned income is $1,000, for a combined family income of $4,500. As earned income rises, negative-tax payments decline until the family's combined income reaches a certain level, such as $6,000, at which the negative-tax payment is zero. If the family income rises higher, tax payments become positive.

This system contrasts sharply with prevailing welfare programs, under which a slight gain in income may cause a family to be ineligible for public assistance. In the language of the negative income tax, welfare programs generally apply a 100 percent rate of reduction; for each additional dollar earned a dollar of welfare benefits is lost.

Difficulties in the negative income tax arise from disagreements about the guaranteed minimum income and the appropriate rate of reduction. But most serious is the question of incentives. Would a negative income tax reduce incentives among the poor to raise their incomes through productive employment? For four years, beginning in 1968, a research organization known as Mathematica Incorporated, working with the Institute for Research on Poverty at the University of Wisconsin, conducted a social experiment in urban New Jersey to test the incentive effects of a negative income tax. Four guarantee levels were tried with four different samples of intact families having able-bodied males present; the lowest guaranteed income was $1,650 per year, and the highest was $4,125 per year. Designers of the experiment tested three rates of reduction: 30, 50, and 70 percent. In brief, the findings suggested that a negative income tax does not significantly reduce the earnings (incentive to earn) of the recipients.

Future Issues

With respect to a guaranteed minimum income for all families, coupled with aid for those with incomes just above the minimum, the critical question involves arriving at the "best" combination of a guarantee level and a rate of reduction. Various guarantee levels have been proposed, ranging from $2,470 annually for a family of four contained in a proposal by the Nixon Administration, to $6,600 per year advocated by the National Welfare Rights Organization. Choice of a reduction rate bears essentially on judgments about incentives. Although the evidence is not conclusive, there is some reason to believe that an appropriately determined rate would not significantly reduce incentives to replace benefits by earned income.

There is a definite movement toward some type of guaranteed income plan. Unless the guarantee were set very low and the reduction rate very high, the resulting redistribution of income would be substantial. Substitution of guaranteed income for many forms of locally administered public assistance means that present federal outlays on welfare would go part of the way toward meeting the costs. The remainder would be covered by reforms in income-tax exemptions and a rise in the overall tax rate. One estimate would entail a redistribution from those who pay more taxes to those who pay less of $43 billion, of which $14 billion would go to those below the official poverty line. For any scheme put into effect, the actual magnitude of income redistribution through taxes would also depend on any cuts that might be made in other government expenditures, such as defense and foreign aid.

CONCLUSION

Four basic developments can be identified in public efforts to reduce poverty. One is incorporated in public assistance legislation and in the comprehensive Social Security Act. This approach focuses upon financial help for the disabled, the aged and their dependents, and others not in the full-time labor force. Income supplements assist those who suffer loss of income previously enjoyed and help them to meet expenses, such as health care, that their incomes cannot bear. A second approach addresses itself to social and personal factors that limit productivity and earnings for those in the labor force. Such programs as those provided for in the Economic Opportunity Act emphasize expanded opportunities for education, training, and retraining which help to raise earned income.

Two new efforts toward poverty reduction are contained in proposals for national health insurance and a guaranteed annual minimum income. National health insurance, which would be financed in a way similar to Social Security, is not aimed exclusively at poverty-stricken families. Rather, publicly sponsored health insurance would encompass citizens generally. But since hospital and medical care is so expensive, those in the lowest income brackets would stand to gain most by a national insurance system. Proposals for a guaranteed annual income seek a single, comprehensive plan to eliminate poverty by means of federal supplements to low income. Most plans would replace existing federal contributions to locally administered welfare programs but would be coordinated with Social Security and manpower training efforts. The costs would be met by a reallocation of funds now spent on a variety of local welfare programs, by income redistribution through changes in the federal income tax, and possibly by some redirection of government expenditures now applied to other areas.

Recent trends suggest that all four methods of poverty reduction will be functioning by the end of this decade. The emphasis is now changing from a "program" approach (College Work Study, Job Corps, VISTA) to a more comprehensive "income situation" approach (health insurance, guaranteed annual income, and so on). But whatever the approach, the results will not be obtained without costs. The costs will be large, and these costs will be borne by the public, both directly through insurance contributions and indirectly through income-tax payments. Assuming a willingness on the part of the nation to undertake such comprehensive social security measures, our ability to carry them forward rests ultimately on the productivity of the economy. The real security of the American people depends upon their capacity to produce in greater abundance and to distribute equitably the needed goods and services.

SUMMARY

1. Whatever reduces one's wealth or income, or deprives one of opportunities to earn income, creates economic insecurity.

2. The lowest income and wealth are found among the very youngest members of the labor force and the oldest members of the population. Older members of the population are in the worst relative income position.

3. It is estimated that approximately 14 percent of our American families have poverty-level incomes.

4. The incidence of poverty is high among certain groups, such as non-whites, the elderly, and those with little formal education.

5. The war on poverty was launched by federal legislation in 1964 in an effort to reduce poverty.

6. Measures to attack poverty among the young center upon education, training, and equal employment opportunity. Measures to attack poverty primarily among the intermediate and oldest age groups center upon social insurance.

7. Social insurance is designed to provide some continuity of income for those unable to make adequate use of private insurance against the contingencies of life.

8. Since 1935 Social Security legislation has embraced retirement benefits, unemployment compensation, disability benefits, and medical assistance.

9. In 1972, amendments to the Social Security Act greatly expanded benefits to recipients and costs to the employed.

10. Two new efforts to ameliorate the effects of poverty are the proposed national health insurance plan and the guaranteed annual income concept.

QUESTIONS FOR DISCUSSION AND ANALYSIS

1. What are the basic types or sources of economic insecurity? Which do you consider the most serious? Why?

2. Is it true that employers who least need unemployment insurance for their workers are contributing the highest amount of taxes toward the payment of unemployment compensation? Explain.

3. Do you think that a merit-rating system for employer unemployment compensation taxes is justifiable? Why or why not?

4. What provisions have been made for the development of reserves under OASDHI? How are these reserves secured?

5. Should the aged not eligible for OASDHI benefits be given some type of assistance? Why or why not?

6. It has been proposed by various government agencies and certain individuals that the federal government should guarantee to each American family an annual income of at least $4,000. Do you agree or disagree with this proposal? Why or why not?

7. Explain how a negative income tax would work.

8. Are you in favor of national health insurance? Why or why not?

9. Are national health insurance and a guaranteed annual income consistent with a private enterprise economy? Why or why not?

SUGGESTED READINGS

Elling, Ray H. (ed.). *National Health Care: Issues and Problems in Socialized Medicine*. Chicago: Aldine-Atherton, Inc., 1971.

Ginsburg, Helen. *Poverty, Economics and Society*. Boston: Little, Brown and Company, 1972.

Harrington, Michael. *Other America: Poverty in the United States*. New York: The Macmillan Company, 1970.

Leacock, Eleanor B. (ed.). *The Culture of Poverty*. New York: Simon & Schuster, Inc., 1971.

Lubove, Roy. *Poverty and Social Welfare in the United States*. New York: Holt, Rinehart, and Winston, Inc., 1972.

Myers, Robert J. *Medicare*. Homewood, Ill.: Richard D. Irwin, Inc., 1970.

Pauly, Mark V. *National Health Insurance: An Analysis*. Washington: American Enterprise Institute for Public Policy Research, 1971.

Roach, Jack (ed.). *Poverty*. Baltimore: Penguin Books Inc., 1972.

Schiller, Bradley R. *The Economics of Poverty and Discrimination*. Englewood Cliffs, N.J.: Prentice-Hall, Inc., 1973.

Social Security Administration. *Social Security Handbook*. Washington: U.S. Government Printing Office.

——————. *Social Security Yearbook*. Washington: U.S. Government Printing Office.

Theobald, Robert. *The Guaranteed Income*. Garden City, N.Y.: Doubleday & Company, Inc., 1967.

41

Population and Manpower Problems

PREVIEW   The rate of population growth has a pronounced impact on any economy. The United States population stood at over 212 million in 1974. Projections, based on differing fertility rates, estimate that the population will be in the vicinity of 240 million by 1985. Changes in the birth rate and age structure of the population influence business activities, government services, the environment, and the labor force. A zero population growth rate, ZPG, would stabilize the United States population sometime in the 2020s. With the growing population, irrespective of the rate, a number of challenging manpower problems exist for the United States economy, especially in regard to employment. High rates of unemployment resulting from economic factors and social prejudices occur among minority groups such as blacks, Spanish-Americans, and American Indians. A separate group requiring special attention are the criminal offenders. In addition, the new and growing role of women in the American economy requires solutions to a new set of issues.

Elsewhere in this text population problems of the world are discussed. Consequently, in this chapter we will concern ourselves only with population and manpower problems of the United States. In 1974 the U.S. had a population of over 212 million. This is neither a minimum nor a maximum population. Whether it is an optimum population is a point of contention. Fortunately the problems associated with the U.S. population growth are not as acute as those found elsewhere in the world, particularly in those areas where foodstuffs are scarce relative to population and where widespread poverty prevails. Before turning to our manpower problems, some notion of our population growth and its structure can be beneficial in understanding the issues.

POPULATION GROWTH

The first official national census taken in 1790 revealed that there were about 4 million people in the territorial United States. In colonial times and the early years of our nation, the population doubled approximately every 25 years up to the time of the Civil War. Subsequently the population growth rate slowed down. On the basis of census statistics then available, President Lincoln calculated that the U.S. population would reach 251 million by the year 1930. After the Civil War it took 30 years for the population to double. In the first 30 years of this century, the population increased by 64 percent, increasing by only 16 percent in the decades of the 1910s and the 1920s. By 1930 the population was 123 million, not 251 million as extrapolated by President Lincoln. The population then increased by a mere 7 percent in the decade of the 1930s, and it was anticipated that the rate would diminish in the future. In fact, it was estimated by the Census Bureau at that time that the population of the United States would stabilize somewhere between 180 million and 200 million sometime between 1980 and the year 2000.

Secular Stagnation

The declining rate of population growth was a basic factor in the secular stagnation concept that became popular in the 1930s. *Secular stagnation* in this case referred to the belief held by a number of noted economists that the economy had reached a point of maturity and that we were going to experience little future economic growth. In short, they were predicting that the economy was stagnant and would remain so for years or decades. This prediction was based on several factors, the most important of which was the estimate of meager population growth. Other factors included the disappearance of the geographic frontier, the conservatism of investors, and a dearth of new heavy industries.

Unfortunately few, if any, demographers could foresee at that time the sudden change in population growth that was to take place in the subsequent decades. In fact, the population increased at such a fast pace that the original 180 million estimate for the 1980-2000 period was reached in 1960, and the 200 million level was attained in 1968. As a result, the dire predictions of the secular stagnationists did not come to pass. Their error, however, was not so much one of method but of assumption.

Growth 1940-1970

The population growth of the United States increased from a rate of 7 percent in the 1930s to 14.8 percent in the 1940s and to 18.6 percent in the 1950s. This, of course, led to some very rosy predictions about the future of our economy. But the rate of population growth slowed down a bit in the 1960s, increasing by about 13.3 percent for the decade. Subsequently some of the bright economic forecasts for the mid-1970s and the 1980s were toned down a bit. In addition, population growth projections for the U.S. have been adjusted even further downward in the past few years.

Population Projections

As late as 1968 the U.S. Bureau of the Census was showing four possible *population projections* for the year 1985. The projections showed a wide range in population estimates, with a high of 274.7 million and a low of 241.7 million. These projections were based on different completed rates of fertility among childbearing women. Series A, for example, assumed that there will be 3,350 children per 1,000 women; Series B, 3,100; Series C, 2,775; and Series D, 2,450. The projections also assumed an immigration factor of 400,000 persons annually. As a result of the 1970 census and a modified birth rate, the projections were amended. It can be seen from Table 41-1 that the range of population estimates for the year 1985 made in 1972 were somewhat lower than those shown in 1968. In fact, the Bureau of the Census dropped the Series A projection as being unrealistic, because of the slowing rate of population growth, and added Series E based on a new lower fertility rate (2,110). In 1972 it also dropped Series B as being unrealistic in light of recent changes in the annual birth date and added Series F (1,800). At that time Series C, D, and E were scaled downward. First, the population base was updated from July 1, 1970, to July 1, 1972. Second, and more important, fertility assumptions were revised downward, due to both the sharp decline in fertility since 1970 and to the sharp decline in the birth expectations of young women in the previous five years. There is, however, no previous demographic precedent for setting such a low rate of fertility for American women. Consequently, today the estimates for the U.S. population for the year 1985 range from a high of 249 million to a low of 231 million, as shown in Table 41-1. This is substantially lower than the range of projections of 275 million to 242 million for 1985 that were made in the late 1960s.

TABLE 41-1

U.S. POPULATION PROJECTIONS FOR THE YEAR 1985

Series	1968 Estimates	1972 Estimates	Completed Fertility [1]	Fertility Rate [2]
A	274,748,000	—	3.4	—
B	264,607,000	—	3.1	114.1
C	252,871,000	248,711,000	2.8	102.7
D	241,731,000	243,935,000	2.5	91.3
E	—	235,701,000	2.1	79.3
F	—	230,913,000	1.8	—

SOURCE: *Statistical Abstract of the United States*, 1970; and U.S. Bureau of the Census, "Current Population Reports," Series P-25, No. 493 (December, 1972).

[1] Average number of children per woman at completion of childbearing period.
[2] Annual births per 1,000 females 15 to 44 years of age.

Of course, the U.S. Census Bureau is always cautious in pointing out that its long-range projections are projections rather than actual forecasts. They are calculations of what can happen under certain assumptions and not judgments of what will happen. Longer range forecasts to the year 2020 are shown in Table 41-2 and Figure 41-1.

TABLE 41-2

SUMMARY OF PROJECTIONS OF TOTAL POPULATION

1960-2020

Year (July 1)	Series C	Series D	Series E	Series F
Estimates				
1960		180,671		
1965		194,303		
1970		204,879		
1972		208,837		
Projections				
1975	215,872	215,324	213,925	213,378
1980	230,955	228,676	224,132	221,848
1985	248,711	243,935	235,701	230,913
1990	266,238	258,692	246,639	239,084
1995	282,766	272,211	256,015	245,591
2000	300,406	285,969	264,430	250,686
2005	321,025	301,397	273,053	255,209
2010	344,094	318,156	281,968	259,332
2015	367,977	335,028	290,432	262,631
2020	392,030	351,368	297,746	264,564

SOURCE: U.S. Bureau of the Census, "Current Population Reports," Series P-25, No. 493 (December, 1972).

General Note: Population in thousands. Total population includes armed forces abroad.

FIGURE 41-1

PROJECTIONS OF THE POPULATION OF THE UNITED STATES

1972-2020

Population projections differ depending on the fertility rate assumed. Notice the wide range of projections for the year 2020, with a high of 392 millon to a low of 264 million.

SOURCE: U.S. Bureau of the Census, "Current Population Reports," Series P-25, No. 493 (December, 1972).

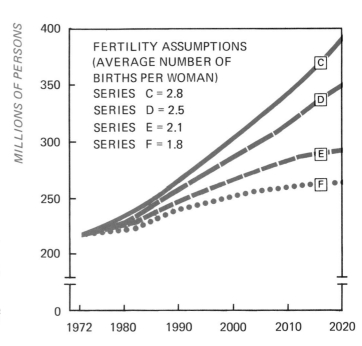

MILLIONS OF PERSONS

FERTILITY ASSUMPTIONS (AVERAGE NUMBER OF BIRTHS PER WOMAN)
SERIES C = 2.8
SERIES D = 2.5
SERIES E = 2.1
SERIES F = 1.8

PART TEN / CURRENT DOMESTIC PROBLEMS

Changes in the nation's population depend on the birth rate, the death rate, and net immigration. Net immigration is steady at about 400,000 people annually. The death rate is fairly constant, having stabilized in recent decades at less than one percent annually. Consequently, the key variable is the birth rate, which has fluctuated widely during the past several decades. As a result population projections, as depicted in Figure 41-1, will vary with periodic changes in the birth rate.

Using an average of the four projections for the year 1985 yields a population estimate of 240 million compared to 205 million in 1970. Although the total population of the United States will increase by approximately 17 percent in the period 1970-1985, or a little over one percent annually, the population will not grow at the same rate throughout the country. One economic growth study indicates that some areas of the nation will grow at much faster rates than others. Furthermore, the trend toward urbanization of the population will continue but at a slower pace. Figure 41-2 indicates that large population increases will occur in the Mountain, Pacific, and South Atlantic states. Much smaller increases will take place in the

FIGURE 41-2

REGIONAL POPULATION GROWTH 1970-1985

During the period 1970-1985 population will grow at different rates throughout the nation. Some areas will grow as much as 25 to 30 percent, while others will be closer to a 10 percent rate of population growth.

SOURCE: *The American Economy—Prospects for Growth to 1985,* McGraw-Hill Economics Department, 1972.

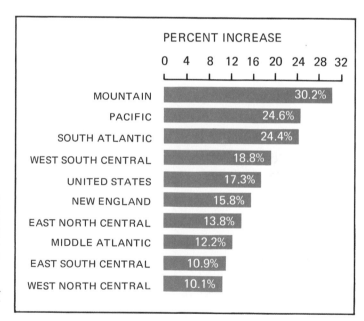

PERCENT INCREASE

0 4 8 12 16 20 24 28 32

MOUNTAIN — 30.2%
PACIFIC — 24.6%
SOUTH ATLANTIC — 24.4%
WEST SOUTH CENTRAL — 18.8%
UNITED STATES — 17.3%
NEW ENGLAND — 15.8%
EAST NORTH CENTRAL — 13.8%
MIDDLE ATLANTIC — 12.2%
EAST SOUTH CENTRAL — 10.9%
WEST NORTH CENTRAL — 10.1%

other regions of the nation. With these changes the center of population for the U.S. will continue to move westward, as shown in Figure 41-3.

The *age structure of the population* also will change somewhat by 1985. The largest increase in population will come in the 22-64 age bracket, with other substantial increases in the 65 and over category and in the under 5

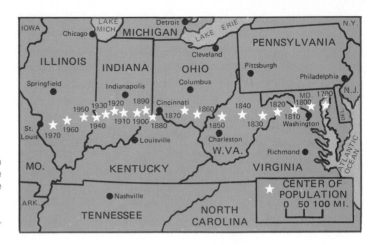

Figure 41-3

CENTER OF POPULATION

1790-1970

As the West Coast and mountain areas increase in population, the center of population will move further westward.

SOURCE: *Statistical Abstract of the United States,* 1973.

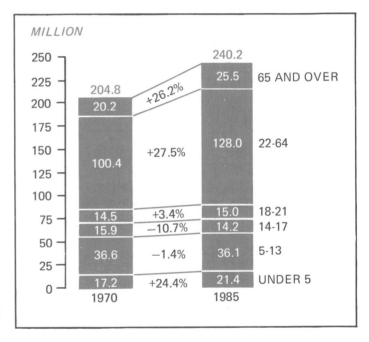

FIGURE 41-4

AGE STRUCTURE OF U.S. POPULATION

1970-1985

There will be a difference in the age structure of the population by 1985. A big increase will come in the 22-64 age bracket, while the percentage of teen-agers will decline.

SOURCE: *The American Economy—Prospects for Growth to 1985,* McGraw-Hill Economics Department, 1972.

years of age category. On the other hand, there will be an actual decrease in the number of people in the 5-13 and the 14-17 age brackets. These changes are shown in Figure 41-4.

ZERO POPULATION GROWTH (ZPG)

In the past decade or more some Americans, concerned about congestion, food supplies, natural resources, energy, and ecology, have advocated limits to the population growth in the United States. In the middle and late 1960s, when population projections were at their highest, a formal organization known as *Zero Population Growth* (ZPG) was established. Its members suggested various measures to stabilize the population at some date in the near future. In order to eventually stabilize the population, the total fertility rate of American women would have to be reduced to 2.1 and remain as such. At that rate each generation would replace itself. A 2.1 instead of a 2.0 figure is used because 1,000 women of childbearing age would have to give birth to 2,098 children in order that there would be 1,000 females for the next generation. This is so because more males than females are born, and some females do not live to childbearing age.

Declining Birth Rate

Even if the goal of ZPG were pursued, it is not easily attained. If the *birth rate* dropped to 2.1 this year, for example, and remained at that level, and net immigration was retained at 400,000 per annum, the population would not stabilize until the year 2022, at a level of approximately 300 million. That is about 40 percent over the 1974 population figure. The lag between the date of attaining a 2.1 birth rate and stabilization of the population results from the fact that a large number of youngsters already born will reach the family formation age between now and the 1990s. This means that there will be more families in the next few decades. Consequently, even if the birth rate is lower, the population will continue to rise until the 2020s. ZPG, of course, could be attained somewhat earlier if a ban were placed on immigration.

To stabilize the population at present levels (1974) with the current immigration factor, the fertility rate would have to drop drastically to 1.0 and hold steady at that level through the 1980s. It could then revert to 2.1 and maintain ZPG. If immigration were banned, however, the birth rate would need to drop to only 1.3, or if reduced and held at 1.0 the population would eventually decline.

In 1972 the U.S. birth rate was actually 2.1, down from 2.3 in 1971, and it dropped a bit lower in the first half of 1973. Whether it will remain at such a low level remains a matter of conjecture. Fertility rates are very sensitive and fluctuate widely. Some demographers suspect that the recession of 1970 was the basic cause of the 1971-1972 downturn in fertility rates. Others attribute the lower rates to national customs and mores. More women are attending school, entering careers, and postponing marriage. Likewise, birth control measures and legalized abortion in several states have had an effect on the fertility rate.

Economic Effects of ZPG

One of the most obvious effects of the attainment of ZPG at some time in the future is that long-run forecasts for the economy, such as discussed in Chapter 21, would have to be reduced. Expectations in terms of total production, employment, and income would have to be adjusted downward, although per capita figures would not necessarily be affected.

Private Sector. A stable population with a higher and growing income still would lead to increased demand and production. But the nature of demand, and consequently production, would differ if higher demand came more from an increase in per capita income rather than from a growing population. Various industries would be affected differently depending on the income elasticity of demand for the products or services of each industry.

The nature of demand would be affected also by the change in the age structure of the population. Some industries would be affected almost immediately and would have a limited time to adjust or diversify their production. Those industries that produce goods and services for preschool children, such as dolls, pull toys, games, tricycles, and diapers, would feel the impact first. Soon thereafter the impact would be felt by the elementary school group. One would anticipate that the demand for toys, games, bicycles, school equipment, clothing, and children's furniture would decline noticeably. Subsequently as the number of teen-agers decreased, producers of records, motorcycles, and automobiles would be affected. Eventually the diminishing rate of new family formations would influence the demand for housing, appliances, and other durable goods. Services, likewise, would be affected. In the field of medicine, for example, the services of obstetricians would be first affected, followed by pediatricians, and then orthodontists.

Public Sector. The attainment of ZPG would certainly reduce the growing economic pressures at all levels of government for the extension of current services necessary to provide for a growing population. It would not remove, however, the growing demand by the populace for new and/or additional services from the government. On the one hand, with an older population there would be a larger percentage of taxpayers, while the percentage of school-aged children would be declining. Trends such as this could lead to a number of fiscal surpluses in the public sector. These surpluses would permit fiscal dividends to be allocated for improvement in the quality of life for Americans.

On the other hand, the increase in the number of aged persons in our economy would have an adverse effect on the Social Security System. The System relies, in large part, on working taxpayers financing the old age and retirement needs of its members. If the population becomes top-heavy with older people, it could put some strains on Social Security financing. Furthermore, with the aging population there would be some problems in channeling resources to other uses. To some extent a large number of institutions have been built in anticipation of a growing population. Consequently, with the event of ZPG a number of schools, maternity hospitals, and other institutions may have to be converted to new uses that would be of more benefit to a society where the number of aged persons is high and increasing.

Labor Force. The increased ratio of aged persons in the population caused by ZPG would bring about some changes in the structure and *participation rate of the labor force*. The female participation rate, for example, would swing upward as women had fewer children. These women would be freer to enter the labor force in large numbers. In addition, they could remain in the labor force longer if family formation were delayed, or they could return to the labor force sooner if the span of family formation years were reduced. Advocates of ZPG contend that the labor force of the 2020s would be of better quality and thus more productive and that a stabilized population would lead to better medical facilities and higher quality medical treatment. This would result in a healthier and more efficient labor force. Workers, moreover, would be better educated and more skilled. Critics of ZPG retort that such advantages could occur readily even with a growing population and that we may need the additional workers to satisfy the increasing demand for goods and services that results from higher per capita income.

From another point of view, ZPG would highlight the need for occupational mobility and worker retraining programs among certain members of the labor force. As the demand for teachers, nurses, and child psychologists declined, some of these workers would have to seek other lines of employment. The necessary transition could cause hardship to some individuals and to society as a whole.

Environment. A strong argument is made that ZPG and the attainment of a stable population would arrest the growing environmental deterioration. There would be fewer people polluting the air and water, less solid waste, and less noise pollution. This view is based on the premise that population density is a major factor contributing to our present rate of environmental deterioration. But this is not the only factor contributing to pollution. Another major factor is economic affluence. Consequently, as the real income of families rises, even with a stable population, there will be an inclination to purchase more of the types of goods and services that contribute toward pollution. ZPG itself would not drastically reduce pollution. It would have a tendency to slow the rate of deterioration, but ZPG could be offset by our growing affluence. In either case, as we saw in Chapter 23, a national commitment and the allocation of sufficient resources to do the job are necessary if we desire to preserve the environment and assure clean air, pure water, the absence of solid waste, and noise abatement.

LABOR FORCE PROJECTIONS

The size and structure of the U.S. labor force will be affected by current and future changes in the rate of population growth. The labor force can be projected more accurately than population, particularly when making a 5-20 year estimate, because those who will be entering the labor force are already born. Using Series E population projections, the Department of Labor estimates that the size of the total force will be 107.7 million in 1985. This will be an annual average growth of 1.6 percent compared to the average annual increase of 1.0 percent in the Series E population projection. The reason for the faster rate of growth in the labor force compared to population, of course, is the fact that the individuals who will enter the labor force during the coming decade were born in the past 15 years or so when the birth rate was considerably higher than it is now or will be in the next decade. The labor force growth rate, however, will slow down considerably in the 1980s compared to the 1970s. The average annual rate for the decade of the 1980s is projected to be only 1.1 percent annually compared to a 1.7 percent annual increase for the decade of the 1970s. By 1990, the labor force is projected to have 112.6 million members, as shown in Table 41-3. Major changes in the age-sex composition of the labor force will occur during the interim period. These changes are as follows:

1. The teen-age labor force, which rose by 300,000 annually in the past decade, is expected to increase only moderately between now and 1985. This trend reflects the present initial effect of the recent decline in the birth rate.
2. The number of young adult workers, age 20-34, will increase dramatically, with an average growth rate of over a million annually. This is a result of the post-World War II baby boom. Three fourths of this increase will be concentrated in the 25-34 year age group, as can be seen in Figure 41-5.
3. The largest number of workers, which are in the middle-aged group, 35-54, is expected to continue between now and 1985, rising at a rate of approximately 150,000 per year.
4. The number of older workers, 55 and over, is projected to rise about 200,000 annually between now and 1985, compared to 150,000 per year during the past decade. Increases for various groups of workers for the next few decades are shown in Table 41-3 and Figure 41-5.

TABLE 41-3

DISTRIBUTION OF
TOTAL LABOR
FORCE BY AGE
AND SEX

(Actual 1960 and
1970 and Projected
1980, 1985, and
1990)

Sex and Age Group	Number (Thousands)				
	Actual		Projected		
	1960	1970	1980	1985	1990
Both Sexes					
Total, 16 Years and Over	72,104	85,903	101,809	107,716	112,576
16 to 24 Years	12,720	19,916	23,781	22,184	20,319
16 to 19 Years	5,223	7,645	8,337	7,165	7,089
20 to 24 Years	7,497	12,271	15,444	15,019	13,230
25 to 54 Years	46,596	51,487	61,944	69,202	76,421
25 to 34 Years	15,099	17,678	26,779	29,739	30,531
35 to 44 Years	16,779	16,789	18,720	23,177	27,617
45 to 54 Years	14,718	17,020	16,445	16,286	18,273
55 Years and Over	12,788	14,500	16,084	16,330	15,836
55 to 64 Years	9,409	11,280	12,787	12,929	12,310
65 Years and Over	3,379	3,220	3,297	3,401	3,526
Median Age	39.9	38.2	35.2	35.8	37.0
Men					
Total, 16 Years and Over	48,933	54,343	62,590	66,017	68,907
16 to 24 Years	8,101	11,773	13,520	12,458	11,305
25 to 54 Years	31,962	33,279	39,282	43,761	48,160
55 Years and Over	8,870	9,291	9,788	9,798	9,442
Median Age	39.7	38.2	35.2	35.8	36.9
Women					
Total, 16 Years and Over	23,171	31,560	39,219	41,699	43,669
16 to 24 Years	4,619	8,143	10,261	9,726	9,014
25 to 54 Years	14,634	18,208	22,662	25,441	28,261
55 Years and Over	3,918	5,209	6,296	6,532	6,394
Median Age	40.3	38.2	35.1	35.9	37.1

SOURCE: *The U.S. Labor Force: Projections to 1990,* Special Labor Force Report 156 (Washington: Department of Labor, Bureau of Labor Statistics, 1973), p. 5.

5. The proportion of women in the labor force, which rose dramatically in the past decade, is expected to continue but at a more moderate pace. This trend is based on the assumption that the decline in fertility rates occurring in the latter part of the 1960s and early 1970s will moderate in the future and remain stable at a 2.1 norm. In 1960 women made up 32.3 percent of the labor force. By 1973 women accounted for over 37.4 percent of the labor force. By 1980 they will constitute 38.7 percent of the labor force. Furthermore, it can be seen from Figure 41-6 that the labor force participation rate, particularly for women in the pre-marriage age and for those of a maturing age, 40-55, will rise in the future.

6. It is expected that the number and participation rate of nonwhite workers will increase in the near future. Sheer numbers will rise

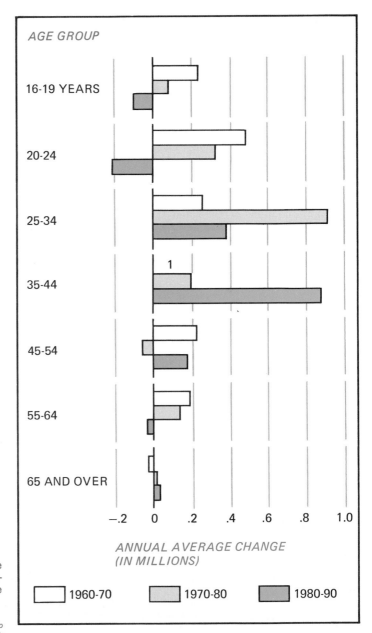

AGE GROUP

ANNUAL AVERAGE CHANGE
(IN MILLIONS)

1960-70   1970-80   1980-90

FIGURE 41-5

CHANGE IN THE LABOR FORCE (ANNUAL AVERAGE) BY AGE GROUP

(Over Successive Decades, 1960-1990)

During the decade of the 1970s, the largest increase in labor force membership will be in the 25-34 and the 35-44 age-group brackets.

SOURCE: *The U.S. Labor Force: Projections to 1990*, Special Labor Force Report 156 (Washington: Department of Labor, Bureau of Labor Statistics, 1973), p. 8.

[1]An increase of one thousand per year, on average.

because of the fact that minorities, particularly blacks, constitute a larger percentage of the population today than they did a few decades ago. According to the 1970 census, for example, nonwhites comprised

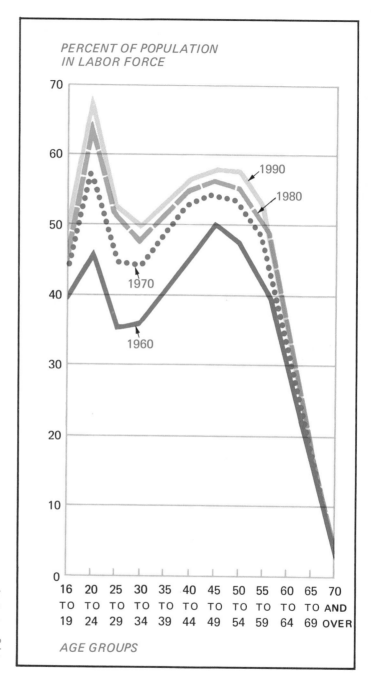

FIGURE 41-6

**LABOR FORCE PARTICIPATION
RATES OF WOMEN, BY AGE
1960-1990**

The labor force participation rate for women of all ages will increase noticeably in the next two decades.

SOURCE: *The U.S. Labor Force: Projections to 1990*, Special Labor Force Report 156 (Washington: Department of Labor, Bureau of Labor Statistics, 1973), p. 11.

11.1 percent of the U.S. population compared to less than 10 percent in 1950. The participation rate of these minority groups will increase as they obtain a higher level of education, more training, and better skills. In addition, the opening of more job opportunities for minority workers should encourage them and, therefore, raise their labor force participation rate.

MANPOWER PROBLEMS

With the growth of the population and the labor force, there will continue to be pressing manpower problems for the U.S. economy. Conditions of nagging unemployment will occur from time to time. Shortages of skilled manpower will occur at other times. Even with full employment, sore spots will appear that are difficult to heal; higher than average rates of unemployment will continue to exist among the elderly, the youth, the nonwhite, the unskilled, and those with limited formal education, as indicated in Chapter 10. Special training and retraining programs will be needed to alleviate and remedy some of these sticky areas of unemployment. More tolerance and assistance for minority workers will be necessary. Workers, too, will have to be more mobile and flexible, both geographically and vocationally.

Black Workers

Blacks form the largest single minority group of workers, comprising about 11 percent of the labor force. For decades large numbers of workers in this group lacked skills and training, possessed limited formal education, and were often discriminated against in the job market. Many of them have been forced to take jobs at relatively low pay and/or have worked in jobs very susceptible to layoffs. The position of the black worker has been improved in recent years, especially since the establishment of the Equal Employment Opportunity Commission through the Civil Rights Act of 1964. It can be seen from Figure 41-7 that blacks have made some advances in white-collar and skilled jobs. The average income of black families, however, is only about two thirds that of white families, and the unemployment rate among blacks is about twice the unemployment rate among whites. Even at full employment conditions of 4 percent unemployment for the total civilian labor force, unemployment among blacks runs about 7 percent.

Particularly distressing is the unemployment problem among black teenagers. During periods of full employment, unemployment among black teenagers is usually 20-25 percent, about double the rate among white teenagers. Moreover, unemployment among black teen-age females is usually 30 percent or more. This problem of high rates of unemployment among black teenagers is likely to be aggravated in the next decade. Because of the higher fertility rate among nonwhites compared to whites in the post-World War II years, a significant proportion of those entering the labor force in the 1970s and 1980s will be young members of minority groups, particularly blacks. In

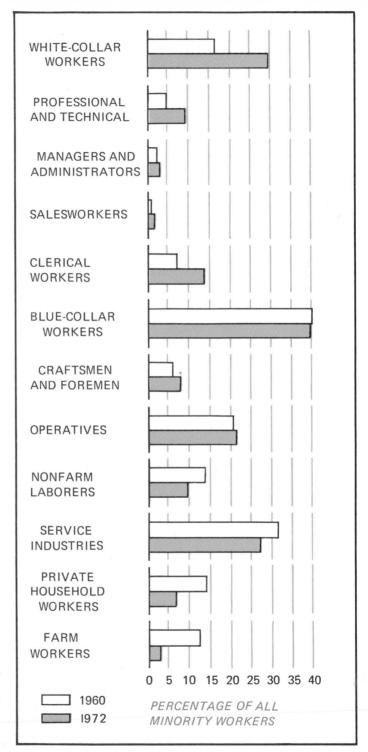

FIGURE 41-7

OCCUPATIONAL SHIFTS OF BLACKS AND OTHER MINORITY WORKERS

1960 and 1972

The proportion of black and other minority workers in white-collar and skilled jobs increased during the decade of the 1960s.

SOURCE: *Statistical Abstract of the United States, 1973.*

fact, in the next decade the black teen-age segment of the labor force will increase four times as fast as the white teen-age segment. Many of these black youngsters will be from disadvantaged sections of the population lacking skills, work experience, or a higher level of education.

There is often a wide gap between the skills required by employers and the actual skills of job applicants from the various minority sectors. In addition, the job scene for minority youngsters is further complicated by the general practice of requiring a high school diploma as a prerequisite for a job. This trend, resulting from the rising level of education of the general population, may become even more widespread, making it more difficult for high school dropouts, particularly minority youths, to find jobs. In fact, some of them may be pushed out of the hard-to-employ category into the mass of unemployables. To overcome and prevent this catastrophe, more effort needs to be exerted to encourage and guide disadvantaged youths through conventional high school programs. Moreover, a major effort must be made to develop new high school curricula and programs related to the needs of these youths. On the other hand, there is need for employers to examine more closely the real skills, education, and work experience requirements necessary to fill some of their less skilled job positions.

Spanish-Americans

The second largest minority group in the United States, Americans of Spanish-speaking heritage, constitutes 5 percent of the total population. Many of these 10 million Spanish-Americans now living on the U.S. mainland face serious social and economic problems because of a variety of employment barriers, such as language difficulties, lack of skills, inadequacy of formal education, and outright ethnic discrimination. Despite their common Spanish heritage and background, the Spanish-Americans are a heterogeneous group. They are a microcosm of American ethnic diversity. Some are recent immigrants or first generation Americans, while others come from families that were living in the American Southwest or Puerto Rico before those areas became part of the United States. The largest group of Spanish-Americans, over 5.3 million, are of Mexican origin or descent. About 1.5 million are Puerto Ricans residing on the U.S. mainland; over 630,000 are Cubans, primarily refugees who have entered the United States since 1959. About 2 million trace their lineage to some other Spanish origin, generally in Central or South America.

Three distinctive groups of Spanish-Americans are concentrated in different parts of the United States. The majority of Mexican-Americans live in the Southwest; Puerto Ricans are heavily concentrated in New York City; and most Cubans live in Florida. Within each group many of these people live in close-knit neighborhoods. Although this is sometimes by choice, often it is because they are barred from, or cannot afford to, live elsewhere. Many of these neighborhoods are in city slums or in poverty-stricken areas on the fringe of urban areas.

In recent years the federal and state governments have taken steps to reduce the cultural isolation and language-barrier problems of these people. Although English literacy among younger Spanish-speaking Americans is relatively high, it is not so prevalent among some of the older age groups, as shown in Figure 41-8. Furthermore, many have inadequate formal education. All this, of course, contributes toward their high rate of unemployment, which is considerably above the national average. In March, 1972, for example, a survey indicated that the rate of unemployment among Spanish-Americans was 8 percent, about one third higher than the national average. Probably the best single measure of social and economic disadvantage of these families is manifest in their median family income of $7,500 per year compared to $10,300 for all Americans. However, this is still higher than the $6,400 for black families, as shown in Table 41-4. Those of Puerto Rican background, however, had a median income of $6,200 per annum.

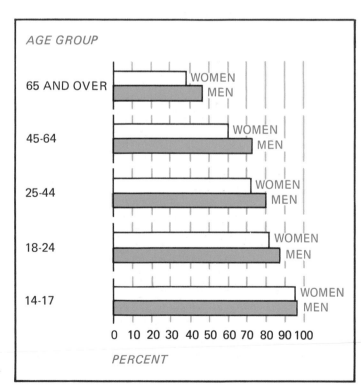

FIGURE 41-8

ENGLISH LITERACY AMONG SPANISH-SPEAKING POPULATION, BY AGE GROUPS, FOR THE UNITED STATES

Nearly all teen-agers of Spanish background are literate in English. In older age groups inability to read and write is a prevalent problem.

SOURCE: *Manpower Report of the President,* 1973, p. 95.

TABLE 41-4

FAMILY INCOMES

1971

Race and Spanish Origin	Median Income	Percent of Families with Incomes—	
		Under $5,000	$15,000 or More
All Families	$10,285	18.5	24.8
White	10,672	16.2	26.4
Black	6,440	38.6	10.6
Families of Spanish Origin	7,548	30.4	10.3
Mexican	7,486	31.2	9.1
Puerto Rican	6,185	38.5	5.3
Cuban	9,371	22.4	21.4
Other	8,494	24.5	13.0

SOURCE: Adapted from *Manpower Report of the President*, 1973, p. 100.

Employment aid has been extended to a number of Spanish-Americans through conventional programs, such as the Work Incentive Program (WIN), the Concentrated Employment Program (CEP), the Public Employment Program (PEP), and Job Opportunities in the Business Sector (JOBS). Other programs have been designed specifically for Spanish-American workers. These include: Service, Employment and Redevelopment (SER), aimed largely at disadvantaged Mexican-Americans in the Southwest; the National Migrant Worker Program, inaugurated in 1970 to aid crop workers; the Spanish-American Basic Education Rehabilitation program (SABER), to aid Cuban refugees; and the Basic Occupational Language Training program (BOLT), designed to teach job-related English to Puerto Ricans in New York City.

The federal Equal Employment Opportunity Commission (EEOC) recently has stepped up its activities to overcome discrimination barriers to the employment of Spanish-Americans. In addition, the U.S. Civil Service Commission, in cooperation with the Cabinet Committee on Opportunities for Spanish-speaking people, in 1970 launched a 16-point program to improve opportunities for Spanish-Americans in the federal job market. Within two years the number of Spanish-Americans working for the federal government had increased to 76,400, or 3 percent of the federal work force.

American Indians

The plight of American Indians in the areas of unemployment, income, health, and education is still severe today, even though public awareness of Indian problems has been increasing in recent years. The Bureau of Indian Affairs estimates that unemployment among the labor force on reservations averages about 40 percent, and in the winter months unemployment reaches 90 percent on some reservations. Annual income for reservation families is approximately $1,500. According to the 1970 census, there are 792,700

American Indians. About one half of these live in urban areas, while most of the remainder live on reservations. Although Indians are widely scattered throughout the United States, one half live in western states, particularly in Oklahoma, Arizona, California, and New Mexico. Only seven major U.S. cities have Indian populations in excess of 5,000.

Some Indians have been enrolled in Neighborhood Youth Corps and Job Corps programs, and 68,000 were enrolled in 1972 in the Employment Assistance Program operated by the Bureau of Indian Affairs. After several months of discussion with Indian leaders during early 1972, more than $3 million of Manpower Development and Training Program (MDTA) funds were allocated for special programs for Indians. These programs included skill-training projects for construction trades, health services, and clerical opportunities. Other Indian programs are sponsored by the Department of Labor, the Department of Health, Education and Welfare, the Department of Housing and Urban Development, and the Office of Economic Opportunity. Model Urban Information Centers in several states attempt to help Indians adjust to urban life without destroying their unique cultural heritage.

The Public Employment Program provided $8.4 million in 1972 to establish jobs on reservations. New uses are also being explored for the use of resources on reservations. On some reservations cash crops are being cultivated and harvested, copper is being mined, aquaculture is being used by Indians in the state of Washington, and an Indian national bank is soon to be established.

Women in the Economy

One of the most important changes in the American economy in recent decades has been the presence of an increasing number and proportion of women in the labor force. Prior to World War II, in 1940, women comprised 25.2 percent of the labor force. This increased to 28.8 percent by 1950, 32.3 percent by 1960, and in 1973 women made up over 37.4 percent of the labor force. This figure will rise to 38.7 percent by 1980.

In spite of the growing contribution of women to our total productive efforts, they have not had equal treatment in regard to wages, promotions, and job opportunities. Historically, many professions and occupations were not open to women. The creation of the Equal Employment Opportunity Commission, established by the Civil Rights Act of 1964, however, has been instrumental in reducing discrimination against women in the job market. The activity and authority of the EEOC was intensified through the passage of the Equal Employment Opportunity Act of 1972. The activities of the Women's Liberation movement, likewise, have had some impact on the employment status of women in the United States. In addition, in

January, 1973, the President established an Advisory Committee on the Economic Role of Women. Among the topics to be explored by this committee are women's work performance, the extent of job discrimination, women's access to financial credit, the need for child care for working mothers, the impact of Social Security differences between men and women, and the special problems of minority women.

The growing presence of women in the labor force, particularly married women, reflects a major change in the life-style of Americans. This is especially true since over 60 percent of the 33 million women in the labor force are married. This means that over one fourth of the total labor force is composed of married women. Currently 44 percent of all women of working age are active in the labor force, and the labor force participation rate of married women has doubled in the past 25 years. Furthermore, the labor force participation rate of women with children, even those with very young children, has increased rapidly in the past ten years. Thus, the old adage that "the woman's place is in the home" can stand scrutiny.

In spite of the fact that women have made substantial gains in some professions, less than 10 percent of the physicians, 3.5 percent of the dentists, and 5 percent of the lawyers in the United States are women. The low representation of women in professional and managerial occupations is shown in Table 41-5. Just how much of this situation results from a voluntary adjustment of balancing home life with work requirements and how much may be due to societal predilections, or prejudice, regarding the role of women is difficult to ascertain. Women may be voluntarily deterred, for example, from undertaking the long training required for many professions

TABLE 41-5

WOMEN AS A PERCENT OF PERSONS IN SEVERAL PROFESSIONAL AND MANAGERIAL OCCUPATIONS

1910-1970

Occupational Group	1910	1920	1930	1940	1950	1960	1970
Clergymen	0.6	1.4	2.2	2.4	4.0	2.3	2.9
College Presidents, Professors, and Instructors [1]	18.9	30.2	31.9	26.5	23.2	24.2	28.2
Dentists	3.1	3.3	1.9	1.5	2.7	2.3	3.5
Editors and Reporters	12.2	16.8	24.0	25.0	32.0	36.6	40.6
Engineers	([2])	([2])	([2])	.4	1.2	.8	1.6
Lawyers and Judges	.5	1.4	2.1	2.5	3.5	3.5	4.9
Managers, Manufacturing Industries	1.7	3.1	3.2	4.3	6.4	7.1	6.3
Physicians	6.0	5.0	4.4	4.7	6.1	6.9	9.3

SOURCE: *Economic Report of the President*, 1973.

[1] Data for 1920 and 1930 probably include some teachers in schools below collegiate rank. The Office of Education estimates the 1930 figure closer to 28 percent.
[2] Less than one tenth of one percent.
General Note: Data are from the decennial censuses. Data for 1910 and 1920 include persons ten years of age and over; data for 1930 to 1970 include persons 14 years of age and over.

simply because of the time involved vis-á-vis their marital intentions. On the other hand, some women may be deterred because of a general feeling of discrimination. As a result, women do not have as broad an occupational distribution as do men.

Not only have women been restricted in certain occupations and professions, but their pay scales are generally lower than those of men. Particularly irritating is the practice of paying women a lower wage than men for doing identical work. Some of this, however, has been reduced or eliminated through activities of the federal Equal Employment Opportunity Commission and through state acts requiring equal pay for equal work. Still, within occupational groups, women tend to hold lower paying jobs than men. This is caused by a number of reasons, such as differences in skills, education, training, job experience, work experience, the desire for temporary as opposed to permanent employment, and outright discrimination. From Table 41-6 it can be seen that earnings of women workers are only about two thirds that of men for various occupations in the civilian labor force. Figure 41-9 shows the striking differences between annual incomes for male and female workers. Of course, if an imputed income for services rendered by housewives were added to the earnings of female members of the labor force, the income of women would skyrocket.

TABLE 41-6

RATIO OF TOTAL MONEY EARNINGS OF CIVILIAN WOMEN WORKERS TO EARNINGS OF CIVILIAN MEN WORKERS

Selected Years, 1956-1971

Occupational Group	Actual Ratios					Adjusted Ratios [1]	
	1956	1960	1965	1969	1971	1969	1971
Total [2]	63.3	60.7	59.9	58.9	59.5	65.9	66.1
Professional and Technical Workers	62.4	61.3	65.2	62.2	66.4	67.9	72.4
Teachers, Primary and Secondary Schools ...	([3])	75.6	79.9	72.4	82.0	([3])	([3])
Managers, Officials, and Proprietors	59.1	52.9	53.2	53.1	53.0	57.2	56.8
Clerical Workers	71.7	67.6	67.2	65.0	62.4	70.0	66.9
Salesworkers	41.8	40.9	40.5	40.2	42.1	45.7	47.4
Craftsmen and Foremen	([4])	([4])	56.7	56.7	56.4	60.8	60.2
Operatives	62.1	59.4	56.6	58.7	60.5	65.4	66.6
Service Workers Excluding Private Household Workers .	55.4	57.2	55.4	57.4	58.5	62.5	63.2

SOURCE: *Economic Report of the President*, 1973.

[1] Adjusted for differences in average full-time hours worked since full-time hours for women are typically less than full-time hours for men.
[2] Total includes occupational groups not shown separately.
[3] Not available.
[4] Base too small to be statistically significant.
General Note: Data relate to civilian workers who are employed full time, year-round. Data for 1956 include salaried workers only, while data for later years include both salaried and self-employed workers.

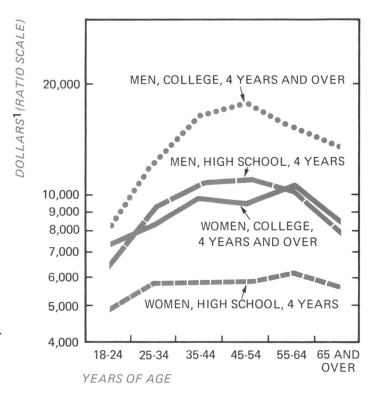

FIGURE 41-9

ANNUAL INCOME BY AGE FOR MALE AND FEMALE HIGH SCHOOL AND COLLEGE GRADUATES

In most age and education categories incomes of male workers are higher than those of female workers.

SOURCE: *Economic Report of the President,* 1973.

Chart labels:
DOLLARS[1] (RATIO SCALE)

MEN, COLLEGE, 4 YEARS AND OVER

MEN, HIGH SCHOOL, 4 YEARS

WOMEN, COLLEGE, 4 YEARS AND OVER

WOMEN, HIGH SCHOOL, 4 YEARS

20,000
10,000
9,000
8,000
7,000
6,000
5,000
4,000

18-24   25-34   35-44   45-54   55-64   65 AND OVER

YEARS OF AGE

[1]Median income of full-time, year-round workers, 1971

Although the income gap between men and women on identical jobs with the same employer has been narrowed, and even eliminated, in many cases, differences do persist within professions and occupations. But even here some studies suggest that after making adjustments for differences in economic factors, such as experience and education, income differentials within occupations can be reduced well below 20 percent. This, however, merely shifts the focus of the problem. Why do women have a different occupational structure than men, and why in different professions are women employed in lower paying establishments than are men?

As mentioned before, women may stay away from certain occupations because of the nature of the work, the education or training required, or because of their desire for temporary work as opposed to permanent employment. There is no doubt, however, about the fact that discrimination against women, particularly in certain professions and occupations, still exists today. Although at one time an oddity, it is no longer uncommon to see women bus, cab, and truck drivers, female commercial airline pilots, car saleswomen, telephone lineswomen, women jockeys, and lady gas station attendants. But there is still prejudice against women in many occupations. Some patients will not select a woman doctor, many clients will not engage a female lawyer, some customers avoid automobile saleswomen, and many workers reject the idea of a woman boss. It may not be possible to determine precisely the degree of inferior economic status of women that results from outright sex discrimination, compared to the role difference created by women who, by choice or necessity, restrict their career opportunities in favor of home duties. Nevertheless, there are a number of obvious cases of outright sex discrimination that must be eliminated in an effort to improve the economic status of women in our economy.

Criminal Offenders

A separate group requiring special study is criminal offenders. Growing unrest within our prisons and the failure to reduce crime and the number of habitual offenders led to accelerated action in the early 1970s to find and develop more effective means of rehabilitating these offenders. Training programs, such as those inaugurated in the late 1960s under MDTA, were improved and expanded, including the adoption of off-site experience. Such programs are needed, as can be seen from Figures 41-10 and 41-11.

An innovation was the pretrial interview project, designed to salvage offenders for employment opportunities through manpower and counseling

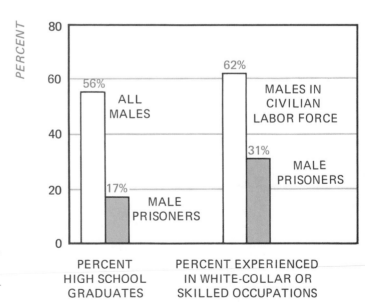

FIGURE 41-10

EDUCATION AND SKILL STATUS OF MALE PRISONERS

In terms of education and skills, offenders rank far below average.

SOURCE: *U.S. Manpower in the 1970's*, Department of Labor, 1970.

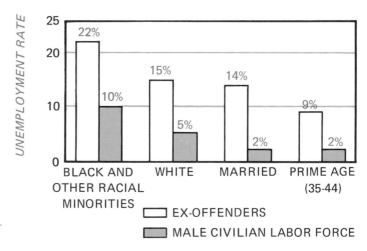

UNEMPLOYMENT RATE

FIGURE 41-11

UNEMPLOYMENT RATES OF MALE OFFENDERS

Unemployment is much higher among all groups of ex-offenders.

SOURCE: *U.S. Manpower in the 1970's,* Department of Labor, 1970.

services rather than subjecting them to the more usual process of arraignment, trial, sentencing, incarceration, release, and a possible new criminal violation.

In addition, a two-year study was inaugurated to analyze the effectiveness of giving financial aid and employment assistance to prisoners released from correctional institutions. Also, in an effort to promote new programs to help rehabilitation, the Secretaries of Labor and HEW, along with the U.S. Attorney General, jointly invited the governors of all the states to work with federal agencies in drafting national guidelines and to plan for the development of comprehensive state programs.

The problem of rehabilitating the offender to become a productive and useful member of society is complex. Several years of research and experimentation have revealed much but, as yet, have yielded no final solution to the problem. A growing awareness of this problem, however, should permit more resources to be devoted to its solution in the future. The need for solution becomes evident when one considers that we have about 196,000 prisoners incarcerated at a given time. Although 156,000 were sentenced to prison in 1970, 154,000 were discharged for various reasons. Moreover, more than one half of the inmates released from prison are rearrested within five years.

SUMMARY

1. After slowing down in the 1930s, the rate of population growth in the United States experienced a definite upturn in the post-World War II decades.

2. By the time the U.S. population reached 200 million in the late 1960s, the rate of population growth had declined noticeably.

3. Based upon varying rates of fertility, current population projections by the Bureau of the Census estimate a population in the range of 231 million to 249 million by the year 1985, with the most probable estimate being in the vicinity of 240 million.

4. Certain groups are recommending that the United States strive for a zero population growth goal. If the ZPG birth rate of 2.1 were attained today, the U.S. population would stabilize around 300 million some time in the 2020s.

5. A ZPG rate and the accompanying change in the population age-structure would have pronounced economic effects on businesses, schools, government services, the environment, and the labor force.

6. Labor force projections, with some modifications, parallel but lag behind those of population esti-mates. In the years ahead there will be fewer teen-agers entering the labor force. A large increase, how-ever, is expected in the 25-34 age bracket, and women will enter the labor force at an increasing rate.

7. The growth of the labor force will highlight some of our future manpower problems. Special prob-lems will continue to exist, and perhaps be aggravated, among minority groups of workers such as blacks, Spanish-Americans, and American Indians. Criminal offend-ers will require special help also.

8. In the future, women will play a more intensive and extensive role in the American economy.

NEW TERMS **Secular stagnation,** *p. 906*

Population projections, *p. 907*

Age structure of population, *p. 909*

Zero Population Growth (ZPG), *p. 910*

Birth rate, *p. 911*

Participation rate of labor force, *p. 913*

Civil Rights Act of 1964, *p. 918*

Equal Employment Opportunity Commission (EEOC), *p. 918*

Equal Employment Opportunity Act of 1972, *p. 923*

QUESTIONS FOR DISCUSSION AND ANALYSIS

1. What happened to the birth rate and the population growth rate in the United States in the late 1960s and early 1970s?

2. Why do U.S. population projec-tions for the future made by the Bureau of the Census differ? What are the high and low projection figures?

3. How will a slowdown in the birth rate affect the age structure of the U.S. population?

4. Will the U.S. population grow uniformly throughout the country in the future? Explain.

5. What is ZPG? If the population reaches a ZPG rate, how long will it take for the U.S. population to stabilize? Why?

6. What effect would a ZPG rate have on the private sector of the economy?

7. Do you favor ZPG? Why or why not?

8. What major changes are ex-pected in the age-sex composition of the labor force in the next dec-ade or more?

9. Why is the unemployment rate higher among nonwhite workers than it is among white workers?

10. What are the three distinctive

categories of Spanish-Americans living in America today?

11. Do you think that special programs should be designed and implemented to reduce unemployment among minority groups?

12. Do you favor the idea of giving American Indians a guaranteed annual income? Why or why not?

13. Should all occupations and professions be open to women? Why or why not?

14. What accounts for the differences in earnings between men and women in the labor force?

SUGGESTED READINGS

"At Last, A National Manpower Policy." *Business Week* (August 7, 1971).

Economic Report of the President. Washington: U.S. Government Printing Office, 1971-1974.

Manpower Report of the President. Washington: U.S. Government Printing Office, 1971-1974.

Moore, Geoffrey H. *How Full Is Full Employment?* Washington: American Enterprise Institute for Public Policy Research (July, 1973).

O'Neill, Dave M. *The Federal Government and Manpower.* Washington: American Enterprise Institute for Public Policy Research, August, 1973.

The American Economy: Prospects for Growth to 1985. New York: McGraw-Hill Book Company, 1972.

The U.S. Labor Force: Projections to 1990, Special Labor Force Report 156. Washington: U.S. Government Printing Office, 1973.

U.S. Department of Commerce, Bureau of the Census. "Current Population Reports; Population Estimates and Projections," Series P-25. Washington: U.S. Government Printing Office (December, 1972).

U.S. Manpower in the 1970's. Washington: Department of Labor, 1970.

PART ELEVEN

International Trade
and Payments

42

International Trade

PREVIEW   Just as domestic trade brings benefits to the parties involved, free international trade can bring mutual economic benefits to nations. Nevertheless, political and military factors play a much larger role in the policies of nations, and these factors have often led to trade restrictions. United States trade policy has passed through an era of self-sufficiency in which high tariffs, import quotas, and other means were used to protect domestic industries. More recently, American policies have aimed at the lowering of restrictions to promote an expansion of world trade. In Europe, and to a lesser extent in other areas of the world, regional associations and trading blocs have come to dominate the trade policies of their member nations.

Many economic problems are international in origin and scope. They are complex, and it is difficult to discover effective solutions. This will continue to be true as long as the people of the earth live in separate nations and, consequently, are motivated by a spirit of nationalism rather than by a spirit of internationalism. Frequently the source of international problems is trade or the lack of trade among the nations of the world. How successful nations will be in solving these problems depends on how well the problems are understood and on the extent to which those who formulate national policies are willing to cooperate in promoting the welfare of all people everywhere.

WHY INTERNATIONAL TRADE?

Trade across national boundaries (between private enterprises presumably) takes place because the parties concerned are free to trade or not to trade as they wish, and they recognize some advantage in trading. Foreign trade may also occur between governments. Private trade may be subject to both restraints and aids by governments. When governments regulate trade, the private advantage, if any, is subject to considerations of national advantages, which may take precedence over private economic gain. In other words, foreign trade is subject to political considerations that are not likely to be found in purely domestic trade, and these political factors cannot be disregarded in any realistic study of international trade.

An international division of labor is only an extension of what occurs here at home. In the United States, North Carolina specializes in the production of tobacco while Wisconsin specializes in the production of dairy products. This division of labor has been found to be mutually advantageous. Wisconsin could cultivate tobacco at great expense. Instead, the people of Wisconsin concentrate on what they can produce more efficiently, trading their dairy products for tobacco. In this way, households in Wisconsin can consume more tobacco, and no less butter, than they could if they were to attempt their own tobacco production. Similarly, North Carolina could devote more of its resources to the production of dairy products (and, therefore, less to the production of tobacco). Residents of North Carolina choose not to do so because they can get more butter from Wisconsin by paying for it with receipts from what they can produce more efficiently, namely, tobacco.

Though the underlying principles of specialization in production are the same, international trade is more complicated. When trade involves two or more nations, the geographic areas not only have different "natural" advantages in producing one or another good, but they also have different currencies, different commercial and financial practices, and different governments. These differences create conditions that call for special attention.

Absolute Advantage

A nation or region is said to have an *absolute advantage* in production when it can produce a product more efficiently than can some other nation or region. Notice that the emphasis is on a single product. For example, if Country X can produce cotton at less real cost (resource use) per bale of cotton than can Country Y, then Country X has an absolute advantage over Country Y in the production of cotton.

Of course, one country may have an absolute advantage over another in the production of two or more commodities. In Table 42-1, by allocating 3 resource inputs to the production of cotton, Country X can produce 30 bales of cotton. Country Y, through the same use of resources, can produce only 15 bales. Thus, Country X has an absolute advantage over Country Y in the production of cotton.

TABLE 42-1

Country	Cotton		Wheat	
	Productive Inputs Used	Output in Bales	Productive Inputs Used	Output in Bushels
X	3	30	2	60
Y	3	15	2	40
Total	6	45	4	100

Notice that Country X also has an absolute advantage in the production of wheat. Employment of 2 units of productive resources in Country X

yields 60 bushels of wheat, whereas the same 2 units generate only 40 bushels of wheat in Country Y. If we assume that each country has a total of 5 productive inputs, does this mean that Country X should produce both products and leave Country Y to shift for itself? The answer cannot be found in absolute advantage.

Comparative Advantage

In the foregoing example it should be noted that both nations together produce 45 bales of cotton and 100 bushels of wheat with a total of 5 productive inputs each. The interesting question is whether the two countries might raise their combined production and their shares in "a larger pie" if each were to engage in more specialized production and trade the "surplus." As we shall see, this hinges not on absolute advantage but on comparative advantage. *Comparative advantage* is the efficiency or cost advantage a given nation has between two products (as opposed to the advantage over another nation in the production of a given product). In general, although one producer has the advantage in the production of both commodities, it is economically more beneficial for that producer to specialize in the production of the commodity in which he has the greater comparative advantage and let the other produce that commodity in which the first has the lesser comparative advantage.

Let us now pose again the question of whether Country X should produce both cotton and wheat. If it were to apply the principle of comparative advantage, Country X would produce the commodity in which it has the comparative advantage. According to our example, Country X should specialize in the production of cotton, for it has a 2 to 1 advantage in the production of this item over Country Y, while it has only a 3 to 2 advantage in the production of wheat. If Country X were to devote all its resources to the production of cotton, it would be able to produce 50 bales. If Country Y channeled its 3 productive units that had been used for cotton into wheat production, it could produce a total of 100 bushels of wheat. Thus, the new schedule of output would be that shown in Table 42-2.

TABLE 42-2

| | Cotton | | Wheat | |
Country	Productive Inputs Used	Output in Bales	Productive Inputs Used	Output in Bushels
X	5	50	0	—
Y	0	—	5	100
Total ...	5	50	5	100

The two countries combined have gained a total of 5 bales of cotton. Now you may ask: Who gets what? That depends upon the exchange between the two countries, but it should work out favorably for both countries. In order to regain its former ratio of wheat to cotton, Country Y would demand 15 bales of cotton, the amount that it gave up in order to specialize, in exchange for 60 bushels of wheat. On the other hand, Country X could afford to give 20 bales of cotton, the amount it obtained through specialization, in exchange for 60 bushels of wheat and still lose nothing compared to what it originally had. It is easy to engage in trade when one country needs only 15 bales of cotton and the other can afford to give as much as 20 bales of cotton for 60 bushels of wheat.

The exchange ratio of wheat to cotton will be set by bargaining between the two countries, and final settlements will depend upon many economic circumstances. If we assume that the countries are of equal economic strength, they might split the difference and set the exchange ratio at 17.5 bales of cotton for 60 bushels of wheat. Trading on this basis, assume that Country X exports 17.5 bales of cotton, reducing its total used domestically to 32.5 bales. This means that each country would have 2.5 more bales of cotton than it had when each country produced both wheat and cotton. In exchange for the cotton, Country Y would have to send to Country X 60 bushels of wheat. The amount of wheat remaining in Country Y would be 40 bushels, which would be the same amount it had under the first plan. Country X

TABLE 42-3

Country	Cotton (Bales)	Wheat (Bushels)
X [1]	32.5	60
Y	17.5	40
Totals	50.0	100

[1] X imports wheat from Y and exports cotton to Y.

would have 60 bushels of wheat, the same amount it had before any specialization and exchange took place. As depicted in Table 42-3, the final position after the specialization and exchange would show a total gain of 5 bales of cotton, 2.5 for Country X and 2.5 for Country Y. Both would have the same amount of wheat as they formerly produced. Both nations have benefited by utilizing the principle of comparative advantage.

Comparative advantage hinges on relative costs of production. Consequently, the principle that expresses the comparative advantage that one nation may have over another is often referred to as the *principle of comparative costs*. This principle expresses the results that follow from specialization as a form of division of labor, and it holds true as definitely for trade between the peoples of different nations as it does for domestic trade.

When the principle of comparative costs is allowed to determine types of production, there are certain beneficial results. In each nation a larger proportion of labor is more efficiently employed. The workers' wages are higher than would otherwise be the case, productivity tends to increase, and actual levels of living are higher than would otherwise be true. When the specialization characteristic of a division of labor is allowed to reach its full development, the result is a maximum gain that is limited only by resources, technology, and the size and quantity of the labor force in a country.

If these economic benefits are desirable, why, then, are there so many limitations and hindrances to international specialization in production?

TRADE RESTRICTIONS

The sentiment of belonging to a particular group that speaks the same language and has the same customs and government, that is, the sentiment of nationalism, is a very important factor that may modify maximum economic advantage. Other objectives are considered equally necessary, such as national security. Furthermore, great differences exist among nations. Some nations are more advanced technologically, some are much larger than others, and all are exposed to worldwide fluctuations in economic activity that in their domestic form are called business cycles.

Under these circumstances, the governments of nations, with or without the consent of their peoples, have developed policies that restrain trade because it is believed that such policies advance the national interest. In this way the international division of labor, which can be most beneficial to all nations when it is free to operate, is limited by political action directed toward particular national objectives. The most important aids and restraints employed by governments to protect their national interests are tariffs, quotas, embargoes, barter agreements, exchange restrictions, and subsidies. What are the nature and effects of these restraints on international trade?

Tariffs

A *tariff* is a schedule of duties or taxes imposed by a government on imports of particular goods into a country (and in some cases on exports from the country). The purpose of the tariff is to increase the cost of the commodity to the importer, whether he is a merchant or a consumer of the good. Some tariff rates are *ad valorem*, that is, the rate applies to the declared value of the article. Other rates are *specific*, that is, the tax applies to the number of units of the good imported and not to its monetary value.

Where free trade is accepted as an economic policy, the schedule of tariff duties may be limited to a few major commodities that are taxed for the purpose of raising revenue, and not for protection. In England the tariff for many years was used primarily for the purpose of raising revenue. The duty on tea, for example, brought revenue to the Crown, but it could not affect the growing of tea in England because there was none grown there. A tariff, however, may be primarily for protection, in which case the rates are made high enough to discourage the importation of the taxed commodity or to prevent entirely the entry of the good. Where protection of the domestic market is a definite policy, the schedule of tariff duties is likely to be extensive and complex and subject to frequent change.

When a tariff rate is set to protect the domestic producer, the question may properly be asked, Why is it necessary to protect him? Firm X, a domestic producer, can make an article at a cost of $20. A foreign competitor, Firm Y, can produce a similar article of the same quality to sell in the American market for $15. A specific duty of $10 per unit is levied, and the foreign article will now sell at not less than $25 in the American market. Firm X can set a price between $20 and $25 and continue to market its product at a profit. If it sets a price of $23, the consumer, who could have bought the article for $15 before the duty was imposed, must now pay $23, and the less efficient American producer is, in effect, receiving a subsidy of $8 per unit to continue his production. Since the foreign producer, Firm Y, cannot compete, its goods do not enter the American market, dollar exchange is not created, and thus the foreigner cannot use dollar exchange to buy other American products. The American exporter and the consumer are taxed in order that Firm X may continue in business. If these are the results, what justification is to be found for a protective tariff?

Many arguments have been developed to justify a tariff imposed for protection of domestic industry, but there are only three that are generally accepted:

1. Protection of industries necessary to the defense of the nation;
2. Protection of young industries that show promise of great expansion; and
3. Emergency protection, as by means of antidumping duties and those imposed to counteract depreciated foreign currency.

Protection of industries necessary for national defense is a most important reason. In a world where opposing political and economic philosophies vie for new recruits, and where wars and police actions continue to break out in spite of searches for reconciliation, nations must often look to their defenses. Since modern war involves practically all industries, this argument can be used to justify protection of any industry that produces a good the supply of which is at least partly obtained by imports, especially if the phrase "necessary for national defense" is interpreted liberally.

The need for protection of young and promising industries is almost as appealing to most people. Not all nations are in the same stage of technological development. Unless protection is devised for the budding industries of the underdeveloped nations, for example, their markets are likely to be dominated by the products of the more advanced countries. In this situation protection leads to a more rapid and diversified industrialization of an underdeveloped nation and at a higher cost to consumers in that nation, for the advantages of international division of labor have been deliberately set aside in order to attain a greater degree of industrial independence. Unfortunately industries that are not really suited to the capacities of that country are thus sometimes developed; they are young but not promising, except at high cost.

Emergency use of protection is even more justified in cases where dumping or exchange depreciation have created disordered market conditions. Dumping implies sporadic unloading of surpluses at low prices by a foreign competitor. By lowering the price of its currency in terms of other currencies, a country can also temporarily stimulate its exports. Both practices can be damaging to the markets of other countries and can create undue hardships for their producers and merchants; hence, the general demand for protection.

Other Restraints on Trade

If a business depression in another country lowers prices in that country, a protective tariff may no longer protect effectively. Then more drastic action—embargoes, quotas, barter agreements, exchange restrictions, and subsidies—may be considered advisable. These are emergency measures to protect a nation's trade from abnormal pressures of foreign commerce. Since all nations can employ them, the result may be worse confusion, with a violent reduction in the volume of international trade.

An *embargo* is complete prohibition of the entry of particular foreign goods; *quotas* are limits on quantities of imports; *barter agreements* provide for limited imports in exchange for limited exports of particular goods; *exchange restrictions* regulate the flow of payments for particular purposes and thus restrain trade indirectly; and *subsidies*, direct or indirect, are government payments intended to aid domestic industry if it is exposed to unfavorable competitive conditions in foreign trade. These emergency measures may provide temporary aid to a nation's commerce, but they can also arouse retaliation that may do more damage than any benefits that may be derived. They must, therefore, be used with great caution.

Subsidies and Countervailing Duties

In order to stimulate the production of certain kinds of goods in the nation, some governments pay subsidies or bounties to domestic producers.

These subsidies may be in the form of property or business income-tax exemptions, the awarding of government contracts for production, outright gifts of cash, or some other method of favorable treatment. The use of such devices has two effects: it protects domestic producers from foreign competition, and it lessens the amount of protection provided producers in a country that imports the goods produced under such subsidies in the exporting country. For example, if Country *A* subsidizes the production of a good, then the good may be sold in Country *B* at a lower price than would be possible without the subsidy.

In order to offset the effect of the subsidy, the importing country may impose a special tariff, or *countervailing duty*, on foreign goods that have been produced under subsidy in the exporting country. In addition, a country may levy an excise, or sales, tax on certain imported commodities similar in amount to the excise taxes levied in the importing country. The importing country may levy a processing or manufacturing tax on certain imported raw materials or semifinished goods. For example, the United States levies a processing tax on imported petroleum products, lumber, greases, oil, inedible animal fats, and some other products.

Protection Through Administrative Devices

By the use of its sovereign power, a nation can intervene in domestic or foreign trade in order to protect the health and general welfare of the people. In recent decades governments have used this right or power to an increasing extent in order to reduce the amount of certain kinds of imports and thereby provide protection for domestic producers. The General Agreement on Tariffs and Trade (discussed later) limits the use of this administrative device to situations in which its use is justified.

National Economic Security

People of every nation seek as high a level of living as possible. They also seek such security in their economic conditions as may make that level of living reasonably permanent. Nations vary as to area and population, and security may therefore be only relative. Nations with great land areas but which are not too large in population, such as the United States, may enjoy a relatively high degree of economic security because they are blessed with adequate amounts of the economic fundamentals, namely, natural resources, manufacturing establishments, and trade facilities, such as rivers, roads, railroads, and efficient means of communication.

Small Nations. Some nations are small in area and large in population. Their economic security is problematical, unless they can cooperate effectively with other people. Belgium, for example, is a small nation of 11,781 square miles (which is only a little larger than Maryland) with a population of 9.7 million, or about 824 persons for each square mile. The density of population in the United States, not including Alaska and Hawaii, by contrast is about 67 persons per square mile. How can the Belgians maintain a relatively high level of living when there are so many of them in such a small area? In the first place, they produce at home as large quantities as possible of foodstuffs and other necessities; then they turn to world markets for raw materials out of which Belgian products are manufactured. These products, in turn, are sold in world markets; and with the profits of their industries, the Belgians import the additional foodstuffs and other necessities of life that are required to maintain their level of living. Thus, the Belgians must turn to world markets in three different connections: (1) for raw materials, (2) for sale of the manufactured products, and (3) for additional quantities of the necessities of life. Because of this dependence on world markets, the people of Belgium can be expected to favor stability of prices in these markets and to welcome any international action that is intended to insure such stability.

Japan, too, is a small nation with high population density. Covering an area of 144,698 square miles (smaller than Montana), it has a population of more than 107 million inhabitants (compared to less than one million in Montana). Traditionally Japan has had to produce what it could at home and manufacture goods for export in order to gain the additional foodstuffs necessary to maintain even the low level of living of its great masses. In the late 1940s Japan was close to bankruptcy and starvation. Since that time, it has maintained a real average growth rate of 10 percent annually—twice the average for the advanced Western countries. Between 1965 and 1973, Japan's growth rate averaged an amazing 12 percent per year. During the same period, Japan's trade with the rest of the world increased annually at a rate of 16.8 percent in real terms, or twice the rate at which total world trade has expanded. Per capita income has risen over the past ten years from $700 to over $2,400. As a consequence of this growth, by 1968 Japan had overtaken West Germany in terms of GNP to become the world's third largest producer after the United States and the Soviet Union. In contrast to its earlier dependence on foreign assistance, by 1971 Japan had become the second largest contributor, among non-Communist nations, of long-term capital to underdeveloped countries. Today Japan's rapid economic growth and the volume of its exports make it perhaps the most dynamic element in the world economy.

Large Nations. Large nations, like the United States, those in the British Commonwealth, and the U.S.S.R., are able to maintain their economic security with less dependence on world markets. Because these larger nations are relatively well provided with economic fundamentals—resources, good agricultural land, and effective manufacturing establishments—they can pursue a policy of self-sufficiency that is impossible for more dependent nations. This policy of self-sufficiency, or *autarky* as it has been called, may be developed by various methods in accordance with the particular economic characteristics of each nation. Although large and well-endowed nations are less self-sufficient today than they were 30 years ago, they are still able to rely primarily on their domestic resources and production for national prosperity.

The British Commonwealth of Nations is a sea empire, for its widely scattered parts are held together by sea routes and ocean transportation. Still comprising nearly 25 percent of the land surface of the earth and accounting for more than one fifth of the total world trade, this large Commonwealth has a highly developed manufacturing center in the United Kingdom and large outlying areas, such as Canada, with extensive resources, including good agricultural land. For more than 75 years, from 1849 to 1932, a policy of complete free trade was maintained by the Commonwealth as a means of promoting its economic security. Since 1932 a preferential tariff with lower rates for members of the Commonwealth than for others has served the same purposes.

By way of contrast, the U.S.S.R. might be called a land empire because it possesses a large united land mass, comprising 17 percent of the land surface of the earth, with very few outlying dependencies. Well equipped with economic fundamentals and with a highly centralized government, this nation can pursue a policy of self-containment impossible for most nations. Because of its highly centralized government, that is, because trade with other people is through government agencies and not through private enterprise, the U.S.S.R. is in a position to employ all the restraints of trade to a degree impossible in most other nations, if it finds such procedure to its advantage.

Between these extremes of relatively free trade and a very high degree of self-containment lies the policy of the United States. Perhaps even better endowed with economic fundamentals but committed to an economy of private enterprise (that is, with foreign trade between private interests rather than between governments), this nation has made extensive use of the protective tariff to insure its domestic markets against intrusion except on its own terms. With its vast territory, however, which comprises approximately 6 percent of the land surface of the earth, the United States has in the past been more concerned with the development of the domestic market than with foreign trade. Domestic trade has usually been more than 90 percent of the nation's total trade. Thus, the United States has sought to maintain its economic security through a policy of protection that has limited trade with other nations in favor of a domestic market where industry has been free to diversify and expand to meet domestic demand.

Here, then, is a variety of policies—policies of necessity in the case of some nations, policies of choice by others—all intended to provide a degree of economic security on the assumption that economic nationalism is the only practical economic way of life in the modern world. Policies that represent restraints of trade, however, usually conflict with the principle of comparative costs. Consequently, they tend to prevent the maximization of world economic well-being.

The Results of Economic Nationalism

Economic nationalism implies that nations in international markets occupy much the same position as private enterprises in the domestic market. In the latter case some enterprises are large and dominate their market; some are small and follow their lead; some enterprises are advanced in organization and technological methods, and some are old-fashioned; but all are in competition, and each is forced to look out for its own welfare. With the ups and downs of business activity, each enterprise will pursue a policy that has as its objective its own maximum benefit, regardless of the effects of that policy on other enterprises or the general welfare. When nations in the international markets are in a position much like this, there is at least one essential difference. There is no international government that can do for nations what a national government can do for the national economy, namely, maintain a high level of welfare by appropriate action or restore it in case of failure to maintain such a level. The purpose of the United Nations is for discussion and persuasion, not for coercion. If the principle of comparative costs points to the ultimate advantage of division of labor among nations and if economic nationalism appears to reduce this advantage greatly, if not destroy it entirely, what other procedures may be employed to preserve and promote the incentives for higher economic efficiency?

INTERNATIONAL COOPERATION

The competitive, capitalistic system, with its division of labor, is also a cooperative system. Insofar as competition leads to a more effective and productive division of labor, the resulting cooperation is likely to mean not only increased welfare but peace as well. Any attempt to achieve greater international prosperity must aim in this direction. The efforts of the great nations, as well as those of the small nations so dependent on international trade, must be in the direction of international economic cooperation and the expansion of trade, national income, and welfare that go with it. Only by such international collaboration can the self-interest of each national group be reconciled with a wider security for all. If such deliberate cooperation can be attained and maintained, a new economic internationalism will develop and reduce to some extent the frictions that result from economic nationalism.

The development of new international agencies for the promotion of greater cooperation has been one of the notable consequences of the great economic breakdown of the 1930s and World War II. These agencies are notable for their objectives and for the promising beginnings that have been made in spite of the opposition or indifference of those who think only in terms of national interests. But these international agencies will be of little significance if nations pursue policies that are focused entirely on national survival without regard to the common welfare. This problem of cooperation or conflict constitutes the fundamental issue that underlies present-day international relations.

The Point Four program of technical assistance to underdeveloped areas of the world and the Marshall Plan to aid in the reconstruction of Europe after World War II represent major contributions of the United States in the same direction.

Among people who accept the principle of international cooperation, the first and perhaps the most important thing that any nation can do is to attain and maintain a high level of domestic prosperity. This fact is particularly important in the case of the United States because of the influence that this nation exerts on the economies of smaller nations. As was indicated in Chapter 9 on business cycles, a continuous high level of economic activity is entirely possible and can be made a reality if the proper degree of adjustment can be made by the federal government as circumstances dictate.

Business fluctuations may be international in their effect. Therefore, any measures taken by one country, however large and important the country may be, to stabilize its economic activity at full employment will not be adequate in the face of international depression, unless it pursues a policy of autarky. Direct attack on international business cycles by way of international conventions is likewise inadequate in view of the variety of economic systems in a world of many nations. But efforts can be directed toward the expansion of trade between nations on the assumption that expansion will mean more employment, larger national income, and greater prosperity.

UNITED STATES TRADE POLICY

In its early history, the United States endeavored to be a leader in the promotion of world trade, but its attitude has changed from time to time. In its first few decades the new nation used the tariff primarily for revenue purposes. Tariffs were necessarily low in order to encourage the importation of goods so customs duties could be collected. At that time 90 percent or more of the revenue obtained by the federal government came from tariffs. About 1815, as a result of the effects of British and other import competition on our infant American industries, which had been given a fillip during the War of 1812 and the prewar embargo acts, the federal government began to shift from a revenue to a protectionist tariff policy.

High-Tariff Era

Although protection became more important in United States tariff policy thereafter, the tariff continued to be a major source of federal revenue until the Civil War. Since then, it has declined in relative importance as a source of federal funds. As protection became more predominant with the growth of American industry, tariff rates continued to climb, at least intermittently. Politically it appears that high tariffs are associated with the Republican and lower tariffs with the Democratic administrations. After World War I, tariff rates were at their highest level in history, but they were pushed still higher by the Hawley-Smoot Tariff Act of 1930. Shortly thereafter, there was hardly an import commodity that did not have a customs duty, and some rates exceeded 100 percent of the original value of the commodity. The average tariff as a percentage of the value of all imports was about 33 percent.

Reciprocal Trade Agreements

The great depression of the thirties and the inauguration of the New Deal ushered in a new policy of lower tariffs. Under the Reciprocal Trade Agreements Act of 1934, the President of the United States was given authority to lower tariffs by as much as 50 percent, without further Congressional approval, provided other nations would make reciprocal concessions. As a result of this Act, more than 30 separate agreements have been made with foreign nations. Tariff rates have been reduced on nearly 2,000 commodities, and the average level of American tariffs has been cut by more than 50 percent under the Act. Included in the Act was the famous "most favored nation" clause by which concessions made in bilateral agreements were generalized to all nations. This requires that if we lower our tariff on wool imports from Australia, this lower rate must apply also to the importation of wool from any other nation that does not discriminate against the United States. In short, we had to extend to all nations the same tariff benefits we gave to most-favored nations. On the other hand, we would not enter into any trade agreement with a foreign nation unless it extended to us the same tariff concessions on various commodities that it gave to its most-favored nation(s).

Although tariff rates were reduced substantially under the Reciprocal Trade Agreements Act in its first 10-15 years, the reductions and coverage permitted by the Act were later weakened by various amendments and revisions. In 1948, for example, the "peril-point provision" gave the Federal Tariff Commission the authority to specify the rates below which tariffs could not be reduced in certain industries without injuring domestic producers. In 1951 the "escape clause" became a part of the Act. This clause permits the raising of tariff rates if the Tariff Commission finds that existing tariffs are causing harm or seriously threatening domestic producers. A 1954 amendment prohibits any tariff reduction that might threaten national security.

General Agreement on Tariffs and Trade

After World War II several of the Allied nations, exclusive of the Soviet Union, met in an effort to form an International Trade Organization (ITO) for the purpose of promoting free trade among nations of the world. Although the move to establish the ITO failed, negotiations did lead to agreements about tariffs, quotas, and other forms of trade restriction. The outcome was the formulation of the General Agreement on Tariffs and Trade (GATT), which was drawn up at Geneva in 1947 and accepted by 23 signatory nations, including the United States. The General Agreement called for equal and nondiscriminatory treatment for all nations in international trade, the reduction of tariffs by negotiations similar to the method used in reciprocal trade agreements, and the easing or elimination of import quotas. One of the main provisions of the Agreement was that of extending the most-favored-nation principle to all signers. At the present time some 80 nations have adopted the General Agreement on Tariffs and Trade.

The original agreement covered 45,000 items, involving about two thirds of the import trade carried on by the 23 signatory nations. Subsequently the United States has entered into agreements with several nations and benefits substantially from the generalization of bilateral agreements between other nations as a result of the implementation of the most-favored-nation provision. Although some progress toward liberalizing trade had taken place under GATT, it was rather limited until the so-called Kennedy Round of negotiations from 1964 to 1967. Since GATT is not a formal agreement, but rather an informal one, there is nothing compelling a nation to eliminate or reduce any of its trade restrictions.

Trade Expansion Act of 1962

The policy toward lower tariffs was reinforced by the passage of the Trade Expansion Act of 1962. This Act was designed for three purposes: (1) to stimulate the economic growth of the United States and to enlarge foreign markets for its products; (2) to strengthen economic relations with foreign countries through the development of open and nondiscriminatory trading in the free world; and (3) to prevent Communist economic penetration. The Act authorized the President to enter into international trade agreements between 1962 and 1967 with foreign nations and to decrease tariff rates on particular commodities by as much as 50 percent below the rate existing on July 1, 1962. On the other hand, the President could raise tariff rates, but by no more than 50 percent above the rate existing on July 1, 1934. The Act contained special provisions for dealings and agreements with the European Economic Community (Common Market).

To ease any hardship that may have resulted from liberalizing trade restrictions, the Act provided relief for import-injured industries. Individual firms could under certain conditions be eligible for adjustment assistance. This could take the form of technical assistance, financial aid (primarily loans), or tax relief singly or in combination. Workers laid off or displaced because of increased foreign imports resulting from implementation of the Act were also eligible for assistance. A displaced worker, for example, could receive unemployment compensation equivalent to 65 percent of his average weekly wage for a period of 52 weeks. These benefits could be extended to 78 weeks for a displaced worker who entered a government-approved training program. Provision was also made under the Act for retraining adversely affected workers. This could include retraining in connection with the Area Redevelopment Act or the Manpower Development and Training Act. Under certain conditions, adversely affected workers could also apply for relocation allowance in connection with training or taking a new job.

Until 1964, very little trade development had taken place under the Act because of the time-consuming procedure necessary to implement a tariff reduction. The President, for example, had to first present the Tariff Commission with a list of articles to be considered for tariff reductions. The Commission then had six months in which to notify the President of the probable economic effect of a tariff reduction with respect to each article or commodity. Before any trade agreement could be made, the President had to seek advice from the Departments of Agriculture, Commerce, Defense, Interior, Labor, State, and Treasury. Subsequently public hearings were held by a designated agency on any tariff reduction proposal. Final negotiations on the agreement with the foreign nation(s) involved typically took many, many more months or years. As a result of this prolonged process, tariff reductions under the Act did not appear before 1965 or later. Furthermore, since tariffs were to be reduced over a five-year period, the full impact of the Trade Expansion Act was not felt until the decade of the 1970s.

On the basis of the authority given to the President under the Trade Expansion Act of 1962, the United States entered negotiations with other nations at Geneva in an effort to bring about substantial reductions in world tariffs. After three years of difficult negotiations in the Kennedy Round, one of the most massive assaults on tariffs in history was agreed upon by the 53 nations participating in the talks under the auspices of the General Agreement on Tariffs and Trade. The United States, for example, granted tariff concessions on thousands of items ranging from automobiles, steel, and chemicals to nuts, cameras, and toupees. These items accounted for $8 billion of the United States total import trade value of $25 billion at that time. Before the agreement, United States tariffs averaged about 11 percent of the foreign value of its imported goods. According to the Kennedy Round agreement, the United States was to reduce its tariffs almost 35 percent, with a few items dropping by the full 50 percent President Kennedy was originally seeking. According to the agreement, the United States and other nations reduced duties by one fifth of the agreed amount on January 1, 1968. The remainder has come in four equal annual installments. These tariff reductions have been a great inducement to world trade and have helped bring many nations closer together economically as well as politically.

The Export-Import Bank

In the past few decades, not only has the United States endeavored to promote freer trade by direct internal legislation and by cooperation through international organizations and agreements, but it has also given substantial financial assistance in an effort to promote world trade. In addition to membership in the World Bank, the International Monetary Fund, and other financial organizations, the United States has its own bank for financing world trade. As a financial aid to the development of world trade, in 1934 the federal government established a government instrumentality known as the Export-Import Bank. The bank was inaugurated during the depression for a number of purposes, primarily for financing exports from the United States. It was anticipated that the bank would aid in the financing of an expected increase in trade with the Soviet Union, officially recognized by the United States in 1933, and with various Latin American countries. The trade with Russia, however, did not materialize. Nevertheless, the bank has been a source of aid in trade with numerous other nations.

The bank under certain conditions guarantees American exporters that they will be paid for the sale of their goods to foreign nations. Sometimes the bank makes loans to foreign importers to buy American goods. The bank mainly finances private exports and imports between the United States and other nations. Such trade cannot be financed at reasonable rates through regular international financial channels. In recent years, however, the bank, as a result of growing financial resources, has been making loans for private and government development projects in underdeveloped nations.

In this regard it does not attempt to compete with national and international financial agencies, such as the World Bank and the International Finance Corporation.

Multilateral Negotiations

The world trading system was seriously unsettled on August 15, 1971, when the United States temporarily suspended the full convertibility of the dollar (see Chapter 43), imposed a 10 percent surcharge on imports, and took a series of other measures to discourage the flow of foreign capital into U.S. markets. The actions were taken in part to curb an increasing volume of imports, especially from Europe and Japan, and in part to induce foreign nations to be more responsive to American appeals for greater economic and financial cooperation. After five months of conferences with major trading nations and international trade organizations and after threats of retaliatory surcharges or tariff increases, the atmosphere of tension was relieved by an international meeting held at the Smithsonian Institution in Washington.

The Smithsonian agreement, reached on December 18, 1971, led the United States to remove its import surcharge and to repeal its policy of tax credits on domestic investments which had discriminated against imports of foreign capital equipment. In addition to monetary reforms, the agreement fostered multilateral negotiations designed to reduce barriers to world trade. Bilateral consultations involving the U.S. and European countries and the U.S. and Japan, begun before the Smithsonian agreement, continued into 1972. By February of that year, joint statements were released and communicated to all contracting parties to GATT. The statements amounted to a declaration that the United States, Japan, and several European countries would open trade negotiations in 1973 on the basis of mutual advantage with overall reciprocity by all participants. These negotiations were to cover a very broad spectrum of agricultural and industrial goods. Moreover, all GATT members were invited to participate.

At the November, 1972, meeting of GATT, the organization went on record as expressing a collective intent to join in multilateral trade negotiations. The first round of meetings, attended by representatives of 102 countries, was held in Tokyo during September, 1973. These meetings closed with what has come to be called the Tokyo Declaration. Under the Declaration, further negotiations, to be conducted in 1974 and 1975 within the procedural framework already established by GATT, would aim for trade expansion by two means. One is the progressive dismantling of direct obstacles such as tariffs and quotas; the other is improvement of the functioning of the world monetary system. If these meetings are successful, policies of self-sufficiency by large, wealthy nations are likely to end and a significant liberalization of world trade can be expected by the later half of the 1970s.

EUROPEAN ECONOMIC INTEGRATION

One of the most significant developments in world trade since the end of World War II has been the movement toward economic integration in Europe. This has come in a series of steps involving coordination and cooperation among members of *regional trade associations.*

Organization for Economic Cooperation and Development

In 1948 eighteen European nations joined together to form the Organization for European Economic Cooperation (OEEC). One important function of the organization was to administer aid under the Marshall Plan. But its general purpose was the joining together of European nations to use their individual capacities and potentialities to increase their production, to develop and modernize their industries, and to expand trade among themselves by reducing tariff barriers.

The OEEC was replaced in 1960 when the United States and Canada joined the 18 European nations of the OEEC in signing a pact setting up a new agency known as the Organization for Economic Cooperation and Development. The stated objectives of this organization, OECD, are to promote prosperity, to maximize economic growth, to establish financial stability in the nations of the industrial West, and to help underdeveloped nations obtain sound economic growth and, thus, contribute toward the expansion of world trade.

European Coal and Steel Community

In 1952 a more definite step toward economic integration was taken with the formation of the European Coal and Steel Community. The purpose of this Community was to pool coal and steel resources of six nations and to eliminate trade barriers on coal, iron ore, iron, and steel. The six nations that joined in the agreement were France, West Germany, Italy, Belgium, the Netherlands, and Luxembourg. The last three nations had previously formed Benelux, a customs union, which had reduced and eliminated tariffs and import quotas among the three nations.

European Common Market

The success of the European Coal and Steel Community led to the formation in 1958 of the European Economic Community. This coalition of the same six nations was promoted in part by the United States. The goals of the Common Market, as it is usually called, are as follows: (1) to reduce and eventually abolish tariff and import quotas among member nations; (2) to establish a common tariff applicable to all imports from outside the Common Market area; (3) to eventually attain the free movement of capital and labor within the Common Market nations; and (4) to adopt a common policy regarding monopolies and agriculture.

The first tariff reduction, 10 percent on industrial goods, was made in January, 1959, and was invoked without any serious difficulty. Subsequently the member nations agreed in May, 1960, to accelerate tariff reductions in an attempt to eliminate tariffs by early 1966, four years ahead of schedule. By January 1, 1967, internal tariffs had been reduced by 85 percent among member nations, and two years later only minimal tariffs on a few goods remained. The movement toward the common external tariff, however, has advanced at a slower pace. Progress has been made toward common internal policies regarding monopoly control, transportation, and social security systems. Furthermore, labor-force training and mobility have received increased coordination. The existence of the Common Market has contributed greatly toward economic growth and prosperity in Western Europe. The bulk of economic barriers among the six nations had been removed by the end of the 1960s; and in the process of tariff reductions, trade among the member nations more than tripled between 1959 and 1973.

Twice during the 1960s Great Britain made serious overtures toward membership in the EEC, but neither succeeded. Then in 1972 European integration made an important breakthrough, perhaps the most important since the founding of the Common Market in 1958. On January 22, Great Britain, Denmark, Ireland, and Norway signed treaties in Brussels opening the way for their membership in the Community. By October, following a negative popular vote, Norway had dropped out of the group. In the other three countries, however, popular referenda ratified the treaties. Therefore, effective January 1, 1973, Great Britain, Ireland, and Denmark joined the Common Market to enlarge its membership to nine.

The importance of this expansion is two-fold. First, it strengthened the Common Market as a trading block vis-à-vis the rest of the world. The enlarged EEC accounts for two fifths of world trade (compared to 15 percent for the U.S.) and has a combined GNP second only to that of the United States. Secondly, in the October, 1972, summit conference, the expanded Common Market nations pledged their commitment to the formation of a "European union" by 1980. If established, this customs union would represent all of Western Europe as a single unit in international trade.

European Free Trade Association

Great Britain did not join the Common Market when it was formed because of its reluctance to abandon its preferential treatment of other members of the British Commonwealth. But discrimination and the threat of competition from the Common Market led Britain to take the initiative in the formation of another economic organization in 1959 known as the European Free Trade Association. In addition to Great Britain, other members were Austria, Denmark, Norway, Portugal, Sweden, and Switzerland. The EFTA differed from the Common Market insofar as it called for the reduction and elimination of internal tariffs and quotas among member nations, but it did not propose the establishment of a common external tariff. Nations were left to establish their own external tariffs and to conduct outside trade negotiations.

During the early 1960s, the two European organizations—the "Inner Six" and the "Outer Seven" as they were often called—existed side by side. At the time, although their formation created the appearance of freer trade, many feared that the EEC and the EFTA might promote disunity, especially if they were to decide to compete vigorously against each other. However, recent history has shown that the situation was more complicated. In the late sixties Finland and Iceland joined the Association, but, as we have seen, Great Britain and Denmark left the Association for membership in the Community beginning in 1973. With two of their member states having transferred membership, the remaining EFTA states gave serious consideration to their trading posture toward Europe and the rest of the world.

High priority was therefore given to negotiations with the EEC Commission. The result was a set of treaties signed in July, 1972, establishing a free trade area for all of the 16 nations belonging to the two organizations. In effect, the treaties initiated a process which would merge the EEC and the EFTA. Agreements provided for mutual reductions of tariffs on industrial goods by 20 percent each year until 1977 and somewhat longer transition periods for certain other goods, such as paper, fish, and some agricultural commodities. The United States protested these agreements on the grounds that special trade arrangements by limited subsets of its members are contrary to GATT policy. It will be the responsibility of GATT to review these agreements, as part of its program of multilateral negotiations during 1974-1975, and possibly to impose modifications.

WORLD TRADING BLOCS

Since the early 1960s there has been a growing tendency for world trade to be conducted among groups of nations acting in concert. Following the lead of the EEC and the EFTA, other regional associations have been formed. Emergence of an expanded East-West trade hinges on negotiations between dominant countries and regional customs unions. Therefore, the present trend toward liberalization of world trade is marked not by a complex of nations each acting independently, much like individual firms in a purely competitive market, but rather by large trading blocs, each of whose exports and imports influence the pattern of international trade.

Other Regional Trade Agreements

The success of the European Common Market and the EFTA has encouraged similar organizations throughout the world. One such organization, the Council for Mutual Economic Assistance (CMEA or Comecon), entered the planning stage at about the time the Common Market was established. Founded in 1960, Comecon had an initial membership of seven: the Soviet Union and the six Communist countries of Eastern Europe. Membership was extended to Mongolia in 1962 and to Cuba in 1972. By 1973 the Comecon countries represented 32 percent of the world's total production. Their combined exports exceeded $86 billion, or about 10 percent of the world total. Approximately 65 percent of their exports and imports arise from trade with each other.

The Montevideo Treaty signed in 1960 created the Latin American Free Trade Association. Comprised of Argentina, Brazil, Chile, Mexico, Paraguay, Peru, and Uruguay, this Association is patterned after the EFTA with the exclusion of an external tariff. Five Central American nations—Costa Rica, El Salvador, Guatemala, Honduras, and Nicaragua—have entered into two treaties calling for integration of industries, removal of internal trade barriers, and the eventual establishment of a common external tariff. Now known as the Central American Common Market, this group has recently encountered many political obstacles to economic integration. Nevertheless, internal tariff reductions have been accelerated.

European influence has been felt in other areas as well. The Association of Southeast Asian Nations aspires to trade liberalization among its members and a common policy with respect to all nonmembers. So, too, does the Organization of African Unity and the Common Organization of Africa. Members and associates of the Caribbean Free Trade Area are now referred to as the East Caribbean Common Market. Indeed, this organization and the Association of Southeast Asian Nations sought associate member status in the EEC in 1973. As a response, the EEC initiated negotiations early in 1974 for a trade agreement between its members and 42 African, Caribbean, and Asiatic nations.

East-West Trade

Because the cold war inhibited relations between Eastern and Western nations during the fifties and sixties, East-West trade was restricted. By 1972, however, the emergence of new trade relations was suggested by a detailed agreement between the United States and the Soviet Union. Its terms stipulated that the U.S. would grant most-favored nation treatment to Soviet imports, and there would be an estimated threefold increase of trade between the two countries, which would reach approximately $1.5 billion within three years. The early 1970s also witnessed signs of expanding trade between Eastern and Western Europe. Japanese competition in European markets has led the EEC countries to seek greater exports to Eastern Europe, which is still short of capital equipment and consumer goods.

Efforts at reconciliation with China have opened new vistas of trade for the decade of the seventies. In spite of rising industrial output, China has experienced critical shortages of capital equipment and essential raw materials. Bottlenecks in production have induced the Mainland Chinese government to reconsider its policies aimed at regional self-sufficiency. In its continuing effort to modernize agriculture and industry, by early 1973 China was actively seeking trade with the United States, Europe, and Japan.

Dominant Trading Blocs

When variations on the European Common Market are formed and when major trading nations enter into bilateral trade agreements, the configuration of world trade is affected. Within each large nation and within the boundaries of trade associations, free trade is prevalent. The extent to which trade flows across the boundaries of associations and large countries not tied to associations depends largely on negotiated reductions in external tariffs and other obstacles to international trade.

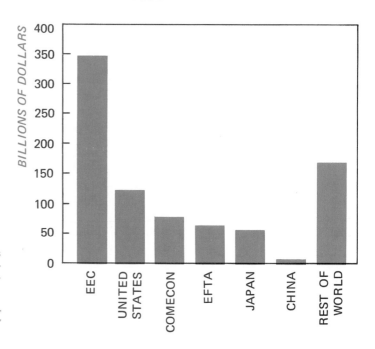

FIGURE 42-1

VALUE OF INTERNATIONAL TRADE, MAJOR TRADING BLOCS 1973

Almost 80 percent of world trade is conducted by the three major regional associations and two nonassociated countries.

SOURCE: *U.N. Monthly Bulletin of Statistics* (April, 1974); and OECD, *Overall Trade by Countries,* quarterly.

Figure 42-1 shows the value of foreign trade (value of exports plus imports) for the world's dominant trading blocs. It can be seen immediately that the nine countries now comprising the European Economic Community constitute the world's largest single trading unit. Next in dollar magnitude is the United States, but the following two in sequence of dollar magnitude are customs unions, namely the Western European EFTA and the predominantly Eastern European Comecon. Except for Japan, all other countries, taken singly, represent only a very small part of world trade. However, it must be remembered that Chinese trade will likely expand significantly in the 1970s and that within the "rest of the world" category are a number of smaller regional associations which formulate trade policies in concert.

Since, with some exceptions, free trade exists within each trading bloc, the formation of trade associations has been a force contributing to an expansion of world trade. National policies aimed at self-sufficiency have been giving way to international cooperation. Nevertheless, national self-sufficiency could be replaced by a spirit of regional or associational self-sufficiency. Whether trade liberalization will spread from a regional orientation to a global orientation depends on both political and economic factors. It will be negotiations among strong trading blocs rather than many individual nations which will set the course for further expansions of world trade; global trade expansion depends principally on reductions in external association tariffs and tariffs imposed by the most important trading nations that are not linked to regional associations.

SUMMARY

1. In the long run the greatest advantage in international trade for all nations is to be found when comparative costs are free to operate.
2. A nation often attempts to gain maximum advantage from foreign trade in the short run through various restraints designed to favor its nationals at the expense of others.
3. When a tariff fully protects, it brings in no revenue; when it brings in revenue, it does not fully protect. Protective tariffs subsidize inefficient industries and slow up technological advance. They may be necessary, however, to preserve industries essential to national defense or to protect new industries capable of great expansion.

4. In the mid-1930s a new policy of lower tariffs was inaugurated in the United States under the Reciprocal Trade Agreements Act, which gave the President the authority to lower tariffs by as much as 50 percent.
5. In 1947 we entered the General Agreement on Tariffs and Trade with several other nations of the world.
6. The Trade Expansion Act of 1962 gave the President further power to reduce tariffs. Substantial progress in tariff reduction was made under this Act as a result of the Kennedy Round negotiations with other GATT nations.
7. One of the most significant economic developments since the end

of World War II has been the trend toward elimination of trade barriers through economic integration. This has been promoted through a series of organizations including the European Coal and Steel Community, the Common Market, the European Free Trade Association, and other regional combinations.

8. Great Britain, Ireland, and Denmark joined the European Common Market in 1973, enlarging its membership to nine. The EEC is now the world's largest regional trade association, accounting for two fifths of total world trade.

9. The bulk of international trade has come to be represented by major trading blocs rather than by a multitude of individual nations acting independently. These blocs are the EEC, Comecon, the EFTA, the U.S., and Japan.

NEW TERMS

Absolute advantage, *p. 934*
Comparative advantage, *p. 935*
Principle of comparative costs, *p. 936*
Tariff, *p. 937*
Ad valorem rate, *p. 937*
Specific rate, *p. 937*
Embargo, *p. 939*

Quotas, *p. 939*
Barter agreements, *p. 939*
Exchange restrictions, *p. 939*
Subsidies, *p. 939*
Countervailing duty, *p. 940*
Autarky, *p. 942*
Regional trade associations, *p. 950*
World trading blocs, *p. 952*

QUESTIONS FOR DISCUSSION AND ANALYSIS

1. It is said that international trade is, in effect, a division of labor. Explain what is meant by this statement.

2. What is the difference between absolute advantage and comparative advantage?

3. The revenue and protection purposes of a tariff are basically incompatible. Explain.

4. Why has a protective tariff been used so persistently by the United States?

5. What is the difference between *ad valorem* tariff rates and specific tariff rates?

6. What are the effects of international depression upon the trade of nations?

7. What are some of the things that the United States has done to promote economic world trade?

8. Shortly after the Kennedy Round negotiations were completed in 1967, the chemical and steel industries, among others, were lobbying for import quotas on their products. Comment.

9. Explain how the Common Market trade policy could put the United States at a disadvantage in trading with an individual member nation.

10. What are some of the consequences of Great Britain's joining the Common Market?

11. What effects would likely follow a merger of the EEC and the EFTA?

12. Do you believe the growth of major trading blocs promotes free trade? Explain.

SUGGESTED READINGS

The Suggested Readings for this chapter are included in Chapter 43, pages 983-984.

43

International Payments

PREVIEW   International trade requires international payments. Importers and others having obligations abroad create the demand for foreign currencies; exporters and others in receipt of claims on foreigners generate a supply of foreign currencies. Thus, a country's balance of payments—the total of all receipts minus all payments—affects its monetary reserves and the exchange value of its money on the international market. Stabilization of exchange rates has been a principal goal of international organizations. American foreign aid, though contributing to a deficit in the United States balance of payments and a gold outflow, has helped to stabilize exchange rates while assisting the development of other economies.

Ordinarily when we buy goods or services or contribute to a nonprofit organization, we make payment in cash or write a check. When the buyer and the seller live in different countries, however, the process of making payment is more complicated. The reason is that two kinds of money are involved: the buyer quite naturally thinks of the value of what he buys in terms of the money of his own country; the seller thinks of the value of what he sells in terms of the money of his country. Thus, a problem arises. How can the buyer obtain money in the seller's country to pay for what he buys there?

FOREIGN PAYMENTS

The seller of goods or services wants to be paid in the kind of money to which he is accustomed and which he can use in buying goods or paying his debts. In domestic trade buyers and sellers use the same kind of money. But the money of an English buyer of American merchandise is in pounds, shillings, and pence. In order to make payment in American money, the English buyer must convert his money into dollars and cents.

The term *foreign exchange* may refer either to the credit instruments used in paying for purchases made abroad or to the process by which balances resulting from transactions between countries are settled. Such instruments constitute promises to pay or orders to pay.

For example, suppose that Jones in London buys 100 typewriters from Smith in New York. The lot of typewriters is valued at $20,000. Jones has funds, but the value of his funds is expressed in terms of pounds, just as purchasing power in the United States is counted in terms of dollars. Since each country has its own monetary system, Jones must convert some of his pounds into dollars and pay the dollars to Smith; that is, Jones uses his pounds to buy dollars.

Conversion of Monetary Units

Since certain banks and exchange houses buy and sell foreign exchange, Jones could purchase the dollars he needs from one of these agencies, which has dollars on deposit in an American bank. What he must pay would depend upon the price of dollars in terms of pounds. If £1 is worth $2.50, Jones would be able to buy the number of dollars he needs for £8,000. Therefore, he would give an English bank £8,000, plus a small fee; the bank would give him a draft, payable to Smith, on the American bank in which it has dollars on deposit. Jones would then send the draft to Smith, who would present it to the American bank and receive his money. The American bank would deduct the amount from the balance of the English bank's account with it.

Thus, the export of typewriters would reduce the number of dollars the British bank has on deposit in the American bank. The fundamental banking principles involved are the same as those that relate to domestic transactions.

Letters of Credit

A *letter of credit* is a formal written statement by a bank that it will accept drafts aggregating not more than the amount named in the letter. Suppose that, instead of buying a draft from his bank and sending it to Smith, Jones had previously deposited funds (pounds) in his bank and obtained a letter of credit stating that the bank would accept drafts up to a certain maximum amount. The letter of credit would be sent to Smith, and the American bank would be notified by the British bank that the letter of credit had been issued.

Then when Smith shipped the typewriters, he would draw a draft on the British bank for $20,000 and take it, together with the letter of credit, to his bank. His bank would buy the draft, pay for it with dollars, and send it to the British bank. When the British bank received the draft, it would subtract £8,000 from Jones' account and add the same amount to the account of the American bank. Thus, the supply of pounds belonging to the American bank would be increased as a result of the export of typewriters.

Exports Pay for Imports and Imports Pay for Exports

The funds—in pounds—in British banks that arise from the export of American goods may be purchased by American importers to pay for the goods and services they buy from British exporters. The reverse is true with respect to funds in American banks belonging to British banks that result from our purchase of imports from Great Britain. This is an important fact because, if a nation is to continue to buy and pay for goods produced in other nations, it must be able to export goods. Indirectly, exports pay for imports and imports pay for exports.

SUPPLY OF AND DEMAND FOR FOREIGN EXCHANGE

A nation increases its supply of foreign exchange by selling goods and services to other nations. The funds in banks in other countries credited to the accounts of American banks, firms, and individuals constitute the supply of our foreign exchange. This supply consists of deposits against which American banks may draw drafts for sale to their customers or to anyone wishing to send funds abroad.

The source of the supply of our foreign exchange consists of all transactions that build up credit in foreign banks—deposits belonging to American banks, firms, and individuals. These transactions include: (1) sales of merchandise, sometimes called visible exports; (2) sales of services to foreigners, sometimes referred to as invisible exports; (3) sales of corporate and other securities; (4) shipments of gold; and (5) any other transactions or conditions that call for payment to Americans.

By selling goods and services to us, other nations acquire American exchange (dollars), which is deposited in our banks and can be used to pay for goods and services that foreigners buy from us.

A demand for foreign exchange arises whenever individuals or business concerns in this country need funds with which to make payment abroad; that is, the sources of demand for foreign exchange are the exact opposite of the sources of the supply of foreign exchange. Transactions that increase the demand for foreign exchange include: (1) the purchase of merchandise from foreigners, visible imports; (2) the purchase of services from foreigners, invisible imports; (3) the purchase of securities from abroad; (4) the receipt of gold from other countries; and (5) any other transactions or conditions that call for payment by Americans to foreigners.

FOREIGN EXCHANGE RATES

A *foreign exchange rate* is the price of the currency of one country in terms of the currency of another country. It is the practice of the monetary authorities in most nations to establish *official exchange rates*, which are the prices that they will pay for the currencies of other nations. These rates often vary from those in the free market, which are prices offered for currencies that are determined by demand and supply.

For a long time—when the advanced commercial nations were on the gold standard—the rate of exchange between American and British money was approximately $4.87 for £1. Also, the rates of exchange between American money and the money of France, Germany, Italy, and other nations were very different from what they are today. The rate of exchange between dollars and pounds was approximately 4.87 to 1 because the weight of the dollar was 23.22 grains of gold and that of the pound, 113.0015 grains. Hence, 113.0015 divided by 23.22 was equal to 4.8665. Therefore, $4.87 for £1 was the *gold-par rate of exchange* between the United States and Great Britain. Ordinarily the actual rate remained at about the gold-par rate.

The Gold-Par Rate of Exchange

To understand how exchange rates are determined when nations are on the gold standard, let us say that the United States and Great Britain are on the gold standard (as they were in 1931). Suppose the gold-par rate is $4.8665 for £1. Now assume that Smith in New York sells to Jones in London $4,866.50 worth of typewriters and that a letter of credit is used in the way we have described before. Smith is paid $4,866.50, less a fee, by the American bank; and the American bank draws a sight draft on the British bank for £1,000, the equivalent of the amount of dollars paid to Smith. When the draft is received, the British bank deducts the amount from Jones' account and adds it to the account of the American bank. Thus, the American bank now has an additional £1,000, which it can sell to anyone.

Now suppose that Wesson and Company in New York owes Sheffield and Sons in London £200 for a purchase of cutlery. As we know, the American firm must buy the £200 with dollars and transfer the amount to the British concern.[1] It can do this by purchasing a part of the amount of pounds that the American bank has on deposit in the British bank. At the gold-par rate of exchange, the £200 would cost $973.30 ($4.8665 × 200) plus a small fee. The American bank could not charge much more than this amount. If the bank were to charge, say, $985, and assuming that the cost of shipping that amount of gold is not more than $6 or $7, Wesson and Company would simply buy 22,600.30 grains (113.0015 × 200) and ship it to its creditors. Because debtors had the privilege of paying their foreign debts in either foreign exchange (drafts) or in gold, the rate of exchange could not deviate very far from the gold-par rate.

---

[1] Actually, when nations were on the gold standard, shipments of gold needed to maintain gold-parity rates were not made by individuals and business concerns—although they could have done so—but by banks that bought foreign exchange and made payment in gold.

Gold Points: Export and Import

Even when nations were on the gold exchange standard, comparatively little gold was used in making international payments. Only when the price of exchange in the form of bank drafts rose to a point where it became more economical to buy and ship gold was gold used in the settlement of foreign obligations. This point was called the *gold export point.* To the country receiving the gold, the price that caused gold to flow into the country was called the *gold import point.*[2] For example, if the cost of shipping gold to England was 3 cents per English pound, $4.8965 was the gold export point, because any price for pounds above that price would cause gold to be used in making remittances.

In practice, when two countries were on the gold standard and the price of exchange rose to or above the gold export point, banks shipped gold and thus increased their balances. Therefore, it was the action of the banks, and not that of debtors, that caused the outflow of gold.

The Flow of Gold and Foreign Trade

The supply of gold does not change rapidly. If there were only two countries between which trade was carried on, exports and imports to and from each country would, in the long run, have to be approximately equal. Otherwise trade between the countries would cease because the country whose exports consistently exceeded its imports would come into possession of all the available gold. The only arrangement whereby further trade could be carried on after this happened would be by means of barter or loans. The countries must abstain from the use of money, or the country whose volume of exports is larger must sell on credit to the one whose volume of exports is smaller.

Of course, where many countries are involved in foreign trade, it is not necessary that exports and imports between any particular two be equal in order that trade may continue. For example, suppose Country *A* exports more to Country *B* than it imports from Country *B*. If Country *C* exports more to Country *A* than it imports from *A* and if *C* imports more from *B* than it exports to *B*, the balance of payments of the countries as a total may be equal. The excess imports of *B* from *A* may be equaled by the excess exports from *C* to *A*. Then a settlement of the differences between *A* and *B* may be effected if Country *B* uses the excess value of its exports to Country *C* with which to pay what it owes to Country *A*. This three-way exchange is illustrated in Figure 43-1.

---

[2] The inflow of gold results in an increase in the amount of money and credit in the gold-importing country, which causes a rise in prices and a decrease in the value of money, which, in turn, results in a decrease in the exchange rate for the money.

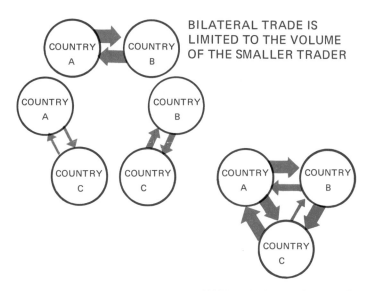

BILATERAL TRADE IS
LIMITED TO THE VOLUME
OF THE SMALLER TRADER

WHEN COUNTRIES TRADE
MULTILATERALLY, THE
TRADE OF EACH EXPANDS

FIGURE 43-1

BILATERAL AND MULTILATERAL INTERNATIONAL TRADE

Under multilateral trade, it is not necessary that exports and imports between any two nations be nearly equal.

SOURCE: Department of State.

WORLDWIDE
MULTILATERAL
TRADE
MAXIMIZES
THE VOLUME
OF TRADE FOR
EVERY COUNTRY

If, however, the total exports of Country *A* are consistently greater than the total of its imports, other countries can continue to buy from Country *A* only if they can find gold to fill the "gap." Otherwise Country *A* must sell the goods on credit or cancel the excess of its exports over that of its imports.

Irredeemable Paper Standards

Let us assume that the currencies of all countries engaged in international trade but one are not redeemable in gold. Then the prices of all other currencies will fluctuate around the value of the monetary unit of the country that is on the gold standard. The value of the currencies of the other countries for exchange purposes will be determined by the amount of such currency that must be given in exchange for a given unit of money of the country on the gold standard. This was the situation during most of the decade between 1930 and 1940. During much of this time, the value of other currencies tended to be stated in terms of the dollar because the United States was on a form of gold standard (which was explained in Chapter 12).

When all countries are on paper standards, there is no commodity-price norm (for example, gold) around which exchange rates will fluctuate. The rate of exchange between two national currencies is determined by the world demand for and supply of each. What underlies the demand and supply of each? One early explanation was the *purchasing-power parity* theory, which concluded that any monetary unit will tend to have the same purchasing power in other countries that it has at home. Thus, equalized purchasing power determines the exchange rate. What would be the value of American dollars in terms of British pounds? If on a given date $3 will buy a specified kind and amount of goods in the U.S. and £1 will buy exactly the same kind and quantity of goods in Great Britain, the purchasing power of $3 equals that of £1, and the exchange rate will be 3 to 1. Now suppose prices double in the U.S. while prices in Great Britain remain unchanged. Then $3 will buy half as much, that is, it will take $6 to purchase in the U.S. what £1 will purchase in Great Britain. The purchasing power of $6 equals that of £1, and the exchange rate will move to 6 to 1.

Monetary experts today do not accept the purchasing-power parity theory. The theory takes no account of other important variables that influence the demand for and supply of national monies on the international market—such variables as national incomes and interest rates. It also ignores the practical reality that national governments attempt to control the supply of their own money on international financial markets. Nevertheless, most monetary experts do concede the principle on which the theory rests, namely, that national price levels exert an effect on exchange rates.

As in the example offered previously, suppose our domestic price level rises relative to prices abroad. Foreign exporters are induced to take advantage of higher American prices by selling more in the U.S., and American importers cooperate by a greater willingness to purchase the relatively cheaper foreign goods. Similarly, foreign buyers of American goods restrict their purchases at higher American prices, and potential American exporters find the domestic market more attractive for the sale of their wares. The consequent drop in American exports and rise in imports act to raise American demand for foreign currencies and to reduce foreign demand for dollars. Hence, dollars will command fewer units of foreign currencies. This happens whether countries are on a gold standard or on irredeemable paper standards. Under irredeemable paper standards, however, there is no gold flow to impose limits on the adjustment in exchange rates. Purchasing-power parity may be regarded as an extreme form of this adjustment process, because there is no assurance that a new equilibrium exchange rate will equalize purchasing power among countries. Rather, adjustments of trade to price changes under irredeemable paper standards may be construed as the effects of national price levels on exchange rates in perfectly free markets, assuming no offsetting or reinforcing changes in other variables (such as national incomes and interest rates) that influence the world demand for and supply of each national currency.

Managed and Floating Currencies

From the end of World War II until 1971, the world monetary system could have been described as a dollar standard. The entire structure rested on the cornerstone of universal acceptability of the dollar and its convertibility into gold. Foreign governments and central banks held a substantial part of their monetary reserves in the form of dollars. International financial markets operated on the reasonable expectation that the dollar would not depreciate in value and the assurance that dollars could be freely converted into gold at a stable dollar price of gold.

Until quite recently, all industrialized countries had *managed currencies* that usually bore little direct relationship to the quantity of gold they possessed. Their governments relied on the so-called *par value system*—regulated exchange rates adjustable only in cases of fundamental trade disequilibrium. Otherwise margins of fluctuation were held within a few percentage points. National monetary authorities used the dollar to intervene in exchange markets, buying and selling in order to control the price of their own currency against others. Then, with a shift in the pattern of world trade (leading to a depreciation of the dollar, to be discussed later in the chapter), several countries abandoned the policy of managed exchange rates. By the mid-1970s the Canadian dollar, the Italian lira, the Japanese yen, and the Swiss franc were *floating currencies*. That is, these currencies have no controlled exchange rate at all; they sell at prices determined primarily by supply and demand. Other exchange rates are flexibly controlled. The German mark, the British pound, the Dutch guilder, and the French and Belgian francs rise and fall in unison with the dollar.

What determines exchange rates today? Some are fixed by rigid exchange control, as will be described shortly. Most are subjected to the forces of demand and supply which reflect patterns of international trade, but these market forces are modified, either by agreements among nations or by compensatory unilateral buying and selling on the part of national monetary authorities. Finally, some exchange rates are left free to float in response to changes in demand and supply without national intervention.

EXCHANGE CONTROL

Exchange control implies governmental action for the purpose of regulating exchange rates. It may also mean the restriction of international payments for certain purposes that are approved by government.

Reasons for Exchange Control

Control over exchange rates may be adopted for any of several possible reasons. For example, during the 1930s the fascist European countries controlled foreign exchange rates for the purpose of encouraging imports and production needed to build a strong military machine. At about the same time, the United States and Great Britain, working together, adopted policies of buying and selling dollars and pounds sterling for the purpose of keeping the value of the two kinds of currency in a stable exchange relationship. The first example illustrates control for the purpose of controlling the nature of foreign trade; the second, for the purpose of preventing fluctuations in exchange rates.

Extreme Methods of Exchange Control

It will be helpful to consider two attempts to control exchange rates by means of drastic methods.

First, during World Wars I and II England found it necessary to "peg" the price of sterling exchange. In both instances she was not on the gold-exchange standard. Her imports were far greater than her exports. Therefore, without support, the price of the pound in terms of dollars would have dropped to a level that would have made it practically impossible for her to pay for the supplies that she desperately needed. In order to prevent financial disaster, England established for the pound an "official" price of $4.76 in World War I and $4.025 in World War II. The price was maintained at these figures in both cases because the British stood ready to buy or sell exchange at these prices.

For the dual purpose of encouraging her exports and discouraging her imports, Great Britain in 1949 devalued the pound to the rate of £1 for $2.80. At about the same time, nearly all nations, other than the United States, took similar action. As a result, Britain's exports increased, her imports decreased, and the "dollar gap" became narrower. But it is difficult to see how, in the long run, political manipulation of exchange rates can overcome trade disadvantages that lie deeper than artificial money rates. This has been proven several times over in the past few years.

Second, during the Hitler regime in Germany, the government exercised complete control over foreign exchange. Germany's chief concern in international trade was to acquire raw materials needed in preparation for war. She had little gold. To achieve her purposes, a system of exchange control was instituted. The system included import quotas, which determined the kinds and the amounts of goods that could be imported; export subsidies; allotments of exchange, which required permission from the government to buy exchange; and "blocked" marks. The last term meant that exporters of goods to Germany acquired marks that could be spent only in Germany. Hence, exporters to that country could use their funds only by purchasing German goods or by selling them to someone who wished to buy German goods or services.

Can Exchange Rates Be Stabilized?

The answer to this question is "yes," provided that each nation's exports and imports, on the average, be equal in money value. When it is recognized that money is an expression of the exchange value of goods, it is easy to understand that what a nation buys from another must be paid for in reality with that which it sells, and vice versa. If the credits obtained from the sale of goods in international trade are used to offset the debits incurred by the purchase of goods from abroad, the exchange rate of the monetary units of two or more nations will tend to remain unchanged.

If either total exports or total imports exceed the other over a long period of time, the unequal flow of goods must be restored to a balance in some way or other. The device that signals balanced exports and imports, and the one that eventually compels readjustment, is the change in exchange rates. When trade is not in balance, a change in the value of a nation's money is sure to arise, regardless of whether nations are on the gold standard or some other standard. Artificial measures (for example, government limitations on the use of foreign exchange and the fixing of exchange rates by agreement between two or more countries) may be provided for the purpose of overcoming temporary variations that will prevent any change in the rate of exchange. If the welfare of all the nations concerned is to be best served, however, no artificial method of stabilization of exchange rates can prove permanently successful.

As in the case of domestic trade, the exchange of goods between nations tends to result because of differences in the cost of producing certain goods in various regions. The rate at which goods are exchanged for each other in international trade—as in domestic trade—in the long run is determined by production costs, although official exchange rates may be controlled temporarily. Changes in production costs are sure to affect exchange rates because foreign exchange, in the long run, can be obtained only by the sale (export) of goods and/or services.

At present there is much argument regarding the establishment of flexible exchange rates—rates that may be changed by agreement as a result of the forces of demand and supply. Those who favor such rates feel that under a "pseudo gold standard" reliance upon gold reserves and heavy borrowing from abroad has proven most unsatisfactory.

Those who favor fixed rates contend that the adoption of a flexible dollar would bring about similar action by other countries, and a worldwide acceleration of inflation would follow. Domestic inflation reduces the value of a nation's money in terms of the currencies of other nations and acts to reduce exports and raise imports.

The period 1972-1974 has been described as a time of rapid world inflation. Depreciation of money, or the decline in domestic purchasing power of a national currency, reflects inflation.[3] From 1962 to 1972, the U.S. annual rate of dollar depreciation averaged 3.2 percent; from 1972 to 1973, the rate was 5.6 percent. Among other industrial countries the comparable ten-year average ranged from 2.6 percent per year in Greece to 6.6 percent yearly in Spain, except for Iceland and Yugoslavia, which averaged 10.5 percent and 11.4 percent respectively. During the one-year interval, 1972-1973, the range was 6.1 percent in Sweden to 10 percent in Japan—all greater than the United States—with Greece at 10.2 percent and Iceland at 14.8 percent.

Several underdeveloped nations recorded depreciation rates lower than that of the U.S., but most were higher. Argentina, for example, experienced a 20.4 percent annual depreciation of money from 1962 to 1972, and Chile 14.1 percent. In the single year from 1972 to 1973, Argentina's depreciation rate rose to 42.2 percent, while Chile's climbed to 54.7 percent. Brazil, which averaged 27.8 percent yearly over the same ten-year interval, has been able to control inflation to the extent that its depreciation of money dropped to 14.1 percent between 1971 and 1972. Yet, the Brazilian depreciation rate rose to 25.7 percent between 1972 and 1973. In general, these statistics reflect world-wide inflationary pressures.

BALANCE OF PAYMENTS AND BALANCE OF TRADE

The international *balance of payments* for a nation is a statement of financial dealings with all other nations during a given period of time. By "nation" in this case, we mean the citizens or their government. The balance of payments shows the transactions that call for payments of money to the nation and those that call for payment by the nation to others. These

---

[3] Depreciation of money is the reciprocal of a cost-of-living or a consumer price index; for example, a rate of inflation of 100 percent is equivalent to a 50 percent rate of depreciation of the buying power of money. Depreciation rates permit international comparisons among different national indexes.

transactions include, but are not limited to, payments for the current sale and purchase of goods and services.

The term *balance of trade* refers to the difference between the value of a nation's exports and its imports of merchandise and services. At one time it was the aim of commercial nations to try to sell more merchandise than they imported, which would result in a flow of gold into the country. As you will recall, this was the policy of *mercantilism*. If a nation sold more merchandise to other nations than it bought from them, it had a favorable balance of trade; if it bought more than it sold, it had an unfavorable balance of trade. The terms "favorable" and "unfavorable" balance of trade are still used; but in calculating the difference between the value of exports and imports, the purchases and sales of service items play a more important part than formerly.

Every transaction has at least two effects on the financial position of each party involved. Every selling transaction gives rise to a claim by the seller for payment; that is, until the payment is made, the seller becomes a creditor of the buyer. In recording the effects of an export of goods or services in the balance of payments, the amount is "credited." The value of the export represents income to the country selling the goods or services. The import of a good or service, on the other hand, results in making the buyer a debtor until the final payment is made. On the balance of payments, the value of imports is "debited."

An attempt is made quarterly by the Department of Commerce to determine the balance of international payments of the United States. The Department keeps account of the country's exports and imports, both visible and invisible, and collects data on capital movements. As Table 43-1 shows, American merchandise exports exceeded imports by $700 million in 1973. However, the sum of the first three items on the left, $81.9 billion, is less than those on the right, $82.5 billion, by $600 million. Therefore, the U.S. in 1973 showed an unfavorable balance of trade of $600 million.

Similar to the flows of private trade are goods, services, and payments generated by American military commitments in various areas of the world. Spending on military establishments abroad plus grants of military assistance amounted in 1973 to $7.1 billion. Partially offsetting these outlays were sales and transfers of planes, tanks, and other military hardware aggregating $5.0 billion, leaving a net deficit from military transactions of $2.1 billion. The final item of current flows is yearly income earned from American investments made abroad in the past ($18.6 billion) and, on the right-hand side, income payments to foreigners on investments they have made in the United States ($8.8 billion). The net difference shows receipts over expenditures in the amount of $9.8 billion. The sum of all these items yields the balance on current account, namely a surplus of $3.2 billion in 1973.

TABLE 43-1

U.S. BALANCE
OF PAYMENTS

1973

(Billions of Dollars)

Receipts (+)		Net	Payments (−)	
Exports .... $ 70.3		+ .7	Imports .... $ 69.6	
Travel and Transportation ..	8.7	− 2.3	Travel and Transportation ..	11.0
Other Services	2.9	+ 1.0	Other Services	1.9
BALANCE OF TRADE ...... $ 81.9		− .6		$ 82.5
Military Sales and Transfers	5.0	− 2.1	Military Expenditures and Grants	7.1
Investment Earnings	18.6	+ 9.8	Payments on Foreign Investments in U.S.	8.8
		− 3.9	Unilateral Transfers (excluding military)	3.9
BALANCE ON CURRENT ACCOUNT $105.5		+ 3.2		$102.3
Foreign Investments in U.S. .	7.8	− 2.6	Private Investments Abroad .	10.4
		− 2.6	U.S. Gov't Capital Flows ...	2.6
		− 5.8	Other Payments (including errors and omissions)	5.8
BALANCE OF PAYMENTS .. $113.3		− 7.8		$121.1

SOURCE: Adapted from *Survey of Current Business* (March, 1974).

Another outflow of dollars appearing on the payments side of the ledger is the result of capital exports. The $10.4 billion in private investments abroad take several forms. One is the purchase of securities such as the stocks and bonds of foreign business firms or governments. Another is loans by American banks and other financial institutions. The building or purchase of factories abroad by American firms is yet another form. The corresponding item on the left, capital investments in the U.S. by foreigners, amounted to $7.8 billion. Thus, private capital exports (payments) exceeded capital imports (receipts) by $2.6 billion, as might be expected of a wealthy nation.

Our government also engages in capital exports, primarily in the form of loans for foreign aid. These totaled $2.6 billion. Finally, other net payments and receipts, including recording errors and items on which it is impossible to obtain data, add up to $5.8 billion.

The nation's overall balance of payments is the final outcome of private and public decisions to buy, sell, lend, or borrow abroad. In 1973 the total of all receipts, both current and capital, fell short of combined payments, resulting in a $7.8 billion deficit in the balance of payments. As in several previous years, the overall deficit could be traced principally to private and governmental capital loans and other investments abroad. In 1973 the deficit in capital flows accounted for approximately two thirds of the deficit in the balance of payments.

This deficit in the balance of payments was met primarily by an increase in dollar IOUs owed to foreigners, that is, an expansion in short-term liquid claims on dollars held by foreigners. More precisely, the deficit in the balance of payments represents a decline in U.S. monetary reserves, including the sale of gold abroad.

THE PROBLEM OF GOLD OUTFLOW

Since World War II our government has extended loans and gifts of money and credit to many other nations; we have spent billions of dollars to maintain military posts in many parts of the world; the armed forces and their dependents spend a great deal for foreign goods and services; American business firms have built factories and made similar investments in other countries because of the opportunities for making profit or for obtaining high rates of interest; and spending by American tourists abroad has increased. All these types of spending in other countries by American firms, individuals, and the government have combined to create a total of more claims for our dollars than is the total of our claims for the money of other nations. This puts a strain upon our gold reserves because the deficits in our balance of payments have resulted in an outflow of gold from this country to other countries over the past several years. And, since the developed nations of the world had settled on a *de facto* dollar standard (as explained earlier), gold out-migration has been spurred by the U.S. Treasury policy of freely selling gold to foreign nations and central banks in exchange for their excess dollars.

The Sixties: Emerging Crisis

By 1964, the deficit in our balance of payments had become smaller than it was at the turn of the decade, and the demand for our gold was much less than it had been in the early 1960s. Foreign creditors were more willing to accept payment in the form of bank credit or convertible currencies of different kinds. Nevertheless, the continuous drain of gold had reduced our gold reserves to less than $15 billion by 1965. Early that year Congress voted to remove the 25 percent gold cover on Federal Reserve Bank deposits. It did, however, retain the 25 percent gold reserve requirement for our federal currency.

The net result of this Congressional action was to free approximately $5 billion more of our gold supply in order that it might be used to meet gold payments in exchange for American dollars held by foreigners. British devaluation of the pound put further pressure on the U.S. dollar and accelerated the gold outflow. Amid speculation that the United States might devalue the dollar, Congress early in 1968 removed the 25 percent gold cover behind the dollar in order to free all of our gold for international transactions.

The continuing gold drain led the President to recommend to the Congress additional measures in the spring of 1968. The Administration proposed that a tax of 5 percent be imposed permanently on air travel and temporarily on sea travel. The Administration also proposed a temporary graduated expenditure tax on travel outside the Western hemisphere. Congress approved the tax on transportation, but the expenditure tax was not voted into law. Thus, further piece-by-piece restrictions on travel were favored over a devaluation of the dollar as a means of combating the gold drain.

The Seventies: Bold Action and International Compromise

Through 1970 the United States had been running a surplus in its private balance of trade. Nevertheless, primarily because of military and economic assistance to foreign nations, our overall balance of payments showed a deficit in all but a few years. These relationships are depicted in Figure 43-2, where it can be seen that the trade surplus declined steadily from 1964 through 1970. After a very modest balance-of-payments surplus ($200 million) in 1966 and a deficit of $3.6 billion in 1967, the following two years generated first a surplus of $1.6 billion and then a surplus of $2.7 billion.

In 1971 the U.S. balance of private trade took a sharp downturn, converting a previous surplus into a deficit of $4.3 billion in that year and an even larger deficit of $8.7 billion in 1972. This reversal of the trade balance was instrumental in producing the largest deficits ever experienced in the American balance of payments. As reflected in Figure 43-2, the trade deficit, together with private capital outflows and government expenditures abroad, generated an overall deficit of almost $22 billion in 1971 and $14 billion in 1972. Although the trade deficit and the total payments deficit both diminished in magnitude between 1972 and 1973, the serious problem of a deficit in the balance of payments continued into 1974.

These trends describe, in effect, a shrinkage of American monetary reserves, especially gold reserves for international settlement of debts. To counteract the loss of reserves, dramatic action was taken by the U.S. government. In August, 1971, the United States suspended convertibility of dollars into gold, imposed a 10 percent surcharge on imports, and introduced other measures to stem the outflow of payments for capital equipment. After a period of tension and unrest, the Smithsonian agreement of December, 1971, led to removal of the import surcharge, relaxation of restrictions

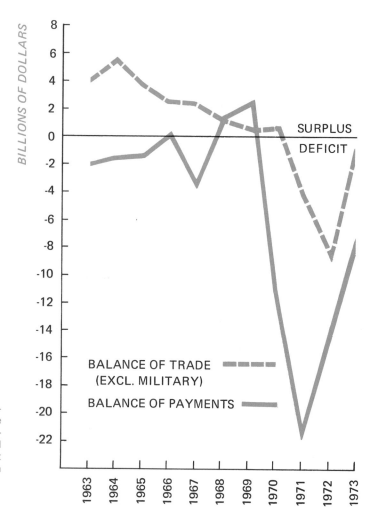

FIGURE 43-2

A DECADE OF AMERICAN TRADE AND PAYMENTS BALANCES

The U.S. balance of trade has declined from a surplus to a deficit. The American balance of payments, normally a deficit since the close of World War II, has reached alarming deficit proportions since 1970, especially in 1971 and 1972.

SOURCE: *Survey of Current Business,* monthly.

against capital imports, and, most importantly, an official devaluation of the dollar. That is, the price of gold in terms of dollars was changed from the almost immutable $35 per ounce which held since 1934 to $38 per ounce. Devaluation meant that exchange rates were altered such that dollars would buy less of other currencies, thus discouraging imports and encouraging exports.

Within 14 months the United States again devalued the dollar. In February, 1973, the dollar was devalued another 10 percent—a total reduction of 17.9 percent since December, 1971. Whereas many governments responded to the 1971 actions by agreeing to greater flexibility in official exchange rates (the official "band" allowed without devaluation was widened from one to 2.25 percent), by allowing their currencies to float, or by devaluation as a counter-offensive, response to the 1973 devaluation was more orderly. By prior agreement, the German mark, the French franc, the Dutch guilder, and the Soviet ruble (all powerful currencies) remained unchanged. The dollar dropped by more than 10 percent against some currencies; for example, the Swiss franc and the floating Japanese yen. It dropped by less than 10 percent against others and remained unchanged for a number of national monies that were also devalued by 10 percent.

Responding to disorder in world money markets, the Board of Governors of the International Monetary Fund established the Committee of Twenty, which was charged with formulating international monetary reforms. The Committee, meeting in Kenya in September, 1973, produced a document entitled *First Outline of Reform*, which recorded preliminary agreements and set a deadline of July 31, 1974, for the completion of basic proposals. By early 1974 the basic proposals included a strengthening of international organizations, an exchange mechanism based on stable but adjustable par values, and establishment of a single world reserve asset, other than gold or any one national currency, in terms of which par values among currencies would be expressed.

The circumstances that led to devaluation of the dollar cannot be considered as less than a world monetary crisis. Having relied on a dollar standard based on a stable rate of convertibility into gold, by the early 1970s most countries found their currencies pegged to an inconvertible dollar. Subjected to a gold outflow and unable to preserve free convertibility into gold at a fixed dollar price, the U.S. changed its policy. Trade relations that led to this result left the world without a coherent monetary system. Ultimately, international monetary reform cannot be achieved by devaluation or by adjustments in official exchange rates but only by the commodity and capital-equipment flows that underlie financial payments. We will return to this topic in discussing American foreign policy and the balance of payments.

UNITED STATES FOREIGN AID

In addition to its endeavor to promote world trade through direct efforts and through international organizations and agencies, the United States has extended a considerable amount of direct economic aid to other countries. In earlier years funds were utilized especially for reconstruction purposes, but in more recent years much aid has been given to underdeveloped nations. Here again aid has been both direct and indirect through international financial institutions.

Bilateral Aid

During World War II we exported nearly $40 billion in military and nonmilitary goods under the Lend-Lease program. About two thirds of this amount went to Great Britain; Soviet Russia received almost $10 billion; and France received approximately $2.5 billion. Smaller amounts were shipped to other nations, such as Belgium, China, the Netherlands, and several Latin American republics. In dollar terms, or on a quantitative basis, this was the largest grant program ever carried on in history.

When World War II ended and lend-lease shipments came to an abrupt halt, the principal source of foreign aid was the United Nations Relief and Rehabilitation Administration, which dispensed several billion dollars in aid to war-injured nations, especially in Western Europe. In addition, the British government in 1946 negotiated a $3.5 billion long-term loan from the United States for purposes of reconstruction.

Economic Cooperation Administration. In 1948 the United States Economic Cooperation Administration program, otherwise known as the Marshall Plan, went into effect to aid the nations of Western Europe. In total, 16 nations became members of ECA, including Great Britain, France, Denmark, Italy, Belgium, and Sweden. In addition to receiving financial aid from the United States, the various nations agreed to take domestic steps necessary to improve their respective economies, and they agreed to participate and cooperate with one another in seeking solutions to their common economic problems. Between 1948 and 1952, the United States contributed $12 billion in goods and services to Western Europe under the Marshall Plan.

Subsequently the name of the Economic Cooperation Administration was changed a number of times. But the objective remained the same, and aid continued to pour into Western Europe during the 1950s. The largest recipient was Great Britain, which received $6.5 billion in aid during the period 1945-1965. Other large beneficiaries in Europe were France with $4.1 billion; West Germany, $3 billion; Italy, $2.8 billion. In other parts of the world, India received $5.9 billion; Korea, $4 billion; Japan, $2.6 billion; and such nations as Australia, the Netherlands, Greece, Yugoslavia, Pakistan, Turkey, China, Vietnam, Brazil, and the Philippines each received aid in excess of $1 billion during that period. During that time aid to Latin American republics was about $6 billion, and to Africa we sent about $2.6 billion. During the past several years some of these loans and grants have in part been repaid.

Technical Assistance. In his inaugural address in 1949, President Truman laid the foundation for a new type of foreign-aid program designed to encourage the advancement of underdeveloped nations through the extension of technical assistance from the United States. The establishment of the "Point Four Program" of technical assistance was initiated in the fourth point of his speech when the President stated:

> Fourth, we must embark on a bold new program for making the benefits of our scientific advances and industrial progress available for the improvement and growth of underdeveloped nations.
> Our aim should be to help the free people of the world, through their own efforts, to produce more food, more clothing, more materials for housing, and more mechanical power to lighten their burdens.

Thus, Point Four stressed the need for a new concept in foreign aid—that to underdeveloped nations. Most previous aid had gone to developed nations in need of reconstruction. Although the aid to underdeveloped nations concept was implied in the formation of the International Bank for Reconstruction and Development in 1946, little had been accomplished in that area by 1949. Point Four was put into effect in 1950 when Congress approved the Act for International Development, which stated:

> It is declared to be the policy of the United States to aid the efforts of the peoples of economically underdeveloped areas to develop their resources and improve their working and living conditions by encouraging the exchange of technical knowledge and skills and the flow of investment capital to countries which provide conditions under which such technical assistance and capital can effectively and constructively contribute to raising standards of living, creating new sources of wealth, increasing productivity, and expanding purchasing power.

In order to implement the objectives of the Act, Congress appropriated $31.9 million for technical assistance. Additional millions have been applied since for technical assistance, and today there are more than 5,000 American technical experts throughout the world giving advice and assistance to foreign nations endeavoring to improve their agricultural and industrial production.

Development Loan Fund. As a further indication of the increased emphasis on economic development as the principal goal of our foreign aid program, in 1957 Congress established the Development Loan Fund and appropriated nearly $1.5 billion for its operation. The Fund was empowered to guarantee or make loans to persons, businesses, governments, or other entities in foreign nations for various industrial, financial, and commercial development projects. Between 1958 and 1962, the Fund authorized loans in excess of $3 billion in more than 50 different countries. About two thirds of the money loaned involved projects in the Near East and South Asia. Another $400 million went to Latin America, and less than $150 million went to Europe. The Development Loan Fund was combined with the

International Cooperation Administration as part of the Agency for International Development on November 4, 1961.

In the 27-year period, 1945-1972, the United States distributed $148.8 billion in foreign assistance to more than 120 nations. Of this total, $56.1 billion was in the form of military grants, $2.5 billion was contributed to four separate international financial institutions (exclusive of IMF), and the remaining $90.2 was used primarily for economic and technical aid.

Aid Through International Organizations

There are a number of international financial institutions the operations of which greatly affect international trade, the balance of payments, and the development of nations. The existence of these institutions emphasizes the degree of international financial cooperation practiced today. Since World War II, the United States has been the world's largest contributor to these financial institutions, both on a worldwide and regional basis. At present there are at least five such major organizations to which the United States contributes.

The International Monetary Fund (IMF). During World War II plans were being made for stabilizing domestic currencies and international exchange ratios. Most important of these plans were those formulated at an international monetary conference held at Bretton Woods, New Hampshire, in 1944, by the representatives of 44 nations. This conference resulted in an agreement for the establishment of the International Monetary Fund and the International Bank for Reconstruction and Development. By 1973, membership in the IMF included 124 nations.

The purposes of the Fund may be summarized briefly as follows: to provide an organization for international consultation and cooperation on monetary matters; to encourage the development of a balanced and permanent international trade; to discourage competitive exchange depreciation and to bring about exchange stability; to promote conditions that will eliminate artificial exchange restrictions; to provide members temporarily with funds with which to meet unfavorable trade balances; and to reduce or to eliminate the violent fluctuations that have occurred in business as a result of disequilibrium in international balances of payments.

One function of the Fund is to fix exchange rates in terms of gold or the U.S. dollar, establishing a par value for the currency of each member nation. These rates may be changed upon the request of a member only if the purpose is correction of a "fundamental disequilibrium" in the official parity. This does not mean, however, that members may not devalue their currencies or allow their exchange rates to float such that market exchange rates determined by demand and supply may deviate from the parity rate.

Another main function of the IMF is the administration of Special Drawing Rights (SDRs) introduced in 1970. SDRs are a collectively managed asset of the Fund, sometimes referred to as "paper gold." They are now a principal source of international reserves. A country with a balance-of-payments deficit can draw upon these reserves to settle its indebtedness to others rather than transferring ownership of gold. In effect, what a nation does is buy the needed exchange with its own currency. It is intended that ordinary transactions between nations will continue to employ private agencies. Only when a nation has a shortage of foreign exchange is it expected to resort to this form of borrowing from the Fund. Similarly, nations with balance-of-payments surpluses may accumulate these drawing rights much as they would accumulate gold reserves.

Since fixed exchange rates must be supported by convertibility of national currencies into internationally agreed-upon reserve assets, expanding trade relies upon regular growth in total world reserves. Because of increased demand for commercial uses of gold and the scarcity of gold as an international reserve, it is probable that SDRs will play a far more important role in the world's monetary system of the future.

The International Bank for Reconstruction and Development (World Bank). This institution, now usually referred to as the World Bank, is intended "to supplement private investments in foreign countries by nations and individuals having capital to lend." The present subscription of member nations amounts to $25 billion. The United States has subscribed almost $8 billion, slightly less than one third of the total.

This bank can issue and sell bonds and use the proceeds for loans to "any business, industrial, or agricultural enterprise in the territory of a member," and it can guarantee loans by private investors. The overall purpose is to develop world production and trade by stimulating investment in enterprises that may be considered "good risks." Obviously the objectives of the bank are predicated on the assumption of a policy by nations of lowering most of their tariff restrictions and other impediments to trade between nations. Over 110 countries had become members by 1973, and loans totaled more than $12 billion.

The International Development Administration (IDA). This institution is an affiliate of the World Bank. The purpose in establishing IDA was to enable a growing number of the underdeveloped nations to borrow funds. According to the terms of IDA, development credits and loans are intended to impose less burden on the balance of payments of borrowing countries than do the usual or conventional types of loans. IDA came into existence in 1960 and began operations the same year. Membership in the organization is open to members of the World Bank. By the middle of 1973, 107 countries had joined and total subscriptions amounted to more than a billion dollars.

The International Finance Corporation (IFC). The IFC, which was formed in 1956, is an international financial institution and an affiliate of the International Bank for Reconstruction and Development. By 1973 it had over 90 members and a subscribed capital of over $100 million. The general objective of IFC is to stimulate economic development by encouraging the growth of private productive enterprise in its member countries, and especially in the less developed areas. To accomplish its objective, the IFC proposes (1) to invest in productive private enterprises along with private investors but without government guarantees of repayment; (2) to serve as a clearinghouse for bringing together foreign and domestic private capital and management; and (3) to help stimulate the growth of domestic and foreign capital.

The Inter-American Development Bank (I-ADB). The Inter-American Development Bank came into existence in 1960. The general purpose of the Bank is to stimulate the economic development and the cohesion of the Latin American nations. It originally had capital resources amounting to $1 billion, which could be increased by the sale of the Bank's own resources. Of its total capital subscriptions, $850 million was available for usual lending purposes, while $150 million could be used for special or unusual lending purposes.

The Bank's Board of Governors in 1964 increased the authorized capital of the Bank to $2.15 billion. By 1973 its capital subscription equaled $3 billion, which had been contributed by 25 nations. With its own resources it furnishes funds for business capital with charges for interest and special reserve of less than 6 percent. From the fund itself, long-term loans with low interest rates are available for hydroelectric power, agricultural, and reclamation projects.

The I-ADB resembles the World Bank as to structure, organization, and general purposes, and both operate in the American regions. But certain differences as to the requirements for loans enables I-ADB to supplement the loans of the World Bank in this part of the world.

AMERICAN FOREIGN POLICY AND OUR BALANCE OF PAYMENTS

During most of its history, the United States has lived in comparative economic isolation. For the most part, the people were busy developing the natural resources of the nation and expanding its territory. Most of our national policies could be adopted or changed without much concern as to what would be the international economic consequences or as to what others might think about what we were doing.

The days of economic isolation are gone forever. For better or worse, we now live in a world where each nation is, so to speak, just "across the border" as far as its proximity to every other nation. As a consequence, the line of demarcation between national and international economic problems is much less clear than it once was. To complicate the matter still further, the struggle of competing economic ideologies has divided the peoples of the world into groups the common purposes of which affect the form of foreign policy that each may be inclined to adopt for itself.

Some General Aspects of Our Economic Foreign Policy

Since World War II we have, in general, come to accept and pursue certain broad objectives with respect to international affairs. This has largely shaped our overall foreign policy. It is generally felt that the promotion of this policy is conducive to the welfare of the nation as a whole and to the other peoples in the free world.

Four principal objectives have guided the role of the United States in international affairs. First, we have sought to maintain our position of leadership by providing for the defense of the Western world. Second, we have encouraged the economic development of those underdeveloped nations which are not antagonistic to the fundamentals of our social, economic, and political way of life. Third, we have supported an expansion of international trade and an easier flow of capital from one country to another. Finally, we have promoted greater efficiency in production and an increase of total world production.

These objectives have led to specific programs and policies which have affected our balance of payments. Foreign military and economic assistance more than offset our favorable balance of private trade. In recent years the efficiency, volume, and variety of production in other industrialized nations has increased markedly. As a consequence, we find ourselves in a much more competitive world, and our trade balance has turned to a deficit. During this entire post-World War II period, the world operated on a system of fixed exchange rates tied to the U.S. dollar that in turn was tied to a stable price of gold.

International Monetary Reform

Temporary suspension of dollar convertibility into gold in 1971 and the devaluations of the dollar in 1971 and 1973 had the effect of changing the world's monetary system. When these actions were taken, American officials insisted that comprehensive reform in the world's monetary system was needed. Moreover, a report prepared by the President's Council of Economic Advisers argued that trade reform and monetary reform should be carried out together. The Council's report spelled out the principles underlying the U.S. negotiation position, namely that trade agreements should be addressed to the removal of all forms of trade barriers so that maximum reliance could be placed on market-directed trade. Similarly, a report issued by the Organization for Economic Cooperation and Development in late 1972 called for reform of the world monetary system.

Gold reserves of the U.S. Treasury declined from a record high of $24.5 billion in 1949 to $10.5 billion at the beginning of 1973. The official U.S. position holds that gold should be deemphasized and that more progress is needed along the path of "degolding." The United States proposes that the International Monetary Fund's SDRs—rather than gold or the U.S. dollar— be built into the principal international reserve asset. According to a plan advanced by the Secretary of the Treasury, SDRs would become the common denominator for national currencies; currency changes would be geared to shifts in the size of this monetary reserve that each nation accumulates in its transactions with the rest of the world. Countries that either persistently lose reserves or accumulate reserves would be obliged by international agreement to bring their accounts closer to balance. Nations could alter their trade practices, devalue, or revalue as a more or less routine procedure.

Not all nations agree to these proposals, especially those holding relatively large gold stocks, such as Japan and the Western European countries. Certain key countries view SDRs as remaining linked to gold and supplementing rather than supplanting gold. Most monetary experts now predict that the dollar will continue to operate as an international yardstick in the foreseeable future and that gold will be retained as an international monetary instrument. However, it is expected that the importance of gold will gradually diminish.

Increasing American Exports

Despite improvements in the American balance-of-payments position stemming from devaluation, economists do not forecast a trade surplus under present conditions. The international meetings begun in late 1973 under the sponsorship of GATT (see Chapter 42) may eventually lead to comprehensive new trade agreements tied to long-range reforms in the world monetary system. But these changes will not come quickly. In the meantime, what course can be recommended in an effort to increase American exports?

1. We should pursue a domestic anti-inflationary policy, which would help to prevent rises in production costs and prices. This would enable us to compete more effectively in the world markets.

2. Efficiency in American production should be encouraged in order to keep the prices of our goods on a competitive level with goods produced in other highly industrialized nations.

3. Irrespective of the effects of inflation, unit costs in American production should be controlled. This can be accomplished, at least to some degree, if employees exhibit a reasonable attitude with respect to wage contracts and if management is also reasonable as to the prices it asks for its products.

4. Government policies that raise the prices of our exports, such as agricultural prices and quotas on imports, should be reexamined.

5. We should encourage other nations to reduce their existing obstacles to foreign trade, including such devices as import quotas, limits of expenditures for foreign travel by their citizens, and limits on private investments abroad.

6. It would seem that some of the other Western nations and Japan are now in a position to assume a larger amount of financial burden incidental to our mutual defense and to the assistance given to the underdeveloped areas of the world.

7. West European nations should be encouraged to understand that appropriate measures by us to prevent deficits in our balance of payments are in the interests of all the nations of the free world. Too great an accumulation of our gold and dollars by other nations as a result of such deficits weakens the value of the dollar. Since the dollar is the most widely accepted medium of exchange in the Western world, such a weakening of it is harmful to international trade and to the internal welfare of those nations with which we are most closely associated.

The United States Department of Commerce has put forth a number of suggestions for solving—or preventing—our balance of payments deficit problem, including:

1. Expand and increase our exports by means of industry-government cooperation;

2. Reduce the drain of military expenditures by (a) encouraging military personnel to buy U.S. goods rather than foreign goods, (b) cutting down on our purchases of foreign-made strategic goods and services, (c) increasing our sales of military equipment to our allies, and

(d) encouraging certain other industrial nations to assume a larger share of the military defense burden;

3. Encourage foreign tourists to visit the United States;

4. Adjust interest rates in this country so as to encourage American investors to invest their money at home, rather than abroad; and

5. Encourage spending of foreign-aid funds and grants for American-made goods and services.

SUMMARY

1. Apparent dissimilarities between trade at home and abroad arise because of differences in monetary units and because of restrictions on trade.

2. A nation must import goods and services if other nations are to acquire the money needed to pay for the goods they want to buy from that nation.

3. The rate of exchange is the ratio at which units of the currency of one country exchanges for those of another country. It is the price paid in the domestic currency for foreign currency. When nations are on a gold-par rate of exchange, the rate is fixed by the ratio of the weight in gold of the monetary unit of one country to that of another country.

4. Any transaction with another nation or foreigner that calls for a payment of money is of the nature of an import; and any transaction abroad that results in a receipt of a claim for money is of the nature of an export. A balance of international payments is a statement of a nation's total exports and imports of visible and invisible items together with an explanation of how the difference between the amount of total exports and imports is reconciled or balanced.

5. The United States has given almost $150 billion in foreign aid since the end of World War II. Much of this aid has been given directly under such programs as the Marshall Plan, the Economic Cooperation Administration, and the Development Loan Fund. Technical assistance, as well as direct loans and grants, is a part of American foreign-aid policy.

6. Several international financial institutions that are intended to promote trade between nations are the International Monetary Fund, the World Bank, the International Development Association, the International Finance Corporation, and the Inter-American Development Bank.

7. In spite of the fact that the value of our exports of goods and services usually exceeds that of our imports, since World War II we have usually had a deficit in our balance of payments. In recent years both the trade balance and the payments balance have shown a deficit.

8. Because of these deficits, the United States has devalued the dollar and taken other measures to improve our competitive position in world trade.

QUESTIONS FOR DISCUSSION AND ANALYSIS

1. Explain the meaning of "foreign exchange" and its use in international transactions.

2. What are the sources of (a) the supply of and (b) the demand for foreign exchange?

3. A nation can manipulate its exchange rates in an attempt to increase its exports and decrease its imports. Explain.

4. Is it correct to say that "exports pay for imports and imports pay for exports"? Why or why not?

5. Distinguish between credits and debits in the international balance of payments. Give examples of each.

6. How are deficits in the balance of payments usually settled?

7. Historically U.S. foreign aid, although large in dollar amounts, has been less than one percent of our national income. Comment.

8. What does devaluation of a currency mean? Explain how devaluation tends to affect exports and imports.

9. In deciding what our trade and financial policy toward other nations should be, what factors should be taken into consideration? Why?

10. Do you favor U.S. participation in the various international financial institutions that have been established since World War II? Why or why not?

11. Do you believe gold should be retained as an international monetary reserve? Why or why not?

SUGGESTED READINGS

Cohen, B. J. *Balance of Payments Policy*. Baltimore: Penguin Books Inc., 1970.

Fleming, J. Marcus. *Essays in International Economics*. Cambridge, Mass.: Harvard University Press, 1971.

Grubel, Herbert G. *International Monetary System*. Baltimore: Penguin Books Inc., 1970.

Hinshaw, Randall (ed.). *Economics of International Adjustment*. Baltimore: The Johns Hopkins University Press, 1971.

IMF Staff Papers, and *Balance of Payments Yearbook*. Washington: The Secretary, International Monetary Fund, current.

Kaser, Michael. *Comecon: Integration Problems of the Planned Economies*, 2d ed. New York: Oxford University Press, Inc., 1967.

Kenen, Peter B. *International Economics*, 3d ed. Englewood Cliffs, N.J.: Prentice-Hall, Inc., 1973.

Kindelberger, Charles P. *International Economics*, 5th ed. Homewood, Ill.: Richard D. Irwin, Inc., 1973.

Liesner, Han. *Britain and the Common Market*. New York: Cambridge University Press, 1971.

Loomis, John E. *International Finance: Official Agencies and U. S. Business*, 2d ed. Washington: Bureau of National Affairs, Inc., 1970.

Robson, P. (ed.). *International Economic Integration*. Baltimore: Penguin Books Inc., 1972.

Root, Franklin R. *International Trade and Investment*, 3d ed. Cincinnati: South-Western Publishing Co., 1973.

Staley, Charles E. *International Economics; Analysis and Issues*. Englewood Cliffs, N.J.: Prentice-Hall, Inc., 1970.

Swann, D. *Economics of the Common Market*. Baltimore: Penguin Books Inc., 1972.

Symposium on International Monetary Problems, Proceedings. Washington: American Enterprise Institute for Public Policy Research, 1972.

Weil, Gordon L., and Ian Davidson. *Gold War: The Story of the World's Monetary Crisis*. New York: Holt, Rinehart and Winston, Inc., 1970.

Wexler, Imanuel. *Fundamentals of International Economics*, 2d ed. New York: Random House, Inc., 1972.

PART TWELVE

Economic Development and Comparative Systems

44

Economic Development

PREVIEW Economic development is broader in scope than economic growth. Development entails the building of new institutions and the creation of new cultural patterns. Consequently, economic development depends upon economic, political, and sociological factors. The Classical and Marxist theories were early attempts to explain economic development. More recent theories stress innovation, steady growth conditions, and social and cultural factors in the process of modernization.

The chapters on trade and finance among nations provide a theoretical and institutional background for analysis of comparative economic development. The determinants of economic growth, discussed in Chapter 21, are part of the process of *economic development*. However, development may be more broadly interpreted. It includes the building of a market structure, the founding of financial institutions, and the creation of new cultural patterns in addition to quantitative expansion of capital and labor or technological innovation. Development objectives may require 100 or more years to be realized. Indeed, the emergence of markets, an entrepreneurial class, new industries, and a network of financial institutions are generally regarded as a prerequisite to fiscal and monetary policies designed to accelerate the growth rate of national income.

The extraordinary advance of Europe during the Industrial Revolution and of the New World in the nineteenth and twentieth centuries are primary examples of economic development. Political and cultural as well as economic factors combined to generate an environment conducive to development. Analysis of the development process has forced economists into a host of peripheral fields, such as sociology and political science.

Since the end of World War II, governments in other parts of the world have demonstrated a growing concern about economic development. Many have embarked upon 5-year plans or 20-year plans designed to accelerate the development process. The Western world has shown its interest by providing technical assistance and capital on a scale unheard of in the past. The prospect of converting poor economies into prosperous and progressive ones by means of a joint effort on the part of developed and underdeveloped countries has excited the imagination of statesmen the world over.

Before proceeding, it should be said that no single term can accurately describe the economic conditions existing in a particular country or area of the world. Those nations with relatively high per capita incomes, advanced technologies, and mature market structures have been called economically developed. Nations lacking these characteristics in various degrees have been described by different terms: underdeveloped, less developed, or developing. The nomenclature now being used by the United Nations is "developing nations." However, any one of these adjectives could be used and has been used in the past. For the sake of consistency, we use the term *underdeveloped*.

FACTORS IN ECONOMIC DEVELOPMENT

National development is more than an economic phenomenon. The factors affecting development can be classified as economic, political, and sociological.

Economic Factors

Economic factors determining development are basically those that influence the growth rate of a nation's per capita income. The four interrelated factors are capital accumulation, population growth, discovery of new natural resources, and technological progress. Without these four economic factors, increases in national output and income would be improbable.

Capital Accumulation. Capital accumulation stands at the core of economic development. In Chapters 5 through 8 and in Chapter 21, we have seen how capital investment can lead to higher income. Saving, or unconsumed current output, is the domestic source of expansion in the economy's stock of physical capital equipment. This saving may be provided directly by the private sector as income rises. If the government provides part or all of the increased saving, it does so by means of tax revenues allocated to the funding of capital projects or by borrowing from the private sector. In an open economy, one that trades with the rest of the world, foreign investment can be crucial. In such an economy, capital expansion is funded from the savings of some other economy.

The construction of irrigation systems; use of better fertilizers, seed, or livestock; land reclamation; building of dams, bridges, factories, railways, airports, and harbors—all the produced means of production associated with high levels of productivity—are essential to economic development. Nevertheless, the *type* of capital accumulation may be at least as important as the quantity of new capital. At a certain stage of economic development, investments in agriculture may produce more results, bringing about a greater increase in output and income, than larger investments in steel mills or transportation.

Many underdeveloped countries have a pressing need for so-called social capital. *Social capital* is equipment utilized by society at large rather than particular sectors or enterprises, such as schools, hospitals, and public utilities. Therefore, the capital mix and its breakdown by kind of equipment and industry of employment are decisive in determining the effects of a given increase in the total stock of capital on economic development.

Nevertheless, in a private enterprise economy or in a socialistic system the process of building up the stock of capital and simultaneously determining the capital mix has its inescapable financial counterpart. A part of national income must be saved or relinquished in taxes in order to purchase or produce the additional capital goods. If this is not done, the necessary funds must be borrowed abroad or obtained as a gift from a foreign country.

Population Growth. Additions to the stock of physical capital will not bear fruit unless the added units are combined with labor to produce greater output. Consequently, a second economic factor in development is growth in the size of the labor force. As we saw in Chapters 32 and 36, a nation's population is not the only determinant of the size and quality of the labor force. Subject to the reservations pointed out in those chapters, reservations that affect primarily short-run changes in the labor force, the changing labor force over long periods, such as 50 or 100 years, may be traced to changes in a nation's population.

Each member of the labor force is both a consumer and a producer. Larger populations bring more mouths to be fed as well as more hands to produce. Moreover, unless population growth remains within a limit dictated largely by the rate of capital accumulation, there may be unemployment because of an excess labor supply relative to the stock of capital. This suggests that there is some optimum or "best" rate of population growth, namely one that will maximize the increase in per capita output. That is, given the rate of capital accumulation, the rate of population growth should not be so small as to result in a labor shortage. Neither should the rate of population growth be so large as to create unemployment or otherwise act to decrease per capita output and income.

An economy may be in any one of several situations. First, population may be less than optimum so that per capita income could be raised merely by increasing the population without changing any other factors. There is a shortage of labor in the sense that population expansion, *in itself*, promotes more rapid development. Second, population growth would stimulate development only if it is combined with capital accumulation or other economic changes, such as technological progress or discovery of new resources. Third, an increase in population may raise national output, but *per capita* output may drop. That is, the marginal productivity of labor is positive so that added inputs of labor raise output; however, the increment to output is so small that the output per person (average output) declines. This result would follow if there already exists a large ratio of labor to capital. The labor supply is "too large" relative to the amount of available capital, so population growth retards development. Only by means of enormous capital expansion can development proceed along with population growth, but the necessary rate of capital expansion may not be feasible.

Discovery of New Resources. Exploitation of new natural resources operates to promote economic development. A nation endowed with navigable waterways has an inexpensive source of transportation. Vast forests provide the raw materials for lumber and paper industries. The existence of abundant mineral resources or fossil fuels, such as coal and oil, also are sources of raw materials or industrial power. Fertile agricultural land practically assures high food or fiber productivity. Nations blessed with rich natural resources have an obvious advantage in promoting development. Those with few natural resources face serious problems.

The "opening up of frontiers" is the means by which nations take advantage of available natural resources. The opportunity of moving to virgin land that is richer than the land being occupied, or the opportunity to mine valuable minerals, plays a prominent role in the development process. However, opportunities do not in themselves cause growth and development. The "frontier spirit" has been described as the mental and emotional outlook of a people who seize the opportunities and exploit the natural endowments of the earth.

Technological Progress. An increase in the rate of technological progress is a fourth factor that produces economic expansion. A nation with given natural resources can expand output per capita by expanding its stock of capital and its population (labor force). Essentially, by raising the input of productive factors, the resulting output is increased. The greater the rate of increase in inputs, the greater the rate of increase in output. But there is a limit to the rate at which output can grow. Greater inputs of capital are constrained by the willingness to save, and greater inputs of labor are constrained by population growth. Growth of output beyond the limit imposed by these constraints hinges upon changes in the productive *quality* (rather than the quantity) of inputs. This qualitative improvement is known as technological advance.

An increase in the rate of output per capita is dependent upon an *increase in the rate* of technological progress. It is not sufficient that there exists some technological advance; the rate of advance must be increasing. A high rate of technological progress requires both inventions and their implementation. New productive techniques must not only be discovered but also brought into use.

Inventions and other discoveries are a function of research and human imagination. Therefore, little can be said about social forces affecting this aspect of technological progress. Even when new techniques are discovered, their implementation often proves difficult, for productive implementation of discoveries requires not only effective entrepreneurship but also a labor force that possesses managerial, technical, and white-collar skills. Unless education and the willingness to assume risk are sufficiently widespread in the population, discoveries with great potential will have little immediate impact on economic development.

Political Factors

Political instability is not conducive to economic development. A prerequisite to economic advancement is a relatively stable system of law and order. Private citizens and foreign lenders who finance capital investment, for example, must feel sure that returns on investments will not be expropriated as the result of a change in the political regime. Revolutions, or other forms of instability, increase the risk associated with investment and, thereby, retard development.

Even though a government is stable, its specific policies may either stimulate or impede economic development. Tax policies that protect concentrated capital ownership by a small, powerful group tend to discourage private initiative and prevent the growth of a widespread entrepreneurial class. Excess profits that accrue to the elite may be reinvested in other countries rather than used to increase capital accumulation, train workers, or promote technology at home.

In Chapter 42 the political phenomenon of nationalism was mentioned as a force that can modify the economic benefits of international trade. Thus, a nation's foreign trade policy is an important political instrument for effecting its own development or the development of other nations. If a large, prosperous nation follows a high tariff policy, the development of poorer nations with which it trades will tend to be retarded. Conversely, poorer nations may adopt a policy of nationalism that is antipathetic to foreign capital because of fear of outside political influence. As a consequence, the flow of capital investment from abroad is reduced.

Trade unions supported by government arbitration boards may possess enough political influence to command higher wages, additional fringe benefits, and shorter work hours. Unless expanded compensation is accompanied by proportionate rises in labor productivity, economic development will suffer. Yet political realities may call the tune. Indeed, the national government itself may insist upon a comprehensive welfare state before the productivity of the economy is capable of carrying the burden. Old-age pensions, unemployment insurance, family allowances, and health insurance can be supported only when the economic system has achieved a relatively advanced stage of development. Nevertheless, the popular appeal of welfare programs may offer a political temptation that the government cannot resist.

On the other hand, the government administration may pursue policies that encourage economic development. Efforts toward stable political change, tax policies, and foreign trade can be effected with the objective of promoting development. In any event, it is apparent that the political structure of a nation and the public policies of the political administration are crucial variables in the development process.

Sociological Factors

Accompanying the growth of new industries and technological advance is a modernization in the style of living. Urbanization normally goes hand-in-hand with industrialization. Factory work entails a more systematic organization of a worker's time and effort than that which exists in an agricultural community. These changes require adjustments in people's style of living as they move from rural to urban areas or transfer employment to more mechanized forms of production.

More rapid development may rely upon a change of the family structure. Incentives differ between a society organized around the undivided family (several living generations and relatives closely tied together) and a society organized around the immediate family unit (parents and their children). Choices between income and leisure, between consumption and saving, between more children and a higher level of living are all affected. These choices in turn influence the rate of development. Under the immediate family unit a man's harder work will bring benefits to himself, his wife, and his children. Under the undivided family system, a man who works harder and earns more may find himself supporting a larger number of distant relatives without gain to himself or his children. Similarly, his own children benefit from the sacrifice he makes in saving more under the immediate family system. Therefore, the incentive to save is greater. It is apparent, then, that the existing family structure affects development and that the process of development may necessitate acceptance of change in the family structure on the part of the populace.

Other cultural patterns, customs, and forms of social organization likewise influence economic development, for they determine the prevalence of work incentives, the desire to amass wealth from profits, attitudes toward risk-taking ventures, the preference for consumption over saving, the educational status of persons, and the mobility of labor. Actual operation of the economic, political, and sociological factors that determine economic development can be seen most clearly from an outline of the course of advancement in the developed nations. The impact of these same factors can also be identified in the underdeveloped nations.

THE DEVELOPED NATIONS

The economic history of the Western world from 1700 to the present time reveals a conjuncture of economic, political, and sociological factors conducive to rapid growth and development. Europe's development during the Industrial Revolution and that of the New World in the nineteenth and twentieth centuries were not the result of one, or even a few, predominant factors. Rather, many factors acted simultaneously and reacted one upon another to produce a remarkable period of sustained growth.

First, among the economic factors, net saving and investment averaged between 10 and 20 percent of national income. This is a much higher rate than exists today. Furthermore, rapid capital accumulation was not centered in a few industries but occurred over a wide complex of public and private enterprises.

Second, population growth constituted a stimulus rather than an impediment to development. In the phraseology of the previous section, population expanded from levels that were less than optimum. Work opportunities were plentiful, and per capita output rose. Moreover, population expansion brought additional demand for increased output and new products without outstripping the capacity of the productive machinery to supply the desired goods and services.

Third, the opening of frontiers and the discovery of new natural resources had two effects. They offered opportunities for even greater capital investment, and they provided opportunities for people to "move West" to regions of more fertile land or more abundant minerals. Capital accumulation and population growth were accompanied by, and further stimulated by, migration to areas richer in natural resources.

Fourth, the period was characterized by a remarkable rate of technological innovation. New technologies encouraged the search for yet more new resources, instigated further population movements, and created incentives for faster capital accumulation.

The coincidence of these economic factors was supported by political and sociological phenomena of the period and the areas affected. During the eighteenth century new industries and urban centers emerged within the borders and jurisdiction of each nation. Thus, each nation's government had the advantage of being able to exert a significant influence on the direction of change. During the nineteenth century, when the pace of development quickened, the technically superior countries were the United Kingdom, France, Holland, and Germany. These countries, especially the United Kingdom, followed a policy of free trade. Manufactured goods were exported in exchange for agricultural raw materials and foodstuffs. Imports from the New World provided markets for the production of those areas and thereby enhanced their development. In addition, exports of manufactured goods to the underdeveloped areas provided these areas with the ingredients for building new industries.

Foreign investment in the New World during the nineteenth century was carried out on a scale unmatched before or since. Although large-scale foreign investment was dictated largely by private economic interests, this flow of capital was consistent with government policies in both the developed and underdeveloped nations. Europe wanted cheap food, and frontier developments using European capital made cheaper food possible. The frontier nations wanted a greater stock of operating capital and welcomed the flow of capital from Europe.

Finally, the technically advanced countries of Europe were able to engender and, if necessary, enforce political stability in the developing areas. In the early stages of the Industrial Revolution, the emerging industries were within their own borders. At a later stage, when development of the New World began, the underdeveloped areas became colonies of European powers. After the colonies acquired independence, political traditions had already established a climate favorable to receipt of foreign investment. Moreover, the European nations had the military strength to police investments abroad. Even if military power was not used, the mere existence of superior military strength contributed to political stability and safer investments in the developing areas.

In addition to economic and political factors, sociological factors in the Western world favored rapid development. It has been argued that the Reformation and the emergence of Puritanism increased the propensity to save. Thrift and saving were advanced as virtues. This attitude helped to generate a flow of saving sufficient to finance foreign investment and the implementation of newly discovered production techniques.

Europe and the New World were characterized by the immediate family form of social organization. As pointed out in the previous section, this form of social organization is conducive to a spirit of entrepreneurship and pursuit of monetary gain. It also helped to promote a flow of both capital and labor to the New World.

THE UNDERDEVELOPED NATIONS

The underdeveloped areas today exist primarily outside the Western world. In terms of the factors affecting economic development, it is useful to compare these areas with the now advanced nations during their period of most rapid growth.

Whereas net saving and investment in the Western nations averaged between 10 and 20 percent of national income during the eighteenth and nineteenth centuries, in most (but not all) presently underdeveloped nations net saving and investment average between 2 and 6 percent of national income. Generally speaking, underdeveloped countries have such low national incomes that a larger volume of domestic saving and investment out of income is very difficult indeed. A major problem is one of somehow raising income to a level at which saving and investment can be increased to promote further expansion.

With respect to population change, the Latin American countries appear to be in such a situation that population growth in itself will not raise output per capita. If population growth is accompanied by sufficient capital accumulation and technological progress, expansion of the population would stimulate development and raise per capita income. Unfortunately in most of the Middle Eastern, African, and Asian countries, further growth in population would act to reduce per capita output and income. The marginal productivity of labor is so low with the present capital stock that total output would rise by less than the increase in persons. This situation is in sharp contrast with conditions that prevailed in the New World 100 or more years ago.

Most underdeveloped nations of today do not have "frontiers" in any way similar to those of the Western hemisphere in the eighteenth and nineteenth centuries. People do not have the opportunity of moving to richer virgin land. In Libya, for example, moving from settled areas means moving out into the Sahara Desert. In Southeast Asia, migration can be made to areas once intensively cultivated and later abandoned, or into the jungle. Little is known about access to new mineral deposits, and the outlook is uncertain as to how long the working mineral reserves can be exploited before they are exhausted.

Prospects for technological progress appear to be more favorable. Underdeveloped countries can "import" new technical methods from the advanced countries. Nevertheless, there are serious problems. Rapid technological progress requires invention (which may be carried out elsewhere) and implementation of new techniques. Implementation is one function of the entrepreneur, and in underdeveloped areas entrepreneurship is scarce. Although the central government may replace private enterprise as an innovator, most underdeveloped nations are short of trained people needed to operate complex technical equipment.

Political and sociological factors in the underdeveloped areas of today also differ from those present in the Western world 100 years ago. Whereas free trade and foreign investment were integral parts of political policy during the nineteenth century, the world situation has changed. On the one hand, the United States and other developed nations pursue policies of high tariffs on imports of consumer goods. In spite of recent efforts to lower tariffs, these barriers to international trade have not yet been scaled down on a broad array of goods. Exports from underdeveloped to developed countries tend to be limited primarily to raw materials. On the other hand, political nationalism in underdeveloped nations commonly assumes a form that curtails foreign investment in these areas. Any suggestion that Western powers are attempting to exercise control over industries may cause trouble for foreign investors. As a consequence, capital inflows are restricted. Furthermore, governmental policy is often designed to redistribute income from rich to poor. Desirable as these policies may be on social and ethical grounds, they tend to reduce saving and investment, for income is transferred from those with a relatively high propensity to save to those with a low propensity to save. In contrast, during the early stages of development in Western countries, taxes consisted mostly of customs and excise duties which were borne primarily by the poor, who consumed the largest fraction of income. The redistribution from poor to rich encouraged greater saving.

Sociological factors in present-day underdeveloped countries are often the reverse of those characteristic of the Western countries during their stage of rapid development. The undivided family structure is usually the basis of social organization. Hence, the incentive for harder work or greater saving is dampened. The spirit of entrepreneurship and the desire for monetary gain through risk taking are rare. The sociological phenomenon of "keeping up with the Joneses" appears to be a Western custom. There is frequently a strong attachment to the village or the peasant way of life. Consequently, the labor mobility necessary for large-scale industrialization is absent.

In summary, the presently underdeveloped nations lack almost all of the advantages enjoyed by the Western countries during their stages of rapid growth and development. It might seem, then, that the task of their achieving a higher rate of growth in the near future is an impossible one. Certainly it is a difficult one. Nevertheless, if both the advanced countries and the underdeveloped countries come to understand what actions are needed to speed development and if they cooperate to carry out these actions, then a greater rate of development is feasible. We shall have more to say about this in Chapter 45.

GENERAL THEORIES OF DEVELOPMENT

Theories of economic development have occupied economists since the earliest days of the science. However, the problems of short-run fluctuations in national income and employment (business cycles) assumed such drastic proportions in the first half of the twentieth century that the problems of long-run development receded into the background. After World War II, with the advance made in our knowledge of the causes of cyclical fluctuations and with the emergence of new political states in underdeveloped areas, the explanation of development again came to the forefront of economic problems. No one theory has been able to explain completely the development process. As we have seen, the variables are many and the causal factors are broad in scope. We shall review some of the theories that have attempted to take into account the various factors and how they operate within the economy.

The Classical Theory

The Classical economists lived during the early and middle development stages of the Western world. According to the *Classical theory*, development was in essence a race between the rate of technological innovation and the growth of population.

Technological progress was a function of capital accumulation, for a larger stock of capital would allow greater mechanization and a further division of labor. In turn, the rate of capital accumulation depended upon profits. Thus, greater profits led to a faster rate of capital investment and further technological advance.

On the other side of the ledger, so to speak, was the rate of population growth. As the population increased, diminishing returns would appear in agriculture. Since agriculture was assumed to be a predominant industry, profits would tend to decline. The decline in profits would slow down the rate of capital accumulation and thus the rate of technological advance. Bursts of technological change would stimulate more rapid development from time to time. The Classical economists predicted, however, that in the long run population growth would win out. Therefore, the economy would settle at a no-change level; stagnation would set in.

The Marxist Theory

The *Marxist theory of economic development* is very similar to the Classical theory. Basically, Karl Marx agreed that technological advance is a function of capital accumulation and that capital accumulation depends upon profits. He also agreed that profits tend to fall in a capitalistic system. However, he denied that population growth caused profits to fall. Marx differed from the Classical economists also in that he argued that attempts to maintain the level of profits would require a decrease in the share of wages in national income. As workers are further exploited, consumption declines, goods go unsold, and profits decrease after all.

Marx recognized technological progress as the only possibility for delaying or preventing the natural decline of profits. Indeed, unlike the Classical economists, he did not predict stagnation of the system. As a prophet of the doom of capitalism, he did predict an overthrow of the capitalistic system. But revolt would result from the exploitation of workers rather than the interplay of economic variables. In the Communist society that purportedly would succeed capitalism, the process of economic development was not clearly spelled out by Marx.

The Entrepreneurial Theory

Joseph Schumpeter followed in the tradition of the Classical economists and Marx by stressing the importance of technological change. In his *entrepreneurial theory*, Schumpeter emphasized the dual aspects of technological progress: invention plus implementation. The latter he called innovation.

Schumpeter theorized that capital accumulation depends upon new resource discoveries and technological progress. These two, in turn, depend upon the supply of entrepreneurs. The supply of entrepreneurs is a function of expected future profits (not past or current profits) and a host of sociological factors that determine personality traits.

The entrepreneurial role is crucial to the Schumpeterian system of thought. The entrepreneur raises money to build an enterprise, organizes the factors of production, takes risks, and innovates. Although he admired greatly the capitalistic system, Schumpeter feared that it would eventually stagnate. He argues, rather vaguely, that the social climate which produces dynamic entrepreneurs will change. Society will become hostile toward the egocentric, ambitious, and untraditional nature of the innovator. Therefore, technological progress will slow down, capital investment will increase more slowly and eventually reach zero, and economic development will come to a standstill.

Steady-Growth Theories

The Classical economists predicted that capitalist development would end in a steady state or stagnation. Marx believed that capitalism would completely break down, and Schumpeter likewise feared gloomy prospects for the capitalistic system. Schumpeter's major writing on economic development extended over the period 1911 through 1939. Post-World War II theories have been much less pessimistic. Some maintained that full employment without inflation is a difficult goal to achieve in a private enterprise economy. Cumulative long-run movements away from full-employment equilibrium were seen as a constant threat but not an inevitable trend. Others sought to identify the conditions that would produce a stable yet constantly growing capitalist economy. They argued only that attainment of short-run stability and long-run growth require proper monetary and fiscal policies, carefully timed.

Most modern theoretical analysis has been constructed with advanced economies in mind. The theoretical models attempt to incorporate the various economic factors determining development and to assess their relative importance. Many economists have concluded that there is a tendency for private capital investment to fall for several reasons: population growth has tapered off; the frontier, with the incentives and opportunities it offered, has disappeared; and the rate of new resource discovery has diminished. More rapid technological innovation could offset the effects of these changes upon investment, but in fact (it is argued) the rate of technological progress has not increased. Therefore, there is a tendency for national income to drop, or to rise at a slower rate, and for chronic unemployment to set in. The government can promote greater development by increasing public investment, by reducing taxes, by redistributing income from savers to spenders in order to increase the demand for goods and services, or by some mixture of these policy actions.

It must be admitted that there is no consensus among economists on the "natural" long-run tendencies of a capitalistic system or the need for more aggressive monetary and fiscal policies. The more elaborate theories allow for more than one conclusion, depending upon the relative force exerted by different economic variables. Further research is required before a predominantly pessimistic or predominantly optimistic attitude will be found among economists.

Historical Theories

Economic historians have devoted a great amount of research to the economic development of the Western world and, much more recently, to present-day underdeveloped areas. Without too much oversimplification these studies can be classified under two categories: (1) the rise of capitalism in the West, and (2) takeoff into sustained growth.

The Rise of Capitalism. Werner Sombart and Max Weber are typical of those who sought historical explanations of economic development in Europe in terms of changing institutions. Sombart perceived capitalism as a particular form of social and economic organization characteristic of a definite period of history. The capitalistic economy has three primary features. The first is technical progress in contrast to static production techniques bound by custom. The second is economic freedom and individualism rather than a corporate community. Third is the profit-seeking spirit. Sombart advances the argument that the Middle Ages were dominated by the opposite characteristics, which impeded development. Capitalism emerged as commercial capitalists were able to displace feudal landlords as holders of economic and political power. Sombart argued further that capitalism, as he defines it, grew from about 1500 to the mid-eighteenth century, reached its highest form of development from about 1750 to 1914, and is now declining. He does not explain what form of economic organization is replacing laissez-faire capitalism.

Max Weber attributes the rise of capitalism to the Reformation. The acquisitive instinct is common to all times and places. Roman Catholicism during the Middle Ages held in check the pursuit of profit and the accumulation of wealth. These activities were regarded as shameful avarice. According to Weber, the Reformation provided the philosophical and moral foundations for the emergence of a *capitalistic spirit*. Profit making, entrepreneurship, and acquisition of wealth became respectable, especially among the lower middle classes; these classes produced the sober bourgeois society in which private enterprise flourished. According to Weber it was this spirit, rather than money flows or other "objective" economic variables, that produced economic development. The spirit provided entrepreneurs, blessed hard work, and praised saving. Thus, the basis for capital accumulation and technological advance was laid.

Takeoff into Sustained Growth. More recently, W. W. Rostow proposed a synthesis of historical explanations of the early stages of economic development. The synthesis is intended to be applicable to any country at any historical point in time. He divides the process of economic development into three stages. The first stage is a century or more during which the preconditions for "takeoff" are being established. The second stage is the takeoff itself, which absorbs only a few decades of time. The final stage is a very long period of sustained economic progress subject to short-run fluctuations in business activity but exhibiting a trend of normal growth.

The *takeoff* is essentially a burst of economic growth that carries an economy into a path of normal and semiautomatic further development. The most important aspect of Rostow's scheme is a definition of the conditions required to achieve takeoff. He specifies three conditions necessary (but not sufficient in themselves) for takeoff. Net investment must rise from near 5 percent of national income to well over 10 percent. The volume of investment must be sufficient to overcome the impediment of population pressure if population growth exceeds the optimum. In addition, one or more substantial manufacturing sectors with high growth rates must appear.

Finally, there must exist a political and social climate that encourages the natural impulse to expansion in the most modern sectors of the economy.

In the takeoff process, three sectors will be found in the economy. Primary growth sectors are those with favorable opportunities for technological progress and new resource discovery. Supplementary growth sectors expand in response to the primary sectors by supplying raw materials, utilities, or transportation. Derived growth sectors advance as a result of rising national income and overall demand for output.

CONCLUSION

The most important factors that determine economic development can be identified. But some of these—such as political and, even more so, sociological factors—cannot be specified in detail. The direct impact of capital accumulation and technological progress upon economic growth can be specified and even measured. However, what causes investment and technology to change, and by how much in the long run, is more difficult to explain. Underlying these changes may be an emerging spirit, an evolving social climate, and other sociologically determined attitudes.

Economic theories of development are applicable for the most part to the development process of current advanced Western countries with given (historically established) institutions. Attempts to adapt these theories to presently underdeveloped nations have not met with striking success. Historical theories, such as Rostow's, are very general descriptive statements rather than systematic causal explanations. Therefore, they are of very limited assistance in devising policies that will promote growth in underdeveloped areas.

SUMMARY

1. Economic, political, and sociological factors determine a nation's economic development.

2. Among the economic factors are capital accumulation, population growth, discovery of new resources, and technological innovation.

3. Underlying rates of change in these economic factors are political and social forces that mold attitudes toward entrepreneurship, profit seeking, and wealth accumulation.

4. The institutions in present-day underdeveloped areas differ radically from those prevalent in the early stages of development of Europe and the New World.

5. Early theories of development (the Classical, Marxist, and entrepreneurial theories) predicted eventual stagnation or breakdown of the capitalistic system.

6. Contemporary theories of advanced economies are more optimistic. Tendencies toward stagnation can be offset by appropriate monetary and fiscal policies so that stable and sustained growth can be achieved in a private enterprise economy.

7. Economic theories have been less successful in interpreting or explaining the forces affecting development in presently underdeveloped areas.

QUESTIONS FOR DISCUSSION AND ANALYSIS

1. What are the differences between short-run stabilization of the economy and long-run economic development?

2. How do the underdeveloped areas of today differ from Europe between 1500 and 1700? How do they differ from the New World in the late eighteenth and nineteenth centuries?

3. What are the economic factors in development? What are the political and sociological factors?

4. Do you believe the spirit of entrepreneurship is on the decline in the United States? What are your reasons?

5. How does the Classical theory of economic development differ from the Marxist theory? From Schumpeter's theory?

6. How do contemporary theories of economic development differ from earlier economic theories?

7. In what way do the historical theories help us to understand the problems and processes of economic development? What are their shortcomings?

8. How does the discovery and industrial use of nuclear energy affect economic development in advanced Western countries? In underdeveloped areas?

9. Is there a potential conflict between faster economic development and environmental protection? Explain.

SUGGESTED READINGS

The Suggested Readings for this chapter are included in Chapter 45, page 1022.

45

The Emerging Nations

PREVIEW Although economic conditions alone do not determine the quality of life in a society, many nations of the world are burdened by a very high incidence of poverty. Such economically underdeveloped areas are characterized by high fertility rates, agriculture as the dominant industry, modest technological progress, low educational attainment, and, in some cases, underutilized resources. Several theories have been advanced to explain differing rates of economic development, but none has yet received general acceptance among social scientists. Planning for development requires both an adequate capital budget and carefully designed public policies.

Many people in the United States have come to regard the nearly continuous rise in per capita income in Europe, North America, and Australia as the normal course of history. If it were possible to record the level of living of all parts of the world over the past 2,000 years, however, the record would show a different story. Instead of continuous growth the data would reveal very long periods of dreary stagnation interrupted by relatively brief intervals of dramatic progress in a few areas of the world.

Since the end of World War II, many new nations have come into being. Almost all of these emerging nations—in Africa, Asia, and Latin America—are considered to be underdeveloped economically. Their governments have become increasingly development oriented, and their political stability is of great importance to the entire world. Therefore, a closer examination of their problems is called for.

WHO ARE THE UNDERDEVELOPED NATIONS?

Economic conditions represent only one facet of a culture or a society. To classify a country as an economically underdeveloped nation tells us nothing about its level of civilization, culture, or spiritual values. Americans can learn a great deal from the people of underdeveloped countries in order to lead more personally rewarding and socially useful lives. Our social relations might be more genial if we adopted some of the manners of the Orientals. We might imitate the capacity some foreign peoples have for complete relaxation and meditation. Grace and poise, food preparation, and art appreciation could be imported by means of experts sent from underdeveloped to advanced nations as a type of foreign aid on the part of these countries.

Nevertheless, it is a brutal fact that many of these nations face poverty. This poverty is not found in isolated pockets but exists on a broad scale affecting well over half the population in many instances. If we were to seek a single measure of underdevelopment, it could be found in a nation's per capita income. Of course, incomes vary among nations, and it is difficult to choose one income figure below which a country is classified as "underdeveloped." We encountered this same problem in defining poverty in the United States, as shown in Chapters 37 and 40, where the somewhat arbitrary figure of $4,000 per year was used as a minimum. In spite of this problem, it is useful to indicate some of the lowest per capita incomes in foreign lands.

TABLE 45-1

PER CAPITA INCOMES BY NATIONS

Per Capita Income	Africa	Asia	Americas
$500 to $1,000	Union of South Africa	Singapore	Venezuela Argentina Chile
$300 to $499	Ivory Coast Southern Rhodesia	China Malaya Lebanon Turkey Iran Philippines	Brazil Cuba Colombia Guatemala Mexico Peru
Under $300	Egypt Senegal Republic of the Congo Kenya Uganda Morocco Tanzania	Ceylon Thailand Korea Pakistan India Burma Indonesia	Dominican Republic Ecuador Honduras Paraguay El Salvador

SOURCE: *United Nations Statistical Yearbook*, 1972.

Table 45-1 lists some of the nations in Africa, Asia, and the Americas by per capita income range. What the table does not reveal is just how small the per capita income is in some nations. In Africa the per capita income is less than $200 per year in the Congo, Kenya, Morocco, and Tanzania. In Asia the per capita income is below $200 per year in Burma, India, Ceylon, Indonesia, and Thailand.

It must be kept in mind, however, that these incomes are not directly translatable into U.S. dollars. An income of $200 does not mean that a person would suffer what an American would suffer with a comparable dollar income, for only the output of those goods and services traded on the market are used to compute national income estimates. Some real income is consumed directly outside the monetary sphere and, therefore, does not enter the statistical tabulations. Nevertheless, this accounting difficulty simply means the degree of poverty is overstated in the statistics. Actual poverty is real and persistent.

Much of the world's population lives under conditions of extreme poverty measured by contemporary standards. An indication of the numbers involved can be obtained from the distribution of world population shown in Figure 45-1 on page 1006.

A population census is conducted every ten years in most countries, and the latest census was completed for 1970. In that year the people of South America, Africa, Oceania, and Asia outside of the Soviet Union numbered 2.61 billion out of a world population of 3.64 billion. Moreover, some of the fastest population growths appear in these same areas. By the year 2,000 it is estimated that these areas will include 5.20 billion people out of a 6.68 billion world population. This is an increase from 72 to 78 percent of world population over a period of 30 years.

Reference to Table 45-1 clearly indicates that, with few exceptions, countries having the lowest per capita incomes are located outside the North American continent, Europe, and the Soviet Union. Thus, the most populated areas of the world exhibit the highest incidence of poverty. Whether the material welfare of people in poor nations is likely to improve or worsen in the near future is suggested in Table 45-2.

TABLE 45-2

A COMPARISON OF POPULATION GROWTH RATES AND GROWTH RATES IN GNP

Country	1970 Population (Millions)	1963-1970 Population Growth Rate (Percent Per Year)	1970 Per Capita Income (Dollars Per Year)	1961-1969 Growth Rate in Real GNP (Percent Per Year)
China	759.6	1.8	364	.3
India	550.4	2.1	92	1.0
Indonesia	121.2	2.8	107	.8
Pakistan	114.2	2.1	139	3.1
Brazil	95.3	3.2	341	1.6

SOURCE: *United Nations Statistical Yearbook*, 1972; and *World Bank Atlas*, 1972.

Each of the countries listed in Table 45-2 is a high population, low income nation. Population and per capita income figures are recorded in the first and third columns respectively. Column two shows the recent growth rate of the population in each country, and the fourth column displays each country's growth rate in GNP over approximately the same period. Comparison of the second and fourth columns reveals that in four of these five

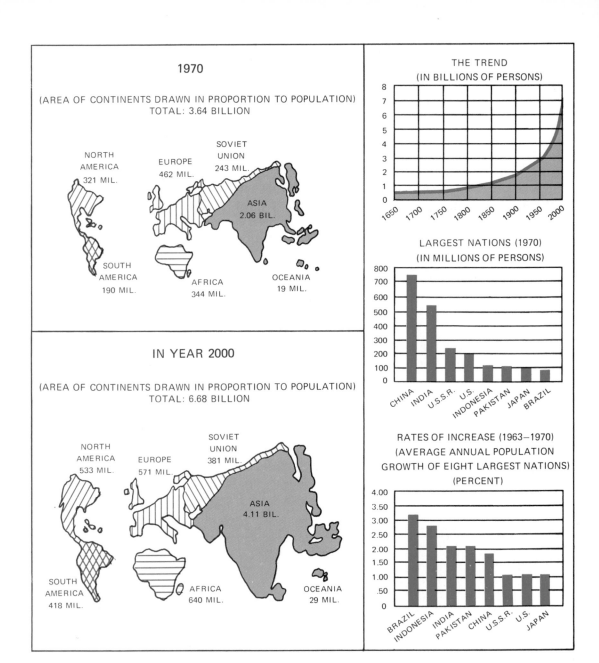

1970

(AREA OF CONTINENTS DRAWN IN PROPORTION TO POPULATION)
TOTAL: 3.64 BILLION

NORTH AMERICA 321 MIL.

EUROPE 462 MIL.

SOVIET UNION 243 MIL.

ASIA 2.06 BIL.

SOUTH AMERICA 190 MIL.

AFRICA 344 MIL.

OCEANIA 19 MIL.

IN YEAR 2000

(AREA OF CONTINENTS DRAWN IN PROPORTION TO POPULATION)
TOTAL: 6.68 BILLION

NORTH AMERICA 533 MIL.

EUROPE 571 MIL.

SOVIET UNION 381 MIL.

ASIA 4.11 BIL.

SOUTH AMERICA 418 MIL.

AFRICA 640 MIL.

OCEANIA 29 MIL.

THE TREND
(IN BILLIONS OF PERSONS)

LARGEST NATIONS (1970)
(IN MILLIONS OF PERSONS)

CHINA INDIA U.S.S.R. U.S. INDONESIA PAKISTAN JAPAN BRAZIL

RATES OF INCREASE (1963–1970)
(AVERAGE ANNUAL POPULATION
GROWTH OF EIGHT LARGEST NATIONS)
(PERCENT)

BRAZIL INDONESIA INDIA PAKISTAN CHINA U.S.S.R. U.S. JAPAN

FIGURE 45-1

**WORLD POPULATION—
THE PICTURE NOW AND A
LOOK TOWARD 2000**

SOURCE: *United Nations Statistical Yearbook,* 1971; and *United Nations Demographic Yearbook,* 1971.

Population growth rates are highest in the poorest areas of the world.

countries, the population growth rate has exceeded the growth rate of GNP. Unless population growth can be retarded or GNP can be raised markedly, or both in combination, the prospects for a significant rise in per capita income in the foreseeable future are not highly encouraging.

Among the nations listed in Table 45-2, one exception is Brazil. A nearly miraculous leap in development began in 1968. Over a period of six years, Brazil's national output rose 9 percent or more every year, exceeding Japan's 1960 GNP of $50 billion in 1973. Per capita income reached the $500 level in the same year. Unlike most underdeveloped countries, manufacturing rose markedly in the early seventies, and exports nearly tripled between 1963 and 1973.

This success story illustrates two important points. One is the diversity among nations classified as underdeveloped. Some are experiencing notable progress, while, for most, material gains are painfully slow. Africa and South Asia have been considerably below the average growth rate for all underdeveloped areas combined, while the Middle East has been well above the average. The second point has to do with income distribution. Although Brazil's national production and per capita income have nearly doubled in five years, 40 percent of Brazilians still receive only 10 percent of national private income, the same share they received in 1960. This would seem to indicate that when a country does reach a point of dramatic development, there is no assurance that the majority of citizens will share appreciably in national gains.

CHARACTERISTICS OF UNDERDEVELOPED NATIONS

Aside from the prevalence of poverty, reflected in very low per capita income statistics, what are the general characteristics of underdeveloped countries?

Economic Characteristics

Subject to exceptions in relatively few countries, underdeveloped areas are marked by a high proportion of the population—usually 70 to 90 percent—in agriculture. Agricultural output is comprised mostly of cereals and primary raw materials. The output of protein foods, such as meat products, is quite small because they require more land per calorie produced. Most studies show that there is overpopulation in agriculture in the sense that the number of workers on farms could be reduced without a decrease in total output.

There is insufficient development of manufacturing and commerce. Thus, few employment opportunities exist outside agriculture, and the evidence suggests there is considerable *disguised unemployment* in those that do exist. Related to the structure of industries is the fact that exports consist primarily of food and raw materials.

Since incomes are so low, per capita saving is nearly zero for the large mass of people. Practically all income goes into current consumption, and consumption expenditures are absorbed by food and necessities rather than new products. Whatever savings do exist are concentrated among a small number of landowners. These landowners do not possess the values that are favorable to investment in industry or commerce.

Much output is consumed directly, so there is a low volume of trade per capita. Credit facilities are poor, housing is far below minimal standards in technically advanced nations, and marketing facilities are rudimentary.

Technological Characteristics

The state of technology and the rate of technological progress are both low in underdeveloped areas as contrasted with industrialized nations. Communication and transportation suffer from the same lack of investment that retards the growth of industry and commerce. Rural areas especially have crude means of communication and inadequate transportation. Although communication and transportation are more effective in urban centers, most of the population is located in the rural areas.

Implementation of advanced technology requires a skilled work force. In order to develop skills, training facilities are needed. Underdeveloped areas typically have inadequate schools and on-the-job training centers for the production of engineers, technicians, statisticians, office workers, and other types of skilled laborers. Indeed, some areas have no facilities whatsoever.

As a consequence, labor productivity is low. In agriculture, the predominant industry, yields per acre of land are low. The number of tractors and mechanized threshers in use in the United States is 5.2 million, whereas there are less than one million in use in all of Africa and Asia combined. In manufacturing and commerce—to the extent that these industries exist—hand labor is common and output per capita remains small. Scientific and technical manpower in the United States numbers over 3.0 million; in Malaysia the number is about 25,000; in Mexico, about 4,500; and in the Congo, less than 1,000.

Demographic Characteristics

High *fertility rates* are found in almost all underdeveloped areas. Live births per 1,000 persons are usually above 40, whereas the world average is 34 births per 1,000 persons. A common measure of fertility (regarded as more accurate than birth rates for international comparisons) is the gross reproduction rate, defined as the number of live daughters per woman. In underdeveloped areas, these rates are in the range of 2.5 to 3.5 as compared to a range of 1 to 1.5 in the United States and most European countries.

High *mortality rates* are also evident in poor nations. General mortality, though higher, does not differ vastly from what has been observed in economically advanced countries, however. Deaths per 1,000 persons in the population range from about 11 to 15; these rates are in the neighborhood of 8 or 9 in industrialized countries. But great differences are observable in infant mortality rates. Measured by deaths of children under one year of age per 1,000 live births, infant mortality rates of 40 to 60 are not uncommon. The rate even exceeds 100 in a few countries, and these numbers gain more importance when they are compared to an infant mortality rate of 20 in the United States.

Sanitation facilities are rudimentary in the underdeveloped countries, and methods of hygiene are often primitive. Public health services are extremely limited. The population suffers from inadequate nutrition and dietary deficiencies. It is not uncommon to find rural areas that are overcrowded. Overcrowding, combined with poor sanitation and health facilities as well as dietary deficiencies, contributes to low labor productivity and limited life expectancy. Compare, for example, a life expectancy of 75 years for an American female one year of age (68 years for a one-year-old American male) to a life expectancy of 33 to 56 years, depending on the country, for a nonwhite African female one year of age (34 to 61 years for a one-year-old African male).

Political and Sociological Characteristics

Only a small fraction of the population receives a full elementary education. Consequently, a high degree of illiteracy exists among the masses. With respect to secondary education, school enrollments are even lower. In Peru only 4 percent of all 16-year-olds are in secondary schools; in Ethiopia, less than 3 percent. By comparison, almost 68 percent of all 16-year-old Canadians are enrolled in secondary school. Since education is a precondition for the learning of skills and the emergence of a widespread middle class, there is a general weakness or absence of a middle class from which entrepreneurs may be drawn.

Child labor is prevalent in most underdeveloped areas. Women generally hold a social position inferior to men. In addition, the great bulk of the population is guided by tradition. Behavior tends to be bound by custom. As a consequence, experimentation and innovation in the economic sphere are discouraged.

Types of Underdevelopment

Although each country is unique and no one country exhibits the general characteristics of underdevelopment exactly, it is possible to distinguish four types of underdevelopment. First, there are nations with per capita incomes low enough to warrant the label "underdeveloped" but with unutilized resources that are known to exist. Argentina, Brazil, Colombia, Mexico, Peru, Venezuela, Ceylon, the Philippines, and Turkey appear to be in this category. These nations are undergoing sufficient agricultural improvement and industrialization to bring about significant rises in per capita income. Their problems are those of sustaining growth and distributing the benefits of growth more widely among the population.

Second, there are nations with low per capita incomes and few resources relative to population size. Burma, Pakistan, China, and Thailand appear to be in this category. The per capita income in these countries is on the rise. The increase in income, however, must be accelerated rather than merely sustained.

Third, there are countries in which per capita income is low and shows no increase over the long run. Yet these nations have rich natural resources. Indonesia is an example. The prospects for these countries are much more favorable than for those with poor resources. If population growth can be controlled, a planned development program holds promise of producing a cumulative rise in per capita income.

Fourth, there are nations with low per capita incomes that show no rising trend and with poor resources. Libya, Jordan, and Yemen seem to fall in this category. Such nations cannot rely upon untapped natural resources. Improvement of existing economic enterprises rather than a change in the structure of the economy appears to offer the only hope for development.

THEORIES OF UNDERDEVELOPMENT

Several efforts have been made to explain, in part at least, why some nations have developed more rapidly than others or why some nations are presently underdeveloped. These theories can be separated into four categories: geographic determinism, sociological patterns, terms of trade, and balanced growth.

Geographic Determinism

Before the Second World War, *geographic determinism* was an influential hypothesis. According to this theory, underdeveloped countries are either too hot or too cold. In the tropics, diseases unknown in temperate climates and hot or humid weather prevent labor productivity from rising. In icy countries natural resources are lacking, and frigid temperatures limit possibilities for development. Geographic determinism holds that temperate climates are conducive to high agricultural productivity, to hard work, and to a frame of mind favorable to economic development.

In fact, recent empirical studies show that the impact of climate on human behavior is the least important of the various factors affecting development. The attitude toward work, leisure, and income is little different between Indonesians living at sea level and those living in the much more temperate climate of the mountains. There is no great difference between the attitudes and the productivity of Australians in subtropical Darwin, which is very hot, and those in chilly Hobart. A number of other examples could be cited. In general, geography does not appear to be important as an explanation of underdevelopment.

Of course, freezing temperatures or tropical climates do have economic consequences. Advanced countries located in temperate zones do have a comparative advantage in agriculture over industry. Whereas technology can be exported or imported, soil and climate cannot. Tropical soils tend to be poorer than soils in temperate regions. Consequently, one cannot expect levels of productivity comparable to those in advanced nations. But there is no reason why many underdeveloped nations cannot be as efficient as the advanced countries in many other industries. The spread of scientific knowledge and technological innovations are reducing economic disadvantages to which tropical underdeveloped countries are subject.

Sociological Patterns

Some writers have attempted to find the most important causes of underdevelopment in social and cultural patterns. *Sociological dualism* holds that social systems are imported into underdeveloped countries from the outside. Most often the imported social system is private enterprise, profit-seeking capitalism—although it may be socialism or communism. In any event, the imported social values and attitudes clash with the indigenous social system, which causes a form of disintegration. Social unity is disrupted, and advancement in the imported social system is prevented.

Others who have done research on underdeveloped nations turn to cultural and psychological factors as primary explanations of underdevelopment. The values are those of a peasant society. Attitudes toward wealth, leisure, and income are at odds with those found in the economically advanced nations. The family structure and the role of tradition are not favorable to economic growth.

Few would doubt that cultural and social patterns influence the rate of economic development. Economic theories formulated by European and

North American economists have implicitly assumed the existence of Western mores and attitudes. It should not be surprising, then, that these theories are less than satisfactory when applied to other areas of the world. It is very unlikely, however, that social and cultural patterns provide a full explanation of underdevelopment. From a policy point of view, the required attitudes cannot be created, so development policies must operate within the framework of existing social patterns.

Terms of Trade

International trade promoted the economic development of the Western world. The expansion of international trade, however, does not seem to have stimulated the growth of presently underdeveloped countries. Several economists have argued that there is a long-run tendency for the terms of trade to turn against exporters of food and raw materials. As we have seen, these are the most important exports of the underdeveloped nations.

According to this theory, trade between advanced countries and underdeveloped countries does not lead to a tendency toward equality of productivity and incomes. Rather, trade acts to widen the disparity. The theory relies upon regional differences within a single country. The growing sectors impose stagnation upon other sectors of the country. Poorer regions tend to have higher fertility rates. They also are typically rural. When growth occurs in the industrialized urban centers, migration into these centers makes the age distribution in the poorer rural areas unfavorable. These rural areas do not attract capital investment. As a consequence, the overall growth of a country is the result of high growth in a relatively few regions and stagnation in others.

International trade speeds the process of regional disparity. Industries in already established centers of expansion derive the benefits. Thus, international trade encourages further shifting of economic activity from stagnating to progressive regions. Although the country as a whole experiences a rise in per capita income, the per capita income of large masses of the population (those in stagnant rural areas) remains unchanged or actually declines.

In addition, the poorer regions are exporters of foodstuff and raw materials. If it is true that the terms of trade tend to turn against these exports as a long-run trend, the rural sectors will lose whatever benefits are derived from these exports. The facts are not clear on this issue. Indeed, the entire argument about the effects of international trade are still debated. More careful investigation will be required before definite conclusions can be drawn.

Balanced Growth

One set of theories has applied the basic tools of economic analysis to the problem of underdevelopment. The process of development and the actions needed to promote more rapid development are phrased in terms of economic models using the familiar concepts of the law of diminishing returns, consumption function, demand and supply, and so on. For lack of a better single term to describe these various development models, they can be described as *balanced-growth* theories.

The distinguishing feature of these theories, in contrast to the usual marginal analysis, is their emphasis upon *discontinuities* or "jumps" in the development process. Their proponents argue that the relationships among causal variables in economic growth are not smooth. Rather they are characterized by bulges, lumps, jumps, or discontinuities. These irregularities are in turn traceable to so-called *indivisibilities* in economic decision making. As a consequence, an all-out effort or big push is needed to overcome the inertia of a stagnant underdeveloped area.

Indivisibilities on the supply side of the economy center upon social overhead capital and the supply of savings. It is argued that *social overhead capital*—housing, educational facilities, transportation, power, communications, and so on—must precede other more immediately productive investments. Savings are required to finance investment which will generate the wage income that is the source of a cumulative increase in the demand for output. Indivisibilities in this connection mean that vast additions to saving (perhaps from outside the area) and enormous investments in social overhead capital are needed to promote development. Gradual or incremental increases are not sufficient to realize "takeoff" in the phraseology of W. W. Rostow.

Indivisibilities on the demand side of the economy mean that investment decisions are interdependent. Individual investment decisions are very risky because the final product may not find a sufficiently large market. The size of the market for new or more products is severely limited in underdeveloped countries. Hence, the market must be enlarged if investment is to be carried out under tolerable risk conditions.

According to these modifications of the usual economic analysis, removal of indivisibilities (of both demand and supply) entails a large-scale concentrated effort. If this effort is made, significant external economies will very likely be realized. That is, benefits will accrue not only to the investor directly concerned but also to others more distantly affected by the investment and to society as a whole. It must be admitted that the adaptations of modern Western economic theory do not constitute a general theory of development from which policies could be derived with great confidence. Although they represent an advance over speculations based on conventional theory, they remain as interesting hypotheses that have not been rigorously tested.

PLANNING FOR DEVELOPMENT

The customary tools of monetary policy, fiscal policy, and foreign exchange policy can be useful in promoting economic development. In order that they be useful, however, attention must be paid to the difference between the economic, political, and social institutions of advanced Western countries and those of underdeveloped countries. Effective planning for economic development requires that the nature of underdevelopment be understood and that the process of transition to a state at which economic growth can be sustained be analyzed at least in part. As we have indicated in the previous section, social scientists have not formulated a general theory of underdevelopment on which concrete development plans can be based. Still, the various theories do provide some guidelines for policy proposals. Within the framework of these guidelines, the development plan of each nation must be tailor-made to the culture, institutions, and attitudes of that nation.

Requirements of Development Planning

A plan for economic development has three fundamental components. The first is a capital budget. This budget consists of a number of capital investment projects with priorities assigned to each. Some will be public investment projects, such as roads, harbors, bridges, hospitals, and communication facilities. Others will be projects in agriculture, manufacturing, and commerce.

The second component of a development plan is a budget for investments in human capital (see Chapter 36). These government expenditures are not usually classified as capital outlays in the conventional sense; yet they contribute measurably to economic and social development. Expenditures on health facilities, education, and manpower training are of foremost importance.

Finally, development planning requires legislation and government regulation conducive to the success of capital expenditures. Political stability is essential to development, as we have seen. In addition, the program should include proposals for new institutions, markets, and industrial structures— and for the reorganization of old ones.

All three components entail decisions that affect the allocation of resources in the underdeveloped economy. In order that these decisions may stimulate development, the objectives of the plan must be clearly defined. A plan for development is not a once-and-for-all program. Rather, it is subject to constant revision as conditions change or partial objectives are attained.

Aspects of Development Planning

Decisions and behavior of large groups, as opposed to decisions and behavior of individuals, are distinguishing features of development planning. If the balanced-growth theories of development contain significant components of truth, and it appears that they do, then these choices of large groups must be made in terms of big pushes or jumps. Widespread structural changes rather than marginal adjustments are necessary. In turn, structural changes in the economy of the underdeveloped area may well involve social reorganization or alteration in prevailing attitudes among the population.

Aside from the general government budgetary requirements of planning, several secondary objectives must be specified in concrete terms. A goal for the balance-of-payments equilibrium position of the country is necessary. Production of food and raw materials should be assigned a target. The target should be defined quantitatively for the expansion of domestic production and the reduction of food imports. A desired increase in total industrial production, and its breakdown into particular industries, is an important aspect of planning. Likewise, a program of capital accumulation—both nonhuman capital and human capital—must be programmed in amounts or percentages of national income for each year of the entire planning interval. Population migration (usually from agriculture to other industries) should be taken into account in development planning, and allowances must be made for the resettlement of people who do move.

These various aspects of development planning do not define a plan appropriate to a particular country. Social and economic characteristics peculiar to the nation must be taken into account. Neither will attention devoted to these aspects assure successful development. Nevertheless, they do provide guidelines within which successful planning can be carried out.

FOREIGN ASSISTANCE IN DEVELOPMENT

A resolution passed by the United Nations General Assembly in 1970 stressed the importance of external assistance in the economic growth of underdeveloped nations. From the end of World War II until 1960, this assistance had been furnished almost exclusively by the United States and, to a somewhat lesser extent, by the Soviet Union. During the sixties, as other developed nations became more self-reliant, the base of support expanded to incorporate contributions from a variety of countries whose per capita incomes were well above the world average. Then, in the early

1970s, a new direction was emphasized in the form of multilateral grants and loans rather than unilateral aid extended by one country to another on the basis of the giver's political self-interest.

American Interest in Underdeveloped Nations

Underdeveloped nations are important to Americans for three primary reasons. First, as human beings we care about the condition of other humans wherever they may live on the planet. This humanitarian concern may not be stronger in our society than in others, but it certainly influences the many public and private American efforts to alleviate suffering among economically less fortunate peoples.

Second, as an economic unit we are interested in the development of other nations because they are economic markets. Some can supply resources of one kind or another that we need. Others provide consumer markets for our products. As their wealth and purchasing power expand, these areas of the world will become more profitable markets for the sale of our goods.

Third, underdeveloped nations have a political importance exceeding their economic potential. After 25 years of cold war, both the Communist and non-Communist countries now appear to be on the brink of a new era in which tolerance will replace confrontation or open warfare. With the end of American involvement in the Vietnam War and with President Nixon's personal visits to China and the Soviet Union, there has come into international relations a new tenor of mutual accommodation. This does not mean that powerful capitalist and Communist nations will refrain from expanding their spheres of influence or that local tensions will disappear. But it does mean that American political interests in so-called third world nations may now focus more on their economic progress as political allies than on their military prowess in "limited wars" or local American "police actions."

From the end of World War II to 1972, the United States extended to other nations a total of $148.8 billion in grants and loans. Of this amount, $146.3 billion assumed the form of *official* foreign aid, that is, grants or credits designated specifically as foreign aid by governmental agencies. Military grants amounted to $56.1 billion, and other types of assistance totaled $90.2 billion. American foreign assistance was extended to 125 countries and five international organizations.

Military grants are channeled through the Department of Defense. Those earmarked for particular regions amounted to $16.8 billion to Western Europe, $7.8 billion to the Near East and South Asia, $29.5 billion to the Far East and Pacific area, $1.3 billion to the Western hemisphere, and $352 million to Africa.

However, our main interest is not military grants but economic aid and technical assistance. These government appropriations are administered by the Agency for International Development (AID) and are governed by such legislation as the Agricultural Trade Development and Assistance Act of 1954 and the Foreign Assistance Act of 1961. We have offered aid to underdeveloped countries on a direct basis by means of loans and grants as part of the Point Four program, indirectly by loans from the Export-Import Bank and the World Bank, and in many other ways. In addition, official economic aid is supplemented by private donations to agencies such as CARE, the National Catholic Welfare Conference, and the Lutheran World Relief.

TABLE 45-3

AID EXPENDITURES BY WORLD AREAS

Fiscal 1948 Through Fiscal 1972

(Millions of Dollars)

Area	Number of Countries	Marshall Plan Period 1948-1952	Mutual Security Act Period 1953-1961	AID Period 1962-1972	Total 1948-1972
Near East and South Asia ...	19	1,088.5	4,681.6	6,888.2	12,007.1
Latin America ...	24	19.5	825.0	5,463.7	5,926.2
East Asia and Vietnam ..	12	705.9	6,470.9	6,381.5	12,810.4
Africa	39	3.8	804.0	2,158.9	2,724.8
Europe	24	12,469.3	2,786.0	31.9	15,239.0
Nonregional		217.6	1,317.5	3,361.0	4,825.4
Total *	119	14,504.8	16,884.6	24,286.0	53,532.8

SOURCE: Agency for International Development, *Operations Report*, 1972.

* Totals may not agree because of rounding.

Foreign economic assistance by the United States is reflected in Table 45-3. According to the Agency for International Development, the major purpose of U.S. foreign economic aid is to give assistance to other countries seeking to maintain their independence and develop into self-supporting nations. Cultivation of a community of free nations, it has been argued, is the best long-run protection for the security and peace of all nations, including the United States. The central objective of our aid has been to help other nations utilize their own resources and attract investments which stimulate growth.

In accordance with this principle, the United States has directed aid toward those areas of the world in which American interests were most critical at the time. As Table 45-3 shows, during the period of the Marshall Plan our economic (as well as military) assistance was concentrated on the rebuilding of Western Europe. Later, following the Mutual Security Act, a much larger share was allocated to Asia. Throughout the sixties and early seventies, foreign aid was more evenly distributed among Asian, African, and Latin American countries—with very little given to Europe because the strength of the European economy had been restored. Recent investments in other nations, especially investments in the middle and late 1960s, reflected continuing commitments to South Vietnam and heightened American recognition of the international political importance of underdeveloped countries not immediately threatened by communism.

A New Multilateral Objective

Because of expanding economic assistance made available to underdeveloped areas, the United Nations designated the 1960s as the Decade of Development. Investments in development brought notable gains. For all underdeveloped countries combined, gross production grew at an average rate of 5 percent per year, compared to about 4.6 percent in the 1950s. This combined production rose to a rate of 6.1 percent in 1971 and 5.9 percent in 1972. However, the average figure conceals wide variations among countries. Some, such as Brazil, made impressive gains, while others have lagged behind, and in some areas economic improvements have hardly been perceptible.

Although per capita income had been rising at an average rate of about 2.5 percent per year in all underdeveloped countries combined, the late sixties and early seventies saw signs of increasing reluctance to provide unilateral development assistance. AID expenditures dropped from $2.3 billion in 1967 to $2.0 billion in 1969 and to $1.8 billion in 1972. Resistance toward larger grants and loans was not limited to the United States. The Development Assistance Committee (DAC) of the Organization for Economic Cooperation and Development represents all major contributors to underdeveloped areas: the United States, Canada, Europe, Australia, and Japan. In 1968, technical assistance disbursements by DAC members reached a record $1.5 billion, an 11 percent increase over 1967, but then declined slightly. Indeed, the total net flow of all financial resources from DAC countries to underdeveloped countries and *multilateral agencies*, which had increased from $8 billion in 1960 to $16 billion in 1970, rose to less than $18 billion in 1971 and to just over $19 billion in 1972.

With respect to American foreign aid, there were three main reasons for a weakening of interest. First was the immensity of problems in capital formation and the very modest increases in agricultural output relative to population growth. In spite of investments in manufacturing and rising output, unemployment persisted at high levels. Between 1960 and 1972, GNP per capita grew less in the underdeveloped countries than in any of the developed countries. As a consequence, many legislators questioned the efficacy of growing foreign-aid expenditures. Second, the U.S. was beginning to experience difficulties in its balance-of-payments position, as described in Chapter 43. Finally, foreign aid had been justified earlier by the argument that assistance strengthened democratic institutions and helped poor nations to resist communism. With the spread of neutralism in the third world and the inability of democratic institutions to flourish in an environment of dire poverty, this argument lost convincing force.

In October of 1969, the Report of the Commission on International Development gave a new impetus to investments in underdeveloped areas. The Commission, headed by Lester B. Pearson, had been created by the World Bank to study the effects of external aid over the preceding 20 years and to propose guidelines for the future. The Pearson Report underlined the need for development finance in order to help poor nations attain faster growth in per capita income. It recommended raising the level of official development assistance to at least seven tenths of one percent of the developed countries' combined GNP by 1975 and strongly favored channeling all aid through multilateral agencies.[1]

The Pearson Report was widely discussed. One result was the U.N.'s resolution establishing the Second Development Decade, covering the 1970s, which stressed the importance of better long-range planning. This resolution called for external assistance amounting to seven tenths of one percent of the combined GNP of developed countries, as recommended by the Report. Underdeveloped countries were exhorted to formulate longer-term development strategies and to adapt shorter-term plans to these strategies. Added assistance would be related to these overall plans rather than to individual projects, and multilateral agencies would be responsible for assuring that the planning criteria were met.

Figure 45-2 depicts the flow of economic assistance from DAC countries to underdeveloped countries from 1958 through 1972. It can be seen that financial resources specifically designated as official assistance have remained well below the U.N. target. Total official assistance in 1972 represented less than one third of one percent of the GNP of the donor countries. Aid from all sources, both public and private, comes much closer to the U.N. target but does not reach the target in any year. Indeed, the gap between U.N. target aid and actual aid has widened since 1961.

In 1971 there was a marked increase in the flow of long-term financial resources to underdeveloped countries, up from about $14 billion in 1970 to $18 billion. As in prior years, the U.S. was the largest single source, providing $7 billion. Japan was the second largest with $2.1 billion; West Germany,

[1] These include the World Bank, the International Development Association, the Inter-American Development Bank, the Asian Development Bank, various U.N. agencies, and others.

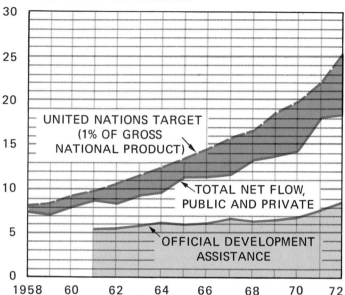

BILLIONS OF U.S. DOLLARS

FIGURE 45-2

NET FLOW OF FINANCIAL RESOURCES FROM DAC COUNTRIES TO UNDERDEVELOPED COUNTRIES IN RELATION TO GNP 1958-1972

Economic assistance to underdeveloped countries has been increasing but falls short of levels proposed by the United Nations.

SOURCE: Organization for Economic Cooperation and Development; and International Bank for Reconstruction and Development.

UNITED NATIONS TARGET (1% OF GROSS NATIONAL PRODUCT)

TOTAL NET FLOW, PUBLIC AND PRIVATE

OFFICIAL DEVELOPMENT ASSISTANCE

France, and the United Kingdom each contributed between $1.6 billion and $1.9 billion. Then, in 1972 the total net flow nearly levelled off. The so-called "October War" of 1973 between Israel and the Arab countries, combined with domestic concerns over energy shortages in the advanced industrial countries which extended well into 1974, has contributed to a more cautious attitude with respect to the granting of foreign aid.

Multilateral agencies have come to play a more important role in allocating development assistance, particularly the World Bank Group (the World Bank, the International Development Association, and the International Finance Corporation). During their fiscal year ending June 30, 1972, the World Bank and IDA approved loans totaling nearly $3 billion, and lending operations for the Group as a whole had expanded 136 percent over the 1964-1969 average.

Since 1971 there has been evidence of continuing American concern over the level and probable effectiveness of foreign aid. Nevertheless, expenditures have not been cut. Bilateral economic assistance declined slightly in 1973, but larger American contributions to multilateral development banks and other agencies more than offset the reduction in bilateral aid, resulting in a modest increase in total commitments. If this trend toward multilateral control continues and if underdeveloped nations do formulate carefully designed long-term development strategies, economic relations between developed and underdeveloped countries will move closer to those proposed by the United Nations.

SUMMARY

1. Emerging political states are typically underdeveloped countries.

2. Although each of these areas has characteristics peculiar to itself, they have in common several economic characteristics.

3. These economic characteristics include low per capita income, predominance of agriculture, overpopulation in agriculture, low saving, disguised unemployment, and poor credit and marketing facilities.

4. In addition, there are common demographic and technological characteristics. These include inadequate nutrition, poor health facilities, rudimentary education, and crude technology.

5. Theories of underdevelopment have not been successful in producing a general explanation of underdevelopment. However, they have provided some useful guidelines in planning for development.

6. Development plans should establish government budgets for investments in human and nonhuman capital, as well as legislation that is conducive to successful investment.

7. The underdeveloped nations are important to the United States because their citizens are fellow human beings, because they can supply resources that our nation needs, and because we value them as political allies.

8. In recent years there has been a shift of emphasis from unilateral development assistance to multilateral assistance managed by such agencies as the World Bank.

NEW TERMS

Disguised unemployment, *p. 1008*
Fertility rates, *p. 1008*
Mortality rates, *p. 1009*
Geographic determinism, *p. 1010*
Sociological dualism, *p. 1011*

Balanced growth, *p. 1013*
Discontinuities, *p. 1013*
Indivisibilities, *p. 1013*
Social overhead capital, *p. 1013*
Multilateral agencies, *p. 1018*

QUESTIONS FOR DISCUSSION AND ANALYSIS

1. What are the main characteristics common to most underdeveloped areas? How do they differ from economically advanced areas?

2. How does population growth affect economic development in underdeveloped areas?

3. Why, in your opinion, have economists and other social scientists been unable to formulate a general explanation of underdevelopment?

4. What are the main features of balanced-growth theories? Do you believe these theories are reasonably complete explanations of underdevelopment? Why or why not?

5. What are the principal components of a plan for economic development? Which component do you regard as most critical?

6. Can you identify any particular underdeveloped countries and apply the principles of development planning to those countries?

7. For what reasons did the United States assume world leadership in granting foreign assistance to underdeveloped countries?

8. What arguments would you make in favor of unilateral foreign assistance? What arguments would you make for multilateral assistance?

9. Do you agree with the recommendations of the Report of the Commission on International Development? Why or why not?

10. What responsibilities, if any, do the developed nations have toward the underdeveloped nations? Explain in full.

SUGGESTED READINGS

Baldwin, Robert E. *Economic Development and Growth,* 2d ed. New York: John Wiley & Sons, Inc., 1972.

Bauer, P. T. *Dissent on Development: Studies and Debates in Development Economics.* Cambridge, Mass.: Harvard University Press, 1972.

Bhagwati, Jagdish, and R. S. Eckaus (eds.). *Foreign Aid.* Baltimore: Penguin Books Inc., 1970.

Cameron, Rondo E. (ed.). *Banking and Economic Development.* New York: Oxford University Press, Inc., 1972.

Culbertson, J. M. *Economic Development: An Ecological Approach.* New York: Random House, Inc., 1971.

Gill, Richard T. *Economic Development: Past and Present.* Englewood Cliffs, N.J.: Prentice-Hall, Inc., 1973.

Helleiner, G. K. *International Trade and Economic Development.* Baltimore: Penguin Books Inc., 1972.

Johnson, Walter L., and David R. Kamerschen (eds.) *Readings in Economic Development.* Cincinnati: South-Western Publishing Co., 1972.

Kuznets, Simon S. *Economic Growth of Nations.* Cambridge, Mass.: Harvard University Press, 1971.

Myrdal, Gunnar. *Challenge of World Poverty: A World Poverty Program in Outline.* New York: Pantheon Books, Inc., 1970.

Pearson, Lester B. *Crisis in Development.* New York: Praeger Publishers, Inc., 1970.

Rostow, Walt W. *The Stages of Economic Growth,* 2d ed. New York: Cambridge University Press, 1971.

46

A Comparative System— The Soviet Economy

PREVIEW From our previous study we know how decisions are made in a market economy such as the United States. Now we turn to a command economy, most often represented by the Soviet Union. There, basic decisions are made by a central authority—the Gosplan. Five-year plans are formulated, with goals and quotas developed and implemented for the entire economy, for each ministry, and for individual enterprises. A sizable portion of Soviet total output is devoted to investment as a means of increasing their productivity.

The Soviets have many problems with certain aspects of their economy, particularly in agriculture. There is need, too, for industrial expansion. The Soviets are endeavoring to alleviate food shortages through huge purchases of grains from other nations, and they are striving to improve technology through increased trade with the United States and other Western economies.

We learned in the beginning of this book that certain basic decisions must be made in every economy regardless of the type of economic system being employed. Whether conditions of capitalism, socialism, communism, or some combination thereof prevails, the questions are the same. What is to be produced? How much of each commodity or service is to be produced? Who gets what out of the total production? Lastly, will resources and labor be employed to produce for current consumption or diverted to future use via savings and investment? Although the questions are the same, the manner in which they are answered differs with various types of economies. In spite of the difference in answers, each economy generally seeks to obtain maximum effectiveness in the utilization of scarce resources in an attempt to satisfy the needs of its citizens.

Throughout this book we have learned and analyzed how these decisions are made in a market economy—the United States. We learned that a market economy affords consumers an important, if not predominant, influence in the decision-making process. We saw that business firms, through the profit system, are motivated to produce goods and services for the satisfaction of consumers' demands. It was evident, too, that apart from providing a political and legal environment in which consumers and businesses could exchange goods and money, the government, except during emergencies, played a relatively small part in the day-to-day decision-making process.

Not all economies of the world operate the same as the United States economy. There are numerous variations along the economic continuum, from an almost completely laissez-faire economy to an almost completely controlled economy. Consequently, before concluding our study of economics, we should gain some insight into how these decisions are made elsewhere. Since the Soviet economy is somewhere near the "command" end of the economic continuum, it will serve well as an example of an economy in which the state decides what and how much to produce and who gets what. Before launching into the operation of the present Soviet economic system, however, a little background on the nature and evolution of economic systems should prove beneficial.

IDEOLOGIES AND INSTITUTIONS

Underlying every society is a system of ideas that purports to identify and explain fundamental values and the meaning of human existence. Such a system of ideas is an *ideology*. An accepted ideology or basic social philosophy gives meaning to human existence, provides criteria as to what constitutes the "good life," and leads to the establishment of institutions or customary social practices that seem logically to provide the most appropriate way of implementing the principles that compose the ideology. For example, acceptance of the basic idea that individuals should be equal before the laws and that the people are capable of self-government leads to the institutions of popular suffrage and democratic government. On the other hand, the adoption of the idea that men and women are incapable of self-government leads to the establishment of a dictatorship.

An accepted ideology which holds that individuals have the capacity to deal successfully with their economic problems leads to diversity of control over the factors of production. Productive resources and consumer goods are allocated by means of a system of free markets. In contrast, centralization of control of the factors of production results from the acceptance of an ideology that emphasizes the importance of the group, instead of the individual, and denies the ability of individuals to solve most of their economic problems through personal and direct effort. Real national income is distributed in accordance with a prearranged plan.

An ideology that recognizes the importance of the individual and, at the same time, acknowledges the interdependence of individuals in society will create institutions founded on these beliefs. Obviously these institutions will consist of some that are intended to promote the idea of individualism, such as that of limited private property, and some that partake of the nature of collectivism, such as that of public education or a formal system of social economic security. These are the types of social and economic institutions that exist in the United States and in several other nations of the Western world.

The basic economic institution in any society relates to the ownership and control of material productive resources, including natural and man-made resources. This is true because ownership and control of these resources confer upon the owner the power to initiate and to direct production. Conceptually, the degree of control may range all the way from that of exclusive and absolute control to that of no control. Moreover, the owner may be a private individual, a private group, or a government. Property, when the term is used to imply the exclusive right and power of control, may be compared to a bundle of rights. The imposition of limitations upon the absolute right to control is equivalent to a removal of one or more of the elements that compose the bundle.

CAPITALISM

The preceding chapters have been devoted to a consideration of economic facts and principles as they exist under our form of capitalism. In the discussion in this chapter, therefore, we shall refer only briefly to the institutions that are basic to the ideological concept of capitalism.

The social philosophy from which the doctrines of capitalism emerged was that of individualism, that is, the goal of society should be the greatest good or happiness of the greatest number of people. To achieve this goal—so it was argued by John Locke, David Hume, Jeremy Bentham, and other moral philosophers—individuals should be allowed the greatest possible degree of freedom. To secure and to maintain this freedom, only a bare minimum of governmental controls are allowed. Acceptance of this idea naturally led to an amplification of the rights of private property and to the adoption of the practices of free enterprise and of free markets. It was assumed that in economic affairs men are motivated solely by their desire to maximize their gain at the least cost in terms of effort or money. At the same time, it was also taken for granted that individuals are rational and that, therefore, reason and circumstances operate to restrain personal acts that would prove detrimental to one's personal good. The result, so it was concluded, would be the greatest possible human happiness.

The basic institution of capitalism is that of private property. Associated with or resulting from the practice of private property are the customary practices of inheritance of property, freedom of individual initiative in economic activities, competition in the production and sale of goods and services, and the quest for profit as the motive for production.

Individualism and the idea of laissez-faire were accepted with enthusiasm by the people of the United States, although the practice of absolute non-interference by government in business was never entirely realized. As a result, for more than a century economic life in this country was characterized by fewer restrictions on individual choices and activities than was true of any other major nation.

About 80 years ago, there developed a noticeable tendency for the people to impose more and more governmental controls over business. In addition, people in capitalistic countries are inclined to invoke the power of government to solve certain economic problems that formerly were regarded as being wholly of a personal nature. In the United States measures of this kind include laws providing for social security, medicare, unemployment insurance, workmen's compensation, public health facilities, rent subsidies, slum clearance, guaranteed income, and the elimination of poverty. As a result, ours has become more and more a mixed economy.

SOCIALISM

Like capitalism, socialism implies a way of life, as well as a system under which men make a living. Therefore, it is impossible to convey an adequate concept of socialism by means of a simple, concise definition. We can appreciate the difficulty involved in any attempt to define socialism when we consider all that is involved in the meaning of capitalism. As we now know, it is a simple matter to say that capitalism is that form of economic order in which most productive property is privately owned and is utilized by the owners for the purpose of producing goods to be sold in the market at a profit; where there are comparatively few restrictions upon the right to enter or to leave a field of production; where demand and supply determine prices; and so on. These facts are descriptive of particular aspects of capitalism. But they do not tell us everything that is needed for a true understanding of capitalism. From these facts alone we do not know how incomes and wealth are actually distributed; the extent to which economic opportunities exist; how economically secure individuals are; whether freedom is more of a theory than a condition; or whether competition or monopoly is the greater factor in the determination of prices.

With reference to its fundamental economic aspect, we may say that socialism, as an organized system, is that form of social order in which the chief instruments of production—mines, factories, banks, merchandise establishments, transportation facilities, and farmlands—are owned or controlled by society as a whole and are operated to produce goods under the direction of the state (that is, government) rather than under the direction of private individuals and groups, as is the case under capitalism. In short, under socialism the government owns, controls, or directs most of the means of production.

COMMUNISM

Communism is the radical socialist doctrine founded by Karl Marx (1818-1883) and developed by Nikolai Lenin (1870-1924). Marx was born in Prussia. His theories and teachings are set forth in the *Manifesto of the Communist Party*—the "handbook" on communism—which he and Friedrich Engels published in 1848, and *Das Kapital*, the first volume of which was published in 1867. The declared ultimate objectives of communism are (1) the establishment of a classless society and (2) the elimination of the state as a means of social control.

As to proposals for the ownership of capital and the control of production, the theory of communism closely resembles that of all types of socialism. Otherwise, however, there are important distinctions between the implications of communism and socialism. These distinctions refer to (1) the methods of abolishing capitalism, (2) the method of distributing the national income, and (3) the function of government.

As a rule, Communists accept Marx's teaching that aggressive, even violent, methods must be used to overthrow capitalism and to establish "dictatorship by the working class." Most socialists believe that democratic means may be used for replacing capitalism and that democracy in government is possible. Ultimately Communists would distribute all consumer goods according to need. Wage differentials would play a minor role in the apportionment of the national income.

The Materialistic Economic Interpretation of History

Marx stressed the point that the way people make a living at any given time depends upon the natural resources, capital equipment, techniques of production, and labor available and in use. He insisted that these factors eventually determine the nature and form of government. He contended, for example, that changes in "the modes of production," which also embraced social and political institutions, have constantly been undergoing change. As the processes and possibilities relative to production change, the form of the social order also changes. Slavery, feudalism, capitalism—these have been transitory phases in the evolution of economic society that have been induced by changes in the ways by which people make a living.

Marx pointed to the changes that had taken place in government in the past and contended that all such changes were merely reflections of changes in the needs of economic society. He contended that changes in the productive processes and conditions make economic society dynamic and not static. There is always an irresistible tendency for changes in the methods of production to bring about changes in social relationships, both as to the relations between individuals and between government and individuals. Social conflict and change are inevitable, he contended, until universal communism is realized.

The Class Struggle

According to Marx, the establishment of a political government stabilizes a society and is intended to perpetuate the status quo. Under feudalism, the gradations of society were recognized and accepted. Moreover, he claimed, it was the function of government to see that these gradations were observed and retained. Under a system of capitalism, he asserted, it is the purpose of government to preserve the institution of private property and to enact laws predicated on the assumption that the relations, rights, and responsibilities between employers and employees must remain essentially the same in the future as they have in the past. But, he insisted, changes in methods and conditions of production call for corresponding changes in government. He contended that government under capitalism is intended to retain relationships as they are.

Marx concluded that employees would remain a submerged and suppressed class. As time goes on, the economic status of this suppressed class would become more and more intolerable, until the workers freed themselves by a successful revolution. It was his argument that capitalism, which served well its historic function for a time, had outlived its usefulness. It was destined to pass away because of changes in the "mode of production." However, because of their vested interests, the propertied class would resist long-overdue changes in economic society. In order to achieve freedom for the workers and to set up a form of social order where opportunities for oppression will disappear, it was necessary, according to Marx, to smash capitalistic governments, establish a dictatorship by the workers, and set about building a classless society.

Marx contended that the bourgeois class would become increasingly rich, while the poor would sink deeper and deeper in poverty. After a while, as capital became more and more concentrated in the hands of the few, competition would be supplanted by monopoly; profits would decline with the greater accumulation of capital; recurring business depressions would become more severe; and the search for investment opportunities would lead to a race of imperialism among capitalistic nations that would result in destructive wars.

FASCISM

Fascism rejects capitalism, communism, and democratic socialism. It accepts in modified form some of the institutions of capitalism and socialism, but it combines these institutions—with others—in such a way that the completed structure bears little resemblance to either of the other two economic systems. Fascism emphasizes nationalism, glorifies war, holds that "might makes right," and relies on propaganda and force—not information and reason—as methods of social control. It uses political controls in an attempt to direct economic forces and holds that "the end justifies the means." On occasion, it poses as the defender of the Christian religion; at other times and in other places, it scorns religion as a sign of weakness and hypocrisy. In Italy it adopted one name; in Germany, another; in Spain, another; and in Argentina, still another. In each instance the name chosen was one that possessed high emotional potentialities. The external appearance of the system varies from country to country, but the underlying nature of fascistic systems is alike everywhere. The one apparent and constant characteristic of fascism, wherever it occurs, is an emphatic and determined opposition to the objectives and practices of communism and democratic socialism.

Following World War I, fascism, in its modern form, developed first in Italy. Then it took root in Germany, under the name of Nazism. Within two decades the fascist nations challenged the "decadent" capitalistic nations of the West and the "barbaric" Soviet Union of the East. The fascist nations were overthrown in World War II; but the ideas of fascism are not dead, as is attested by elections in Europe, by the continued existence of certain governments in Europe and South America, and by the nature of some of the proposals that have been made for coping with certain current economic problems in this country.

THE SOVIET ECONOMY

The Constitution of the U.S.S.R. declares that "The Union of Soviet Socialist Republics is a Socialist state of workers and peasants." It further states that the political foundation was established by "the conquest of the dictatorship of the proletariat." This implies that a state of communism has not yet been achieved. Meanwhile the social and economic order operates under a dictatorship.

At the time of World War I, from 80 to 90 percent of the Russian population was rural. Industrially the whole nation was backward. A majority of the people were illiterate. The greater part of the farming land was held by the nobility or other large landowners. In 1905, after a wave of strikes and uprisings, a manifesto from the Tsar theoretically brought the absolute monarchy to an end and established, in name, a constitutional monarchy. But in fact the government remained corrupt, bureaucratic, and practically absolute. When World War I came, Russia found herself on the side of the Allies. Lack of preparation, continued graft on the part of officials, the presence of foreign agents in strategic positions—all combined to weaken the military forces. Finally, defeats of the soldiers on the battlefield and war-weariness of the people at home brought about disintegration of the army and of the government.

At this juncture a few thousand trained Communists seized their opportunity. Lenin, Trotsky, and other leaders who had been exiled came home secretly, aided in part by Germany who hoped that they would foment further dissension among the Russian people.

A provisional government was set up. Strife between various groups continued, particularly between the Bolsheviks and the Mensheviks.[1] Finally, after much strife, the Bolsheviks secured control of the government and proceeded to organize the political and economic life of the people along communistic lines. Control of the factories was turned over to the workers, and the tillers of the soil were told to take possession of the farms. In other words, the private property rights of former owners were abolished. Throughout the country, councils, called Soviets, were elected by the masses of the people. The central government was to function through these Soviets, which were to be, in theory, democratic. In fact, they became the organizations through which the ruling spirits of the Communist Party were to operate.

An attempt was made to establish immediately a real communistic society. Ownership of private property was abolished; the use of money was largely discarded; and an attempt was made to organize production and distribution according to communistic theory. The attempt met with discouraging results. Production fell below the prewar level, internal strife continued in many places, and other nations regarded the experiment with disfavor and suspicion. By 1921 Lenin executed a "strategic retreat." The practice of paying wages in money was reinstated, small business concerns operated for profit

---

[1] The terms "Bolshevik" and "Menshevik" are derived from Russian words which mean, respectively, majority and minority. They came into use in 1903, when the faction of the Social Democratic Workmen's Party, led by Lenin, was slightly larger than the other faction.

were permitted, and peasants were allowed to sell their produce directly to consumers. In 1923 the "autonomy" of each of the several Soviet republics was recognized and organized into a federation, which gave rise to the name Union of Soviet Socialist Republics. But the Communist Party remained in control.

The New Economic Policy (NEP), as Lenin's "retreat" was labelled, produced favorable results in the way of increased production. By 1927 the level of production was about equal to that of 1913. As a result, the hold of the Communist Party was strengthened. Under Joseph Stalin in 1928, NEP came to an end, and a determined drive was instituted to make Russia a truly socialistic dictatorship.

Political Organization of the U.S.S.R.

In theory the Russian people are living under a "dictatorship of the proletariat," which might be called "dictatorial socialism." Some refer to it as "state capitalism." The U.S.S.R. has been in this state since Lenin gained control after the revolution in 1917. The leaders say that the dictatorship will have to continue until the people have learned to get along without governmental controls. Then the state will "wither away." It is not surprising that no one has any idea when that will be.

Each of the constituent republics of the U.S.S.R. possesses certain autonomous powers with respect to local government. Under the constitution the central or federal government exercises jurisdiction over all political and commercial international relations, the armed forces, fundamental labor laws, transportation and communication, the conduct of planning methods and operations, federal taxes, budgetary procedures, banking, industry and agriculture, interstate trade, and other matters. One large republic, the Russian Soviet Federated Socialistic Republic, is authorized to occupy a predominant place in the exercise of government authority.

Organizational Structure of the Economy

Industry and commerce in the Soviet Union are divided into both functional and regional sectors. Each sector is placed under the control of a minister (formerly called a commissar). Thus, there are ministers for railways, communications, public health, defense, power, foreign affairs, agriculture, ferrous metals, motor vehicle industry, gas industry, lumber industry, aviation industry, and numerous other industries. Each ministry is a functional group and is composed of a number of trusts that in turn contain and control the individual plants. The ministries are of two types: the all-union ministries, which control matters of major national importance; and the union-republic ministries, which control activities of a more local nature.

The more important ministers make up the greater part of the Council of Ministers, a body that possesses much power over the planning and production of the nation. Large and/or complex ministries have an intermediate level of authority called the chief administration (*glavak*). Thus, a minister may have one or more chief administrators to help manage his operations. The Ministry of Ferrous Metals, for example, encompasses a huge industrial structure, involving control over hundreds of ore mines, coal mines, coke plants, blast furnaces, lumber mills, and both a research and a marketing organization, scattered throughout the vast Russian land empire. It would be difficult, if not impossible, for one man to manage such a huge network of industrialization without some help. It is the job of the glavak to deal directly with the business enterprises regarding the allocation of inputs, the establishment of an output quota, and the measure of plant efficiency.

Planning. The economic decisions in the Soviet economy are made primarily by central authority. Instead of relying on the operations of markets, the price system, and profit maximization to allocate resources and incomes, the Soviets, through the use of planning, command what is to be produced, how much of each commodity is to be produced, and how goods and services are to be distributed. Through a rather complex system a plan is evolved or formulated that allocates inputs to various subunits in the economy. The planning process starts with the Council of Ministers, which sets the general goals for industrial and agricultural production, determines the ratio of consumer to investment output, and the allocation for government and military expenditures. At the heart of the planning system is the State Planning Commission, commonly called the *Gosplan*. On the basis of general goals determined by the Council of Ministers, the Gosplan has to construct the detailed mechanics of the plan. This involves working indirectly with hundreds of thousands of subunits gathering information about available resources, manpower, finances, and input-output flows for the entire economy. Plans are usually drawn for a five-year period but with enough flexibility to permit periodic changes. Once the plan is completed and approved by the Council of Ministers, the Gosplan implements the plan through the ministers, chief administrations, managers of the business enterprises, and the workers. As directives are passed downward, more details are filled in at each of the lower levels. Resources, manpower, and finances are directly or indirectly allocated, and production quotas are assigned to the various 200,000 or more state-owned enterprises in the economy. In implementing the plan there may be some conflicts and some haggling and bargaining between various levels of authority.

Industry. Each factory or enterprise is presided over and directed by a state-appointed manager. Nearly all trade is conducted in state-owned stores.

Foreign trade is a government monopoly, so that all import and export is carried on by state organizations.

The manager of the enterprise has full charge of production and is responsible for achieving the quota assigned to his enterprise. He may at times dicker with the glavak regarding the size of the quota or the allocation of resources, manpower, or finances. However, once the quota is set, it is his goal to fulfill or overfulfill the quota. An incentive system is used to encourage the manager to produce as much as possible. The incentive system has both positive and negative features. On the positive side a manager may earn a salary bonus, an automobile for his personal use, a paid vacation for his family at a seaside resort, or other bonuses if he fulfills or overfulfills his quota. On the negative side, if he fails, he can receive anything from a verbal reprimand to dismissal or reassignment to Siberia. At the extreme, he may be charged with a crime against the state and be penalized with possible imprisonment if he consistently or flagrantly falls short of his assigned quota. With the great stress on the quota, there naturally develops some illegal practices in the operations of enterprises. Thus, just as American executives are sometimes found guilty of fraud, embezzlement, and theft, in the Soviet economy there are also cases of falsification of records and illegal collusion.

Consumer goods are delivered to the 600,000 retail outlets in the Soviet economy. The largest segment of the retail market is the state store system through which 68 percent of the retail goods are sold. Cooperatives account for 28 percent of the retail sales and the collective farm market 4 percent.

Agriculture. Agriculture in the Soviet Union is divided into three distinct sectors. The *state farms* (Sovkhozy) are in a fashion similar to other state-owned enterprises. There are about 12,700 state farms in the Soviet economy, controlled and administered through the planning system. The average state farm is about 17,000 acres and is worked by 600 or more hired laborers, who earn a wage. Generally state farms tend to specialize in the production of such crops as wheat and other grains or in the raising of cattle. Their output, about 25 percent of the nation's total farm output, is intended primarily for delivery to other state agencies or factories in accordance with the plan.

A second important segment of Soviet agriculture is the system of *collective farms* (Kolhozy), which theoretically operate as cooperative enterprises for the benefit of their members. The farmers in a given area or town work the collective with machinery and equipment belonging to the collective. A large portion of their output is required to be sold to the state. The residual can be sold in the collective farm market, which is a relatively free market in which the collective farm can sell its surplus products to urban residents at prices established primarily by supply and demand. The income derived, along with any unsold output, is distributed to the farmers belonging to the collective. There are about 36,000 collective farms in the Soviet economy, and they produce about 44 percent of all Soviet agricultural output. Because the state absorbs such a large part of the collective output and pays such a low price, income of collective farmers has been low, especially compared to income of state farm workers.

The third sector of Soviet agriculture is the private-plot sector. Each collective farm worker, and some others, are given a private plot, usually no more than one acre, which he can cultivate for his personal use. By cultivating these plots intensively, the Soviet farmers have been able to gain considerable output from their plots. This output may be consumed or sold in the collective farm market. Consequently, through maximizing efforts and efficiency on these plots, the collective farm workers have been able to augment their diets and incomes. Although many of the farmers are reluctant workers on the collective farms, they seem to be well-motivated to work on their private plots. Although these plots comprise about 2 percent of the total cultivated farm area of the Soviet economy, they account for nearly one third of Russia's total agriculture production. Not only do they produce about two thirds of the Soviet potatoes, 42 percent of the vegetables, and 60 percent of all the eggs on these small plots, but also nearly one half of the cows, a third of the hogs, and most of the goats are raised on these plots.

In the past few decades there has been a trend toward consolidation of the smaller collective farms and a move toward state farms. In the early 1950s, for example, there existed only 5,000 state farms and more than 250,000 collective farms. The average-size collective today is about 7,500 acres, worked by 400 families spread over several villages, compared to an average-size collective of 1,250 acres in 1950. In the same period the average size of the private plot was reduced by 25 percent.

The inefficiency of Soviet farm production is evident when it is compared to that in America. In the United States with 4 percent of the civilian labor force (3-4 million farmers) engaged in farming, we produce more than enough to feed our 212 million people and to contribute much food to the rest of the world. In fact, our productivity is so high compared to our needs that we sometimes pay farmers for not farming. In the Soviet economy, however, with eight to nine times the number of farmers, 30-35 million, they are hard pressed to produce enough to adequately feed their population of 250 million. In addition, the Soviets have under cultivation nearly double the acreage that is cultivated in the United States. As we said earlier, however, the low level of Soviet agriculture is not all due to waste and inefficiencies. The natural conditions of climate and soil add to their problem. Fertilizers are in relatively short supply, and Soviet farmers do not possess the hybrid seeds we use in America. From a mechanical point of view, the Soviets have only about one third as many trucks and tractors as found on American farms. Moreover, the Soviet collective farm system does not have the research and technical facilities and organizations, such as exist in America, for the development and promotion of new methods and techniques or the dissemination of information to the farms and farmers.

In spite of glorious planning by the Gosplan, there is still considerable lack of progress, so that today productivity is not much above what it was prior to the Revolution over 50 years ago. In an effort to increase output, the Soviets cultivated 100 million additional acres of virgin land in Kazakstan and western Siberia between 1954 and 1961. This expanded their cultivated acreage by 25 percent. In addition, Khrushchev, while Premier, exhorted Soviet farmers to learn as much as they could from farmers in other nations, including the decadent capitalistic America, as a means of bolstering Soviet agricultural output. In the mid-1960s, for example, Khrushchev sent a team of Soviet farmers to America to study some of the American farmers' techniques and methods. Nevertheless, agriculture has been a perennial problem to the Soviets.

Disappointing crop yields in the early 1960s led the Soviets to make large purchases of wheat and other grains from the United States and elsewhere to overcome food shortages. After a number of years of improvement in farm output, the Soviet economy was again plagued with crop shortages in the early 1970s. Consequently, in 1972 the Soviets entered into an agreement with the United States to purchase a record of over $750 million of grain. In addition, to alleviate their food shortages, the Russians purchased grain from other producers of the world.

Size of the Soviet Economy

One method of comprehending the size of the Soviet economy is to compare it with some other country, such as the United States. Although Soviet Russia in area is more than twice the size of the United States and it has a population of 250 million compared to 212 million in the United States, various estimates indicate that the GNP of the Soviet economy is only about one half the size of the GNP of the United States. This, of course, means that output per capita in the United States is more than double that in Russia. A recent analysis of the Soviet GNP shows that sources of this production and national income differ markedly from those in the United States. Noticeable differences occur in the contribution of agriculture, domestic trade, and services, as shown in Table 46-1.

Another way of comparing the size and the efficiency of the Soviet economy is to look at the end-product use of the GNP. In this regard it can be

TABLE 46-1

Sector	U.S.	U.S.S.R.
Industry	32.1	36.1
Construction	5.2	6.9
Agriculture	4.0	26.6
Transportation	4.1	5.1
Communications	2.0	.7
Domestic Trade	16.3	4.4
Other Services	36.3	20.2
	100.0	100.0

NATIONAL INCOME BY SECTORS

(Percent of Total)

observed that the Russian consumer does not share in the total productivity to the same extent that the American consumer does, as can be seen in Table 46-2.

TABLE 46-2

DISTRIBUTION OF GNP

(Percent of Total)

End Use	Share of Total GNP	
	U.S.	U.S.S.R.
Consumption	62.5	55.8
Investment	16.0	33.1
Government	15.2	1.6
Defense	6.3	9.5
	100.0	100.0

The relatively low level of consumer participation in Russia, of course, is the result of planning in the Soviet economy. Russian citizens for years have been asked to make sacrifices, by taking fewer consumer goods and services, in order that the Gosplan could channel more resources and labor into industrial development. The Soviets accomplish this through the use of a *turnover tax*, which provides the funds for government spending and investment. How does it work? Suppose that the Gosplan decided that 90 billion rubles worth of production should be diverted to defense, investment, and other government spending. If the GNP were estimated at 200 billion rubles, it would mean that Russian income would be equal to 200 billion rubles. In order to raise the necessary 90 billion rubles for government investment, a turnover tax of 82 percent would be imposed on the 110 billion rubles worth of noninvestment production. This tax is added to the value of consumer goods and services, usually in a hidden fashion. The higher prices paid for consumer goods, naturally, decreases the discretionary income of income recipients. They have to use their 200 billion ruble income to buy the 200 billion rubles worth (including tax) of consumer goods production. The government can then use the 90 billion rubles received from the turnover tax for investment, defense, and other government spending. The turnover tax is an invisible, indirect tax. With such a large tax bite required, the turnover tax is much easier to impose than an income tax that would allow the people to receive the higher income but then tax it directly away from them.

Through the various decades of five- and seven-year plans, the Russian people were assured that sacrifices currently being made would lead to a greater amount of goods and services in the future. In fact, Khrushchev, in the late 1950s, ran into controversy with his fellow planners when he recommended increasing the consumers' share of total production. More recent plans of the mid-1960s and early 1970s, however, provided for increasing ratios of consumer goods and services production.

The heavy investment programmed via the Soviet planning system brings out another important issue. For years Communists and Socialists have claimed that capitalism exploits the workers. Consequently, many disparaging remarks have been made about capitalism over the years by socialist leaders. Khrushchev in the late 1950s told American audiences that their grand-children would live under socialism. At another time he assured us that the Soviet Union would "bury" us, implying that the U.S.S.R. within a decade or so would outproduce us, thereby showing its economic superiority.

These remarks and other criticisms of the capitalistic system appear strange when one considers that they come from the leaders of one of the largest, if not the largest, capitalistic nations in the world today—the Soviet Union. How can we make such a statement? If we analyze the term "capital," we know that a capital good (or producer good) is a good used to produce other goods. We can extend the word "capital" into capitalism, which can be defined as a system in which a portion of the total output is devoted to the production of capital, or producer, goods. Referring back to Table 46-2, or to past Soviet economic plans, it can be observed that the Soviets through their plans devote 25-35 percent of total output to the production of capital goods. In relative terms this is a much larger capitalistic system than exists in America, where we voluntarily devote 15-20 percent of total production to capital goods. Indeed, the Soviets must like capitalism very well, since they insist on directing such a large segment of the GNP into capital forma-tion. Furthermore, the Soviet planners insist that the state own all of the capital and other means of production.

If the Soviets like capitalism so well, what then is it that they do not like? What they do not like is free enterprise. In the American free enterprise capitalistic system, for example, individuals, business firms, and others may own the means of production and benefit directly from their use. On the other hand, what the Soviets prefer and have is a form of compulsory capitalism in which the state owns, directs, and determines who will benefit from the use of capital.

Growth of the Soviet Economy

There is no doubt that the Soviet economy has been growing at a fairly good rate. In recent years or decades its growth rate has exceeded that of the United States and many other leading nations in the world. Nevertheless, the level of living of the average Russian family is still at a low level. In regard to housing, for example, the average family lives in limited quarters, and black bread is still an important staple in the family meal. There is only one automobile for every 200 persons compared to one for every 2 persons in the United States, where 83 percent of the families own one or more automobiles. Similar comparisons exist regarding washing machines, television sets, telephones, and other basic household appliances. One major reason for the low level of consumer durables despite the high rate of economic growth is the fact that the Soviet families started from a very low base. Consequently, they had a long way to go before approaching the consumption levels in other nations. On the other hand, the initial low level of economic activity has a tendency to exaggerate the rate of growth. Moderate absolute gains on a small base convert into large percentage gains statistically.

The Soviet growth rate is better in some sectors of the economy than it is in others. Agriculture, for example, is poor, whereas construction, machinery, investment, education, and defense have experienced substantial growth rates. The investment sector is faring much better than the consumer sector.

Although there are many estimates of the overall growth for the Soviet economy, a typical estimate indicates that GNP had a growth rate of about 6 percent annually since the end of World War II. This exceeds the growth rate of 3 percent annually over the same period for the American economy.

There have at times been charts and figures presented to demonstrate that at current growth rates the Soviet economy would catch and even surpass the United States in total production sometime in the 1980s. These forecasts, however, have to be taken with a certain amount of reservation. As the Soviet economy moves toward higher levels of production, it is able to adopt and implement methods and techniques employed in other economies. When the economy begins to approach the level of other leading industrial nations, however, it may not be able to gain so much through transfer of knowledge and techniques. Furthermore, in the 1960s the growth rate in the United States economy rose to an annual rate of 4.5 percent in the period 1960 to 1970. This substantially narrowed the growth rate differential between the two economies.

Profit Reform

As the Russian economy grew, especially after World War II, it became evident in the mid-1950s that there was an increasing amount of waste and inefficiency in the system. Much of this was due to the difficulty of managing such a large system by dictate. The inherent inflexibilities in shifting manpower, resources, and capital from one use to another added to the problem. Literature about the operation of Soviet industry is replete with stories of excess production in some areas and shortages in others, the lack of parts for trucks and tractors, abundance of large bolts and shortage of small ones, plenty of bulky furniture but a dearth of trim styles, and the scarcity or opulence of various sizes and styles of dresses, shoes, and other consumer durables. The problem of production imbalance was caused in part by the undue stress placed on the quota system. Frequently quotas are expressed in pounds of production rather than units. Consequently, an enterprise may favor large, heavy units rather than small ones to more easily meet its quota. At other times the quota was expressed in units of production. Consequently, a shoe or dress manufacturer may concentrate on smaller sizes to run up his production record. Sometimes the quota is expressed in rubles of production. As a result of the emphasis on production to meet the quota, rather than to satisfy market needs, there developed a growing amount of unsalable commodities.

This situation in some industries was aggravated by the lack of proper quality control for manufactured goods. Usually when the goods were produced by the enterprise and delivered to the state retail outlet, the producing enterprise was given credit toward its quota. There were no return sales and allowances. In their desire to meet the quota and gain an overfill, many shabby and unsalable items were delivered to the retail outlets.

The pileup of unsalable and unusable commodities was magnified by the rising level of living of the average Russian family. In earlier years, with meager incomes, consumers usually bought the limited selection of goods available in the market. However, as discretionary incomes of the family rose, the Russian housewife became a more sophisticated buyer. She did not want ill-fitting dresses, shabby or bulky furniture, and drab-looking shoes. Today, she demands stylish shoes, fashionable, colorful, and well-fitted garments, and solid, well-designed furniture. With higher income it no longer is a matter of buying what is available or going without. Frequently she can postpone purchases because she owns a current stock of goods. This *embourgeoisement* of the Soviet consumer manifests characteristics of freedom, choice, preference, and satisfaction associated with consumer sovereignty.

Observing the growing inventories of unsalable and unusable goods in some sectors of the economy, Soviet planners began seeking ways of eliminating waste and inefficiencies in the Soviet economy. In the early 1960s Professor Liberman, of the University of Kharkov, and others, such as Kantorovich and Novuzhilov, suggested that the Soviets adopt a profit system as a measure of enterprise efficiency along with a flexible pricing system in some areas of consumer sales. In simple terms, Liberman's proposals recommended that the enterprise be charged for the materials used and the labor employed and that it pay interest on the funds received from the Gosbank. Through an accounting system the cost of production would then be known. It was further proposed to permit the manager of the enterprise, in cooperation with the manager of the retail outlet, to decide the sizes, types, colors, styles, and other characteristics of some of the consumer goods to be produced. A further step was to permit a flexible pricing system, which would allow a higher or lower price for items. In this way inventories could be cleared more readily than with a rigid pricing system. The revenue from the sale of the enterprise's production could then be measured against the production charges of the enterprise to ascertain the profitability of its operation. The more that was sold and the better the price, the greater was the profit, thus bringing about greater efficiency. Goods not moved or those sold at low prices would bring less profit. Under this new system bonuses would be based on profit rather than on a production quota. Thus, it would behoove any enterprise to produce the right style, color, and size of commodities desired by consumers.

This profit system was first introduced in the Soviet economy on a small scale about 1964. A few enterprises in Moscow and Gorkey were given the freedom to make delivery and pricing contracts with retail outlets and gear production accordingly. Amazingly, production increased by 35 to 50 percent in these firms. Subsequently 25-30 percent of the clothing manufacturers, shoe factories, textile mills, and tanneries were brought under the reform profit plan. Later a coal mine reported a production increase of one third after it was put on a profit-making basis. In 1967 a government directive brought 800 additional factories, primarily in the consumer-goods producing market, under the profit system. It was reported that by 1970 about 11,000 industrial enterprises were operating under the profit reform system. Another source indicated that about 75 percent of the industrial enterprises had been converted to the new system.[2] The current emphasis is on goods sold rather than on goods produced as it was under the quota system. Consequently, many new merchandising methods have been introduced into the Soviet economy in recent years. In addition to price reductions, these include full-

[2] *Business Week* (January 31, 1970), p. 110.

scale advertising, the use of more salesmen and the adoption of a bonus system for them, installment selling, expanded home deliveries, and intensified market research.

Similar moves, many of them more drastic, toward economic freedom and a market system have taken place in recent years in the Soviet satellite nations of Yugoslavia, Poland, Rumania, Bulgaria, and especially Czechoslovakia.

Although Professor Liberman maintains that the Soviets are not moving toward Western style capitalism and there is still a very small portion of total Soviet production on a profit basis, the profit reform movement is gaining greater recognition in their economy. It has not, however, reached the investment-goods production area as yet. But in the consumer-goods field it certainly is giving the Russian consumer a better choice in quantity, quality, and variety of products. Interestingly enough, just as the American public has for years heard comments about creeping socialism in America, Russian citizens must be hearing more and more about creeping capitalism in their homeland.

Improved U.S.-Soviet Trade

In addition to the purchase of grain to offset food shortages in the early 1970s, the Soviets also opened up trade for industrial items with other nations, particularly the United States. In the fall of 1971, a U.S. Trade Commission, led by Secretary of Commerce Maurice H. Stans, visited the Soviet Union to lay the groundwork and pave the way for trade liberalization between the two nations. Agreements were signed then and at subsequent meetings in which both nations removed trade restrictions and barriers between the two economies. An important basis for this trade was the Soviet desire for machinery, equipment, tools, and technology, coupled with the United States desire for natural resources, such as oil, natural gas, timber, copper, and other metals. President Nixon's visit to Russia in the spring of 1972, followed by another visit in 1974, further solidified the promotion of trade relations between the two nations.

In 1972 it was estimated that the United States sold only $165 million annually in goods to the Soviet Union, compared to United States merchandise exports of more than $43 billion per annum. Other Western countries combined, however, were doing about $5 billion annually in trade with the Soviet economy. It was estimated that United States trade with the Soviets might grow to $2 billion annually within five years.

By the end of 1973, several United States firms had entered into various types of agreements for the exchange of goods and technology with the Soviet Union. In addition, a number of United States government agencies, business firms, and banks had been given approval to do business with the

Russians and were scrambling for the relatively scarce space for office facilities in Moscow. In 1973 alone, U.S. exports to Eastern European nations, including the Soviet Union, had risen to $1.8 billion.

ISMS OF THE FUTURE

Communism has not followed the rigid and uncompromising pattern predicted by Karl Marx and his immediate disciples. Russian communism has made adjustments to political realities and modified centralized control over the economy when practical circumstances have made change necessary. The form taken on by communism in the so-called satellite nations of Eastern Europe has varied in response to cultural and institutional differences. Recent cries for individual freedoms on the part of the people have altered the very structure of government in some of these countries. In comparison with the decade following World War II—when communism was regarded by many in the United States as an unbending and monolithic enemy of capitalism— the communist bloc of Eastern Europe has become not only more fragmented but also more capitalistic in several respects. Chinese communism until recently followed more closely the aggressive attacks upon private enterprise forecast by the founders of communism. But a reversal of these practices began to appear in the 1970s. President Nixon's visit to Mainland China in 1972 and the opening up of trade relations between the two nations brought them into closer harmony in spite of their ideological, economic, and political differences.

Socialist economies have become a reality in some of the smaller and newer nations. However, the differences among these nations are more marked than the common label of socialism. Some seek to anchor their organization in doctrine, while others abide by no particular economic theory or ideology. Thus, what is called "socialism" or "communism" can mean a great many different things.

At the same time, capitalism has been undergoing change. England, once the home of the staunchest defenders of laissez-faire capitalism, has nationalized several industries. The Western European nations were regarded as typically capitalistic during the nineteenth century. Today, such countries as France, the Netherlands, Sweden, and Germany have prominent elements of government ownership or control of industry. Indeed, the United States, while still the world leader of traditionally capitalistic nations, has a far different form of economic organization than that which existed in this country at the turn of the century. Certainly the American economy of today cannot be described as nineteenth-century capitalism.

Many emerging and developing nations are seeking an economic structure deemed to be most suitable to their customs and life styles. These countries are not committed by historical tradition to either capitalism or socialism, and they often tend to borrow elements from both systems.

Within this context of evolution, of adaptation to change and new forms of economic organization containing elements of old forms, it is natural to ask what the future holds. Of course, we cannot peer into a crystal ball and read the future, but certain trends can be identified and evaluated. Among these trends is the tendency toward more social measures and more state regulation in some of the leading capitalistic nations of the world and the move toward more individual economic freedom in some of the socialistic and communistic nations.

SUMMARY

1. The institutional framework for making basic decisions in an economy varies with the type of economic system. In a command economy the decisions are made by a central authority. In a market economy they are made primarily by the interactions of consumers and businessmen.

2. Socialism differs from capitalism in regard to the extent and degree of government control over the means of production.

3. Communism rejects the institution of private property and has as its ultimate objective a classless society and the elimination of state control over the means of production.

4. The Gosplan is the central economic planning unit for the entire Soviet Union.

5. Industrial production, according to the plan, is attained through a quota system involving 200,000 state-owned enterprises in the Soviet economy.

6. Incentives, both positive and negative, are used by Soviet planners to encourage managers and workers to fill and overfill production quotas.

7. The agriculture sector of the Soviet economy consists of ap-

proximately 12,700 state farms, approximately 36,000 collective farms, and millions of small family plots.

8. Although the Soviets have double the acreage and eight to nine times as many farmers as does the United States, agricultural output in the Soviet economy, on both a total and per capita basis, is much lower than agricultural output in the United States.

9. Because of the stress put on investment production by Soviet planners, Soviet consumers receive a relatively small share of the GNP.

10. In the past few decades the growth rate of the Soviet economy has exceeded that of the United States and several other major nations. Nevertheless, the actual level of living of the average Soviet family is still low compared.to other leading nations.

11. Beginning in the mid-1960s, the Soviet planners instituted a profit-reform system as a means of eliminating some of the waste and inefficiencies in the Soviet economy.

12. In the 1970s the Soviets expanded trade with the United States and other nations in an endeavor to alleviate food shortages and expand their industrial capacity.

NEW TERMS

Ideology, *p. 1024*	Gosplan, *p. 1032*
Fascism, *p. 1029*	State farms, *p. 1033*
Bolsheviks, *p. 1030*	Collective farms, *p. 1033*
Mensheviks, *p. 1030*	Turnover tax, *p. 1036*
Glavak, *p. 1032*	

QUESTIONS FOR DISCUSSION AND ANALYSIS

1. What do you see as the major difference between capitalism and communism? Elaborate.

2. How does socialism differ from communism?

3. Do you think present-day communism in Russia is the same as that advocated by Karl Marx? Why or why not?

4. What is the role of private property in the Soviet economy today?

5. How does the organizational structure of the Soviet economy differ from that of the United States economy?

6. Does the Soviet economy have any free markets? Explain.

7. How are prices established in the Soviet economy?

8. Compare the end-product use in the Soviet economy to that in the United States.

9. What motivated the profit reform of the Soviet economy?

10. Compare economic growth rates of the United States and Soviet Russia. Do you think the Soviets will overtake the United States in total or per capita production?

11. Do you think that creeping socialism and creeping capitalism will ever meet? Explain.

12. Do you agree with the current program of expanded U.S.-U.S.S.R. trade? Why or why not?

SUGGESTED READINGS

Ames, Edward. *Soviet Economic Processes.* Homewood, Ill.: Richard D. Irwin, Inc., 1965.

A New Trade Policy Toward Communist Countries. New York: Committee for Economic Development, September, 1972.

Bernard, Philippe J. *Planning in the Soviet Union,* translated by I. Nove. London: Pergamon Press, 1966.

Brodersen, Arvid. *The Soviet Worker.* New York: Random House, Inc., 1966.

Campbell, Robert W. *Soviet Economic Power.* Boston: Houghton Mifflin Company, 1966.

"Doing Business with Russia." *U. S. News & World Report* (December 20, 1971).

Felker, Jere L. *Soviet Economic Controversies.* Cambridge, Mass.: The M.I.T. Press, 1966.

Nove, Alec. *The Soviet Economy.* New York: Praeger Publishers, Inc., 1965.

"Prospects for U. S.-Soviet Trade." *Business Week* (May 6, 1972).

Schwartz, Harry. *An Introduction to the Soviet Economy.* Columbus, Ohio: Charles E. Merrill Publishing Company, 1968.

Sherman, Howard J. *The Soviet Economy.* Boston: Little, Brown and Company, 1969.

Shershnev, Yevgeni. "A Soviet Viewpoint . . . What's Ahead in U. S.-Russian Trade?" *Industry Week* (April 16, 1973).

U. S. Congress Joint Economic Committee. "New Directions in the Soviet Economy." Washington: U. S. Government Printing Office, 1966.

"U.S.-Soviet Trade Enters a New Era." *Commerce Today* (October 30, 1972).

Wellisz, Stanislaw H. *The Economics of the Soviet Bloc.* New York: McGraw-Hill Book Company, 1964.

Index

base year, changing, 228
Basic Occupational Language Training Program, 922
basing-point pricing, 643-644
basing-point system, 643
Bay Area Rapid Transit System, 868
Benelux, 950
Bentham, Jeremy, 1025
Berman vs. *Parker*, 860
Biddle, Nicholas, 275
bilateral monopoly, 647
bimetallic standard, 244-245, 248-249
bimetallism, compensatory principle of, 245
birth rate, declining, 911
black capitalism, 491
blacklists, 736
board of directors, 62
Bolsheviks, 1030
bonds:
  corporation, 64
  purchase of, by the Federal Reserve, 297-299
  sale of, by the Federal Reserve, 299
book value, 63
border tax, 436
borrowing, 318-319:
  during depression, 179
boycotts:
  primary, 733
  secondary, 733
break-even point, 584
Breech, Ernest, 780
budget:
  as a stabilizer, 372-374
  balanced, 87-88, 371
  deficit, 88-90, 371
  family, income and, 816-818
  full-employment, 373
  surplus, 88, 371
  types of, 371
budgetary policy, 370-374
budget surplus, accumulation of a, 484-485
built-in stabilizers, 316, 342
business:
  optimum size of, 667
  size of, 654-655
  structure of, 59-66
Business Conditions Digest, 192
business corporations, 61-65
business cycle, 174-178:
  causes of, 192-197
  endogenous forces that bring about the, 178
  exogenous forces that bring about the, 178

major, 175
minor, 175
monetary causes of, 195-196
pattern of, 178
phases and measurement of, 176-177
psychological causes of, 194-195
real or physical causes of, 193-194
spending and saving causes of, 196-197
types and length of, 175
business-cycle changes, statistical indicators of, 191
business cycle indicators, 188-192:
  composite, 190
  general, 190-192
  lagging, 191
  leading, 191
  other indexes, 189
  representative, 189
  roughly coincident, 191
business profit, 588
business taxes, 428
Business Week Index, 191
by-products, utilization of, 657

C

capital, 45-49:
  corporation, 62
  demand for, and loanable funds, 768-771
  demand for, defined, 768
  economy in production by the use of more, 656
  fixed, 45
  function of, 45-46
  human, 788
  human, determinants of, 797-804
  marginal efficiency of, 163
  savings and the accumulation of, 46-47
  social, 988
  social overhead, 1013
  supply of, 771
  suply of, and loanable funds, 771-774
  value of nonhuman, 792-794
  working, 45
capital accumulation, 988
capital consumption allowances, 103
capital goods, 37
capitalism, 1025-1026:
  black, 491
  free enterprise, 19-23
  state, 1031
  the rise of, 999-1000
capitalistic spirit, 1000

capitalistic system, 19
capitalization of income, 789-791
capital stock, value of, 63
cartel, 666
cascade tax, 434
cash balance approach, 218
caveat emptor, 492
caveat venditor, 492
Celler-Kefauver Amendment, 669
central bank, 279
central city, 852
Cheves, Langdon, 275
Chicago Board of Trade, 527
circular flow:
  government and the, 86-90
  GNP and the, 109
  in action, 90-92
  model, 80-86
City Worker's Family Budget, 817
Civil Aeronautics Act of 1938, 687
civilian labor force, 200-201
Civil Rights Act of 1964, 918
classical theory of economic development, 997
class struggle, 1028-1029
Clayton Act of 1914, 665-666, 668-669, 688
Clean Air Act:
  of 1963, 517-518
  of 1970, 518
closed shop, 728
Coinage Act of 1873, 249
collective bargaining, 731-732
collective farms (Kolhozy), 1033
combinations. *See* corporate combinations
command economies, 23-25:
  functions of prices in, 534-535
Commission on National Goals, 32
Committee on Industrial Organization (CIO), formation of the, 724
Commodity Credit Corporation, 840:
  and related organizations, 841-842
commodity money, 239
Commodity Stabilization Service, 840
common-law doctrines, 738
Common Organization of Africa, 953
common stocks, 63
communism, 24-25:
  the class struggle, 1028-1029
  the materialistic economic interpretation of history, 1027-1028
Community Action Programs, 334
community of interests, 665-666

more efficient use of, 469-470
participation, 205-207
participation rate, 41, 205, 913
projections, 914-918
size of, 200, 204-205
total, 40, 200
trends in, 202-207
unemployed, 201
Labor Management Relations Act (Taft-Hartley Act), 729, 736, 740-742
Labor-Management Reporting and Disclosure Act (Landrum-Griffin Act), 70, 742-743
labor market equilibrium, 713-715
labor migration, 802-804
laborsaving machinery and processes, use of, 730
labor supply, control of, 731
labor unions. *See* unions
lagging indicators of business-cycle changes, 191
laissez-faire policy, 68
land, 41-45:
  and water resources, conservation of, 43-44
  causes of changes in demand and supply of, 756-758
  demand and supply of, 755
  fertility of, 748
  government-owned, 403-405
  location of, 748
  marginal, 750
  other income from, 754
  productivity of, 747-749
  scarcity of, 749
  submarginal, 750
  supramarginal, 750
  value of, 759-761
Landrum-Griffin Act, 70, 742-743
land values, 792-793:
  reasons for changes in, 761
  rent and, 760-761
large-scale enterprises, advantages of, 656-659
Laspeyres' formula, 227
Latin American Free Trade Association, 953
Law Enforcement Assistance Administration, 874
law of diminishing marginal productivity, 572
law of diminishing marginal utility, 539
law of diminishing returns, 571
leading indicators of business-cycle changes, 191
least-cost combination, 576
legal reserve requirements, of the Federal Reserve System, 288-289

leisure, 115
Lenin, Nikolai, 1027, 1030
Leontief, Wassily, 119
letters of credit, 958
level of living:
  changes in the, 57-59
  rising, 29-30
Lewis, John L., 724
liberal doctrine, 68-69
liberalism, economic, pure and mixed, 68-69
liquid assets, family, 816
liquidity, international, 256
liquidity preference:
  during depression, 179
  during recession, 186-187
liquidity preference theory, 767-768
loanable funds:
  demand for capital and, 768-771
  savings, the source of, 771-772
  supply of capital and, 771-774
loans:
  consumption, 769
  governmental, 770-771
  length of, 301-302
  production, 769-770
local government expenditures, character of, 400
location rent, 752-753
Locke, John, 1025
lockouts, 735
long run, 587:
  price and profit in the, 605-610
long-run cost curve, 608-609
long-run equilibrium, 631-632
losses, minimizing, in the short run, 586-588
lotteries, 447-450

M

macroeconomics, 15
Malthus, Thomas, 706
managed currencies, 964
managerial efficiency theory of profit, 780-781
Manpower Development and Training Act of 1962, 330-331
manpower problems:
  American Indians, 922-923
  black workers, 918-920
  criminal offenders, 927-928
  Spanish-Americans, 920-922
  women in the economy, 923-927
marginal cost, 581
marginal efficiency of capital, 163:
  relationship of, to rate of interest, 164-165

marginal land, 750
marginal outlay, 708
marginal product, 572-573
marginal productivity theory of interest, 765-766
marginal productivity theory of wages, 707-717:
  other complications, 716-717
  reservations on, 715-717
  under imperfect competition, 715-716
marginal propensity to consume, 131
marginal propensity to save, 131
marginal revenue, 583:
  vs. marginal cost, 585-586
marginal revenue product, 709
marginal utility, 539:
  consumption tends to balance, 540
  law of diminishing, 539
Marimont, Martin L., 119
market, 527-528:
  demand, 542-543
  demand schedule, 543-545
  structure, American, 647-648
  why the government interferes with the, 678-679
market price:
  competitive, 567
  interest as a, 768
market rate of interest, 766:
  determination of, 774-776
market ratio, 244
market share elasticity, 555
market supply, 558:
  schedule, 558-559
market value, 63
Marshall, John, 62
Marshall Plan, 974
Marx, Karl, 67, 707, 997-998, 1027-1028, 1042
Marxist theory of economic development, 997-998
mass transit:
  history of, 861-862
  impact of the automobile on, 862-864
  role of the federal government in, 866-868
mass transportation, 490
materialistic economic interpretation of history, 1027-1028
Mathematica Incorporated, 900
mathematical economics, 13
McCulloch vs. *Maryland*, 275
McGuire Act of 1952, 688, 671
Meadows, Dennis, 478
Medicaid, 897
Medicare, 893-894

shifting of the, 419-422
tax duplication, 401-403
taxes, 405-406:
   border, 436
   business, 428
   cascade, 434
   death, 429
   direct, 421
   effect of, 420
   estate, 429
   excess profits, 347
   general property, 423-426
   gift, 429
   hidden, 421
   impact of, 420
   incidence of, 420
   income, 426-427
   indirect, 421
   inheritance, 429
   kinds of, 423-430
   national retail sales, 328
   reduction of, 484
   sales, 428-429
   shared, 407
   shifting of, 420
   Social Security, 430
   trends in the use of direct and
      indirect, 421-422
   turnover, 1036
   value added, 433-438
tax evasion, 422
tax rates, 416:
   degressive, 418
   progressive, 417-418
   proportional, 417
   regressive, 418-419
   structure of, 416-419
tax system, 412
technological progress, 47-48, 990-
   991
Tennessee Valley Authority, 44,
   66
third order or tertiary investment,
   138
throw-away society, 503
time-preference theory of interest,
   766-767
Toffler, Alvin, 502
token money, 240
tool for economic stabilization,
   372
total cost, 581
total labor force, 200
total revenue, 583:
   vs. total cost, 584-585
trade:
   balance of, 968
   balance of, balance of payments
      and, 967-970
   East-West, 953-954

international (*see* international
   trade)
other restraints on, 939
restrictions on, 937-943
terms of, in underdevelopment,
   1012
trade agreements, reciprocal, 945-
946
Trade Expansion Act of 1962,
   946-948
trade policy, United States, 944-
949
Trade-Union Educational League,
   723
trading blocs:
   dominant, 954-955
   world, 952-955
training, on-the-job, 801-802
transactions:
   monetary, 114
   net, time factor and, 118-119
transactions approach, 218
transactions motive for liquidity
   preference, 767
transfer payment, 103
transportation:
   costs of, 865-866
   mass, 490
   public, decline of, 864-865
   urban, 860-869
Treasury notes, 259
trend, 176
Trotsky, Leon, 1030
trusts, 663
Truth-in-Lending Bill, 686
turnover tax, 1036

U

underconsumption theories of the
   business cycle, 196
underdeveloped nations, 988, 995-
996:
   a new multilateral objective for
      assistance to, 1018-1020
   American interest in, 1016-1018
   characteristics of, 1007-1010
   demographic characteristics of,
      1008-1009
   economic characteristics of,
      1007-1008
   foreign assistance in develop-
      ment of, 1015-1020
   political and sociological, 1009
   technological characteristics of,
      1008
   who are the, 1003-1007
underdevelopment:
   balanced growth theories of,
      1013

geographic determinism, 1010-
   1011
sociological patterns, 1011-1012
terms of trade, 1012
theories of, 1010-1014
types of, 1010
underemployment, 26
underinvestment theory of the
   business cycle, 197
unemployed labor force, 201
unemployment, 26, 462:
   disguised, 1008
   frictional, 26
   nagging, 355
   policies to alleviate, 315-324
   rates, in the U.S. and elsewhere,
      212-213
unemployment equilibrium, 154-
159
unemployment insurance, 890-892
Uniform Relocation Assistance and
   Land Acquisition Policies Act,
   856
unionism, industrial, since 1933,
   723-725
union methods:
   boycotts, 733
   collective bargaining, 731-732
   picketing, 732-733
   propaganda and political pres-
      sure, 734
   sabotage, 734
   strikes, 732
union objectives:
   control of the labor supply, 731
   hours of work, 729-730
   increasing and maintaining
      wages, 729
   restriction and regulation of
      output, 730-731
   union security, 728
   use of laborsaving machinery
      and processes, 730
unions:
   company, 736-737
   craft or trade, 721
   ideological, 723
   independent, 725
   industrial, 721
   international, 726
   local, 725-726
   national, 726
   national federations of, 722-723,
      726-728
   political, 722
   structure of, 725-728
union shop, 728
unit elasticity, 548
urban areas, federal aid to, 874-
876

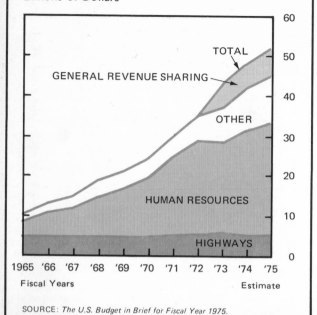

FEDERAL GRANTS TO STATE AND LOCAL GOVERNMENTS
Billions of Dollars

TOTAL

GENERAL REVENUE SHARING

OTHER

HUMAN RESOURCES

HIGHWAYS

1965 '66 '67 '68 '69 '70 '71 '72 '73 '74 '75
Fiscal Years   Estimate

SOURCE: *The U.S. Budget in Brief for Fiscal Year 1975.*

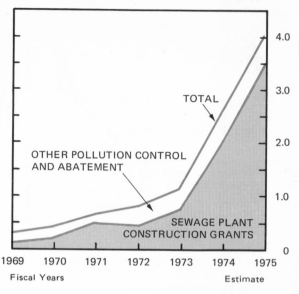

OUTLAYS FOR POLLUTION CONTROL AND ABATEMENT-EPA
Billions of Dollars

TOTAL

OTHER POLLUTION CONTROL AND ABATEMENT

SEWAGE PLANT CONSTRUCTION GRANTS

1969   1970   1971   1972   1973   1974   1975
Fiscal Years   Estimate

SOURCE: *The U.S. Budget in Brief for Fiscal Year 1975.*

FEDERAL OUTLAYS

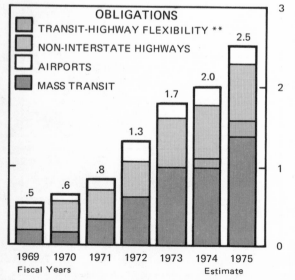

FEDERAL SUPPORT FOR URBAN* TRANSPORTATION
Billions of Dollars (Excludes Proposed Legislation)

OBLIGATIONS
- TRANSIT-HIGHWAY FLEXIBILITY **
- NON-INTERSTATE HIGHWAYS
- AIRPORTS
- MASS TRANSIT

.5 .6 .8 1.3 1.7 2.0 2.5

1969 1970 1971 1972 1973 1974 1975
Fiscal Years   Estimate

*Areas over 50,000   **Highway authority used for mass transit

SOURCE: *The U.S. Budget in Brief for Fiscal Year 1975.*

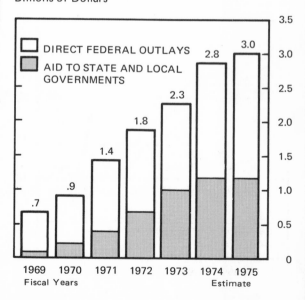

FEDERAL OUTLAYS FOR THE REDUCTION OF CRIME
Billions of Dollars

- DIRECT FEDERAL OUTLAYS
- AID TO STATE AND LOCAL GOVERNMENTS

.7 .9 1.4 1.8 2.3 2.8 3.0

1969 1970 1971 1972 1973 1974 1975
Fiscal Years   Estimate

SOURCE: *The U.S. Budget in Brief for Fiscal Year 1975.*